Ronald N. Check

THE WAY OF THE LORD JESUS

Volume One

CHRISTIAN MORAL PRINCIPLES

THE WAY OF THE LORD JESUS

Volume One

CHRISTIAN MORAL PRINCIPLES

by

Germain Grisez

The *Reverend Harry J. Flynn* Professor of Christian Ethics
Mount Saint Mary's College — Emmitsburg, Maryland

with the help of

Joseph M. Boyle, Jr., Basil Cole, O.P., John M. Finnis
John A. Geinzer, Jeannette Grisez, Robert G. Kennedy,
Patrick Lee, William E. May, and Russell Shaw

Franciscan Press
Quincy University
1800 College Avenue
Quincy, Illinois 62301-2699
Telephone: 217-228-5670 • FAX: 217-228-5672

Nihil Obstat:
Rev. John F. Harvey, O.S.F.S.
Censor Deputatus

Imprimatur:
Rev. Msgr. John F. Donoghue
Vicar General for the Archdiocese of Washington

June 2, 1983

The nihil obstat and imprimatur are official declarations that a book or pamphlet is free of doctrinal or moral error. No implication is contained therein that those who have granted the nihil obstat and the imprimatur agree with the content, opinions, or statements expressed.

Library of Congress Cataloging in Publication Data

Grisez, Germain Gabriel, 1929–
  The Way of the Lord Jesus.

  Includes index.
  Contents: v. 1. Christian moral principles.
  1. Christian ethics— Catholic authors. I. Title.
BJ1249.G74 1983   241'.042   83-1508
ISBN 0-8199-0861-4 (v.1)

CONTENTS

Contents

3:   Conscience: Knowledge of Moral Truth

Conscience is one's last and best judgment concerning what one should choose. Genuine judgments of conscience are derived from sound moral principles. One's knowledge of these principles and of their application develops. This development is the formation of conscience. It is based on natural law and assisted by the teaching of the Church.

4:   Some Mistaken Theories of Moral Principles

Many today reject conscience as the Church understands it. In various ways they deny that judgments of conscience can be derived from objectively true moral principles. Such theories are wholly at odds with Catholic moral teaching. Less subversive, but still inadequate, is the scholastic natural-law theory of classical moral theology. What is needed is an account of how true moral norms are based upon human goods.

5:   The Goods Which Fulfill Persons

Moral norms are based on human goods. "Good" means fullness of being; "bad" means privation of this fullness. There are various sorts of goods which fulfill human persons. Some complete persons in their existential aspect—insofar as they constitute themselves by their choices. Others complete persons in other aspects. The human good as a whole is not only moral goodness; it includes a rich participation in all the human goods.

Contents

8: The Modes of Responsibility Which Specify the First Principle

The modes of responsibility, which are the primary specifications of the first principle of morality, are principles of concrete moral norms. These modes make the first principle applicable to human acts. Each mode excludes a way in which human fulfillment can be blocked, and thus indicates a requirement for integral human fulfillment. The first mode excludes laziness and requires proper ambition. The second mode excludes individualism and requires responsible participation in community. The third mode excludes the quest for mere gratification and requires self-control. The fourth mode excludes frightened failure to pursue goods and requires courage. The fifth mode excludes acting on feelings of partiality toward persons; it requires fairness. The sixth mode excludes seeking the experienced aspects of goods to the detriment of a fuller participation in them; it requires clearheaded pursuit of real goods. The seventh mode excludes a choice out of hostility against any good (that is, against any person); it requires forbearance. The eighth mode excludes any choice to destroy, harm, or impede any one good for the sake of another, or another instance of the same sort of good; it requires reverence for all human goods—that is, for all persons.

9: The Voluntary: What Moral Norms Bear Upon

Moral norms direct human acts, but they primarily bear upon choices. They bear upon the rest of life to the extent that it is shaped by the will. One's life depends on one's will in various ways. Since there are diverse varieties of voluntariness, moral norms bear upon different aspects of human life in diverse ways. By considering the varieties of voluntariness, the nature and extent of moral responsibility is clarified.

Contents

10:   From Modes of Responsibility to Moral Norms

Specific moral norms are derived from the modes of responsibility by considering acts to be evaluated in terms of the goods at stake and the varieties of voluntariness involved. When one tries to use a previously formulated norm to reach a judgment of conscience, one sometimes, but not always, finds it nonabsolute. To say that a norm is "nonabsolute" is to say that it does not apply in some cases. This happens because some cases involve morally relevant features in addition to those of the cases for which the norm was designed. Duties and rights are derived from the modes of responsibility in the same way as other norms; so are the moral responsibilities of communities.

11:   The Moral Authority of Law

Many of the specific norms which direct the lives of people are embodied in law. The moral obligation to obey laws follows from their moral basis. The nature and limits of that obligation can be understood only by distinguishing divine precepts, Church law, and the law of civil society. The latter is of various sorts.

12: Moral Judgment in Problematic Situations

Sometimes a person is in doubt about what is the right thing to do. Such doubts of conscience arise from a variety of sources. Some involve a doubt of fact, others doubt about a norm or its application, and still others a seeming moral conflict. In all doubts of conscience one ought to make a serious attempt to discover what truly is morally good.

13: What Sin Is and What It Is Not

Sins are morally evil acts considered insofar as they disrupt a person's relationship with God. Not every sin is a choice, but every sin is related to a choice contrary to conscience. In most sins, one does not choose precisely to offend God. Rather, one wrongfully prefers one human good to another human good. Yet by violating moral truth and human good all sins do offend God. Although rooted in the choices of individuals, sins—like choices in general—can be social. Christians must resist attempts to explain away the real evil of sin.

14:   Sin of Adam and Sins of Men and Women

Essentially, original sin is the alienation of the human race from God. This state of alienation came about by the immoral choice of the first humans. Death was introduced into the world with sin; with death comes a distortion of all our capacities. Attempts to revise the Church's teaching concerning original sin are not defensible.

15:   Distinctions among Sins; Sins of Thought

Not all sins are equally serious. On a scriptural basis, the Church distinguishes venial sins from mortal sins. Because Christian morality primarily concerns the existential self— rightness of the heart—sins of thought are important. Like other sins, sins of thought can be mortal only if one makes a definite choice.

16: The Distinction between Grave and Light Matter

Why do not all sins involve grave matter? Some suggest that a sin in light matter is one unlikely to subvert a good fundamental option. Current theories of fundamental option must be rejected. However, they offer an insight which can be synthesized with St. Thomas' account of the distinction between grave and light matter to provide a more adequate solution to the problem. Faith is the fundamental option of Christian life; those kinds of acts are light matter which conflict neither with faith nor with its implicit requirements.

17: Sufficient Reflection; Sins of Weakness

The awareness required for sufficient reflection is at the level of moral truth concerning the gravity of the act. This awareness need not include an insight into why the act would be wrong. Emotion can mitigate guilt. However, sins of weakness which meet the usual conditions for mortal sin must be presumed to be mortal sins. With God's grace, every sinner can stop sinning. The sinner through weakness is no exception.

18:   The Way of Sin to Death

Sins are not discrete acts unrelated to the dynamics of one's whole life. Imperfections lead to venial sins, venial sins to mortal sins, and mortal sins to final impenitence and hell. Grace and freedom always can reverse this evil process up to the moment of death. But eternal separation from God is a real possibility for each of us.

19:   Fulfillment in Jesus and Human Fulfillment

The purpose of creation is the glory of God. This purpose will be realized in the fulfillment of all things in Jesus. Human persons are called to share in his fullness. Their share in fulfillment is to be the perfection of the ways in which Christians even now are united with Jesus: in divine life, in bodily life, and in human action. Thus there is an intrinsic relationship between Christian life in this world and in the next.

20:   The Relationship between God and Sinful Humankind

Revelation is God's personal self-communication. By it he invites human persons to intimacy with himself. Faith is our acceptance of this invitation. By faith we commit ourselves to living our lives in friendship with God. Given our sinful human condition, God's revelation is redemptive. God allows us to share in his redeeming work.

21:   God's Redemptive Work: Covenant and Incarnation

God redeems by inviting sinful humankind into a covenant relationship with himself. This relationship both demands of its human participants that they live a morally good life and clarifies what this means. The Incarnation of the Word perfects the covenant relationship by divine sharing in human life in its fallen condition. In Jesus, the human and divine natures are united but uncommingled, distinct but inseparable. The life he lives has the same complex structure.

22: God's Redemptive Work in Jesus' Human Life

Jesus' basic commitment is to do the Father's will by reconciling fallen humankind to God. Jesus began to carry out his personal vocation by his teaching, miracles, and forming of the apostolic Church. He completed his earthly work by making the new covenant on our behalf. In choosing to do this, he freely accepted death and humanly cooperated in the divine work of re-creation by which alone evil is finally being overcome.

23: God's Redemptive Work in the Lives of Christians

We are allowed to share in redemption not only by being redeemed but even by helping to redeem ourselves and others. United in the Mass with Jesus' central commitment and the act by which he most perfectly carries it out, each of us is called to live a unique life which will contribute to the completion of Jesus' redemptive work. Our prophetic responsibility as Christians requires that our deeds carry out and bear witness to our faith in Jesus. To fulfill this responsibility, close adherence to the moral teaching of the Church is essential.

Contents

26: Modes of Christian Response

The modes of Christian response are general determinations of the first principle of morality, which draws Christians to fulfillment in Jesus. These modes include Christian virtues, at least in incipient form. They correspond to the Beatitudes which proclaim the intrinsic relationship between Christian life in this world and heavenly fulfillment. The gifts of the Holy Spirit indicate these modes insofar as they are divinely given powers to live as a child of God. Like Jesus, the poor in spirit are humble, the meek are obedient and resigned, the sorrowing are detached, those who hunger and thirst are faithful, and the merciful are compassionate. The pure in heart grow toward likeness to Jesus in perfect devotion. The peacemakers are like him in reconciliation. Those persecuted for righteousness' sake sacrifice themselves as he does.

27:   Life Formed by the Modes of Christian Response

Christian life is unified by the principle of the modes of Christian response. This principle is the commitment of faith to share in Jesus' redemptive life. This commitment thoroughly transforms the common norms of morality, not by negating them but by completing them. This transformation is effected in each Christian's response to the universal call to perfection and to his or her personal vocation. Because each Christian life is unique, conscience has an important, creative role.

28:   The Practicability of Christian Morality

The modes of Christian response make real moral demands which can be fulfilled. Rigorism is avoided because the modes of Christian response become exigent only gradually as one carries out one's personal vocation. As the requirements of Christian life become clear, it also becomes clear that the alternative to a life of holiness oriented by hope is a worldly existence which inevitably falls short of human dignity.

29:   Prayer: The Fundamental Category of Christian Action

In prayer one develops the intimate relationship with God which one accepts by faith. The liturgy is the center of each Christian's prayer life, because in it the whole Church prays in union with our Lord Jesus. But personal prayer also is essential: all are called to a unique personal vocation which must be lived in conversation with God.

30:   Sacraments in General and Baptism

The sacraments are cooperative acts, designed by Jesus, which permit human persons to share with him and the Holy Spirit in their work of redemption and sanctification. By baptism a member of the fallen human family enters the new family of God and undertakes to live a life like that of Jesus. The other sacraments are principal acts of a Christian's life; they organize the rest of life in several distinct but compatible ways.

31: Confirmation, the Apostolate, and Personal Vocation

Every mature Christian is called to share in redemption not only by being redeemed but also by bearing witness to Jesus. This apostolic responsibility takes the form of a personal vocation. Confirmation strengthens one to bear witness; hence it is the principle of one's whole life organized in response to one's personal vocation.

32: Penance, Anointing, and the Life of Self-Denial

Sin is more than an immoral act which must be amended. All sin requires reparation, and the whole of Christian life requires self-denial. Every act of self-denial can serve as reparation for sin, and such reparation is suitably centered in the sacrament of penance. Moreover, this sacrament is an apt way of overcoming venial sin. The sacrament of the anointing of the sick completes penance by consecrating the Christian for the final act of reparation—suffering and death with Jesus.

33: Eucharistic Life as Fulfillment in the Lord Jesus

By making present to us the sacrifice of Jesus and his whole glorified Reality, the Eucharist nourishes us to everlasting life and transforms our moral lives. Integrated into our Lord's still-continuing human life, our lives are bound together in the fellowship of the Church and drawn within his fullness. In different ways, the Liturgy of the Hours and the sacrament of matrimony extend the Eucharist throughout daily life.

34: Christian Life Animated with Hope of Everlasting Life

The doctrine of the fulfillment of all things in Jesus shows the inadequacy of the other-worldliness of much Catholic moral and spiritual thought, of modern secular humanist thought, and of various contemporary optimistic mixtures of these currents of thought. None of these adequately explains the relationship between the divine and human in Christian life. Nor does any of them rightly understand the continuity and discontinuity between this life and the next. Our heavenly vocation and our earthly duty to bring forth fruit in charity for the life of the world are intrinsically related. Heaven includes the perfection of all the good things of this life, both human and divine. But heavenly fulfillment requires an act of divine re-creation, which alone can finally overcome sin and all its effects.

35: The Truth of Christ Lives in His Church

By the gift of infallibility, the Church is protected from error in recognizing what does and does not pertain to faith. The apostles were infallible in their appropriation of God's revelation in Jesus, and their infallibility extends to the belief and teaching of the Catholic Church. Teaching is proposed infallibly not only in solemn definitions but also in day-to-day authoritative teaching which meets certain conditions. A substantial body of received Catholic moral teaching has been proposed infallibly. Even teaching not proposed infallibly might pertain to divine revelation; it calls for religious assent.

36: A Critical Examination of Radical Theological Dissent

Some theologians dissented from much received Catholic moral teaching, including many norms infallibly proposed by the ordinary magisterium. This dissent was justifiable neither by any principle grounded in faith nor by any rational argument. The claim by some dissenting theologians to a teaching authority superior to that of the pope and other bishops was gratuitous. The attempt by some to represent dissent as mere reformulation of doctrine or as legitimate development of it was specious.

Indexes .

USER'S GUIDE AND PREFACE

General suggestions

Users of this volume might find it helpful to begin by reading the entire table of contents, which includes brief summaries of each chapter. The table of contents is a map of the volume as a whole; it can be used repeatedly for orientation.

Each chapter is constructed of several levels of material. The numbered paragraphs in each question contain what is most essential. With the context provided in these paragraphs, the sentences directly answering the question are highlighted in bold type. The other paragraphs in each question include subordinate material which will be helpful for many readers—examples, further explanations, supporting evidence, and treatment of important tangential matters.

The summary, just after the questions in each chapter, provides a compact but thorough review of the chapter's essential content. The summary may also be read as a preview before studying the questions. Readers with sufficient background may obtain a good idea of the work as a whole by reading straight through the summaries of all the chapters.

In most chapters one or more appendices follow the summary. These contain material of less urgency for the average reader, but necessary for a more scholarly grasp of the subject matter or as additional support of positions stated in the chapter.

The notes at the end of each chapter sometimes amount to small appendices. They also refer to works mentioned or used, other than the sources cited in the text itself. The notes often suggest materials for further study. No separate bibliography is provided.

Directions for use of all the indexes will be found at the beginning of that section. The first index, *Some key words,* will help to minimize the burden of the technical vocabulary peculiar to this work.

Key to references within the text

The chief sources of this work are Scripture, the teachings of the Catholic Church, and the writings of certain Fathers and Doctors of the Church, especially St. Thomas Aquinas. References to these sources are provided within the text rather than in notes.

Quotations from Scripture (except those within other quotations) unless indicated otherwise are from the Revised Standard Version Bible, Catholic

Edition. However, citations other than direct quotations follow the numbering of verses in The New American Bible. A few quotations, labeled "NAB," are from that translation. References are made by means of the following abbreviations:

Acts	*Acts of the Apostles*	2 Kgs	*2 Kings*
Am	*Amos*	Lam	*Lamentations*
Bar	*Baruch*	Lk	*Luke*
1 Chr	*1 Chronicles*	Lv	*Leviticus*
2 Chr	*2 Chronicles*	Mal	*Malachi*
Col	*Colossians*	1 Mc	*1 Maccabees*
1 Cor	*1 Corinthians*	2 Mc	*2 Maccabees*
2 Cor	*2 Corinthians*	Mi	*Micah*
Dn	*Daniel*	Mk	*Mark*
Dt	*Deuteronomy*	Mt	*Matthew*
Eccl	*Ecclesiastes*	Na	*Nahum*
Eph	*Ephesians*	Neh	*Nehemiah*
Est	*Esther*	Nm	*Numbers*
Ex	*Exodus*	Ob	*Obadiah*
Ez	*Ezekiel*	Phil	*Philippians*
Ezr	*Ezra*	Phlm	*Philemon*
Gal	*Galatians*	Prv	*Proverbs*
Gn	*Genesis*	Ps	*Psalms*
Hb	*Habakkuk*	1 Pt	*1 Peter*
Heb	*Hebrews*	2 Pt	*2 Peter*
Hg	*Haggai*	Rom	*Romans*
Hos	*Hosea*	Ru	*Ruth*
Is	*Isaiah*	Rv	*Revelation (Apocalypse)*
Jas	*James*	Sg	*Song of Songs*
Jb	*Job*	Sir	*Sirach (Ecclesiasticus)*
Jdt	*Judith*	1 Sm	*1 Samuel*
Jer	*Jeremiah*	2 Sm	*2 Samuel*
Jgs	*Judges*	Tb	*Tobit*
Jl	*Joel*	1 Thes	*1 Thessalonians*
Jn	*John (Gospel)*	2 Thes	*2 Thessalonians*
1 Jn	*1 John (Epistle)*	Ti	*Titus*
2 Jn	*2 John*	1 Tm	*1 Timothy*
3 Jn	*3 John*	2 Tm	*2 Timothy*
Jon	*Jonah*	Wis	*Wisdom*
Jos	*Joshua*	Zec	*Zecariah*
Jude	*Jude*	Zep	*Zephaniah*
1 Kgs	*1 Kings*		

"FEF" refers to *The Faith of the Early Fathers,* 3 volumes, selected and translated by William A. Jurgens (Collegeville, Minn.: Liturgical Press, 1970-1979). This collection includes many important theological and historical passages from the Christian writings of the patristic period, ending in the West in the mid-seventh century and in the East in the mid-eighth century. Passages 1–910a are in volume 1; 911–1416 in volume 2; 1417–2390 in volume 3. Father Jurgens' scholarly introductions and notes are very useful.

"DS" refers to Henricus Denzinger—Adolfus Schönmetzer, S.I., *Enchiridion Symbolorum Definitionum et Declarationum de Rebus Fidei et Morum*, ed. 34 (Freiburg in Breisgau: Herder, 1967). This volume, as its title indicates, is a collection of "creeds, definitions, and declarations on matters of faith and morals." Texts are in the original languages (mostly Latin) and in chronological order. Two sequences of numbers appear in the margins; both are indicated in references in the present text. The lower numbers are found in earlier editions of the handbook and in many publications which used it. Quotations from this collection, unless otherwise noted, are from: *The Church Teaches: Documents of the Church in English Translation*, translated by J. F. Clarkson, S.J., J. H. Edwards, S.J., W. J. Kelly, S.J., and J. J. Welch, S.J. (Rockford, Illinois: Tan Books, 1973). Texts in the translation are arranged topically rather than chronologically; a table (370–375) correlates with DS.

Quotations from the Constitutions, Decrees, and Declarations of the Second Vatican Council, unless otherwise noted, are from *The Documents of Vatican II*, edited by Walter M. Abbott, S.J., and Joseph Gallagher (New York: America Press, 1966). In some cases the Abbott–Gallagher translation has been amended to conform more exactly to the Council's Latin text, and when minor amendments proved inadequate, a fresh translation usually has been supplied. These facts are indicated with the reference. In a few cases, marked "Flannery translation," the translation is drawn from *Vatican Council II: The Conciliar and Post Conciliar Documents*, ed. Austin Flannery, O.P. (Northport, New York: Costello Publishing Company, 1975).

References to the Vatican II documents use the abbreviations derived from the initial letters of the Latin text of each document and then the numbers of the articles into which the documents were divided by the Council itself.

AA   *Apostolicam Actuositatem* (Laity)
AG   *Ad Gentes* (Missions)
CD   *Christus Dominus* (Bishops)
DH   *Dignitatis Humanae* (Religious Liberty)
DV   *Dei Verbum* (Divine Revelation)
GE   *Gravissimum Educationis* (Education)
GS   *Gaudium et Spes* (Church in the World)
IM   *Inter Mirifica* (Communications)
LG   *Lumen Gentium* (On the Church)
NA   *Nostra Aetate* (Non-Christian Religions)
OE   *Orientalium Ecclesiarum* (Eastern Churches)
OT   *Optatam Totius* (Priestly Formation)
PC   *Perfectae Caritatis* (Religious Life)
PO   *Presbyterorum Ordinis* (Priestly Life)
SC   *Sacrosanctum Concilium* (Liturgy)
UR   *Unitatis Redintegratio* (Ecumenism)

Note that in the Abbott–Gallagher edition only the *italicized footnotes* are part of the Council documents. The notes in Roman type were added by the commentator on each document, whose name appears at the end of the essay introducing the document. Because of the added notes, the official notes are not numbered in the Abbott edition as they are in the official texts.

"S.t." refers to the *Summa theologiae* of St. Thomas Aquinas. This work is cited by its five main divisions: 1 (the first part or *prima pars*), 1–2 (the first part of the second part or *prima secundae*), 2–2 (the second part of the second part or *secunda secundae*), 3 (the third part or *tertia pars*), and sup. (the supplement compiled from an earlier work after Thomas' death). These main divisions are subdivided into questions (cited by "q." with the question number), the questions into articles (cited by "a." with the article number), and the articles into a body ("c." for *corpus*) and replies to objections (cited ad 1, ad 2, and so forth). *"S.c.g."* refers to St. Thomas' *Summa contra gentiles*, which is divided into four books and these into chapters.

Many popes and Vatican II have commended St. Thomas as a model for work in theology. The reflection completed in the present book began from his work. I am far more indebted to him than the numerous citations of his works suggest. Still, the writings of St. Thomas are not theological sources on a par with the teaching of the Church herself. On some important matters, the unfolding teaching of the Church seems to require positions incompatible with those of St. Thomas. In such cases, one must be a better friend of Thomas by disagreeing with him, for he cared far more about the truth of the Catholic faith than about his own theological positions.

A few other sources and some reference works

The following works were used very frequently in the preparation of this book and are often cited in the notes.

"AAS" refers to *Acta Apostolicae Sedis*, the journal of the Holy See in which are published the official texts of documents issued by the popes and the Holy See's congregations. *AAS* began publication in 1909; its predecessor, from 1865–1908, was *Acta Sanctae Sedis* (*ASS*).

Dictionnaire de Théologie Catholique, 15 volumes (Paris: 1899–1950). This work is cited by volume and column. Although sometimes out of date, this magnificent collective work remains indispenable for theological research.

Dictionary of Biblical Theology, ed. Xavier Léon-Dufour, 2d ed. (New York: 1973).

Encyclopedia of Biblical Theology: The Complete "Sacramentum Verbi," ed. Johannes B. Bauer, in one volume (New York: 1981).

Encyclopedia of Theology: The Concise "Sacramentum Mundi," ed. Karl Rahner, in one volume (New York: 1975).

The Interpreter's Dictionary of the Bible: An Illustrated Encyclopedia, 4 volumes and supplementary volume (Nashville: 1962 and 1976).

New Catholic Encyclopedia, 15 volumes and 2 supplementary volumes (New York: 1967, 1974, 1979). The original set meets high standards of scholarship and doctrinal soundness; the supplementary volumes are quite uneven in both respects.

The New International Dictionary of New Testament Theology, ed. Colin Brown, 3 volumes (Grand Rapids: Michigan: 1975, 1976, 1978).

The Papal Encyclicals (1740–1981), ed. Claudia Carlen, I.H.M., 5 volumes (Raleigh, North Carolina: 1981). The English translations of the encyclicals are cited by the numbers assigned them and their sections in this edition.

The Rites of the Catholic Church as Revised by Decree of the Second Vatican Council and Published by Authority of Pope Paul VI (New York: 1976). References are to the page numbers in this collected edition.

Theological Dictionary of the New Testament, ed. Gerhard Kittel and Gerhard Friedrich, trans. Geoffrey W. Bromiley, 10 volumes (Grand Rapids, Michigan: 1964–1976).

The necessary foundation for theological study is sound and comprehensive catechesis. Two fine works not only supply this need but contain a wealth of historical and bibliographical information. Each has its own strengths and the two complement each other very well:

John A. Hardon, S.J., *The Catholic Catechism: A Contemporary Catechism of the Teachings of the Catholic Church* (New York: 1975).

The Teaching of Christ: A Catholic Catechism for Adults, ed. Ronald Lawler, O.F.M.Cap., Thomas Comerford Lawler, and Donald W. Wuerl (Huntington, Indiana: 1976).

The purpose and character of this book

This book is constructed primarily as a textbook in fundamental moral theology for students in Catholic seminaries. Three drafts were used in a two-semester course I have been teaching since 1979 in Mount Saint Mary's Seminary. However, those already ordained to the priesthood, teachers of religion, parents concerned about the catechetical formation of their children, and others may find the book helpful. As I explain in chapter one, questions E through H, the book responds to Vatican II's call for renewal in moral theology.

Why is moral theology so important? Morality is a characteristic of human actions. Human actions are not what is most fundamental in reality or in Christian life, for more basic is the reality and work of God. Nevertheless, God has chosen to create persons who can be like himself in acting intelligently and freely. God ennobles his creatures by making them his able and effective cooperators. Our lives are not passing; they are ourselves. In this passing world we make the selves and relationships which will endure forever. For this reason, the moral quality of Christian life is very important.

The reality of God and the quality of his other works do not depend upon what we think. But the quality of our Christian lives, which also are the work of God, does depend upon what we think. Moral theology helps to improve this thinking. Therefore, moral theology is one of the most important parts of theology. Its study contributes in a unique way to the work of God.

In this book, I assume that the reader accepts everything the Catholic Church believes and teaches. This book is not apologetics aimed at nonbelievers nor is it an attempt to rescue the faith of those who have serious doubts. However, anyone who thinks has many difficulties with respect to the Church's teaching, and I try to help resolve some of these difficulties.

Moreover, here and there notes are supplied to suggest how arguments based on common human experience can help prepare the way for the acceptance of the Church's teaching. These indications are intended, not as proofs in any strict sense, but as helps to understand what the Church believes and proposes for belief.

For the most part I proceed in this work in a constructive way, with minimal attention to positions inconsistent with received Catholic teaching. But sometimes alternative opinions which bear directly on the subject matter could not be ignored. Such opinions are expounded and evaluated critically, using as the standard the constant and very firm teaching of the Catholic Church.

My evaluation of much that has been published by Catholics writing in moral theory since Vatican II is negative. The Council called for a Christ-centered moral theology. Too much of what has been published in recent years, far from being centered upon Jesus, is vitiated by substantial compromises with secular humanism.

My criticism of various recent works ought not to be misunderstood as a judgment upon any person. It is one thing to criticize what someone says (or even does) and quite another to judge persons themselves. When one is convinced that what others are saying is erroneous or what they are doing is wrong one hopes they are sincere and that God, who reads hearts, will find their hearts pure or that, if he does not, will make them so.

Undoubtedly, this work itself includes errors. Vatican II's call for renewal is an overwhelming challenge. I hope no error here will be found contrary to faith and that none will seriously harm anyone. I ask that those who are more able call my attention to any error they find. In what I have written here, as in everything I write—everything I think—I submit gladly and wholeheartedly to the better judgment of the Catholic Church.

Some acknowledgments

This volume on Christian moral principles is only the first fruits of a larger project. In subsequent volumes I plan to take up the specific responsibilities of Christians and to clarify them in the light of these principles.

Three subsequent volumes are projected: the second on the responsibilities common to all Christians, the third on responsibilities proper to Christians in various specific roles and states of life, and the fourth on responsibilities of members of the Church as such toward one another. God willing, this project will be completed before the year 2000.

The antecedents of this project go back to 1968–69. The polemics which followed in the wake of *Humanae vitae* made it clear that classical moral theology could not adequately explain and defend the moral truth the Church teaches. Renewal along the lines called for by Vatican II clearly was urgent. My first plan was to construct a limited work, dealing with only a few questions in fundamental moral theology. Cardinal John Wright encouraged and supported that effort with a summer grant in 1971. However, my work that summer only made it clear that a more thorough systematic work was needed.

After several years, during which I hoped someone else would undertake the task, I outlined the present project in 1976–77, and articulated the conditions necessary to carry it out. These included an opportunity to teach moral theology in a Catholic seminary, a professorship with few other duties, and substantial funds for expenses.

I did not expect these conditions to be met. However, I presented the project to those whom I thought might support it—Cardinal Wright and a number of other bishops. Many responded favorably, foremost among them John B. McDowell, Auxiliary Bishop of Pittsburgh. He obtained the support of more than thirty other bishops for the project, as well as the backing of the Knights of Columbus and other Catholic organizations and individuals. The contributors established a Trust for Theological Studies.

Dr. Robert J. Wickenheiser, President of Mount Saint Mary's College, recognized this project as one way in which the College, which has served the Catholic Church in America for 175 years, can continue to fulfill its vocation as it completes its second century. With the approval of the College's Board of Directors, Dr. Wickenheiser established a new position, dedicated to the execution of this project and to similar work as long as the College exists. Thus the Trust for Theological Studies and Mount Saint Mary's College cooperated as the chief sponsors of this work.

Beginning in the fall of 1980, De Rance, Inc., also supported the project. (De Rance is a foundation whose President, Mr. Harry G. John, devotes all his time and effort to the prudent use of his wealth for the apostolate of the Catholic Church.) The De Rance support made possible the purchase of word-processing equipment, much of the help I received with the research and writing of the book, and its publication by the Franciscan Herald Press.

I thank all who contributed for their generosity and confidence in me. Many persons also supported this work with their prayers, some on a regular basis. I especially thank them for this support and hope they will continue and others join them in it.

Mount Saint Mary's College named my position *The Reverend Harry J. Flynn Chair in Christian Ethics*. Father Flynn returned to pastoral work in his home diocese after many years of devoted service in Mount Saint Mary's Seminary, including almost a decade as its distinguished rector. I am honored to work under the patronage of Father Flynn's name, and hope that this book will duly honor him.

With the help of . . .

The development of this volume owes much to the help of many persons—students, librarians, and fellow scholars who have offered criticism and suggestions on various points. But the nine persons whose names appear on the title page contributed more than anyone usually does to a project of research and writing not his or her own. Of course, while I have usually taken their advice, I have sometimes ignored it and frequently tried to improve on their suggestions. Hence, while this book could not have been written without my helpers, its remaining weaknesses and defects should not be blamed on them.

Joseph M. Boyle, Jr., and I have collaborated on various projects since 1970. Our previous work together taught me much. In the winter and spring of 1977 he helped work out the very first outline of this book. His analytical ability contributed greatly to the fuller outline we developed together in the summer of 1978; at that time, we brought nearly to its present form the ethical theory embodied in chapters seven through twelve. The first draft proved too complex; it needed major reconstruction. Boyle devoted most of the summer of 1980 to intensive work with me on this task. During the summer of 1982, he helped for two more months in a thorough revision of the theological heart of the volume—chapters nineteen through twenty-seven—and improvement of some parts of other chapters. Boyle's work contributed greatly to the logical tightness and clarity of the book. On a project less vast than the present one, his more than six months full time work would ground a just claim to coauthorship.

Jeannette Grisez, my wife, discussed many difficulties of content and presentation with me during the course of the work, and in doing so helped significantly with it. Measured in terms of time and labor, however, her greater contribution was the secretarial work, which she carried out single-handedly. Between December 1980 and August 1981 she learned the use of an electronic typing system and put the entire manuscript on electronic media; she then reworked much of the material six or seven times as rewriting and editing proceeded. Moreover, she did most of the work of duplicating each draft and coding the final manuscript for typesetting. Thus this volume owes much which will make it easier to use to Jeannette Grisez's skill, accuracy, and devoted labor in word processing.

Russell Shaw is a professional writer; he is Secretary for Public Affairs of the United States Catholic Conference—National Conference of Catholic Bishops. In the spring of 1981, he obtained a three-month leave-of-absence and devoted all his time and talent to the complete rewriting of the numbered paragraphs and the editing of the remainder of the manuscript. During 1981–82, Shaw did additional editorial work on the entire manuscript and composed the summaries. In the spring of 1983, he did still further editing and proposed the sentences to be set in boldface. Due to his effort, readers will find the book—especially the material on which students must concentrate their effort—much easier to use than it otherwise could have been.

During 1981-82, John Finnis, Robert G. Kennedy, Patrick Lee, and William E. May provided research assistance.

John Finnis checked every reference to and quotation from Denzinger and the documents of Vatican II, criticized the use of these materials, compared the English translations with the original Latin, and suggested amendments where necessary.

Robert Kennedy checked every reference to and quotation from Scripture, compared every New Testament reference with the Greek, and consulted reliable secondary sources where necessary. His work enhanced the book's accuracy in the use of Scripture and supplied many helpful references to the scholarly literature.

Patrick Lee suggested many specific references to the *Summa theologiae* and *Summa contra gentiles* of St. Thomas; incorporated in the book, these references bear witness to the debt this work owes to St. Thomas and will help introduce students to his thought.

William May made many suggestions for strengthening the manuscript in reference to contemporary Catholic theology; as a result of his help, the book draws on the strengths and criticizes the weaknesses of the works of other Catholic scholars far more effectively than it otherwise could have done.

The Rev. John A. Geinzer and the Rev. Basil Cole, O.P., both read and criticized the entire manuscript in two or three of its full drafts. Reflecting their pastoral sensitivity, their suggestions enhanced the relevance of the book to its primary audience. Each of them made hundreds of suggestions for the manuscript's improvement. Father Geinzer concentrated mainly on refinements of style and Father Cole on points of doctrinal precision. Almost every one of their comments led to some improvement.

For these helpers and all who have contributed in any way to this work, for those whose views are criticized in it, for all who will use it, and for myself, I pray: May the Lord bless us, protect us from all evil, and bring us to everlasting life. Amen.

Emmitsburg, Maryland
2 August 1983

PROLOGUE

Created by the eternal Father, redeemed by the Word made flesh, and offered the gift of their Holy Spirit, we human beings are related to the members of the divine family not only as creatures to creator but as persons to persons. We are called to share in the intimate life of this family, to join its members in an eternal wedding feast (see Mt 22.2; Rv 19.7–9), to know them in fulfilling union even as we are known by them (1 Cor 13.12; 1 Jn 3.2). Communion in heaven will include the enjoyment of divine life itself (Rv 21.6–7); the present gift of the Holy Spirit is, as it were, only the first payment from the inheritance promised us as God's children (see Eph 1.14).

We shall also enjoy fulfillment precisely as human persons. We are not souls only, but human, living bodies. Nor are we only intellects. We have intellects for knowing, but we also have wills for loving the goods we understand, senses for experiencing, emotions for feeling, and hands for making useful and beautiful things for human enjoyment and the praise of the Trinity. We shall give over to the Lord Jesus, our brother, the good fruits of our nature and our work done in the Spirit. In and through him we shall return to the Father all the gifts we have received (see Eph 1.10; 1 Cor 15.24).

Vatican II teaches: ". . . after we have obeyed the Lord, and in his Spirit nurtured on earth the values of human dignity, brotherhood and freedom, and indeed all the good fruits of our nature and enterprise, we will find them again, but freed of stain, burnished and transfigured. This will be so when Christ hands over to the Father a kingdom eternal and universal: 'a kingdom of truth and life, of holiness and grace, of justice, love and peace' [Preface of the Feast of Christ the King]. On this earth that kingdom is already present in mystery. When the Lord returns, it will be brought into full flower" (GS 39). The goods of the kingdom— truth, life, holiness, grace, justice, love, and peace—are divine blessings, but they are also fulfillments of aspects of what human beings can be. Insofar as they are good fruits of our nature and effort, they are created and redeemed; insofar as we who share in them share also in divine life, they are sanctified.

The kingdom will be brought to fulfillment only when the Lord comes. Without him we can do nothing (see Jn 15.5). But with him and with the grace of the Holy Spirit, we can and ought to contribute here and now to the building up of Christ in whose fullness we shall share in the kingdom (see LG 36). We can do this by respecting and defending the human goods of the kingdom insofar as they are

1

goods of our nature, and pursuing and promoting them insofar as they can be good fruits of our work. It is God's wish that our daily contribution to the building up of Christ, made in obedience to him and in the power of his Spirit, have eternal worth. Every morally good act of Christian living through the grace of the Spirit is therefore an act of cooperation in the work of the Trinity.

Here is a central and profound principle of Catholic life. The creative, salvific, and sanctifying love of the divine persons bears directly upon the goods proper to us as human persons; and our love for the divine persons, which is a gift of the Spirit (see Rom 5.5), also bears directly upon our own fulfillment and that of all humanity. As a man, the Lord Jesus has but one human heart to love his heavenly Father and his human fellows. Precisely because we are called to share in his divine life, we ought to strive to realize the fullness of human life in ourselves and others.

The rest of this book will be devoted to explicating this fundamental principle of a human life centered upon the Lord Jesus and embracing all things: "For all things are yours . . . and you are Christ's; and Christ is God's" (1 Cor 3.21, 23).

CHAPTER ONE

INTRODUCTION TO MORAL THEOLOGY AND TO THIS BOOK

Introduction

This chapter explains briefly what moral theology is, how it is related to faith, and how it is related to other theological disciplines. It also explains why renewal is needed in moral theology and how this book is intended to help in that work.[1]

Question A: What is theology?

1. **"Theology" in the most general sense means thought and talk about God. Theology is also about ourselves and everything else, considered in relation to God.** Philosophical theology (sometimes called "natural theology" or "theodicy") is distinct from sacred theology. The former proceeds by the light of reason, while the latter proceeds by the light of faith and uses reason only as a tool of faith (see *S.t.,* 1, q. 1, a. 1; a. 5, ad 2; a. 8, ad 2; *S.c.g.,* 1, 9).

2. Sometimes the word "theology" is used to refer to the systematic features of a scriptural author's appropriation (that is, personal reception) of divine revelation: We speak of the "theologies" of St. Paul, of St. John, and so on. It should not be supposed, however, that Scripture and our reflections on faith are theology in the same sense. Since it was essential to the completion of God's act of communication that revelation be personally received and made their own by persons whom God chose for that purpose, the Scriptures, together with sacred tradition, constitute the supreme rule of faith (see DV 21). We receive Christian faith only by understanding and using the books of the Bible as the Catholic Church understands and uses them in her teaching, liturgy, and life. Hence, the "theologies" in Scripture itself are normative—that is, they set the standard—for our reflections on faith.

The books of the New Testament in particular bear perpetual and divine witness to the effective communication accomplished by the revelation of God in the Lord Jesus (see DV 17). Inasmuch as these books were written by the apostles and their associates, they reflect apostolic belief and teaching, which contains the basic appropriation of the words and deeds of Jesus and the authorized witness to his resurrection (see DV 7–8, 18, 20; LG 18–19).

We cannot rightly read the books of the New Testament if we imagine that they contain mere interpretations of an ineffable "revelation." Revelation is communication, and the communication was not accomplished until what Jesus said and did was appropriated by the apostles under the inspiration of the Holy Spirit (cf. Jn 14.26; 15.26–27; 16.13).[2] Therefore, we have no more direct access to God's revelation in Jesus than the New Testament writings, understood and used as the Catholic Church understands and uses them in her teaching, liturgy, and life. It follows that, for our own thinking and speaking about matters of faith and morals, we ought to regard the various theologies of the New Testament as compatible, mutually complementary, and each a genuine constituent of the supreme rule of faith.

3. **In a narrower sense, "theology" refers to reflection upon the sources in which the truth of faith is articulated. Such theology is subordinate both to Scripture and to certain other documents which bear witness to the faith of the Church.** Among these latter, the documents of the general councils, such as Trent, Vatican I, and Vatican II, have a special place. The present work is theology in this narrower sense. It proceeds in the light of faith, with constant reference to Scripture and other authoritative expressions of the Church's faith.

4. "Interpretation" in a technical sense refers to the spontaneous appropriation of a communication; thus, the inspired writers are said to have interpreted God's message. In the ordinary sense, however, "interpretation" refers to systematic efforts to facilitate communication and overcome misunderstandings. This is where theology as we commonly understand it begins. **The theological interpreter tries to find and state the true and full meaning of texts of Scripture and other authoritative expressions of the Church's faith. This is the task of the part of theology called "positive theology."**

5. Although the study of Scripture is positive theology's most important work, other witnesses to faith must also be studied. This is so because sacred tradition is essential to the handing on of God's word, and the magisterium (living teaching office) of the Church has the unique role of proclaiming this word authoritatively to each generation (see DV 9–10). Moreover, all that the Church *is* belongs somehow to the tradition of revelation and so to faith (see DV 8). The positive theologian, therefore, studies not only documents, such as those containing the Church's teaching, but also the history of the Church, the lives of the saints, the liturgy, and so forth. The purpose is to help people hear and accept God's revelation in all its richness (see DV 23–24; OT 16).

A very important part of the work of positive Catholic theology is to locate the origin of the Church's beliefs in the books of sacred Scripture and in other witnesses, and trace their development up to the present. Part of this task is to show how doctrines defined by the Church, understood in the precise sense in which the Church understands them, already are in some way present in Scripture and tradition, and to show this without reading into these sources anything which cannot be found there (see DS 3886/2314).

6. The method of positive theology is primarily linguistic-literary and historical. A theoretical framework is necessary for this discipline, as for any scholarly study. For Catholic positive theology, however, this framework ought not to be a construct of theories from outside revelation but should be the theoretical framework provided by developed Catholic teaching. This teaching is not extrinsic to revelation, but rather transmits it intact (see DV 10).[3]

7. Besides positive theology, Catholic theology also includes systematic reflection. **Systematic theologians try to determine the relationships between truths of faith and other propositions which are not revealed but seem true.** The goal is fuller understanding of the truths of faith and their implications. A classic formula summing up the work of systematic theology is "faith seeking understanding" (see *S.c.g.*, 1, 8).

St. Cyril of Alexandria, commenting on John 6.70, beautifully expresses the common Christian conviction that faith is intellectually dynamic: ". . . knowledge comes after faith and not before it, according to what is written: 'If you have not believed, neither have you understood [Is 7.9 in the Septuagint].' When we have first within us a kind of basis for the augmentation of faith, then knowledge is built up little by little, and we are restored to the measure of stature in Christ and are made a perfect man and spiritual [cf. Eph 4.13]" (FEF 2111; cf. St. Augustine, FEF 1429, 1486, 1499, 1826). On this view, growth in understanding of what is of faith, which systematic theology attempts to promote, is not an optional extra for Christians, but an essential aspect of Christian life.

8. The following consideration helps to clarify the role and importance of systematic theology. God reveals himself in order to establish a personal relationship with us. Through this relationship he wishes to bring humankind, and indeed all things, into personal touch with himself: "to unite all things in him [Christ], things in heaven and things on earth" (Eph 1.10). This is a work of integration in which we are called to play a significant part. But to integrate realities, we must know and act upon the truth about them (see *S.t.*, 1, q. 1, a. 6). Truths of faith must be integrated with all other truths we can know. Systematic theology helps us do this and so helps us cooperate in the work of restoring all things to God through Christ.

Systematic theologians help the whole people of God to carry out this work of integration; they help especially at the boundary where revealed and nonrevealed truths meet. Here rational reflection upon nonrevealed truths extends to consider those truths which can be known by reason and which also pertain to revelation. The systematic theologian attempts to illuminate and guide rational reflection in order to inform it with the light of revelation, while attempting, in exchange, to borrow from reason enlightened by faith truths which will expand understanding of the truths of faith.

Question B: What is moral theology?

1. Systematic theology is divided into contemplative and moral. Contemplative theology was formerly called "dogmatic theology"; today it is often called simply "systematics." Contemplative systematic theologians try to work out a single, coherent view of reality in the light of faith. Some truths of faith can be known by reason, and contemplative theologians look for philosophical and other theories which seem to fit well with these. The theories are then used to round out the picture of reality provided by revelation itself.

2. To the extent it succeeds, contemplative systematic theology "does reach, by God's gift, some understanding of mysteries, and that a most fruitful one" (DS 3016/1796; translation supplied). But this understanding by no means lessens the need for faith. Rather, it makes it clear that intimacy with God is God's free gift,

whose fullness will wholly surpass human understanding. Thus, genuine contemplative theology leads from talk about God to the "theology" which is talk with God: to prayer.

3. Moral theology is another systematic theological discipline. **Like contemplative theology, it reflects upon the truths of faith, but it is less concerned to round out the Christian view of reality than to make clear how faith should shape Christian life, both the lives of individual Christians and the life of the Church.**

Pagans who have never heard the gospel preached but who strive to live good lives share in some way in the redemption God brings about in Christ (see DV 16). They live Christian lives without knowing it. Persons who have heard and consciously accepted the gospel are not necessarily better or holier persons than such unconscious Christians. Why, then, is moral theology important for us?

Its primary importance is this: Having received the gift of an explicit knowledge of the truth revealed by God in Christ, we have the privilege and responsibility of sharing in the redemptive work of Jesus. He has made us friends and coworkers in carrying out his redemptive work in ourselves and in communicating him to others. Moral theology helps us better to understand and so better to do the work of redeeming which our Lord Jesus has assigned to us.

4. Revelation and faith establish an intimate relationship between God and us. Contemplative theology tries to appreciate the given reality of this relationship; moral theology tries to clarify our part in the relationship, understood as a friendship which we must do our part to maintain and develop. Contemplative theology is mainly concerned with what God has done and promises to do; moral theology is mainly concerned with how we ought to respond and cooperate. In moral theology we study revelation to find its meaning for our lives; from faith we seek guidance for practical thinking, choices, and commitments.

Yet one should not too sharply distinguish contemplative from moral theology. The source of both is the one word of Christ, which dwells by faith in the hearts of believers. It is a dynamic word, with power to perfect both the inner self and the whole of one's life: "Let the word of Christ dwell in you richly, as you teach and admonish one another in all wisdom, and as you sing psalms and hymns and spiritual songs with thankfulness in your hearts to God. And whatever you do, in word or deed, do everything in the name of the Lord Jesus, giving thanks to God the Father through him" (Col 3.16–17). The revelation of God, the divine self-gift in the Lord Jesus, calls for thanks on our part. Thanks is expressed in two ways: praise and performance. By praise we acknowledge the generosity of God; by performance we give him in return for his gift all that we are, all that we have—our very lives (see Rom 12.1; Gal 5.13; 2 Tm 4.6–7; Heb 13.16; 1 Jn 3.16).

5. The most basic part of moral theology is the study of Christian moral principles. These, however, are not only the standards by which we distinguish right from wrong. The central mysteries of faith—the Trinity, the Incarnation, and our adoption as children of God—are also normative, as indeed the whole of revealed truth is. To say revelation is "normative" means that it has practical implications (see *S.t.*, 1, q. 1, a. 4). Invited by the Father, Son, and Spirit to intimate communion, we are to live lives worthy of this calling (see Eph 4.1); but the only style of life worthy of children of God is that exemplified by Jesus. In

clarifying this way of life, the study of Christian moral principles makes clear the practical relevance of the whole of Christian faith.

6. While the study of Christian moral principles comprises the basic part of moral theology, other parts draw out the implications of these principles. A complete moral theology deals with specific moral questions; it includes pastoral theology, a discipline concerned with the living of the Christian life not only by those to whom the pastor ministers but by the pastor himself; and it embraces spiritual theology, which studies the growth of Christian life to its proper perfection.

Moral theology cannot do its full job if it remains at the level of general principles. It also must show the relationship between divine revelation and Catholic teaching on particular issues, such as the morality of choosing one's profession, of paying taxes, of sexual activity, and so on.

Pastoral theology studies the implications of the other parts of theology for the work of the priestly life. Inasmuch as pastoral theology concerns the Christian life—the lives of the faithful and also the life of the priest himself—its principles are those of Christian morals. But pastoral theology is not related to the other disciplines of systematic theology as medicine is related to biology. Pastoral work is not a mere technique. Rather, it is a way of making Jesus present to teach, govern, and sanctify humankind today.

7. Moral theology must be distinguished from two other disciplines: philosophical ethics and canon law. All three of these disciplines have a practical bearing on Christian life. Philosophical ethics, however, proceeds by the light of reason; its concepts and arguments must be accessible to persons who have not heard (or do not accept) the gospel. When the results of philosophical ethics are used by moral theology, they must be evaluated and transformed by incorporation in the more adequate view of reality provided by the truth of faith.

8. Canon law studies the meaning and application of the regulations established by Church authorities to coordinate the common life of the Church's members. Hence, in themselves, the provisions of canon law are rules, not moral truths. Having been made by the Church, these rules can be changed by the Church; moreover, they have moral force for the Christian conscience only insofar as one understands the duty to obey those who enact them.

Question C: What is the role of the teaching of the Church in the method of moral theology?

1. Systematic theology as a whole should proceed by a method which can be called "dialectical."[4] Dialectical method explores from within the reality in which one lives—one tries to understand the meanings and relationships which comprise the expanding and unified framework of one's life.[5] **The use of dialectical method in Catholic theology means that, accepting the truth of Catholic faith present in the living Church of which one is a member, one seeks a better understanding of this truth in which one already lives.**

2. Dialectical method in theology neither calls into question the truth of faith nor attempts to prove it (cf. *S.t.*, 1, q. 1, a. 8; *S.c.g.*, 1, 9). There is no superior

standard by which to criticize or establish the word of God. Moreover, the Church is the living community of faith where God's word is received and handed on. To try to contact this word apart from the Church would be to try to step outside oneself—outside one's real world and history. This is impossible.[6] Because it is, Catholic theology must presuppose the truth of Catholic faith in the word of God.

As Vatican II teaches: "Sacred theology rests on the written word of God, together with sacred tradition, as its primary and perpetual foundation" (DV 24). Again: "The task of authentically interpreting the word of God, whether written or handed on, has been entrusted exclusively to the living teaching office of the Church, whose authority is exercised in the name of Jesus Christ" (DV 10). In mentioning the living teaching office (magisterium) of the Church here, Vatican II incorporates by reference the teaching of Pius XII in *Humani generis,* that theology must defer to the magisterium in interpreting the deposit of faith and that defined doctrines, *understood in the sense in which they have been defined by the Church,* should serve in theology as explanatory principles (see DS 3886/2314).

Of course, even if it be granted that theology ought to proceed from Scripture and tradition as the magisterium interprets them, important questions remain concerning the certainty and permanence of various elements of Catholic teaching. In other words, one can ask whether a particular point of teaching received and handed on in the Church really does belong to the truth of Catholic faith. These questions will be treated in chapters thirty-five and thirty-six. But it is worth noticing here that when Vatican II prescribes that future priests be taught theology "under the light of faith and with the guidance of the Church's teaching authority" (OT 16), the Council also refers to a section of *Humani generis* which includes the statement that "if the supreme pontiffs in their official documents purposely pass judgment on a matter debated until then, it is obvious to all that the matter, according to the mind and will of the same pontiffs, cannot be considered any longer a question open for discussion among theologians" (DS 3885/2313; translation supplied).[7]

3. Dialectical method equally resists any attempt to explain faith scientifically. Although theology can be called a "science" in the sense that it is a careful study which must be accurate about facts and logical in reasoning, it is not a science in the sense that this word connotes comprehension, detachment from a subject matter, and control over it (see *S.c.g.*, 1, 6). Theology tries to understand God's intimate personal relationship with his people. This relationship is not subordinate to anything larger and more important in our experience; it is a mystery in which we share and, as such, is to be accepted and lived, not just analyzed and explained. Nor can it be mastered, made subject to our control.[8]

4. Today, as often in the past, methods which have shown their power in other disciplines are employed in theology. While theologians can make good use of scientific and other methods as tools for limited purposes, difficulties can arise from the uncritical application to theology of methods developed in other fields. A method suited to another subject matter may not be particularly suited to the investigation of faith. There is a danger that the rich and mysterious reality of which Christian life is part will be reduced to some human way of seeing things.

The method which seems appropriate in systematic theology is that of disciplined meditation and discussion, by which one clarifies various relationships among truths of faith and between them and other propositions, develops new concepts and propositions, and achieves a gradually growing understanding of the mysteries of faith and of other things in the light of faith. This method is called "dialectic," but since there are many conceptions of dialectical method, it is necessary to clarify what is meant by this way of doing theology.

Anyone who has studied some of Plato's dialogues will understand what dialectic is. Plato always tries to formulate clear questions and to distinguish the meanings of linguistic expressions. The devices of logic are used to determine whether propositions are compatible or incompatible, to find which propositions imply which other ones, and thus to clarify what is involved in holding a certain position.

In such dialectics, one finds reasoning similar to that required by various models of scientific inquiry. For example, sometimes the properties of something are shown to follow from what it essentially is, as in Aristotelian science; sometimes conclusions are proved from more certain principles, as in a rationalist science; and sometimes hypotheses are developed to account for a certain range of data, as in a modern empirical science. What is peculiar about the dialectical method as Plato uses it is that none of the models of science organizes inquiry as a whole. Each scientific model's characteristic way of proceeding is employed where it seems helpful, but no attempt is made to organize all reflection according to a single model.

Dialectical method proceeds by considering propositions in one another's light. This method of meditation and discussion can lead to some understanding of truths of faith by a comparison of true propositions of faith with other true propositions. But in proclaiming the gospel, the Church also must safeguard the faith by rejecting false propositions incompatible with it (see 2 Tm 4.1–5; 2 Pt 2.1–9; Jude 3–4).

Vatican I teaches that the possibility of disagreement between faith and any other source of knowledge is excluded in principle (cf. *S.t.*, 1, q. 1, a. 8, c.). God cannot be inconsistent, and all knowledge ultimately comes from him either by revelation or by the natural light of reason. Of course, apparent contradictions do crop up. But ". . . the chief source of this merely apparent contradiction lies in the fact that dogmas of faith have not been understood and explained according to the mind of the Church or that contrivances of opinion are taken as deliverances of reason" (DS 3017/1797; translation supplied).

The Church has the mission of proclaiming the gospel, the source of all saving truth and moral teaching (see DS 1501/783; DV 7). To carry out her mission, the Church must safeguard the faith by rejecting false claims to knowledge, so that no one will be misled by faulty theories and sophistical arguments. It follows that Catholic theologians and ". . . all faithful Christians are forbidden to defend as legitimate conclusions of science such opinions that are known to be opposed to the doctrine of faith, especially if they have been censured by the Church; rather, they are absolutely bound to regard them as errors that have taken on the false appearance of truth" (DS 3018/1798; translation supplied). The phrase "doctrine of faith" used here must not be limited to truths solemnly defined. It also includes at least those truths of faith and morals proposed by the ordinary and universal magisterium of the Church as truths to be held definitively, whether as truths divinely revealed or as truths essential to guard as inviolable and faithfully unfold the deposit of divine revelation (see DS 3011/1792; LG 25).[9]

Thus it is characteristic of Catholic theologians to think with the Church, to conform their judgments to the doctrine of faith, and to treat as erroneous every opinion which the Church condemns as such. St. Vincent of Lerins accurately describes the ideal of the theologian: "He is a true and genuine Catholic who loves the truth of God, the Church, and the Body of Christ; who puts nothing else before divine religion and the Catholic Faith, neither the authority nor the love nor the genius nor the eloquence nor the philosophy of any man whatsoever, but, despising all that and being fixed, stable, and persevering in his faith, is determined in himself to hold and believe that only which he knows the Catholic Church has held universally and from ancient times" (FEF 2172).

5. Before one makes a judgment of conscience, one must have factual knowledge of the possibilities open to choice, including the circumstances and likely consequences of carrying out each of them. Moreover, one must proceed logically from basic principles, and these principles come to be understood by children only as they learn about and spontaneously act for human goods. Nevertheless, the judgment of conscience, which characterizes each possible choice as right or wrong, cannot be deduced from facts and logic. How things are cannot finally determine how one ought to live. Moral principles and judgments neither can be established nor overturned by experience or the sciences. Whenever it is argued that some finding of contemporary science undercuts a Christian moral norm, critical examination will show that the argument depends on at least one nonscientific assumption at odds with Christian faith.

For this reason, it is a mistake to think that the Church's rejection of the proposals of a new morality can lead to an embarrassment similar to that which followed from the rejection on their own level of the factual observations included in Galileo's research. Facts can no more show the Church's moral teaching false than they can prove it true. The situation in this matter is strictly parallel to a matter of faith such as the bodily presence of Jesus in the Eucharist: Chemical tests cannot show him present, nor can the results of such tests disprove what faith teaches.

Nevertheless, the moral teaching of the Church and the data of the experience of Christian life—such as the lives of the saints—are mutually illuminating. Likewise, the concrete moral judgments the faithful make are relevant to the reflective work of Catholic moral theology.

Every moral theory, philosophical or theological, reflects upon the moral experience and judgments of a certain community.[10] To the extent that the theory fits the data, the latter are used to testify to the theory's realism and practicability. To the extent that the theory must reject moral judgments commonly made in the community, reasons are given to explain why false moral judgments are made. A moral theorist can disagree with the moral judgments made in his or her own community provided the theory belongs to a view of reality which allows the theorist to transcend the limits of this particular community.

For example, many secular humanists reject racial discrimination. A poll might show that the sense of the community favors racial discrimination in certain instances. The secular humanist who engages in ethical theory does not accept the sense of the community as determinative. Instead, witnesses who favor discrimination are disqualified—as insufficiently informed, say, or as narrow-minded and short-sighted.

In a similar way, Catholic moral theology finds the experience of Christian life and the judgments of the faithful illuminating, but does not allow such data to override the Church's moral teaching. Catholic moral theologians are helped to keep their balance by bearing in mind that the community to which Catholic moral theology is relevant is not merely the present membership of the Church in affluent societies, but the whole People of God, from Abraham to the last man, from Calcutta to Amsterdam, Cracow, New York, Peking, and Rome.

6. Therefore, a sound method in moral theology will not allow the moral experiences and judgments of some of the contemporary faithful to override the constant and very firm moral teaching of the Church. Instead the moral theolo-

gian must go back to the principles of Christian morality—ultimately to the fundamental truths of faith—to find resources for explaining modern experience and criticizing dissenting opinions. In doing so, the Catholic moralist will proceed very much as does the secular, philosophical moralist who, for example, does not allow the fact of racial prejudice to settle its morality. Rather, the secular moralist uses a world view which goes beyond facts and science to criticize such prejudice, no matter how widespread, and to explain why it exists although it is wrong.

7. Since divine revelation does not just convey a set of theoretical truths but establishes a personal relationship, the one gospel is "the source of all saving truth and moral teaching" (DS 1501/783; DV 7). One is called not only to hear God's word but to adhere to it, to do God's will by putting our Lord's teaching into practice (see Mt 7.15–17; Jas 1.23–25; 2.14–26). It follows that the teaching authority of the Church, with the gift of infallibly identifying what God reveals, extends to matters of morals as well as faith (cf. Mt 16.19; 28.20; 1 Jn 3.18; DS 3007/1788, 3032/1811, 3074/1839; LG 25). A sound Catholic moral theology will therefore adhere to the authoritative moral teaching of the Church.

Someone might object that the answer to this question disregards the present pluralism in Catholic moral theology, a pluralism both of methodology and of positions on specific moral issues.[11] It will be pointed out that the absolute solidarity of opinion which existed in Catholic moral theology prior to Vatican II no longer obtains, and one must come to terms with this new situation.

As question D will show, I fully recognize the limitations of the older moral theology, which all the newer approaches, including the present work, seek to overcome. Moreover, theological pluralism compatible with the unity of faith in God's word articulated in the common doctrine of the Church is both inevitable and accepted by the Holy See itself (see appendix 2). In Catholic moral theology, there is room even for a diversity of positions inconsistent with one another on questions about which the Church as such has reached no definite judgment.[12]

However, not all opinions expressed in recent years by Catholics in moral theology can be accepted uncritically as justified and responsible positions. Some writers maintain that there is no specifically Christian ethics, and on this basis more or less limit the role of the Church's teaching authority in the moral field.[13] The following chapters, especially twenty-three through twenty-seven, show that there is a specifically Christian morality and a place in the tradition of faith for concrete moral teaching. Some writers accept as legitimate various theological opinions inconsistent with the constant and universal teaching of the Church.[14] Chapters thirty-five and thirty-six will mark out the narrow limits of responsible dissent and criticize attempts to justify radical dissent.

Most dissenting theologians have adopted the method of proportionalism.[15] Proportionalism is not a method of systematic theology as such, but a method of defending specific moral judgments—for example, that in a difficult case it is right to do something otherwise wrong because in the actual situation it is the lesser evil. Proportionalism is advocated by some nonbelieving moral philosophers as well as by some moral theologians. As chapter six will show, this method can be criticized decisively on purely rational grounds.

11

Question D: Why is renewal in moral theology necessary?

1. Several factors tended to limit the effectiveness of Catholic theology after the Council of Trent.[16] These included contention among rival theological schools, concentration on controversies with Protestants, and the simplification of theology resulting from efforts to adapt it to the seminary program. The most important factor, however, was the fact that philosophy in the seventeenth century was heavily influenced by the ideals of science and mathematics. A rationalistic method developed, emphasizing clarity of concepts, certainty of principles, and the quasi-mathematical proof of conclusions. Though unsuited to systematic theology, this rationalistic method was widely adopted by theologians. Efforts to understand faith often were set aside, their place taken by efforts to reduce faith to as few principles as possible and defend these effectively.

2. Trent's program of reform had the good result of fostering better discipline of the sacraments, especially penance. Yet this encouraged a tendency to limit the study of moral theology to what priests need to know to hear confessions— especially what is and is not mortal sin, and how to resolve doubts of conscience. Rationalistic method meanwhile tended toward the codification of norms. The basic part of moral theology came sometimes to amount to little more than a study of the general notions needed to understand and work with this code.

3. Thus the effort to understand the living of Christian life in the light of the fundamental truths of faith was almost wholly abandoned by moral theologians. Moral and dogmatic theology were divorced, and Jesus ceased to play a significant role in moral theology. Moral theologians more and more ignored Scripture and other sources for systematic theological reflection, or else invoked them only to show that a certain kind of act violates the Christian code.

4. The moral theology which developed after Trent and persisted until Vatican II is here referred to as "classical moral theology." Among the characteristics arising from its attempt to codify Christian morality, two of particular note are rationalism and legalism.[17]

5. Rationalism (see appendix 4) affected classical moral theology's understanding of the objectivity of moral norms. On this view, essential and unchanging human nature is the standard of human goodness. This nature is open to rational observation; good acts conform to it, while bad acts do not. Judgments of fitness are, however, purely speculative, whereas the practical judgment that a certain act is morally licit or illicit requires a further principle: a divine command that human persons do good acts and avoid evil ones.

6. In thus tracing the practical force of moral obligation back to God as lawmaker, classical moral theology tended toward voluntarism. Voluntarism in general is a theory which assigns primacy to the will over reason. Classical moral theology assigned primacy in the genesis of moral obligation to God's will, although it left a subordinate place for human reason. **This limited voluntarism, together with the isolation of moral from dogmatic theology, led classical moralists to pay less and less attention to intrinsic reasons for accepting Christian moral norms as true. Instead, they increasingly tended to treat moral norms as laws which members of the Church must obey because the**

Church insists upon them with divine authority. By keeping these rules one would merit heaven; by violating them one would deserve eternal punishment in hell. In this perspective, an understanding of the intrinsic connection between Christian life in this world and eternal life was far less important than a firm conviction that the disobedience of mortal sin must be avoided.

7. Legalism emphasizes the regulation of behavior. The legalist tends to think of moral norms as if they were merely a body of rules binding members of a society to commonly accepted standards. Today some dismiss as "legalism" several positions characteristic of Christian morality itself—for example, that one may not do evil to achieve good and that even one unrepented mortal sin separates a sinner from God forever. But classical moral theology was legalistic in a more genuine sense; it can be found wanting even by those who accept all the positions characteristic of Christian morality.

8. First, classical moral theology focused on the detailed specification of duties, while ceasing to clarify the meaning of good and bad in terms of the total Christian vocation. Second, it became minimalistic, emphasizing the minimum required to avoid mortal sin. The basic categories of classical moral theology were not the good and the bad, but the permitted and the forbidden. Third, it tended to suggest that what is not forbidden is thereby permitted, in the sense that one is free to do as one pleases in regard to it; thus it tended to ignore the responsibilities of personal vocation. Fourth, classical moral theology tended to liken moral truths to Church laws. The clarification of moral truth in the light of faith was neglected in favor of procedures more like those used in developing a body of law: The opinions of moral theologians were regarded as if they were decisions of lower courts, and the judgment of the Church's magisterium as if it were the decision of a supreme court. The results are now apparent in the suggestion that the Church might or should change its moral teaching, as if it were changeable law rather than unchangeable truth.

9. Legalism often causes the faithful to view the Church's moral teaching as an imposition. The suspicion grows that the Christian life itself is a kind of arbitrary test for which different rules could well be devised if only the test maker chose. In these circumstances, the desire increases to do as one pleases as much as one can. Thus, while setting stringent requirements concerning a few matters, classical moral theology offers little or no helpful guidance for much of Christian life. The temptation to rebel against received teaching is nourished by its seeming arbitrariness, as well as by interests cultivated without reference to Christian faith.[18]

Question E: What does Vatican II say about renewal in moral theology?

1. For a century and more before Vatican II the unsatisfactoriness of classical moral theology was increasingly recognized.[19] There were many criticisms and suggestions for renewal, some extreme but most of them sound and convergent. The Council accepts these sound suggestions and clearly calls for a development which will overcome the limitations and inadequacies of classical moral theology.

2. Vatican II calls for renewal in theology generally. It should be taught "under the light of faith and under the guidance of the Church's teaching authority" (OT 16; translation supplied). Students should learn to draw Catholic doctrine from divine revelation, to understand this doctrine deeply, to nourish their spiritual lives with it, and to teach it to the faithful and proclaim it to the world.

3. Dogmatic theology should start from Scripture. Then it should examine the tradition of doctrine, its history and development. Speculation under the guidance of St. Thomas Aquinas will help students understand the mysteries of faith. Synthesis is important: Students should learn how the mysteries are interconnected and how they are present and active not only in doctrinal expressions but in the liturgy and the whole life of the Church. Vatican II builds a bridge between dogmatic and moral theology by saying that even in dogma students should learn to bring eternal truths to bear upon the human condition: "Let them learn to search for solutions to human problems with the light of revelation" (OT 16).

4. The Council also prescribes renewal for other theological disciplines, especially moral theology.[20] This renewal requires "livelier contact with the mystery of Christ and the history of salvation." Moral theology "should be more thoroughly nourished by scriptural teaching." **In this renewal of moral theology, two things call for equal attention: the nobility of the calling of Christians and "their obligation to bring forth fruit in charity for the life of the world" (OT 16). Christian life should be both other-worldly and this-worldly at the same time** (see LG 48; GS 22, 38–39). **The moral theology for which Vatican II calls must show how such a life can be lived.**

In providing guidance for the implementation of this decree of Vatican II, the Holy See stresses that moral theology must include the dynamic aspect of Christian life. In other words, it is not enough to indicate what is expected of a Christian; moral theology also must consider how Christians can do what is expected. The unfolding of individual vocation and the principles for fully developing the image of God which is perfectly realized in Jesus are included in its concern.[21]

The Holy See recognizes that at present any systematic work in theology involves serious difficulty. Still, the ideal of "unity and synthesis, although it seems difficult, should interest both professors and students." It is vital for the fruitfulness of theological studies. It includes synthesis of doctrines, of levels of theology (positive and systematic), and of disciplines and spiritual formation with the preparation for pastoral work and priestly life as a whole.[22]

Question F: What are the shortcomings of current efforts in moral theology?

1. Most Catholic moral theologians would agree in general with the criticisms of classical moral theology outlined above. Yet many faithful Catholic moralists, finding no better framework, continue to use this unsatisfactory one. Since Vatican II, many others have set aside the purposes and methods of classical moral theology. Few of them, however, really begin to meet the Council's prescription for renewal.

2. Some claim that the resolution of moral issues is a work of human wisdom which can proceed without reference to faith.[23] For them, the normative part of

moral theology is simply ethics. Thus much recent work in moral theology is neither centered on Christ, nor tied to other central truths of faith, nor nourished by Scripture, nor oriented toward the heavenly calling of Christians.[24]

3. This work can be called "theology" only because those who do it hold positions as theologians and pay particular attention to the Church's teaching. They invoke its support when they agree with it, while criticizing it and urging the faithful to ignore it when they disagree.

4. The renewal for which Vatican II calls began even before the Council. Some who then participated in the work of renewal still seek to emphasize Christ, scriptural themes, and some other theological dimensions which most current moral theology ignores. But not even these theologians succeed in clarifying the relationship between the theological dimensions they discuss and the special subject matter of moral theology—namely, human acts, their norms, and the shaping of Christian life to its heavenly-and-earthly end. In many cases their conclusions on specific issues are the same as those of theologians who frankly engage in moral reflection without reference to faith.[25]

5. Many recent works in moral theology emphasize the importance of human fulfillment and the well-being of society. This is in line with Vatican II's emphasis on the obligation of Christians "to bring forth fruit in charity for the life of the world" (OT 16). As it finds expression in these theological works, however, this emphasis is often flawed by the influence of secular humanism.[26] Under Marxist influence, for example, certain liberation theologians have developed a rationale for revolutionary violence, although such violence is hard to reconcile with the gospel.[27] In wealthy, liberal societies like the United States and West Germany, some theologians dissent from the Church's teaching and opt for solutions to personal and social problems involving sexuality and killing which were first proposed by nonbelieving thinkers.

6. One reason for this state of affairs lies in the fact that most contemporary moral theologians were trained in classical moral theology and retain its legalistic orientation. They assume that what is not absolutely and certainly forbidden must be permitted and that the faithful are free to do as they please in its regard. Much effort is spent trying to lessen the obligations of Christian life—for example, attempting to show that certain kinds of acts cannot be proved to be always wrong. Doing as one pleases is then called "following one's conscience."

7. Insofar as the requirement to assent to Catholic teaching is denied, the minimum set by the new moral theology is much lower than that set by classical moral theology. **But the new remains as legalistic as the old.[28] It provides no account in Christian terms of why one should seek human fulfillment in this life, what the specifically Christian way of life is, and how living as a Christian in this life is intrinsically related to fulfillment in everlasting life.**

8. Beginning in the Old Testament and persisting throughout the Christian tradition is a sense of the ultimate seriousness of moral choices (see Gn 3; Jn 1.11–12; 3.17–21; Rv 22.10–11). One can freely choose life or death, and can do so in each choice one makes (see Dt 30.19; Sir 15.11–20; 1 Jn 1.6–10). This Christian moral seriousness is eliminated or greatly reduced by the new moral theology in

its movement toward secular humanism. Some say everyone will go to heaven, without reference to the choices they make; others say one can have a fundamentally right orientation despite particular evil choices; still others, despite Christian hope's specifically other-worldly orientation, simply ignore the question of a life beyond this one.

Question G: What fundamental problem underlies the unsatisfactory development of moral theology?

1. The unsatisfactory character and results of both classical moral theology and the new moral theology point to real problems. The theologians of both groups have been essentially intelligent and decent people who wished to serve the faith. There must therefore be an underlying reason or reasons why nothing approximating the moral theology envisaged by Vatican II was achieved in the past or is now being achieved.

2. It is suggested—and the suggestion will be elaborated in this volume as a whole—that the underlying difficulty is as follows. Jesus is both human and divine, and so, too, is his entire life. In him the human and divine are distinct but inseparable, dynamically integrated but not commingled (that is, mixed with one another). The early Church experienced many difficulties and deviations before this central truth about Jesus and his life was clarified and accepted by all faithful Christians. This truth does not pertain only to Jesus, however. The Christian is to be like Jesus, with both a human nature and an adoptive share in divinity—with a life fully human but also truly divine. **Difficulties analogous to those in Christology appear to have blocked an accurate understanding of the complex make up of the Christian and to have led to many mistakes concerning the structure of Christian life. In short, the underlying difficulty in moral theology has been an inadequate understanding of how Christian life must and can be at the same time completely human and divine** (see GS 22, 43, 45, 92).

3. The Fathers of the Church, especially St. Augustine, gave an account of Christian life which stressed the supernatural and other-worldly but hardly did justice to the human and this-worldly (see 34-A). Medieval thought, even that of St. Thomas Aquinas, failed to resolve the problem.[29] At the time of the Renaissance and Reformation many accepted a false dichotomy. Some opted for a humanism which evolved during the centuries of the modern era into rejection of faith and the supernatural. Others opted for a fideistic supernaturalism which regarded human nature as the corrupt vessel of Christian life rather than an essential part of it. During the last century and one-half, the second option, that of Protestantism of the Reformation, has been more and more widely abandoned, while secular humanism has become dominant. Although the Catholic Church has never accepted this dichotomy and some contemporary Protestants also reject it, the underlying problem has not yet been resolved.

4. Vatican I pointed to a solution in its definitive teaching that reason and faith are not mutually exclusive (see DS 3015–20/1795–1800). Vatican II sketched the

solution without working it out in detail. To make room for divine life, Christians need not set aside anything of their human lives; and to live fully human lives, they cannot aim at anything less than lives of the highest holiness (see LG 39–41; GS 1, 11, 21, 22, 32, 34, 92; AA 7). The call to intimacy with God who definitively reveals himself in Jesus is also a call to protect and promote the flourishing of human persons and societies in the goods which fulfill human nature (see GS 34–35).

5. Without anticipating later chapters, it is possible even at this point to glimpse the underlying reason for the inadequacy of both the classical and the new moral theologies. Classical moral theology remained too other-worldly. Its tendency to commingle the human and the divine caused it to confuse the human good of religion, which is only one human good among others, with the superhuman, adoptive divine life of the Christian. The new moral theology also usually involves commingling; for example, it generally reduces charity to human good will or good deeds. But it also is too this-worldly. Attending insufficiently to the transitory character of this present life, it dispenses in practice with Christian hope for the total re-creation—the new heavens and the new earth—by which alone God will finally overcome evil (see Rv 21.1–4; GS 39).

If there really is no necessary conflict between the divine and human aspects of Christian life, still many people think they perceive some incompatibility here. How does this illusion arise? There are two factors.

First, sin diminishes human nature and makes it seem incompatible with one's sharing in the divine nature (see GS 37). The remedy is to make humanity whole, and Catholic faith teaches that men and women who accept the gift of the Spirit can overcome sin and grow in holiness in this life (see GS 38). By the redemptive work of Jesus, God preserved the Virgin Mary from all sin; by the same redemptive work, he calls every human person to holiness (see LG 48 and 59–65). A good human life in which much effort must be spent in overcoming sin is quite different from what a good human life would be if there were no sin to overcome. But a human life spent in overcoming sin is devoted to the good fruits of human nature and effort; like the life of Jesus, such a life is not less but more fully and perfectly human than a life based on a refusal to acknowledge and fight against sin.

Second, the illusion of inevitable conflict between the divine and human aspects of Christian life arises from the mistake of supposing that the expressions used about God in the language of faith can have the same meaning they would have in other contexts. If one makes this mistake, the divine and human aspects of Christian life are imagined to be on the same level. Then not only sin but even human good itself would have to diminish in order that grace might abound. The Catholic Church teaches the opposite: The call to intimacy with God who reveals himself in a definitive way in the man, Jesus, is also a call to protect and promote the flourishing of human persons and societies in the goods which enrich human nature as such (see GS 34–35).

For precisely this reason, the Catholic Church has insisted—especially during the past century—upon moral teaching which belongs both to natural and to gospel law. The social teaching of the Church insists upon principles demanded both by human fairness and by Christian mercy. The Church's teaching on other subjects, such as marital morality, equally insists upon principles demanded both by the nature of human persons and their acts, and by the eternal destiny to which each human person is called (see GS 51).

Question H: How can a treatise on
Christian moral principles provide a basis
for the needed renewal in moral theology?

1. **An adequate treatise in Christian moral principles needs to clarify what a Christian is and show how Christian life can be at one and the same time both fully human and fully divine. It must explain the dynamic unity of the human and divine aspects of Christian life without mixing the two.** To clarify the life of the Christian, it must clarify the life of Jesus and show how the Christian is united with him. Chapters nineteen to twenty-six and thirty-four of this volume are especially concerned with these matters.

2. Such a treatise needs to explain how human goods determine Christian moral norms. It should show why a life in accord with Christian norms is, in this fallen world, the only life which is really humanly good. Moreover, the contribution of human goods and acts to heavenly fulfillment in the Lord Jesus must be explained. These matters are dealt with here, mainly in chapters five to ten, twenty to twenty-seven, and thirty-four.

3. An adequate treatise also needs to make clear how one can organize and live one's Christian life. While taking realistic account of the fallen human condition and working toward a final resolution in the world to come, Christian life as it is lived in this world must be inherently meaningful and humanly fulfilling. The plan of such a life is described in chapters twenty-eight to thirty-four.

4. The treatise needs a forward-looking perspective. Its primary orientation should be toward preaching, teaching, and counseling, to assist the faithful in living full and rich lives in Jesus. However, it must also provide an adequate basis for studies which will help priests be sound and sensitive confessors. The primary orientation of the present treatise is forward-looking; but such topics as conscience, the principles of right and wrong, and sin are treated, especially in chapters three, eight to eighteen, and twenty-six to twenty-eight.

5. Finally, an adequate treatise on Christian moral principles must explain the authority of the Church's teaching and show the implications of dissent from this teaching. These matters are treated in chapters twenty-three, thirty-five and thirty-six.

The reader of this work should keep in mind that the mysteries of faith are treated here from a moral-theological point of view—that is, from the point of view of human acts. Thus, the treatment of the redemptive work of Jesus, the functioning of the Church, the Christian life itself, the sacraments, and so on, will focus on the human acts involved— those of Jesus and of human persons. This emphasis by no means conflicts with the truth that everything good is the work of God (see Jas 1.17). But the point of view of even an adequate theology of Christian moral principles is limited, and the truth of faith must not be reduced to the limits of this perspective.

Question I: What difficulties can be expected by those
who study moral theology with this book?

1. The study of Christian moral principles makes demands on students as great as those made by any serious theological study. **One ought to proceed with**

personal obedience of faith; one must submit one's experience, insights, and wishes to the judgment of the Church's teaching, prepared to reform oneself according to the mind of Christ (see Jn 12.44–50; Rom 12.2; Gal 2.2). This thorough intellectual conversion is not easy, and one will often be tempted to evade it.

2. It is also necessary to safeguard scholarly integrity in theological reflection. Difficulties should not be ignored or set aside. The elements of each difficulty must be examined patiently, in the confidence that a solution will eventually be forthcoming—if not to oneself, then to someone else—without compromising either fidelity to the Church's teaching or intellectual honesty.

Catholic theologians should take up difficulties which arise and should pursue truth with the full power of their scholarly discipline, wherever that pursuit might lead. The question is: How can one function as a scholar without calling into question any truth of the Catholic faith?

The answer is that neither theology nor any other field of scholarship bearing upon faith deals in obvious matters of fact or in simple self-evident truths such as those of logic. Catholic scholars deal in historical probabilities which can be argued, in interpretations which are never absolutely certain, in theoretical constructions which are only more or less plausible. Therefore, scholarly conclusions never absolutely compel assent. If a conclusion appears to be incompatible with a truth of faith, one asks: Is this conclusion as certain as it seems to be? Is the result really incompatible with faith, or does it only seem to be so because of lack of understanding? Is one's personal understanding of faith really an accurate grasp of the faith of the Church?

Nothing of intellectual rigor need be sacrificed in answering these questions, nor need one in the least doubt the truth of faith. Every apparent conflict is somehow soluble, although solutions do not always come easily (see *S.t.*, 1, q. 1, a. 8; *S.c.g.*, 1, 9). The human mind has in reserve a great capacity for withholding assent. If one has faith, one draws on this capacity to gain time for seemingly insoluble problems to be solved. In this way, not by hasty revisions, real progress is made in understanding faith.

3. Any work in moral theology presents three further difficulties. First, moral theology has a normative orientation; it is concerned not with what is but with what ought to be. This makes it more abstract and thus more difficult than most other subjects, such as history or psychology, which also study human action but do so descriptively or theoretically. Second, in bringing faith to bear upon the life of the person who studies it, moral theology challenges one to live according to one's expressed convictions (see Mt 7.21–23; 23.2–3). Third, many today regard calling upon others to face up to their infidelity to the gospel as the most frightening duty of priestly ministry (see Jer 20.7–18; 2 Tm 4.1–2). The study of moral theology focuses ineluctably on this duty.

The moral methodology articulated in this book is likely to seem very complex Students will wish that a simpler "system" might be used for moral-theological reflection. Unfortunately, the complexity is unavoidable. The situation here is somewhat like that in medicine. There was a time when a physician could learn what was needed rather easily; the practice of medicine was not so complicated. Today, a competent physician must be able to practice in accord with contemporary knowledge of bodily functions, diseases, drugs, and so on.

However, the situation is not so difficult as the analogy suggests. Moral theology articulates faith. The complexity of the methodology is not greater than the richness of faith, upon which one ought constantly to meditate. The present theological reflection is more complicated than the older moral theology mainly because it interprets systematically a wider range of the data of faith, making explicit many connections which formerly were left implicit.

One ought not to be impatient with this explication, which makes for complexity. In part, it is needed today for more effective pastoral work. One can see this to be so, for example, in the obvious unsatisfactoriness of merely insisting on the Church's moral teaching as a set of norms to be obeyed, when it is possible to make their intrinsic sense clearer in the light of fundamental truths of faith.

4. To make good use of this book students will have to possess or acquire the ability to do certain things: to study regularly and effectively, to dialogue with opposing points of view, to face and resolve personal resistances, and to integrate theological reflection into a life of prayer which, for seminarians, is also in a formative stage. They are not likely to meet these challenges unless they dedicate themselves to the well-being of those who will be their spiritual children. To be good students, seminarians must care above all about helping people grow in Jesus toward fulfillment both as human beings and adopted children of God.

Prayer, both personal and liturgical, is essential for one who undertakes theological reflection. The Holy See points out: "Since theology has for its object truths which are principles of life and personal commitment, both for the individual and the community of which he is part, it has a spiritual dimension and, therefore, the theologian cannot be purely intellectual in his research and study, but must always follow the requirements of faith, always deepening his existential union with God and his lively participation in the Church."[30] The Council similarly teaches that seminarians must live the mystery of Christ and of human salvation which they will find present in the liturgy (see AG 16).

The fundamental reason why prayer is needed is that theology reflects on revelation, and revelation is not merely a collection of words, not even merely a collection of statements expressing propositional truths. Rather, revelation is personal communication. The realities and not merely the words which pertain to this communication are made present to us in the Church. The divine communication passed down from the apostles and received by us grows in us: "This happens through the contemplation and study made by believers, who treasure these things in their hearts (cf. Lk 2.19, 51), through the intimate understanding they experience of spiritual things, and through the preaching of those who have received through episcopal succession the sure gift of truth" (DV 8; translation supplied).[31] Theology without prayer is cut off from its real subject of study: God. Theology without prayer turns him into an object, and it turns our personal relationship with him into an interesting, magnificent, but ultimately unreal idea.

Theology only leads to growth in understanding when one who undertakes it attends with full openness to the presence of Jesus in the Church: to his presence in the word of God and especially in the liturgy, to his presence in the successors of the apostles teaching in his name, and to his presence in those for whose service through pastoral activity or other work the study of theology is undertaken.

In the liturgy one experiences bodily and sensible aspects of God's revelation in the Lord Jesus which are not captured—which cannot be captured—in propositions or expressed in language. Moreover, liturgical prayer, because it is communal and public, eliminates the merely subjective and private biases of one who undertakes theological reflection. The Liturgy of the Hours, for example, often does not fit one's individual mood and disposition;

for this very reason, such prayer is invaluable to keep one thinking with the Church at large about God and humankind's friendship with him.

Private prayer also is essential. One can assent to all the truths of faith and wish to hold them firmly, just as the Church believes and teaches them, yet not have a lively sense of the reality grasped in these truths. If one lacks a lively sense of the reality, one also will have an inadequate sense of the importance of each particular truth. One who engages in theological reflection must focus on parts of the truth of faith, one by one, and sometimes must study some single point with great intensity. Only by private prayer can one engaged in theological reflection keep a vivid sense of the importance of every other article of faith, and remain resolved to respect fully even the most minor truth of faith. For only in private prayer can one constantly and systematically ponder all the truths of faith in one's heart, and so keep real for oneself every truth which must be clung to as an indispensable aspect of one's clinging to Jesus.

If theological reflection is to be fruitful, one's clinging to Jesus and to all the truths of faith must be confident, not nervous. Only the confidence and easy familiarity with the Lord Jesus which prayer gives enable one to face every question with fearless faith. The failure to explore difficulties, the refusal to face objections straightforwardly, and the evasion of situations in which one's faith is likely to be challenged are sins against the vocation of one who undertakes theological work. Because there is no growth without struggle, no creativity without the overcoming of obstacles, these sins will block that deeper understanding of faith which a theologian should always seek. One who has a vivid sense of the reality grasped in the truths of faith is less likely to be tempted to commit these sins and is more able to resist the temptation should it arise.

Summary

"Theology" in the most general sense means thought and talk about God, and also about everything else insofar as it is related to God. In a narrower sense, "theology" refers to reflection upon the sources in which the truth of faith is articulated; it is subordinate to Scripture and to other normative documents which bear witness to the Church's faith. Positive theology tries to find and state the true and full meaning of these normative sources, while systematic theology attempts to determine the relationships between truths of faith and other propositions which are not revealed but seem true.

Systematic theology is divided into contemplative and moral. Contemplative theology seeks to work out a single, coherent view of reality in the light of faith. Moral theology also reflects upon the truths of faith, but it is less concerned with elaborating a Christian world view than with making clear how faith should shape Christian life. It includes pastoral theology and spiritual theology.

The appropriate method of theology can be called "dialectical." This method explores from within the reality in which one lives. Its use in Catholic theology means that one who accepts the truth of Catholic faith, present in the living Church of which he or she is a member, seeks a better understanding of this truth in which he or she already lives.

There is a need for renewal in moral theology today.

In the seventeenth century, after the Council of Trent, Catholic theology generally adopted a rationalistic method emphasizing clarity of concepts, certainty of principles, and the quasi-mathematical proof of conclusions. As manifested in the moral theology which persisted until Vatican II, this approach was marked by a legalism which helped give the impression that the Church's moral teaching consists of changeable laws rather than unchangeable truths.

Vatican II called for renewal in theology generally. Regarding moral theology, it prescribed "livelier contact with the mystery of Christ and the history of salvation," a firmer grounding in Scripture, and clear recognition that the Christian calling has a heavenly character while also involving the "obligation to bring forth fruit in charity for the life of the world" (OT 16).

Many, however, view moral theology as essentially a human science which can be carried on without reference to faith. Thus, much recent work in moral theology is neither focused on Christ, nor related to other central truths of faith, nor nourished by Scripture, nor oriented toward the heavenly calling of Christians. While it sets minimum standards of behavior lower than the old moral theology did, its approach is no less legalistic.

The fundamental difficulty of both the classical moral theology of the past and much moral theology of the present is their failure to appreciate the complex make up of the Christian and of Christian life. As the human and divine are distinct but inseparable in Jesus, dynamically integrated but not commingled, so the Christian has a human nature and an adoptive share in divinity, and is to lead a life fully human but also truly divine.

In view of this, an adequate treatise on Christian moral principles, which meets the Council's prescription for renewal, must clarify what a Christian is and how Christian life can be at once and entirely both human and divine. It must explain how human goods determine Christian moral norms and show why a life in accord with Christian norms is the only life which is really humanly good, while also showing how to live such a life. It should be oriented toward preaching, teaching, and counseling, while providing an adequate basis for studies leading to the formation of confessors. Finally, it must explain the authority of the Church's teaching.

Appendix 1:   The importance of this subject

If we must accept and follow the Church's moral teaching in any case, why bother trying to understand the point of the moral norms we must follow? Will not such an inquiry merely produce bad reasons for a life which ought to be lived in the light of faith?

The first point to be noted in reply is that the explanation of moral norms to be presented in this book will itself proceed in the light of faith. Clarifications will be drawn from experience and rational reflection, but these will be subordinate to the data of revelation. If the account I propose is in some respects neither required by faith nor intelligible in itself, then to that extent it ought to be ignored. But if it helps to clarify what we believe, then it can be enriching and useful.

It will be enriching because human action is not simply outward behavior and moral norms are not simply devices for eliciting behavior. Human action fulfills human persons; by it they share in community. Human moral norms make possible truly good human acts and shape them toward human fulfillment. Christian action is destined to last forever in Christ. Christian moral norms make possible our fully conscious and free sharing in the life of Jesus and cooperation in his redemptive work; Christian lives of holiness in this world contribute to the joy of eternal life.

At the Last Supper, our Lord Jesus told the apostles he regarded them, not as slaves, for a slave "does not know what his master is doing; but I have called you friends, for all that I have heard from my Father I have made known to you" (Jn 15.15). An important and wonderful part of God's gift to us in making us sharers in his own life is his showing us the point of the moral norms we must follow, as we live our human lives by following the way which Jesus is. By knowing what God is doing, we understand what we are trying to do; our action has greater inherent richness and has even now the fruit of joy in divine friendship.

Moreover, this same action becomes by deeper insight a better and more perfect gift to God. The more we put ourselves into what we do, the more our lives constitute that rational worship to which St. Paul teaches every Christian is called (see Rom 12.1–2). God wants from us not empty acts of ritual but our very lives (see Is 1.10–20; 29.13; Hos 6.6; Mi 6.6–8; Mt 9.13; 12.7; 15.8–9; Heb 10.5–9; 13.16). Enriched with God's own love and united with the life of Jesus, our lives become a holy and acceptable sacrifice.

By the grace of God we are what we are, and his grace is not fruitless. By it we share the dignity of active and contributing members of the divine family. Being familiar with God, we must be conscious of what he is about and must consider what we are about. In this way, we will grow to maturity as children of God and please our heavenly Father by the richness of our accomplishments (see Mt 25.14–30; Lk 19.11–27; Jn 15.1–8). Thus we may hope to share in the accolade of the heavenly Father: "You are my beloved Son; with you I am well pleased" (Mk 1.11).

In sum, human acts express rational choices. The better one understands what one is doing, the richer in significance one's acts are. The richer in meaning a good act is—other things being equal—the better it is. Goods can be realized in acts, and so can contribute to completion in Christ of themselves, only if they are in some way known by the person acting. Thus lack of understanding when understanding is possible detracts from the gift one could and should be offering to God.

There also are several secondary ways in which an understanding of the general norms of Christian life will be helpful. Study of this work will help answer a question much discussed today: What precisely does Christian moral teaching add to the body of moral truth which could be known by upright persons even without the light of faith? Moreover, the explanations to follow will provide the principles by which the Church in her teaching can explain and defend specific norms of Christian morality when these are misunderstood and called into question. Finally, to a considerable extent, priests in their preaching ought to stress the normative principles of Christian morality. The perceptive student will find the present treatise very helpful in this work.

Appendix 2:   Pluralism, theological synthesis, and the present work

In providing guidance for the implementation of Vatican II's plan for the renewal of theology, the Holy See recognizes legitimate pluralism in theology, which can arise from differences in philosophies used, methods employed, terminologies adopted, purposes pursued, plans of organization followed, and so forth. The Church favors pluralism "provided always that such pluralism is a further enrichment of the doctrine of faith already well and clearly determined and in constant reference to it."[32] But continuity with past theological tradition is important in seminary training.[33] Even more important, unity of faith must be safeguarded: "In theology there is a nucleus of affirmations that are certain,

23

common, and which cannot be given up, constituting the basis of all Catholic dogmatic teaching. These cannot be questioned but only clarified, studied in depth, and better explained in their historical and theological context."[34] Thus it is essential to distinguish matters of faith from matters in which a choice of opinions is legitimate.

The Holy See also recognizes that at the present time there are inherent difficulties in any attempt at theological synthesis:

> The theology of today in its search for new arrangement and new formulae is marked by a transitory and provisional character. Always in search of a new synthesis, it is like a huge construction-site in which the building is only partly completed, while within there is an accumulation of material which must be used in the building.
>
> Consequently, the teaching of theology has in many cases lost its unity and compactness, and presents an incomplete fragmentary aspect so that it is often said that theological knowledge has become "atomized". When order and completeness are lacking, the central truths of the faith are easily lost to sight. Therefore, it is not at all to be wondered at, if, in such a climate, various fashionable "theologies", which are in great part one sided, partial, and sometimes unfounded, gain ground.[35]

As a partial remedy for all these difficulties, a more intense collaboration among persons in various fields is urged.[36] And despite the difficulties, for the sake of effective seminary formation with a preparation in systematic theology which will be sound and complete, "up-to-date textbooks for each of the disciplines are highly to be recommended as the basis of both lectures and private study."[37] The present book is offered in response to this last recommendation.

In attempting to carry out this project, I see a chief obstacle in the transitory and provisional character of current theology, which the Holy See notes. The present flux in thinking about central doctrines on Jesus, original sin, the last things, grace, and so on is especially disconcerting, for I must touch on all of these matters, but can hardly become expert in every one of these fields.

To try to overcome this obstacle, I undertake to expound doctrinal points not so much in a subtle as in an accurate way, for the most part taking for granted positions commonly held by Catholic theologians until recent years. Fresh reflection upon the implications of faith for living the Christian life cannot wait for the settling of all other theological questions.

Also, because this work is intended as an essay at fulfilling the mandate of Vatican II, I must make extensive use of sacred Scripture and other witnesses of faith. Much of what I have just said about the present situation in systematic theology applies analogously to the situation in Scripture scholarship and positive theology in general. While I shall do my best not to abuse Scripture and other witnesses of faith by distorting their meanings, I cannot pretend to handle these materials with the competence of a Scripture scholar. I shall strive only to use Scripture and other witnesses as the Church uses them in her teaching—for example, as they are used in the documents of Vatican II.

Doctrine develops, and theologians must work to probe received teachings, so that the refinement and better expression which are needed can be achieved by the Church. But one must not think of the witnesses of faith in Scripture and in other aspects of the life of the Church as if they were merely past realities. By the service of the magisterium, these witnesses of faith remain present and effective. The unfolding of faith is a living and creative process; the Church as a whole and every one of her active members contributes to this process as the Spirit expands and extends the Mystical Body of the Lord Jesus through spaces and times.

The Church remains one eucharistic fellowship, the communion of those united with one another by being united in Jesus. What we say of him does not come from ourselves; it is the Spirit of his Father speaking in us (see Jn 14.26). In the Lord Jesus, the identity and self-consistency of the Church is assured. What the Church as such proposes as an essential part of Jesus' teaching is affirmed by the Spirit always and everywhere; he does not say yes and no to the same proposition (see 2 Cor 1.18–19). "Jesus Christ is the same yesterday and today and for ever. Do not be led away by diverse and strange teachings" (Heb 13.8–9).

For this reason, I am confident that the more radical proposals for revision of Catholic teaching never will receive the acceptance of the Church as a whole. But undoubtedly many less radical proposals, including some which appear at first glance to be unacceptable, will turn out with proper clarification, qualification, and expression to be important contributions to the Church's knowledge of her Lord. By ignoring these proposals, I lose here the advantage of such eventual developments. However, since they will not contradict what the Church has hitherto accepted as saving truth, I am confident that future developments will not undermine the main outlines of the theology of Christian life presented here, although they will demand improvements and make it possible for others to do better what I am attempting here.

Appendix 3:   Renewal in moral theology and the present crisis in the Church

The need for renewal in Catholic moral theology is indicated not only by the limitations of the older moral theology. Substantial opportunities for ecumenism and evangelization also call for renewal in Catholic moral life and the moral teaching which guides it.

Almost from the beginning, Christian moral thought has been impeded by an unresolved, underlying tension between the supernatural and the natural, between the sacred and the secular. Before Christianity, neither Jews nor pagans sharply distinguished these domains. The gospel introduces a new and sharp distinction: Birth as a human person is distinguished from rebirth as a child of God; flesh is distinguished from Spirit; the things of Caesar are distinguished from the things of God.

In the Christian thought of the Middle Ages, this essential distinction—which in itself clearly is divinely revealed—tended to develop into a separation and even into an opposition between nature and grace. Catholic thought resisted this tendency in many ways, for example, by the doctrine and practice of the sacraments, which unite earthly with heavenly things. Also, the Catholic ideal of society was not one of separation and opposition between Church and state. Still, a strong tendency persisted to regard the pursuit of human goods in this world as an activity in itself pointless. St. Augustine and many others located the point of Christian life more or less exclusively in the vision of God after death (see 34-A).[38] On this view, the realization of human goods is of little importance in itself; it becomes significant only in cases in which one's eternal destiny is at stake.

St. Thomas attempts to integrate the natural and supernatural aspects of Christian life. A leading maxim in his thought is that grace perfects and completes nature and does not nullify it (see *S.t.*, 1, q. 1, a. 8, ad 2; q. 2, a. 2, ad 1; q. 62, a. 5). Thus he firmly denies any opposition between the two, but he maintains their distinction and asserts their real relationship. Unfortunately, he is not able to clarify this relationship beyond a certain point; he leaves many unresolved difficulties as to how the fulfillment of human persons as such is related to their vocation to share in divine life.[39]

The residual tension becomes particularly acute when one considers things by means of the nominalist theological perspective, which developed after the time of St. Thomas, for this perspective emphasizes certainty and sharply separates reason from faith. Certainty about human nature based on experience makes it clear that human life is deeply marked by sin; faith offers assurance of salvation, but this assurance seems incompatible with daily experience. For many minds in the late Middle Ages, the tension between nature and grace degenerated into irresolvable opposition.

The Renaissance and the Reformation were—or at least became—alternative ways of cutting through this opposition. The humanist option of the Renaissance, although initially not against Christian faith, developed into an ideal of humankind "uncontaminated" by grace, and ultimately into the secular humanism of the Enlightenment of the eighteenth century, which rejected the supernatural in favor of human nature and rejected faith in favor of autonomous human reason. The Christian option of the Reformation, although initially not opposed to humanism, developed into an ideal of New Testament Christianity "uncontaminated" by human elements, and ultimately into various forms of fideistic supernaturalism. These rejected corrupt human nature in favor of an altogether passively received grace; they also rejected the use of human reason in matters of ultimate significance in favor of the autonomous faith of the individual before God.

Secular humanism can reject altogether humankind's calling to share in divine fellowship. Fideistic supernaturalism cannot reject altogether humankind's natural condition and duties. The latter fact elicited an effort to isolate the secular from the sacred and to insulate the two domains from each other as completely as possible. The result was the increasing irrelevance of religion to the rest of human life. Catholic Christianity never accepted in principle the option of fideistic supernaturalism, but in practice even Catholics were deeply affected by this movement. Much popular teaching and preaching expressed hostility toward this world and its human goods and emphasized saving one's soul.

Today the Catholic Church is confronted with substantial opportunities for ecumenism and evangelization. The reason is that events are making it clear that the forced option between human fulfillment and intimacy with God, between reason and faith—which led to the dichotomy between secular humanism and fideistic supernaturalism—is a highly unsatisfactory option, no matter which alternative is chosen.

On the one hand, few Christians today actually hold the negative views of human nature and the powers of reason and free choice which generated the doctrines Trent was compelled to condemn. Moreover, Christians today can see clearly the result of allowing the world to go its way without the illumination of faith; few are satisfied with a disincarnate Christianity which isolates faith in the individual relationship of the soul before God. Rationalistic philosophy no longer shapes Protestant theology, and most Protestant theologians who believe in divine revelation realize the difficulty of sustaining the claim that it is enshrined in the Bible, to be found there by individuals without a community whose faith somehow transcends and sustains the individual's faith.

On the other hand, secular humanism is in deep trouble (see GS 18, 21). In all its varieties, individual and society are set against one another. The memory of Christian hope haunts post-Christian individuals and societies; they wish to be more than merely human. Contemporary humankind yearns for perfect liberty and perfect justice: the liberty of the children of God in the fellowship of the divine family—but without God. As a result, societies invent grandiose schemes to try to implement this hope; in so doing, they become totalitarian, attack fundamental values of the person such as life itself, and increasingly infringe upon individual liberty and privacy. Individuals experience the lack of a humane society, and so they suffer from identity crises—a sense of meaninglessness, boredom, alienation, and loneliness.

Post-Christian humankind cannot find its way back to the naiveté of paganism in which religion helped individuals and societies to live tolerable lives in this broken world, where finite persons must face not only their finitude but also their personal guilt and the inevitability of their own death. Having driven out Christian faith, secular humanism condemns nonbelieving persons either to face reality and live intolerable lives, or to evade reality by never adequate means, such as thin veils of individual escapism and rationalization or smothering blankets of social control and ideology. The option of post-Christian humankind for secular humanism has been a choice of death. Individuals and societies kill their unborn to solve their problems; to defend their ideologies, societies and individuals concur in their readiness to kill and be killed in an all-out war.

From this characterization of secular humanism, I conclude not simply that it ought to be rejected, but also that despite its seeming power and vitality, it is weak and dying. Eventually, the inhumanism of secular humanism will become obvious to everyone. At that point, a new phase of history, with new opportunities for evangelization, will begin.

Appendix 4:   Theological method and science

A method is a regular way of doing something. In the work of an intellectual discipline, such as systematic theology, it is helpful to have a method appropriate to the discipline's subject matter and purpose. In many respects, the method of an intellectual discipline consists in many little tricks and bits of information. One learns most of these things by working with someone competent in the field. But in a certain respect, the question of method is a question of how to organize propositions into trains of thought. Only this aspect of method will be considered here.

There are different ways of organizing propositions into a train of thought. A poem does it in one way, a sermon in another, and a scientific treatise in still another. Some of these ways are not appropriate for systematic theology.

There is legitimate and important work to be done in finding more expressive and persuasive representations to use in the communication of divine revelation. This poetic and rhetorical task belongs mainly to liturgy, homiletics, and catechetics. Its need is clear if one realizes that revelation is a personal communication, not exclusively the transmission of propositional truths.

Today some scholars suggest substituting this work for rational reflection upon the truths of faith. In the Catholic Church, however, the poetic and rhetorical task never has been allowed to replace the articulation of propositional truths of faith, nor have doctrinal formulae ever been allowed to be reduced to mere symbolic or persuasive elements of communication (see DS 3426/2026, 3483/2079). The teaching of Vatican II clearly maintains the received view of this matter (see OT 16). Indeed, theology as rational reflection on the truths of faith is the only conception the Council knows.

So much is it the case that Catholic theology takes an intellectualist approach, that in ecclesiastical documents theological disciplines often are called "sciences." In English, the word "science" primarily applies to the supreme kind of autonomous human knowledge about some field of experienced facts. Theology is not a science in this sense. I think it would be best to avoid the word "science" when speaking in English of theological disciplines.

St. Thomas Aquinas probably fulfilled the ideal of Catholic contemplative systematic theology more perfectly than any other single theologian before or since his time. Using an original philosophy which he developed by creative reflection upon both the work of Aristotle and the philosophical content of prior Christian writing, Thomas articulated a systematic theology which begins from God, proceeds to study creation and the fall of humankind, then considers the principles and norms of Catholic morality, and finally treats the Incarnation, redemption, and sacraments as the way by which human persons can return to God.

St. Thomas had a wide and deep knowledge of Scripture and of the writings of the Church Fathers. Thus he was able to bring his philosophical view into contact with many witnesses of faith, which he interpreted with all the accuracy permitted by the historical knowledge and literary techniques of the thirteenth century. In developing his systematic reflection, Thomas followed as far as possible Aristotle's scientific method. The result is that his system does illuminate the mysteries of faith by reason working in the light of faith. His work brings out many important connections among the truths of faith. It also clarifies the relationship between divine revelation and human learning, insofar as the latter can be fit within the framework of Aristotle's philosophy.

The Catholic Church still recommends the approach of St. Thomas as a model for theological work (see OT 16). Nevertheless, even as adapted by Thomas, the scientific method of Aristotle is not altogether appropriate in theology.

For Aristotle, the objective of science is explanation of facts by knowledge of their precise causes. Once one knows the proper cause, one sees that the fact is necessary and could not be otherwise than it is. Since theology is centrally concerned with the acts of God revealing and human persons responding—which are not necessary but free acts—the central facts cannot be explained. Moreover, although fundamental truths of faith do in a way illuminate other truths, causes remain obscure. For example, the main causes of what is brought about in the sacraments belong within the intimate life of the divine persons to whom faith is only an approach.

Thus, as important as is the work of St. Thomas, his attempt to proceed in a scientific way can be criticized. It has been argued, I think justly, that Thomas proceeds too confidently in drawing implications from truths of faith.[40] It seems to me that at times Thomas forgets that the language of talk about God is relational; he proceeds as if the concepts expressed by this language involved an understanding—which Thomas himself expressly excludes—of what God is in himself (cf. *S.t.*, 1, q. 12, a. 12, with q. 14, a. 1; also *S.c.g.*, 1, 14, with 44–59).

St. Thomas was not the only great medieval thinker to attempt a theological synthesis. There were other excellent attempts, notably that of St. Bonaventure.[41] At the same time, some theologians using less adequate philosophical instruments went to the opposite extreme from Thomas. If he was overconfident, they were underconfident.

They began to doubt the ability of the human mind to understand and grow gradually in knowledge of reality. They emphasized the problem and importance of knowing that propositions certainly are true; they gave far less attention to problems of clarification and explanation. This philosophical and theological approach usually is called "nominalism." It had the result of sharply separating the domains of rational inquiry and faith. In the former, certitude was to be sought from sense experience and logical analysis. In the latter, certitude depended entirely on authority.[42] The nominalism of late medieval thought persisted into the beginnings of modern philosophy.

Although much of modern philosophy is a humanist substitute for Christian theology, the first movements of modern philosophy were not opposed to Christian faith. For example, Descartes intended his philosophy to help fundamental theology by securing beyond any possibility of doubt the existence of God, the immortality of the human soul, the freedom of the human will, and other truths which are both revealed and knowable by the natural light of reason.[43] The method of Descartes emphasized the objective of gaining absolute certitude. He believed this could be reached by analyzing cognition to its absolutely unquestionable bases, which he thought consisted in clear and distinct ideas.

The philosophy of Descartes and of others who shared his general approach is called "rationalism," not because it stresses reason in opposition to faith but because it stresses reason in opposition to experience. Descartes was greatly interested in mathematics, and he developed his philosophical ideal on the model of mathematical reasoning, rather than the model of a factual study such as biology or history. Rationalistic philosophy seemed consistent with faith and it seemed to many Catholic theologians to offer a new and promising approach. Therefore, they more or less fully adopted and adapted a rationalistic approach in their work.

A rationalistic philosophy, even if it need not contradict essential truths of faith, has a number of limitations and tendencies which render it less than ideally suited for the work of theology. The rationalist stresses certitude as an objective; this objective does not fit well with the ideal of theology as a work of faith seeking constantly growing—but only gradually growing—understanding. Also, the rationalistic emphasis on clear and distinct ideas tends to distract users of the method from the complexity and richness of human cognition, and thus leads them to overlook the many ways in which linguistic expressions have meaning. As a result, rationalists almost inevitably misunderstand the relational character of the language used to talk about God. Moreover, rationalists often overlook the need for careful interpretation of the witnesses of faith. They generally oversimplify the problem of interpretation even when they realize the need for it.

Rationalist philosophers focus on the intellectually knowing subject; they tend to identify the human person with the mind, the thinking self. Bodiliness and other dimensions of the person are insufficiently appreciated. A theologian using rationalism tends for this reason to ignore many aspects of revelation and to stress almost exlusively the communication of propositional truths. At its extreme, this tendency leads to a conception of faith as acceptance of a certain amount of correct information rather than as a personal relationship of hearing and adhering to God revealing himself.

Rationalist philosophy also makes a very sharp distinction between the knowing subject and the thing known. It thus tends to be unsuited to practical reflection, in which one thinks about oneself and shapes one's becoming by one's thought. A rationalist approach tends rather to look at what is known as if it were a detached object. Any practical problem tends to be looked at on the model of the application of mathematics in engineering.

This approach also takes insufficient account of history, which can hardly be so easily ignored when one begins practical reflection about the lives of real, bodily persons who have diverse abilities and opportunities, and who exist in actual relationships with one another. This aspect of rationalism had the result that the more it became accepted as a method for Catholic theology, the less Christian life could be treated integrally by the same theological inquiry which considered the central truths of faith. The latter were considered much more as dogmas or theoretical truths to be proved from the witnesses of faith than as normative truths shaping Christian life.

Every Christian philosophy is concerned essentially with truths which can be known and defended by the natural light of reason, but which also are included in or implied by divine revelation. The Christian philosopher seeks to understand this set of truths as a unified view of reality, to establish them by various methods without invoking the authority of revelation, and to answer objections from anyone who is willing to engage in a fair exchange of reasoned criticism. Because Christian philosophy is a creative work of reason, there can be many such philosophies which differ on various issues, but which are alike in never denying any proposition whose denial would entail a denial of a truth of faith.

Christian philosophies such as those of St. Thomas and St. Bonaventure are equally Christian but simply different on the philosophical level. Despite any limitations in method, both are flexible and powerful instruments for faith seeking understanding, since both can develop through the interchange of criticism and both are able to deal with the facts of nature and of history.

A rationalistic philosophy is not very adequate. It is a poor instrument for faith seeking understanding. Its ability to deal with data is strictly limited. To the extent that Catholic systematic theology began to use rationalistic philosophy, it tended to become unchanging and sterile.

By 1700, Catholic theology was heavily influenced by rationalism.[44] The belief of the Church was divided into theses to be proved. At this point moral theology was almost entirely separated from dogma—that is, from contemplative systematic theology. Even within dogmatic theology, the relationships among the truths of faith considered in the various treatises tended to be ignored. Although there were exceptions, it was too often the case that Scripture and other witnesses of faith were mined simply as sources of premises to be used in proofs, rather than being studied in their own integrity. The full and accurate interpretation of the tradition in the light of Catholic faith was neglected. The importance of certain sources, such as the Church's history and liturgical practices, tended to be ignored, for although these sources contain aspects of revelation, it is not easy to draw rationalistic arguments from them.

The model of science adopted in modern theology under the influence of rationalist philosophy was even less appropriate than the Aristotelian model of science which St. Thomas had used. The quest for a kind of certitude which is not always available in theology and the ignoring of relationships among the mysteries of faith led quickly to frustration and ultimately to a discipline with minimal relevance for Christian life.

Today, some think that previous attempts to make theology scientific met with grief only because of the unsuitability for theology of the scientific models of Aristotle and rationalism. These models are called "classical" conceptions of science. The suggestion is that theology should adopt the model of modern, empirical science.

Such a science proceeds by gathering facts, noting regularities, and excogitating hypotheses which might account for the observed data.[45] A good hypothesis should logically imply factual truths other than those which first suggested it. Further investigation is conducted to see whether the implications of the hypothesis check out. Eventually, even good hypotheses must be qualified, modified, or discarded in favor of more adequate ones. Chemistry is a good example of a modern science. The data to be explained are chemical changes. The theory that matter is made up of elementary atoms variously arranged into compounds has been extraordinarily enlightening, powerful in accounting for facts, and fruitful in inquiry and application.

The modern model of science seems to me even less suited to theology than any classical model. What are the data to be explained? On the one hand, if they are facts which can be observed by anyone, with or without faith, such as the facts of religious experience or behavior, theology will be reduced to a theory of part of human life. If what faith says about this part of human life is admitted into the theory, there seems to be no reason to ignore what faith says about what has not yet been experienced. If what faith says about human life is excluded from the theory, the result is a merely rational discipline detached from divine revelation. On the other hand, if theology models itself on some modern science but considers as data the truths of faith themselves, then the mysteriousness of God and of his will to draw humankind into intimacy with himself blocks any attempt to develop very wide-ranging hypotheses and to test them by experiment. The model of modern science will be useful within limits, but not for systematic theology as a unified whole.

It is perhaps worth noticing in passing that even those disciplines which usually are called "social sciences" do not conform strictly to the model of modern natural science. It is true that careful workers in these disciplines do proceed with accurate methods to collect, describe, and catalogue data. But instead of developing testable hypotheses, psychology and the social sciences usually must settle for more concrete and limited understandings of human activities and relationships. In attaining these insights, the human sciences more often proceed like humanistic studies than they do like natural sciences.[46]

Almost all the work done in the human sciences proceeds on the assumption that human persons cannot make free choices. Some philosophical theory or ideology which purports to account for unfree human behavior is used to organize and interpret facts about the activity and relationships of persons. Thus psychologists and social scientists offer diverse and incompatible accounts of the evils which afflict humankind, but sin has no place in their accounts. They propose diverse remedies for these evils, but the grace of Christ is not mentioned among these remedies. Because of their inadequate grasp upon the reality of their subject matter, these disciplines do not reach the same consensus as does a science like chemistry, which differs little in the Soviet Union and in the United States.

It follows from the dependence of the human sciences on nonfactual assumptions—especially the assumption of determinism—that while theology cannot ignore the findings of these disciplines neither can it accept their results uncritically. A Christian philosophy must sift these results to separate the important data and sound insights they contain from the assumptions which reflect commitments incompatible with Christian faith.[47]

Appendix 5:   The appropriate method for theology: dialectic

Vatican I speaks about the method of theology. Its words are few, but clear and precious. After pointing out that the mysteries of faith come to us only by God's gift, the Council continues: "It is, nevertheless, true that if human reason, with faith as its guiding light, inquires earnestly, devoutly, and circumspectly, it does reach, by God's generosity, some understanding of mysteries, and that a most profitable one. It achieves this by the similarity [analogia] with truths which it knows naturally and also from the interrelationship of mysteries with one another and with the final end of man" (DS 3016/1796). Even so, the mysteries are not grasped in the way that truths about the natural world are grasped. Faith remains necessary.

It is interesting to notice what the modest statement of Vatican I does not say. It does not say that rational reflection upon the mysteries of faith leads to a knowledge of truths through causes (Aristotle's scientific method), nor that it establishes with certitude which propositions are truths of faith (the method of rationalist science), nor that it develops theories to account for the data of faith (the method of a modern science). Rather it says that reason can gain some understanding of mysteries by comparing one truth with another.

It seems to me that this teaching of Vatican I implies that the proper method for theology is the method called "dialectic" in Plato's sense of the word. By this method, one considers truths of faith by comparison (analogia) with truths of reason, with one another, and with the ultimate fulfillment to which God calls us in the Lord Jesus. As is often said, one truth is considered in the light of another. To understand the dialectical method of theology, it is helpful to consider what is meant by "in the light of."

If one considers the truth that Mary is the mother of Jesus in the light of the truth that Jesus is God, one sees the truth of Mary's motherhood in a new light, for one knows her to be the mother of God. The relationship here is deductive. But nondeductive relationships among propositions also illuminate one truth by another. For example, propositions about revelatory words and deeds corresponding to one another are mutually illuminating. The truth that God made promises to Moses together with the truth that what was promised occurred communicate as neither by itself could do. The relationship in this case is not a deductive one. Again, the truths of the Old Testament illuminate those of the New and vice versa, since the gospel fulfills what God began with the law.

One not only finds the various truths of revelation mutually illuminating; one also comes to some understanding of faith in the light of truths naturally known by reason and vice versa. For example, the truth that human persons can make free choices pertains to faith (see DS 1555/815), but it also can be established by reason.[48] If this truth and the truth that humankind is made in God's image are brought to bear upon the truth that God creates, the mystery of God's creative act is not eliminated, but in some way it is illuminated, for it also is a matter of faith that God creates freely (see DS 3025/1805). Conversely, the truth about human aspirations for freedom and justice is understood in a different way by one who believes that human persons are made in God's image than by a secular humanist.

Divine revelation, as personal communication, contains more than the propositional truths of faith. Tradition has an experiential aspect and also includes ways of living and worshipping whose reality the Church gradually comes to understand more and more perfectly. This development can be aided by theological reflection which brings into fruitful relationship truths of faith already implicitly taught by the Church and truths deeply imbedded in Christian imagery, experience, life, and worship. Thus, for instance, the truth that Jesus is truly a man is greatly illuminated by the practices and experiences related to the celebration of Christmas. This celebration gives us an irreducible awareness of the Incarnate Word's solidarity with us in our human weakness and limitations. We knew the risen Lord of Easter when he was just a babe in arms.

In the ways exemplified and others, a dialectical method of meditation and discussion can lead to some understanding of mysteries of faith. This insight can provide a basis for genuine development of doctrine. Over and over again throughout history, questions are put to the Church which bear upon the realities of faith but which are formulated in concepts not previously in use among believers. For example, whether the human species could have evolved, using the word "evolved" in the precise sense in which it is used in Darwin's *Descent of Man,* is a question which could not have been asked before Darwin.

Faced with such new questions, the Church must consider the possible answers in comparison with truths of faith already articulated, and judge which answer is in harmony with faith (see DS 3896/2327). This judgment is not an arbitrary one, since the Church must be faithful to what God has revealed. Moreover, not even the Church herself can change the meaning or contradict the truth of doctrines she already has taught as belonging to faith, since God's revelation is present in the Church's teaching (see DS 3020/1800).

Appendix 6:   Modern philosophies and theology

When modern philosophers treat of religious matters, they almost always regard an incoherent human theory as if it represented Christian faith. Hobbes, Hume, Spinoza, Kant, Hegel, Feuerbach, Marx, Nietzsche, Dewey, Sartre, and many others deny divine revelation.[49] Yet they retain a residue of what Christians believe, especially in their exalted idea of the human person or, at least, in the ideal by which they criticize human life. Since it is the business of philosophers to articulate their beliefs, to show the reasonableness of holding them, and to answer objections from all sides against them, modern philosophers such as those named have articulated more or less tightly integrated atheistic systems (see GS 19–21).

Modern philosophical systems are plausible, complex, and seemingly powerful. Yet they are ultimately inconsistent. Hume, for example, holds that reality *necessarily* excludes anything which is not contingent—that is, which is necessary; in this way he tries to exclude God. Kant holds that human knowledge cannot extend to God because it is limited to the world of experience; he thinks he shows this by his theory of the sources of knowledge, yet he locates these sources *outside experience*. Hegel maintains that one cannot know anything in a fully true way short of knowing the totality of reality; he believes that at this point knowing and what is known coincide; yet, at the same time, Hegel thinks his own philosophy is *true knowledge* and that he can exclude other philosophies as false. The post-Hegelian philosophers mentioned above and many others hold that the complex of human thought and action is the ultimate source of all meaning and value; at the same time, they try to *exclude as illegitimate* the belief and way of life of Christians, since we do not agree with their view that God is to be replaced by the human mind—and replaced in the particular way each atheistic humanist personally prefers.

The preceding paragraph is not intended as a summary refutation of the leading approaches in modern philosophy. I have treated these matters at length in a previous work.[50] Rather, my intention is to make it clear that Catholic theology must be very careful in borrowing from modern philosophies and from theologies which have been shaped by modern philosophies. Vatican II continues to commend St. Thomas as a guide for Catholic theological speculation (see OT 16). The Holy See continues to point out that modern philosophies are not the apt instruments for Christian reflection which ancient philosophy was for the work of Thomas.[51]

Notes

1. A convenient, brief introduction to theology: G. F. van Ackeren, S.J., "Theology," *New Catholic Encyclopedia,* 14:39–49. A fuller introduction, including but not limited to historical considerations: Yves M.-J. Congar, O.P., *A History of Theology* (Garden City, N.Y.: Doubleday, 1968).

2. A good, general introduction to the theology of revelation: René Latourelle, S.J., *Theology of Revelation* (Cork: Mercier Press, 1966).

3. The Sacred Congregation for Catholic Education, *The Theological Formation of Future Priests* (Washington, D.C.: United States Catholic Conference, 1976), sections 30–33 (hereinafter cited as "CCE" with the relevant section numbers). Concerning the proper methods for the study of Scripture, see three encyclicals: *Providentissimus Deus* (Leo XIII), *Spiritus Paraclitus* (Benedict XV), and *Divino Afflante Spiritu* (Pius XII). These encyclicals received their indispensable complement from Vatican II's constitution, *Dei verbum,* which at crucial points incorporates their doctrine by reference (see esp. DV 11–12). A balanced theological study of theological problems concerning Scripture: Pierre Grelot, *The Bible Word of God: A Theological Introduction to the Study of Scripture,* trans. Peter Nickels, O.F.M.Conv. (New York: Desclee, 1968).

4. Appendix 4 considers and excludes several alternatives to dialectic as the method of theology as a whole, especially alternatives which conceive theology as some sort of science. But what about transcendental method? How is it related to what I call "dialectic?" This question is not easy to answer, for "transcendental method" has various meanings. For Rahner, "transcendental theology is not simply the whole of theology and must not claim to be anything more than one part or one aspect of it" ("Reflections on Methodology in Theology," *Theological Investigations,* vol. 11, *Confrontations I,* trans. David Bourke [New York: Seabury Press, 1974], 84). Moreover, as Rahner makes clear (86), transcendental theology is more than a method, for it includes an acceptance of modern philosophy. For my part, I have argued in a previous work that the major approaches of modern philosophy must be rejected on strictly philosophical grounds, although each of them has something to contribute to an antireductionist, antirationalist metaphysics: *Beyond the New Theism: A Philosophy of Religion* (Notre Dame and London: University of Notre Dame Press, 1975), 94–240 and 343–56. Transcendental Thomism as developed by Coreth and Rahner seems to me an unnecessary hypothesis whose plausibility arises from the inadequate critique by Maréchal and his followers of modern philosophy,

especially Kant. Moreover, this form of Thomism has been expounded with parasitic dependence on St. Thomas, not as a free-standing philosophical effort, yet in important respects it is inconsistent with Thomas' theory of knowledge. See, for instance, James B. Reichmann, "Transcendental Method and the Psychogenesis of Being," *Thomist*, 32 (1968), 449–508; Cornelio Fabro, *La svolta antropologica di Karl Rahner* (Milan: Rusconi, 1974), esp. 87–121. Bernard Lonergan's conception of transcendental method is quite different; for him, this method simply is the process of human knowing as such: *Method in Theology* (New York: Herder and Herder, 1972), 13–14. His discussion of the specific method of systematic theology as a whole is in his treatment (235–353) of four of the functional specialties he enumerates: dialectic, foundations, doctrines, and systematics. Although I do not agree with everything in Lonergan's treatment of these matters, still on the whole what he describes in these four chapters corresponds to what I mean by "dialectic," which I thus use in a wider sense than Lonergan does. Moreover, in maintaining the permanence of dogmas (320–24) and the distinction between doctrine and systematics, with the priority of the former (349–50), Lonergan locates the source of theology as reflection in the living faith of the Church. In this, Lonergan shows himself a Catholic theologian, by contrast with Hans Küng, for example, who also uses a dialectical method in theology, but accepts as sources only two: (1) the historical reality of Israel and of Jesus accessible by historical-critical method, and (2) the contemporary human world of experience as a whole, without the interpretation and criticism of the Church's magisterium: "Toward a New Consensus in Catholic (and Ecumenical) Theology," in *Consensus in Theology? A Dialogue with Hans Küng et al.*, ed. Leonard Swidler (Philadelphia: Westminster Press, 1980), 1–17. Walter Kasper, *The Methods of Dogmatic Theology* (Glen Rock, N.J.: Paulist Press, 1969), 11–21 and 45–48, argues against considering theology a science and, 22–32 and 48–65, in favor of a methodology which incorporates many elements of what I call "dialectic." Unfortunately, Kasper is insufficiently critical of modern and contemporary philosophy, and so even he is in danger of overlooking ideological elements in it which tend toward an inconsistent historicism—the claim that every position except itself is a time-conditioned point of view on reality.

5. See the excellent and brief exposition: Cornelius Ernst, "Theological Methodology," *Encyclopedia of Theology*, 1671–78. I doubt that the "perspective" of *meaning* suggested by Ernst can be worked out in the way toward which he points. But it would be, in any case, a "perspective" for a contemplative system. The "perspective" of the present work is determined by its moral preoccupation to be *divine-human cooperation*.

6. On the relationship between ecclesiastical tradition and Scripture, see Grelot, op. cit., 26–33.

7. The note of Vatican II is numbered 31 in the official notes, and 46 in the Abbott edition. The reference is to *AAS* 42 (1950) 567–69, which includes the passage quoted. On Vatican II's teaching on theological method: José Luis Illanes Maestre, "Teología y método teológico en los documentos del Concilio Vaticano II," *Scripta Theologica*, 12 (1980), 761–86.

8. Thus, as I conceive it, theology does not solve problems, but rather clarifies mysteries, using "problem" and "mystery" in the sense they have for Gabriel Marcel, *Being and Having: An Existentialist Diary* (New York: Harper Torchbooks, 1965), 116–21; see Kenneth T. Gallagher, *The Philosophy of Gabriel Marcel* (New York: Fordham University Press, 1962), 30–49, for an exposition of Marcel's method, which is dialectical in my sense of the word. Because theological reflection is relative not only to the common and objective principle of the faith of the Church and its authoritative articulation by the magisterium, but also to the proper and subjective principle of each theologian's personal and culturally conditioned appropriation of this faith, pluralism in theology is inevitable and in practice insurmountable: see W. M. Shea, "Pluralism, Theological," *New Catholic Encyclopedia*, 17:513–14, and the works cited in his bibliography. Still, such pluralism does not entail the subjugation of faith and the life of faith in the Church to a multitude of mutually inconsistent theological speculations. For, in the first place, authentic Catholic theology recognizes and submits to the antecedent faith of the Church: see International Theological Commission, *Theses on the Relationship between the Ecclesiastical Magisterium and Theology* (Washington, D.C.: United States Catholic Conference, 1977), esp. theses 5 and 8. And, in the second place, genuine Catholic theologians do not present themselves as authorities whose propositions might be believed alongside (or even in place of) truths of faith, but only as fellow believers whose observations and reflections might commend themselves by the inherent cogency they have in the light of faith.

9. Thus it is a mistake to argue: "This point of Catholic teaching has not been solemnly defined; therefore, it has not been infallibly proposed, and it could be false." See John C. Ford, S.J., and Germain Grisez, "Contraception and the Infallibility of the Ordinary Magisterium," *Theological Studies*, 39 (1978), 263–77.

10. Although one cannot agree with the implicit relativism, the procedure of moral theory is decribed with some accuracy by John Rawls, *A Theory of Justice* (Cambridge, Mass.: Belknap Press of Harvard University Press, 1971), 17–22. The use of this method in theology presupposes the infallibility of the Church as a whole: Jesús Sancho Bielsa, *Infalibilidad del Pueblo de Dios: "Sensus fidei" e infalibilidad organica de la Iglesia en la Constitucion "Lumen gentium" del Concilio Vaticano II* (Pamplona, Spain: EUNSA, 1979). Peter Eicher, "Administered Revelation: The Official Church and Experience," in *Revelation and Experience*, Concilium, vol. 113, ed. Edward Schillebeeckx and Bas van Iersal (New York: Seabury Press, 1979), 3–17, sets up a dichotomy between religious experience and dogma, and between the magisterium and experience as a whole. In doing this, he ignores the fact that each new convert or generation of Catholics receives a tradition which includes liturgical practice and a Catholic way of life, and so has a concrete basis for the linguistically expressed propositional content of faith (see DV 8). Eicher is allergic to the authority without which there can be no obedience of faith; he proposes to displace this: "The scientifically explained experience of modern times, the suffering experience of everyday life as illumined by literature, and the unarticulated life-experience of the nameless millions without any apparent relationship with God, is no longer testified to by the authority of lived experience of faith, but is ultimately confronted by the sterile claim of a quite non-experiential and formal authority" (9). One counterexample—e.g., Mother Teresa—falsifies this generalization, and if the whole of the Catholic Church does not bear witness as it should, this fact is due to defects of fidelity and holiness, not to the work of the magisterium. Further, when Eicher invokes the "scientifically explained experience of modern times," it is clear that the real criterion by which he wishes to judge Catholic teaching is not experience, but rather the ideological presuppositions of those academic disciplines which succeed sufficiently in academic politics to retain or acquire the social status marked by the honorific title of "science."

11. See Richard A. McCormick, S.J., *Notes on Moral Theology: 1965–1980* (Washington, D.C.: University Press of America, 1981), 522–29 (cited hereinafter as *"Notes"*). See also Thomas Dubay, S.M., "The State of Moral Theology: A Critical Appraisal," *Theological Studies*, 35 (1974), 482–506, with which I agree in general; Charles E. Curran, *Ongoing Revision in Moral Theology* (Notre Dame, Ind.: Fides/Claretian, 1975), 37–65, to which chapter thirty-six of the present work may be taken as a response.

12. Besides the treatment in chapter thirty-five, see Austin B. Vaughan, "The Role of the Ordinary Magisterium of the Universal Episcopate," *Proceedings of the Catholic Theological Society of America*, 22 (1967), 1–19; Luigi Ciappi, "Crisis of the Magisterium, Crisis of Faith?" *Thomist*, 32 (1968), 147–70.

13. See McCormick, *Notes*, 296–303, 428–29, and 626–38, for a summary of various positions and counterpositions on this issue. Those who deny that there is a specifically Christian ethics hold for the autonomy of human reason in the determination of right and wrong; the role of faith and Church teaching in respect to moral life is in adding a characteristic motivation and significance to what is and can be known to be right and wrong even without faith. The thesis sometimes is expressed by saying that *materially* (that is, in respect to specific moral norms) Christian ethics is nothing but common human morality; my position is that Christian norms further specify the norms which can be known without faith.

14. See Charles E. Curran, *Transition and Tradition in Moral Theology* (Notre Dame and London: University of Notre Dame Press, 1979), 43–55; McCormick, *Notes*, 242–51, 668–82, 737–45, and 817–26. Two essays contributed to one volume can serve as an introductory critique of the attempt to justify dissent: Donald McCarthy, "The Teaching of the Church and Moral Theology," in *Principles of Catholic Moral Life*, ed. William E. May (Chicago: Franciscan Herald Press, 1980), 45–71; Richard R. Roach, S.J., "Moral Theology and the Mission of the Church: Idolatry in Our Day," ibid., 19–43. Also: Dario Composta, "Il magistero di fronte al diritto naturale," *Apollinaris*, 49 (1976), 79–105; Gustav Ermecke, "Die katholische Theologie in der Krise," *Münchener theologische Zeitschrift*, 32 (1981), 194–205; Bernhard Stoeckle, "Flucht in das Humane? Erwägungen zur Diskussion über die Frage nach dem Proprium christlicher Ethik," *Internationale katholische Zeitschrift (Communio)*, 6 (1977), 312–24; Marcelino Zalba, S.J., "Principia ethica in crisim vocata intra (propter?) crisim morum," *Periodica de Re Morali, Canonica, Liturgica*, 71 (1982), 25–63 and 319–57.

15. See McCormick, *Notes*, 648–52; Charles E. Curran and Richard A. McCormick, eds., *Readings in Moral Theology No. 1: Moral Norms and Catholic Tradition* (New York: Paulist Press, 1979). In his own essay in this volume, "Utilitarianism and Contemporary Moral Theology: Situating the Debates," Curran says (354) that "reforming Catholic theologians generally speaking do not embrace utilitarianism" but what "can be described as mixed consequentialism." Curran is correct, but

it remains that the indefensibility of consequentialism vitiates their thought just to the extent that they do make some use of this method. See Germain G. Grisez, "Christian Moral Theology and Consequentialism," in May, ed., op. cit., 293–327; Ferdinando Citterio, "La revisione critica dei tradizionali principi morali alle luce della teoria del 'compromesso etico,'" *Scuola cattolica*, 110 (1982), 29–64; Dario Composta, "Il consequenzialismo: Una nuova corrente della 'Nuova Morale,'" *Divinitas*, 25 (1981), 127–56. The argument that dissenting opinions, defended by partly consequentialist (proportionalist) arguments, ought not to be condoned in the Church has been criticized as uncharitable, and this criticism has been answered: Germain Grisez, "Charity and Dissenting Theologians," *Homiletic and Pastoral Review*, 80 (November 1979), 11–21.

16. See Congar, op. cit., 144–99. On moral theology, see L. Vereecke, "Moral Theology, History of (700 to Vatican Council I)," *New Catholic Encyclopedia*, 9:1120–22; J. J. Farraher, S.J., "Moral Theology, History of (Contemporary Trends)," ibid., 1122–23.

17. St. Thomas Aquinas is not included in what I call "classical moral theology." The view of moral teaching and the role for the moral theologian I call "classical" did not exist before the impact of rationalism. In Thomas, one finds a far less legalistic view, and conscience plays a comparatively minor role. See Thomas Deman, O.P., *La Prudence*, in S. Thomas d'Aquin, *Somme théologique, 2a–2ae, Questions 47–56*, 2d ed. (Paris: Desclée, 1949), 478–523. Moreover, although the fundamental moral theology of St. Thomas is not Christocentric, his Christology includes the principle of the following of Christ, and Thomas never divided contemplative from moral theology as did later scholasticism: Louis B. Gillon, O.P., *Christ and Moral Theology* (Staten Island, N.Y.: Alba House, 1967), 135–41. For an outline of a moral theology based on St. Thomas, in many respects fulfilled by the present work, see S. Pinckaers, O.P., "Esquisse d'une morale chrétienne: Ses bases: la Loi évangélique et la loi naturelle," *Nova et Vetera*, 55 (1980), 102–25.

18. By the mid-nineteenth century, the unsatisfactory condition of Catholic theology was widely recognized. Leo XIII encouraged renewal in the study of Scripture and other areas of theology; he also urged a return to the Christian philosophy of St. Thomas. Before Vatican II much progress was made, especially during the pontificate of Pius XII. See P. de Letter, S.J., "Theology, History of," *New Catholic Encyclopedia*, 14:56–58, for a brief summary with bibliography. Although one cannot agree with him in everything, Jacques Leclercq, *Christ and Modern Conscience* (New York: Sheed and Ward, 1962), 39–68 and 197–204, offers a remarkably insightful analysis of legalistic morality ("code morality") in contrast with a morality of truth ("wisdom morality"). The volume as a whole is useful for the comparisons it makes between Christian morality and many forms of non-Christian morality, including forms from non-Western cultures. Another insightful but not entirely fair dissection of classical moral theology: Marc Oraison, *Morality for Our Time* (Garden City, N.Y.: Doubleday, 1968), 43–63.

19. See John C. Ford, S.J., and Gerald Kelly, S.J., *Contemporary Moral Theology, vol. 1, Questions in Fundamental Moral Theology,* (Westminster, Md.: Newman Press, 1959), 42–79, for an introduction to some of the modern criticisms and suggested new approaches, and 80–103, for an evaluation from the point of view of classical moral theology. For a useful survey of developments in Catholic moral theology, with particular reference to principles, from 1918 to the post-Vatican II period, see Domenico Capone, C.Ss.R., "Per un manuale di teologia morale," *Seminarium*, 16 n.s. (1976), 462–83. An important book published before Vatican II, which also refers to other reforming works: Gérard Gilleman, S.J., *The Primacy of Charity in Moral Theology* (London: Burns and Oates, 1959). An earlier, and I think better, work, to which I owe a considerable debt: E. Mersch, S.J., *Morality and the Mystical Body* (New York: P. J. Kenedy, 1939). Two works first published before Vatican II and again since: Servais Pinckaers, O.P., *La Renouveau de la Morale: Etudes pour une morale fidèle à ses sources et à sa mission présente*, 2d ed. (Paris: Téqui, 1979); Octavio Nicolás Derisi, *Los fundamentos metafísicos del orden moral*, 4th ed. (Buenos Aires: Universidad Católica Argentina, 1980).

20. For an interesting exegesis of Vatican II's call for the renewal of moral theology, see Josef Fuchs, S.J., *Human Values and Christian Morality* (Dublin: Gill and Macmillan, 1970), 1–55. Most of what Fuchs says in this chapter seems to me right, and his thinking was very helpful in the reflection which led to the present work. Fuchs says unequivocally (49) that the mind of the Council on moral theology is that "the time has come at least for a change in the simple and uncomplicated approach to this subject which has prevailed (more or less) throughout a very long period indeed." And he insists (49) that "moral theology has never yet—strictly speaking—attained the ideal contemplated by the Council" and (50) "no real tradition of the ideal moral theology contemplated by the Council exists today." Perhaps the most successful attempt thus far to fulfill Vatican II's prescription for renewal is

the worthwhile, although not entirely satisfactory, work: Anselm Günthör, O.S.B., *Chiamata e risposta: Una nuova teologia moral*, 3 vols., 3d ed. (Rome: Paoline, 1979). Also, a clear exposition of an attempted reworking of fundamental moral by an author of one of the best of the classical manuals: Pietro Palazzini, *Avviamento allo studio della morale cristiana* (Rome: Paoline, 1979). A more elementary, but worthwhile, attempt: Carlo Caffarra, *Viventi in Cristo* (Milan: Jaca Book, 1981). A collective work highlighting problem areas in the renewal of moral theology: José Luis Illanes Maestre et al., eds., *Etica y Teología ante la crisis contemporánea: I Simposio Internacional de Teología de la Universidad de Navarra* (Pamplona, Spain: EUNSA, 1980).

21. *CCE*, 100.

22. *CCE*, 69–70.

23. See McCormick, *Notes*, 296–303 and 626–38, for summaries of the thinking both of those who promote this view and of those who have criticized it. The problem of the distinctiveness of Christian ethics will be treated below (25-E).

24. See J. J. Farraher, op. cit., 433–35, for a summary and bibliography. See also Servais Pinckaers, O.P., "La question des actes intrinsèquement mauvais et le 'proportionnalisme,'" *Revue Thomiste*, 82 (1982), 181–212. Most recent work in moral theology is in essays on various topics, rather than in synthetic works. An exception: Timothy E. O'Connell, *Principles for a Catholic Morality* (New York: Seabury Press, 1978). This work includes brief chapters on biblical morality (20–29) and "Christ and Moral Theology" (30–41). The themes treated in the former chapter yield no fruit in the remainder of the work; the latter chapter is used to reduce moral theology to ethics by way of the humanity of Christ. O'Connell states his position concisely (40): "Christian ethics, like all of the Christian faith, is essentially and profoundly human. It is a human task seeking human wisdom about the human conduct of human affairs. It is therefore not an isolated enterprise. It does not possess any secret sources of information, and it does not lead to any 'mysterious' conclusions. Thus, in a certain sense, moral theology is not theology at all. It is moral philosophy, pursued by persons who are believers. Moral theology is a science that seeks to benefit from all the sources of wisdom within our world. It listens respectfully to all philosophies, and uses them. It accepts and cherishes the evidence and conclusions of the social sciences. It tests its own conclusions against the experience of mankind, not only that of members of the Church. It speaks in the midst of the human community and attempts to speak for and to that whole community." For a sympathetic exposition and critique of O'Connell's book and similar work: Raphael Gallagher, C.Ss.R., "Fundamental Moral Theology, 1975–1979: A bulletin-analysis of some significant writings examined from a methodological stance," *Studia Moralia*, 18 (1980), 149–68.

25. Bernard Häring, C.Ss.R., is typical. His preconciliar work, *The Law of Christ: Moral Theology for Priests and Laity*, trans. Edwin G. Kaiser, C.Pp.S., vol. 1 (Westminster, Md: Newman Press, 1961), 23–33, summarized the reform movement which began in Germany at the beginning of the nineteenth century, and which Häring's work took to its highest point. Unfortunately, this movement never clarified the intrinsic relationship between the requirements of human goodness and the status of Christians as children of God. After Vatican II, Häring joined in dissent concerning points of received Catholic moral teaching, even on matters such as the indissolubility of marriage: "Internal Forum Solutions to Insoluble Marriage Cases," *Jurist*, 30 (1970), 21–30. He then published a new work, *Free and Faithful in Christ: Moral Theology for Clergy and Laity*, vol. 1 (New York: Seabury Press, 1978), which still often mentions Christ and scriptural themes, but now proceeds on the supposition that theological dissent is justified and conscience is autonomous in relation to the Church's teaching (see 4–5, 280–84, 331–33 and 345–48). Häring's second systematic work makes no progress in solving the problem of synthesis. Häring's thought at times seems more Lutheran than Catholic; when he locates himself in respect to the question of the specificity of Christian ethics, he significantly says (27, n. 12): "For those who have followed or are studying this problem I want to indicate that my position comes very close to James M. Gustafson." A brilliant critique of *Free and Faithful in Christ*: Ramón García de Haro, "Vecchi Errori della Nuova Morale: L'ultimo libro di Bernhard Häring," *Studi Cattolici*, 25 (1981), 83–94.

26. For an explanation of the way in which secular humanism has impacted on Christian theology, see Peter L. Berger, *The Sacred Canopy: Elements of a Sociological Theory of Religion* (New York: Doubleday Anchor, 1969), 127–71. For a broader treatment of the modern social and ideological situation as a challenge to faith: Stephen B. Clark, *Man and Woman in Christ: An Examination of the Roles of Men and Women in Light of Scripture and the Social Sciences* (Ann Arbor, Mich.: Servant Books, 1980), 467–540; bibliography, 672–73, 726–35. For a broad historical background concerning the emergence of secular humanism and its influence on Christian faith, leading to the emergence of

liberalized Christianity: James Hitchcock, *What Is Secular Humanism? Why Humanism Became Secular and How It Is Changing Our World* (Ann Arbor, Mich.: Servant Books, 1982), esp. 7–48 and 115–38.

27. See Juan Luis Segundo, S.J., *Liberation of Theology* (Maryknoll, N.Y.: Orbis Books, 1976), 154–75, who argues that truly communitarian and generous-hearted ends can justify any necessary means whatsoever, and who tries to reconcile this with the gospel by the simple expedient of declaring anything in the gospel incompatible with it "ideology." For references to some other relevant literature, see McCormick, *Notes,* 181–86. John Paul II clearly and forcefully rejects the sort of liberation theology I criticize here in his Allocution to the Third General Meeting of the Bishops of Latin America, Puebla, Mexico (28 January 1979), 71 *AAS* (1979) 190–91; *L'Osservatore Romano,* Eng. ed., 5 February 1979, 2. See also Quentin L. Quade, ed., *John Paul II Confronts Liberation Theology* (Washington, D.C.: Ethics and Public Policy Center, 1983).

28. Someone might object that a work such as Häring's *Free and Faithful in Christ,* with its emphasis on responsibility toward God as person and on creative liberty (62–76) really does transcend legalism, as Häring claims (69, 128–29, and passim). A position like Häring's certainly differs from older forms of legalism, and it is a matter of semantics whether one calls it "legalism." It is like the legalism of classical moral theology in locating the force of moral responsibility in a relationship to God's antecedent choice, rather than in the truth about human fulfillment (see DH 2–3); significantly, the freedom Häring emphasizes is liberty, not freedom of choice (see GS 17). For further discussion of the shortcomings in most efforts in moral theology since Vatican II, see Philippe Delhaye, *La Scienza del bene e del male: La morale del Vaticano II e il "metaconcilio"* (Milan: Ares, 1981); Ermenegildo Lio, *Morale perenne e morale nuova nella formazione ed educazione della coscienza* (Rome: Città Nuova, 1979).

29. The unsynthesized fragments of an account of the natural end of human persons, which one finds in St. Thomas' various works, are a clear symptom of the unsatisfactoriness of his synthesis in this respect. See Germain Grisez, "Man, the Natural End of," *New Catholic Encyclopedia,* 9:134–37. Both Aristotle and St. Augustine pointed Thomas in the direction of an overly definite conception of the natural end of human persons. The exigencies of this end—knowledge of the divine—made it hard to treat it in practice as a real end distinct from the beatific vision. Thus in Thomas there is an unresolved tension between a natural desire for beatitude and the gratuity of the supernatural end, which (despite his intentions and efforts) threatens to become the natural end of the human person. It seems to me that a better solution is suggested by Vatican II, especially in *Gaudium et spes;* this view will be articulated in the present work, particularly in chapters nineteen and thirty-four.

30. *CCE,* 22; cf. 73.

31. See 1 Tm 4.14; 2 Tm 1.6–7, 13–14. On the prophetic gift which makes the teaching of revelation certain, see Jerome D. Quinn, "'Charisma Veritatis Certum': Irenaeus, *Adversus Haereses* 4, 26, 2," *Theological Studies,* 39 (1978), 520–25. The concept of Irenaeus seems to provide an important link between Scripture and the teaching of Vatican I and II concerning infallibility in certain acts of the magisterium.

32. *CCE,* 66. Discussions of theological pluralism frequently not only ignore the criterion for legitimate pluralism the Holy See points out, but other necessary distinctions as well. See, for instance, W. M. Shea, "Pluralism, Theological," *New Catholic Encyclopedia,* 17:513–14. Shea never considers the difference between a set of logically inconsistent positions and plural but logically compatible positions; he ignores the difference between propositions and linguistic expressions; he confuses theological speculation with interpretation; and he gratuitously denies the priority of magisterium to theology in judging the soundness of interpretations of Scripture and the creeds.

33. *CCE,* 66–67.

34. *CCE,* 68. A helpful theological study: José Luis Illanes Maestre, "Pluralismo teológico y verdad de la fe," *Scripta Theologica,* 7 (1975), 619–84.

35. *CCE,* 69. For a clear and well-documented treatment of the situation, with a discussion of authentic and false pluralism: Eugene M. Kevane, "The Faith and the Theologies," in *The Teaching Church in Our Time,* ed. George A. Kelly (Boston: St. Paul Editions, 1978), 13–61.

36. *CCE,* 125.

37. *CCE,* 126.

38. St. Augustine was strongly influenced by the Neoplatonic philosophy which he used as an instrument for his theological work. See Robert J. O'Connell, *St. Augustine's Early Theory of Man,*

A.D. 386–391 (Cambridge, Mass.: Belknap Press of Harvard University Press, 1968), 1–28 and 279–89; *St. Augustine's "Confessions": The Odyssey of Soul* (Cambridge, Mass.: Belknap Press of Harvard University Press, 1969), 1–22 and 177–90; John Burnaby, *Amor Dei: A Study of the Religion of St. Augustine* (London: Hodder and Stoughton, 1938), 25–42.

39. See Grisez, "Man, the Natural End of," 9:134–35. Among recent, worthwhile attempts to contribute to the necessary synthesis are two works of D. J. Lallemant, *Vivre en chrétien dans notre temps* (Paris: Téqui, 1979); *Notre besoin de Jesus sauveur* (Paris: Téqui, 1980). Also: Servais Pinckaers, O.P., *La quéte du bonheur* (Paris: Téqui, 1979).

40. On St. Thomas' overconfidence in reason, see Louis Bouyer, *The Eternal Son: A Theology of the Word of God and Christology*, trans. Simone Inkel, S.L., and John F. Laughlin (Huntington, Ind.: Our Sunday Visitor, 1978), 348–55; James F. Ross, "Aquinas and Philosophical Methodology," *Metaphilosophy*, 1 (1970), 300–317. A treatment of the history more sympathetic to St. Thomas: Servais Pinckaers, O.P., "Réflexions pour une histoire de la théologie morale," *Nova et Vetera*, 52 (1977), 50–61; "La théologie morale à la périod de la grande scolastique," *Nova et Vetera*, 52 (1977), 118–31. A useful and not too difficult introduction to the philosophy of St. Thomas: Armand A. Maurer, C.S.B., *Medieval Philosophy* (New York: Random House, 1962), 163–91; with an excellent short bibliography, 404–6.

41. Maurer, op. cit., 137–52 and 400–401, is a helpful introduction to St. Bonaventure.

42. Ibid., 265–91 and 414–15, is an introduction to William Ockham and nominalism in general. See Servais Pinckaers, O.P., "La théologie morale au déclin du Moyen-Age: Le nominalisme," *Nova et Vetera*, 52 (1977), 209–21; digested as "Ockham and the Decline of Moral Theology," *Theology Digest*, 26 (1978), 239–41.

43. A helpful introduction to Descartes: James Collins, *A History of Modern European Philosophy* (Milwaukee: Bruce, 1954), 138–98.

44. See de Letter, op. cit., 55; Servais Pinckaers, O.P., "La théologie morale à l'époque moderne," *Nova et Vetera*, 52 (1977), 269–87.

45. See Irving M. Copi, *Introduction to Logic*, 4th ed. (New York: Macmillan, 1972), 422–68, for an introduction to the method of modern science.

46. The situation in the sciences of man is far from simple, but reflection on them from diverse philosophical viewpoints at least makes it clear that they are not called "sciences" in the same sense as, say, chemistry: Maurice Natanson, ed., *Philosophy of the Social Sciences: A Reader* (New York: Random House, 1963); May Brodbeck, ed., *Readings in the Philosophy of the Social Sciences* (London: Collier-Macmillan, 1968).

47. *CCE*, 99.

48. See Joseph M. Boyle, Jr., Germain Grisez, and Olaf Tollefsen, *Free Choice: A Self-Referential Argument* (Notre Dame and London: University of Notre Dame Press, 1976), 122–85.

49. A very good, critical treatment of the philosophies of Hume, Kant, and Hegel, with special reference to religion: James Collins, *Emergence of Philosophy of Religion* (New York: Yale University Press, 1967), esp. 393–406, for the attitude of these philosophers toward revelation. For a more encompassing treatment, including much post-Hegelian thought: Cornelio Fabro, *God in Exile: Modern Atheism: A Study of the Internal Dynamic of Modern Atheism, from Its Roots in the Cartesian "Cogito" to the Present Day*, trans. and ed. Arthur Gibson (Westminster, Md.: Newman Press, 1968).

50. See Grisez, *Beyond the New Theism*, 93–228. For a critique of the use of modern philosophies by recent theology: Cornelio Fabro, *L'Avventura della teologia progressista* (Milan: Rusconi, 1974).

51. *CCE*, 52. For a further account of the considerations behind the magisterium's decision: Cornelio Fabro, *Breve introduzione al tomismo* (Rome: Desclée, 1960), 69–80.

FREE CHOICE, SELF-DETERMINATION, COMMUNITY, AND CHARACTER

Introduction

Chapter one explained what moral theology is and why it needs renewal. The remainder of the first half of this book will deal with topics, beginning with free choice, traditionally treated in the fundamental part of classical moral theology. This treatment will, however, be a fresh synthesis, shaped by a theological framework which will be made fully explicit in the book's second half.

Question A: In what sense is free choice a principle of morality?

1. Free choice is not a normative principle—one which distinguishes right from wrong—and it is a moral principle only in a wide sense. While the word "morality" is sometimes limited to moral goodness, free choice underlies both goodness and badness. The moral domain in this wide sense, embracing both goodness and badness, can be called "existential." **Free choice is, properly speaking, an existential principle, a source of both moral good and moral evil.**

2. Free choice is the central reality in us by which our acts are present in the moral field—that is, are existential. It might be said that free choices put one in a game whose rules are moral norms. It is true that feeling, thought, behavior, and so on also pertain in various ways to the existential. But what we do is *our* doing and can be *wrong*doing or its opposite only if we freely choose to do it. What we do makes up our moral life only insofar as our choice is free, not something which happens to us as a result of factors outside us (see *S.t.*, 1, q. 83, a. 1; 1–2, q. 1, a. 1; q. 6, a. 1; q. 18, a. 1).

3. If what we do were determined by something other than ourselves, not we but that other something would be responsible for our lives. We are responsible in a full sense only when two conditions are fulfilled: first, when it is in our power to do what is good or bad; second, when we do one or the other by our own choice, a choice which really could be otherwise. Thus free choice underlies existential responsibility.

4. "Responsibility" here does not mean being held responsible. One can

rightly be held responsible only if one really is responsible—if one acts by free choice. Human persons are historical beings who day by day build themselves up by their free choices. One shapes one's own life, one determines one's self, by one's free choices.[1] To be responsible ultimately means to be a self one cannot blame on heredity, environment, or anything other than one's own free choices.

5. Moral norms direct free choices; they indicate which choices are good, which bad. If choices were not free, moral norms would be useless. Christian moral norms direct believers empowered by God's grace to make the free choices by which they share in and contribute to fulfillment in the Lord Jesus. If this sharing and contribution did not depend upon free choices to accept God's grace in Jesus and follow him, Christian moral norms would be senseless.

The idea of the "existential" can be clarified by considering that human persons involve four distinct and irreducible modes of reality: the system of nature, the intentional order, the existential domain, and the world of objective culture.[2] One and the same sensible object can be seen to have fourfold intelligible reality insofar as it can be understood in each of these orders.

For example, a crucifix hanging above an altar can be weighed and measured; as a *natural entity* it is subject to the same physical-chemical laws as the rest of nature, including human individuals. The same crucifix belongs to the intentional order insofar as it concretely presents the *meaning* of the new covenant formed by God's redemptive love and Jesus' human cooperation. Human reasoning relates the symbol to the truth of faith it expresses. The same crucifix, again, belongs to the existential domain, for it can be the *occasion* of conversion or commitment for those who gaze on it with devotion; it brings to mind possibilities for free choice not only by individuals but also by groups—for example, by the congregation choosing to offer the sacrifice of the Mass. And, finally, the same crucifix belongs to the world of objective culture, for it is a *product* of technical skill with certain economic and esthetic values.

Thus the existential domain is not a certain set of things, but all things insofar as they make up the moral universe. This universe centers upon the free choices of created persons, who ought to form a communion sharing in the freely given love of their creator, but who instead form a world of good and evil in tension. Into this conflict free choices draw everything else, and so all things come in some way to share the existential significance of moral good and evil.

The existential center of each human person is the will, insofar as it is the principle of free choices and of the self determined through choices. But morality, although it begins in the heart, is not confined there. The bodily self who belongs to the system of nature, the thinking self who unfolds the intentional order of human meaning, and the performing self who acts out a role in the world of culture—all these share in and complete the moral character of the acting person.

Question B: Can human persons make free choices?

1. The ability of human persons to make free choices is taken for granted throughout the Bible. God does not impose his love—he proposes it: Yahweh offers the covenant; Jesus announces the kingdom; those who hear must respond (see Dt 30.19; Mk 16.16). If they do not accept the divine offer of friendship and intimacy, they reject it (see Mt 12.30; Lk 11.23). How individuals respond depends on themselves, and the nature of their response determines their lives in

this world and the next (see Jn 3.14–21).

2. The reality of free choice is made clear in the book of Sirach (15.11–20), written when Jewish faith came in contact with Greek culture. In general, Greek thought did not accept free choice, and under its influence Jews were tempted to evade moral responsibility by thinking of divine, creative causality as being like the fate in which pagans believed. Sirach rejects this mistake: We cannot blame God for our sins.

Writing about two centuries before Jesus, another man named "Jesus," son of Eleazar, son of Sirach, provided a classic formulation of the sublime truth concerning the human power of free choice.

> Do not say, "Because of the Lord I left the right way";
> for he will not do what he hates.
> Do not say, "It was he who led me astray";
> for he has no need of a sinful man.
> The Lord hates all abominations,
> and they are not loved by those who fear him.
> It was he who created man in the beginning,
> and he left him in the power of his own inclination.
> If you will, you can keep the commandments,
> and to act faithfully is a matter of your own choice.
> He has placed before you fire and water:
> stretch out your hand for whichever you wish.
> Before a man are life and death,
> and whichever he chooses will be given to him.
> For great is the wisdom of the Lord;
> he is mighty in power and sees everything;
> his eyes are on those who fear him,
> and he knows every deed of man.
> He has not commanded any one to be ungodly,
> and he has not given any one permission to sin. (Sir 15.11–20)

Human persons are not simply subject to fate, to natural necessity, or to their heredity and environment. In what is most important, human persons are of themselves.

3. Much later, at the time of the Reformation, Luther and others rightly wished to emphasize sinful humankind's total dependence on God's grace. But they made the mistake of supposing that, in crediting salvation entirely to God, we must exclude the sinner's responsibility for his or her conversion and justification. Thus these Protestants denied human free choice. **Against them, the Council of Trent solemnly defined the truth that human beings, even after Adam's sin, can make free choices** (see DS 1555/815). Good free choices also are God's gift, yet they are truly our own free choices (see DS 1525/797; also see *S.t.*, 1–2, q. 111, a. 2).

Free choices are created entities. There would be no free choices if God did not cause them. The free choice to believe in God and to keep his commandments is the work of God's grace; sinners and saints alike can do nothing without God.

If God's causality were like any causality we understand, then for something to be both created and a free choice would make as much sense as for something to be both square and not-square at the same time and in the same respect. But we do not understand what God is in himself, and we do not know what it is for him to cause. The existence of free choices in the world is part of the existence of the whole of creation which is accounted for by referring everything to God the creator. There is no contradiction in God creating human-persons-making-free-choices. We know there is no contradiction, because it is a fact that there are free choices, and they could not exist if God did not cause them to be (see *S.t.*, 1, q. 19, a. 8; q. 83, a. 1, ad 3; 1–2, q. 6, a. 1, ad 3; q. 10, a. 4; *S.c.g.*, 3, 67, 70, 73, 89). Similarly, we do nothing salvific without God's grace, but part of God's grace is our freely seeking him, accepting him, and living in his love. (For a fuller explanation of this point, see appendix 3.)

4. The ability to make free choices is one important way in which human persons are somewhat like God. God is not determined in any way by anything other than himself. Moreover, he creates all else by his free choice (see DS 3002/ 1783, 3025/1805). Similarly, in choosing freely one is not determined by anything other than oneself, although as a creature one remains dependent upon God even for one's free choices. Moreover, as a real cause through freedom, a human person also is like God. **In choosing freely, however, one not only brings about things other than oneself, one is one's self-maker under God.** Thus we have the great dignity of being, in a limited but true sense, of ourselves (see *S.t.*, 1–2, Prologue; q. 1, a. 2; q. 9, a. 3).

From this point of view, free choice and morality are not humankind's burden, but humankind's dignity—our natural similarity to God the creator and our natural power of sharing in the work of creation. Vatican II stresses that the power of free choice "is an exceptional sign of the divine image within man" (GS 17).

The Council does not apply the word "dignity" to human persons in any loose and popular way. "Dignity" means inherent worth; the high status which belongs to those made in God's image and called to share his likeness as his adopted children: "It is in accordance with their dignity as persons—that is, beings endowed with reason and free will and therefore privileged to bear personal responsibility—that all men should be at once impelled by their nature and also bound by a moral obligation to seek the truth, especially religious truth. They are also bound to adhere to the truth, once it is known, and to order their whole lives in accord with the demands of truth." (DH 2; translation supplied). Dignity: the power to be of oneself, to live not in a limited world but in the truth of boundless reality, to bring oneself to exist not as stunted but as fulfilled. Morality is a privilege.

Free choice is not only a principle of Christian morality in making us responsible and able to be of ourselves, but also a principle of the act of faith, by which we accept God's offer of love and become his adopted children (see *S.t.*, 2–2, q. 1, a. 4; q. 2, a. 2). Vatican II insists upon the relevance of free choice to the act of faith: "The act of faith is of its very nature voluntary. Man, redeemed by Christ the Savior and through Christ Jesus called to be God's adopted son, cannot give his adherence to God revealing himself unless the Father draw him to offer to God the reasonable and free submission of faith" (DH 10; translation supplied). The same point is made by many of the Fathers of the Church, including St. Irenaeus (see FEF 245), St. Clement of Alexandria (see FEF 417), Arnobius (see FEF 622), and St. Augustine (see FEF 1734 and 1821).

In sum, there are three important ways in which freedom of choice is a principle of Christian morality. It is a necessary condition for moral responsibility. It is the central subject matter which moral norms are about; in this respect, the power of free choice is the principle of human dignity, insofar as human persons are like God in being of themselves what they morally are. And, finally, free choice is that by which we accept God in faith, and so enjoy his love and can live as his children.

5. Experience and philosophical reflection agree with faith that human beings can and do make free choices. Everyone capable of thinking about the matter has had the experience of making choices, including wrong ones by which moral guilt was incurred. Yet determinists deny that choices can be free.[3]

6. Since this denial runs counter to experience, determinists bear the burden of proving their case. In attempting to do so, they must appeal to our reasonableness and try to show that we ought to accept their position. The difficulty is, however, that this "ought" itself embodies an appeal to freedom. Determinists are asking us to be loyal to the pursuit of truth, and such a commitment is impossible if we cannot make free choices. **Thus any attempt to prove that the experiences of choice and moral guilt are illusory is self-defeating.**

The reality of free choice and the availability of this reality to experience and reason are of great importance in pastoral work. On the one hand, calling attention to free choice emphasizes something essential to faith and incompatible with practically every other world view. A consideration of this sort is very valuable when one proclaims the faith, for it supports the credibility of faith and makes evident the unreasonableness of alternative world views. On the other hand, free choice must be emphasized constantly or the faithful begin to misconceive their lives in some way incompatible with faith, often coming to rationalize sin without avoiding real moral guilt.

7. Underlying most deterministic arguments is the assumption, usually unstated, that nothing can come to be without a "sufficient reason" which accounts for it.[4] A "sufficient reason" would be one which makes clear why the thing has come to be rather than not coming to be, and has come to be precisely as it is rather than otherwise. Of course, a free choice has an adequate cause: the person choosing. But the idea of sufficient reason involves more than that of adequate cause, for it adds the notion that everything can be completely explained. Thus a sufficient reason for a choice would make clear why just this choice, not some other, had been made. But the assumption that there must always be a sufficient reason is not self-evident; and if any free choices are made, either by God or by us, it is false.

8. God does act freely—that is, without a sufficient reason—for example, in creating and redeeming. Of course, God always acts in accord with his own wisdom, but his love is not determined by his wisdom. As for human persons, they also have reasons, but not sufficient reasons, for their choices. To explain why they chose as they did, people point to the good promised by the possibility which they chose. Yet if they had chosen otherwise, they would also have explained their different choice in a similar way (see *S.t.*, 1–2, q. 13, a. 6). Thus there are reasons but never sufficient reasons to account for human free choices.

9. Determinists also point out, quite correctly, that many factors limit the possibilities open to us, and we are not usually even conscious of some of these. They are, however, mistaken in thinking that factors beyond our control which limit our possibilities also settle what we will choose within these limits. Because there are limits on what one can choose, it does not follow that one cannot choose freely within the limits.

Question C: How is free choice distinguished from other realities called "freedom"?

1. While the word "freedom" has many meanings, all share certain common elements. With reference to persons, the meaning of freedom includes as its elements someone who is or could be acting, the action, and something which might be but in fact is not blocking the action. **To distinguish meanings of "free," one must specify various factors which might block action.**

2. In one sense "freedom" means physical freedom. Some physical force or constraint might interfere with action; in its absence, action proceeds naturally and spontaneously. Someone who is not fettered or bound is physically free. In a second sense "freedom" means doing as one pleases. The orders or demands of another person or persons might prevent one from acting as one wishes; in their absence, one is free to do as one pleases. When they are out of school, children are free to do as they please. In a third sense "freedom" means the emergence of novelty. Various factors might keep things as they are and prevent originality; in their absence, one is free in the sense that one has a share in authorship, originality, innovation. James Joyce was free in writing *Ulysses*.

Some degree of physical freedom nearly always is given; one who is outwardly forced generally can still control to some extent his or her own focusing of attention on this or that. At the same time, physical freedom always is limited. So physical freedom is a matter of more and less; it is subject to degree. Physical freedom is important for moral life in this way: The more physical freedom one has, the more possible courses of action there are among which one might choose.

In a second sense, "freedom" means freedom to do as one pleases. A slave, to the extent that he or she is a slave, has no freedom in this sense. Adolescents who demand their freedom are primarily interested in freedom to do as they please. Almost everyone has some scope for doing as he or she pleases. But this scope is limited in two ways: by one's own sense of duty and by the impositions from others which one regards as arbitrary.

Correspondingly, there are two ways of increasing one's freedom to do as one pleases. The more one pleases to do as one ought, the less one's sense of duty is an obstacle to doing as one pleases. Jesus is just as free to do as he pleases as is the Father, for Jesus desires nothing apart from the Father. Again, the more one can evade the force of alien wills which really are arbitrary, the more one is free to do as one pleases. Thus, the weaknesses of antireligious secularism allow Catholics in Poland and the United States some scope to do as they please in practicing their faith.

Freedom to do as one pleases is morally ambiguous; it means rather different things to good and bad persons, who differ in what they find pleasing.

Emergence of novelty is another sense of "freedom." In creating, God is free in this sense; to the extent that we share in his creative and redemptive work, we also share in this freedom. Goodness is in an open and expanding realization of potentialities. The immoral life is unnecessarily self-limiting, and tends to be dull and repetitious. Wherever there is free choice, of course, there is something really new. In this respect, even the sinful act is somewhat creative. It tends, however, not to be very creative, both because sinners merely follow given inclinations and because they do not wish to admit free choice and responsibility. Hence, they view goods and possibilities in such a way that sin will seem to be—and more and more will come to be—almost inevitable.

3. Freedom in each of these senses is also present in social contexts. Thus "political freedom" refers to nothing other than these sorts of freedom. The freedom for which revolutions are fought is the liberty of a group to do as it pleases; the freedom prized in democratic societies is the liberty of individuals to live as they wish within the framework of a common social order.

4. **It is possible to affirm the reality of freedom in any of the preceding senses yet deny the reality of free choice.** Actions performed by physical freedom can spring from a natural, inner necessity, as in the case of a dog which chases a cat (see *S.t.*, 1–2, q. 6, a. 2). Disobedient three-year olds want freedom to do as they please, yet are quite incapable of making free choices. And, although every free choice does involve a certain creativity, novelty is possible without free choice.

5. After the Reformation, some theologians did not accept the truth of faith concerning free choice. They asserted that human persons are free, not in the sense that they could choose otherwise than they do, but only in the sense that they are not compelled to choose. In other words, while admitting that moral responsibility requires physical freedom for human acts, they held that grace or some other cause determines precisely what one will do. A formula for the erroneous position that physical freedom suffices for moral responsibility is: "What comes about voluntarily, even if it comes about necessarily, still comes about freely." The Church condemns this error (see DS 1939/1039). This teaching is important today, because most contemporary social scientists, psychologists, and nonbelieving philosophers admit freedom in human choice only in this sense, which the Church teaches is insufficient for moral responsibility.[5]

6. There is another, important sense of freedom: the freedom of the children of God (see *S.t.*, 2–2, q. 183, a. 4; 3, q. 48, a. 4; q. 49, aa. 1–3). Factors such as Satan, sin, death, the flesh, and the law confined the lives of fallen human persons. Our Lord Jesus overcame sin and won freedom for us, the Christian freedom which rightly belongs to members of God's family (see Rom 6.6–23; 7.24–25; 8.21; 1 Cor 7.22; 15.24–26; 2 Cor 3.17; Gal 4.26, 31; 5.1, 13).[6]

7. The freedom of the children of God presupposes free choice but is distinct from it. This freedom cannot be badly used, but one can make bad free choices. The freedom of the children of God is the liberation we receive in Jesus by God's gift, a gift to be perfected in heavenly fulfillment; free choice is the principle of one's living of a Christian life.

8. **The New Testament clearly distinguishes Christian liberty from freedom to do as one pleases** (see Gal 5.13; 1 Pt 2.16–17). Christian liberty is not license, for, like the freedom of the Son and the Spirit, it operates out of divine love and so always in accord with this love. Vatican II reaffirms this point (see GS 17). People need room to act upon their responsible judgments, but they should not "use the name of freedom as the pretext for refusing to submit to authority and for making light of the duty of obedience" (DH 8).

Free choice is the beginning of one's own action in Christian life; the freedom of the children of God is the end. Even now we share in this end, although not as perfectly as we hope to do in heaven. The more we love God, the less sin has a hold over us, the less fearful we are of death, the less we even notice that there is a moral law. Nothing is impossible for God, and so nothing is impossible for those who act out of the love—which is the power—of God (see Lk 1.37; 11.13; 18.27).

In talking about free choice and moral responsibility, it is important always to make it clear that the two go together. So-called freedom of conscience often means a claim to do as one pleases in disregard of moral norms. The freedom of God's children is not a license to ignore God's commandments, whose truth the Church explains and defends; rather, the freedom of God's children, received by the gift of the Spirit, liberates conscience by divine love (see Rom 5.5; 8.1–17). Thus the law of God is written on one's heart (see Jer 31.33; Rom 6.15–23), and one can do as one pleases, for nothing is pleasing but what pleases God (see Gal 5.13–26).

Question D: How does a person experience free choice?

1. **The experience of choice begins in an awareness of conflict. One finds oneself in a situation where it is impossible to pursue all the goods one is concerned with, fulfill all the wishes one has.** There are definite, incompatible possibilities—at least the possibilities of acting and not acting—each of them attractive in some way but also limited. This conflict causes hesitation; the continuous flow of behavior is blocked. Thus the first stage of the experience of choice is conscious thinking about alternatives (see *S.t.*, 1–2, q. 9, a. 4; q. 13, a. 6; q. 14, a. 1). Instead of being drawn by some unopposed motive into spontaneous action, as usually happens, one begins to deliberate.

2. Normally, the first step in deliberating is to ask oneself two questions. Isn't it possible after all to have both (or all) of the apparently incompatible possibilities? Or, isn't it the case that all the alternatives but one are already ruled out and so are not really possibilities which one could choose? In other words, one tries to obviate the need for choice. Not infrequently this attempt is successful: Either one can have all the possibilities, or only one of them is actually possible.

To one who is faced with the need to make a choice, the prospect has a certain negative aspect. No matter what one chooses, one must give up what one does not choose, at least for the time being. To face the need to choose is to confront one's own finitude. If one does not make the choice, one will not be fulfilled in any of the possible, appealing ways which one is considering. But it would be preferable to be fulfilled in all the possible ways. As it is, the choice will open a way to fulfillment, but also will set aside a way or ways to alternative fulfillment.

In this respect, human free choice is very different from God's choice. Since his action is not self-fulfilling—he being perfect in goodness whether or not he causes anything—God in choosing need only accept the limitedness of creatures, not limit himself (see *S.t.*, 1, q. 19, a. 3; *S.c.g.*, 1, 81). This negative aspect of human choice is one reason why people naturally try to avoid making choices when they consider alternatives in deliberation.

3. An especially interesting case of resolving deliberation without choice is that in which one compares the alternatives initially presented and finds that one possibility definitely promises more good (or less bad) than any other. In this case, one's interests will so clearly be better satisfied by the superior alternative that the others lose their appeal. Upon inspection, one finds that one's previously settled wishes and interests foreclose the apparent openness of the situation which initially led to hesitation and reflection.

An example of an apparent choice-situation which is resolved without the need for free choice is a family's selection of a new residence. Initially, they look at many places. But some are too expensive; they are not real possibilities. Others are taken off the market by sale to someone else. The family has a checklist of "musts," and many of the seeming possibilities do not meet one or another of their requirements. They drop out. Finally, only a few possibilities remain.

If each has its own diverse appeal, which cannot be measured and weighed against the appeal of the others, then a choice finally must be made. For example, if one house has a better location while the other will more satisfactorily accommodate the family's possessions and activities, one must be chosen and the other given up. But sometimes as they reach the last few possibilities, a family happily finds that one prospective property has all the good features of the others. In that case, the others lose the appeal they initially had. The family closes the deal and need not later think: "It would have been nice if we could have had X but this house does have Y which we also wanted, and you just can't have everything."

When investigation eliminates apparent alternatives or shows that one can enjoy them all, no free choice is needed. In a sense, of course, one can say that the fortunate family "chose" their new residence. But a well-programmed computer could have done the same thing. Given their assumptions and the actual conditions, there was only one thing to do, although initially there seemed to be many live options. Notice also that people who find they do not have to make a choice proceed with a sense of freedom—meaning physical freedom and freedom to do as they please. Indeed, in a case of this kind one feels free in a sense in which one does not when one must set aside one possibility in order to realize another.

In cases in which one finds choice unnecessary, the factors which eliminate some of the initial options can themselves have been established by one's prior choices. A person who lives up to his or her commitments often is able to reduce a range of possibilities to one: I cannot do otherwise. The moral significance of such acts arises from the prior and continuing commitments which they express. As people get older and settle into a regular life, they often find themselves deliberating and choosing much less frequently than they did in late adolescence and early adulthood, when many important decisions had to be made.

4. When reflection does not eliminate all alternatives but one, we conclude that we face real and incompatible possibilities. "I can make this choice or that one." The word "can" does not express mere contingency (objective possibility) here (see *S.c.g.*, 3, 73). It is not as if we expected one thing or another to happen, regardless of or even despite ourselves. Rather, the possible choices appear to be really within our power. **"It's really up to me what I'm going to do."**

When one sees an animal or infant vacillate between courses of action, one realizes that it can do this or that. But this "can" merely expresses the contingency of physical freedom: Nothing is compelling or constraining behavior. One need not suppose that the animal or infant is considering possibilities and is about to choose between them. Rather, one supposes that inclinations will settle the issue.

By providing appropriate sensory stimulation, we can control the behavior of animals and infants. In doing this, we arouse an impulse strong enough to prevail over any other inclination which might otherwise be operative. Human adults, however, cannot be controlled so easily. As long as they are able to choose, they can resist every stimulation one can apply. And even when behavior is elicited without choice—for example, by torture—it is alien to the person. Only when we are about to choose do we have the awareness that we are making up our own minds, that our chosen action will be our doing, our life, our self.

5. While the act of choice involves focusing attention on one possibility—the one chosen—there is more to choice than just focusing attention. Even in choosing, one is aware of what one is setting aside. At the same time, one is not aware of anything happening which one can identify as the choice itself. **One does not encounter choices, one makes them.**

In sum, the experience of choice has three aspects. First, one is aware of a situation in which one's desires or interests are aroused by alternative possibilities, and one cannot find any way of eliminating the incompatibility or limiting the possibilities to one: "I could do this or that, but I cannot do both; these are real and incompatible possibilities."

Second, one is aware that it is within one's own power to take one or the other alternative, and that nothing but the exercise of this power will realize one possibility and set aside the other (or others): "It's up to me what I'm going to do; nothing and nobody else is going to settle this for me."

Third, one is aware of making the choice, and aware of nothing making one make it: "I made up my own mind; the limitation I've accepted by choosing is my own self-limitation." One who has this experience has a sense of freedom and of being responsible for his or her own life. If one is honest, one looks for excuses only in factors beyond one's control which limited the possibilities one was able to consider and choose among.

Although the experience of choice has been described with some care, the word "experience" can be misleading here. Choice is not a datum of consciousness. There is nothing experienced passively at the moment of choosing, as there is when one sees or hears, feels pain or dizziness, dreams or remembers, and so forth. Choosing is like reasoning; one is aware of doing it and of the outcome, but is not aware of any thing before one's mind which is this doing (see *S.t.*, 1, q. 87, a. 1).

Of course, as soon as one has made a choice, one is aware that one has made it. One is aware of having proceeded from indecision to the state of having made up one's mind; one realizes that choice divided the two. Thus one's knowledge of one's own choices is immediate, not inferential. In this sense, one has an experience of choice, but in choosing, one simply chooses. One does not choose and also perceive something which is a choosing. The reason is that choice is not something which happens to oneself; choice is one's settling of one's self.

Question E: What are the essence and the most important properties of free choice?

1. One makes a choice when one faces practical alternatives, believes one can and must settle which to take, deliberates, and takes one. The choice is free when choosing itself determines which alternative one takes. Right up to the moment of choice one is able to do this or that, and only one's very choosing determines which. True, factors beyond one's control both supplied and limited one's possibilities. But within these limits, nothing but oneself could determine what one would do. One chooses and in choosing determines oneself to seek fulfillment in one possibility rather than another. Inasmuch as one determines oneself in this way, one is of oneself.

2. **Free choice is not outwardly observable; it is making up one's mind or settling oneself in one's heart** (see *S.t.*, 1–2, q. 6, a. 4). It is possible to make a choice and then not act on it. Hence morality, which is centered in choice, is not so

much in one's behavior as in one's inner self (see Mt 15.10–20; Mk 7.15–23; Lk 6.45; also see *S.t.*, 1–2, q. 20, aa. 1–2). Nevertheless free choice cannot be separated from action. One chooses to do something. What is in view is generally a positive and appealing fulfillment of some capacity, whether of inner activity or outward behavior. Having chosen, one usually proceeds to do what was chosen. The outward performance shares in and completes the goodness or badness of the choice (see *S.t.*, 1–2, q. 20, aa. 3–4).

3. The most obvious cases of choice are those in which one does something which is a positive fulfillment. But one can also choose not to do something, to omit something which might have been done. Inaction can be chosen as a way of either avoiding evil or allowing factors apart from oneself to have their own effect.

4. One can choose to accept another's proposal, to put up with something, or to remain aloof from a problem. Moreover, one can choose indirectly—by choosing to put off choosing or by making little choices, aware that they will lead to an important outcome but never fully facing up to what one is doing.

5. Choices are concerned with what is judged to be good, not simply with what is felt as appealing or repelling; choices are acts of the will, not emotions of the sentient self (see *S.t.*, 1, q. 83). They are spiritual realities, not physical entities, and as such are not subject to space, time, and other physical conditions. If they were subject to such conditions, they would not be what they are—free acts by which persons are of themselves.

The conflicting possibilities which make one hesitate, deliberate, and choose initially present themselves as particular possibilities: for example, to do this or that particular thing this evening. From one point of view, the need to choose arises simply because of factual limitations—for example, one cannot be in two places at once. But from another point of view, the need to choose more truly arises from the multiplicity and incommensurability of human possibilities. One wants to be in both places because possible aspects of one's fulfillment can be found in each, and the fulfillment possible in either leaves out something of the fulfillment possible in the other. The real issue which is settled in choice is, then, whether one will fulfill oneself in one way and forgo the fulfillment promised by the other possible way of acting, or vice versa.

Someone might object that one can choose a particular, sensibly appealing object—for example, one pastry from a tray. But "choose" here is used simply to mean "pick out," and such choice can be a spontaneous performance of the sort that even animals and small children do. Free choices, as explained in D above, follow hesitation and deliberation. Blocked from acting on spontaneous inclination, a person begins to consider the reasons in favor of and against various possible resolutions of the problem. These reasons are understood goods and bads. Even sensibly appealing and repelling aspects of possibilities under consideration count in deliberation only insofar as they are intelligible factors in making possibilities more or less suitable to one's self according to a self-concept, not merely as they correspond to one's current feelings. For this reason, the very freedom of free choices often is explained by their relationship to rational deliberation (see *S.t.*, 1, q. 83, a. 1; 1–2, q. 13, a. 6).

Whichever way one chooses, then, one has some reason—the promised fulfillment—for one's choice. But prior to choice, one also would have had a good reason for choosing the other way. Once the choice is made, a certain aspect of one's self is involved in the good one has chosen which is not involved in the alternative. One is as one has chosen to be. If the very same alternatives were to present themselves again—everything one judges to be good or bad being the same—one could have no reason for choosing otherwise. And so no new choice would be necessary. This is why previous choices provide fixed points of reference to resolve further situations without new choices, and why people therefore usually make fewer choices as they settle down in life.

6. Since they are spiritual entities, not particular events or processes or things in the world, free choices must be distinguished from the particular acts one chooses to do. Particular acts come and go. **But a choice, once made, determines the self unless and until one makes another, incompatible choice.** That is why choosing to commit sin is said to put one in a "state of sin." This state is not something other than the sinful choice; it is the choice, not as a choosing, but as a self-determination—that is, as a settling of oneself in regard to the morally good alternative and the other alternative which one chooses. This way of being persists; it is one's "state," unless and until one repents—has a change of heart—by making another and incompatible choice.

7. The fact that free choices as self-determining last is the key to understanding many of the central issues treated in the remainder of this volume. One who thinks of choices as transient cannot expect to understand sin, the redemptive life of Jesus, the act of faith, personal vocation, or the sacraments. Moreover, the intrinsic relationship between our present lives and heavenly fulfillment in Jesus is intelligible only if we grasp the connection between what we make ourselves now by our choices and what we will be forever by the persistence of these same spiritual acts.

In discussing the stain of sin, St. Thomas notes that besides privation, a sinful act leaves in the soul a positive disposition or habit (cf. *S.t.*, 1–2, q. 86, a. 2). The same idea is expressed here by saying that choices last. To understand fully the point Thomas is making, one must set aside the notions of disposition and habit normally used in psychology today, and grasp the conception of potency and act Thomas developed from Aristotle. This conception is difficult and perhaps unnecessary for the understanding of the truth about the lastingness of choices.

Some understanding of the "habit" which choice leaves in the self can be gained by analogy with intellectual learning and knowing (cf. *S.t.*, 1, q. 79, a. 6). Learned people usually are consciously thinking of only a fragment of what they know. But the knowing involved in learning something lasts as a development of one's knowledge as a whole. As lasting, knowledge is more than a power to recall what one previously thought; one's store of knowledge is the systematic context of further inquiry and judgment which continually expand one's view of reality. Similarly, choices as self-determinations last, not simply as dispositions to act similarly in similar situations, but as developments of the existential self, which will continue to unfold itself in further deliberation and choice.

Classical moral theology tended to confuse the analysis of action by assuming that choices are essentially events or processes which are done and left behind. Yet the moralists, reflecting upon revelation and carefully attending to the facts of Christian life— particularly insofar as these facts concern the conscientious confessor—constructed many categories to take account of the reality of choice, including its self-constituting aspects. So the older manuals talk about a "state" of sin, "habitual intentions," and "states of life." All of these expressions signify perfectly valid ideas, and these ideas are reducible to an adequately articulated conception of choice.[7]

Question F: In what ways can free choices be social or communal?

1. Modern individualism diminishes the sense of human life as communal. Social actions often are thought of as mere accumulations of individual acts. The assumption is that there are no social choices. But there are: **Some choices can only be made by two or more people.** Marriage is an example. The man and the woman must both choose, and each is responsible. Yet neither's choice to take the other as spouse is effective without the other's. The two choices are operative only within the common, mutual commitment.[8]

2. People are naturally inclined to society; they need one another to exist and be fulfilled (see *S.t.*, 1, q. 96, a. 4; 1–2, q. 94, a. 2; 2–2, q. 129, a. 6, ad 1; *S.c.g.*, 3, 117). Among the reasons for this need is the fact that every choice involves self-limitation as well as self-fulfillment. Some possibilities must be set aside in order to pursue others. To realize oneself as much as possible, one must accept limitation. Only genuine community can make up for this limitation. **In such community one identifies with others by love and so is fulfilled in them in ways in which one can never be fulfilled in oneself.** Any genuine community is one body with many members (see 1 Cor 12.12–13.13).

The point made here about community—that in it one finds compensation for one's own limitedness—is an obvious fact of daily experience. Members of a family are pleased when one of their number does well. A whole nation experiences fulfillment when its representatives win gold medals in some international competition. Persons who are generous applaud the accomplishments of someone who does what they could not do themselves: "More power to you." Every Christian who truly believes in and loves the Lord Jesus rejoices in his victory: "We've won."

3. A social choice is required when a person comes into an already existing community. When, for example, a person becomes a Christian, he or she makes an act of faith and the Church administers baptism. The two acts are parts of one common act, in which God adopts the new Christian and he or she accepts the status of a child of God.

4. In any community certain persons can make choices on behalf of the community as a whole (see, e.g., Ex 32.30). If those who do so act within the limits of their authority, their choices involve every member of the community willy-nilly. It is true that besides supporting or acquiescing in acts of communities of which they are members, individuals can resist. But such resistance to a legitimate act of a community partly or wholly nullifies the individual's existential membership in that community.

5. The social dimension of choice is very important in moral theology. The story of salvation begins with the promise to Abraham, that all nations will find salvation through him, and this promise is fulfilled in the Lord Jesus (see Gn 12.1–3; Acts 3.25; Rom 4.13; Gal 3.8, 16).[9] It is by social choices that the relationship among God, the Lord Jesus as man, the Church, and the individual Christian is established and lived. Furthermore, one cannot understand original sin without bearing in mind that in any community someone can and does make the choice which is decisive for the social choice and responsibility of the whole community.

Question G: How are an individual's choices related to one another?

1. There are large choices and small choices.[10] Some large choices bear upon such acts as accepting a status, entering a relationship, undertaking a way of life: the choice to get married, the choice to be a priest, and so on. Small choices usually bear directly upon a particular course of action which involves specific behavior: the choice of where to take one's vacation, for instance.

2. While large choices and small ones are plainly different, the dividing line is not clear and distinct, for there are also intermediate choices. For instance, between the choice to get married (large) and the choice to celebrate their anniversary in a certain way (small), a married couple must make intermediate choices, such as the choice to live in a certain neighborhood.

3. It seems natural to say that by large choices one chooses to be this or that, while by small choices one chooses to do this or that. But this view is mistaken, because being and doing are not really distinct. In one's largest choices one chooses to do something, while in one's small choices one chooses to be the sort of person who does that sort of thing.

4. Sometimes choices are made without reference to one another. A small choice can settle a particular issue which has no bearing on anything else with which one is concerned. Even large choices, which perhaps should be related to each other, can be made in isolation. For example, some Christians choose their profession without considering its possible relevance to their act of faith.

5. **Large choices place one in the position of having to carry them out by many small choices.** In other words, large choices open possibilities which must be settled by small ones; large choices are undertakings which small ones implement. Thus, smaller choices articulate and, as it were, nest within larger ones. For example, a married couple's choices to celebrate their anniversary in a certain way and to live together in a certain place both nest within their choice to get married, although the two subordinate choices do not nest within one another.

6. Some choices are incompatible with others. One sort of incompatibility, already mentioned in question E, is the conflict between two choices which cannot exist together in the same person. For instance, a choice to spend one's vacation in a certain way cannot last if one changes one's mind and spends it in a different way. Again, a choice to reform one's life cannot stand with a subsequent choice to sin again. Another sort of incompatibility is the tension which arises in a person who makes a choice inconsistent with what is appropriate to implement a previous choice. For example, a choice to gamble the savings one needs for an expensive vacation is incompatible in this way with a choice to take the vacation. Again, the choice to commit adultery is incompatible in this way with one's marital commitment. In such cases, the incompatible choices coexist, but they are in tension.

7. **Certain large choices which organize one's life are called "commitments."** They will be treated later (9-E). But it is worth noting here that faith, insofar as it depends on our choice, is a commitment. The choice to accept

Christian faith opens up certain possibilities, excludes others, and affects one's whole life.

Question H: How are choices constitutive of one's self and of community?

1. The power to make free choices, precisely insofar as they really are free, is the power to be of oneself, as was explained in question B. **It follows that in making and carrying out choices, a person constitutes his or her own identity.**

2. Reflection on what it means to know a person helps show that this is so. To know a person is to know his or her life. The person's heredity and environment are interesting just to the extent that they at once open up a certain range of possible choices and exclude others. Outward behavior, its effects, and the reactions of others are interesting in knowing a person just insofar as they relate to previous choices or call forth additional ones—either a change of heart or a consistent unfolding of the self-identity laid down by the basic choices.

Perhaps the clearest approach is by thinking of someone—for example, Pope John Paul II. If one were to try to know this man well, what would one have to find out? One would begin with his childhood. He was born in 1920, his mother died when he was nine, and so on. From this one would learn something about his abilities and inherited dispositions, about the factors which were simply givens for him. These facts will help one understand how the young Karol saw things, why certain options occurred to him, why others never appealed to him at all. Then one would go on to examine some of the important decisions he made as a young man, to see what obstacles he encountered and how he undertook to overcome them, what relationships he entered into with others and which ones he avoided, and so on. After the Nazi invasion in 1939, he acted in an underground theater group, read St. John of the Cross, worked in a chemical factory, became a seminarian in 1942, and so forth. All this information would help one understand the man Cardinal Wojtyla was when he became Pope. Finally, one would study the problems he confronted upon becoming Pope, would consider what he has tried to do, how the effort is succeeding or failing, and what his responses are.

3. People make themselves the persons they are by their choices in two ways. First, as was explained in G above, in some large choices a person accepts a status, undertakes a way of life, or enters into a relationship. The consistent carrying out of such large choices gives an individual's life obvious continuity. Second, as was explained in E above, choices are not natural events or processes but spiritual realities which endure. They actualize and limit the self and so settle one's orientation toward further possibilities. Choices would be unnecessary if one were already so settled in one's way that only one path through life could meet one's requirements. But choices are needed to resolve the indeterminacy which is present when one might still find various goods fulfilling. Hence, in making choices one brings it about that some possible goods rather than others will be fulfilling for oneself—the self, that is, whom one constitutes by these choices.

4. Of course, when one chooses, one must have in view the particular goal which will be reached by carrying out the choice. But one also must understand why that goal is good. One can be interested in this good not only insofar as it will

be embodied in the particular goal, but also for itself. Its very goodness is appealing. One can wish to share in and serve this good, and can consider this particular choice and action as a way of doing so.

5. The particular goal realized by successful action is sensibly good and experienced as such; by contrast, the appealing goodness with respect to which one determines oneself in choosing is intelligible and transcends experience. In many successful human actions, the goods concretely realized can also be realized by natural processes or spontaneous human acts without choice; by contrast, the sharing in and service to goods to which one determines oneself by choice can only occur in one's self-determining choice. Whether an action is appropriate to the goal one has in view is a technical question; by contrast, whether an action is appropriate to the self one constitutes by a free choice is a moral question.

6. People often think of actions as if they were units of transitory behavior, related to themselves much as clothing is. To the extent, however, that actions are from the heart—are the carrying out of choices—what one does cannot be taken off, set aside, or replaced as clothing can.

7. There are several reasons why people fail to realize that they are what they do. Particular performances come and go, and it is these which are present in sense experience; the choices, which last, are less tangible and so seem less real. Again, children learn to think and talk about action in infancy, before they make choices. Later they continue to think and speak of action according to a model which does not do justice to fully personal action. Also, one's constituted self seems like a reality which not only is stable but has always been there; one tends to forget how unformed one once was and how one's choices constituted one's present self. Finally, to the extent that people act immorally, they prefer to think of their actions as something apart from their selves—as something they can do and enjoy but also cast off and leave behind, much as they would soiled clothing.

Karl Barth, probably the most important Protestant theologian of the twentieth century, very clearly states and rejects the common but erroneous account of actions: "It is for the whole man, man in his unity of being and activity, for whom He [Christ] has died—in the ordered integrated unity in which he does what he is and is what he does. This disposes of the idea that actions are merely external and accidental and isolated. They are not, as it were, derailments. A man is what he does. Their wickedness and folly counts. They are his wicked works and by them he is judged. As the one who does them, who produces these wicked thoughts and words and works, he is the man of sin who would perish if Jesus Christ had not taken his place. Nothing that he does or leaves undone is neutral or indifferent or irresponsible or outside the sphere of his accountability. He is inwardly the one who expresses himself in this way outwardly. And this disposes of the idea of an Ego which is untouched by the evil character of its actions, an Ego in which a man can remain neutral because he, too, is not touched or touched only remotely by the evil character of his actions."[11]

8. **Choices have constitutive implications not only for individuals but for communities.** A social choice such as marriage begins when the couple marry but it makes them permanently a married couple. The mutual commitment is the enduring entity we call the "bond of marriage." Similarly, although political societies often lack essential features of real community, they do generally use the

form of self-constitution by a common choice. For example, the Preamble to the United States Constitution expresses a common commitment to a certain set of goods, such as justice, peace, and liberty. This commitment makes the people of the United States a political unity organized by the provisions of the Constitution as a whole.

Scripture scholars have pointed out that the Old and New Testaments do not take the individualistic view of human persons and communities which is typical of the modern, Western world. Rather, in Scripture a single individual is capable of gathering up and acting for a whole group; and the group is regarded as if it were the extension of one individual. Jesus, for example, is the one man who dies for the Church whom he makes his wife, while the Church is a part of the whole Christ, for she is the embodiment of him who is her head. This conception of the relationship between individuals and groups is called "corporate personality."[12]

Corporate personality is partly explained by the paradigmatic character of the family for all community in biblical times. A family has natural solidarity; children are extensions of their parents, who do act for the family as a whole. But corporate personality also must be understood in light of the reality of communal choices and their power to constitute communities. For this reality means that a community is not merely a collection of individuals but an existential unit. It also means that someone really can act in such a way that the whole community acts in and through him or her. Corporate personality is thus not as mysterious as it appears to those who regard society with a modern, individualistic bias.

In the Old Testament, a living man was very conscious of his relationship with his ancestors and his descendants. He shares in the honor of his forefathers, but suffers the hardships of his children. Similarly, children extend a family into the future, and to die without heirs is to be annihilated, to have one's name blotted out from Israel (see Gn 38.8; Dt 5.9–10; 25.5–10). The unity is conceived realistically. For this reason, it is useless to ask whether the mysterious son of man (see Dn 7.13) is a single individual or the whole of Israel; he is both at once (see Dn 7.27).

After Abraham, the covenant which God offers is never between himself and individuals, who might enlist if they wish one by one. The nation-forming covenant of Sinai is made with the people of Israel, through the mediation of Moses (see Ex 19.2–8; 24.3–8). The covenant also is renewed in a social act (see Jos 24.14–28; Neh 8). Each individual has an obligation to remain faithful to the covenant and somehow shares in the guilt of ancestors who have broken it (see Neh 9.1–2). The prophets emphasize individual responsibility (see Ez 18), but still look to a communal redemption (see Ez 37 and 40–47).

Because the sense of community is strong, individuals do not act in a merely individualistic way. In the Psalms, personal prayer and prayer by and on behalf of a whole community are virtually indistinguishable. An outstanding individual or the whole covenant people interchangeably are Yahweh's "son," and such a son can act toward Yahweh on behalf of the whole people (see Hos 11.1; Zec 3.1–10; Neh 1.6). A prophet is the nation, pleading with God not simply for himself but for the whole (see Am 7.2, 5). The suffering servant of Yahweh is both identified with Israel and distinct enough from the people as a whole to be dissatisfied with them (see Is 42.1–4; 49.1–6; 50.4–10; 52.13–53.12).

What is called "corporate personality" appears to be a more adequate view of the relationship of human persons in communities than that of modern, Western individualism. The individualistic view tends to ignore the communal aspects of choice described above. But more than this, it involves the dualism of modern Western philosophy. That dualism considered the person to be the thinking subject, distinct from the body, and so concluded to a multiplicity of individuals isolated from each other, rather than joined in the flesh-and-blood communion of bodily, sexual persons. By making us think we are not our own bodies, modern individualism thus gives us an illusion of insulation from the persons of others, inasmuch as personal union always is accomplished in bodily contact of some sort.

Question I: How are the virtues and vices which make up character related to free choices?

1. The stability of moral persons which is called "character" has traditionally been attributed to virtues and vices. Even to speak of virtues and vices is to acknowledge that one's existential self is lasting and structured and that one's acts are not a mere series, like pearls on a string. **Virtues and vices are considered to be both a residue of one's previous acts and dispositions to engage in further acts similar in moral quality to those which gave rise to the dispositions.**

St. Thomas and many later Catholic writers called virtues and vices "habits," but in an unusual sense. In ordinary speech a habit is what shapes an unthinking routine of behavior. Thomas and his successors did not mean that virtues and vices are habits in this sense; they considered them aspects of character which make for consistency in deliberate behavior done by free choice (see *S.t.*, 1–2, q. 49, aa. 1–3; q. 55, aa. 1–2).

To understand the general notion of virtue, one must recall that persons have several naturally given capacities.[13] These are active potentialities, abilities to become by some sort of action. Due to a variety of factors, the whole range of possible action tends to become limited, and the limited range of action, at the same time, facilitated. The limitation and facilitation of actuations of capacities occurs by dispositions, which are acquired and more or less lasting qualities (see *S.t.*, 1–2, q. 51, a. 2). One knows the disposition from the regularity and facility of the actuations of particular capacities.

Dispositions of one type are habits, such as motor skills. For example, a person who engages in a sport or carries out a task such as driving a car has a disposition (or a set of dispositions) which both limit and facilitate the actuations of the various capacities involved in the activity. The disposition persists; one does not lose it at once when one is not engaged in the activity. In English, we call dispositions "habits" only when they limit possible action to definite, recognizable patterns of behavior; habits are acquired by repetition of behaviors of empirically describable sorts, and habits lead to further instances of the same types of behavior. For example, one gets into the habit of drinking coffee each morning by drinking coffee many mornings, and the habit disposes one to go on doing the same sort of thing.

Although in Latin "habitus" extends to the whole range of dispositions, so that a virtue is a kind of "habitus," in English a virtue is not a "habit." Virtues are dispositions which limit action to that which is (at least in some sense) humanly fulfilling and which facilitate such good action. A person who has a virtue is disposed to act in a way which is good. Vices are dispositions similar to virtues, except that they dispose to bad action (see *S.t.*, 1–2, q. 54, a. 3).

2. As was explained in question H, choices constitute one's identity, and large choices organize one's life and give it continuity. The constitutive and organizing power of choices provides the basis for explaining the data referred to as "character."

3. A person's existential dimension—that is, the capacity for free choices, the

choices one makes, and whatever exists through choices—does not exist alone. A person has other dimensions as well, including a natural bodily dimension, an intellectual dimension, and a cultural, behavioral dimension. All become engaged in making and carrying out any choice. Hence the dispositions of all these dimensions affect one's actions. And all the other dimensions of the self share in the goodness or badness of the existential self.

Thus, for instance, the dispositions of imagination and feeling which are present in a chaste person are very different from the dispositions of imagination and feeling present in one who is unchaste. Central to the virtue is one's commitment—for example, to be a true husband or to be a playboy. However, the dispositions of other aspects of the self are important too. To the extent that they contribute to virtue, they do so not so much by habituation—that is, determination to behavioral routine—as by the disposition of imagination and feelings to conform to virtuous choices. Thus, a truly chaste married person will feel differently about sex with his or her partner than about other sexual stimulation, and will feel differently when sexual activity is appropriate and when it is not.

4. This suggests what is meant by "character." **It is the integral identity of the person—the entire person in all his or her dimensions as shaped by morally good and bad choices—considered as a disposition to further choices.**[14] Good character is simply a matter of morally good choices together with dispositions in all parts of the person to continue making and carrying out such choices. Because persons of good character are well integrated, they not only do what is right, but do it easily: Virtue lends facility to good will.

5. One who consistently acts according to a well-organized set of fundamental choices becomes a very unified and stable person. But he or she need not respond in stereotyped ways. Stable concerns and consistent evaluations give rise to very different responses to new opportunities and challenges. Thus choice accounts for both the stability and the flexibility rightly emphasized by St. Thomas' theory of habit.

One can distinguish among virtues (or vices) in different ways, by using as a principle of distinction any intelligible set of factors relevant to choices. Thus virtues (or vices) can be distinguished by the different dimensions of the acting person, by different fields of behavior, and so on. No one of these accounts is definitive to the exclusion of others. Each is a way, helpful for some purposes, of dividing the same whole into intelligible parts.

6. Character is not merely individualistic. Good or bad communal choices comprise part of every individual's life. So, for example, an expression like "the American character" is meaningful if it refers to those aspects of the characters of Americans which arise from their communal choices. However, communal "character" also refers to factors of common heredity and environment which have nothing to do with free choice. Moreover, the communal "character" popularly assigned to members of a particular group often expresses prejudice against them.

Summary

Free choice is a source, a principle, of both moral good and moral evil. By the ability to make free choices human persons live in the existential world, that is, the world of moral good and evil. Thus free choice is an existential principle.

The ability of human persons to make free choices is taken for granted throughout the Bible. At the time of the Reformation, Luther and others, rightly wishing to emphasize sinful humankind's total dependence on God's grace, mistakenly denied human free choice. Against them, the Council of Trent solemnly defines the truth that, even after Adam's sin, human beings can make free choices. This ability is one important way in which human persons are like God. They have real causal power in respect to themselves; in choosing freely, they are their own self-makers.

Determinism denies free choice, but in doing so it is self-defeating. Determinists argue that one ought to accept their position, but this "ought" itself embodies an appeal to freedom of choice.

"Freedom" has various meanings—physical freedom, the freedom to do as one pleases, the emergence of novelty, political freedom—but all have certain common elements. With reference to persons, the meaning of freedom includes someone who is or could be acting, the action, and something which might be but in fact is not blocking the action. Different meanings of freedom are distinguished according to the factors which might block action. Freedom in one important sense, the freedom of the children of God, presupposes free choice but is distinct from it. This freedom cannot be badly used, but one can make bad free choices.

The experience of free choice begins in an awareness of conflict. One finds oneself in a situation where it is impossible to pursue all the goods which attract one. The act of choosing involves focusing attention on one possibility, putting aside others, and setting out on a definite line of action. But one is not aware of anything which is the choice itself, nor is the experience of choosing that of undergoing something. One does not encounter choices, one makes them.

Although in many important ways factors beyond one's control supply and limit the possibilities for choosing, one is really free to choose among the alternatives one considers interesting and possible. Furthermore, although outward action often follows upon choice, free choice itself is not outwardly observable; it is a settling of oneself in one's heart. Free choices are spiritual entities, not particular events or processes or things in the world. A choice therefore lasts (in the sense that one continues to be self-determined by it) until one makes another, incompatible choice. This is why the choice to commit sin is said to put one in a "state" of sin.

Social actions are often thought of as mere accumulations of individual acts. But there are social choices—choices, that is, which can only be made by two or more people. Marriage is an example. Community of this sort—the community of common, mutual commitment—compensates for individual self-limitation. One is fulfilled in others in ways in which one can never be fulfilled in oneself.

There are large choices and small choices. The difference is not that by large choices one chooses to be something and by small choices one chooses to do something. Rather, although many choices can be made without reference to one another, large choices place one in the position of having to carry them out by many small choices. Moreover, some choices are incompatible with one another. Certain large choices which organize one's life are called "commitments." Faith, insofar as it depends on choice, is a commitment: It opens up some possibilities, excludes others, and affects one's whole life.

There are two ways in which people make themselves the persons they are by their choices. First, in some large choices one accepts a status, undertakes a way of life, or enters into a relationship. Second, because choices are spiritual realities which endure, they actualize and limit the self, and so settle one's orientation toward further possibilities. Choices have constitutive power not only for individuals but for communities. A community is not merely a collection of individuals but a unit; someone really can act in such a way that the whole community acts in and through that person.

Virtues and vices are both residues of previous acts and dispositions to engage in further acts similar in moral quality. This suggests what is meant by "character." It is the integral existential identity of the person—the entire person in all his or her dimensions as shaped by morally good and bad choices—considered as a disposition to further choices. Insofar as its identity is constituted by communal choices, a community as a whole also has character.

Appendix 1:   The Fathers of the Church on free choice

Because we can make free choices, we are responsible for ourselves. Not God but we ourselves go astray. Empowered by God, the blessed make themselves sharers in his life. All by themselves, the damned make themselves what they are (see *S.t.*, 2–2, q. 24, a. 10, c.). Since this truth is so alien to the minds of all who lack the light of faith, the ancient pagans had a hard time grasping and accepting it. Hence, the Fathers of the Church constantly affirm it. Writing in the second century, St. Justin the Martyr states:

> We have learned from the Prophets and we hold it as true that punishments and chastisements and good rewards are distributed according to the merit of each man's actions. Were this not the case, and were all things to happen according to the decree of fate, there would be nothing at all in our power. If fate decrees that this man is to be good, and that one wicked, then neither is the former to be praised nor the latter to be blamed.
>
> Furthermore, if the human race does not have the power of a freely deliberated choice in fleeing evil and in choosing good, then men are not accountable for their actions . . ..
>
> Neither would man deserve reward or praise if he did not of himself choose the good; nor, if he acted wickedly, would he deserve punishment, since he would not be evil by choice, and could not be other than that which he was born. (FEF 123)

Similarly, Tatian says that the wicked person is "depraved of himself" while the good person does God's will by "his free choice." Persons are "created free, not having the nature of good, which pertains only to God, and which is brought to perfection by men through their freedom of choice" (FEF 156). St. Theophilus of Antioch affirms that God made man neither mortal nor immortal, but capable of being either: "For God made man free and self-determining" (FEF 184).

Not only the earliest Fathers but the later ones as well continually reaffirm the same truth. St. John Chrysostom says that "everything depends, after grace from above, upon our own choice" (FEF 1151; cf. 1165, 1188, 1219), and so we deserve the reward or punishment we receive. St. Augustine likewise affirms moral responsibility based on freedom of choice: "If, with divine grace assisting the human will, a man is able to be without sin in this life, I can tell you very easily and most truthfully why such does not happen: men do not will it" (FEF 1722). Moreover, while always careful to assert the necessity of grace for doing good, Augustine also defends free choice as a principle of good acts: "Let us take care not to defend grace in such a way that we would seem to take away free choice; nor again can we insist so strongly on free choice that we could be judged, in our proud impiety, ungrateful for the grace of God" (FEF 1723; cf. 1710, 1883, 1890, 1954). St. Cyril of Alexandria points out that Adam and Judas sinned by their own fault, since the Creator gave human persons the power of "choice and permitted them to follow whatever spontaneous inclinations each of them might wish" (FEF 2113). Inclinations are spontaneous; temptations are a given. But what one does is up to oneself.

Free choice is related to morality, not only as a condition of responsibility, but also as a source of the dignity of the person as moral agent. This fundamental aspect of the relevance of free choice to morality also is stressed by the Fathers. St. Irenaeus says: ". . . God made man free from the beginning, so that he possessed his own power just as his own soul, to follow God's will freely, not being compelled by God. For with God there is no coercion; but a good will is present with him always. He, therefore, gives good counsel to all. In man as well as in angels—for angels are rational—he has placed a power of choice, so that those who obeyed might justly possess the good things which, indeed, God gives, but which they themselves must preserve" (FEF 244).

The Fathers often emphasize how like God human persons are by virtue of the power of choice. Tertullian, for example, says: "I find that man was constituted by God with a freedom of both his own will and his own power; for I observe in him the image and likeness of God by nothing so clearly as by this, the characteristic of his estate. . . . That such is his estate has been confirmed even by the fact of the law which was then imposed upon him by God. For a law would not be imposed upon one who did not have it in his power to render the obedience due to law" (FEF 335). St. John Damascene affirms the same truth about humankind made in God's image (see FEF 2357), and St. Thomas Aquinas, continuing the teaching of the Fathers, cites Damascene in the Prologue to the moral section (the Second Part) of the *Summa theologiae:* "Because, as Damascene says, man is said to be made in the image of God inasmuch as by 'image' is meant one who has intellect, is free in choosing, and through himself able to act . . . it remains for us to consider this image—namely, man—insofar as he is the principle of his own acts as one who has free will and control of his acts." By endowing human persons with free choice, God has made them his image even according to their nature, and this image is perfected when they freely accept grace.

Appendix 2:   Further clarifications of the experience of choice

To talk clearly about free choice, one must avoid confusing "freedom" in this sense with other uses of the word. But one also needs to be clear about what free choice itself is. The starting point for this clarification is an accurate description of the experience of making a choice.

The experience is also sometimes called "deciding," "making up one's mind," "making a commitment," "agreeing to a proposal," "accepting one's vocation," and so forth. All these expressions refer at times to something other or more than the experience of making a choice. "Deciding" and "making up one's mind" sometimes refer to purely cognitional operations of making judgments and drawing conclusions. The other expressions often refer to some outward (or at least inward) behavior consequent upon a choice, and they apply only to certain special cases of choice.

One sometimes uses "make a choice" to mean the outward act of picking one item from a group—for instance, one apple from a basket. Such picking sometimes does carry out a free choice, but animals and small children also can pick an item from a group without making any free choice. Moreover, the experience of making a choice can occur without any observable, outward expression at all.

One naturally is interested in and cares about basic human goods. No one who understands one of the basic human goods can fail to love it, and this love is the disposition of human nature toward its own fulfillment. This fundamental love, which St. Thomas calls "simple willing," does not by itself result in any action, but it is the underlying thrust toward every possible human action (see *S.t.,* 1–2, q. 8, a. 2; q. 10, a. 1).

As soon as a child begins to understand some possible way of acting for one of the goods, simple willing—the underlying interest in that good—generates a spontaneous desire to do the act for the sake of that good. If no other impulse or distraction intervenes, the child consciously, purposefully, and intelligently proceeds to act for the good and, if the act is successful, to enjoy it. Notice, for instance, the efforts of small children to satisfy their curiosity.

Older children and adults also continue to act in this spontaneous way. Such acts are human; animals do nothing like them, and they are directed to specifically human goods. But they are not initially and in themselves morally significant acts, since they are done without reflection and consent. However, if one finds that one has done something spontaneously which one ought not to do, then the awareness of the moral norm will alter a future situation in which one thinks of doing the same sort of thing. One now will confront the possibility with an offsetting awareness that proceeding to act would be wrong. One will hesitate. This situation is that of temptation.

Adults hesitate not only when they are tempted, but in many other cases, because they are aware of various aspects of possible courses of action and usually are aware of other possibilities. Nevertheless, even adults do many things voluntarily—that is, consciously, purposefully, and intelligently—not by free choice but by spontaneous willing. A student who thinks of a question and notices nothing which would make it inappropriate to ask the question, asks as spontaneously as the small child, simply to satisfy curiosity.

It is important to notice the role which physical freedom and knowledge have in relation to free choice. No one ever chooses anything without having considered it a possibility. Moreover, one never chooses anything unless one finds it appealing. That something is appealing—that it is a live possibility worth thinking about—always depends upon one's knowledge and past experience. Thus, causal factors determinists notice do limit the range in which one can make free choices. Alterations in circumstances and knowledge can enlarge the range very greatly. For example, while one who proclaims the gospel cannot cause those who hear it to make an act of faith, neither can one choose to believe what he or she has never heard effectively proclaimed (see Rom 10.14). It follows that while people are morally responsible for the free choices they make, they often are not morally responsible for the good choices they do not make—because conditions beyond their control prevent them from considering (and so from choosing) as ideally they should. Moreover, the moral significance of a bad choice partly depends upon the alternatives one actually confronted.

Appendix 3:   The compatibility of God's causality with free choice

To clarify this point, one must consider human cognition concerning God, and as a basis for this consideration one must note certain features of human cognition in general.

One can say both of human persons and of other primates that they see and hear, perceive things as units, remember and dream, learn by experience, tell the helpful from the threatening, love and hate, fear and become enraged, strive after things and enjoy satisfactions. Such experience is common to the higher animals, including rational animals. This form of consciousness is preconceptual and lacks reflective discrimination between subject and object, between self and other.

This level of awareness is called "sentient" to distinguish it from the properly human functions of thinking and willing. These properly human functions and their level of awareness are called "rational," using the word in a wide sense. Even sentient awareness in human persons is permeated by reason and will, for while the two levels are distinct, they are not separate. They make up a single system of human conscious life.

Human persons are created in God's image (see Gn 1.26–27). For this reason, men and women are not only valuable; they are beings of dignity, of inherent worth (see Ps 8.5–7). The capacities of intelligence and free choice raise human persons above the rest of material creation and make them like God (see *S.t.*, 1, q. 93, a. 2). These same capacities are the ground of human moral responsibility and of the openness of human existence to share in divine life (see GS 12–17; also *S.t.*, 1–2, q. 5, a. 1).

Human persons know themselves as selves; they know everything else as a world of other persons and of things. The rational capacity to distinguish oneself as a knowing subject from other persons and the objects one knows is exercised in reflective intelligence, by which one knows oneself knowing. In this reflection, one can distinguish what one knows from one's knowing of it and the conditions of this knowing; in making this distinction one knows the truth of one's knowing and posits the content known as other: So it is, not merely in my know*ing*, but in *what* I know, in reality (see *S.t.*, 1, q. 16, a. 2).[15] Truths known in reflection are propositions, "pro-positions" because we put forth and posit as real what we know to be true. We call a truth a "proposition" precisely insofar as it is known and present in our knowing; the reality attained in propositional knowing is some state of affairs.

Something of the reality which will be known in this objective way must first be understood (see *S.t.*, 1, q. 27, a. 1; q. 34, a. 1; q. 85, a. 2; *S.c.g.*, 4, 11). Understood aspects of a reality are concepts. We call these aspects "concepts" precisely insofar as reality is grasped in our understanding of it. We often construct tentative propositions and then seek to determine whether any state of affairs corresponds to them; to do this is to ask a question. A proposition which picks out a state of affairs which is not real is a false proposition.

Human rational awareness is based upon sentient awareness (see *S.t.*, 1, q. 84). Our first understandings are of aspects of things given in experience; the first truths we know are about the reality of states of affairs in the world of experience. Already in knowing truth we know ourselves with an awareness other than sentient awareness, and so from the start our knowledge of the world of experience points beyond this limited domain. By reasoning we come to know order among things. In investigating the order of things we discover loose ends in things experienced, and seek after causes—factors not yet experienced—to complete the pattern which is grasped rationally as incomplete.[16]

Sometimes it is said that human persons have some direct and preconceptual awareness of the world and even of God—a sort of direct look at or undifferentiated contact with reality. It is true that sentient awareness is preconceptual and undifferentiated. Also, very basic truths are known in propositions which are so obvious and familiar that it is hard to express them in language; it is easier to talk about aspects of reality which vary and are differentiated.

However, there is neither evidence nor any teaching of the Church that human persons have any intellectual awareness of anything prior to concepts (see *S.t.*, 1, q. 88). The self-awareness which is incidental to knowing truths about the world of experience is not preconceptual, for it arises from the understanding of experienced things and takes form in the concept of the self who knows, the self one calls "I" (see *S.t.*, 1, q. 87, a. 1). Preconceptual awareness would be without understanding of any aspect of reality and would be awareness of no state of affairs as real. It is unnecessary to posit such awareness. To do so leads to avoidable mystifications.[17]

Still, as already indicated, human rational knowledge is not limited to the world of experience and the knowing self, since reason follows the pointing of these beyond themselves: "Ever since the creation of the world his invisible nature, namely, his eternal power and deity, has been clearly perceived in the things that have been made" (Rom 1.20). Vatican I defines: "If anyone says that the one and true God, our creator and lord, cannot be known with certainty with the natural light of human reason by means of the things that have been made: let him be anathema" (DS 3026/1806).

The general form of the reasoning by which one comes to know God from experience is simple enough. In many ways humankind experiences the world as incomplete, as in need, as somehow unsatisfying to the human mind and heart. Part of this unsatisfactoriness no doubt is based upon our awareness that we will die; this fact seems absurd to persons, who have an inherent sense of their own dignity. Another factor is our awareness of solidarity and community with ancestors and descendants; this suggests another dimension of reality, outside worldly time and space, in which we remain with others. Yet another factor is our poignant sense of evil, especially of our own guilt, which cries out for salvation and forgiveness. Shaping all this experience is the realization that the world of things which come to be and pass away needs as a principle of its reality something independent in being.

Nothing within the world of experience nor even the human self grasped in knowing this world is able to remove the absurdity of death, unite the community of humankind, overcome evil, and account for the reality of things not real of themselves. And so an Other, apart from the world of experience but required by it, is posited as an invisible and higher reality. This Other almost inevitably is thought of as a person or as something like a person. Virtually every human group seeks ways to live without tension and in harmony with this quasi-personal Other. The ways diverse peoples find and use constitute their religions. Thus, religion of some sort is almost a universal phenomenon.

The formulation of Vatican I and the common aspects of efforts by Catholic philosophers to articulate reasoning toward the existence of God point to a precise argument which follows the general form of reasoning already described but leads to a very careful way of thinking and talking about God. Elsewhere I have attempted to lay out this precise argument in detail.[18]

The reasoning begins from the distinction between understanding propositions and knowing them to be true. Wherever this distinction holds, it implies that the states of affairs picked out by propositions are not real of themselves, but require conditions beyond themselves to be real. An infinite regress (in the series of conditions of conditions of . . .) is meaningless; some explanation is rationally required for the reality of everything which has borrowed reality. Thus, there must be a principle of reality which is other than any state of affairs having borrowed reality; this principle must have its own reality of itself.

In this reasoning one reaches a principle which really is wholly other than anything we understand. For our understanding proceeds by concepts which grasp aspects of entities which cannot be real of themselves. It follows that whatever we understand about anything else will not be an understanding of the Other whose reality is of itself. The attributes we predicate of everything else must be denied of this principle of reality. It is neither one nor many, neither changing nor unchanging, neither animate nor inanimate, neither bodily nor mental—using these words in the same senses in which they are used to describe entities having borrowed reality. We do not know what the Other is; we know what it is not.[19]

Can we even say of this principle that it is "real," that it is "other?" Not if these words are used in the same sense in which they are used when we talk of familiar entities. As St. John Damascene teaches: "Concerning God, it is impossible for us to say what he is in his essence; it is more fitting, rather, to discuss how he is different from everything else. For he belongs not among things that exist, not because he does not exist, but because he is beyond all existing things, and beyond even existence itself. For if all modes of knowledge are concerned with what exists, that which is beyond knowledge must be beyond existence and likewise, what is beyond existence must be beyond knowledge" (FEF 2340). We can say "God exists" only because in the context of the reasoning by which one reasons beyond existing things, the word "exists" takes on a special meaning, which does apply to that Other on which they depend for their reality.

Even words such as "principle" and "cause" do not express what this Other is in itself, for they cannot be used of it in the sense in which they are said of anything else without eliminating the uniqueness which must belong to the Other. The Other must be unique to fulfill the requirement for which it is posited—to account for the reality of everything else. Rather, in saying that the Other is "principle" or "cause" we are saying that whatever it is in itself, it is in some way, which we do not understand, what it must be to supply reality to everything having borrowed reality. Thus, while we do not know what the Other is, but only what it is not, we do know that things of our experience and we ourselves are related to it, and that, in a way beyond our comprehension, it has in itself what it must have to sustain this relationship (see *S.t.*, 1, q. 12, a. 12; *S.c.g.*, 2, 11–14).

Do we have reason, even apart from faith, to think of this Other as quasi-personal? I think we do (see DS 3892/2320). While we must deny that it either is a mere object or a personal subject like ourselves, entities having borrowed reality depend upon the Other in a way somewhat similar to that in which free choices depend upon the person whose choices they are. For no one can choose freely if there is a sufficient reason apart from the choice for making it, and the Other cannot be the principle of all else if there is a sufficient reason apart from its causing things for them to have the borrowed reality they enjoy. On the basis of this similarity, we are entitled to think of the Other as if it were a free agent, and so as intelligent, for choice presupposes understanding of options.[20]

At this point it becomes clear that the "Other" about which we have been talking can only be the God in whom we believe: he who freely creates heaven and earth, things visible and things invisible (see 1 Cor 8.4–6).

However, even the characterization of God which is provided by Christian faith is not a description of him in himself but an understanding of him only insofar as he draws us into personal relationship with himself in the order of salvation. Once this point is understood, one realizes that it is a mistake to take expressions which Christians use in talking about God to have precisely the same meaning they would have in uses outside the context of faith.

Nonbelievers constantly make this mistake. For example, they ask how Christians can reconcile their belief that God is a good and loving Father with all the evil and misery in the world. Again, they ask how human persons can be free if God causes everything and directs all things according to the plan of his providence. Believers sometimes make these same mistakes. Some believers also wonder whether the reality of humankind's personal relationship with God in the order of salvation does not entail that God mutually depends on his creatures.

While a great deal can be said about these questions, the fundamental principle for replying to them is that they all assume that one knows God in himself, that one's thought and talk about him is not after all very different from one's thought and talk about everything and everyone else.[21]

We Christians do not know how to reconcile our belief in God's goodness with our experience of evil. We do know that we do not understand God and cannot expect to justify his ways (see Jb 42.2–6). We also believe that in the death and resurrection of Jesus, God gives us a sign of his love which does not lessen the reality of evil but does promise to overcome it (see Rom 8.18–39; Jn 11.17–44).

Similarly, we do not know how God can cause the very reality of our free choices without determining what we choose, nor do we know how his providential design can include our lives without reducing us to the status of puppets playing roles in a drama in no way our own. But the difficulties dissolve if we keep in mind that we do not understand God's causality and providential direction. God "causes" in a unique sense; his plan is not the merely superhuman design of a grand puppet master (see Rom 11.33–36). The life of good deeds is a gift of God's grace (see Eph 2.10), yet we can choose either life or death (see Sir 15.11–20).[22]

Appendix 4:   Only believers accept the reality of free choice

Apart from those who share in the truth of divine revelation, virtually all of humankind either ignores or denies that there is a power of free choice.

One reason for this is that free choice is unique. In general, everything that happens in the world of experience has a cause, and the precise way things happen is determined by definite features of their causes. One imagines that if one knew at a given moment the whole state of the universe—what everything is, where it is, what it is doing—then one could in principle predict the state of the universe at every future moment. This supposition is the theory of physical or natural determinism.

True, most things can be accounted for by antecedent causal conditions. If this were not so, there could be no natural science, for the world would not have the order it has. But determinism does not hold true of everything. It is not true of God the creator, because nothing in any sense causes him to create. Nor is determinism true of the miracles God does in the world to signal us, in order to initiate or to call attention to his revelation. Nor, of course, is determinism true of our own free choices.

People who hold a deterministic view are likely to look at human behavior as if it were the behavior of a subhuman animal or even as if it were the output of a complicated machine. Such entities do not have the God-like ability to be of themselves. They are what they are, and they become only what they are caused to become by their own internal programming and by external factors. If their behavior or output is abnormal, this "evil" has to be accounted for as sickness, malfunction, or breakdown of some kind.

Even Aristotle sometimes thought of human life in this way, although it is inconsistent with other aspects of his philosophy. What human persons ought to be is settled entirely by their nature. If one is brought up properly, lives in a good environment, and has a healthy disposition, one will naturally understand what is good. Understanding it, one will want it and act for it, thus to fulfill oneself. Choices—not free choices—come in for Aristotle only because there are diverse ways of attaining one's good, due to the complexity of the world.[23] A god would not have this problem and would have no choices to make.

Many modern and contemporary thinkers accept essentially the same view. One finds it almost everywhere in psychology and the social sciences. Not only individual but also social moral difficulties are considered as if they were problems in the ways things "work," not results of wrong choices people make. So, just as individuals seek treatment to get rid of guilt, married couples want therapy for their broken-down relationships, and nations try to find ways to "tune up" their economies.

An obvious reason for the attractiveness of this view of human life is that it is a true picture of a great deal of human behavior, for not everything people do follows from free choice, and choices themselves can only be between options which occur to one and seem interesting. To the extent that determinism is true, the individual and social human condition can be treated and tinkered with so that it is healthier and works more smoothly. When one is somewhat successful in improving matters on a deterministic approach, there is a natural tendency to suppose that one has the key to complete human liberation and progress. It is hard to admit that much human evil simply cannot be fixed.

Determinism also is attractive because it excludes real moral responsibility and denies real moral guilt. It therefore functions as a means of rationalizing, which allows one who holds it to act immorally while pretending not to be able to do otherwise.

Another reason why free choice is overlooked or denied is that it seems in one way to be inconsistent with one's own experience of deliberating and choosing. One does not make a choice for no reason at all. One always chooses for the sake of some good (see *S.t.*, 1–2, q. 13, aa. 5–6). Thus one always can give a good reason—or at least a plausible reason— why one has chosen as one has. Moreover, after a choice is made, it often seems in retrospect that what one chose was obviously the better (or best) alternative. One could hardly have chosen otherwise. This impression will be especially strong if one has done something morally evil, because then it is comforting to feel that one did the only reasonable thing.

It is obvious that one can affect one's own choices and the choices of other persons by getting or providing information. One cannot choose unless one thinks of something, sees it as interesting, and considers it possible (see *S.t.*, 1–2, q. 14, a. 1). In many cases, people who lack necessary knowledge make very poor choices, but begin to make better choices when they learn better. This situation suggests (falsely) that whenever bad choices are made, the problem is a lack of knowledge. So on this approach, moral evil is reduced to ignorance, and salvation is sought by education. If sin always is a matter of mistakes and ignorance, knowledge is virtue.

Plato perhaps held a view along these lines.[24] Much Eastern religion seeks to overcome illusion and to help people to accept the way things are. A great deal of modern and contemporary Western thought—with its tremendous confidence in science and in education—is based upon a very similar view of human life.

The difference between Eastern mystical passivity and Western pragmatic activism is due to a difference in assumptions about reality and knowledge. The view of Eastern religion is that reality is one; knowledge reveals the impossibility of changing anything; and so knowing liberates by eliminating useless desire and effort. The view of Western pragmatism is that reality is a struggle; knowledge reveals how things work and gives power to obtain wanted results; and so knowing liberates by showing how to get what one wants.

A naturalistic determinism and some sort of theory that sin is ignorance and knowledge saves often are mixed together in contemporary thought. Such a view is appealing for reasons analogous to the appeal of naturalistic determinism. It is especially appealing to intellectuals, since it makes that in which they are superior (intellectual activity) a guarantee of their quality as persons—that is, of moral superiority.

Not everything in experience seems to follow from natural necessity, nor does every inclination seem to arise from some definite knowledge. Against both naturalistic determinism and the view that knowledge is virtue, many people today do notice and make much of the reality of the unpredictable. Evolution seems to mean that really new things somehow emerge; nature is not simply a big machine forever grinding on in the same way. Similarly, human creativity is real. The genius is "inspired"; human art and science constantly innovate. When these facts are considered, one might suppose that the reality of free choice would be noticed and accepted, not ignored or denied.

But the great emphasis upon evolution and creativity during the past century has not led to a reaffirmation of free choice. For the emergence of novelty in nature and in the work of genius essentially is a nonrational, nonaccountable process. If human moral action is thought of in one of the nondeterminist ways provided by theories of evolution and innovation, no antecedent standards can be admitted as valid for such moral action. Nietzsche developed a theory along these lines.

While a free choice is not like a determined natural event, nor like the behavior which necessarily follows upon certain knowledge, neither is it like a stroke of genius or something which emerges inexplicably in the course of evolution. Free choices are made by persons; they are in our own power, while emergents and strokes of genius are not. Free choices do introduce novelty into the world, but the person choosing introduces and controls this novelty (at least initially) and so is responsible for it. There are antecedent standards for human free choices, because the power of choice is a power to fulfill or to stunt oneself in respect to the possibilities of human and divine fulfillment.

Thus, the great emphasis upon evolution and creativity in recent thought has not led to a reaffirmation of free choice. Instead, it has led to a denial both of moral standards and of the responsible persons to whom such standards would provide relevant guidance. Contemporary philosophies of evolution and creativity deal with some facts, but they overgeneralize from them.

In sum, only those who accept the Judeo-Christian account of creation are likely to admit the reality of free choice. Naturalistic determinists acknowledge prior reality, but conceive it in a way which excludes novelty. Gnostics acknowledge knowledge, but conceive it in a way which excludes love which surpasses understanding—including the love involved in free choices for which there can never be a sufficient reason. Contemporary theorists of evolution and creativity acknowledge novelty, but conceive it in a way which precludes its being a purposeful expression of an antecedent self to whom it belongs.

Only in the case of the creator and his pro-creators can novelties emerge from and in harmony with an antecedent, real principle, emerge shaped by wisdom and expressed by love: emerge through *Logos* and *Agape*. Only the three divine persons and created persons can be authors (the Father; the human self as moral agent) of novelty (creation; the self-determined human person) by wisdom (the Son; the plan for human fulfillment we call "moral norms") and love (the Spirit; the very making of free choices). In making free choices, human persons display the image of God in which they are made.

Notes

1. See John Paul II, *Familiaris Consortio,* 74 *AAS* (1982) 123; Eng. ed. (Vatican City: Vatican Polyglot Press, 1981), 66 (sec. 34): "But man, who has been called to live God's wise and loving design in a responsible manner, is an historical being who day by day builds himself up through his many free decisions; and so he knows, loves and accomplishes moral good by stages of growth." Also: Karol Wojtyla, *The Acting Person,* trans. Andrzej Potocki, ed. Anna-Teresa Tymieniecka (Dordrecht: D. Reidel, 1979), 169–74.

2. The metaphysics of four orders of reality, suggested in certain passages in St. Thomas, is developed by Germain Grisez, *Beyond the New Theism: A Philosophy of Religion* (Notre Dame and London: University of Notre Dame Press, 1975), 230–40 and 343–56. Although he does not explicitly make these distinctions, Wojtyla, op. cit., 189–258, provides a phenomenological description of the

integration of the acting person who includes the natural as the somatic and psychic presupposition of action, the intentional and existential as the transcendent subject of action, and the cultural as the bodily medium and outcome of action.

3. See Joseph M. Boyle, Jr., Germain Grisez, and Olaf Tollefsen, *Free Choice: A Self-Referential Argument* (Notre Dame and London: University of Notre Dame Press, 1976), 122–77.

4. Determinists often suggest that actions done by free choice would be unintelligible, mysterious, random, accidental, causeless, contingent, chance happenings. This whole line of argument reduces to the argument from sufficient reason, which received its classic formulation from Laplace. See ibid., 77–90.

5. In recent philosophical literature, those who hold that moral responsibility is saved by freedom other than free choice are called "compatibilists" or "soft determinists," while those who reject both free choice and moral responsibility are called "hard determinists." Various forms of compatibilism are criticized in ibid., 104–21. Social scientists and psychologists who deny free choice can say people are morally responsible, but they tend to adopt a conception of responsibility very different from the traditional Christian one. A sign of this is that wrongdoers are thought to need enlightenment, treatment, and so on, rather than a witness of faith and hope together with an invitation to repentance.

6. The freedom of the children of God also is taught in the Johannine writings; for a careful exegesis of relevant texts: Matthew Vellanickal, *The Divine Sonship of Christians in the Johannine Writings*, Analecta Biblica, 72 (Rome: Biblical Institute Press, 1977), 286–94.

7. With respect to the lastingness of choices as self-determination, also see Wojtyla, op. cit., 149–52. In his early work, Karl Rahner clearly indicated the self-determining and lasting character of free choices: *Hearers of the Word*, rev. by J. B. Metz, trans. Ronald Walls (London: Sheed and Ward, 1969), 104–5. But later he loosened the relationship between free choices and self-determination, downgraded the former and identified the latter with fundamental option, while holding for "unity in difference" between the fundamental option and individual acts of man: *Theological Investigations*, vol. 6, *Concerning Vatican Council II*, trans. Karl-H. and Boniface Kruger (Baltimore: Helicon, 1969), 183–86. Theories of fundamental option will be treated in chapter sixteen.

8. Gabriel Marcel has done much to illuminate the relationships among individuals and communities. See, for example, *Creative Fidelity*, trans. Robert Rosthal (New York: Noonday Press, 1964).

9. See Gerhard von Rad, *Genesis: A Commentary*, rev. ed. (Philadelphia: Westminster Press, 1972), 152–61.

10. Some theologians hold that one's fundamental "option," which gives one's life its basic moral and spiritual orientation, is not a large choice at all, but rather an actuation of a freedom more basic than freedom of choice (although somehow mysteriously related to it). Theories of fundamental option will be examined in detail in chapter sixteen. But one point may be noticed here. Even the free choice by which one accepts the gift of faith is sometimes considered only a superficial expression of something deeper: Pierre Fransen, S.J., "Towards a Psychology of Divine Grace," *Lumen Vitae*, 12 (1957), 208, 217, 224, and 231. This position is hard to reconcile with Scripture, where faith is presented as the foundation of one's right orientation toward God, and nothing is said of any more basic option underlying it. That the human act accepting the gift of faith is a free and deliberate consent is taught expressly by Vatican I and II: DS 3009–10/1790–91; DH 2.

11. Karl Barth, *Church Dogmatics*, vol. 4, *The Doctrine of Reconciliation*, part 1, trans. and ed. G. W. Bromiley; ed. F. Torrance (Edinburgh: T. and T. Clark, 1956), 405.

12. See the very rich study by an Anglican Scripture scholar, Ernest Best, *One Body in Christ: A Study in the Relationship of the Church to Christ in the Epistles of the Apostle Paul* (London: S.P.C.K., 1955), esp. 184–207. Jean de Fraine, S.J., *Adam and the Family of Man* (Staten Island, N.Y.: Alba House, 1965), is an extensive study, with references to many earlier works; note the references (285) to H. Wheeler Robinson, who was one of the pioneers in using this notion. Robinson, however, introduced psychological elements on the basis of information from primitive anthropology: J. W. Rogerson, "The Hebrew Conception of Corporate Personality: A Re-examination," *Journal of Theological Studies*, 21 (1970). 1–16. Setting aside these elements, it seems to me, one still can profitably notice that in Scripture there is a greater sense of communal solidarity and moral responsibility than in modern, individualistic thinking.

13. See George P. Klubertanz, S.J., for an extensive treatise on habits and virtues, with an emphasis on the Thomistic tradition, references to much secondary literature, and also to modern psychology: *Habits and Virtues* (New York: Appleton-Century-Crofts, 1965). He follows (97–101) Thomas in defining habit. Like Thomas, Klubertanz does not notice that choices of themselves last,

and that the disposition established by a freely chosen act is nothing other than the persistent choice and the modifications of the personality it integrates.

14. Stanley Hauerwas, *Character and the Christian Life: A Study in Theological Ethics* (San Antonio, Tex.: Trinity University Press, 1975), 114–26, provides an analysis of character very close to mine, although he does not distinguish and relate the existential and other dimensions of the person. Because of the similarity of concept, much of what he says in his study about current action theory and Protestant ethics could be brought to bear to fill out the present, necessarily brief summary. Even some of Hauerwas' critique (68–82) of the concept of character in Aristotle and St. Thomas brings out certain difficulties—ones I think arise mainly from their too definite conception of the end of the human person—while at the same time clarifying the manner in which, for them, character is the self, determined through morally significant action.

15. See also St. Thomas, *De Veritate*, q. 1, a. 9; q. 10, a. 5; *In libros Metaphysicorum Aristotelis*, vi, 4.

16. The theory of knowledge summarized here is based on St. Thomas Aquinas. A useful summary of this theory: L.-M. Regis, O.P., *Epistemology* (New York: Macmillan, 1959). For clarifications of the notions of proposition, state of affairs, truth, and obtaining, see Grisez, *Beyond the New Theism*, 40–52, and references to additional materials, 390, nn. 12–14.

17. The theory criticized here is found in the movement stemming from Joseph Maréchal, called "transcendental Thomism"; see W. J. Hill, "Thomism, Transcendental," *New Catholic Encyclopedia*, 16:449–54. It is precisely the epistemological realism of members of this school, who reject the idealistic aspects of Kant's critical philosophy, which leads them to posit preconceptual knowledge—the intellectual intuition Kant rejected. The most accessible presentation of the argument for such cognition: Emerich Coreth, S.J., *Metaphysics*, ed. Joseph Donceel (New York: Herder and Herder, 1968), 45–76. For an account of the genesis of the epistemological problem and critique of Maréchal's approach, see Regis, op. cit., 32–108. Once the empiricist presuppositions of Kant's critique are set aside, so that the irreducibility to concepts of propositions and reasoning is understood, the knowledge of God possible to us can be accounted for without the primordial intellectual intuition of being (implicitly of God) transcendental Thomism assumes. See Grisez, *Beyond the New Theism*, 230–72.

18. See St. Thomas Aquinas, *De ente et essentia*, chap. 4; Grisez, *Beyond the New Theism*, 36–91.

19. See A. D. Sertillanges, O.P., *Dieu*, in Thomas d'Aquin, *Somme théologique* (Paris: Desclée, 1926), 379–89. In Scripture, the impossibility of saying what God in himself is often is expressed by saying he is "hidden" and "mysterious." The Church likewise teaches that God is ineffable—that is, indescribable in language (see DS 800/428, 3001/1782).

20. See Grisez, *Beyond the New Theism*, 268–72.

21. Ibid., 273–324, for a fuller treatment of these questions.

22. See Ramón García de Haro, "La Libertad Creada: Manifestación de la Omnipotencia Divina," *Atti del VIII Congresso Tomistico Internazionale*, vol. 6, *Morale e Diritto nella prospettiva tomistica*, Studi Tomistici, 15 (Vatican City: Libreria Editrice Vaticana, 1982), 45–72; *Cuestiones fundamentales de Teología Moral* (Pamplona, Spain: EUNSA, 1980), 169–242. It has been argued that the Old Testament accepts a fundamental determinism by divine causality, with only "relative freedom" (that is, voluntary action determined by psychic and circumstantial factors). See David Winston, *The Wisdom of Solomon*, The Anchor Bible, 43 (Garden City, N.Y.: Doubleday, 1979), 46–58. It seems to me that the ancient writers neither accepted nor rejected such a position. Rather, they held both God's universal causal initiative and lordship, and the initiative and responsibility of persons made in God's image; they did not articulate the problem which was formulated by subsequent metaphysical reflection, perhaps partly because they thought of the relationship between God and created persons existentially rather than ontologically. In any case, the teaching of the Church, developed to reject determinism by divine causality, controls the issue for Catholic theology.

23. Aristotle certainly maintains that vices are voluntary and that persons are morally responsible: *Nichomachean Ethics* iii, 1109b30–1115a6. But his handling of the problem of incontinence makes clear that competing psychic factors determine action: vii, 1146b6–1147b19. For a good, concise analysis of the relevant texts, see David J. Furley, *Two Studies in the Greek Atomists* (Princeton: Princeton University Press, 1967), 210–26. Writing in his own name but with evident inspiration from Aristotle, the Aristotelian scholar W. David Ross proposed a deterministic theory of moral responsibility: *Foundations of Ethics* (Oxford: Oxford University Press, 1939), 230 and 250–51. This treatment of free will seems to me to extrapolate Aristotle's views very neatly to deal with a question he never explicitly treats.

24. In such dialogues as the *Protagoras*, Plato seems to accept the thesis that no one voluntarily

does evil. Yet the interpretation of Plato's dialogues always is difficult; it is hard if possible to derive his position from them. It might be argued that for Plato, as for the Bible, wisdom has a strong moral component, such that the fool is not so much ignorant as a rationalizing sinner (see Ps 53.2; 74.22), and so "the fear of the Lord is the beginning of wisdom" (Ps 111.10; cf. Prv 1.7; 9.10). But it seems more likely that Plato, like Aristotle, falls short of understanding the radical initiation present in human free choice, modeled as it is on divine free creation. The *Republic* ends (614–21) with the myth of Er, an exhortation to moral seriousness, yet in this passage Plato fails to articulate the principle of free choice this seriousness presupposes.

CHAPTER THREE

CONSCIENCE: KNOWLEDGE OF MORAL TRUTH

Introduction

Because we can choose freely, we can be of ourselves and so are responsible for what we make of ourselves. The ability to make free choices would be useless, however, if we could not know which choices are good ones. But we can; judgments distinguishing good choices from bad ones are called "conscience." As an essential prerequisite of moral good and evil, conscience is a basic existential principle, just as free choice is.

Question A: What are the different senses of the word "conscience"?

1. Sometimes "conscience" is used to refer to feelings and judgments which have no direct relationship with moral truth. **The feelings arising from superego and the awareness of social conventions are both often called "conscience," but they need not correspond to moral truth.**[1]

2. "Superego" refers to the subconscious source of one's sense of requirement and guilt at the emotional level. This is formed by early training. The child who misbehaves experiences inner conflict, which is repugnant. As a consequence, the demands of parents and others on whom the child depends become internalized as an authority over (super) the conscious self (ego). Parents are not always reasonable, however, and the child's own inclinations are distorted by the inherited effects of sin; thus superego tends to be rigid, nonrational, sometimes oppressive, and often irrelevant to what is truly humanly good and bad.

3. People are also aware of the requirements set by society, and they generally call violations of social conventions "wrong." Authority at this level is located in the group. To the extent one is identified with a group, one makes its demands one's own; to the extent one is not wholly identified with a group, one feels its demands to be impositions. Even in the latter case, though, the demands may be accepted as the price of belonging. Most social requirements have at least some basis in moral truth. Yet because various groups have interests which are not always reasonable and which often conflict with one another, social convention also is often at odds with what is truly humanly good and bad.

4. Many people of limited maturity of conscience perceive the Church's moral teaching at the legalistic level of social convention. They do not clearly under-

stand that it is more than a God-given body of rules one must accept in order to enjoy the benefits of Church membership. Compulsive and guilty feelings at the level of superego are also sometimes very strong in such persons.

It is unnecessary here to investigate the complex psychology of guilt feelings. The important point is that superego has to do with guilt only in a secondary and derivative sense, for it is tied to the whole premoral phase of personal development. Genuine conscience is an awareness of responsibility assessed by a judgment derived from some principle one understands in itself or accepts from a source (such as the Church's teaching) to which one has intelligently and freely committed oneself. Once conscience is developing and the personality is being integrated in a mature way, feelings of guilt will more and more coincide with choices one knows to be wrong and will be in proportion to how serious one judges the wrong to be.

Such maturing takes time and is achieved in some areas of life more easily than others. Adolescent rebelliousness consists in part of an attempt to overcome childish principles of right and wrong, and the superego guilt which enforces them. To the extent that the superego persists without being integrated into mature morality, people remain in an adolescent posture toward all authorities. Thus many Catholics feel childish guilt when they violate the Church's moral teaching, especially in the area of sex, and resent the Church's authority much as rebellious adolescents resent parental authority.

This resentment shapes and colors the entire attitude of many Catholics to the Church. They fail to see moral teaching as a gift of truth; they entirely miss their responsibility to share in a common task of communicating God's truth and love to others. They want the Church to change her teaching, for they think such a change would relieve their feelings of guilt, and they consciously or unconsciously assume that the teaching could be changed, much as a parental decision that it is time to go to bed can be changed.[2]

5. **Conscience in a full and strict sense is an awareness of moral truth.** Only at this level are moral good and evil fully understood and rightly located in the freely choosing person who confronts the reality of the world and human possibilities. Wrongdoing is seen to lie either in refusing to make the commitments and enter into the communities in which one might hope to be fulfilled, or in betraying commitments and failing to meet responsibilities once they are accepted.

6. Judgments of right and wrong by a person with a mature conscience express more than early training or awareness of what is socially required. They say what ought to be required, what one will require of oneself if one is reasonable. To think of morality as an area in which one is made to feel guilty or as a set of rules someone else imposes expresses an immature conscience. By contrast, a person of mature conscience thinks of morality as a matter of real human goodness and reasonableness. For such a person, to do what is wrong is a kind of self-mutilation.[3]

7. The forbidden and the permissible are not the exclusive or even primary concerns of a mature conscience. A person of mature conscience does not ask, "What is the minimum I have to do? How far can I go in doing what I please?" These questions express at least a residue of superego and social convention. Rather, a mature Christian conscience seeks to determine the implications of faith for one's entire life: "What is the good and holy thing to do? What is Christ's mind

on this matter? How can I do God's will in my life?" (see Mt 5.38–48; Rom 12.1–2; Phil 4.8–9; Col 3.12–17).[4]

One may sum up the distinction between the three senses of "conscience" as follows.

First, the superego is not really moral at all, in the sense that it offers no reason for acting as distinct from a feeling. Social convention is moral in the sense that it offers reasons for acting as distinct from nonrational determinants of action. However, at this level reasons for acting need only be grounded in one's actual desires, not in human goods understood as valuable in themselves. By contrast, moral truth is based on reasons which are fully intelligible, not merely factual.

Second, the superego is concerned only with a certain area of behavior, namely, behavior subject to disapproval, which leads to guilt feelings. The remainder of the infant's behavior is free. Social convention also is limited to a restricted field, namely, that in which a reason for acting is backed by a social sanction. Apart from this, choices seem morally indifferent. Moral truth in its full development is not restricted to any area of behavior, although it comes to bear only when there is some possibility of free choice.

Third, the superego is most concerned with outward performances, which can cause trouble. Social convention is primarily concerned with good intentions; the individual must accept the authority. Moral truth is concerned with integral human fulfillment, which primarily exists in existential goods—that is, in various forms of peace and harmony within persons and among them.

Fourth, the superego generates a sense of compulsion; one has to abide by its dictates or suffer the pain of violating them. Social convention generates a sense of obligation; one either abides by the rules or is criticized and cut off from what one wants. Moral truth generates responsibility; fulfillment of others and of oneself depends on oneself, and consistency with one's own care for fulfillment requires one to act reasonably for it.

Fifth, the superego defines the self as a person of others—for example, the child of these parents. The little child tries to be like and to fit in with the parents. Conventional morality defines the self in part negatively, by efforts to be different from others, and in part affirmatively, by the set of goals it encourages one to pursue in the society—for example, the adolescent tries to accomplish certain things and to make something of himself or herself. Moral truth defines the self by commitments and communion—for example, "I am a Christian."

Still, these three stages are not in watertight compartments. Even small children already have some understanding of basic human goods, and this understanding shapes their action. By the time they are six or eight, most children are somewhat aware that fairness is not merely a device, but something of an ideal. Conversely, the superego can and should continue to develop in all one's personal relationships; it provides an immediate sense of the cost of being offensive to those one cares about. Similarly, conventional morality, to the extent that it is grounded in moral truth, can be incorporated in a mature conscience as the legal embodiment of norms.

Question B: What is conscience according to the teaching of the Church?

1. Church documents never use the word "conscience" to mean superego or awareness of social convention.[5] **The Church is interested in conscience only in the third sense, as the ability to know moral truth.**

2. In Scripture the judgment of conscience often is attributed to the "heart"

(see Jb 27.6; Ps 16.7), which receives and retains God's law (see Dt 6.6–9; Ps 37.31; 40.9; Prv 7.1–3) and which can be enlightened by his gift of wisdom (see Ps 90.12; Prv 2.9–11). Again, the work of conscience in Christian life is assigned to the renewed "mind" (see Rom 12.1–2). But the technical term "conscience" seldom is used; indeed, no Hebrew word exists for this specific concept. In the New Testament "conscience" refers mainly to awareness of wrongdoing, especially the pangs experienced after one has done wrong.[6]

3. Although they lack divine revelation, even the Gentiles are said to have this awareness of right and wrong; it is part of the human make up created by God. Conscience, which is joined to knowledge of moral norms written in the heart, serves the Gentile as the demand of the revealed law serves the Jew (see Rom 2.14–16).

4. As a source of warnings, conscience is helpful for Christians, too, much as law is. But it is not infallible. A clear conscience does not necessarily mean one is justified (see 1 Cor 4.4–5); and one's heart can charge one with something even though one is at peace with God (see 1 Jn 3.19–20).

5. Vatican II emphasizes the dignity of conscience, a dignity rooted in the law written in our hearts. We do not make this law; we discover it (see *S.t.*, 1–2, q. 91, a. 3, ad 2). It consists of a group of moral principles which God gave us in creating us and which we can know naturally. Although this law written in our hearts is made up of general principles, it has implications for particular moral issues (see GS 16).

6. **As used by Vatican II, "conscience" refers at once to awareness of principles of morality, to the process of reasoning from principles to conclusions, and to the conclusions, which are moral judgments on choices made or under consideration.** St. Thomas uses a particular word for each: "synderesis" for awareness of principles, "practical reasoning" for the process of moving from principles to conclusions, and "conscience" for the concluding judgment only (see *S.t.*, 1, q. 79, aa. 12–13; 1–2, q. 94, aa. 2, 6).

7. According to St. Thomas, conscience is an intellectual act of judgment. This judgment is primarily practical and forward-looking, corresponding to and guiding each choice one is about to make. Conscience is one's last and best judgment concerning what one should choose. With this judgment in mind, one chooses, either in agreement with conscience or against it (see *S.t.*, 1, q. 79, a. 13).[7]

8. Conscience plays a further role after choice. One compares the choice one actually made with one's judgment as to the choice one ought to have made (for example, in examining one's conscience). Even here, conscience is an act of knowledge, not to be confused with feelings of guilt or security, which may also be present.

9. **Given this understanding of conscience, it is true by definition that one ought to follow one's conscience.** As one's best judgment concerning what is right and wrong, an upright person has no alternative to following it. "Follow conscience" does not indicate one possible source of moral guidance in contrast to some other possible source or sources; supposing one thought in some case that it

was better to follow a norm other than that previously provided by conscience, by that very fact the new norm would become one's real judgment of conscience.

The teaching of Vatican II on conscience is mainly contained in one article of the *Pastoral Constitution on the Church in the Modern World* (GS 16). It deserves close reading. "In the depths of his conscience, man detects a law which he does not impose upon himself, but which holds him to obedience. Always summoning him to love good and avoid evil, the voice of this law can when necessary speak to his heart more specifically: do this, shun that. For man has in his heart a law written by God. To obey it is the very dignity of man; according to it he will be judged" (GS 16; translation supplied). At this point the Council refers to what is probably the most important passage in Scripture in which "conscience" occurs: "When Gentiles who have not the law do by nature what the law requires, they are a law to themselves, even though they do not have the law. They show that what the law requires is written on their hearts, while their conscience also bears witness and their conflicting thoughts accuse or perhaps excuse them. On that day when, according to my gospel, God judges the secrets of men by Christ Jesus" (Rom 2.14–16).

The law mentioned here is called "natural law" in Catholic teaching. It is known by everyone, even persons who do not have faith, for its demands are "written in their hearts"—that is, known spontaneously. Conscience here is a co-witness with the law. The two together will accuse or defend, which implies that they must agree with each other. Vatican II expresses the same idea in its image of conscience as a voice of the law written by God in the heart—God writing it by creating persons of human nature.

The use of the scriptural word "hearts" does not mean that conscience is considered by St. Paul or Vatican II a power of feeling what is right or a disposition to love what is good. "Heart" in the Bible has a much wider reference than in current English. The reference includes the whole of one's interior life, including one's mind and will.[8]

Vatican II continues with a metaphorical description of conscience taken from a document of Pius XII: "Conscience is the most secret core and sanctuary of a man. There he is alone with God, whose voice echoes in his depths. In a wonderful manner conscience reveals that law which is fulfilled by love of God and neighbor" (GS 16). Here the Council refers to the precept of love formulated in the New Testament (see Mt 22.37–40; Gal 5.14). Implicit is the statement: The law Christian love fulfills and must fulfill is the natural law (see *S.t.*, 1–2, q. 99, a. 1, ad 2; q. 100, a. 3, ad 1; q. 105, a. 2, ad 1; *S.c.g.*, 3, 117).

Since conscience expresses the natural law, which can be known by everyone, and since this law is objective, the Council proceeds to point out: "In fidelity to conscience, Christians are joined with the rest of men in the search for truth, and for the genuine solution to the numerous problems which arise in the life of individuals and from social relationships. Hence the more that a correct conscience holds sway, the more persons and groups turn aside from blind choice and strive to be guided by objective norms of morality" (GS 16). Here the Council speaks of "correct conscience." When correct, conscience demands that one be reasonable, not arbitrary; that one conform to objective or true norms, not to subjective substitutes chosen arbitrarily. But conscience is not always correct; the Council distinguishes two ways in which conscience goes wrong. (These will be considered in question C below.)

Vatican II teaches that every human person has a right to religious freedom (DH). This teaching often has been misunderstood and sometimes has been exploited to promote a false conception of freedom of conscience. John Courtney Murray, S.J., the theological expert whose work was most fruitful for the development of this document, comments: "It is worth noting that the Declaration does not base the right to the free exercise of religion on 'freedom of conscience.' Nowhere does this phrase occur. And the Declaration nowhere lends its authority to the theory for which the phrase frequently stands, namely, that I have the right to do what my conscience tells me to do, simply because my conscience tells me to do it. This is a perilous theory. Its particular peril is subjectivism—the notion that, in the end, it is my conscience, and not the objective truth, which determines what is right or wrong, true or false."⁹ Vatican II does teach about conscience in this document (DH 3 and 14), but in a very traditional way.

Question C: What is one's moral responsibility for errors of conscience?

1. Experience, Scripture, and the Church's teaching agree that judgments of conscience can be in error. The law of God written in one's heart can be misapplied in one's judgments. Mistakes are possible in formulating principles, reasoning from them, and considering the facts involved in the possible choices which are to be morally evaluated (see *S.t.*, 1–2, q. 19, aa. 5–6; q. 94, aa. 4, 6; cf. 2–2, q. 48, a. 1).¹⁰

2. **According to common Christian teaching, one must follow one's conscience even when it is mistaken.** St. Thomas explains this as follows. Conscience is one's last and best judgment as to the choice one ought to make. If this judgment is mistaken, one does not know it at the time. One will follow one's conscience if one is choosing reasonably. To the best of one's knowledge and belief, it is God's plan and will. So if one acts against one's conscience, one is certainly in the wrong (see *S.t.*, 1–2, q. 19, aa. 5–6).¹¹

Thomas drives home his point. If a superior gives one an order which cannot be obeyed without violating one's conscience, one must not obey. To obey the superior in this case would be to disobey what one believes to be the mind and will of God (see *S.t.*, 1–2, q. 19, a. 5, ad 2; 2–2, q. 104, a. 5).¹² It is good to abstain from fornication. But if one's conscience is that one should choose to fornicate, one does evil if one does not fornicate. Indeed, to believe in Jesus is in itself good and essential for salvation; but one can only believe in him rightly if one judges that one ought to. Therefore, one whose conscience is that it is wrong to believe in Jesus would be morally guilty if he or she chose against this judgment.¹³

3. Still, one is not necessarily guiltless in following a conscience which is in error. **If the error is one's own fault, one is responsible for the wrong one does in following erroneous conscience.** As Vatican II teaches: "Conscience frequently errs from invincible ignorance without losing its dignity. The same cannot be said when someone cares but little for truth and goodness, and conscience by degrees grows practically sightless as a result of a practice of sinning" (GS 16; translation supplied).

St. Thomas asks: Does erring conscience excuse? Is one who conforms to conscience when it is mistaken nevertheless sometimes morally guilty of the wrong choice? The answer is: Sometimes, yes. One must follow one's conscience, since it is one's last and best judgment as to what one should choose. But the error in judgment can be one's own fault. This is so if one somehow chooses to stay in ignorance about one's responsibilities or if one fails in any way to do all one should to know what is right and bring this knowledge to bear in one's judgment of conscience. If one's erroneous conscience is in any way one's own fault, to that extent one's action in conformity with erroneous conscience is one's fault. One has an obligation to avoid mistakes in conscience so far as possible by informing oneself fully and by conscientiously thinking out what one should choose.[14] If one does not fulfill this obligation, one's choice in accord with an erring conscience is not blameless (see *S.t.*, 1–2, q. 6, a. 8; q. 19, a. 6; q. 74, a. 5; q. 76, aa. 2–3).

This conclusion seems to entail that in some cases one is damned if one does and damned if one does not follow conscience. Thomas points out that if one's mistake is in no way one's own fault—if ignorance is invincible—then one is not damned if one does follow conscience. There is no moral fault here at all. If one's erroneous conscience is somehow one's own fault, then one has a way out: Ignorance is vincible and voluntary. One can inform oneself and ought to do so (see *S.t.*, 1–2, q. 19, a. 6, ad 3).[15]

4. Errors in conscience are one's own fault if one chooses to remain ignorant of one's responsibilities or fails to do all one should to know what is right and bring this knowledge to bear upon one's choices. Conscience entails moral responsibility. **One's first responsibility is to form conscience rightly so that one's moral judgments will be true.**[16]

5. Sometimes people who are in error through their own fault suspect the possibility of error and are in a position to correct it. In such cases, where ignorance is voluntary and vincible, there is an alternative to remaining in bad faith and following erroneous conscience: Replace the false judgment of conscience with a true one and then follow correct conscience in an upright way.

6. Sometimes, however, people who are voluntarily in error eventually become insensitive to the possibility that their consciences are erroneous (see *S.t.*, 1–2, q. 79, a. 3; q. 85, a. 2). Rationalization and self-deception make it almost impossible for them to acknowledge error about a particular matter. People whose consciences are in error through such a process are responsible for the erroneous judgment. Although they must follow the erroneous judgment as long as it seems certainly correct, doing so does not entirely free them from guilt.

7. The condition of a conscience voluntarily fixed in error through rationalization and self-deception is what Vatican II has in mind in speaking of a conscience "practically sightless as a result of a practice of sinning" (GS 16). The possibility that this state of conscience might actually exist in anyone is often ignored today. Nevertheless Scripture speaks of such guilty blindness, which is closely related to hardness of heart (see Is 6.9–10; Prv 28.14; Jn 3.19–21; 9.39–41; 12.35–43).

Christians should realize that if they care little for the truth of Christ and for living lives like his, even their consciences can become blind and unreliable. The process by which this comes about might, for example, include studying only those theological opinions which dissent from the Church's teaching and purposely seeking direction and support from confessors or other spiritual advisors who apply dissenting opinions.

Those who do this are not blameless, yet they cannot easily overcome their error. At times their conscience probably bothers them, but they are locked in the box of their own "conscience," for they hardly can admit that their judgment and ongoing way of life, supported by the opinions of others, are erroneous. "Why doesn't the Church change her teaching? Pope John Paul II seems to be such a fine man; why must he be so rigid on this matter?"

In the present cultural period the reality of moral evil is somewhat hidden. This general climate of opinion makes it very difficult for Christians to recognize and admit their own moral guilt. Such recognition and admission are important not only for moral improvement, but even more because we cannot accept and be thankful for God's merciful love if we do not acknowledge everything on our consciences and seek his forgiveness.

A priest working as a pastor of souls ought to be very careful to help people realize and admit their true state of conscience. Even if a priest were personally convinced that certain kinds of acts can be done blamelessly, he would endanger those entrusted to his care if he led them to hide from themselves the fact that their actions are at odds with their own consciences. Today there is real danger of this happening. John Paul II teaches:

> Priests and deacons, when they have received timely and serious preparation for this apostolate, must unceasingly act towards families as fathers, brothers, pastors and teachers, assisting them with the means of grace and enlightening them with the light of truth. Their teaching and advice must therefore always be in full harmony with the authentic Magisterium of the Church, in such a way as to help the People of God to gain a correct sense of the faith, to be subsequently applied to practical life. Such fidelity to the Magisterium will also enable priests to make every effort to be united in their judgments, in order to avoid troubling the consciences of the faithful.[17]

This teaching was necessary, because some had pressed dissenting opinions upon the faithful, contrary to the Church's teaching and to the great detriment of the faithful. This procedure would be wrong even if the teaching were mistaken; all the more so if it is true. (The authority of the Church's teachings and the very narrow limits of any justifiable dissent will be treated in chapters thirty-five and thirty-six.)

Some who urge priests to condone practical dissent from the Church's moral teaching say that under certain conditions a penitent in error but good faith should be left in good faith. This may be so, but great caution is needed, for it is one thing to leave someone in good faith and another to encourage someone to continue in bad faith.

Question D: What is the ideal way to make a judgment of conscience?

1. Considering how a judgment of conscience is ideally reached helps clarify both what "blindness of conscience" means and what the goal of formation and refinement of conscience is—a goal which is more than the acquisition of a body of knowledge.

2. The practical intellect operates best in a person who is good, mature, and integrated. A good person has no reason to evade moral truth, to hide from the light. A mature person goes beyond superego and social convention and judges moral issues by moral principles. A well-integrated person is not excessively distracted by a disorganized multiplicity of thoughts and inclinations arising from various parts of the self and clamoring for attention.

3. Such a person has a virtue traditionally called "prudence" or "practical wisdom." Prudent people easily tell what is right; they are precommitted to it; and the various elements of their personalities are harmoniously integrated with their upright commitments. In considering possibilities for action, they usually find it easy to judge what is the appropriate thing to do.

4. They usually do this by perceiving the harmony between what is right and their own established commitments and other dispositions integrated with them. **For prudent persons, in other words, their own character is a standard of morality because it embodies moral norms.** Since character is like a second

nature, they can be said to judge "by connaturality."

St. Thomas teaches in a number of places that a virtuous person makes moral judgments by affective connaturality. For example, a chaste person easily detects anything which is immodest and avoids it (see *S.t.*, 2–2. q. 45, a. 2). This teaching of Thomas has been used by some to bolster the claim that individuals can make moral judgments as if by inspiration, even against the general moral truths proposed by the Church.[18]

However, this is a misinterpretation of the teaching of Thomas, for he does not suggest that affective connaturality replaces moral norms, moral reasoning, and the judgment of conscience. Rather, he holds that a virtuous person has integrated the moral norms, so that his or her moral reasoning is facilitated and made certain (see *S.t.*, 1–2, q. 57, aa. 5–6).[19] Nowhere does Thomas suggest that cognition by affective connaturality could authorize anyone to set aside the moral norms proposed by the Church. Thomas always assumes that a good Christian knows these, and even accepts and integrates them into the self to the point that they are second nature.

5. When prudent persons reflect upon practical possibilities and judge by connaturality, they ignore or set aside without choice possibilities which are not morally acceptable, since such possibilities are not appealing to them insofar as they are upright. The appropriate thing to do usually comes to mind without prolonged inquiry and is accepted without deliberation; love both shows the virtuous the best way to proceed and inclines them to follow it. In such cases, the practical judgment of a prudent person is not conscience indicating what ought to be done, but an effective judgment determining what will be done (see *S.t.*, 2–2, q. 47, a. 8). A person already fully ready to do what is good need only see what that is to put practical insight into effect.

6. Sometimes even prudent persons must deal with factors extrinsic to their own existentially integrated personalities. They must, for example, take a stand with respect to a wrong communal act in which they find themselves involved or must resist morally unacceptable suggestions from others. Also, even the prudent must sometimes choose contrary to normal, existentially undistorted inclinations. For example, Jesus had to resist a normal, emotional repugnance to dying (see Lk 22.40–44). In such cases the prudent usually have little difficulty recognizing what is morally upright; they need only choose to reject wrong possibilities which thrust themselves before consciousness and appeal for acceptance.

7. No one perfectly realizes the ideal of the prudent person, and many Christians, especially those who are younger or weaker, hardly realize it at all. All morally earnest persons are aware that their personalities are only partly integrated and their unreflective insights on moral questions can thus be mistaken.

8. Whenever one's prudence is adequate, one has no doubts; one has confidence in one's judgment. **But when doubt and hesitation are present, they signify a defect of prudence and cannot be removed by some supposedly direct personal insight into moral truth.** One does wrong in such cases to fall back upon a subjective impression. Nor does it help matters to call a resort to feeling by some other name—"discernment of prudence" or "my personal conscience judgment."

81

9. Moreover, although immoral people cannot be as perfectly integrated as those who are prudent, an individual who is morally bad, mature, and well-integrated also judges by connaturality. A thoroughly vicious person, like a saintly person, sees what is appropriate and acts without doubts or hesitations (cf. *S.t.*, 2–2, q. 47, a. 13). Not psychological ease and immediacy, but agreement with moral truth—which, if necessary, can be reflectively and critically articulated—is the hallmark of sound practical judgment.

10. Thus, one whose conscience is blind because of sin often proceeds with the self-assurance of an upright person and refuses to be criticized by anyone (see Prv 5.12–13; 1 Cor 2.14–15). However, all who are children in Christ need help in forming their consciences (see 1 Cor 3.1–3).[20] The Church's teaching contributes to this formation.

Conscience will be quiescent whenever one operates within a framework of previous choices one is sufficiently satisfied with and integrated around. One makes fresh choices but they do not raise new issues, and so they do not elicit moral reflection. This type of situation arises for both morally good and bad people. For example, good parents might deliberate at length and finally make a choice with respect to their child's education, yet not confront any judgment of conscience, because all the possibilities considered are morally acceptable. Again, criminals can make many choices to settle the means to be used in pursuit of their objectives without ever confronting a judgment of conscience, because they are interested only in what effectively leads to their ends, and make choices only because of the impossibility of settling rationally among options.

Question E: What is meant by "formation of conscience"?

1. The will to live a good life is the indispensable foundation of an upright conscience. In its submission to God's word, the act of living faith provides this foundation. Still, on the level of knowledge, three things are needed to make a sound judgment of conscience. **First, one must be clearly aware of the norms which distinguish right from wrong. Second, one must have sufficient factual knowledge to see practical possibilities, including at least one which is morally acceptable. Third, one also must attend to the relationship between the norms and the practical possibilities.**

2. Ignorance and error are possible in regard to all these matters, and instruction and learning are therefore needed in regard to all. The formation of a Christian conscience thus relates to three areas: clear understanding of norms, accurate and adequate information about possibilities, and readiness to engage in moral reflection before every choice.

3. Help in achieving a clear understanding of norms takes the form of clarification of the principles of natural law, the law written in our hearts (see Rom 2.15). In this clarification Catholics are assisted by the teaching of the Church (see DH 14). Chapters five through ten of this volume will articulate the principles of natural law and show how one can reason validly from them. Question F, below, will say a little more about the help which the Church's teaching gives; and much more will be said about this matter in chapters twenty-two through twenty-eight. Chapter thirty-six criticizes the opinion that tries to justify dissent from the Church's constant and very firm moral teaching.

4. Instruction about practical possibilities is an important part of the preaching of the gospel. Only in the gospel can we learn how it is possible to live a morally good life in this fallen world. More specific instruction about practical possibilities is an essential part of catechesis, spiritual direction, vocational guidance, and counseling. Until their lives are well organized by commitments and their personalities are integrated with these commitments, people need help in thinking of the right thing to do. Often, in a difficult situation, the morally good possibility simply does not occur to a person.

5. Directing attention to the relationship between moral norms and practical possibilities is a very important part of conscience formation. The use of conscience only really begins with the asking of moral questions. Yet children and morally immature adults often act spontaneously, with no moral reflection, and when they do engage in reflection, it often enough concerns only the promptings of superego and social convention. Thus it is a basic step in the formation of conscience to encourage those who are morally immature to ask moral questions, including whether the demands of superego and social convention are reasonable.

6. Existing desires and accepted projects must also be called into question. Indeed, a fully mature Christian conscience comes into being only when all merely assumed goals and standards have been examined in the light of faith, and faith itself has been accepted by a commitment which one confidently holds to be reasonable and right. So St. Paul urges: "Do not be conformed to this world but be transformed by the renewal of your mind, that you may prove what is the will of God, what is good and acceptable and perfect" (Rom 12.2).

In trying to form consciences, Christians customarily have concentrated on exhortation. For example, most of the Epistles of the New Testament include straightforward efforts to call attention to moral truths. These exhortations usually take the form of lists of good deeds and attitudes, contrasted with their opposites. Christians are urged to put aside their old ways, be vigilant, resist the devil, and submit to the demands of their state of life.[21]

Today, many question the effectiveness of such exhortation and suggest instead a more dialectical method for forming consciences. For example, values clarification tries to elicit moral reflection in children without authoritatively proposing any correct answer to the moral questions on which the children are asked to reflect.

Traditional exhortation surely has been part of the good news suitably directed towards Christian converts, who are enabled by the power of the Holy Spirit to live a new life in Jesus. Without downgrading such exhortation, one can admit some real advantages in a more dialectical approach to the formation of the consciences of Christians. After all, the principles of morality are available to them by natural insight; what they need is a stimulus to reflect morally, to bring to mind and put to work what they already somehow know. This is true especially of children brought up in a Christian environment, for their experience and habits of behavior will not block sound moral insight.

But if a more dialectical approach in the formation of consciences might be advisable, the movement of values clarification cannot be accepted uncritically. Much of the pedagogical material and literature of this movement is defective by Christian standards. For example, there often is a suggestion, at least implicit, that every individual should choose his or her own values, and that the only real duty is to be consistent. Similarly, the suggestion often is made that sufficiently good consequences can justify virtually anything.[22]

In a Christian educational context, a method somewhat like that used in secular programs of values clarification could be developed, but only after the approach is thoroughly criticized and reconstructed. Questions should help children to articulate objective moral principles and to appropriate the truth they find, truth which they will realize does not depend upon their own choices. Faith will illuminate the real but limited significance of every human good to be realized in this world. Attitudes of submission to values and of absolute respect for the dignity of persons—a respect which excludes some choices regardless of consequences—need to be cultivated. The lives of Jesus and of saints should be used as models, so that children will be encouraged to shape their own lives according to these exemplars.

Question F: How can the Church's teaching form conscience from within?

1. It is apparent to anyone who understands what natural law is that there can be no inconsistency between the objectivity of its norms and the personal quality of conscience. Natural law is our understanding of the basic principles of our fulfillment as human persons, and these principles are the premises from which we reason to judgments of conscience. Hence, natural law cannot be regarded as an imposition.

2. By contrast, the Church's moral teaching seems to come from outside oneself. Many think of it as if it were a set of imposed social standards, much like a civil society's body of law. This view is false. Here we shall see how the Church's moral teaching forms conscience from within. Later (23-G) we shall see why Catholics must conform their consciences in detail to this teaching.

3. The act of faith is the accepting of a personal relationship with God revealing himself. One can enter this relationship only by free choice and remain in it only if one is willing. This choice and willingness ought to be in accord with one's own conscience. In other words, people ought to make the act of faith and live up to it because all human persons have a responsibility to seek the truth, "especially religious truth. They are also bound to adhere to the truth, once it is known, and to order their whole lives in accord with the demands of truth" (DH 2).

In the next paragraph of the same document, Vatican II goes on to explain that while the divine law—which is God's wise and loving plan for all creation—is the highest standard for human life, human persons have been created with the ability to grasp for themselves the relevant implications of this plan for their lives. "Hence every man has the duty, and therefore the right, to seek the truth in matters religious, in order that he may with prudence form for himself right and true judgments of conscience, with the use of all suitable means" (DH 3). Naturally, the quest for truth will be social, but it should be a matter of free cooperation, not one of public imposition, because genuine religion depends on personal assent. Hence compulsion to accept and practice religious faith is excluded. One "perceives and acknowledges the imperatives of the divine law through the mediation of conscience" (DH 3), and so "it is by a personal assent that men are to adhere to [religious truth]" (DH 3).

4. Thus, in making the act of faith, one conforms to one's own conscience. Moreover, this judgment of conscience is rooted in an appreciation that the life of faith is not opposed to human goods and one's own true fulfillment, but is a necessary way of serving human goods and fulfilling oneself. In particular, faith

and the life of faith are essential to sharing in the goods of friendship with God and redemption from the wounds of sin and its consequences. These are great human goods; those who lose themselves in their service most truly fulfill themselves.

5. The act of faith makes one a member of the Church, the communion of those in friendship with God through friendship with Jesus. Since one is a member of the Church by one's own commitment of faith, identity as a Catholic is part of one's existential self-identity. This is an example of the self-constitution by choice explained previously (2-H). **For her committed members, therefore, the Church is not a society from which they are more or less alienated. For such people, to accept the Church's teaching is to be self-consistent.** To wish to be a Catholic while refusing to accept the Church's teaching would be rather like wishing to have a friend without being a friend.

6. Moral teaching is an important part of the Church's teaching. Faith makes practical demands precisely because it involves a personal relationship. But the moral demands of the Church's teaching are not additions over and above the requirements of morality which one can know naturally; rather, they specify the moral implications of natural law.

7. By Jesus' will it is part of the Church's duty to state authoritatively "those principles of the moral order which have their origin in human nature itself" (DH 14). In carrying out this duty, the Church calls attention to principles of the natural law, rejects formulations which distort them, and spells out many of their implications. This work is necessary because sin leads individuals and societies to rationalize their immoral choices and policies, and such rationalizations cloud insight into moral principles. This part of the Church's teaching does not form conscience by conveying information or giving orders, but by calling attention to truths one can know for oneself.

8. The Church's teaching also provides a great deal of information about the human condition and human possibilities, particularly about the fall, redemption, and our vocation to fulfillment in the Lord Jesus. This information does not comprise a set of commands but a set of facts which cannot be known apart from faith. One can ignore them if one wishes, but it is folly to do so. These facts about the human condition and human possibilities also specify the moral implications of natural law. Because the human predicament and the solution which faith proposes limit morally acceptable choices, a merely general knowledge of what is right and wrong simply does not provide sufficient moral guidance.

If they do what they ought, teachers in the Church have no choices to make concerning what to teach; their choices instead concern how most clearly and effectively to teach the truth entrusted to the Church by Jesus. Anyone who chooses to teach something other than what has been received and is believed simply ceases to act as a Catholic teacher. Teaching is not making or enforcing rules. Rules can be changed or softened; but where it is a question of the Church's teaching, there is no room for the Church to "ease the ban on X" or for those who minister in the Church's name to "relax the Church's rules on Y."

Question G: How is conscience misunderstood in the modern world?

1. **Today conscience often is confused with arbitrariness.** For instance: "My conscience tells me it is all right to do X—so it is all right for me, and nobody else can tell me I am wrong." Or: "I do not see that doing X really hurts anybody, and it does not bother my conscience. So doing X is all right." Or again: "I know a lot of decent people who are doing X, and I would not presume to pass judgment on them, so it would be all right for me to do X, too. Of course, I never do—well, hardly ever."

John Henry Newman observed the beginning of this view of conscience and criticized it bitingly in the *Letter to the Duke of Norfolk,* written in 1874. "Conscience has rights because it has duties; but in this age, with a large portion of the public, it is the very right and freedom of conscience to dispense with conscience, to ignore a Lawgiver and Judge, to be independent of unseen obligations. It becomes a license to take up any or no religion, to take up this or that and let it go again, to go to church, to go to chapel, to boast of being above all religions and to be an impartial critic of each of them. Conscience is a stern monitor, but in this century it has been superseded by a counterfeit, which the eighteen centuries prior to it never heard of, and could not have mistaken for it, if they had. It is the right of self-will."[23]

The situation today is very like that described by Newman. Ironically, some even invoke his authority to justify subjectivism.

2. **This popular erroneous conception of conscience amounts to moral subjectivism** (see 4-A and 4-C). The subjectivist account of conscience is to some extent simply a rationalizing attempt to justify refusal to submit to moral norms; but subjectivism is also to some extent a mistaken theory which follows from certain confusions.

3. The first of these concerns the sense in which conscience is personal. Although conscience is one's own grasp of moral truth, this does not make it one's own wish or fiat. Conscience is personal just as seeing something for oneself is personal. What one sees truly for oneself is an objective fact which others, too, can see. And the moral truth grasped by one's conscience is true apart from one's grasping of it.

4. The second confusion concerns the role of conscience in relation to legal impositions on the one hand and moral principles on the other. Because it knows moral requirements, conscience is a locus of personal dignity for the individual confronted with arbitrary, morally unacceptable legal impositions. But the situation is different when conscience faces moral principles: Here it confronts the source of its own authority. Those whose consciences are at odds with these principles need to correct their error, not withstand moral truth in the name of personal freedom.[24]

5. In appealing to freedom in such a situation, one is claiming the liberty to do as one pleases. A person who supposes that the basic moral categories are the permissible and the forbidden is inclined to do this. One whose practical judgments are affected by a residue of superego and awareness of social convention is likely both to confuse moral norms with legal impositions and to suppose that the basic moral categories are the permitted and the forbidden.

Hence, such a person is likely to appeal to liberty against moral norms which are not felt to be personally acceptable.

6. **Unlike persons of immature conscience, those whose consciences operate maturely do not perceive objective norms as standing apart from personal conscience.** Thus, faithful Catholics with mature consciences will not regard the Church's teaching as a burden to be eased as much as possible, but as a bright light to be gratefully accepted and followed. As Leo XIII teaches, this light is liberating: "For the truth which proceeds from the teaching of Christ clearly demonstrates the real nature and value of every being; and man, being endowed with this knowledge, if he but obey the truth as perceived, will make all things subject to himself, not himself to them; his appetites to his reason, not his reason to his appetites. Thus the slavery of sin and falsehood will be shaken off, and the most perfect liberty attained: 'You shall know the truth, and the truth shall make you free (Jn 8.32).'"[25]

After the publication of the encyclical, *Humanae vitae*, in July 1968, many episcopal conferences issued pastoral statements.[26] Most discussed conscience. While virtually everything said in these statements about conscience has a true sense, still many people were misled by them. Why this happened can be understood from the following general observation, which holds equally in any pastoral situation.

Normally, conscience becomes a subject of reflection when one is thinking about one's past action or someone else's action. In forming one's conscience here and now, one pays attention to the relevant moral truth, not to conscience. It follows that when someone seeks pastoral guidance, he or she wants to know what the Church believes is truly the right thing to do. If one responds by saying that a person who follows a sincere conscience is morally blameless, the remark can be misleading. It is true, but the truth about conscience is not what is being asked for. The question is: What should I think I may do? The question is not: If I do what I think I should do but happen to be mistaken, then how do I stand?

Thus, when an advisor in a pastoral situation talks about conscience and about the moral norms proposed by the Church at the same time, the talk about conscience is likely to be mistaken for talk about one's substantive moral responsibilities. The teaching on conscience does not form conscience; it merely says that if one blamelessly thinks doing X is right, then choosing to do X is blameless.

But this truism is likely to be taken as significant and to be misinterpreted to mean: "If you think that doing X is morally unobjectionable, and if you are blameless in having come to think so, then I, as your pastor, assure you that you may do X blamelessly." In other words: "If you think it is right, then it is right for you." Thus, inappropriate talk about conscience is likely to be understood by the faithful who need formation of conscience as an endorsement of subjectivism. Subjectivism is completely alien to a Christian conception of moral principles.

Summary

The word "conscience" is sometimes used to refer to feelings and judgments which have no direct relationship with moral truth—to manifestations of the superego, which, arising from early training, give a sense of requirement and guilt at the emotional level, and to awareness of social conventions imposed by a group with which one identifies. In a full and strict sense, though, conscience is awareness of moral truth.

The Church is interested in conscience only in this latter sense. As Vatican II uses it, "conscience" refers at once to awareness of moral principles, to the process of reasoning from principles to conclusions, and to the conclusions—moral judgments on choices already made or under consideration. St. Thomas' classic account concentrates on conscience in this last aspect, as an intellectual act of judgment. When conscience is regarded in this way, as one's best judgment of what is right and wrong to choose, it is true by definition that one ought to follow one's conscience; but this truism provides no specific moral guidance by itself.

Judgments of conscience can be mistaken. Although one ought to follow conscience even when it is mistaken—since it is one's last and best judgment as to the choice one ought to make—one is not necessarily guiltless in doing so. If the error is one's own fault, one is responsible for the wrong one does in following erroneous conscience. Thus, one's first responsibility is to form conscience rightly so that one's moral judgments will be true. Rationalization and self-deception can, however, produce a conscience which is voluntarily fixed in error. This is what Vatican II means in speaking of a conscience "practically sightless as a result of a practice of sinning" (GS 16).

Conscience functions best in Christians who are good, mature, and integrated. They have the virtue of prudence or practical wisdom; as a result of their established commitments, they find it easy to make moral judgments. Evidently, then, when one is in doubt, one's prudence is not adequate to the occasion, and it is wrong to fall back on a subjective impression, calling it an "insight of prudence" or something of the sort.

The formation of conscience requires learning and thinking about three areas: the principles of natural law, practical possibilities, and the application of the principles to the facts of each situation of choice. A great deal of conscience formation, especially in children, consists simply in getting people to think about their behavior from a moral point of view and to question the reasonableness of the demands of superego and social convention.

Some people regard the Church's moral teaching as an imposed set of social standards similar to civil law. This view is false. The act of faith is a free personal commitment by which one becomes a member of the Church. For one who makes this act, such membership is part of his or her existential self-identity. Thus, to accept what the Church teaches, including its moral teaching, is to be self-consistent. Moreover, the moral demands of the Church's teaching are not alien to the requirements of morality which one can know naturally. Rather, they specify the moral implications of natural law, the law written in our hearts (cf. Rom 2.15). Thus the moral teaching of the Church forms conscience from within, not by external imposition.

All the same, conscience today is often confused with arbitrariness. This is expressed by such statements as, "My conscience tells me it's all right to do this, so it is all right for me." Such moral subjectivism rests on two confusions. First, the fact that conscience is one's own grasp of moral truth is taken to mean that moral truth itself is whatever one makes it. Second, moral principles, which are the source of conscience's authority, are mistaken for legal impositions, which it is the task of conscience to judge. By contrast, persons of mature conscience do not perceive objective moral norms as standing apart from personal conscience.

Appendix 1:   Three levels in the development of conscience

Conscience does develop. The meaning of "right," "wrong," and "permissible" changes as a child grows up. The levels of this development can be distinguished in various ways, but at least three levels must be recognized.

First, the physical environment conditions small children; for example, they learn quickly by experience not to touch hot radiators. The social environment, usually principally the parents, also teaches children, not simply conditions them. Their relationship with other persons is interpersonal; the child feels the importance of the bond. Imitating and conforming to others wins their reassuring approval. To behave in a way which brings a negative reaction from persons to whom the child is strongly bonded is to experience not-being-loved, insecurity, aloneness, being cut off, being bad.

In effect, the child experiences something of the reality of the evil which is disharmony in the existential domain. Even at an infantile level, interpersonal disharmony sets up inner conflict. The child quickly learns that misbehavior engenders this experience of inner conflict—an experience obviously much more repugnant to the child than many other negative experiences which it begins to accept in order to avoid this one. This initial level is called "superego," since the authority of good and bad is interiorized in the child as a personal authority overseeing the child's own desiring and scheming ego.

Second, growing children meet and mingle and begin to interact with one another. For each other they constitute a new type of social environment. Here the relationships are more on a par; the children need one another. They have certain common interests and begin to form a voluntary association to pursue them. In doing this, they learn the necessity of a certain level of norms centered in fairness and the control of impulses necessary to attain desired ends. To behave in a way the group disapproves both threatens participation and elicits criticism.

At a new and more articulate level, the child experiences disharmony in the existential domain. Interpersonal disharmony and inner conflict again are linked, but since the relationships are shaped by discourse, the child experiences the stupidity of its own wrongdoing. To avoid this sort of stupidity, to maintain solidarity with the peer group, the child once more must limit its impulses, accept certain objectives as its own, and affirm its identity as a member of society. This second level of conscience can be called "social convention," since the authority of good and evil is located in the group and in those who speak and act for it.

Third, if all goes well, the young person in adolescence begins more and more to understand basic human goods and the principles of responsibility. These are not tied to existing interpersonal relationships, but they open up the possibility of new and deeper relationships. There arises a desire to share in commitment to a worthy cause; to love and be loved in ways which go deeper than the rather superficial relationships of most groups formed by accident (children in a neighborhood, in a school class, and so on). The model of persons who are or were dedicated to human goods and lived heroic lives has vibrant appeal.

Once more, the young person experiences disharmony in the existential domain, but only now in its full depth and reality. One finds one's inner self torn, with feelings at odds with reason. One realizes that one's ideals are not expressed in one's life. One often is disappointed in love and disillusioned with the imperfections of one's heroes. One knows one must come to terms with reality and is reluctant to do so.

The preceding summary of the distinction between the superego and conventional morality finds support in common observation of the difference between the self-control of infants and that of children who understand and more or less follow rules to balance their own desires and the demands of others. The summary of the distinction between conventional morality and the morality of truth is supported by the philosophical and religious tradition which has sought objective grounds to criticize accepted standards. This three-level structure also finds some support in the work of psychologists, such as Jean Piaget and Lawrence Kohlberg, who hold a cognitive-developmental view of the awareness of right and wrong.[27]

The implications for moral education of the development of conscience cannot be treated here. But the following points should be noted. Chapter four will make it clear that a cognitive-developmental view of the awareness of right and wrong is defensible against those psychological and sociological theories which reduce conscience to principles below the level of reason and leave no room for the conception of conscience as awareness of moral truth. Still, work done along this line is subject to certain limitations which need to be taken into account.

First, a definite conception of moral truth is assumed. For instance, Kohlberg maintains a formalistic theory of justice, along the lines of Kant's and Rawls' theories. Sometimes he suggests that moral goodness is simply cognitive maturity: "He who knows the good chooses the good."[28] This view would reduce moral evil to inevitable immaturity, exclude free choice, and thus undermine moral responsibility. At other times he suggests that ultimately moral principles are in force because they are self-chosen—a position similar to R. M. Hare's prescriptivism, which will be criticized (4-C).[29] An ethics combining the elements Kohlberg's does can be criticized in many ways. Justice surely is a requirement of morality, but it is not the only nor even the highest requirement of Christian morality, as will be explained in chapters seven and twenty-six. But even more important than theoretical criticisms is the fact that the limits of Kohlberg's ethical theory limit the questions he asks, thus shaping and limiting the value of his conclusions.

Second, a further limitation arises from the experimental approach itself. Piaget, for example, assumed that morality is a matter of rules, for this assumption permitted him to investigate an empirical question: What reasons can children state for following rules?[30] Similarly, Kohlberg's work makes use of standardized problems or stories.[31] Such methodological limitations mean that what actually is investigated is children's verbal behavior expressing their thinking about theoretical moral questions, not their practical thinking forming their own present choices. To know when children become morally responsible in a full sense, one would like to know when they themselves begin to understand that they ought to obey, not because disobedience is naughty or might be risky, but because parental knowledge, love, and care deserve a willing response. But Kohlberg's results can at most reveal what children can say about obedience, and what children can say is limited by what adults do say.

Third, Kohlberg's elaboration of stages and his conclusions about their relationships depend on evidence which is hardly conclusive and which has been subjected to severe criticisms from a scientific viewpoint.[32]

Thus, while the distinction between three levels of conscience—preconventional, conventional, and post-conventional or principled—is well-grounded, beyond this, one can at present only say that there is some evidence (which is disputed) concerning the ability to talk theoretically (not the ability to think practically) about certain areas of morality, especially questions of justice (but not about questions even more critical to the emergence of Christian moral responsibility).

Appendix 2:   How conscience can make blameless mistakes

Sometimes people do things on the basis of mistakes of fact; they would have acted otherwise had they known better. One has a moral obligation to try to determine facts in important matters, and also to proceed on the safe side in guesses about factual matters when important moral obligations are to be fulfilled (see 12-B). However, one can and often does make mistakes of fact. In cases of this sort, the judgment of conscience based on false information is not itself in error.

For example, a woman takes what she thinks to be a safe sleeping pill, prescribed by her doctor, because she is restless during the early weeks of pregnancy. The pill turns out to cause severe, congenital defects in the child whom she wished only to protect by caring for her own health. Had she only known, she would have done otherwise. However, her conscientious decision to go to a physician about her difficulties in early pregnancy and to follow the prescription she received was perfectly sound. The error was not at all in conscience.

The error of fact can be about a moral fact. For example, a child is sent by parents to what is recommended as an excellent Catholic school. The parents decide to do this at great sacrifice out of a sense of duty, because of the bad moral atmosphere of the local public school. At the Catholic school, some of the teachers who are depraved seduce the child. The parents wrongly feel somehow at fault.

It is easy for persons who are developing a genuine conscience to mistake the deliverances of superego or social convention for moral truths. For example, some good Germans who had developed but imperfectly integrated consciences rightly judged (as a matter of moral truth) that they had to resist certain Nazi decrees, yet felt guilty and unpatriotic about it. In some matters, these lower levels of conscience probably confused their judgments, so that they did not see clearly how little responsibility they had toward that regime. Thus they were restrained from more bold action by blameless confusion of conscience.

Within the sphere of moral reasoning itself, blameless errors also are possible. For example, one can easily absolutize a nonabsolute norm, failing to notice that additional intelligible factors call for reconsideration. Again, one can notice that an action is consistent with several basic principles of morality and mistakenly conclude it is morally right, although further inquiry would have indicated that it is not. For instance, one who notices that killing in self-defense is not otherwise immoral might consider it justified in a case in which a Christian should accept death rather than kill in self-defense.

To the extent that one must supplement one's moral reasoning by appeal to a moral authority, one tends to perceive the norms proposed by that authority as if they were rules of law. Most Catholics thus rely upon the Church's teaching for normative guidance in some matters in which the norm proposed would not in itself be recognized as a moral truth. This situation is a necessary stage in the development of a fully mature Christian conscience—a stage from which most of us never totally emerge. However, it has its own hazards, which create possibilities of innocent mistakes.

Specific norms which are proposed can be misunderstood. For example, people easily misunderstand the commandment to obey proper authority, not observing that the authority must operate within its due bounds (see *S.t.*, 2–2, q. 104, a. 5). Conversely, they easily misunderstand the duty to make exceptions in the fulfilling of laws, thinking this to be a right to exempt oneself whenever one honestly thinks the lawmaker, if informed of the facts, would consider an exception reasonable (see *S.t.*, 1–2, q. 96, a. 6; 2–2, q. 120, a. 1). Thus, people often are both too strict and too lax, too subservient to laws and not sufficiently submissive to them.

Perhaps even more important, one who looks to a moral authority needs procedural rules for determining in doubtful cases when the authority is proposing a binding norm and what this norm is. This is the role fulfilled by probabilism and the other moral systems. One such procedural rule is: If there is a real doubt whether a binding norm has been proposed, then one is not morally obliged to assume that it has been: "A doubtful law does not oblige."

This procedural rule (explained in 12-D) presupposes that one has tried to resolve the doubt by investigation and that the doubt is within the framework of the Church's teaching. However, people informed of this maxim in the course of superficial moral guidance often misunderstand it to mean that moral matters debated by theologians automatically become open questions, so that the norms lose their force.

Even in the cases discussed here, "blameless" mistakes are not always in fact completely blameless. One perhaps failed somewhere to do something one could and should have done; one perhaps was in too much of a hurry to deal with a certain matter and did not give it quite enough attention. However, such faults would be venial sins. Perhaps there is little or no moral error without a basis somewhere in at least a venial sin.

Appendix 3:   Failures of conscience through some fault

Traditionally, this subject was called "the culpably erroneous conscience" or "vincible ignorance"—a lack of knowledge one could overcome. By my analysis there are three distinct situations: (1) conscience which is quiescent or not operating on the level of moral truth as it could and should; (2) conscience which delivers an erroneous judgment which one could and should question, but does not; (3) conscience which delivers an erroneous judgment which one is psychologically incapable of questioning at present due to one's own prior, grave fault.

In the first case, one is responsible morally only for one's prior wrong acts or omissions which block the operation of mature conscience. Here and now there is no genuine judgment of conscience which is ignored or violated.

In the second case, one's moral state is rather similar to that of a doubtful conscience, in the sense that one ought to investigate before acting. However, the duty to investigate is not so clear, because the unsatisfactory state of one's conscience is not directly before one's mind.

For example, a businessman once heard that in many cases one is not morally obliged to pay all of the taxes which would be required by a strict interpretation of the law. He has cut corners for some time, but not investigated whether his corner-cutting falls within the boundaries of the moral teaching of the Church. Now and then it occurs to him that he ought to think this matter through, but when it comes time to prepare taxes he is always busy and inclined to assume that the vague moral formation he once received is adequate to cover what he is doing. This is a typical case of vincible ignorance; to the extent that the judgments the businessman makes are false, he also is in culpable error.

This state of mind can have two quite different moral backgrounds. In one, there earlier was a mortal sin—for example, a serious act of fraud—which was never repented. In such a case, the conveniently ignorant and probably erring conscience belongs to the sinful pattern of life. But in another moral background, there was no earlier, unrepented mortal sin, and the man never clearly faced and violated a judgment of conscience in a grave matter. In this latter case, until he becomes aware that he has a grave obligation to resolve the moral issue of his tax evasion, the businessman has not committed a mortal sin, even though his ignorance might be culpable and the evasion of taxes grave matter.

The third case—that of a person at present psychologically unable to uncover the error of conscience initiated by a prior act of his or her own—likewise divides into two morally different subtypes.

One of these is the bad faith of a person whose false conscience is generated by a persistent state of mortal sin. "For every one who does evil hates the light, and does not come to the light, lest his deeds should be exposed" (Jn 3.20). Truthful preaching and teaching arouse resentment in such persons, because they are forced to encounter the truth they could not bring to the surface for themselves, and they will not consider submitting to the truth when they are forced to face it (see Jn 12.37–43).

Quite different is the error of the simple person who tries to avoid and overcome grave sin, who perhaps is not well instructed or very intelligent, but who by many venial sins of commission and omission has a conscience filled with unsuspected misinformation. Such a person might do things gravely evil in themselves without realizing their character. The error in conscience is culpable and subjectively correctable, but there is no mortal sin.

Perhaps, also, one might include here the erroneous consciences of generally upright people who accept without question the moral errors of their times, although they should be sophisticated enough to see through them. Those who burned heretics ought to have known better. Why didn't they? Perhaps because of many venial sins, some serious, of prejudice, vindictiveness, anxiety about the faith (a sin against hope), arrogant overconfidence in the system of which they were functionaries, insufficient diligence to think the matter through, and so on.

Notes

1. For an introduction to psychological aspects of conscience and its development, one may study two essays in *Conscience: Its Freedom and Limitations*, ed. William C. Bier (New York: Fordham University Press, 1971): Dorothea Miller, "Development of the Normal Conscience," 39–61; Robert J. Campbell, "Superego and Conscience," 82–91. (Neither essay can be recommended without qualification from the point of view of Catholic doctrine.)

2. John W. Glaser, S.J., "Conscience and Superego: A Key Distinction," *Theological Studies*, 32 (1971), 30–47, treats the distinction between conscience and superego (but does not distinguish the level of conventional morality) and some of the problems which can be generated by superego's confusion with conscience. Unfortunately, Glaser's treatment is marred by ambivalence toward ecclesial authority.

3. For a treatment of conscience in general along the same lines presented here, see Karol Wojtyla, *The Acting Person*, trans. Andrzej Potocki, ed. Anna-Teresa Tymieniecka (Dordrecht: D. Reidel, 1979), 152–74. There are at least two differences. First, Wojtyla thinks of conscience more broadly, including not only the judgment in which one is aware of moral truth, but the process of the mind striving for truth in the sphere of values (159–61). Second, and more significantly, Wojtyla attributes to conscience the role of transforming insight into values into the force of obligation (165–66). As will be explained in chapter seven, even the principles of practical reasoning in general and of morality have of themselves a normative force, which Wojtyla does not seem sufficiently to recognize; note his remark (162) on duty and normative power, manifested in conscience, which he seems to wish to distinguish from truth itself. Wojtyla's treatment of conscience at times—for instance, in the emphasis on striving for truth—seems insufficiently to distinguish the working of conscience as such (including the conscience of the person who disregards it) from the working of the conscience of the upright person, whose ideal moral cognition is discussed in question D.

4. Walter E. Conn, *Conscience: Development and Self-Transcendence* (Birmingham, Ala.: Religious Education Press, 1981), stresses throughout that genuine conscience is concerned with moral truth, not with conformity to mores. Summarizing the developmental psychology of Erikson, Piaget, and Kohlberg, and the philosophical theory of Bernard Lonergan, he rightly rejects minimalism and legalism in favor of a primary focus on full human development (208). Unfortunately, Conn's work is defective in at least two respects. First, he wishes to make a contribution to theological ethics, but he pays no attention to the teaching of Scripture and Vatican II concerning conscience; against these sources, Conn denies that conscience is a principled judgment (205) and instead says: "Quite simply, conscience is the fullest expression of the personal subject's fundamental exigence for self-

transcendence" (208). Conn wishes to identify "is" and "ought" in the human person (12); he says that conscience is "the fundamental, dynamic reality of the personal subject who has committed, dedicated, indeed, surrendered her or himself to the radical demands of the human spirit" (208). Thus, he seems to leave no room for the radical moral evil of a choice against mature conscience. Second, near the end of his book, without any basis in what has preceded it, Conn gratuitously claims that ethics can best be compared to esthetics (209). On the basis of this analogy, he suggests that "because the ethical analyst realizes that decisions are made in particular situations according to the subject's best *creative* understanding of the complex concreteness of the situation, he or she does not regard interpretations of general problem areas like abortion as applicable in a *deductive* way to particular cases, any more than a literary critic pretends to offer the author a formula on how to compose a fine poem or a first-rate novel." Apart from the fact that critics do articulate ways guaranteed to result in wretched poetry and third-rate novels, Conn here seems to adopt a mistaken theory of moral principles (see 4-B).

5. For a rich summary of the scriptural and patristic sources which underlie the teaching on conscience of St. Thomas and Vatican II: Philippe Delhaye, *The Christian Conscience* (New York: Desclée, 1968), 36–99. For a concise statement of the meaning of "conscience" and criticism of certain prevalent errors: William B. Smith, "The Meaning of Conscience," in *Principles of Catholic Moral Life,* ed. William E. May (Chicago: Franciscan Herald Press, 1980), 361–82. For a more extensive systematic treatment, rooted in classical moral theology but not entirely confined by it: Pietro Palazzini, *La coscienza,* Studi cattolici (Rome: Ares, 1961).

6. See C. A. Pierce, *Conscience in the New Testament* (London: SCM Press, 1955), 108–9. Pierce's study, considered as a whole, suggests that, although the sacred authors spoke in a variety of ways concerning matters relating to conscience, no developed doctrine on conscience emerges. Some aspects of Pierce's treatment need to be amended: Margaret E. Thrall, "The Pauline Use of *Syneidesis," New Testament Studies,* 14 (1967), 118–25; also Ceslaus Spicq, O.P., "Conscience dans le Nouveau Testament," *Revue Biblique,* 47 (1938), 50–80; W. D. Davies, "Conscience," *Interpreter's Dictionary of the Bible,* 1:671–76; and two articles in *Encyclopedia of Biblical Theology:* Ceslaus Spicq, "Conscience," 131–34; J. B. Bauer, "Heart," 360–63.

7. Also see St. Thomas Aquinas, *De veritate,* q. 17, a. 1. Anthony Battaglia, *Toward a Reformulation of Natural Law* (New York: Seabury Press, 1981), in a study which makes use of St. Thomas, fails to distinguish between social convention and moral truth, and thus reduces the moral "ought" to the "is" of cultural practices (134). As part of his reconstruction of natural law as a natural, psychosocial principle of conventional morality, Battaglia suggests that the objective reference of moral judgment, which takes us beyond "feeling good about ourselves" (69), is reached by a sense of fitness analogous to the aesthetic sense (79). Battaglia makes no distinction between the judgment of conscience and choice. In individual decision making, one arrives at "what makes sense," he explains, by balancing the inputs of senses, emotions, intelligence, and intuition, to see what best satisfies these various and contradictory inclinations as a whole (102–9). The trouble with this is that it so generously and indiscriminately takes into account all aspects of human motivation that it is hard to see how one could possibly choose contrary to conscience—that is, commit a sin. Indeed, Battaglia says: "We must over and over again assert that human beings act according to what makes sense to them in the particular circumstances of their particular lives—or at least they try to" (104). The only possibility of immoral action he recognizes is a practice which does not arise out of social consensus (135), for such a practice violates the universalizability criterion as Battaglia understands it, and he thinks this criterion is the specific contribution of reason to moral judgment (108). Thus, even on this theory, conscience in the genuine sense emerges solely and precisely at the point where a rational requirement is violated.

8. In addition to Bauer's article on "heart" cited above, see Johannes Behm, "kardia," *Theological Dictionary of the New Testament,* 3:605–13. Since "heart" in the Bible embraces the whole inner self of the person, it can sometimes be replaced by "conscience." But frequently such a substitution would be erroneous or at least questionable. Hence, one must be extremely careful about drawing conclusions concerning the scriptural teaching on conscience from passages in which "heart" occurs. One must be even more careful in using the word "heart" in teaching about conscience, since in English "heart" usually means sentiment rather than awareness of truth.

9. John Courtney Murray, S.J., n. 5 to his edition of "Declaration on Religious Freedom," in *The Documents of Vatican II,* ed. Walter M. Abbott, S.J. (New York: America Press, 1966), 679.

10. See also St. Thomas Aquinas, *De veritate,* q. 17, a. 2.

11. Ibid., q. 17, aa. 3–4.

12. Ibid., q. 17, a. 5.

13. Ibid., a. 3 and a. 5. Timothy E. O'Connell, *Principles for a Catholic Morality* (New York: Seabury Press, 1978), 91–93, rightly emphasizing the obligation to follow one's certain conscience, mistakenly confuses the subjective absoluteness of this obligation with the objective truth of the judgment of conscience, and declares the latter "ultimately infallible conscience." This confusion obscures the facts that conscience can be in error and the error can be one's own fault. Following conscience in such a case does not free one from guilt, and so the awakening of such consciences in unconscious bad faith is important.

14. St. Thomas Aquinas, *Quodlibet,* 8, q. 6, a. 3.

15. Ibid.

16. See *De veritate,* q. 17, a. 4. St. Thomas does not consider the study of the formation of conscience to belong to moral principles. He deals with it in his treatise on prudence: *Summa theologiae,* 2–2, qq. 47–56. I think he is correct in this view.

17. John Paul II, *Familiaris Consortio,* 74 *AAS* (1982) 170–71; Eng. ed. (Vatican City: Vatican Polyglot Press, 1981), 138 (sec. 73).

18. See, for example, John W. Glaser, S.J., "Authority, Connatural Knowledge, and the Spontaneous Judgment of the Faithful," *Theological Studies,* 29 (1968), 742–51. Glaser assumes that St. Thomas' judgment by connaturality is the same as Karl Rahner's "preconceptual knowledge," but Thomas, in the passage Glaser cites (748) from *S.t.,* 2–2, q. 45, a. 2, speaks only of a *judgment* made without the complete use of *reason*—that is, without working out the argument from principles to conclusions.

19. For a summary of St. Thomas' doctrine on prudence: H. D. Noble, "Prudence," *Dictionnaire Théologie Catholique,* 13:1023–76. On knowledge by connaturality: W. E. May, "Knowledge, Connatural," *New Catholic Encyclopedia,* 8:228–29. On the logic of moral judgments involving connatural knowledge: Germain Grisez, "The Logic of Moral Judgment," *Proceedings of the American Catholic Philosophical Association,* 36 (1962), 67–76. Joseph Owens, C.Ss.R., "The Ethical Universal in Aristotle," *Studia Moralia,* 3 (1965), 27–47, shows that prudence in Aristotle does not make for a subjectivism which would qualify the universal norm, but since the norm is specified formally in terms of the virtues, its material application is conditioned by recognition. The latter is limited and guided by the culture. Thus, Aristotle's prudence entails cultural relativity in respect to material norms; if it is accepted in a Christian context, the implication is that a person fully formed in a Christian way of life will recognize by connaturality what will embody the Christian (and underlying common human) virtues—e.g., mercy and justice.

20. See Rudolf Schnackenburg, "Christian Adulthood According to the Apostle Paul," *Catholic Biblical Quarterly,* 25 (1963), 354–70.

21. See Marcus Barth, *Ephesians, 4–6,* Anchor Bible, 34A (Garden City, N.Y.: Doubleday, 1974), 453–62, 550–53, and (bibliography) 824–25.

22. A widely used text for values clarification, which contains many things unacceptable by Christian standards: Sidney B. Simon, Leland W. Howe, and Howard Kirschenbaum, *Values Clarification: A Handbook of Practical Strategies for Teachers and Students* (New York: Hart Publishing, 1972). An official state publication which exemplifies the pragmatic, proportionalist approach of the new value instruction: *Valuing: A Discussion Guide* (Albany, N.Y.: The Board of Regents, 1976). A revealing work directed toward teachers: Ronald G. Havelock, *The Change Agent's Guide to Innovation* (Englewood Cliffs, N.J.: Educational Technology Publications, 1973), which assumes that the function of the school is to lead children beyond traditional moral views they bring from their homes.

23. John Henry Newman, *Certain Difficulties Felt by Anglicans Considered . . . a Letter addressed to the Duke of Norfolk* (London: Longmans, Green, 1897), 250. Defenders of dissent from the Church's moral teaching often quote the sentence at the end (261) of this section: "Certainly, if I am obliged to bring religion into after-dinner toasts (which indeed does not seem quite the thing) I shall drink—to the Pope, if you please—still, to Conscience first, and to the Pope afterwards." They do not mention that the immediately preceding discussion concerns a possible duty in conscience to disobey an *order,* not a *moral teaching,* of the pope. Gladstone had suggested that since the papacy is a foreign power, Catholics might not be loyal citizens, for they might feel bound to follow the pope's orders in case of a political dispute between England and Rome.

24. Max Scheler, *Formalism in Ethics and Non-Formal Ethics of Values* (Evanston, Ill.: North-

western University Press, 1973), 317–28, provides a cogent analysis and critique of subjectivism based on "freedom of conscience" analogous to that offered here. But Scheler distinguishes between (1) universally valid and nonformal moral propositions, which cannot be played off against conscience, and (2) the adaptation of moral insight to what is good as such for me. The second Scheler thinks in principle irreplaceable by any possible norm (324–25). This position in part depends on Scheler's inadequate account of the essential relation between values and personal fulfillment, which makes him imagine one must move from the former to the latter. It also depends in part on his overlooking the fact that in comparison with any social context, each individual has added personal considerations (for example, my prior commitments and personal vocation, my abilities and opportunities) which require normative judgments no one else can supply. Such judgments, if true, still will be universally valid, although in fact they might be relevant only to a single instance; they will bear on what is good simply, which also is good for me insofar as I share in an intelligible existential order of interpersonal communion open to all who can be fulfilled in the goods of human persons.

25. Leo XIII, *Tametsi futura prospicientibus,* 33 *ASS* (1900–1901) 281; *The Papal Encyclicals,* 153.9.

26. For a brief discussion of these statements and references: John C. Ford, S.J., and Germain Grisez, "Contraception and the Infallibility of the Ordinary Magisterium," *Theological Studies,* 39 (1978), 308–12. It should be noticed that insofar as some of these statements disagree with received Catholic teaching on conscience, they also disagree with one another. Certain conferences which published rather questionable statements under the pressures immediately following the publication of *Humanae vitae* later issued more deliberate and far sounder treatments of relevant points. See, for example, Canadian Catholic Conference, *Statement on the Formation of Conscience* (1 December 1973), in *Catholic Mind,* 72 (April 1974), 40–51. The bishops of the United States also published a later statement which provides an adequate, brief summary of common Catholic teaching on conscience and many other general and particular questions in Christian morality: *To Live in Christ Jesus: A Pastoral Reflection on the Moral Life* (11 November 1976). This letter was drafted with great care after wide consultation; it accurately presents common Catholic teaching in a contemporary form and format.

27. See Jean Piaget et al., *The Moral Judgment of the Child* (New York: Free Press, 1965); Lawrence Kohlberg, "Stage and Sequence: The Cognitive-Developmental Approach to Socialization," in *Handbook of Socialization Theory and Research,* ed. David A. Goslin (Chicago: Rand McNally, 1969), 347–480; "Stages of Moral Development as a Basis for Moral Education," in *Moral Education: Interdisciplinary Approaches,* ed. C. M. Beck et al. (Toronto: University of Toronto Press, 1971), 23–92; "Moral Stages and Moralization," in *Moral Development and Behavior,* ed. Thomas Lickona (New York: Holt, Rinehart and Winston, 1976), 31–53; "The Cognitive-Developmental Approach to Moral Education," in *Readings in Moral Education,* ed. Peter Scharf (Minneapolis: Winston Press, 1978), 36–51.

28. Lawrence Kohlberg, *Essays on Moral Development,* vol. 1, *The Philosophy of Moral Development: Moral Stages and the Idea of Justice* (San Francisco: Harper and Row, 1981), 189.

29. See Kohlberg in Beck et al., eds., op. cit., 31–53; in Scharf, ed., op. cit., 50–51; in Lickona, ed., op. cit., 34–35.

30. See Piaget, op. cit., 13–15 and 361.

31. See Kohlberg, in Scharf, ed., op. cit., 38–47.

32. See "Part V: Criticism and Controversy," ibid., 248–307 (and note especially the concessions of those who defend Kohlberg's work); William Kurtines and Esther B. Greif, "The Development of Moral Thought: Review and Evaluation of Kohlberg's Approach," *Psychological Bulletin,* 81 (1974), 453–70; Robert T. Hall and John U. Davis, *Moral Education in Theory and Practice* (Buffalo, N.Y.: Prometheus Books, 1975), 98–106.

CHAPTER FOUR

SOME MISTAKEN THEORIES
OF MORAL PRINCIPLES

Introduction

As chapters five through eight will explain, moral principles are truths which shape one's judgments of conscience toward human fulfillment. But there are also various mistaken theories of moral principles. Some deny that there are any general truths from which to draw judgments of conscience. Others admit that there are general principles, but deny that they shape moral judgments toward human fulfillment. Such theories have impeded Christian thought in the past and do so today. It is therefore useful to examine erroneous theories rather carefully.[1]

Question A: Are judgments of conscience
mere expressions of moral feelings?

1. As we saw (3-A), children learn to feel guilt and distinguish acceptable and unacceptable behavior even before they are old enough to make judgments of conscience and choices. This childish sense of the required and the forbidden is superego. Some people reduce conscience to superego; judgments of conscience, in their view, are no more than expressions of internalized pressures.[2]

2. Although no Catholic theologian denies that there is moral truth, much popular opinion, reflected in the modern confusion already criticized (3-G), implies such a denial. There is also something close to a denial of moral truth in the current tendency to devalue careful reflection upon moral issues and substitute, as a moral guide, a sense of being at peace with oneself or in agreement with others.

3. Some philosophers have in fact defended the view that there is no moral truth. Influenced by psychological theories such as Freud's, they lay great emphasis on the fact that morality does involve feelings and they argue from people's frequent use of moral language—for example, "That's unfair!"—simply to express their feelings.[3]

4. This philosophical view has some plausibility because disagreements about what is right and wrong are often hard to resolve. In science, disagreements can generally be settled by experimentation and logic. When it comes to profound moral disagreements, however, experience and logic by themselves settle nothing, since the question at issue is always what ought to be, not what is. Thus it

can seem that morality is a matter of taste, and that there is nothing beyond the superego to serve as a guide or monitor of behavior.

5. Nonetheless, this view must be rejected. **If correct, it would leave no room for moral reflection, moral teaching, or even reasoned dissent on moral issues. It is plainly incompatible with Catholic teaching, for it would undercut the Catholic conception of a conscience which can be really correct or really mistaken.** That conception is grounded in a still deeper truth of faith—that the created order of things embodies meanings and values placed there by a wise and loving creator. As was explained (3-B), according to the Catholic understanding of conscience these meanings and values, spontaneously understood by human beings, are for them a law written in their hearts (see GS 16).

6. Difficulties in settling moral disputes bring out the special character of moral principles, which are neither matters of fact nor logical requirements. But these difficulties do not show that there are no moral truths. Agreement is sometimes reached in moral disputes. People admit that their previous judgments were in error and correct them. Such admissions would make no sense if conscience were nothing more than superego. It is also worth noticing that agreement is not always easily come by in fields other than morality. Psychologists, economists, and physicists also have their seemingly unresolvable differences, but no one concludes from this that there are no truths of psychology, economics, and physics.

Question B: Are judgments of conscience derivable from any general principle?

1. The view that they are not, reduces conscience to isolated acts of insight. Although these insights are thought to embody moral truth, it is denied that there are any general principles from which rational reflection can draw them.

2. Some hold that judgments of conscience are direct inspirations from God. This claim has been pressed most with respect to certain especially important questions of conscience, such as the discernment of one's personal vocation.[4]

3. The view that judgments of conscience cannot be derived from any general principle has a certain plausibility. To some extent, this plausibility arises from the fact that the deliverances of superego, which are often confused with conscience, do not follow rationally from principles, but rather follow from early conditioning. Even at the level of moral truth, as was explained (3-D), people who have sufficiently appropriated and integrated moral principles do make immediate, sound, practical judgments by connaturality.[5] Moreover, one often reasons from principles to conclusions without being clearly aware that one is doing so and without making explicit the principles and steps of the reasoning process. This can lead one to suppose that a judgment of conscience is an isolated act of insight when actually it is a reasoned conclusion.

4. Some aspects of Protestant theology incline toward this view of conscience.[6] It suits the thesis that fallen humankind is so thoroughly corrupt that we can put no trust in anything proper to our nature. Direct divine inspiration would relieve us of having to trust our corrupted nature, since conscience would have

nothing to do except receive the message passively. In recent years some Catholic theologians have been influenced by these beliefs.

5. This view must be rejected. **If one takes from human persons their understanding of moral principles, their ability to reason from them, and their capacity to judge according to them, one takes away their ability to act humanly.** Further, if all moral judgments were isolated acts, life would lack organization and continuity; no one could be a person of principle. **Moreover, if all moral judgments were unique personal insights, no group of persons could hope to discover true solutions to their differences through reasonable discussion in the light of shared principles.**

Christian life is a communal sign, as will be explained (23-F). The communal character and sign-value of Christian life would be lost if each Christian judged and acted by private inspirations, rather than by a common and publicly preached moral teaching which belongs to faith. Faith must be articulated in the words which complete the sign of Christian life and make it effective in communicating divine revelation to the world.

6. This view is also theologically unacceptable. In attributing everything exclusively to the Holy Spirit, one is not crediting more to grace but failing to credit grace with its full effect: the raising of human persons to the status of children of God, able to live lives like that of Jesus. Furthermore, individuals are prone to take the deliverances of their personal urges or superego or some social group for the voice of God; discernment with respect to moral judgments thought to come immediately from the Holy Spirit consists in examining them for their conformity or nonconformity to the teaching of the Church. Finally, the Church has condemned the view that conscience consists of isolated acts of insight suited to each situation and underivable from general principles (see DS 3918–21).

Some argue: The Spirit illumines the Christian; the spiritual person can judge everything. Why cannot a Christian simply receive by inspiration whatever guidance is needed to form a correct conscience? At the concrete level one would grasp which choice is to be made and would see the limits of general guidelines, thus being able to set them aside when appropriate. Sometimes this idea is supported by the argument that what really should bind the Christian is God's holy will, not some rational norm.

The work of the Spirit is not the communication of the content of faith, but evidence of God revealing, so that one can accept on divine testimony the content one receives by hearing (20-E). Because morality is not extrinsic to faith, the same is true of basic moral principles. Of course, faith's implications must be continuously unfolded and the practical demands it makes must be defended against competing demands. In this work, the Christian community is sustained by the continuing light of the Spirit. However, this process cannot negate truth already received, nor can it be an individualistic process.[7]

Someone might object that special divine inspiration cannot be excluded in principle. After all, some especially holy souls attest to receiving direct divine guidance. One ought to attend to the promptings of the Spirit. One ought indeed. The difficulty is to discern which spirit is prompting one (see 1 Thes 5.19–22; 1 Jn 4.1–3). Promptings must be put to the test of their conformity to revealed truth; one also must discern supposed promptings by the fruit to which they lead.[8]

One of the greatest mystics, St. John of the Cross, takes a very dim view of supernatural means of obtaining practical knowledge: "There is no necessity for this kind of knowledge, since a person can get sufficient guidance from natural reason, and the law and doctrine of the Gospel. There is no difficulty or necessity unresolvable or irremediable by these means, which are very pleasing to God and profitable to souls."[9] John would discard anything which is not in perfect harmony with the Church's teaching. God wants human persons to be guided by other human persons; he does not want us to accept any private revelations not confirmed "through the human channel of the mouth of man."[10]

Vatican II teaches that the responsibility for judging the genuineness and proper use of the gifts of the Spirit belongs to those who preside over the Church (see LG 12). This position has its foundation in the fact that the Spirit builds up the Church by working not only in every member but also in the authorities Christ set over it (see Acts 20.28–31; Eph 4.11–13; 2 Tm 1.14).

Question C: Are moral norms in effect only if they are validated by personal choices?

1. The view is that moral norms are in force only if they are adopted or accepted by choices. In one version, these choices are personal decisions of principle by which one sets one's course in life.[11] In another, they are acts of consent to social policy decisions.

2. If the Church's moral teaching is thought of as policy proposed by Church leadership, it is not difficult to suppose that it must be validated by the consent of the faithful. Some who appeal to the *sensus fidelium* against the Church's teaching seem to have something of this sort in mind.[12]

3. Three things help explain why some find this view plausible. First, moral norms indeed make no practical difference unless one is willing to be guided by them, and one can always choose to violate them. Second, moral principles do resemble laws in many ways, so that it is easy to imagine they are the same. If moral principles were laws, it would seem reasonable to suppose that they lacked force if they were not popularly accepted. Third, since moral norms are not a matter of facts and logic, the source of their force is obscure; locating this source in personal choices seems to solve the problem.

4. But this view must be rejected. **It makes the human person's choice stand on its own without any ultimate measure, for it ignores the requirements which arise from the meanings and values God has embodied in creation, including human persons.** Therefore, it allows grossly immoral ways of life equal moral status with the way of Jesus, and even makes it difficult to see how a clever person, careful about adopting moral norms, can go wrong. Some proponents of this view suggest that one can go wrong if one is inauthentic—inconsistent with one's self-constituted standards. But they do not show why such inconsistency should be immoral, nor do they recognize the ease with which one can avoid inconsistency by being careful not to make decisions which truly tie one down.

5. This view loses its plausibility when three confusions are removed. First, although it is true that one can avoid or assume some duties by choice, this does not mean one can avoid moral responsibility for wrongdoing merely by refusing to endorse the norm one is violating. For example, if one does not choose to marry, one has no duties to a spouse; but if one does marry, one cannot do away with such

duties merely by not choosing to acknowledge them.

6. Second, arguments to support this view are often based on equivocations. For example, "decide" means both "judge" and "choose." Judgments of conscience and choices can both be called "decisions," but they are decisions in very different senses. One can decide that something is wrong (conscience) and decide to do it anyway (choice). When "decide" refers to judgment, it is a matter of detecting what is right or wrong; when it refers to choice, it is a matter of doing what is right or wrong.

7. Third, though moral norms are like laws in some ways, the two also differ. Moral norms can be true even if they are widely ignored. To be sure, one can render moral norms ineffective in one's life by choosing to be immoral. Even so, they do not lack their proper force. A violated moral norm remains a moral truth and condemns as immoral the choice which violates it (see Rom 2.12; 3.9–20).

Question D: Are moral principles established by God's arbitrary choice?

1. According to this view, the principles of our judgments of conscience are arbitrary demands made upon us by God. They might, for instance, be rules invented by God simply to test our obedience. If so, any judgment as to what is right could be reversed if God changed the rules. In this view, moral principles are not truths but commands.[13] They do not express an intrinsic relationship between what is required and what is humanly fulfilling; fulfillment, rather, is a sort of prize awarded for passing a test which is otherwise unrelated to the prize.

2. This view, too, has a certain plausibility. We owe our existence and everything else to God—we are entirely dependent on his choice. Obedience to him thus seems inescapably necessary. Moreover, since we are his children, obedience seems altogether right. The view that moral principles are established by God's arbitrary choice seems to fit these facts. Furthermore, it is more acceptable to a Christian than any of the views examined up to now. Thus, in the absence of a better account of normative principles, it appeals to a believer.

3. Still, this view must also be rejected. It is inconsistent with the truth of faith that God directs all things wisely and lovingly, not arbitrarily and despotically. The normative force of his commands cannot follow from the mere fact that he commands, any more than from the fact that we choose (see Dt 4.5–8). God's will ought of course to be followed, but faith provides a cogent reason for doing so: that he is leading and guiding us toward our true good (see Ps 23).[14]

4. God's will is not some sort of irrational force. By choice, he freely creates and redeems all things according to a wise plan. His wisdom settles what is good and bad for us and all creatures. **By wisdom God makes us what we are and thus determines the true requirements for our fulfillment** (see Gn 1.26–30; 2.18–24; Wis 7.21–8.1; DS 3002–3/1783–84; see *S.t.*, 1–2, q. 71, a. 2, ad 4; q. 91, a. 2; q. 93, aa. 1–2; q. 100, a. 8). **He does not make things right and wrong by an additional, arbitrary choice.**

5. In short, moral norms are truths about how to act in ways that are humanly good (see *S.t.*, 1–2, q. 99, a. 1; *S.c.g.*, 3, 122). It is not the case that any judgment

of conscience could as well be reversed if God chose to reverse it. Human nature being what it is, it simply cannot be humanly fulfilling to act contrary to a correct judgment of conscience; and since God is wise and loving, he could not direct us to act against our own well-being (see *S.t.*, 1–2, q. 100, a. 8; *S.c.g.*, 3, 129).

The view that existential principles are established by God's arbitrary choice is a serious obstacle to evangelization and catechesis. Even those who issue ukases have some end in view—if not the good of their subjects, then their own good. To suggest that God determines right and wrong arbitrarily thus generates the suspicion that God creates us to exploit us. This idea, rejected by Vatican I (see DS 3002/1783), underlies much modern and contemporary rebellion against God, especially the systematic atheism of the various forms of secular humanism (see GS 19–20). The good toward which God directs creation will be treated more fully (19-A).

Question E: Are moral principles the requirements for the functioning of particular societies?

1. This view is cultural relativism. It argues as follows. People in different societies desire somewhat different goods. True, all wish at least to survive, but even the requirements of survival vary greatly under diverse conditions. Societies articulate their own sets of norms as means to their own somewhat different ends. Thus, moral norms vary according to cultures, though each culture's own norms provide a more or less true way for it to attain its ends.[15]

2. Several factors lend plausibility to this view. First, children initially think of morality in terms of social norms, and many adults retain a notion of morality which is scarcely more adequate. Second, every society does have some norms, not all have the same norms, and each society's accepted norms seem to be more or less effective means of achieving its purposes. Third, any society's norms include some genuine moral requirements, such as fairness in at least certain relationships.

3. Cultural relativism must be rejected. **It involves a confusion between social facts—what actually is required in various societies—and real moral norms.** The latter concern what individuals and societies ought to require, not what they consider necessary to achieve their purposes. Furthermore, cultural relativism leaves no grounds for moral criticism of socially accepted norms, including those of one's own society.[16]

In every society, some norms are proposed and generally accepted as standards of morality. Human fulfillment is defined in terms of a rich enjoyment of the goods understood and appreciated in the society. Accepted social goals provide the criterion by which various patterns of action are considered more or less acceptable, or altogether unacceptable. Norms of behavior reflect commonly accepted limits which are necessary if society is to function. Anything meeting these norms which is acceptable to the individuals involved and not unfair to others seems of little moral significance.

Any society must establish and defend a certain level of fairness; even among thieves there must be mutual honor. Modes of behavior which express selfish impulses, contrary to accepted standards of fairness, are considered immoral. So are modes of behavior based on impulse contrary to the rational requirements of the pursuit of the common good, even if these modes primarily have their adverse effects only on those who engage in them. Thus, laziness, drunkenness, and excessive fearfulness are frowned upon in any society, particularly when they lead to unfairness according to its standard.

Of course, not everyone lives up to the conventional standards of morality. Moreover, some who are reflective and critical always find the conventional standards more or less seriously defective.[17] Such persons seek a higher standard; they wish to criticize accepted moral norms and to find true moral norms, grounded in reality rather than in the mere fact of social acceptance. The Greek and Roman quest for natural law beyond the law imposed by social authority is an example of this movement from sociological fact toward principles. Socrates also set out from conventional morality in his quest for wisdom and an examined life, which he considered would be worth living in a way that life lived according to uncriticized conventional norms cannot be.

Moral truth goes beyond any conventional morality in demanding openness to all human goods, not merely to certain commonly accepted objectives, and in aiming at perfect harmony on all levels, not merely at some level of fairness among persons belonging to a particular group. Moral truth extends to the whole of the person, to the whole of life, to the whole of humankind, and to the whole of reality by way of the human relationship to God.

4. Most important, cultural relativism is at odds with Christian awareness of the broken human condition and the Christian prescription for its restoration. Humankind is fallen and redeemed; both facts transcend all diversity of cultures in different times and places. The redemptive community, Christ's Church extended through space and time, has in some important respects its own culture which is one and universal. Judged by Christian standards, each society's culture is more or less defective. To the extent that any culture falls short, it is simply the "world" and the "present age" which Christians should not conform to but redeem.

St. Paul points out that without belief in the resurrection, human life in the fallen world would hardly seem worth living. If death is the end, one must obtain what fulfillment one can in the present life (see 1 Cor 15.19, 32; Is 22.13). The wisdom of the world is absurdity with God (see 1 Cor 3.19); worldly liberty is slavery to sin (see Rom 6.16–22; Gal 4.8; 2 Pt 2.19). Conventional morality is part of that world which defines itself by opposition to the Lord Jesus (see Jn 17.14–17). Redemption from the defects of conventional morality and its service to human stuntedness is an important part of the liberating work of Jesus. The world as we know it is passing away, and so the good Christian will no more conform to it than a fashionable person will adopt styles just as they are going out (cf. 1 Cor 7.31).[18]

Even those who do not explicitly believe in Jesus are able to transcend conventional morality to some extent, for if they do what they can to pursue human goodness, their good will is assisted by the grace of the Spirit (see GS 22). This help explains why in various times and places some higher level of moral truth and goodness has begun to emerge despite the limits of conventional morality. The work of a Socrates or a Buddha is the fruit of cooperation of some group of good men who happen to be able to break through the limits of their own society. However, without the integral gospel of Jesus and the fulfilling and stabilizing order of his Church, such moral breakthroughs suffer from the limitations of human error and extreme fragility.

Question F: Are moral principles laws of human nature?

1. Until recently, the view that they are was common in classical moral theology and scholastic philosophy, and it is still held by some Catholic theolo-

gians and philosophers trained in the older approach. It was developed by Francisco Suarez, S.J., and became dominant in the seventeenth century. Though actually quite different from St. Thomas' understanding of natural law, many believed it to be his position.[19] It can be called "scholastic natural-law theory," to distinguish it from the more adequate account of natural law which will be presented in chapters five through ten.

2. What is most characteristic of scholastic natural-law theory is its notion of the objectivity of moral norms. The basic moral standard is simply human nature as it is given—given, of course, not to sense experience but to intellectual knowing. Moral goodness or badness can be discerned merely by comparing the essential patterns of possible human actions with the intelligible structure of human nature considered both in its inner complexity (human persons are vegetative, sentient, and rational in themselves) and in its extrinsic relationships (human persons are creatures, fellow creatures, and rulers of lower creation in their essential relationships). When compared with human nature, actions are seen either to conform or not conform to the requirements set by nature.

3. According to scholastic natural-law theory, knowing whether or not a possible action conforms with human nature is a matter of making a comparison. Thus, this judgment is a piece of theoretical knowledge and has the kind of necessity enjoyed by a fundamental law of nature. When the action is compatible with human nature, the judgment registers conformity; it registers nonconformity, intrinsic evil, when the action is incompatible with human nature in any of its essential aspects.

4. Of course, to become aware of one's obligations it is not enough to observe the conformity or nonconformity between the action and one's nature. More than this theoretical knowledge, one needs a basic requirement. According to the theory, this can be expressed in various ways: *Follow reason, Act in accord with nature,* or *Do good and avoid evil.* However formulated, the demand's full meaning is grasped only when one sees it to be a message to the created subject from God's sovereign will. And one sees nature itself as an effective moral norm only when one sees it as a sign of God's will.[20]

5. This theory is unlike the divine command theory, criticized in question D above, in two ways. First, it provides a reason for God to require what he does—namely, that it suits our nature. Second, it claims to provide a way by which we can know what is good, so that morally upright choices are more than blind obedience. Thus scholastic natural-law theory is far more plausible and acceptable than a simple divine command theory.

6. Moreover, because it grounds morality in human nature, it is an improvement over all the other views considered up to now. Unlike the view criticized in A, which reduces moral judgment to feeling, it makes judgment a matter of knowledge and truth. Unlike the view criticized in B, which excludes the possibility of moral reasoning by reducing moral judgments to isolated insights, scholastic natural-law theory indicates a source of principles from which one can reason. Unlike the subjectivist theory criticized in C, this theory confronts our freedom with objective norms. And unlike the cultural relativism criticized in

question E, it gives morality a basis which transcends the diversity of cultural norms in different places and times and makes it possible to criticize the standards of every society, including one's own.

7. Furthermore, nature does indeed have a certain normativity. A stomach, for instance, is made for digesting. From such natural normativity certain requirements follow: for example, the laws of diet. Thus one can know, for example, that it is appropriate for monkeys to eat bananas. It seems reasonable to imagine that, studying human nature by a similar though more complicated process of inquiry, one can determine what is existentially right and wrong for human persons.

8. This theory takes on still more plausibility in a theological context. It seems to fit the truth of faith that human persons are made in God's image and so are by nature like him. It seems to explain the natural law written in our hearts by God when he made us.

9. But scholastic natural-law theory must be rejected. **It moves by a logically illicit step—from human nature as a given reality, to what ought and ought not to be chosen.**[21] Its proponents attempt to reinforce this move, from what is to what ought to be, by appealing to God's command. But for two reasons this fails to help matters. First, unless there is a logically prior moral norm indicating that God's commands are to be obeyed, any command of God considered by itself would merely be another fact which tells us nothing about how we ought to respond. **Second, even leaving this problem aside, the difficulty remains that human persons are unlike other natural entities; it is not human nature as a given, but possible human fulfillment which must provide the intelligible norms for free choices.**

10. By such choices, human persons are of themselves. Human existence is more than conforming to a built-in pattern, as monkeys do when they eat bananas and otherwise do what comes naturally. Scholastic natural-law theory tells human persons: "Here you are—here is your nature—now be what you are." Such advice can have a true sense, but unless human persons have possibilities which are not yet defined, there is no room for them to unfold themselves through intelligent creativity and freedom.

It is a sign of the basic flaw in scholastic natural-law theory that it provided only question-begging arguments for specific norms of Christian morality. Against contraception, for instance, it argued that this practice perverts the generative faculty by using it while frustrating its natural power to initiate new life. In reply, people reasonably note that perverting faculties in this sense cannot always be wrong—no one objects to the use of earplugs or chewing sugarless gum. As people chew sugarless gum for the pleasure of chewing, apart from nutrition, why should they not also engage in sexual activity for some human purpose such as celebrating marital unity, while excluding other purposes which at the moment cannot appropriately be pursued?

Question G: How does the preceding critique of scholastic natural-law theory help to explain the inadequacy of classical moral theology?

1. **Scholastic natural-law theory's use of nature as a norm helps explain the negativism and minimalism of classical moral theology.** What does not

conform to human nature can be forbidden absolutely. What does conform cannot be absolutely required, since people cannot possibly do everything which is permissible; affirmative precepts can require only kinds of action which are specified in such a way that their omission would be wrong. Thus scholastic natural-law theory is far more adept at issuing a few prohibitions than at directing people's lives toward growth and flourishing. However, an adequate Christian moral theory must not be merely negative. One needs to know affirmatively how to fulfill God's will; conscience must indicate what is good, pleasing, and perfect (see Rom 12.2).

2. Classical moral theology tends to reduce Christian moral life to a means of gaining heaven and avoiding hell. The absence from scholastic natural-law theory of any intrinsic relationship between the basis of moral norms in human nature and what truly is humanly fulfilling helps explain why. As sanctions for legalistically conceived moral law, heaven and hell can motivate obedience, but they cannot give this present life an inherent meaning. Yet only such meaning can make life in this world intrinsically worthwhile and make Christian life joyful despite inevitable suffering and necessary self-denial.

3. Scholastic natural-law theory's use of nature as it is given as a source of moral norms helps also to explain the static character of classical moral theology. However, although essential human nature does not change, in the course of human history new possibilities do open up and humankind acquires powers to act in new, more complex ways. An adequate moral theory must look toward possible human fulfillment, and its vision of this must be as dynamic as humankind itself.

4. Classical moral theology is vulnerable to the charge that it is too much concerned with laws and too little with persons. Scholastic natural-law theory's failure to ground moral norms in human fulfillment explains why. Only an account which shows how morally right acts contribute of themselves to the fulfillment of persons can rebut this charge.

Question H: How do this chapter's critical reflections contribute to a more adequate theory of moral principles?

1. The result of this chapter's examination of inadequate theories is not entirely negative. From this criticism one can draw an outline of a more adequate theory, which articulates what the Church means by natural law but is not legalistic or otherwise inadequate in the manner of scholastic natural-law theory.

2. **Against the moral-feelings theory, an adequate theory must show how conscience judges. Against the view which reduces judgments of conscience to isolated insights, it must show how conscience starts from principles and proceeds by rational reflection. Against the view that moral principles are in force only if accepted by personal choices, it must show how principles are objective—they hold true whether one likes them or not. Against the view that moral principles are established by God's arbitrary choice, an adequate**

theory must show how they can be truths which cannot be otherwise. Against cultural relativism, it must show how moral norms are more than facts concerning the necessary conditions for attaining the ends which people have in view. Against scholastic natural-law theory, it must show how moral norms provide us with guidance toward goods which fulfill human persons more and more abundantly.[22]

Summary

Today, as in the past, a number of mistaken theories of moral principles enjoy currency.

One is that judgments of conscience are essentially expressions of feelings. This has a certain plausibility, since disagreements over moral questions always concern what ought to be, not what is, so that it can seem as if morality itself is a matter of taste. But such a view rules out moral reflection, moral teaching, and even reasoned dissent. Moreover, it is incompatible with Catholic faith because it confuses superego with conscience. The difficulties, by no means insuperable, in settling moral disputes reflect the special character of moral principles—that they are neither matters of fact nor logical requirements—but do not show that there are no moral truths.

Again, it is said that judgments of conscience cannot be derived from any general principle. This reduces conscience to isolated acts of insight, sometimes thought to be divinely inspired. It is true that people of mature conscience do make immediate moral judgments and that people generally reason without being aware of doing so. But neither fact supports a view of conscience as intuition or inspiration. Besides being theologically unacceptable, this theory in effect takes away from human beings their ability to act humanly and radically undermines community.

Another theory has it that moral norms are in effect only if they are validated by personal choices, either one's own individual decisions of principle or acts of consent to social policy. This, too, has a certain plausibility, since moral norms make no practical difference in one's life unless one is willing to be guided by them, and moral principles do resemble laws in some ways. However, while it is true that one can assume or not assume some duties by choice, one cannot do away with the duties one really has merely by refusing to acknowledge them. A moral norm which is ignored or violated remains a moral truth.

According to yet another view, moral principles are established by God's arbitrary choice. They are as they are, but they could be different; they are not truths but commands. It is certainly true that God's will ought to be followed. But faith provides a cogent reason for doing so: that he is guiding us to our true good. By his wisdom he makes us what we are and so determines the requirements for our fulfillment. Moral norms, rather than being arbitrary demands made upon us by God, are truths about how to act in ways that are humanly good.

Cultural relativism is another mistaken view of moral principles. According to this account, moral principles are expressions of conditions for the survival and more or less satisfactory functioning of particular societies; they vary as these conditions vary from society to society. This, however, confuses social facts (what various societies actually do require) with true moral norms. It removes all basis for moral criticism of society. And it is contrary to the Christian awareness of the human condition, as fallen and redeemed, and the transcultural character of the Church.

The view which may be called "scholastic natural-law theory" holds that moral principles are laws of human nature: Moral goodness or badness can be discerned by comparing possible actions with human nature to see whether or not they conform to the requirements which nature sets. Nature does indeed have a certain normativity, from which certain requirements follow: for instance, the laws of diet. But this theory must be rejected because it proceeds by a logically illicit step—from human nature as a given reality to what ought and ought not to be chosen, from what is in fact to what morally should be. Scholastic natural-law theory's use of nature as a norm helps explain the negativism and minimalism of classical moral theology. What does not conform to human nature can be absolutely forbidden, but what does conform cannot be absolutely required.

This critique indicates what an adequate theory of moral principles must show: against a theory of moral feelings, how conscience is a judgment; against intuitionism, how moral reflection starts from principles and proceeds by reasoning; against a personal-choice theory, how moral principles and norms are objective; against a divine command theory, how norms are truths; against cultural relativism, how norms are more than social facts; against scholastic natural-law theory, how norms guide persons to act for human fulfillment.

Appendix: Immanuel Kant's theory of moral principles

The ethical theory of Immanual Kant, who wrote around the beginning of the nineteenth century, has greatly influenced subsequent philosophical and theological reflection on moral principles. Kant attempted to transpose into philosophical terms the traditional, Protestant moral outlook. The product of his effort was very heavily conditioned by his peculiar metaphysics and theory of knowledge, which almost no one today accepts. But this framework aside, Kant's view of moral principles is not so much false as grossly inadequate. Hence, it is not treated in this chapter as a mistaken theory. Still, a brief treatment of Kant might help the reader to understand the relationship between his theory of morality and the one to be presented in the coming chapters.[23]

Kant would reject all the theories of moral principles criticized in this chapter and also any view which would base morality on the effectiveness of actions for promoting human happiness. He thinks that any such theory would reduce morality to a mere technique and thus depersonalize human persons. He especially notices that if the rightness of an action depended upon its effectiveness in realizing limited objectives (a theory to be criticized in chapter six), then human freedom and thus morality itself would be impossible.

Kant assumes that the natural world is thoroughly deterministic; he thinks that all observable human acts, including inner thoughts and choices, are determined by natural, including psychological, laws. To ensure that this universal determinism will not preclude morality, Kant separates the moral self absolutely from the world of experience. Goodness, Kant thinks, is centered wholly in a good will—that is, in the uprightness of one's attitude in choosing.

But what constitutes an upright attitude? Kant cannot answer this question except in terms of the inner standards of the rational work of the mind itself, for to go beyond these standards (even by taking psychological factors into account) would mean that something else was imposed upon the moral self. Such an imposition would not be a moral "ought" but a freedom-destroying "must." Therefore, Kant says that the uprightness of moral attitude, good will, consists in acting for the purpose of doing what is morally right. In other words, our action is morally good only if it springs from a will bent on doing what we ought to do.

What ought we to do? Kant explains that whenever we act, our action implies a rule. Human action is meaningful with a meaning which our own intelligence puts into it. Implicit in the fact that we are acting intelligently there is the thought: "Since such-and-such is what I want to accomplish and the factors in the situation I am up against are so-and-so, an act like this is the appropriate thing for me to do." Now, Kant says, if the rule we have in mind is consistent with itself and if it could fit into a system of rules that we could really want everyone to follow consistently, then actions shaped by the rule may be done. But if the rule we have in mind cannot meet this test, then it cannot reasonably be adopted, and action shaped by that rule ought not to be done and will not be done by a person of good will.

Kant believes that if human persons were only their reason, then they never could be unreasonable and so never would do anything immoral. But since persons also exist as objects in the world of experience, natural feelings can get the better of reason. Individuals act by a private rationale for action, which means that they are acting intelligently and deliberately in view of their actual desires. But reason could not approve their private rationale, for they would not be able to adopt it as a general rule for everyone to follow consistently. In this way immoral acts can be chosen. For instance, individuals can decide to lie when it is convenient to themselves, but could not want lying to be a general rule, for that would render affirming meaningless and so remove the very possibility of either lying or affirming truthfully. Hence, telling a lie as a matter of convenience is wrong; people who do this act intelligently but unreasonably, sanely but immorally.

Moral uprightness is essential to human goodness (see 5-F); and the rightness of action is not settled by its efficiency in promoting human well-being (see 6-F). But chapter seven, developing points to be outlined in chapter five, will explain that the ultimate principle of morality—that which makes for a good will—is much more inclusive of human good than Kant thought. The good will must be open to a continuing unfolding of human fulfillment in all the basic goods of persons—including life and health, skill in work and play, and knowledge of truth—not just to moral uprightness.

Moreover, chapter eight will show that there are eight basic requirements for right choices of which Kant's consistency test is only one. There are more ways of acting unreasonably than he realized, and so his test for morality is too loose. One who is inclined to lie might not be able to want everyone to do the same whenever it is convenient. But attention to specific features of the situation usually will reveal factors which will provide a much narrower justification which will seem rationally acceptable. Kant himself points out that a general rule—for example, excluding suicide—might well not hold in situations in which individuals have special reasons for choosing to kill themselves.[24]

There are other difficulties in Kant's theory, including the supposition that human persons could not sin if they were pure spirits, free of the supposed determinism of the world of nature. Immorality also has roots in the ability of finite freedom to limit its own unfolding. Moreover, Kant's effort to separate the world of freedom and morality from the world of nature and determinism ultimately is incoherent in itself and inconsistent with the unity of human action.[25]

Notes

1. For the history of moral theories, see Vernon J. Bourke, *History of Ethics* (Garden City, N.Y.: Doubleday, 1968); Alasdair MacIntyre, *A Short History of Ethics* (New York: Macmillan, 1966). Philip B. Rice, *Our Knowledge of Good and Evil* (New York: Random House, 1955), gives a useful summary and critique of the positions developed in Anglo-American ethics from about 1900–1950. For a critique of many modern, continental theories from a Thomistic viewpoint, see Jacques Maritain, *Moral Philosophy: An Historical and Critical Survey of the Great Systems* (New York: Charles Scribner's Sons, 1964). A useful work for clearing away many mistaken theories and moving in the direction of a modified Aristotelianism: Mortimer J. Adler, *The Time of Our Lives: The Ethics of Common Sense* (New York: Holt, Rinehart and Winston, 1970). Henry B. Veatch, *For an Ontology of Morals: A Critique of Contemporary Ethical Theory* (Evanston, Ill.: Northwestern University Press, 1971), systematically criticizes contemporary theories and points in the direction of a modified Thomism somewhat similar to the theory to be articulated in chapters five, seven, and eight. There is no properly theological, thorough critical study of modern and contemporary moral theories. For the most part, theologians have either ignored the development of moral theory or accepted uncritically some modern theory.

2. See Sigmund Freud, *Civilization and Its Discontents,* trans. and ed. James Strachey (New York: W. W. Norton, 1961), 70–92, esp. 83, where conscience is reduced to superego as function to inferred faculty.

3. The most important statement of the emotive theory in the philosophical literature: C. L. Stevenson, *Ethics and Language* (New Haven: Yale University Press, 1944). For a summary of arguments against emotivism, see Richard B. Brandt, *Ethical Theory: The Problems of Normative and Critical Ethics* (Englewood Cliffs, N.J.: Prentice-Hall, 1959), 225–31, bibliography (items marked "criticism"), 239–40.

4. Karl Rahner, S.J., "On the Question of a Formal Existential Ethics," *Theological Investigations*, vol. 2, *Man in the Church,* trans. Karl-H. Kruger (Baltimore: Helicon, 1963), 217–34; *The Dynamic Element in the Church* (New York: Herder and Herder, 1964), 84–170; proposed that a process of nonconceptual intuition or discernment is required to determine what affirmative choice is appropriate in matters such as vocation. In these arguments, Rahner always assumed the scholastic theory of natural law which is criticized in question F; thus his proposal was a somewhat confused effort to make up for the inadequacy of this theory. A telling critique of Rahner's proposal: Donal J. Dorr, "Karl Rahner's 'Formal Existential Ethics,'" *Irish Theological Quarterly,* 36 (1969), 211–29. Still, it must be credited to Rahner that in these works he was careful to separate himself from the situation ethics condemned by the Church; he firmly maintained that there are intelligible, general principles taught by the Church which hold true in every case, so that discernment is limited to possibilities tested by these general principles and found morally permissible or good (*Dynamic Element*, 91, 101, and 169). (In 27-C the work of conscience in such judgments will be explained without appeal to mysterious intuitions and inspirations.) More questionable is Rahner's subsequent positing of a "moral instinct of faith" which is supposed to deliver universal moral judgments irreducible to principles: "The Problem of Genetic Manipulation," *Theological Investigations*, vol. 9, *Writings of 1965–67, I,* trans. Graham Harrison (New York: Herder and Herder, 1972), 238–43. One must agree with Rahner that in the light of faith and with the help of the Church's teaching, Catholics often can grasp moral truths for which they cannot articulate reasons. But this is not all he has in mind. One also must admit that people reasonably hold moral norms without being able to articulate the reasoning by which they follow from first principles; the situation is analogous to the rational knowledge of God's existence, where the general line of reasoning is clear enough but the articulation of a tight argument is difficult. However, Rahner claims that the analysis is impossible. For this claim he provides little support except his supposition that the "conceptual" falls short of aspects of the "experienced" and of "practice" which nevertheless essentially determine moral goodness (239). Underlying this supposition is a voluntarism which makes moral judgment rest on choice (similar to the position examined in question C). Thus, Rahner suggests that "'is' and 'ought' *mutually* determine each other," and "what is 'objectively' right only becomes transparent to the person who has already embraced the correct attitude toward it" (239); and explicitly (later in the same essay): "The 'instinct' justifiably has the courage to say *Stat pro ratione voluntas* because such a confession need not be overcautious about making a decision" (251).

5. Thus, in arguing for an intuitionist theory at the level of specific moral norms, William A. Luijpen, *Phenomenology of Natural Law* (Pittsburgh: Duquesne University Press, 1967), 156, uses examples: "Anyone who is at least a little bit human knows that it is unjust to pluck out the eyes of

children solely because they happen to be blue; and whoever disagrees with this statement is simply wrong. Anyone who is at least a little bit human knows that it is unjust to burn widows or to offer children in sacrifice; and whoever disagrees with this is simply wrong." A minimally decent person in our culture does know such things by connaturality, but this fact does not show there is an implicit knowledge identical with the "being of man" as Luijpen thinks. His criticism (86–111) of the "Thomistic" doctrine of natural law, which he attempts to better with this intuitionism, is full of misconceptions; he distorts St. Thomas' view into something akin to the theory criticized in question F.

6. See Rudolf Bultmann, *Jesus and the Word* (New York: Charles Scribner's Sons, 1958), 72–98; Helmut Thielicke, *Theological Ethics*, vol. 1, *Foundations*, ed. William H. Lazareth (Philadelphia: Fortress Press, 1966), 648–60, who conducts a polemic against the Catholic notion of natural law, under the title: "The Guidance of the Holy Spirit in the Given Situation"; Paul L. Lehmann, *Ethics in a Christian Context* (New York: Harper and Row, 1963), 124–61 (esp. the last five pages) and 287–367 (esp. 348–52). Other references to this tendency can be found in Edward LeRoy Long, Jr., *A Survey of Christian Ethics* (New York: Oxford University Press, 1967), 146–64.

7. See William F. Orr and James Arthur Walther, *I Corinthians*, Anchor Bible, 32 (Garden City, N.Y.: Doubleday, 1976), 165–67. A valuable treatment by a philosopher who argues against both intuitionism and illuminationism and for reasons in the light of faith: Basil Mitchell, *Morality: Religious and Secular: The Dilemma of the Traditional Conscience* (Oxford: Clarendon Press, 1980).

8. See Thomas Dubay, S.M., *Authenticity: A Biblical Treatment of Discernment* (Denville, N.J.: Dimension Books, 1977), for an excellent treatise on this matter.

9. St. John of the Cross, *The Collected Works of St. John of the Cross*, trans. Kieran Kavanaugh, O.C.D., and Otilio Rodriguez, O.C.D. (Garden City, N.Y.: Doubleday, 1964), 174.

10. Ibid., 182.

11. For a clear account and critique of one version of this sort of ethics, systematically proposed by R. M. Hare, see Joseph M. Boyle, Jr., "Aquinas and Prescriptive Ethics," *Proceedings of the American Catholic Philosophical Association*, 49 (1975), 82–95.

12. One finds tendencies in this direction in much popular discussion of conscience and the authority of the magisterium, but Catholic theologians generally explicitly reject this theory of conscience and moral principles, since they hold to the traditional view that the task of conscience is to discern truth. Still, the theory is fairly clearly assumed by Jean-Marie Aubert, "Pratique canonique et sens de l'humain," *Revue de droit canonique*, 28 (1978), 91–104. It seems implicit in the argument of Andrew Greeley on the effect of *Humanae vitae* in Andrew Greeley et al., *Catholic Schools in a Declining Church* (Kansas City, Mo.: Sheed and Ward, 1976), 313–27. And although the exposition is very ambiguous, a theory along these lines seems to underlie the treatment of commandment and conscience in *A New Catechism: Catholic Faith for Adults* (New York: Herder and Herder, 1967), 371–76. For a clear distinction between "sense of faith" and the vulgar misunderstanding of it as "sensus fidelium," see John Paul II, *Familiaris Consortio*, 74 AAS (1982) 85–86; Eng. ed. (Vatican City: Vatican Polyglot Press, 1981), 9–11 (sec. 5). An impressive monograph on this point: Jesús Sancho Bielsa, *Infalibilidad del Pueblo de Dios: "Sensus fidei" e infalibilidad organica de la Iglesia en la Constitucion "Lumen gentium" del Concilio Vaticano II* (Pamplona, Spain: EUNSA, 1979).

13. Perhaps the clearest example of a theory of the sort considered in this question is that of William of Ockham; see Kevin McDonnell, "William of Ockham and Situation Ethics," *American Journal of Jurisprudence*, 16 (1971), 25–35. See also Emil Brunner, *The Divine Imperative: A Study in Christian Ethics*, trans. Olive Wyon (Philadelphia: Westminster Press, 1947), 53, 83, 114–15, and 120.

14. An excellent exegetical study clarifies the nonarbitrariness of God's commandments: Matthew J. O'Connell, S.J., "The Concept of Commandment in the Old Testament," *Theological Studies*, 21 (1960), 351–403.

15. For a discussion and criticism of relativism, see Brandt, op. cit., 92–99, 271–94, and 402–3; Morris Ginsberg, *On the Diversity of Morals* (London: Mercury Books, 1962), 97–129.

16. Anthony Battaglia, *Toward a Reformulation of Natural Law* (New York: Seabury Press, 1981), mistakenly thinks that the point of natural law is to explain how the diverse and changing conventions of morality are grounded in the more basic reality of human nature and the human condition. Hence, while he uses the language of natural law and makes some use of St. Thomas Aquinas' treatise on it, Battaglia's "reformulation of natural law" actually is a version of cultural relativism. Throughout his work, Battaglia reduces moral oughtness to psychosocial fact. Thus, he thinks that "good is to be done" means that people naturally desire to be good (5), that natural law is de facto conformity of human persons to eternal law and that synderesis is a knowledge of this conformity (51), that the good

111

is what works and has worked (72), that the universalizability requirement means that one can learn about morality by seeing what has worked (108), that notions of happiness as an ultimate end are testable against experience (122), that a moral system must account for basic human needs as a science accounts for data (128), that the morality of producing babies in test tubes might be determined by trying the process out to see whether it works to the satisfaction of the parents, society, and the children themselves (130), and that the "is" and the "ought" are given together in culture (132–34). His account of moral judgment and action (106–8) is so thoroughly psychologically reductive that it is hard to see how anyone could make a morally wrong choice.

17. By treating conventional moral standards as beyond objective criticism, Hegelian and Marxist theories take a position very similar to the cultural relativism described here. By offering a wider, metaphysical framework which relativizes each historical era, such theories repudiate the moral truth of tradition. Recent Catholic moral theology which appeals to historicity and changing human nature has been strongly influenced, sometimes without knowing it, by such thinking. For a useful summary of Hegelian and Marxist thinking: Rodger Charles, S.J., and Drostan Maclaren, O.P., *The Social Teaching of Vatican II: Its Origin and Development* (San Francisco: Ignatius Press, 1982), 99–103. Christian teaching presents its own dialectic (see GS 10), but salvation history does not relativize the moral truth of divinely revealed moral norms.

18. Despite the strong thrust of the gospel against cultural relativism, some Catholic theologians verge toward this theory in their efforts to justify revision of received teaching in conformity with dominant contemporary opinions. This tendency is especially obvious in those who defend a practice such as polygamy, despite Trent's condemnation of it (see DS 1802/972). See, for example, Joseph Fuchs, S.J., "The Absoluteness of Moral Terms," in *Readings in Moral Theology, No. 1: Moral Norms and Catholic Tradition,* ed. Charles E. Curran and Richard A. McCormick, S.J., (New York: Paulist Press, 1979), 112–16, and 135, n. 29. A critical discussion: Gustav Ermecke, "Das Problem der Universalität oder Allgemeingültigkeit sittlicher Normen innerweltlicher Lebensgestaltung," *Münchener theologische Zeitschrift,* 24 (1973), 1–24. Also: Theo G. Belmans, O.Praem., *Le sens objectif de l'agir humain* (Vatican City: Libreria Editrice Vaticana, 1980), 310–22.

19. An accessible presentation of scholastic natural-law theory, by a proponent: Thomas J. Higgins, S.J., *Man as Man: The Science and Art of Ethics,* rev. ed. (Milwaukee: Bruce, 1958), 14–146. The chief source of this type of theory is Francisco Suarez, S.J., *De legibus ac de Deo legislatore;* the most relevant passages are in: Suarez, *Selections from Three Works,* ed. J. B. Scott, The Classics of International Law, 20 (Oxford: Clarendon Press, 1944). A good historical study of natural law, which divides Catholic theories from others, although still confusing Thomistic and Suarezian approaches: Heinrich A. Rommen, *Natural Law: A Study in Legal and Social History and Philosophy* (St. Louis: B. Herder, 1947). For an account of the differences between the Suarezian and Thomistic theories: Germain Grisez, "The First Principle of Practical Reason: A Commentary on the *Summa theologiae,* 1–2, Question 94, Article 2," *Natural Law Forum,* 10 (1965), 168–201. The historical roots of scholastic natural-law theory as distinct from that of Thomas are traced more fully by John Finnis, *Natural Law and Natural Rights* (Oxford: Clarendon Press, 1980), 43–47, 54–57, and 348–50, who shows that Gabriel Vasquez and Francisco de Vitoria probably contributed to the development of the displacement of moral obligation from human practical reason to divine will.

20. According to Suarez, law is "the act of a just and right will by which the superior wills to oblige the inferior to do this or that" (*De legibus ac de Deo legislatore,* I, 5, 24). Thus the eternal law of God, which is the supreme norm of morality, is an act of God's will decreeing observance of a certain order (II, 1, 5; II, 3, 1; II, 3, 5–6). In God, natural law is identical with the eternal law, decreeing that creatures conform to their natures (II, 5, 14). But in the rational creature, Suarez distinguishes between the nature as the foundation of the law and reason itself, which observes what agrees or disagrees with nature; the latter is the law (II, 4, 3; II, 5, 9 and 14). Thus for Suarez, natural law is not identified with human will, but rather with human reason; yet the obligatory character of the norms imposed by reason—which makes mere observations of conformity to or disconformity from nature into precepts—derives not from human reason but from the divine will (II, 6, 8).

21. St. Thomas was careful to explain that practical conclusions always must be resolved into practical principles which are distinct from and irreducible to theoretical ones: *S.t.,* 1, q. 79, a. 12; 1–2, q. 94, a. 2; 2–2, q. 47, a. 6. To try to derive propositions containing "ought" from premises none of which contains or implies "ought" is a formal, logical fallacy. Counterexamples often suppress a premise: "The house is on fire; therefore, you ought to get out," assumes that one ought to leave a burning house. Other counterexamples work by smuggling an "ought" into an apparently descriptive premise: "This act is uncharitable; therefore, you should not do it," follows because the uncharitable

by definition is to be avoided. Arguments from what is natural to what should be done are notorious examples of equivocation; "natural" is used descriptively in the premises but normatively in the conclusions, and so these arguments have four terms. The fact that nature can be understood (as it is by Aristotle) purposively does not help matters, for the normativity characteristic of nature is that of a type for its instances, while moral normativity is a requirement set by a judgment upon free choice between open alternatives.

22. The theories discussed in this chapter share the defect of overlooking the relationship between moral norms and human goods. MacIntyre, op. cit., 84–86, draws out some of the implications of the difference between theories defective in this way and those which ground moral norms in human goods. His discussion, although marred by conceptual relativism, clarifies some of the difficulties involved in theories which fail to ground norms in goods.

23. The following summary is based primarily upon Immanuel Kant, *Foundations of the Metaphysics of Morals* (Indianapolis, Ind.: Bobbs-Merrill, 1959); see also Warner Wick, "Introduction: Kant's Moral Philosophy," in Immanuel Kant, *The Metaphysical Principles of Virtue: Part II of the Metaphysics of Morals* (Indianapolis, Ind.: Bobbs-Merrill, 1964), xi–lxii.

24. Ibid., xl–xli (for Wick's observation on Kant's casuistry); 84–85 (for Kant's opening toward situation ethics on suicide).

25. See Joseph M. Boyle, Jr., Germain Grisez, and Olaf Tollefsen, *Free Choice: A Self-Referential Argument* (Notre Dame and London: University of Notre Dame Press, 1976), 112–18, 165–66, and 180; also Brandt, op. cit., 27–36.

CHAPTER FIVE

THE GOODS WHICH FULFILL PERSONS

Introduction

As the preceding critique of scholastic natural-law theory suggests, a sound account of normative existential principles must show how they are grounded in human goods. If they are not so grounded, there is no adequate answer to the question, "Why should I be morally good?" The answer is not that God commands this, for the moral obligation to obey divine commands, although rightly accepted by believers, is not self-evident. Indeed, nothing clarifies the force of moral norms except the relationship of morality to human goods.

The present chapter therefore focuses on human goods. It first takes up the meaning of "good" and "bad" in general, setting aside the specific question of the existential good and bad—that is, the morally right and wrong. It then clarifies the human goods, including the fact that the goods which fulfill human persons are not yet of and by themselves moral principles—they do not directly tell one which choices to make and which to avoid. However, as chapters six through twelve will explain, moral principles are indeed grounded in human goods, since these principles generate judgments of conscience which direct action in line with love of all such goods.

Question A: What is the central meaning of "good" and "bad"?

1. As it comes from the hand of God, all creation is good. "God saw everything that he had made, and behold, it was very good" (Gn 1.31). Even things touched by sin can be redeemed, for their original goodness is not wholly corrupted. "For everything created by God is good, and nothing is to be rejected if it is received with thanksgiving; for then it is consecrated by the word of God and prayer" (1 Tm 4.4–5). Made in God's image, human persons as created, fleshly beings are completely good.

2. This truth of faith seems at odds with the reality of the bad—a word used here in preference to "evil" since the latter is generally taken to refer to moral badness only. Of course, some have held that the bad is only an illusion, the appearance of multiplicity and disunity created by human desire and striving. But this view, common in Eastern religious thought, is unacceptable. Even if the bad were only an illusion, the real situation which gives rise to this illusion would still

have to be explained. And escape from the bad, whether illusion or reality, into nirvana (an extinction of personal existence) seems little different from annihilation. This view is in any case incompatible with the Christian account of what is bad, of redemption, and of everlasting life.[1]

3. There is another account of the bad which conflicts with the teaching of faith that God creates everything good. It is metaphysical dualism—the view that the good and the bad are basic categories dividing reality into two realms. If, as dualism supposes, badness were a positive reality, there would either have to be a bad god to create it or God would have created something bad. Faith excludes both positions. Moreover, badness does not appear to have the autonomy which dualism attributes to it; rather, it appears to be parasitical on something good. For example, a victim of cancer no sooner dies than the disease also ends.

4. According to Jewish and Christian belief, badness is real, not merely apparent, but is not on a par with the good. Reality is God the creator and his creatures, a multiplicity with a single source. The bad is present in what is distorted, damaged, and corrupted in creatures. **The badness of what is bad is precisely the distorting, damaging, or corrupting factor. This factor is a privation, a real lack of something which should be present and perfect.** There must, however, be something to undergo this privation, and, insofar as this "something" remains what God intended it to be, it is good (see *S.t.*, 1, qq. 48–49; *S.c.g.*, 3, 4–15).

The account of badness as privation and of the origin of the bad in the sin of creatures raises many questions. Only a few can be mentioned here.

A first difficulty is that in many cases badness seems hardly to be merely incidental to something positive, as the privation theory requires. Often badness appears instead to have a positive character of its own. For example, if one is robbed, one undergoes a positive, bad experience. Again, if a child is born with a birth defect, the abnormal development is a positive state of affairs.

Being robbed is certainly a bad experience. However, in saying this, one is characterizing the whole experience by what is defective in it. Bad as it is, the whole experience nevertheless does include elements which are good. Concentrating on what is bad in it, one overlooks the fact that the robber is engaging in an intelligent action, that one is able to have and is having an experience, and many other aspects of the encounter which, to the extent that they are real, are good.

The example of the abnormal development which is a positive state of affairs brings out another important point. A privation in a cause can lead to a positive state of affairs in its effect which is other than the state of affairs which should exist (see *S.t.*, 1, q. 49, a. 1; *S.c.g.*, 3, 10). The account of badness as privation does not mean that nothing is positively other than it would be if there were no badness. The abnormal development, to the extent that it involves some life and functioning, remains good. What is given is a more or less diminished good, which can be called "bad" in a secondary sense, just to the extent that its difference from the norm is a consequence of some privation in the cause.

Another question concerns the origin of the bad. Many things in nature seem to fall short of a norm without the intervention of any sin; indeed, it seems natural that bad things occur. For example, one animal eats another, and every organism dies. Two points must be made in response to this question.

First, the determination of what ought to be, and so of what is bad, is relative to a norm, and the norm is relative to an orderly whole whose integral being is in question. If one considers disruptions in nature from the point of view of very limited segments of the whole process—for example, from the point of view of a particular organism—then one will see as bad the inevitable interference of small systems with one another. Such relative badness does not have to be accounted for by reference to sin; in a sense it is natural, as is clear if one considers the whole process of nature as a unity (see *S.t.*, 1, q. 48, a. 2; q. 49, a. 2).

Second, Scripture suggests that much of what we might take to be merely relative disruption has a mysterious relationship to sin. "We know that the whole creation has been groaning in travail together until now" (Rom 8.22; cf. 5.12). Perhaps demonic forces have some responsibility for this (see 1 Cor 15.24–26; Eph 6.12). Of course, it is altogether possible for the same state of affairs to be determined both by natural causes and by sin; it will be a merely relative bad in the former relationship and something more significant in the latter. For example, people who grossly neglect care for their health die both from natural causes and from sin.

5. Because badness is privation, the Church teaches "that there is no such thing as a nature of evil, because every nature insofar as it is a nature is good" (DS 1333/706). In other words, there is no sort of thing which is bad, as there are sorts of things which are dogs, straight lines, loud noises, and so on (see *S.t.*, 1, q. 48, a. 1; *S.c.g.*, 3, 7–9). Badness is a gap in something which remains good to the extent that it remains the sort of thing it is. Some things bad from a limited point of view are reducible to good in a wider perspective. Thus, the death of any organism is bad for it, but part of an orderly natural process. However, among the things created by God there are beings—angels and human persons—so real and powerful that they can introduce disruption into the good creation by their own free choices; this disruption, springing from the abuse of created freedom, is the real source of the irreducibly bad (see *S.t.*, 1–2, q. 75, a. 1; q. 79, a. 2; *S.c.g.*, 3, 10).

Negative states of affairs are real, not merely apparent. The emptiness of one's gasoline tank, for example, is hardly an illusion. Yet this emptiness is not a "nature" on a par with a full tank of gas. Not every negative state of affairs is bad, of course. The holes in one's sweater through which one puts one's torso, head, and arms are not defects. The bad is a negative state of affairs in which something is missing which ought to be present. Thus badness is privation, for it deprives that on which it is parasitical of some part of the full reality it should enjoy.

6. **As badness is privation, goodness is fullness of being.** Creatures do not have absolute fullness of being, but they can have real fullness according to their kind and condition—according to their specific and actual possibilities for becoming and being more. Creatures do not exist fully from the beginning; they develop. They have careers, and their goodness depends on their coming to be what they can be at each stage of their existence. Yet not every realization of potentialities is good. **Goodness lies in a fulfillment of potentialities which leads to being and being more; badness lies in the realization of a potentiality which cuts off further possibilities and tends to limit opportunities for self-realization which would otherwise be open to an entity.**

Because God is infinite in being, he also is infinitely good; in him there can be no lack. God creates to express and share something of his incomprehensible perfection (see DS 3004–5/1785–86). While in God there can be no distinction between what he is and what he ought to be, each creature has a role in the order of things which it ought to fulfill. Its fulfillment and fullness of being will be that share in the expression of the divine goodness which God intended for it in creating it. Badness is privation of something of the fullness to which a creature is called. But what, positively, is this fullness? Clearly, it is not the boundless perfection of God himself, for creatures are not bad merely by being limited as God meant them to be.

The fullness of being, the goodness of each creature, is that fullness of which it is capable, insofar as it is a creature of a certain sort, with certain capacities and opportunities to be and be more. A turtle is not defective inasmuch as it lacks the ability to run like a gazelle, nor is an ape defective because it lacks a sense of justice. Goodness is the fullness appropriate to each entity. Badness is not simply lack, it is privation—lack of what ought to be.

In a certain respect, each creature is good just by having the reality which makes it the kind of entity and the particular thing it is. But this fundamental goodness is not what is usually meant when we call something "good." Normally, a good X is an X which has a fullness which not every X has. "Good" commends some X in comparison with another X (see *S.t.*, 1, q. 5, a. 1, ad 1). This is the goodness we need to understand.

Unlike God, creatures—at least the ones we are concerned with—do not exist all at once, but come to be gradually. They grow and develop. Their fullness in being depends upon their realizing potentialities.

Thus, goodness is in the fulfillment of potentialities (see *S.t.*, 1, q. 5, aa. 4–5; *S.c.g.*, 3, 1–3, 18–22). Yet not every fulfillment of potentialities is good. People who get sick and die, who make mistakes in reasoning, who burn the potatoes, or who hurt others are fulfilling potentialities just as truly as people who live healthily, who think straight, who make good dinners, and who help others. Various forms of badness are objectively possible, and the bringing about of privations as such is not good. Goodness is in that fulfillment of potentialities which leads to being and being more. By comparison, we consider bad that fulfillment of a potentiality which cuts off further possibilities and tends to restrict the realization which otherwise would be open to an entity. This point can be illustrated with examples from various orders of reality.

First, consider the bodily dimension of a person. An organism can function in a good or bad way; "health" and "sickness" mark this difference. How are they distinct? Both are ways of functioning; both fulfill some of the potentialities of one's body. But health describes a way of functioning which is compatible with and leads to functioning further and more fully, while disease is a way of functioning which interferes with and closes off further possible functions. Disease tends toward death—the cessation of all functioning. Health keeps possibilities of organic life open; the healthier one is, the more one as an organism is able to do. Thus the good of an organism (health) is to live and live more fully; what is bad (disease) is what diminishes possible fullness of life.

A similar pattern exists in other dimensions of the person. In the field of thought and inquiry, logic distinguishes good and bad reasoning. Good reasoning requires clarity, consistency, certitude, and explanatory power. Bad reasoning is marked by confusion, inconsistency or looseness, inconclusiveness, and lack of illuminating insight. When the former characteristics are present, understanding grows and expands, new areas for inquiry open up, and one continues to learn more and more. When reasoning has the latter characteristics, the processes by which we know are blocked and hampered. Thus, in the field of thought and inquiry, as in that of bodily life, the good is that which makes possible further growth, while the bad is that which blocks further growth.

The same pattern exists in the fields of work and play, art and technology. Creativity, efficiency, success, and the like are good because they fulfill possibilities and open up further possibilities. Dull conformism, wastefulness, and failure are bad because they lead to dead ends—they realize some restricted possibilities in ways which unnecessarily limit further possibilities of human self-expression and achievement.

The remainder of this chapter and chapter seven will show how this same pattern of good and bad is present in the existential domain and how it helps to clarify moral right and wrong.

Question B: How are sensible goods and bads distinct from intelligible goods and bads?

1. The central meaning of "good" clarified in question A refers to what is understood as fulfilling. The corresponding meaning of "bad" refers to what is understood as a privation of fulfillment. But "good" and "bad" are used with secondary meanings to refer to what is sensibly appealing and repugnant. In both senses, whatever is called "good" provides a positive motive for behavior, and whatever is called "bad" provides a negative motive. However, what is good or bad in the secondary sense is not always good or bad in the primary sense.

2. This complexity in the uses of the words "good" and "bad" arises from the complexity of the human person. By nature, human persons are both sentient and intelligent. Their sentient nature is similar to that of other animals; their intelligence and freedom of choice are distinctive. Emotions are aroused by sentient awareness of what is suited or unsuited to the person as organism. Free choices are made on the basis of judgments about what will fulfill or prevent the fulfillment of the person as a whole.

3. Although complex, the acting person is one self. A person lives in a single world, and behavior must be adapted to all aspects of the reality of this world. Hence, normally a person's outward behavior is motivated at once by both emotion and will, directed both toward sensible pleasure (or the avoidance of its opposite) and intelligible fulfillment (or the avoidance of its privation).

4. For example, a person imagines good food and experiences the emotional appeal of eating it. If there is no reason not to eat, one sees the point of doing so and proceeds without having to make a choice. If a choice is necessary, in addition to the emotional appeal of the imagined food, there will be some reason for eating—some respect in which doing so will be considered fulfilling. Again, a martyr has a good reason to choose to suffer rather than be unfaithful. But in addition to the intelligible good of religious fidelity, the martyr needs motivation at the emotional level, such as affection for Jesus, attachment to others who are suffering, or fear of the pains of hell.

5. In many cases, emotion and will work together harmoniously in motivating action. Emotion advances possibilities, intelligence considers reasons for acting on the possibilities proposed, and will initiates action. If all goes well, what is done brings about results which are both pleasant (the sensible good is experienced) and fulfilling (the intelligible good is served). For example, a person takes pleasure in eating a meal, and the meal also serves health, sociability, and other human concerns which provide reasons for eating.

6. Choices are necessary only if emotions advance two or more possibilities, which are considered in deliberation. Thus, when one acts by choice, some emotional impulses are integrated as motives of the action and satisfied if it succeeds. But others, which advanced options other than the one chosen, remain unsatisfied, with more or less attendant frustration. For example, if a person on a diet chooses to eat a rich meal, the emotional appeal of the food is satisfied, but the emotional repugnance toward one's shameful obesity is overridden.

7. **The distinction between sensible and intelligible goods and evils is most obvious when a choice for an intelligible good overrides emotional repugnance to a sensible evil which will be experienced in the chosen act itself.** For example, one chooses to undergo painful dental treatment for the sake of the intelligible good of healthy, functioning teeth. But in undergoing the treatment, one experiences pain. Unlike the intelligible evil of the loss of one's teeth, the sensible evil of pain is a positive reality. **Thus, sensible evils are not privations, and sensible goods are only partial aspects of the intelligible goods which fulfill a human person as a whole.**

Felt pleasure and pain evoke strong emotional reactions and shape behavior, generally in a way which has survival value for the organism affected. As a positive sensation, pain is real; however, pain is no less beneficial to the organism than pleasure. In other words, in general the experience of pain ought to occur; it belongs to a healthy organism as part of its survival equipment. Thus pain does not have the character of privation, and so it is not intelligibly bad.[2]

Question C: How do mistaken views of the good and the bad lead to false accounts of what is good for human persons?

1. The view that badness is an illusion leads to the theory that human goodness is enlightenment. Certain Eastern religions hold that this enlightenment ends in nirvana, loss of self, absorption into the ultimate unity. According to Gnostic heresies, enlightenment transforms one's attitude and raises one above the seeming conflict of good and bad. Spinoza and Hegel among modern philosophers and Christian Science among modern religious movements are examples of a Gnostic approach.

2. The view that badness is a positive reality also leads to mistaken theories.[3] The Pharisees, taking this view of evil, thought that it could be avoided by separation and purification. In the Middle Ages, the Manichaean heresy identified badness with bodiliness. Currently, secular humanist ideologies which seek human good in empowerment imply that badness is a positive reality to be overcome. For example, pragmatists like Dewey regard the bad as the challenge to human ingenuity set by various environments; revolutionaries like Marx think of the bad as social structures which must be destroyed so that others can emerge.

3. **Hedonism is the most widespread view which considers badness a reality on a par with goodness. In this view, the good is pleasure and the bad is pain. This view rests on a confusion between sensible and intelligible good and bad.** Moreover, hedonism is incompatible with Christian faith (see *S.t.*, 1–2,

q. 2, a. 6; *S.c.g.*, 3, 27). St. Paul emphatically rejects it, ascribing its appeal to lack of hope for resurrection (see 1 Cor 15.32–34). Christian spirituality has always stressed the importance of being ready to forgo pleasure and endure pain for the sake of higher and more genuine goods.

4. Rational reflection confirms the previous analysis and Christian wisdom's evaluation of hedonism. Suppose a device were invented which could create experiences somewhat like motion pictures, but communicated directly to the brain, so as to make the experience a total one in which the individual's awareness of being a spectator was eliminated. Suppose, further, that one could select a lifelong program on this device and consign oneself—or one's child or best friend—to this pleasurable and all-absorbing existence. Would there be any point to doing so? Evidently not. No amount of guaranteed pleasure and avoidance of pain would make up for the fact that one was not really living a life. Living is more than experience; it is real relationships, which mean involvement with other real persons in a real world. For human persons, these real relationships come to be in and by acting. As we shall see, they are an important part of what is humanly good. Thus hedonism is to be rejected along with other mistaken views of the good and the bad.

If one confuses sensible and intelligible sources of motivation and takes pleasure and pain to be basic principles of human action, one's conception of action will be distorted. There is an intelligible aspect under which one can choose pleasure and seek to avoid pain, namely, the lessening of tension or increase in harmony among various parts of oneself. This good, especially in its conscious aspect, is peculiarly individualistic. Thus, emphasis upon pleasure and pain tends to focus concern upon oneself and to distract attention from the larger possibility of finding one's fulfillment by participation in community, ultimately in heavenly fellowship.

Question D: What are the goods which fulfill human persons?

1. Since human goodness is found in the fullness of human being, one begins to understand what it is to be a good person by considering what things fulfill human persons. Things which do so are human goods in the central sense—that is, intelligible goods.

2. **These goods are aspects of persons, not realities apart from persons.** Property and other things extrinsic to persons can be valuable by being useful to persons. But the basic goods by which they enjoy self-fulfillment must be aspects of persons, not merely things they have (see *S.t.*, 1, q. 5, a. 6; 1–2, q. 2, aa. 1–3).

Frequently in the Old Testament blessings extrinsic to persons themselves are understood to follow from God's promise to Israel: full warehouses, huge flocks, oxen loaded with goods, strong city walls, and so on (see Ps 144.13–14). Such things surely are human goods, but they are not directly and in themselves fulfillments of persons. They are extrinsic things persons can possess and use, but they do not guarantee personal fulfillment even in the bodily, intellectual, and cultural dimensions, much less in the existential or moral dimension (see Ps 73).

Thus, in many cases, something is not understood to be good or bad in itself, but by its relevance to something else. An empty gasoline tank is understood as bad by a person who wishes to drive somewhere, not because the empty tank is itself humanly bad, but because it prevents the person's doing as he or she wishes. Getting to the desired destination normally seems good not in itself but for the sake of what can be done there. For example, a man wishes to get home to eat dinner. As in this example, any intelligible chain of human purposes always ends in some goods appealing in themselves, because they contribute directly to the fulfillment of persons. Similarly, what interferes with, damages, or destroys good at any level is considered bad. But all humanly significant bads in the end are reduced to privations of the basic human goods.

Here we are concerned not with useful goods which are only means to personal fulfillment, but with goods which are appealing and can be sought on their own account, because they directly contribute to the fulfillment of persons.

Goods which are sought after on their own account are called "ends" to distinguish them from merely useful, instrumental goods which are called "means." John Dewey and others have denied that there ever are final ends for human activity; they say that any good always is a means to some further good.[4] This view is sound to the extent that it focuses on the open and dynamic character of good. Furthermore, goods which can be sought for their own sake also can be regarded as means to an ulterior purpose or, more importantly, as contributions to a larger whole, all the way to the largest whole which is the consummation of everything in Christ (see Eph 1.9–10).

But the view that there are no final ends for human activity is unsound to the extent that it breaks down the distinction between what persons are and what they have, between things constitutive of the fulfillment of persons and things merely instrumental to it. Moreover, heavenly fellowship in no way is for the sake of anything ulterior; the fulfillment of God's plan is an end which in no way is a means to anything else.

3. One can distinguish human goods by noticing the assumptions implicit in one's practical reasoning and that of other individuals and deliberative assemblies. In considering reasons in favor of proposals, deliberation quickly reaches some good which is taken to be not merely a means to an end but an aspect of personal fulfillment. Much effort is directed, for example, toward preserving life and health, and one needs no reason beyond themselves for concern about these goods. True, they can be considered means to other goods intrinsic to persons, but they can also be sought for themselves.

4. There are different senses in which a good can be said to be "sought for itself." The human goods which fulfill persons should not be considered mere outcomes one wants and seeks—as the goals one will enjoy if action is successful. Such outcomes have the character of accomplishments rather than of self-fulfillment—that is, they remain extrinsic to the person. Basic human goods must instead be considered aspects of what one might call human "full-being." They are sought for themselves in the sense that they are judged to be humanly fulfilling. They provide reasons for intelligently wanting something and choosing to act for it as a goal.

5. Persons and groups can take an interest in basic human goods and commit themselves to their service. For example, the human good of peace is not simply the resolution of a particular conflict; it is the harmony of persons which peacemakers commit themselves to and seek to serve by working for the resolution of conflicts. Basic human goods are thus greater than the particular things people do to participate in them.

6. The early chapters of Genesis suggest what the basic human goods are. Sin

is presented as making people worse in every aspect. In their bodily reality, they are doomed to die—the great good of life is forfeited. In their intellectual life, they are ready to believe lies and think crookedly—the good of truth and knowledge is surrendered. In their reality as cooperators with God in the work of procreation and dominion over the earth, they are condemned to experience pain in their labor—fruitfulness now carries with it burdens as well as fulfillment. Moreover, harmony is lost on all levels in the existential domain. There is inner conflict, manifested by ashamed self-consciousness; there is discrepancy between the capacity for intelligent action and what is actually done, a discrepancy which issues in self-deception, rationalization, and untruthfulness; there is interpersonal conflict, expressed in the shirking of responsibility, the hint of male-female tensions, and murder; and there is alienation from God.

God is depicted in Genesis as giving an order: "You may freely eat of every tree of the garden; but of the tree of the knowledge of good and evil you shall not eat, for in the day that you eat of it you shall die" (Gn 2.16–17). (It is worth noticing that this "order" sounds more like a bit of good advice than like an arbitrary edict. From the outset, God is pictured more as a lawgiver than as a lawmaker.) The man and woman disobey, and so disrupt their harmony with God (see Gn 3.6).

The committing of the sin and its subsequent rationalization entail elements of self-deception and self-betrayal: "The woman saw that the tree was good for food, and that it was a delight to the eyes, and that the tree was to be desired to make one wise" (Gn 3.6). The first point is wishful thinking, the second irrelevant, and the third an irresponsible belief. The serpent had lied (see Gn 3.4–5). When questioned, the man blames the woman—and God for giving her to him—and the woman blames the serpent (see Gn 3.12–13).

There is some disruption of the harmony between man and woman in this account (see also Gn 3.16); a more radical interpersonal conflict is depicted when Cain's disturbed relationship with God leads to his killing Abel (see Gn 4.6–8). For this, Cain is exiled from God's presence (see Gn 4.16). The sin of the man and woman also immediately leads to their loss of innocence and thus to an uneasy self-consciousness: "They knew that they were naked" (Gn 3.7). Pain and frustration become part of the experience of the procreative and creative work of woman and man (see Gn 3.16–19). And from this painful and frustrating labor there will be no rest "till you return to the ground, for out of it you were taken; you are dust, and to dust you shall return" (Gn 3.19).

7. One can infer the basic human goods from the privations which mutilate them. **Harmony is the common theme of several. We experience inner tension and the need to struggle for inner harmony; the good is self-integration. Our practical insight, will, and behavior are not in perfect agreement; the goods are practical reasonableness and authenticity. We have strained relationships and conflicts with others; the goods are justice and friendship. We experience sin and alienation from God; the goods are the peace and friendship with God which are the concern of all true religion.**

8. These forms of harmony on various levels can be called "reflexive goods," in the sense that choice is included in their very definition: Part of the meaning of self-integration is choice which brings aspects of one's self into harmony, part of the meaning of practical reasonableness and authenticity is choice and performance consistent with our insights, and so on. **These are existential goods**

because they fulfill persons insofar as persons make free choices and are capable of moral good and evil.

9. Religion is a great blessing, for nothing in life is more important than liberation from sin and friendship with God. However, harmony with God should not be confused with God himself nor with the divine life in which Christians share by adoption. The human good of religion—that harmony with God which perfects human persons as human—is only one human good alongside others (see GS 11). St. Thomas Aquinas makes this point by distinguishing the virtue of religion from the theological virtues. The former, concerned with specifically religious acts, such as prayer and sacrifice, does not bear upon God himself as the latter do (cf. *S.t.,* 2–2, q. 81, a. 5).

10. **There are other goods in whose definitions choice is not included; they fulfill dimensions of persons other than the existential one. Life and health fulfill persons as bodily beings; knowledge of truth and appreciation of beauty fulfill persons as intellectual beings; and playful activities and skillful performances in general fulfill persons as makers and sharers in culture.**

11. In sum, there are seven categories of basic human goods which perfect persons and contribute to their fulfillment both as individuals and in communities. Four of these can be called "reflexive," since they are both reasons for choosing and are in part defined in terms of choosing. These are: (1) self-integration, which is harmony among all the parts of a person which can be engaged in freely chosen action; (2) practical reasonableness or authenticity, which is harmony among moral reflection, free choices, and their execution; (3) justice and friendship, which are aspects of the interpersonal communion of good persons freely choosing to act in harmony with one another; and (4) religion or holiness, which is harmony with God, found in the agreement of human individual and communal free choices with God's will. The reflexive goods also can be called "existential" or "moral," since they fulfill human subjects and interpersonal groups in the existential dimension of their being. The other three categories of basic human goods fulfill persons in the other three dimensions of their being. These goods can be called "nonreflexive" or "substantive," since they are not defined in terms of choosing, and they provide reasons for choosing which can stand by themselves. These are: (1) life itself, including health, physical integrity, safety, and the handing on of life to new persons; (2) knowledge of various forms of truth and appreciation of various forms of beauty or excellence; and (3) activities of skillful work and of play, which in their very performance enrich those who do them.

One can supplement simple observations of the assumptions implicit in practical reasoning by directly asking questions: "Why are you doing this?" and pushing the line of inquiry until one comes to a normative principle which seems obvious. "Why do you work?" "To make money." "Why do you want money?" "I have to eat." "Why bother about eating?" "Don't be silly. I'll die if I don't."

The results of this sort of inquiry cannot be accepted uncritically. The raw data must be examined and sifted. One answer which is likely to appear is: "For fun." It should not be taken at face value. In some cases, it merely indicates that someone is acting for the good inherent in the action, not for some extrinsic goal. In other cases, it more particularly indicates that the person is acting for a certain aspect—some experience—of the good of self-integration. One reduces tension, at least temporarily, by doing something one feels like doing.

Other responses to questions about reasons for actions also can be seen to indicate some part or aspect of one or several of the basic forms of human goodness. One drinks because one is thirsty. The behavior sometimes is spontaneous and unthinking; in such cases, thirst is a motive rather than a reason. But if one deliberately chooses actions which satisfy normal organic needs, one is acting for life (which includes health, safety, and so on). Again, a person acts out of patriotism. Patriotism is reducible to specific aspects of certain goods; it presupposes a particular view of what constitutes a good community and personal integrity.

Very often highly vague and obscure language is used to refer to human fulfillment. For example, someone might talk about acting in accord with reason, or living for self-realization, or acting out of love. Such notions work in one of three ways. Sometimes they summarize many or all of the basic forms of human goodness, as "peace" in the Bible and "happiness" in Greek philosophy do. Or a very broad concept can simply be a way of articulating the notion of good itself, as is the case with "self-realization" and "creative growth toward fulfillment." Or, finally, a large concept can express a certain view about how human fulfillment is best pursued and most likely realized. "Love" often works this way, and it is given very different practical contents by different theories in which it plays a part.

Question E: What are the principal inadequate theories of the human good as a whole?

1. Unlike the views criticized in C above, there are several inadequate theories of human good which do not go wrong in their understanding of the meaning of "good" and "bad" but which fail to recognize the richness and complexity of human fulfillment. They err by mistaking a part for the whole.

2. **Some think the human good consists in getting what one wants—that is, in the aspect of human goods which is their realization in accord with one's wishes.**[5] People who get what they want are considered happy. This is not the same thing as hedonism, since it takes more than pleasure into account. But it is inadequate all the same. For on their theory, what one wants is settled either before one's choices or by one's choices. If the former, then, supposing "what one wants" constitutes the good of human persons, the whole existential domain (the domain of freedom and choice) is thereby reduced to serving desires which are given before choice. If, on the other hand, what one wants is settled by choice, then, again supposing it constitutes the good of persons, morality is subjective; since the rightness of choices depends on their relationship to human good (see 4-H), and human good in this case is whatever one chooses. Hence, the view that getting what one wants constitutes the human good as a whole is not adequate.

As definite possibilities of the fulfillment of human persons, goods have a real objectivity, even though they are not actual entities. Many subjectivistic and relativistic theories suggest that whatever one wants or chooses, or whatever a particular group of people happen to care about is "good for them."

True, the plurality and richness of human possibilities and the openness of human goods to development leave room for pluralism, diversity, and creative initiative. However, human goodness is the fullness of which human persons are capable, insofar as we are creatures of a certain sort, endowed with some definite capacities and opportunities for being and being more.

Although God had a choice whether to create human persons or not, even he could not make us what we are—which includes a definite set of possibilities—and then arbitrarily decide what sorts of things would be our goods (see *S.t.*, 1, q. 21, a. 1, ad 3; q. 25, a. 6). For instance, God cannot create an organism for which mortal illness is a good. Much less can individuals and groups arbitrarily determine what is "good for them."

The objectivity of human goods led some thinkers in the idealistic tradition—Nicolai Hartmann is an example—to make an opposite mistake. They supposed that the goods, because they are objective, must be real apart from and prior to human persons.[6] While it is true that all created goods preexist in the perfection and the wisdom of God, the basic human goods considered in their own being are created realities. As created, human goods have no reality apart from the individuals and groups of persons in whom they can be and are realized, for these goods are nothing but certain realizations of the possibilities of persons.

3. **Some think the human good consists in the full exercise of one's properly human capacity, the ability to reason.** Aristotle is the best example of this view. Aware that human fulfillment is not simply the realization of some state of affairs, he holds that the human good is a lifetime of action. But he fails to accord adequate recognition to human goods other than the exercise of reason. Thus he thinks that fulfillment consists simply in the reasonable ordering of life and the use of reason in philosophical reflection of the highest sort.[7]

4. This view, and any similar to it, is inadequate. Either one can opt for a good other than the exercise of reason or one cannot. If one can, human fulfillment is not reducible to the exercise of reason—it must include the other good for which one can opt. If one cannot, any basic shortcoming in one's life must be due to ignorance, disease, or some other factor beyond one's control which has impaired the use of reason—not to wrong choice. But in this case, radical moral evil is impossible.

5. **Some think fulfillment consists in living a life which executes a difficult project in an excellent way.** Nietzsche is the best example of this view. It makes no difference what the project is. What count for him are the effort, creativity, and skill which go into carrying out whatever it may be. On this view, life should be a work of art; the greater the art, the better the life.[8]

6. Although Nietzsche does see that human fulfillment must consist of more than getting what one wants and being what one is, his account also is inadequate. It is vulnerable to a dilemma similar to that used against Aristotle. Nietzsche denies the reality of moral evil, but he bitterly criticizes those who do not accept his notion of the human good—pointless criticism if there is no objective standard of morality to support it. Moreover, Nietzsche's theory is essentially individualistic, with no room for community, and is incompatible with the Christian belief that human fulfillment depends on cooperation with God's work.

The appeal of the three theories criticized here can be accounted for as follows. The satisfaction of basic needs is of service to the good of life and is likely to be of service to human fulfillment in its other aspects. Those who idealize liberty and who wish to create the conditions for its uninhibited exercise assume that in the right situation people will use liberty to fulfill themselves individually and communally in all the basic goods. The exercise of intelligence is related to at least two of the basic human goods: namely, truth and practical wisdom. Creative work also is a human good, and all the human goods, in their open-endedness, call for a creative approach to life.

Yet all three of these approaches fall short. None takes into account the whole variety and richness of human fulfillment. Human freedom of self-determination is essential to all of the existential goods; the three approaches ignore or deny this freedom, and so they misconceive and oversimplify the personal and interpersonal, existential dimension of humankind.

Moreover, none of these three approaches has a conception of human fulfillment which really fits the requirements of faith. Just as the Incarnation did not annul the human nature of Jesus but perfected it (see GS 22), so sharing in divine perfection cannot annul human fulfillment for us. But if one attempts to reconcile the Christian vocation with any of the three approaches (including Aristotle's), the attempt will be blocked at once. All of them involve such limited conceptions of human good that they leave no room for its transformation by grace into an integral part of the heavenly fulfillment of all things in Christ.

Question F: What is St. Augustine's theory of the human good as a whole?

1. St. Augustine holds that the human good consists in peace. By this he means harmony, the tranquillity of order, in oneself, with others, and especially with God. **By focusing on peace, he calls attention to the existential dimension of persons and their fulfillment.**

2. However, Augustine primarily thinks of peace as an ultimate, desirable condition which is to be realized in heaven. In this respect his view is similar to that which considers fulfillment to consist in satisfying one's desires. Against versions of this conception of fulfillment other than his own, he makes the point that one's deepest desire, for which one's heart is always restless, is for union with God beyond this life.[9]

One can state Augustine's position on the human good as a whole by beginning with God. God alone is the human person's good, and he is good for persons in their possessing him. The possessing will be by a mental grasp, which will yield perfect enjoyment. Lacking this enjoyment, the soul longs for it restlessly. Thus, the good for human persons essentially is peace—that is, the eternal rest of the now restless heart.[10]

This theology, frequently mistaken for Christian faith itself, narrows human life to its religious dimension and renders problematic the very possibility of a Christian humanism. The conception of happiness as the enjoyment of an intellectual possession of God will be criticized (34-A).

3. As Aristotle showed, a good life must be a whole life lived out. As Nietzsche argued, it must have room for self-realization and creativity. Augustine's account of human fulfillment does not include these things. However, his treatment of peace as an other-worldly goal might be expanded into a more open view. Instead of a particular goal to be realized definitively, peace can be considered an inexhaustible good really shared in during this life, and shared in also, in another and superior way, in heaven.[11]

4. Even so, there are human goods which are not simply aspects of peace as Augustine understands it: life and health, knowledge of the truth, and skill in

performance. An adequate account of human good must find a place for these substantive goods and their realization in this life.

5. Inadequate as it is, however, Augustine's theory of the human good is suggestive. Peace in oneself, with others, and with God is an essential and special part of the human good, a part by which one who shares in it is called "good" without qualification—that is, good not in some limited respect, but simply as a person. Thus it is worth considering next what "peace" more precisely means, then indicating how the other human goods are included in the complete fulfillment of human persons.

"Peace" in the Old Testament has a much richer meaning than it does in St. Augustine, yet its sense is not indefinite.[12] It signifies utter fulfillment, completion, perfection—a condition of well-being and flourishing in which nothing is lacking. The prophets foretell a Messiah who will be prince of peace (see Is 9.5–6).

About to die, Jesus leaves his followers peace: "Peace I leave with you; my peace I give to you" (Jn 14.27). Newly risen, he repeatedly greets the disciples: "Peace be with you" (Jn 20.19, 21). The proclamation of the gospel is of peace: "Let the peace of Christ rule in your hearts, to which indeed you were called in the one body" (Col 3.15). God will answer every prayer of Christians, and so they have nothing to worry about: "The peace of God, which passes all understanding, will keep your hearts and your minds in Christ Jesus" (Phil 4.7). As the alienation of sin brings death, so peace brings life (see Rom 5.12; 8.6–11).

It is clear that this promise and hope of peace include every aspect of human fulfillment (see GS 39 and 93). The sending of the Spirit at Pentecost begins to build up the new creation in Christ (see 2 Cor 5.17; Eph 2.10); God has sent forth his Spirit and the face of the earth is renewed (see Ps 104.30). Thus, in the end, sin and all its effects will be overcome; the evils initiated at the beginning will be healed. God creates a new heavens and a new earth, and from heaven sends to earth a new Jerusalem, which also is a new Eden (see Rv 21.1–6).

Question G: What does it mean to say without qualification that a person "is good"?

1. "Good" is not said of people without qualification—that is, without specifying a limited aspect or role of their lives—merely because they flourish in health and strength, in knowledge and esthetic appreciation, or in any form of excellent performance (see *S.t.*, 1–2, q. 56, a. 3; q. 57, a. 5). One can be a good specimen of the human male or female, a good scientist or an individual of good taste, a good violinist or a good linguist, without being a good person.

2. **We say without qualification that people "are good" if and only if they are morally good.** Moral goodness resides centrally in a person's choices. One is not considered morally good merely for having made a few good choices, but for making a set of morally upright commitments and living by them consistently. Since moral goodness depends on free choices, it is in one's own power. For fallen humankind, of course, the right use of freedom is impossible without grace; but by the redemptive work of Jesus, grace is won for fallen humankind—men and women can be good.

The notion of moral goodness will be clarified in chapters seven and eight. For the present, it is enough to notice that the moral challenge arises from the multiplicity and distinctness of creator and creatures, self and others, and the various dimensions and capacities within oneself. One can act in ways which preserve and harmonize all this richness or in ways which are exclusive of some constituents and disruptive of community and integrity. The former ways of acting point to more abundant life; the latter to a constricted existence. As in other domains, goodness in the existential domain is on the side of fulfillment; moral evil is a kind of existential self-mutilation.

3. Of the various basic human goods, the reflexive ones, which pertain to the several levels of harmony, also pertain to the existential dimension of the person. In other words, peace within oneself, with others, and with God is essential to being a good person, because peace is the goodness of the person as moral—that is, as free in self-determination and in relating to others.

4. **It follows that moral uprightness is an essential part of human fulfillment. It leads to harmony on all levels.** In living a morally good life, one utilizes and respects all the aspects of the self which are given prior to choice; the distinctiveness and unity of one's experience, feelings, intelligence, interests, and powers of execution are simultaneously furthered. Similarly, in living a good life, powers and gifts one has prior to choice are in harmony with the life which executes one's choices. Likewise, in living morally good lives, distinct persons become intimately united in communion without losing those things which make their personalities distinctive; rather, they make the most of their different gifts. Last but not least, in living morally good lives in communion with others who will to do the same, persons are gathered together from fallen humankind into a family in friendship with God. (The formation of this family, primarily the work of God in Jesus, will be considered in chapters twenty through twenty-three.)

5. The other human goods—the nonreflexive or substantive ones such as life and health, knowledge, and skilled performance—are realized in definite states of affairs distinct from one's choices. For instance, the dedicated physician is interested in health in his or her patients' bodies, the scientist in knowledge in the thought and discourse of a scientific community, the athlete in skillful performance in a game. **By contrast, the various levels of harmony are not primarily realized in definite states of affairs which result from the carrying out of choices.** Rather, the existential goods (self-integration, practical reasonableness and authenticty, justice and friendship, and friendship with God) are personal and interpersonal spiritual realities which primarily exist in upright individual and communal choices themselves.

According to the explanation given, moral goodness is only one aspect of the total fulfillment of human persons. Moral goodness primarily pertains to the will, by which one makes choices which either contribute to or detract from the various forms of personal and interpersonal harmony, which are most essential to the fulfillment of persons as persons. Someone can be physically sick, mentally retarded or ignorant, and inept and unsuccessful, yet be morally good. Such an individual will be recognized as a good person, although he or she might be considered unfulfilled. A morally good person need not be one whom the Greeks would have called "happy" and contemporary secular humanists would say has "adequate quality of life."

6. These existential goods do have psychological and symbolic-expressive dimensions. Friends, for example, feel friendly and make friendly gestures. But

feelings and gestures cannot substitute for mutual good will; sincerity and sound commitments are essential. Peace in the sense of sharing in the existential goods can thus be present even when appropriate feelings and gestures are not. To put it more concretely, people whose feelings are inappropriate because of psychic illness or whose gestures are socially and culturally inept may indeed be more or less crippled and limited personalities; but if they make upright use of their freedom, they are nevertheless called "good persons" without qualification.

The relationship between moral uprightness and human fulfillment has been considered in answering this question. Moral goodness—participation in the existential goods—is an intrinsic part of integral human fulfillment. The normative principles of morality have not yet been articulated. Thus, this treatment might appear circular, but it is not. The effort here has been to explain the role which moral goodness, whatever it may be, plays in the overall full-being of persons; chapters seven and eight will be devoted to clarifying what moral goodness is.

Question H: How are existential and substantive goods related to one another?

1. As was explained in question F, persons are called "good" without qualification if they make morally upright choices and so share in the existential goods. But what about the other basic human goods—the substantive ones—which also can be loved for themselves and can be ultimate reasons for choices? One can, for example, choose to jog for the sake of one's health, with no concern for anything beyond health. How do the substantive goods fit into the overall fulfillment of a good person?

2. The existential goods are realized primarily in right choices, but something more than choices is needed if substantive goods are to be realized. It is necessary to do things which bear upon them—to jog for one's health, to study in order to learn, to practice in order to perform and then actually to perform well. Nor will fulfillment as a whole be achieved by one who is indifferent to substantive goods or slack in carrying out choices which bear upon them.

3. Although primarily interested in cultivating the goods of the existential domain, the upright person fully appreciates the goods of the other domains. Necessarily so. One simply cannot have a friendly relationship with another person unless one shares common interests with that person and does things together with him or her. Similarly, one cannot pursue religious fulfillment apart from activities in which one seeks to promote bodily well-being or skillful performance or thoughtful reflection; religion which does not make a difference in daily life is meaningless (see Jas 1.23–25; 2.14–17). As one cannot make music without sound, so there must be some substance to the harmony which existentially perfects persons and communities. **This is to say that the substantive goods are the "stuff" of a morally good life—they are vehicles for the existential goods.**

4. Similarly, one will not enjoy real self-integration if one does not care about one's nonexistential dimensions. And the integration of these other dimensions into one's existential self requires that one fulfill them in concert. It is true that no

one can give precisely the same attention to health, to intellectual knowledge, to skillful performance, and so on; the emphasis will be different for different people. But everyone must at least give appropriate attention to all these dimensions—it will not do to neglect any. Similarly, those who really care for others will not stop at having good will toward them. They will be concerned and will seek to remedy the situation if others are hungry, ignorant, unskilled, or needy in any other way. To love others means being concerned about everything from which they suffer and interested in every good which will fulfill them (see Mt 25.31–46; Rom 13.10).

Justice is concerned with the impartial distribution of burdens and benefits pertaining to means to all human goods, and also directly to the fulfillment of nonmoral aspects of persons—for example, health, education, opportunities for play, and so on. Similarly, if one wishes to express one's love for another, one gives a gift, shares a meal, or something of the sort. All such friendly acts involve some contribution to or sharing in human goods other than love itself. Interpersonal relationships, including the religious relationship of humankind to God, would lack substance if they did not center around substantive goods such as life and truth, which are realized and experienced when a group of persons eat and converse together as at a banquet.

The immediate reason for this complex relationship between the existential and the substantive goods is that the former are forms of harmony—that is, various levels in which unity and diversity are perfected by love. Harmony cannot be a mere form; it requires some definite content. Music cannot be harmony without harmonious sounds; sounds have many characteristics studied by physics which human art can only respect and cannot change; yet the art and beauty of music centers upon harmonies which human art creates among sounds. Similarly, the harmonies in which moral goodness consists must have some real content, and this content is drawn from the other domains in which persons participate.

5. The goods of the existential domain can only be realized in and through human actions. For example, justice is realized only in choices which are just, in the justice which is done in carrying out such choices, and in resulting arrangements and institutions. By contrast, there are two distinct ways in which the substantive goods can be realized.

6. First, they may come naturally. Health, for instance, can be a blessing one enjoys without deliberately doing anything to promote or protect it. In such cases, the good is not present in any peculiarly human act but only in the functions which occur naturally in the bodily self.

7. Second, these goods also come about through choice and action. One is healthy, for instance, because one is careful to exercise, gets needed medical care, and so on. In such cases, the fulfillment of the person who acts, lies in being the cause of the good; while the fulfillment of the person in whom the good is realized (who may or may not be the same one who acts) lies in some condition or state which is an instance of the good. For example, the fulfillment of one who feeds the hungry lies in voluntarily feeding them, while the fulfillment of the hungry lies in being fed. This makes it clear why it is possible to do morally upright acts in the service of substantive goods yet fail to realize them; one can be faithful in doing what is good yet not successful in bringing about what is good.

8. Still, the substantive goods remain basic forms of human goodness, and they are closely connected with the existential goods. Ordinarily, for example,

one cannot consistently pursue goods such as life and truth, without at the same time taking care to promote goods such as self-control and social justice. Conversely, an attack on a good such as life violates existential goods as well: Abortion not only kills an unborn child but also violates its right to life.

9. Faith, specifically the doctrine of the resurrection, makes it clear that life is itself one of the basic goods of the human person. Life is no less a personal good for being a gift prior to one's choice. And one can make choices with respect to it—to protect it or attack it, to hand it on to others or impede its transmission, and so on. There is an implicit dualism in the view that bodily life is not an intrinsic good of persons but only an instrumental good; for this implies that the real human "person" is one thing and the body something else, apart from the person.

10. Integral human good thus includes both existential and substantive goods. **The existential goods primarily are realized in and through choices themselves. Since choice has a communal dimension, however, existential goods cannot be perfectly realized in an imperfect community. Thus, given the imperfect character of the world, the world cannot give perfect peace. As for the substantive goods, such as life and truth, they require effective action, which is not always possible even for persons of good will. People can therefore be morally good yet unfulfilled. But the Christian promise of fulfillment includes the realization of all the goods; in heaven the upright will be happy.**

11. This account clarifies the role of morality in human life. Moral requirements are supreme in human life; there is nothing more important than choosing rightly. But other human goods are also basic. A sound morality will guide choices toward human fulfillment in all its aspects. The upright person is concerned not only to choose rightly but also to serve all the human goods.

Insofar as they perfect persons called to everlasting life, basic human goods belong not merely to the passing world but to the heavenly communion of fulfillment in the Lord Jesus. The fulfillment for which Christians hope will be clarified in chapters nineteen and thirty-four. Here these clarifications may be briefly anticipated.

The Christian promise is of a fulfillment which includes the satisfaction of a great desire, unending joy, a noble life of individual excellence, a perfect community with interpersonal intimacy and personal liberty, and everlasting life after death. And this promise excludes—except during the brief span of this life—frustration, misery, failure, and loneliness. Moreover, the Christian promise is open not only to an elite (Aristotle and Nietzsche) and not only to future generations (Marx), but to every human person.

What is more, the fulfillment which is promised is for flesh and blood persons, not disembodied spirits; for persons who share a common life, not souls merged into the One or isolated in ecstasy; for persons whose present lives in this world can make lasting contributions to the promised fulfillment, not those mystics and philosophers who consider life here and now a necessary evil which offers nothing of true human fulfillment.

The Christian promise of fulfillment calls upon individuals to establish their own identities by free commitments: by the commitments of faith and personal vocation. The Christian is to live a rich life in which potentialities are realized in an orderly and ever-expanding way. Even the frustration, misery, and failure which are inevitable in this life can be made to contribute to fulfillment, and whatever contributes to fulfillment here and now is treasure which will last forever.

Summary

Faith teaches that all creation as it comes from God's hand is good. Yet this seems in conflict with the reality of the bad. Some explain the bad as an illusion, others as a positive reality.

To suppose that badness is an illusion leads to the theory that goodness lies in enlightenment. To suppose that badness is a positive reality leads variously to the notions that good consists in separation or segregation from evil, in gaining power to limit or control evil, or, in the case of hedonism, in having pleasure and avoiding pain. None of these views is rationally defensible or compatible with Christian faith.

Using "good" and "bad" in their central senses, Christian faith instead understands badness as a privation, a real lack of something which should be present; while goodness is fullness of being. For limited and imperfect beings, goodness lies in realizing their potentialities in a way which leads to being and being more.

The sensibly good and bad must be distinguished from the intelligibly good and bad. Only the intelligibly good and bad are so in the central sense according to which the good is fulfillment and the bad privation. Nevertheless the sensibly appealing and repugnant also are factors in motivating behavior, because the human person not only differs from other animals by having intelligence and the power of free choice, but is like them in having a sentient nature. In many cases, an action leads both to pleasure and to fulfillment. But sometimes the two sources of motivation are at odds, for example, when one chooses painful treatment for the sake of health. In such a case, it is clear that the sensible evil of pain is not a privation.

Since human goodness (using "good" in its central sense) consists in the fullness of human being, one naturally asks what things fulfill human persons. These basic human goods are not apart from persons, not extrinsic goals which people desire and hope to reach. Rather, they are aspects of persons in their individual and communal flourishing. Basic human goods can be distinguished by noticing the assumptions implicit in people's practical reasoning; when the question is why to do something, deliberation quickly arrives at a good which is not just a means to an end but itself an aspect of individual and communal personal fulfillment.

Scripture and reflection both point to the same basic goods. Harmony is the theme of several: self-integration (harmony among aspects of the self), practical reasonableness and authenticity (harmony among moral reflection, free choices, and their execution), justice and friendship (harmony among human persons), and religion (harmony between humankind and God). This latter, the good of religion, should not be confused with God himself, nor with the divine life in which Christians share by adoption; it is by itself only one human good alongside the others. Besides these, there are also goods which fulfill dimensions of the person other than the existential: life and health, knowledge of truth and appreciation of beauty, satisfaction in playful activities and skillful performances.

Some err in their understanding of the human good by underestimating the

133

richness and complexity of human fulfillment. It is often supposed, for instance, that human good consists in getting what one wants; but this either reduces free choice and moral effort to serving desires given before choice, or else renders morality subjective. Again, Aristotle and others maintain that human good lies in the full exercise of one's properly human capacity, the ability to reason; but a human being is more than an intellect, and fulfillment consists in more than reasoning. Others, such as Nietzsche, say fulfillment lies in the individualistic execution of a difficult project in an excellent way; but this leaves no room for community or for cooperation with God's work.

St. Augustine's view is that the human good consists in peace, by which he means harmony in oneself, with others, and especially with God. However, he understands peace as an ultimate desirable condition, to be realized in heaven, and so takes too narrow a view of fulfillment. His account is nevertheless important for the place it gives to various forms of personal and interpersonal harmony.

The human goods which are forms of harmony pertain to the existential domain. This is to say that "peace" is the goodness of the person as moral. It follows that moral uprightness is an essential part of human fulfillment. A person is called "good" without qualification if, and only if, he or she is morally good. Moral goodness resides centrally in choices, and especially in making and living by morally upright commitments. The human goods of self-integration, practical reasonableness, friendship, and religion therefore primarily exist in upright individual and communal choices.

While always concerned about the goods of the existential domain, the morally upright person will also necessarily be interested in the goods of the other domains (life and health, knowledge, skillful performance). For these latter not only are humanly fulfilling in themselves, but also are, in effect, the vehicles for the existential goods. Yet even one who chooses rightly and acts on their behalf cannot always realize these goods in practice—for example, one cannot always be healthy, cannot always be successful in one's work, and so on. Christian hope therefore looks forward to integral human fulfillment in heaven in regard to these goods as well as the goods of the existential domain.

Appendix 1:   Vatican II's indication of the human goods

Vatican II teaches that the laity has a special role in the kingship of Jesus. By his obedience he becomes the Lord of creation, subjecting everything to himself (see Phil 2.6–11). He passes on this power to his disciples so that they might both share in their own redemption and lead others to his kingdom:

> For the Lord desires to spread his kingdom by the laity too—a kingdom of truth and life, a kingdom of holiness and grace, a kingdom of justice, love, and peace. In that kingdom, creation itself will be liberated from its slavery to corruption into the glory of the freedom of the children of God (cf. Rom 8.21). Clearly, a great promise, a great mandate is given to the disciples: For "all these are yours, and you are Christ's, and Christ is God's" (1 Cor 3.23).

The faithful, therefore, must recognize the inmost nature and the value of the whole of creation, and its ordination toward the praise of God. They ought to help one another toward a holier life in their secular occupations too, so that the world may be imbued with the Spirit of Christ and more effectively attain its destiny in justice, love, and peace. The laity hold the chief role in the universal fulfillment of this task. (LG 36; translation supplied)

This passage refers to some of the principal human goods which I identify: truth and life, holiness, justice, love, and peace. (I omit grace, for this is the divine good shared by human persons insofar as they participate in divine life, rather than a properly human good.)

It should not be supposed that the Council—or the Preface of the Feast of Christ the King to which the Council refers—means to provide an analytic list of the goods of human persons. For our purposes, such a list is necessary. Also, because the Council is at pains to insist that the worldly goods of human persons, which are the proper concern of the laity, are intrinsic and not incidental to Christian life, it does not here make another point important in what follows: that human friendship with God and human life—and all the other goods of human persons—are alike in being fulfillments of human persons to be pursued and protected in this life and contributed to fulfillment in Jesus. But Vatican II does make this point elsewhere (cf. GS 39), and it will be developed at length in chapters nineteen through thirty-four.

Appendix 2: The reflexive or existential goods explained more fully

All people experience tensions within themselves. Their concern with getting-it-all-together points to the fact that people generally sense that they are not able to get it all together. Various aspects of the given self seem to be at odds with one another. There is a need to struggle for inner harmony. The objective sought is the integration of the competing components of the self. This good is quite appropriately referred to as "self-integration," in its basic meaning of order within the self.

St. Paul refers to the relevant sort of conflict; he calls it a war between the law of the body's members and the law of the mind. Only Christ liberates one from this conflict (see Rom 7.15–25). Gifts such as chastity, mildness, patience, courage, and self-control are aspects of this single existential good (see Gal 5.22–23). These aspects are distinguished by different areas of activity in which the well-integrated Christian functions in a characteristic way.

Tension also exists between the moral reflection of individuals, their free choices, and the behavior by which they carry out their choices. It is true that an action always is the act of a person who does it, yet the action is somehow other than the actor. Conflict is possible here, and it is expressed in comments such as "I could kick myself for having been such a fool as to have done that." The harmony which is disrupted by this sort of conflict can be called "practical reasonableness and authenticity." This good is manifested in the life of a person such as Mother Teresa, who chooses in accord with her convictions and expresses her commitments clearly in all she says and does. This good is part of what Scripture means by "wisdom" (see Ps 14.1–3; Sir 1.22–25). A person who lacks this good is double-minded (see Jas 1.8).

Looking beyond the individual, it is obvious that we experience tensions in our relationships with others. We seek in many ways to overcome these tensions and to establish harmony between ourselves and other people. Justice and friendship between individuals and groups are aspects of this good. In Scripture, words such as "justice" and "peace" often are used in such a broad sense that they refer to all the levels of existential fulfillment, and even to the whole of human well-being. However, there can be no doubt that interpersonal harmony, just cooperation, and fraternal communion are great goods of persons, celebrated throughout Scripture and the Christian tradition: "Behold, how good and pleasant it is when brothers dwell in unity!" (Ps 133.1).

In the existential domain there is, finally, the level of harmony with which all religion is concerned: peace and friendship between humankind and God. We tend to think of friendship with God as something too elevated to list alongside other human goods, and of sin as if it were an injury to God rather than a deprivation of human fulfillment. Thinking this way, we tend to draw the conclusion that what we suffer as a consequence of sin is a punishment arbitrarily imposed on the sinner by God.

But although communing with God in Christ does go beyond a merely human good, human fulfillment also is sought and found in the human relationship of peace with God.[13] Sin does deprive the sinner of this fulfillment; separation from God is logically entailed by sin, not an imposed harm (see *S.t.*, 1–2, q. 71, a. 2; 2–2, q. 24, a. 12).

As the account of sin in Genesis already suggests, the various levels of human fulfillment in the existential domain are closely interrelated. This partly explains the tendency to use expressions such as "peace" and "justice" in a wide sense to cover all or many aspects of these personal goods. The various levels of existential fulfillment can be distinguished from one another, but in reality they are not separable. All are realized or damaged together. We know this well by experience; for example, when we are angry with someone else we are troubled within ourselves, we do things we do not approve of, and we cannot pray with a good heart. The scriptural teaching about the inseparability of love of God and neighbor emphasizes one important aspect of this same point (see 1 Jn 2.10; 3.11–18; 4.20–21).

Appendix 3:   Substantive goods explained more fully

Human fulfillment in the intellectual dimension is knowledge of truth, particularly that truth which is sought for its own sake. Considered from the point of view of the activity, this good is knowing, while considered from the point of view of the perfective content, it is truth. Theoretical knowledge—truth sought for itself—is not limited to professional intellectuals such as philosophers and scientists. The curiosity of a child also is aimed at this good. Esthetic experiences, which are engaged in for their own sake, involve a great deal of sensory activity, but this activity is formed and given its peculiar value by the influence of intelligence. Thus, such activity also pertains to the fulfillment of human persons in the domain of intellect.

In Scripture, explicit mentions of truth and knowledge usually refer to the practical or existential fulfillment previously described, called "wisdom" (see Prv 3.13–18). However, the fulfillment of persons by theoretical truth and esthetic experience is not ignored, even if it is seldom explicitly discussed. It is implicitly recognized and commended in various contexts, including that of the praise of God the creator (see Ps 104). The beauty and order of God's universe are acknowledged and acclaimed with childlike wonder (see Jb 38–41).

Vatican II explicitly commends work in philosophy, history, mathematics, and the sciences, as well as cultivation of the arts, because this effort "can do very much to elevate the human family to a more sublime understanding of truth, goodness, and beauty, and to the formation of judgments which embody universal values" (GS 57).

In the field of external activity, one might suppose there is no good directly perfective of human persons, but only goods instrumental to properly personal fulfillment. But this supposition would be a mistake. Playful activities are engaged in for their own sake, and so are many forms of skillful performance which also are productive of fruitful results.

An important aspect of human dignity is cooperation with the creative work of God (see Gn 1.28; Ps 8.7). If work is not fulfilling, this situation arises not from any necessary irrelevance of external behavior to the fullness of personal being, but rather from the conditions which make work into labor (see Gn 3.17–19). Vatican II explicitly teaches that work is not merely instrumental and that human fulfillment demands culture, including external activity (see GS 53 and 67). Activities which are merely playful in a special way reflect the utter gratuitousness of God's creative act, for such activities express a person and seek to acquire nothing.

The fulfillment of persons in their bodily dimension is acclaimed as a great blessing throughout the Bible. Creation is crowned by life and this good is specially blessed to insure its growth and continuance (see Gn 1.22, 28). In the covenant with Noah, there is a permission to kill animals, but an explicit protection of human life (see Gn 9.1–7). The position that life is precious and death a great evil is strongly asserted in Wisdom (see 1.12–16; cf. GS 18). That life itself is a good is presupposed in all of the cases in which life is miraculously preserved or restored.

Vatican II clearly teaches that whatever is opposed to life itself or to bodily integrity is a great crime (see GS 27). Procreative fruitfulness, good health, and bodily integrity are aspects of the human good of life (see 2 Kgs 4.12–16; Ps 127.3–4; 128.3–4; 144.12). Considered as an intelligible value, the avoidance or treatment of pain belongs to this same general category of human well-being.

Appendix 4:   Bodily life a basic human good

Many today argue that human life is falsely considered an intrinsic good of human persons, if by "life" one means simple bodily existence. This reality, they argue, is an important one, since it is a necessary condition for all other goods. But in itself life, understood in this strict way, is only an instrumental good. A full life, a life of real quality, is good—so the argument goes—but this goodness is from other intrinsic goods of the person which build upon the foundation of mere existence.

However, the truth is that bodily life in itself is a basic human good, as the following discussion will make clear.[14]

One reason some think life is not an intrinsic good of persons is that they think life is common to all living things. In a sense this is true, of course, but in a deeper sense it is false. Biological life is different in humans, in other animals, and in plants. This is a matter not of speculation but of fact, which is established in works on human embryology, human physiology, and so on.

Although animals can perform many of the kinds of functions performed by plants, they perform their functions in a way proper to them. Animals assimilate food, grow, and reproduce, but they carry out these so-called vegetative functions in an animal way. To be able to do some of the things plants can do is not to be a plant; to be partly perfected by functions generically common to plants and animals is not to be partly a plant.

The same is true of humans. Human persons can do many of the things which other animals can do and many of the things plants can do. But this does not mean a human person is partly an animal or a plant. Even biologically, a human being is a specific kind of organism. To be one finite kind of thing, by definition, is not to be any other finite kind of thing. An individual of a certain kind is of that kind through and through. Human life, then, is properly human, for every aspect of it is specific to human persons (see *S.t.*, 1. q. 18, aa. 1–2; q. 76, aa. 3–4). In reality there is no life in general; this is merely an abstract concept.

The proposition that life is only instrumentally good implies that the human person or some parts of the human person are one thing and a person's living body is quite another thing. This implied position splits the person in two, and so it is called "dualism."

The Christian doctrine of the resurrection points to the falsity of dualism.[15] Resurrection life is bodily life. When Jesus was dead, he was not without divine life, but he did lack human, bodily life. Eternal life means much more than the good of human life, but the importance of bodily resurrection can only be grasped if one accepts the intrinsic goodness of human bodily life, and so its real necessity for ultimate completion in Jesus. Paul makes clear how important resurrection is (see 1 Cor 15.13–26). At the same time, Paul himself seems to have envisioned the possibility of disembodied existence (see Phil 1.20–24; 2 Cor 5.2–10). The Church teaches the immortality of the soul (see DS 1000/530, 1440/738). Therefore, one cannot say that the resurrection is important only because one could not conceive any manner of communing with God unless bodily life were given as a necessary condition. Rather, resurrection is so important because bodily life is an intrinsic good of human persons; their human fulfillment would be incomplete without it.

One aspect of the unity of Christians with Jesus is a real, bodily unity. The resurrection of Christians is to a radically new form of life, grounded in their unity with the risen Lord (see 1 Cor 15.20–49). As one shares natural life and death with Adam, one shares in the death and resurrection life of Jesus (see 1 Cor 15.20–23). "He who raised the Lord Jesus will raise us also with Jesus and bring us with you into his presence" (2 Cor 4.14).

Now, if one firmly rejects dualism and takes seriously the Christian's bodily union with Jesus, then the sanctity of human bodily life here and now is clear. The great concern in the Christian tradition about the sources of life and sexual activity which touches upon life's beginning also is obviously appropriate—see, for example, Paul's argument against fornication (see 1 Cor 6.15–20). Moreover, the real effectiveness, not mere symbolic value, of the sacraments is clarified, for they are means of conferring and nourishing the resurrection life one shares with Jesus. However, if one is imbued with a dualistic view of the human person, these important matters are greatly obscured.

Rational reflection supports the truth faith teaches. First, the instrumental view of the good of human life implies dualism. As already explained, intrinsic human goods are not possessions of persons, but the fulfillment of their being. On the instrumental view of life, life is not part of the intrinsic good of persons. However, life certainly is not separable from the living body, as if it were a mere possession. Thus, on the instrumental view of the good of life, the living body will be one thing and the fulfilled person something else. Thus the instrumental view of the good of human life implies dualism.

Second, dualism is indefensible (see *S.t.*, 1, q. 75, a. 4; q. 76, a. 1). Life is not merely one process among others, a process which can be distinguished from breathing, feeling, choosing, talking, and so on. The life of a person is indistinguishable from the person's very reality. Life must pervade every part and activity of a person, or something of the person would be unreal. Moreover, one's fulfillment is the completion of one's given self. If the personal goods which constitute fulfillment were other than one's given self, one could not fulfill oneself by acting.

If the dualist conception of the human person and the instrumentalist view of the good of bodily life are false, why do so many people think this way? The question is not easy to answer. Modern Western culture has developed a peculiar view of human persons, considering them to be incommunicable conscious subjects, encased in body objects which conceal them from, rather than communicate them to, one another.

In part, this peculiar view must be due to factors proper to modern Western culture—for example, the felt separation from nature experienced by persons who live in cities, work with inanimate objects, and deal constantly in artificial symbols. In part, however, sins against bodily life and sexuality lead to a distorted consciousness of one's self. For example, one can sin more comfortably in killing the unborn if one can separate human life from the person; similarly, one can abuse sexuality for gratification with less unease if one thinks of one's true self as the gratified consciousness and one's sexuality as a lower form of life with its own dynamism.

Notes

1. An excellent theological treatment of evil: Charles Journet, *The Meaning of Evil* (New York: P. J. Kenedy and Sons, 1963).

2. Roger Trigg, *Pain and Emotion* (Oxford: Oxford University Press, 1970), 166, describes the case of a young woman who did not enjoy a normal sense of pain: "As a result she suffered considerable physical damage regularly, and it merely went unnoticed or was regarded with indifference."

3. Max Scheler, *Formalism in Ethics and Non-Formal Ethics of Values* (Evanston, Ill.: Northwestern University Press, 1973), 23–30 and 81–85, like many others who give values an ontic status prior to entities which bear or participate in them, allows disvalues including moral evil the same metaphysical status as values. However, this mistake is a consequence of his failure to recognize principles beyond the value phenomena he was exploring, together with his effort to absolutize the phenomena in order to exclude various reductionistic theories of values.

4. John Dewey, *Human Nature and Conduct* (New York: Henry Holt, 1922), 210–77.

5. See Ralph Barton Perry, *General Theory of Value: Its Meaning and Basic Principles Construed in Terms of Interest* (Cambridge, Mass.: Harvard University Press, 1954), 115–45. Though Perry defines value as any object of any interest, his ultimate moral theory moves a long way in the direction of a satisfactory account of human fulfillment. Others who adopt a view similar to his elaborate it less plausibly.

6. See Nicolai Hartmann, *Ethics*, vol. 1, *Moral Phenomena*, trans. Stanton Coit (New York: Humanities Press, 1932), 183–244.

7. Aristotle, *Nicomachean Ethics* i, 1098a5–19; x, 1177a12–1178b32.

8. Friedrich Nietzsche's thought is diffuse and frequently expressed poetically; thus, it is difficult to cite a single source in his work to illustrate his position as summarized here. However, I think my summary a fair reflection of his later position, as represented, for example, by *Twilight of the Idols; or, How One Philosophizes with a Hammer*, in *The Portable Nietzsche*, ed. Walter Kaufmann (New York: Viking Press, 1954), 463–563. For a critique of atheistic existentialism, including Nietzsche: Cornelio Fabro, *God in Exile: Modern Atheism: A Study of the Internal Dynamic of Modern Atheism, from Its Roots in the Cartesian "Cogito" to the Present Day*, trans. and ed. Arthur Gibson (Westminster, Md.: Newman Press, 1968), 867–967.

9. The clearest and most systematic treatment by St. Augustine of the question of the human good as a whole: *The City of God*, xix, esp. chaps. 10–11, 17, 20, and 25–28.

10. For a sympathetic study of Augustine's thought centering on this view, see Etienne Gilson, *The Christian Philosophy of Saint Augustine*, trans. L. E. M. Lynch (New York: Random House, 1960), esp. 3–10; for a brief summary: Eugène Portalié, S.J., *A Guide to the Thought of Saint Augustine*, trans. Ralph J. Bastian, S.J. (Chicago: Henry Regnery, 1960), 271–73. Augustine's theology is heavily influenced by a particular metaphysics, namely, Neoplatonism: Robert J. O'Connell, *St. Augustine's Early Theory of Man, A.D. 386–391* (Cambridge, Mass.: Belknap Press of Harvard University Press, 1968), esp. 217–18 and 279–89.

11. There is some basis for such an expansion in Augustine himself, and more in the Augustinian tradition: Thomas Renna, "The Idea of Peace in the Augustinian Tradition: 400–1200," *Augustinian Studies*, 10 (1979), 105–11.

12. See Heinrich Gross, "Peace," *Encyclopedia of Biblical Theology*, 648–51; H. Beck and C. Brown, "Peace," *New International Dictionary of New Testament Theology*, 2:776–83.

13. See Mariasusai Dhavamony, *Phenomenology of Religion* (Rome: Gregorian University Press, 1973), 291–316, for evidence on this point from comparative religion.

14. I have dealt more fully with the subject of this appendix in two previous works, which provide additional clarifications and references: Germain Grisez and Joseph M. Boyle, Jr., *Life and Death with Liberty and Justice: A Contribution to the Euthanasia Debate* (Notre Dame and London: University of Notre Dame Press, 1979), 372–80; "Dualism and the New Morality," *Atti del Congresso Internazionale Tommaso d'Aquino nel Suo Settimo Centenario*, vol. 5, *L'Agire Morale* (Naples: Edizioni Domenicane Italiane, 1977), 323–30. Cf. Georges Cottier, O.P., "La conception chrétienne de la

sexualité," *Nova et Vetera,* 52 (1977), 1–21; summarized: "The Christian Conception of Sexuality," *Theology Digest,* 26 (1978), 218–22.

15. The modern, dualistic conception of the human person must be contrasted with the scriptural view. See John A. T. Robinson, *The Body: A Study in Pauline Theology* (Philadelphia: Westminster Press, 1952), esp. 11–16, for a concise summary of the Old Testament background of St. Paul's theology of the body. Again, although marked by Protestant assumptions, Ernst Käsemann, *Perspectives on Paul* (Philadelphia: Fortress Press, 1971), 17–29, brilliantly clarifies Paul's conception of the human person as body.

CHAPTER SIX

CRITIQUE OF THE PROPORTIONALIST METHOD OF MORAL JUDGMENT

Introduction

Chapter four explained that moral norms direct choices toward human goods, and chapter five clarified these goods. Chapters seven through twelve will give an account of norms consistent with Catholic teaching on natural law in general and on specific moral questions. Before proceeding with this constructive work, however, we need to examine and criticize an alternative view which has been accepted by some Catholic moral theologians.[1] Although sometimes called "consequentialism" because it focuses upon states of affairs consequent upon choices and their execution, this theory is here called "proportionalism" because what is most central to it is its appeal to the proportion of good and bad as a basis for moral judgment.

Question A: What is the proportionalist method of moral judgment?

1. Proportionalism is a theory of moral norms; it rightly considers them truths which direct action toward human goods. What is peculiar about proportionalism is the way it does this. According to a simple version of proportionalism, a moral judgment is a comparative evaluation of the possibilities available for choice. Each is examined to see what benefit and harm are likely to come about if it is chosen and the choice is carried out. Suppose one possibility promises considerably more benefit than harm, while another promises less benefit than harm. One ought to choose the first possibility, according to proportionalists, because it gives a better proportion of good to bad.[2]

2. Many who accept a more or less restricted version of proportionalism object that they do not advocate a merely quantitative calculus. **However, the theory, and indeed the very notion of "proportion," requires some method for comparing possibilities with respect to benefit and harm to determine which promises the most attractive proportion.**[3]

3. Suppose pregnancy endangers a woman's life. If she dies, so will the unborn baby. Those who are not proportionalists might approve abortion in some such cases, but the point here is not the moral judgment, but the method for

reaching it. Typically, proportionalists would approve abortion in such a case by arguing that it is better—that is, less bad—to have a dead baby and a live mother, than to have both die. Since the proportion favors abortion, on this view one ought to choose to kill the baby. Although this is a choice of something bad, in the sense that the baby's death is contrary to the good of human life, the choice will be morally good according to the proportionalist precisely because one is choosing what is less bad.[4]

4. Because it requires attention to consequences, proportionalism is also called "consequentialism." However, proportionalists can take into account the benefits and harms which are inherent in acts, independent of the results they cause. The acts-consequences distinction is not crucial for them; what matters is the overall proportion of benefit and harm promised by each possible choice.[5] To make sure all areas are considered, some proportionalists suggest that one attend to the object of the act, the circumstances, and the end in view, then do a cumulative summing-up of harm and benefit in all areas. Still, provided everything is considered and nothing counted twice, precise distinctions between the parts of a moral act are unimportant to proportionalists.[6]

5. Proportionalism has many forms and variations.[7] Noticing some of these sheds light on various attempts to introduce proportionalism into moral theology.

6. Some—Jeremy Bentham and Joseph Fletcher, for instance—apply proportionalism directly to all morally significant choices. This is called "act utilitarianism" or "act consequentialism." Others—for example, proponents of what is called "rule utilitarianism"—apply proportionalism to the justification of norms but wish to exclude its use for choices other than those by which norms are accepted.

7. Some admit proportionalism only in more or less restricted areas, while excluding its use in certain other areas—say, in regard to acts directly against religion such as false swearing or particularly unfair acts such as racial discrimination. Or they may use proportionalism only to limit the application of certain received norms, such as those pertaining to sex and innocent human life. Or they may restrict its use to conflict situations—cases where choosing to violate some received norm would seem to bring about less harm than choosing to act in accord with it. Moreover, a proportionalist can hold that acts of certain kinds will always be wrong.[8]

8. One accepts proportionalism just to the extent that one thinks the moral judgment concerning which possibility a person ought to choose can and should be reached by making a comparative evaluation of benefits and harms promised by available possibilities. As will be shown, the essential problem with proportionalism is this comparative evaluation. None of the variations and limitations noted above avoids it. Even if proportionalism is used only to judge whether to act in a certain way or to refrain from acting in that way, a comparative evaluation must be made of the benefits and harms expected in either case.

9. Herein lies the key issue between the theory of natural law to be articulated in chapters seven through twelve and any version of proportionalism.[9] Although the moral theologians who use proportionalism may hold a defensible account of

moral judgment on many matters (for example, that one should attend to received Christian moral wisdom with respect to them), all who accept even a limited or restricted version of proportionalism are vulnerable insofar as they think that some moral judgments should be made by a comparative evaluation of benefits and harms promised by available possibilities.

Question B: What account of human goods does proportionalism presuppose?

1. The utilitarians were both proportionalists and hedonists. Reasons of history and methodology underlie this connection. Like Marxists, they were mainly interested in alleviating social misery caused by the industrial revolution. By reducing human good to pleasure, they hoped also to find a way of calculating proportions—something which seems impossible if there are many goods of different kinds. Unlike the utilitarians, however, most proportionalists today hold nonhedonistic theories of the human good, and some theological proportionalists accept a list of basic human goods similar to that proposed above (5-D).

In explaining how a moral code is developed, Richard A. McCormick, S.J., says he follows the school of J. de Finance, G. de Broglie, G. Grisez, John Finnis, and others, by using basic human inclinations to identify the goods to which action is directed: "With no pretense at being exhaustive, we could list some of the following as basic inclinations present prior to acculturation: the tendency to preserve life; the tendency to mate and raise children; the tendency to explore and question; the tendency to seek out other men and obtain their approval—friendship; the tendency to use intelligence in guiding action; the tendency to develop skills and exercise them in play and in the fine arts. In these inclinations our intelligence spontaneously and without reflection grasps the possibilities to which they point, and prescribes them."[10]

The British utilitarians treated preferred states of human consciousness as the only self-validating value. On this theory, moral norms must yield whenever necessary to promote the enjoyment or lessen the misery of most people (see 5-C). No Catholic theologian adopts the utilitarian, hedonistic conception of what is good. But some theologians tend to demote some of the goods of persons to a merely instrumental status. For example, some do not always regard bodily life as a personal good; they consider the misery a seriously defective child can suffer and cause others a significant personal disvalue, and so tend to regard such a life as if it were merely instrumental. Thus proportionalism can be used to justify infanticide as a lesser evil in some cases.[11]

2. Interested as they are in measurable benefits and harms, proportionalists focus on one aspect of the realization of human goods, namely, their instantiation—their being concretely present—in the definite and limited states of affairs which arise from making and carrying out choices. **The human goods (and bads) whose proportions are to be compared exist for proportionalists only in the sum total of their concrete instances.**[12]

3. However, this is not an adequate account of the realization of any of the human goods, although it is partly correct for substantive goods such as life and health. While the latter have a certain reality in the dedication of persons who strive to promote and protect them, their more proper realization is in living and healthy bodily persons. Nevertheless, when people choose, they really determine

themselves in respect to goods and form community with one another (see 2-E and 2-H). Thus all of the basic human goods have a certain reality—they determine persons existentially—simply in being chosen.

Consider, for example, a dedicated nurse. She is committed to the care of those who cannot care for themselves. At least two basic human goods give meaning to her work: the bodily well-being of her patients and the personal bond (somewhat like the bond between mother and child) she has with each patient.

Bodily well-being, which pertains to the category of human life, is realized in two ways. It has a certain reality in the nurse's commitment to it. In the heart of a person dedicated to serving this good of persons, health is more than a mere idea or possibility. The dedication itself gives that to which one is dedicated a more than ideal status. But the more proper realization of a substantive good, such as bodily well-being, is in its instantiations—that is, in its realizations/expressions in concrete states of affairs distinct from the mind and will—in healthy bodies.

The personal bond between the nurse and her patients, which is an existential good in the category of interpersonal harmony, primarily exists in their human acts, most centrally in the choices by which nurse and patient are mutually committed to the common cause of the patient's bodily well-being. The existential good also is realized outwardly in its psychological and symbolic expressions, but these are secondary to the spiritual, interpersonal bond (see 5-H).

Thus both categories of goods have part of their reality prior to their instantiations. This prior, existential reality of the goods is important, although secondary, for the substantive goods, but is primary for the existential goods, including religion and friendship. Here what matters most is not any measurable benefit or harm, but what is in the heart and comes forth from it.

4. Like any coherent moral theory, proportionalism regards the moral goodness of the person as an absolute; thus, there is no place for justifying the choice of what is admitted to involve moral evil. To avoid approving the choice of moral evil, proportionalism requires that the goods which can be sacrificed for proportionate reasons not include moral specifications. Instead, the good is defined independently of moral considerations, and what is right and wrong is determined by benefits and harms in respect to the good thus defined. This way of defining the goods other than moral goodness itself is expressed in the language proportionalists use; the basic goods are often called "premoral," "nonmoral," "ontic," or "physical."[13]

5. **Thus, proportionalists have two reasons for omitting from consideration the aspect of the reality of human goods which resides in people's choices and commitments: first, their assumption that goods exist only in concrete instances of their realization; second, their need to define the goods which can be sacrificed for proportionate reasons entirely independently of moral specifications. However, it is precisely in choices and commitments that existential human goods, such as marital friendship, have their primary and proper reality.** The basis for the realization of marital love is a faithful commitment, which is a spiritual reality, not a definite, limited state of affairs. Particular acts done by couples in accord with their marital commitment simply express and flesh out the existential reality of the bond of marriage. The same is true for all the existential goods.

6. Because of this, proportionalists tend to limit proportionalism to cases in which existential goods are not at stake—for example, by excluding absolutely acts which are scandalous or irreligious.[14] Proportionalists sometimes also redefine existential goods in such a way that their whole realization is in nonexistential expressions and embodiments. So, for example, instead of locating the central reality of marriage in a commitment, a proportionalist may reduce marriage to psychological experience and satisfactory performance, and declare the relationship dead if these are absent.[15]

7. In sum, proportionalism presupposes a sharp distinction between moral goodness and other goods which fulfill human persons. These other goods usually are called "premoral," "nonmoral," "ontic," or "physical." Because proportionalism focuses on measurable benefits and harms, it overlooks the reality even substantive goods take on in a person's self-determining free acts bearing upon them. Moreover, if proportionalist justifications are proposed for choices to destroy, damage, or impede existential goods, these must be reduced to their nonexistential expressions and embodiments. Hence, although theological proportionalists might accept a list of goods similar to that proposed here (5-D), they would not agree with the account of the structure of the human good proposed in the remainder of chapter five.

Question C: Why is proportionalism plausible?

1. Like most basic questions, problems about the primary principles of morality can be settled neither by deduction from prior principles nor by induction from facts. Hence, there are no direct arguments in favor of proportionalism. Instead, its philosophical and theological proponents commonly propose indirect considerations.

2. Thus, proportionalists often criticize the theories evaluated in chapter four, state that proportionalism meets the criteria for a moral theory which emerge from such criticism, and conclude without further argument that their theory is the correct solution.

Proportionalism has some plausibility. It does relate morality to some aspects of human fulfillment—namely, to the goods of persons which are affected by human actions. Proportionalists are certainly right in thinking that the fulfillment of persons has to settle what is morally good. After all, moral goodness is one dimension of human goodness—in other words, moral fulfillment is part of total human fulfillment.[16] Thus, compared with any of the theories discussed in chapter four, it sounds plausible to say that what is right is what really minimizes harm and maximizes benefit to persons.

3. **Many think the basic idea of proportionalism is undeniable and irrefutable; it seems to be a self-evident truth.** Bentham and Mill take this position, correctly pointing out that what is most basic cannot be demonstrated. Richard McCormick similarly holds that in conflict situations, the alternative to the judgment that the lesser evil should be chosen is the absurdity that the greater evil should be chosen. (In the discussion which follows, McCormick will be taken as representative of contemporary Catholic proportionalists because of his commendable willingness to clarify and argue for his views, a willingness not universally present among other proportionalists.)

In arguing for proportionalism (in application to certain moral problems) McCormick says: "... the rule of Christian reason, if we are governed by the *ordo bonorum* [the basic human goods], is to choose the lesser evil. This general statement is, it would seem, beyond debate; for the only alternative is that in conflict situations we should choose the greater evil, which is patently absurd."[17] Although McCormick limits proportionalism to conflict situations, his position shares the general characteristics of this approach. He is not saying that one might morally choose to do what one thinks is morally evil. But he is saying that in conflict situations one may will human nonmoral evil in choosing to destroy, damage, or impede some basic human good, such as life, provided one has a proportionate reason. Like other proportionalists, McCormick understands "proportionate reason" in terms of a comparison of benefits and harms, which he assumes one can make, to identify the lesser evil. (An appendix deals with the restricted theory of proportionate reason McCormick adopted in 1978.)

4. **Moreover, proportionalists think their view uniquely accounts for the fact that many moral norms admit of exceptions.** Here is a classic case: "One ought to return to the owner on demand anything left in one's safekeeping subject to this condition." But suppose the owner of a gun arrives in the middle of the night, drunk and bent on revenge against somebody—should one return his gun to him? Obviously not.[18] When they break promises and do other things which they consider justifiable exceptions to accepted norms, people often explain themselves in a way which sounds like proportionalism. "I broke my promise to my friend and wouldn't let him have his gun because, regardless of any harm to our friendship, it would have been much worse if I had let him go out and kill somebody."

5. **Catholic proportionalists claim also to find instances of the use of proportionalism in the theological tradition.**[19] McCormick argues, for example, that contraception can be justified by "concurring" personal values; he says this is an instance of a sort of reasoning adopted by many contemporary theologians. Then he adds a quotation in which St. Thomas says that, although killing a person as such involves a disorder, it can be made right by a particular circumstance—for example, the circumstance that it is capital punishment for the sake of justice. "By reason of particular circumstances" McCormick takes to mean "by reason of the good of the person or persons"; on this basis, he claims that Thomas supports proportionalism.[20]

6. Many people find proportionalism's flexibility attractive. They dislike absolute norms—for example, "Adultery is always wrong"—and say these require one to disregard the benefit and harm to persons in actual situations. Some proportionalists argue further that, while moral absolutes could be maintained in an ideal universe, compromises are in order in this real universe broken by sin.[21]

Part of proportionalists' impatience with moral absolutes is rooted in their reaction to an inadequate conception of moral obligation. If God is not being simply arbitrary in stamping "forbidden" on acts, there must be some plausible reason for his doing so—such as that they cause more harm than good. Similarly, when proportionalists insist, as they often do, on the dynamism of human nature—its historical character and openness to real change—they are rejecting the static human nature envisaged by scholastic natural-law theory. Imagining that the best reasons which can be offered in support of received Catholic moral teaching are the question-begging arguments of scholastic natural-law theory, many

Catholics brought up on such arguments are tempted to dismiss the moral norms the Church teaches along with the bad arguments for them.

Question D: Why do these considerations, which render proportionalism plausible, fail to constitute sound arguments in its favor?

1. Proportionalism is not the only alternative to the theories criticized in chapter four, and it has difficulties of its own. As those theories are incompatible with one another yet all inadequate, so there is no reason why proportionalism, though incompatible with all of them, should not also be inadequate. It can meet many requirements for a sound theory yet be unsound, as a person can meet almost every criterion of good health yet be mortally ill.

2. If an expression like "lesser evil" could have a definite meaning in the contexts in which proportionalists want to use it, proportionalism would be self-evident. **However, as we shall see in question F below, goods and bads cannot be comparatively measured as proportionalism requires, and proportionalism therefore is not self-evident.** Moreover, in a conflict situation, choosing a truly greater evil need not be the alternative to choosing what a proportionalist calls a "lesser evil." The alternative may instead be to appraise the possibilities differently than a proportionalist does. Suppose, for instance, a pregnant woman has been told she must have an abortion, lest she and her unborn child both die. She can reject the calculus and refuse the abortion; in doing so, she can hold against proportionalism that purposely destroying her baby would be an act of unfaithfulness to it, and as such a greater evil than accepting the risk of a natural disaster in which she and the baby will both die.

Of course, proportionalists will deny that there can be any unfaithfulness in a choice to kill a child in circumstances of this sort. But this denial is not self-evidently correct, and a parent who took the opposite view could hardly be summarily judged irrational or immoral. This can be clarified by considering other cases in which parents, unable to save their children in situations of disaster, choose to remain with them to the death rather than abandon them to improve their own chances for survival.

If McCormick were right in thinking that the only alternative to "Choose the lesser evil" is "Choose the greater evil," then proportionalism would be self-evident and its alternative absurd, as he claims. Of course, if this really were the case, then one could hardly violate this "rule of Christian reason." However, if goods could be weighed as the proportionalist thinks, then there would be no choice to make. (This point will be explained in question F.)

In any morally significant choice, there are at least some aspects of good and bad which cannot be measured by any available common standard. So one is not reduced, as he imagines, to a choice between a measurably lesser and greater evil. For example, if one has a choice between (1) caring for a very severely defective child as fully as one would for a normal child and (2) withholding all care so that the child will die quickly, on what scale does one weigh whatever goods and bads one recognizes in these alternatives?

3. Most moral norms do admit of exceptions. **But this nonabsoluteness (this openness to exceptions) can be explained without adopting proportionalism, by pointing out the absolute norms in which others are grounded.** For

instance, the Golden Rule—treat others as you would have them treat you—both grounds the norm that one should keep promises and justifies exceptions. But the Golden Rule itself is absolute (not open to exceptions) and it does not operate by comparing benefits and harms.

The plausibility proportionalism derives from the nonabsolute character of many moral norms only shows that there must be some absolute norms, not that "Always choose the greater good" or "In conflict situations choose the lesser evil" is an absolute norm. There are better candidates for this role, and the Golden Rule is only one of them.

Many standards of social behavior admit of exception when the Golden Rule demands that one make an exception. For example, one who breaks a promise when the Golden Rule requires this judges that fairness is a greater good than dependability. This judgment is by no means proportionalist; it does not involve the proportionalist's weighing and balancing of goods and bads prior to a moral norm in order to justify a judgment that some goods can be attacked for the sake of promoting others or preventing "greater evils." Fairness is a greater good than the dependability of keeping promises because the latter has moral value from the former: One ought (usually) to be dependable because it is (usually) unfair not to be. The Golden Rule itself does not admit of exceptions. What could justify one who treated others in a way he or she would not want to be treated in a similar situation?

Similarly, just law can never authorize acts of certain kinds against persons (see GS 27). If a society sets about to improve the condition of some of its members by killing others, or by enslaving them, or in any other way by using them rather than treating them as members of the society with rights like everyone else, then the legal arrangements made to carry out such projects do not deserve the cooperation of upright citizens.

4. **It is not true that the theological tradition endorses proportionalism.** Although some classical moral theologians no doubt occasionally proposed arguments which look like proportionalism, this is very different from articulating and defending the method. St. Thomas' defense of capital punishment clearly does not rest on a proportionalist rationale (see *S.t.*, 1–2, q. 46, a. 6; q. 87, a. 1; 2–2, q. 64, a. 2). Rather, he thinks that the moral disorder usually involved in killing a person can be removed entirely in the case of capital punishment, so that the killing is rendered upright. Whether or not this position is correct, it is not the same as the proportionalist claim that the harm of a death might be outweighed by some benefit.

Even if it were shown that traditional Catholic theologians used arguments really proportionalist in form, this could be regarded much as we regard the widespread use of certain invalid forms of syllogism. It is one thing to use an argument of a faulty type. It is quite another thing to articulate and systematically employ a faulty form of reasoning. When a form of reasoning has been articulated and an instance of it is being criticized, it is a very weak defense to point out that in the past it has been used by able and upright people. The whole point of critical reflection is to prevent mistakes which are very likely without such reflection.

St. Thomas never sets out a proportionalist theory (see *S.t.*, 1–2, q. 18, a. 4, ad 3; q. 20, a. 2; 3, q. 68, a. 11, ad 3). He does not say that capital punishment and killing in just wars are justified by a "proportionate reason." His handling of these matters may not be sound, but it certainly is not proportionalist. One reason why it is not, is clear in the very article from which McCormick quotes. Thus McCormick:

> In the *Questiones quodlibetales*, St. Thomas laid the foundation for this type of

assessment. He wrote: "There are some actions which, absolutely considered, involve a definite deformity or disorder, but which are made right by reason of particular circumstances, as the killing of a man . . . involves a disorder in itself, but, if it be added that the man is an evildoer killed for the sake of justice . . . it is not sinful, rather it is virtuous." Here something which is a "deformity" is "made right by reason of particular circumstances." Contemporary moral theology would say *amen* to that and would add that the Thomistic phrase "by reason of particular circumstances" can be translated "by reason of the good of the person or persons."[22] But St. Thomas goes on to explain that supervening circumstances can totally empty out the disorder and make the act upright.[23] On a proportionalist account, by contrast, the nonmoral evil is not eliminated; it remains, but is outweighed. The deformity or disorder Thomas speaks of is not nonmoral evil; rather it is the moral evil usually involved in killing a human person, but not in those cases which Thomas accepts (on nonproportionalist principles) as exceptions.

McCormick also neglects to inform his readers that, unlike proportionalist theologians, St. Thomas (in the very article McCormick uses) describes another class of human acts: "For there are some which have deformity inseparably annexed to them, such as fornication, adultery, and others of the sort, which in no way can be done morally." (True, even in the case of such acts, Thomas considers that the *behavior* could be justified if it were done in the carrying out of a divine command, for then he thinks the behavior would not require a choice of fornication or adultery.[24])

5. Logically, the proportionalist's polemic against moral absolutes and appeal to flexibility are question-begging—that is, they actually take for granted what they claim to prove. They are persuasive mainly because they agree with prevalent secular humanism and appeal to everyone's desire to do as he or she pleases. Although there are indeed difficulties with the account of moral absolutes given by scholastic natural-law theory, these need not attend every account of absolute moral norms.

6. In setting aside absolute prohibitions of such acts as adultery, proportionalism is at odds with Christian moral teaching. However, the revision of received teaching is precisely the aim of the theologians who use proportionalism, and so, to avoid begging the question against them, the case presented in this chapter is not based on the assumption that such revision is unacceptable. Chapters thirty-five and thirty-six criticize theological dissent from received Catholic moral teaching. The use of proportionalism, here shown indefensible on other grounds, will tell against the dissent it is invoked to support.

The theory that moral compromises are necessary because the world is broken by sin implicitly contradicts both God's strategy in redeeming humankind and denies the success of this strategy. The theory of compromise derives from a conception of redemption, according to which grace does not inwardly transform Christians, so that they actually can fulfill the law of God, but only covers over their sinfulness.[25] This position was explicitly and definitively condemned by the Council of Trent (see DS 1536–39/804, 1568/828).

Classical moral theologians did agree that if someone is determined to act immorally, he or she may rightly be advised to choose the lesser evil. For example, an upright person might advise someone determined to take revenge on an enemy to beat up rather than kill him or her. One can accept this position without making any concessions to proportionalism or the theory that compromises are necessary. "Lesser evil" is determined in this case by antecedent moral norms, not by proportionalist balancing of premoral goods and bads. And the advice to choose a lesser evil was considered legitimate not because sin was thought to be unavoidable but because people sometimes freely limit themselves to morally unacceptable alternatives for choice. One who counsels the "lesser evil" in a case of this sort hopes that the more serious sin will be avoided and so accepts the doing of the less serious one, but in no way approves or tries to justify it.

Question E: Do practical experience and language provide evidence for proportionalism?

1. One often has the experience in deliberating of finding one possibility definitely better overall than the others. The latter then simply drop out of consideration. When only one possibility remains, deliberation ends and one does what is clearly best.

2. This experience seems to verify the proportionalist account of moral judgment. But in fact it does not. If the conclusion that one possibility is best determines action, there is no need for free choice and there is none. If there is no choice, there is no judgment of conscience either; it, too, is unneeded. In such cases, one cannot do otherwise than one does. **What is perceived as definitely less good or more bad simply cannot be chosen, because one can only choose what appeals to intelligent interest, and that which is seen as being definitely less good or more bad than something else has no appeal.** It is as if, all other contestants having been disqualified in advance, someone were to win a race without running.

3. This choice-less reduction of possibilities to one happens in two sorts of cases: first, in technical reasoning about instrumental goods; second, in moral judgments which follow necessarily from one's prior and now unquestioned choices.

4. In cases where one has a definite, firmly accepted goal in view, deliberation seeks to determine the easiest or least costly route to this objective. After considering the possibilities, one often finds only one remaining and proceeds to take it. Here "more good" and "less bad" have definite meanings, for one is not thinking morally but technically: Only instrumental good is at stake. The morality of what one is doing and of the various ways of doing it is either taken for granted or ignored for the time being. One reaches a conclusion about the best course from a comparative evaluation of premoral goods, but the conclusion is not a moral judgment. For example, if someone is only concerned to reach a destination as quickly as possible, "I ought to take I–95 North to New York" is not a judgment about moral rightness but about efficiency.

5. In other cases, one makes a moral judgment, eliminating possibilities by using previously recognized moral norms. For instance, a mother who believes she ought to divide her estate evenly among several children may consider and reject several possible ways, until she finally finds the way which seems least inequitable. She then makes the division in this way, saying it is less bad than the alternatives—that is, less uneven than the discarded possibilities. Here the moral good of fairness is at stake, and reflection concludes in a moral judgment. But the judgment is different from those proposed by proportionalists. The proportion

here is determined by a moral principle (fairness); by contrast, the proportionalist thinks moral judgments are reached by a comparative evaluation of human goods, without assuming a moral principle to settle the proportions.

6. In sum, practical experience and language do seem to offer support for proportionalism, since people plainly deliberate, find proportions, and talk meaningfully about "greater good" and "lesser evil." But these facts do not support the procedure advocated by the proportionalist, namely, the determination of moral right and wrong by the comparison of benefits and harms promised by alternative possibilities before choice, where the comparison of possibilities is not made in light of prior moral evaluations.[26]

Proportionalists point out that upright people often explain their conscientious judgments by saying they chose the lesser evil or made the best choice possible, all things considered. People who normally respect the property rights of others will make an exception if someone's life is at stake, saying that life outweighs property rights—the one good is greater than the other.

The language people use, although it sounds proportionalist, does not show proportionalism correct. Sometimes people use proportionalist language because they are engaged in rationalizing choices they otherwise would have to admit immoral. More often, people talk about "lesser evils," "proportionate goods" and the like, using these expressions to refer to higher moral principles of judgment.

For example, when an upright person breaks a promise, the consequences of keeping it and of breaking it are evaluated in the light of the Golden Rule; if one would not want others to keep a similar promise to oneself in similar circumstances, then one is released from keeping the promise. Again, when a person says that life outweighs property rights, an appeal is being made to the merely instrumental status of property, which morally ought to serve the intrinsic goods of persons, and to the moral fairness which establishes property rights and so can make exceptions to them.

Question F: Why is proportionalism unacceptable as a theory of moral judgment?

1. One who accepts both unrestricted proportionalism and the Christian doctrine of divine providence (God permits what is bad only to draw good from it) should also accept the following as a moral principle: If in doubt about what is right, try anything. For if one accomplishes what one attempts, one can be certain that on the whole it is for the best, since it must fit into the plan of providence (see *S.t.*, 1, q. 19, a. 6; *S.c.g.*, 3, 71). **This suggests unrestricted proportionalism's theological inadequacy: It confuses human responsibility with God's responsibility.** We, however, are not responsible for the overall greater good and lesser evil—the good and evil of "generally and in the long run"—for only God knows what they are.

2. There are many philosophical arguments against unrestricted proportionalism. For instance, in appraising the good and bad consequences of proposed choices, whose interests are to be considered? To what extent must one try to think of other possible courses of action? How far must one go in investigating consequences? Although these questions have been asked for a century and more, no cogent answers have been given up to now.[27]

3. Partly because of unrestricted proportionalism's vulnerability to the preceding criticisms, many proportionalists have limited the application of the method in various ways. McCormick, for example, has limited it to justifying the evil done to achieve good in respect to a single category of value, where both the good and the evil are brought about in a conflict situation through one and the same act.[28] **But even in so restricted a form, proportionalism is rationally unworkable. Its proponents are unable to tell how benefits and harms can be measured so that proportions can be settled.** Yet benefits and harms in alternatives must be commensurable if there is to be any reasonable judgment as to what is the lesser evil. Although proportionalists are aware of this problem, none has solved it or even offered the plausible beginning of a solution.[29]

Nor is it helpful to say that, while precise measurements of benefits and harms are impossible, rough but adequate estimates can be made. In order to estimate—or even guess at—more and less, one needs a method by which in principle measuring might be done, since an estimate is a guess based on experience with measurements. Hence, one cannot estimate proportions unless one can measure, or at least describe how measurements might be made, and this proportionalists are unable to do.

4. This problem is in principle insoluble, because proportionalism requires that two conditions be met, and the two conditions are incompatible. The two conditions are: first, that a moral judgment is to be made, which means both that a choice must be made and a morally wrong option could be chosen; second, that the option which promises the definitely superior proportion of good to bad be knowable. The following consideration makes it clear that these two conditions cannot be met at the same time.

5. If the first condition is met and the morally wrong option could be chosen, then its morally acceptable alternative must be known. Otherwise, one could not choose wrongly, for one chooses wrongly only when one knows which option one ought to choose and chooses a different option.

6. But when the first condition is met, the second cannot be. The option which promises the definitely superior proportion of good to bad cannot be known by a person who chooses an alternative which promises less. If the superior option were known as superior, its inferior alternative simply could not be chosen. Any reason for choosing it would be a better reason for choosing the superior option. Whenever one really knows that one possibility is definitely superior in terms of the proportion of good to bad it promises, any alternative simply falls away, as explained in question E above, and there is no choice to make.

7. **Thus, although proportionalism is proposed for cases in which one must choose between morally significant alternatives, all that proportionalists really say is that it would be wrong to choose precisely that which practical judgment (as they understand it) would exclude as a possibility for free choice, namely, an alternative measurably inferior in terms of the relevant good and bad.** The truth of the matter is that when such an alternative is recognized in deliberation, no choice about it is possible; it drops out of consideration. Hence, whenever proportionalist judgments are possible, they exclude choices contrary to them by preventing them, not by forbidding them. But a judgment which prevents one from choosing otherwise is not a moral judgment.

Therefore, proportionalism is inherently unable to serve as a method of moral judgment.

One condition—that the alternatives really be morally significant—entails that the one choosing be able to choose the morally evil possibility. There is no moral significance in a choice between right and wrong proposals unless one is in danger of making the wrong choice. By itself, this first condition poses no problem. However, the other condition—that the one about to choose has reached a definite conclusion as to which alternative is preferable in proportionalist terms—requires a knowledge which would preclude the choice the proportionalist claims is wrong.

Why is this so? Because nothing is chosen except insofar as it seems good. If one alternative is seen to promise definitely greater good or lesser evil, then no other can be chosen. This sort of case was described in question E above (also see 2-D). Alternatives under consideration which one sees to promise less, simply drop out of consideration. What reason could there be to choose the less good or the more bad? None.

A proportionalist might object that "reason" is ambiguous. In one sense it means a rational ground for choice; in another sense it means an intelligently grasped but nonrational moving cause—for example, the fear of pain which tempts weak-willed people to choose contrary to their better judgment. The objector might argue that there cannot be a reason in the first sense for choosing anything other than the possibility which promises the definitely greater good or lesser bad, but there can be a reason—a contrary motive—in the second sense. In this way, a proportionalist could claim, immoral choices are made inconsistently with a true moral judgment reached by the proportionalist method.

This objection fails for two reasons. First, it assumes a thesis which is debatable, namely, that one can deliberately choose to follow a nonrational motive without finding some rational ground for adopting it. Second, even granting this thesis for the sake of argument, this sort of choice would be irrelevant to the proportionalist method. This method claims to solve moral problems which arise due to conflicting rational grounds for choices—alternatives which promise diverse proportions of benefit and harm. One does not need proportionalism to support reasons in general against nonrational motives which, by hypothesis, are interesting not for the sake of their promise of benefit and/or mitigation of harm, but somehow without such rational ground. Rather, according to proportionalists, one needs proportionalism to decide for possibilities supported by weightier reasons against those supported by less weighty reasons.

8. **In requiring that two incompatible conditions be met, proportionalism is not false but absurd, literally incoherent.** It is like telling someone to prove a point, but only the most obvious point (logically, one can only prove a conclusion from premises more obvious than itself). Similarly, one can only be morally required to choose one possibility, when another possibility can remain tempting because it promises to yield some benefit or avoid some harm not commensurable with the human goods, including the moral goodness, promised by the morally right choice.

Genuine moral judgments govern free choices. Whenever a free choice must be made, the options between which it is made are incommensurable with each other in respect to relevant intelligible goods. No morally significant option promises a definitely superior proportion of good to bad in any sense interesting to the morally concerned person unless the superiority is measured by a norm which contains a moral "ought." As has been explained, such a norm cannot be derived from a set of premises all of which consider premoral goods and bads and the proportion in which they will be realized by adopting various proposals. When one can proceed from such premises to a practical conclusion, no choice is made and so no moral choice is possible.

People who really think, because of previous choices they have made, that it is better to kill a baby than to risk both its own and its mother's life do not hesitate. If the problem arises, no choice need be made. They say: "It is sad to have to kill babies, but at times it is necessary." Someone who wonders whether it is right to do an abortion to save the mother's life and who must choose whether to do (or to have or "give permission for") an abortion does not see clearly what is the greater good or the lesser evil. On the one hand, such a person sees the-death-of-the-baby-and-my-killing-it. On the other hand: the-likely-death-of-both-mother-and-baby-and-my-allowing-it. Which of these is right is the question moral reflection must help to settle.

9. Proportionalism, though incoherent, is plausible because what it advocates is easily confused with the sound, nonmoral reasoning described in E above. More important, it is plausible because it provides a form for arguments on behalf of morally wrong choices. One who follows emotion against conscience is tempted to say afterward: "I had to make that choice—it was obviously the lesser evil."

One must be careful not to claim that a proportionalist necessarily will approve some violation of a received norm in a difficult case. One never knows what proportionalists will hold to be right and wrong. That is so because, although proportionalism is presented as a rational method for making moral judgments, it really is no such thing. Rather, it is no more than a framework in which each proportionalist expresses his or her own personal judgments, reflecting the preferences settled by the proportionalist's own emotions and prior choices.

Suppose a priest, in hearing confessions, is moved by the very natural, human pity he feels for his penitents to try to make life easier for them by giving them permission (a strange idea, but one intelligible in a legalistic context) to do something forbidden by the moral truth which the Church teaches. In doing this, the priest is making a choice—usually with much struggle and soul-searching at first—which determines his own self with respect to the human goods involved in the matter at issue. When confirmed, unrepented, and integrated into his character, this choice will lead the priest to regard the relevant good or goods differently than does one who is faithful to the moral truth. This different regard will affect his personal judgments on matters where the same goods are at issue, not only on the particular question he directly chose about.

Question G: How does proportionalism misconstrue the nature of morality?

1. Morality is primarily concerned with the fulfillment of persons in their existential dimension, an ongoing fulfillment which resides mainly in individual and communal choices, not in the definite states of affairs caused in carrying out choices (see 5-G; *S.t.,* 1–2, q. 57, aa. 4–5). However, as question B above points out, proportionalists leave out of consideration the reality human goods have simply in being chosen. **Thus they misconstrue the nature of morality, reducing it to effectiveness in bringing about benefit and preventing harm.** At the same time they ignore the personal and interpersonal significance choices have apart from the tangible benefit or harm they lead to.[30]

2. Proportionalists are correct in believing that the beneficial and harmful implications of choices are morally important. Right choices and commitments

are directed to human goods, including substantive goods like life and truth whose realization is mainly apart from choice itself. There is no genuine love of self, of neighbor, or of God which does not embrace and serve the goods of all dimensions of persons (see 5-H).

3. As the argument from providence in question F above makes clear, however, human persons have limited responsibility. We are responsible for choosing rightly and carrying out right choices; in doing so, we serve human fulfillment in a responsible way.[31] However, for the realization of human good on the whole and in the long run, we must trust God. We do not have the same responsibility God has for the good he wills. That is why St. Paul teaches that we may not do evil that good may come of it (see Rom 3.8).[32] We do God's will by being faithful; he will accomplish the total good he wills by bringing all things to fulfillment in the Lord Jesus.

4. The faithfulness required of Christians is an essential part of their prophetic style of life (see 23-E). For example, a woman who refuses an abortion which she has been told is medically indicated to save her life can bear outstanding witness to her faith and hope in God: faith if her refusal is based on her willingness to live by the Church's teaching and to leave in God's hands the risk of the disaster which might occur; hope if her choice shows her confidence that disaster accepted in Jesus is not final. By contrast, a woman who chooses to kill her unborn child to save her own life gives no such witness to faith and hope in God, even if she acts in good faith.

5. Misunderstanding morality as they do, proportionalists think of an upright choice as a mere means to an end beyond itself. **They overlook the self-creativity of choices by which persons, individually and in communion, constitute themselves participants in goods which continue to unfold as they are responsibly pursued.** Many proportionalists attack absolute norms—for example, "Adultery is always wrong"—as legalistic impositions which subordinate persons to rules. They fail to see that such absolutes make possible the commitments which are essential for genuine development. For instance, the absolute prohibition of adultery is essential to the authenticity of marital commitment; this prohibition defines marriage by what it excludes, while leaving its positive reality to each couple's creative unfolding of their unique marital friendship. To limit human goods as proportionalism does, by focusing on their realization outside choice itself, tends to exclude such creativity. Instead married couples are reduced to pursuing fixed goals, such as "happiness" predefined in psychological terms or "optimum sexual adjustment" predefined in physiological terms.

Human acts are not just ways of getting results, as proportionalists tend to think. As was explained (2-H), to make a free choice is to determine oneself. Human action is soul-making. Moral acts are ultimately most important insofar as they make a difference to the self one is constituting by doing the act. Ultimately, it would profit nothing if one saved the mortal lives of everyone in the world by committing one mortal sin.

Proportionalism also undermines unconditional commitments, which are essential to Christian personal vocation. Those who have lived in any state of life for a few years have a very different awareness of its good and bad points than they had upon entering it. Marital and religious vows often are set aside today with the encouragement of proportionalist theologians, who suggest that in some cases the choice to set them aside is a lesser evil than continuing fidelity without any apparent benefits.

Question H: Do proportionalists respond successfully to criticism?

1. One response to the argument that human goods are incommensurable is the claim that there is a hierarchy of goods. This is true; in fact, there are several senses in which goods form a hierarchy. But none provides the common denominator proportionalism needs to make commensurable the human goods and bads one understands in the alternatives available for a free choice.

Is there an objective hierarchy of values or not? There certainly is a hierarchy of values in one sense: Sentient satisfactions as such are not adequate human goods. They are valuable only insofar as they contribute to some aspect of intelligible human fulfillment. Moreover, extrinsic and merely instrumental goods, such as money, are not in themselves fulfillments of the human person. They can be means; they also can be obstacles.

There is a second sense in which one can correctly say there is an objective hierarchy of values: What is morally good is superior to what is morally bad. Very often when people talk about a proper scale of values, they mean that one ought not to act for goods in immoral ways, but ought rather to prefer moral uprightness even when it requires that one give up something, perhaps even forgo something which would be genuinely fulfilling. Analogous to this is the ranking of things which the Christian carries out, even within the field of what is morally acceptable. For example, according to a Catholic sense of values, celibacy or virginity for the Lord is superior to marriage (see DS 1810/980; LG 42).

Moreover, within the perspective of faith—since faith itself is an act which fulfills human persons by forming their relationship with God—the religious level of the existential domain is most important. Nothing is more important for the Christian than to be in unity with the love of God which comes to us in our Lord Jesus (see Rom 8.35–39).

However, there are two senses in which there is not a hierarchy among the basic human goods. In the first place, they are all essential and closely related aspects of human fulfillment. In the second place, when it comes to making choices, there is no objective standard by which one can say that any of the human goods immanent in a particular intelligible possibility is definitely a greater good than another. For example, parents who deliberate the evening before Thanksgiving whether to spend the next morning having a leisurely family breakfast or to use it to join in a special liturgy (which would mean getting up at a certain time, dressing the children, and so on) cannot reach a conclusion by comparing goods or bads to find which alternative is measurably better. The same thing holds in much more important matters, such as determining one's personal vocation; if a choice must be made, no comparison of the goods and bads one sees in the alternatives will settle what one ought to do.

2. McCormick points out that in making choices people adopt a hierarchy and so in fact commensurate goods. This is true; but the commensuration here is not that required by proportionalism. Proportionalism requires comparison of goods in a moral judgment antecedent to choice; when commensuration occurs in choice itself, the time for moral judgment is past. (A theory which tries to ground moral norms in choices was criticized in 4-C.)

For a long time opponents of proportionalism have been pointing out the problem of incommensurability to its proponents. Most of the latter make no attempt to answer this objection. McCormick does try. Part of his answer to the problem of the noncommensurability of goods is that one makes the noncommensurable commensurable by choice: "... What do we do? *Somehow or other,* in fear and trembling, we commensurate. In a sense we *adopt* a hierarchy. We go to war to protect our freedom. That means we are willing to sacrifice life to protect this good. If 'give me liberty or give me death' does not involve *some kind* of commensuration, then I do not know what commensurating means" (italics his).[33] And McCormick goes on to add several examples like this one. (He also gives examples—such as the assertion of Jesus that there is no point in gaining the world if one loses one's soul in the process—in which the comparison is not proportionalist, but is based on presupposed moral standards.)

Commensuration does occur once one adopts a hierarchy. About this McCormick is right. People do choose to go to war; having done so, they say it is a lesser evil than loss of liberty (unless they have some other justification for war). The commensuration is in the choice. Choices do determine the limits of options to be considered, consequences to be inquired about, and persons to be taken into account; when choice cuts off deliberation, these boundaries are drawn automatically. Moreover, choice does determine which good henceforth will be considered greater and which evil lesser, because the good with which one identifies in choosing becomes part of one's personal scale of value.

But by locating commensuration in choice, McCormick implicitly admits that proportionalism has failed. It was to have been a rational method of moral judgment, and a rational method should determine what is right and wrong before one chooses. In other words, one should reach a judgment of conscience first and then choose afterwards. By locating the commensuration in choice, McCormick admits that the process of proportionalism is just the opposite: First one makes a choice and then one finds a reason for it. When this process is followed to justify an action one otherwise would have to admit immoral, it has a proper title: rationalization.

But there are cases in which antecedent choice does determine true moral duties. McCormick refers to them, saying: "I mean to suggest that we do all possible to reduce the incommensurability. In ordinary daily living this reduction occurs via personal aims, vocations, life commitments, possibilities."[34] Again, McCormick is correct in thinking that prior commitments can determine what is better. But this fact is of no help to a proportionalist, for they do it by introducing a moral principle of judgment, not by rendering premoral benefits and harms commensurable. For example, a man who is deliberating whether to divorce the wife of his youth and marry his young secretary can reduce the incommensurability by choosing according to his marital commitment. Of course, he also can abandon this commitment and rationalize that by doing so he is on the whole and in the long run giving the best possible service toward the single good of creative growth toward integration of all concerned.[35]

3. Proportionalists claim that commensurating the incommensurable is a problem for every moralist who is at all reasonable. But this is question-begging; it assumes that all reasonable moralists make at least some use of proportionalism. However, sound moralists who seem to make use of proportionalism can often be understood as proceeding in a very different way. Rather than making moral judgments by what is proportionate in premoral terms, they determine what is proportionate by moral standards.

In response to the argument that proportionalism requires comparison of incommensurable goods, McCormick says that a proportionalist "might urge that if proportionate reason involves measuring the unmeasurable, then what is the meaning and function of proportionate reason in the standard understandings of the double effect?"[36] My answer to this challenge is that when traditional moralists talked about "proportionate good" in their discussions of the principle of double effect, they perhaps slipped into proportionalism (which they had never articulated as a general theory). But I think that in many cases they referred to moral norms which govern the acceptance of side effects. Thus a physician prepared to accept the harsh side effects of some form of therapy for his patients when he would not approve the same sort of treatment for his or her loved ones shows immoral partiality. In such a case, although the other conditions of a standard understanding of double effect would be fulfilled, there would be lack of proportionate reason for accepting the harmful side effects, and so the choice of that type of therapy would be immoral.

McCormick admits that there are serious and unresolved theoretical problems in the use of expressions such as "lesser evil" and "proportionate reason." But he claims that anyone who accepts as morally licit any killing, in the face of the prescription "Thou shalt not kill," has the same problem.[37] This claim is false. In various works I have articulated a consistent account of the ethics of killing, which excludes absolutely any choice to bring about death, but does not exclude absolutely other choices whose execution causes death as a foreseen and accepted side effect. Such other choices will be justified, not by a proportionalist weighing of values, but by moral norms such as impartiality.[38]

In his discussion of self-defense, St. Thomas Aquinas says: "An act done with a good intention can still be rendered illegitimate if it is not proportioned to the end. And so if someone uses greater violence than necessary in defending his own life, it will be illicit" (*S.t.*, 2–2, q. 64, a. 7, c.). This text has been used to claim Thomas for the cause of proportionalism.

But this claim misinterprets the text. Thomas is not comparing benefits and harms as proportionalism requires; he is not trying to balance the harm to the attacker against the benefit of preserving one's life. The proportion is between the force used and the purpose of self-defense, which Thomas considers justifiable on other grounds. His point is that if the damage to the attacker is truly to be an acceptable side effect, then it must be no more than necessary to defend oneself. Thus, a store owner who fired a shotgun toward the heads of a pair of robbers instead of toward their legs, when he considered either adequate for self-defense, would violate the requirement of proportion Thomas states.

4. Some proportionalists suggest that commensuration can be achieved by using communally accepted standards of comparison. To use communally accepted standards after criticizing them in the light of moral truth is sound procedure, but it is not proportionalism. For in this case, moral principles, not a comparison of premoral benefit and harm, determine the moral judgment. But to make uncriticized community standards the basis of moral judgment is to adopt another theory criticized above (4-E). Christians who accept commonly held estimations of values as the basis for their moral judgments are conforming to the "world" rather than renewing their minds by conforming to Christ.

Joseph Fuchs, S.J., says that the value of acts is settled by weighing the priority and urgency of different values "for the individual, for interpersonal relations and for human society, in connection, of course, with the total reality of man and his society and in view of his whole culture."[39] While this phrasing is ambiguous and the remainder of the essay is far from clear, Fuchs seems to think that the given culture enables one to weigh.[40] If he does mean this, he is adopting the nonrational principle of the choices people have made in the past in a particular society—choices morally good and morally bad alike—as the basis for morality.

In a somewhat similar move, McCormick suggests that in some cases we know by experience what is right and in others "we must proceed to normative statements gradually by trial and error."[41] He does not notice that experience and experiment cannot settle any moral issue unless a moral principle is presupposed. To ignore this requirement amounts to inviting people to accept the personal or communal satisfactoriness of the results of various ways of acting as a standard for judging their rightness—in other words, what we do is right if it gets us what we want.

5. In an implicit admission that there is no rational way of determining proportions, McCormick fell back upon spontaneous and instinctive moral judgments as a test. Joseph Fuchs, S.J., similarly suggested that we somehow commensurate without being conscious of it and so are unable to explain how we do it.[42] In making moves such as these, proportionalists retreat into another faulty theoretical position (see 4-B).

McCormick holds that the relationship underlying a proportionalist judgment "is often grasped spontaneously, nondiscursively, and therefore obscurely to a large extent." He goes on: "I believe and do not apologize for the fact that our emotions and religious commitments do function in our value judgments in a way that is sometimes beyond reduction to reasoning processes or analytic arguments."[43] He sums up: "I would say that, even though our spontaneous and instinctive moral judgments can be affected by cultural distortions and can be confused with rather obvious but deeply ingrained conventional fears and biases, still they remain a more reliable test of the humanizing and dehumanizing, of the morally right and wrong, of proportion, than our discursive arguments."[44]

Now matters become clear. Over the years one had supposed that McCormick wished Catholics to follow the judgment of dissenting theologians rather than the Church's teaching because in his view their judgments were based on good reasons while the Church's teaching is not rationally defensible. According to this account by McCormick, however, it turns out that at bottom moral norms depend on spontaneous and instinctive moral judgments. This sort of view was criticized (4-B). But even if it were right, it would at least make more sense to entrust oneself to the accumulated wisdom of the Church, proposed with bad reasons by the magisterium, than to the consensus of dissenting theologians, proposed with bad reasons by Richard McCormick.

6. Thus an irony emerges. **Proportionalism begins by claiming to be a reasonable method of moral judgment, opposed to irrational moral norms for which no cogent argument can be provided; it ends in intuitionism, unable to provide any rational grounds at all for the exceptions to traditional norms which it proposes.** People who set aside the teaching authority of the Church as insufficiently reasonable on the basis of theological dissent grounded in proportionalism are making an act of faith in the untestable and rationally unsupportable intuitions of dissenting theologians.

Summary

Some Catholic moral theologians have adopted a theory called "consequentialism" or "proportionalism." This is the view that a moral judgment is based on a comparative evaluation of benefits and harms promised by the possibilities for choice; one ought to choose the possibility which offers the best proportion of good to bad. There are many varieties of proportionalism, but this comparative evaluation of benefits and harms is central to all.

Because they are interested in measurable benefits and harms, proportionalists focus on the instantiation of human goods—their concrete realization in states of affairs—which comes about in making choices and carrying them out. This, however, is not an adequate account of the realization of human goods. It overlooks the fact that because choice is self-determining, goods rightly chosen fulfill persons existentially simply in being chosen. Furthermore, to avoid approving the choice of moral evil, proportionalism requires that the basic human goods which can be sacrificed for a "proportionate reason" not include moral specification. Thus it regards them as "premoral," "nonmoral," "ontic," or "physical."

The plausibility of proportionalism arises in part from the inadequacy of the moral theories criticized in chapter four; its proponents claim that it meets the criteria of an adequate moral theory. A basic proportionalist recommendation, "Choose the lesser evil," seems self-evident; it would be absurd to say, "Choose the greater evil." Proportionalism also seems necessary to account for the fact that many moral norms admit of exceptions. Finally, some Catholic proportionalists claim to find instances of the use of proportionalism in the theological tradition.

However, proportionalism is not the only alternative to the theories criticized in chapter four; another is set forth here in chapters seven through twelve. Proportionalism also involves difficulties of its own. "Choose the lesser evil" would be a workable principle only if goods and evils could be comparatively measured as proportionalism requires; but this cannot be done. As for the fact that most moral norms admit of exceptions, this does not show that proportionalism is at work; rather, it simply shows that at times one appeals from norms which admit of exceptions to absolute, exceptionless principles (such as the Golden Rule) in which nonabsolute norms are grounded. Finally, although some classical moral theologians occasionally proposed arguments which look like proportionalism, they did not articulate and defend the method.

Proportionalism seems to be verified by the experience one sometimes has in deliberating of finding one possibility definitely better overall than the others; the others simply drop out of consideration. In fact, however, this experience does not support the proportionalist account of moral judgment. For when all options but one drop out of consideration, there is no need to make a free choice, and none is made. This happens in two sorts of cases: technical reasoning about instrumental goods and moral judgments which follow from one's prior and now unquestioned moral judgments and choices.

This suggests why proportionalism is unacceptable as a theory of moral judgment. Its proponents cannot say how to measure benefits and harms in the options so that their proportion can be settled. Moreover, it involves two incompatible conditions: first, that a morally wrong choice be possible; second, that the alternative which is superior in terms of the proportion of good to bad be known. But this cannot be, for if the alternative which is superior in these terms is known, other possibilities fall away, and there can be no morally wrong choice. In other words, proportionalism simply says it would be wrong to choose what its account of moral judgment would render it impossible to choose. Since proportionalism is inherently unworkable, it is not false but incoherent.

Morality is primarily concerned with the fulfillment of persons in their existential dimension—a fulfillment which resides mainly in individual and communal choices, not in the definite states of affairs which result from carrying them out. But proportionalism thinks of choice merely as a means to an end beyond itself. Proportionalists mistakenly view as legalistic impositions norms which admit of no exceptions (such as "Adultery is always wrong") rather than recognizing them as essential conditions for the commitments necessary for creative human living.

Their attempts to respond to criticism have led some proportionalists to say that, ultimately, a moral judgment is based on a prior choice or on an instinctive, intuitive perception of right and wrong. Hence, an irony: Proportionalism begins by claiming to be a more reasonable method of moral judgment than supposedly unreasonable traditional norms; but it ends by admitting itself unable to provide rational grounds for the exceptions it proposes to traditional norms.

Appendix: A restricted theory of proportionate reason

In "A Commentary on the Commentaries," in *Doing Evil to Achieve Good,* McCormick tried to bypass the problem of noncommensurability of values by limiting his proportionalism. He abandoned the attempt to evaluate long-term effects beyond the act itself, distinguished "proportionate reason" from "net good," and agreed that proportionalism is incoherent if it means weighing all the values (including goods of diverse categories) against one another in an attempt to produce the greatest net good.[45] He suggested that there is a proportionate reason for doing evil to achieve good when the good sought will not be undermined by the proposed action; there is lack of proportionate reason when the good sought "is being pursued in a way calculated in human judgment (not without prediscursive elements) to undermine it."[46] "Thus, where there is a question of taking life, such taking is proportionate only if it is, all things considered, the better service of *life itself* in the tragic circumstances."[47] McCormick maintained that the only question to be answered by his limited proportionalism is the modest one: ". . . is the good end being sought by means involving nonmoral evil promoted and not undermined in this action or is it undermined?"[48]

Consideration of this question makes it clear that McCormick has not succeeded in bypassing the problem of noncommensurability. A calculated judgment whether the good is promoted and not undermined still would require comparison of the alternatives of acting and not acting, to see which promises a better proportion of benefit to harm (the lesser evil). But the central argument in question F above shows that where there can be a choice, there is noncommensurability of the goods in the possibilities open to choice. For example, a person who hesitates to take life in the service of life may question whether any other realization of life can make up for the destruction of this life here and now. Again, such a person may think that in judging what is a "better service to life itself" one cannot leave out of account the difference between serving-life-by-choosing-to-kill and serving-life-by-allowing-to-die. If so, this perceived difference blocks commensuration, requires a moral judgment by a method other than proportionalism, and makes a morally significant choice both possible and necessary.

McCormick's subsequent assimilation of his own view to that of Peter Knauer, S.J., also shows that McCormick's restricted theory of proportionate reason has not bypassed the problem of noncommensurability. In an article published in 1967, Knauer seemed to circumvent the problem of the noncommensurability of goods by reducing the concept of commensurate reason to that of a genuinely efficient means to a definite goal.[49] I criticized this position by pointing out that it omits moral considerations other than efficiency, and so leaves an opening for fanaticism. For example, a mad but efficient scientist could defend any sort of human experimentation really necessary to obtain some piece of knowledge he sought. But I also pointed out that Knauer might reply that "the fanatical investigator would really damage the cause of scientific inquiry by giving it a bad name."[50]

The point of this remark was that Knauer could avoid the implication of reducing morality to efficiency by reverting to a consideration of noncommensurable goods—for example, the cause of scientific inquiry as such, which is indeterminate in reference to the definite goals of specific inquiries, which can be more or less efficiently pursued. I pointed out this inconsistency in Knauer's article by citing the way he handled the question of whether a woman may rescue her children from a concentration camp by committing adultery. Knauer responded to this problem with a question: "Does life or freedom have any value if in the end one is forced to give up all human rights and in principle be exposed to every extortion?"[51] The argument implicit in this question clearly involves an appeal to noncommensurable goods.

In 1980 Knauer returned to the topic of his earlier essay, but now emphasized again and again that there is no proportionate reason if the action involving harm will "generally and in the long run" undermine the good being sought here and now. McCormick reported this development of Knauer's position and identified his own restricted proportionalism with it. Recalling my criticism of Knauer's earlier effort, McCormick suggested that Knauer's consideration of the good "generally and in the long run" adequately handles my objection concerning fanaticism.[52] But McCormick did not notice that the price Knauer pays is a renewed acceptance of the onus of commensurating the incommensurable, namely, the specific goal sought here and now and the value in general, whose indeterminate set of instantiations is referred to by the phrase "generally and in the long run."

An example will help to make clear that the benefit and harm present in a particular choice directed toward a definite objective are incommensurable with the benefits and harms which might be brought about in the same category of value in the indeterminate set of its future instantiations. The point of the nuclear deterrent is to prevent the use of nuclear weapons, and their likely destruction of life, by potential enemies. Clearly, there is no way to determine whether the present threat to destroy enemy noncombatants is or is not undermining the value of human life generally and in the long run. Opponents of the deterrent probably would say so; they might claim that the commitment to nuclear deterrence has corrupted people's hearts and paved the way for the worldwide acceptance of easy abortion and other antilife practices. Defenders of the deterrent probably would deny this. The latter also might insist that freedom from Communist domination, seemingly ruled out of consideration by restricted proportionalism, must be taken into account, even though it is a value of a different category.

This brings us to another aspect of McCormick's attempt to salvage proportionalism. As initially stated, the restricted theory applies plausibly to only a few cases, such as abortion to save the mother when otherwise both mother and child are expected to die.[53] But McCormick and other theologians had invoked proportionalism to justify the revision of received Catholic moral teaching in other, more complex cases, in which values in diverse categories must be compared. For example, they argued that contraception can be justified because the premoral evil of preventing new life can be outweighed by the good of marital love. McCormick suggests that in such cases the incommensurability is reduced by the causal connections among the various goods. For example, sexual abstinence can harm marital love and thereby the procreative good itself, and so by this route a proportionalist assessment might be made.[54]

In making this suggestion, McCormick even more clearly undertakes to calculate net good by weighing long-term effects beyond the act itself. For example, in and of itself the choice to contracept does absolutely nothing but determine the one who makes it to try to prevent the coming to be of a new person. The end in view (which is claimed to be the offsetting good) can be realized only beyond the contraceptive act itself. (This point is clearest when a contraceptive like the pill is used, and the contraceptive behavior is altogether separated from sexual intercourse. But the same is true of all contraceptive choices, regardless of the contraceptive method used.) In complex cases of this sort, even more than the simpler ones, it is clear that there is no objective way to assess proportions of benefits and harms, and judge what is the best service to the good sought. McCormick himself sometimes seems to sense this difficulty, for it is this which leads him to speak of commensurating by the adoption of a hierarchy. He sums up his position: "Thus, I see 'association of basic values,' 'proportionate reason,' and 'adoption of a hierarchy of values' as attempting to say the same thing, or at least as very closely related."[55]

The constraints of McCormick's reconstructed proportionalism also led him to offer some implausible accounts of perfectly sound positions. For instance, it often is argued that the bombing of Nagasaki was justified because fewer people were killed by it than would have died on both sides had the war dragged on. McCormick, commendably, wished to show against this view that obliteration bombing is immoral. Applying his theory of associated goods, he argued that this manner of saving life tended to undermine it in the long run by injuring the associated good of human liberty: "Making innocent (noncombatant) persons the object of our targeting is a form of extortion in international affairs that contains an implicit denial of human freedom. Human freedom is undermined when extortionary actions are accepted and elevated and universalized. Because such freedom is an associated good upon which the very good of life heavily depends, undermining it in the manner of my defense of life is undermining life itself—is disproportionate."[56]

McCormick could not say that terror bombing is evil simply because those who engage in it choose to destroy human lives, for his proportionalism requires that choices to destroy human lives be justifiable if there is a proportionate reason. Many would accept the saving of a larger number of lives as a proportionate reason, but McCormick rightly rejects their view. Hence he is reduced to this argument. It is quite implausible, because it is not clear that extortion undermines freedom, that the good of life depends on freedom (in the same sense of the word "freedom"), or that the lives that perhaps were at stake later on made the bombing of Nagasaki wrong if it were not wrong in itself.

From McCormick's further explanations, it becomes clear that the freedom he thinks implicitly denied by extortion is the moral liberty of the enemy: "If a nation is wrongfully aggressing, once again it is the Christian's faith—and a well-founded one—that that nation can and must cease and desist from wrongful aggression without our harming innocents to make that nation do so. There is no *necessary connection* between our doing harm to noncombatants (for example, killing innocent civilians to stop that nation) and that nation's ceasing unjust aggression. To say that there is would be to insult the humanity of the aggressor by denying his liberty. For unjust aggressors are free to cease unjust aggression."[57] The freedom on which he argues that human life itself heavily depends is political liberty, "on the grounds that a real threat to that is tantamount to a threat against an individual's life."[58]

But the moral liberty of the enemy and the political liberty on which life is said to depend differ. The former is freedom of self-determination, while the latter is a specific form of the freedom to do as one pleases. The difference is demonstrated by the fact that slaves can be morally good or bad persons. Thus McCormick's attempt to argue against obliteration bombing within the constraints of his reconstructed proportionalism falls into equivocation. The argument also is implausible in resting the immorality of destroying the lives of noncombatants upon the alleged insult to the humanity of the aggressor. It is not clear that terror bombing denies liberty, for extortion leaves those against whom it is used a morally free choice, though a different choice than they would have had otherwise.

Still, McCormick's introduction of the requirement of necessary connection was laudable to the extent that it limited proportionalism. One would not have a proportionate reason for doing a nonmoral evil which would not be necessary except for another's wrongdoing. Unfortunately for consistency, the requirement of necessary connection invalidates other arguments, such as the one on contraception. Christian couples have the morally free choice to express and cultivate their love (and thus indirectly serve the good of procreation) in many nongenital ways, and also by sexual abstinence. There is no necessary connection between preventing the coming to be of a new person and these goods, which are allegedly served by the use of contraceptives.

Moreover, many of McCormick's proportionalist colleagues will deny that there must be a necessary connection—that is, a causal relationship apart from another's free choice—between the doing of a nonmoral evil and the overriding value for which it is done. Thus, although McCormick made this requirement central in his 1978 reconstruction, by 1980 he had received criticism of it from persons whose views he respected. Although he thought he could deal with this criticism to some extent, he no longer felt certain that there must be a necessary connection to justify the use of force as such: "The necessary-connection requirement—if it is valid, and I am far from sure that it is—pertains . . . ."[59]

Notes

1. Some typical examples of proportionalism are in a collection: Charles E. Curran and Richard A. McCormick, S.J., eds., *Readings in Moral Theology, No. 1: Moral Norms and Catholic Tradition* (New York: Paulist Press, 1979), esp. the articles by Louis Janssens, Joseph Fuchs, S.J., and Bruno Schüller, S.J. McCormick summarizes the position, counting himself among those who hold it: *Notes on Moral Theology: 1965–1980* (Washington, D.C.: University Press of America, 1981), 709–11 (hereinafter cited as "*Notes*"). McCormick's evolution can be followed. In *Notes,* 349–67, McCormick showed reserve and called the method "consequentialism" (see esp. 359). By *Notes,* 529–44, McCormick defended Fuchs against critics of the method he then accepted.

2. Timothy E. O'Connell, *Principles for a Catholic Morality* (New York: Seabury Press, 1978), 152–53, argued that as finite, social, temporal entities, human persons cannot act without bringing about both good and bad, and asserted as if it were a conclusion: "We do evil that good may come of it." He then enunciated a simple version of proportionalism (153): "These reflections upon experience, then, lead us to the answer to our questions. What ought we to do? We ought to do that action which maximizes the good and minimizes the evil. How do we discover the right thing to do? We discover it by balancing the various 'goods' and 'bads' that are part of the situation and by trying to achieve the greatest proportion of goods to bads. What constitutes right action? It is that action which contains the proportionally greatest maximization of good and minimization of evil."

3. Charles E. Curran, *New Perspectives in Moral Theology* (Notre Dame, Ind.: Fides Publishers, 1974), 19, summed up the requirement: "The newer approaches call for a weighing and comparison of all the values involved so that I perform the action which brings about the greatest possible good. Note the obvious consequentialist calculus in such a determination but also the fact that the relative importance attached to the different values involved transcends the present limited situation and can be verified only in the context of the fullness of Christian experience." Curran did not explain how this fullness is brought to bear in setting aside norms accepted in the entire Christian tradition.

4. McCormick, *Notes,* 718, began by suggesting that Paul Ramsey and I would agree with the practical judgment of the proportionalists in all such cases (which is not entirely true) and that the only issue is the reason for the conclusion. He then proceeded more accurately: "The defenders of the

traditional distinction would argue that the conclusion is correct in so far as, and only in so far as, the death of the fetus can be said to be indirect. The revisionists, so to speak, would argue that the real reason for the conclusion is that *in such circumstances* the abortion is proportionately grounded, is the lesser evil. When one is faced with two options both of which involve unavoidable (nonmoral) evil, one ought to choose the lesser evil." Many theologians who have adopted proportionalism have gone beyond justifying abortion to save the mother when otherwise both would die. See McCormick, *Notes,* 515–16; John F. Dedek, *Human Life: Some Moral Issues* (New York: Sheed and Ward, 1972), 86–90; Charles E. Curran, *Contemporary Problems in Moral Theology* (Notre Dame, Ind.: Fides Publishers, 1970), 144–45; *New Perspectives in Moral Theology,* 190–93; note the concise formulation, 191: "Thus abortion could be justified to save the life of the mother or to avert very grave psychological or physical harm to the mother with the realization that this must truly be grave harm that will perdure over some time and not just a temporary depression."

5. Richard A. McCormick, S.J., in *Doing Evil to Achieve Good* (cited hereinafter as *"Doing Evil"*), ed. Richard A. McCormick, S.J., and Paul Ramsey (Chicago: Loyola University Press, 1978), 234–35, says that his approach does not involve considering all the relevant values and comparing them quantitatively. Rather, when the object of an act includes harm to a basic human good, one needs a proportionate reason for doing the act. One should do it only if it gives the "best service" possible in the circumstances to that good. Nevertheless, McCormick continues (232–33) to use expressions such as "overrides" and "lesser evil," which imply quantitative comparisons if they mean anything at all. Also consider the language McCormick uses (*Notes*, 710) to explain how some acts are always wrong: They are so "because when *taken as a whole*, the nonmoral evil outweighs the nonmoral good, and therefore the act is disproportionate" (emphasis McCormick's). Moreover, once one allows the willingness to damage some human good to be overridden by some other relevant good, one stops reflection arbitrarily if one could and does not carry out similar comparisons with respect to other relevant benefits and harms.

6. See McCormick, *Notes,* 530–35 and 717; "Current Theology: Notes on Moral Theology: 1981," *Theological Studies,* 43 (1982), 83–86.

7. For an introduction to some of the more important philosophical variations and an interesting critical discussion of consequentialism: Alan Donagan, *The Theory of Morality* (Chicago: University of Chicago Press, 1977), 189–209.

8. McCormick, *Notes,* 710, says that if a kind of act is specified sufficiently—"For instance: abortion of a fetus in order to avoid a medical (delivery) bill. That is always wrong"—one can be sure it never will be right, "because when *taken as a whole*, the nonmoral evil outweighs the nonmoral good, and therefore the action is disproportionate" and will be so in "*any* conceivable circumstances." But he provides no criterion by which one can be sure that in some case there will not be a "proportionate reason" (assuming for the sake of argument that this expression makes sense). What if the person saving the money were a very poor widow living in a slum in a backward country, who faced these alternatives: (1) accept a free abortion from U.S. AID; (2) carry the baby to term and die for lack of medical care (if, for instance, she were unable to deliver without surgery); or (3) spend all she has, which she needs for her children's very survival, on the surgery?

9. Some proportionalist theologians claim that proportionalism simply is natural law, but they provide no justification for this assertion. See O'Connell, op. cit., 144–54. Virtually nothing O'Connell says (125–43) about the history supports this identification. See also Gerard J. Hughes, S.J., *Authority in Morals: An Essay in Christian Ethics* (London: Heythrop Monographs, 1978), 26–63, whose version of proportionalism is notably different from O'Connell's, but who also wishes to identify proportionalism with natural law.

10. Richard A. McCormick, S.J., *How Brave a New World: Dilemmas in Bioethics* (Garden City, N.Y.: Doubleday, 1981), 5. Comparison of this statement by McCormick with Germain G. Grisez, *Contraception and the Natural Law* (Milwaukee, Wis.: Bruce, 1964), 62, shows the extent to which there is agreement in identifying the goods. All in the "school" McCormick mentions are influenced by St. Thomas Aquinas.

11. See Richard A. McCormick, S.J., "To Save or Let Die: The Dilemma of Modern Medicine," *Journal of the American Medical Association,* 229 (1974), 175; A. R. Jonsen, R. H. Phibbs, W. H. Tooley, and M. J. Garland, "Critical Issues in Newborn Intensive Care: A Conference Report and Policy Proposal," *Pediatrics,* 55 (1975), 760–67; Richard A. McCormick, S.J., "A Proposal of 'Quality of Life' Criteria for Sustaining Life," *Hospital Progress,* 56 (September 1975), 79. In the first of these articles, McCormick opened the door, by suggesting potentiality for human relationships as a criterion for saving the lives of severely defective newborns; Jonsen and his coauthors went further, quoting McCormick; and McCormick responded by quoting their conclusions and endorsing them as

similar to his own proposal, which he was willing to formulate in terms of potentiality for "meaningful life." Admitting the phrase to be packed with implications and claiming the individual still has a value, McCormick nevertheless concluded that life might not be worthwhile if the individual does not stand to gain from it.

12. An inadequate account of human goods along these lines is the object of criticism by those value theorists who hold values to be a priori, nonformal principles. See, for instance, Max Scheler, *Formalism in Ethics and Non-Formal Ethics of Values: A New Attempt toward the Foundation of an Ethical Personalism* (Evanston, Ill.: Northwestern University Press, 1973), 9–23; Dietrich von Hildebrand, *Ethics* (New York: David McKay, 1952), 95–105. Unfortunately, such theories of value go too far in the direction of making values entities independent of persons fulfilled by them. The truth is in a middle position, which recognizes both the transcendence of values to the concrete instances in which they are realized and their metaphysical status as aspects of the fulfillment of persons.

13. See McCormick, *Notes,* 529–43, esp. 534; 643–49; 693–97.

14. See McCormick, *Doing Evil,* 219–20 and 257–59, with respect to intending the sin of another. With respect to blasphemy, see *Notes,* 581, where McCormick treats blasphemy, theft, adultery, and murder as similar in presupposing that if they are always wrong, it is because they are defined to include the value judgments that the nonmoral evil is not justified by an adequate good end.

15. For an explicit use of proportionalism and its distinction between ontic and moral evil to justify divorce and remarriage, see Philip S. Keane, S.S., *Sexual Morality: A Catholic Perspective* (New York: Paulist Press, 1977), 144–46 and 218–19, nn. 108–9.

16. Aware of the strength of their position insofar as it takes account of this important truth—as, for instance, scholastic natural-law theory fails to do—many proportionalists call their approach "teleological" (an ethics of fulfillment) and label all alternatives to proportionalism "deontological" (ethics of arbitrary commandments and of duty). The division is inadequate; the theory laid out in chapters seven through ten falls into neither category.

17. McCormick, *Doing Evil,* 38. There is a legitimate sense, recognized by classical moral theology, in which it is right to "choose the lesser evil." If someone erroneously supposes that he or she has no morally right option (including delaying choosing), his or her conscience is perplexed. In reality, there must be a morally right possibility, but if a person sincerely trying to see what is right and do it cannot discern any way to avoid choosing what seems morally evil, then what seems to be the lesser moral evil should be chosen. See Bernard Häring, *The Law of Christ: Moral Theology for Priests and Laity,* trans. Edwin G. Kaiser, C.Pp.S. (Westminster, Md.: Newman Press, 1961), 1:156. "Choose the lesser evil" in this sense plainly is another matter altogether from McCormick's "rule of Christian reason," which purports to guide one in forming a correct conscience by comparing nonmoral evils, not counsel an erroneous conscience to minimize moral evil when it is mistakenly regarded as inevitable.

18. See St. Thomas Aquinas, *Summa theologiae,* 1–2, q. 94, aa. 4–5; 2–2, q. 51, a. 4; q. 120; *De malo,* q. 2, a. 4, ad 13; *In decem libros Ethicorum,* v, 16.

19. See McCormick, *Notes,* 701, for the claim that the proportionalists are merely extending a method traditionally accepted in Catholic moral theology.

20. See Richard A. McCormick, S.J., "Moral Theology Since Vatican II: Clarity or Chaos," *Cross Currents,* 29 (Spring 1979), 21.

21. See Charles E. Curran, *Catholic Moral Theology in Dialogue* (Notre Dame, Ind.: Fides Publishers, 1972), 209–19, where compromise is applied to homosexual relations and Curran distances himself from more radical, Protestant theories; *New Perspectives in Moral Theology,* 191–92, where compromise is applied to some instances of abortion; *Ongoing Revision in Moral Theology* (Notre Dame, Ind.: Fides/Claretian, 1975), 104–5, where compromise is presented as a resolution only for those conflicts arising from prepersonal sinfulness; *Themes in Fundamental Moral Theology* (Notre Dame and London: University of Notre Dame Press, 1977), 19–20, 31–32 and 140–41; *Transition and Tradition in Moral Theology* (Notre Dame and London: University of Notre Dame Press, 1979), 71–78.

22. McCormick, "Moral Theology Since Vatican II," 21. For my treatment of St. Thomas' handling of these matters, see Germain G. Grisez, "Toward a Consistent Natural-Law Ethics of Killing," *American Journal of Jurisprudence,* 15 (1970), 66–73. For an excellent and profound critique of proportionalism from a more strictly Thomistic viewpoint, see Servais Pinckaers, O.P., "La question des actes intrinsèquement mauvais et le 'proportionnalisme,'" *Revue Thomiste,* 82 (1982), 181–212; in the course of this article, Pinckaers makes unmistakably clear how far St. Thomas is from the entire outlook of the proportionalists.

23. St. Thomas Aquinas, *Quaestiones Quodlibetales*, 9, 7, 2 (15). On the proportionalist account, by contrast, the nonmoral evil remains but is outweighed.

24. See *Summa theologiae*, 1–2, q. 100, a. 8; *De malo*, q. 15, a. 1, ad 8. There is some confusion in St. Thomas' ethical theory on this question. This is not surprising, since he did pioneering work in the area of moral theory. The matters on which he is confused do not touch Catholic moral teaching itself, but only the theological account of it. Here, as Thomas himself says, authority is no argument.

25. Charles Curran, *Catholic Moral Theology in Dialogue*, 209–19, distances himself from Protestant positions by saying (211) that they make the effect of sin too total and unnuanced, and imply that sin totally destroys or disfigures the order of creation. But not all Protestant theologians hold such extreme views. See, for example, Dietrich Bonhoeffer, *Ethics*, ed. Eberhard Bethge (New York: Macmillan, 1965), 110–19 and 240–41. Bonhoeffer writes dialectically; one must read his whole work to understand any of it accurately. His position as a whole is deeply Christian, although defective in respects determined by the errors of Lutheranism.

26. For a fuller treatment of this question, see Germain Grisez, "Against Consequentialism," *American Journal of Jurisprudence*, 23 (1978), 49–62.

27. Secular philosophers generally realize the failure of every sort of proportionalism; much effort has been expended and no progress made in making some such approach practicable. See Dan W. Brock, "Recent Work in Utilitarianism," *American Philosophical Quarterly*, 10 (1973), 241–69. Donagan, op. cit., 172–209, sets out several objections to proportionalism, especially showing (199–209) how ignorance blocks the required calculation. See Grisez, "Against Consequentialism," 30 and 35–36, for admissions by proponents of the method that the calculation it requires is impossible; these admissions make it clear that proportionalist "judgments" are determined by feeling or by choice.

28. See McCormick, *Doing Evil*, 201–3, 233–35, and 261–65, where under criticism he considerably restricted the proportionalism articulated in "Ambiguity in Moral Choice," especially in treating noncombatant immunity (42–44), and proportionate reason (45–46): "To see whether an action involving evil is proportionate in the circumstances we must judge whether this choice is the best possible service of all the values in the tragic and difficult conflict" (46). Richard M. Gula, S.S., *What Are They Saying about Moral Norms?* (New York: Paulist Press, 1982), favors a restricted consequentialism, which he limits in two ways: (1) that the chosen means do more good than harm (thus excluding as an option which is a lesser but preponderant evil), and (2) the universalizability principle (80). Gula honestly states (97–98) the argument against proportionalism based on the noncommensurability of goods and bads, and offers no answer to it. Gula oversimplifies my own position, mistakenly suggesting (84) that the principle by which I would reject masturbation and several other kinds of acts is the same as that by which I reject contraception and abortion, and falsely claiming (85) that this same principle absolutizes affirmative norms. Underlying these errors is a fundamentally legalistic orientation; Gula's ultimate position is that revisionist theology should be regarded as probable and admitted in practice on the basis of probabilism (101–4).

29. See "Against Consequentialism," 29–41, for the failure of philosophical efforts; also Robert Spaemann, "Wer hat wofür Verantwortung? Zum Streit um deontologische oder teleologische Ethik," *Herder-Korrespondenz*, 36 (1982), 345–50, 403–8; "Nochmals: deontologische oder teleologische Moralbegründung?" *Herder-Korrespondenz*, 37 (1983), 79–84. McCormick's attempts, criticized throughout the present chapter, are as serious as those of any theologian. Most do not even mention the argument based on noncommensurability of goods against their position. Franz Böckle, *Fundamental Moral Theology* (New York: Pueblo, 1980), 239, mentions only aspects of opposing positions that would be question-begging if offered as arguments: (1) the obvious point that proportionalism undercuts absolute norms; (2) my articulation of the mode of responsibility excluding choices to destroy, damage, or impede basic human goods. I reject proportionalism in defense of this moral principle, but not by invoking it, and it is hard to understand how Böckle could have overlooked this fact. In any case, he never explicitly mentions the problem of the noncommensurability of goods; he only implicitly suggests a solution to it (207–22), namely, that experience and social communication should lead to a consensus to be articulated into binding norms by social scientists. This solution is implausible, for it either amounts to accepting conventional morality as moral truth (the cultural relativism criticized in 4-E) or projects an ideal of community falsified by the reality of human moral disagreement. In practice, to require universal consensus for the recognition of moral truth is to espouse nihilism, since there is no such consensus.

30. See Pinckaers, op. cit., for a critique of proportionalism's understanding of morality rooted in more strictly Thomistic insights, but very similar to that proposed here. Some additional theological critiques of proportionalism: John R. Connery, S.J., "Morality of Consequences: A Critical

Appraisal," *Theological Studies,* 34 (1973), 396–414; "Catholic Ethics: Has the Norm for Rule-Making Changed?" *Theological Studies,* 42 (1981), 232–50; Ferdinando Citterio, "La revisione critica dei tradizionali principi morali alle luce della teoria del 'compromesso etico,'" *Scuola cattolica,* 110 (1982), 29–64; Dario Composta, "Il consequenzialismo: Una nuova corrente della 'Nuova Morale,'" *Divinitas,* 25 (1981), 127–56; Marcelino Zalba, S.J., "Principia ethica in crisim vocata intra (propter?) crisim morum," *Periodica de Re Morali, Canonica, Liturgica,* 71 (1982), 25–63 and 319–57; Gustav Ermecke, "Das Problem der Universalität oder Allgemeingültigkeit sittlicher Normen innerweltlicher Lebensgestaltung," *Münchener theologische Zeitschrift,* 24 (1973), 1–24.

31. On the central bearing of morality upon the acting person's self-determination in choice and self-fulfillment in action, see Karol Wojtyla, *The Acting Person,* trans. Andrzej Potocki, ed. Anna-Teresa Tymieniecka (Dordrecht: D. Reidel, 1979), 149–74.

32. Proportionalists deny the relevance of this verse of St. Paul as a proof text against their position. They claim that Paul only excludes the choice of a moral evil, not of a premoral evil proportionalism seeks to justify. However, the preceding verse is raising precisely the question whether what otherwise would be evil—a lie or refusal of truth—might not be justified if it promotes God's glory. Still, I do not use Rom 3.8 as a proof text against proportionalism, for without an independent and conclusive critique of proportionalism, its proponents could plausibly argue that Paul's rejection of violating truth to promote God's glory is a specific norm whose extrapolation into a general principle is question-begging. However, Rom 3.8 has been cited by the magisterium for the general principle that "it is never lawful, even for the gravest reasons, to do evil that good may come of it." See Paul VI, *Humanae vitae,* 60 AAS (1968) 491; *The Papal Encyclicals,* 277.14.

33. McCormick, *Doing Evil,* 227; also 251–53.

34. Ibid., 228.

35. See Anthony Kosnik et al., *Human Sexuality: New Directions in American Catholic Thought* (Garden City, N.Y.: Doubleday, 1979), 106. This work does not deal with the specific question of divorce and remarriage, and takes a somewhat reserved attitude toward adultery: "In general, it seems difficult to imagine a situation where such activity would be considered to be good for all involved" (170).

36. For the challenge: McCormick, *Notes,* 718. Classical authors do not offer a thorough analysis of the determination of proportionate reason. But they do not simply reduce everything to commensuration of premoral goods and bads. E.g., Arthurus Vermeersch, S.J., *Theologiae Moralis: Principia, Responsa, Consilia,* tomus 1, *Theologia Fundamentalis* (Rome: Apud Aedes Universitatis Gregorianae, 1947), section 117, invokes principles of justice, charity, and piety; I. Aertnys and C. Damen, C.Ss.R., *Theologia Moralis secundum Doctrinam S. Alphonsi de Ligorio,* ed. 17, vol. 1 (Rome: Marietti, 1956), section 58, suggest that one consider what virtue would be violated if the bad effect were not merely accepted but willed. Thus, for these authors, moral norms must be assumed to judge what is proportionate. For the proportionalist, who often is arguing for exceptions to received norms, the judgment of proportionate reason would involve weighing nonmoral goods and evils, as McCormick, op. cit., 710, clearly indicates: A kind of act is always wrong "when taken as a whole, the nonmoral evil outweighs the nonmoral good, and therefore the action is disproportionate."

37. *Notes,* 647.

38. See Grisez, "Toward a Consistent Natural-Law Ethics of Killing," 64–96. McCormick might find other difficulties with my earlier work, but he finds the difficulty of commensurating the incommensurable only by reading it into a theory in which commensuration has no place; see McCormick, *Doing Evil,* 23–29. Compare McCormick's hypotheses about my position (28), with what I actually say (94–95), which clearly excludes McCormick's interpretation. In "Current Theology: Notes on Moral Theology: 1982," *Theological Studies,* 44 (1983), 102, McCormick once again attempted this sort of counterattack: "Grisez does not seem to realize that his arguments bite back." McCormick ignored the distinctions, similar to those made in question E, above, by which I answered this objection in "Against Consequentialism," 49–62, an article mentioned in the notes of the one to which he was trying to respond: "The Moral Implications of a Nuclear Deterrent," *Center Journal,* 2 (Winter 1982), 24, n. 6. Indeed, McCormick was loathe to deal with "Against Consequentialism," which he knew well, for it had been prepared and accepted for publication in *Doing Evil* and included in the first draft of McCormick's response to his critics in that book. The specific answer to McCormick's counterattack in its latest reformulation is that "unduly burdensome" means *unfairly* burdensome, and fairness is determined not by proportionalism but by the fifth mode of responsibility; people do determine what they do not want done to themselves by emotion and spontaneous willing, which *are* among the sources of proportionalist pseudojudgments, but that determination is only the

subject matter to which fairness applies. The "ought" of a moral judgment based on fairness derives from the mode of responsibility, not from the factual situation to which it applies.

39. Joseph Fuchs, S.J., "The Absoluteness of Moral Terms," in Curran and McCormick, eds., op. cit., 113.

40. Ibid., 114, where he suggests that missionaries perhaps should not expect members of an African tribe to accept Christian marriage. John Paul II, *Familiaris Consortio*, 74 *AAS* (1982) 85–86; Eng. ed. (Vatican City: Vatican Polyglot Press, 1981), 10–11 (sec. 5), carefully distinguishes between the sense of faith and the results of sociological research, and asserts: "The 'supernatural sense of faith' however does not consist solely or necessarily in the consensus of the faithful. Following Christ, the Church seeks the truth, which is not always the same as the majority opinion." He also reaffirms without compromise Catholic teaching on marital morality, including the teaching on contraception, "in continuity with the living tradition of the ecclesial community throughout history" (*AAS* 144–45; Eng. ed., 54; sec. 29). Someone might say that St. Thomas' theory of natural law shows how the conventional moral standards of each society are grounded in human nature and thus somehow justified. But grounded does not entail justified. A recent study overlooked this point: Anthony Battaglia, *Toward a Reformulation of Natural Law* (New York: Seabury Press, 1981), 87–102. Referring to the given system of morals in each society, Battaglia says: "It is by acting rightly or wrongly within the system that we merit eternal life" (134). To Battaglia, Thomas' treatment of natural law "appears to be a discussion of the permanent elements of any system of ethics that works" (131). Battaglia accepts a thoroughgoing reduction of the moral "ought" to the sociocultural "is" of the practices of any functioning society (132–35). To attribute this to Thomas, Battaglia makes several remarkable moves. He identifies "per se nota" in Thomas' sense with Wilfred Sellars' language-bound "ex vi terminorum nota" (96–100); he also gratuitously claims that analogy in Thomas means "theoretical reformulability" (101) and bases this on the claim that human knowledge, being analogous, is for Thomas "neither wholly true nor wholly false" (33). Paradoxically, unlike Fuchs, Battaglia does not seem ready to approve polygamy, for while he holds (consistently with his cultural relativism) that one possible explanation of it "is that if it does not appear to the people who live within it to be a bad paradigm, then it is not one," he goes on to say: "A more persuasive explanation might be the fact of human sinfulness. A situation where a given practice does not arise out of consensus but is forced on a group as a result of power, for example, would be such a situation" (135). The underlying principle of this concession to moral truth is that Battaglia identifies social consensus with univer-salizability, which he suggests is the specific contribution of reason to moral decision making (108), the remainder of the process being left to an estheticlike balancing of the imputs of senses, emotions, intelligence, and intuition (102–7). With this notion of moral judgment, Battaglia suggests that the way to determine the moral acceptability of producing babies in test tubes would be to try it out and see whether it is satisfactory to the parents, society, and the children themselves (130). He does not explain how he would apply this approach to problems such as abortion.

41. McCormick, "Current Theology: Notes on Moral Theology: 1980," *Theological Studies*, 42 (1981), 89.

42. Josef Fuchs, S.J., "'Sin of the World' and Normative Morality," *Gregorianum*, 61 (1980), 67: "Causing an 'evil for man' is not necessarily wrong in every case. All that seems necessary is that it be justified by a comparative evaluation of all the elements of the total concrete situation, without such evaluation necessarily having to take place on the plane of conscious reflection." Garth L. Hallett, *Christian Moral Reasoning: An Analytic Guide* (Notre Dame and London: University of Notre Dame Press, 1983), 167–68, similarly is reduced to intuitionism when he tries to answer the objection from noncommensurability by suggesting that one assign numbers to all relevant values and disvalues and reach moral judgments by simple arithmetic. Hallett virtually avoids stating the objection to which he is trying to reply, coming nearest to acknowledging the problem in one footnote reference (247, n. 40). Hallett's method in this work is dialectical; he first surveys (45–72) a variety of Christian judgments of various sorts (but ignores their distinctions), then claims (73–105) that only proportionalism consistently covers the data. But though aware (113–14) of my moral theory, Hallett exempts himself from even considering it, on the ground that it supports traditional conclusions but not a traditional principle. In arguing thus, Hallett begs the important question concerning what counts as a principle; in my view, the eighth mode of responsibility is *the* traditional principle underlying, say, the rejection of contraception, and the trouble with a perverted-faculty argument is that it fails to articulate this principle accurately, not that it assumes (in Hallett's sense) something else as a principle.

43. McCormick, *Doing Evil*, 250.

44. Ibid., 251. McCormick also invokes Karl Rahner for "what he calls a 'moral instinct of faith.'" This instinct can be called by any number of different names; but the point is that there is a component

to moral judgment that cannot be adequately subject to analytic reflection. But it is this component that is chiefly responsible for one's ultimate judgments on concrete moral questions" (250–51). The reference is to Karl Rahner, S.J., "The Problem of Genetic Manipulation," *Theological Investigations*, vol. 9, *Writings of 1965–67, I*, trans. Graham Harrison (New York: Herder and Herder, 1972), 243. Rahner posits, not proves, that there are aspects of the essential morality of human acts which are nonconceptual, but belong to experienced reality and to practice which is in a "darkness" beyond theory. Apart from this metaphysics, Rahner supports his positing of this "instinct" only by pointing out that people (including moral theologians) have a hard time articulating good arguments for their moral convictions. One must admit that there can be moral truths contained in revelation which remain opaque, but such truths, unfolded by the magisterium of the Church in the light of the gospel, do not seem to be what Rahner has in mind, and they would be of no help to McCormick. Rahner's thinking on this "instinct" is somewhat confused, for he says it deals with the particular situation and yet is a judgment in principle (239). But, on the whole, it seems he intends to propose a version of prescriptivism or individual voluntarism, for in the summary he says that "this 'instinct' justifiably has the courage to say *Stat pro ratione voluntas* because such a confession need not necessarily be overcautious about making a decision" and that the whole theoretical argument is based on "we do not *want* to manipulate" (251). Rahner does not seem to notice that if one approves will's replacing reason, the will of some to manipulate also is approved. Nor does McCormick seem to notice that in adopting Rahner's "instinct" to solve his problem of the noncommensurability of goods, he is reducing his whole, elaborate effort to deal with moral problems, such as contraception, to an antecedent decision, for example: "Contraception is morally acceptable because we want to contracept."

45. McCormick, *Doing Evil*, 201, 233–34, and 265. In *Notes*, 715, McCormick admits modifying his position: "In other words, there is another understanding of proportionate reason than the one I gave."

46. *Doing Evil*, 265; cf. 201 and 261.

47. Ibid., 201.

48. Ibid., 223.

49. Peter Knauer, S.J., "The Hermeneutic Function of the Principle of Double Effect," *Natural Law Forum*, 12 (1967), 140–50. An inspection of McCormick's *Notes*, 8–13 and 355–59, shows that elements of McCormick's own earlier criticism of Knauer might be used against the position to which McCormick's reconstructed theory marks his conversion.

50. Germain Grisez, *Abortion: The Myths, the Realities, and the Arguments* (New York: Corpus Books, 1970), 331.

51. Knauer, op. cit., 162.

52. McCormick, "Current Theology: Notes on Moral Theology: 1980," 85–89.

53. *Doing Evil*, 208–9.

54. Ibid., 223–31.

55. Ibid., 253.

56. Ibid., 236.

57. Ibid., 237.

58. Ibid., 252. Note that McCormick goes on (253) to argue: "And because they are associated values, the community may make this association, namely, adopt a hierarchy (or better, a policy with regard to interrelatedness) of values." Thus the association is not discovered by conscience but created by an act which, one had supposed, was to be shaped by the moral truth of "proportionate reason."

59. McCormick, *Notes*, 812. McCormick's continuing amendments to his theory remind one of a medieval astronomer's efforts to save the Ptolemaic system by endowing the planets with queer dynamical properties. On the arbitrariness of McCormick's use of language: John Hill, "The Debate between McCormick and Frankena," *Irish Theological Quarterly*, 49 (1982), 121–33. McCormick was not alone in withdrawing from a straightforward position, clearly requiring impossible commensuration of incommensurable goods and bads, to a more qualified view. Philip S. Keane, S.S., *Sexual Morality*, 49, explained proportionate reason simply: "In the total story of the action, are there factors that make the level of ontic evil present in the action reasonably acceptable?" In a subsequent article, "The Objective Moral Order: Reflections on Recent Research," *Theological Studies*, 43 (1982), Keane eschewed reducing proportionate reason to weighing or calculating of harms and benefits, and said "proportionate reason asks what defines an action, what gives the action its meaning or *ratio*" (267). If this were true, the account of moral determination proposed below (10-B) would qualify as

proportionalism. But there still would be an opposition between such proportionalism and that of the proportionalist authors Keane cites (265, n. 17), whose supposed method would require the commensuration of the incommensurable. Significantly, in his summary of objections against proportionalism (269–71), which includes several straw men, Keane omits the decisive objection based on incommensurability; he mentions it only in a note (272, n. 36) as perhaps showing overtones of concern that people might not be wise or mature enough to use the approach properly.

CHAPTER SEVEN

NATURAL LAW AND THE
FUNDAMENTAL PRINCIPLES OF MORALITY

Introduction

We saw in chapter three that judgments of conscience are based on principles which the Church calls "natural law." Scholastic natural-law theory was criticized in chapter four; one of its faults is its failure to ground moral norms in human goods. Proportionalism was criticized in chapter six; while it tries to base moral judgments on human goods, it provides no workable method for doing so.

In chapter five human fulfillment was clarified by examining the goods which fulfill us. With the present chapter, we begin to see what natural law is and how it directs choices toward these goods. Since this account is a product of theological reflection, it commences by considering what the Church teaches concerning natural law. The intent is both to point out the data to be understood and to avoid confusing what is essential to the Church's teaching with what belongs to theological reflection.

Question A: What does "natural law" mean in Catholic teaching?

1. According to St. Paul, even the Gentiles find the requirements of morality which conscience discerns written in their hearts. Although Gentiles do not have the law divinely revealed to the Jews, they naturally do have this given standard of conduct (see Rom 2.14–16).[1]

2. The Church calls these naturally known principles "natural law." They are *natural* in the sense that they are not humanly enacted but are objective principles which originate in human nature (see GS 16; DH 14).[2] Thus, in speaking of natural law, we are not contrasting "natural" meaning "physical" with "intellectual." As a matter of fact, natural law does pertain to intellect. Nor is the contrast primarily that of "natural" with "supernatural," for natural law overlaps divinely revealed law.

3. Much Catholic teaching on natural law refers to the work of St. Thomas Aquinas (see DH 3, note 3).[3] Vatican II continues to commend him as a guide for theologians (see OT 16). It is therefore legitimate to examine his treatment of natural law, in order to find out how the Church views this subject.

4. St. Thomas begins from what he calls the "eternal law" (see *S.t.*, 1–2, q. 91, a. 1; q. 93, a. 1). This simply is God's plan, according to which he carries out his whole work of creating and redeeming. In current English, "law" refers mainly to rules and commands of people in authority; God's plan of action is not a law in this sense.[4] But Thomas thinks of law primarily as a reasonable plan of action (see *S.t.*, 1–2, q. 90, aa. 1, 3; *S.c.g.*, 3, 114). Since God knows well what he is doing, he must be acting according to a law. And since no one forms God's plan of action for him, the law of his creative and redemptive work must be his own wisdom, by which he directs everything to the fulfillment he has in mind (see *S.t.*, 1, q. 21, a. 1; q. 22, a. 1; 1–2, q. 90; q. 91, a. 1; q. 92, a. 1).

5. Since eternal law embraces the whole of creation, any other law—any other reasonable plan of action—must somehow derive from it (see *S.t.*, 1–2, q. 19, a. 4; q. 71, a. 6; q. 91, aa. 1–2; q. 93, a. 3). **People can plan their lives reasonably only because, in one way or another, they share in the universal plan perfectly present in God's eternal law** (see *S.t.*, 1–2, q. 91, a. 2; *S.c.g.*, 3, 113). If they try to follow a plan not somehow derived from eternal law, their lives will be unrealistic, as would be the behavior of workers on a large project who departed from the project's master plan in order to follow some other plan.

6. According to Thomas, people are naturally disposed to understand some basic practical principles. He calls these the "primary principles of natural law." Since everyone knows them naturally, no one can make a mistake about them. **They are the law written in one's heart of which St. Paul speaks—the law whose voice is conscience, according to Vatican II.** Interpreting the text he had of Psalm 4 ("Who will show us any good? Lift thou up the light of thy countenance upon us, O Lord"), Thomas says natural law is a "light of reason which is in us, inasmuch as it can show us goods and direct our will, because it is the light of God's countenance—that is, a light which derives from his countenance" (*S.t.*, 1–2, q. 19, a. 4; cf. q. 91, a. 2; q. 94, a. 2; 2–2, q. 47, a. 6).

Vatican II teaches that human persons find in their conscience a law they do not impose on themselves which demands their obedience: "For man has in his heart a law written by God" (GS 16; see 3-B). This law not only calls the person to do good and avoid evil, but it also when necessary speaks "to his heart more specifically: do this, shun that" (GS 16). The Council makes its own the explanation of St. Thomas, that this natural law is the human participation in the eternal law: ". . . the highest norm of human life is the divine law— eternal, objective, and universal—whereby God orders, directs, and governs the whole world and the ways of the human community according to the plan of his wisdom and love. God makes man a sharer in this his law, so that, by divine providence's sweet disposing, man can recognize more and more the unchanging truth" (DH 3; translation supplied).

In the context, "unchanging truth" has a double reference. It refers back to the previous section of this document, where the Council lays the basis of its declaration on religious liberty by emphasizing the moral duty, imposed by human nature, to seek religious truth and to live by it (see DH 2). But "unchanging truth" also refers to the eternal law itself, as is clear from one of the texts of St. Thomas to which Vatican II refers (a reference omitted in the Abbott edition): "The eternal law is unchanging truth . . . and everyone somehow learns the truth, at least the general principles of the natural law, even though in other matters some people share more and some less in the knowledge of the truth" (*S.t.*, 1–2, q. 93, a. 2).[5]

The Council makes it clear that this unchanging truth serves as the principle for judgments of conscience: "On his part, man perceives and acknowledges the imperatives of the divine law through the mediation of conscience. In all his activity a man is bound to follow his conscience faithfully, in order that he may come to God, for whom he was created" (DH 3). Consciences must be free of any coercive imposition by public authority; in their liberty they are supported by the Church's teaching: "The Church is, by the will of Christ, the teacher of the truth. It is her duty to give utterance to, and authoritatively to teach, that Truth which is Christ himself, and also to declare and confirm by her authority those principles of the moral order which have their origin in human nature itself" (DH 14).

That the principles of natural law to which Vatican II refers are not only general ones is clear by its teaching on specific points, such as genocide: "Contemplating this melancholy state of humanity, the Council wishes to recall first of all the permanent binding force of universal natural law and its all-embracing principles. Man's conscience itself gives ever more emphatic voice to these principles. Therefore, actions which deliberately conflict with these same principles, as well as orders commanding such actions, are criminal. Blind obedience cannot excuse those who yield to them. Among such must first be counted those actions designed for the methodical extermination of an entire people, nation, or ethnic minority" (GS 79).

In teaching like this, the Church carries out her divine mission of service: "In pursuit of her divine mission, the Church preaches the gospel to all men and dispenses the treasures of grace. Thus, by imparting knowledge of the divine and natural law, she everywhere contributes to strengthening peace and to placing brotherly relations between individuals and peoples on solid ground" (GS 89).

Although we are naturally disposed to know basic practical principles and can make no mistake about them, they are not by themselves sufficient for the judgment of conscience which we must make. Our ultimate end is to share in fulfillment in the Lord Jesus, and we do not judge rightly what to do unless we judge in light of this end. So we must supplement natural law with faith, by this means drawing on the eternal law in a way that goes beyond reason (see DS 3005/1786; *S.t.*, 1–2, q. 91, a. 4; q. 98, a. 1; q. 106, aa. 1–2).

Moreover, we must bring both the basic practical principles of natural law and the way of Jesus which faith teaches to bear upon the particular possibilities we consider in our deliberation. This application of principles to possibilities under consideration is a process of reasoning, and only at the end of it do we reach our best and last judgment as to what choice we should make. So the judgment of conscience must be reached by conscientious reflection on the possibilities before us in the light of the moral standards we have from natural law and faith (see *S.t.*, 1, q. 79, a. 13; 1–2, q. 94, a. 2; 2–2, q. 47, a. 6).

Question B: Are natural law and revelation completely separate sources of moral guidance?

1. Vatican I teaches that God, although he can be known naturally as creation's source and goal, still chooses to reveal himself and his decrees, in part so that "even in the present condition of the human race, those religious truths which are by their nature accessible to human reason can readily be known by all men with solid certitude and with no trace of error" (DS 3005/1786; translation supplied). Otherwise, our wounded nature would prevent our knowing certainly and accurately some important truths concerning human fulfillment, even though in principle these truths are naturally knowable.

In this matter Vatican I adopts the position of St. Thomas (*S.t.*, 1, q. 1, a. 1; 1–2, q. 98,

a. 5; *S.c.g.*, 1, 4). Thomas expands on the general position with respect to the particular question: Can the natural law be wiped from the human heart? His answer is that the most common principles in themselves cannot be ignored, but their application in the concrete can be ignored due to unruly passions; and norms which must be derived from the most general principles by any sort of reasoning can be ignored due to bad customs and corrupt habits (*S.t.*, 1–2, q. 93, a. 6; cf. q. 77, a. 2; q. 85, a. 3).

Pius XII refers to Vatican I and expands upon it, in line with the teaching of St. Thomas:

> . . . though, absolutely speaking, human reason by its own natural force and light can arrive at a true and certain knowledge of the one personal God, Who by His providence watches over and governs the world, and also the natural law, which the Creator has written in our hearts, still there are not a few obstacles to prevent reason from making efficient and fruitful use of its natural ability. . . .
>
> It is for this reason that divine revelation must be considered morally necessary so that those religious and moral truths which are not of their nature beyond the reach of reason in the present condition of the human race, may be known with a firm certainty and with freedom from all error.[6]

Thus the Church teaches that truths of natural law are included in revelation. It follows that they belong to the proper sphere of the Church's authority to teach, and that if one does not find cogent arguments for them, they must be accepted on faith. One cannot expect people who refuse to accept such moral norms on faith to see all of them to be true.

In the place where St. Paul alludes to natural law, he also points out that Gentiles in fulfilling it were fulfilling the law—that is, the requirements of the covenant (see Rom 2.14–15). Obviously, he does not mean that the Gentiles could know and keep the precepts peculiar to Mosaic law, which are abolished in Christianity. Rather, he means that moral content common to the Old and the New Testaments—such as the Ten Commandments and their foundation in the law of love—constitutes natural law. The *Decretum* of Gratian, compiled in the middle of the twelfth century and authoritative as canonical law until 1917, begins with the famous definition: "Natural law is what is contained in the law and the gospel"—that is, in both the Old and New Testaments.

Hence, St. Irenaeus, St. Thomas Aquinas, and the whole Catholic tradition consider the Ten Commandments to pertain to natural law and, at the same time, to divine revelation.[7] St. Thomas maintains that all moral precepts of the old covenant are included, in one way or another, in natural law (see *S.t.*, 1–2, q. 100, a. 1). He also holds that the law of Jesus, in its moral aspects, is an expression of the requirements of human virtue which pertain to natural law (see *S.t.*, 1–2, q. 108, aa. 1–3).

2. **Thus the Church teaches that revelation includes truths of natural law.**[8] This provides a premise for rejecting certain conclusions which today are often drawn—mistakenly—from the fact that natural law is naturally knowable. For instance, some theologians claim that the Church cannot authoritatively teach specific moral norms pertaining to natural law, but can only endorse norms agreed upon by people of good will, Christians and others.[9] Indeed, some theologians hold that the authority of any specific moral norm received and handed on in the Church can be no greater than the rational arguments which can be offered to support it.[10] Thus they conclude that while the Church can firmly teach the very general principles of morality with which no believer disagrees and may tentatively commend specific norms supported by consensus and rational arguments, the Church cannot authoritatively teach specific moral norms pertaining to natural

law in such a way that the faithful ought to accept them as moral truths even if consensus and cogent rational arguments are lacking.[11]

3. The teaching of Vatican I concerning the help given to fallen humankind by revelation explains why many people of good will do not see the truth of moral norms of natural law. The Church's teaching, based on divine revelation, gives us a motive to accept as true those norms of Christian morality for which we may not have completely satisfying arguments. Moreover, as part of her divine mission the Church calls attention by her sacred and certain teaching to the principles of the moral order, which we can ignore or badly articulate despite knowing them naturally (see DH 14; GS 89). (The issues concerning theological dissent from the Church's moral teaching will be examined in chapter thirty-six.)

4. The argument that revelation contains no specific moral norms but only very general principles is at odds with the entire history of Christian moral teaching. Christians always have handed on specific norms as revealed truths and offered scriptural warrants for them.[12] For example, the Council of Trent cites St. Paul to show that several kinds of acts other than sins against faith itself are mortal sins (see DS 1544/808). Similarly, Vatican II proposes specific norms concerning forgiving injuries and loving enemies as the teaching of Christ, citing Matthew's account of the Sermon on the Mount (see GS 28).

5. Moreover, both Trent and Vatican II teach that the gospel which Jesus proclaimed and commissioned the apostles to spread is the "source of all saving truth and moral teaching" (DS 1501/783; DV 7; note that the "omnis" comes before the first "et").[13] How the gospel contains all moral teaching will be made clear in chapter twenty-six. The key point is that God reveals in Jesus how men and women in a sinful world should respond to his love and live good human lives which necessarily will be redemptive like the life of Jesus himself.

6. Thus Vatican II teaches that Christ "fully reveals man to man himself and makes his supreme calling clear" (GS 22). "Whoever follows after Christ, the perfect man, becomes himself more of a man" (GS 41). By Christian holiness, "a more human way of life is promoted even in this earthly society" (LG 40).

7. Vatican II's understanding of the relationship between divine and natural law is exemplified in its teaching on birth regulation. According to the Council, the Church authoritatively interprets divine law in the light of the gospel to make clear objective standards based on the nature of human persons and their acts (see GS 50–51). Again, the Council teaches that the Church contributes to international peace and friendship by imparting knowledge of divine and natural law, and that this work belongs to the Church's divine mission of preaching the gospel and dispensing the treasures of grace (see GS 89, Latin text). This teaching would be unintelligible if, as some wish, divine law and natural law were separated, with the Church's teaching authority limited to the former while all specific moral issues were consigned to independent rational reflection on experience.[14]

8. **It follows that natural law and divine law can be distinguished from each other and even contrasted, as they are in many documents of the Church, without being separated and opposed to each other.[15] In the actual order of things natural law does not stand apart from the law of Christ. The**

dictates of natural law and the truth of divine revelation are two agreeing streams from the same divine font; the Church is the guardian of the single supernatural Christian order, in which nature and grace converge.[16] In this Christian order, natural law is restored, completed, and elevated, so that it now serves to direct humankind to heavenly as well as earthly fulfillment.[17] A real Christian life is a humanly good life—the only completely fulfilling life for persons who, called to share in divine life, have fallen and been redeemed.

Richard A. McCormick, S.J., held this same view and articulated it very clearly in 1965. He held that in becoming man, God reveals the dignity of man. Also, Jesus and Paul insist on natural-law prescriptions. Paul presents them as part of the gospel. The natural law is within the law of Jesus. McCormick also argued that in any case the Church can teach infallibly the whole of the natural law:

> . . . even if (*per impossibile,* I should think) the natural law was not integral to the gospel, the Church's prerogative to propose infallibly the gospel morality would be no more than nugatory without the power to teach the natural law infallibly. One could hardly propose what concerns *Christian men* without proposing what concerns *men.* The Church could hardly propose *Christian love* in any meaningful way without being able to propose the very suppositions of *any love.* In other words, and from this point of view alone, to propose the natural law is essential to the protection and proposal of Christian morality itself, much as certain philosophical truths are capable of definition because without them revealed truths are endangered. Furthermore, charity has no external act of its own. It can express itself only through acts of other virtues. But natural-law demands constitute the most basic demands of these virtues, simply because we can never escape the fact that it is *man* who is loving and to be loved. Would not, therefore, the ability to teach infallibly the dignity of man (certainly a revealed truth) without being able to exclude infallibly forms of conduct incompatible with this dignity be the ability infallibly to propose a cliche?[18]

Question C: What is the first principle of practical reasoning?

1. Practical reasoning has two phases, one concerned with what might be done, the other with what ought to be done. Although these phases are not usually separated in practice, for purposes of analysis this question and the next will consider the principles of practical reasoning in general (what might be done). Good and bad people alike use these principles in considering what they might do. Then, questions E through H will consider moral principles, the starting points for thinking out what one ought to do—that is, for making judgments of conscience.

2. Even in its general phase, practical reasoning is thinking and judging about what is to be, not about what already is.[19] It does not simply report and explain; it entertains possibilities and projects lines of action (see *S.t.,* 1, q. 79, aa. 11–13; 2–2. q. 47, a. 2). It is within the wider context of this first phase of practical thinking that moral thinking takes place, since moral reflection is concerned with what is to be done and is not to be done. Even retrospective moral thinking—as when one examines one's conscience—is concerned with what was to have been done or avoided.

3. According to St. Thomas, the very first principle of practical reasoning in general is: *The good is to be done and pursued; the bad is to be avoided (S.t.,* 1–2,

q. 94, a. 2). This is a directive for action, not a description of good and evil. "Good" here means not only what is morally good but whatever can be understood as intelligibly worthwhile, while "bad" refers to whatever can be understood as a privation of intelligible goods. Thomas' formulation—"Good is to be done and pursued" rather than "Do good!"—suggests that he thinks this principle extends to and governs all coherent practical thinking.[20]

Since this very first principle is so extremely broad, of what use is it? It does not settle what is good and bad morally. Even immoral choices and their rationalizations depend on this principle, for the immoral choice is not insane, and though arguments for it are unreasonable, they are understandable. What the first practical principle does provide is a foundation for practical thinking.

The first principle of practical reason directs thinking toward the fulfillment which is to be realized in and through human action. It concerns anything a person can understand that would make a possible course of action seem appealing and worth deliberating about, or make it seem unappealing and perhaps to be excluded from further consideration. All human practical reflection—whether it leads to morally good action, to bad action, or to no outcome at all—presupposes the first practical principle.

4. The first principle of practical reasoning is a self-evident truth. One understands it to be true as soon as one understands its terms. Although someone might suggest that for this very reason it is simply a matter of juggling words and tells one nothing at all, this is not the case. True, the first principle does not say what is good and what is to be done, but it does play an important role. To explain this role, St. Thomas compares the first principle of practical reasoning with the principle of noncontradiction.

To understand the meaning of the terms of a principle is not only to know something about words; it is also to have some knowledge of the realities to which the words refer by way of concepts. The very first principle of practical reasoning is a grasp upon the necessary relationship in existential reality between human goods and appropriate action bearing upon these goods.

This necessary relationship is not one we find in the world, since we do not find our own actions in the world; rather we put them there. What the first principle of practical reason tells us is that we must act—we must do things—to be fully the human persons we can and ought to be. In telling us this, the first principle provides human fulfillment as the basis for all of the normative demands which reason ever will make upon us. When at a later stage of practical reflection one wonders, "But why should I do this?" one is asking about the intelligible good to be achieved. One asks this because one knows one's action would be absurd if it were not directed to some good or other.

To say this is not to exclude that in a particular case the right answer to "Why should I do this?" might be "Because God wills it, as the Church teaches." Such an answer is not ultimate. It assumes that what God wills is wise, and that his wisdom orders all things to good (see Wis 8.1; DS 3003/1784; DH 3). It also assumes that it is humanly good to trust and obey God, who has shown his love and faithfulness—for example, in the resurrection of Jesus (see DS 3009/1790).

5. The principle of noncontradiction states that the same thing cannot both be and not be at the same time and in the same respect. It asserts the intrinsic relationship between reality and its own definiteness. One cannot consciously proceed to think and talk in disregard of the definiteness of reality. In this sense,

the principle of noncontradiction always controls one's thinking. Yet one can find oneself in a muddle or talking nonsense, and then the principle of noncontradiction makes its demand.

6. **Similarly, the first principle of practical reasoning articulates the intrinsic, necessary relationship between human goods and appropriate actions bearing upon them** (see *S.t.*, 1–2, q. 94, a. 2; cf. q. 90, a. 1; q. 99, a. 1; 2–2, q. 47, a. 6). In thinking and speaking about what one might do, it is impossible to disregard entirely the goods and bads to which one's possible acts would be relevant. Thus the first principle of practical reasoning always controls practical thinking. Yet one can find oneself doing something which cannot attain any intelligible good; then the first principle makes it clear that one's action is pointless and this leads to a cessation of effort. Thus the principle is normative, even though it does not specify the relationship of actions to goods in such a way that deliberation and choice among possibilities are at all limited.

7. In scholastic natural-law theory, the first principle of practical reasoning was misunderstood, formulated not as St. Thomas did but as a most general moral imperative: *Do good and avoid evil.* However, the first principle is not a moral norm; it governs morally good and morally bad thinking alike. Moreover, an imperative to do good and avoid evil would not be self-evident. Confronted with this command, one could reasonably ask: Why?

Question D: What are the general determinations of the first principle of practical reasoning?

1. The first principle of practical reasoning directs one toward the fulfillment to be realized in and through human acts: *Good is to be done and pursued.* Since, as St. Thomas points out, people grasp as goods all the fulfillments to which they are naturally inclined, it follows that there is a basic precept of natural law corresponding to each natural inclination (see *S.t.*, 1–2, q. 94, a. 2; sup., q. 65, a. 1). Thomas very briefly sketches these inclinations and the goods to which they call attention, while in chapter five of the present work the basic human goods are described and distinguished in greater detail. **The general determinations of the first principle of practical reasoning are these basic precepts of natural law.** They take the form: Such and such a basic human good is to be done and/or pursued, protected, and promoted.

2. The practical principle which directs thinking to each basic human good is a self-evident truth. It proposes that particular good as something to be pursued and protected, while directing that what is contrary to it be avoided and prevented. For example, life is naturally understood as a good to be preserved, death as an evil to be prevented. Since, however, basic human goods have many distinct aspects (for example, life can be understood in terms of survival, health, safety, and so on), it is impossible to make a simple, exhaustive list of the basic precepts of natural law.

3. Although these general determinations of the first principle of practical reasoning are self-evident, people usually do not advert to them even when thinking in light of them. A man seeking food for his family or a woman caring for her baby is proceeding on the assumption that life is a good to be preserved, but the

principle is taken for granted, not articulated. How the basic human goods can be defended in theoretical reflection has been treated previously (5-C). But there is another question to be considered: How do they come to be known naturally, so that people take them for granted and use them as starting points in practical thinking?

4. Basic themselves, these principles cannot be learned as conclusions from more basic truths. People do "learn" them, but in a different way. As they develop, individuals experience their natural inclinations and the things which fulfill these inclinations. This experience begins at the sensory level but goes beyond it (see *S.t.*, 1–2, q. 94, a. 2; cf. q. 51, a. 1; q. 57, a. 4). For example, infants are naturally curious, and their curiosity is initially satisfied as a result of instinctive behavior, with intellectual satisfaction the reward. In time, insight into the total experience of natural inclinations and their fulfillment prompts children to project goods as possibilities which can be realized by their own action. Thus, even before they make choices, small children spontaneously act to realize goods they understand. Finally, the experience of free choice itself becomes part of the data for understanding existential goods such as justice and friendship. (Appendix 1 provides a fuller discussion of how one comes to know the basic human goods.)

The principles of practical reasoning clearly are understood by small children. They can consider them one at a time. Simple willing is the disposition toward the good which responds to the basic practical principles; acts done by spontaneous willing require only the further understanding that some possible manner of acting will participate in one of the goods.

The fact that small children in their premoral acts proceed according to the principles of practical reasoning thus far described helps to make clear that an additional principle is required to account for the distinction between moral good and evil. The basic principles of practical reasoning make possible all human acts. Morality is in choices, in acts consequent upon choices, and in forms of voluntariness somehow conditioned by choices or by the failure to make them when one could and should make them. To determine questions of morality, a principle is needed which will refer to choices and indicate how they are to be made.

The process of experience and insight by which we come to know the basic principles of practical reasoning is very different from the process by which we come to have and articulate wants for specific goods, which sometimes are adopted as objectives of freely chosen acts. The latter process (of having and articulating specific wants) presupposes and follows from the former process (that of understanding goods as fields of practical possibility and being disposed to them by simple willing).

One can have a want for a specific good merely in virtue of its appeal to sensory experience and feeling—for example, a sexually stimulating image can arouse sexual desire. Such a want can be articulated as an intelligible objective by thinking of ways in which satisfying the desire might contribute to virtually any of the basic human goods. For example, one can think of the possible experience as an experiment which might satisfy curiosity, as a performance which might be carried on with more or less skill, as a way of lessening pain (sexual tension), as a way of having a feeling, at least, of self-integration (getting rid of temptation by giving in to it), as a way of being true to oneself (a rationalization of perversion used by some), as a way of experiencing and celebrating interpersonal relationship (one of the reasons for marital intercourse), or as a ritual act (such as temple prostitution). One can understand the same possible behavior under two or more goods simultaneously, and thus have multiple reasons which could make it a possible object of choice.

5. These general determinations of the first principle of practical reasoning concern goods which are definite as natural human inclinations are; yet these same goods are to be realized indefinitely—that is, they are always to be realized, and new ways of realizing them can always be found. **In acting for a good, one gradually comes to perceive its possibilities more and more fully. Thus, human nature and natural-law morality are both stable and changing** (cf. *S.t.*, 1–2. q. 94, aa. 4–5). Stable, in that the givenness and fundamental unalterability of natural inclinations account for the unalterability of the principles of natural law; but also changing, in that the dynamism of the inclinations, their openness to continuing and expanding fulfillment, accounts for the openness of natural law to authentic development.

6. Examples clarify this important point. Since people always know that human life is a good to be acted for, they always know that sickness is to be resisted. The natural inclination toward health and what protects and promotes it is constant and unchanging. Modern medicine, however, has given "health" a much richer content for us than for people of any previous era. Thus, even with regard to the basic good of life, the possibilities of human fulfillment are only gradually specified as humankind realizes and experiences them, then presses on to expand them further. This is even more clear in the case of friendship. One begins to understand what it means before adolescence, and thereafter the basic inclination—to get along with other people—does not change. But as one grows and matures, so does one's understanding of the possibilities for human fulfillment present in friendship; and specifically Christian friendship has a far richer meaning, modeled on Jesus' friendship for us, than friendship which is unformed by gospel values.

It often is suggested today that human nature changes. If so, actions appropriate in one time and place would no longer be appropriate in another. Moral truths would be transient.[21] How does the account of natural law articulated here help to deal with this question?

One point to notice is that the basic forms of good open up the possibilities which make for all sorts of cultural solutions under varying historical conditions. But one does not find a human culture in which death is considered good and life bad, or one in which conflict within the group is regarded as humanly fulfilling. The problems are basically the same for people always and everywhere.[22] The beliefs about what will help solve them are different. Insight into human possibilities is more or less extensive and accurate in some places and times than in others.

From the perspective of Christian faith, the effect of sin cannot be overlooked. Without the light of divine revelation, humankind is incapable of consistently grasping and accurately following out the implications of what truly is humanly good. The New Testament authors were well aware that the conventions of societies do not always direct persons to their true fulfillment, and so they warned against the temptation to conform to conventions at odds with the gospel (see Rom 12.2; Eph 4.17–19; 5.3–8; 1 Pt 4.2–3). Very often, whole societies settle for solutions which mutilate human nature. This mutilation is a kind of change, but not one which sets new and better standards.

At the same time, the open-endedness of human goods, their multiplicity, and the extremely varied opportunities provided by diverse natural and cultural environments for participating in them do make for a great deal of variety and invite a creative approach to human life.[23] Human nature in its historical actuality can be changed for better or for worse—this is a fundamental assumption of Christian morality with its awareness of the impact of sin and grace. Thus Vatican II teaches that Christ, the perfect man, reveals to human persons what human nature can and should be. All human persons can be united to him and perfected in him (see GS 22, 29, 41, 45; LG 13, 40).

The human nature which is a standard for morality is not a formal essence and set of invariant relationships, as was suggested by inadequate, scholastic natural-law theory. Rather, the standard is the basic possibilities of human individuals as bodily creatures, endowed with intelligence, able to engage in fruitful work and creative play, psychically complex, capable of more or less completely reasonable action, in need of companionship, capable of love, and open to friendship with God in whose image they are made. If these possibilities in their basic givenness are what is meant by "human nature," then human nature does not change. Thus, after an extended description of cultural changes through history, Vatican II teaches: "The Church also maintains that beneath all changes there are many realities which do not change and which have their ultimate foundation in Christ, who is the same yesterday and today, yes and forever" (GS 10; cf. Heb 13.8).

Indeed, when "nature" is understood in terms of basic human possibilities, the very notion that human nature could change is logically absurd, for "change" not only in respect to actuality but also in respect to basic possibility would no longer be change but simple loss of identity. Thus, those who use human historicity to support the new morality need not be taken seriously, for they cannot show that there are human persons for whom life, knowledge, friendship, and so forth are not basic goods.

Question E: What is the function of the first principle of morality?

1. The principles of practical reasoning considered so far do not tell us what is morally good. Rather, they generate the field of possibilities in which choices are necessary. At the same time, when choices are made, the goodness of goods is never directly challenged. In making life and death decisions, for instance, no one assumes that life as such is bad and death good; choices to let die or even to kill are instead made on other grounds, such as the limitation of suffering or the justice of punishing criminals. Evidently, then, there is a need for moral norms which will guide choices toward overall fulfillment in terms of human goods.

2. The proportionalism criticized in chapter six is one proposal for guiding choices. But although it appears plausible at first, the suggestion that the right choice is the one which promises the most good (or least evil) is unworkable in principle.[24]

3. St. Thomas holds that the precepts of charity (see Mt 22.37–39) are the primary and general moral principles of natural law, and the Ten Commandments, which he also thinks belong to natural law, follow from these primary precepts as conclusions from principles (see *S.t.*, 1–2, q. 100, a. 3, ad 1; cf, q. 98, a. 1; q. 99, a. 1, ad 2; q. 99, aa. 2–3).[25] As St. Paul points out, love fulfills the law because one who loves certainly avoids harm to any neighbor and seeks the neighbor's good (see Rom 13.8–10; 1 Thes 5.15).

4. Vatican II also has a formulation of the basic moral principle. The Council notes that human activity is important not only for its results but because it

develops persons. The person is more important for what he or she is, than for what he or she has. Justice and friendship are more important than technical progress; the latter is only instrumental. Growth in human fulfillment is more important than any sort of riches. "Hence, the norm of human activity is this: that in accord with the divine plan and will, it should harmonize with the genuine good of the human race, and allow men as individuals and as members of society to pursue their total vocation and fulfill it" (GS 35). This has the merit of reflecting a nonproportionalist understanding of morality. Good human acts will harmonize with—not necessarily realize—the true good of humankind.[26] Besides trying to realize some good in fact, one must maintain a dynamic openness to fulfillment, since the total human vocation goes beyond measurable goods.

5. The functions of a first principle of morality are indicated by the formulations proposed by St. Thomas and Vatican II. **It must provide the basis for guiding choices toward overall human fulfillment.** As a single principle, it will give unity and direction to a morally good life. At the same time, it must not exclude ways of living which might contribute to a complete human community.

6. Still, the formulations of St. Thomas and Vatican II are not entirely satisfactory for purposes of ethical reflection and moral theology. **To serve as a standard for practical judgment, a formulation must refer to the many basic human goods which generate the need for choice and moral guidance.** In short, there appears to be a need for a formulation which is related more closely to the principles of practical reasoning.

The meaning of Vatican II's formulation of the norm of human activity is clarified by consideration of the context of this formulation and some of its applications. The Council's effort in *Gaudium et spes* is to clarify the service the Church offers to humankind. Hence, the hinge of the treatment is "man himself, whole and entire" (GS 3). It belongs to God's plan that human persons flourish and build up their world (see GS 34). Hence, objective standards of morality in respect to the regulation of births are based upon the nature of human persons and their acts (see GS 51). "In the socio-economic realm, too, the dignity and total vocation of the human person must be honored and advanced along with the welfare of society as a whole. For man is the source, the center, and the purpose of all socio-economic life" (GS 63). Productivity must serve integral human fulfullment: Its purpose ". . . must be man, and indeed the whole man, viewed in terms of his material needs and the demands of his intellectual, moral, spiritual, and religious life. And when we say man, we mean every man whatsoever and every group of men, of whatever race and from whatever part of the world" (GS 64).

Question F: How is the first principle of morality to be formulated?

1. The basic principle of morality might best be formulated as follows: *In voluntarily acting for human goods and avoiding what is opposed to them, one ought to choose and otherwise will those and only those possibilities whose willing is compatible with a will toward integral human fulfillment.*

In his encyclical, *Populorum progressio*, Paul VI teaches about authentic development. It must include the development of each person, the whole of the person, and every person. Every individual has a personal vocation and is called to self-fulfillment in it. Each one is responsible for his or her own self-fulfillment, for all are endowed with intelligence and freedom. Moreover, self-development "is not left up to man's option. Just as the whole of creation is ordered toward its Creator, so too the rational creature should of his own accord direct his life to God, the first truth and the highest good. Thus human self-fulfillment may be said to sum up our obligations."[27]

Understood in context, "human self-fulfillment may be said to sum up our obligations" expresses the same propositional formulation of the first principle of morality as that stated here. For the Pope stresses that this harmonious integration of human nature is destined for a higher fulfillment in Christ, a fulfillment in divine life; that human fulfillment must be both personal and social; and that development must not only increase material goods, but serve the values of life, knowledge, culture, friendship, love, mutual respect, peace, prayer, contemplation, faith, and loving unity in Christ.[28]

Moreover, although Paul VI did not explicitly deal with proportionalism in *Populorum progressio,* the way he later dealt with the question of birth regulation made it clear that "human self-fulfillment may be said to sum up our obligations" as he understood it, excluded a proportionalist conception of human good and moral action. For many who criticized *Populorum progressio* and some who misread it believed the Pope would have to approve contraception as a method of population control if he were serious about international economic development. Instead, the following year he issued *Humanae vitae.*

There he takes note of real and widespread concern about the rapid growth of population,[29] but firmly teaches that "it is never lawful, even for the gravest reasons, to do evil that good may come of it" and cites St. Paul (see Rom 3.8) on this point.[30] Moreover, explaining that the Church has no choice about teaching the moral law, since she did not make and cannot change it, Paul VI confidently explains that in reaffirming the teaching on contraception he is acting for the fulfillment indicated in *Populorum progressio* as a principle by promoting the creation of a truly human civilization, defending the dignity of husband and wife, and helping men and women live up to their calling as children of God.[31]

2. To the first principle of practical reasoning, *Good is to be done and pursued,* this first moral principle adds a reference to choice. While the first principle of practical reasoning underlies even spontaneous, intelligent acts where no choice is needed, the first moral principle comes into play only when a choice must be made. Thus, the first moral principle underlies the differentiation of moral responsibility, for one can will otherwise than it directs.[32] **Moreover, in referring to human goods, the first moral principle envisages them not merely as constituting diverse possible fields of action but as together comprising the stuff of integral human fulfillment.** The ideal of integral human fulfillment is that of a single system in which all the goods of human persons would contribute to the fulfillment of the whole community of persons.

In general, goodness is in fullness of being—that is, in realization of potentialities by which one is open to further and fuller realization of potentialities. This general notion of goodness also applies in the moral domain. By freely chosen human acts one determines oneself; in choosing one settles the thrust of one's own will. Moral goodness is in choices which not only lead to some participation in particular human goods—as all choices do— but which maintain a constant disposition toward all human possibilities. In other words, moral goodness is characteristic of choices in which one avoids unnecessary human self-limitation.

Apart from faith, humankind cannot know that integral human fulfillment is possible, and faith teaches that this possibility can be realized only by the divine act of re-creating all things in Jesus (see Eph 1.3–10; Col 1.15–20). However, reason does not exclude the possibility of integral human fulfillment, and a generous and reasonable love of human goods will lead one to act in a way compatible with this ideal. In so acting, some degree (and a concretely expanding degree) of human sharing in goods will be achieved and openness to integral fulfillment will be maintained; at the same time, unnecessary self-limitation will be avoided.

3. Integral human fulfillment is not individualistic satisfaction of desires; it is the realization of all the human goods in the whole human community. But in the course of human history—even in the course of each person's life—new dimensions of human goods unfold and new possibilities of serving them emerge. Moreover, the human community is not some limited group, but all human persons, past, present, and future. Thus, integral human fulfillment is an ideal corresponding to total human responsibility. Like the ideal of perfect love, it is something toward which one can work but which one can never reach by human effort. In other words, "integral human fulfillment" does not refer to a definite goal to be pursued as a concrete objective of cooperative human effort.

4. **The guidance which the ideal of integral human fulfillment offers to choice is to avoid unnecessary limitation and so maintain openness to further goods.** True, here and now one must pursue this or that; but one who chooses in a morally right way cares no less for the goods involved in the alternative not chosen. Constant openness to these goods is important for one's future choices, for one's attitude toward other people's choices, and for one's readiness to accept a share in divine life, which includes in a higher mode all the created goods of human persons.

5. This formulation and the one proposed by Vatican II (discussed in E above) are very close. The Council adds theological specifications: a reference to eternal law ("the divine plan and will") and a reference to the complete fulfillment in Jesus to which humankind actually is called ("their total vocation"). The present formulation makes reference to the general principles of practical reasoning based on the many human goods. Thus the Council's formulation, which benefits from the light of faith, presupposes and adds to the formulation proposed here, which can be understood by anyone, even without faith.

6. Because it is basic, the first principle of morality cannot be proved directly by being deduced from prior truths. However, several considerations indirectly support this formulation.

7. First, it shows the basis of morality in human goods. Proportionalism also wishes to show this, but the subordination of moral reflection to specific objectives, inherent in proportionalism, is here avoided. So, too, is the need to do the impossible by measuring and comparing goods as proportionalism requires. At the same time, the upright person is directed to remain open to goods beyond all the ways they can be embodied in courses of action which one could now pursue or even imagine. In short, the basic moral standard articulated here gives their due to aspects of morality which proportionalists tend to misconstrue.

A sound, nonproportionalist principle of morality will indicate how to make choices in such a way as to shape oneself in the light of the whole range and depth of the human possibilities opened up by the intelligible goods. The upright person will maintain openness to goods beyond his or her understanding of them as they are embodied in presently possible—or even presently thinkable—courses of action. This fact has two important implications for Christian morality.

First, the moral principle which shapes the life of every person of good will does not limit human fulfillment beforehand to a specific set of human satisfactions—for example, to the pattern of the "good life" taken for granted by the conventional morality of one's particular culture. An upright Greek was not limited to the ideal of wisdom proposed by Greek philosophy, but was open to the wisdom of the cross (see 1 Cor 1.18–25). An upright American is not limited to the ideal of prosperity and success which is proposed as the middle-class standard of the American way of life. Hence, the moral principle to which every person of good will adheres maintains openness to goods beyond everything human persons can ask or imagine, including openness to the heavenly fulfillments which are promised by God, fulfillments both in human and in divine goods: life and more abundant life (see Jn 10.10).

Second, sound morality can make sense of choices which have the character of commitments. By a commitment one determines oneself in reference to the basic human goods. By a basic commitment one accepts a certain place in the community of persons striving together to realize and share in the whole range of human possibilities. But commitments go beyond any particular objective; indeed, they provide one with the power to creatively think out objectives which one without commitment would not even consider. (Commitments are discussed more fully in 9-E.)

Choice inevitably involves a certain self-limitation. One actualizes one's possibilities through choice only by pursuing some and setting aside others. Choices made according to a principle which is logically independent of any particular objectives (any determinant set of wants) do not involve any self-limitation arising from the set of wants one happens to have at a given time. Choices made on a principle which logically depends upon the specification of goods by particular objectives do involve self-limitation by the limits of the set of wants one happens to have at a given time.

Thus, the choice to marry is inevitably self-limiting in excluding other possible partners. But if the choice is an upright commitment, one does not limit oneself to satisfying the specific desires one happens to have at the time. Thus one can continue to carry out the commitment as its meaning unfolds and one's desires change. But if the choice is not really a commitment, one limits oneself to carrying out a definite project. When marriage is found to be different from what one expected or when one's desires change, the project will be abandoned as too demanding or as pointless.

8. A second consideration which indirectly supports this formulation concerns the fact that many in the Catholic natural-law tradition have said the standard of morality is right reason (e.g., *S.t.*, 1–2, q. 18, a. 5; q. 19, a. 3; q. 71, a. 2). The present formulation articulates what is meant by "right reason." Even the immoral person reasons; one cannot violate conscience without reasoning to form it and rationalizing to violate it. But a morally upright person is reasonable in a way an immoral person is not (see *S.t.*, 1–2, q. 56, a. 3; q. 57, a. 4). He or she consistently follows reason, acknowledges all the goods, and accepts the openness of human possibility. By contrast, those who are immoral must curb reason and bring it into conformity with their choices; they must ignore or deny the openness of human possibility, in order to justify arbitrary limitations on human fulfillment.

9. Third, this view of the foundation of morality is reinforced by considering various ideas of moral evil with which it is consistent. Thus, moral evil is thought of as sin, as the violation of the rights of others, as a kind of practical folly, and as a sort of self-mutilation. It is sin (alienation from God), because it detracts from love of the goods God loves and prevents us from being open to him. It is likely to violate our neighbor's rights (or at least to lessen his or her well-being, which is unfriendly even when not unjust) inasmuch as it detracts from a will to integral human fulfillment, which includes our neighbor's good. It is surely a sort of folly, since it aims at unnecessarily restricted goods, while reason prescribes integral human fulfillment as self-evidently worthwhile, and to ignore in one's action the clear claim of reason is folly. And it plainly is a kind of self-mutilation, inasmuch as it detracts from the existential fullness of human persons who choose wrongly, since by such choices they determine themselves to be less—and to be less open to goods—than they might be.

The correctness of what has been said about the first principle of morality can be confirmed by considering in greater detail its relationship to the conceptions of immorality.

First, rejection of God. Immoral action is considered sinful. A genuinely religious attitude acknowledges that human purposes and possibilities have meaning which transcends their particular significance for the individual—meaning related in some way to God's goodness. However, when one chooses in a way incompatible with integral human fulfillment, one asserts in effect that the good is simply what one chooses, and that "goodness" means no more than what one causes it to mean by one's choices. To choose immorally is to set up an idol. By contrast, choices which conform to the primary principle of morality—a will to integral human fulfillment—leave open the possibility that the meaning of human life is not limited to what persons actually choose and attain, but derives at least in part from humankind's greater possibility of fulfillment in Jesus. Even without faith, one could see that immoral choice implicitly assumes that goods have no higher principle which sustains them when they are not chosen; morally upright choice, guided by the principle of a will toward integral human fulfillment, affirms (at least, in an implicit way) the reality of a more-than-human ground of human possibilities.

Second, violation of community. When one chooses a possibility which is not compatible with integral human fulfillment, one in effect makes a statement not only about the value for oneself inherent in the alternatives but about one's determination as to their value in themselves. If, then, others confronted with similar alternatives make a different choice, it follows that they have chosen wrongly. Presumably an individual who chooses wrongly is either stupid or immoral. Thus, in making an immoral choice, one inherently creates conflict between oneself and others who make different (morally right or wrong) choices. By contrast, one who chooses rightly, because he or she maintains a constant will toward integral human fulfillment, is also able to acknowledge the reasonableness and decency of others who make other choices consistent with the same basic moral standard. Morally upright people genuinely appreciate the value of diversity; they rejoice in the richer community it brings about, since this richer community is a better approach to the ideal: integral human fulfillment.

Third, unreasonableness in action. If one chooses a possibility which is not compatible with integral human fulfillment, one deafens oneself to an appeal to which no one can possibly be deaf, because it comes from within oneself. It is necessary to deny the reality of that of which one is perhaps all too aware—since it is part of oneself. To put the point abstractly: In choosing immorally, one treats as nongood (or as less good than it seemed) what is not chosen, but what is not chosen had a chance to be chosen only because one recognized in it and was attracted by the good it offered. Here there is a kind of inconsistency which is not logical contradiction, but which is unreasonableness in action.

Fourth, self-mutilation. When we are confronted with a choice, each possibility expresses something in us reaching out for realization. In any choice, something inevitably goes unrealized. But if one chooses a possibility which is not compatible with integral human fulfillment, some aspect of the self is suppressed and denied. It is told in effect not only that it is not going to be satisfied here and now, but that it is in principle not entitled to the satisfaction of a part of the self sharing in the dignity of the whole. When one chooses thus, part of one's personality is alienated.

Question G: What are the primary specifications of the first principle of morality?

1. By itself, the first principle of morality is obviously too general to provide practical guidance. Even if acts are defined in terms of choices and human goods, the principle's bearing on them remains obscure. Specifications of the first principle are needed. They must have a clear bearing on possible choices, so that the relationship—positive or negative—between the choices and integral human fulfillment will be clear. The principles of practical reasoning in general—for example, *Life is a good to be preserved*—do not specify the first principle of morality, for each refers only to one basic human good, not to integral human fulfillment.

2. The primary specifications of the first principle of morality are intermediate principles which stand midway between the first principle and the completely specific norms which direct choices. Here these principles are called "modes of responsibility," because they shape willing in view of the moral responsibility inherent in it. **The modes of responsibility specify—"pin down"—the primary moral principle by excluding as immoral actions which involve willing in certain specific ways inconsistent with a will toward integral human fulfillment.** An example of a mode of responsibility is the principle of impartiality which the Golden Rule expresses. This and seven other modes will be treated in the next chapter.

The principle of impartiality requires one not to favor oneself and those with whom one is identified by sympathy (for example, those who are near and dear) over others, unless one has a reason for discriminating which would be valid against oneself and those with whom one is identified by sympathy. In other words: "So whatever you wish that men would do to you, do so to them" (Mt 7.12; cf. Lk 6.31). The first principle of morality is specified by the principle of impartiality because the latter is only one intermediate-level moral truth among others. This is obvious because one does not violate the Golden Rule if one chooses wrongly in a way not unfair to anyone else.

The principle of impartiality generates completely specific moral norms such as the following: Parents who act as judges in a game should not favor their own children over other children. This norm is based on the mode of responsibility and the way of willing involved in a particular kind of action. All modes of responsibility work in a similar general way. One must consider the basic human goods involved in a possible action, and see how one responsible for the act would be related by choice (or some other mode of voluntariness) to the goods.

3. A classic explanation of temptation is based on New Testament teaching, interpreted in the light of a particular Christian philosophy of the human person. According to this explanation, emotion and intelligible good compete to shape behavior. Insofar as they are based on sentient nature, emotions are not bad; but they do move us toward very limited fulfillments of our concrete, sentient self as it actually is (see *S.t.*, 1–2, q. 71, a. 2, ad 3). By contrast, left to themselves, intelligent love and unrestricted reason would move us toward integral human fulfillment.

4. Despite having reasons for choosing otherwise, one can choose to follow one's feelings. The modes of responsibility exclude various ways in which feelings might lead one astray. In other words, if the primary principle of morality articulates what is meant by "right reason," the modes of responsibility exclude specific ways of acting unreasonably.

St. Paul suggests that there is a law in our members which struggles against the law of the mind (see Rom 7.22–23). Again, he talks of natural passions and desires which must be crucified so that Christians can walk according to the Spirit (see Gal 5.24–25). Denying that God tempts anyone, the Epistle of James points to an inner source of temptation: "But each person is tempted when he is lured and enticed by his own desire" (Jas 1.14). Accepting the position that the activity of reason is the specific perfection of human persons, St. Thomas takes "passion" in such texts to refer to sensuality and the "law of the mind" to refer to the principles of reasonable judgment. According to this view, human persons are tempted because emotion competes with intelligible good for the role of determinant of behavior, and one can choose to allow oneself to be determined by emotion to the detriment of a fully reasonable judgment of conscience.[33]

If temptation begins from emotion, so does interest in every morally acceptable possibility. Emotions as such are not morally evil; Jesus himself experienced them and was tempted as we are but did not sin (see Heb 4.15). Sin begins only when one freely chooses to satisfy emotion even at the cost of restricting reason. In sinning one excludes from consideration some aspects of human fulfillment which were in view before the wrong choice was made. Thus, in the context of unrepented sin, not only emotion but bad will and rationalization contribute to further temptation.

Someone might object that sometimes people cooly and calmly choose to do what is morally wrong, moved by rational calculation rather than emotion. For instance, merchants sometimes make a policy of cheating customers to improve profits, and military planners sometimes adopt terror tactics to break an enemy's will to fight.

This objection perhaps assumes that emotions operate only when people are so aroused and disturbed that they do not proceed cooly and calmly. But this is not so. Emotions are operative whenever anyone is concerned with a particular instance of good, whether experienced or imagined. Thus emotions play a role in every human choice, just as inner sensory cognition plays a role in every human thinking process. Normally, the emotional component of action does not call attention to itself; it does so only if it is not entirely integrated or brings about unusual physiological symptoms. Fear is not limited to cases in which a terrified person shakes, stammers, and so on. One who takes care in crossing a busy street also is moved by it.

Merchants who cheat and military planners who use terror usually are carrying out previous immoral commitments. Thus, their current immoral acts express bad will and twisted thinking. But the nonrational appeal of certain goods made possible the initial morally wrong choices and continues to play a role. The good of me and mine has an emotional appeal greater than that of the faceless public and the depersonalized enemy. The goods to be purchased with fraudulent profit or the status quo to be preserved by terroristic force can have emotional appeal greater than that of justice in competition or integrity in defeat.

The role of reason in such cases is clarified by the fact that one invokes against unfairness the rational principle of universalizability and against unprincipled pragmatism the rational noncommensurability of goods. The immoral merchant or military planner will allege their own "realism" against moral "idealism." Contrary arguments will be set aside by an appeal to unanalyzable feeling, perhaps dignified with the title "common sense" or "the community's scale of values."

5. The definite goals people pursue appeal to imagination and emotion, while the intelligible goods to which upright persons are committed do not directly make such an appeal. For example, the goal of sexual satisfaction has an immediate appeal which faithful marital communion lacks. Hence, a temptation to act immorally often takes the form of an impulse to violate or neglect one's commitments by pursuing some particular goal. One is tempted to subordinate being (interpersonal communion) to having—for example, being a Christian to having the rewards of worldly success, being a husband or wife to having pleasure in an extramarital relationship. All the modes protect commitments in line with integral human fulfillment against such subversion by inappropriate goal seeking.

6. The modes of responsibility take the form of negative propositions. This does not mean that morality itself is negative; the principles of practical reason in general are affirmative, and the first principle of morality calls for openness to integral human fulfillment. **Each mode of responsibility simply excludes a particular way in which a person can limit himself or herself to a quite partial and inadequate fulfillment.** Their negative form precludes conflict among them. Their demands cannot be incompatible, for one can always simultaneously *not make* any number of possible choices.

7. People are ordinarily interested in completely specific moral norms, not in the modes of responsibility which generate them. Thus, although the modes are more definite than the first principle of morality, one usually does not think about them by themselves. For this reason, in the history of ethics and moral theology modes of responsibility have not been discussed systematically up to now.

8. If not systematically discussed, however, most have been articulated—for example, as the principle of impartiality is articulated in the Golden Rule (see Mt 7.12; Lk 6.31).[34] Many proverbs embody or are based on modes of responsibility. Also at one time or another, almost every one of these modes has been taken by some philosopher as the first principle of morality—an understandable error, since the modes embody the first principle. Finally, as chapter eight will show, there is some basis in Scripture for each mode of responsibility.

The modes of responsibility do not exclude the fulfillment of emotional needs and the pursuit of suitable goals. One's concrete sentient self is part of one's whole self; emotional fulfillment is part of integral human fulfillment. However, the demands of feeling and desires for particular goals can be satisfied rightly only insofar as they are included within some intelligible good, and that good, in turn, is chosen compatibly with integral human fulfillment. For example, parental affection should not be satisfied by unreasonable partiality among one's children, but may be satisfied by carrying out parental responsibilities toward all of them. A desire to obtain rectification of particular injustices should not be satisfied by revolutionary terrorism, but may be satisfied by a campaign of nonviolent resistance to make the truth of the injustice clear to all concerned.

As explained above, the first principle of morality can be formulated in terms of right reason in action. The explanation in the present question further clarifies this formulation of the moral principle, since modes of responsibility exclude various ways of being unreasonable in action. Thus, stated negatively, the first principle is: Do not be unreasonable in acting. The modes of responsibility are: Do not be unreasonable in such and such ways (for instance, by partiality) in acting.

Since the first principle of morality is broader than any one of the modes of responsibility, a moral system based exclusively on one mode would be too loose. For example, the Golden Rule is not adequate as a general principle of morality, for it is exclusively concerned with the way one treats others. One might commit suicide without violating the Golden Rule. Suicide violates a different mode of responsibility. The commendatory saying of Jesus about the Golden Rule (see Mt 7.12) must be understood in context; it summarizes the law and the prophets only as to their moral implications for human interpersonal relationships, not, for instance, as to their implications for our relationship with ourselves.

Question H: How are the modes of responsibility related to the virtues?

1. Much that Scripture and Christian teaching say about morality is cast in the language of virtues. Furthermore, the normative content of statements about virtues can be organized and clarified by the modes of responsibility. Hence, an explanation of the relationship between the modes of responsibility and the virtues will be helpful.

2. The modes of responsibility are, to repeat, propositions which specify the first principle of morality. They are understood and generate judgments of conscience prior to choice. Thus, they are present in the thinking of the child who first chooses with or against conscience, and they remain present in the thinking of immoral people as long as they are aware of the moral truth they violate.

3. Like the modes of responsibility, virtues are not concerned with specific kinds of acts. Virtues are aspects of personality as a whole when all the other dimensions of the self are integrated with morally good commitments (see 2-I). Commitments establish one's existential identity; a whole personality integrated with a morally good self is virtuous. **Since such a personality is formed by choices which are in accord with the first principle of morality and the modes of responsibility, the virtues embody the modes.** In other words, the modes of responsibility shape the existential self of a good person, this self shapes the whole personality, and so good character embodies and expresses the modes.

As was explained (5-A), goodness is a realization of potentialities which tends to further and fuller realization; badness is in a realization of potentialities which blocks further and fuller realization. Thus a virtue is a disposition to goodness, and a vice a disposition to badness. Because of the dynamic character of goodness, dispositions defined in terms of it do not lead to habits—that is, to repetitive patterns of behavior of the same sort. Rather, a virtue will dispose one to a constantly changing pattern of behavior, whose only regular feature will be that it realizes potentialities in any given instance in a way consistent with the openness and growth which define goodness. Because immorality is limiting, vicious dispositions do involve elements of habit.[35]

This point can be illustrated in the nonmoral sphere. (English barely recognizes the existence of nonmoral virtues.) A great painter, such as Monet, had the dispositions to do excellent work in his art. The result of these virtues is not empirically describable constancy in his work, although Monet was limited by certain aspects of his style and techniques, which can be described. Rather, the effect of the artistic virtues of Monet was that his performance continued to improve and his works continued to show unexpected freshness and originality.

4. Discussion of virtues is thus helpful in describing what is required by the various modes. Furthermore, one who understands the virtues sees the essential point of being morally good, since good action of itself makes one virtuous, and being virtuous signifies fulfillment of the person with respect to the existential goods.

5. Insofar as character is a unified whole, distinct virtues are not separate entities but only aspects of a good person. They, and their corresponding vices, can therefore be distinguished in various ways. In chapter eight, the modes of responsibility will be used for this purpose. Furthermore, since the modes correspond to the Beatitudes, as chapter twenty-six will explain, a discussion of the virtues in the framework provided by the modes escapes the limitations of a conventional, worldly morality.

6. During the classical period of moral theology, some theologians, reacting against too narrow a view of human acts and too minimalistic an understanding of moral norms, called for an ethics of virtue rather than law. As the preceding explanation of the relationship between virtues and modes of responsibility makes clear, however, virtues do not provide a normative source distinct from propositional principles such as the modes and the completely specific norms they generate (cf. *S.t.*, 1–2, q. 51, a. 1; q. 94, a. 3; 2–2, q. 47, a. 6). The account given here and above (2-I) makes it clear that there is no dichotomy between propositional moral principles, the choices which realize them existentially, and the virtues which body them out in the personality as a whole. Chapter twenty-six will show the even more intimate relationship between specifically Christian modes and virtues.

Those who wish to emphasize character and the general trend of one's life, rather than particular human acts, are partly correct. Not all particular acts are of equal significance. Some sins are only venial, and there are various reasons why this is so. Moreover, even mortal sins are not all equally grave, and a mortal sin from which one is quickly converted by God's grace is less important than the act of faith which maintains the continuity of one's Christian life.

Theories which emphasize character and the general trend of one's life nevertheless suffer from a major defect: They fail to realize that character itself—which is one's virtues or vices as a whole—is chiefly (although not solely) the enduring structure of one's choices. Choices are self-determinations to do something or other; they are the most central principle in oneself of one's acts. The enduring, spiritual reality of one's choices, especially the larger ones which mainly shape one's identity, is the principle of an integrated moral self. Character simply is this self, regarded as the source of further acts.

Thus, those who wish to emphasize character rather than particular acts are setting up a false dichotomy between them. Character itself essentially is particular choices, and it manifests itself in further particular acts. Of course, one who has a developed character often acts with no need for further choices, since the self is well enough defined by past choices. Most possibilities which suggest themselves or are suggested by other people seem uninteresting or definitely less appealing than lines of action which express one's character.

Summary

Much Catholic teaching on natural law refers to the work of St. Thomas Aquinas, and Vatican II commends him as a guide. We can therefore examine his treatment of natural law to see how the Church views the subject.

"Law" for St. Thomas primarily means a reasonable plan of action. He begins from what he calls the "eternal law"—God's plan in creating and redeeming. Any other reasonable plan of action must somehow derive from it. People can plan their lives reasonably only because, in one way or another, they share in the universal plan present in God's law; to the extent they try to follow some other plan, their lives are unrealistic.

Human beings, according to St. Thomas, are naturally disposed to understand some basic practical principles. These are the primary principles of natural law— what St. Paul calls the law written in one's heart (see Rom 3.14–16). However, truths of natural law, including specific norms, are also part of revelation. As Vatican I says, this is in part so that "even in the present condition of the human race, those religious truths which are by their nature accessible to human reason can readily be known by all men with solid certitude and with no trace of error" (DS 3005/1786; translation supplied). Thus natural law and divine law can be distinguished, but not separated and opposed.

Practical thinking is reasoning and judging about what might and ought to be. According to St. Thomas, its first principle is: The good is to be done and pursued; the bad is to be avoided. Scholastic natural-law theory formulated this as a moral imperative: Do good and avoid evil. But, as Thomas' formulation shows, the first principle is not a moral norm. It expresses the intrinsic, necessary connection between human goods and actions which bear upon them; in thinking about what one might do, it is impossible to disregard entirely the goods and bads involved.

People grasp as goods all the fulfillments to which they are naturally inclined. Corresponding to each natural inclination, therefore, is a basic precept of natural law: Such and such a basic human good is to be done and/or pursued, protected, and promoted. These are general determinations of the first principle. In their light we can see why human nature and natural law morality are both stable and changing: stable because they are based on fundamental, unalterable natural inclinations; changing because these potentialities are open to continuing, expanding fulfillment.

But such principles of practical reasoning do not tell us what is morally good. Moral norms are needed to guide choices toward the fulfillment of persons in relation to human goods.

The first principle of morality might best be formulated as follows: In voluntarily acting for human goods and avoiding what is opposed to them, one ought to choose and otherwise will those and only those possibilities whose willing is compatible with a will toward integral human fulfillment. Note that this conceives human goods not simply as diverse fields for possible action, but as together comprising the totality of integral human fulfillment. This avoids subordinating moral reflection to specific objectives; instead, the upright person is to remain open to goods which go beyond his or her present capacity for realizing them in action.

There is also need for intermediate principles of morality, midway between the first principle and the completely specific norms which direct particular choices. These are the modes of responsibility. An example is the principle of fairness or impartiality expressed by the Golden Rule. These modes exclude choices involving various unreasonable (immoral) relationships of willing to the human goods. People who are thinking in a morally sound way commonly take them for granted. But for the most part they have not been systematically discussed up to now, though at one time or another almost every one of them has been mistaken for the first principle of morality.

Scripture and Christian moral teaching do not speak of modes of responsibility but of virtues. However, the virtues do not constitute moral norms distinct from the modes; rather, virtues embody modes. For virtues are aspects of a personality integrated around good commitments, and the latter are choices in accord with the first principle of morality and the modes of responsibility.

Appendix 1:   How one knows the basic human goods

How does one come to know the general determinations of the first principle of practical reasoning? This question can be considered on two levels. On one level, the question is how anyone directly and practically knows that human life, for example, is good and death is bad. On another level, the question is a methodological one: How is a definite list arrived at? How could it be checked? This second, methodological question was treated above (5-D).

As to the first question, practical insight into the various forms of human fulfillment cannot be derived from any more general knowledge. One does not come to know these goods by deducing them from prior principles. But neither is knowing them a matter of experience in the sense that knowing fire burns is a matter of experience. To know that fire burns is to understand something which is the case. To know that life is a good is to understand something of human possibility. In practice life is understood as good only insofar as it is to be realized or is threatened and needs to be protected. How can one understand on the basis of experience what is not actual but only potential?

This question can be answered only if one realizes that human intelligence does not become practical merely by its subject matter, nor merely by being moved by will or inclination. Reason is practical by nature just as much as it is theoretical by nature. And just as theoretical thought by its very nature is thinking *that-it-is,* so practical thinking by its very nature is thinking *that-it-would-be-well-to-be.* Facing the world, one not only wonders, "What is so and not so?" but also, "What might I bring about or not bring about?" Underlying the theoretical question is a frame of mind which can be expressed: What is so must be affirmed, and what is not so must be denied. Underlying the practical question is a frame of mind which can be expressed: Good is to be done and pursued, and evil is to be avoided.⁵⁶

With this practical presupposition in mind, people experience their tendencies and understand in them possibilities which could be satisfied by action. The tendencies, simply as psychic facts, are not themselves knowledge of human goods. Tendencies might move one to action, but they are no more reasons for acting than are any other facts. However, in the experience of tendencies, human understanding which is oriented toward possible action grasps the possible fulfillments to which the tendencies point. Thus one forms, naturally and without reflection, the truth: Such-and-such is a good.

A practical truth grasped in this way is so basic and so obvious that it is seldom stated expressly or considered by itself. People who become aware that food is becoming scarce think they must try to ensure their supply. Underlying this thought is awareness of a fact— food is necessary for survival—and the practical truth: Life is to be preserved.

Some tendencies can be at least partly satisfied by nature and by the action of other persons. The process of gaining insight into goods partly depends upon this fact. In experiencing a tendency and its satisfaction, one learns factual truths which provide a background for the practical insight. Thus, for instance, children are naturally curious and naturally grow in understanding as they ask and answer questions. Insight into this process provides a basis for the practical insight that knowledge is a good which can be pursued by one's own deliberate action. However, this insight cannot be derived from nonpractical awareness. Practical awareness is an irreducible starting point of self-actualization, which is a creative process of exploring and realizing one's own possibilities by one's own initiative.

To the extent that the understanding of basic forms of human goodness is a projection of possibilities implicit in one's naturally given tendencies, this understanding is stable and invariant. Thus the concept of truth as a good remains an invariant framework insofar as this practical insight corresponds to natural curiosity, for such curiosity does not change.

However, any experience of fulfillment in any basic form of goodness leads to some specification of interest. The child at first asks questions about everything, but later wonders only about certain subjects. Moreover, experience of fulfillment together with theoretical inquiry leads to more or less detailed practical sketches of the basic goods. Truth, for example, is articulated into a set of fields of study. The secondary parts of the understanding of the basic forms of human goodness can develop and vary, and they can include mistakes and thus be open to correction.

What is true of goods such as life and truth also is true, mutatis mutandis, of the personal and interpersonal goods of the existential domain. The various levels of existential harmony are understood as good on the basis of human tendencies no less fundamental than the urges to survive, to play, and to understand. For everyone wants peace of mind, friends, and a favorable relationship with unseen Power. But differences in experience and in theoretical beliefs make a great difference in how people conceive these goods in specific detail.

Appendix 2:   Further clarification of the first moral principle

Since the first principle of morality is at once so important and so difficult to grasp, further reflection might be helpful to clarify its precise meaning and so to help make its truth comprehensible. To some extent this clarification will come about in later discussions, as the principle is shaped into general modes of responsibility and specified by the human condition understood in the light of faith. However, even at the present level of abstractness, some additional explanation of the first principle is possible.

Any ethical theory based upon the ordering of human actions to human fulfillment must account for the fact that not every choice is morally evil, yet every choice responds to the appeal of the human goods promised by one possible course of action and leaves unanswered the appeal of the equally basic and incommensurable goods promised by one or more other courses of action. That each of these goods is to be realized and protected is a starting point for deliberation about possibilities which would realize or protect it. Such a starting point is a (premoral) principle of practical reasoning. Corresponding to the whole set of basic human goods is the whole set of principles of practical reasoning.

The whole set of principles directs that all the goods be realized and protected. But even morally evil acts depend upon and respond to some of these principles. Therefore, none of the principles of practical reasoning is a moral norm merely by being a principle of practical reasoning. That human life is a good to be protected, for example, does not by itself dictate that killing is always wrong.

The distinction between moral good and evil is a distinction between ways in which proposed courses of action are related to the whole set of principles of practical thinking. Some proposals comport well with all of the human goods. Others comport well with some of the principles of practical thinking—those which direct action to the goods promised by these proposals—but are inconsistent with or inadequately responsive to one or more others. It is morally good to adopt proposals of the former sort and morally bad to adopt proposals of the latter sort.

One about to choose in a morally right way respects equally all of the basic human goods and listens equally to all of the appeals they make through the principles of practical thinking. Because of the incompatibility of concrete possibilities—one cannot do everything at once—choice is necessary. No single good, nothing promised by any single possible course of action, exhausts human possibilities and realizes integral human fulfillment. But just as two propositions which have no common terms cannot be inconsistent with each other, so any proposed course of action is consistent with those principles of practical thinking to which it is merely irrelevant. Moreover, one who chooses cannot be inadequately responsive to a principle of practical thinking if the principle in question has played no role whatsoever in the deliberation leading to that choice.

Thus, one can choose in a morally upright way. One can choose one possibility which promises certain goods and is irrelevant to other goods promised by an alternative, without violating the practical principle which directs action to these other goods. One does not adopt a restrictive standard of human fulfillment. One's understanding of all the human goods, one's appreciation of the special contributions they can make to integral human fulfillment, remains the same after the choice as before.

One about to choose in a morally wrong way does not respect and respond equally to all of the basic human goods, does not listen equally to all of the appeals they make through the principles of practical thinking. The proposal he or she is about to adopt involves detriment to some human good, or at least it involves slighting some good. One is tempted to accept this detriment to or slighting of a good for the sake of another good which will thereby be possible. Such a proposed course of action is responsive to at least one principle of practical thinking, and it might be irrelevant to—and so consistent with—some others. But it is both relevant to and inconsistent with (or, at least, inadequately responsive to) the principle which directs to the good with which the choice comports less well. Yet the goods represented by these different principles are equally basic and equally essential to the ideal of integral human fulfillment.

Thus, one can choose in a morally wrong way. One is wholly or partly voluntarily unresponsive to the appeal of some of the basic human goods. In making such a wrong choice—a procedure which might be called "exclusivistic choice"—one's understanding of the various goods is itself affected. The good which is violated or downrated is no longer considered equally basic and incommensurable with the good which is preferred. The preferred good is considered a "greater good" while the other becomes a "lesser good." The choice, which is partly irrational insofar as it is inadequately responsive to some principle of practical thinking, is rationalized by reappraising the value of the good one has rejected or whose appeal one has partly ignored.

Although the fair treatment of persons is itself a question within morality, one can understand the preceding explanation by analogy with fairness and unfairness. The principles of practical reason which are in play during deliberation are like the appeals for consideration made by a number of different persons. When one is confronted with many different and incompatible requests, one cannot satisfy all of them. One must choose. An upright person will be impartial in making this choice. One appeal will not be preferred and another set aside out of motives which have nothing to do with the content of the various appeals. If one were to do this, one would have to ignore or even deny part of the intrinsic force of the appeal one rejected. After making such a choice, one could not continue to regard all of the persons involved as equal. One would have to pretend the person one treated unfairly was of less worth, thus to justify the unfair treatment. In making immoral choices, we deal in a similar way with the various basic human goods and the principles of practical reason which represent them in deliberation.

Appendix 3: Natural law, the magisterium, and dissenting theologians

Dissenting theologians often criticized the magisterium's references to natural law. Such criticism was especially prevalent after *Humanae vitae*. Charles Curran and his associates rejected "some of the specific ethical conclusions contained in the Encyclical. They are based on an inadequate concept of natural law: the multiple forms of natural law theory are ignored and the fact that competent philosophers come to different conclusions on this very question is disregarded."[37]

In fact, the moral teaching of *Humanae vitae* is not based on any concept of natural law or any philosophical argument at all. It is received teaching in the Church, and it originated (probably before Christ) before there was any natural law theory to articulate and defend it. Natural law theories are theology; the Church's moral teaching is part of the Judeo-Christian heritage.[38]

Curran and his associates also attacked what they called "biologism" in *Humanae vitae:* "Other defects include: overemphasis on the biological aspects of conjugal relations as ethically normative; undue stress on sexual acts and on the faculty of sex viewed in itself, apart from the person and the couple . . . ."[39] Richard A. McCormick, S.J., urged that the moral criterion must be the whole person, not part of the person, and reported that many held similar views; they often cited Vatican II's statement that the moral criteria for birth regulation must be based on "the nature of the human person and his acts" (GS 51).[40]

The argument about biologism can be taken as an expression of self-body dualism. In the Birth Control Commission, proponents of contraception implicitly asserted such dualism by saying that biological fecundity "ought to be assumed into the human sphere and be regulated within it."[41] This implied that the fecundity of human persons is in itself outside the human and personal, since one need not "assume" what one already is. I have treated this matter elsewhere.[42]

The dissenting theologians could grant that human sexuality is personal of itself, yet claim it is only one part of the person, whose fulfillment can be outweighed by other parts. This move was made by talking about the whole person and by referring to Vatican II. The Council teaches that there must be objective criteria for birth regulation, and it does say these should be based on the "nature of the human person and his acts." But it adds immediately that these acts must "preserve the full sense of mutual self-giving and human procreation in the context of true love" (GS 51). This last phrase, with its reference to procreation, was regularly omitted by dissenting theologians. They likewise omitted what the Council immediately adds about the need to cultivate the virtue of marital chastity and to conform one's conscience to the teaching proposed by the magisterium. In short, dissenting theology built its argument on a selected phrase from the Vatican II document.[43]

Correctly interpreted, what the Council teaches cannot support the approval of contraception unless one reads into the Council a proportionalist theory of moral judgment. If one does, one can suppose that the full sense of procreation in conjugal acts can be preserved in marriage as a whole while being excluded from some of its acts, on the supposition that this exclusion is a premoral evil outweighed by the overriding value of the contribution regular orgasms make to marital love. Again, since proportionalism is indefensible, the argument collapses.

Notes

1. See C. Spicq, O.P., *Théologie Morale du Nouveau Testament*, 14th ed., vol. 1 (Paris: J. Gabalda, 1970), 394–406.

2. See also John XXIII, *Pacem in terris*, 55 *AAS* (1963) 258–59; *The Papal Encyclicals*, 270.4–9, for the contrast between natural law—an order inscribed by God in human nature and known by conscience—and the laws of lower nature. This moral order is prior to positive law and it sets the standard for all human interpersonal relationships. The encyclical goes on to develop in detail a catalogue of the rights and duties which flow directly from human nature.

3. In his encyclical, *Libertas*, 20 *ASS* (1888) 594–97; *The Papal Encyclicals*, 103.4–8, Leo XIII, who so highly commends the teaching of Thomas in general, closely follows his treatment of natural law and its relationship to free choice. A useful introduction to St. Thomas' natural-law theory, with good bibliographies: Jean-Marie Aubert, *Loi de Dieu, Lois des Hommes* (Tournai: Desclée, 1964), 31–116.

4. St. Thomas Aquinas, *Summa theologiae*, 1–2, q. 96, a. 4, makes it clear that much we call "law" is not law at all for him; he considers rules and commands laws only if they conform to morality, and so to God's law.

5. See also John XXIII, *Pacem in terris*, 55 *AAS* (1963) 266–67; *The Papal Encyclicals*, 270.37–38, where the universal, absolute, and immutable principles of natural law are identified with the unchanging truth which is the foundation of the moral order, and this truth is grounded in the reason of the true, personal, and transcendent God. A recent statement of moral objectivity with reference to current confusions about conscience: "Conscience et morale: Déclaration doctrinale de la Conférence épiscopale irlandaise," *Documentation catholique*, 78 (1981), 31–40. A systematic theological treatment of this point: Ramón García de Haro, *La conciencia moral*, 2d ed. rev. (Madrid: Rialp, 1978).

6. Pius XII, *Humani generis*, 42 *AAS* (1950) 561–62; *The Papal Encyclicals*, 240.2–3. See also Pius XI, *Casti connubii*, 22 *AAS* (1930) 579–80; *The Papal Encyclicals*, 208.102–3, for a development of the same point, and the foundation of the competency of the Church in marriage morality in God's supplementation of the light of reason by revelation, whose interpretation is entrusted to the Church's teaching office.

7. *S.t.*, 1–2, q. 100, aa. 1 and 3; St. Irenaeus, *Adversus Haereses*, iv, 13, 1 and 4. See Dario Composta, "Il diritto naturale in S. Ireneo," *Apollinaris*, 45 (1972), 599–612. See the brief, cogent exegetical study of the fathers: Guy Bourgeault, "La spécificité de la morale chrétienne selon les Pères des deux premiers siècles," *Science et Esprit*, 23 (1971), 137–52. Classical Lutheran ethics did not take a different point of view on this matter: Theodore R. Jungkuntz, "Trinitarian Ethics," *Center Journal*, 1 (Spring 1982), 48–51.

8. Sound exegetical studies confirm the truth of the Church's teaching with respect to Scripture. See, for example, the brilliant summary by a leading, non-Catholic Scripture scholar: W. D. Davies, "Ethics in the New Testament," *Interpreter's Dictionary of the Bible*, 2:167–76. In the Old Testament, too, God's law is presented as an expression of wisdom recognizable in principle as valid by the nations (see Dt 4.5–8); for a helpful analysis: Jon D. Levenson, "The Theologies of Commandment in Biblical Israel," *Harvard Theological Review*, 73 (1980), 17–33.

9. See summaries in Richard A. McCormick, S.J., *Notes on Moral Theology: 1965 through 1980* (Washington, D.C.: University Press of America, 1981), 251–58 and 684–87 (hereinafter cited as *"Notes"*). Also: Timothy E. O'Connell, *Principles for a Catholic Morality* (New York: Seabury Press, 1978), 96–97.

10. Besides the materials cited in the preceding note, see Richard A. McCormick, S.J., "Moral Theology since Vatican II: Clarity or Chaos," *Cross Currents*, 29 (Spring 1979), 25; he says that a fresh notion of the magisterium has emerged and within its perspective "much more attention is given to evidence and analyses in evaluating authentic teaching. Only persuasive arguments command assent." Gerard J. Hughes, S.J., *Authority in Morals: An Essay in Christian Ethics* (London: Heythrop Monographs, 1978), denies that "appeal to revelation will enable us to solve moral dilemmas to which there is no other adequate solution" (10). He holds "that there is no specifically Christian authority in ethics by appeal to which we can effectively hope to foreclose any moral argument," and that any moral authority "owes its status as an authority to the success with which it interprets the facts, and it is to these alone that any ultimate appeal can be made" (123–24).

11. The position is sometimes put in terms of an injunction that the magisterium's role is to ask questions on moral issues rather than to answer them, or to conduct a dialogue to elicit the insights of the faithful: Charles E. Curran, *Themes in Fundamental Moral Theology* (Notre Dame and London: University of Notre Dame Press, 1977), 118: "Too often in the past the teaching or prophetic role of the Church has been seen in giving answers or pronouncements to particular questions. This approach wedded to a claim of absolute certitude actually hindered the Church from properly fulfilling its teaching and prophetic function." Cf. Bernard Häring, *Free and Faithful in Christ: Moral Theology for Clergy and Laity*, vol. 1, *General Moral Theology* (New York: Seabury Press, 1978), 331–33.

12. For example, the story about Onan (see Gn 38.9–10) was very often cited as the basis of the Church's teaching on contraception. No matter what anyone today thinks this passage means, the fact that it was used as it was shows that those who handed on the teaching believed it was divinely revealed—see, e.g., *Casti connubii*, quoting St. Augustine, 22 *AAS* (1930) 559–60; *The Papal Encyclicals*, 208.55. In a symposium conducted after the publication of *Humanae vitae*, Joseph Coppens, an Old Testament scholar, made this precise point: "All moral textbooks, theological and philosophical, from the earliest centuries on, speak of Onan's sin as contraception. (Whether this agrees with contemporary scholarship, which sees Onan's sin as a refusal to obey the levirate law, is not at issue here.) Onan's sin has been constantly and universally condemned; this is the constant teaching referred to in the encyclical" ("A Symposium on 'Humanae vitae' and the Natural Law," *Louvain Studies*, 2 [Spring 1969], 224).

13. It has been argued that the phrase, "faith and morals," has shifted its meaning in the course of history: Piet Fransen, S.J., "A Short History of the Meaning of the Formula, 'Fides et Mores,'" *Louvain Studies*, 7 (1979), 270–301. Up to Trent, "morals" denoted (Always? Or, perhaps, only sometimes?) legal institutions we would not include in that category today. But it is not shown that Christian moral norms ever have been outside the reference of one or the other term, for since Trent "morals" came to refer to them, while in earlier times "faith" was less limited (to assent to propositional truths) and had a more inclusive, existential sense. Prior to the Reformation, all Christians believed that saving faith included both assent to the truths of faith and a real effort to live up to them. See Teodoro López Rodriguez, "'Fides et mores' en Trento," *Scripta Theologica*, 5 (1973), 175–221; Marcelino Zalba, S.J., "'Omnis et salutaris veritas et morum disciplina': Sentido de la expresión 'mores' en el Concilio de Trento," *Gregorianum*, 54 (1973), 679–715.

14. The continuity between the papal magisterium and Vatican II on the Church's competency in teaching natural law is shown by John J. Reed, S.J., "Natural Law, Theology, and the Church," *Theological Studies*, 26 (1965), 40–64. See also the helpful discussion by McCormick (at the time in agreement with Reed and critical of Gregory Baum's views): *Notes*, 16–20. For a commentary on Vatican II's teaching on natural law with a critique of some current theological positions at odds with it, see John Finnis, "The Natural Law, Objective Morality, and Vatican II," in *Principles of Catholic Moral Life*, ed. William E. May (Chicago: Franciscan Herald Press, 1980), 113–49. A critique of views which attempt to separate autonomous morality from faith: Ferdinando Citterio, "Morale

autonoma e fede cristiana: Il dibattito continua," *Scuola cattolica*, 108 (1980), 509–61, esp. 542–61; 109 (1981), 3–29, esp. 26–29.

15. See Josef Fuchs, S.J., *Natural Law: A Theological Investigation* (New York: Sheed and Ward, 1965), 10. This book, written before Fuchs became a proportionalist, is reliable in general, although it is imbued with scholastic natural-law theory. See also Edouard Hamel, S.J., *Loi Naturelle et Loi du Christ* (Bruges: Desclée de Brouwer, 1964), 11–43.

16. Pius XII, "Nuntius Radiophonicus" (1 June 1941), 33 *AAS* (1941) 197; see Fuchs, op. cit., 12. In his inaugural encyclical, *Summi Pontificatus*, 31 *AAS* (1939) 423–25; *The Papal Encyclicals*, 222.28–32, Pius XII, writing at the outbreak of World War II, traces the descending darkness back to the Reformation, with its "abandonment of that Christian teaching of which the Chair of Peter is the depository and exponent." "Cut off from the infallible teaching authority of the Church, not a few separated brethren have gone so far as to overthrow the central dogma of Christianity, the Divinity of the Saviour, and have hastened thereby the progress of spiritual decay." Secularization—the emergence of a new paganism—resulted in the stilling or weakening of conscience, due to "the inability of all human effort to replace the law of Christ by anything equal to it." Thus the cause of the deplorable evils of modern society "is the denial and rejection of a universal norm of morality as well for individual and social life as for international relations; We mean the disregard, so common nowadays, and the forgetfulness of the natural law itself, which has its foundation in God." In sum: "With the weakening of faith in God and in Jesus Christ, and the darkening in men's minds of the light of moral principles, there disappeared the indispensable foundation of the stability and quiet of that internal and external, private and public order, which alone can support and safeguard the prosperity of States."

17. See Leo XIII, *Tametsi futura prospicientibus*, 33 *ASS* (1900–1901) 279; *The Papal Encyclicals*, 153.7; "By the law of Christ we mean not only the natural precepts of morality and the Ancient Law, all of which Jesus Christ has perfected and crowned by His declaration, explanation and sanction; but also the rest of His doctrine and His own peculiar institutions." See also Pius IX, *Qui pluribus*, *Pii IX Acta* (1846–54), I, 1:10; *The Papal Encyclicals*, 40.10: "God Himself has set up a living authority to establish and teach the true and legitimate meaning of His heavenly revelation. This authority judges *infallibly* all disputes which concern matters of faith and morals, lest the faithful be swirled around by every wind of doctrine which springs from the evilness of men in encompassing error." Pius XI, *Mit brennender Sorge*, 29 *AAS* (1937) 158–59; *The Papal Encyclicals*, 218.29: "It is on faith in God, preserved pure and stainless, that man's morality is based." Pius XII, *Ad Apostolorum Principis*, 50 *AAS* (1958) 608; *The Papal Encyclicals*, 261.33: "By God's appointment the observance of the natural law concerns the way by which man must strive toward his supernatural end. The Church shows the way and is the guide and guardian of men with respect to their supernatural end." Among the theologians who explain and defend this position: Carlo Caffarra, *Viventi in Cristo* (Milan: Jaca Book, 1981); Ermenegildo Lio, *Morale e beni terreni: La destinazione universale dei beni terreni nella "Gaudium et spes"* (Rome: Città Nuova, 1976), 18–29; Jean-Marie Aubert, "La morale chrétienne selon saint Thomas," *Seminarium*, 29 (1977), 780–811.

18. McCormick, *Notes*, 20.

19. Anthony Battaglia, *Toward a Reformulation of Natural Law* (New York: Seabury Press, 1981), systematically ignores both the distinction between the two phases of practical reasoning and that between the theoretical and the practical. Overlooking the latter, he thinks that "good is to be done and evil is to be avoided" means that "ordinary human beings ordinarily want to be good" (5; cf. 63) and that natural law properly is a de facto conformity of man to eternal law, which synderesis and inclination only bring us to know (51). Except for a suggestion that social practices should be established by consensus rather than force (108, 135), he also overlooks the distinction between the two phases of practical reasoning and accepts a thoroughgoing cultural relativism (132–35) as well as a reduction of moral judgment to a process analogous to aesthetic intuition (79, 108). To impose all this on St. Thomas, Battaglia has to make him out to be a sceptic. Thomas' theory of analogous predication is distorted to mean that "our knowledge is analogical—neither wholly true nor wholly false" (33; cf. 41, 101, 116). Moreover, Thomas' theory of morality is reduced to a simple pragmatism in which the good is what works and what has worked in the past (72, 128–32).

20. See Germain G. Grisez, "The First Principle of Practical Reason: A Commentary on the *Summa theologiae*, 1–2, Question 94, Article 2," *Natural Law Forum*, 10 (1965), 181–86. Also: Ignacio de Celaya, "La Sindéresis, Principio de Rectitud Moral," in *Etica y Teología ante la crisis contemporánea: I simposio internacional de Teología de la Universidad de Navarra*, ed. J. L. Illanes et al. (Pamplona, Spain: EUNSA, 1980), 127–43.

21. For a typical statement of the view being evaluated here, see Charles E. Curran, *Contemporary Problems in Moral Theology* (Notre Dame, Ind.: Fides Publishers, 1970), 116–36. See also Michael Bertram Crowe, *The Changing Profile of the Natural Law* (The Hague: Martinus Nijhoff, 1977), 258–59, 266–75, and 286–89. In part, Crowe bases his position (289) on St. Thomas' statements that human nature is mutable, but Crowe himself had shown in a previous article that these statements only mean that human nature exists in diverse conditions which leave human persons (unlike angels) open to change: Michael B. Crowe, "Human Nature—Mutable or Immutable?" *Irish Theological Quarterly*, 30 (1963), 204–31. In part, Crowe's grasp on natural law is defective, since he interprets the first principle as a moral imperative (*Changing Profile*, 177) and in general thinks of human nature's role according to scholastic natural-law theory (criticized in 4-F). With its formalistic understanding of nature, this theory cannot accomodate the dynamism of history; hence, Crowe, Curran, and others imagine that human nature and natural law must be thought to change to make room for this dynamism. If one understands human nature as an open-ended set of possibilities for personal and communal self-creation, then this dynamism can be explained in terms of unchanging human nature expressed in a basically unchanging understanding of goods to be realized in ever new ways. Against the historicism of post-Hegelian thought: Dario Composta, "Anchora sul diritto naturale: l'antropologia classica di fronte al diritto naturale, in un confronto con le recenti filosofie negatrici," *Euntes Docete*, 32 (1979), 117–38.

22. See Alexander MacBeath, *Experiments in Living: A Study of the Nature and Foundations of Ethics or Morals in the Light of Recent Work in Social Anthropology* (London: Macmillan, 1953); Morris Ginsberg, *On the Diversity of Morals* (London: Mercury Books, 1962), 130–48; Robert H. Lowie, *An Introduction to Cultural Anthropology*, new and enlarged ed. (New York: Rinehart, 1940).

23. From this point of view, cultural evolution is seen to be as essential and constant as any of the other unchanging aspects of human nature. See David Bidney, *Theoretical Anthropology* (New York: Columbia University Press, 1953), 120–24, and subsequent chapters; A. Irving Hallowell, "Self, Society, and Culture in Phylogenetic Perspective," *Evolution after Darwin*, vol. 2, *The Evolution of Man*, ed. Sol Tax (Chicago: University of Chicago Press, 1960), 309–71; Charles Fay, "Human Evolution: A Challenge to Thomistic Ethics," *International Philosophical Quarterly*, 2 (1962), 50–80. Fay's work is helpful, but one cannot always agree with him. In particular, he seems (63–64) to consider the underlying constant factors to be universals; in one sense, this is true: They hold for all humankind. But they also are concrete realities of the order of potentiality. The potentialities which are constant are no more abstract than the actualizations which vary.

24. Max Scheler, *Formalism in Ethics and Non-Formal Ethics of Values: A New Attempt toward the Foundation of an Ethical Personalism* (Evanston, Ill.: Northwestern University Press, 1973), 23–30, 42, and 206, proposes a basic moral principle radically opposed to proportionalism, namely, that moral goodness is in a preference for the positive value of a higher ranking. Dietrich von Hildebrand, *Christian Ethics* (New York: David McKay, 1952), 39–45, rightly objects that this proposal leaves out of account the pivotal distinction between the objectively valuable and the merely subjectively satisfying and is inherently unworkable. Von Hildebrand himself distinguishes (280–81) between moral values as such and other morally relevant values (such as human life itself) and proposes that moral goodness is in appropriate response to morally relevant values together with a will to be morally good. With this position one cannot quarrel, but its circularity makes it an unhelpful way of formulating basic moral principles.

25. In *Summa theologiae*, 1–2, q. 100, a. 11, c., St. Thomas suggests that there are other very general moral principles on a par with the precepts of charity. It is impossible to tell for certain what he had in mind, but one possibility is that he was aware that the fundamental principle of morality can be formulated in other propositional forms. Another possibility is that he had some inkling of the intermediate principles I call "modes of responsibility," recognizing, for instance, that the Golden Rule is more basic and obvious than the specific norms of the Ten Commandments.

26. Hans Küng, *On Being a Christian*, trans. Edward Quinn (New York: Doubleday, 1976), 534, states a criterion of morality: "The *morally good* then is what 'works' for man, what permits human life in its individual and social dimensions to succeed and to work out happily in the long run, when freedom and love are engendered." On this basis, he affirms proportionalism and reduces all specific norms to hypothetical imperatives: "All these precepts and prohibitions are valid therefore, not however for their own sake, but for the sake of realizing the greater good" (537). Of course, proportionalism is unworkable, so in practice Küng opts for a form of cultural relativism (540–41). In this way Küng attempts to justify his endorsement as normative for the Church of secular conceptions of social organization, women's rights (including a "right" to ordination), and the new sexual morality for young and old (526–27).

27. Paul VI, *Populorum progressio*, 59 *AAS* (1967) 263–65; *The Papal Encyclicals*, 275.16, with introductory material, 275.13–15.

28. Ibid., *AAS* 265–68, 278; 275.17–21, 42.

29. Paul VI, *Humanae vitae*, 60 *AAS* (1968) 482; *The Papal Encyclicals*, 277.2.

30. Ibid., *AAS* 491; 14.

31. Ibid., *AAS* 494–95; 18.

32. It must be remembered that freedom primarily means self-determination and that conscience in the genuine sense is a grasp upon truth. Hence, responsibility primarily is for oneself and for the possible goods one can help to realize; only derivatively is it to anyone, and even then primarily to oneself, insofar as one's free choices are self-determining. See Karol Wojtyla, *The Acting Person*, trans. Andrzej Potocki, ed. Anna-Teresa Tymieniecka (Dordrecht: D. Reidel, 1979), 169–74. Much recent religious ethics, in stressing responsibility, has sought to transcend legalism, but by taking responsibility-to (God) as basic has failed to do so, and at the same time by softening the sharp edges of obligation legalistically conceived has introduced an element of subjectivism, sometimes articulated in a theory that moral norms themselves are to be generated by a communal exercise of proportionalist rationality—in other words, are merely human laws. See Albert R. Jonsen, *Responsibility in Modern Religious Ethics* (Washington: Corpus Books, 1968), 173–228, for a development of this line of thought on the basis of a summary of various ideas of responsibility in Karl Barth, Bernard Häring, Dietrich Bonhoeffer, H. Richard Niebuhr, and Robert Johann.

33. The key text in which St. Thomas takes this view is *S.t.*, 1–2, q. 71, a. 2 (esp. ad 3), where he explains that every vice is against nature inasmuch as it is against reason. The position demands that concupiscence be understood in terms of disordered sensuality, and Thomas understands it thus (*S.t.*, 1–2, q. 82, a. 3; q. 91, a. 6). He interprets Rom 7.22–23 in terms of conflict between disordered sensuality and reason: *Super Epistolam S. Pauli ad Romanos Lectura*, vii, 4. This view was commonly accepted in classical modern Catholic theology, and the magisterium of the Church often assumed and developed it. See, for example, Leo XIII, *Exeunte iam anno*, 21 *ASS* (1888) 327–28; *The Papal Encyclicals*, 108.10. Yet this view has been challenged: Karl Rahner, S.J., "The Theological Concept of Concupiscentia," *Theological Investigations*, vol. 1, *God, Christ, Mary and Grace*, trans. Cornelius Ernst, O.P. (Baltimore: Helicon, 1961), 347–82. Rahner thinks the opposition is between the whole of desire prior to free decision (a whole both sentient and volitional) and what one becomes as person by this decision; concupiscence is the residue of naturally given desire, morally neutral in itself, undetermined by freedom (368–69). This view also involves a particular philosophy of the human person, one in which what is proper to person as spirit is the dynamism of freedom, while nature is thought of as inert in comparison with spirit's dynamism toward the transcendent. It seems to me that the data of deliberation (including temptation) and choice (including sin) are covered better by Thomas' than by Rahner's philosophy of the person.

34. St. Thomas has no general discussion of modes of responsibility. One finds in his works formulations which might be taken as expressive of the fifth (*S.c.g.*, 3, 117; *S.t.*, 1–2, q. 100, a. 8, ad 1), and perhaps of the seventh and the eighth: One ought not to harm anyone (*S.c.g.*, 3, 129; *S.t.*, 1–2, q. 95, a. 2). Sometimes he moves quite directly from a general principle (love of neighbor) to specific moral norms (the Ten Commandments), as question E explains. But in general the place which would be occupied by modes of responsibility is filled in his general moral theory by the virtues. However, without propositional articulation, the virtues cannot generate specific norms, and so in most of his treatment of specific moral questions, Thomas argues in ways which neither proceed clearly from his general moral theory nor depend essentially upon the concept of virtue, although the division of virtues serves to schematize the treatise (see, e.g., *S.t.*, 2–2, qq. 151–54, where the treatise on sexual ethics is organized in terms of the virtue of chastity, but the arguments—e.g., q. 154, a. 11—are independent both of what he says about the virtue and the moral theory of *S.t.*, 1–2).

35. Although "habit" in Aristotle has a somewhat different meaning than it has in modern psychology, the position taken here is deliberately at odds with Aristotle's view. Aristotle's thinking on virtue is mainly to be found in his *Nichomachean Ethics*. A useful introduction: David Ross, *Aristotle* (London: Methuen, 1964), 187–234. The notion of the voluntary is a key one for Aristotle and it often is mistakenly confused with that of free choice. On voluntariness, see *Nichomachean Ethics* iii, 1109b30–1111b3. In fact, Aristotle's voluntariness is consistent with soft determinism, and some who hold that position use Aristotle to support their claim that free choice is unnecessary for moral responsibility. In treating virtue, Aristotle stresses certain features which moral dispositions have in common with habit—for example, that it is acquired by repeated acts. Actually, the repetition of acts is important only for the secondary aspect of virtue—that is, the integration of other dimensions of the personality with one's commitments. Aristotle also was heavily influenced in his analysis and

description of virtues by conventional morality. The conventional morality of the time presented a somewhat too definite ideal of human perfection, since it lacked the distinction between what is naturally given and what is existentially possible. The notion of moderation probably was adopted in ethics from medicine, which considered health to consist in a proper balance of organic factors. This model is plausible for the organism. It is not as plausible for the existential self.

36. See Grisez, op. cit., 190–96.

37. Charles E. Curran et al., *Dissent In and For the Church: Theologians and "Humanae Vitae"* (New York: Sheed and Ward, 1969), 25. Rejection of radical dissent by no means precludes recognition of a need for a more integrated mode of fulfilling the prophetic responsibility of the Church; see, for instance, Philippe Delhaye, "La collaboration de la Hiérarchie et de tous les chrétiens dans la formulation des normes morales," *L'Année canonique*, 22 (1978), 43–60.

38. With respect to the morality of sex and innocent life, one can confirm the antiquity of the norms very easily by comparing Catholic teaching with the beliefs of Orthodox Jews. Curran, *Contemporary Problems in Moral Theology*, 105, recognizes that Catholic teaching antedated its theological explanation: "Many erroneously believe that Catholic theology is committed to a particular natural law approach to moral problems. In practice, however, the vast majority of Catholic teaching on particular moral questions came into existence even before Thomas Aquinas enunciated his theory." Curran, however, tries to argue from the teaching's independence of any particular theory of natural law to the acceptability of theories inconsistent with the received teaching. The conclusion does not follow. What does follow from the teaching's priority to theory is that criticism of the theory (even if it were telling) would not call into doubt the teaching itself.

39. Curran et al., *Dissent In and For the Church*, 25.

40. McCormick, *Notes*, 678–79 and 806–7.

41. This revealing phrase is found in the so-called majority report as published: Robert G. Hoyt, ed., *The Birth Control Debate* (Kansas City, Mo.: National Catholic Reporter, 1968), 71. The leaked documents are not precisely what they were purported to be, but the document in question does represent the view of the proponents of contraception. The very expressions, "majority" and "minority" presuppose a conception of the Commission very different from that of Paul VI, who made it clear that he wanted a thorough study of the question and who appointed to the study group a number of moralists who were convinced at the outset that in some way they could make a case for contraception. It seems clear he was anxious to find out if anyone in any way could make a convincing case that the received teaching is not binding on the Church—at least that a different view might be true with respect to oral contraceptives. But virtually the entire Commission agreed that there was no morally significant difference between oral contraceptives and barrier methods. Thus, not having obtained from the Commission what he expected, Paul VI finally came to the conclusion that nothing he could find put the received teaching in any doubt whatsoever.

42. See Germain Grisez, "Dualism and the New Morality," *Atti del Congresso Internazionale Tommaso d'Aquino nel Suo Settimo Centenario*, vol. 5, *L'Agire Morale* (Naples: Edizioni Domenicane Italiane, 1977), 323–30. Cf. Georges Cottier, O.P., "La conception chrétienne de la sexualité," *Nova et Vetera*, 52 (1977), 1–21; summarized: "The Christian Conception of Sexuality," *Theology Digest*, 26 (1978), 218–22.

43. An example: Louis Janssens, "Artificial Insemination: Ethical Considerations," *Louvain Studies*, 8 (1980), 3–29. He detaches the phrase "objective standards which are based on the nature of the person and his acts" from its context (4), takes proportionalism for granted (16), preempts the title of "an ethics of responsibility on a personalist foundation" by pretending that the only alternative is a formalistic type of scholastic natural-law ethics (13–19), and reaffirms a dualistic conception of the person in attacking "biologism" (20): ". . . nature, both in and outside of us, is rather the material which we must deal with in a human way." On this basis, Janssens goes on to defend, subject to various conditions, the moral acceptability of artificial insemination, whether by husband's or donor's semen, and in vitro fertilization (17–29). While Janssens comments on the final amending of the text of *Gaudium et spes*, 51 (4), he ignores the much more significant development by which the May 1965 draft was amended to introduce references to objective moral criteria and the magisterium into the version approved in principle 16 November 1965. See Francisco Gil Hellín, ed., *Constitutionis Pastoralis "Gaudium et Spes": Synopsis Historica: De Dignitate Matrimonii et Familiae Fovenda, II Pars, Caput I* (Pamplona, Spain: EUNSA, 1982), 110–16.

CHAPTER EIGHT

THE MODES OF RESPONSIBILITY
WHICH SPECIFY THE FIRST PRINCIPLE

Introduction

The basic principle of morality (formulated in 7-F) is: *In voluntarily acting for human goods and avoiding what is opposed to them, one ought to choose and otherwise will those and only those possibilities whose willing is compatible with a will toward integral human fulfillment.* This formulation articulates the moral requirement that one act in accord with reason in the pursuit of true human good. Derived from this basic principle are its primary specifications, here called "modes of responsibility" (treated in general in 7-G). These modes are more definite than the basic principle of morality, yet they are more general than the moral norms regarding specific kinds of acts to which they lead. Each mode excludes a certain unreasonable way of willing, a particular way of acting which is inconsistent with a will toward integral human fulfillment. The present chapter will explain in detail how each mode does this and will indicate the virtues in which it is embodied.

As will be explained (26-A), the modes of responsibility correspond to the eight Beatitudes (see Mt 5.3–12). Although the relationship will not yet be apparent, the modes are listed in the present chapter in the order of the Beatitudes to which they correspond, with the Beatitude concerning the lowly (or meek) taken as the second and that concerning the sorrowing taken as the third.[1]

Question A: What is the first mode of responsibility?

1. The first mode is this: *One should not be deterred by felt inertia from acting for intelligible goods.* **One who violates this mode fails, without any real reason, to act for some human good and so does not proceed in a manner consistent with a will toward integral human fulfillment.**

2. Sometimes a person feels sluggish, lazy, depressed, unenthusiastic, or the like. One thinks of doing something worthwhile, sees no reason for not doing it, but refrains out of sheer emotional inertia. This is not the same as the situation in which a person refrains from an activity which might actually be too taxing or chooses to take a needed rest. A person who violates the first mode has no such reason for inaction.

3. Here is an example of the violation of this mode: Simply out of laziness, a man sleeps past the time when he had decided to get up and so fails to do something he had judged worth doing. Again: A woman in authority realizes that a particular situation requires attention but somehow just doesn't get around to dealing with it.

4. The virtuous disposition corresponding to this mode has various aspects and is usually named in reference to some particular sphere of action. Various aspects are referred to by certain uses of words like "ambitious," "energetic," "diligent," "industrious," and "enthusiastic." Words which name the opposed vice include "lazy," "sluggish," "lackadaisical," "slothful," and "dilatory."

5. Even before Jesus, divine revelation deepens the foundation for this mode of responsibility. In making himself known as always active and creative, God provides a model for human energy. Revelation also shows the dignity of human activity within the plan of providence and makes clear God's readiness to support good work. The greatest deterrent to human effort is the sense of hopelessness induced by evil, when opportunities to do good are cut off and efforts on behalf of human fulfillment come to naught. By making God known as liberator, revelation counteracts hopelessness. With faith comes a renewal of hope, and with hope comes energy to act.

The sluggard is advised to learn from the industrious ant (see Prv 6.6–8) and is compared with a stone in the mud or a lump of dung (see Sir 22.1–2). Sleepiness is disparaged: "How long will you lie there, O sluggard? When will you arise from your sleep?" (Prv 6.9). While the sluggard naps, poverty and want will sneak up like bandits (see Prv 6.10–11). Torpor is characteristic of fools; to teach them is like trying to talk with someone in a deep sleep, who at the end of the lesson says: "What is it?" (Sir 22.8).

St. Paul urges his converts to work hard and to encourage the listless (see 1 Thes 4.10–12; 5.14; 2 Thes 3.7–12). He clearly regards laziness as a vice. He claims credit for himself and his fellow workers for their hard work and sleepless nights (see 2 Cor 6.5; 11.27). Christian life is urgent business: "Besides this you know what hour it is, how it is full time now for you to wake from sleep. For salvation is nearer to us now than when we first believed" (Rom 13.11). The Christian who grows lazy (as part of a general pattern of lukewarmness) is crucifying the Son of God a second time (see Heb 6.6, 12).

The parable of the silver pieces teaches a similar lesson. Servants are to be reliable and industrious, not merely to keep safe the gifts they receive. The servant who failed to make a gain on the funds left in his care is condemned as worthless and lazy (see Mt 25.26). A false sense of caution and nervous reluctance to take minimal risk of acting is no excuse. The unprofitable servant loses what little he had (see Mt 25.29–30).

Question B: What is the second mode of responsibility?

1. The second mode is this: *One should not be pressed by enthusiasm or impatience to act individualistically for intelligible goods.* One who violates this mode acts alone or without adequately considering the possibilities and needs of common action, even though individualism is not really called for. **Unnecessary individualism is not consistent with a will toward integral human fulfillment, which requires a fellowship of persons sharing in goods.**

2. Sometimes enthusiasm, eagerness for results, or impatience with the delays and cumbersomeness of cooperative action incline one to act by oneself, although

knowing that responsible cooperation with others would cause the good to be attained more perfectly and allow others to share in it. This is not the same as the situation in which a reasonable need—an emergency, say—requires prompt, individual action. Nor is it the same as cases in which individuals responsibly take initiative on others' behalf, with a view to proceeding in cooperation with them.

3. One can violate this mode without actually being unfair to anyone and without being overly attached to the good one pursues too individualistically. Violation lies simply in acting upon nonrational motives which lead one to overlook or dismiss some communal aspects of what one is doing.

4. Examples are often found in the tendency of a community's more active members to appropriate functions to themselves instead of fostering wider, active participation, because the latter is more trouble and leads to uneven performance. Again: A person with many interests easily becomes overcommitted; this will lead to mediocre performance and to conflicts of responsibilities which eventually will affect others adversely.

5. Possibly because people today have more scope to choose between individualistic and sociable styles of action, the virtuous disposition corresponding to this mode is more widely recognized in our culture now than in the past. In one aspect it is called "team spirit," meaning openness to sharing, to mutual and responsible action, and to participation by others in the activities in which one is engaged. The virtue also includes having a well integrated set of commitments, reflected in the simplicity and orderliness of life of a person who has "got it all together." The opposed vice is indicated by such expressions as "going it alone," "having a star complex," and "being overcommitted."

6. The foundation for this mode of responsibility is deepened by divine revelation even before Jesus. God makes it known that humankind had an original common life and calling—of which marriage is the paradigm (see Gn 1.26–28; 2.15, 18, 21–24)—to fill the earth and subdue it. The experience of Israel, whose communal life is shaped by the covenant, makes clear the need for coresponsibility among God's people.

Obedience is related to this mode of responsibility. The notion of obedience is not unitary but multiple. In one set of cases, it is a duty which members of a constituted community owe to decisions made for the common good. One who fails to obey is being unfair. But in another set of cases, the disposition to obey is antecedent to any constituted relationship. It is a docility and submissiveness which are an important part of openness to community. In Scripture, obedience often is commended, and in many instances the disposition is less that of strict dutifulness than that of a ready, cooperative spirit.

By original sin, humankind is isolated from God and enclosed in darkness (see Rom 11.32). This alienation leads to a breakdown in human community symbolized by the dissolution of language at Babel (see Gn 11.1–9). The beginning of salvation, with Abraham, is marked by his readiness to leave his land (see Gn 12.1) and follow God's command even at the sacrifice of his son, on whose life the fulfillment of the promise depended (see Gn 22.1–16). The spirit of service, of readiness to accept responsibility within a framework of cooperation, is perfectly expressed by Samuel's "Speak, for your servant hears" (1 Sm 3.10) and by Mary's "Behold, I am the handmaid of the Lord; let it be to me according to your word" (Lk 1.38).

A clear example of the violation of this mode of responsibility is the situation at Corinth which Paul attempts to correct by his teaching about the unity of the Church as the single body of Christ (see 1 Cor 12). Members of the Church were fascinated with their own gifts. There is no indication they were acting unfairly to one another or violating other modes of responsibility. But they needed a sense of team spirit, a disposition to shared responsibility. The situation could be improved only by a spirit of obedience and service which would lead to greater community consciousness and less individualism.

Question C: What is the third mode of responsibility?

1. The third mode is this: *One should not choose to satisfy an emotional desire except as part of one's pursuit and/or attainment of an intelligible good other than the satisfaction of the desire itself.* Violations occur when a person deliberately chooses to act upon impulse, habit, or fixation on a particular goal. The proposal one adopts in making such a choice appeals by promising some sense of inner harmony through tension-reduction. Thus, one's reason for acting is the very satisfaction of the emotional desire rather than some intelligible good whose instance has features which arouse the desire. A choice to act on this basis sets aside whatever reason there was for restraint, and the action at least wastes time and energy one might otherwise use for the pursuit of goods in line with upright commitments. **In deliberately settling for mere emotional satisfaction, one's choice is not that of a will toward integral human fulfillment.**

2. A person sometimes is aware that his or her desire, instead of pointing to some reason to choose to satisfy it, offers only its own satisfaction as a reason for choosing. Yet one can be drawn—and perhaps almost driven—to choose, for example, by a quasi-compulsive desire, by habitual routine, or by a particular goal on which one's heart is fixed. (It sometimes happens that goals which were reasonable at the outset lose their point with the passage of time yet retain their emotional appeal.) This is not the same as the situation in which one spontaneously does reasonable things without having reasoned about them. Nor is it the same as cases in which one acts for an intelligible good and gains emotional satisfaction in its concrete, sensibly pleasant aspects.

3. This mode is violated by the person who sees no point in having another drink, or smoking, or eating a rich dessert, or spending the evening in idle chatter, yet does so in response to an urge. Again: People spend much of their daily lives unreflectively following routines; sometimes doing so is pointless, yet they choose to continue to follow the routine merely for the sake of the feeling of security and accomplishment they gain from doing so. Again: Some people work hard to enjoy a constantly rising standard of living, yet they know that more wealth and material things will yield no more real satisfaction.

4. Some deny the truth of this mode. Their argument is based on the principle that the pleasure accompanying an act shares in the act's own moral quality, good or bad. From this they conclude that if what one does is not otherwise wrong, choosing to do it for the sake of pleasure alone does not make it wrong. The principle is sound, but the conclusion does not follow. The principle applies to acts

whose moral quality already is settled, whereas the conclusion concerns possible choices whose moral quality is in question.

5. Moreover, one violates this mode only by making a choice. One has no choice to make unless one hesitates and deliberates, and so one never has occasion to act for the mere satisfaction of an emotional desire unless there is some reason for restraint. Thus, whenever one violates this mode, one acts despite some reason or other. The reason might not be weighty, but any reason inherent in what one chooses for making the choice is better than none, for any such reason will have a basis in intelligible goods.

If a person chooses to engage in some sort of sexual behavior merely to experience pleasure and still desire, this mode is violated. But it is not violated when a married couple spontaneously take pleasure in marital intercourse. If they do not hesitate and deliberate, it is because there is no reason why they should not engage in intercourse. In their situation, it has an inherent intelligible significance, for it expresses and celebrates the larger, intelligible good to which they are committed—namely, their marriage itself as a special sort of friendship. Loving marital intercourse contributes to faithful communion in this relationship, which is structured in a way that integrates sexual behavior in the service of life and its transmission. This substantive good provides the vehicle for the reflexive good of marital friendship, and so it helps distinguish authentic marital friendship from its counterfeits, and love-giving marital intercourse from the use of the marital relationship for self-gratification.

6. The virtuous disposition corresponding to this mode is most appropriately called "self-control" (see *S.t.*, 1–2, q. 61, aa. 2, 4; 2–2, q. 141, aa. 1–2). Violators are not in control of their own lives but are slaves to nonrational motives. Self-control includes at least some aspects of many traditionally recognized virtues, such as temperance, modesty, chastity, and simplicity of life. Also, if "discipline" is used to refer to a virtuous disposition rather than an imposed regimen, a person free from positive nonrational motivation can be called "disciplined." The opposed vice includes at least certain aspects of lustfulness, gluttony, greed, jealousy, envy, shortsightedness, impetuosity, and so on.

7. The foundation for this mode, too, is deepened by divine revelation before Jesus. God makes human persons aware that, being made in his image, they should share in his excellence. Also, in clarifying the reality of free choice and moral responsibility, revelation sharply distinguishes what one does by reasonable choice from what one is moved to do by nonrational drives and habits. Moreover, the life proposed by the Jewish law requires self-discipline.

Scripture is filled with condemnations of vicious dispositions which more or less clearly pertain to this mode of responsibility, but in many cases one cannot be sure that the irrational lack of self-control is the precise evil in view.

However, certain chapters of the wisdom literature seem to be concerned with this mode, for they gather the criticism of many relevant vices and treat them as forms of foolishness. For example, one chapter in Proverbs criticizes striving to be rich, wasting time with foolish people, neglect of discipline of the young, drinking wine, consorting with prostitutes and adulterous women (see Prv 23). Ecclesiastes contains two passages (see Eccl 2.1–12; 5.9–6.9) in which the vanity of pleasure and riches is underlined; their precise point is that desire for such things leads to no true human good.

Sirach specifically commends self-control: "Whoever keeps the law controls his thoughts" (Sir 21.11), and advises: "Do not follow your base desires, but restrain your appetites" (Sir 18.30). He proceeds to condemn satisfaction of lustful desires, momentary pleasure, wine bibbing, gluttony, harlotry, and useless talk (see Sir 18.31–19.11). Other passages point out the uselessness of pursuing riches and the self-punishing character of miserliness (see Sir 31.1–11; 14.3–10). Again, the self-destructiveness of indulgence in goods is stressed (see Sir 37.26–30).

St. Paul takes up an important idea from the wisdom literature, that sin and idolatry are at the bottom of a foolishly dissolute life. The pagans were able to know God yet they did not glorify and thank him, so their pretense of wisdom ended in foolishness. They practiced idolatry: "Therefore God gave them up in the lusts of their hearts to impurity, to the dishonoring of their bodies among themselves" (Rom 1.24). He instructs Christians to be different: "The night is far gone, the day is at hand. Let us then cast off the works of darkness . . ... But put on the Lord Jesus Christ, and make no provision for the flesh, to gratify its desires" (Rom 13.12, 14).

That Christians must put aside fleshly desires is a standard element of New Testament instruction (see 2 Cor 7.1; 1 Thes 4.1–5; Jas 1.21; 1 Pt 2.11). What the world offers is not from the Father: "For all that is in the world, the lust of the flesh and the lust of the eyes and the pride of life, is not of the Father but is of the world. And the world passes away, and the lust of it" (1 Jn 2.16–17).

Question D: What is the fourth mode of responsibility?

1. The fourth mode is this: *One should not choose to act out of an emotional aversion except as part of one's avoidance of some intelligible evil other than the inner tension experienced in enduring that aversion.* **Violations occur when one chooses to refrain or desist from acting, or changes a reasonable course of action, because of repugnance, fear of pain, or other concerns about obstacles which involve nothing intelligibly bad.** Choices contrary to this mode, like those which violate the third mode, aim to reduce tension by yielding to the emotion. The emotion is not aroused by sensible features of an intelligible evil whose avoidance one judges appropriate; moreover, acting on the emotion inhibits pursuit of intelligible goods. In accepting such a limitation, one does not proceed with a will toward integral human fulfillment.

2. Sometimes one is aware that there is an intelligible point to acting in a certain way—perhaps that such action would serve a good to which one is already committed. Yet one chooses not to act—perhaps even chooses to act in a contrary fashion—because of negative feelings such as repugnance toward something disgusting, squeamishness, fear of pain, desire to avoid criticism, anxiety about possible obstacles, and so on. This is different from the situation in which a person spontaneously avoids what reasonably should be avoided. In particular it must be distinguished from cases where an upright person is restrained by moral sensitivity from doing things which someone less morally sensitive would do boldly and with moral recklessness.

3. This mode is violated by those who choose to neglect or abandon their vocational responsibilities when these prove unpleasant and unrewarding. Again: People put off exercise and care of their health because they fear pain and

discomfort. Or again: Fear of failure leads people to choose security instead of possibly significant achievement.

The soldier who chooses to leave his post to avoid being killed does not violate this mode of responsibility. His choice is not merely to escape fear itself. Rather, he seeks to escape the fearful and intelligible evil of death. His choice can be morally wrong—for example, because the call of duty is a genuine one. Or the choice to flee can be morally right—for example, because he is ordered unreasonably to stand and fight by a leader who realizes defeat is inevitable but wants his army to fight to the death.

4. The virtuous disposition corresponding to this mode is signified by many uses of words like "courage," "mettle," "fortitude," "resolution," "tenacity," "backbone," "perseverance," and "guts" (see *S.t.*, 1–2, q. 61, aa. 2, 4; 2–2, q. 123, aa. 1–3). The vice is signified by uses of "cowardice," "squeamishness," "irresolution," "being a quitter," "being a worrywart," and so forth.

5. The ways in which divine revelation before Jesus deepens the foundation for the third mode are equally relevant here. Moreover, revelation provides assurance that God supports and rescues his people; God shows himself the model of faithfulness. Furthermore, in fostering love of fellow Israelites, the law forms social solidarity and encourages people to give one another mutual moral support, which in turn fosters their endurance.

Several of the Scripture passages cited in question C also make reference to the fourth mode, because it is parallel to the third. Because confidence in God is the chief basis of courage, fearfulness is a sign of defect in faith and trust in God's faithfulness. Knowledge and experience are valuable in dangerous situations, but steady confidence is primarily based upon hope (see Sir 34.9–17). For this reason, the entire story of faith and hope throughout the Old Testament is essentially also a story of courage. Abraham, for example, leaves his home for the promised land, not knowing where he is going, lives under adverse conditions, and is ready to sacrifice the one who is the bearer of the promise—all because of his unshakable confidence in God (see Heb 11.8–11, 17–19).

Fear is useless; what is needed is trust, which instills courage (see Mt 9.22; Mk 5.36; Lk 8.50). During Jesus' earthly life, the apostles often show their lack of courage, which manifests the inadequacy of their faith (see Mt 8.26; Mk 4.40; Lk 8.25). After Pentecost, their faith was firm and they proclaimed the gospel boldly (see Acts 2.4, 23). The exhortation to faithfulness is a constant of New Testament instruction (see 1 Cor 15.58; Gal 5.1; Phil 4.1; Col 1.23; 2 Thes 2.15; Heb 12.12; Jas 4.7–8). The Christian must stand firm in faith and with patient endurance wait in hope for Jesus' coming.

Question E: What is the fifth mode of responsibility?

1. The fifth mode is this: *One should not, in response to different feelings toward different persons, willingly proceed with a preference for anyone unless the preference is required by intelligible goods themselves.* Violations occur when, responding to feelings of partiality, one adjusts one's choices in such a way that one does not act altogether in accord with the possibilities for realizing intelligible goods; that is, in making a choice which affects two or more persons, one subordinates the good of all to the advantage of some. This also obstructs the formation and smooth functioning of community, without which integral human fulfillment is impossible. **Instead of proceeding in a manner consistent with a**

will toward integral human fulfillment, one who acts with partiality settles for an unnecessarily limited fulfillment of certain people.

2. Sometimes one is aware—or could and should be aware—that what one is doing or omitting affects others in ways one would consider unreasonable if the positions of various people involved (perhaps including oneself) were reversed. Still, one is moved to act or deterred from acting—by self-interest, or sympathy (say, toward those near and dear), or antipathy (for instance, toward people different in some way from those one identifies with). This is different from cases in which one makes distinctions among people on a basis which has some intelligible relationship to the action in which one is engaged. It must also be distinguished from fulfilling responsibilities which arise from commitments to particular people—for example, of parents to their own children. Impartiality does not dictate egalitarianism, nor does it detract from the special responsibility which individuals have for themselves and their dependents.

3. Although partiality is often expressed as selfishness, simple egoism is only one form. Possibly more common, and certainly as unreasonable, is allowing one's choices to be shaped by personal likes and dislikes, jealous love of one's own family, group prejudices, culturally established patterns of bias, and so on.

4. Philosophical moral theorists have tried to clarify the concept of fairness by investigating the principle of fair rule making, called the "principle of universalizability." This says that a fair rule is one which can omit proper names and apply equally well to any and all persons who meet its intelligible conditions. Such a rule is not composed on an ad hoc basis to serve partiality in a particular situation.

5. Here are some examples of violations. Somebody accepts favors but always finds excuses when asked to do them. People resent gossip about themselves and their loved ones but gossip freely about others. Professional people give better treatment to more respectable and congenial clients than to others with similar needs and claims to their service. Lawmakers favor powerful interest groups which support them, rather than working for the laws and policies they think best for the people as a whole.

6. The virtuous disposition corresponding to this mode is most appropriately called "fairness"; a person who violates it acts unfairly. Although fairness is an important aspect of justice, justice is a wider concept, since it includes other modes of morally right action toward others (see *S.t.*, 2–2, q. 61; q. 63, a. 1). Often, people who are fair are said to be "disinterested." They do not lack interests, but in acting on interests they are not motivated by partiality. The vice opposed to fairness is variously called "unfairness," "bias," "partiality," "selfishness," "favoritism," "prejudice," and so on.

7. Divine revelation deepens the foundation for this mode of responsibility even before Jesus by making it clear that human beings all stand in a similar relationship to God, who is fair to all. Humankind is universally weak, helpless, in debt, yet God acts toward this fallen humanity with faithfulness and loving kindness. One desires mercy from God (and from those in power) for oneself and one's dear ones. The covenant assures such mercy. Hence, under the covenant,

fairness tends to demand mercy toward others; there is no clear line between justice and mercy. The Jewish law also rectifies much unfairness common in other conventional moralities.

God has no favorites and accepts no bribes; his people must act in a similar manner (see Dt 10.17–19). The judges especially are enjoined to imitate God in this respect (see 2 Chr 19.7). Jesus is complimented on the same quality (see Mt 22.16; Mk 12.14; Lk 20.21). God is not "unduly partial," even to the weak (see Sir 35.13). St. Paul repeats the teaching that God plays no favorites (see Rom 2.11; Gal 2.6; Eph 6.9; Col 3.25). James insists on the necessity of fairness, nondiscrimination, and social justice (see Jas 2.1–9; 5.1–6). The prophets often denounce injustice and oppression (see Is 5.7, 23; Jer 22.13, 15; Am 5.7; 6.12); James writes in this tradition.

Frequently in Scripture, "justice" means the rightness of the action of one who fulfills the law. This concept is common to all conventional moralities; people consider someone just if he or she commits no crimes and fulfills all legal obligations. The difference in the biblical context is that one who fulfills the law is being faithful to the covenant, and so fulfills God's will and can hope for God's reciprocal faithfulness in keeping his promises. "Justice" used in this sense does not specifically characterize the disposition proper to the fifth mode of responsibility, since law-abidingness can extend to all sorts of responsibilities, and good law presupposes a generally sound moral foundation.

One formulation of the Golden Rule, which undertakes to express this mode of responsibility in an explicit way, is found in the Old Testament: "What you hate, do not do to anyone" (Tb 4.15). An affirmative formulation is found in the Sermon on the Mount: "So whatever you wish that men would do to you, do so to them; for this is the law and the prophets" (Mt 7.12; cf. Lk 6.31). It sometimes is argued that the affirmative formulation substantially extends the negative one, but whether it does depends upon the precise interpretation one gives the various formulae. As they stand, both can be taken to express the requirement of impartiality, which extends to all actions and omissions.

In establishing the covenant, God acts freely, with no obligation to do so, but rather out of pure generosity and mercy (see Ex 33.19; 34.6–7). Within the context of the covenant, God has assumed obligations which he fulfills out of faithfulness. Yet, the people are unfaithful and God still continues in mercy (see Mi 7.18–20). Eventually it is recognized that only the sinner's refusal of pardon blocks God's tender compassion (see Is 9.12, 16; Jer 16.1–13). Mercy extends even to those altogether outside the covenant (see Jon 3.10; 4.2; Sir 18.1–13; Ps 103).

This extension of mercy stretches the terms of the covenant, as it were, and by fairness itself demands that those who experience God's mercy show mercy also to others (see Is 58.6–11; Jb 31.16–23). The sage, Sirach, teaches:

> Forgive your neighbor the wrong he has done,
> and then your sins will be pardoned when you pray.
> Does a man harbor anger against another,
> and yet seek for healing from the Lord?
> Does he have no mercy toward a man like himself,
> and yet pray for his own sins? (Sir 28.2–4)

One who has become a recipient of mercy and wishes mercy in the future for his or her own self and friends must also forgive others.

Jesus demands of his followers perfection precisely in this: that they be merciful as the Father in heaven is merciful (see Lk 6.36). The parable of the prodigal son drives home the lesson and justifies Jesus' associating with sinners (see Lk 15.11–32). The parable of the merciless official—who refuses to forgive a small debt after having been forgiven a great one—makes the same point as that made by Sirach (see Mt 18.23–35).

Question F: What is the sixth mode of responsibility?

1. The sixth mode is this: *One should not choose on the basis of emotions which bear upon empirical aspects of intelligible goods (or bads) in a way which interferes with a more perfect sharing in the good or avoidance of the bad.* **Violating this mode means sacrificing reality to appearance, as is done, typically, by someone more interested in the conscious experience of enjoying a good or avoiding an evil than the reality.** This blocks some realization of intelligible human goods and leads to self-deception, which distorts one's appreciation of what is good. Hence, one who violates this mode does not proceed consistently with a will toward integral human fulfillment.

2. Sometimes one is aware—or could and should be aware—that what one is doing interferes with possible ways of serving goods or avoiding evils more perfectly and effectively. But, eager to experience some measure of satisfaction or enjoy some alleviation of a bad situation, one substitutes a less appropriate action for a more appropriate one. Whether for one's own sake or another's, one settles for an appearance of a good instead of pursuing its reality. This is not the same as a situation in which one acts for a limited aspect of an intelligible good without impeding a possible alternative. Nor does this mode rule out seeking "experience" as part of one's action for the integral good, or even rule out acting for an empirical aspect of an intelligible good alone when nothing more can be attained.

3. Here are some examples of violations. A sick man who could have treatment which would really cure his condition prefers less effective treatment which offers a feeling of quick relief. A girl engaged to be married spends all her time and energy planning her wedding and has none left for adequate spiritual preparation for married life. A bishop, anxious to reconcile those alienated from the Church, holds penitential services to which he invites persons unwilling to amend their lives, gives all who come general absolution without individual confession, and thus fosters an appearance of reconciliation as a substitute for the reality.

4. There is no one name for the virtuous disposition corresponding to this mode of responsibility. It is referred to by various uses of such expressions as "having a sound sense of values," "sincerity," "seriousness," "clearheadedness," and "practical wisdom." Expressions sometimes used to signify the opposed vice include "self-deception," "superficiality," "insincerity," "lacking a sense of values," "frivolity," and "childishness."

5. Even before Jesus, divine revelation deepens this mode's foundation by establishing the primacy of divine reality which transcends experience. The new hope offered by God draws interest away from the more superficial to the more profound aspects of human goods. Moreover, living out the covenant requires sincerity. It is more a matter of doing than of feeling.

The primary expression of this mode of responsibility in the Old Testament is in the criticism of idolatry as a kind of foolishness, since idols are vain. Yahweh alone is great,

"For all the gods of the peoples are idols; but the Lord made the heavens" (1 Chr 16.26). Elijah provides a proof by experiment that Baal is a nondeity, incapable of acting (see 1 Kgs 18.18–40). Since idols are nonentities, they can neither help nor save anyone (see 1 Sm 12.21).

Detailed descriptions of the making and use of idols help to drive home the point that they are powerless (see Is 44.18; Wis 13.11–14). As a last blow in this line of criticism, a very plausible anthropological explanation of idolatry is provided; it is a practice which originates in an effort to maintain the illusion that the dead still are present. Once begun, the illusory practice is extended (see Wis 14.12–21; 15.7–15).

The critique of idols is broadened to include wrong ways of worshipping the true God. The prophets insist on the primacy of interior sacrifice; this offering is not merely a substitute for ritual sacrifice, but is the heart of all sacrifice (see Is 1.11–16; Jer 7.22–23; Hos 6.6; Mi 6.7–8). None of the prophets rejects the rite as such; what is rejected always is the tendency to substitute apparent religiosity for true religion. This point is expressed with clarity in Psalm 51 (see Ps 40.7–11).

St. Paul summarizes both lines of criticism in his argument that prior to redemption in Jesus no one is justified (see Rom 3.10–12). All religion is vain, until Jesus makes possible a real communion with God. Likewise, Greek philosophy is a sham, and the eloquence of rhetoric is useless, for neither provides anything but an appearance of wisdom (see 1 Cor 1.18–2.5).

Apart from instances in which the appearance of religion becomes a substitute for its reality, there are few cases in Scripture where it is clear that this mode of responsibility is at work, for it easily blends in with others. For example, when wealth and status seeking are condemned (see Ps 62.10–11; Col 3.5), one cannot be sure that anything more than the need for detachment and fairness is in view. To the extent that the whole of human life in the fallen condition is unsatisfactory, everything can be reduced to vanity, as it is in Ecclesiastes. However, such a reduction does not show that every action is a pursuit of apparent goods in violation of this mode of responsibility, since it is violated only if one's chosen action somehow blocks an alternative which would lead to participation in a true good.

Question G: What is the seventh mode of responsibility?

1. The seventh mode is this: *One should not be moved by hostility to freely accept or choose the destruction, damaging, or impeding of any intelligible human good.* **Violations occur when people deliberately will out of anger or hatred (or milder feelings of the same sort, such as distaste or resentment) the destruction, damaging, or impeding of any instance of any intelligible human good.** In acting on such negative feelings, they reduce human fulfillment without reason, and so proceed in a manner which is inconsistent with a will toward integral human fulfillment.

2. One sometimes knows that acting in a certain way will not be conducive to any intelligible human good—nothing positive will be achieved. Still, negative feelings move one to act in a destructive, and possibly self-destructive, manner. This is different from the situation in which hatred of evil moves one to act reasonably to protect a good or limit an evil (see *S.t.*, 2–2, q. 123, a. 10). It is also different from cases in which people vent hostile feelings by actions which are otherwise useless but not destructive of any human good.

3. Here are some examples. A nation which is losing a war launches all its nuclear weapons against its enemies to make their victory as costly as possible. Children who have been outvoted in planning a party stay away in order to detract from the joy of the event. A wife who resents her husband's infidelity has an affair to get even.

4. The virtuous disposition corresponding to this mode is signified by at least some uses of "forbearing," "patient," "longsuffering," "forgiving," "easygoing," "gentle," and so on. The vice is variously called "vengeful," "vindictive," "spiteful," "impatient," "resentful," "grudging," and "unforgiving" (see *S.t.*, 2–2, q. 157, aa. 1–2; q. 158, aa. 1–2).

5. The foundation of this mode, too, is deepened by divine revelation before Jesus. God reveals himself as forgiving. Revelation also makes it clear that no one is secure of himself—everyone needs to be forgiven. Finally, revelation teaches that God will rectify evil; human revenge is uncalled for (see Dt 32.30–43).

The first violence against another described in the Bible, Cain's murder of Abel, is an act of resentment (see Gn 4.5). As part of the law of love, hatred in one's heart toward a brother is excluded: "You shall not take vengeance or bear any grudge against the sons of your own people" (Lv 19.18). The control of anger is taught in the wisdom literature (see Prv 15.18, 16.32, 17.27). The destructive act is to be replaced with an act of kindness, which will open the way to divine justice (see Prv 25.21–22).

Paul teaches that it is characteristic of love not to be angry and not to brood over injuries; to be forbearing, patient, kind, and not jealous; to rejoice with the truth, not with what is wrong (see 1 Cor 13.4–7). The quarrel among the Corinthians which he was attempting to settle apparently involved a good deal of petty spitefulness and resentment. Anger and quick temper, malice, insults, and foul language are among the pagan ways which Christians must put aside (see Col 3.8).

It is important to recognize that if the Bible makes it clear that God can be angry, there is a distinction between mere vindictiveness and divine vindication. God's vengeance is not destruction for its own sake, but is a rectification of sin, required by justice (see Ex 32; Ps 51.6; Is 9.7–16; Ez 5.11–16; Hos 5.1–14; and so on). The nations are punished in proportion to their guilt (see Is 10.5–15; Ez 25.15–17).

The threat of God's anger leads sinners to repent (see Mi 7.9). With a view to repentance, God is longsuffering, slow to anger and quick to forgive (see Ex 34.6). He uses a strategy of gradual punishment, to induce sinners to repent and to provide them with a real opportunity to do so (see Wis 11.26–12.2; 15.1–2). Thus, God's wrath and his patience balance each other (see Na 1.2–3). And his longsuffering extends, to the dismay of some, even to alien peoples who are the enemies of Israel (see Jon 4.1–2, 11). God understands the misery of the human condition, and so he is patient and merciful, "He sees and recognizes that their end will be evil; therefore he grants them forgiveness in abundance" (Sir 18.12).

Question H: What is the eighth mode of responsibility?

1. The eighth mode is this: *One should not be moved by a stronger desire for one instance of an intelligible good to act for it by choosing to destroy, damage, or impede some other instance of an intelligible good.* This mode is violated by one who deliberately brings about something humanly bad, in order to prevent something else bad or to attain something humanly good. In such a case, one is moved to act according to the comparative strength of one's various desires. **Thus**

one subordinates some possible elements of human fulfillment to others, even though there is no reasonable basis for doing so. In placing a nonrational limit on fulfillment, one proceeds in a way not consistent with a will toward integral human fulfillment (see *S.t.*, 1–2, q. 18, a. 4, ad 3; q. 20, a. 2; 3, q. 68, a. 11, ad 3) [2]

2. At times one is aware that acting in a certain way would bring about the bad, either for the sake of the good or to prevent something else bad. Practical reason provides the same sort of grounds for respecting the good one proposes to injure as for pursuing the good one proposes to pursue. Still, one is moved by the desire which is stronger at the emotional level, that is, the desire which draws one to this rather than that imagined outcome. (This experience—of being drawn—is the intuition which the proportionalist thinks justifies choosing what one feels to be the lesser evil or the greater good.) This situation is different from that in which a person chooses to act for a good while foreseeing that executing the choice will incidentally bring about unwanted human evils—which, however, can be accepted without violating any other mode of responsibility. Nor is it the same as the situation in which someone subordinates goods which are not basic human goods to the attainment of such goods.

3. This mode of responsibility is not violated by one who freely accepts death rather than leave an important duty unfulfilled. Nor is it violated by killing animals for food, since animals' lives are not instances of a human good. Nor is there a violation in setting aside the letter of legal requirements for the sake of fairness, since law is simply a means to this human good. Violations are present in the following. To obtain a grant to continue his research, a scientist falsifies data to make the project's initial results appear more promising than they are. To obtain information which will save many lives, a military commander tortures children. To bring about what he considers a necessary change in moral teaching, a theologian encourages people to do something they believe wrong.

4. The virtuous disposition corresponding to this mode is signified by "reverence." For instance: "Out of reverence for life, she refused the abortion which her physician said was medically necessary"; or: "Out of reverence for the consciences of those who thought it wrong to eat idol-meat, St. Paul chose not to use the most efficient means of correcting their false view." "Craftiness" is one name for the opposed vice. Those who deny this mode's validity often appeal to what they call "prudence" or "common sense realism." In public affairs, the vice is sometimes called "pragmatism" or, if criticism is intended, "machiavellianism" or "amoral expediency."

5. As with the others, the eighth mode's foundation is deepened by certain aspects of divine revelation even before Jesus. God's revelation that humankind is made in his image tends to enhance reverence for the goods which fulfill human persons. Moreover, a deep awareness of human sinfulness makes one skeptical that feelings can be trusted to measure good and evil.

A few passages in the Old Testament condemn cunning or craftiness, but usually there is no clear indication that the reason for the condemnation is the violation of this mode of responsibility (see Gn 3.1; Jb 5.12; 15.5; Ps 83.4). Perhaps nearest to the point are a few passages in Sirach, for example:

> There is a shrewdness that is detestable,
> while the simple man may be free from sin,
> There are those with little understanding who fear God,
> and those of great intelligence who violate the law.
> There is a shrewdness keen but dishonest,
> which by duplicity wins a judgment. (Sir 19.19–21; NAB)

Again, Sirach suggests: "A man may be shrewd and the teacher of many, and yet be unprofitable to himself" (Sir 37.19). These passages could refer to the craftiness of the person who uses bad means to good ends, but the point is not clear, because there is no context or application.

6. Before Christian revelation, however, there was a tendency, as a side effect of certain other aspects of divine revelation, for people to misunderstand this mode.[3] God reveals himself by participating in human history; he participates in history through sinful human beings, precisely to save fallen humankind. Presupposing and working within the framework of their conventional morality, the people who received the revelation of the Old Testament assumed that it provided a divine sanction for their moral convictions. This assumption caused social norms to be taken as guides, not to human fulfillment as such, but to the fulfillment of Israel's specific aspirations. In the pursuit of this fulfillment, whatever seemed necessary was considered justified, even if it involved violating the eighth mode of responsibility.

7. Thus, in Old Testament times the eighth mode was accepted with a condition: *The end does not justify the means—unless God commands or authorizes otherwise.* This can be illustrated in the case of human life. Israel's law recognizes life as sacred and establishes protection for it, but its sacredness is qualified by the presumption that God authorizes killing in some cases. In the last analysis, even innocent human life is subordinated to the good of religion realized in the covenant relationship. Carried over into Christian thinking, this mentality justifies killing—in violation of the eighth mode of responsibility—in capital punishment and war.

In the perspective of the Old Testament, God is the absolute Lord of life. All blood (which is identified with animal and human life) belongs to God, for he is its source. All humans must treat it as sacred, but God may dispose of it according to his sovereign will. In consequence, certain crimes demand punishment by the shedding of blood, which can have the character of expiation, purification, or both. Moreover, the wars of Israel, although not holy wars fought for specifically religious objectives, are the wars of Yahweh, Israel's king.[4]

This Old Testament perspective, while coherent in itself, should not be used to justify choices to kill within the more adequate perspective of Christian morality. The unacceptable implications of using the Old Testament in this way become apparent if one considers the whole range of killing considered justified, rather than looking only at selected texts; for instance, to defend capital punishment: "Whoever sheds the blood of man, by man shall his blood be shed; for God made man in his own image" (Gn 9.6).

In the law of Israel the death penalty was mandatory for murder, for offenses having a specifically religious character, and for bearing false witness in a capital case (see Ex 21.12–14; 31.14; Nm 35.31–33; Lv 20.2–5; 24.14–16; Dt 13.2–10; 17.2–7; 19.11–13, 21). But also subject to the death penalty were kidnapping in certain cases (see Ex 21.16; Dt

24.7), bestiality (see Ex 22.18; Lv 20.15–16), male homosexual behavior (see Lv 20.13), various incestuous relationships (see Lv 20.11–19), and adultery involving a married woman (see Lv 20.10; Dt 22.22). Both parties involved in these sexual offenses, including the animal in cases of bestiality, were subject to the death penalty.

A man who raped a betrothed girl could be punished by death, and so could the victim of such a rape, if the rape occurred in the city and she was not heard to cry out for help (see Dt 22.23–27). A bride accused by her husband of not being a virgin, who could not provide evidence that she was a virgin, might be punished by death (see Dt 22.20–21). The death penalty also was prescribed for striking a parent (see Ex 21.15) or cursing a parent (see Ex 21.17; Lv 20.9). A stubborn and rebellious son, if incorrigible, could be denounced by his parents to the elders of the city and punished by being stoned to death by the populace (see Dt 21.18–21).

In war, enemies of Israel were regarded as enemies of God. Hence, killing in war was taken for granted as justified: "Saul has slain his thousands, and David his ten thousands" (1 Sm 18.7; cf. Dt 20.10–18). For certain religious crimes, a family or a city as a whole was to be destroyed utterly under the penalty of the ban (see Dt 13.13–18; Jos 7.10–26).

The absolute subordination of human life to religion is expressed in the story of Abraham's sacrifice of Isaac. Within the context of the covenant relationship, the killing of the child to fulfill what was taken to be a divine command is not seen as presenting any moral problem, although Isaac clearly is innocent. The difficulty is that Isaac is the medium of the fulfillment of the promise, and so Abraham must trust God sufficiently to hope against hope that the promise will be fulfilled despite the destruction of the necessary medium to fulfill it (see Gn 22.1–19; Heb 11.17–19).

8. At that stage of salvation history, the inadequacy of the mentality of God's people was virtually inevitable. In the Old Testament, friendship with God was understood strictly in terms of human fulfillment rather than sharing in God's own divine life. Compared with other goods, the covenant relationship appeared of overriding importance. By the terms of the covenant, God was Israel's legal and political sovereign. Taking on the sanctity of God himself, the law came to be considered holy. In consequence, other human goods were accorded respect only insofar as the law embraced and protected them.

9. The people of Old Testament times, thinking of their acts simply in terms of obedience to God, did not violate human goods as they would have done had they engaged in the same deeds while focusing on human goods as the direct determinants of morality. Sharing in the fallen human condition and living in the early stages of the divine pedagogy which culminates with Jesus, the Israelite conscience was necessarily somewhat immature and cannot be criticized as if it had perfect access to moral truth.[5] Their general error in conscience was sincere, and God's people were not set against human goods in trying to do his will as they understood it. Eventually Israel was defeated in war, and this experience led to the prophets' recognition of the ultimate significance of infidelity and the need for a new and more profound kind of covenant relationship. Thus, in God's providence the defects of ancient morality prepared the way for Jesus.

10. The Christian tradition has not firmly required socially authorized killing in violation of the eighth mode of responsibility. But Christians too often have overlooked the fact that the warrior God of the old covenant has become the crucified king of peace of the new. Now it appears that a true development of

Christian understanding on this matter is possible and even is occurring. It is like the development by which Christians came to recognize slavery as always unjustifiable, even though for many centuries it was widely considered morally acceptable.[6] True development does not involve contradicting anything the Church has firmly believed and handed on as essential to Christian faith and life. Its movement is not toward accepting something previously considered wrong, but toward seeing the unacceptability of something previously considered permissible.

Christian teaching has not insisted upon capital punishment, but has defended the licitness of such killing.[7] This defense, I believe, does not constitute teaching infallibly proposed by the ordinary magisterium.[8] As for war, although very restricted, it still can be justified if the war is defensive and the killing involved is incidental to just self-defense, not chosen for its utility as a means to an end.[9]

It seems that a development of Christian understanding concerning the morality of killing in capital punishment and in war is occurring, much like the development which Jesus carried out with respect to divorce and the development which the Church has carried out with respect to slavery. Divorce seems to be authorized in the Old Testament (see Dt 24.1), but Jesus corrects this view (see Mt 19.3–9; Mk 10.2–12). In many places, the New Testament seems to authorize slavery by taking it for granted and by regulating the moral relationships of masters and slaves (see Eph 6.5–9; Phlm; Ti 2.9–10; 1 Pt 2.18–25), but the Church's teaching firmly excludes this view (see GS 27).

This latter teaching is based on human dignity, and is closely joined with the exclusion of what is opposed to human life itself (see GS 27). I think the full implications of this principle for all killing which violates the eighth mode of responsibility soon will be drawn by the Church, in a legitimate development of doctrine. True, Leo X condemned Martin Luther's proposition that the burning of heretics is against the will of God (see DS 1483/ 773). But this condemnation was not proposed infallibly, and Vatican II clearly excludes the practice (see DH 6).

11. As St. Paul's teaching concerning the law makes clear, there is an important discontinuity between the Old Testament and the New. The law did not justify; it only pointed out what is sinful (see Rom 3.20). Justification comes through faith in God revealing himself in Jesus, a faith by which one accepts God's gift of his own transforming Spirit (see Rom 5.1–5). Because of this difference between the Old Testament and the New, the norms assumed in the Old Testament did not have to be completely correct or altogether rightly understood; for example, Moses permitted divorce (see Mt 19.8). But the fallen human condition really is transformed by Jesus, and the morality of the New Testament, the law of Jesus, follows from the gift of the Spirit (see Gal 5.22–6.2).

12. The divine life which Jesus enjoys and communicates by the gift of the Spirit is not just one human good among others. It is beyond all human goods. Hence there is no competition between the requirements of the new law and any human good. Nor can God's covenant with humankind in Jesus be served by any act which destroys, damages, or impedes a human good. **Hence, the limitation of the eighth mode of responsibility taken for granted in the Old Testament is removed in the New.** Thus St. Paul explicitly excludes rationalizations which would seek to justify evildoing for the sake of religion (see Rom 3.7–8; 2 Cor 4.2; Eph 4.14–15).

It is worth noting that although the gospel contains a reaffirmation of the ancient protection of human life (see Mt 5.21–26; 19.18), the New Testament does not mention capital punishment. St. Paul's teaching on the moral obligation to obey civil authority is not to be read as doing so (see Rom 13.4).[10]

Jesus undermines the traditional understanding of the subordination of other human goods to the good of religion. Of course, he does not deny that friendship with God is the supreme good, but he refuses to accept the reduction of friendship with God to the keeping of the law of Israel and the reduction of all other human goods to the fulfillment of Israel's quite determinate, this-worldly hopes. This refusal is shown in his relationships both with the Pharisees and with the zealot inclinations among his own close followers.

Jesus declares himself as Son of Man to be Lord even of the Sabbath, and asserts the subordination of the Sabbath to human fulfillment (see Mt 12.1–8; Mk 2.23–28; Lk 6.1–5). The supposed absoluteness of the prescriptions of the law is undercut. A human good, such as saving life, takes priority and is wholly in accord with the forgiveness of sin and integral friendship with God (see Mt 12.9–13; Lk 6.6–10).

At the same time, while Jesus consigns to human authority the keys to God's kingdom, he refuses to accept his followers' tendency to reduce this kingdom to earthly fulfillment (see Mt 16.13–23; Mk 8.27–33). Having come not to destroy human lives but save them, he will not destroy enemies (see Lk 9.52–56). Swords are not to be used even in his defense (see Lk 22.38, 49–51). Who lives by the sword will perish by it (see Mt 26.51–54). The kingdom of Jesus is not of this world (see Jn 18.36). His closest followers could not understand this point, and even after his resurrection looked to him to restore Israel's political autonomy (see Acts 1.6).

In place of the legal perspective of the Old Testament, Jesus puts himself. In him divine life is present and available to humankind. By this life, men and women really do share in a new and everlasting covenant. This good is not a limited set of human goods, such as Israel hoped for. Hence, the relationship with God no longer demands the constrictions upon human fulfillment which were taken for granted as acceptable both by the Pharisees and the zealots. For Jesus, the criterion for entry into or exclusion from the kingdom is how one treats one's human brothers and sisters, for the Son of Man is in solidarity with them (see Mt 25.31–46).

What is at stake here is Christian humanism. Once this Christian perspective is fully unfolded and accepted, it becomes clear that God cannot will that human persons choose to destroy, damage, or impede any of their other proper goods, even for the ulterior good of religion itself. The love of God is not itself the medium of the fulfillment of a promise of some limited set of human goods, and the love of God requires not the negation but rather the fulfillment of all the basic human goods (see GS 22–39). (This point will be treated in 24-E.)

Jesus is both the image of the invisible God and the perfect man (see Col 1.15; 2 Cor 4.4). "Since human nature as he assumed it was not annulled, by that very fact it has been raised up to a divine dignity in our respect too" (GS 22). From the moment of the Incarnation, it became impossible to fulfill the law of God except by the fulfillment of human persons. The divinization of human persons—their sharing in the Spirit—demands reverence for the basic goods of persons.

The mentality which was common in Old Testament times finds its ultimate expression in the very drama of the killing of Jesus. His activities threaten the safety of Israel and the temple. To protect the nation, Caiphas urges and justifies the killing of Jesus: "You know nothing at all; you do not understand that it is expedient for you that one man should die for the people, and that the whole nation should not perish" (Jn 11.49–50). Caiphas, of course, was correct. The death of Jesus was the salvation of his people (see Jn 11.51). However, though human evildoing cannot frustrate—and in the end even promotes—the divine plan (see Rom 11.25–36), this fact does not justify the craftiness of a Caiphas.

Subsequently, the eighth mode of responsibility is found in the teaching of St. Paul. Paul applies it only in contexts where it serves to exclude rationalizations of evildoing for the sake of religion.

In the primary text, the question is why there is anything wrong in falsehood if it is useful to promote God's glory. Paul states that some accuse him of teaching that we may do evil that good might come of it. He firmly rejects this accusation (see Rom 3.8). The clear implication of this text is that the suggested justification of doing evil to promote good, even the supreme good of God's glory, must be rejected. Not merely the end, but also the means, must be good.

This holds true of missionary practice. One might be tempted by discouragement to cut corners. But Paul rejects this temptation: "We have renounced disgraceful, underhanded ways; we refuse to practice cunning or to tamper with God's word, but by the open statement of the truth we would commend ourselves to every man's conscience in the sight of God" (2 Cor 4.2). Heresy springs from the desire to accommodate, to make the Christian message more acceptable. Such a technique is excluded. Christians instead should stick to the truth and propose it with charity (see Eph 4.14–15). Worldly wisdom is wholly unprofitable with God. He catches the wise in their own craftiness.

Question I: How do the eight modes of responsibility shape the life of a good person toward integral human fulfillment?

1. The first principle of morality was stated (in 7-F), and each of the modes considered individually in the previous questions of this chapter. Here we gather together the elements of the analysis. Doing so will help make clear how the modes of responsibility are related to one another and how they direct moral reflection in a positive way, not merely forbidding evil but encouraging the pursuit of good. The present description of the humanly good life also will serve as the skeleton to be fleshed out by the account of Christian life beginning in chapter nineteen.

2. **Integral human fulfillment means a single system in which all the human goods would contribute to the fulfillment of the entire human community.** It is not a goal to be reached by human effort. Humanity has been and remains socially divided, and many who might have been members of a human community already have died. Human power cannot raise the dead or even make peace on earth among living men and women. As chapter nineteen will show, integral human fulfillment will be realized by God's action; human persons can pursue it as a real goal only insofar as they can cooperate with God by a life of faith in Jesus. Considering integral human fulfillment in relation to human moral effort alone, however, it remains an ideal, not a goal toward which we can project our lives.

3. Still, as an ideal, integral human fulfillment does guide action. **It does this by calling for a life which would contribute to integral human fulfillment if it could be realized and excluding action inconsistent with its realization.** No

one can act for all the human goods and avoid accepting every evil. However, if one follows this ideal articulated by the first principle of morality, one can and will act for some of the basic human goods and avoid choosing against any of them. Similarly, no one can live in community with all other men and women. However, one can cooperate with some other people and avoid creating barriers to community with anyone.

4. Thus, one lives as an upright person who follows the ideal of integral human fulfillment only if one acts in the service of intelligible human goods. If one instead acts on the basis of the urges and aversions of sentient nature as such, one is not contributing to the realization of the human goods. Indeed, to that extent one's life amounts to little more than the life of a subhuman animal, except that one uses reason at the bidding of one's animal nature. The third and fourth modes of responsibility forbid us to settle for an existence so far beneath our dignity. They require that what one chooses at least include some intelligible good which provides a reason for the choice.

5. Without violating either the third or fourth mode, one could fail to act in the service of intelligible goods simply by not acting at all. Someone too lazy to do anything worthwhile certainly would make no contribution to integral human fulfillment. In a sense, such a person would be more a vegetable than an animal. The first mode of responsibility rules out inertia and requires one to pursue some intelligible good or other.

6. In pursuing goods one is reasonably concerned with success. Unfortunately, not only the limits of human power and the effects of sin, but the sheer complexity of reality itself sometimes makes it difficult to succeed in achieving the goals one is reasonably pursuing. Often, a goal cannot be realized unless one chooses to destroy, damage, or impede some instance of a human good. A person whose will is set upon integral human fulfillment will not make choices incompatible with it by acting against any good. The eighth mode forbids doing so.

7. Without violating any mode mentioned thus far, an individual could pursue exclusively a certain aspect of the good of self-integration. The quest for personal fulfillment often means consistently trying to attain what one wants and prevent or avoid what one does not want. Such a quest is self-centered in a very radical way. Aspects of human goods which would be realized in other people and, in general, human concerns beyond one's own experience are ignored except insofar as they touch oneself. Pursuit of so partial a good blocks openness to the larger possibilities of integral human fulfillment. Those whose hearts are fixed on the ideal will not adopt such a style of life. The sixth mode excludes it.

8. If there is to be any real human community, one must be fair to others. Without fairness, interpersonal relationships involve exploitation, and this prevents the real cooperation in the pursuit of goods characteristic of genuine community. This requirement of the ideal is specified by the fifth mode.

9. Without violating fairness, one can deliberately repay injury with injury, engage in retribution. To do this directly attacks some substantive good, such as life, and also obstructs the building up of community. The ideal of integral human fulfillment demands that when one suffers harm through another's action, one try

to limit the harm by not responding in kind. The seventh mode specifies this requirement.

10. Community requires still more. It is not enough to avoid a self-centered plan of life, to be fair, and to forgive injuries. If a person's life really is to be in accord with the ideal, positive effort to help others and readiness to benefit from their help are needed. One must be open to community in the sense of being ready to undertake and extend it whenever possible. The second mode requires that one not ignore or set aside such possibilities through an individualistic way of acting.

11. To avoid individualism and meet the requirements of all the modes, one must make at least some large choices which will guide one's day-to-day moral reflection. For one can fulfill one's sentient nature within the larger context of an intelligent plan of life only by directing one's life to the service of some of the substantive goods. Moreover, willingness to cooperate with others when possible implies openness to community with all human persons, for none are ruled out. Such openness is necessary to ensure one's own attention to possibilities of cooperation which one might otherwise overlook.

12. Children who are well brought up can begin to adopt an intelligent plan of life by particular choices even before they are mature enough to make any commitments. By spontaneous goodness they can be willing to enter into community with all persons. But in our society such moral development in harmony with the ideal of integral human fulfillment is sure to be directly challenged. A person of normal intelligence can hardly grow up without being tempted not only to make particular immoral choices but even to reject moral truth and adopt some subjectively satisfying world view. This temptation will take different forms according to each individual's previous moral formation. But whatever its exact form, in setting aside the alternative, those who meet the challenge freely submit themselves to moral truth and make a commitment to integral human fulfillment as they understand it.

13. **This commitment shaped by the modes of responsibility will be basic in a person's life—that is, it will be large enough to shape his or her whole life.** At least implicitly it will bear upon all the goods and extend to all people. The concept of basic commitment will be articulated more fully (in 9-E).

14. The act of faith can be such a basic commitment. Faith will be treated as the fundamental option of Christian life (16-G and 23-A). As for the upright person who has not already heard the gospel, he or she implicitly makes an act of faith by the basic commitment to serve genuine goods and build up community. If subsequently such a person accepts the gospel with grace and faith, it transforms his or her following of the moral ideal of integral human fulfillment into the following of Jesus by showing how heavenly fulfillment in him can be realized through human cooperation in God's plan of salvation. Chapters twenty-three through twenty-eight will show how the basic commitment of faith shapes the whole of Christian life.

Summary

These are the eight modes of responsibility:

1. *One should not be deterred by felt inertia from acting for intelligible goods.*
This happens when one refrains from doing something worthwhile out of
laziness, conquerable depression, or the like. Words like "energetic" and "diligent" signify the virtue corresponding to this mode; words like "sluggish" and
"slothful" name the vice. Revelation deepens the first mode by making God
known as a liberator and so counteracting the hopelessness induced by evil.

2. *One should not be pressed by enthusiasm or impatience to act individualistically for intelligible goods.* This happens when one acts by oneself, although
knowing that by cooperation with others the good would be more perfectly
attained insofar as others could share in it. In one aspect, the corresponding virtue
is called "team spirit"; the vice is named by expressions like "going it alone" and
"overcommitted." Revelation deepens this mode by making known humankind's
original common life and vocation, and the need for every person to play a
particular role in God's plan.

3. *One should not choose to satisfy an emotional desire except as part of one's
pursuit and/or attainment of an intelligible good other than the satisfaction of the
desire itself.* Violations occur when people act for no good reason, on account of
impulse, craving, routine, or the continued lure of goals which no longer make
sense. The virtue is called "self-control" or "discipline"; the vices "lustfulness,"
"greed," "fanaticism," "jealousy," "impetuosity," and so on. Revelation
deepens this mode by manifesting the dignity of human persons and by clarifying
the reality of free choice and moral responsibility.

4. *One should not choose to act out of an emotional aversion except as part of
one's avoidance of some intelligible evil other than the inner tension experienced
in enduring that aversion.* This happens when one is deterred from reasonable
action by feelings of repugnance, fear of pain, anxiety, and so forth. Words like
"courage" and "perseverance" signify the virtue, while the vice is expressed by
words like "irresolution" and "squeamishness." Revelation deepens this mode by
making it clear that evil has a limited reality and that God is dependable.

5. *One should not, in response to different feelings toward different persons,
willingly proceed with a preference for anyone unless the preference is required by
intelligible goods themselves.* This mode is violated when one's treatment of
others is marked by partiality toward some (including partiality toward oneself).
The virtue is called "fairness" and "disinterestedness"; the vice "favoritism,"
"selfishness," "prejudice," and so forth. Revelation deepens this mode by making
it clear that all human beings stand in a similar relationship to God, who is fair and
merciful to all.

6. *One should not choose on the basis of emotions which bear upon empirical
aspects of intelligible goods (or bads) in a way which interferes with a more
perfect sharing in the good or avoidance of the bad.* This happens when people act
for the conscious experience of a good rather than its fuller reality. The virtue is
named by expressions like "sincerity," "clearheadedness," "having a sound set of

values"; the vice by words like "superficiality," "frivolity," and "childishness." Revelation deepens this mode by making clear the primacy of divine reality which transcends experience.

7. *One should not be moved by hostility to freely accept or choose the destruction, damaging, or impeding of any intelligible human good.* Violations occur when negative feelings cause people to act destructively (including self-destructively). The virtue is named by words like "patient" and "forgiving"; the vice by words like "vengeful" and "resentful." Revelation deepens this mode in that God is shown to be long-suffering and forgiving.

8. *One should not be moved by a stronger desire for one instance of an intelligible good to act for it by choosing to destroy, damage, or impede some other instance of an intelligible good.* This happens when one deliberately acts to bring about something bad, either for the sake of a good or to prevent something else bad. The virtue is signified by the word "reverence"; the vice by "craftiness," "expediency," and so on. Revelation deepens this mode by enhancing reverence for the goods of human persons made in God's image. The acceptance of certain practices (for example, killing in warfare or capital punishment) both in the Old Testament and by Christians does not tell against this mode. For one thing, the people of Old Testament times did not have perfect access to moral truth; for another, there is reason to think an authentic development of doctrine may be occurring in regard to just these matters.

The eight modes of responsibility together guide action positively toward integral human fulfillment. An ideal rather than a goal, integral human fulfillment shapes a good life by requiring that one's actions be suited to its realization (if that were possible) and ruling out actions incompatible with this. The third and fourth modes direct one away from a life of sentient satisfaction toward intelligible human goods. The first and eighth modes require one to pursue some of the goods and not act against any. The sixth mode excludes a life focused on mere self-satisfaction, and the fifth requires one to treat others fairly. The seventh mode forbids revenge and so conduces to community despite the wrongs people do one another. And the second mode calls for a will toward cooperation with others in genuine community.

Alternative world views tempt people to turn from the vision of moral truth; one who deals uprightly with this temptation makes a more or less explicit commitment to integral human fulfillment. Such a commitment is basic in the sense that it shapes the whole life of one who makes it. For Christians, their act of faith constitutes such an upright commitment; for those who have not heard the gospel, their basic commitment serves as an implicit act of faith.

Notes

1. The opposite order of the second and third Beatitudes is perhaps preferable, and nothing vital will depend on this point. The order indicated is accepted here because, being that of the Vulgate, it is found in most past Catholic discussions of the Beatitudes. Readers familiar with my earlier works in which the modes of responsibility were articulated in a strictly philosophical way will notice that they are considerably reworked here. This has been done in the light of faith, especially the relationship I

think I have found between the modes of responsibility (and their corresponding natural virtues) and the Beatitudes or Christian modes of response (and their corresponding Christian virtues, exemplified in the character of Jesus).

2. In my early treatments of modes of responsibility, I formulated this mode by saying one should not "act directly against any of the basic human goods" or one should "never act against them with direct intent": *Contraception and the Natural Law* (Milwaukee: Bruce, 1964), 83; *Abortion: The Myths, the Realities, and the Arguments* (New York: Corpus Books, 1970), 319. Richard A. McCormick, S.J., in *Doing Evil to Achieve Good: Moral Choice in Conflict Situations*, ed. Richard A. McCormick, S.J., and Paul Ramsey (Chicago: Loyola University Press, 1978), 213–14, confuses this with Paul Ramsey's "turning directly against" and foists upon me a confusion not mine. "To act directly against" and "to act against with direct intent" are equivalent to "to choose to destroy, damage, or impede," as the analysis of choice (in 9-C) will help to clarify. It is important to notice that as in the present work, so in earlier treatments, I never propose this mode of responsibility as an argument against proportionalism or any other theory, and so there is no question-begging, as McCormick erroneously claims (213). Rather, having disposed of proportionalism on the grounds of its incoherence (in 6-F) and proposed a coherent formulation of the first principle of morality commended by the light it throws on the Church's teaching and common conceptions of morality (in 7-F), I now derive the modes of responsibility from that moral principle and theologically commend them by the sense they make of received Christian moral teaching, including what appears to be its potential for legitimate development—for example, in the matters of capital punishment and war.

3. For a very helpful, brief explanation of the limitations of Old Testament morality, see L. Johnston, "Old Testament Morality," *Catholic Biblical Quarterly*, 20 (1958), 19–25.

4. See Josef Scharbert, "Blood," *Encyclopedia of Biblical Theology*, 75–79; M. Greenberg, "Crimes and Punishments," *Interpreter's Dictionary of the Bible* 1:733–44; Roland de Vaux, *Ancient Israel*, vol. 1, *Social Institutions* (New York: McGraw-Hill, 1965), 10–12, 158–63, and 247–65.

5. On the progressive character of the divine pedagogy with special reference to morality in the Old Testament, see the brief but clear remarks of Pierre Grelot, *The Bible Word of God: A Theological Introduction to the Study of Scripture* (New York: Desclee, 1968), 124–26.

6. For further discussion of capital punishment and killing in war, see Germain Grisez and Joseph M. Boyle, Jr., *Life and Death with Liberty and Justice: A Contribution to the Euthanasia Debate* (Notre Dame and London: University of Notre Dame Press, 1979), 191–99 and 396–401, with accompanying notes.

7. See, for example, St. Augustine, *City of God*, i, 21; xix, 6; St. Thomas Aquinas, *Summa theologiae*, 2–2, q. 64, a. 2; *Summa contra gentiles*, 3, 146; Collegii Salmanticensis, *Cursus theologiae moralis*, vol. 3 (Venice: 1728), tr. 3, cap. 2, 157–58. Augustine thinks the judge would show greater refinement if he shrank from involvement in capital punishment (xix, 6). Thomas obviously has in view real, heretical opponents who argue from New Testament texts. The Salamancans mention one doctor who holds an unusual position: Scotus (I, d. 15, q. 3, sec. 2); he treats all Old Testament legislation on the death penalty as divine positive law, and so limits the use of the death penalty to crimes specifically mentioned in Scripture. Thomas (*S.t.*, 2–2, q. 64, a. 4) holds that clerics should not serve as executioners, since they are ordained to serve in the commemoration of the passion of Christ, who did not strike back, and since their assigned work serves the new covenant which prescribes no penalty of mutilation or death. It seems to me that some intuition of the wrongness of such killing probably underlies this restriction.

8. In 1210 Innocent III prescribed a declaration of faith for some who had accepted the Waldensian heresy, which included: "We assert concerning the secular power that it can carry out the death penalty without mortal sin, so long as it proceeds in imposing the death penalty not from hatred but from judgment, not carelessly but prudently" (DS 795/425). This statement seems to be the most formal teaching in defense of the death penalty, and it might be argued that it is definitive. If so, one must note that it concerns the subjective morality of the act. No doubt, at that time a Christian ruler of the best sort—a King Saint Louis, for instance—could carry out the death penalty with a good conscience. And this is all the statement required those who accepted the declaration to assert.

9. On early Christian attitudes toward war, see Jean-Michel Hornus, *It Is Not Lawful for Me to Fight* (Scottdale, Pa.: Herald Press, 1980), esp. 158–99. It is noteworthy that the statements of recent pontiffs have sounded an increasingly negative note concerning war, and that Vatican II allows for justifiable war only when it is a defensive last resort (see GS 79). I can accept certain forms of self-defense, including communal self-defense, which do not involve direct killing. Vatican II forcefully condemns the direct killing involved in terror bombing: "Any act of war aimed indiscriminately at the

destruction of entire cities or of extensive areas along with their population is a crime against God and man himself. It merits unequivocal and unhesitating condemnation" (GS 80). Building on the Council's teaching, the American bishops—National Conference of Catholic Bishops, *To Live in Christ Jesus: A Pastoral Reflection on the Moral Life* (Washington, D.C.: United States Catholic Conference, 1976), 34—have taught: "As possessors of a vast nuclear arsenal, we must also be aware that not only is it wrong to attack civilian populations but it is also wrong to threaten to attack them as part of a strategy of deterrence."

10. Pius XII, while insisting on the legitimacy of vindicative punishment imposed by public authority, states: ". . . the words of the sources and of the living teaching power do not refer to the specific content of the individual juridical prescriptions or rules of action (see particularly, Rom 13.4), but rather to the essential foundation itself of penal power and of its immanent finality" (47 *AAS* [1955] 81). Thus the New Testament text usually cited in defense of the death penalty is mentioned by Pius XII precisely to exclude specific reference to it. This statement is understandable, perhaps, if one notes that the address was to Italian jurists; Italy renounced the death penalty in 1889, reintroduced it in 1928, and abolished it in 1944.

CHAPTER NINE

THE VOLUNTARY
WHAT MORAL NORMS BEAR UPON

Introduction

The modes of responsibility are normative principles by which we can determine the morality of our acts. Acts themselves are existential principles in a different way; they make up one's morally significant life. Before seeing how the modes determine the morality of acts, we must see clearly what human acts are. For this purpose, the present chapter distinguishes and clarifies choice and several other sorts of voluntariness.

This chapter is one of the most important. At every step of the way, readers should try to relate what is being discussed to their own experience. Although some classical terms are retained in their traditional senses, those who have studied human acts in a previous course in ethics or moral theology will find that the present analysis differs from what they previously learned. The reason is that previous analyses of human acts included obscurities and confusions avoided here—although defects probably remain in the present effort, too.

Question A: Why is it necessary to study various sorts of voluntariness?

1. **Moral theology is concerned with how we constitute ourselves. Choices evidently play a large part in this, for they are actuations of the will, guided by moral norms, by which we determine ourselves with respect to human goods.** Chapter two treated free choice at length; questions C through F below will clarify our responsibilities in choosing. (Questions C and D deal with choice in general; question E treats commitment, which is an especially important kind of choice; question F treats the accepting of side effects of a choice.)

2. However, choices are not the only acts of the will. Choice presupposes intelligent interest in a good; such interest is itself a form of willing. **There are also other actuations of will allied with or consequent on choices; and, by bearing on choices, moral norms bear also on these other forms of voluntariness. Moral theology must consider these, too, insofar as they dispose persons well or badly with regard to human fulfillment.** (Question B treats the modes of voluntariness which precede choice, while question G treats those which are consequent upon it.)

3. If the modes of responsibility are followed, they shape life as a whole by their bearing on choices and other sorts of voluntariness. Acts of the will do not exist in isolation, somewhere deep inside us. They energize both one's inner activities and one's outward behavior, and so determine the existential quality—the moral goodness or badness—of one's whole life.

4. Classical moral theology spoke simply of the bearing of moral norms on "human acts," which were distinguished from nonvoluntary behavior—"acts of man" (cf. *S.t.*, 1–2, q. 1, a. 1). Although human acts were analyzed by reference to choice, the analysis began with those things accepted by common sense as human acts of various sorts—for example, killing a person. While this focus—on conventionally defined human acts—seems appealingly simple at first, the present analysis proceeds differently. Beginning with the sorts of voluntariness, the analysis of this chapter and the next considers the bearing of the modes of responsibility upon choices and other sorts of voluntariness.

5. This approach has the advantage of beginning with what is morally relevant about human acts: their voluntariness. By contrast, the older approach tended to obscure what is morally relevant by focusing on features which are significant for common sense or legal or metaphysical reasons. Such considerations call attention to many distinctions which have nothing to do with morality, while failing to point out others which make a difference to one's responsibility. For example, right and wrong tend to be obscured if one begins by considering killing in a common sense way, homicide in a legal way, or the various metaphysically distinct causes of death. The work of moral analysis proceeds more easily if one first distinguishes between choosing to kill and freely accepting death, and then examines the morality of each.

As will become clear in the analysis, "morally significant human acts" is not a general class-name (a genus) univocally predicated of specifically different instances of kinds of human acts. Rather, "morally significant human acts" refers to an ordered set (a grouping of analogy) of diverse sorts of things, which are human acts and morally significant in diverse but related ways.

Chapter two explained that free choice, because it is self-determining, is central for morality. The primary sort of things (the prime analogate) called "moral acts" consists of executions of free choices. In other words, the basic and most obvious morally significant action is a choice to do something and its execution. The whole—choice and performance together—is the human act. Since doing by choice is central, the analysis in this chapter focuses on this kind of human acts.

One might suppose that the only morally significant acts are those which carry out choices. In fact, while the execution of a choice always is morally significant, there are other morally significant aspects of human action. Moral selfhood and the responsibility which goes with it belong to persons just insofar as they have the power to make choices. Thus, moral responsibility extends beyond acts done by choice—for instance, to omissions and foreseen side effects. It follows that even in its full moral sense, "responsibility" does not refer to a single existential reality. For example, responsibility for what one does by choice is not the same as responsibility for side effects one accepts. Yet both are real and the latter can be as serious as the former.

Question B: Which sorts of voluntariness are presupposed by choice?

1. **Simple willing—a simple and basic caring about human goods—is presupposed by every volitional desire, choice, voluntary action, and volitional enjoyment.** It is based on two things: first, one understands that the basic human goods are possible fulfillments; second, in a practical frame of mind, one grasps them in the primary principles of natural law as fulfillments to be promoted and protected. Given this practical insight, simple willing naturally follows. **It is the constant, underlying disposition toward the goods.** It is natural and necessary that one be interested in what makes a difference to human survival and health, to knowledge of truth, to living in harmony with others, and so on (see *S.t.*, 1–2, q. 8, aa. 2–3; q. 10, a. 1; q. 94, a. 2; 3, q. 18, a. 3).

Someone might object that simple willing is not a natural and necessary disposition toward all of the basic human goods. For one can choose to act in ways destructive of these goods, knowing full well that one is doing so. For example, one can choose to kill another person or oneself, and so set oneself by choice against the supposedly basic good of life.

The answer to this objection is that one can indeed do this, for there are various other human goods, and in a choice situation one cannot act for all of them at once. By choice one determines oneself toward fulfillment in one aspect, setting aside possible fulfillment in another. By a choice to kill, one sets oneself toward whatever good one has in view which makes the killing seem desirable. One not only sets aside but sets oneself against the good of a particular human life. Yet the underlying simple volition of the good of life remains. There is then an inconsistency in one's willing introduced by one's own choosing. Notice that this is not logical inconsistency: the incompatibility of two propositions. It is existential: the incompatibility of a fundamental prolife disposition and a particular antilife self-determination.

2. Another sort of voluntariness presupposed by choice is spontaneous willing. **Given the basic disposition of simple willing, when people think of some definite way of proceeding in order to realize a concrete possibility and reach a fulfillment, they spontaneously will to proceed.** If no other factor prevents it, spontaneous willing leads into action (see *S.t.*, 1–2, q. 14, a. 4).

3. Human voluntariness makes raising children very different from training animals. Even children younger than six understand goods, are interested in them (simple willing), spontaneously will to realize them in definite ways, and act on this intelligent desire. The process is clearest in cases where they overcome repugnance to something (for example, taking bitter medicine) for the sake of an understood good (getting better).

What the child does by spontaneous willing, whether as a means or an end, is done voluntarily—"on purpose." In this sense, it is done intentionally. However, "intend" has at least two distinct meanings here, as is clear if one considers the case of taking medicine to get well. In this case, one intends to get well as an end, while one intends to take the medicine only as a means. Taking the medicine is intentional in the sense that it is done on purpose, but is not one's intention in the sense that it is not wanted for itself and would not be done except for the sake of something else.

If a boy at play gets muddy, he does not intend to get muddy in either of the preceding senses. Mother might say: "You're all muddy, again. Now, take your shoes off." The boy replies: "I didn't get muddy on purpose." And mother says: "But you knew you were getting muddy, didn't you?" The boy is reduced to silence. He did know, but simply was not concerned about it. In a third, weaker sense, one might say that the boy got muddy intentionally, not meaning "on purpose," but rather that he did get muddy knowingly and carelessly.

Children can be blocked from spontaneously doing what they spontaneously will by emotions incompatible with the emotions aroused by the spontaneous willing. For example, on a family hike, a small girl begins to tire. The parents say: "Come on, it's only a little farther, and then we'll stop and eat lunch." The child's understanding of lunch leads to spontaneous willing; this focuses imagination, which in turn arouses desire and leads to continued behavior: trudging along. But as she tires still more, the emotions aroused by pain and fatigue distract the girl's attention from lunch, and she stops walking. At some point, additional talk about lunch no longer is effective. Even at this point a new and effective motive sometimes can be supplied: "And where we are going to eat lunch there are swings and slides and a merry-go-round. We'll play while lunch is cooking." The little girl, spontaneously wishing to play, trudges on.

4. However, small children do not make choices. They act by spontaneous willing; but if there is to be a free choice, spontaneous action must be blocked— not merely by distraction and emotion but by the awareness that two or more incompatible alternatives are simultaneously real possibilities for the one who is to choose. Children under six, however, do not seem able to understand two possibilities at once and to compare them. Doing so requires not only understanding and judgment but reasoning. Small children can be responsible in a sense— their action is their own, and their naughtiness and good behavior express human capacities—but they are not morally responsible.

5. Adults also frequently act by spontaneous willing, but when they do, their action has moral significance. Capable of reflecting on every aspect of their lives, adults can notice what they spontaneously do and take control over it. If they can and should choose to do something to prevent themselves from doing what comes naturally and nevertheless fail to take control, adults have some responsibility for the omission.

It is worth noticing that certain aspects of willing and acting are present both in actions done by choice and in those done by spontaneous willing.

First, spontaneous willing includes a double relationship to the good. Underlying all spontaneous willing and still present in it as its spiritual energy is simple volition. Spontaneous willing thus is related to the understood good as to that in which one might share by action. But spontaneous willing also is directed to the specific, concrete realization understood as possible by one's action. This understood good is a definite state of affairs which actually is (expected to be) fulfilling. This state of affairs either is realized in one's very action or is subsequent to one's action, which is a partial cause of it.

Thus, a child's spontaneous willing to play is a willing to share in the good of play and also is a willing to do the very things which count as play. This latter willing can unfold into spontaneous acts of play. It also can unfold into a spontaneous act of trudging along, in order to arrive at the playground.

Second, what is done spontaneously is defined by what one understood and spontaneously willed to do. A child at play brings about many states of affairs other than its play activity. For example, children dirty their clothing, fall down occasionally, and so forth. A child of four or five can be well aware of some of these effects. But what it is doing is what it does "on purpose"—that is, what expresses its understanding and willing.¹ That which is done on purpose includes not only activity which is directly fulfilling, but also activity done to bring about a fulfilling state of affairs. For example, the sick child purposely takes the bad-tasting medicine to get well.

Thus, what a child does spontaneously is done either for its own sake or for the sake of something ulterior. What is done for its own sake—for example, playing—is in itself a good; it can be called an "end" in the sense that it is in itself a purpose of human action. What is done for the sake of something ulterior—for example, taking bitter medicine—is not in itself an intelligible good. It can be called a "means" in the sense that it is done as a way of bringing about an end—in this case, getting well.

Question C: How are choices related to what one chooses?

1. We turn now to choice. If one makes and carries out a choice, what one does—one's human act in the strictest sense—is precisely the unified whole: one's choice and what one has chosen to do. By choice one adopts a proposal to do something. Individuals deliberate about doing what they consider possible and interesting much as members of a deliberative body debate motions (see *S.t.*, 1, q. 83, a. 3; 1–2, q. 13, aa. 3–5; q. 14, aa. 1–3). Adopting a proposal to do something is a choice, just as a motion which is adopted is a decision of the group. The doing carries out the choice, much as the executive carries out a legislative body's enactments. **The action of an individual is defined by the proposal adopted by a choice, just as the action of a group is defined by the motion adopted by a vote.** In both cases, execution of what is decided completes the action (see *S.t.*, 1–2, q. 16, a. 1; q. 17, aa. 3–4).²

2. Thus, a person who chooses to play golf is playing golf, while a person who chooses to take painful treatment for a disease is taking painful treatment. A man who considers the proposal to kill himself, adopts the proposal, and carries it out, kills himself. If Mary chooses to lay down her life rather than yield to a rapist, then she is resisting rape, not killing herself like Peter, who adopts a proposal to hang himself.

3. **Since one's action is defined by the proposal one adopts, one not only does what one chooses to do as good in itself** (playing golf for its own sake) **but also does what one chooses to do as a means** (taking painful treatment for the sake of health) (see *S.t.*, 1–2, q. 8, aa. 2–3). A person who chooses to kill a defective child so that the child will not have to endure a miserable life is perhaps a misery preventer but certainly a child killer. The fact that reluctance, regret, and so on accompany a choice does not substantially alter what one is doing (see *S.t.*, 1–2, q. 6, a. 6; q. 78, a. 1, ad 2).

The expression, "the proposal adopted by choice," has more or less the same meaning as St. Thomas' expression, "the object of an action." The point made here by saying, "The action is defined by a proposal adopted by choice," often is expressed in his language, "The action is specified by its object" (cf. *S.t.*, 1–2, q. 18, a. 2).³

However, the classical moralists sometimes used "object of the act" to refer to the outward deed without clearly including its relationship to deliberation and choice. Thus, when they said that the object of the act is a determinant of its morality, they seemed to be trying to ground morality directly in nature considered physically and metaphysically, rather than in human goods. (The sort of ethical theory which fostered this confusion was criticized in 4-F.)

This confusion offered an opportunity for theologians who adopted proportionalism to denounce as "physicalism" or "biologism" the thesis that some kinds of acts are always wrong—wrong *ex obiecto* or intrinsically evil—regardless of the foreseen goods which might be intended in choosing to do them.[4] The present analysis provides a way of understanding "object of the act" which is not physicalist, but which does allow certain kinds of acts to be always wrong, for example, when a choice would violate the eighth mode of responsibility. (In proposing this analysis, no question is begged against proportionalists, since their position has been examined in chapter six and found indefensible in virtue of its inherent unworkability.)

4. People are responsible not only for what they do but for what they fail to do, that is, their omissions. Not everything called "omission" is a moral failing, however. To say someone "ought" to do something may express the judgment that he or she is morally required to do it, but it may also indicate some other sort of requiredness (see *S.t.*, 1–2, q. 6, a. 3; q. 71, a. 5). For instance, consistency requires people to do what they usually do, and the failure to do this can be called an "omission." But it is a moral omission only if there was a moral requirement to do what was not done.

5. **Analyzed from the point of view of voluntariness, omissions are seen to be of several kinds. One kind corresponds to the sort of actions which carry out proposals adopted by choice.** In such omissions, one chooses not to engage in certain performances precisely in order to bring about a desired state of affairs.

6. Thus, parents or medical personnel sometimes choose to kill a defective infant by withholding food and water until it dies. The voluntariness of this omission is the same as the voluntariness of choosing to kill the child by giving it an overdose of narcotics. Only the technique and the outward state of affairs are different. The choice in both cases is to kill—in one case by not doing something, in the other by doing something. (Other kinds of omissions will be dealt with in questions F and G.)

Actions expected because people usually do them, because consistency requires them, or because they seem appropriate can be said to be "omitted" if they are not done; but they are omissions from a moral point of view only if there is some moral norm indicating that they should be done, despite which they in fact are not done. Thus, a person who skips lunch on a certain day has omitted it, but has done a moral omission only if there was some moral requirement to have lunch. A priest who leaves out appropriate but optional items in a liturgy omits in a certain sense, but not in a moral sense, since he uses the option; however, a priest who omits what is prescribed by the Church omits in a moral sense, since the faithful have a right to the Church's liturgy.

Question D: How are choices related to human goods?

1. As was explained (in 6-B), choices are related to human goods in two ways. First, in choosing one determines oneself in respect to human goods (see *S.t.*, 1–2, q. 1, a. 3; q. 26, a. 2; q. 28, a. 6; q. 86, a. 1, ad 2). One establishes one's moral

identity as open to the good in its fullness or as open only to limited aspects of goodness, not to integral human fulfillment. Second, there is a causal relationship: In choosing, one sets oneself to bring about certain states of affairs (see *S.t.,* 1–2, q. 17, a. 1). In these states of affairs, human goods are to some extent realized or manifested. In more figurative language, by choosing one makes one's soul and also sets the course of one's life. In deciding to play golf, for example, one integrates the good of play rightly or wrongly into one's moral self, while at the same time setting oneself to perform the playing of the game.

2. These two relationships to the goods are distinct. They can coincide, but they need not. One can choose to look at a beautiful sunset and then look at it. But one can also see the sunset without choosing to see it (the second relationship to the good exists without the first) or choose to see it but be prevented (the first relationship without the second).

3. There are different kinds of actions, distinguished by the simplicity or complexity of various elements of the action as a whole.

4. **In the simplest kind of action, the only relevant good actually affected is that actualized in the state of affairs brought about in carrying out the choice.** If, for instance, one chooses to play and plays golf simply for the sake of play, the only human good directly affected is the good of play. One determines oneself in respect to it in choosing, and one realizes it in the playing of the game.

5. Slightly more complicated in outward structure, yet morally the same, is a case where the deed one chooses to do is the cause of a desired effect. One chooses, for example, to take medicine for the sake of health; the only relevant good is health, not the taking of medicine. Here the complexity of the cause-effect sequence does not affect the act's moral simplicity. From the point of view of medical technique, taking medicine is a means to health. From a moral point of view, the act is as simple as playing golf for the sake of play. There is a real difference between the cause and the effect, but it is morally unimportant, since the two are humanly inseparable and both are included in one actuation of the will—the choice to do a health-giving action.[5] The choice determines the person only in respect to the single good: health.[6]

6. Some actions, however, are morally more complicated. Although carrying out a proposal will have an effect upon a human good, one makes this choice for the sake of some good other than that involved in the carrying out of the choice and the unfolding of its humanly inevitable effects. For instance, one might choose to play golf, even though one detests the game, for the sake of making a business deal.[7]

7. In such cases, the action or omission one chooses is a means from the existential point of view; thus the means-end distinction has ethical significance here. **One has some responsibility not only in regard to the good one pursues, but also in regard to the goods one willingly affects in using the means one chooses.** Still, it makes a difference whether the effect on a human good of the use of the means is or is not part of one's proposal. Effects of carrying out a proposal, if foreseen but not included in the proposal, are side effects. (The voluntariness involved in accepting side effects will be considered in question F.) **But the**

impact on a human good which is part of one's chosen proposal is not a side effect. Even though one's action affects this good only as a means one is using to attain one's end, still one determines oneself—not simply in respect to one's end, but in respect to any good affected as means.

8. For example, the United States, in order to protect freedom and peace, has adopted a policy of nuclear deterrence which includes a real and continuing choice to destroy an enemy's noncombatant population if deterrence should fail.[8] This policy involves a fourfold relationship to human goods. If deterrence works, the goods which are its end, peace and freedom, are realized. But if execution of the policy becomes necessary, this also will affect a human good: life. Furthermore, the moral self of everyone who cooperates in and supports this policy is also doubly determined. Love of peace and freedom is part of one's identity; but so, too, is irreverence toward human life, implicit in the readiness to kill for peace and freedom's sake. (In misunderstanding human goods and misconstruing the nature of morality, proportionalists overlook the "soul-making" aspect of one's choice in cases of this sort, as was explained in 6-B and 6-G.)[9]

In addition to the object of the human act done by choice, classical analyses mention the "end of the agent." The present analysis clarifies this conception, both by distinguishing between the two ways in which one's choice is related to a good, and by making explicit the relevance of both the good which pertains to the end and the good affected by an act chosen as a means.

Obviously, the end of the agent is very important, especially insofar as it is that to which one commits oneself, for in this aspect the end constitutes the person acting. But in choosing and acting one also constitutes oneself by one's relationship to a good which is relevant only to a means adopted in pursuit of an ulterior end. One who chooses to kill as a means wills to be a killer in wanting the particular death, not of course for its own sake, but for the sake of the ulterior good for which killing is chosen. The ulterior good is intended both as that to which one commits oneself and as that which one hopes to realize by killing.

One who chooses to kill one person to save the life of another constitutes himself or herself both by the intentional killing and by the intended saving of life. The inconsistency involved can exist in one's moral self only if one makes some sort of distinction between life worth saving and life which is expendable. In making such a distinction, one is qualifying one's basic love of life, limiting it to love of life of a certain quality, or something of the sort.

It is worth recalling that the good to which one determines oneself and in which one thereby shares is wholly distinct from the concrete good brought about by one's action only in the case of goods pertaining to domains other than the existential. In the existential domain, to determine oneself to a true good is to begin to effect what one wills; to seek some satisfaction in a mere appearance of the good is to constitute oneself accordingly. For example, one who gives a gift out of friendship thereby begins to realize the good of friendship; one who does favors only for selfish purposes brings into existence a manipulative relationship.

Question E: What are the special characteristics of commitments?

1. The word "commitment" has many meanings. In the sense in which it is used here, commitments are among the large choices described previously (2-G).

Here commitment will be explained more fully and its special voluntariness will be clarified. The act of faith, marriage promises, religious vows, oaths of allegiance, a decision to reform one's life—these are examples of commitments.[10]

2. **Commitments bear directly upon goods of the existential domain.** One commits oneself in view of religion, justice and friendship, practical reasonableness and authenticity, and/or one's own self-integration. Since these are interrelated, commitments can bear upon all at once. Moreover, since existential goods are understood practically as possible forms of harmony in personal and interpersonal relationships, one commits oneself both to a particular person or persons, and to some goods which will be shared.

Many of the interesting characteristics of commitments depend upon the goods of domains other than the existential which provide a common substance for the personal and interpersonal relational harmonies of the existential domain. For instance, the commitment of Christian faith has certain characteristics which arise from its specific relationships to life and truth. Marriage has characteristics which follow from the fact that this type of companionship makes possible a service to new life impossible by any other cooperation.

3. Ordinarily, in making a commitment, one initially makes only a symbolic gesture toward realizing the goods to be shared. Their fuller realization will depend on making and carrying out many additional choices consistent with the commitment. Still, the commitment also is a choice, and one has the same general sort of experience in making it as in making other, lesser choices (see, e.g., Jos 24.14–28).

4. **At the time the commitment is made, it is impossible to foresee precisely what observing it will require; the concrete implications unfold only as it is lived out.** Even at the outset, however, the commitment excludes certain choices which might otherwise be acceptable. In this way, one marks out negatively the good which will be creatively realized by living out the commitment, continually reaffirming it, and growing in it. When, for example, a couple marry, they do not—for they cannot—know what life together will be like. Only in living their married life will they creatively unfold the reality of this sort of friendship in their particular case. But even though they cannot fully understand marital love in advance, from the beginning they can grasp the meaning and wrongness of adultery. By pledging fidelity they are not choosing negatively. Rather, they are affirming, in the only way they can, the yet-to-be-conceived, unique good of their life together.

5. **Thus, to make a commitment is not simply to decide upon a long-range goal for oneself.** In pursuing a definite goal, however long range, one can follow a method for selecting and using proportionate means, and can measure progress toward the goal. In carrying out a commitment, one cannot proceed efficiently— for example, there is no recipe for making a good marriage. One who faithfully serves a commitment continues to discover new depths in the good—growth in marital love leads to a corresponding enrichment of the ideal—which is always being realized yet never becomes exhausted. Service of any morally upright commitment is a gift of oneself, and the fulfillment one receives in service is a merited response to this gift. Such fulfillment must be distinguished from the good one achieves by successfully pursuing any definite goal.[11]

6. Although making a commitment is not choosing a long-range goal, commitments do organize one's life somewhat as goals do. Commitments can require or exclude choices not only of particular actions but also of goals. Moreover, commitments themselves differ in scope. Some bear upon more human goods than others, and some are to a wider community of persons than others. A more inclusive commitment will shape a greater part of one's life. Morally mature persons make some basic commitment which organizes their entire life, including all other commitments and goals. Morally upright mature persons at least implicitly establish a relationship with all other human persons and with God. (This point was treated in 8-I.)

7. One who has made a commitment faces the realm of possibilities in a new way. Before, he or she was limited to possibilities which suggested themselves and so, usually, to lines of action which others had set and followed. For the creativity of a person without commitments is in respect to thinking or performance, but not in respect to the existential goods themselves. Having made a commitment, however, one is now in a position to reflect upon the goods to which one has committed oneself and upon one's powers in relation to all possible ways of serving those goods. In short, a person with a commitment can think of altogether new ways of acting in the service of goods and realizing them in the context of the commitment.

Thinking creatively about how to realize goods to which one is committed is extremely important in living a Christian life. Very often, the only apparent possibilities are the alternatives of committing a sin or accepting some very bad consequences. One who is without commitments and creative reflection based on them is likely to use this common occurrence as an argument for proportionalism. A person faithful to commitments very often (not always) can find possibilities no one else would have dreamed of. Love finds a way. This is one reason why the lives of saints are more varied and original than the lives of sinners.

8. **The freedom of choice with which one makes a commitment pervades what one does in carrying it out.** Often, even creative activity in the service of commitments requires no further choice. Caring, one looks for a way to help; love finds a way, and one takes the way love has found. Such actions, generated by commitments, are no less free and morally responsible than those which carry out additional acts of choice. When one acts spontaneously but willingly under a commitment, even without a further act of choice, one is acting freely, with the freedom of the commitment itself.

9. Unfortunately, this is as true of sinful commitments as virtuous ones. One who persists in sin and acts spontaneously but willingly to carry out a sinful commitment—for example, an ongoing adulterous relationship—is responsible for further sinful acts, even if these are done without any additional choice. The freedom of the unrepented sin persists in the life one knowingly lives in accord with it. This kind of voluntariness, here called "executive willing," is discussed in G below.

Question F: What is the difference between voluntariness in choosing and in accepting foreseen consequences distinct from what is chosen?

1. We are responsible for more than just what we aim at and choose. In making a choice, one usually foresees many effects of carrying out the proposal. Some, although not included in the proposal, can have an important bearing on human goods. A person has some responsibility for such side effects. For instance, one who chooses to drink and drive foresees possible harm to the lives and property of others. Though drunken drivers do not aim at this harm or include it in the proposal they adopt, they nevertheless bear some responsibility for this foreseen side effect. An accident which is due to their condition is their fault.

That one can bear responsibility for foreseen consequences which are no part of one's proposal is clearly indicated by examples. A person who enjoys very loud music might decide in the late night hours to play his or her favorite records, realizing that the sound will disturb others. The proposal simply is to listen to music; the disturbance to others might even be regretted. Still, one who thus disturbs others is responsible, and others are justified in complaining that such a person is selfish.

Many injustices are like this one. People often are not interested in harming others, but they foresee harm to others occurring along with benefit to themselves and proceed to act selfishly. In a case of this sort, the moral responsibility is not in self-determination against some good—for example, the health of others damaged by their lack of sleep. Rather, the responsibility is in lack of commitment to community with others, since such commitment would incline one to treat their interests on a par with one's own.

2. **Although one bears responsibility for foreseen side effects, one does not have the same sort of responsibility for them as for what one chooses** (see *S.t.*, 2–2, q. 43, a. 3; q. 64, a. 7). Moral responsibility is to be found first and foremost in one's choosing. For example, a man, such as Jesus, who freely accepts certain death as a side effect of continuing to carry out his upright commitments does not choose to kill himself; thus he is not guilty of the destruction of his life. But a man who chooses to kill himself is guilty of the destruction of his life, even if he is killing himself for the sake of some human good which he rightly desires to serve.

Still, in many cases the effects one foresees and accepts have a great significance for human goods. Although in some cases one may accept effects which significantly inhibit or damage some human good, this possibility is not unlimited. If one really is as committed to community as one ought to be, one will not accept effects selfishly. Nor will one bring about effects which it is one's duty to avoid.

Firefighters, for example, will try to fight fires, not always in the easiest way, but in ways which minimize loss of life, since it is their duty to save lives. The law also reflects this sort of responsibility by prohibiting various cases of homicide which involve no premeditation. For instance, the responsible drunken driver might be convicted of manslaughter. Hence, although one is not responsible for side effects one accepts in the same way one is responsible for what one does by choice, responsibility for the former can be just as grave as responsibility for the latter.

3. What one does in the strict sense is what one chooses to do—that is, what is sought for its own sake and/or included as a means in the proposal one adopts (see *S.t.*, 1–2, q. 1, a. 3; q. 6, a. 1; q. 19, a. 5). What one brings about, including all

foreseen side effects, is far more extensive than what one chooses to do and "does" in this strict sense. One determines oneself primarily in choosing. In choosing one establishes one's existential identity by settling one's personal priorities among the goods on which the choice bears. One does not determine oneself in the same way with respect to foreseen side effects, which are neither sought for their own sake nor included in the proposal one adopts.[12]

The goods in which one is interested and on which one's choice directly bears are much more limited than the whole state of affairs one actually brings about by executing the proposal one adopts. For instance, if two boys play catch, they are interested in the good of playing the game. Perhaps the boys have been told to do chores instead of playing catch, and they know they might be caught and punished for their delinquency. This foreseen consequence, though understood as part of the state of affairs their action will bring about, is not precisely what they choose. Their self-determination is to play, not to being punished. Punishment, if it comes, will be an unwanted side effect of having done as they pleased.

It might be assumed that the foreseen consequence in this example lies outside the precise boundaries of the boys' choice only because the consequence occurs by parental fiat. But this assumption is false. The boys might also realize that they are wearing out their gloves. Even if they consider this natural and inevitable consequence of using their gloves, it is no part of the proposal they adopt in choosing to play. They are interested in play; they accept wear on their gloves as an unwanted consequence of using them.

4. At the same time, one bears responsibility for foreseen side effects. Since they are foreseen, these effects are voluntary. One could avoid them by not choosing what one chooses. One might not want them, but one does accept them. Thus, while primarily responsible for choices, which directly determine oneself and shape one's character, one is secondarily responsible for the foreseen consequences of carrying out one's choices. **Since side effects are freely accepted, it makes sense to ask whether one ought to accept them. Several of the modes of responsibility help to answer this question.**

5. Freely accepted side effects must be distinguished from chosen means to one's ends. Means are adopted as at least useful goods; they are included in one's proposals. Thus one determines oneself in regard to the goods upon which they bear.[13] As has already been explained, in adopting a proposal to destroy, damage, or impede any instance of any of the goods intrinsic to persons, one determines oneself against that good, in violation of the seventh or eighth mode of responsibility. By contrast, to accept side effects contrary to a human good is not to determine oneself against it.

Many documents of the magisterium distinguish between direct and indirect action— for example, direct sterilization and indirect sterilization. This distinction is the same as that clarified here between what one chooses and what one accepts as a foreseen side effect. For example, direct sterilization is an action in which one chooses to sterilize, while indirect sterilization is an action in which one chooses something else and accepts sterility as a foreseen side effect.

In cases where this distinction is invoked, the direct action usually is rejected as always wrong, whereas the indirect action might sometimes be upright. The so-called principle of double effect is an attempt to formulate the conditions under which an indirect action would be upright if the corresponding direct action would be wrong. (For this problem and a discussion of the classical handling of it, see 12-F.)

6. Among the foreseen consequences of one's choices, those conducive to one's own or another's subsequent immoral acts are especially important for moral theology. Having some responsibility for the foreseen side effects one accepts, often obliges one to refrain from otherwise innocent choices, precisely because one foresees that they will create occasions of sin for oneself or someone else (see *S.t.*, 2–2. q. 43, aa. 6–7). (In creating an occasion of sin for another when one could and should avoid doing so, one is said to give scandal.)

7. **Many omissions are voluntary in the following way: Rather than simply choosing to omit what one should do, one instead chooses something else, with the omission accepted as a side effect.** For example, a student chooses to watch television when he or she should be studying. The neglect of study is not regarded as a good or included in the proposal of amusement which the student adopts; but it is a foreseen side effect, freely though perhaps reluctantly accepted. Responsibility for such omissions is the same as responsibility for positive foreseen consequences, which are accepted even though they could and should be avoided.

Question G: What varieties of voluntariness presuppose choice but are distinct from any act of choice?

1. **One such variety of voluntariness is executive willing—the willing acceptance at a time subsequent to choosing of effects of one's action.** A person chooses and begins to do something; while carrying out the choice, he or she discovers that its execution is having certain effects; the person makes no additional choice, but knowingly and willingly proceeds to bring about these significant effects. For example, a woman takes a job outside the home, finds that her absence is having serious effects on her children, makes no additional choice, but knowingly continues with her career and willingly accepts these side effects.

Executive willing can occur not only where one executing a choice accepts a previously unforeseen side effect, but also in cases in which one executing a choice willingly does an act other in kind from that which one had chosen to do. For example, a gangster, Ma Fia, decides to get revenge on a rival by burning down her rival's warehouse. As she executes this plan, she perhaps notices that a strong wind is blowing in the direction of other nearby buildings, and foresees that the fire will spread, but proceeds nevertheless without any further choice. Here the executive willing is of something which would have been a foreseen side effect had it been taken into account during deliberation. But in executing the plan, Ma might also discover, to her delight, that her rival unexpectedly is in the warehouse, and is likely to die in the fire. Had this effect been foreseen, it would have been part of the proposal adopted since it serves the purpose even better than the original proposal. Thus, Ma Fia kills her rival, does it voluntarily, and is responsible for doing it, but never chose to do it.

Executive willing is not the same as the voluntary in cause, since the voluntary in cause involves willing acceptance of foreseen results of one's chosen actions. Executive willing concerns unforeseen aspects or results of one's actions, which come to light as one executes one's proposals. Without further deliberation and choice, one willingly continues to carry out the action despite its unforeseen aspects or willingly accepts the unforeseen results.

2. Plainly, one is responsible for what one does by executive willing. If the

significant consequences fall within the scope of the original purpose or proposal, their subsequent acceptance seems to be a development or extension of the choice and to be voluntary as it is. If the significant consequences are such that they would only have been side effects if they had been foreseen, accepting them by executive willing is an extension of the free acceptance of foreseen consequences involved in the choice and is voluntary in that way.

3. **Corresponding to the executive willing of unforeseen consequences of choices is a type of omission without choice.** Aware that one should choose and act, one deliberates about what to do and about doing it—but fails to make a choice to do anything. In some cases, there is another choice—to put off (but not omit) decision and action. In other cases, there is no choice at all, but deliberation is broken off by something which distracts attention from the problem.

Here is an example. Parents notice that one of their children seems to have a health problem. They begin to discuss the situation, knowing they ought to do something about it. Ideally, they investigate and seek advice until they formulate a reasonable plan of action, and then adopt the plan and carry it out. But often parents fail to take the action they should for a child's well-being. Perhaps they think they should make an appointment with their physician, but put off making it. Perhaps they are not sure what to do and put off looking into the matter. Perhaps at times they worry over the problem rather aimlessly, but always are interrupted by work, sleep, or something else before coming to a conclusion.

Although very different from the voluntariness and responsibility involved either in choosing to do something or in accepting foreseen consequences of one's acts, the moral responsibility in cases of omissions without choices also is real. The responsibility is for failure to use one's freedom when one could and should use it. By such omissions, one certainly can be morally responsible. If the child dies of the condition, the parents will realize the death is their fault: "We knew Mary was not well; we ought to have taken her to the doctor. We did talk about it, but we just never got around to doing anything until it was too late." This sad story is very different from that of parents who decide to kill their defective infant by starving it, and also different from that of parents who abandon a child, accepting the possibility of its death but hoping someone might care for it.

4. **There are still other varieties of voluntariness. Sometimes one's choices have unforeseen consequences which could and should have been foreseen and avoided.** Such consequences can include behavior which would be recognized as immoral if it proceeded from choice or willing acceptance at the time it is done. They also can include inaction which would be omission if one were aware of one's responsibilities. For example, a person who wrongly neglects studies while preparing for a profession is likely sooner or later to do and omit many things which could and should have been foreseen and avoided by diligence in studying. This responsibility clearly is derivative from what one has previously done and failed to do. It is less than the previous varieties of voluntariness.

A priest fails to do adequate preparation of his homilies, although he could and ought to prepare them carefully. Let us imagine the priest never even thinks about how he is preparing his homilies and is not in the least worried about obligations in this area. Where is the responsibility here? It lies in other actions and omissions which have not been as they should. In the seminary, perhaps he did not study much, because he did not enjoy it. Entering upon the pastoral ministry, he realized he should allocate his time with some care in order to be able to do the job well, but he never got around to making and following a regular schedule. The result is that he divides his time between doing things he finds enjoyable and responding to urgent pastoral demands, and so never has time to prepare the Sunday homily carefully. If he had fulfilled his other responsibilities, he would be able to do this, would see that he ought to do it, and probably would do it. Thus there is some responsibility for the ill-prepared homilies this priest gives, and for the fact that the faithful—most of whom never receive instruction otherwise—receive little solid teaching from him.

5. **Readiness and unreadiness to choose can also be voluntary.** One should, for example, be ready for martyrdom and unready to do anything immoral. The voluntariness of readiness and unreadiness follows from one's responsibility to make and live out commitments which will generate these dispositions.

6. The preceding distinctions among varieties of voluntariness help render intelligible certain scriptural notions, such as unconscious faults, the inevitable sinfulness of the upright, and so on. They also help in understanding problems of pastoral practice and spiritual development. For example, a person whose omissions without choices lead to very serious consequences—say, someone's death—will be helped if the confessor or counselor clarifies both the reality and the limits of the responsibility. Similarly, someone whose conscious conversion and commitment are vitiated by the continuing effects of past sins can be helped to understand and persevere in the task of growth in holiness.

Summary

Choices are morally good or bad acts of the will by which we settle what we shall do and so determine ourselves with respect to human goods. But choices are not the only forms of morally significant voluntariness. Consideration of the several varieties of voluntariness is important not only for the theoretical analysis of human acts but also for pastoral practice by counselors and confessors.

Two forms of voluntariness precede choice. The first, simple willing, is the constant, underlying disposition toward human goods; the second, spontaneous willing, occurs when, seeing some definite way to reach a fulfillment, one wills to proceed. Small children act by spontaneous willing without choice, and so without moral responsibility. While adults often do the same, their ability to anticipate and take control of spontaneous willing gives their spontaneous actions a moral significance lacking in those of a child.

As for choices, they deserve consideration in several respects. To begin with, if one makes and carries out a choice, what one does—one's act in the strictest sense—is precisely one's choice together with what one has chosen to do. An action is defined primarily by the proposal adopted by a choice. One does, not only what one chooses to do for its own sake as a good in itself, but also what one chooses to do as a means to some other good. Among the several kinds of omissions, too, there is one which corresponds to the action which carries out a proposal adopted by choice: that is, one chooses not to do something precisely in order to bring about a desired state of affairs.

Choices are related to human goods in two ways. First, in choosing one determines oneself in respect to human goods and so establishes one's moral identity. Second, in choosing one sets oneself to bring about certain states of affairs in which goods are realized or infringed on. In the simplest kind of choice, the only good affected is that realized (or infringed on) in the state of affairs brought about in executing the choice. Slightly more complicated, but morally the same, is the case where one's performance causes a desired effect, and only the latter bears upon a human good. More complicated still are cases where executing a proposal will have an effect upon one good but this choice is made for the sake of some other good realized in some other state of affairs. Here the means-end distinction has ethical significance; one has a responsibility for goods which are implicated in the means one uses to attain yet other goods one desires.

Although a commitment is a choice, at the time it is made it is impossible to foresee precisely what it will entail; only in living it out do its concrete implications become apparent. Nevertheless, the freedom of choice with which one makes a commitment pervades what one does in carrying it out. In acting spontaneously but willingly under a commitment, even without a further choice, one is acting freely with the freedom of the commitment itself, and one's action is morally responsible.

Passing on from choice to other aspects of voluntariness, we turn next to freely accepted side effects. These must be distinguished from means to an end. In adopting a means which does harm to a good, one determines oneself against that good; this is not the case when one accepts a side effect harmful to a good. Still, people do have some responsibility for foreseen side effects. Since they are foreseen, they are voluntary. (Drunken drivers, for instance, are responsible for the unintended—but foreseen—harm they do.) Several of the modes of responsibility help answer the question whether one should or should not accept particular side effects.

Finally, there are some varieties of voluntariness which presuppose choice. One of these is executive willing—the willing acceptance at a time subsequent to choosing of effects of one's action. (A person chooses to do something, discovers while doing it that it has unexpected aspects or is having unforeseen effects, and knowingly and willingly continues to do it.) One is responsible for one's executive willing. Corresponding to this is a type of omission without choice. (Aware that one should choose and act, one deliberates about what to do, but either makes no choice or chooses to put off the decision.)

One also is responsible for consequences which could and should have been foreseen but were not; such consequences include behavior and omissions not now considered wrong due to some earlier sin. Readiness and unreadiness to choose can also be voluntary; for instance, one ought to be ready to accept martyrdom and unready to choose anything immoral.

Appendix 1:   Why human acts must be described so precisely

In the first place, Christian life must be both like and unlike the life of Jesus. Our lives must be both united to his and distinct from his. Often, traditional spiritual guidance talks about imitating or conforming to Christ. As chapters nineteen through twenty-seven will show, this approach is sound. But what does it mean to imitate or conform to Jesus? He lived a long time ago, in a culture very different from ours, was unmarried. Most people have abilities, opportunities, and responsibilities very different from his. How can they live as he did? The only way to answer this question is to make some very precise distinctions concerning human acts. The necessary distinctions are made in this chapter. (The question is answered in 23-C.)

In the second place, because human acts are much more complicated than at first they seem, whole areas of Christian life which could be cultivated very fruitfully are ignored. For example, inadequate understanding of spontaneous human acts, which are done intelligently and willingly by small children, has led to an almost complete absence of ministry to children under six or seven years old. Only at this age do children begin to make choices. But their earlier Christian life is important, too, and the Church could do a great deal to foster its growth. Again, too exclusive a focus upon the outward acts of individuals has made it difficult to understand even them very well, and has led to insufficient attention to omissions, cooperative acts, the voluntary readiness of a person ιo act, and many other important aspects of Christian life.

In the third place, the correct application of the moral teaching of the Church demands that one understand human acts with some precision. For example, God commands us not to kill. This norm cannot be applied unless one knows exactly what a human act of killing is. Are parents who refuse to allow very painful treatment for their child, aware that the child will die without it, killing the child? Is a nurse who prepares a patient for abortion killing the unborn baby? Questions similar to these must be answered by priests in the confessional and by them and others outside the confessional. Their answers will be poor if they do not understand human acts with precision.

Classical treatises on action usually begin by making a distinction between "acts of man" and "human acts." "Human acts" is said to refer to those acts done voluntarily, or to those done through deliberation and choice. All others are called "acts of man" and dismissed as morally insignificant. This distinction points one's thinking generally in the right direction, for it suggests that one should examine for moral purposes the acts which are involved in and express choices and other operations of the will. However, the distinction is not altogether clear, for it does not take account of spontaneous acts. What is more important, the scholastic treatises proceed to try to analyze for moral purposes many diverse sorts of acts, just as one finds them jumbled together in ordinary language. This approach is confusing, for it tends to conceal relevant moral differences.

Because of these difficulties, for the purposes of moral theology the analysis of human acts should start by considering various sorts of willing. Instances of willing are called "acts" in ordinary language; we speak of "acts of choice." In scholastic terminology, instances of willing, or at least certain of them, were called "elicited acts" to distinguish them from acts done in accord with one's willing. The latter were called "commanded acts," because they are performed at the direction of the will. Because instances of willing are not "acts" in any ordinary sense, it would be better if we referred to them by another name, such as "actuations." But "acts" is not objectionable and may be used, with the proviso that the distinction must be kept in mind.

Appendix 2:   The moral significance of spontaneous willing

Are the child's spontaneous willing and acting morally significant? They certainly are not morally significant as actions done by free choice are. Children acting spontaneously do not determine themselves in respect to goods. For three-year-old Stephen to swipe baby sister's bottle is naughty, not immoral. But there are two ways in which a child's spontaneous willing and acting are morally significant.

In the first place, the child's spontaneous willing and acting are specifically human. The action is voluntary. The child has a certain responsibility for it, diverse both from the "responsibility" of a pet and from the moral responsibility of a person who makes and acts on free choices. Small children are praised and blamed for what they do on purpose; these responses would make no sense were there no responsibility. Yet this responsibility is not moral responsibility in a full and proper sense. The child's human acts are premoral, not so much in the sense that they are prior in time to moral acts, but rather in the sense that they are incipient realizations of the human person's capabilities.

In the second place, the child's life of human action cannot be understood in its full significance if it is viewed in an individualistic framework. The child acts within an acting community: its family. Its own spontaneous willing and acting are shaped to a great extent by the moral life of its family. The child, as it were, lives the life of a human moral person embryonically, exercising some functions for itself, depending for some essential functions—the free choices—upon those who are bringing it up. The life of the child is a participation in the life of its family. By way of this participation, the child's life really has moral significance, although the child bears no moral responsibility for this significance until he or she begins to make free choices.

The Christian child, who has received the gift of God's love, surely makes an act of living faith by spontaneous willing prior to its choice to affirm this faith—a choice which might not be necessary until adolescence. The child's act of faith participates in the freedom of its parents' and ultimately of the Church's act of faith. With faith and love, the child can act for many human goods for Jesus. Children of three, four, and five live a Christian life which needs to be fostered.

Whatever spontaneous willing and acting make up the life of the child, whatever adult choices it participates in, and whatever Christian development it enjoys—these all provide the context for its subsequent full and independent life of Christian moral action. The self of the child is not determined by spontaneous willing as it will be by free choices, but such willing provides some experience of human fulfillment, and thus shapes the child's later appreciation of goods and grasp of possibilities.

The adult choices in which the child participates constitute its existence in a moral community; the child must later either reaffirm or rebel against this existence. Such affirmation or rebellion will not be a choice without antecedents; in some way, it will be like an adult's choice confirming or repenting of a previous choice of his or her own. The Christian development the child enjoys can unfold into a mature life of holiness.

Appendix 3:   The voluntary in cause

A special case of foreseen effects is that in which one looks ahead and expects with greater or lesser probability that if one chooses to do X now, then later one is likely to do Y, when Y is something one ought not to do. If one nevertheless does X, one assumes some responsibility for doing Y, even if in the event one does not do Y. This mode of voluntariness was named "the voluntary in cause" by St. Thomas (see *S.t.*, 1–2, q. 77, a. 7; 2–2, q. 43, aa. 1–3; q. 46, a. 2, ad 2).

There are at least two modes of voluntariness in cause. In one case, one foresees the likelihood that one's choosing to do X now will lead to one's choosing to do Y later. For example, a man might consider whether to stop at a stand where magazines containing immodest photographs are for sale, foreseeing that if he chooses to do so, he is likely to choose to buy one, look at it, and masturbate. In another case, one foresees the likelihood that one's choosing to do X now will lead to one's proceeding without choice to do Y later. For example, an alcoholic woman might consider whether to have a drink with an alcoholic friend, foreseeing that if she chooses to do so, they are likely without further deliberation to get drunk.

Voluntariness in cause also can apply to the foreseen consequences of one's choices for the actions of another person or persons. For example, those who oppress others might foresee that their choice to do so is likely to lead to a choice by the oppressed to do violence. Again, one who chooses to tease an irascible person might foresee that the person is likely to react violently.

In principle, one's responsibility for that which is voluntary in cause, whether in oneself or in others, is the same as one's responsibility for other foreseen consequences of one's acts. The difference is that, whereas the voluntary in cause bears upon goods of the existential domain, most foreseen consequences involve goods of other domains. In other words, in the present case, one is dealing with foreseen consequences which have in themselves an immediate moral significance, since they are cases of human action or of behavior which ordinarily can and ought to be avoided. The treatment of occasions of sin is concerned with voluntariness in cause in respect to one's own foreseen actions and behavior; the treatment of scandal is concerned with voluntariness in cause in respect to the foreseen consequences of one's acts for the actions and behavior of other persons.

Notes

1. Thus the distinction between what one does and foreseen side effects is independent of a moral judgment of conscience and freedom of choice in acting. This fact becomes clear by analysis of ordinary language: see G. E. M. Anscombe, *Intention,* 2d ed. (Oxford: Basil Blackwell, 1963), 72 and 89.

2. Proportionalists typically deny the moral significance of the distinction between object, end, and circumstances of an act, and in doing so take advantage of confusions in the use of this terminology in classical moral theology. See, for example, Richard A. McCormick, S.J., "Current Theology: Notes on Moral Theology: 1981," *Theological Studies,* 43 (1982), 83–86. In the criticism of proportionalism in chapter six, I did not use this denial as an argument against proportionalism, for such an argument would be question-begging. However, proportionalism having been shown inherently incoherent, the present analysis helps clarify its faulty and implausible attempt to merge the voluntariness of choice and free acceptance. Since the eighth mode of responsibility bears only on choices, the distinction between choice and other modes of voluntariness is vital for some moral questions, but not for all. For example, when only fairness is at issue, close analysis of actions is unnecessary, for the fifth mode of responsibility bears upon every mode of voluntariness.

3. In scholastic terminology, what one does by choice—one's action as defined by the proposal it executes—was called the "object of one's act" (see *S.t.,* 1–2, q. 18, a. 2). Sometimes the same thing was called "finis operis" or "the end of the work." However, many classical moralists took this terminology to mean that the natural teleology of behavior considered by itself is morally significant. Thus the language has become confusing, and probably is best avoided. From the point of view of moral analysis, the human act is not a chunk of outward behavior, with an inherent sense prior to deliberation and choice, which is merely projected into existence by one who chooses it. Rather, human behavior has a definite sense precisely because it executes a proposal excogitated by deliberation and adopted by choice. Theo G. Belmans, O.Praem., *Le sens objectif de l'agir humain: Pour relire la morale conjugale de Saint Thomas* (Vatican City: Liberia Editrice Vaticana, 1980), 175–88, provides many references to texts of St. Thomas and attempts a synthesis. I do not claim to reproduce Thomas' thought precisely on "object of the act," since I do not think his distinction between the exterior act and the act of the will is altogether clear or coherent. In general Thomas does think of the object of the act as a complex understood by practical reason and chosen or able to be chosen. Nevertheless, Thomas often includes in its object anything which makes an act definitely wrong, for this settles its moral species (cf. *De malo,* q. 2, a. 6, ad 2). On my account, the object only includes what one chooses even if the wrongness of the act arises elsewhere. For example, the object of an act of driving somewhere in an automobile is determined by the choice *to travel to that place,* and this remains so even if the auto belongs to another, is used without permission, and in using it one accepts the side effect of grave partiality toward oneself against the other.

4. See Belmans, op. cit., 327–411, for an examination of many different authors, some of whom

clearly identify morality "ex obiecto" with moral "determination by physical nature," and most of whom wish to derive the objective morality of the act from a good end (or ends) which one might uprightly pursue, while setting aside as morally irrelevant or outweighed the choice to destroy, damage, or impede a good by which the good end is pursued.

5. I have made this point in previous works. Joseph A. Selling, "The Problem of Reinterpreting the Principle of Double Effect," *Louvain Studies*, 8 (1980), 53, n. 17, criticizes it (without citing any particular work) by saying: "Grisez will not allow for the existence of a cause-effect relationship in anything other than his indivisible—read physical—process," and providing examples of causes and effects which are not in an indivisible process. But Selling has missed my point, and the claim that I do not allow such relationships is false. My point rather is that some cause-effect relationships need not be means-end relationships in a moral sense. Selling's entire argument in this article presupposes the acceptance of proportionalism, for he maintains that only the agent's intention of an end and proportionality determine morality (57). Since proportionalism has been refuted (6-F) independently of the analysis of action, analyses of action which assume proportionalism may be rejected precisely on that ground. Selling also refers to his general theory as "an ethics of responsibility" (62), as if proportionalism has an exclusive claim on that title.

6. W. Van der Marck, O.P., *Love and Fertility: Contemporary Questions about Birth Regulation*, trans. C. A. Jarrott (London: Sheed and Ward, 1965), 42–60, says that the means-end distinction simply is between a piece of outward behavior and the total human act determined by the good one intends. In saying this, he makes two mistakes, both of which can be seen by analyzing examples. First, he fails to notice that the mere outward behavior cannot in any case be regarded as a means or act (in any sense), for just as such it can be picked out only by a naturalistic description which is altogether neutral with respect to categories such as "means." This point is clear from the work of empiricists who attempt to reduce action to categories acceptable in their metaphysics; they are compelled to introduce beliefs and wants to distinguish even the most basic acts. See, for instance, Arthur C. Danto, *Analytical Philosophy of Action* (Cambridge: Cambridge University Press, 1973), 18 and 72–78. Second, Van der Marck assumes that all acts are as simple as those in which the means-end distinction is merely technical, and thus overlooks the more complex case in which one adopts a certain proposal by choice, realizing it to bear upon certain human goods in certain ways and willing that bearing so far as it is included within the proposal, but directs the entire action to some other purpose—for example, one plays golf for the sake of making a sale. Here, regardless of what one thinks about its morality, the chosen means is such from an existential point of view, and an analysis which leaves no room for this is obviously inadequate.

7. This distinction explains why descriptions of acts from a moral point of view can vary within limits in characterizing by consequences what one is doing, but cannot plausibly vary beyond certain limits. Once a description includes a bearing upon some human good, a redescription specified by further consequences which conceals that bearing will seem implausible, especially if doing the act as involving that bearing is morally arguable, even if acceptable. See Eric D'Arcy, *Human Acts: An Essay in their Moral Evaluation* (Oxford: Clarendon Press, 1963), 10–39.

8. See Robert S. McNamara, *The Essence of Security: Reflections in Office* (New York: Harper and Row, 1968), 52–53; The Organization of the Joint Chiefs of Staff, *United States Military Posture for FY* [fiscal year] *1983* (Washington, D.C.: U.S. Government Printing Office, 1982), 19. For quotations from and references to other statements of the threat and a history of the evolution of American strategic doctrine, see Donald M. Snow, *Nuclear Strategy in a Dynamic World: American Policy in the 1980s* (University, Ala.: University of Alabama Press, 1981), 48–85, with notes, 253–56.

9. Richard A. McCormick, S.J., accepted the view of Bruno Schüller, S.J., that with respect to nonmoral goods (such as human life) one need no more "approve" the evil (destruction of life) when one chooses to kill as a means to some ulterior end than when one accepts death freely as a side effect. Thus for nonmoral goods both authors denied the significance of the distinction between direct and indirect killing, sterilizing, and so on. ("Approve" is equivocal to emotion and will; Schüller gained some plausibility from this since one's emotional attitude can easily be the same in the two cases although the volitional self-disposition is very different.) See McCormick, in *Doing Evil to Achieve Good: Moral Choice in Conflict Situations*, ed. Richard A. McCormick, S.J., and Paul Ramsey (Chicago: Loyola University Press, 1978), 254–62. McCormick admitted that this position makes it difficult to understand why the direct-indirect distinction is vital in the case of causing another's sin, where both authors wish to retain it (258–59). The explanation of the difficulty is that they and others who have embraced proportionalism overlook the existential character of moral acts in general and so do not see the self-determination with respect to basic goods in every free choice. With respect to substantive goods, they think of upright choices as if they were nothing but efficient means of bringing

about their realization in concrete instances. But they do see that one cannot will that another do evil even in only a particular instance without willing—and so being—morally evil oneself.

10. The conception of commitment, as distinct from acceptance of a long-range goal, has hardly been analyzed up to now. However, some contemporary philosophical work points in this direction. See, for example, Charles Fried, *An Anatomy of Values: Problems of Personal and Social Choice* (Cambridge, Mass.: Harvard University Press, 1970), 87–101, on the concept of "life plan" and life as an ordered set of rational acts; Gabriel Marcel, *Creative Fidelity*, trans. Robert Rosthal (New York: Noonday Press, 1964), 104–19, for the notion that the life of a person is a unique act; John Rawls, *A Theory of Justice* (Cambridge, Mass.: Belknap Press of Harvard University Press, 1971), 407–16, for the idea of life plans, and 548–67, for arguments against reducing the human good to a single dominant goal.

11. In an earlier work, the points being made here about commitment were made by distinguishing between "second level" and "third level" action, and between contractual and communitarian relationships: Germain Grisez and Russell Shaw, *Beyond the New Morality: The Responsibilities of Freedom*, rev. ed. (Notre Dame and London: University of Notre Dame Press, 1980), 8–9, 16–23, 30–32, and 45–50. Gabriel Marcel clearly develops the distinction between commitment and setting objectives, although he uses different terminology. See, for example, *Being and Having: An Existential Diary* (New York: Harper and Row, 1965), 154–74; *The Mystery of Being*, vol. 1, *Reflection and Mystery* (Chicago: Henry Regnery, 1960), 182–270.

12. Even God foresees and permits evils which he does not directly will. See St. Thomas, *S.t.*, 1, q. 49, a. 2; 1–2, q. 79, aa. 2–4; *S.c.g.*, 1, 96; 3, 71. To deny this would be to deny either that there really is any evil or that God's will is holy or that his providence and causality are all-embracing. The point is reflected in the Church's solemn teaching (e.g., DS 1556/816) and essential for making sense of Scripture, e.g., on predestination: see Ceslaus Spicq, "Predestination," *Encyclopedia of Biblical Theology*, 694–700. Hence it is an error to suppose that the distinction between choosing to bring about evils and accepting them as side effects becomes necessary only in virtue of the limitations of human causality or the brokenness of the fallen human condition.

13. This is a key position rejected by many proportionalists. Since proportionalism has been refuted (6-F) independent of the analysis of responsibility, the presupposition of proportionalism in arguments against this point can provide a premise for criticizing such arguments without begging any question. By contrast, proportionalists' efforts to analyze action to fit their theory generally are question-begging and often lead to bizarre positions. See, for example, Selling, op. cit., who tried throughout to settle substantive issues by mere stipulation, argued (51) circularly that a chosen act is unintended inasmuch as it is not done for its own sake, attributed (53, n. 17) to me an absurd position I nowhere take, and made (56) the bizarre claim that an act which executes a proposal adopted by choice, if not done for itself, is permitted—e.g., that giving alms in order to do penance involves permitting, not intending, the giving of alms (n. 24). On this basis, murderers whose reason or purpose in acting is not the death of their victims but some ulterior end permit rather than intend killing them!

CHAPTER TEN

FROM MODES OF RESPONSIBILITY TO MORAL NORMS

Introduction

The modes of responsibility and their corresponding virtues are normative principles—they direct and incline one to live a morally good life—but they are not specific enough to serve as norms. Told to act impartially, one finds oneself asking whether or not one is guilty of partiality in adopting a particular proposal. Even someone fully disposed to do what is fair can be uncertain what that is. In asking what is right, one is asking for a more specific moral norm. This chapter explains how more specific norms are drawn from moral principles. These more specific norms are judgments of conscience or contribute to such judgments. Hence, this discussion begins to round out the inquiry commenced in chapter three; chapters eleven and twelve will complete the treatment of moral principles and their application in judgments of conscience.

Question A: Do all the modes of responsibility have normative force in the same way?

1. The answer is both yes and no. All the modes of responsibility exclude unreasonable grounds for acting. Their normative thrust comes from the priority of intelligence, which comprehends the whole of human possibility, over emotion, which is limited to some parts and aspects of what a human person can be. **Thus, all the modes have normative force in the same way in this sense: All are requirements of practical reasonableness** (see *S.t.*, 1–2, q. 18, a. 5; q. 21, a. 1; q. 71, a. 2, ad 3).

2. Furthermore, all the modes embody the same first principle of morality. This unitary first principle makes a single demand: that one live in a way consistent with openness to integral human fulfillment. This human ideal is the ultimate normative principle of the requirements of human morality. (As chapter nineteen will show, integral human fulfillment is part of the fulfillment of all things in the Lord Jesus, which is the purpose of the plan of eternal law.) **Thus, the modes of responsibility all have normative force in the same way in this sense, too: Their thrust comes from integral human fulfillment, and they shape life toward this fulfillment.**

3. **However, the eight modes also differ in their normative force, since they exclude somewhat different unreasonable grounds of action.** For example, laziness, excluded by the first mode, is plainly different from favoritism, excluded by the fifth. In disregarding any mode of responsibility when one makes a choice, one determines oneself in a way which does not comport well with all the basic human goods. In not responding fully to all the principles of practical reason which correspond to these goods, one is more or less unreasonable. But violations of different modes comport badly with human goods in somewhat different ways—there are different ways of being unreasonable.

4. In other words, unreasonable self-determination can dispose one badly toward integral human fulfillment in a variety of ways, depending on which mode of responsibility is violated. But the normative thrust of the modes comes precisely from their orientation toward integral human fulfillment. Thus, the normativity of the different modes is somewhat different. In disregarding various modes, one's disposition—or, more properly, indisposition—toward human goods and integral fulfillment is diverse; and this indisposition is more or less radical, depending on which mode one violates.

5. Reflecting upon the modes and upon one's dispositions toward human goods in disregarding them, one can see the variety of ways in which violations dispose (or indispose) one toward integral fulfillment. Thus: A person deterred from acting by emotional inertia lacks adequate commitment to the good, but is not determined against it. A person pressed by impatience or enthusiasm to act individualistically is disposed favorably to the good, but not committed enough to respect the social conditions for integral human fulfillment. A person moved to act out of reasonless desire lacks adequate commitment to the goods to prefer reasonable action for an intelligible good. A person deterred by fear from acting is disposed to the good, but not committed enough to persist in acting for it. A person moved to act or deterred from acting by partiality is disposed to the good, but more concerned that certain people enjoy it than that its realization contribute to integral human fulfillment. A person moved to act or deterred from acting by apparent goods or evils is disposed to the good, but more concerned with the conscious experience of it than with its full reality. A person moved to act destructively out of hostility is committed against the good, and there is no relevant commitment to a human good. A person moved to act for an emotionally qualified "greater good" or "lesser evil" is committed against one good, but there is some disposition toward another good. Plainly, the relationships of unreasonable choices to goods are not all alike.

6. This point can be illustrated by considering different modes of responsibility and violations of them whose actual effects on a human good are similar. For example, even though one's immoral actions in several different cases are equally likely to lead to someone else's death, one's immorality can nevertheless be more or less grave depending on the mode of responsibility in question in each case. Thus, it would be worse to try to hurt somebody one hates (a violation of the seventh mode) than to assign somebody to hazardous duty unfairly (a violation of

the fifth mode), and worse to do the latter than fail to help somebody in distress (a violation of the first or fourth modes).

7. All the modes of responsibility bear upon choices, and some of them bear only upon choices. In choosing, one can violate any mode, and often one violates two or more at the same time. The fifth mode of responsibility, impartiality, bears upon every sort of voluntariness—simple and spontaneous willing aside—including that with which one accepts foreseen consequences of choices and that with which one is limited by former choices (see 9-F). How the other modes of responsibility bear upon the acceptance of foreseen consequences and the other varieties of voluntariness which presuppose choice can be worked out in analyzing various moral questions.

8. **Even in their bearing upon choices, different modes of responsibility set different requirements. Some demand appropriate acts, others forbid inappropriate ones, and some do both.** This difference is important because, as will be seen shortly, only negative specific moral norms can hold without exception.

9. Because different modes have a normative character which is also different and because they set different sorts of requirements for choices, a sound conscience does not experience all specific moral norms as having the same degree of definiteness and force. There is a moral obligation to help starving children and a moral obligation not to kill unwanted children; but the second obligation is more definite and exigent than the first.

To show that modes of responsibility differ in normative force, the following example compares the guilt of a person who brings about three deaths by acts chosen in disregard of three different modes of responsibility. In all three cases, there is responsibility for someone's death, which is foreseen as having the same degree of likelihood.

In the first instance, an individual—call him "Titus"—is driving along an expressway before the morning rush. Driving in the left of the two lanes, as is his custom, Titus notes in passing a woman lying in the middle of the right lane waving frantically. Titus is too surprised to stop at once; by the time he does, he realizes he probably is more than a half-mile beyond the woman. He could walk back or he could proceed to the next exit and drive back on the other side or he could summon emergency help. He decides that the third course is safe and reasonable, and sets off for the next exit.

But as Titus drives toward it, it occurs to him that summoning help will be a nuisance and is likely to lead to questions, which will waste more time. He did not come near the woman. Even if he does not summon help, someone else might help her, although she is likely to be struck soon if no one does. Titus is having a hard time making up his mind as the exit looms. He decides not to turn off. The next day he reads in the morning paper that the woman was killed on the expressway.

In the second instance, Titus is at work, doing his job as an assistant fire chief directing operations at a large fire. The fire is threatening to spread to a wide area, and it would be useful for one man to do an especially hazardous job. Titus cannot do it himself, but there are two men who can. As is his custom, Titus asks them if either will volunteer, but neither will, although both say they will do the job if ordered to. Titus recalls the morning when he did not summon help; the chances of the man who does this job are about the same as were the chances of the woman on the road. "Decisions, decisions!" Titus thinks, "Who if anyone will I order to do this?" The one more likely to do the job successfully and survive—but more likely only by a slight margin in Titus' judgment—is a man Titus likes. If he were the only person available, Titus thinks he would not order the job to be done. The other is a man Titus does not know well, who somehow gets under his skin. Titus orders this man to do the hazardous job. He does it successfully, but does not survive.

In the third instance, Titus has been spending a night drinking with a group of relatives, including his father-in-law, whom Titus detests. The older man is a very unpleasant drunk, but quite strong; he also has a bad heart. Father-in-law tries to pick a fight with Titus, who brushes him aside several times. But eventually Titus begins to think that he will teach the old so-and-so a lesson, and if he has a heart attack, that will serve him right. Recalling the two previous incidents, Titus is aware that there is about the same likelihood that his father-in-law will not survive the strenuous exertion of a fist fight. However, Titus relishes the thought of pasting the old so-and-so. Finally, he says: "Okay. If you want to fight, come on outside." They fight; the older man is amazingly tough, but Titus gets the better of him. In the morning Titus receives a call; his father-in-law is dead of a heart attack.

In all three instances, the death for which Titus is responsible follows upon a choice Titus makes. In the first instance, his failure to help violates the fourth mode of responsibility; in the second instance, his choice of the fellow he likes less violates the fifth mode of responsibility; in the third instance, his decision to fight violates the seventh mode of responsibility. In all three cases, there are various distractions and pressures; let us assume they even out. In all three there is the same chance of a death, which Titus is willing to take.

Intuitively, it seems that in the first instance Titus is not so guilty as in the second, and in the second not so guilty as in the third. In all three cases, Titus makes a choice which does not comport well with the principle of practical reason: Life is a good to be preserved. But in the first instance, Titus just does not care enough about life; in the second instance, he cares, but he cares more about one life than another; in the third instance, any concern about life is submerged by hostility, so that the destruction of life has some appeal.

Question B: How are specific moral norms derived from the modes of responsibility?

1. Usually people do not personally derive moral norms from the modes of responsibility. Rather, having a stock of moral norms on hand, they reach a moral judgment by applying one or more to the act in question. A student tempted to slip a book out of the bookstore without paying recalls that this is theft and theft is wrong; the norm forbidding theft is "on hand." If such a norm is a moral truth, not merely a rule of conventional morality, it is derived from the modes of responsibility, even if the process by which this is done is not repeated each and every time the norm comes into play.

2. How, then, are such norms derived? In answering this question, it is best to begin with the conclusion to be reached—a specific moral norm. It is a proposition about a kind of action; the predicate characterizes the kind of action normatively, as wrong, good, obligatory, or permissible. For instance: "Trying to teach someone a lesson by beating him with a definite, foreseen risk to life is wrong," "Feeding a hungry person is good," "Keeping promises is obligatory," "Excluding all meat from one's diet is permissible."

3. Since specific moral norms refer to kinds of actions and apply to them moral determinants, one obviously needs something common to kinds of action and to moral principles as the middle term of the reasoning by which a specific norm is drawn from a mode of responsibility. **What is common to both are relationships of the will to basic human goods. The modes of responsibility indicate the moral exclusion of certain relationships, and various kinds of action are morally significant insofar as they involve such relationships.**

Of course, as a matter of historical fact, specific moral norms have not been derived by people who had clearly articulated the basic human goods and the modes of responsibility, and who then set about to formulate norms for various kinds of acts. Rather, the principles of practical reasoning and the normative principles were understood by direct insight, but not explicitly formulated. Consideration began from deliberation about possibilities for choice, and also (perhaps even more) from criticism of actions which in one way or another led to trouble and second thoughts. Reflection often refined previous formulations. (However, in the fallen human condition, criticism also encounters blocks which eventually confine the moral reflection of the vast majority of people within the limits of the conventional morality of their society.)

4. Thus, a specific, negative moral norm can be derived as follows. First one considers how the voluntariness involved in a certain kind of action is related to basic human goods. Next one considers the moral determination which the modes of responsibility indicate for this relationship. From these two premises one deduces the negative moral determination of that kind of action. For example, beating a man to teach him a lesson, with a definite risk to life, is a kind of act which involves a will hostile to the good of life. "To teach a lesson" in the sense intended here brings this kind of act under the seventh mode of responsibility, for one is acting out of hostility and accepts the destruction of a basic human good. Therefore, this kind of act is wrong.

5. A specific, affirmative moral norm logically depends on the affirmative first principle of morality, which directs the choice of those and only those possibilities whose willing is compatibile with a will toward integral human fulfillment. Thus, a certain kind of act is morally good if it offers a way of voluntarily serving a human good and involves no voluntariness excluded by any of the modes of responsibility. Not all morally good acts are obligatory—for example, feeding the hungry is good yet not obligatory. The reason is that an act of this kind can have an alternative itself morally good. However, whenever a morally good kind of act is such that its alternative is excluded by one or more modes of responsibility, then that sort of act is obligatory.

6. Promise keeping is an example. Promise keeping is a kind of act that bears upon the good of interpersonal harmony. One sets up expectations in others by making a promise, and one fulfills or disappoints these expectations by keeping or breaking it. Mutually creating and satisfying expectations is a very important part of interpersonal harmony; without it, cooperation is impossible. Among the various modes of responsibility, the fifth will certainly be relevant to making and keeping promises. If one allows the keeping and breaking of promises to be determined by one's own convenience, one violates this mode. By contrast, one

who keeps promises is plainly not doing so because of differences in feelings toward different people. Therefore, keeping promises is obligatory; breaking them is wrong.

7. In everyday speech, "permissible" sometimes is used to refer to the morally good but nonobligatory act. In a narrower sense, kinds of acts which can be characterized neither as wrong, good, nor obligatory are called "permissible." In this sense, "permissible" is not a moral determinant on the same level as the others. To call a kind of act "permissible" is merely to say it has not been specified sufficiently to tell whether willing it would or would not be consistent with openness to integral human fulfillment.

8. For example, excluding all meat from one's diet is permissible. But the description of the act, although it specifies certain behavior, is insufficient to specify a moral act. Does excluding meat promote or damage health? Is it an act of religious abstinence? To begin to characterize the act morally, one needs to know something about the proposal under consideration. Only then could one say what modes of responsibility might be relevant and how they would determine the morality of the act.

Question C: Why are some specific moral norms absolute and others nonabsolute?

1. If people always personally derived specific moral norms directly from the modes of responsibility, the present question could be omitted. The exposition could proceed at once to question D, where the relationship between general moral principles and judgments of conscience will be explained, and the role of specific norms clarified.

2. Of course, most people, for good reasons, do not personally derive specific moral norms directly from the modes of responsibility. Rather, they reach moral judgments by drawing on a stock of moral norms they have on hand. Most of these norms are not absolute. For instance, St. Paul teaches: "Let every person be subject to the governing authorities. For there is no authority except from God, and those that exist have been instituted by God" (Rom 13.1). But the people who carried out the Nazi policy of genocide surely should not have obeyed orders. Norms which admit of exceptions are here called "nonabsolute."

3. **Most specific moral norms are nonabsolute because they are open to further specification by recourse to the same principles from which they were derived. The basic human goods, the first principle of morality, and the modes of responsibility generate norms in the first place, and they can generate more refined norms when necessary.**

4. For example, a specific norm such as "Keeping promises is obligatory" is true and guides choices as long as the only thing in question is the aspect of interpersonal harmony underlying the making of promises and the norm that they should be kept. However, promises and the cooperation they foster very often concern other goods besides. When keeping a promise would affect these other goods in a way which can be taken into account without partiality, one faces a choice which is more specified than that involved in simple promise keeping. A

more specific norm is needed to govern this more specific action, and this second norm limits the comparatively general norm that promises should be kept.

5. Suppose a person makes a promise and afterwards discovers it cannot be kept without violating the eighth mode of responsibility. The promise ought not to be kept. On this basis, German officials were not bound by allegiance to the nation to carry out orders to kill the innocent. They were bound by reverence for life not to carry out their orders.

6. Again, if the choice one makes in breaking a promise involves no partiality, the foundation of the obligatory character of promise keeping is undercut. For instance, if one promises a friend to go sailing on a certain day but wakes up on the appointed day with what seems an attack of appendicitis, one should break the promise. Normally one should keep one's promises because one wants others to keep theirs, and it is unfair to expect this of them if one is not reciprocally steadfast. But no reasonable person would want a friend with an apparent attack of appendicitis to keep a promise to go sailing; so the fairness which usually demands promise keeping does not demand it in this sort of case.

7. **However, some specific moral norms are absolute. In some cases, an already-given determination settles a kind of act as morally wrong.** Thus, "One should not get rid of unwanted children by killing them" is a norm expressing the moral determination of this kind of act by the good of life and the eighth mode of responsibility. No matter what further specifications might be added in a particular case of killing an unwanted child, an act of this sort is necessarily incompatible with openness to integral human fulfillment.

8. Even so, the absoluteness of certain specific moral norms will not be apparent if the actions they morally determine are described behaviorally rather than morally (see *S.t.*, 1–2, q. 20, a. 6). For example, "Killing is wrong" does not express an absolute moral norm if "killing" is taken to mean "behaving in any fashion which brings about someone's death." On this behavioral definition, Jesus "killed" himself, for he behaved in a manner which brought about his death. Absolute moral norms—which are generated by the third, fourth, sixth, seventh, and eighth modes of responsibility—must be formulated with respect to the moral act, which includes the wrongful choice. Jesus did not choose to kill himself; he freely accepted death as a foreseen consequence of carrying on his mission.

Those who deny that there are any absolute, specific moral norms often divide norms into two kinds: (1) nonabsolute rules concerning kinds of acts described behaviorally (which they sometimes call "material norms"); (2) absolute truisms concerning kinds of acts described and characterized morally (which they sometimes call "formal norms"). "Killing is wrong" is of the first type; "Murder is wrong" (where "murder" means wrongful killing) is of the second type. The second does not settle the problems raised by the first, for in disputed cases—for example, the abortion of unwanted children—the problem just is whether this killing is wrongful and so appropriately rejected as murder.[1]

By contrast, the position explained here focuses upon another type of specific moral norm. The description of the act goes beyond mere behavior, yet does not go so far as to build in the moral determinant. "Getting rid of unwanted children by killing them" is specified sufficiently to make clear that the act involves a choice to destroy their lives, yet the description is morally neutral in itself. The application of the moral determinant, "is wrong," comes through the logical step of bringing this kind of act under the eighth mode of responsibility. The absolute norm follows from the fact that killing of this sort includes in itself a will incompatible with openness to integral human fulfillment.

A proportionalist might say that the norm about getting rid of unwanted children by killing them is virtually exceptionless, since such killing is hardly ever likely to be the lesser evil. However, the proportionalist cannot admit a genuinely absolute specific norm in this case, because proportionalism rejects the eighth mode of responsibility.

The thesis that norms using concepts such as "murder" and "adultery" are mere truisms ("formal norms") useful only for exhortation also is questionable. According to received Christian teaching, "murder" limits the concept of killing in two ways. The killing is deliberate killing of a human being, and there is no divine authorization of it. The first sets aside behavior which results in death accidentally or as a side effect. The second sets aside capital punishment, war, and killing in obedience to divine commands.[2] This second limitation is theologically questionable (see 8-H). As for adultery, Christians of earlier centuries probably would have been amazed by the suggestion that "adultery" means wrongful—but not necessarily all—extramarital intercourse involving at least one married person.

9. An analogy with the norms of diet illustrates the distinction between absolute and nonabsolute norms. There are general principles of good diet, and a dietitian applies these in making the judgments involved in drawing up menus. Although many specific norms are formulated, most are nonabsolute. For example, children should have milk—but not if they are allergic to it. However, some norms of diet are absolute. A diet of pure strychnine is, for example, to be avoided, and this norm will hold good no matter what one's special problem or condition. Now, as the point of eating is health, so the point of acting is integral human fulfillment. As some sorts of diet can never be healthful, some kinds of action can never be right. Therefore, as some norms of dietetics are absolute, so some norms of morality are absolute—although most norms of both dietetics and morality are nonabsolute inasmuch as they can be refined to fit actions more specific than those envisaged in formulating them.

10. Not only most specific affirmative norms but most specific negative ones are nonabsolute. For instance, it is wrong to drink oneself into a stupor. This norm is generated by the third and sixth modes of responsibility and by the goods of health, rational functioning, and genuine self-integration. (The latter requires that one seek real solutions to problems, not escape into drunkenness.) Nevertheless, one might rightly choose to drink oneself into a stupor—if, for example, one's leg had to be amputated and no other anesthetic were available. It is not that getting drunk is a lesser evil here. Rather, one has a different state of affairs and so a different norm. Although the outward behavior might be the same, the moral act is simply not the usual act of drinking too much. One is motivated not by a mere craving nor by escapism but by a reasonable wish to facilitate the operation required for one's health. The third and sixth modes of responsibility do not rule out this choice. In dietetics, an analogous case would be: Do not consume barium sulfate. Generally a sound rule of diet, yet subject to exception when one needs a stomach X-ray.

11. The preceding explanations clarify a point made previously (6-D): **Proportionalism is not needed to account for the nonabsoluteness of most moral**

norms. Nonabsolute norms simply are those which can be specified further, with the result that the moral determination changes. But the change is not dictated by some impossible weighing of goods and bads promised by various alternatives, to see which will yield the greater good or lesser evil. Rather, it is dictated by the basic human goods and the modes of responsibility, which generated the nonabsolute norm to begin with.

12. Still, an upright person who correctly judges that a nonabsolute norm requires further specification is likely to talk in a way that sounds like proportionalism. A German physician who refused to obey a Nazi decree to kill the innocent might well have said that disobeying constituted authorities is a lesser evil than killing the innocent. But "lesser evil" is defined here by a moral principle, not by a comparison of premoral goods. Disobeying authorities in such a case is not an evil at all. Instead, it is the morally good act of an upright person who has subjected a nonabsolute norm (obedience to authority) to appropriate further specification.

Question D: Is the method of deriving specific moral norms adequate for conclusive criticism of every judgment of conscience?

1. Conscience is primarily a practical judgment, one's last and best judgment of the moral quality of a choice one is about to make (see 3-B). Question C has shown that some judgments of conscience can be criticized conclusively. A true moral absolute holds in every case. If it is wrong to kill unwanted children, any particular choice to do so will be wrong, no matter what additional factors complicate the situation.

2. But can judgments of conscience other than those which follow directly from absolute norms be criticized conclusively? If the preceding account of moral principles is correct, nothing determines the moral rightness or wrongness of an act except the relationships between the will and basic human goods involved in it. If this is so, then the method explained in question B of deriving specific moral norms seems adequate to criticize conclusively every judgment of conscience. For, while a judgment of conscience must refer to individuating factors, these do not affect the intelligible relationships between varieties of voluntariness and the basic human goods. (In the remainder of this question, these intelligible relationships will be called "moral determinants.")

3. However, many philosophers and theologians have thought that some judgments of conscience cannot be conclusively criticized by any rational procedure. The reasons which make their view plausible will be examined here. **The conclusion will be that although many factors can block conclusive criticism of judgments of conscience, nothing can do so except by making it difficult or impossible to discover and articulate the relevant moral determinants.**

4. The personal character of conscience seems to many to block conclusive criticism of its judgments. No one is in a position to assume another's view and criticize his or her judgments of conscience. No two persons share the same prior commitments, level of maturity of conscience, clarity about principles, awareness

of relevant goods, creativity in generating alternatives, and ability to reason accurately. Hence, it seems that if conclusive criticism of judgments of conscience is attempted, the result can only be an intrusion into the heart. Systematic reflection should limit itself to general principles and stop short of this intrusion.

5. This concern to respect the interiority of others is sound. But the present question does not call for a judgmental project. The issue, rather, is whether the method which has been explained is adequate to develop and criticize judgments of conscience for oneself or for a group in which one participates. The present discussion will not concern subjective factors which often limit moral responsibility by limiting moral reflection. Rather, the point here is that there are no factors other than the moral determinants which could block attempts to make and criticize judgments of conscience by the method proposed in questions B and C.

6. Again, the theory of natural law articulated thus far in this work seems at least incomplete. Although the method is grounded in divine revelation and its unfolding by the Church's teaching, thus far no moral determinants proper to Christian life have been described. It seems that if there is to be a specifically Christian morality, some factors knowable only by faith must be brought into play.

7. Indeed, as we shall see (25-E), there are specific norms, knowable only by faith, whose fulfillment is strictly required by Christian love. These are generated because faith brings to light new options for fallen men and women, ones they would not otherwise think of and find appealing. But the present question is: If one does think of these options with the help of faith, can the judgment of conscience that they ought to be adopted be conclusively criticized and found sound by the method of deriving specific moral norms explained here? This methodological question can be answered without examining the content of specific moral norms.

8. The way people actually carry on moral reflection also seems to block any effort to criticize conclusively every judgment of conscience. For, normally, people make use of principles such as the basic human goods and modes of responsibility without reflecting upon them. In trying to reach a sound judgment of conscience, one focuses on the problem to be solved, not on the intellectual tools one uses. Just as people can reason deductively without being able to criticize their results conclusively by the canons of syllogistic reasoning, so they can reach judgments of conscience without being able to criticize them conclusively by the method described here.

9. This point is well taken. If one has not articulated the principles and procedure of reasoning, so that these are available to reflective examination, conclusive criticism of the results of reasoning will be impossible. However, the principles and process of moral reasoning have been articulated more and more fully in the course of the history of moral philosophy and theology. As this work has proceeded, progress has been made toward conclusive criticism of judgments of conscience. If the present account were entirely adequate, then the method described here would make it possible to criticize judgments of conscience as conclusively as possible. But even if, as is likely, the present account is imperfect in some respects, it still will make possible a closer approximation to the theoretical ideal of conclusive criticism of all judgments of conscience.

10. The seemingly decisive obstacle to conclusive criticism of many judgments of conscience is that the principles of moral reasoning are intelligible factors known in universal propositions, while judgments of conscience must fit choices. Choices are unique, individual realities, not only inasmuch as they are made by a certain person (or group) at a certain time and place, but inasmuch as they bear upon a unique performance in a unique situation. **True, absolute norms which exclude certain ways of willing hold in every single instance, and so conclusively falsify judgments of conscience which violate them. However, most judgments of conscience cannot be conclusively criticized by any absolute norm.** Conscience must judge: "I (or we) ought to do this here and now." Plainly, it is logically impossible for such a judgment to follow from any set of universal propositions.

11. This point has been emphasized by Thomists, who see clearly that whenever a person makes a judgment of conscience, the choice it guides is a concrete instance of a kind of action, embedded in a unique set of circumstances. In the circumstances, the action might have side effects which should be considered; there might be significant alternatives; and so on. Such factors are morally relevant and cannot be dismissed, and no general norm can anticipate them. Thus, prudence is needed, not to override absolute moral requirements which are known, but to generate the affirmative judgment: This is what I ought to do. For the good person not only avoids evil, but does and pursues the good.

12. This position is acceptable if it is correctly understood. **Judgments of conscience are reached by nondeductive reasoning.** The final step in this process has two premises. One of these is the specific norm one has developed to guide this choice—often a norm far more complex and richly specified than any of the norms one has on hand as one begins to reflect seriously on a moral problem of a kind not previously considered. The other is a judgment that no morally relevant factor will be overlooked if this specific norm is followed in the present case. The conclusion of this reasoning—the judgment of prudent conscience— directs choice as an instance of the kind characterized by the specific norm one has developed and now ought to follow.

13. Some theories of prudence suggest that this final step in moral reflection utterly defies articulation. This is only partly so. In deliberating together, two or more people often reason to a single judgment of conscience concerning what they ought to do cooperatively. In deliberating, they can rationally articulate everything involved in the proposal they are considering which affects its morality. Still, as experience teaches, there is an element which defies complete analysis in ending reflection and reaching a judgment of conscience. This element is in the judgment that reflection has proceeded sufficiently—that no further effects, possibilities, or aspects of the action which should be considered will come to light if reflection is widened or a decision delayed. Still, if a judgment of conscience is made, nothing nonrational enters into its moral characterization of the choice. Rather, the judgment of conscience simply determines the choice under consideration to be an instance of the moral norm—usually a richly specified one—which makes it morally acceptable or not.

14. After moral reflection is terminated, one sometimes discovers something which would have led to a different judgment of conscience. This happens in two ways. Sometimes errors in the reasoning which led to the judgment of conscience come to light. But if the reasoning was sound, nothing will overturn the judgment of conscience except the discovery of additional moral determinants which should have been taken into account. Morality primarily is in willing; willing bears upon goods one understands; so unique features of a situation only make a moral difference insofar as they affect these moral determinants. Had the moral determinants taken into account been different, they would have led to a different, more specific norm. Nothing could lead to a different judgment of conscience in any other way.

15. Thus, Thomists are correct in holding that a prudent judgment must take into account all the circumstances of an action. In reaching judgments of conscience other than those determined by an absolute norm, one cannot directly settle the choice's moral character by treating it as an instance of a norm one has on hand. One must first ask if there are not other morally relevant factors in the situation.

16. **However, if the norm one uses in making a judgment of conscience really is adequate to a given situation, no matter how complex, then the same norm would be true in any other situation whose intelligible features were exactly the same.** If all the ways in which will is related to basic human goods are the same in two actions, then the actions will be morally the same no matter how greatly they differ in other respects.

17. This explanation of the possibility and limits of conclusive criticism of all judgments of conscience also helps account for the creativity of people who are prudent in the genuine sense. Such persons go beyond legalism. They not only conform to recognized norms but direct all their lives toward integral human fulfillment. To do this, in many situations they refuse to choose among the options which initially present themselves. Instead, examining factual possibilities more thoroughly and extensively in the light of human goods and moral principles, they think of new options. Proposing new approaches and plans, they circumvent the seeming necessity of choosing either an immoral or humanly repugnant option. Thus, they think out a new option in better conformity with their will toward integral human fulfillment and choose it as an instance of a new specific norm. They generate this norm in the very process of prudent deliberation which fashions the action to fulfill it.

People who talk about the need to allow for exceptions in "unique situations" always offer examples, and these examples lend their argument some plausibility. But the examples are effective only because of some intelligible features which in principle can occur over and over.

For instance, a woman in a concentration camp committed adultery with a guard in order to become pregnant, since pregnancy would gain her release and allow her to return to her family. The action described is a specific kind, potentially repeatable ad infinitum. It is not a morally unique act in a unique situation. The example is proposed with the information that the woman's name was "Bergmeier," that the concentration camp was

Russian, that the woman already had three children named "Ilse," "Paul," and "Hans," and so forth. None of this is relevant, nor does it do anything for the rational plausibility of the argument.[3] (The particular details do stir one's sympathy.)

What makes the argument plausible is nothing unique, but something specific. This woman was not committing adultery in violation of the third and/or sixth modes of responsibility (which probably usually is the case); one might plausibly argue she is not committing adultery in violation of the fifth mode of responsibility (fairness), since she rightly presumed that her husband would be pleased that she acted as she did. Usually adultery does violate fairness; it clearly is wrong to the extent that it does.

The question is: In the very specific kind of case exemplified by Mrs. Bergmeier's act, do any of the modes of responsibility exclude what she did? If so, which human good is at stake here?[4]

Question E: How are rights and duties derived from the modes of responsibility?

1. All the modes of responsibility apply to each person's acts which have an effect upon others. This is especially clear in the case of the second and fifth modes, which concern community responsibility and fairness. Also, it is obvious that among the actions against human good which the seventh and eighth modes forbid are those which destroy, damage, or impede the goods in others as well as in oneself. As for the other modes, they clearly apply to the acts of those whose laziness, cowardice, lack of self-control, or pursuit of the mere appearance of goods would have bad effects on others besides themselves.

That all the modes of responsibility apply to acts of one person toward another (or others) can be seen from the following examples. A person who thinks it would be good to help a stranger in distress (Titus in the first instance) and who fails to do so out of laziness violates the first mode of responsibility. The second mode precisely shapes one's action to the needs and possibilities of community; a person who makes multiple commitments without considering conflicts among the responsibilities to others which might arise from these commitments violates this mode of responsibility. A mother who resists the marriage of a favorite child whom she does not wish to give up to another violates the third mode of responsibiltiy. A coward who unreasonably abandons companions in a dangerous situation violates the fourth mode of responsibility. The fifth mode precisely bears upon interpersonal allocation of burdens and benefits; a child who takes all the candy supplied for several children violates this mode of responsibility. A person who treats another with superficial cordiality instead of allowing real friendship to develop by engaging in more serious communication violates the sixth mode of responsibility. A person who reveals a damaging truth about another out of spite violates the seventh mode of responsibility. A person who kills a defective child to prevent its living a wretched life violates the eighth mode of responsibility.

2. **Duties are responsibilities which one person or group has toward another or others.** They include the mutual responsibilities of groups and their members. Since not all moral responsibilities concern others, not all are duties (see *S.t.*, 1–2, q. 60, aa. 2–3; 2–2, q. 57, a. 1; q. 122, a. 1). (Note, however, that some do use the word "duty" to refer to all moral responsibilities, including even those which bear directly only upon oneself.) Since all modes of responsibility can apply to the acts of individuals or groups toward others, all can generate

duties. As was explained in A above, not all modes have normative force in the same way; thus, not all duties are duties in the same way.

For example, one who fails through laziness to help another who needs help, but who has no other claim to help, violates a duty in one sense of "duty." Titus had a duty to help the woman lying in the road. One who acts unfairly toward another violates a duty in a different (and many people would say "stricter") meaning of "duty." Titus had a duty to order his friend, if anyone, to do the dangerous job, since his friend was the person better qualified to do it, but he was passed over out of favoritism. One who chooses to act against the good of another in violation of the seventh or eighth modes of responsibility violates a duty in still other senses of "duty." Titus had a duty to restrain himself from fighting with his father-in-law.

In very many cases, two or more modes of responsibility will be violated simultaneously if one acts wrongly. In many, but not all, acts affecting others, if one acts wrongly, one also acts unfairly. Not all, because, for instance, one can treat others badly in the same ways one treats oneself badly, by engaging in agreeable modes of self-destruction. In such cases, one violates a duty—in some sense of "duty"—to the other without being unfair. An example would be a person who fairly shares dope with his or her addict friends.

3. Not only is "duty" sometimes used more loosely than here, it is sometimes used more strictly. This is so when its meaning is restricted to instances where nonfulfillment of a responsibility would involve unfairness. These differences in usage are not important, provided they do not cause confusion.

4. Even if "duty" is used in the stricter sense—to refer only to responsibilities whose nonfulfillment is unfair—duties must be distinguished according to the other modes of responsibility involved. For instance, it is one thing to be unfair to others by enthusiastically overcommitting oneself and something different to be unfair by spitefully harming others.

5. **Since duties have diverse moral sources, they differ as do specific moral norms generally. Many are nonabsolute** (for example, the general duty to keep promises), **while others are absolute** (for example, the duty not to kill unwanted children). **Many exist prior to anyone's making any choice.** This is true of duties grounded in the eighth mode of responsibility. Duties existing prior to any choice whatsoever can be said to pertain to human nature itself; thus a duty of this sort can be called a "natural duty."

6. Many duties, however, arise from one's own commitments and/or the decisions of authorities. Since they have a moral foundation and there are nonabsolute norms requiring that they be carried out, such commitments and decisions generate moral responsibilities. If these responsibilities bear upon other persons, they always involve—at least—a requirement of fairness. Yet these duties do not exist without a choice and so do not pertain to human nature itself. They can be called "positive duties," for they are posited or placed upon one by one's own commitment or the decision of someone in authority.

7. The word "rights" is used as a correlative to "duties." Rights are not separate entities.[5] **Rather, right and duty are the same reality, "right" signifying its bearing upon the person or group affected by the action which the duty specifies** (see *S.t.*, 2–2, q. 57, a. 1; cf. 1–2, q. 100, a. 2).[6] Thus, my right to life is nothing other than the duties of others not to kill me, to help me to

survive, and so forth. Consequently there are as many meanings of "rights" as of "duties," and all distinctions made concerning duties must also be made concerning rights.

8. It follows that, just as "duty" is often restricted to cases where the failure to fulfill a duty would be unfair, so it is often asserted that a "right" exists only where failure to perform the relevant duty would be unfair. Since one cannot be unfair to oneself, those who take this view think of rights as claims, or the bases for possible claims, to fair treatment.

The distinction between natural rights and positive rights is of great importance (see *S.t.*, 2–2, q. 57, a. 2; q. 60, a. 5). This is evident when one considers the various entities called the "right to life." The right to life which is based on the seventh and eighth modes of responsibility is a natural right. It is also absolute, because the duty not to choose to kill is absolute. However, one also speaks of the "right to life" of a person who needs help to survive (that is, the right to the help others can give). Such a right also is natural, yet it is nonabsolute—in response to further specification, it admits of exceptions, (for instance, in the case of a terminally ill patient taken off the respirator close to death).

Again, one speaks of the "right to life" of a patient who has a right to competent medical care based on a physician's commitment to supply it. In many places, there is a legal cause of wrongful death if the physician negligently causes the patient's death. But this violation of a right, though it leads to wrongful death, is not against a natural right, since the expectation of competent treatment is based only on the physician's undertaking to provide it.

Such distinctions make it clear why one cannot argue from the positive and/or nonabsolute character of some things called "right to life" to the positive and nonabsolute character of everything called "right to life." On the contrary, the right to life which is grounded in the duty not to choose to kill is natural and absolute.

From the preceding analysis it follows that one ought not to think of rights as basic moral principles, even though today many appeal to rights as if they were basic. Usually such appeals go nowhere, because rights are not self-evident, and what is gratuitously claimed can be summarily denied. Rights are intelligible only in terms of duties, and duties must be reduced to principles—namely, to the basic human goods and modes of responsibility. That anyone has a right of any sort is always a moral conclusion, never a moral principle.

Question F: Are communities governed by moral norms other than those which govern individuals?

1. All of the modes of responsibility can apply to the acts of communities. Groups, like individuals, can make decisions which involve giving in to nonrational motivations against reasonable considerations. The modes direct those who participate in making group decisions not to do this—to proceed instead in line with a will toward integral human fulfillment.

That all the modes of responsibility apply to acts of communities can be seen from the following examples. A parish which carries on a minimal liturgy because there is not enough interest and enthusiasm to plan and arrange, practice, obtain necessary things, and participate violates the first mode of responsibility. Ecclesiastical administrators who discourage the people's involvement in church affairs in favor of more efficient management violate the second mode of responsibility. A nation which does not abandon war aims which it realizes are unreasonable violates the third mode of responsibility. A society which abandons its weaker members out of reluctance to bear the burden of caring for them violates the fourth mode of responsibility. A nation which goes to war in order to seize for itself the natural resources of another country violates the fifth mode of responsibility. A university which develops curricula aimed at providing its students with an educational "experience" instead of the reality of education violates the sixth mode of responsibility. A nation which takes revenge in kind against enemy attacks on its civilian population violates the seventh mode of responsibility. A nation which threatens the total destruction of a potential adversary in order to deter war violates the eighth mode of responsibility.

2. Moreover, cooperative acts do not involve any form of voluntariness other than those available to individuals. Although group acts should not be reduced to an artificial structure of individual choices, still the acts of a group do arise from the willing of individuals. These individuals often act on behalf of others, sometimes as their representative. But even when a whole group fully participate in common action, the group's act depends on its individual members, united in common spontaneous willing, choice, acceptance of consequences, and executive willing.

3. The basic human goods, the human capacities for action, and the norms of reasonable action are the principles of morality. They are the same for individual and for group action. **Therefore, the moral principles of the actions of groups are the same as those of the actions of individuals; and, since responsibilities follow from the principles, there is no difference in principle between the moral responsibilities of groups and those of individuals.**

4. "In principle" means that the same specific norms apply to the extent they are relevant. Obviously, the possible acts open to individuals and groups are not the same. No group can have an obligation to remember its wife's birthday; no individual as such can have an obligation to levy taxes fairly. Thus, there are some specific norms which apply only to individuals and others which apply only to certain groups. If, however, a certain kind of action is always wrong for any individual, it is always wrong for any group. For instance, if it is wrong for individuals to kill one another for the sake of revenge, it is wrong for nations to do the same. If it is wrong for an individual freely to accept another's death when there is no basis for doing so in a common good and common commitment, then it is wrong for a corporation freely to accept the death of its employees or its customers in order to increase its corporate profits.

5. **This conclusion is at odds with the view that reasons of state justify nations in doing whatever they must to survive and maintain public order** (international and national security). The notion of "reasons of state" is clearly articulated by Machiavelli and accepted almost universally in modern politics. It is simply an instance of proportionalist rationalization in the service, often, of a kind of mystique of the state. A similar rationalization is used by the administrators of many other groups, including ecclesiastical leaders and business executives. Not uncommonly, for example, people who consider lying in self-interest wrong take lying to be a necessary and justified part of their social responsibilities.

6. Aristotle thought of the state as a quasi-organic whole, its parts the individual citizens.[7] Individuals could rightly be treated by the state as one treats

parts of one's body: Much as one cuts off a diseased limb, the state might cut off a criminal by capital punishment (cf. *S.t.*, 2–2, q. 64, a. 2). But this conception of the state is false, and any notion of the common good based on it will have unacceptable implications (e.g., *S.t.*, 2–2, q. 11, a. 3). Rather, the common good of a civil society is only that part of human fulfillment which its citizens should cooperate in pursuing and serving. But the modes of responsibility articulate the requirements of openness to integral human fulfillment. Thus, they define what truly furthers the common good, while the common good cannot justify violating any of them.

Summary

The modes of responsibility are normative principles but not specific moral norms. It is necessary to see how specific norms are drawn from the modes of responsibility.

All the modes exclude unreasonable grounds of acting, and all embody the same first principle of morality. To this extent, all have normative force in the same way. But their normative force also differs, since different norms exclude different nonrational motives (laziness, unreasonable partiality, and so on), and violations dispose one differently toward integral human fulfillment. Similarly, although all of the modes bear upon choices, they do so in different ways—some demanding appropriate acts, others forbidding inappropriate ones, and still others doing both.

Specific moral norms can be derived, first, by considering the voluntariness involved in the kind of action under consideration in relation to relevant basic human goods, then considering the moral determination which the first principle of morality and the modes of responsibility indicate for such volition; from these two premises one deduces the moral determination of that kind of action.

Most specific moral norms nevertheless admit of exceptions (are not absolute). This is so because most norms are open to further specification by the same principles—basic human goods and modes of responsibility—from which they were derived. It is true, for instance, that promises ought to be kept; but one is justified in breaking a promise—for instance, if keeping it would involve violating the eighth mode. However, some moral norms are absolute—that is, an already-given determination settles a kind of action as morally wrong.

Proportionalism is not needed to account for nonabsolute moral norms. Such norms are simply those which can be specified further, with the result that the moral determination changes. But this does not come about by some proportionalist weighing of goods and bads to ascertain the greater good or lesser evil; rather, it is dictated by the basic human goods and the modes of responsibility, which generated the norm in the first place.

Some judgments of conscience can be criticized conclusively by absolute moral norms. Others cannot, but the method of deriving norms described here is adequate for criticizing these as well. This is so because all the morally relevant features of the unique acts which conscience judges are found among the principles from which specific norms are derived. Thus, if a judgment of conscience is defective, its defect can be discovered and rectified only by developing a more fully specified norm which is adequate to the situation.

What bridges the gap between a fully specified norm (which still is logically universal) and a judgment of conscience (which is logically singular) is a judgment that all the moral determinants in the situation have been sufficiently considered, and one may proceed in this situation by treating one's choice as an instance of a specific moral type. This judgment—that reflection has gone far enough—defies articulation and so requires prudence. Likewise, the prudent person often solves difficult moral problems by thinking of new options, which fulfill new specific norms corresponding to them and conform better than any of the options initially available to a will toward integral human fulfillment.

All of the modes apply to those acts of a person which have an effect upon others. Duties are responsibilities which one person or group has toward another or others. Arising from diverse modes, duties differ as they do. Many are not absolute; others are. Some exist prior to any choice and can be called "natural duties." But others ("positive duties") arise from one's own commitments and/or the decisions of authorities.

Rights are not separate entities. Rather, right and duty are the same reality, "right" signifying its bearing upon the person or group affected by the action which the duty determines. Rights also are both natural and positive, absolute and nonabsolute. But they are not basic moral principles. They are intelligible only in terms of duties, and duties must be reduced to moral principles—to human goods and the modes of responsibility.

The actions of groups are governed by the same moral principles as those of individuals. It is true of course that the acts open to individuals and to groups are not the same; thus there are some specific norms which apply only to individuals and some which apply only to groups. If, however, a certain kind of action is always wrong for any individual, it is always wrong for any group. The notion that "reasons of state" justify a nation in doing whatever is necessary to survive and maintain public order is simply an instance of proportionalist rationalization. Similarly, the idea that individuals can be sacrificed for the common good of society, much as one amputates a diseased limb from a body, is based on a notion of the state as a quasi-organic whole. But this view of the state is false, and the common good, which is defined in terms of moral principles, cannot justify violating any of the modes of responsibility.

Appendix 1:   St. Thomas on the nonabsoluteness of norms

In articulating his theory of natural law, St. Thomas Aquinas asks about the unity of its norms in application to cases. To answer this question, he borrows a distinction from Aristotle's physics between what is universal and necessary, and what is particular and subject to chance variation. Applying this distinction, he says the basic principles of natural law are the same for all, but at the concrete level the proper principles which guide action hold for most cases, yet because of special conditions can be subject to exceptions (*S.t.*, 1–2, q. 94, a. 4; cf. q. 100, a. 8). Some dissenting theologians quote or cite this one article of Thomas to support their view that one must decide in each case whether a received moral norm must be fulfilled or is overridden by other considerations.

The first thing to notice about this argument is that the point Thomas is making can be true with respect to most specific moral norms, which must be applied and limited by basic moral principles. The next thing to notice is that Thomas in his actual moral thinking—as distinct from his reflection upon natural law—holds that there are norms which do not admit of exception (e.g., *S.t.*, 2–2, q. 41, a. 1; q. 64, a. 6; q. 70, a. 4; q. 100, aa. 2–3; q. 153, a. 2, with q. 154). In any case, Thomas does not articulate a proportionalist theory.

Beyond these considerations, I think it must be said that this particular position of Thomas is a mistake and that his Aristotelian argument for it is fallacious. The structure of the existential domain is not exactly parallel to that of the natural world. The whole morally significant content of one's action must be intelligible, since one is responsible only for what one understands. For this reason, proposals one adopts by choice never are morally particularized by unique, unrepeatable, material, contingent factors. The really unique aspects of one's action make no difference whatsoever to the morality of what one does.

Hence, Thomas is confusing the specificity of moral acts with the uniqueness of physical particulars. Although one's dog Fido has individual traits which no branch of science ever studies, one's morally significant act of mistreating Fido on a particular day due to particular irritations has no morally relevant features which will not be considered by a complete Christian ethics. For one's morally significant act will include only what one deliberately chooses to do and permit—that is, what one understands about what one is doing—and one's practical understanding can be wholly determined by moral principles.

Appendix 2:   Limitations of the language of rights

According to the explanation given in question E, the language of rights is wholly reducible to the normative principles set out in previous chapters. Anyone who has examined the literature on rights knows that rights have proved very resistant to theoretical analysis. Initially, one's rights seem to be a set of moral levers by which one can move others (or a society) to act or refrain from acting as one wishes. All the levers in the set appear homogeneous. But on closer examination, rights turn out to be a very heterogeneous collection of moral entities, whose reality cannot be denied but whose precise nature and sources become more mysterious the more closely they are examined.

Nevertheless, in modern times the language of rights has been very widely used in social and political philosophy, in moral theology, and even in the social teaching of the Church. If this language is theoretically opaque and if (as I hold) it is reducible to the more basic modes of responsibility, why has it been adopted so widely?

To begin with, everyone makes claims which he or she considers justified, and many such claims are widely acknowledged, sometimes even by those against whom they are made. Therefore, rights are immediately present in social experience and are explicitly conceptualized and discussed. For this reason, their reality is obvious and vital to everyone. Furthermore, people can talk about rights and reach some agreement about them without having any theory of morality. Indeed, even those who disagree about the foundation of rights can agree that there are rights and can even agree concerning some specific rights— although this agreement is easier when one is formulating a document such as the United Nations Declaration of Human Rights than when one is dealing with a real issue. However, in a political context one can occasionally reach practical agreement about actions required to protect or promote commonly recognized rights. Finally, the language of rights is an appealing one for leaders, since it calls the attention of those addressed to their own stake in society.

There is one sense in which the language of rights is unavoidable in moral reflection and teaching concerning human life in society. Since rights correspond to duties, and since duties are social responsibilities, one must talk about rights more or less explicitly if one is going to talk about social morality at all. Moreover, since modern thought about society makes heavy use of the language of rights, in many cases an important moral point can best be articulated by beginning from an acknowledged right and then clarifying the responsibilities which constitute the moral basis of that right. Vatican II does precisely this in its teaching on religious liberty; it asserts the right to religious commitment and practice against the infringements of political society, but the Council explains this right by the various responsibilities which underlie it (see DH 2–3).

However, the use of the language of rights often is very confusing. One reason for the confusion is the many meanings of "rights"; there is a tendency to suppose that all are similar in ways they are not. Again, because talk of rights focuses on claims, the language of rights is easily exploited by those who overlook or conceal essential qualifications, such as against whom and to what the claim is directed. Thus, the right to religious liberty often is misunderstood or misrepresented to mean that people are justified in teaching heresy or practicing it.

All things considered, Catholic moral theology and social teaching should be cautious in using the language of rights. In reading the New Testament, one finds a great deal about the responsibilities of Christians, very little about rights. Sound talk about rights should move quickly from the modern focus upon justifiable claims to the traditional focus upon the principles which underlie them, by generating the responsibilities to which they correspond.

Appendix 3:   The notion of the "common good"

A full examination of the notion of the "common good" belongs to the treatise on justice. However, certain misunderstandings of this notion will lead to objections to the conclusion reached in question F. Here I explain "common good" sufficiently to raise and answer these objections.

In the teaching of the Church and in older treatises on moral theology, it often is said (and always taken for granted) that in social matters the principle of moral rectitude in action is the common good. One might suppose that "common good" signifies a principle other than the basic human goods which contribute to integral human fulfillment or that it signifies certain categories of these goods exclusively—in other words, that some of them are common and that others are strictly individual.

"Common good" sometimes is used to signify something other than the basic human goods. For instance, one sometimes refers to common property or tools as a "common good"; it sometimes is said that shared natural resources, public facilities such as roads, and a shared body of national cultural objects are components of the common good of a political society. These things can pertain to the common good, but they are not principles of morality, for they are merely instruments to or expressions of common life and the humanly fulfilling actions and realities which perfect it. Hence, the common good which is a principle of the moral rectitude of action should not be identified with such goods.

There is no good which helps to shape morally right action except goods which can be sought for their own sake as a basis for a choice to act. The basic human goods precisely are all the kinds of good which can be sought for their own sake, whether in an individual's or a group's decision to act. Hence, the common good as a principle of moral rectitude cannot be a good other than the basic human goods.

Nor are some categories of the basic human goods common and others strictly individual. All the basic human goods can be purposes of both individual and communal acts; moreover, all of them have both individual and communal dimensions in their realization.

A person can individually choose and act for any of the goods. One might suppose that one could not individually choose and act for a good such as interpersonal harmony, but that supposition is a mistake. A private citizen who summons others to be concerned about what seems a social injustice is acting individually for justice, although such a person hopes that this individual action will lead to social action. One also might suppose that a group of persons could not communally choose and act for a good such as individual self-integration, but this supposition also is a mistake. A community of monks can choose and act together according to a rule of life, an important part of whose purpose is the development of self-control and detachment in each member of the community, since personal sanctification is part of the common purpose.

Moreover, there are individual and communal dimensions in the realization of all the basic human goods. Harmony in the existential domain is an interconnected whole; one does not have inner peace if one is at war with one's fellows, and vice versa. Justice is realized in persons whose individual lives are perfected in community. Individuals are fulfilled by knowledge of the truth, but the truth of any field of study is known only by a scholarly community, with its many experts and specialists. Human life itself belongs to individual organisms, but it also exists in the common functions of sexual intercourse and procreation. Thus, there are no categories of human good inherently private or inherently social.

What, then, does it mean to talk about the "common good" as a principle for the moral rectitude of action in a social context? The common good of a particular society is the set of basic human goods insofar as members of that society are commonly committed to them and pursue them by cooperative action. The common good also can be thought of as including instrumental goods, such as public property. But these are not morally determinative. When the moral rectitude of an action in a social context is in question, an emphasis on the common good ordinarily means three things. First, that the principle of moral rectitude is found in intelligible human goods, not in empirical goods which appeal to emotion (considered simply as such). Second, that the relationships which constitute the society must be structured in a fair way, and this just order must be constantly reestablished when it is disturbed. Third, that actions which affect many must be directed by impartial (fair, just) judgments, not by partial (unfair, biased, selfish, prejudiced) decisions.[8]

As for the first of these points, morality as a whole depends upon intelligible goods. Still, in the case of individuals acting in respect to their own affairs and the concerns of small, intimate groups, such as the family, emotion normally is more or less integrated with reason, and in many cases one need not think much about what is truly good. However, in social affairs which involve larger groups, such as a whole political society, feelings seldom can be trusted. If upright judgments are going to be made, there must be constant attention to the fact that action must be directed to what is intelligibly good, not simply to particular, appealing states of affairs. For example, the policy of a nation at war ought to be directed to the intelligible good of peace, not merely to the empirical good of the euphoric day when the war will be brought to a successful end.

In general, the basic human goods are not good precisely insofar as they are realized in this or that individual or group; they are good because they are humanly fulfilling. There is a constant danger that my or our experience of sharing in a good will become an empirical objective whose emotional appeal will override reasonable judgments about the pursuit of that which is good—for example, peace and justice. The appeal to the common good in part attempts to forestall this danger.

271

However, the second point—the demand for fairness—is more precisely what it means to say that in social matters the principle of moral rectitude in action is the common good. Most large-scale societies are a complex of various sorts of interpersonal relationships, some of them based on morally evil acts. However, to the extent that there really is community and cooperative action, people are committed to the same goods and (in most cases) work so that these goods will be realized in such a way that all will share to some extent in their realization. For example, insofar as a political society has the character of a real community, its members are committed to justice among themselves and try to establish a form of life such that all will share in this good, by treating others justly and by being treated in the same way.

Of course, the precise states of affairs for which a community undertakes common action usually cannot be achieved without such common action—which is why common action is undertaken. However, in many cases individuals or smaller groups can enjoy many of the rewards of the common undertaking although they do not contribute fairly to bearing its burden. Moreover, individuals often can prefer objectives other than the common ones; their action for these can be unfair merely because they are pursued selfishly to the detriment of the common undertaking. Further, some individuals relate to others on a completely amoral basis; they consider only their own satisfactions and care nothing for others except insofar as they can use them or must beware of them. Hence, there is much unfairness in the life of any large-scale society. The appeal to the common good is an appeal for fairness in the conduct of every communal undertaking.

On the basis of the preceding explanation, it is easy to grasp two senses in which it is correct to say: "The common good is superior to the goods of individuals."

In one sense, this means that intelligible goods are humanly superior to empirical goods, and thus the human good itself is more important than whose good it happens to be. For example, that truth be known is more important than that I know it or you know it. Of course, truth is not known unless some individuals and groups participate in it. But the whole possible fulfillment is larger than any participation, and each participation is humanly good because of what it is, not because of whose it is.

In another sense, the superiority of the common good means that the fulfillment of the group by its cooperative action has priority over any unfair individual satisfaction. Any individual who views common life selfishly, any group which views public life solely in terms of its partisan interests, will seek unfair satisfactions and violate the primacy of the common good, understanding "common good" in this sense.

Aristotle's conception of the common good was that individuals are related to society as parts to a whole. The common good, on this view, is the only true and complete good of the individuals, just as the common life is the only real life they have. On this view, as Aristotle says: To attain the common good is greater and more godlike than to attain the good of an individual.[9] Unfortunately, by way of St. Thomas and others, this conception has found its way into Catholic moral and social thought (see *S.t.*, 2–2, q. 47, a. 10; q. 64, a. 2; q. 141, a. 8).

The trouble with this view is obvious. It simply is not true that individual persons are subordinated to communities as parts of an organism are subordinated to the whole organism. Parts of one's body as such do not have moral standing of their own. For example, the life and health which is a human good is that of the person as a whole. Hence, not only may one cut off a cancerous part for the life of the whole, one may cut off an organ healthy in itself to protect the well-being of the whole—for example, one may amputate healthy testicles to impede breast cancer in a man, because the normal hormonal product of the testicle contributes to the virulence of such cancer. But one may not kill members of society—particularly innocent ones—for the welfare of the whole. To do so is to violate the eighth mode of responsibility.

Needless to say, St. Thomas does not develop Aristotle's dictum into a justification for Machiavellianism. For Thomas, human persons are not ordered to political society according to all they are and have, but rather to God (cf. *S.t.*, 1–2, q. 21, a. 4, ad 3). Faith teaches that subordination to divine goodness requires not the destruction of persons but their fulfillment.[10] Hence, in Catholic social teaching, passages abound in which the primacy of persons is declared. For example, Vatican II teaches that the political community exists for the common good, and "the common good embraces the sum of those conditions of social life by which individuals, families, and groups can achieve their own fulfillment in a relatively thorough and ready way" (GS 74).[11]

Notes

1. See Richard A. McCormick, S.J., *Notes on Moral Theology: 1965 through 1980* (Washington, D.C.: University Press of America, 1981), 576–81, for some references and discussion.

2. See *Catechismus ex decreto Ss. Concilii Tridentini ad Parochos, Pii V., Pont. Max., iussu editus* (Rome: Propagandae Fidei, 1839), 2:125–31.

3. See Joseph Fletcher, *Situation Ethics: The New Morality* (Philadelphia: Westminster Press, 1966), 164–65.

4. Paul Ramsey, "The Case of the Curious Exception," in *Norm and Context in Christian Ethics*, ed. Gene H. Outka and Paul Ramsey (New York: Charles Scribner's Sons, 1968), 74–93, argues the same point (although he also makes several incidental points with which I do not entirely agree). Regardless of one's moral theory, if a specific moral norm is to admit justifiable exceptions, then there must be some feature which is morally relevant on which the specification can be based rationally. But if there is such a feature, then one really is articulating another specific norm, which might not in fact apply to many instances, but still is logically universal—that is, open to any instance of an indeterminate set which meets the intelligible condition that grounds the justified exception.

5. See John Finnis, *Natural Law and Natural Rights* (Oxford: Clarendon Press, 1980), 198–230, esp. 205–10, for a discussion of various aspects of the concept of rights within a perspective very like that of the present work.

6. See John XXIII, *Pacem in terris*, 55 AAS (1963) 264; *The Papal Encyclicals*, 270.30, on the relevant reciprocity of rights and duties arising from natural law. The encyclical also stresses the tie between rights and duties in one and the same person (28–29). A right is a claim and opportunity to share in a human good, openness to which generates some specific responsibilities (duties in a broad sense) on the person who has the right.

7. Aristotle, *Nichomachean Ethics* i, 1094b7–10; *Politics* i, 1253a19–28. Although Aristotle's social philosophy is unsatisfactory, his view must be distinguished from the modern conception of the organic state, which makes it into a supraindividual reality and endows it with characteristics of the divine, thus setting up an idol which claims to justify negating the dignity of individual persons. Aristotle never dreamed that the human could be divine; only a post-Christian society can adopt this distortion of Christian faith. This modern conception was fully articulated by G. W. F. Hegel, *Hegel's Philosophy of Right* (Oxford: Clarendon Press, 1942), 215 and 279–86. With modifications it is continued in the thinking of subsequent totalitarians. The Catholic critique of totalitarianism has rightly rejected this conception of the common good, but has not been so critical of the comparatively innocuous Aristotelian view.

8. Usually "common good" is used in the Church's teaching as if the sense of the expression were obvious. Hence, it is impossible to verify the point made here by reference to any single place. However, comparison of many references to the "common good"—for example, in the two great social encyclicals of John XXIII—does point to the conclusion that appeal to the common good is nothing more than appeal to justice in the social pursuit of the genuine human goods of persons in communion. See *Mater et magistra*, 53 AAS (1961) 410, 417, 421, and 438–39; *The Papal Encyclicals*, 267.40, 65, 78–81, and 151; *Pacem in terris*, 55 AAS (1963) 272–73, 280–81, 293–94, and 298; *The Papal Encyclicals*, 270.55–56, 84–85, 136–39, and 154–55. For additional references and a summary:

Jean-Yves Calvez, S.J., and Jacques Perrin, S.J., *The Church and Social Justice: The Social Teaching of the Popes from Leo XIII to Pius XII* (Chicago: Henry Regnery, 1961), 114–24.

9. See Aristotle, *Nichomachean Ethics* i, 1094a28–b10.

10. See St. Thomas, *In Decem Libros Ethicorum Aristotelis ad Nicomachum Expositio*, i, 2, where the dictum of Aristotle is qualified doubly: first, that what is in question is the pursuit of the same good for many or for one; second, that politics is not supreme absolutely. See also Jacques Maritain, *The Person and the Common Good* (New York: Charles Scribner's Sons, 1947), 5–20; Carlos Cardona, *La metafísica del bien común* (Madrid: Rialp, 1966).

11. This statement of Vatican II need not be taken as a definition of the common good, reducing it to a purely ancilliary role. In a generally sound treatment of common good, Johannes Messner, *Social Ethics: Natural Law in the Western World*, rev. ed. (St. Louis: B. Herder, 1965), 123–50, considers the common good attained in social cooperation to be only auxiliary to the fulfillment of distinct persons (143) although he holds this order to be of intrinsic value (149). Messner seems not to understand clearly that at least the good of justice in the society, which is the formal aspect of anything that can be called "common good," not only requires cooperation for its attainment, but can only exist in the community. For although interpersonal harmony is not real apart from persons, it is real only in persons-in-communion, not in many individual persons as a mere aggregate. (See Pius XI, *Mit brennender Sorge*, 29 AAS [1937] 158–59; *The Papal Encyclicals*, 218.30, for an explicit recognition of properly social goods.) Behind Messner's difficulty (and also Maritain's) is no doubt a reaction against the organicism of totalitarian theories and perhaps also a residue of a religious individualism, which sought the fulfillment of the person more in individual salvation (union of each soul with God by a private act of beatific vision) than in social liberation (communion of divine and human persons in the perfected kingdom).

CHAPTER ELEVEN

THE MORAL AUTHORITY OF LAW

Introduction

As was explained in chapter seven, moral principles can be called "natural law." But here "law" is used in the more usual sense to refer to various types of positive law—that is, law made or posited (put in place) by a legislator. Divine law, the law of human societies, and the law of the Church specify a large part of a Christian's clear moral responsibilities. Genuine laws of all these types have a moral foundation and thus deserve to be obeyed. Even so, the moral basis of law and the obligation to obey laws are limited. This chapter examines the moral foundation of laws and the limits of their moral force.

Question A: What is meant by "authority"?

1. In general, an authority is a source whose judgments and/or choices provide a reason for thinking and/or acting otherwise than one would if left to judge and/or choose for oneself.[1] Beyond this very general core of meaning, the word "authority" is used in two quite different ways.

2. Authority in one sense is competence to make judgments which reasonable persons of lesser competence will accept as certainly or probably true. One speaks of the authority of experts, of scholars in their fields, and also of the teaching authority of the Church—each in its own domain and according to its own competence. **Authority in another sense is a social capacity to give directions which generate a nonabsolute moral duty to obey. This is the authority of law.**[2] (The distinction between the Church's teaching authority and law-giving authority will be clarified in question F.)

Authority in the second sense includes the capacity to make choices on behalf of a group. In a famous definition, St. Thomas says that law is a "certain ordinance of reason, directed to the common good, promulgated by one who has the care of the community" (*S.t.*, 1–2, q. 90, a. 4, c.). This ordinance of reason is a directive for activity, a command, which itself presupposes an act of will, namely, a choice (*S.t.*, 1–2, q. 17, a. 1 and a. 3, ad 1). This choice itself must be in accord with moral principles if the directive is to be a genuine law with moral force (*S.t.*, 1–2, q. 96, a. 4).

The choices of the authority specify what those directed by the law ought to choose to do as cooperative members of the group. But the will of an authority making choices is not the source of law's moral force. Rather, members of groups ought to obey the laws which are specified by the choices of authorities because such obedience is necessary for just cooperation toward the common good.

St. Thomas' definition of law can be applied only by extension to the set of moral principles called "natural law." As was explained (7-A), these principles are directions for action. They are given human persons as truths about how to live good lives so that they can cooperate intelligently in God's plan for the fulfillment of his whole creative undertaking. In this case, the specifying choice of the divine authority is to create intelligent beings such as human persons. Human persons being what they are, the principles of morality could not be other than they are.

3. In a loose sense, all who are able to exact conformity to their wills are called "authorities," even when their power lacks a moral basis, provided there is some appearance of lawful authority. Thus, the Nazis were "in authority" in Germany until the end of World War II, although their directives as such ceased to have moral force some time before then. Although the behavior of those in control in such situations may generate obligations—for example, the obligation to cooperate with them up to a point in order to avoid evils which they will otherwise perpetrate—their directives, having no moral basis, do not of themselves generate any duty to obey. In a strict sense, those in control in such situations have no authority, and their directives are not laws. Rather, they resemble the orders of outlaws, which are backed only by threats.

4. There are other cases besides obeying authorities where one should act on another's decision. In exchanging marriage vows, for instance, each party undertakes, within limits, to engage in marital relations at the other's request. But a request for what has been promised is not lawmaking, and granting such a request is not obeying authority.

5. Still, in some lasting relationships, something analogous to law and authority does arise from promises. Employees who contract with their employers are, for example, bound within certain limits to carry out the orders of superiors. The latter have the capacity in such cases to give directions which ought to be followed. Yet this power, "managerial authority," is not that of law. One is subject to managerial direction only by one's morally free promise in accepting a position. By contrast, the authority of law has, as we shall see further below, a moral basis independent of any commitment which those subject to it are morally free to omit.[3]

Question B: How can people be morally obliged to act on decisions they do not participate in making?

1. In some cases, the directions given by those in authority call attention to already-existing moral responsibilities. Thus criminal law forbids many acts which would be morally wrong even if the law did not forbid them. In other cases, however, authorities require something which would not otherwise be morally required.

2. Even when an authority is only calling attention to an already-existing obligation, the obligation's backing by authority generates an additional moral duty, the duty to obey. This, furthermore, is the only moral duty generated when

authority directs something which is not otherwise morally required. In other words, the only new moral responsibility arising in either case from the decision of an authority is the duty to obey. Thus the question comes down to this: Why should persons sometimes obey other persons? **The obligation to obey is grounded in two distinct ways** (see *S.t.*, 1, q. 96, a. 4; 1–2, q. 95, a. 1; 2–2, q. 57, a. 4; q. 104, aa. 1–2).

3. First, if two or more people are morally obliged to cooperate but not all are capable of deciding what to do, fairness (the fifth mode of responsibility) requires that those in a better position to decide for the good of the whole community do so, and that all follow the directions to carry out such decisions. **Thus, authority and obedience can have a moral grounding in the differing abilities of people who are morally bound to live in community and engage in common action.**

4. Authority of this kind is present in a family, which is a natural society. Parental authority is not based on the children's consent or on common commitment. But neither does it simply come down to the fact that parents were there first and are stronger. Rather, a family must live a common life; moral judgments and choices must be made; children are more or less incapable of making these judgments and choices. Even as children grow, decisions are often required about matters where no consensus can be obtained. Even then parents can judge and choose in a sense that children cannot, since they are responsible for the whole family and have scope for action which the children lack.

5. The second way in which the obligation to obey is grounded is found in societies created by a common commitment. In making such a commitment, people unite to cooperate for goods which they cannot pursue by themselves. The commitment must be implemented by an indefinite series of choices, and these choices must be carried out cooperatively for the sake of the common purpose.

6. The many diverse communities based on common commitment have no single locus of authority. In many friendships and purely voluntary associations, all the parties share authority and decide together what to do, then obediently carry out the common plan of action together. Although this might seem the ideal arrangement, it is not practical in a complex society, where not all can share authority on all matters because decision making itself is a full-time job. In such cases, the locus of authority is frequently part of the understanding on which the common commitment constituting the society is made.

7. In societies based on common commitment, the obligation to obey has a twofold moral basis. First, one is morally required to make commitments, for people must pursue goods and, as the second mode of responsibility makes clear, they should not do this in an altogether individualistic way. Moreover, once one has made commitments, they must be carried out despite obstacles. **Second, once a person has entered into a community formed by mutual commitments, fairness (the fifth mode) requires one to carry out even those decisions one finds burdensome and personally unrewarding.** This is so because one wants others to carry out decisions which benefit oneself. All should do their part; those who do not, impose on others.

8. Despite the real moral ground of authority, the duty to obey is nonabsolute (see *S.t.*, 1–2, q. 96, a. 4; 2–2, q. 104, a. 5). First, a person convinced that what authority directs cannot be done without moral wrongdoing must not violate conscience out of obedience. Thus children should not obey when their parents tell them to act spitefully or tell lies. Second, cases arise in which duties conflict and it is impossible to carry out all of them at once. Third, there are cases in which legitimate decisions should be overridden. This happens when a member of the community is in a position to know that an exception to an authoritative rule is urgently required by the very goods to which members of the community have made their common commitment (see *S.t.*, 1–2, q. 96, a. 6; 2–2, q. 120).

Question C: What is the basis of one's moral obligation to obey divine precepts?

1. In most cases we can see, with the help of faith, the wisdom of norms proposed in divine revelation, for they can be reduced to human goods and the modes of responsibility. Integral human fulfillment itself requires that we observe these norms. When we do God's will in such cases, we clearly act for the human good in which he wishes us to flourish.

2. However, only revelation tells us of some norms. For example, we are to participate in the liturgy; to protect, live within, and hand on the structure of the Church; to carry on and extend the redemptive work of Jesus to all places and times. If these norms had not been revealed, we could not have formulated them (see *S.t.*, 1–2, q. 91, aa. 4–5). They make up what is called "divine positive law."[4] Why should we obey them?

3. The question should not be brushed aside by saying one obviously should do whatever God commands. The mere fact that God commands, considered apart from any moral ground, does not generate moral responsibilities (see 4-D). That we ought to obey divine positive law is itself a specific moral norm. In asking why, we are seeking this norm's basis in human goods and modes of responsibility.

4. Religion—harmony with God—is a basic human good. Once God reveals himself as personal and extends his invitation to intimate friendship, humankind has a moral reason to cooperate with him. The moral basis for accepting God's invitation by making the act of faith will be explained later (20-D). Briefly, however, it may be said here that interpersonal harmony and the development of friendship always depend on compliance with the wishes of others. Moreover, the covenant relationship is proposed by God only after he shows it to be in line with human fulfillment.

5. In making an act of faith, one enters into communion with God by a mutual commitment. At the same time, however, one is aware of one's radical and unique dependence on God. **Thus, while the covenant relationship requires our cooperation, only God is in a position to make certain decisions for the life we share with him. These decisions, which determine the requirements of divine positive law, therefore have authority for us—we ought to obey.** The precise point of doing as God directs remains to be seen, but we have reason to believe that there is a point and we will understand it in due time. It is reasonable to comply

with God's directions—with divine positive law—even when we do not discern the intrinsic point of doing what he directs (see *S.t.*, 1, q. 21, aa. 1–2; 2–2, q. 104, a. 4).

6. Divine positive law does not require us to do anything inconsistent with openness to integral human fulfillment: We are not asked to offer human sacrifice, to tell lies, or anything of that sort. Taking into account what we know by faith of the redemptive act of Jesus and our role in it, we can see even now that the precepts of divine positive law are fitting. Obedience does contribute to completing God's redemptive work in our lives and the world at large.

7. Compared with God's people in the Old Testament, Christians are asked to do little that is not clearly needed for human fulfillment (see *S.t.*, 1–2. q. 98, aa. 1–2; q. 107, a. 4). Though the old law had many detailed requirements, it was of limited help to friendship with God and thus was burdensome. Not only is the law of Jesus much simpler, but by the power of the Holy Spirit it is effective, for we can fulfill it with the new hearts he gives us (see Rom 7.1–6; Gal 4.21–5.6). God treated the Jews with loving care, but only as trusted servants.[5] Christians are treated as friends and members of God's household (see Rom 8.14–17; Jn 15.14–15). Thus the law of Jesus is not burdensome (see Mt 11.28–30).

Question D: What distinctions among the laws of civil societies are necessary for moral reflection?

1. Many societies are more or less completely based on common commitments: for example, civil societies, universities, labor unions. Although the authorities in all such societies make "laws" in the sense to be considered here, the laws of communities other than civil societies are usually called by some other name—"bylaws," "policies," "rules," or simply "decisions." According to the position explained in question B above (and in 10-E), there is an essential moral similarity between the authoritative decisions of civil societies and those of other communities.

2. These legal obligations are very important. Many of one's affirmative duties arise from the obligation to obey laws (taking "laws" in the wide sense it has here). Unfortunately, many people today fail to see the moral force of such legal duties. The former awe of public authority has faded, but it has not been replaced by a more intelligent respect (see GS 30).[6] This lends added importance to the discussion which follows. Although its focus is on the law of civil society, the implications for the law of other societies can be gathered by analogy.

3. The law of civil society can be divided in various ways.[7] Here the division will be from the moral point of view. Without such a division, the various responsibilities of citizens are likely to be confused.

4. **Constitutional law articulates the common and accepted plan by which a community exists.**[8] It indicates common purposes, the locus and structure of authority, and the limits of public authority. Its moral authority toward its members insofar as they are incapable of consent is similar to that of parents toward children. To the extent people ought to consent, however, the constitution establishes a just power to govern them as a community of free men and women.

Once the commitment is made, fairness requires that it be upheld. This duty—to uphold the constitution—is especially incumbent upon those who accept positions of trust under it.

5. Civil law provides a public facility for regulating private affairs according to the public purpose of mutual justice and common peace. For instance, the law of contracts and the law of torts (damages) help people make binding agreements to facilitate cooperation and minimize conflict through the settlement of disputes. One must use the facility of civil law when other moral obligations require its use. Fairness normally requires one to cooperate when others initiate the use of this facility. For example, a person who takes family responsibilities seriously might be morally obliged to make a will; those affected by a will normally are required by fairness to cooperate in carrying out its provisions.

6. Criminal law generally marks out certain acts which would be immoral—usually due to serious unfairness—even if they were not illegal. Even wrongful acts which are possible only because of the existence of the society—treason, say, or deliberate tax evasion—would be immoral even if they were not legal crimes. Authority does not create the wrongness of such criminal acts, and they cannot be made morally right by repealing criminal laws.[9] Besides specifying criminal acts, criminal law also determines by authoritative decision how the community will react to them; in other words, it determines criminal processes and punishments (see *S.t.*, 1–2, q. 95, a. 2).

A proper understanding of criminal law is important. In this area, a political society is less the maker of norms than their protector. No society can exist unless there is widespread outward compliance with some basic moral norms—for example, those forbidding killing. However, a society can permit the killing of certain classes of its weaker members, such as the unborn and the aged who lack the support of relatives and friends. To introduce such differences in legal protection is unfair. This consideration about fairness—not the sanctity of life as such—points to what is basically objectionable about the legalization of abortion, though not about abortion itself.

Because criminal law generally presupposes the wrongness of the acts with which it deals, the legalization of such acts previously and rightly considered criminal does not alter their moral wrongness. Moreover, the argument that one ought not to try to enforce moral standards by criminal penalties is fallacious. Not every immoral act can be the concern of society, since most immorality is hidden. Moreover, much of it is slight, and even serious immorality may not be directly related to the common good of civil society. Society can concern itself only with more serious wrongs, about which evidence is available, and which interfere with the common purpose of the society, usually by their injustice (see *S.t.*, 1–2, q. 96, a. 2). However, within these limits, morality is precisely what criminal law is concerned with. Those who object to certain criminal laws as impositions of morality really mean that they hold a different moral position and wish to impose it.

7. With respect to the criminal act itself, the moral force of criminal law is chiefly in one's antecedent responsibility not to do such an act. With respect to criminal process and punishment, one is bound by the same duty of obedience which requires conformity to laws of the type to be discussed next.

8. Law of this last kind is the regulation by statute and ordinance of the common life of the community at large, of some of its more important subgroups,

and especially of the government itself and its agencies. Morally, such regulation is like the process and legal sanction for civil and criminal law. **Regulatory law directs public policies and programs, the working of security forces, the public control of businesses, public administration, and many other matters of common life, such as the flow of traffic.** Some regulatory laws are general—they direct frequently repeated behavior into commonly accepted patterns. Others are single public acts—for example, a declaration of war.

Question E: To what extent does one have a moral obligation to obey human laws which are purely regulative?

1. The moral force of this sort of law comes from the moral foundation of the authority of the community, discussed in B above. To the extent civil society really is a community, its members have a nonabsolute duty to obey the decisions of its authorities.

2. But civil society is complex even insofar as it is a community. For some of its members—those incapable of making a free commitment—it functions wholly as a natural society, an extended family as it were. As far as others are concerned, it derives at least part of its character as a community from their morally upright commitment to its common purposes. The extent to which the authority of governments is grounded in the consent of the governed varies at different times and places, and also with different groups of citizens. And aliens voluntarily present in a civil society share in a limited way in its community, on a contractual basis, perhaps with no commitment at all to the society's common purposes.

3. Yet civil society is not without moral force even in regard to those of its members who do not consent; its authority can morally bind those who wrongfully refuse to commit themselves to community. Also, under some conditions—when common action is morally required and only certain persons are in a position to direct it—civil society rightfully functions in the manner of a "family" toward more of its members than usual. That the consent of the governed is absent at such times does not deprive government of its just power or nullify the responsibility of citizens to obey the law.

4. **The duty to obey the kind of laws under consideration here can be qualified in two ways. First, a law can lack authority due to some defect in it or in the way it was arrived at. Second, a law can be nonapplicable in particular cases.**

5. An authoritative decision of civil society contains a defect which causes it to lack moral authority if it would require a person to do something inconsistent with a moral absolute or would involve a person in a social action inconsistent with any of the modes of responsibility (see *S.t.*, 1–2, q. 96, a. 4). For example, Nazi laws which directed people to kill the innocent and carry on a useless war to the death were morally defective in a radical way.

6. Less radically, a decision can be morally defective in regard to the process by which it was reached. This can happen in three ways. First, the constitution which it implements can be defective, as was the original United States Constitu-

tion in its acceptance of slavery. Second, the decision can be inconsistent with the constitution, as laws enforcing racial segregation in the United States were (and were found to be in 1954 and subsequently). Third, the procedure by which the decision was made can be unfair, as is often the case in the formulating of tax laws, which reflect political pressures and favoritism more than judgments concerning what is fair and best for the society as a whole.

Even so, a morally responsible citizen will realize that life in political society is inevitable, that the society in which he or she lives is not altogether unjust, that many of its activities ought to be supported, and that other citizens, including those in worse economic condition, will suffer if one does not contribute one's legally specified share. This consideration shows that one cannot easily be morally certain that a defect in the process by which a law is made is sufficient to undermine its moral force.[10]

7. A law of civil society also lacks moral authority if it is inapplicable. Although not defective in itself, an authoritative directive sometimes need not be obeyed because of specifying factors, which can be of three kinds.

8. First, sometimes a law requires one to do something incompatible with another duty one has. (Conflicts of duties will be discussed in 12-E.)

9. Second, sometimes a law originally made for a reasonable purpose is undercut because changed conditions render compliance irrelevant to its purpose. Antiquated ordinances which a government could not reasonably try to enforce need not be obeyed (see *S.t.*, 1–2, q. 97, a. 3).

10. Third, a law can be inapplicable because of exceptions—that is, under specific conditions, not mentioned and perhaps not even anticipated by the lawmaker, it could not reasonably have been meant to apply. In emergencies, for example, property laws can be set aside to save human lives, for no authority can reasonably wish the system of ownership to block the more basic good of human life to whose service property mainly is directed. In such a case, one violates the letter of the law to preserve its spirit. Such a reasonable judgment to act against the law's letter is called "epikeia" (see *S.t.*, 2–2, q. 120).

11. **Lacking moral certitude that a law is without moral authority or is inapplicable, an upright person will observe the nonabsolute norm requiring obedience.** One must bear in mind that a law is not altogether defective and nonbinding merely because it is not perfectly and ideally just. Moreover, although the practice of epikeia can be sound, it is very often misunderstood and grossly abused. Then too, even if there is no duty to obey, Christians will often find reason to comply with laws when it is not wrong to do so, because a law-abiding style of life generally furthers their Christian vocation.

Although analogous to the qualification of nonabsolute moral norms by the addition of further specifications, epikeia really belongs only in the area of positive law, when one is morally obliged to make an exception to an authoritative decision, which one has no authority to revise and refine.[11]

Those subject to law are not justified in making exceptions simply because they personally would have made a different law. If such individualism were permissible, social authority would mean nothing. Nor are those subject to law justified in making exceptions whenever they think a different course of action would be considered reasonable by the authority if it knew all the conditions. For members of a society to make such judgments would produce too much diversity and leave the community without a common framework for its common action.

The condition which justifies exceptions is more stringent: One must be able to say sincerely that if the lawmaking authority knew the circumstances, it would surely want the exception to be made (see *S.t.*, 1–2, q. 96, a. 6; q. 100, a. 8).

Question F: What is the difference between the Church's moral teaching and her law?

1. The teaching authority of the Church, although unique, is called "authority" in the first of the senses distinguished in A above. The Church's competence to teach is different in various ways from that of experts and scholars; but its authority is like theirs insofar as it is a competence to make judgments which reasonable, believing persons should accept as true. At the same time, its teaching authority is unique in that it deals with the interpersonal truth of faith and has the task of shaping the Christian community and its life in the light of faith. This situation will be explained more fully in chapters twenty and thirty-five.

2. As for the Church's authority to make law, it is special insofar as it is conferred by divine positive law upon the pastors of the Church (see LG 18–22, 27, 37). However, this pastoral authority is analogous to the ruling authority of any human society. It is a social capacity to give directions to members of the Church.[12]

3. Those with teaching authority in the Church have no choice about whether and what to teach but only how to teach. Their teaching communicates a truth they did not create and cannot modify, namely, the truth of Jesus whom they are committed to serve (see *S.t.*, 2–2, q. 1, aa. 9–10). In exercising governing authority, however, the pastors of the Church do have a choice about what directives to give. Their decisions direct the Church's common life to the common good of completing Jesus' work throughout the world. With the light of faith and within the framework of divine positive law, how the Church is to complete this task has been left to the discretion of the apostolic pastoral authority (see *S.t.*, 2–2, q. 88, a. 12).

4. **When a Catholic violates a moral norm taught by the Church, the wrongful act is not of itself disobedience to the Church. The act is wrong because it violates a moral truth and the goods which this truth represents.** For instance, when wealthy Catholics violate the Church's teaching that they should pay their employees fair wages, the sin is not of itself disobedience to the Church; it is a violation of justice and of the well-being of those who are cheated.

5. **When a Catholic violates a pastoral directive, however, the wrongful act is disobedience.** For instance, those who do not bother to observe prescribed days of fast and abstinence fail primarily in obedience. At the same time, some laws of the Church forbid acts which, even apart from the Church's law, should be recognized by all as immoral. Such acts include canonical crimes: for example, the procuring of abortion. Those who deliberately and freely procure abortion are doubly guilty, for they not only violate justice and life, but also disobey the law of the Church.

Question G: To what extent do Catholics have a moral obligation to obey the Church's law?

1. In general, what has been said in questions D and E about the law of civil societies applies here, too. However, although law in the Church and law in other human societies are similar, the Church herself is essentially different from any other human society. Thus, certain points concerning the moral foundations and force of Church law deserve special notice.

2. The Church's constitutional law is divine positive law, discussed in C above. All of the Church's law rests on this foundation and shares in its sacred character. Moreover, since the common life of the Church is directed toward the great good of completing Jesus' work, the obligation to obey the Church's law is rooted not only in fairness but also in the good of religion.

3. **The act of faith itself is the baptismal commitment by which one shares in the life of the Church as community. This baptismal commitment, and nothing less, grounds the duty to obey Church law** (see DS 1621/864). **Deliberate disobedience is therefore a sin against faith.**

By way of the divine precepts and their act of faith, Christians are in a relationship of cooperation with the redemptive work of God. In this work, God has authority because decisions are necessary which only he can make. Divine authority was given to Jesus, and he transmitted it to the apostles, led by Peter, and their successors. Therefore, members of the Church are unreasonable and impious if they do not obey ecclesiastical authority.

4. Hence, although the part of the Church's law which regulates her common life by authoritative decision has only the moral force of the authority from which it comes, this authority is different in kind from that of any other society. The Church's law can be changed by the same authority which makes it, but while it is in force the members of the Church should treat it with reverence.

5. **It is unlikely that the laws of the Church will be defective by requiring anything immoral or issuing from an abuse of authority.** Several factors militate against this: the nature of the Church, the subject matter of her laws, the character of those who make them, and the care with which they are made. The likelihood of defect is further reduced in the case of laws issued by the pope's authority. Moreover, even if there were a substantial defect in the procedure by which a Church law was made and issued, one subject to the law could hardly be morally certain of this. For all practical purposes, therefore, the possibility of moral defectiveness, which sometimes undercuts the authority of the laws of other human societies, can be discounted in the case of the law of the universal Church.

6. **Like similar law in other societies, however, the Church's law, which is made by authoritative decisions and could be changed by them, has limits in its application.** Church laws can lose their point and fall into general disuse. Conflicts of duties can demand that an individual not fulfill some requirement of the Church's law. And, within the very narrow limits of its legitimate use, epikeia applies to Church law.

7. Still, it should not be assumed too quickly that any of these conditions is fulfilled. Certain cases in which laws can be considered inapplicable are discussed in treatises on canon law; in other cases, dispensations can be obtained from the

proper authority. It is a very common but grave abuse of epikeia to substitute one's own judgment for the law of the Church. Epikeia is properly used only when one is morally certain that the very authorities who made a law would wish its letter set aside so that the common good which is its spirit might be better served (see *S.t.*, 1–2, q. 96, a. 6, ad 2). Moreover, one ought not to suppose that a law is a dead letter merely because it is widely violated. Here only the practice of those who are most experienced, conscientious, and holy is a safe guide.

8. One widespread confusion among Catholics is failure to distinguish between the Church's moral teaching and her law. Moreover, many take seriously neither the duty to form their consciences by the Church's moral teaching nor the duty to obey the Church's law. In this situation, exact obedience to the Church's law is especially important; any disobedience is likely to be taken by some as an example and justification not only for contempt toward the Church's law but also for dissent from her teaching.

There are several reasons why priests ought to be especially conscientious in observing Church law. First, compliance with the law maintains unity among the clergy and solidarity with the bishop; noncompliance is divisive. Division seriously impedes the work of the Church. Second, compliance (except in the rare case in which a law truly is inapplicable) serves the people; noncompliance arrogantly imposes upon them personal judgments instead of the proper authority of the Church. Third, compliance sets a good example of obedience; noncompliance sets a bad example of self-will.

These points can be illustrated by the many arbitrary, usually minor, and seemingly insignificant variations in the liturgy one encounters today. Such variations lead to disagreements, irritation, and uncooperativeness among priests. Virtually all of them are ill-considered, and they often compel the faithful to tolerate things they rightly find repugnant. Finally, an easygoing approach to the liturgy detracts from its sacred character, while at the same time suggesting that Christians may do as they please in very important matters.

This last suggestion is applied by some of the faithful to moral issues. There is a difference between canon law and moral norms, but not all members of the Church understand this difference.

Summary

In one sense, authority is competence to make judgments which reasonable persons of lesser competence will accept as probably or certainly true. In another sense, it is a social capacity to give directions which generate a moral duty to obey; this is the authority of law. (Note, however, that the authority of law is not the only source of a duty to carry out another's wishes. Such a duty also arises in other relationships ranging from marriage to the freely contracted relationship of employee to employer.)

Sometimes, as in the case of criminal law, the directions of authorities call attention to already-existing moral obligations. Here the backing of an obligation by authority generates an additional moral duty—to obey. In other cases, authorities direct something which would not otherwise be a moral obligation. Here the duty to obey is the only moral duty.

There are two distinct bases for the duty to obey. First, those in a community who are in a better position to make decisions have a duty to do so, while the others have a duty to act upon their decisions. Second, in societies created by a common commitment, members are obliged by their commitment to cooperate for the sake of goods, and fairness requires that each do his or her share. In neither case, however, is the duty to obey absolute. If one is convinced that what authority directs cannot be done without wrongdoing, one should not obey.

Generally it is clear how integral human fulfillment itself requires obedience to divine precepts, but in the case of certain norms revelation is required. These latter make up what is called "divine positive law." Here the basis for obedience lies in the human good of religion. Interpersonal harmony of any kind always involves compliance with the wishes of others, and this is no less true of our relationship with God. Furthermore, awareness of our radical and unique dependence on God underlines the fact that only he is in a position to make certain decisions for the life we share with him—the decisions which constitute divine positive law.

The law of civil society can be divided in various ways. (Many societies besides civil societies also make laws in the sense considered here, though they call them by other names such as "policies" or "rules.") Constitutional law articulates the common and accepted plan by which a community exists. Civil law regulates private affairs according to the public purpose of mutual justice and common peace. Criminal law shapes a public response to certain acts which would be immoral even if they were not illegal. Regulatory law directs the common life of the community at large, especially the government and its agencies.

The members of a civil society have a nonabsolute moral duty to obey purely regulative laws to the extent the society is truly a community. However, the duty to obey such laws can be qualified in two ways: first, if a law lacks authority due to some defect (for example, it requires something inconsistent with the seventh or eighth mode of responsibility) or in the way it was arrived at; second, if a law is inapplicable in a particular case. Lacking moral certitude that a law is without moral authority or is inapplicable, however, an upright person will obey it. The too-ready resort to what is called "epikeia" is an abuse; violating the letter of the law to preserve its spirit is only justified if one can say sincerely that the lawmaking authority would want one to make this exception (not just consider it reasonable) if it knew the circumstances.

The Church's teaching authority must be distinguished from its governing authority. The former is the capacity of the apostles and their successors to make judgments in matters of faith and morals. The latter is the capacity of these same persons, acting as pastors of the Church, to direct all of her members in their common life. When a Catholic violates a moral norm taught by the Church, the act is wrong not as disobedient but because it is at odds with a moral truth and the human good this truth represents. When a Catholic violates a Church law, the act is wrong because it is disobedient. The Church's teaching authority cannot change what it teaches, but the Church's pastoral authority can alter the directions it gives, except insofar as these directions themselves express moral truth or divine positive law.

In general, what has been said about the duty to obey the laws of civil societies applies also to the laws of the Church. However, the Church's constitutional law is divine positive law; all Church law rests on this foundation and shares its sacred character. Moreover, the act of faith is the baptismal commitment by which one shares in the life of the Church; this baptismal commitment grounds the duty to obey the Church's law, and deliberate disobedience is thus a sin against faith. Considering the source of Church laws, their subject matter, and the care with which they are made, it is hardly likely that they will be defective by requiring anything immoral or issuing from an abuse of authority. Nor should it be assumed too quickly that the conditions are fulfilled which might justify setting aside a law of the Church as inapplicable—for example, by using epikeia.

Notes

1. On the general notion of authority, see John Finnis, *Natural Law and Natural Rights* (Oxford: Clarendon Press, 1980), 231–37.

2. On authority, see Yves Simon's work, for instance, *Philosophy of Democratic Government* (Chicago: University of Chicago Press, 1951), 144–94.

3. Lon L. Fuller, *The Morality of Law*, rev. ed. (New Haven: Yale University Press, 1969), reaches a concept of law (145–51) including its distinction from managerial direction (207–13) remarkably similar to the basically Thomistic theory stated here, although Fuller begins his study from the phenomena of contemporary Anglo-American legality, rather than from the different data and metaphysical-theological framework of Thomas.

4. St. Thomas Aquinas, *Summa theologiae*, 1–2, q. 108, a. 2, seems to limit the positive precepts of the new law to those pertaining to the sacraments. Perhaps Thomas thought the other matters I mention pertain to the sacraments reductively by pertaining to baptism, confirmation, and orders. Or perhaps he was thinking only of precepts fulfilled by individuals individually, not the precepts of Jesus which govern the life and work of the Church as a whole.

5. *S.t.*, 1–2, q. 107, a. 4; and in general qq. 98–108.

6. See John XXIII, *Pacem in terris*, 55 AAS (1963) 269–71; *The Papal Encyclicals*, 270.46–52, for a compact magisterial treatment of the authority of political societies, including its moral foundation by which it comes from God, its ground in and limitation by the common good, and its nonabsolute character.

7. St. Thomas distinguishes two ways in which positive laws are derived from natural law: *S.t.*, 1–2, q. 95, a. 2. Some are derived as conclusions which follow necessarily from principles; others by a specifying choice between open possibilities. Although the close relationship of law to moral norm in certain cases (for example, criminal law) cannot be ignored, this distinction is not used as a principle of organizing the present analysis, because even the most obvious moral requirements for life in society become legal provisions in a particular system only by determination through a specifying choice or choices which establish the legal offense. See Finnis, op. cit., 281–89 and 294–96.

8. At this point one must take a position on the difficult question of the role of consent of the governed in the constitution of civil society. For a more extensive articulation of the view proposed here, see Germain Grisez and Joseph M. Boyle, Jr., *Life and Death with Liberty and Justice: A Contribution to the Euthanasia Debate* (Notre Dame and London: University of Notre Dame Press, 1979), 25–46. For a different view, see Finnis, op. cit., 245–52. To be realistic, any consent theory must recognize that even insofar as it is just the same government is different things to different people: a quasi-parent to the incompetent, a host to aliens, a moral community defending itself as best it can against immoral members who ought to consent but refuse to do so, and a community of free persons to its members who rightly consent to its constitution and cooperate in the common life it organizes for the sake of liberty and justice for all.

9. In the development of Anglo-American common law, knowledge of what acts are objectively

wrong always was presupposed. (For a brief introduction to common law and a helpful bibliography: Peter Stein, "Law, Common," *Dictionary of the History of Ideas*, 2:691–96.) The legal development—which proceeded case by case—did not concern what is right and wrong, but only how the community would deal with wrongful acts. Because of its moral foundations, the common law did not punish as crimes acts lacking the conditions for moral imputability—malicious choice and sufficient reflection. However, in criminal codes of many societies one finds prohibitions of certain kinds of acts which, the prohibition apart, would not be immoral. On my analysis, such laws belong to the purely regulative type, treated in question E. Thus, "criminal law" in the present analysis does not mean exactly the same thing as it does in the descriptive language of lawyers, for whom criminal law simply means what is in the criminal code.

10. Proponents of natural law often argue that an unjust positive law is no law at all. In one sense this is surely true, but in another not. On this point, see Finnis, op. cit., 354–66, esp. 361–62, 367, for a discussion of collateral sources of obligation to obey unjust laws. See also *S.t.*, 1–2, q. 96, a. 4.

11. See Lawrence J. Riley, *The History, Nature, and Use of Epikeia in Moral Theology* (Washington, D.C.: Catholic University of America Press, 1948), 276–85.

12. For a concise general introduction to canon law, see J. M. Buckley, "Canon Law," *New Catholic Encyclopedia*, 3:29–34. A fuller treatment of Church law in the context of a general theology of law: Jean-Marie Aubert, *Loi de Dieu, Lois des Hommes* (Tournai: Desclée, 1964), 177–234. A clear treatment of the distinction between the Church's teaching and law: Alvaro del Portillo, *Faithful and Laity in the Church: The Bases of Their Legal Status*, trans. Leo Hickey (Shannon, Ireland: Ecclesia Press, 1973), 56–60. A brief theological treatment of the obligation of obedience to bishops, including the universal law of the Church: Joseph Lécuyer, C.S.Sp., "Obedience to the Bishop," in Karl Rahner, S.J., et al., *Obedience and the Church* (Washington: Corpus Books, 1968), 57–74.

CHAPTER TWELVE

MORAL JUDGMENT
IN PROBLEMATIC SITUATIONS

Introduction

This chapter considers cases of several kinds in which there is a special difficulty in arriving at a judgment of conscience. Some involve doubts of fact, while others concern difficulties in applying moral principles to facts.

Question A: What should be the objective of reflection by those with doubts of conscience?

1. Those who confidently think they know what is right should act accordingly (see 3-B). Sometimes, though, one is unsure what to do—conscience is doubtful. In such cases, one should try to resolve the doubt. A person willing to proceed while in doubt about what is right—assuming the doubt could be resolved with reasonable effort—is willing to do what is wrong; and one who is willing to do wrong does wrong (see Rom 14.23; *S.t.*, 1–2, q. 19, aa. 3–6).

2. For people with doubts of conscience, the objective of moral reflection should be to discover what is truly the right thing to do. If, having made a reasonable effort, one still cannot be sure what that is, one may consider right that which seems most likely to be so. **It is never allowable to act in doubt which might be overcome by reasonable effort.** But people may follow their best judgment, though aware it could be mistaken, provided they have made every reasonable effort to find out what is right. **When uncertain, an upright person will be ready and eager to find a more solid basis for judgment.**

3. Because doubts of conscience are of diverse sorts, efforts to resolve them must be similarly diverse. Some doubts arise because of uncertainty about facts—what was, is, or will be the case. Others arise because one is unsure what the relevant moral norm is. Sometimes a norm comes to mind or is proposed by somebody else, but one is not sure it is adequate to the act one is considering (see *S.t.*, 1–2, q. 100, a. 8). Still other doubts arise because there seem to be conflicting moral requirements.

4. In all the cases which follow, it is assumed that the person desires to know what is right and to do it, has been instructed in the Church's moral teaching, is willing to conform to it, has tried to resolve the doubt by direct personal

reflection, and has failed in that effort. Thus deliberation has reached the point where a definite proposal for choice is being considered, and one has some reason to hesitate about its moral acceptability.

5. People who do not desire to do what is right, are not instructed in the Church's moral teaching, or are not willing to conform to this teaching sometimes say or are told that they have doubts of conscience. Although the problem presented by such claims is real and important, it is not considered in this chapter; instead it will be treated in chapters twenty-three, thirty-five, and thirty-six.

Question B: How can one resolve doubts of conscience which arise because of uncertainty about relevant facts?

1. At times doubts of fact lead to difficulties in applying rules of positive law, which have moral force only insofar as they specify the duty to obey law. The law itself sometimes provides for ways of settling such doubts; while at other times they can be obviated by a procedure of legal inquiry or by obtaining a dispensation from the law.

2. **If a doubt of fact must be resolved without help from the law itself, one may resort to reasonable presumptions.** This method is based on a general consideration of fairness: No one can be expected to do more to abide by the law than reasonable, law-abiding people do. Hence, one may resolve doubts of fact by any judgment of probability which such persons would accept.

3. Laws are not made to immobilize people but to guide common life. If doubts of fact are not readily resolved, however, law does tend to immobilize rather than help people cooperate fruitfully. Therefore, reasonable, law-abiding people who must resolve doubts of fact without the help of the law itself proceed on whatever judgment of fact seems probable.

4. Sometimes, however, a doubt of fact leads to difficulty in applying a specific moral norm.

5. In some cases, uncertainty about matters of fact leads to doubt about the gravity of an act recognized to be immoral. Perhaps one does something spiteful, in doubt about how much damage the act will do. Or one takes a pill to prevent birth, not knowing whether it works by abortion. When the doubtful fact bears on settling an issue of this sort, one should assume that the true state of affairs is that which renders the act more seriously wrong. For a person who purposely does what might destroy, damage, or impede a particular human good is willing actually to do so; and, morally speaking, anyone who is willing to do a wrong does that wrong. **In general, a person who is willing to do what is wrong and is uncertain because of a doubt of fact how grave that wrong will be, is willing to do the more serious wrong.**

6. In other cases where a doubt of fact leads to difficulty in applying a specific moral norm, the issue is whether any of the modes of responsibility will be violated if one acts in that state of doubt. In such cases, one can reach a judgment of conscience despite lack of certainty about the facts. **The state of doubt itself is a matter of fact to be considered together with other relevant facts of the situation to which moral norms must be applied.**

7. For instance, if one is not sure whether a side effect which one usually ought not to accept will occur, the doubt of fact should be resolved in the affirmative—expect the worst—if resolving it in the negative would be unfair, unfaithful, or against any other mode. Normally, for example, one should assume that drunken driving will lead to someone's injury or death; almost never should one assume that the bad side effects will be avoided. The reason is that very seldom can one take such risks with the well-being of others without being grossly unfair to them.

8. Still, a level of doubt about the safety of driving which normally would indicate that one ought not to drive might be accepted without violating any of the modes—for example, if there is no other way to save someone's life. In such a case, reasonable persons would wish others to take some unusual risk on their own behalf or on behalf of those they love, and so in fairness would approve acting with a certain level of doubt.

Question C: How can one resolve doubts of conscience which arise because of uncertainty about relevant norms?

1. Doubts of conscience which arise because of uncertainty about relevant norms are of two kinds: (1) whether a norm exists; (2) whether a norm which comes to mind is true and adequate to the proposal about which one is deliberating.

2. Supposing the norm, if any, is a rule of positive law, whether it exists is a question of fact, and whether it is relevant to the proposal under consideration is a question of legal interpretation. These questions should be distinguished from whether a law is morally defective and whether it is applicable. The latter are not under consideration here. (Questions of applicability were treated in 11-E.)

3. **Every system of positive law provides some way of determining whether rules of law exist and are relevant to one's actions.** These means take priority in settling such questions. When the procedures provided by law do not settle questions about the existence and relevance of rules of law, one may follow the axiom which allows liberty. One's moral duty is to obey laws, not anything and everything which might be a law; thus, a rule of law which is doubtful does not bind one to obedience.

4. When, however, there is a preponderance of expert opinion that a norm exists and is relevant, the rule of law is not truly doubtful. Rather, it is probable. The contrary opinion, even if held by some who are competent, is not truly probable, only plausible but improbable. The reason is that the questions at issue are suited to expert observation and interpretation. In such matters, the nonexpert should accept as correct the preponderance of competent opinion.

5. **If the norm in question is not a rule of law but a specific moral norm, doubt can arise for a Catholic only in the absence of clear Church teaching on the matter under consideration.** If, lacking clear Church teaching, there is a consensus of theologians, one should be guided by it, for when theologians agree their reflection very likely articulates true moral norms in the light of faith. If, however, faithful theologians disagree, one reasonably disregards all theological

opinions, for as a body they provide no ground for assuming that one or another of the disagreeing opinions is true.

6. Lacking both clear Church teaching and a consensus of theologians, Catholics doubtful about the truth and adequacy of a moral norm should ask themselves whether or not they would have any responsibility to do the act if it is permissible. If the answer is no, an upright person will instead choose to do something which is certainly good.

7. **But if the answer is yes (one should do the act if it is permissible), then one should accept the judgment—it is permissible or it is not permissible—which seems more likely true.** Those unable to make a judgment for themselves should act on the advice of others whom they trust: children on the judgment of their parents, simple souls on the judgment of their confessors, and so forth.

Question D: How is the position taken in the preceding question related to probabilism?

1. The way of resolving doubts about rules of positive law proposed above is what has been called "equiprobabilism." If the preponderance of expert opinion is that one is bound by a rule of positive law, one is bound. But if there is no discernible preponderance of opinion that one is bound—that is, if opinion seems equal on both sides of the question or if the preponderance of opinion is that one is not bound—one is not bound.

2. **The way of resolving doubts about moral norms, proposed in question C, is analogous to what has been called "probabiliorism," but it also differs significantly from the probabiliorism of classical moral theology.**[1] To see why, one must understand probabilism in its context.

3. As was explained (in 1-D), in the legalistic perspective of classical moral theology, moral norms were regarded as if they were rules of positive law rather than normative truths. The magisterium of the Church was thought of as a governmental authority setting outer limits to the liberty of the faithful. Where the magisterium set no clear and definite boundary, both confessors and penitents often were perplexed when confronted with diverse theological opinions. It became urgent to determine how one in doubt about what the moral law requires should select an opinion to follow. Different systems were proposed in the latter part of the seventeenth century.

4. According to one view, "laxism," a person might consistently adopt the most permissive and least well-grounded theological opinions. The Holy See rejected this approach in 1679 (see DS 2101–67/1151–1216). The next year the Holy See allowed two widely supported views to stand without definitely embracing either (see DS 2175–77/1219). According to one, called "probabilism," a solidly probable permissive theological opinion could be followed in practice; according to the other, called "probabiliorism," only a permissive opinion more likely to be true than a more restrictive alternative might safely be followed. Another view, called "tutiorism" or "rigorism," held that the strictest opinion was the only safe one to follow; it was rejected by the Holy See in 1690 (see DS 2303/1293).

It is important to keep in mind the conditions under which probabilism and probabiliorism were approved. Moral theologians were regarded as if they were appellate courts, and their opinions as if they were legal decisions. But no moral opinion had the slightest ground at all if it conflicted with a clear decision made by the supreme authority—the Holy See.

This view of moral teaching and this role for the moral theologian did not exist before the impact of rationalism. In St. Thomas, for example, one finds a much less legalistic conception of moral judgment.[2]

5. This entire debate presupposed a legalistic focus on the possible conflict between the obligatory demands of law and the desire of those subject to law to enjoy the liberty to do as they please. Proponents of various positions often treated doubts about positive law and doubts about moral norms without distinction, as if they presented the same problem. Obligation was thought to characterize isolated acts in virtue of their falling under norms. The acts were considered one by one, in abstraction from reflection upon a person's overall responsibility to live a good life.

6. Probabilism eventually became the dominant method in classical moral theology. The probabilists defined "probable" in such a way that incompatible opinions could both be probable—that is, plausible and competently defended. Probabilism was applied indiscriminately to settling doubts about rules of positive law and norms of morality alike. A familiar slogan sums up the probabilists' legalistic view: *A doubtful law does not bind.*

7. The way of resolving doubts about moral norms (proposed in C) is analogous to probabiliorism in three respects. First, the impact on theological opinion is the same, insofar as both approaches set aside theological opinions which articulate norms unless there is a definite teaching of the Church or a solid theological consensus in favor of one position. Second, both probabiliorism and the present approach discourage the arbitrary multiplication of supposed obligations which might well not be true moral responsibilities. This was especially important in a legalistic context, when many Catholics simply trusted their confessors to define their moral responsibilities. It kept people from being completely smothered by paternalism and so left them room to mature in Christian responsibility. Third, both probabiliorism and the present approach differ from probabilism by using the likelihood of truth as a criterion for resolving doubts of conscience.

8. Still, the position proposed here differs fundamentally from probabiliorism. **In the present view, seeking the minimal limits of strict obligation—reflected in such a question as, "How far can I go without committing a mortal sin?"—is not the appropriate context for resolving doubts of conscience. Instead, the correct context is the effort to discern moral truth as a guide for whatever choice one will make.**

9. A person with doubts of conscience should consider the possibilities available for choice in the light of his or her existing commitments and an overall orientation toward the basic human goods. The question is not, "Am I bound by a law or free to do as I please?" but, "What, all things considered, is the right way for me to act?" If one norm does not determine conscience, some other will. If there is no adequate reason for thinking oneself subject to one responsibility, it

remains to take account of other responsibilities—at least, the general responsibility to seek and pursue human good in ways consistent with integral human fulfillment.

10. Hence, people with doubtful consciences should not proceed on the legalistic assumption that a doubtful law leaves one free to do as one pleases. Rather, they should proceed on the nonlegalistic assumption that one ought to act in pursuit of human goods in ways which seem appropriate, even though one is aware of possible contrary responsibilities whose reality cannot be ascertained.

11. Thus, persons who resolve a doubt by concluding that a possible moral norm need not prevail are not left free simply to do as they please. Rather, they find themselves directed by some other norm to choose as they had feared it might be wrong to do. For example, having rightly set aside the possibility that it would be wrong to accept a certain job, one accepts it—as a way of fulfilling the responsibility to support oneself and others, as a way of doing something worthwhile in itself, or for some other upright reason.

Probabilism has value in that it is the more reasonable solution to the precise question it addresses. One who confronts a just legal system and wishes to obey it must try to find out what it requires; one must submit when its requirements are clear, but one cannot submit when it sets out no clear and definite requirement. In practice, as long as the Church's moral teaching was generally regarded as if it were a system of law—and for those who continue to regard it as such, to the extent that and for as long as they do—probabilism offers a lifesaving limit to moral obligation.

If the Church had not allowed probabilism, the faithful would either have been paralyzed by irresolvable doubts of conscience whenever unsettled moral issues arose or would have been more and more suffocated by restrictive norms proposed by theologians. For without probabilism, whenever there was a good reason for supposing oneself obligated, one would be obligated, and there is good reason for supposing oneself to be obligated whenever some expert thinks so. Probabilism allowed one to take the less restrictive alternative: Expert opinions do not of themselves generate obligations unless they are opposed by no solidly probable opinion in favor of liberty.

The limits of probabilism are in its underlying assumption that morality is simply a system of law. True laws are necessary, and there are moral grounds for obeying them. But morality itself can be identified with law only by being limited to the social-convention level of the development of conscience.

In reality, the Church did not restrict morality to the legalistic system. Although "moral" was restricted to the narrow boundaries of the minimal, common requirements of Christian life, the Church continued to propose the fullness of Christian morality without calling it "moral"; instead it was called "ascetical," "spiritual," and so on. Limiting the legalistic moral system left room for souls who satisfied minimum requirements to proceed toward Christian perfection without a straitjacket of law.

The problem of resolving doubts of conscience takes on a different character when one begins to think about it outside a legalistic framework—in other words, on the level of moral truth rather than social convention. On the level of moral truth, one wants to live in the truth and toward fulfillment; the committed Christian wishes to live toward God and to share in the redemptive work of Jesus. Hence, when one's conscience is unsettled, one asks which judgment is more likely true.

This position is not merely a stricter alternative to probabilism. What is more likely true is determined by an honest appraisal of the available sources of moral knowledge; the judgment more likely true sometimes will seem more restrictive, sometimes less so. However, for the mature, good person there is no free (that is, nonmoral) area; every act of one's life is morally significant. One's act of faith is a responsible commitment. Personal vocational commitments are made to carry out faith in one's life. Fresh questions of commitment are settled by how well a new commitment comports with one's already-articulated personal vocation. Finally, all particular questions are settled by reference to one's personal vocational commitments.

Even so, doubts of conscience still arise. If one cannot think them through for oneself in the light of faith, one seeks counsel. But one looks to one's pastors for enlightenment about the way of Jesus, not for legal norms at the level of social convention. Concretely, one is interested in finding the implications of divinely revealed truth and human wisdom for one's life. Therefore, one would like intrinsic grounds for considering one's judgment correct. If one cannot understand the intrinsic grounds, one nevertheless trusts the Church's teaching authority because it is endowed with an unfailing gift of truth, not as if it had legislative authority in moral matters.

Question E: How can one resolve a doubt of conscience which arises from the appearance of conflicting responsibilities?

1. **Since the first principle of morality is one and the various modes of responsibility are negative, there can be no conflict at the level of moral principles.** Faced with an apparent conflict of responsibilities, one should first consider the facts and the relevant norms, to see whether there has been an error in identifying possibilities or in applying moral principles to arrive at specific norms. Usually, apparent conflicts are cleared up by careful reflection.

2. If one has mistakenly assumed a false norm, conflict is likely, and it cannot be resolved until the false norm is corrected. For example, if attaining certain goods or avoiding certain harms is taken to be an unconditional responsibility, there can seem to be a conflict with a norm derived from the eighth mode of responsibility. Excessive attachment to certain goods and failure to rely on divine providence often lead people to think they must do things which are always wrong. In such cases, proportionalism is often invoked to rationalize the wrongdoing.

3. If a person accepts a sinful commitment—for example, a promise to do something wrong—as normative, conflict cannot be resolved until the sinful commitment is set aside. Conflicts will also arise if a person takes received norms simplistically: for example, by reading Scripture without sound, traditional interpretation. Similarly, conflict is inevitable if one erroneously absolutizes rules of conventional morality, etiquette, or law.

Perplexity is the condition of a conscience doubtful about a specific question: Which of these two possibilities, both of which seem wrong, is right? An example is the situation of a child who thinks it wrong to tell on other children and also thinks it obligatory to inform adults that another child is doing something very dangerous, such as playing with matches and gasoline. Since the principles of morality reduce to an ultimate unity, incompatibility between two true moral judgments is not a possible source of perplexity. However, the complexity of some moral issues in the fallen human condition and the limits of moral insight lead to perplexity as a subjective experience.

The experience of perplexity often indicates that one has acted immorally and in doing so created a situation within which no morally good possibilities can be chosen. In such cases, the perplexed individual can resolve the problem only by repenting the immoral act which is at its basis. However, the experience of perplexity also can arise for individuals who are personally upright but are caught within the somewhat false demands of a conventional morality, which has been adapted to the fallen human condition. The child in the example is perplexed because of the false absoluteness which children give to the norm forbidding telling on one another.

4. If no false norm has been assumed, the appearance of conflicting responsibilities arises from the fact that nonabsolute norms have not been sufficiently specified. There are different kinds of cases. In one sort, two definite responsibilities arising from some law or social role—duties in a strict sense—make incompatible demands: They require one, say, to be in two places at the same time. In another sort, a definite responsibility arising from law or one's social role conflicts, not with another duty in the strict sense, but with some other perceived moral responsibility.

5. When duties in the strict sense conflict, one must bear in mind that fairness is the moral ground of both definite responsibilities. One's task is therefore to formulate a more specific norm which resolves the conflict in accord with fairness. Sometimes the best one can do is simply to fulfill one or the other of the conflicting duties, choosing between them on the basis of inclination or chance.

6. Similarly, when a duty requires a choice contrary to what a nonabsolute norm would indicate if the requirement of duty did not exist, one must resolve the conflict by formulating a more specified norm in accord with fairness. For example, a person who ought to go to work but who stops to help someone desperately in need of help, even though there is no specific duty to render such help, acts rightly if he or she judges impartially—if, that is, any reasonable and impartial person affected by the behavior would approve what is done. It is necessary to bear in mind in such a case that one's duties in the strict sense also serve the needs of others and cannot usually be set aside without partiality. If there is doubt, one ought to fulfill one's definite responsibilities rather than substitute other good works.

7. **When duties would require one to do something inconsistent with an absolute norm, the latter prevails.** For example, St. Thomas More could not fulfill his family responsibilities without taking what he believed to be a false oath. He rightly judged that, despite the consequences for his family, he should not take the oath. Such cases involve no true conflict of duties, for duty can never require a person to do what is morally evil.

In practice, many conflicts of duties can be avoided by being careful not to overcommit oneself (the second mode of responsibility) and by planning one's schedule. Incipient conflicts of duties can be forestalled by arranging to fulfill one of them at another time or by another means—for instance, through someone else's help. Most laws which require the regular fulfillment of a duty at a precise time—Sunday Mass attendance, voting, participation in an academic exercise—carry at least implicit exception clauses. Moreover, in cases of conflict one often can solve the problem by obtaining a permission or dispensation.

Still, there remain certain conflicts. For example, a professor might have a conflict between a professional duty to meet his or her classes, which cannot be taken over by someone else or made up, and a family duty to participate in the funeral of a parent, which would require a day's absence. (The latter, it is to be noted, is a definite duty, for although it is not prescribed by law, it does pertain to one's role in the family.) If there were no conflict, it would be wrong to omit either act. Because it is impossible to do both, only one can be morally required.

In cases of this sort, one must be careful not to act with partiality. To avoid unfairness, one must ask oneself how one's omission of either duty would affect everyone involved, and one must try to put oneself in the place of the various persons or sorts of persons affected. Having done this, one possibility is likely to be identifiable as the proper duty to fulfill. If not, one may blamelessly omit either duty.

Question F: How can one resolve a doubt of conscience which arises when one seems obliged to do an act of a kind which is always wrong?

1. As has been explained, a duty must be left unfulfilled if its fulfillment would require doing something forbidden by a norm derived from the eighth mode of responsibility. The same is true if any other norm seems to require an act excluded by an absolute norm. By definition, nonabsolute norms yield to absolute ones.

2. Today, many try to override norms derived from the eighth mode. They argue, for instance, that the choice to kill an unwanted child is sometimes justified as a lesser evil. This is an example of the proportionalism criticized in chapter six; what was shown there need not be repeated here.

3. In many cases, apparent conflicts are removed when the morally right course, previously ignored because it is unappealing, is accepted as a practical possibility. For example, persons who have divorced and remarried need not really choose between committing adultery and renouncing their responsibilities to their second family. They can choose instead to live together in celibacy, in accord with the moral truth that they have no marital rights but do have familial responsibilities.[3]

At other times a certain creativity would resolve apparent conflicts. Thus, a person seemingly compelled either to lie or violate a serious obligation of secrecy might simply refuse to answer questions, while pointing out that the refusal was a matter of policy (for example, in the case of the confessional) and could not be taken as indicating anything for or against the proposition about which questions were being asked.

4. In other cases, an apparent conflict of responsibilities involving the eighth mode can be dissolved by clarifying how relevant norms apply to the choices under consideration. It is virtually impossible to do anything without bringing about some humanly bad effects, and these can often be foreseen. But, as was explained (in 9-F), there is a difference between what one brings about as a chosen means to one's end and what one brings about as a freely accepted side effect of carrying out one's choice. **The eighth mode of responsibility precludes only a**

choice to destroy, damage, or impede a human good. It does not rule out accepting foreseen side effects which it would be wrong to choose. Hence, such side effects may be accepted, unless some other mode of responsibility requires the contrary.

Even the best acts bring about some bad effects, at least indirectly. For example, preaching the gospel brings about the effects of belief and disbelief, and so leads to division, which ultimately leads to conflict and persecution. Going for an automobile ride may add to the traffic death toll and certainly adds to pollution (which causes various diseases) while using up an energy resource, and so forth. Even the most innocent acts use time and energy which thereby are not available for service to various human goods. Thus, in an indirect way, an hour's meditation contributes to the misery of those whom an hour's labor could have helped.

This situation is not a consequence of our fallen human condition, nor is it essentially a result of our finitude.[4] Even God could not create without bringing about foreseen bad consequences; he knew that freedom could and would be abused. His proposal, however, was not that creatures should sin, but that they should be able to love freely. He accepted sin as an unwanted side effect of the creaturely freedom by which love was refused (see *S.c.g.*, 3, 71).

According to the seventh and eighth modes of responsibility, it is wrong to choose to destroy, damage, or impede any instance of an intelligible human good. One is tempted to make such choices either out of a nonrational hostility or out of a nonrational preference for some good which is to be realized through the act chosen. To bring about humanly bad effects out of such nonrational motives always is wrong.

But there are other modes of responsibility. The fifth, for instance, is concerned with fairness. If a gardener uses a poison to protect a crop with a possible side effect of poisoning a neighbor's children, the acceptance of the possible ill effect probably is unfair. The gardener would object if someone took such a risk with his or her children. Likewise, an upright person will not accept foreseen bad effects to a real good in acting for a merely apparent one, in violation of the sixth mode of responsibility, although such bad effects normally are no part of one's proposal.

Therefore, the problem of when one may act in a way which one foresees will have humanly bad effects can be solved only by considering all of the intelligible features of that about which one is deliberating, referring to all the modes of responsibility, and articulating a norm for the act under consideration. The act will be right if and only if in choosing it one violates none of the modes of responsibility.

Thus, if one's proposal is to destroy, damage, or impede any of the basic human goods, the act will be excluded by the seventh or eighth mode of responsibility. If one is inclined to accept the bad effects out of partiality and would not accept them otherwise, one violates the fifth mode. If the bad effects are consequent on an omission to which one is inclined out of laziness, one violates the first mode. And so forth. If the foreseen bad effects are accepted without violating any mode of responsibility, one simply accepts them as incidental to the good one is doing. One does not need any reason for so accepting them, except the reason provided by the intelligible goodness of that for which one acts.

5. There might appear to be a conflict of responsibilities involving the eighth mode when, for example, one must choose between removing a nonviable ectopic embryo and allowing the pregnancy to continue, with a definite threat to the mother's life and little hope for the embryonic child's survival. In choosing to remove the ectopic embryo, however, one need not be choosing to kill it, in

violation of the eighth mode of responsibility. The embryo's death is not a means and is in no way helpful to solving the problem. Rather, one can make this choice—to remove the ectopic embryo—simply to remove its threat to the mother's life, accepting the embryonic child's certain death only as an inevitable side effect.

6. Apparent conflicts of this sort arise because acts conventionally classified in one way (for example, as killing an attacker) must be morally classified in another way (for example, as stopping a violent attack) (see *S.t.*, 1–2, q. 1, a. 3; q. 18, a. 5). The behavior involved in bringing about another's death in self-defense is outwardly similar to that involved in morally impermissible acts in which one chooses to kill and carries out the choice. However, one who brings about another's death in self-defense need not be choosing to kill in violation of the eighth mode of responsibility (cf. *S.t.*, 2–2, q. 64, a. 7). If there is no choice to kill, the morality of what is done depends upon fairness and other modes of responsibility. One's act will be right if one violates no mode of responsibility.

The Catholic teaching condemning all direct killing of the innocent certainly excludes any choice to kill them. There also is a received teaching condemning direct abortion, and "direct abortion" is taken to mean the expulsion of a nonviable fetus otherwise than as a side effect of some other legitimate act. Usually direct abortion has been considered a species of direct killing of the innocent. While I do not wish to deal with specific normative problems here, I admit that my analysis points to the permissibility of certain operations which classical moralists would have excluded. I do not think this position is in significant conflict with received Catholic teaching.[5] However, if my theory and the Church's teaching should in a particular case lead to inconsistent conclusions, I would follow and urge others to follow the Church's teaching rather than my theory. If the Church's teaching is open to legitimate refinement in the details of its application, the refinement must be completed by those who exercise teaching authority in the Church.

7. **Since problems of this sort are dissolved by analyzing the human act more closely and applying norms to it, it is misleading to formulate the solution in language suggesting that justifiable exceptions are being made to absolute moral norms.** For instance, the moral rightness of removing an ectopic embryo and performing certain other operations which result in the death of the unborn should not be summarized by saying: It is wrong to kill the unborn except when the mother's life is at stake. To choose to kill is always wrong, and choosing anything else while freely accepting another person's death usually violates one of the modes, especially fairness. But sometimes it is morally right to choose to do good and accept bad side effects.

8. Classical moral theology dealt with this sort of problem by the so-called principle of double effect.[6] Double effect is not a normative principle but a somewhat cumbersome attempt at clarifying what one is morally responsible for in freely accepting side effects which it would be wrong to choose.

9. In most formulations of double effect, one stated condition is that there be a proportionate reason for accepting the bad side effect. Some proportionalists maintain that this shows that classical moral theology was committed to proportionalism. If so, however, the classical moralists would not have required a double

effect analysis. They did so because in fact they held that certain things are always wrong, regardless of ulterior good consequences.

When the classical moralists required a "proportionate reason" for freely accepting bad side effects, they implied that the good sought and the evil accepted could be rendered commensurate. They did not say how this might be done. But the commensuration they required can be explained without admitting the commensuration of premoral goods and bads the proportionalist requires. For one can say that the reason for accepting bad side effects is "proportionate" if their acceptance does not violate any of the modes of responsibility. For example, by this criterion one who risked the death of healthy children in medical experiments would lack a proportionate reason, for to take such a risk would be unfair.

In a case of a pregnant woman with a cancerous uterus, the analysis proposed here leaves open the question of the morality of surgical treatment which would lead to the child's death. If both mother and child were likely to die without the treatment, then the choice to treat with its foreseen bad consequences certainly can be accepted without unfairness. But if the child has a chance for survival if the treatment is not initiated, it is not clear that the choice to carry on treatment to save the mother does not involve partiality.

When a soldier on a battlefield shoots an enemy, the proposal executed by this performance need not include killing. (Of course, very often the shooting is precisely to kill; dead bodies are viewed as a good means to ending the war.) A soldier who is involved in a defensive action against an unjust attack could be trying only to inactivate the attackers and limit the injustice. The shooting at the enemy could be effective for its real objective if the shot missed, but caused the enemy to surrender or to flee and cease engaging in the unjust action; it also could be effective if the enemy was wounded only minimally but sufficiently to be incapable of further participation in the unjust action. This example begins to indicate both the possibility and the limits of justifiable war on the theory presented here.[7]

Question G: How can one resolve a doubt of conscience concerning the permissibility of cooperating with someone who is doing something wrong?

1. The question of cooperation has considerable practical importance. People often seek the help of confessors and other moral advisors in resolving problems of this sort. In her teaching, furthermore, the Church speaks of "formal cooperation" and "material cooperation," and these expressions must be clarified. For all that, cooperation does not raise any theoretical problems distinct from those already treated in question F.

2. A person who commands, directs, advises, encourages, prescribes, approves, or actively defends doing something immoral is sometimes said to cooperate in the immoral act. The morality of cooperation is clear enough in such cases—one who instigates immorality gives scandal and cannot be free of guilt. For example, physicians who refer for abortion are directing that it be done. Abortion is included in the choice they make, and so, morally, it is what they do.

3. The cases which present problems are different. Here the one who cooperates is in a secondary or subordinate role, and cooperating does not mean instigating anything but helping another to do something. The doubt of conscience arises typically because one is asked or expected to help family members, friends,

employers, government officials, or others toward whom one has duties do things which one would regard as immoral to choose to do oneself.

The cases of cooperation and communal action which pose the fewest complexities are those in which two or more persons freely associate and cooperate in a common life and common actions. Partners in marriage or in business are examples. To the extent that they are partners, nothing different from the responsibility of the individual will be revealed by analytic reflection. Their deliberations and decisions will go on in discourse expressed in language; even their acceptance of consequences, their putting off of problems, and so on will belong to their common life.

Things begin to become complicated when one considers cases in which persons are involved in something other than an ideally communal and cooperative relationship. Traditional moral treatises often dealt, under the present heading, with the problems of Christian slaves whose masters involved them in a variety of unseemly activities. The problem was: To what extent could the slave contribute to the activities which executed immoral proposals without himself or herself committing sin? In other words: At what point must a person who is subservient take a stand and accept some level of martyrdom?

Since no human relationship is perfect and no authority altogether upright, we still have essentially the same problem. May the nurse who considers abortion evil prepare a patient scheduled for abortion? Must an employee of a business which is hiding dangerous defects in its products resign and/or publicize the practice?

4. The Church has tried to clarify such problems by using the distinction between formal and material cooperation. **Formal cooperation in a gravely sinful act is always excluded as gravely sinful; material cooperation is sometimes, but not always, permissible.** The idea of the distinction is that one who formally cooperates participates in the immoral act in such a way that it becomes his or her own, whereas one who materially cooperates does something which facilitates the immoral act but does not make it his or her own.

5. For example, associates of a criminal mob who wish its enterprises to flourish so that they, too, will prosper formally cooperate in all the immoral acts which the mob does, even though some of them (accountants and lawyers, say) never personally carry out any of the mob's dirty work. By contrast, people forced against their wills to do something which substantially facilitates a crime (to open a safe, carry out the loot, or the like) only materially cooperate.

6. While material cooperation can sometimes be morally acceptable, one can also have a moral responsibility to avoid it. For instance, instead of cooperating materially in criminal acts, citizens might have a duty to help law enforcement agents, even at some personal risk, by informing on mobsters and seeking the protection of the law.

If a nurse who favors abortion adopts a proposal to kill unborn babies and participates in abortion procedures in execution of the proposal, she is killing unborn babies, and it matters not whether outwardly she does no more than fill out forms. On the other hand, if a nurse is threatened with loss of employment unless she assists a surgeon who is doing abortions, she could be assisting in surgery to keep her job without ever adopting a proposal to kill any unborn baby. The acts of the nurse herself need be no different than what she does in any morally good operation. The acts of the surgeon and the death of the babies not only are no ends of hers, they are not even means she chooses. They are only foreseen consequences.

The fact that one does not adopt any proposal which is morally excluded, however, does not free one from moral responsibility—perhaps grave responsibility—for what one helps to bring about. For example, a nurse who prepares patients for abortion not because this behavior carries out any proposal of hers but merely as part of her job perhaps ought to look for a different job or refuse to do these preparations by way of testimony to the truth. The abortions she assists really are a foreseen and accepted consequence of her own chosen actions; perhaps she is obliged not to accept this consequence.[x]

7. Classical moral theologians did not explain the distinction between formal and material cooperation as clearly as they might. Their explanations often reveal confusion between outward behavior and morally specified human acts, as when they take into account such factors as how physically close the help is to the wrongful performance.

8. The preceding analysis makes it clear that no special moral principle is needed to resolve doubts of conscience regarding cooperation. Apparent difficulties arise mainly because it is supposed that being involved in unseemly behavior or bringing about unacceptable consequences has a moral significance of its own, apart from the morality of one's choices and other volitional principles of personal responsibility. But that is not the case. One's responsibility for what one is involved in is determined by what one personally chooses, freely accepts, and so on.

9. According to the present analysis of the foundations of moral responsibility and the varieties of voluntariness, the distinction between formal and material cooperation and its normative implications can be explained as follows. People who help others do something wrong are responsible for what they themselves choose, accept, omit, and so forth. Cooperation is formal and is altogether excluded in the following two cases: (1) one's purpose is or includes that another commit sin; (2) one's proposal—what one chooses—is identical with or includes the immoral proposal of the person with whom one is cooperating.

10. Whenever cooperation is not formal, it is material. However, the fact that cooperation is material does not excuse one from responsibility—perhaps grave responsibility—for what one·helps bring about. **Material cooperation is often ruled out by other moral considerations, especially fairness.** The conditions under which Christians may cooperate even materially in evil are especially stringent, because refusing to cooperate in evildoing is often an important way of bearing witness to the truth.

Individuals who act as agents for others (called "principals") usually have responsibility as formal cooperators. One who merely contributes behavior to wrongful schemes—for example, by delivering messages—without adopting any wrong proposal is not doing the evil act, but might well be accepting consequences which he or she ought not to accept. Agents are not passive instruments; they have their own responsibilities. An agent given wide discretion is unlikely to be able to serve without adopting as his or her own the proposals which the principal wishes to execute, for the agent with discretion will be unable to do anything except by proceeding with the principal's own end in view.

There is a good side to this situation if the principal's purposes are noble ones. Agents told precisely what to do might carry out instructions for their own, less noble purposes. Agents given a broad mandate and a wide field of discretion, but provided with a good idea of the intentions of the one for whom they act, become in a full sense cooperators. The apostles and all Christians who share in the redemptive work of Jesus are not mere instruments; they are friends and fellow workers with God.

It is worth noting that Christian standards leave less room to act in ways which in fact facilitate evil, especially when that evil involves serious harm to others. The demands of mercy and self-oblation require Christians to avoid cooperation when the immoral act which is facilitated harms another and the only consideration which might justify cooperation is the good of the Christian himself or herself. Christians not only must avoid partiality in their own favor; they also are called to act with partiality toward others.

Summary

A person whose conscience is in doubt should try to resolve the doubt. One willing to proceed while in reasonable doubt about what is right is willing to do wrong, and to be willing to do wrong is itself wrong.

Doubts arise from uncertainty about facts, uncertainty about norms, and the appearance of conflicting responsibilities.

Where doubts about facts make it difficult to apply a rule of positive law and the law itself offers no help in resolving the doubt, one may resort to reasonable presumptions. But where a doubt of fact leads to difficulty in determining the gravity of an act recognized to be immoral, one should assume that the facts are such as to make the act more seriously wrong. Where the doubt affects the judgment whether the act is right or wrong, what one ought to do depends on whether acting in a state of doubt will involve a violation of any of the modes of responsibility.

Other doubts arise from uncertainty about norms. Where the norm is a rule of positive law, it is a question of fact whether it exists and a question of legal interpretation whether it applies to the action under consideration. In the case of a truly doubtful law, one has no obligation to obey; but a law is not truly doubtful when a preponderance of expert opinion holds that it exists and is relevant. Where the norm is not a rule of law but a specific moral norm, doubt can arise for a Catholic only in the absence of clear Church teaching on the matter. Then one should be guided by the consensus of theologians, if one exists; if not, one should refrain from the action if one would not otherwise have any responsibility to do it; or, supposing such a responsibility, one should perform the action if one judges it more likely to be permissible but refrain from it if one judges it more likely to be impermissible.

The method of resolving doubts about rules of positive law described here is what has been called "equiprobabilism." The method of resolving doubts about moral norms is analogous to "probabiliorism." Both probabiliorism and the present approach set aside theological opinions when there is a clear teaching of the Church and also when, lacking such teaching, particular theological opinions are not part of a solid theological consensus; both also discourage the arbitrary multiplication of supposed obligations. Moreover, both differ from probabilism by taking as a criterion the greater likelihood of truth.

However, the present approach is also fundamentally different from probabiliorism. In the legalistic context in which probabiliorism developed, the central question was whether one was bound by a law or free to do as one pleased. By contrast, the nonlegalistic assumption of the present approach is that one ought always to act in pursuit of human goods; thus, the conclusion that one possible norm is not operative in a particular case simply makes it clear that one has a responsibility to choose and act according to some other norm.

The third way in which doubts of conscience arise is from the appearance of conflicting responsibilities. There can, however, be no such conflicts at the level of moral principles, and cases of apparent conflict are usually cleared up by reflection on the facts and the relevant norms.

Where one has assumed a false norm, the conflict cannot be resolved until the error is corrected. Where no false norm is involved, the appearance of conflicting responsibilities results from the fact that nonabsolute moral norms have not been sufficiently specified. As for conflicts of duties in the strict sense, they are resolved by formulating a norm in accord with the principle of fairness. But when duties would require one to do something contrary to an absolute norm, the latter prevails.

In many cases, apparent conflicts impelling one to do something contrary to an absolute norm are resolved when the morally right course, previously ignored because it is unappealing, is accepted as a practical possibility. In other cases of apparent conflict involving the eighth mode, the resolution lies in clarifying how relevant norms apply to the choices under consideration. The eighth mode rules out a choice detrimental to a human good, but it does not rule out accepting foreseen side effects detrimental to a good (although some other mode may do so in a particular case). Classical moral theology dealt with this question—when one may accept side effects which it would be wrong to choose—by what is called the "principle of double effect."

Cooperating with someone who is doing something wrong raises the same issues as those just considered. "Formal" cooperation is altogether excluded; it is present when one's purpose includes the committing of sin by another, or when what one personally chooses is identical with or includes the immoral proposal of the person with whom one is cooperating. Other cooperation is "material." In some cases it may be permitted, but very often it is ruled out by other moral considerations, especially fairness. The conditions under which Christians may cooperate even materially in evil are especially stringent, since refusing to cooperate is often a requirement of mercy and an important way of bearing witness to the truth.

Appendix 1:   Probabilism considered in its context

Probabilism is one of several so-called moral systems; these are methods of resolving doubts of conscience.[9] A person is not sure what is right; to act with one's conscience in this state certainly is a sin, for to do so is to be ready and willing to do what is wrong. One must find some way of reaching a confident judgment that what one proposes to do is legitimate.

Probabilism is proposed as a way of reaching this confidence. However, it is a way which only makes sense within a certain context, namely, the context in which the Church's moral belief and teaching are regarded as a body of law, and this body of law becomes morally obligatory by way of one's responsible acceptance in faith of the Church as a moral authority. While faithful Catholics have never confused the Church's moral teaching with mere social convention, in modern times theological reflection proceeded in a way more consistent with legalism than with a clear appreciation of the status as truths of received Christian moral norms.

In the Church after Trent there was a great tightening of discipline in general and of the practice of the sacrament of penance in particular. At the same time, because of the cultural transformation worked by the dawn of modern economics and social structures, new and often difficult moral questions rapidly proliferated. Rationalism, an outgrowth of medieval nominalism, took hold in philosophy and theology, and legalism took hold in moral theology.

How the level of social convention is a necessary one in the development of conscience was explained previously (3-A). Every normal child goes through this stage, especially during the period between about seven and fourteen; probably few decent persons ever wholly emerge from it. The mentality of conscience at this level is highly legalistic. Virtually the only real sin is disobedience. Moral norms are felt as limits on one's behavior imposed by parents, teachers, society at large, the Church, and ultimately God, who authorizes and backs up all the other authorities.

Where no moral norm is in force, one is free to do as one pleases, and no moral issue arises. If one is not sure whether something is morally acceptable or not, one simply asks someone in authority: "Is it all right if I . . .?" If the answer is affirmative, one proceeds with confidence; one is okay; the superego, still operative and more or less integrated, allows one to proceed without anxiety. Thus, this legalistic system of childhood limits one's moral responsibility. There is no moral responsibility about most matters—namely, about all those questions which authorities do not seem to care about one way or another. Where there is moral responsibility, one can fulfill it by obtaining a suitable approval: "Mommy said it was all right for me to . . .."

Classical modern moral theology organized the whole of the Church's moral belief and teaching into a body of law. The truth of Christian moral norms always was affirmed. Nevertheless, the intrinsic relationship between right action and basic human goods, and the inherent reasonableness of acting morally tended more and more to be ignored. Moral theology extended only to moral issues, and these were thought to concern only some aspects of one's life. In effect, morality was limited to matters concerning which strict and more or less general precepts can be laid down. Most of these necessarily are negative, because it is much easier to determine what is morally wrong than what is morally right. Where the moral law was silent, the faithful were free—free to do as they pleased, but also free to be caught up in the Christian life and to grow in holiness according to the guidance of systems of asceticism and spirituality, which were quite separate from the legalistic moral theology.

In this context, the faithful looked to confessors for advice concerning doubts of conscience. Confessors looked to their bishops and/or teachers of moral theology. The latter looked to the "doctors"—the more eminent moral theologians who published works which gained recognition and respect in the Church. Eventually a certain number of more systematic works in moral became widely used and accepted for seminary training; these works were the "approved authors." The doctors and, later, the approved authors not only systematized and summarized received Christian moral teaching, which had been handed down from the Middle Ages; they also developed the Church's moral teaching. They refined it in regard to innumerable questions which had been treated before and expanded it to settle innumerable questions—especially in the area of justice—which never had been treated, because they had not arisen prior to the development of modern business, politics, and law.

The teaching authority of the Church functioned, largely through the activity of the Holy See, as a supreme court overseeing this legal system. The various commended doctors and approved authors came to have the function of lower courts; they could settle cases within the boundaries of the body of moral law and the authority conceded to them by the magisterium. Moral theology and canon law came close together; sometimes they merged into one.

There were various difficulties in this situation. One was that the approved authors and commended doctors did not always agree with one another. Every child is familiar with this difficulty. What must one do when mother says one thing and teacher says the opposite? A method for resolving this type of question is essential. Hence the problem of moral systems, which emerged in the Church in the sixteenth century. Some thought one always is obliged to accept the strictest view in favor of law and against doing as one pleases. This position is tutiorism; it is rigoristic, and the Church rejected it. Others thought one might always adopt the view most favorable to liberty. This position is laxism; it is like allowing a child to go from authority to authority until it finds one who absentmindedly gives approval. The Church also condemned this position.

In this way the problem which probabilism and probabiliorism answer was framed.[10] These are not methods of forming one's conscience independently of the Church's teaching authority. Far from it. One who knew for sure what is right and wrong did not have a doubtful conscience; one who had a doubtful conscience was expected to find an authoritative solution to obey. The only sources of authoritative solutions were moral theologians approved by the magisterium and working within the unquestioned body of her already-definite moral tradition. The problem is: When these sources of authoritative solutions to doubts of conscience disagree among themselves, how can one settle the doubt?

The theses of probabilism and probabiliorism are ones freely held and disputed in Catholic theology. Neither Scripture, nor tradition, nor the documents of the magisterium either approve or reject them.[11] They are only tacitly approved by the magisterium, in that many approved authors defend one of them, probably including St. Alphonsus Ligouri, who is a doctor of the Church especially commended in moral theology.[12]

Appendix 2:   Legalism, dissent, and the current abuses of probabilism

The old, legalistic order in which probabilism made sense largely has collapsed in the Catholic Church since the beginning of Vatican Council II. The Council itself signalled this fact: "Laymen should also know that it is generally the function of their well-informed Christian conscience to see that the divine law is inscribed in the life of the earthly city. From priests they may look for spiritual light and nourishment. Let the layman not imagine that his pastors are always such experts, that to every problem or even every serious problem which arises they can readily give him a concrete solution, or that such is their mission. Rather, enlightened by Christian wisdom and giving close attention to the teaching authority of the Church, let the layman take on his own distinctive role" (GS 43; translation amended).

This very important paragraph makes it clear that the Church's role is to help form conscience by communicating truth. Where one has formed one's conscience in conformity with what the Church teaches, one is then on one's own to discern moral truth in doubtful cases. The opinions of moral theologians are no longer to be taken as authoritative. Moralists can be useful only insofar as they help one to learn and understand what moral truth is.

Quite providentially, this dissipation of legalism occurred at the same time one party of professional moral theologians, including many who publish books and articles, declared its own autonomy from the magisterium. This portion of the moral-theological community, by engaging in dissent, eliminated the apparatus required for the working of the legalistic system. By pursuing moral truth as each one sees it, often in the light of secular wisdom and apart from the light of revelation unfolded by the Church's teaching authority, dissenting theologians made unmistakably clear that Christian morality must be considered a matter of truth, not of law, and that a good Christian life will be one lived in the light of Christ, not merely in conformity with the rules of the Church as a society.

It is ironic although not surprising that in the present new, and still transitional, situation many—among theologians, priests, teachers, and the ordinary faithful—both gladly reject legalism insofar as it is restrictive and cling to it insofar as it limits responsibility. Herein is the present great danger of probabilism, a danger not arising from the system itself, properly understood and applied in its appropriate (but now largely past) context, but from the system's abuse.

Thus some now appeal to probabilism in favor of dissenting theological opinions against the teaching of the Church. If one were a consistent legalist, one would recognize dissenting opinions as illicit; if one were consistently seeking moral truth, one would look at dissenting opinions only on their intellectual merits, just as one looks at the opinions of any moral commentator, whether nonbeliever or believer. However, the abuse is to reject legalism sufficiently to allow moral theology to proceed without regard for the supreme judgment of the magisterium, yet to cling to legalism sufficiently to allow the opinions of dissenting theologians some weight of authority which goes beyond the cogency of their arguments.[13]

Appendix 3:   The principle of double effect

In the older treatises on moral theology, one finds a treatment of a difficult type of moral problem in which there might seem to be but really is not a conflict of moral responsibilities. For instance, a pregnant woman is diagnosed as having cancer of the uterus. Treatment of the disease is likely to result in the death of her child; nontreatment, in the spread of the disease and the woman's death after the delivery of the child. At first glance, both treatment and nontreatment seem justifiable in view of the goods sought and unjustifiable in view of the harms expected. Cases of this type were resolved by clarification of the moral act rather than by clarification of the relevant norm.

The clarification of the moral act began by noticing that in cases of this sort, the same act has two effects, one good and the other bad.[14] The clarification, called "the principle of double effect," usually was summarized along the following lines:

One may perform an act having two effects, one good and the other bad, if four conditions are fulfilled simultaneously:

1) The act must not be wrong in itself, even apart from consideration of the bad effect. (Thus the principle was not used to deal with the good and the bad effects of an act admittedly excluded by an absolute norm.)

2) The agent's intention must be right. (Thus if one's precise purpose is to destroy, damage, or impede some basic human good, the deed carrying out this purpose could not be justified by the principle.)

3) The evil effect must not be a means to the good effect. (Thus if one chooses to destroy, damage, or impede some basic human good, although one chooses this for the sake of a good one might otherwise rightly pursue, the deed carrying out this choice could not be justified by the principle.)

4) There must be a proportionately grave reason to justify the act. (Thus, even if all the other conditions were fulfilled, one still might be obliged by the moral significance of the expected bad effect to abstain from the action.)

A moralist working in the classical framework would have applied this principle to the case of the cancerous uterus as follows. The treatment of the cancer itself is not a bad act. If the woman were not pregnant, no doubt it would be obligatory. The purpose is not to damage or kill the unborn child. The operation is unlike one done to get rid of an unwanted child; if possible, the child will be saved. Moreover, whatever harm comes to the child is not a means to the good sought by the treatment. If the woman were not pregnant or if the child were miraculously preserved from harm, the treatment of the cancer would be every bit as effective. The case is unlike one in which the child is killed in order to lessen the load it is putting on the mother's system. Finally, there is a very serious reason for going on with the treatment despite its bad effect; the mother's life is just as much at stake as the child's. Thus the case is unlike one in which a pregnant woman has a medically indicated but not urgently necessary hysterectomy (removal of uterus) despite her pregnant condition, thus bringing about the death of the child merely to do something which could be done later.

As formulated, the principle of double effect gives rise to three sorts of difficulties.

First, what is to count as "the act" mentioned in the first condition? Are abortionists killing babies? Or is the act something else? For example, does an abortionist who injects saline into a pregnant uterus precisely do the act of injecting saline, with the death of the baby as an effect of the act? Again, if a soldier in battle takes dead aim at an enemy soldier, is the act one of killing?

Second, what is to count as "a means" mentioned in the third condition? Is every cause of a desired effect a means to the end sought? For instance, if the effect desired by the soldier is his own safety, and if the death of the enemy soldier in fact secures this, then is the enemy's death a means to the good end?

Third, what is to count as a "proportionately grave reason" mentioned in the fourth condition? Does the physical proximity or probability of the bad effect have something to do with this? Is the justification in the cancerous uterus case simply that one life is as good as another? Should one take into account the probability that the child could live many more years than the mother? Or can one consider here factors such as the woman's responsibilities for other children?

It seems to me there are two sources of these difficulties. First, the older moral theologians started out by thinking of human acts in a commonsense way, as chunks of behavior having some moral significance because of their inherent characteristics and their being done on purpose. If one takes this view, one literally never knows exactly what anyone is doing, and so one will not be able to deal with precision with difficult cases of the sort for which the principle of double effect was designed.

Second, the classical moralists also lacked an explicit understanding of the modes of responsibility. Hence, they could not define "proportionately grave reason" simply in moral terms, and they sometimes talked in ways which have provided an opening for proportionalism.

Nevertheless, it is worth noting that many of the older moralists, in talking about what is proportionately grave, suggested that its meaning at least included the following consideration. In doing something which brings about unintentional bad consequences, one still might be acting irreverently with religious things, unfairly toward other people, or recklessly with one's own well-being. If so, one's reason would not be proportionately grave. This consideration clearly avoids anything like proportionalism, since it brings into play other relevant moral norms rather than proposing to weigh and balance the good and bad effects considered prior to moral specification—that is, taken simply as basic human goods.

Notes

1. A clear statement of the problem of conscience and the moral systems as understood by the classical moralists: Henry Davis, S.J., *Moral and Pastoral Theology*, vol. 1, *Human Acts, Law, Sin, and Virtue*, ed. L. W. Geddes, S.J., 7th ed. (London: Sheed and Ward, 1958), 64–115.

2. See Thomas Deman, O.P., *La prudence*, in S. Thomas d'Aquin, *Somme théologique: 2a–2ae, Questions 47–56*, 2d ed. (Paris: Desclée, 1949), 478–523.

3. See John Paul II, *Familiaris Consortio*, 74 *AAS* (1982) 184–86; Eng. ed. (Vatican City: Vatican Polyglot Press, 1981), 160 (sec. 84).

4. As is maintained by some Protestants, for example: Helmut Thielicke, *Theological Ethics*, vol. 1, *Foundations*, ed. William H. Lazareth (Philadelphia: Fortress Press, 1966), 279–97.

5. I do not accept direct killing in any instance, but do question whether everything which has been considered direct abortion is direct killing. In the latter part of the nineteenth century, an extensive and rather unsatisfactory controversy developed among Catholic moralists, all of whom rejected direct killing, concerning certain problems in this area. The Holy See ended the controversy by determining what might and might not be taught. An extensive summary of this controversy: John R. Connery, S.J., *Abortion: The Development of the Roman Catholic Perspective* (Chicago: Loyola University Press, 1977), 214–303. Have the fine determinations of what counts as direct killing been proposed universally by the magisterium as judgments to be held definitively? I do not think so, and if they have not, they are open to refinement (as will be explained in 35-G). But I do consider these judgments normative unless they are reconsidered by the magisterium itself.

6. For a historical summary, see Joseph T. Mangan, S.J., "An Historical Analysis of the Principle of Double Effect," *Theological Studies*, 10 (1949), 40–61; J. Ghoos, "L'Acte à Double Effet: Etude de Théologie Positive," *Ephemerides Theologiae Lovaniensis*, 27 (1951), 30–52. Ghoos is unjustifiably negative about the work of others; he does not show Mangan's study to be in error, although he does add material useful for additional insight into the history.

7. See Germain Grisez, "Toward a Consistent Natural-Law Ethics of Killing," *American Journal of Jurisprudence*, 15 (1970), 91–94, for further discussion of the limits of killing in war.

8. For a typical discussion of this problem of cooperation, see Gerald Kelly, S.J., *Medico-Moral Problems* (St. Louis: The Catholic Hospital Association, 1958), 332–35.

9. The classic treatise on probabilism: Thomas Deman, O.P., "Probabilisme," *Dictionnaire de Théologie Catholique*, 13:417–619. Deman gives a complete historical analysis; his conclusions are soundly drawn from the perspective of the moral theology of St. Thomas.

10. A careful description of the various moral systems, and the arguments for and against each: John A. McHugh, O.P., and Charles J. Callan, O.P., *Moral Theology: A Complete Course*, vol. 1 (New York: Wagner, 1958), 245–78.

11. See Marcelino Zalba, S.J., *Theologiae Moralis Compendium*, vol. 1 (Madrid: B.A.C., 1958), 393–97.

12. On St. Alphonsus, see Deman, "Probabilisme," 580–92. Alphonsus is commended mainly because he steers a safe, middle course between laxism and rigorism; this commendation does not imply that the commonly assumed conception of moral theology Alphonsus confronted was sound, but only that he did well in a bad situation.

13. An example of this confusion through ambivalence: Richard M. Gula, S.S., *What Are They Saying about Moral Norms?* (New York: Paulist Press, 1982), 101–4. Gula also uncritically accepts the arguments for radical theological dissent which will be examined in chapter thirty-six and ignores the case which has been made that much received Christian moral teaching has been proposed infallibly by the ordinary magisterium (see 35-D–E).

14. For a clarification of the principle beyond what is provided by the manuals, see Mangan; for defense against current objections, see Joseph M. Boyle, Jr., "Toward Understanding the Principle of Double Effect," *Ethics*, 90 (1980), 527–38.

CHAPTER THIRTEEN

WHAT SIN IS AND WHAT IT IS NOT

Introduction

Up to this point we have considered free choice and the norms which direct it toward the well-being of persons. Some choices, however, violate moral norms—they are morally evil.[1] Since it assumes that in knowing good one sufficiently knows evil, philosophical ethics contains no detailed examination of evil choices. But moral theology must give close attention to evil. For one thing, Christian life is a work of redemption, and redemption is liberation from sin and its effects. For another, a priest is a physician of souls, and sin is the "disease" he treats—although, unlike most diseases, humankind freely afflicts itself with this one.

The present chapter explains what sin is. Because many today give an account of the phenomena of sin incompatible with Christian faith, it also explains with some care what sin is not.

Chapter fourteen treats original sin, which put humankind in the condition of alienation that the redemptive act of Jesus rectifies. Not only do human persons, with the exception of Mary, share the common condition of sin, but also each contributes by his or her personal sins to the evil from which Jesus redeems us. Thus, Jesus not only is the "Lamb of God, who takes away the sin of the world" (Jn 1.29)—that sin in which the whole world shares together—but also is the priest who pours out his own blood "for many for the forgiveness of sins" (Mt 26.28). The sacrifice of Jesus brings acquittal and life to overcome the sin and death first brought into the world by the sin of Adam (see Rom 5.12–18); the blood of Jesus frees us not only from the sin of Adam but from our sins (see 1 Cor 15.3; Rv 1.5; *S.t.*, 3, q. 49, a. 5).

Chapter fifteen explains the different kinds of sin and makes many important distinctions which must be kept in mind if one is to deal effectively with sin in one's own life and help others deal with it in theirs. Chapter sixteen explains what constitutes grave matter, which is one of the conditions for mortal sin, and criticizes certain theories of "fundamental option." Chapter seventeen deals with the effects of ignorance, inadvertence, and false conscience on sin and moral responsibility, and also examines sin of weakness. Chapter eighteen clarifies the dynamics by which a Christian can move along the broad and easy road from imperfection through venial sin and mortal sin of various degrees of gravity to eternal damnation.

Unfortunately, although we are redeemed, growth toward perfection is not a smooth process of maturation from imperfect to perfect goodness. Evil remains in us. In this world, each of us must bear this fact constantly in mind: "If we say we have no sin, we deceive ourselves, and the truth is not in us" (1 Jn 1.8). Hence, we must battle against evil throughout this life (see GS 22). We must "lay aside every weight, and sin which clings so closely, and let us run with perseverance the race that is set before us" (Heb 12.1). The fight against sin can require even the shedding of our own blood according to the example of Jesus (see Rv 6.9–11). Having died with Jesus and been raised with him to new life, we now face, by reason of the gift of redemption, the task of destroying the rule of sin in ourselves (see Rom 6). The present treatise on sin is primarily oriented toward this task.

Question A: What does Scripture say about sin?

1. **Scripture never identifies sin with the state of being a creature as such.**[2] All creatures come from God, and as such all are good. Otherness from God, limitations, the need to develop, even the capacity for sinning—these are not sin. **At the same time, sin is no illusion but a terrible reality. It arises in the abuse by created persons of their power of free choice** (see Sir 15.11–20).

2. Apart from a very few passages in the Old Testament arguably suggesting a more primitive view (see 2 Sm 6.6–7), Scripture never regards sin as the mere breaking of a taboo. There is more to sin than forbidden behavior.

3. **The Old Testament teaches that the act of sin involves a personal, inner, and enduring wrong** (see Ps 51). As Jesus himself confirms, sin is in the heart (see 1 Sm 16.7; Jer 4.4; Ez 11.19; Mk 7.20–23). To sin is to be stiff-necked and resistant to God (see Ex 32.9; Dt 10.16; 31.27; 2 Chr 30.8; Is 48.4; Jer 17.23). St. Paul fully develops the implications of this understanding of sin and shows that legalism means slavery; only the holiness of living faith liberates one from sin (see Rom 7.7–8.2; Gal 3.19–29).

The dimensions of sin and redemption are marked out in the *Miserere* (Ps 51). Sin offends God and spoils a person's true self. Repentance depends upon God's love and one's own sincerity. Redemption requires not merely the washing away of a superficial stain, not only a thorough cleansing of ground-in dirt, but even a re-creation of the entire, inner self. Created anew by God's saving act, the sinner gives thanks and praise, communicates God's ways to others, and offers God acceptable outward sacrifices which manifest the renewed inward relationship.

The description in Genesis of the paradigmatic sin contains important elements representative of sins in general. A known precept of God is violated (see Gn 3.3–6). The violation in outward behavior proceeds from an inner act of disrespect. The inner act is motivated in part by suspicion concerning God's disinterestedness, in part by impatience with the limits imposed by the norm, and in part by desire for the immediate good to be realized in the sinful act. The sin engenders its own negative consequences in the sinners themselves (see Gn 3.7).

It also damages their relationship to God (see Gn 3.8–24). (One often hears today that sin breaks one's relationship to God; this is not entirely accurate, since the sinner remains God's child, though a prodigal one.) In defense, sinners rationalize (see Gn 3.8–13), but these rationalizations help not at all to forestall the disastrous consequences which follow from their sin (see Gn 3.14–24). Still, God cares for Man and Woman; his care foreshadows redemption (see Gn 3.15, 21; DS 3901/2331).

4. As a result of communal solidarity, there is a sense in which the sins of ancestors affect their descendants; this is most striking in the case of original sin. Responsibility for sin is nevertheless a personal matter. One may not escape personal guilt by passing it on to the larger society (see Dt 24.16; Jer 31.29–30).

The rich treatment of this subject in the prophets (e.g., Ez 18) makes it clear that each person is responsible for his or her own heart and acts.

5. Even when it primarily takes the form of injustice to other people, sin is still more basically against the Lord (see 2 Sm 12.13). A psalm has David, repentant for his sins of adultery and murder, praying: "Against you, you only, have I sinned, and done that which is evil in your sight" (Ps 51.4). Within the context of the covenant, all sin is hatred of God, while all upright life is love of him (see Dt 5.9–10).

6. **Still, sin hurts not God but sinners** (see Jb 35.5–8; Is 59.1–2; Jer 7.8, 19). Insofar as one sinfully chooses to act in opposition to the will of God, one is a fool (see Prv 1.7). Conversely, the fool, characterized by denial of God, seems inevitably to sin (see Ps 53.1–4). God's commands are given for the good of his human children (see Dt 6.24; 10.13; Sir 16.22–28). The persistent suggestion that God's concern for morality is self-concern is a typical aspect of temptation (see Gn 3.5) and must be firmly set aside.

To the suspicion that God rules in his own interests rather than in the interests of his creatures, one of the participants in the dialectic of Job replies:

> Look at the heavens, and see;
> and behold the clouds, which are higher than you.
> If you have sinned, what do you accomplish against him?
> And if your transgressions are multiplied, what do you do to him?
> If you are righteous, what do you give to him;
> or what does he receive from your hand?
> Your wickedness concerns a man like yourself,
> and your righteousness a son of man. (Jb 35.5–8)

7. Catechetical materials often call sin a violation of the covenant. It is true that, once the covenant is established, sin does violate it; the sin of idolatry now becomes a sort of adultery (see Ez 23; Jer 3.20; Hos 2). But sin is not limited to covenant violations. The idolatry of the chosen people was sin even before the covenant was established (see Ez 20.7–8). The prophets denounce the sins of pagan nations who have no special covenant relationship with God (see Am 1.3–2.3). St. Paul also makes it clear that pagans living outside the covenant know enough of God, simply by the natural light of reason, for their immoral acts to have the character of true sin (see Rom 1.18–22; 2.14–16).

God as creator, not only as covenant maker, has provided a wise order of things. Violation of this true order of reality begins by a refusal to acknowledge that God is God and creatures are only creatures, and this refusal leads to all other sins. This intrinsic connection between God and created goods leads to the great insight: "He who does not love his brother whom he has seen, cannot love God whom he has not seen" (1 Jn 4.20).

Immorality, then, is a self-imposed privation which blocks love of God, since he is all goodness. When God reveals himself and offers his love, those whose deeds are evil flee the light to avoid exposure. Thus the rejection of faith has a basis in prior immorality, to which individuals can cling, even when Jesus invites humankind to abandon immorality and death in favor of immortality and life (see Jn 3.16–21). The revelation of God in Jesus provides an adequate opportunity for sinners to accept divine love; the rejection of this opportunity is a reconfirmation in sin which is utterly inexcusable (see Jn 15.21–25).

8. The New Testament's deeper understanding of the intimacy God wishes to share with his creatures underlies its similarly deeper understanding of sin as separation from God. As light and darkness have nothing in common, so neither do uprightness and iniquity (see 2 Cor 6.14). Jesus and the devil, belief and unbelief, God and idols are absolutely opposed; therefore, so also are uprightness and iniquity (see 2 Cor 6.15–16). One who believes must walk according to the Spirit, who makes the faithful believer a child of God (see Gal 5.16). One must not walk according to the flesh, which obliterates divine life (see Rom 8.1–17).

9. **Thus, in the New Testament sin is much more the unitary reality of one's single state of alienation from God than the multiple reality of one's numerous immoral deeds.** Sins are sins because they give rise to and prolong life apart from God.

To sin is to do iniquity—that is, to alienate oneself from divine life. The Word became flesh to take away sins; for him alienation from God is impossible. Therefore: "No one who abides in him sins; no one who sins has either seen him or known him. Little children, let no one deceive you. He who does right is righteous, as he is righteous. He who commits sin is of the devil; for the devil has sinned from the beginning. The reason the Son of God appeared was to destroy the works of the devil. No one born of God commits sin; for God's nature abides in him, and he cannot sin because he is born of God" (1 Jn 3.6–9). To cling to Jesus is to remain God's child, and to remain God's child is to be incapacitated for acting sinfully. Sinful deeds express the godlessness of iniquity.[3]

Considered in this way, sin is to be found not so much in the millions of transgressions as it is in the one privation of divine life from a person's heart. Thus, in the Johannine writings "sin" tends to be used in the singular rather than in the plural. The descent of the Holy Spirit upon Jesus reveals him to John the Baptist as the Lamb of God who takes away the sin of the world (see Jn 1.29). This sin is the alienation of creation which has separated itself from God. Similarly, St. Paul speaks of sin as a unitary reality opposed to divine life, a reality which entered the world with the sin of Adam, and which is overcome by the obedience of Christ (see Rom 5.12–19). Needless to say, these sacred writers never minimize the sinfulness of the deeds of iniquity; rather, they deeply realize the sinfulness of each single sinful act, for they see godlessness in it.

Question B: What is sin?

1. The first principle of morality (see 7-F) makes it clear that moral evil is privation in the existential domain of openness to integral human fulfillment. Sin really is the same thing as moral evil, but the concept of sin considers moral evil under a certain aspect.[4] **Sin is moral evil considered precisely insofar as it is contrary to the good of religion—contrary, that is, to the fulfillment of humankind's potential for harmony with God.** Moral evil blocks human fulfillment on every level of existence (see GS 13), disintegrating the self, disrupting personal life, dismembering community, and distorting the relationship of humankind with God. Thus every morally evil act offends God, and sin is immorality considered under this specific aspect (see *S.t.*, 1–2, q. 71, a. 6, ad 5).

2. A person who chooses according to a nonrational principle of self-determination need not intend to offend God (see *S.t.*, 1–2, q. 72, a. 1; q. 73, a. 1; q. 75, aa. 1–2; q. 78, a. 1). Perhaps one wishes only to enjoy oneself (see *S.t.*, 1–2,

q. 71, a. 2, ad 3; q. 77). Even so, moral evil cannot be without sin (see C below for further clarification).

3. Moral evil is privation in the existential domain. One might say that moral evil precisely is in the free choice which is not as it should be (see *S.t.*, 1–2, q. 79, a. 2). St. Augustine sometimes speaks this way (see FEF 1558 and 1560). More broadly, sin not only is in free choice but in all the varieties of voluntariness, to the extent that willing is not as it should be (see *S.t.*, 1–2, q. 71, a. 5). Sometimes sinful willing affects and involves others besides those who sin by their own choice. Hence, as Augustine teaches, one person can be in sin by another's choice (see FEF 1454). Such is the case with original sin, to be treated in chapter fourteen.

4. Prior to free choice one understands the human goods and spontaneously wills them, but one's will is not determined to respect all of them fully in every instance. In making an evil choice, one responds to some principles of practical reason but not all; one determines oneself in regard to some good but fails to determine oneself in a manner consistent with openness to integral human fulfillment. The privation which constitutes the evil of immorality is precisely this lack of reasonableness and openness which could and ought to be present in every free choice. To put this another way, one's choice could and ought to conform perfectly to God's law made known through one's conscience; a morally evil choice does not; this lack of due conformity is the privation which constitutes the moral evil of the act (see *S.t.*, 1–2, q. 71, a. 6; q. 79, a. 2).

5. The privation is the evil. A sin centrally is a choice subject to this evil. The privation is not imposed on choice from without. Rather, it is freely accepted in the free choice by the free choice itself (see FEF 1549). **A sin is therefore something real (in the primary instance, it is a choice); it is a sin because of something real, namely, a real privation of right order. Yet this privation is not a positive reality; it is not something which needs a causal explanation, as if it were a distinct creature.** For this reason, sin as such in no way depends on God (see *S.t.*, 1–2, q. 79, a. 2; *S.c.g.*, 3, 162). Instead its source is altogether one's own bad will (see Jas 1.13–15).

Evil will and good will are not counterparts. Only the good has positive reality from God. Augustine explains: "Let no one, therefore, seek the efficient cause of an evil will; it is not efficient but deficient, because the will in this case is not an effecting of something but a defecting. To defect from that which supremely exists to that which has less being is to begin to have an evil will. But to try to find causes of those defections, since, as I said, they are not efficient but deficient, is as if someone tried to see darkness or to hear silence" (FEF 1754).

6. Insofar as a choice is morally evil, the behavior which carries it out shares in moral evil. Thus the sinful deed, the deviant behavior, has the character of moral evil not from its positive reality but from the sinfulness of the choice it executes. Sin is from the heart (see *S.t.*, 1–2, q. 74, aa. 1–2). And the choice itself is not evil by what it positively is but by the privation one accepts in making it. Sin is unnecessary, unreasonable self-limitation and self-mutilation (see *S.t.*, 1–2, q. 29, a. 4; 2–2, q. 25, a. 7).

For this reason, it is a mistake to base moral criticism and exhortation on any positive qualities of sinful behavior. Sexual immorality, for example, is not sinful because it is ugly, or because it can lead to disease, or because it might end in unwanted pregnancy. Murder is not sinful because it gets blood on the floor. Criticism and exhortation based on such grounds distract attention from real moral concerns, and encourage people to find more acceptable ways of sinning—for example, sexual indulgence which is not ugly, unhealthy, or unwantedly fruitful, and murder which is bloodless.

7. **Sin primarily is in sinful choices, and sinful choices are of themselves spiritual entities which persist.** Hence, as St. Augustine notes (see FEF 1873), the guilt of sin—which is sin itself—lasts even after the sinful behavior is past and forgotten. Anyone who understands what immorality is knows that no sin is a mere passing event or temporal process. In every free choice, one makes oneself be what one is by choosing. In every sinful choice, one makes oneself guilty (see *S.t.*, 1–2, q. 86; q. 87, a. 6). There is no need to think of a state of sin, a habit of sin, or a condition of guilt distinct from the sin itself. Sin is of itself a state, a habit, a condition of guilt.

8. Moral evil spreads from sinful choices throughout the other forms of voluntariness. Gradually but inevitably, it pervades and perverts the whole existential domain of personal and interpersonal relationships, engendering disharmony and alienation on every level (see *S.t.*, 1–2, q. 85, aa. 1–3; q. 87, a. 1). From the existential domain, the perversity which begins in free choice introduces disorder even into the other dimensions of individual and social reality. It leads to disease and death, confusion and error, shoddiness and breakdown.

9. The expressions "formal sin" and "material sin" mark a useful distinction. Any choice which is not what it morally ought to be can be called "sin," but sometimes such a choice does not violate conscience because one is unable to make a judgment of conscience or one's conscience is in error. **A choice which conforms to an erring conscience or a wrong choice made without moral reflection is called a "material" sin, while one which violates conscience is called a "formal" sin.** Those who make choices but are simply unable to make relevant judgments of conscience are blameless—for example, children and persons who are mentally ill can lack the capacity to discern moral truth, at least in some matters. One is not always blameless in following an erring conscience, for the error can be one's own fault (see 3-B). Material sins which are in conformity with a culpably erroneous conscience are thus not free of guilt.

Question C: In what sense is sin an offense against God?

1. Certain sins, such as idolatry, obviously infringe upon religion, but it is not so clear what bearing most immoral acts have upon the relationship with God. How do immoral acts which do not directly involve religion nevertheless offend God?

2. St. Augustine defines sin as "anything done, said, or desired against the eternal law" (FEF 1605). The eternal law is God's wise plan by which he directs all things to their fulfillment: integral human fulfillment, in our case. Every immoral act, however, involves lack of openness to integral human fulfillment.

Thus, one who acts immorally always deviates from the loving plan of the eternal law, regardless of which particular human good is directly at stake (see *S.t.*, 1–2, q. 71, a. 2, ad 4; a. 6). This can be seen more clearly if one considers the various ways in which people know what is right.

3. The people of the old covenant and we of the new accept God in faith as our Lord. It is his plan and will that we should worship him alone, for other worship is senseless and degrading; that we should treat one another as persons made in his image and called to share in his life; that we should be liberated from self-imposed limitations and brought to share in Jesus' glory. Whenever the law of Moses forbade something, the pious Jew knew it to be against God's wisdom and love; similarly, when the Church teaches that something is a sin, the faithful Catholic knows it to be against God's wisdom and love. Every immoral act deviates from God's plan for our fulfillment. In doing so, it also violates covenant friendship with God, for as part of this covenant relationship he wishes us to cooperate in carrying out his plan. But violation of friendship with God alienates us from him, and such alienation is sin. Therefore, every immoral act is sin.

4. However, even the pagans, although not within the covenant, know what is right and are capable of sin (see Rom 1.18–22). For even without faith, people can realize that immorality offends not only against reason and, often, the rights of one's neighbor but also against the more-than-human source of meaning and value called "God." One who violates moral requirements refuses to accept his or her limitation as a creature and implicitly aspires to be beyond boundaries, as God is.[5] Thus, in sinning, one implicitly rejects God's wisdom and love, the source of meaning and value in creation at large and in human life in particular. But those who reject God's wisdom and love in effect declare their independence of God and so alienate themselves from him. This alienation, implicit in every immoral act, is sin.

5. An unreasonable, morally evil act can be recognized as sin in two ways, for there are two distinct routes by which we know immorality to be against God's mind and will. **First, in acting against a conscience formed in the light of faith, one violates the covenant of faith and so violates the eternal law which faith makes known.** In other words, when one offends against the Church's teaching, one offends against the divine truth of the gospel, which is the source of the Church's teaching. **Second, in violating one's conscience, one violates natural law and so violates the eternal law in which natural law participates** (see 7-A). In other words, in violating human reason, one violates the light of divine wisdom which shines there. When they act immorally, Christians are more or less clearly aware in both of these ways of sinning.

Noticing the first way in which sin is against the eternal law and mistakenly thinking it to be the only possible way to relate moral evil to God's plan, some have taught that there is a real distinction between "theological sin" and "philosophical sin." Theological sin, on their account, is a deliberate transgression of God's law, done by one who is aware of God and conscious of the fact that the act is a violation of his will. Philosophical sin is a morally evil act done by one who does not know God or is not thinking about him—the immorality, for instance, of a pagan who does not know God or a Christian who knows that something is wrong but has never heard that this kind of act is a mortal sin. Those who held this view wished to deny that "philosophical sin" could be mortal. The Church firmly condemns this position (see DS 2291/1290).

6. If Christians commit mortal sins, their offenses are worse than those of nonbelievers. To sin after receiving the truth is infidelity, as the prophets, especially Hosea, make clear. In the old law, infidelity was punishable by death. "How much worse punishment do you think will be deserved by the man who has spurned the Son of God, and profaned the blood of the covenant by which he was sanctified, and outraged the Spirit of grace?" (Heb 10.29). In sinning gravely, Christians exchange the life and liberty won for them by Jesus for renewed death and slavery (see Rom 6; Gal 5). Since the Christian is a member of Christ's body and a temple of the Spirit, a sin such as fornication takes on the character of sacrilege (see 1 Cor 6.12–20). And since Christian life is not merely individual, every grave sin violates a Christian's responsibility to Christ and the Church (see Rom 14.7–8; Gal 5.13–6.10). (The last point will be developed in 16-G.)

7. Since we determine ourselves by our choices and these last, in sinning more gravely than nonbelievers Christians also harm themselves more radically. Even though not chosen as a good, sin's offensiveness to God and injuriousness to the Church, which a Christian willingly accepts in committing grave sin, affect his or her very being unless and until the sin is repented and forgiven. Therefore, "If, after they have escaped the defilements of the world through the knowledge of our Lord and Savior Jesus Christ, they are again entangled in them and overpowered, the last state has become worse for them than the first. For it would have been better for them never to have known the way of righteousness than after knowing it to turn back from the holy commandment delivered to them" (2 Pt 2.20–21).

8. St. Augustine tries to clarify how sin offends against God by saying that in every immoral act one turns from God to a creature and loves oneself to the point of contempt for God (see appendix 1). These things—turning from God and contempt for God—can be understood in terms of the implications of moral evil which have already been explained. One who refuses to follow God's wise guidance in the matter of true human fulfillment does turn from him and contemptuously prefers his or her own arbitrary satisfaction to the full good proposed by God's love.

9. Still, St. Augustine's clarification of sin as a turning away from God and contempt for him is easily misunderstood. This happens, for instance, if it is supposed that one does not sin unless one purposely offends God (cf. *S.t.*, 3, q. 88, a. 4). In fact, however, sinners generally do not advert to the fact that their sins are offenses against God or, if they are believers, only reluctantly accept this implication of their sinning.

10. Augustine's clarification is also misunderstood if taken to mean that the nonreligious aspects of sin are in themselves unimportant and only the offense against God is evil. On the contrary, the self-mutilation involved in sin, its social implications, and its incompatibility with integral human fulfillment are of themselves important aspects of its evil. It is because immorality does involve these evils that God's commandments are not arbitrary restrictions on our

freedom but wise and loving guides directing us toward true human fulfillment.

The self constituted by immoral choices is insubstantial; it is the "I" in search of its own emotional peace, security, success, and satisfaction—in short, it is the sinful self St. Augustine so well analyzed. This is the self which Jesus teaches one must lose to find one's true self (see Mt 16.24; Mk 8.34; Lk 9.23). Therefore, in this sense of "self-love," all sin is perverse self-love, for it is the pursuit of a "me" defined by sinful passion, not the pursuit of the "we" in which divine and human persons will be united in the fulfillment of all things in Jesus.

Question D: How can a person choose to do what is morally evil?

1. **In committing sin one does not choose its sinfulness as such. Rather, one chooses a certain good.** A man who steals a watch chooses to enjoy the watch; he accepts the injustice of taking what belongs to somebody else. Even in violations of the seventh and eighth modes of responsibility, where one does choose something bad (the destruction, damage, or impeding of a human good), one does not choose the sin as such. Rather, one accepts its sinfulness, while pursuing revenge or seeking, through violating some good, to attain some other good or avoid some evil (see *S.t.*, 1–2, q. 73, a. 1; q. 78, a. 1).

There are exceptional cases in which someone does choose moral evil as a means to some ulterior end. For example, Hamlet thinks of avenging himself on the king at a time when the king is in sin, in order to send him to hell. A choice to do this would include sin in the proposal adopted. Similarly, a wife outraged by her husband's adultery might choose to commit adultery to get even with him. In making this choice, she might include the very immorality of her own act in the proposal she adopts, for she can wish not only to make her husband suffer but even to wound the marital relationship itself.

2. To a person who is not conscious of living in a religious framework which embraces every choice, it seems that all or most morally evil acts are only violations of the dictates of reason. In the fallen human condition, however, consistent reasonableness is likely to seem pointless. For one thing, although being reasonable is a human good, it is only one good among others and it is incommensurable with the others. Furthermore, one may very well question the point of being always reasonable, for no matter how reasonable one is, one is faced with tension and conflict, disappointment and unfulfillment, suffering and death. This explains the Church's teaching that apart from the light of faith and the help of grace, morally evil choices are inevitable (see DS 241/132, 383–85/186–88, 389/192, 391/194, 393/196).

3. Even one who considers the possibilities in a situation of temptation in the light of faith does not face a choice between God and the wrongly desired good. True, one fully realizes in the light of faith that every morally evil choice is an offense against God. But the choice is between the wrongly desired good and one's actual, present relationship with God. This relationship is not God himself. It appeals to us as one human good among others, and usually we think that in sinning we will disrupt it only for the time being, not forever.[6]

4. Thus, when tempted to sin, we do not see our relationship with God as absolutely and in every respect a greater good than that which tempts us. In fact,

here and now the relationship with God does not offer something promised by the tempting alternative. If it were otherwise, if the relationship with God were understood as being absolutely and in every respect better than anything else we might choose, there would be no choice, and sin would be impossible (see *S.t.*, 2–2, q. 34, a. 1).

5. Although in sinning one does not choose the sin as such, still one does choose to do what is in fact sinful. How does one come to do this? If this question asks for the reason why one chooses sinfully rather than uprightly, no answer is possible, because one sins by free choice. But if the question asks only about the genesis of the sinful choice, the answer begins with sentient awareness and emotion. (This was considered in 7-G.) Emotions, although good in themselves, are not in themselves rational, and these nonrational motivations can make sinful possibilities appealing (see *S.t.*, 1–2, q. 75, a. 2).[7] (The many ways in which they do this were described in chapter eight, where the modes of responsibility were articulated.)

6. Still, emotional appeal is not enough for choice. One only chooses what one understands as good in some respect. Thus, some aspect of intelligible goodness must be found in the possibility which emotion urges in its own nonrational way (see *S.t.*, 1–2, q. 74, a. 4). But this is not difficult: Sinful possibilities always offer at least a certain realization of the good of self-integration, specifically the satisfaction of the emotional drive itself.

7. To the extent a possibility is sinful, however, its choice cannot be consistent with all the principles of practical reason (see 7-F). **Thus, by giving in to temptation one gains some aspect of self-integration at the expense of a certain self-mutilation.** The peace, the temporary inner harmony, which comes in sinning is only an apparent good, for it blocks the attainment of a deeper and more inclusive self-integration (see *S.t.*, 1–2, q. 75, a. 2).

8. In sum, one does not choose moral evil as such. Rather, one chooses to do that which is morally evil only by choosing a certain good and accepting the immorality of the choice as something accompanying it. Emotion promotes the morally excluded possibility, urging it on one's attention and encouraging its acceptance. One who is tempted understands this possibility as offering a certain good—at least the experience of temporary inner peace which comes with emotional satisfaction. In a morally evil choice, however, such peace is only an apparent good. One satisfies part of oneself but sacrifices the more inclusive integration of one's whole self.

Question E: In what sense does sin extend beyond individual sinners?

1. Scripture often speaks of sin almost as if it were an autonomous power at work in the world. Thus St. Paul: "Sin will have no dominion over you" (Rom 6.14); sin misused the commandment so that it "might become sinful beyond measure" (Rom 7.13); the very cosmos is in "bondage to decay" (Rom 8.21). According to St. John, the world shares a common condition of sin (see Jn 1.29); it hates those who believe in Jesus (see Jn 15.18–20). Such passages have a true and

important meaning, but one must be careful not to misunderstand what this is.

2. Clearly, sin is not simply deviation in isolated pieces of behavior. Sin is evil in the existential domain (see B above). It extends to all that exists by or is affected by sinful choices. **Thus, of itself moral evil persists in the being of the person who sins, and one morally evil commitment can lead to many morally evil acts.**

3. Moreover, sins in social acts affect members of the community who do not personally participate in them. When, for example, a nation does an injustice, all its citizens become involved whether or not they wish to be; to the extent they approve or needlessly tolerate the injustice, they share in doing it. **Social injustices also tend to become institutionalized as part of the fabric of common life.** Social processes and structures, cultural forms and products are marred by sin and embody more or less profound injustices.

4. Once embodied in social and cultural reality, such injustices take on a life of their own, independent of the primary modes of voluntariness of individuals, yet voluntary in some of the secondary ways previously described (9-G). For example, the civil rights movement of recent decades has made us aware of much racial unfairness which we long shared in unawares. Furthermore, such injustices often lead to disease, generate anxiety, and prompt people to seek various escapes from the harsh realities of life.

5. **Humankind is thus confronted not only with the particular sins of individuals but with a whole system of evil deriving from both original sin and actual sins, individual and social.** In consequence, not only are there individual souls to be saved—there is a world to be redeemed (see GS 13 and 25).[8] People need also to be saved from the slavery of fear of death (see Heb 2.14–15) and from the malaise which accompanies sin (see Lk 5.17–26; Jn 5.14).

6. Although an individual's suffering cannot always be explained by the fact that he or she has sinned (see Jn 9.2–3), still moral evil and the other miseries which afflict us cannot be neatly compartmentalized. The perception that there are some intimate connections between sin and palpable human suffering constitutes a permanent temptation to accord to sin a reality in itself. Some erroneously elevate sin to the status of a superhuman power, sometimes identified with the devil, and consider evil a primary reality apart from and opposed to God. This line of thought leads to Manichaeism. Evil is objectivized, and the reality of personal moral responsibility is denied. Much modern secular humanist ideology moves in this direction.

7. Christian faith makes it clear that, while there is a moral element to all human misery, this can be explained without positing a source of evil independent of sin. The doctrine of original sin clarifies this matter. Similarly, it does not follow from the fact of social sin that because all share responsibility, no one is guilty. Every social sin originates in and is perpetuated by people's personal wrong choices—which, however, are sometimes only materially, not formally, sinful. Particular persons are responsible, for instance, for initiating such social sins as unjust wars, the oppression of minorities, the waste of natural resources, and needless damage to the environment.

A serious Christian analyst of complex social problems must refrain from the easy moralism common among less committed social critics and the deterministic analysis of secular humanists. Christian social reflection must trace the lines of responsibility back to the many and diverse wrong choices in which they originate. The choices which contribute to social sins can be of very different kinds, yet share in common effects. For example, various businesses might collaborate in carrying on an industry which unjustly exploits the poor in an underdeveloped nation; consumers in industrialized nations might indulge themselves with the products of such an industry with no concern for the source of supply; government officials might collaborate to make the system work; many people who could bring the matter to light and help rectify it instead choose to spend their time in idle chatter and pointless amusements.

Question F: How do unbelievers try to account for sin?

1. Although the world views of those who do not believe in God have no place for sin as separation from God, the reality of moral evil in the world still demands an explanation. **For most modern nonbelievers, some form of secular human-ism takes the place of Christian faith, and secular humanist ideologies explain away moral evil by denying free choice.**[9] The evil which Christians consider irreducibly moral is accounted for in nonmoral terms.

2. Many provide a naturalistic account of the human condition and of human action. Some say humankind has only recently evolved from lower forms, and all nonrational tendencies are exclusively a residue of earlier stages. Some, Sigmund Freud among them, claim that the pressures of civilization—an environment literally without precedent in biological history—generate the conflicts we experience.[10] Others, such as John Dewey, hold that what Christians consider moral evil should be regarded as a crisis of development, which poses a challenge for human intelligence. If we solve our problems, evolution will continue; if not, the human race will become extinct.[11]

3. Marxists also explain evil in deterministic terms—that is, they deny wrong free choices. Marxism has a naturalistic basis; it claims to be a science of history and society, and places special emphasis on social structures and economic factors. In its view, the source of all difficulty is scarcity, which has led to economic systems with class divisions and oppression.[12] More than other natural-ists, Marxists analyze in great detail—and sometimes with acuteness—the permeating distortions which social injustices bring into every aspect of life.

4. Many secular humanists try to account for the unsatisfactory character of the human condition mainly in terms of ignorance and error. Thus knowledge is the solution. For Freud, insight can cure neurosis. For Dewey, progressive education can liberate intelligence to solve problems. For many other modern thinkers, the obliteration of religious belief and superstition—similar forms of error, in their view—will enable science to prevail over human misery. In the age of science, it is believed, what formerly was considered sin and the effects of sin will be subject to healing and repair, much as one heals an infection with an antibiotic or repairs the heart by replacing a valve.

5. Atheistic existentialists also deny free choice and personal responsibility.

Some talk extensively about freedom, but "freedom" in one of the other senses distinguished earlier (2-C), not the freedom of self-determination. Nietzsche, for instance, is mainly concerned with creative freedom; for him, what is bad are the mediocrity and stodginess routinely accepted by most people.[13] Heidegger develops an elaborate metaphysical description of the human in which he uses traditional moral language; but his thought has no place for objective moral norms based on human goods, and he substitutes aesthetic for moral responsibility, demanding that humankind make something of itself. He attributes failure to respond to this demand for creativity to lack of metaphysical insight rather than wrong choice.[14]

6. No matter how they explain the phenomena of sin, when they speak of immorality contemporary nonbelievers are usually thinking of conventional morality. They equate morality with the norms more or less generally accepted in a given society. "Sin" is deviant behavior. Although they criticize conventional morality to some extent—as a product of collective neurosis (Freudians) or a tool of oppressors (Marxists)—to some extent they also reinforce it. For example, both Marxists and liberal secular humanists reinforce the conventional morality which justifies killing unborn babies to solve personal and social problems.

For the most part, the social sciences in the liberal, democratic nations are dedicated to helping the established social order solve its problems and maintain itself more or less intact. From this point of view, what formerly was considered sin appears as deviant behavior. A person who does not fit into the society, who annoys others, who behaves contrary to the common norms of conventional morality is a nuisance and a trouble maker. Various methods of social control, both formal (such as the criminal process) and informal (such as public education), are used to try to engineer the desired level of conformity.

In carrying out this undertaking, several of the accounts of sin discussed above are very widely used. For example, psychology is widely used to treat supposed ills; information is provided to help people satisfy their desires in socially acceptable ways (for example, children are taught to avoid venereal disease and pregnancy); social and economic structures are tinkered with by the use of government funds and agencies of regulation (for example, in adjusting welfare programs).

This state of affairs is not as absurd as it appears to many persons of Christian faith who view the inept efforts of social engineering as presumptuous Pelagianism—that is, as an effort to attain salvation from sin by purely human means. In the first place, social engineering is not directed to salvation; it is based on a denial of free choice and the reality of sin. The aim of those working for social control is simply the elimination of troublesome, deviant behavior. No Christian ought to confuse this objective, whatever one thinks of it, with the redemption accomplished by God in Jesus. In the second place, much of the deviation which the social engineer wants to eliminate is not immoral human action. The standards of conventional morality diverge greatly from moral truth; they establish the workable, livable level of immorality necessary for a moderately satisfactory, this-worldly existence for fallen humankind. Deviation from these conventional standards often is the result of psychological illness, ignorance, especially unfavorable environment, and so on.

Conventional morality also is criticized by proponents of contemporary philosophies and ideologies. In many cases, conventional morality has a mixture of Christian moral teaching, and many people utterly confuse the two. Secular humanists tend to confuse Christian morality with whatever they were told was Christian morality when they were young. Hence, criticism of conventional morality often is thought to be criticism of

Christian morality, and defects discovered in conventional morality often are mistakenly regarded as errors in Christian teaching.

Christians ought to examine in the light of faith the argument between critics and defenders of conventional morality. Some behavior which is deviant by the standards of conventional morality does manifest sin; some of the social order protected by conventional morality also manifests sin; the philosophies and ideologies used by secular humanist critics of conventional morality themselves serve as elaborate systems for rationalizing sin. Marxism, for example, serves to rationalize the dehumanization it works—amply documented by critics such as Solzhenitsyn. Freudian psychology owes its fascination partly to its utility in rationalizing sexual sins.

Question G: How should Christians evaluate deterministic accounts of sin?

1. The denial of the reality of God and of free choice must be rejected.[15] It is a divinely revealed truth, solemnly defined by the Church, that human persons have a capacity to make free choices (see 2-B). Free choice is both an essential principle of Christian moral responsibility and an integral part of what it means for human persons to be made in God's image.

2. It is quite true that people often act without choosing. Experiments show, for example, that people can be led to act spontaneously, without any choice, by hypnotic suggestion. Psychological case studies by Freud and others further suggest that many people have emotional urges which they do not understand and which limit them in making choices, including such very important choices as that of a marriage partner. Furthermore, it hardly needs saying that, in choosing, people are often unable to consider possibilities they might choose if they considered them. For example, children raised in a slum simply do not face the same set of practical possibilities as children raised in a middle-class neighborhood.

3. Such evidence points to the conclusion that some people are not in a position to make the choices others might think they morally ought to make. Thus, a comfortable, middle-class, psychologically healthy Christian, who is in a good position to live in accord with Christian norms of morality, might well fail to appreciate the narrow limits within which others, lacking such advantages, make their choices.

4. We ought not, however, to make the nonbeliever's mistake of generalizing from limited data to deny free choice and moral responsibility. **The data show that people often act without choosing and often choose without being in a position to give serious consideration to possibilities others regard as morally right. But these data do not show that people who have the experience of making choices could be mistaken in thinking their choices free. Despite all modern attempts to explain away sin, free choice and radical personal responsibility remain intact.** Moral responsibility ends where free choice becomes impossible, but where there is a possibility of free choice for a person in his or her actual condition, moral responsibility is present.

5. Christians should therefore reject deterministic theories of moral evil. Some of the data which they cover—namely, data arising from free choices—

should be attributed to free choices, and the irreducible character of free choice should be defended. To the extent that sins depend on the freedom of free choices, it is a mistake to try to give explanations for them, for freedom simply cannot be explained by something other than itself. Otherwise, it would not be freedom.

Deterministic theories remain tempting for two reasons. First, we would like to think we are not as responsible as we are. We talk about "falling" into sin, as if we sinned by accident, rather than admit that we sin by freely choosing a path apart from God. We also become very "charitable" in explaining away the apparent sins of others—not only to avoid condemnation but presumptuously to render an acquittal—because this sort of indulgence allows us to excuse ourselves: "If Titus, who commits murder, cannot help it, how could I be held responsible for a bit of malicious gossip?" Second, a deterministic theory remains attractive because it seems to explain human action; free choice leaves human action ultimately mysterious. We not only could distance ourselves from sin but could feel sin to be in our power if we could point to an adequate cause which would explain it. However, no free choice as such can be fully explained.

6. Where determining factors are really operative, rather than denying their operation, one should appeal to them to explain what they actually explain, but only that. For example, alcoholism has many determining factors; it is a disease of sorts. But it is also a condition which continues to rule people because they freely refuse, when sober, to seek the necessary help, such as joining Alcoholics Anonymous.

7. Many psychological and social determining factors invoked by modern theories of moral evil have moral roots. For example, it is easy enough to see how social conditions do limit choices for many people who are subject to oppressors; to this extent, Marxism's deterministic account of some aspects of people's behavior can be justified. But on the further account of Marxism, the behavior of the oppressors is due to morally questionable motives such as greed, and there is nothing in the theory which compels one to accept a deterministic account of this greed or the oppression to which it leads.

8. Similarly, one can at times accept a psychological account attributing certain behavior of individuals to neurotic compulsion. Yet the compulsion itself might be traceable to moral guilt on the part of the individual. If Lady Macbeth could not help washing her hands, there nevertheless was a time when she freely chose to bloody them.

9. Insofar as human misery has its moral roots in freedom, hope remains for conversion and redemption. By contrast, Marxists propose to improve the human condition by violent revolution, liberal secular humanists by technocratic manipulation. Both approaches infringe upon the inner integrity and intimate relationships of persons; both undermine appreciation for human dignity. For its part, the gospel calls for repentance, offers forgiveness, and promises the grace to live a life worthy of one made in God's image. It respects inner integrity and intimate relationships; it promotes true personal dignity.

Secular humanists usually propose their accounts of sin in the name of science. Attempts to explain away sin are often found in psychological and sociological writings. Drawing upon such sources, many Catholic writers, including theologians, religious educators, and popular writers on spirituality, have become imbued with a false account of sin. To repeat: It is necessary to guard against attempts to explain sin. They are appealing for, if successful, they would eliminate responsibility and allow one to sin with impunity. But sin cannot be explained in terms of anything else. I alone am responsible for my sin.

Summary

Scripture neither identifies sin with creatureliness, nor reduces it to illusion or the breaking of a taboo. Rather, the sacred writers show sin to be a terrible reality involving a personal, inner, and enduring wrong. Even when it involves injustice to other people, sin is more basically against the Lord. Yet it is not God whom sin hurts but the sinner. The New Testament regards sin not primarily as the multiple reality of many immoral deeds but as the unitary reality of the sinner's state of alienation from God.

Moral evil and sin are really the same thing, considered under different aspects. Sin is moral evil considered precisely as it is contrary to the good of religion. Every immoral act disrupts harmony in the relationship with God as well as within the self and in the relationship with other people.

All sin is an offense against God. This is so because sin is moral evil, and moral evil is contrary to integral human fulfillment—the fulfillment to which we are directed by God's eternal law, in which both natural law and revealed moral truth participate. The sins of Christians are more serious than those of nonbelievers; the Christian offends Jesus, wounds the Church, and consciously sins against God in choosing some other good in a way incompatible with continued friendship with him. Understood this way, St. Augustine is correct in saying that every immoral act involves turning from God and contempt for him; but this is misunderstood if it is taken to mean that one does not sin unless one purposely offends God or that the evil of sin is only in disruption of one's relationship with God.

Moral evil resides precisely in a privation—lack of openness to integral human fulfillment. As a privation, moral evil is real but not a positive reality. It does not require a causal explanation, as if it were a distinct creature, and therefore in no way depends on God.

While the behavior which executes an evil choice shares in its evil, sin is primarily in the choice; and because choices are spiritual realities which determine the self and which last, the guilt of sin—which is sin itself—lasts after the sinful behavior ceases. Moral evil spreads from sinful choices through other forms of voluntariness. It pervades interpersonal relationships and introduces disorder into all the dimensions of individual and social reality.

A wrong choice which conforms to erroneous conscience or one made by a person unable to make a relevant judgment of conscience is called "material" sin, while a choice which violates conscience is "formal" sin. To the extent erroneous conscience is culpable, however—that is, to the extent one is responsible for being mistaken—material sins also involve guilt.

Although in sinning one does not choose moral evil as such but a certain good, one nevertheless accepts the moral evil. To persons without faith, moral evil generally appears unreasonable at most. But because consistent reasonableness is likely to seem pointless in the fallen human condition, morally evil choices are, as the Church teaches, inevitable apart from faith and grace. Sinful possibilities can be appealing to emotion; furthermore, they invariably offer at least some aspect of intelligible goodness, namely, a certain realization of the good of self-integration effected by satisfying an emotional drive (though at the expense of a deeper and more inclusive self-integration).

Sins in social acts affect even members of a community who do not personally participate in them. Original sin, the prototype of social sin, affects the entire human situation. Humankind is confronted not only with the sins of individuals but with a whole system of evil deriving from original sin and actual sins. In working for redemption, Christians must strive to overcome the sin which pervades society and culture. Pervasive as this is, however, one ought not therefore to accord to sin a reality, an autonomy, in itself.

In attempting to account for the reality of moral evil in the world, secular humanist ideologies seek to explain sin away by denying free choice and proposing solutions which do not depend on freedom. This is true in their various ways of Freud and Dewey, of Marxists, of Nietzsche and Heidegger. Regardless of their preferred explanation, when they speak of immorality most contemporary nonbelievers are thinking of conventional morality; and while to some extent they criticize conventional morality, to some extent they also reinforce it.

Christians cannot accept the atheism and determinism of secular humanist ideologies. True, people's capacity for exercising free choice is often limited by pyschological factors or social and cultural circumstances. But this does not take away the reality of free choice and personal responsibility. It is a mistake, furthermore, to try to explain sins; for sins are free choices, and freedom cannot be explained by anything but itself.

A great deal of human suffering has its moral roots in sin and thus in freedom; to the extent this is so, there is hope in the possibility of conversion and redemption. By contrast, Marxism sees the solution to human suffering in violent revolution and liberal secular humanism in technocratic manipulation. Some Catholic writers and educators have been influenced by false accounts of moral evil which attempt to explain it away and, in the process, do away also with freedom and personal responsibility.

Appendix 1:   Misunderstandings of sin to be avoided

St. Augustine undertakes to clarify the notion of sin in terms of turning: It is an inordination by which one turns from the creator toward inferior, created things.[16] There is a sense in which this formulation is correct, but it also is likely to lead to misunderstandings.

The formulation is correct in the sense that sin does violate the law of God in the ways indicated in question C. One who sins settles for a possibility marked out by nonrational desire; the sinful choice is not in line with consistent openness to integral fulfillment in Jesus. Moreover, a well-instructed Christian who is tempted to commit a sin is acutely aware that the immoral choice also means accepting a violation, more or less serious, of friendship with God. In choosing between the object of one's wrong desire and the morally upright alternative to it, one therefore can be said to be choosing between a certain created, quite transitory good and the goodness of God, whose friendship one freely violates.

327

But Augustine's formulation is likely to lead to misunderstandings because of the particular theological framework in which he worked—a kind of Neoplatonism.[17] As will be explained (in 34-A), Augustine did not sufficiently appreciate the inherent importance of created goods and of human life in this world. He tended to think of the human soul as if it were naturally oriented to the divine as to its only adequate fulfillment. Thus, for him the human person about to choose stands between the infinite goodness and beauty of God, on the one side, and the very limited beauty and defective goodness of creatures, on the other. Sin consists in turning from God toward the creature—a turning so hard to understand that it can only appear either insane or utterly perverse.[18]

In our day-to-day experience, sin is by no means so dramatic. A woman whose husband has abandoned her must choose between lonely faithfulness to him and a new chance at happiness, in the form of an appealing man who wishes to marry her. A businessman must choose between losing his investment and using methods of competition which he considers fraudulent. Even Thomas More's choice was between pleasing the king with the empty gesture of an oath and giving his life to avoid perjury. In none of these cases would one who does not share Augustine's metaphysics be inclined to formulate the issue as whether to turn from God to a created good.

Augustine refined his formulation by contrasting the two loves: "Two loves, therefore, have made two cities. There is an earthly city made by the love of self even to the point of contempt for God, and a heavenly city made by the love of God even to the point of contempt for self" (FEF 1763). Here, again, the formula has a sound sense. To sin is to violate the mind and will of God, and so to express contempt for him; a morally upright life, by contrast, is the fruit of charity, which is divine love. Still, charity does not require contempt for oneself absolutely, but only contempt for one's sinfulness which separates one from God and from one's own fulfillment.[19]

Sinners are not great lovers of themselves; saints who love God perfectly love themselves far more richly than do sinners, for saints seek the finest good for themselves (see *S.t.*, 1–2, q. 29, a. 4; 2–2, q. 25, a. 7). Moreover, not all sin is selfishness. Certainly one can sin by egoism, by lack of sympathy for others, by partiality which prefers oneself and those with whom one is identified to others equally or more deserving of one's concern (see *S.t.*, 1–2, q. 77, a. 4, ad 4; 2–2, q. 63, a. 1). But one also can sin in many other ways— for example, by a fanatical act of revenge which destroys not only one's hated enemy but oneself. No doubt, one who chooses such an act seeks a certain self-fulfillment in it, namely, the satisfaction of revenge itself. But such satisfaction cannot be called "selfish" in any ordinary sense of the word.

Appendix 2:   Emphases on self and law to be avoided

In Christian teaching today, it probably would be wise not to stress selfishness or self-love as a danger. Even more, it is important to avoid emphasis on law.

To say that self-love and selfishness should not be stressed as a danger is not to say that lack of sympathy and unfairness should be ignored. Especially in dealing with children, one must confront rather gross forms of egoism. However, the effort must be to help children understand that their genuine self-fulfillment is in Jesus rather than elsewhere. It is a mistake to overcome egoism by transforming it into irrational partiality toward a group; sin resides more securely in such partiality than in the fragile egoism of the selfish little child.

When one deals with adults, one must try to help them understand that their group biases and prejudices, their partiality to selected classes and types of people, can have a nonrational ground which is much more seriously immoral than the naive egoism of the child or the social misfit. However, in our culture, which is both individualistic and dominated by social controls necessary to keep selfishness in check, to stress self-love and selfishness as a moral danger is in practice to put Christian moral teaching in the service of socialization into mass culture as it is. It is more important to stress the inadequacy of the self-love of the sinner, to point out his or her failure to move toward true self-fulfillment which can be found only in Jesus.

In short, where "self" for Augustine and most medieval thinkers pointed to a center of resistance to communion in intelligible goods, "self" for people living in our time points to unenlightened and immature egoism. In earlier times, warnings against self-love might turn sinners toward God; today, warnings against self-love turn everyone toward the organization, the group, the lonely crowd—the mass society in which individuals surrender personal dignity for a feeling of community and in return gain only participation in a larger and less self-conscious center of resistance to communion in intelligible goods.

Likewise, any emphasis on law is likely to be confusing. "Law" has a bad name, for it is much abused as an instrument of formal social control and an enforcer of conventional norms, regardless of whether they have a moral foundation. Hence, the aspect in which law is an alien imposition upon one's freedom is paramount in most people's thought. Moreover, small children necessarily view morality in a rather legalistic way, and adolescents inevitably rebel against this childish view. Today, such rebellion is in full flower, with the whole culture selectively setting law aside as an encumbrance of childhood.

For these reasons, I do not speak of "natural law," but rather of human modes of responsibility, human moral principles, and so on. One must understand what "law" means in Scripture, in traditional teachings, in the Fathers, and in recent documents of the magisterium. But one can hardly hope to bring the faithful at large to understand the realities to which the Church refers by "law" if one constantly uses the word itself.

Enlightened by true moral norms, a Christian is not confronted with a set of arbitrary choices, made for some purpose which he or she might or might not share. Rather, moral norms in Christian instruction clarify the truths which everyone more or less knows at heart and add the light of faith which makes clear the way of Christ for finding both human and divine fulfillment. To sin is not to break a law (taking "law" in any ordinary sense); to be punished for sin is not to experience the sanction imposed upon lawbreakers. Rather, to sin is to limit oneself unnecessarily, to damage one's true self and block one's real fulfillment; the punishment of sin is the sin itself and its inevitable consequences, as will be explained more fully (in 18-I).

Notes

1. In its main lines the treatment of sin in this and the next five chapters depends on St. Thomas Aquinas, to whose work references are supplied where appropriate. The consensus of modern classical moral theology is followed when it consistently develops Thomas and fits into the theological framework of the present work. For a study of a key work of St. Thomas on sin and evil: Carlos Cardona, "Introducción a la questión disputata de Malo: Contribución al diagnóstico de una parte de la situación contemporánea," *Scripta Theologica*, 6 (1974), 111–43. For a systematic survey which usefully notes certain problem areas and developments, see Thomas Deman, O.P., "Péché," *Dictionnaire de Théologie Catholique*, 12:140–225.

2. Still fundamental for the study of sin in Scripture: Gustav Stählin et al., "hamartanō, hamartēma, hamartia," *Theological Dictionary of the New Testament*, 1:267–316. An excellent brief treatment of sin in Scripture: Stanislas Lyonnet, S.J., "Sin," *Dictionary of Biblical Theology*, 2d ed., 550–57. Although not perfect, a generally helpful introduction: Eugene H. Maly, *Sin: Biblical Perspectives* (Cincinnati, O.: Pflaum/Standard, 1973); for greater depth and bibliography: Stanislas Lyonnet, S.J., and Leopold Sabourin, S.J., *Sin, Redemption, and Sacrifice: A Biblical and Patristic*

Study (Rome: Biblical Institute Press, 1970), 1–57; Albert Gelin (Old Testament) and Albert Descamps (New Testament), *Sin in the Bible* (New York: Desclée, 1965).

3. See Ignace de la Potterie, S.J., and Stanislas Lyonnet, S.J., *The Christian Lives by the Spirit* (Staten Island, N.Y.: Alba House, 1971), 174–96. For an excellent, general summary of "sin" in 1 John: Eugene J. Cooper, "The Consciousness of Sin in 1 John," *Laval Théologique et Philosophique*, 28 (1972), 237–48.

4. Some scholars who write on sin lack insight into any nonlegalistic concept of moral evil. They have no understanding of authentic natural-law theory. Hence, they think that a "moralistic" conception of sin is mere legalism—deviation from externally imposed norms. To this they contrast a theological, "personalistic" conception—personal alienation from God. See, for example, S. J. de Vries, "Sin, Sinners," *Interpreter's Dictionary of the Bible*, 4:362–63, where such a defect mars an otherwise helpful article. To some extent, to use responsibility, conceived as answerability to God, as the basic category of religious ethics is a sign of the same defect. See, for instance, Charles E. Curran, "Responsibility in Moral Theology: Centrality, Foundations, and Implications for Ecclesiology," *The Jurist*, 31 (1971), 113–42, where the responsibility motif is advanced in contrast to the institutional motif, in a framework where the moral teaching of the Church is misconceived in a thoroughly legalistic way.

5. Lyonnet and Sabourin, op. cit., 5.

6. In the case of mortal sin, one's participation in divine life, which is more than a merely human good, also is implicitly at stake. But this fact is known only by faith, since grace does not present itself as something humanly fulfilling except insofar as it affects the human good of religion. Thus, only the latter appears directly threatened when one is tempted to commit a mortal sin.

7. See St. Thomas Aquinas, *S.t.*, 1–2, q. 71, a. 2, esp. ad 3; in showing that every vice is against nature, he explains that emotion provides the natural foundation for the irrationality of sin. One might object that angels also can sin, and that Thomas elsewhere (*S.c.g.*, 3, 109) suggests that human beings can sin as the angels do, by refusing to subordinate their proper good to divine goodness itself, which is the ultimate end. I think that Thomas is inconsistent in this matter. For in the same work (*S.c.g.*, 3, 122) he holds that "we do not offend God except by doing something contrary to our own good." To refuse to subordinate one's proper good to divine goodness will not be contrary to our own good unless this subordination is essential for an immanent order constitutive of one's proper good. But if ordering one's proper good to God is essential to one's proper good itself, then there can be no choice between standing in one's proper good and ordering that good to God—the two are not genuine alternatives. So one will naturally love God more than oneself provided one does not violate one's proper good, and Thomas teaches precisely this to be the case, both with respect to angels and human persons (*S.t.*, 1, q. 60, a. 5). In dealing with the angels and with human persons in the condition of original justice, Thomas holds that sanctifying grace is required to order the created will to the supernatural end (*S.t.*, 1, q. 62, a. 2; q. 95, a. 1). Here the subjection of human reason to God is a matter of grace, and one might suppose that sin in the case of the angel (and the parallel case for human persons) is simply a refusal of grace, without any immanent violation of a proper, natural good (cf. *De malo*, q. 16, a. 5). But there can be no choice without an alternative, and so if grace can be rejected without a violation of the natural good of the creature, then that good itself must be an alternative to grace; in that case, grace would not perfect nature, but annul it. I think that this inconsistency in Thomas underlies the unsatisfactory situation among Thomists on the sin of the angels. See Jacques Maritain, *The Sin of the Angel* (Westminster, Md.: Newman Press, 1959), v–vii; but his own resolution is inadequate, since he supposes (30) that in opting for God the proper good of the creature must be set aside and (90) that the violation in angelic sin is simply disobedience, for obedience is always required by nature. How, then, can angels sin? I think we must stop assuming that we know what angels are—simple spiritual substances. This is only a theological hypothesis. If we assume in them some complexity of nature, analogous to that of our own, then we can suppose that they might sin as we do, by preferring their own partial good. Supposing this, we no longer need suppose either that there can be an option with no genuine alternative or that grace is a genuine alternative to the perfection possible to finite persons according to their nature. Chapters twenty-four and twenty-five propose a resolution to the underlying difficulty about the distinction and unity in created persons of nature and grace.

8. See Dionigi Tettamanzi, "La Dimensione Ecclesiale e Sociale del Peccato del Cristiano," *La Scuola Cattolica*, 107 (1979), 516–44; Patrick Kerans, *Sinful Social Structures* (New York: Paulist Press, 1974), 5–7 and 55–82.

9. On determinist theories and their account of morality: Joseph M. Boyle, Jr., Germain Grisez, and Olaf Tollefsen, *Free Choice: A Self-Referential Argument* (Notre Dame and London: University of Notre Dame Press, 1976), 48–103. A splendid treatment of the metaphysical foundations of

contemporary atheism: Cornelio Fabro, *God in Exile: Modern Atheism: A Study of the Internal Dynamic of Modern Atheism, from Its Roots in the Cartesian "Cogito" to the Present Day*, trans. and ed. Arthur Gibson (Westminster, Md.: Newman Press, 1968), 629–938.

10. For an introduction to the thought of Sigmund Freud as an alternative world view to Christian morality, see Luther J. Binkley, *Conflict of Ideals: Changing Values in Western Society* (New York: Van Nostrand, Reinhold, 1969), 84–106; Erich Fromm's contemporary development of Freud's thought also is summarized by Binkley, 106–23. Freud himself summed up his view: *Civilization and Its Discontents* (New York: W. W. Norton, 1961), 64–80 (chaps. 6 and 7).

11. A very readable introduction to his entire system of thought: John Dewey, *Reconstruction in Philosophy*, enlarged ed. (Boston: Beacon Press, 1957). A more technical work, essential to understand Dewey's thought as an alternative to Christian morality: *Human Nature and Conduct: An Introduction to Social Psychology* (New York: Henry Holt, 1922), esp. 248–332.

12. Binkley, op. cit., 44–83, provides a basic introduction to Marxism from the relevant viewpoint, with helpful references to primary and secondary literature. Unfortunately, no single work of Karl Marx or Friedrich Engels summarizes their world view as an alternative to Christian morality. A more sophisticated introduction to Marxist thought, with critique: Louis Dupré, *The Philosophical Foundations of Marxism* (New York: Harcourt, Brace and World, 1966), 213–30.

13. Binkley, op. cit., 144–59, provides a simple introduction. The most relevant and representative work of Nietzsche for comparison with Christian morality: *The Antichrist*, in *The Portable Nietzsche*, ed. Walter Kaufmann (New York: Viking Press, 1954), 565–656.

14. For an introduction to Heidegger: Thomas Langan, *The Meaning of Heidegger: A Critical Study of an Existentialist Phenomenology* (New York: Columbia University Press, 1959), esp. 201–38. The central, relevant segment of the basic work: Martin Heidegger, *Being and Time* (New York: Harper and Row, 1962), 312–48. The most relevant brief work of Heidegger, "Letter on Humanism," in *Martin Heidegger: Basic Writings*, ed. David Farrell Krell (New York: Harper and Row, 1977), 193–242.

15. I know of no thoroughgoing critique of post-Hegelian world views considered precisely as proposals alternative to Christian morality's understanding of sin and redemption. A helpful beginning toward such a critique: Jacques Maritain, *Moral Philosophy: An Historical and Critical Survey of the Great Systems* (New York: Charles Scribner's Sons, 1964), 209–447. Some suggestive reflections on certain post-Hegelian thinkers' inadequate reactions to legalism: Wilhelm Korff, "Dilemmas of a 'Guilt-Free Ethic'," in *Moral Evil under Challenge*, Concilium, 56, ed. Johannes B. Metz (New York: Herder and Herder, 1970), 69–89.

16. See M. Huftier, "Péché Mortel et Péché Veniel," in *Théologie du Péché*, ed. Ph. Delhaye et al. (Tournai: Desclée, 1960), 315.

17. The heavy influence of Neoplatonic philosophy in Augustine's conception of sin is shown by M. Huftier, *Le Tragique de la Condition Chrétienne chez Saint Augustin* (Paris: Desclée, 1964), 34–91. For a brief, clear, and very helpful summary of the difference between Augustine's more Neoplatonic view and Thomas' view, see Maurice Huftier, "The Nature of Actual Sin," *Theology Digest*, 9 (1961), 121–25. In a purely Neoplatonic view, there is no sin, because the human individual is alienated from God simply in coming to be as an individual, and reunited to God by an intellectual knowing rather than conversion of heart. Even in his early work, *On the Free Choice of the Will*, Augustine clearly recognizes the role of freedom and so affirms the characteristically Christian conception of moral responsibility. But in that work (1, 16; 2, 20) he defines sin as a turning from the immutable to the changeable, from the intelligible to the sensible good, and in this way preserves as much of the Neoplatonic view as he can. This conception of sin makes it hard to understand how anyone is tempted to choose to sin; it also leads to false accounts of the sinfulness of real sins, for example, in the domain of sex. A good deal of what was defective in the classical theology's account of the evil of sexual sins can be traced to the Neoplatonic element in Augustine: William M. Alexander, "Sex and Philosophy in Augustine," *Augustinian Studies*, 5 (1974), 197–208.

18. See Frederick L. Miller, "The Fundamental Option in the Thought of St. Augustine," *Downside Review*, 95 (1977), 271–83, esp. 282, where Miller captures the near irrationality of sin in Augustine's framework: "For a man who participates in the divine intellect through faith to repudiate the order he finds therein (viz. natural law, divine revealed law) is tantamount to an act of deliberate insanity." But Miller also makes it clear (283) that Augustine is too consistent and faithful a Christian to doubt that every gravely disordered choice against a divine commandment is a mortal sin. Also see the rich and sympathetic account of Augustine's view of sin by D. J. MacQueen, "Contemptus Dei: St. Augustine on the Disorder of Pride in Society and its Remedies," *Recherches Augustiniennes*, 9

(1973), 227–93, esp. 253–56; "Augustine on Superbia: The Historical Background and Sources of His Doctrine," *Mélanges de Science Religieuse,* 34 (1977), 193–211; 35 (1978), 78. The basic trouble with Augustine's Neoplatonism is that it requires one to cease being human in order to become fully human by the possession of God: Robert J. O'Connell, *St. Augustine's Early Theory of Man, A.D. 386–391* (Cambridge, Mass.: Belknap Press of Harvard University Press, 1968), 217–18.

19. Augustine himself was aware of the ambiguities of "self-love": Oliver O'Donovan, *The Problem of Self-Love in St. Augustine* (New Haven: Yale University Press, 1980), 93–111. Yet Augustine's view is shown by the same study (60–92) to be shaped by a transformed Neoplatonism which posits the self initially as a substance midway between God and created goods, between the One and the many.

CHAPTER FOURTEEN

SIN OF ADAM AND SINS OF MEN AND WOMEN

Introduction

Pius XI provides a brief summary of Catholic teaching on the subject of this chapter. "Original sin," he explains, "is the hereditary but impersonal fault of Adam's descendants, who have sinned in him (Rom 5.12). It is the loss of grace, and therefore of eternal life, together with a propensity to evil, which everybody must, with the assistance of grace, penance, resistance and moral effort, repress and conquer. The passion and death of the Son of God has redeemed the world from the hereditary curse of sin and death."[1]

This summary indicates why the treatment of original sin does not belong exclusively to dogmatic theology. Rather, it must be considered in the treatment of Christian moral principles, for it conditions the whole of Christian life. The central principle of that life is the redemptive life of Jesus, whose obedience is related to original sin as an antidote to a poison. The specific demands of Christian life are hard; an understanding of original sin helps make it clear why they cannot be easy. Finally, the effects of original sin set many of the problems which Christian life must solve. For all these reasons, original sin must be considered and rightly understood, in order to grasp what Christian living is.[2]

To understand the redemptive work of Jesus, one must understand what faith teaches concerning original sin. Otherwise, the mystery of the redemption will seem absurd, because the suffering and death of Jesus will seem pointless—as if it were an arbitrary price exacted by a cruel Father, rather than an appropriate price paid by a Father whose merciful love is boundless. This brutal misperception of the sacrifice of Jesus can be an important obstacle to the acceptance of Christian faith.

Question A: For what aspects of the human condition does original sin account?

1. **Although death is natural and inevitable, it hardly seems appropriate to us that we and those we love should die. Even worse than death is the general condition of conflict—of inner turmoil, of falling short of one's ideals, of striving against others. The situation is no better, indeed is often worse, when one looks beyond the individual to society.** Social structures which should promote justice foster oppression and war; races, nations, classes, and groups of all sorts struggle constantly for supremacy at one another's expense. As

for powers beyond the human, their attitude toward humankind, as attested by the various religions, seems ambiguous—by no means always benign and, to judge from many manifestations, in some respects distinctly hostile.[3]

2. Accounts of evil incompatible with Christian faith are common. As we have seen (5-C), some posit an ultimate duality of good and evil principles, with human existence their battleground. Others suggest that evil is an illusion. Secular humanists, both Western liberals and Marxists, write off evil as a stage of evolutionary development and expect increasing knowledge or the unfolding dialectic of history eventually to overcome it. These false accounts of human misery fail to take into account people's abuse of the power to choose freely.

3. Jews and Christians cannot consistently accept such accounts of evil. According to their religious tradition, God created everything good, and evil is a privation which arises primarily from the abuse of the God-like gift of freedom. Our misery is not inevitable; we have somehow brought it upon ourselves (see S.t., 1, q. 48, a. 5). Still, the account of evil given by the Jewish and Christian religious tradition does not eliminate its mysteriousness.

4. A Jewish writer near the time of Jesus remarks: "God did not make death, and he does not delight in the death of the living. For he created all things that they might exist" (Wis 1.13–14; cf. Is 45.18). Yet death seems to be natural. If so, it must have been "made" by God; in that case, how can God be truly good? Death also lends a kind of support to sin, since the wicked seek oblivion in death (see Wis 1.16–2.9). Thus sin and death are essentially related. But as death is a universal feature of the human condition, so, too, must sin be in some sense universal.

5. The data of experience testify to this, as also to the fact that sin is, in some sense, inevitable. One sins freely; one also sins inevitably (see DS 228–30/106–8). **We find ourselves preconditioned in a sinful situation, distracted by anxiety about death, driven by temptations we seem too weak to resist for long.**

6. **Even if this situation confronts all humankind, however, it could not have been this way at the beginning** (see GS 13). **For God is good, and sin cannot have originated with him.** If, then, we cannot account for these universal features of the human condition by referring them to God, we must look instead to the beginning of humankind (see S.c.g., 4, 52). The problem requires us to consider the condition of Man in the innocence in which our race emerged from the hand of God. How did human beings first commit sin? Only in an abuse of freedom by Man at the beginning can we find an explanation for the misery which still afflicts the whole of humankind.[4]

The data of experience make clear the universality of sin. As St. Paul points out, those who do not believe in God are sunk in evil; this evil follows from all sorts of sins, which in turn issue from idolatry and nonbelief (see Rom 1.18–32). The situation cannot be blamed on God; he gave even the pagans sufficient knowledge to be aware of him, whom alone they should worship, and he gave them an adequate grasp on right and wrong (see Rom 1.20 and 2.14–16). How, then, does sin originate among the pagans, who do not break the law of God, yet fall into wickedness by abusing their freedom?

The Jewish sage suggests explanations for the origin of idolatry. For example, "For a father, consumed with grief at an untimely bereavement, made an image of his child, who had been suddenly taken from him; and he now honored as a god what was once a dead human being, and handed on to his dependents secret rites and initiations" (Wis 14.15). The ambition and greed of artisans and artists make idolatry flourish (see Wis 14.18–19; 15.11–13). And from idolatry flood all sorts of sins (see Wis 14.22–31). God is kind and gentle even with such sinners, for he provides them with the motive and opportunity for repentance (see Wis 12.2–10). Yet the pagans fail to seize the opportunity; their malice is ingrained; "they were an accursed race from the beginning" (Wis 12.11).

But is Israel free of sin? Not at all, despite being chosen by God and favored with his word of guidance and his faithful help. Jesus, after excoriating the scribes and Pharisees, says: "Thus you witness against yourselves, that you are sons of those who murdered the prophets. Fill up, then, the measure of your fathers" (Mt 23.31–32). No more than the pagans do the Jews avoid sin. "None is righteous, no, not one" (Rom 3.10). Solomon prays, with wise consciousness of human sinfulness: "If they sin against you—for there is no man who does not sin . . ." (1 Kgs 8.46), taking for granted the inevitability of sin.

Question B: What does the Church teach about original sin?

1. The Council of Trent teaches definitively on original sin in a decree devoted to this subject.[5] In doing so, it prescinds from the case of Mary (see DS 1516/792). Its essential teaching is in five articles (see DS 1511–15/788–92).

2. **First, the Council asserts that the first man, Man (Adam), was constituted in justice and holiness, that he disobeyed a divine command, that he thereby lost justice and holiness and incurred as punishment the death with which God had threatened him.** The Council teaches that with death Man became a slave to the devil, and that he was as a whole, both body and soul, changed for the worse by the offense of this sin (cf. *S.t.*, 1, q. 95, a. 1; 1–2, q. 80, a. 4; q. 83; 2–2, q. 164, a. 1; 3, q. 49, a. 2).

The proposition that Man was changed as a whole for the worse is partially quoted from a definition of the sixth-century Second Council of Orange, which explicitly holds a point Trent does not explicitly mention: that the freedom of Man's soul did not remain untouched by this sin (see DS 371/174).

3. Second, Trent asserts that Man's sin was injurious to his descendants as well as to himself, that he lost holiness and justice for us as well as himself, and that he passed on to the whole of humankind sin itself, which is death of the soul, and not merely death and punishment of the body (cf. *S.t.*, 1–2, q. 81, a. 1; q. 82, aa. 1, 3; q. 83, a. 3; *S.c.g.*, 4, 50). Trent holds that the contradictory of this teaching is incompatible with the teaching of St. Paul (Rom 5.12).

4. **Third, Trent asserts that the sin of Man is one in origin and is communicated to all men and women by propagation, not by imitation, that this sin is in all humankind and also is each individual's sin.** The Council teaches that this sin is not taken away by the powers of nature, that its only remedy is the unique mediator and Lord Jesus Christ who reconciles us to God in his blood, and that the merit of our Lord is applied to adults and infants alike through the sacrament of baptism (cf. *S.t.*, 1–2, q. 81, aa. 1, 3; q. 82, aa. 1, 4; 3, q. 1, aa. 2, 4; q. 49, aa. 1–5; q. 69, aa. 1, 5; *S.c.g.*, 4, 50).

5. Fourth, Trent asserts that it is right to baptize infants and cleanse them of original sin, for they really do contract it; it is sin in the true sense, and it must be expiated (cf. *S.t.*, 3, q. 68, a. 9). This article also asserts that the Church has always understood St. Paul (Rom 5.12) to teach the universality of original sin, and so the universal need for redemption.

6. Fifth, Trent asserts that through the grace of our Lord Jesus original sin really is taken away, not merely covered over, that concupiscence (a tendency to sin) remains in the baptized, but that concupiscence is not sin in the true and proper sense of the word; it is only an effect of sin which inclines to sin (cf. *S.t.*, 1–2, q. 82, a. 3; q. 110, a. 1; q. 113, aa. 1, 6).

In support of its teaching that baptism really takes away sin, the Council also inserts in this article an argument based on various passages of Scripture. This argument is aimed against those who did not recognize the full effect of the redemption worked by God through our Lord Jesus.

7. The Second Council of Orange, which Trent intends to follow, makes explicit one further, important point.[6] It gives a reason, not mentioned by Trent, why it would be inappropriate to say that the punishment for original sin, but not sin itself, was transmitted to Man's descendants: namely, that this would be to attribute an injustice to God (see DS 372/175). In other words, if we share in the punishment for Man's sin, we must also somehow share in the sin itself, since otherwise God would be punishing us unfairly for a sin in no way our own (cf. *S.t.*, 1–2, q. 81, a. 1; q. 83, a. 1; *S.c.g.*, 4, 52).

Trent stresses the exclusivity of Christ's mediatorship, leaving no question that no one is saved except in him. Our Lord Jesus saves us from sin, from death, and from the power of the devil. By Jesus' redemptive work, effective in us through baptism, we truly are freed from sin, although unruly desire, which is an effect of sin, remains in us.

Although Vatican II has no extensive treatment of original sin, the recent Council in many places takes for granted the traditional teaching, which Trent defined, and alludes to its various aspects (see LG 2, 55–56, DV 3, AA 7, and GS 13, 18, 22). In the "Credo of the People of God," Paul VI summarized Trent's teaching in all its essentials, and very clearly reaffirmed it.[7]

Question C: Are current attempts to revise the Church's teaching defensible?

1. In what follows, three separate questions will be devoted to three important areas of difficulty concerning the teaching on original sin: the evolutionary account of human origins (question D), the seeming naturalness of death (question H), and the question of how a sin can be hereditary (question I). The present question considers attempts to revise the Church's teaching in view of these difficulties.[8] The unsatisfactoriness of the new approaches should reinforce our determination to resolve the difficulties without contradicting any element of the Church's teaching.

2. Modern Scripture studies make it clear that less is asserted about original sin in the Bible—for example, in Genesis—than might appear to be the case. The revealed truth is communicated by a linguistic-literary vehicle which includes picturesque details that need not be taken as part of revelation. Moreover, theories

of an original golden age influenced many of the Church Fathers in their descriptions of the condition of Man at the beginning, while St. Augustine linked the transmission of original sin with the vehemence of sexual passion.[9] Although such literary and theological elaborations are sometimes confused with the essential teaching of the Church, they are not part of it. Missing this point, defenders of the tradition sometimes burden themselves unnecessarily, while critics often focus their attack on points not essential to the Church's teaching.[10]

Awareness of the distinction between the propositions expressed and the linguistic-literary vehicle of their expression was not always clear prior to the nineteenth century, and probably was not clear to those who participated in Trent. Therefore, it seems appropriate to some contemporary theologians to limit the faith-requirement concerning original sin to what scholars today think can be established from Scripture, and then to reinterpret the definitions of Trent accordingly. This strategy also offers promise for resolving other difficulties, while still maintaining a doctrine of original sin sufficient to make clear what is wrong with humankind prior to personal sins.

However, while sound studies make it clear that Scripture says less about original sin than might have been thought in times past, they do not show that anything in the Bible is incompatible with Catholic faith concerning original sin as defined by Trent.[11] Moreover, while Catholic faith teaches more about original sin than could be established by cautious modern exegesis of Scripture, the definitive teaching of the Church on original sin is far more modest than popular impressions and past theological speculations.

Scripture must be interpreted in the light of living faith. The sense of Scripture which the Church has held and still holds is its true sense. In the matter of original sin, Trent explicitly specifies the meaning of Romans 5.12. Moreover, the Church's teaching helps greatly to sort out revealed truth from literary vehicle in passages such as the account in Genesis of the origin of human sinfulness.

3. One approach to revising the Church's teaching begins by emphasizing that human persons are destined for fulfillment in Christ, but require grace and a free decision for Christ to come to this fulfillment. This fulfillment is sharply contrasted with human nature considered by itself, apart from Christ. Hence, according to those who take this approach, original sin need not be considered a pervasive or primordial moral evil, but can instead be identified with such inevitable aspects of the human condition as our creaturely status, our vulnerability to temptation, or the fact that we are only gradually evolving toward the status we shall eventually enjoy.[12]

4. **Because God is responsible for these aspects of our condition, however, this approach faces a dilemma: Either these are not evils or God is responsible for evil.** If they are not evils, then it is a denial of original sin, not an explanation, to reduce it to such factors. If they are evils for which God is responsible, we have a new theory of original sin at the expense of denying God's goodness.

The teaching of Trent makes it clear that the first humans were constituted in holiness, but lost it by their disobedience. This proposition is central, as will become clearer in what follows, since it points to what is primary in the privation which original sin is: the lack of that grace in human persons which by God's generosity could and should have been in them merely by their coming into being as members of the family of humankind.

Yet it is a mistake to proceed from this point in isolation and try to account for original sin by assuming in human persons simply as created and as human a true resistance to participation in divine life—a resistance which must be overcome by grace. This would mean that there is some inherent incompatibility between fulfillment in human goods and fulfillment in divine goods—an inevitable clash between the natural and the super-natural—so that a perfectly natural thrust toward human fulfillment would entail a choice against supernatural life. There is no such incompatibility. It is not necessary that the human decrease so the divine might increase. Therefore, an adequate account of original sin must make clear how this condition affects the will, making every human person, until fully healed by grace, prone to immoral acts by which human goods are violated.

Much recent Catholic theology has been influenced in respect to original sin and evolution by the writings of Teilhard de Chardin. He sought to include all reality in a single evolutionistic scheme. Teilhard's vision is not a scientific hypothesis; rather, it is specula-tive metaphysics and theology. In Teilhard's system, neither free choice nor sin is fully recognized, and original sin is dismissed as an obstacle to the evolutionist optimism with which Teilhard replaces the traditional doctrine of the redemption.[13]

5. Another approach to revising the Church's teaching identifies original sin with the complex product of personal sins, which comprise a situation of evil impinging on every individual. Some claim this situation is referred to by the Scriptural expression "sin of the world." **However, while "sin of the world" might refer either to the pervasive situation of evil in the world or to original sin as the Church understands it, the expression cannot possibly refer to both.** For although baptism remits original sin, it clearly does nothing to alter the environment of sin for those who are baptized.[14] Evidently, then, original sin and the complex product of personal sins must differ.

Many of these attempted theological reconstructions fail to explain why humankind cannot in principle be redeemed by the combined natural powers of human persons, as all secular humanists propose. In this way, they rejoin the Pelagian heresy which evoked the most significant development of the traditional doctrine of original sin and of grace (see DS 222–30/101–8).

Some theologians who propose revisions of the Church's teaching go beyond careful exegesis and theological reflection, to reject—not merely interpret and develop—what the Church has definitively taught. In doing so, they set aside faith. But faith is an essential presupposition of true theology. It is not surprising that no one has proposed any cogent principle by which revisions are to be limited or graded once the requirement of faith is set aside. A question such as original sin is simply not like an issue in science or philosophy, where experience and reason can support some opinions and rule out others. Once the Church's teaching on such a matter is set aside, one opinion is as groundless as another.

6. **Radical revisions of Catholic teaching on original sin threaten a far more important doctrine: that on redemption.** If it is difficult to understand how sin was introduced into the world by the sin of one person and has been passed on from him to us, it is no easier—indeed, it is more difficult—to understand how grace is restored to humankind by the redemptive work of Jesus and com-municated from him to us. Again, if it is incredible that there was a conditional gift of immortality to a faithful humanity at the beginning, it is more incredible that there should be the actual gift of resurrection to redeemed humanity at the end. If, finally, one cannot accept a break in the continuum of nature to allow for

the special creation of human persons, one will find it far more difficult to accept the total transformation of nature into the new heavens and new earth.

7. The Council of Trent insists on the link between original sin and redemption (see B above). In doing so, it relies on and authoritatively interprets the doctrine of St. Paul, who explains the unity of redemption accomplished in Jesus by analogy with the unity of sin initiated by Man. Certainly, Paul's main interest is in reconciliation through Christ. However, contrary to what is often said, Paul does not simply project original sin as a kind of shadow of the redemption. Rather, he assumes it as the starting point for clarifying the redemption: "Therefore as sin came into the world through one man and death through sin, and so death spread to all men because all men sinned . . ." (Rom 5.12).[15]

In speaking of the sin of the first man, Trent refers to Genesis, chapters 2 and 3. Taken as it stands, the story in Genesis pictures the first humans as part of God's good creation. They disobey a divine command and are worsened in every aspect of human goodness.

One interesting feature of the story is the serpent's argument against the divine threat of death: "You will not die. For God knows that when you eat of it your eyes will be opened, and you will be like God, knowing good and evil" (Gn 3.4–5). Scripture here suggests a basic temptation: Sin has the appeal of freedom to do as one pleases, regardless of moral norms.[16] Before one encounters the consequences, it seems that sin, rather than being an obstacle to fulfillment, is a requirement if one is not to be limited arbitrarily. The appeal of sin is to one's desire to do and experience everything, to know—that is, to experience and enjoy—both what is recommended as good and what is forbidden as evil. The self-limitation inherent in choice is restrictive enough. Why must one also submit to moral norms, which appear to be additional and arbitrary limits?

Considerations along these lines support the view that the Man of Genesis 2 and 3 is every man, not simply the first man. But while these chapters clearly are not history in any ordinary sense, we should not conclude that they are myth. There is another possibility, namely, that in the concrete form of story they propose an inspired hypothesis. This hypothesis accounts not only for the general features of individuals' sins, but also for the common human situation of existential evil and mortality in a world God had created and deemed "very good" (see Gn 1.31).[17] For St. Paul, an expansion of the hypothesis becomes an element in his account of how faith in Christ justifies while nothing else does.

Question D: Does the theory of evolution present a serious difficulty for the doctrine of original sin?

1. The idea of evolution is popularly applied in various contexts. It is extended to the natural world generally, as when people speak of the "evolution" of the cosmos. In this wide sense, "evolution" simply means orderly process. Again, "evolution" is often used to refer to development in every sphere of culture and human life. This is a loose and inappropriate use of the term, for history is not a natural process but rather unfolds through human reflection, argument, and conflicts of power determined by human plans and choices. Popular usage aside, the only theory of evolution which is well established pertains exclusively to the unity and diversity of organic life.

The biological theory of evolution can be summarized as follows. Organisms reproduce; reproduction is not replication, but continuity with difference; differences which enhance reproductive potential tend to predominate; but what enhances reproductive potential differs under diverse conditions; therefore, organisms with common ancestors differ greatly under diverse conditions. Clearly, this theory applies neither to the natural world generally nor to human history, for they do not involve reproduction.

2. In light of these distinctions, one sees that only a pseudoscientific ideology supports the view that everything human can be accounted for in a single, all-embracing, naturalistic scheme of evolution. On the contrary, evolution as a biological theory can account only for the organic existence and attributes of humankind.

3. Intelligence and the capacity for free choice are not merely organic, however. As we experience and exercise them, these capacities involve self-reference and self-causation. These, in turn, presuppose the personal self which, in the natural world, only human beings possess. Nor can these capacities be accounted for as modifications of organically based functions. Thus evolution cannot account for human persons (see *S.t.*, 1, q. 16, a. 2; q. 75, aa. 2–6; q. 82, a. 2).[18]

4. The capacity for free choice either is or is not present. One cannot have a partial ability to make a slightly free choice. It follows that, if one admits the spiritual reality of human persons including their capacity for free choice, one also must admit that their emergence in the world had to be a sudden event.[19] **Whether from the dust of the earth or from some group of subhuman primates, human persons had to be brought into being by a special act of the divine, creative power** (see *S.t.*, 1, q. 90, a. 2; *S.c.g.*, 2, 87).

5. Following Genesis, Christians have usually thought of the human race as being descended from a single pair of individuals. This view is called "monogenism." However, evolution theory points to the need for a sizable, interbreeding population at the origin of any organic type as complex as the human.[20] This theory is called "polygenism." Both Pius XII and Paul VI warn that polygenism, which evolution theory seems to demand, appears incompatible with the Church's teaching. However, it is not clear that either of these popes proposed monogenism as the position to be held definitively.[21] Hence, if a Catholic can show how polygenism is compatible with the essential elements of the Church's teaching on original sin, then he or she may admit polygenism on the evidence for it.

6. There is nevertheless no evidence requiring us to suppose that the present human race descended from more than one interbreeding population. Like Genesis, biological theory points to a single group at the beginning of humankind. Question F below will explain why the size of this group is not important.

7. **Thus, there is no incompatibility between the Church's doctrine concerning original sin and the scientific view that, insofar as they are organisms, human beings had subpersonal antecedents.** Nor does the theory of evolution either require one to think or offer evidence for thinking that the first humans were semibestial or childlike, and incapable of serious sin. Whatever their antecedents, they were able to sin as soon as they were able to make free choices. If there were earlier, childlike, human beings, not yet capable of free choice, we have no social and moral solidarity with them.

Since anyone who accepts a Christian account of human persons must assume that they emerged by a sudden event inexplicable through natural causes alone, there can be no reason to suppose that the intelligence of the first person who was able to make a free choice was in any important way less than our own. In any case, one who can make a free choice can commit a sin; the Church's teaching on original sin requires no more than this of the first persons. If they did not have this ability, then they simply were not persons relevant to our moral situation.

This last point is important to bear in mind when various data about human origins are considered. Fossil remains, even the remains of primitive tools, do not necessarily show that the creatures which left these remains were morally responsible persons. Subhuman primates today evidence some tool-making ability; extinct species might well have had more of this ability. Some species too advanced for our ancestors' comfort may well have been extinguished by their competition.

Question E: What does faith teach about the initial human condition?

1. As was noted in question C, many Fathers of the Church added more than is needed to their description of humankind's original condition.[22] Following their lead, classical theology elaborated on the extraordinary knowledge, virtue, and power with which Man was said to have been endowed (see *S.t.*, 1, q. 95, a. 3; q. 96, aa. 1–2; q. 97, a. 2; q. 102). But the Church's teaching does not propose all of this supposed endowment as essential to faith. The concern in what follows is to give a minimal, essential description of what faith requires one to hold concerning the original human condition.

It often was suggested that Man was immune from pain. The argument for this is that Trent teaches that the sin we inherit is more than death and bodily pain (see DS 1512/789). But this argument is weak, since Trent does not assert here that we inherit susceptibility to bodily death and pain from Man, but that what we inherit as sin affects the soul and cannot be reduced to these bodily consequences. (Trent does assert in the previous article that sin leads to death; therefore, nonmortality must be considered part of the original human endowment, although immunity from pain need not be.)

2. **It is basic to everything else that God created Man good, without sin, and with the power of free choice** (see DS 239/130). Man was constituted in holiness and justice—that is, in friendship with God and moral uprightness (see DS 1511/788, 1901–26/1001–26). Moreover, by God's special gift, not by nature, Man would have been immortal had he not sinned (see DS 222/101, 1978/1078; *S.t.*, 1, q. 97, a. 4; 2–2, q. 164, a. 1). The Church's teaching leaves it open whether nonmortality was given and lost or whether it was only promised if Man remained in God's friendship.

3. Man cannot be envisaged as unconscious of the initial situation of friendship with God. Not only does God make himself known in the things he has made, but, as Vatican II teaches, "planning to make known the way of heavenly salvation, he went further and from the start manifested himself to our first parents" (DV 3). The bond of friendship between God and humankind was a real relationship in the experience of the first human persons. It has been fully restored

only through Jesus (see Rom 5.10–21; Col 1.20). One who thinks it incredible that there was a divine revelation to primitive humankind will think it no less incredible that there was revelation through Abraham, Moses, or Jesus.

4. Trent says concupiscence is a result of sin.[23] Implicit in this teaching is the proposition that Man in the beginning was free of unruly desire which might positively tend toward sin. Instead of the inner conflict we experience, Man was at first well disposed toward integral human fulfillment (see *S.t.*, 1, q. 95, aa. 1–2). Yet this disposition obviously could not have ruled out natural human desires or a normal inclination toward a good which it would be wrong to choose. Otherwise, sin would have been impossible.

Question F: How might the first humans have sinned?

1. According to the account of original sin in Genesis, a minimal human community, a man and a woman, was involved. Although the woman's sin was first, it was not decisive. The man's was, so that the common responsibility was primarily, although not exclusively, his.

2. For the sake of argument, the theory of polygenism, according to which the minimal human community must have been a sizable group, is granted here. It is also assumed that this was one interbreeding population with a potentiality for communication and social cohesion. Note, finally, that any social group can act as a group (see 2-E).

The Church's teaching about this initial human condition has been stated above. What does theological speculation appropriately add to this picture?

First, it seems appropriate from a theological point of view to add that Man not only emerged from the hand of God but also organically emerged from subpersonal antecedents. A subpersonal creation which is like God not only in existing but also in causing other things to exist is a more perfect manifestation of God's goodness than a subpersonal creation which simply exists as a setting for these other things. In particular, a subpersonal creation which has a share in causing the very image of God to come to be in the world is more noble than one which has no such share. Just as Mary and the whole of Israel are ennobled by the role which they play in the Incarnation of the Word, so the natural world (including our primate antecedents) is ennobled by doing its part, albeit nonconsciously, in the coming to be of persons within nature (see *S.c.g.*, 3, 69).

Second, it is appropriate to assume that the condition of primal humans was no more different from our condition than must be assumed. The basis is Ockham's razor. On this assumption, we ought to suppose that the primal Man's awareness of God was much like our own: faith in revelation. He had ground enough to believe in God and his promises, but no knowledge of what immortality and everlasting life might be like. He knew the difference between right and wrong, but saw no more clearly than we the implications for his friendship with God of doing what is wrong.

Third, while the biological evidence indicates that humankind emerged from a very large, widely scattered, interbreeding population, theology must assume that the spiritual capacity for free choice was given initially by a special divine intervention, which completed hominization, to a group of individuals small and cohesive enough to function socially as a single body. In this way, solidarity in sin by the whole of humankind was possible at the beginning. As additional groups were hominized, they emerged into an already-given existential situation, and so shared prior to any personal act in the moral condition of humankind. In this sense, they shared "by propagation not by imitation" (DS 1513/790), even if not all humans were lineal descendants of a single couple.

3. No matter how a group is organized, someone's action is decisive. (In a group which operates by simple majority voting, for example, the vote which makes the majority is decisive.) Primate hordes are structured socially, with a single dominant leader; supposing the transformation of a primate group into a human extended family, it is reasonable to suppose that it would have a similar social structure. **Thus, there is no obstacle to thinking the original human community had a single leader whose action was decisive for its action as such.** We can call this individual "Man."

4. As was explained in D above, the primitive condition of the first humans cannot be supposed to preclude free choice and sin. Once there were humans, they could make free choices and so could sin. It is a mistake to suppose initial goodness would have ruled out the possibility of temptation and, thus, of sin. Even emotional inclinations which are natural and in themselves good cannot always be followed reasonably, because they are not always consistent with integral human fulfillment.

5. It is evident that a large group of people can be carried away by a common wave of emotion and unreasonable thinking and so go wrong together. Moreover, factional conflict, in which questions of social control are settled by power with unfairness on all sides, is very common. Even in such factional contention there is common responsibility for accepting the use of unfair means; at the same time, the individual with primacy in the society has the primary responsibility for any general resort to violent means of settling issues.

All sorts of possible temptation situations which will meet the requirements of the original condition can be imagined. For example, leaders of groups and their followers often have disagreements in judgment about what is best for the group. Perhaps such a disagreement arose—for instance, about whether the time was ripe for Man to turn over leadership (changes in leadership do occur in all groups). Not out of any unruly passion or selfish inclination established by previous sin, for these are excluded by hypothesis, but out of a judgment that the problem threatened the whole group's well-being, Man may well have decided to cripple his brother.

The wrongness of such an act would have been obvious to Man. But all the consequences of doing wrong need not have been clear. Moreover, human freedom in this case would first have encountered its own paradoxical character. If the wrong is done, human good—the well-being of the group—seems to be promoted. The choice to do wrong does have a negative aspect with respect to human good, but so does the choice not to do wrong! True, God had warned against doing it. But the warning was not an evident truth. Perhaps—in this "perhaps" is a role for Satan—the submission to moral limits is something God demands for his own good, not for ours? In that case, one can assert one's human dignity by rejecting God's warning to do only what is morally right (see *S.t.*, 2–2, q. 163, a. 2).

6. Every morally evil act is a sin, even though there is no direct choice of something else in preference to God (see 13-D). To act against reason is to alienate oneself from God in whose wisdom and goodness human reason and fulfillment are participations. Moreover, as faith teaches, some sort of revelation and covenantlike relationship existed at the beginning between God and humankind.

Thus it is reasonable to assume that Man was aware that moral evil would disrupt friendship with God.

7. It is not necessary to suppose that humankind in general and Man in particular fully comprehended the significance of the sin they were tempted to commit. Indeed, Genesis suggests that, inasmuch as the comprehension of evil comes from experiencing its consequences, it was only by experience that Man learned the whole human meaning of evil. **Thus, those who first sinned could have known right from wrong without fully appreciating in advance the significance of their wrongdoing.**

8. Nor, to have involved us all in his sin, need Man have thought of himself as acting on behalf of humankind at large (see I below). Our existential involvement follows from our natural solidarity with humankind at the beginning, for whose social act the sin of Man, the leader of the first human social group, was decisive. One in species, humankind could and should have been one community in friendship with God, but by sin from the beginning instead constituted the broken human world.

Question G: What were the consequences of the first sin?

1. **Humankind as a group was no longer in friendship with God.** The human family was no longer God's earthly family. Moreover, whatever the matter of the first sin was, it inevitably disrupted harmony at every level of existence; it generated inner tension, insincerity, and interpersonal conflicts.[24]

2. **As faith teaches, Man would not have died had he not sinned, but with sin, death became inevitable.** Question H will consider how death is a consequence of sin. Here we need to consider some of the implications of introducing death into human existence. This consideration will explain why fear of death makes fallen men and women lifelong slaves of Satan (see Heb 2.14–15).

3. The fear of death has an effect on all human emotion. Were it not for this fundamental anxiety, our emotional reactions would be as naturally well adjusted as those of a healthy animal. Given this anxiety, however, the whole human emotional make up is distorted, radically biased toward intense pleasure, which helps offset fear. This distortion is documented by modern psychiatry, with its description of the subsconscious and of neurotic behavior.[25]

4. **The fundamental processes of human experience are affected by the distortion of emotion brought about by anxiety concerning death.** As psychology makes clear, memory and learning are very heavily conditioned processes. Therefore, emotions skewed by anxiety about death necessarily generate a very different experiential world than would have been generated by emotions without this basic anxiety.

5. Intellectual judgments, especially of a practical sort, are also distorted. They are based on experience to some extent and are also influenced by one's choices. Rationalization, together with the impact of distorted experience, generates moral opinions which often are false.

6. **As a result of distortions in knowledge, especially in practical judgment, language and the other products of culture are deprived of the**

rationality and pure usefulness they should have. Tools are made to serve not only good purposes but sinful ones. Language is used not only to communicate but to deceive. Everything human, as Marx helped show, is perverted by injustice.

7. Once begun, this whole situation is perpetuated in a vicious circle. Each sin of one person against another intensifies anxiety. Each immorality adds its bit to the pollution of the whole human system. Nothing of an individual's make up is what it would otherwise have been. The whole person, body and soul, is changed for the worse. This change, a result of sin, gives rise to temptations which would not have occurred in the condition of innocence. From this point of view, human desires as affected by sin and its consequences are called "concupiscence."[26]

The social impact of original sin can be clarified by considering the question: How can parents have any real effect upon their children's future free choices? In other words, how can one posit any real influence of parents on children without implicitly denying the children's own true freedom and moral responsibility?

One way parents make a difference is by their conditioning of children's spontaneous willing (discussed in 9-B). Such conditioning shapes the way in which the child will come to see human goods and his or her own possible fulfillment in them. Moreover, parent's choices to a great extent limit the options of children. Thus parents very largely predetermine the conditions under which their children's moral battle will be fought.

Some children, when they begin making free choices, have little reason to choose what is morally right even to the extent that they correctly judge what that is. Without any fault of their own, they can be strongly tempted to do things they know to be immoral. Supposing they make some morally evil choices under such conditions, then even if at some point they are converted and begin to live upright lives, their early immoral acts can continue to reverberate throughout the rest of their lives. Years later, such persons still will be insensitive to some of their obligations and to many of the consequences of their acts, and so will be responsible—in one of the weak modes of voluntariness—for things they cannot any longer do anything about. Thus, parent's failures can affect their children's lives.

8. Insofar as the will is a spiritual power, its weakening seems difficult to explain. If one can make a free choice, what does it mean to say one's will is weak? The answer is that as a capacity for free self-determination the will cannot be weakened in itself. However, choices are among diverse possibilities, and some possibilities—not necessarily the morally right ones either—can be far more attractive than others to the person as a whole, especially given the change for the worse in this "person as a whole" described above. This accounts for the evident fact that some temptations are harder to resist than others. And so we can understand the total phenomenon to which we refer in speaking of the weakening of the will.

9. Every choice involves self-limitation. There is compensation for this in the fact that choices in accord with integral human fulfillment open us to community, where our individual limitations are transcended. But sin lessens the likelihood of genuine community. Thus it worsens the possibilities confronting every human person. Once sin is at large in the world, the morally upright person is as likely to suffer from others as to find fulfillment in them. Virtue becomes its own punishment, as Scripture teaches (see Wis 2.10–20, aptly applied to Jesus in Mt 27.41–44). **Thus, too, in creating a situation in which right choices are harder, original sin can be said to weaken the will.**

345

The primal human group lost something—perhaps virtually all—of its character as genuine community when its members sinned. After sin was committed, anyone considering making a choice faced worse alternatives than those initially confronted by Man. For now the self-limitation involved in all choice was not offset by participation in community, and so moral goodness did not have on its side one of its most appealing fruits.

Question H: How could death be a consequence of sin?

1. Insofar as human persons are bodily, death is a natural, physically necessary process. Of all organisms, however, only human beings foresee their own death. Although death's inevitability is universally recognized, refusal to accept death as appropriate also is universal. Most people yearn for and project some kind of survival beyond death.

2. This yearning for survival is not without reason. People are not exclusively bodily realities, as is clear from the fact that free choices cannot be accounted for as organic functions. People realize, more or less clearly, that they are more than bodies and that, since they are *more,* bodily death, though naturally inevitable, is an affront to personal dignity.

The relationship between sin and death has always been felt to pose a difficulty for the doctrine of original sin. If death truly is a result of sin, it seems to follow that there would have been no death had Man not sinned. Yet human organisms are not very different from other organisms in respect to organic life and death, and it is hard to imagine a natural world without death. Therefore, it seems that human death is natural and inevitable. In that case, there would have been death regardless of sin, and so death hardly can be a punishment for sin.

Yet people universally yearn for and project some sort of survival; even some secular humanists speculate about the possibility of eventually finding a "cure" for death—something which would prevent the degenerative processes associated with aging. Death is not accepted. As Vatican II teaches:

> It is in the face of death that the riddle of human existence becomes most acute. Not only is man tormented by pain and by the advancing deterioration of his body, but even more so by a dread of perpetual extinction. He rightly follows the intuition of his heart when he abhors and repudiates the absolute ruin and total disappearance of his own person.
>
> Man rebels against death because he bears in himself an eternal seed which cannot be reduced to sheer matter. All the endeavors of technology, though useful in the extreme, cannot calm his anxiety. For a prolongation of biological life is unable to satisfy that desire for a higher life which is inescapably lodged in his breast.
>
> Although the mystery of death utterly beggars the imagination, the Church has been taught by divine revelation, and herself firmly teaches, that man has been created by God for a blissful destiny beyond the reach of earthly misery. In addition, that bodily death from which man would have been immune had he not sinned [note 14: cf. Wis 1.13; 2.23–24; Rom 5.21; 6.23; Jas 1.15] will be vanquished, according to the Christian faith, when man who was ruined by his own doing is restored to wholeness by an almighty and merciful Savior. (GS 18; translation amended)

The Council then proceeds to spell out the Christian hope, which answers human anxiety about death and even now maintains a communion between us and our dead loved ones.

3. Considered according to a purely naturalistic world view, the fact that death is a physical necessity makes the Christian teaching that it is a consequence of sin seem absurd. But according to such a world view, the hope of resurrection also seems absurd. If, then, we can hope for resurrection, there is no reason to deny that, except for sin, we would have been immune from death.

4. Although the purely naturalistic world view is presented as scientific, it generalizes beyond empirical evidence. Science, in its proper domain, tells only about how the world works as it is. No empirical data can show that humankind would have been subject to death even if Man had not sinned. **Death is naturally inevitable in the world as it is, and faith does not question this.** It teaches instead that the world could have been different than it now is, just as it also teaches that the world will be different when God completes the re-creation which he has begun with the resurrection of Jesus.

5. Considered in the perspective of faith, it seems fitting that bodily persons should have been created with a power to avoid death. Their appeal to God's creative imagination presumably concerned ways in which they can manifest his goodness—for example, in being parents and children—which are not open to angels. Bodiliness itself, however, carries with it the possibility of corruption, which hardly seems to manifest God's perfect life. **Hence, it was fitting that in creating bodily persons, God also somehow provide them with a power of avoiding death.** Human beings, children of God by being members of the family of Man, would have enjoyed the immunity from death suitable to those who share in divine life (see *S.t.*, 1–2, q. 85, aa. 5–6; 2–2, q. 164, a. 1, ad 1).

In this way, human persons would have been preserved from the implications—now physically necessary—of their organic nature. The affront we sense to our personal dignity, which is doubly an affront to the dignity of children of God, would have been avoided. As St. Athanasius teaches: "God not only made us out of nothing, but he also gave us freely, by the grace of the Word, a life divinely oriented. But men rejected the things of eternity and, on the prompting of the devil, turned to the things of corruption. They became the cause of their own corruption in death; for, as I said before, they were by nature corruptible, but were destined, by the grace of the communion of the Word, to have escaped the consequences of nature, had they remained good. Because of the Word and his dwelling among them, even the corruption natural to them would not have affected them" (FEF 750). Similarly, St. Theophilus of Antioch argues that God made human persons neither mortal nor immortal, but open to either destiny, according to the use they would make of their freedom. God is not the cause of death; rather, death follows from sin as immortality would have followed from human self-determination to obey God (see FEF 184).

6. This explanation helps clarify the sense in which death is a punishment for sin. It need not be supposed that God chose death and imposed it on humankind, answering evil with evil. Rather, the evil of death is a punishment only in the sense that it is a deserved consequence of sin. This consequence follows naturally when Man's sin alienates humankind from God and so causes the loss of divine life as something which would have accompanied human nature itself. **In other words, we need suppose that God punishes sin with death only in the sense that, Man having sinned, God does not prevent nature from taking the course on which sin set it.**

Some theologians suggest that perhaps sin might have changed only the human attitude toward death, not the fact of death.[27] Neither Scripture nor tradition offers grounds for this view.[28] On the contrary, the logic of faith is that, since resurrection is entailed in the share in divine life won for us by the redemptive death of Jesus, immortality must have been entailed in the share in divine life lost for us by the sin of Man.

Moreover, the notion that only our attitude is different as a result of sin implies that attitudes float free of profound realities like death, in some sort of metaphysical stratosphere. Man in innocence would have been no more sanguine about death than Jesus was. He faced death obediently and confidently—but with utter horror.

If human persons would in any case have been subject to death, on what ground are we to suppose that God did not create us in exactly that mortality in which we find ourselves and will not also leave us in it? The truth of faith hangs together: If the share in divine life won for us by the redemptive death of Jesus entails bodily resurrection and eternal life, then the share in divine life lost for us by the sin of Man would have entailed a like immortality.

Question I: How can those who come after the first humans inherit original sin?

1. There is another perennial difficulty about original sin. If it has the character of true sin and somehow affects the will, how is it also transmitted by propagation as part of the human heritage? How can true sin be inherited? Sin seems of all things the most personal, while what is inherited by all alike seems to belong to humankind as a species. The problem is to account for our involvement in guilt prior to our personal self-involvement, without reducing guilt to the status of illusion or attributing its source either to a superhuman power other than God or to God himself.

2. The response to this difficulty is as follows. If Man and the rest of the initial human community had not sinned, the family of Man would ipso facto have accepted its role as God's human family. Human creatureliness supplied a natural basis for communal fulfillment in friendship with God, while God for his part extended to humankind as a natural community a divine calling to intimacy. This possibility could and should have been realized through the cooperation of the initial human group.[29] Their sin blocked its realization. In the beginning, humankind fell short of its common responsibility by a communal sin.

3. It follows that, precisely insofar as one shares humanity with Man, one shares something which is not as it could and ought to have been. **One does not inherit the initial sinful choice. The positive reality which is transmitted is human nature itself. This nature ought to be handed on in a human community in friendship with God. Every human person ought to voluntarily share in that community. Instead, human nature is handed on in a humankind divided in itself and so also religiously divided.** The central privation which constitutes the evil of original sin is simply the absence of grace from concrete human nature.[30]

4. This absence of grace has the character of sin because humankind's present privation of a common will to genuine religious community is a consequence of social irresponsibility from the beginning. For each new person, this existentially defective social situation is not a personal, actual sin, however, since the original

possibility of the human family's cooperating with God no longer exists. Still, if we sin seriously, we personally endorse and contribute to the human heritage of sin.

5. We come to be in this condition of privation simply by coming to be as human persons. By nature we are members of a human family which lacks natural solidarity in genuine religious community and has lost its opportunity for heavenly citizenship. This loss affects each human being merely by his or her natural membership in humankind; thus the privation of original sin accrues to each by propagation, not by personal imitation of a prior sin (see *S.t.*, 1–2, q. 81, aa. 1–3; q. 82, aa. 1, 4; *S.c.g.*, 4, 52).[31]

The children of Man are like the children of a displaced person who has a chance to apply for American citizenship. If he does so, he may immigrate to the United States and his children will be born American citizens. However, he fails to apply and loses his chance to immigrate. His children are born outside the United States and are deprived of the citizenship they should have enjoyed. Similarly, the children of Man are born outside the genuine religious community of which they should have been members just by being human persons.

But in this case, there would be no genuine religious community to which any human person could belong apart from God's redemptive work. It is as if the displaced person's failure to apply for American citizenship had prevented the United States from coming to be. However, by the grace of Jesus, the People of God is constituted and all human persons are called to be citizens of it.

6. The reality of original sin must not be distorted by considering it outside the context of God's persistent love. God does not leave men and women to their fate: ". . . after their fall his promise of redemption aroused in them the hope of being saved (cf. Gn 3.15), and from that time on he ceaselessly kept the human race in his care, in order to give eternal life to those who perseveringly do good in search of salvation (cf. Rom 2.6–7)" (DV 3).

Someone might object that St. Paul's teaching that the gift of redemption is greater than the offense seems inconsistent with his teaching about the universality of sinfulness, both among pagans and among Jews, apart from faith in Jesus. For, it might be argued, even if grace is available to all, the remedies Christianity provides against the consequences of original sin are not available to all. Hence pagans did in fact fall into idolatry, and Jews were in fact unfaithful. In the actual conditions, without the full benefit of Christian faith and life, the works of human persons hardly can be what they ought to be, yet God renders to each according to his or her works (see Jer 17.10; Mt 16.27; 1 Cor 3.8; Rv 2.23; and so on).

The answer is that God also assesses works according to the talents each one is given (see Mt 25.14–30)—that is, with full consideration for all of the circumstances in which one lives one's life.[32] Sin by anyone, Jew or Greek, deserves punishment, "but glory and honor and peace for every one who does good, the Jew first and also the Greek. For God shows no partiality" (Rom 2.10–11). No partiality: It makes no difference when one is called to God's vineyard; what matters is one's willingness to do as best one can what one is called to do when one is called to do it (see Mt 20.1–16).

7. The difference between the human condition before original sin and since the redemption is this: Before, friendship with God was given with human nature itself; now it depends on membership in the community of faith. Had it not been

for original sin, the family of Man would have been the human family of God. As it is, God offers membership in his family to each person individually. The possibility of a family of God grounded in nature and therefore centered upon Man is lost by sin. In its place, by divine generosity and the human cooperation of Jesus, is the possibility of realizing a family of God grounded in free commitment and centered upon Jesus, the Son of Man (see *S.t.,* 1–2, q. 81, a. 3, ad 3; 3, q. 1, a. 4; q. 8, a. 3).[33]

8. We do not inherit humanity without grace but with everything else intact (see *S.t.,* 1–2, q. 85, aa. 1–5). On the contrary, the human world itself resists God's love more or less extensively and maliciously (see Jn 15.18–20). Moreover, concrete human nature carries with it sin's consequences, including death, and the cumulative effects of the fear of death. Among these are concupiscence and weakness of will. Thus, without the special help of God's grace, no human being can long avoid falling into grave personal sin.

9. But God's grace is given in Jesus. Faced with the need to overcome death and other evils, redemptive Christian life is harder than human life would have been if Man had not sinned, yet holiness is not less possible. The life of Jesus is more noble than Man's could have been, and Christian life is more noble than human life would have been without original sin.

Toward the end of the first part of the Liturgy of the Easter Vigil the Church exultantly proclaims Easter. The Proclamation praises God the Father and our Lord Jesus, and then explains why:

> For Christ has ransomed us with his blood,
>> and paid for us the price of Adam's sin to our eternal Father!
> This is our passover feast, when Christ, the true Lamb, is slain,
>> whose blood consecrates the homes of all believers.
> This is the night when first you saved our fathers:
>> you freed the people of Israel from their slavery
>> and led them dry-shod through the sea.
> This is the night when Christians everywhere,
>> washed clean of sin and freed from all defilement,
>> are restored to grace and grow together in holiness.
> This is the night when Jesus Christ broke the chains of death
>> and rose triumphant from the grave.
> Father, how wonderful your care for us!
>> How boundless your merciful love!
>> To ransom a slave you gave away your Son.
> O happy fault, O necessary sin of Adam,
>> which gained for us so great a Redeemer![34]

The Church then offers to the Father the liturgy to follow, together with the Easter candle, which represents Jesus.

The most important truth about original sin is that we are redeemed from it. Jesus redeems us from all defilement, from the chains of death, from slavery, from alienation from God. He restores us to grace, gives us the power to grow in holiness, restores our innocence, brings us joy, weds heaven to earth, and reconciles humankind to God. Somehow all of the evils which our Lord Jesus overcomes sprang from original sin; all redemption from these evils comes from the Father through our Lord Jesus. And so Man's sin is called a "happy fault" and a "necessary sin," not as if in itself a fault were a good or a sin inevitable, but because in Man humankind misspoke itself in the dialogue between its freedom and God's freedom, and in doing so evoked from him the splendid response of so great a redeemer: the Word made flesh in glory.

Summary

Evil is a privation arising primarily from the sinful abuse of freedom. Yet, although we sin freely, in a sense we also sin inevitably. Somehow our condition is such that we are preconditioned to sin. It cannot have been this way at the beginning, however, for sin cannot have originated with God. Only an abuse of freedom by Man at the beginning can account for the present misery of humankind.

The Council of Trent teaches definitively that Man (Adam) was constituted in justice and holiness, disobeyed God, lost justice and holiness, incurred the punishment of death, and was changed for the worse in body and soul; that Man passed on sin to the whole of humankind; that this sin is communicated by propagation, not imitation, and is remedied only by Christ; that therefore even infants contract original sin, and it is right to baptize them; and that original sin is really taken away in baptism, but concupiscence remains. The Council of Orange adds that it would be wrong to say the punishment for sin, but not sin itself, was passed on to us, since in that case God would be unjust.

Various unacceptable attempts have been made to revise the Church's teaching on original sin. One identifies original sin with inevitable aspects of the human condition, another with the sociocultural environment of sin in which we live. Theological revisions which set aside faith remove the essential presupposition for theology itself. They also threaten a doctrine far more important than original sin—redemption.

There is no incompatibility between the doctrine of original sin and the biological theory of evolution as an account of the organic existence and attributes of humankind. But intelligence and the capacity for free choice are not merely organic. They—and therefore human persons—can be accounted for only by a special act of divine, creative power. While Pius XII and Paul VI cautioned that polygenism appears to be incompatible with faith, it is not clear that they proposed monogenism as the position to be held definitively. Thus there is room for an account of original sin compatible with polygenism.

It needlessly complicates the task of understanding and defending the doctrine of original sin to add nonessential details to the account of the initial human condition. What is essential is that God created Man good, without sin, and with the power of free choice, in friendship with himself, and with the potential to be immortal. Man was free of unruly desire tending toward sin; he was well disposed toward integral human fulfillment; yet this did not rule out a normal inclination toward a good which it would be wrong to choose, for otherwise he could not have sinned.

Scientific evolutionary theory suggests the need for an initial human community of some size. Granting polygenism for the sake of argument, therefore, it is still possible to give an account of Man's sin which protects the essentials of the Church's doctrine. Even supposing polygenism, there is no reason to deny the original human community had a single leader (Man) whose action was decisive for the community's action; furthermore, it is obvious that groups can be carried away by emotion and go wrong together, particularly at the instigation of a leader. As for our involvement in the sin of the original human community and Man in particular, it follows from our solidarity with them, a solidarity which is not only biological but also existential.

As a result of sin, death became inevitable. Fear of death distorts the whole human emotional make up, and this distortion affects the fundamental processes of human experience. This in turn generates false moral judgments and deprives language and other products of culture of the rationality and pure usefulness they should have. Once begun, the entire process is perpetuated in a vicious circle. Each individual and the whole human system are changed for the worse. Even the will is weakened, in the sense that some possibilities which should not be chosen are now more attractive—and so more tempting—than they would have been. Also, the disruption of community by sin makes persons less inclined to pursue the good disinterestedly and more inclined to do as they please.

It remains a question how death can be a consequence of sin, since it is a natural, physically necessary process. The problem is insoluble according to a purely naturalistic world view. But science tells only how the world is; it tells nothing about how the world would have been without sin. Faith does not deny that, as the world is now, death is inevitable; it only says that, without sin, the world would not have been as it is now. Supposing faith's view of God's purpose in creating, it seems fitting that bodily persons should have been created with a power to avoid death.

The guilt of original sin is transmitted by propagation. For the positive reality which is transmitted is human nature itself; and, as a result of Man's sin, concrete human nature is not as it could and ought to have been. Each new human person comes to be without thereby sharing in a human family united as a peaceful community in friendship with God. Sin thus accompanies human nature; grace is absent from it, and this absence is the central privation which constitutes the evil of original sin.

But God has not simply left human beings to their fate. His love persists, redemption is a reality, and, where originally the family of Man would have been the human family of God, God now offers membership in his family to each of us individually.

Appendix 1:   St. Paul and Trent on original sin

The teaching of the Council of Trent on original sin clearly and explicitly relies far more upon St. Paul than it does upon Genesis. Luther and others had relied heavily upon the Epistle to the Romans for their account of justification. Trent appeals to the same text, together with other New Testament books, to buttress Catholic teaching.

Romans begins by showing how disastrous the human condition without Jesus would be. Paul points out that the pagans worshipped idols and in consequence fell into all sorts of sins, although the true God is knowable even by the light of reason (see Rom 1.18–31).

Moreover, the pagans are not excused by their lack of guidance from a revealed law, for conscience and natural knowledge of the law written in one's heart are sufficient to make clear that wrong acts are sins and deserve punishment (see Rom 1.32; 2.12–16).

Paul also points out that although the Jews enjoy the gift of God's word, which protects them from idolatry and gives them sound moral guidance, they are hardly better than the pagans. They do not fulfill the requirements of God's law, which serves only to make clear their sinfulness (see Rom 2.1–11, 17–29; 3.1–20).

The only escape from sin is faith, and this way out is available both to pagans and to Jews (see Rom 3.21–31). Even Abraham is saved not by observing a law, but by faith in God, a faith which implicitly stretched forward to redemption through Jesus (see Rom 4). Christians likewise are saved by living faith in God, faith received through the sacrificial and redemptive work of Jesus (see Rom 5.1–11). Saved by faith, Christians have a solid hope of heavenly glory, because the love of God has been poured forth in our hearts by the Holy Spirit (see Rom 5.5).

In this context—after reviewing the universal disaster of sin and asserting the universal redemptive power of faith in God—Paul brings up original sin in order to show that like Man, Jesus is a unique and universally significant principle in humankind's relationship to God, and, in fact, that Jesus is a far more powerful principle than Man. Paul begins: "Therefore as sin came into the world through one man and death through sin, and so death spread to all men because all men sinned . . ." (Rom 5.12).[35] This is the verse on whose significance Trent was to insist. One person introduces sin and death, and in doing so truly is a principle of sin and death for all. At this point, Paul breaks off to comment upon the situation of humankind between Man and Moses, when there was no law but there was sin and death (see Rom 5.13–14).

It seems clear enough that Paul is proceeding here from the causality of sin and death by Man to the causality of grace and life by Jesus. Paul takes it that the story of Man's sin is well known and accepted. The analogy would not work unless Man is as truly a principle of sin and death as the Lord Jesus is of grace and life. If, for instance, one assumed that Man merely initiated sin as a bad example which others follow, the conclusion could not be stronger than that Jesus provided a unique example of obedience for others to imitate.

Paul goes on to point out the limits of the parallel. The gift is far more powerful than the offense; Man's sin only spoiled things, whereas our Lord's redemptive work is constructive (see Rom 5.15–17). In indicating the limits of the parallel, Paul would be omitting a very powerful point, which he hardly would have ignored, had he thought but not said that Man's sin is inefficacious for us without our willing consent. Instead of saying any such thing, Paul goes on to reaffirm the parallel within the limits he has indicated. "Then as one man's trespass led to condemnation for all men, so one man's act of righteousness leads to acquittal and life for all men. For as by one man's disobedience many were made sinners, so by one man's obedience many will be made righteous" (Rom 5.18–19). If the universal human disaster of evil has a unitary principle, the act which introduced sin and death for all humankind, so much more does the universal grace of redemption have a unitary principle: the redemptive work of God in our Lord Jesus, which Paul proposes for acceptance in faith.

Trent's definition says a good deal more than Paul, but says nothing inconsistent with what Paul says. Paul's expression of faith makes clear that the whole of humankind became sinners and so subject to death, because of the sin of one man. The context makes it clear that this basic condition of every human person as sinner is only the beginning of universal human sinfulness, which the basic sin helps to explain.

Another important passage in Paul on original sin is his treatment of the resurrection in First Corinthians. Insisting that Jesus really lives, Paul says: "But in fact Christ has been raised from the dead, the first fruits of those who have fallen asleep. For as by a man came death, by a man has come also the resurrection of the dead. For as in Adam all die, so also in Christ shall all be made alive. But each in his own order: Christ the first fruits, then at his coming those who belong to Christ" (1 Cor 15.20–23). The parallelism here makes clear Paul's belief that the death which came through Man includes precisely that biological process which Jesus underwent and from which he rose.

Appendix 2:   Responses to some objections

A careless reader might object that the present account is implausible in assuming that God constituted the original persons as unelected representatives of the whole human race and that they formed by social contract a community in friendship with God. Such an objection would show incomprehension of the theory of action set out in chapter nine and of the account of original sin proposed here. For no such juridical assumptions are required. The entire theory moves on a different plane altogether, one which takes full account of both the social character of human acts and the conditioned character of personal moral responsibility. The persons in the primal situation no more represented us than parents represent their children when, in living foolishly, they squander what should be their children's heritage.

Someone might object that the present account of original sin still leaves standing a difficulty in any account of it: A universally inherited sin is hard to reconcile with God's universal salvific will. The response is that the two data of faith are not hard to reconcile. God creates the human race, endows human persons with freedom, permits sin, and allows it to have its inevitable consequences. But at the same time he provides remedies. If all who come to be as humans are in sin insofar as they are children of Man, all also can be redeemed insofar as they are brothers and sisters of our Lord Jesus. As St. Paul teaches, the gift is greater than the offense (see Rom 5.15–17).

What about unbaptized children? Revelation and faith bear primarily upon the situation of those who can hear the word and believe it. In insisting upon the reality of original sin, the Church teaches the necessity of baptism (see DS 1514/791). But the Church does not say when and how baptism begins. One can hold that absolutely everyone has an opportunity for salvation, inasmuch as any real relationship to Jesus is a bridge over which life in him can come, and everyone at all times and places has some real relationship to Jesus.[36] (This view does not render the completion of baptism in its full, sacramental rite less necessary when it becomes possible, nor does it at all suggest that anyone who freely refuses God's grace and persists in this refusal is saved despite this personal sin.)

If this is so, how is Mary, conceived immaculate, different from anyone else? The answer is that for every other human person, the beginning of existence is without grace, for the sin of Man obtains. Subsequently, grace is given overcoming an existing state of sin. In Mary's case, redemption is preventive rather than curative. She is God's child even in the first instant of her being.

However, someone might object that, this fine distinction apart, the very social character of original sin, as it has been described, would entail that Mary too—and for that matter even Jesus himself—is caught up in it. The answer is that they truly were caught up in the condition and consequences of original sin, but original sin was excluded for them personally. In other words, they never exist as humans-without-divine-life. Moreover, certain effects of original sin in their very humanity were prevented. Thus it is false to suppose that either Jesus or Mary was subject to concupiscence. It also seems inappropriate to suppose that Jesus could have died had he not permitted himself to be killed (see *S.t.*, 3, q. 47, a. 1) or to suppose that Mary did die (a point the Church has left open).[37]

Notes

1. Pius XI, *Mit brennender Sorge*, 29 *AAS* (1937) 157; *The Papal Encyclicals*, 218.25.

2. A rich and helpful historical study: A. Gaudel, "Péché Originel," *Dictionnaire de Théologie Catholique*, 12:275–606. A useful treatment of the Church's teaching on original sin: T. C. O'Brien, O.P., "Appendix 2" and "Appendix 3," in St. Thomas Aquinas, *Summa theologiae*, vol. 26 (New York: McGraw-Hill, 1965), 110–20. The other appendices also are helpful; O'Brien clearly explains St. Thomas' theology of original sin. Also see C. J. Peter, "Original Justice" and "Original Sin," *New Catholic Encyclopedia*, 10:774–81. Karl Rahner, "Original Sin," *Encyclopedia of Theology* (New York: Seabury Press, 1975), 1148–55, provides a summary treatment of original sin which, allowing for differences in metaphysics, comes very close to that given here. Rahner's treatment seems weak in respect to human action and its material component, and so leaves some ambiguity about the existential (in my sense) reality of original sin and the realism of death as its punishment.

3. The starting point in experience for treating original sin (and much of the rest of the approach in this chapter) was suggested by the original text and supplement authorized by the Holy See to the "Dutch" catechism: *A New Catechism: Catholic Faith for Adults* (New York: Seabury Press, 1973), 259–70; Edouard Dhanis, S.J., and Jan Visser, C.Ss.R., "The Supplement to 'A New Catechism': On Behalf of the Commission of Cardinals appointed to examine 'A New Catechism,'" 519–38.

4. Walter Kasper, *Jesus the Christ* (London: Burns and Oates, 1976), 203–4, presents an argument like that given here for taking seriously the substance of the traditional Catholic doctrine of original sin, concluding (204): "If someone for the sake of freedom wants to sail between Scylla and Charybdis, if he does not want either to define metaphysically the power of sin or to minimize it and if he wants to be able to justify his solution intellectually, he must see that the traditional doctrine of original sin—not in its misleading terminology, but in the sense in which it is really meant—is one of the greatest achievements in the history of theology and one of the most important contributions of Christianity to the history of ideas."

5. The following studies by A. Vanneste are helpful in understanding the decree of Trent in its historical context: "La Préhistoire du Décret du Concile de Trente sur le péché originel," *Nouvelle Revue Théologique*, 86 (1964), 355–68, 490–510; "Le Décret du Concile de Trente sur le péché originel," *Nouvelle Revue Théologique*, 87 (1965), 688–726.

6. On the source of this position and the relation between Second Orange and Trent, see John P. Redding, *The Influence of St. Augustine on the Doctrine of the II Council of Orange Concerning Original Sin* (Washington: Catholic University of America, 1939), 50–68.

7. See 60 *AAS* (1968) 439; for a helpful commentary on this section of Paul VI's Credo, see Candido Pozo, S.J., *The Credo of the People of God: A Theological Commentary*, trans. Mark A. Pilon (Chicago: Franciscan Herald Press, 1979), 103–18.

8. For a clear summary of a spectrum of revisionist approaches: James L. O'Connor, S.J., "Original Sin: Contemporary Approaches," *Theological Studies*, 29 (1968), 215–40. A less technical summary of many positions: George J. Dyer, "Original Sin: Theological Abstraction or Dark Reality?" *Chicago Studies*, 17 (1978), 385–98. Also: B. O. McDermott, "Original Sin," *New Catholic Encyclopedia*, 17:471–72; "The Theology of Original Sin: Recent Developments," *Theological Studies*, 38 (1977), 478–512. One of the more helpful recent theological attempts: Maurizio Flick and Zoltan Alszeghy, *Il peccato originale*, 2d ed. (Brescia: Queriniana, 1974). The authors summarize other current views (179–226) and present their own view (273–374) which, if not altogether satisfactory, does include most of what is helpful in other recent works. A critical examination of a few of the most important revisionist approaches: G. Vandervelde, *Original Sin: Two Major Trends in Contemporary Roman Catholic Interpretation* (Amsterdam: Rodopi N.V., 1975), 313–34 (summary of criticism). The multiplication of theories of original sin inconsistent with one another and the Church's teaching is a prime example of theological disarray: José Luis Illanes Maestre, "Pluralismo teológico y verdad de la fe," *Scripta Theologica*, 7 (1975), 619·84.

9. See J. N. D. Kelly, *Early Christian Doctrine*, rev. ed. (San Francisco: Harper and Row, 1978), 346–66. Origen was strongly influenced by Neoplatonism, and his thought influenced many others: Antonia Tripolitis, "Return to the Divine: Salvation in the Thought of Plotinus and Origen," in *Disciplina Nostra*, Patristic Monograph Series, 6, ed. D. Winslow (Philadelphia: 1979), 171–78. Gregory of Nyssa also supposed that humankind's original paradise was more spiritual than natural, and extramundane: Ernest V. McClear, S.J., "The Fall of Man and Original Sin in the Theology of Gregory of Nyssa," *Theological Studies*,(1948), 175–212, esp. 177–85. Although sometimes questionable as to interpretation, George Arkell Riggan's dissertation includes a great wealth of scholar-

ship, not only on St. Augustine but on other Church Fathers and a variety of ancient literature: "Original Sin in the Thought of Augustine," Ph.D. diss., Yale University, 1949, esp. 44–166.

10. For a plausible attempt to disengage the essential from the nonessential: Anthony T. Padovano, "Original Sin and Christian Anthropology," *Proceedings of the Catholic Theological Society of America*, 22 (1967), 93–132, summary 120–22. But some critics of received treatments of original sin focus on nonessential features. For example: Herbert Haag, *Is Original Sin in Scripture?* (New York: Sheed and Ward, 1969), 23–63 and 101–6; a less extreme example: Peter de Rosa, *Christ and Original Sin* (Milwaukee: Bruce, 1967), 80–86.

11. For a brief exposition: Michael J. Cantley, "The Biblical Doctrine of Original Sin," *Proceedings of the Catholic Theological Society of America*, 22 (1967), 133–71; this is generally sound, although the author accepts (148–50) the view—at odds with Trent and difficult to reconcile with other truths of faith such as the bodily resurrection of Jesus and the bodily assumption of Mary— that even if Adam had not sinned, still he would have died. A book-length treatment: A. M. Dubarle, *The Biblical Doctrine of Original Sin* (New York: Herder and Herder, 1964), 45–200. This work is well-argued, clear, and helpful, except for the final chapter, where the author's speculations are hard to square with Catholic teaching.

12. A rather straightforward example of this approach: A. Hulsbosch, O.S.A., *God in Creation and Evolution* (New York: Sheed and Ward, 1965), 24–49. Alfred Vanneste, *The Dogma of Original Sin* (Louvain: Vander/Nauwelaerts, 1975), reduces original sin to the universality of personal sin in adults (83–92) and strongly criticizes views such as Hulsbosch's (180–82). All the same, Vanneste himself denies that creation has any goodness in itself apart from relation to the Christian economy of salvation (157–59), and thus seems to imply that an initial condition of personal, freely chosen sin is (despite its freedom) an inevitable moment of created persons' reality in themselves antecedent to their incorporation into Christ. For a detailed analysis and critique of Vanneste's view: Vandervelde, op. cit., 259–88 and 322–24.

13. See Pierre Teilhard de Chardin, *Christianity and Evolution*, trans. René Hague (New York: Harcourt, Brace, Javanovich, 1969), esp. 36–55, 79–86, 133–37, 162–63, 189–98, and 212–20. For some links between Teilhard and revisionist accounts of original sin: Robert T. Francoeur, *Perspectives in Evolution* (Baltimore: Helicon, 1965), 145–229. One cannot proceed far in the direction Teilhard takes without embracing a monistic theory (some sort of pantheism) in which evil becomes an illusion; the dialectic of freedom, so central to Christian faith, simply drops out. Still, Teilhard's concern to emphasize the positive side of the redemption—the fulfillment of everything in Christ—and our role in it is sound and important, as is made clear by Robert L. Faricy, S.J., "Teilhard de Chardin's Theology of Redemption," *Theological Studies*, 27 (1966), 553–79. Chapters nineteen through twenty-three below will show how this concern can be satisfied without compromising the dialectic of freedom and the essential character of fulfillment in Christ as a communion of persons.

14. Piet Schoonenberg, S.J., *Man and Sin: A Theological View* (Notre Dame, Ind.: University of Notre Dame Press, 1965), 177–81, suggests that original sin might be reduced to the "sin of the world," which he describes as an actual sinful situation (111–18). Still, he holds that infants need baptism, even if they are in a Christian family, and that this sacrament is effective (190–91). He simply does not consider how baptism, which does not change the situation of sin he describes, is effective. For an analysis and critique of Schoonenberg's theory in its various stages, see Vandervelde, op. cit., 57–84, 107–11, 149–65, 187–234, 241–48, and 313–22. The baptismal liturgy itself, viewed in the light of Scripture and the teaching of the Fathers, strongly supports the traditional teaching: G. M. Lukken, *Original Sin in the Roman Liturgy* (Leiden: E. J. Brill, 1973), 266–96; Manuel Garrido Boñano, O.S.B., "El pecado original en los ritos bautismales," in Consejo Superior de Investigaciones Cientificas, *El Pecado Original: XXIX Semana Española de Teologia* (Madrid: 1970), 78–125. In the volume last cited, Joaquín M. Alonso Antona, C.M.F., "Schoonenberg y su teoria del pecado original," 357–96, provides an incisive critique not only of Schoonenberg's theory but also of his theological methodology.

15. This is not to say that because St. Paul presupposes Adam as original sinner and principle of human sin and death, he asserts the reality of Adam. The text must not be pressed too far. But Trent's interpretation of it cannot be ignored, nor can Trent's teaching be subjected to "interpretation" which denies hereditary alienation without contradicting at least one of the following: (1) all humankind is in a common situation of existential evil, not merely defective development or the like; (2) God did not put humankind in the condition of evil; (3) by baptism into Christ individuals really are freed from the common situation of existential evil and reconciled to God. Careful exegesis admits an interpretation of Rom 5.12 consonant with Trent and consistent with the three essential truths stated above: S. Lyonnet, S.J., "La Doctrine du péché originel en Rom., V, 12," in *Dictionnaire de la Bible*,

Supplément, 7:524–63; C. E. B. Cranfield, "On Some of the Problems in the Interpretation of Romans 5.12," *Scottish Journal of Theology*, 22 (1969), 324–41; A. J. M. Wedderburn, "The Theological Structure of Romans V. 12," *New Testament Studies*, 19 (1972–73), 339–54.

16. See W. Malcolm Clark, "A Legal Background for the Yahwist's Use of 'Good and Evil' in Genesis 2–3," *Journal of Biblical Literature*, 88 (1969), 266–78. Clark shows that "good" and "evil" refer to those things or possibilities which happen to be one or the other; they are real alternatives; the "knowledge" of both is the autonomous choice of either and rejection of the limitations to which the divine order subjects creatures.

17. See Louis F. Hartman, C.Ss.R., "Sin in Paradise," *Catholic Biblical Quarterly*, 20 (1958), 24–40.

18. Various naturalistic reductions (explainings away) of the nonnaturalistic aspects of human personhood are so common in contemporary opinion that even faithful Christians continually fall into this line of thought, completely incompatible with Christian faith. Those who engage in no Christian philosophical reflection but do read scientific works and theology are likely to miss the dogmatic and ideological character of all but the most technical writing about evolution. Except in purely scientific contexts, where they are harmless, evolutionist views express a speculative metaphysics of an indefensible sort. For an introduction to philosophical anthropology: James E. Royce, S.J., *Man and His Nature* (New York: McGraw-Hill, 1961); Mortimer J. Adler, *The Difference of Man and the Difference It Makes* (New York: Holt, Rinehart, and Winston, 1967). Against metaphysical reduction of the human person: Germain Grisez, *Beyond the New Theism: A Philosophy of Religion* (Notre Dame and London: University of Notre Dame Press, 1975), 230–40 and 343–56; Joseph M. Boyle, Jr., Germain Grisez, and Olaf Tollefsen, *Free Choice: A Self-Referential Argument* (Notre Dame and London: University of Notre Dame Press, 1976), 57–97.

19. This point often is overlooked in theological discussions. See, for example, J. P. Mackey, "Original Sin and Polygenism: The State of the Question," *Irish Theological Quarterly*, 34 (1967), 106 and 110. Mackey also seems to confuse (112) polygenism (the evolution to human status of a substantial group, rather than a single pair) with polyphyletism (the origin of present humankind in two or more independent evolutionary processes, with later merging into a genetically unified species). The latter is not required by evidence and poses obvious biological problems of its own. See G. E. Kennedy, *Paleo-Anthropology* (New York: McGraw-Hill, 1980), 372–73; the possibility of different lines evolving into contemporary homo sapiens is "exceeding small" (373).

20. For a readable summary of the evidence, see Melvin Konner, *The Tangled Wing: Biological Constraints on the Human Spirit* (New York: Holt, Rinehart and Winston, 1982), 31–58, notes and references, 454–58; Theodosius Dobzhansky, *Mankind Evolving* (New Haven: Yale University Press, 1962); Claude Heddebaut, "Biologie et péché originel," in *La culpabilité fondamentale: péché originel et anthropologie moderne*, ed. Paul Guilluy (Gembloux: J. Duculot, 1975), 153–64; but also see Jérôme Lejeune, "Adam et Eve ou le monogénisme," *Nouvelle Revue Théologique*, 90 (1968), 191–96.

21. On monogenism: Pius XII, DS 3897/2328; Paul VI, "Original Sin and Modern Science: Address of Pope Paul VI to Participants in a Symposium on Original Sin," *The Pope Speaks*, 11 (1966), 234 (58 AAS [1966] 649–55). Commentary: O. W. Garrigan, "Monogenism," *New Catholic Encyclopedia*, 9:1063–64; Karl Rahner, S.J., "Evolution and Original Sin," in *The Evolving World and Theology*, Concilium, 26, ed. Johannes Metz (New York: Paulist Press, 1967), 61–73. Dhanis and Visser, "The Supplement to 'A New Catechism,'" 534–37, offer a speculative account similar to mine which renders the Church's essential teaching on original sin and polygenism compatible. The teaching of Paul VI on polygenism ought not to be overstated; see Pozo, op. cit., 108–12.

22. It is worth noticing that not all the Fathers took this direction. Some are uninfluenced by its metaphysical presuppositions and others reacted to excesses. See Robert F. Brown, "On the Necessary Imperfection of Creation: Irenaeus' *Adversus Haereses* iv, 38," *Scottish Journal of Theology*, 28 (1975), 17–25; John Boojamra, "Original Sin According to St. Maximus the Confessor," *St. Vladimir's Theological Quarterly*, 20 (1976), 19–30.

23. A theological reflection on concupiscence: Karl Rahner, S.J., *Theological Investigations*, vol. 1, *God, Christ, Mary and Grace*, trans. Cornelius Ernst, O.P. (Baltimore: Helicon, 1963), 347–82. Although suggestive, this reflection is weakened by the assumption, common since Augustine, that one can choose directly contrary to divine goodness. (Against this assumption, see 13-C and 24-E.)

24. Not only does the Church teach that humanity as a whole, body and soul, is changed for the worse by original sin (see DS 1511/788), but the image of sick and wounded humanity frequently recurs in the liturgy: Lukken, op. cit., 305–51. For a theological treatment of the pervasive effects of

original sin: Enrique Colom Costa, *Dios y el obrar humano* (Pamplona, Spain: EUNSA, 1976), 130–81.

25. See Ernest Becker, *The Denial of Death* (New York: Free Press, 1973), for an introduction to the relevant psychiatric literature.

26. For a study of concupiscence, chiefly according to Augustine, see John J. Hugo, *St. Augustine on Nature, Sex, and Marriage* (Chicago: Scepter, 1969), 39–78.

27. For example, Schoonenberg, *Man and Sin*, 183; also John B. Endres, O.P., "The Council of Trent and Original Sin," *Proceedings of the Catholic Theological Society of America*, 22 (1967), 51–91, raises doubts about this point (82–83), although he admits that the Council of Carthage's strong affirmation of corporeal death as a result of sin (see DS 222/101) has been "generally taught" (75). Karl Rahner, *On the Theology of Death* (New York: Herder and Herder, 1964), 42–43, sometimes is cited in support of the view that sin only changes the way death affects or is experienced by people, for they would in any case have suffered biological destruction. But Rahner, at least in the passage cited, does not seem to be saying this. Rather, he seems to be making a point with which I would agree: that even had Man not sinned, still his life in this world would have ended "without suffering any violent dissolution of his actual bodily constitution through a power from without" (42). I would say: One can imagine that if Adam had not sinned, what in our situation is the last moment of mortal life and the first moment of resurrection life would have been in immediate succession. (Other aspects of Rahner's conception of death which follow from his idea of the human person as spirit in the world raise further questions.) Bruce J. Malina, "Some Observations on the Origin of Sin in Judaism and St. Paul," *Catholic Biblical Quarterly,* 31 (1969), 33, says quite confidently that St. Paul (in Rom 5.12) is uninterested in the "speculative question of physical death," but Wedderburn, op. cit., 340–48, provides reasons for thinking the opposite. It seems to me decisive that Trent was following Carthage, and not only assumed but asserted that bodily death is an hereditary consequence of original sin.

28. It is a mistake to suppose that "death" in relevant texts of Scripture, the Fathers, and the liturgy must refer either to physical death alone or to the loss of salvation alone. It embraces both: Lukken, op. cit., 99–156. For a good summary of the data of Scripture: Pierre Grelot, "Death," *Dictionary of Biblical Theology,* 2d ed., 114–19.

29. This point—that a group can have responsibilities which ought to be fulfilled through certain definite persons whose failure therefore puts the whole group in the wrong—is the essential truth in the notion of corporate personality (see 2-H). Problematic aspects of that notion have been pointed out: J. W. Rogerson, "The Hebrew Conception of Corporate Personality: A Re-examination," *Journal of Theological Studies,* 21 (1970), 1–16. But these aspects are not essential to understand the inheritance of original sin.

30. See St. Thomas, *Summa theologiae,* 1–2, q. 82, aa. 1–2; also O'Brien, op. cit., 133–43. More radical than the view presented here, but in many respects similar: Jesús Cordero Pando, O.P., "La naturaleza del pecado original: Ensayo de formulación teológica," in Consejo Superior de Investigaciones Cientificas, op. cit., 425–62.

31. Trent's teaching that original sin is communicated to all human persons by propagation does not demand a specific mode of transmission, but rather excludes transmission by example only and requires a universal, automatic communication: Segundo Folgado Florez, O.S.A., "La transmisión del pecado original en el Magisterio de la Iglesia," in Consejo Superior de Investigaciones Cientificas, op. cit., 295–324. Hence, the formulation I provide concerning transmission is purposely constructed with sufficient openness to accommodate the polygenetic origin of humankind. There is no need to suppose that all of us are lineal descendants of the original sinners, but only that they created a human situation into which all subsequent humans naturally come to be without the human community the original sinners could and should have initiated.

32. Dubarle, op. cit., 201–17, deals well with this point.

33. For an analysis of the essence and transmission of original sin somewhat like that presented here, see Karl Rahner, S.J., "The Sin of Adam," *Theological Investigations,* vol. 11, *Confrontations I,* trans. David Bourke (New York: Seabury Press, 1974), 247–62.

34. From the "Short form of the Easter Proclamation," the Easter Vigil, *New Roman Missal.* The Christological perspective of the Easter proclamation on original sin is not the only instance, though it is the most splendid one, in which the liturgy clarifies this important link of the truths of fall and redemption: see Lukken, op. cit., 352–94.

35. See Cranfield, op. cit., 331–41. See also F. Prat, *La Théologie de Saint Paul,* vol. 1 (Paris: Beauchesne, 1961), 223–68; Lucien Cerfaux, *Christ in the Theology of St. Paul* (New York: Herder and Herder, 1958), 230–43.

36. See Peter Gumpel, S.J., "Unbaptized Infants: May They Be Saved?" *Downside Review,* 72 (1953–54), 342–458; "Unbaptized Infants: A Further Report," *Downside Review,* 73 (1954–55), 317–46; P. J. Hill, "Limbo," *New Catholic Encyclopedia,* 8:762–65.

37. See Bonaventura Kloppenburg, O.F.M., *De relatione inter peccatum et mortem* (Rome: Liberia "Orbis catholicus," 1951), 155–200, for a survey of theological opinions. The definition of the dogma of the Assumption (see DS 3903/2333) uses a formula which carefully leaves open the question whether Mary died.

CHAPTER FIFTEEN

DISTINCTIONS AMONG SINS
SINS OF THOUGHT

Introduction

Having considered both sin in general and original sin, we now begin a closer examination of actual sin, the sin one personally commits. This chapter considers the distinction among sins based on their seriousness, especially the distinction between mortal and venial sins. It also deals with sins of thought. Chapters sixteen and seventeen take up in detail problems about the conditions for mortal sin. Chapter eighteen describes the dynamics by which a life of sin can decline from imperfection to everlasting death.

Question A: Are all sins equally serious?

1. It has sometimes been argued that all sins are equally serious. All violate the same first moral principle, all are unreasonable, and so all seem alike in evil. Moreover, all sins offend God's infinite goodness and so seem somehow infinite in their own right.

2. **Nevertheless, common sense and divine revelation agree that not all sins are equally serious** (see *S.t.*, 1–2, q. 73, a. 2). In his trial before Pilate, Jesus remarked that the one who handed him over was guilty of a greater sin than Pilate's (see Jn 19.11). Similarly, warning against officiousness, Jesus says: "You hypocrite, first take the log out of your own eye, and then you will see clearly to take the speck out of your brother's eye" (Mt 7.5). Beam and mote are both sins, but the sin of the hypocrite is greater than the fault he or she would correct in another.

St. Basil makes the point that even among serious sins, not all are equally grave. Circumstances can make a sin more or less grave. "Suppose it is fornication that is brought to judgment. But the one who committed this sin was trained from the beginning in wicked practices; for he was brought into life by licentious parents and was reared with bad habits, in drunkenness, reveling, and with obscene stories. If someone else, however, had many invitations to better things,—education, teachers, hearing more divine discussions, salutary readings, advice of parents, stories which shape character to seriousness and self-control, an orderly way of life,—if he falls into the same sin as the other, how were it possible, when he is called to account for his life, that he would not be regarded as deserving of a more severe penalty than the other?" (FEF 957). This analysis also develops a saying of our Lord: "Every one to whom much is given, of him will much be required" (Lk 12.48).

3. **The difference in the seriousness of sins can arise from the following sources: what one does (sometimes called the "matter" of the act), one's awareness of wrongdoing in acting, whether one actually makes a sinful choice, and the appeal of a morally acceptable alternative to the sinful choice.** The more serious the matter, the more clear the knowledge which forbids the act, and, assuming consent, the easier a right choice of an appealing alternative, the worse the sin.

4. The following considerations make it clear why not all sins are equally serious. Although moral evil does consist in unreasonableness, unreasonableness is not simply the violation of a unitary principle. One violates the first principle of morality by violating various goods in various degrees and also by violating various modes of responsibility whose violation is more or less radically at odds with a will toward integral human fulfillment. Hence, while all sins are unreasonable, their unreasonableness is subject to degree.

5. Similarly, morally evil action is sinful not by violating divine goodness in itself—for it is inviolable—but by violating what participates in divine goodness. Although all sins offend God, not all are equally offensive to him, since not all encroach to the same degree upon the human good he loves.

It is worth considering how sins differ in seriousness according to differences in the seriousness of what one does, setting aside, for the present, differences arising from degrees of awareness or the appeal of the good alternative.

The modes of responsibility have normative force in various ways (see 10-A). In three different ways, Titus brings about the death of another person, and in each case other factors are assumed constant. The sin which violates the seventh mode of responsibility is more serious than that which violates the fifth, and the sin which violates the fifth mode is more serious than that which violates the first. The difference is not in the damage done, yet it is in what Titus does; for what he does is not simply bring about three deaths, but wrongly determine himself in three diverse ways with respect to the good of human life.

It is important to bear in mind that the same act can violate several modes of responsibility at once. If so, its seriousness is increased. For example, many violations of the seventh and eighth modes of responsibility also involve a violation of the fifth mode. Most abortion and euthanasia of defective persons violate both sanctity of life and fairness; such acts are more seriously wrong than would be the mercy killing of a person who really wished to be killed; for such a killing would not be unfair although it would violate the sanctity of life.

The seriousness of what is done also differs according to the good violated. In the light of faith and within its perspective, acts which directly violate the religious relationship are more serious than those which of themselves violate only a relationship among human persons or groups, and the latter are more serious than those which of themselves violate only the harmony within oneself.

In comparing the seriousness of what is done according to differences in the good violated, one must bear in mind that the same act often violates several goods at once. For example, a Christian who commits adultery violates the religious good of the sacrament, fairness to the injured spouse or spouses, and the good of authentic sexual communion.

The seriousness of what is done also differs according to the extent to which the relevant good is violated (see *S.t.*, 1–2, q. 73, a. 3). For example, those who seek revenge act in a more seriously wrong way if they intend to kill than if they intend only to injure. Injuries to a person are more serious than comparable injuries to an extrinsic good of the person—for example, it is worse to scratch an enemy's face than to scratch the finish on his or her car. Such differences generally can be distinguished easily enough by asking which injury one would prefer to avoid to oneself. The extent of violation of a relevant good also can be measured by the number of persons adversely affected. For example, the vindictive killing of a whole family is worse than the killing of a single member of the family.

Considering seriousness from a properly Christian perspective, what one does is more seriously wrong if it is more clearly inconsistent with the teaching of the gospel; likewise, what one does is more seriously wrong if it more greatly impedes the life and activity of the Church.

The preceding distinctions—which are not necessarily exhaustive—do not form a single system. Differences in seriousness can be measured in many incomparable ways. One might imagine that if all of these could be applied simultaneously, one could discern a gradation in seriousness proceeding by very small steps from the most grievous to the least serious matters. However, we are in no position to construct such a hierarchy, nor is there any real need to attempt it.

Someone might suppose that comparisons between sins according to the seriousness of what is done involve proportionalism. This supposition would be false. Proportionalism consists in an effort to commensurate the incommensurable—to determine what possibility morally ought to be chosen by comparing various human goods without the use of a prior moral standard to measure them. The comparisons made in the present section involve no such effort. Moral standards are used in making the comparisons.

Question B: What are the theological sources of the distinction between mortal and venial sin?

1. Ethical theory ignores the difference between mortal and venial sin. Although philosophers are aware that there are degrees of seriousness in moral evil, immoral acts considered apart from faith seem to comprise a continuum, from the slight to the very serious. Ethics does not observe the sharp break marked by theology: the distinction between mortal and venial sin.

2. While there are degrees of seriousness in each category, the worst venial sin differs altogether in its significance from the least grave mortal sin (see *S.t.*, 1–2, q. 88, a. 1). As we shall see in the present question, faith requires that this sharp division be acknowledged. Mortal sin will be formally defined in the next question, and the problem of gravity of matter will be more fully explored in chapter sixteen.

3. In the Old Testament, an expiatory offering was required for sins of human frailty and inadvertence (see Lv 4–5). However, other sins, having the character of crimes against the covenant community and its God, could not be expiated. They were punished by death or by cutting the sinner off from the community (see Lv 7.25; 17.8–10, 14; 19.7–8; 20.3; and so on). The words "venial" and "mortal" were not used, but some such distinction is obviously implicit in the difference between faults which could be expiated ("venial" means "pardonable") and crimes which could not.

4. The New Testament maintains this distinction. In teaching his disciples to pray, Jesus directs them to seek forgiveness for their daily transgressions (see Mt

6.12; Lk 11.4). By contrast, he threatens his determined opponents with the condemnation of Gehenna (see Mt 23.33). Certain sins exclude one from the kingdom forever (see Mt 25.43–46); some are unforgivable in a way that others are not (see Mt 12.31–32; Mk 3.28–30).

5. Similarly, the Epistles mention daily sins of which everyone can be guilty (see Jas 3.2; 1 Jn 1.8). By contrast, there is the slavery to sin which leads to death (see Rom 6.16). Certain sins call for excommunication (see 1 Cor 5.13). The grave sins exclude from the kingdom (see 1 Cor 6.9–10; Gal 5.19–21).

A long tradition has taken a passage in St. Paul as marking the distinction between venial and mortal sin. Paul says people build differently on the foundation which is Jesus, some with gold, silver, and jewels, others with wood, hay, or straw. Judgment will test the quality of each one's work; one whose building burns because of its poor material can be saved, but as fleeing through a fire. But others utterly destroy God's temple, for they separate themselves from Jesus; at judgment, these will be destroyed, not saved (see 1 Cor 3.10–17).[1]

Among the Fathers of the Church, the distinction between venial and mortal sins is clearly marked.[2] St. Jerome, for example, says: "There are venial sins and there are mortal sins. It is one thing to owe ten thousand talents, another to owe but a farthing. We shall have to give an accounting for an idle word no less than for adultery. But to be made to blush and to be tortured are not the same thing; not the same thing to grow red in the face and to be in agony for a long time" (FEF 1382). Augustine points out that it is a mistake to make light of lesser sins; they can lead to grave sin. Hence, lesser sins should be confessed and overcome with works of mercy (see FEF 1846). The lesser sins, for which everyone needs pardon, are distinguished from crimes; every crime is a sin, but not every sin is a crime (see FEF 1918). St. Caesar of Arles, writing before the mid-sixth century, briefly lists mortal and venial sins, basing himself on the lists in St. Paul and on the sense of the faithful. Those dominated by mortal sins must do penance, give alms, and amend their lives. The lesser sins can be remitted, even if one dies with them, through purgatorial fire; Caesar identifies this with the fire which according to St. Paul will burn away the wood, hay, and straw of those who nevertheless build on Jesus (see FEF 2233).

6. The Church's teaching, rooted in Scripture, insists on this distinction. Against the Pelagians, the Church teaches that even the upright Christian sins (see DS 228–30/106–8). The Council of Trent teaches that not all sins take away grace; some are venial (see DS 1537/804). Without a special divine privilege, like that given Mary, not even a justified person can altogether avoid venial sin (see DS 1573/833). St. Pius V condemns the severe view that every sin of its nature deserves hell (see DS 1920/1020). Thus the Church insists firmly on the reality of the category called "venial sin."

7. No less firmly does the Church insist upon the reality of the category called "mortal sin." The Council of Trent teaches that one can lose the grace of justification not only by sins directly against faith, which cause faith to be lost, but also by a variety of sins which, if unrepented, exclude even believing Christians from the kingdom. Sins other than infidelity also can be grave and enormous; Trent invokes St. Paul (see 1 Cor 6.9–10) in support of this teaching (see DS 1544/808, 1577/837).

8. Trent also insists on the distinction between mortal and venial sin in its teaching on the sacrament of penance. Catholics must confess all mortal sins they

can remember after a careful examination of conscience. These can include sins of thought without any external act. Mortal sins have the character of crimes. They must be submitted to the Church, in the person of the confessor, for judgment. Venial sins also may be confessed but they do not have to be (see DS 1679–81/899).

Already in the time of St. Thomas, centuries before Trent, there was substantial agreement among the Church's teachers not only on the points concerning which Trent insists but also on the sorts of acts which constitute mortal sins. In the centuries since Trent, moral theologians whose works were authorized for use in the formation of confessors reached even more detailed and precise agreement concerning the kinds of acts which are grave matter. This common body of Catholic moral teaching seems to meet the conditions for teaching infallibly proposed by the ordinary magisterium (see 35-E). Therefore, it not only is a matter of faith that there is a definite line to be drawn between mortal and venial sins; the faithful Catholic in many cases is in a position to say whether a certain kind of act falls on one side of the line or on the other.[3]

Question C: What is a mortal sin?

1. **It is clear from the preceding that a mortal sin is a sin which is incompatible with divine life.** Those who commit and remain in mortal sin are excluded from the kingdom of God; they are separated from Jesus; they evict the Holy Spirit from their hearts. They incapacitate themselves for life in the Church, particularly for the reception of Holy Communion, which expresses and nourishes the living unity of humankind redeemed in Jesus.

2. **The conditions required for mortal sin are three: grave matter, sufficient reflection, and full consent** (see *S.t.*, 1–2, q. 88, aa. 2–6). Explained briefly here, these conditions will be examined in greater detail in the next two chapters.[4]

3. It is common theological teaching that certain kinds of acts are of themselves light matter—for example, idle talk, lack of diligence in prayer, and so on. Other kinds of acts are of themselves grave matter—killing the innocent, adultery, lying, theft, and so on. Of the latter, however, some necessarily bring about great harm: In killing the innocent the victim cannot be only somewhat dead, and in adultery the marriage bond cannot be only slightly defiled. Others can sometimes involve slight harm: In stealing, one can take a newspaper without paying for it or one can take somebody's entire livelihood; in lying, one can make a harmless joke or one can practice deception in a matter of life and death.

4. Acts of kinds which admit of smallness in the harm done (parvity of matter) are not necessarily grave. They will not be matter for mortal sin if the parvity of matter makes a particular instance so light that it simply cannot count as an act of that kind. For example, to sample one grape as one passes by a vineyard is too slight a matter to count as theft.[5]

For practical purposes, Catholics must consider grave matter what the Church teaches is such, since they ought to conform their consciences to the Church's teaching. When the precise teaching of the Church is not clear, two points should be borne in mind.

First, when the Church teaches that a certain kind of act always is wrong, then any more specific kind of act which includes all the characteristics of that general sort of act also is always wrong. For example, since the Church teaches clearly that any positive act intended to impede procreation from following upon marital intercourse always is gravely wrong, the more specific act of impeding procreation by anovulant drugs in order to limit the size of the family to a reasonable number also is always gravely wrong. Similarly, since the Church teaches clearly that any act intended to kill the innocent always is wrong, the more specific act of intending to kill millions of innocent persons by a retaliatory strike in case of nuclear war also is always gravely wrong.

Second, when the Church's teaching is not clear—for example, when there is disagreement even among the classical theologians—that something is grave matter, then no one, except a bishop or pope, on his or her own judgment ought to tell anyone else that the matter is grave. For example, a priest who is convinced that his parishoners ought not to vote for a candidate who favors euthanasia nevertheless should not tell his congregation that such a vote would be a mortal sin. Again, although failure to do works of mercy can be mortally sinful, the obligation in any particular instance is not easy to determine; therefore, someone urging contributions to a special collection to alleviate starvation should not say failure to contribute is grave matter.

5. For a sin to be mortal, it is enough that a person who is willing to sin believe the matter to be grave. One willing to violate conscience in what he or she thinks a grave matter is guilty of the degree of moral evil willingly accepted. Similarly, a person who suspects that the matter might be grave and acts without taking reasonable care to eliminate doubt is guilty of the grave moral evil he or she suspects.

6. Sufficient reflection requires more than just awareness of what one is doing. Without this there is no human act at all. Sufficient reflection also requires awareness that the act is gravely wrong. In other words, reflection sufficient for mortal sin exists only if two conditions are met: (1) one acts in violation of one's conscience, and (2) one's conscience is that the matter either is grave or might be grave.

7. At the relevant time, one must actually be aware of the act's wrongness. It is not sufficient simply that one could and should be aware, for in such a case one is primarily responsible for the failure to form conscience but is not gravely responsible for each unrecognized evil consequent upon this failure.

8. The relevant time is the time of decision, not of execution. For example, realizing that he or she has a grave obligation to seek help and foreseeing future neglect of family responsibilities otherwise, an alcoholic nevertheless decides now not to seek help. The relevant time is the time when this decision is made. The decision is made with sufficient reflection, although the neglect consequent on the choice will occur later, when the alcoholic is no longer able to think or care about family responsibilities.

9. Reflection can be insufficient when one's state of consciousness is such that one does not attend clearly to what one is about to do: in cases of extreme fatigue, semiwakefulness, partial sedation, great pressure, distraction, and so on. In such circumstances it can be a sign of insufficient reflection that the individual in no way planned the act in that situation, that the act was out of character, and that it was firmly rejected as soon as it was considered with full attention.

10. It is not necessary for sufficient reflection that one think specifically of what the act's wrongness consists in. For example, a candidate for public office might realize that there was something seriously questionable about accepting a certain campaign contribution, without knowing exactly how it would be corrupt to take it.

11. Similarly, it is not necessary for sufficient reflection that one think explicitly that the act is an offense against God or will damage one's relationship with him. At the same time, no well-instructed Catholic is likely to recognize an act as seriously wrong without having some awareness of this most important implication of sin. If this awareness is really lacking in such a person, it is a sign that the act's wrongness was probably not clear enough for sufficient reflection to have taken place.

12. Full consent is a definite choice. Even when aware that an act would be gravely evil, one has not sinned until one has made a definite choice. The choice itself need not bear only upon a wrongful performance, but can carry out an immoral commitment, can bear instead upon an omission, or can involve (without bearing upon) the acceptance of consequences one is gravely obliged to avoid.

13. One can make a choice without expressing it in words or carrying it out in any sort of behavior. One can also make a choice which leaves open a range of possibilities to be settled by additional choices. For example, a person can decide to indulge in some form of illicit gratification and only then deliberate about specifics. In such cases, the choice required for a mortal sin is made as soon as a proposal involving grave matter, however generally understood, is accepted with sufficient reflection.

14. Judgments of conscience can bear upon the process of deliberation itself as well as upon other acts. If an individual is sufficiently aware of a grave obligation to deliberate and decide a certain matter yet chooses not to do so, or is sufficiently aware of a grave obligation to set aside a certain deliberation (for instance, by directing attention to something else) yet chooses to persist in it, then an actual choice which is mortally sinful has been made.

A member of a community, aware that another is doing something seriously wrong, can be aware of an obligation to deliberate about possible ways of remedying the situation. Although this obligation might be recognized as grave, the possible unpleasantness of fulfilling it could lead to a temptation to set the problem aside. Such a choice, inconsistent with a judgment of conscience recognizing the seriousness of the obligation to deliberate, would be a mortal sin.

15. If a mortally sinful choice is not repented, subsequent voluntary acts and omissions in grave matter, supposing them to be sufficiently known as such, can continue the initial sin and, as it were, unfold its implications in new circumstances. This can occur by executive willing, even without further, distinct choices in each new instance of sin.

Question D: How can an individual become guilty
of a mortal sin by involvement in a group
which acts in a seriously wrong way?

1. Groups can sin. But to what extent do members of a group share personally in its sins? In particular, how can one be guilty of mortal sin by involvement in a group which does serious wrong?[6] Earlier we saw how one individual can be responsible for the actions of another (see 2-F, 12-G, and 13-E). At issue here is the responsibility of a group member for his or her involvement in the group's action.

2. Societies engage in no positive acts except by the personal acts of some of their members. Those who do what constitutes an immoral social act are responsible both for their personal wrongdoing and for the wrongdoing of society to which they contribute. For example, the leaders of a nation which wages an unjust war are guilty both of abusing their office and of the injustices which make up the unjust war.

3. For a society to fail to do something will be a grave omission only if some of its members could and ought to act in a manner which would constitute a required social act. Those who choose to omit acts which would cause the society to fulfill its grave responsibilities, or who deliberately choose in ways which will make it impossible for society to do so, can be gravely responsible for both their own omissions and the social omissions which they cause.

For example, if a student in a boarding school is becoming deranged, other students have a collective responsibility to inform the rector of the problem. If the situation is serious enough (always assuming sufficient reflection and the relevant choice), those who could and should act but fail to do so are gravely responsible not only for their personal failing but for the irresponsibility of the student body to which they belong.

4. Often a society engages in an action which some of its members consider immoral or omits something which some think it has a serious obligation to do. **The responsibility of members in such cases cannot extend beyond their power to affect their society's actions.** If, for example, one's country carries on an unjust war, one's responsibility cannot extend beyond one's power to stop the war or, at least, to withhold personal involvement in it.

5. Individuals do have a responsibility to rectify the actions of groups to which they belong, but this responsibility is nonabsolute. Conscientious people in particular may be aware of innumerable wrongs by groups of which they are members; actively attempting to rectify them all would exhaust their time and talent. In such cases, the norms of resolving conflicts of duties (discussed in 12-E) apply. Those whose lives are already organized by upright commitments which they strive to fulfill and which include no special commitment to righting social ills generally have no responsibility to take an activist stance toward social wrongs.

For example, a cloistered nun or the mother of a large family probably is not morally responsible for doing the political work which might be necessary and useful to change unjust public policies toward underdeveloped nations. However, a person whose life is not organized by personal vocational commitments and who spends much time and energy in self-gratifying amusements could have a grave responsibility to become politically active in the cause of justice.

6. Sometimes an individual can avoid contributing to a group's immoral action simply by not doing something. Even in such cases, the responsibility not to act is nonabsolute, provided the socially required act can be done for some good. For example, paying taxes furthers many evil acts of a society, and a citizen might avoid involvement in these acts by refusing to pay taxes. Most societies, however, also do many good acts, and citizens can be justified and even obliged to pay taxes to further these and avoid imposing heavier burdens on those less able to bear them. Similarly, one who thinks a war unjust has a nonabsolute obligation to refuse to register for service; but such a person could be justified in registering to avoid the legal penalties for draft evasion.

7. **Nevertheless, no group member can rightly do things which directly contribute to the group's wrongdoing and of themselves do nothing else.** Thus, a person who thinks a war immoral has a grave obligation not to take part in any military action in that war. The fact that refusal might entail criticism, legal penalties, even death, does not justify doing what one believes immoral.

Question E: How important to Christian morality are sins of thought?

1. The Ten Commandments forbid not only evil deeds but evil desires (see Ex 20.17; Dt 5.21). In stating that love fulfills the whole law, St. Paul includes the sin of coveting as part of the law (see Rom 13.9). Thus evil desire violates the law of love, even though it does no outward damage. Jesus, deepening the commandments in the Sermon on the Mount, emphasizes that sins of murder and adultery are already committed when one nurses anger and lustful thoughts (see Mt 5.22, 28).[7]

In commenting upon the Sermon on the Mount, St. Augustine describes the psychology of sin which begins in the heart: "For there are three steps in the commission of sin: suggestion, pleasure, consent. Suggestion comes about either through memory or a sense perception as when we see, hear, smell, taste or touch anything. If to enjoy any of these sensations brings pleasure, the pleasure, if forbidden, must be checked. . . . Were we to yield consent to it, we would commit sin surely, a sin in the heart known to God, though actually it may remain unknown to man."[8] Augustine goes on to explain that if a habit has not been formed, the pleasure is less intense and more easily resisted. If one carries through and puts the consent in the heart into action, desire at first seems satisfied, but a habit is formed, and pleasure becomes more intense and harder to resist.[9] Thus, on Augustine's account, the sinful deed must be avoided more for the sake of preventing sins of thought than sins of thought must be avoided for the sake of preventing sinful deeds.

2. One must avoid evil thoughts because they are the beginning of evil deeds; to refrain from the deeds, one must nip the thoughts in the bud. There is, however, a more profound reason for emphasizing the morality of thoughts. **Morality essentially pertains to thought; evil is much more in the heart than in outward behavior** (see Mt 23.25–28; see *S.t.*, 1–2, q. 74, a. 1). Jesus emphasizes that the moral distinction between clean and unclean cannot be drawn by legalistic

standards for outward behavior; rather, impurity emerges from the heart (see Mt 15.17–20; Mk 7.18–23).

3. In its definitive teaching on the sacrament of penance, the Council of Trent explicitly teaches that even completely interior sins, which violate only the last two of the Ten Commandments, can be mortal and must be confessed (see DS 1707/917). Indeed, the Council teaches that these sins "sometimes wound the soul more grievously and are more dangerous than those sins which are committed openly" (DS 1680/899).

4. Evil's moral significance lies not so much in the harm done in outward fact as in the privation introduced in the existential domain (see *S.t.*, 1–2, q. 73, a. 8, ad 2).[10] This privation is less obvious but just as real in sins of thought as in gross, outward immorality. Morally evil choices mutilate sinners, and this mutilation at once and of itself brings disharmony into their relationships with other people and God. As soon as a man commits adultery in his heart, for instance, his relationship with his wife is damaged and so is his relationship with Jesus, in which the sacramental marital relationship participates.

5. One who tries to avoid sinful outward behavior while freely indulging in grave sins of thought inevitably takes a false, legalistic attitude toward morality. If one's heart is not pure, the attempt to avoid impure behavior becomes a pharisaic pretense. In such a case outward conformity to moral standards can only be the result of a nonmoral motive, such as shame or fear of punishment. Moral standards will seem arbitrary, irrational impositions, while inward love of goods and the attitude of openness toward integral human fulfillment will be lacking.

Inaccurate teaching concerning sins of thought can lead to morbid self-consciousness, inappropriate anxiety and feelings of guilt, and an inversion of the priority from doing good to avoiding evil. But to ignore or condone sins of thought is to undermine the inwardness of Christian morality, to encourage pharisaism, and ultimately to pave the way for a total abandonment of Christian moral standards in the interest of "honesty"—that is, the reintegration of people's covetous hearts and their outward behavior. The only remedy is timely, careful, and accurate teaching about sins of thought. In this area there is much work to be done, because in times past instruction about sins of thought often was vague and confused, and in recent years it often has been omitted or lax.

Question F: At what point does mortal sin begin in sins of thought?

1. Spontaneous emotional reactions are a determined aspect of sentient nature—they cannot be prevented. In themselves they no more have the character of human acts than do reflexes, such as being startled by a loud noise. Nor is their character altered by their duration, intensity, or recurrence. Thus there can be no personal sin in the mere experience of an emotional reaction (see *S.t.*, 1–2, q. 74, a. 4; q. 89, a. 5). For example, a person working in the prolife movement who feels hatred toward abortionists is not guilty of personal sin by reason of that feeling as such; one who notices an attractive individual of the opposite sex and feels sexual desire has not committed sin merely by feeling desire.

2. At the same time, the psychologically normal play of emotion is not beyond moral criticism. In the fallen human condition, normal emotion has the character

of concupiscence. It not only lacks but resists reasonable integration into the pattern of a humanly good life (see *S.t.*, 1–2, q. 82, a. 3; q. 89, a. 3; 2–2, q. 164, a. 1). In this way the effect of original sin on human emotionality inclines to sin (see DS 1515/792).

3. Moreover, each individual's emotional reactions can be badly conditioned by inappropriate habituation in childhood and by personal sins. The resulting lack of emotional integration is a privation in the existential domain and so is sin of a sort. But such sin cannot be mortal, because the usual conditions for mortal sin are not met; there is no choice contrary to conscience.

4. In confronting situations, courses of action (proposals for possible choice) come spontaneously to mind. There can be no mortal sin in the mere coming to mind of proposals, no matter what they are. Furthermore, one naturally begins— without any actuation of the will beyond simple willing, for which we have no responsibility—to consider the good and bad aspects of any proposal which comes to mind. In itself, this spontaneous beginning of deliberation can involve no sin either.

5. However, one who begins deliberating about a morally unacceptable proposal is in a condition of temptation. Temptation as such is not sin.[11] Without committing any sin, one can be drawn into this process and compelled to terminate it by choosing between doing what is right and doing what is wrong. Jesus himself "in every respect has been tempted as we are, yet without sinning" (Heb 4.15). One can be tempted without the slightest evil will, because temptation can arise due to the natural and good functioning of practical reasoning itself and due to the intelligible goodness present even in choices it would be wrong to make.

6. It might be supposed that there must be something wrong in proceeding to begin deliberating about a possibility one recognizes as morally wrong to adopt. However, while this sequence can involve venial sin, it need not involve sin at all. This is so because practical reason naturally and necessarily begins to consider the case for and against any proposal which comes to mind. True, a person can block such consideration—but only when the possibility of blocking it comes to mind. It comes quickly to the mind of a virtuous person, but not so quickly to someone whose thought processes are not so well integrated with morally upright commitments (see *S.t.*, 1–2, q. 74, a. 6, ad 3).

In many cases, incipient deliberation about a possibility which initially is thought to be morally wrong leads to—and is absolutely necessary to achieve—insight into the morally right thing to do. For incipient deliberation can lead to conscientious reflection which will make it clear that in reality the adoption of the possibility which at first seemed wrong is not so. For instance, not keeping a promise, which might initially seem wrong, can be found to be obligatory. Again, incipient deliberation often leads to the replacement of the possibility one should not adopt by a possibility which is upright. For example, an unmarried young couple who begin to deliberate about fornicating can replace the unacceptable possibility with the upright plan to get married.

7. Thus deliberation can occur, desires and wishes can come to mind, and one can experience some emotional satisfaction in imagining acts which it would be wrong to choose—all without making any choice. All these things can occur without mortal sin.

8. If one ought not to have such thoughts, desires, wishes, and experiences of satisfaction but has them due to some prior sin, then they are sinful. But only venially so, unless they are voluntary by executive willing consequent upon some prior, unrepented mortal sin. Likewise, one can sin in failing to turn one's attention to other matters. But unless the failure follows by executive willing from an unrepented mortal sin, one commits only venial sin until there is a wrong choice.

9. The qualification with respect to executive willing is important. Often, temptations and sins of thought occur after one has freely chosen to adopt a mortally sinful proposal. A person who deliberately seeks sexual excitement from pornographic entertainment or who has decided to take revenge on another by inflicting serious harm might, for instance, experience subsequent temptations and sinful thoughts. Even if these do not proceed from additional distinct choices, they can share in the character of mortal sin to the extent that they unfold the previous mortally sinful choice in subsequent actuations of the will.

10. **When one's present experience and thinking do not follow upon a prior, unrepented mortally sinful choice, a mortal sin of thought begins only when the usual conditions for mortal sin are fulfilled. One must be aware of a grave moral obligation to do something (for example, to focus attention on some innocent matter) or not to do something (for example, not to continue deliberating about an immoral proposal), and one must choose contrary to the awareness.**

The following example will illustrate the preceding distinctions. A businessman who has lost a contract to a competitor might think of a legal but gravely unjust way to destroy the competitor's business. Hatred and an angry desire for revenge could make the plan attractive, and the businessman might elaborate it in detail, taking considerable satisfaction in the prospect of his competitor's downfall.

Under what conditions does the businessman commit a sin of thought? At what point will the sin be mortal? Four possibilities should be distinguished.

First, this entire process could occur without any personal sin. This would be so if it unfolded spontaneously, without dependence on any prior personal sin, although conditioned by the concupiscence which results from original sin. When the businessman reflects in conscience that he is entertaining a gravely wrong possibility and that he ought to set aside these thoughts and desires, he has experienced temptation but commits no sin provided he chooses to follow this judgment of conscience.

Second, the process described might result from some personal sin, yet not unfold in the course of living out an unrepented mortally sinful choice. Perhaps the businessman has accepted the grasping and merciless standards of the world in which he moves, yet without ever deliberately violating his conscience in a grave matter. Or perhaps he is simply not as conscientious as he should be in guarding his thoughts. In such cases, even before sufficient reflection and consent, there will be venial sin. Venial sin in these cases involves only the derivative modes of voluntariness (see 9-G). Many classical moralists, who overlooked these modes of voluntariness, would find only temptation and imperfection here, but St. Thomas rightly teaches that there can be a privation of moral rectitude in sensuality itself (see *S.t.*, 1–2, q. 74, a. 3). Thus, the moral defect in spontaneous thoughts and desires for revenge can be venial sin of a genuine though analogous sort insofar as the defect is in some way voluntary.

Third, the process described might unfold in the mind of a man who has made and not repented a mortally sinful commitment to succeed in business and destroy his competition by every expedient means. In this case, his developing plan and desire for revenge unfolds in the course of executing this prior, mortally sinful choice. Even without any new and specific judgment of conscience that the revenge would be wrong and choice contrary to such a judgment, his mortal sin continues in the executive willing with which he entertains vengeful plans and desires.

Fourth, the process described might unfold into a mortal sin of thought in the mind of a businessman who is not guilty of any relevant, unrepented mortal sin. In this case, there will be no mortal sin until he chooses contrary to a judgment of genuine conscience that the wish and plan for revenge is gravely wrong and ought to be set aside. Without sufficient reflection and choice at odds with it, there can be no mortal sin of thought, no matter how grave the injustice, how detailed the planning, and how intense the hatred and desire for revenge.

Thomas expressly holds (S.t., 1–2, q. 74, a. 8) with respect to *delectatio morosa* that the mortal sin is in the choice: "When one thinks about fornication and delights in the activity, this occurs because his affections are bent to the act of fornication itself. When one consents to this type of delight it is equivalent to consent to affection for fornication. Nobody delights in a thing unless it suits his desire. If one deliberately chooses (*ex deliberatione eligat*) to fix his desire on something that is gravely sinful, it is a mortal sin."

11. Choosing is a conscious act; one cannot make a choice without knowing it. Moreover, one cannot make a choice and an instant later forget having made it. A person uncertain of having made a choice a moment before can be sure he or she did not make it.

12. Of course, unreflective people often have no clear understanding of what choices are and cannot recognize their own choices in reflex awareness after having made them. Such people should not be given false reassurance—for instance, by telling them: "Unless you know you have made a choice, you have not sinned mortally." They can sin mortally without being able to point to anything they would call the "choice."

13. It is possible to make a choice and later forget having made it. However, there is no need for anxiety and minute introspection concerning possible sins of thought on the part of people who try constantly to avoid mortal sin and regularly examine their consciences, if, upon doing so some time after a temptation, they find themselves not clearly aware of having committed such a sin.

Question G: What are the most common kinds of sins of thought? (skip)

1. **The primary case of a sin of thought is a sinful choice.**[12] Even if it is a choice to say or do (or omit) something, the sin is already present in the choice itself, and one who is prevented from executing the choice or repents before doing so has nevertheless committed a sin of thought (see S.t., 1–2. q. 74, a. 7). (Other things being equal, of course, a sinful choice which is not carried out is less evil than one which is.)

2. Sometimes one makes a sinful choice subject to a contingent condition not in one's own power: I will do X if I have the chance, if it does not seem too risky, if

somebody else does Y, and so on. The sin of thought is committed whether or not the condition is fulfilled and the choice carried out.

3. **The wish to do or have something evil is itself evil.** The desire to commit a mortal sin one cannot commit or to have committed a mortal sin one can no longer commit is grave matter. Persistence in such desires and wishes is a mortal sin if one reflects sufficiently and chooses to entertain them.

4. If, however, one experiences desires contrary to a firm choice to set them aside, such experiences are emotions and not wrong choices. Moreover, to know as a matter of fact that one would like to commit certain sins or that one feels sad at having forgone the pleasure of sinning is not to desire deliberately to commit sin. A person who thinks "I would do X if it were not a sin" ordinarily does not will to commit the sin but is unwilling to do so.

5. **It is evil to consider with satisfaction and approval the doing of something evil, whether by oneself or another.** Hence, such consideration of the actual or possible doing of a mortal sin is itself grave matter. One aware of taking satisfaction in or approving sin ought to choose to stop doing so. If, having sufficiently reflected, one instead chooses not to set aside this sinful attitude, the continuing satisfaction or approval is mortally sinful (see *S.t.*, 1–2, q. 74, a. 8).

6. It is possible, however, to enjoy knowing about evil without taking satisfaction in it. One may, for instance, enjoy a story about a robbery and be delighted with the robber's skill, without taking satisfaction in the sin or approving it.

7. One can also take satisfaction in and approve the residual good aspects of an evil act, without approving of the evil. So one might be pleased by the acquittal of a woman who murders her brutal and unfaithful husband and happy about the deterrent effect which the act will have on other men of this sort, without approving homicide.

8. One can also consider with satisfaction and approval an act which it would be wrong to carry out now but which will be or was good at the time to which one refers it. Thus, an engaged couple can blamelessly look forward to marital intercourse while a widow can blamelessly look back on her intimacy with her husband.

It does not follow that people can rightly choose to take emotional satisfaction in thinking about doing things under conditions in which they would be right, when these things may not now be done without sin, and when there is no real necessity to think about them. One usually should judge that to engage in such thinking is wrong, because it will lead to temptations to do something wrong; to choose to engage in it despite such a judgment is a sin.

Satisfaction in the knowledge or in good aspects of sinful acts one would not oneself be tempted to choose can be distinguished readily enough from satisfaction in or approval of the evil as such. Thus, most people can read stories of robbery written from the point of view of the criminal without adopting a frame of mind which is wrong.

If, however, one considers immoral acts one would oneself be tempted to choose, supposing they seemed to be real possibilities, then satisfaction in the knowledge or in good aspects of the subject matter cannot easily be distinguished from satisfaction in or approval of the evil as such. One who thinks a state of mind could be wrong yet chooses to enter or persist in it is willing to do what is wrong. Thus, most people cannot read stories of illicit sexual activities without adopting a frame of mind which is wrong.

Summary

Common sense and divine revelation agree that not all sins are equally serious. Differences in their seriousness arise from differences in what is done, in the awareness of wrongdoing, and in the appeal of a morally acceptable alternative. The more serious the matter, the clearer the judgment of conscience, and the easier the choice of a morally acceptable alternative, the worse the sin.

The significance of the worst venial sin is altogether different from that of the least serious mortal sin. Faith requires this sharp distinction between venial and mortal sin—a distinction which is clear in Scripture and the teaching of the Church.

A mortal sin deprives one of divine life; mortal sinners exclude themselves from God's kingdom, separate themselves from Christ, and evict the Holy Spirit from their hearts. The conditions required for mortal sin are grave matter, sufficient reflection, and full consent. Certain kinds of acts are of themselves light matter, while other kinds are of themselves grave matter. Even among the latter, gravity sometimes can be lacking due to the smallness of the harm done. Sufficient reflection requires awareness at the time of decision that the act is or may well be gravely wrong. Full consent is a definite choice.

Individuals can become guilty of mortal sin by involvement in a group which acts in a seriously wrong way. But the responsibility of individual members cannot extend beyond their power to affect the group's actions. Similarly, although individuals have a responsibility to rectify the group's wrongdoing, this responsibility is not absolute: The norms for resolving conflicts of duty apply. Likewise, even when it would take only inaction to avoid contributing to the group's immoral action, the individual's responsibility is not absolute, provided the socially required act can be done for some good. For example, taxes are used for evil purposes and also for good purposes; citizens may be justified in paying their taxes and even obligated to do so, in order to support the good purposes and avoid imposing heavier burdens on others by the nonpayment of taxes by which they might otherwise seek to avoid involvement in the society's wrongdoing.

Sins of thought are very important to Christian morality. Scripture and the teaching of the Church testify to this. Evil thoughts are important not only because they are the starting point for evil deeds but, more profoundly, because morality primarily pertains to the mind and the will. Evil is much more in the heart than in outward deeds; its greatest moral significance does not lie in the harm done by outward behavior but in the privation in the existential domain. Legalism and pharisaism are natural consequences of attempting to avoid sinful behavior while freely committing grave sins of thought.

Sins of thought must be distinguished from what precedes them. Spontaneous emotional reactions are not themselves sinful (although, in the fallen human condition, even normal emotion has the character of concupiscence, and each individual's emotional reactions often reflect a further lack of integration arising from upbringing and personal sins). Nor is spontaneous deliberation about an immoral course of action sinful, since proposals for choice naturally come to mind when one confronts a situation, and one naturally begins to consider their good and bad aspects.

However, in beginning to deliberate about an immoral proposal, one is in a situation of temptation. Also, thoughts, desires, and experiences of satisfaction arising from some prior sin are themselves sinful—though only venially so, unless they arise in implementing a prior, mortally sinful choice. Where prior, unrepented mortal sin does not play a role, however, mortal sins of thought begin only when the usual conditions are fulfilled: grave matter, sufficient reflection, and full consent. Choice is a conscious act, and a person uncertain of having made a choice a moment before can be sure he or she did not make it. Still, unreflective people can and do make choices without being able to point to anything in their experience which they would call a "choice."

The primary case of a sin of thought is a sinful choice. There is sin here whether or not the choice is carried out, though carrying it out makes the sin worse. Evil wishes are also matter of sin, as is considering with satisfaction and approval the doing of evil, whether by oneself or another. However, it is possible to enjoy knowing about evil and to approve good consequences of evil without taking satisfaction precisely in the evil itself.

Appendix 1:   Mortal sin and the modes of voluntariness

In chapter nine, I distinguished diverse modes of voluntariness. The doing of a positive act by free choice is the central mode of voluntariness, but there are several others. In which of these is mortal sin possible? In the following examples, I always assume sufficient reflection prior to the relevant choice.

Obviously, mortal sin is possible in the voluntariness with which one adopts a proposal, whether that proposal is adopted for its own sake or as a means to an ulterior end. For example, mortal sin is present in adopting the proposal to kill a person out of revenge or to kill a person one otherwise would have to support in order to avoid this burden.

Mortal sin also is possible in the voluntariness with which one accepts foreseen consequences one ought not to accept. For example, to market a product which one foresees will imperil the life and health of many who use it could be a mortal sin, although one neither intends this peril as an end nor chooses it as a means. (Whether the sin is mortal or not—indeed, whether there is any sin at all—will depend upon whether and how great an injustice one is willing to do.)

The voluntary in cause can involve mortal sin. One who needlessly and deliberately enters the occasion of mortal sin commits mortal sin; one who gives easily avoidable scandal which will likely lead to mortal sin commits mortal sin. For example, ordinarily people who produce and people who consume pornography commit mortal sins in this way, since the choice to do either ordinarily responds to no moral requirement and is likely to lead to mortal sins (at least of thought) in oneself or others.

Executive willing is the acceptance without an additional choice of significant aspects of one's actions which come to attention only in performing them. Because there is no mortal sin without sufficient reflection and full consent, there will be no mortal sin in executive willing unless it occurs in the performance of an act already mortally sinful. For example, if a person venially sins by deliberately getting into a quarrel with another, and knowingly but without a further choice carries the quarrel to the point that the matter is grave (begins to inflict serious harm), the voluntariness involved in executive willing does not make the deliberate venial sin into a mortal one.

However, executive willing in the carrying out of a mortally sinful choice can specify the sin, making it worse than it otherwise would be. For example, when Ma Fia, bent on mortally sinful revenge, is glad to carry it out when she learns it involves homicide, then her sin becomes murder, although her original choice was not specifically to commit murder, and in the press of action she makes no new choice. A person who makes a mortally sinful choice to embark upon a certain way of life will be responsible for the gravely wrong acts done in the course of unrepentantly living that life, even though many of these acts will be done without further thought about their sinful character or a distinct choice to do each wrong act.

Omissions in which there is a choice can be mortal sins. For example, if one chooses to kill a baby by withholding food and fluids, then one is guilty of homicide just as one would be if one chose to kill it by drowning it in the bath. (One who chooses to kill by the purposeful omission also might be guilty of an additional sin of cruelty, to the extent that the child's suffering is foreseen and accepted as a means of avoiding the legal implications for oneself of straightforward homicide.) Also, omissions foreseen as consequences of choices to do something else can involve mortal sin. For example, people who foresee that they are likely to miss Sunday Mass altogether if they do not get up for an early Mass can commit a mortal sin if they choose to stay up very late partying, knowing they never will be able to get up for early Mass.

Omissions which in no way depend upon a mortally sinful choice cannot be mortal sins, since mortal sin requires the full consent present only in choice. Thus, the parents who know they should do something about their child's health and fail to make up their minds to do (or not to do) anything are morally guilty of neglect but the sin is not mortal, unless it is an outcome of some earlier, unrepented, mortally sinful choice. Again, the person who is being tempted by lustful desire can be at fault for failing to resist the temptation, but there will be no mortal sin if there is not a choice—for example, an earlier, unrepented, mortally sinful choice which has led to the present temptation and failure of resistance, or a current choice to continue to entertain a temptation one knows one should set aside.

Other modes of voluntariness (discussed in 9-G) can involve venial sin but not mortal sin. Those whose spontaneous willing is disorderly because of past mortal sins of commission or omission, those who do wrong with no present awareness because of past mortal sins which led to present obtuseness or error, and those who are ready to sin seriously but have not chosen to do so were guilty of mortal sin in the past or might be guilty of it in the future, but are not guilty of it now by these derivative modes of voluntariness. Of course, one who has not repented a past mortal sin remains guilty of it now.

In sum, the inadvertent faults and unknown sins which arise in voluntariness apart from choice cannot be mortal sins. However, one who chooses to commit a mortal sin and who, by executive willing, does something specifically more serious than what was chosen is guilty of what he or she knowingly and willingly does in carrying out the original, mortally sinful choice. Similarly, one who makes a mortally sinful choice which leads to subsequent, gravely evil acts and/or omissions can be guilty of these grave sins even if sufficient reflection and/or an actual choice are not given in each and every instance of sin which makes up a sinful life.

Appendix 2:   The distinction of sins according to species and number

The question of the distinction of sins in species is the question: What sin was committed? The question of the distinction in number is the question: How many times was it committed? The theoretical discussion of these questions could be very complicated and will not be undertaken here. However, these questions have a certain practical importance, since Catholics are obliged, as the Council of Trent definitively teaches, to confess mortal sins not only in general—"I have sinned mortally"—but in species and number (see DS 1679/899, 1707/917). Therefore, I treat these questions from this practical point of view.[13]

Sins differ in species not by the difference in external behavior but by the difference in the intelligible aspects of the human act which are defective and so render the act evil. It follows that details of a sin which involve proper names, places, and times do not alter its species.

Generally, penitents will have been instructed to consider certain kinds of acts mortally sinful by being taught a set of specific moral norms. For example, a penitent will have learned that adultery and theft are mortal sins and will confess in these terms. What is fundamentally morally relevant about sins is the precise goods which are violated and the modes of responsibility in respect to which they are violated. However, penitents do not think in these categories and cannot be expected to do so.

Penitents might need help in reaching a reasonably adequate specification of their confession. Confessors should provide such help, not only to fulfill the requirement for integral confession, but also to provide a reasonable basis for instructing and counseling the penitent.

For example, sins of adultery differ specifically according to whether both parties to the adultery are married or only one is married. The appropriate advice to be given also might be somewhat different. Similarly, sins of theft differ in species according to the likely injury which will accrue to the person whose property is stolen; the confessor's guidance about the duty of restitution also requires more information than the generic indication that theft was committed.

Perhaps the penitent has an erroneously strict conscience which needs to be corrected; such correction will not be given if the confession is permitted to stand at a level of vague generalities. Moreover, no helpful guidance can be given about avoiding occasions of sin without an adequately specific confession. In any case, while the sincere contrition of the penitent and genuine purpose of amendment are far more important than the details of sins, the Church's clear and definitive teaching about the requirement for specific confession must not be ignored.

From a theoretical point of view, moral acts are individuated by actuations of the will—by choices and by acts of willing implementing prior choices. Thus, the act of machine-gunning fifty persons is one homicide if it carries out a single choice; the complex act of kidnapping might involve dozens of distinct morally evil acts if it requires dozens of distinct choices and acts of executive willing.

In practice, penitents generally count sins by counting external performances, whose individuation is by standards used by common sense. Such an estimation ordinarily can be taken as adequate to fulfill the requirement of integral confession. Moreover, in many cases a penitent can only guess at the frequency with which a certain sin was committed; an estimate of the instances per unit of time over a certain period is sufficient—for example, "about three times a year for the last ten years."

If a penitent seems to need help to make a judgment concerning the number of sins, the point to keep in mind is that quantity or extent is what is at stake here. Thus, a person involved in a prolonged adulterous relationship should confess the duration of the relationship as well as the approximate frequency of specific acts; a person involved in drug traffic should estimate the volume of business and the number of persons probably harmed; a person who neglected to help support aged parents should indicate the duration of the neglect and the portion of support which was omitted.

In the case of purely internal sins, penitents are likely to count the episodes or discontinuous periods of sin; strictly speaking, the number of sins is determined by the number of immoral choices and subsequent implementing will actuations. Generally, many such sins are committed in the course of any complex act, but if the complex proceeds to an external performance, the penitent ordinarily does not distinguish the numerous sins involved. Nor need such distinctions be pressed; an honest estimate of the extent of sin according to common criteria is sufficient.

A point to notice is that the obligation to be specific and precise in confession is an affirmative one; as such it is limited by one's reasonable ability to fulfill it. Thus, penitents are held only to examine their consciences with due care and to confess truthfully according to their ability. In exceptional circumstances, where a penitent cannot confess with precision because of a handicap, a language barrier, unavoidable lack of privacy, or simply lack of time (for example, in a disaster situation), then the requirement for specific confession does not hold; the sacrament can be completed without it, although a person absolved under such exceptional circumstances must make good the confession of sins when an opportunity presents itself.

Notes

1. See St. Thomas Aquinas, *Summa theologiae*, 1–2, q. 89, a. 2; St. Augustine, *Expositions on the Psalms*, 81 (80), 19–20. The fire by which the wood, hay, and straw are consumed is identified by the tradition with the fire of purgatory. See Thomas Deman, O.P., "Péché Mortel et Péché Veniel," *Dictionnaire de Théologie Catholique*, 12:225–26.

2. See Hubert Louis Motry, *The Concept of Sin in Early Christianity* (Washington, D.C.: Catholic University of America, 1920), for a tracing of the concept up to and including Tertullian; summary, 157–58.

3. See Ronald Lawler, O.F.M.Cap., "The Love of God and Mortal Sin," in *Principles of Catholic Moral Life*, ed. William E. May (Chicago: Franciscan Herald Press, 1980), 193–219.

4. The practical implications of what is said here and in the remainder of this question, if not evident from reflection or established from other sources, have the weight of the consensus of the classical theologians. To the extent that this consensus was accepted by bishops as a norm in the formation of confessors, it remains a safe guide for pastoral practice. See Arthurus Vermeersch, S.J., *Theologiae Moralis: Principia, Responsa, Consilia*, tomus 1, *Theologia Fundamentalis* (Rome: Apud Aedes Universitatis Gregorianae, 1947), sections 381–402; I. Aertnys and C. Damen, C.Ss.R., *Theologia Moralis secundum Doctrinam S. Alphonsi de Ligorio*, ed. J. Visser, C.Ss.R., ed. 17, vol. 1 (Rome: Marietti, 1956), sections 233–38; Benedictus Henricus Merkelbach, O.P., *Summa Theologiae Moralis ad Mentem D. Thomae*, vol. 1, *De Principiis* (Paris: Desclée de Brouwer, 1942), sections 538–50.

5. The conception of acts in themselves grave in kind but falling short of gravity due to parvity of matter is in St. Thomas, *De malo*, q. 10, a. 2; cf. q. 12, a. 3; q. 13, a. 2. St. Thomas does not admit parvity of matter in sexual sins except for those incidental to marital intercourse open to procreation: q. 15, a. 2, c. and ad 18. Many theologians categorize venial sins otherwise than indicated here, the most common alternative being to consider sins venial by parvity of matter to constitute a category in themselves, rather than to reduce such sins to objective imperfection of the act, as is done here following St. Thomas. See Marcelino Sánchez, O.P., "Las Categorias del Pecado Venial," *Studium Revista de Filosofia y Teologia*, 12 (1972), 319–32.

6. For a survey of relevant literature: Dionigi Tettamanzi, "La Dimensione Ecclesiale e Sociale del Peccato del Cristiano," *La Scuola Cattolica*, 107 (1979), 516–38.

7. For a good summary of scriptural teaching relevant to sin of thought, see H. Schönweiss, "epithymia," *New International Dictionary of New Testament Theology*, 1:456–58.

8. St. Augustine, *The Lord's Sermon on the Mount*, trans. John J. Jepson, S.S. (New York: Newman Press, 1948), 43.

9. Ibid., 44.

10. With the acceptance of proportionalism and its emphasis on what is brought about in making and executing choices, many Catholic moralists have tended to ignore or condone sins of thought. See, for example, Philip S. Keane, S.S., *Sexual Morality: A Catholic Perspective* (New York: Paulist Press, 1977), 46–51 and 57–59.

11. On temptation, see St. Francis de Sales, *Introduction to the Devout Life*, part 4, 3–10.

12. In some respects, the treatment of sins of thought here depends upon the common views of the classical moral theologians. See Vermeersch, op. cit., sections 429–35; Aertnys and Damen, op. cit., sections 241–47; Merkelbach, op. cit., sections 452–60.

13. For treatments of these questions, see Vermeersch, op. cit., sections 406–19; Aertnys and Damen, op. cit., sections 233–38; Merkelbach, op. cit., sections 538–50.

CHAPTER SIXTEEN

THE DISTINCTION BETWEEN GRAVE AND LIGHT MATTER

Introduction

The three requirements for mortal sin were stated in chapter fifteen. Here the notion of grave matter will be clarified, with particular reference to current theories of fundamental option and to St. Thomas Aquinas' discussion of the question. The conclusion will be that the act of faith is a Christian's fundamental option, and that the distinction between grave and light matter can be explained by the different ways in which immoral acts can be related to faith. Problems about sufficient reflection and full consent will be considered in chapter seventeen.

Question A: What problem is raised by the distinction between grave and light matter?

1. Everyone is aware that there are degrees of seriousness in immorality. We have seen why not all immoral acts are equally serious (15-A). We have also seen that the Church teaches not only that there are degrees of seriousness but that there is a sharp break between grave matter, required for mortal sin, and light matter (15-B). This teaching articulates Christian understanding developed from divine revelation and in its light. The question to be answered here is why there is an absolute break between grave and light matter and so between fully deliberate venial sin and mortal sin.

2. A person who loves God ought by that very fact to love every human good, since every created good is a participation in divine goodness. One who loved every human good to the full extent of its goodness would proceed in perfect consistency with integral human fulfillment. But one who commits an immoral act is not acting in a manner consistent with integral human fulfillment. There-fore, it seems that every immoral act is at odds with the love of God.

3. Yet a venial sin is not incompatible with love of God. This is not difficult to understand if it is venial because of a lack of sufficient reflection or full consent, for the lack of either reduces or eliminates responsibility. However, one can also commit sins which are fully deliberate yet venial because of light matter—for example, cheating someone of a very small sum (see *S.t.*, 1–2, q. 88, aa. 2, 5, 6).

Consider a man who would like a morning paper. Checking for change, he discovers that he lacks the coins necessary to purchase a paper from a vending box. However, he notices that the box is not latched tightly. The thought occurs: "I could take a paper without paying for it, but that would be wrong. However, the newspaper company will not be seriously hurt if I take a paper and close the box, so that subsequent customers will pay." He hesitates momentarily, realizing the wrongness of the act, but is inclined to choose to do it anyway. A quick look about assures him there is no one to notice his pilferage. He filches the paper.

In a case like this, one might suppose that he did not reflect sufficiently and consent fully. However, the supposition of the example precisely is that he did. One also might suppose that he entertains some thoughts which could justify the act—for example, that he would pay double next time or that on some previous occasion the box has taken his coins without opening. But let us suppose he had no such thoughts.

Catholic moralists and the faithful in general would agree that, despite the sufficient reflection and full consent in this case, the act was not a mortal sin. What the man did is light matter.

4. A few theologians have held that of itself every kind of immorality would be grave matter, but God by a merciful fiat simply decrees that many sins people are likely to commit will not be mortal. This view is unsatisfactory, since it presupposes a legalistic conception of the relationship between moral action and one's share in divine life. If God determines by fiat which immoralities remain mortal sins, there seems to be no intrinsic connection between living an upright life and remaining in his friendship. The requirement to avoid mortal sin becomes an arbitrary test.

5. This unsatisfactory position nevertheless does help clarify the essential point. **The question is not why some moral evils constitute grave matter, but why some do not—why not all matter is grave. Charity is love of divine goodness; every evil is incompatible with divine goodness; even a small sin is a real evil; yet this real evil and love of God can coexist in one's heart.**[1] How?

6. There is also a subordinate problem. Why is the division between grave and light matter made where it is and maintained so rigidly? Why, for instance, is the seeking of sexual orgasm apart from marital intercourse always grave matter, while many minor offenses against one's neighbor—for example, slighting another—are only light matter?[2]

Question B: What are the current theories of fundamental option?

1. In recent years, some Catholic theologians have taken a position along the following lines. Even on our side, the relational bond of the Christian's soul to God is not constituted by an ordinary act of free choice; a person in friendship with God is disposed toward him not simply by a particular act but in his or her whole being. This comprehensive orientation is a fundamental option, which is somehow different from and much deeper than any ordinary choice.[3]

2. From this the proponents of this view conclude that no ordinary choice of itself can reverse one's fundamental option. Where sufficient reflection and full consent are lacking, a sin is imperfect even as a choice. In other cases, although the sin is perfect as a choice, the bad will which it involves might not be sufficient to reverse the whole thrust of one's being.

3. Beyond this general framework, current fundamental-option theories take two different forms. One treats fundamental option as a basic commitment. Commitment is thought of either as an extraordinary choice or an aspect of many choices. This approach begins with a fact: Many people do make central commitments which organize their lives. From this fact proponents proceed to the conclusion that everyone must make a most fundamental commitment, for or against God (for, by explicit love of God or a commitment to live the moral life; or against, by an opposite love or commitment). The basic commitment is supposed to establish a predominant thrust or momentum, such that occasional acts incompatible with it usually cannot radically alter or reverse it.[4] (This approach is expounded more fully in appendix 1.)

4. **The second form regards fundamental option as something more mysterious than a basic commitment: a total self-disposal, attributed not to free choice but to another freedom, often called "fundamental freedom" or "basic freedom."** Most who take this approach overlook the existential dimension of free choice and attribute self-determination to fundamental option.[5] Some do realize that freedom of choice and self-determination are linked together. But, supposing them nonidentical, they think one can freely choose in a way inconsistent with one's fundamental option without altering that option.[6]

Joseph Fuchs, S.J., talks about a "basic" or "transcendental" freedom, contrasted with what he calls psychological freedom of choice: "Basic freedom, on the other hand, denotes a still more fundamental, deeper-rooted freedom, not immediately accessible to psychological investigation. This is the freedom that enables us not only to decide freely on particular acts and aims but also, by means of these, to determine ourselves totally as persons and not merely in any particular area of behaviour. It is clear that man's freedom of choice and his basic freedom are not simply two different psychological freedoms. As a person, man is free. But this freedom can, of course, be considered under different aspects. A man can, in one and the same act, choose the object of his choice (freedom of choice) and by so doing determine himself as a person (basic freedom)."[7]

John W. Glaser, S.J., summarizes the thinking of a number of authors in the following typical formulation: "According to this theory, man is structured in a series of concentric circles or various levels. On the deepest level of the individual, at the personal center, man's freedom decides, loves, commits itself in the fullest sense of these terms. On this level man constitutes self as lover or selfish sinner. This is the center of grave morality where man makes himself and his total existence good or evil."[8] With this "core" freedom, Glaser contrasts "peripheral" freedom which is "shallower" and does not have the "same degree of stability as core freedom." On this basis, Glaser thinks a person can with core freedom be constantly committed to doing God's will, yet with peripheral freedom quickly fluctuate between affirmation and rejection of God's will in particular acts.[9]

Fundamental freedom sometimes is said to belong to individuals as persons, not as agents; the assumption is that personhood is something much more than agency. One way of putting this is to say that the person is subject, not object, and that fundamental freedom disposes the subject in respect to everything objective at once. Timothy E. O'Connell writes as follows of fundamental freedom's unique act—the fundamental option: "It is the decision to accept or reject reality as I find it. The central core of myself, the 'I' which is my personhood, is confronted with a reality that transcends all categories. It is confronted with the reality of my world, my situation, my body, my feelings, my attitudes and prejudices. In fact it is confronted even by the condition of the possibility of that reality: namely, God.

And from the perspective of my own core, the subjectivity that I am, this cosmically inclusive objectivity presents itself for decision. A simple, singular decision: yes or no. The freedom of the human person, then, is not categorical freedom at all. Rather it is a freedom that transcends all categories, it is 'transcendental freedom.'"[10]

Karl Rahner, S.J., explicitly asserts that one is not aware of when one takes one's fundamental stance.[11]

5. One can gather several properties of this supposed fundamental freedom from the descriptions offered by its proponents. First, it is thought to be exercised at the very core of the human person; therefore, it is the locus of self-determination and so of grave moral responsibility. Second, particular possibilities to be adopted by choice are not its object, but rather the relationship of the whole self to God or to morality as such. Third, exercising fundamental freedom is not an action in any ordinary sense of the word. There is an option in some sense, but an option to take a stance or assume an attitude rather than do anything whatsoever.[12]

6. While insisting that free choice and fundamental option are not the same, proponents of fundamental freedom do not clearly explain how the two are related.[13] They usually suppose that one's fundamental option is outside one's conscious awareness; unlike one's free choices, it cannot be located in consciousness. For this reason, fundamental option remains mysterious.

This mysteriousness is very helpful to the theory that free choice can be consciously and busily deployed in one direction (for example, sexual self-indulgence) while fundamental freedom is unconsciously and peacefully deployed in another (loving submission to the will of God).

Fundamental-option theories in general are appealing for three other important reasons. First, they reject a legalistic emphasis on correct performance and focus instead on the person's general orientation. Second, they focus attention on Christian life considered as a unified and developing whole, rather than on particular choices considered in isolation. Third, they seem to explain how people act out of character at times without permanently changing their character.

Question C: How do current theories of fundamental option try to account for the distinction between grave and light matter?

1. The human person is self-determining, and this self-determination accounts for the structure and unity of one's life. Chapter two treated self-determination as a necessary aspect of free choice and showed how choices can organize life by constituting the moral self and community. Although proponents of current theories of fundamental option do not understand free choice as it is understood here, they are aware of self-determination and its existential implications, and they invoke fundamental option to try to account for them.

2. Thus they find in the person's potentially self-determined identity a principle by which to distinguish acts which are radically important from those which are not. Radically important acts are ones which establish, develop, significantly alter, or reverse one's fundamental option. Acts which do not relate

in one of these ways to the fundamental option are thought to have only marginal importance. Proponents of current theories of fundamental option claim this difference of importance has an important religious significance for a Christian. They believe one's fundamental option should be a total self-disposition toward God, either by loving him or, if one does not explicitly know him, by committing oneself to a morally upright life.

3. **On this approach, grave matter is the sort of thing which is likely to be an occasion for making or reversing one's fundamental option.** Actions not likely to affect one's basic orientation toward or against God are light matter. "Grave" and "light" are thus used with regard to good acts as well as bad. Many fundamental-option theorists speak of grave and light virtuous acts.

4. Most proponents of fundamental option hold that even a free and deliberate choice of grave matter involving immorality need not always break one's friendship with God. Inasmuch as they distinguish fundamental option from an ordinary choice, they are reluctant to admit that any specific kind of act, even assuming it to be done with sufficient reflection and a free choice, is always incompatible with the love of God. Something traditionally considered a mortal sin is, they hold, likely to be incompatible with a fundamental option toward God, but the incompatibility is not inevitable.[14]

Question D: Why do such theories fail to account for the distinction between grave and light matter?

1. The basic question which a fundamental-option theory must try to answer is: Why are some matters grave and some light? Or, as a fundamental-option proponent would formulate it: Why are some morally excluded possibilities such that choosing them is likely or certain to subvert one's good fundamental option, while others are such that choosing them probably or certainly will not subvert it?

2. The various current theories do assert that some matters are such that choosing them is likely or certain to subvert a good fundamental option. These are morally excluded possibilities traditionally considered grave matter. At the same time, most proponents also assert that in some and perhaps many instances, immoral acts traditionally considered to involve grave matter can be done with sufficient reflection and full consent without subverting a good fundamental option.[15]

3. **However, they do not explain why some matters are likely to subvert a good fundamental option and others are not.** Much less do they explain why some immoral acts traditionally considered to involve grave matter can be done with sufficient reflection and full consent without subverting a good fundamental option. These explanations are lacking because, as was pointed out above, fundamental freedom is mysterious.

4. Besides failing to clarify the distinction between grave and light matter, current theories of fundamental option aggravate the problem. For the fundamental option of a Christian is supposed to be love of God or, in the case of anyone who is morally upright, an undertaking to live a morally upright life.[16] But the puzzle

about grave and light matter arises precisely because any deliberate sin seems incompatible with these standards (see A above). What needs to be explained is how any moral evil can be a light matter—how it can coexist in one's heart with love of God or a commitment to moral goodness.

5. In sum, current theories of fundamental option recognize the need for a principle to distinguish the morally more and less important, as the traditional distinction between grave and light matter has done. They propose fundamental option as this principle. In their view, fundamental option is a disposal of the whole self in reference to God or to morality as such. Hence, the principle proposed to distinguish the more and less important is equivalent to the first principle of morality or embodies it.

6. Yet all deliberate sins are incompatible with the principle thus proposed— all are contrary to moral rectitude and to the perfect goodness of God. The implication is that the difference among immoral acts can only be one of degree, not of kind. But this implication is both contrary to the intentions of proponents of fundamental option and inconsistent with the data of the problem. Thus, current theories of fundamental option aggravate the problem as to why some moral evils constitute grave matter and some do not.

Question E: What other reasons tell against current theories of fundamental option?

1. Besides failing to explain the distinction between light and grave matter, current theories of fundamental option have logical difficulties. Also, most of these theories seem to conflict with the teaching and longstanding pastoral practice of the Church.

2. **Those who think of fundamental option as a basic commitment try to show that everyone makes such a commitment. However, they fail to demonstrate this.** One argument proceeds from psychological and sociological descriptions which show that many people make commitments, to the conclusion that everyone makes a most basic commitment. But the fact that many people make commitments which can be either compatible or incompatible with love of God and moral uprightness by no means shows that everyone makes a further, most basic commitment. (This type of fundamental-option theory is criticized more fully in appendix 1.)

3. A second argument begins from the true premise that every morally good or bad act implicitly affects one's relationship with God. But the argument moves too quickly from this to the conclusion that everyone, in making morally significant choices, implicitly makes a fundamental option which establishes a single, comprehensive orientation. The possibility that some people might have no such integrating orientation is overlooked.

There also are principles other than commitments by which people order their lives. A definite, more or less structured set of desires or interests can order the life of a person who lacks real commitments. For example, a man can direct most of his time and energy to creating opportunities for sensory gratification; a woman can direct most of her time and energy to attaining a position of power and prestige. Such life-styles manifest what the sociologists and psychologists might take to be a fundamental orientation; these are lives of a definite form. But such lives do not require some sort of mysterious, implicit fundamental option for oneself or for the created good. Moreover, if such an option is posited and is thought to be a disposal of the whole self, radical conversion to the opposite option becomes inexplicable.

4. Those who think fundamental option is total self-disposal by a freedom distinct from free choice never make it clear what such opting might be. It is true that free choices are limited—they dispose one only with respect to human possibilities within one's power—but it does not follow that there is a more fundamental freedom by which one can utterly dispose oneself.

Free choices are not as limited as most proponents of fundamental freedom suppose. Choices are not passing events; they are of themselves lasting self-determinations. Although they are made throughout life, one's consistent set of free choices can constitute and articulate an enduring self. There is no need for fundamental freedom to explain how a saint by many acts carries out his or her personal vocational commitments, which are made to fulfill the basic commitment of faith. Animated by the gift of charity, such a life is a unified whole, intelligible as a humanly good life and recognizable in the light of faith as the life of a child of God.

A person who has Christian faith but fails to live up to it—perhaps even to think seriously about it—can undergo an experience of radical conversion very similar to the experience of those initially converted to Jesus. But to account for this experience, one need not postulate a fundamental option or personal act of conversion distinct from the act of faith itself. Commitments once made can be reaffirmed and deepened, as most married couples reaffirm and deepen their marital commitment on many occasions throughout their life. Likewise, the conversion of a slack Christian, if it is genuine, most centrally is an intense reaffirmation of the fundamental commitment of life with Jesus: the act of faith. This reaffirmation, especially if made in a penitential context, naturally will have experiential components which lend it an especially intense quality.

The act of faith itself is made by a free choice. Although one's act of faith is not total self-disposition toward God, it can be the beginning of such total self-disposition. One must proceed from this principle to work out one's Christian life, to seek perfection by a gradual growth in holiness accomplished by many day-to-day acts.

5. There is no reason to suppose any sinner is ever as fully integrated in alienation from God as a person with a fundamental option directly against God presumably would be.[17] Not even the worst sin destroys God, ends all relationship with him, or utterly corrupts the self. On the other hand, while it is true that the love of God poured forth in the hearts of fallen persons does utterly transform them (see Rom 5.5), still this love is not a human act, not self-disposal by an exercise of human freedom (see 25-A).

6. **Those who think there is a fundamental freedom distinct from free choice usually have an impoverished idea of free choice.** We do determine ourselves in making free choices (see 2-H), and we experience ourselves making them (see 2-D). Although choices and the self-determination included in them are not given in experience as sense data are, still we are aware of choosing.

7. Some who posit fundamental freedom argue that one cannot be aware of self-determination, because the subject and object of awareness must always be

distinct. But this claim is a bit of metaphysics falsified every time we are aware of making up our minds about anything.[18]

8.   Another argument often proposed for fundamental freedom is that one cannot oscillate as rapidly between mortal sin and grace as people with a habit of sin oscillate between the choice to commit the sin and a routine of repentance. The argument begs the question. Perhaps such oscillation does occur. Or perhaps the person with the "habit of serious sin" does not commit a mortal sin on every occasion; defects in reflection or consent may render some falls venial. Or perhaps the person with the practice of routine "repentance" does not really repent on every occasion; defects in the purpose of amendment render some acts of contrition insincere.

Some point out that one does not observe rapid oscillation between intimate friendship and deep alienation in human interpersonal relationships such as marriage. This argument by analogy is not cogent. For in marriage a couple are concerned only with certain goods and aspects of their lives, and they are able to conceal many things from each other. At the same time, repeated forgiveness is difficult, although possible with the help of grace. One's relationship with God is different: Everything affects it, nothing is hidden, and God's mercy is generously given. Hence, human interpersonal relationships can persist despite deep ambivalence and ambiguity. One's relationship with God cannot; instead, it is subject to oscillations which would destroy any possibility of relationship between human persons.

9.   Proponents of current theories of fundamental option focus on the transcendent, religious aspect of morality. But moral goodness is not just a matter of avoiding mortal sin and staying in friendship with God. The morally good person who is mature should live a harmonious life open to integral human fulfillment. The great nobility of the Christian, as we shall see in chapters twenty-three through twenty-six, lies in cooperating consciously with Jesus in the redeeming work of God. Such cooperation depends upon awareness of one's basic commitment of living faith, which shapes one's personal vocation and thereby organizes one's whole life. **If, as many fundamental-option theories require, there were a mysterious and individualistic basic self-orientation, inaccessible to conscious awareness, Christians could hardly undertake consciously to shape their whole lives so as to fulfill their commitment of faith in Jesus.**[19]

This conclusion is perfectly consistent with the teaching of the Council of Trent (see DS 1534/802) that one cannot know with the certitude of faith that he or she has obtained God's grace. Grace is not a human act; hence, one could be perfectly aware of every human act, no matter how profound an act of self-disposal, yet remain unaware of grace itself.

Moreover, Trent excludes only the certitude of faith. This certitude is superior to every other certitude, including that of immediate experience. Therefore, without denying Trent's teaching, one could maintain that one is aware by immediate experience of having obtained grace.[20] No one has the certitude of faith even about a free choice one is making, which certainly is experienced. Furthermore, Trent is talking of certainty about being in grace; the impossibility of such certainty is compatible with the possibility of being certain that one is not in grace. This point is important, because one's own act is sufficient for mortal sin, but not for grace. Hence, what Trent teaches by no means excludes what the fundamental-option proponent wishes to exclude. One can be aware of committing a sin which removes one from God's love.

10. **As a practical matter, the significance of most current theories of fundamental option is to allow some acts traditionally considered mortal sins not to be such.** Proponents acknowledge the distinction between grave and light matter made by the common teaching of the Church, but they deny that grave matter, sufficient reflection, and full consent really suffice for a mortal sin, one which necessarily subverts a good fundamental option.[21] For them, "grave matter" is rather like the Surgeon General's warning on a pack of cigarettes: These things could kill. Still, most people can smoke a bit without dying from it.[22] Likewise, according to most current theories of fundamental option, some people at times can do with sufficient reflection and full consent acts traditionally considered grave matter, without necessarily suffering the specific consequences of mortal sin.[23]

Some claim support for this position from the *Declaration on Certain Questions Concerning Sexual Ethics,* published by the Holy See in 1975. This document does state: "In reality, it is precisely the fundamental option which in the last resort defines a person's moral disposition." But this sentence is the beginning of a critical evaluation of certain theories. The document continues: "But it [one's fundamental option] can be completely changed by particular acts" and concludes that "it is wrong to say that particular acts are not enough to constitute mortal sin." Thus, although the document affirms the reality of fundamental option, it does not support every theory of it, but firmly teaches that a person "sins mortally not only when his action comes from direct contempt for love of God and neighbor, but also when he consciously and freely, for whatever reason, chooses something which is seriously disordered."[24]

11. The Council of Trent teaches that we must examine our consciences and confess all the mortal sins we find, according to species and number, and that we may but need not confess venial sins (see DS 1679–81/899, 1706–8/916–18).[25] In saying this, Trent obviously takes for granted its own teaching on mortal sin (see DS 1544/808), which certainly reflects the prior, common, scholastic tradition.

12. Clearly it would have been misleading for Trent to teach the faithful the duty of confessing every mortal sin discovered in a diligent examination of conscience if examination of conscience, no matter how diligent, were unable to discover any mortal sin. **This would be the case if a real mortal sin required change in a fundamental option in principle inaccessible to conscious reflection.** However, the teaching of Trent on penance cannot mislead, for this teaching is solemn and definitive.[26]

A theory of fundamental option often leads to a threefold categorization of sins. Instead of the distinction between mortal and venial sin, understood in the traditional way, those who hold for fundamental freedom often distinguish between the sin of the wrong option (which can be called "mortal" or "sin unto death" or something else) and the sin which traditionally would have been considered mortal, since it had all three of the traditional conditions (which still may be called "mortal," or may be renamed if "mortal" is assigned to the sin of wrong option). They usually also distinguish the latter from the sin traditionally considered venial.

In some cases, authors who adopt a theory of fundamental freedom avoid adopting a threefold categorization of sins by treating only sins of wrong option as mortal and considering all other sins, including some which meet all the traditional criteria for mortal sin, as more or less serious venial sins.[27]

Either of these approaches has the same result: Sins which would traditionally have been considered mortal turn out not to be so; they do not exclude one from the kingdom, separate one from Jesus, evict the Holy Spirit from one's heart, and so forth.

Someone will object that if the argument based on received teaching is sound, there will be no possibility for new insights which would reclassify any acts or make any new distinctions among sins. But the objection is not cogent. Developments and reclassifications compatible with the definitive teaching of the Church and with constant pastoral practice are not ruled out.

The argument against current theories of fundamental option on the basis of their inconsistency with Trent's teaching on the sacrament of penance can be clarified by considering some practical implications of these theories.[28] I wish to make a good confession, and so I undertake to examine my conscience. I am aware of a multitude of particular free choices, but whatever their moral quality, they are not determinative of my state of soul. What is determinative underlies the whole drift of my life. Presumably, if I had made a basic option against morality and God, I would not be interested in going to confession. Since I am interested, it seems to follow that I have not made such an option. Therefore, I need not go to confession. But perhaps I made a fundamental option of which I have not the slightest suspicion, by a fundamental freedom of which I am not at all aware? In this case, I cannot find it no matter how long I examine my conscience. The result is that, although I may have a vague sense of sinfulness, I no longer can identify guilt with particular wrong choices, and the confession of such choices becomes pointless.[29] And so, as the doctrine of fundamental freedom has waxed, the use of the sacrament of penance has waned.

One further point. Proponents of fundamental freedom tend to be optimistic. They generally assume that one's fundamental option might be good even though one's free choices meet the traditional conditions for mortal sin. Logically, they ought equally to entertain the opposite possibility. In that case, they would have to admit that just to the extent an evil fundamental option is something very different from an ordinary free choice, one might find oneself in hell without ever having made a definite free choice with sufficient reflection in grave matter, and so without ever having had an opportunity to accept the grace of repentance.[30]

Question F: How does St. Thomas explain the distinction between grave and light matter?

1. **According to St. Thomas, some kinds of acts have about them something specific and intelligible which makes them incompatible with the harmony engendered by charity between humankind and God, and within human society.** Blasphemy and idolatry are simply not compatible with reverence for God and subjection to him; theft and homicide are simply not compatible with a good community. But there are other kinds of acts which involve some disorder yet are compatible with maintaining these harmonious relationships. If, for instance, somebody tells a lie which does not infringe upon faith or hurt anyone, perhaps to help someone or just for fun, or if somebody eats or drinks a little too much, then an act venial in kind is done (see *S.t.*, 1–2, q. 88, a. 2).

Thomas holds that any kind of disordered act can be made into a mortal sin by the sinner's bad intent, for one can take the occasion to alter one's ultimate end, or one can do an act venial in kind for a mortally sinful purpose—for example, tell small lies to further seduction. Also, lack of sufficient reflection and full consent can render a disordered act which is mortally sinful in kind so imperfect as a human act that it becomes a venial sin (see *S.t.*, 1–2, q. 88, aa. 2, 5–6). But Thomas is insisting upon a principle which goes beyond these considerations.[31]

2. In his explanation of venial sin, Thomas observes that when one wills what of itself is incompatible with charity, one's sin is mortal by virtue of what one is doing. Thus blasphemy, perjury, and the like are against the love of God; homicide, adultery, and so on are against the love of neighbor. By contrast, idle talk, joking lies, overeating, and the like are somewhat disordered, but they are not against the love of God or neighbor (see *S.t.*, 1–2, q. 88, aa. 1–2).

According to Thomas, sin is like a disease of the soul; mortal sin is like death. The principle of upright spiritual life is order to the ultimate end. If this order is lacking in one's life, then one has no place to begin putting oneself straight. The disorder in one's life is not reparable from within one's life itself. Therefore, sins which destroy order to the end are of themselves irreparable, although even they can be overcome by the re-creative power of God. But sins which involve disorder only in respect to something subordinate to the ultimate end are reparable. The power of the Spirit being available, one can repent of venial sins by reorganizing according to the principle of the end, which still is in control of one's life. Such sins are like sicknesses that do not cause death, ones which the body can overcome by its inherent vitality (see *S.t.*, 1–2, q. 72, a. 5; q. 88, a. 1; 2–2, q. 24, a. 12).

3. Thomas further explains that venial sin is called "sin" only in a derivative and mitigated sense. Somehow related to mortal sin, it shares by this relationship in the significance of sin, but in itself is not sin in the same sense as mortal sin. "For venial sin is not against the law, since one who sins venially does not do what the law forbids or fail to do what it requires by a precept; but he or she behaves apart from the law by not keeping to the reasonable mode which the law points out" (*S.t.*, 1–2, q. 88, a. 1, ad 1).[32]

4. Consistently drawing out the implications of this position, Thomas holds that, although a venial sin is not referred to God and his glory, neither is it directed to a different ultimate end. Rather, by the constant order of one's life to God as ultimate end, even the venial sin itself—though not, of course, precisely as sin— is directed toward God. Venial sins only interfere with means, that is, with things ordered to an end (see *S.t.*, 1–2, q. 88, a. 1, ad 2; cf. q. 72, a. 5; q. 88, a. 2; q. 89, a. 3).

5. Although Thomas' explanation is suggestive, it does not appear to solve the problem. It suffers to some extent from conceptual difficulties analogous to those of current theories of fundamental option.

6. One of these difficulties is that although it might be true that mortal sins are contrary to the ultimate end while venial sins only interfere with things ordered to the end, this does not explain matters. The sins which Thomas considers mortal because they are violations of charity also interfere with means: the good of religion and the good of justice. At the same time, even a light matter such as the theft of a very small amount is immoral because one proceeds unfairly; but to act unfairly is not consistent with integral human fulfillment and so, it would seem, is at odds with love of divine goodness, in which the particular good violated by this act is a participation.

7. Moreover, the position that the mortal sinner acts against the law while the venial sinner only behaves apart from the law seems questionable. The immorality involved in a very small theft surely is forbidden by the norm which prohibits theft. If not, in what sense would it be true that it deviates, as Thomas admits it does, from the reasonable mode of action indicated by the law?

8. Again, the distinction Thomas makes is plausible as long as one thinks only of the examples he offers. However, according to the Church's teaching, which he accepts as determinative, many acts which do not obviously violate the goods of religion and justice ("charity" toward God and neighbor) nevertheless are classed as acts grave in kind (see GS 27). Among these are suicide, mercy killing of a willing person, and many sexual sins, including acts of simple fornication and homosexual acts between consenting adults. At the same time, certain acts which can be quite disruptive of society, such as nonmalicious gossip and the forming of cliques, are not usually regarded as grave matter.

9. **Still, despite its weaknesses, there is something helpful in Thomas' discussion of the way mortal sins disrupt existential harmony on its various levels and venial sins do not.** Unlike the theories criticized in questions D and E, Thomas' account of grave matter shifts the focus away from the ultimate end and charity considered in themselves to human goods such as religion and justice. It seems almost self-evident that if they are fully deliberate, acts such as blasphemy and perjury, which violate the good of religion, thereby exclude charity. Moreover, one feels that it makes sense to say killing and adultery are grave matters because of what they do to interpersonal human relationships, while idle talk and white lies are venial because they have no such impact. The question is how to relate these sensible insights to the theological distinction between grave and light matter, namely, that a deliberate choice of the first is incompatible with charity while a deliberate choice of the second is not.

The account proposed by Thomas has caused his commentators a great deal of difficulty. The Carmelites of Salamanca, for instance, realize that some sins mortal in kind are not directly contrary to charity. Their explanation is that such sins are disruptive in ways God in his wisdom and goodness wills to forbid; therefore, the moral norms which express God's mind and will strictly prohibit such acts. But one who loves God does his will; therefore, such acts are mortal sins.[33]

Again, there has been a long debate about the ultimate end of venial sins. One plausible view is that such acts simply have no ultimate end, but this position is not compatible with Thomas' general theory of action (see S.t., 1–2, q. 1, aa. 4–6).[34] However, his theory of action also has its problems. For instance, according to Trent's definitive teaching, a sinner prior to justification does good, preparatory acts aimed at fulfillment in divine life, but only after doing them receives charity (see DS 1526/798, 1528/799). How could Thomas account for the possibility of such acts?

These difficulties are rooted in Thomas' conception of humankind's last end. He tends to think of the ultimate end as if it were a goal, rather than the ideal of integral fulfillment in all goods, and to think of charity as if it were somehow more specified than it really is (see S.t., 1–2, q. 1, a. 7; 2–2, q. 23, a. 4; cf. qq. 37–43). Thomas tries to show that one person cannot simultaneously direct acts to diverse ultimate ends, and he supposes that sinners seek absolute fulfillment in some definite goal, such as acquiring wealth (see S.t., 1–2, q. 1, aa. 5–7).

But, as a matter of fact, people can pursue diverse goods without ordering them to one another and without ordering all of them to anything ulterior. For example, a dissolute man can seek both sentient pleasure and status as a political leader. Similarly, a Christian girl of fourteen can sincerely try to live her faith insofar as she is aware of its requirements, yet simultaneously and without reference to her faith (and without serious sin) try to become a cheerleader for the sake of the activity itself and the status it will give her with her schoolmates. Hence, Thomas seems to have made a mistake in assuming that an ultimate end must promise integral fulfillment (see *S.t.*, 1–2, q. 1, a. 5). At least, this premise needs to be proved; Thomas does not prove it; and his failure to do so renders question-begging his use of it to show that a person can have only one ultimate end.

Furthermore, Thomas teaches that one living in mortal sin can do good acts and can have genuine Christian faith.[35] The Council of Trent also teaches definitively that by some mortal sins one can lose grace without losing faith (see DS 1544/808, 1578/838). It hardly seems possible that a person can act for one and the same end in sinning mortally and in doing nonmeritorious but morally good acts, including the act of faith.

Consider the case of a person living in a pseudomarital relationship. Reflecting upon the sinfulness of his or her situation, such a sinner might deliberate: "I could give up this illicit relationship, I could give up my faith, or I could persist in this relationship and admit that I am living in sin." If the third possibility is chosen, the sinner reaffirms both his or her faith and the pseudomarital commitment. Clearly, these two simultaneous acts cannot be directed to one and the same ultimate end.

The truth seems to be as follows. Anything sought for its own sake, not for something ulterior, is an ultimate end in a given situation of choice. Any such ultimate end must be or include an intelligible good spontaneously willed. But there are several such goods, which are organized into a single ideal of integral fulfillment only when one accepts and consistently lives by a single world view. Many people have no such coherent world view. Christian faith serves this organizing function in Christian life, yet one can, and the mortal sinner does, fail to live it consistently. Thus, one person at the same time can be self-determined in respect to two or more goods, without willing these for some one ulterior good.

If this criticism of Thomas' theory of the end is right, and if the account of charity as a principle of Christian life in chapter twenty-five also is correct, then there must be something very important short of charity and integral human fulfillment which mortal sin violates and venial sin does not. Moreover, this principle needs to have the specificity and intelligibility (at least, in the light of faith) of a norm or source of specific norms. Thomas has failed to make clear the necessity for such a principle and has offered no account of what it might be.

Question G: How can some kinds of morally evil acts be compatible with charity?

1. The solution of the problem of grave and light matter appears to require a synthesis of certain insights of fundamental option theories and St. Thomas' account. **Those who hold that fundamental option is a basic commitment seem correct in thinking that a basic commitment of the right sort can render certain immoral acts compatible with charity. Thomas seems correct in suggesting that the difference between grave and light matter is to be found in the depth to which various kinds of immoral acts can disrupt existential harmonies.**

2. With these insights as basic, the following solution is proposed to the problem of the distinction between grave and light matter.

3. There is a fundamental option in Christian life, namely, the act of living faith. Jesus says: "Believe in God, believe also in me" (Jn 14.1). Although Scripture does not use the language of fundamental option, it teaches that the act of faith is the basis of salvation.[36] Faith is God's gift: "No one can come to me unless the Father who sent me draws him" (Jn 6.44; also 3.11–21; 12.44–50). It is all-important to be united with Christ "and be found in him, not having a righteousness of my own, based on law, but that which is through faith in Christ, the righteousness from God that depends on faith" (Phil 3.9; cf. Rom 3.28–30; 4.2–12; 9.30–33; 10.8–12; Gal 2.16; 3.5–9; and so on).

4. Besides being God's gift, faith also is a human act: Abram "believed the Lord; and he reckoned it to him as righteousness" (Gn 15.6; also Rom 4.3; Gal 3.6; Heb 11.8–12; Jas 2.22–24). Since faith is a human act, the believer puts faith in God: "He who believes in me, believes not in me but in him who sent me" (Jn 12.44; also Mk 16.16; Acts 14.23; Rom 10.8–17). Christians "follow the example of the faith which our father Abraham had" (Rom 4.12), and faith shapes the remainder of Christian life: "The life I now live in the flesh I live by faith in the Son of God" (Gal 2.20; also 2 Cor 13.5; Jas 2.14–26). Maintenance of one's faith requires effort (see 1 Cor 16.13; 2 Cor 13.5; Col 1.23; 1 Tm 1.18–19; 6.11–12; and so on).[37]

5. Following Scripture, the Catholic Church also teaches definitively that faith is the foundation of all justification and the beginning of our salvation, that it is God's gift, and that it is accepted by a free human act (see DS 1528–32/799–801, 1552–54/812–14, 3035/1814; DV 5; DH 2–3), which must shape a life of good works (see DS 1532–39/801–4; LG 35; DH 10). The "split between the faith which many profess and their daily lives deserves to be counted among the more serious errors of our age" (GS 43; cf. GS 21). Indeed, Vatican II comes close to saying that faith is the fundamental option of Christian life when it teaches that by the obedience of faith "man entrusts his whole self freely to God" (DV 5). Hence, if anything can be called the fundamental option of Christian life, the act of faith deserves this title.[38]

Bernard Häring says some questionable things about fundamental option, but he seems correct in suggesting that the fundamental option of Christian life is faith. By faith one accepts God's truth and love; faith includes gratitude and self-commitment. ". . . Christian life is the creative and faithful concretization of the basic act of faith. Faith means wholeness and salvation to the extent that it is filled with hope and trust and bears fruit in love for the life of the world. If it is active in love, faith is truly a fundamental option. Hope and love do not belong only to the later unfolding of faith; they are an essential part of faith as a fundamental option. The unfolding of these three virtues—faith, hope and love— understood as integration of faith and life, occurs in the choir of virtues."[39] In other words, the act of living faith is the formative principle of Christian moral life. The sin for St. John is lack of faith in Jesus (see 13-A); iniquity or godlessness and living faith are the two basic states in which human persons can be, now that the Word has come into the world.

6. In considering the basic commitment of living faith to be a fundamental option, the present theory nevertheless differs in an important way from current

theories of fundamental option. Because it is faith in Jesus, who is not only God but man, Christian faith is specified by a definite content: One accepts revealed truth and the offer of a share in divine life from and within Jesus' Church. Although one's baptismal commitment of faith makes some specific demands, it does not immediately organize one's whole life. Hence, although a perfectly holy Christian would never act without reference to faith, many actions, both good and bad, of faithful pilgrim Christians have no direct reference to their fundamental option of faith.

7. Thus, the act of faith is not simply an option for God or for moral goodness. Rather, it is an option for Jesus as Lord, and so faith has both explicit and implicit specific determinations. **Some morally evil acts are incompatible with faith's specific requirements; such acts thereby involve grave matter. Other morally evil acts are not incompatible with the specific requirements of faith, and these, though incompatible with perfect charity, are only light matter.** One does not determine one's self against or turn away from the life of Christian faith even in deliberately choosing an act involving only light matter.

8. Since faith specifies that certain harmonious relationships must be protected in certain ways, as St. Thomas pointed out, it violates charity to infringe upon these relationships in ways which are excluded. Charity is violated because such infringement violates the requirements of the faith by which charity is accepted.

9. To sin against faith itself is an act of infidelity. By such a sin one loses faith, since willingness and unwillingness to accept God's self-revelation cannot coexist. But as the Council of Trent definitively teaches (see DS 1577/837), not all mortal sins are sins against faith. This is so because the commitment of faith has definite implications which extend beyond faith itself. One who makes the act of Christian faith accepts responsibility for living as a member of the Church and for cooperating in its apostolic and eucharistic life.

10. **It follows that faith implicitly excludes kinds of acts which are inconsistent with living as a member of the Church.** Among these are all the kinds of acts which would be disruptive of any human community whatsoever and all the kinds of acts which are specifically disruptive of communion and cooperation in the Church. The implications of faith for ecclesial communion exclude not only acts against God, such as idolatry, and acts against human community in general, such as homicide, but also acts which abuse one's own body, such as fornication (see 1 Cor 6.15–20).

11. Some morally evil acts violate neither the specific requirements of faith itself nor any of its implications for ecclesial life. The life of faith and the work of the Church can go forward despite the presence of such sin in her members. Of course, to will any moral evil is inconsistent with complete openness to integral human fulfillment and so, indirectly, is at odds with perfect love of divine goodness. However, the deliberate choice of an immorality which does not violate faith or any of its implications—except, of course, the general implication that living faith points toward perfection in charity—does not displace or qualify the self-commitment of faith, by which one abides in the gift of divine love. The self-

determination of the venially sinful choice constitutes an isolated, secondary self which limits without displacing the primary self; the self which is determined by the fundamental option of Christian faith remains the primary self of the deliberate venial sinner. Hence, some morally evil acts are light matter.

12. Because faith is commitment to the covenant relationship, grave sins violate this relationship. Hence, idolatry and lack of faith are called "adultery" in Scripture (see Hos 2.4; 3.1; Mt 12.39; 16.4; Mk 8.38). The faithlessness to the covenant involved in serious injustice toward one's neighbor can be viewed in the same way (see Jer 9.1–5). However, just as spouses fall short of perfect love in many ways without violating their marital covenant, so God's people fall short in many light matters of Jesus' holiness without committing mortal sin.

Thus, a deliberate act of stealing a newspaper is only a venial sin because it neither is incompatible with faith itself, nor incompatible with one's standing in the Church, nor incompatible with the communion of the Church, nor detrimental to her mission. It is simply immoral. Of itself it would imply that one does not love divine goodness; but the act of faith blocks this implication.

By contrast, homicide or substantial theft will disrupt human relationships; such acts among members of the Church will be destructive of its human unity, and against outsiders will block their inclusion in the redemptive community. Because of the special characteristics of the community which the Church is, kinds of acts are grave matter which would hardly be important enough to consider crimes in any other society. In particular, the Church is not a society only of outward relationships, but of inward communion. For this reason, grave matter extends into the heart. Even sins of thought have a deep communal significance.[40]

In sum, the act of living faith is a Christian's fundamental option. This act excludes as inappropriate not only everything not compatible with faith itself but also everything not compatible with specific conditions of the life of faith. It does not exclude all immorality, and so there is light matter. However, anything which the Church clearly and firmly teaches to be mortal sin certainly is incompatible with the act of living faith. If one deliberately chooses to do such an act, one is unfaithful to one's commitment of faith, even though one does not commit a specific sin against faith itself, such as heresy.

13. As St. Augustine points out, even in the light of faith one cannot always easily see why some matters are grave and others light.[41] Still, in general the distinction has an intelligible foundation. In particular cases, the Church's conviction and constant teaching can be based on an insight, born of long experience, which perhaps defies easy articulation. If the Church teaches that a certain matter is grave, we can be sure there is some reason why it is grave, though the reason might not be obvious. **And given that a certain kind of act is considered grave matter, one who deliberately chooses to do an act of that kind cannot be living the life of a faithful member of the Church.**

14. Someone might object that some matters traditionally considered grave seem to be purely personal—they have nothing obvious to do with the Church or one's relationship with God. But one cannot decide independently what is purely personal. The theological distinction between grave and light matter is rooted in Scripture's distinction between expiable faults and crimes which cut one off from the People of God, between the failings of those who faithfully follow Jesus and the malicious hearts of those who reject or turn aside from his way (see 15-B). As

St. Paul points out, Christian life is not purely individualistic; it is life in and for Jesus, and this has implications even for "purely personal" actions: "None of us lives to himself, and none of us dies to himself. If we live, we live to the Lord, and if we die, we die to the Lord; so then, whether we live or whether we die, we are the Lord's" (Rom 14.7–8).

15. The definitive teaching of the Council of Trent on the sacrament of penance helps make clear the ecclesial dimension of serious sin. The faithful must confess their mortal sins to a priest ordained and given jurisdiction to hear their confessions; certain sins may be reserved to episcopal or pontifical authority (see DS 1679–85/899–902, 1686–88/903). Underlying this system is the truth that sacramental absolution is a juridical act (see DS 1685/902, 1709/919). A person who is contrite and has a firm purpose of amendment—conditions which should be fulfilled prior to confession—already is morally upright and may indeed already be in grace. Yet sacramental confession remains necessary, because sin does not simply concern the relationship between one's will and God, as if this relationship were a purely spiritual and individualistic one. Every serious sin affects one's whole relationship to God in and through Jesus; but this relationship for its part arises and endures, is injured and restored, in the human communion of the Church (see LG 11; PO 5).[42]

A man living openly in incest is not committing a merely private sin; he is corrupting the community (see 1 Cor 5). St. Paul teaches: "If any one has caused pain, he has caused it not to me, but in some measure—not to put it too severely—to you all" (2 Cor 2.5), thus making clear the significance of an offense for the community as a whole.

Private judgment concerning sin is excluded (see Rom 14.4, 10; Jas 4.12). The leaders of the Church are responsible for rebuking sinners in the presence of the assembly (see 1 Tm 5.20). After several attempts at correction, a person can be given up as perverse and self-condemned (see Ti 3.10). However, this judgment is reserved to the Church (see Mt 18.17). The power of binding and loosing, of forgiving or retaining sins, has been assigned by the Lord to the Church, and her judgment is valid in heaven (see Mt 16.19; 18.18; Jn 20.23). The communal or ecclesial significance of sins underlies the injunction that Christians, though personally responsible each for his or her own life, bear one another's burdens (see Gal 6.2–5). It also underlies the practice of mutual confession and prayer for forgiveness (see Jas 5.16).

The ecclesial significance of serious sin is brought out most clearly by two things. First, the Eucharist is the actuation of the unity of the Church in the redemptive act of Jesus (see 1 Cor 10.16–17). Sin and participation in the Eucharist are at odds; the sinner falls under judgment for unworthy participation (see 1 Cor 11.26–34). Second, since communion in the Church overcomes sin and since the Church has power to forgive sin, separating oneself from the Church puts one beyond the possibility of repentance and forgiveness (see Heb 6.4–6).

St. Augustine develops in many ways the understanding of the relationship between grave sin and the Church. In some sense, grave sin cuts one off from the Body of Jesus; for this reason, one in grave sin is excluded from the Eucharist. Yet the separation is not total. The practice of penance is available to the grave sinner, and for one who is baptized, no sin is absolutely unpardonable (see FEF 1532, 1536, 1874, and 1919). Mortal sin means spiritual separation from the Mystical Body of Christ; one does not abide spiritually in Jesus, and so is unfit to share Holy Communion.

Still, there is a difference between such sin and the separation from the Church of heretics and schismatics.[43] The difference between grave and light matter thus holds for persons within the Church who still have faith; some continue to build their lives on the foundation of faith in Jesus, and these commit only venial sin, but others build in a way which cannot at all stand upon this foundation, and these commit mortal sin (see *S.t.*, 1–2, q. 89, a. 2).[44]

Summary

It is by no means self-evident why there is an absolute break between light and grave matter and so between venial and mortal sin. Any immoral act is contrary to integral human fulfillment and so, as we have seen, to divine goodness; yet a venial sin is not incompatible with love of God, and some sins are venial because of light matter. The explanation that God simply decrees that some sins will not be mortal cannot be accepted. But how can the real evil of venial sin coexist in one's heart with love of God?

In recent years some Catholic theologians have proposed versions of fundamental-option theory. The basic idea is that a person is disposed toward or against God, not by any ordinary free choice, but by a comprehensive orientation of the whole self. Some treat fundamental option as a basic commitment, others as something more mysterious—a total self-disposal attributed not to free choice, but to a freedom outside experience, often called "fundamental freedom" or "basic freedom."

Fundamental-option theory distinguishes between those acts which establish or alter fundamental option and those which do not. The matter of acts of the first sort is grave, while the matter of acts of the second sort is light. (Thus there are grave and light good acts as well as bad ones.) Many current theories suggest that even a fully deliberate immoral choice of grave matter need not break one's friendship with God.

Rather than explaining why some matters are likely to subvert a good fundamental option and others are not, however, current theories aggravate the problem. The fundamental option of a Christian is supposed to be love of God (in the case of a nonbeliever, a commitment to moral uprightness); but the problem about grave and light matter arises precisely because any deliberate sin seems at odds with these standards.

Besides failing to resolve this problem, current fundamental-option theories have factual and logical difficulties. It is not demonstrated that everybody makes a fundamental option or that there is a fundmental freedom apart from free choice. The love of God poured forth in the hearts of believers, which transforms fallen human beings, is a divine gift, not an act of human self-disposal. Many proponents of fundamental option have an impoverished view of free choice which fails to do justice to its self-determining character. And the assertion that repeated oscillation between mortal sin and repentance is impossible is simply question-begging. As a practical matter, the main point of current fundamental-option theories has been to allow that some acts traditionally considered mortal sins need not be; such theories cannot be reconciled with the teaching of the Council of Trent on penance and mortal sin.

St. Thomas Aquinas explains grave matter and light matter on the basis that some kinds of acts are incompatible with charity between humankind and God or within humankind, while some are not. His treatment does not solve the problem. Still, it is helpful in calling attention to the fact that mortal sins disrupt existential harmony on its various levels as venial sins do not.

The solution to the problem seems to lie in a synthesis of his account and certain insights of fundamental-option theory. The fundamental option of Christian life is the act of faith. This is not simply an option for God or moral goodness; it has specific determinations, a definite content. This commitment excludes not only sins against faith but, implicitly, acts of any kind inconsistent with living as a member of the Church: These involve grave matter. Anything which the Church herself clearly and firmly teaches to be grave matter certainly is at odds with the act of living faith. Light matter, by contrast, is the matter of morally evil acts which violate neither the specific requirements of the act of faith nor any of its implications for ecclesial life.

Finally, there is an objection that some matters traditionally considered grave seem "purely personal" and have nothing to do with one's relationship with God or the Church. The answer is that Christian life, as St. Paul points out, is not individualistic but is life in and for Jesus, and this has implications even for "purely personal" actions.

Appendix 1:   Flick and Alszeghy on fundamental commitment

In 1960, M. Flick, S.J., and Z. Alszeghy, S.J., published an article which has greatly influenced discussion of fundamental option.[45]

The authors begin by pointing out that everyone seeks self-fulfillment, but also seeks goods which will be realized in others. Thus, to be an end of affective life is not to be the end of the whole affective life. A strong personality has a single, all-embracing end of his or her whole life; for example, the revolutionary or the mother of a family centers virtually everything around one basic interest. Activities which do not contribute are merely incidental, hardly part of life. To have some such fundamental orientation of life is not the exception but rather the rule; most people have a more or less definite orientation, of one or another sort, which constitutes a form of life for them. It provides an organizing norm to which their particular activities are related.[46]

Psychologically, the fundamental option is prepared by childhood and adolescent experience and matured in the subconscious mind. It need not be expressed in a distinct, explicit act, but can be in a particular, significant deed which is a turning point in an individual's life. Once made, the fundamental option tends to shape every subsequent act; it tends to last through life. Yet it can be reversed. The fundamental option tends to be confirmed as it is made explicit and worked out in particular situations, particularly when it requires difficult acts. However, it can be changed either by a sudden, tragic break in a person's life, or by a gradually maturing process of conversion.[47]

The love of God, Flick and Alszeghy go on to assert, can be such a fundamental option. The love in question is willing God's goodness with charity, not simply to enjoy God for oneself, but to will his goodness for his own glory and its expression in creation. One can love another person genuinely without this love becoming a fundamental option, but such is not the case with God. One either tries to use God or one must subordinate one's whole being and life to him. To love him is to dedicate oneself to his will, not merely to direct an act to him as ultimate goal. This is an act of personal liberty, yet it need not be conceptually distinct from a choice on some particular issue.[48]

The authors claim the authority of St. Thomas for the view that this option must be made by a child at the outset of its moral life. They argue that the self-orientation of the child can be gradually prepared and can be implicit in a decision by which the child accepts God's will, not for some extrinsic reason (such as wishing to please mother) but because of a love which is willing to direct the whole self to God. The child who is not brought up in a religious context also makes a fundamental option for or against God, according to Flick and Alszeghy, but in this case the option is implicit in the acceptance or rejection of moral norms as making an objective and absolute demand to which one must submit. The child who takes the stance that moral demands are merely a set of factual obstacles and restraints to be dealt with realistically—avoided and neutralized and used as one can to suit oneself— takes an immoral stance and opts against God. The child who recognizes and responds to the claim of moral demands to personal reverence and submission implicitly acknowledges in the moral law its divine source and opts for God.[49]

The authors go on to argue that one or the other absolutely fundamental option is inevitable. Either one accepts the glory of God (at least implicitly in accepting moral claims) as one's principle, or one takes one's own interest or that of another creature with which one identifies oneself as one's highest law. The former option renders one morally good and makes one tend to do what is right in every instance; the latter option, while it leaves one free in each instance to do what is right, guarantees that in some instances one will choose what is morally evil. The habitual option for God is inconsistent with a grave transgression of moral law; such a transgression remains possible, but it would mean changing one's fundamental option. However, Flick and Alszeghy state, the habitual disposition can coexist with acts which do not agree with it.[50]

What sort of acts are these? According to the authors, they are acts which either are not fully deliberate or are not of their nature such as to engage the whole person. They are acts which, even if they do not agree with the prior fundamental option, still "are not of such degree as to alter the prevailing tendency toward it. This is why the fundamental option, of its nature, does not exclude venial sins."[51]

I turn now to criticism of the views proposed in this influential article.

The sociological and psychological evidence Flick and Alszeghy cite to indicate that people have some basic interest or fundamental orientation in life is beside the point. A revolutionary might be wholly dedicated to a cause; most people are not like this. The mother of a family can have a single focus for her emotional life, her family; many people are not like this. More important, while both the revolutionary and the mother can be morally upright and oriented toward God, both also can be vicious people. Since that concerning which sociology and psychology provide evidence can be determined without that with which Flick and Alszeghy are concerned being determined, it is clear that the two things are different, and the existence of the former does not establish or help clarify the latter.

If people understood all the implications of their choices, it might follow that one's initial, morally good or bad choice would establish one's general stance toward moral norms and their divine source. However, people often do not understand the implications of their choices. Usually a person can genuinely respect and submit to some norms of morality, respect others as valid claims but violate them in practice, and treat still others as mere factual nuisances.

People implicitly commit themselves to much more than they consciously choose. A choice determines the person who makes it with respect to certain goods and conditions subsequent acts of spontaneous willing with respect to possibilities which involve these goods. Morality as such, however, is not a specific good. A person can do acts of kindness in a very unselfish way, thus affirming implicitly the transcendence of the principles of morality to self, yet act with destructive self-indulgence, thus affirming implicitly a power of absolute self-disposal. What is more, a Christian can remain oriented toward God by a genuine act of faith while alienated from him by mortal sin (see DS 1544/808, 1578/838). Human persons generally (there are exceptions) are far too ambivalent to support the belief that everyone has a fundamental option which establishes a single, comprehensive life-orientation.

Flick and Alszeghy certainly are correct in thinking that one who loves God with charity has a principle by which the whole of life is oriented toward human fulfillment. But charity is not a human act; rather it is the gift of divine love. Although fundamental in Christian life, the love of God is not a fundamental option, and so it has no contrary as any true option does.

Much of the Christian theological tradition suggests this erroneous root of contemporary fundamental-option theories, namely, the supposition that love of charity is a disposition of our freedom rather than a gift poured forth in our hearts by the Spirit. On this view, charity is a preferential love for God over created goods.[52] However, as Vatican II teaches, the true opposition is not between created goods as such and divine goodness, but rather between created goods perverted by sin and divine goodness (see GS 37). The latter embraces in perfect harmony the true fulfillment of every creature, and this harmony is destined to be accomplished in the ultimate fulfillment of all things in Jesus. Hence, no option between God and creature, between God and self, is necessary.

The alternative to love of God is the privation of sin, which is not a unitary principle which can organize anyone's life and be chosen for its own sake. One sins not on principle, but for the diverse residual goods one can experience through each different sinful act. Thus, there is no positive reality contrary to charity which can organize the life of a sinner as charity animates and organizes the life of a saint.

Flick and Alszeghy, like many theologians who write on fundamental option, were working out of a very impoverished understanding of human acts.[53] They tended to think of acts as passing events. For them, one of the unique aspects of a fundamental option is that it is an enduring disposition. But every choice of itself is lasting, since a choice is a spiritual actuation, not a physical or psychological event or process.

While Flick and Alszeghy claim the support of St. Thomas for the position that a child must make a fundamental option at the outset of its moral life, the article to which they refer in Thomas is concerned with a much more limited question: Whether venial sin can exist in someone with original sin and without mortal sin (see *S.t.*, 1–2, q. 89, a. 6). Thomas thinks not. His explanation is that until a child reaches the age of moral responsibility, it cannot commit any personal sin. When it does, it first deliberates about itself. If it directs itself to a due end, then grace is given and original sin removed; if it does not order itself to a due end, to the extent possible at that age, it sins mortally, since it does not do what it can toward the good. Thus, without mortal sin there will be no venial sin in one still in the condition of original sin.[54]

Thomas here is considering only the case of a child who is not baptized and brought up in the faith. He is not discussing the case of the child in grace, who begins to deliberate in the light of faith, by an act of faith willed out of love of God and by spontaneous willing of relevant human goods. Moreover, Thomas is taking for granted his theological theory of the end of the human person, a theory which must be criticized (see 34-A). According to a more adequate account of human fulfillment and of the primary principle of morality, a child without grace by its first choice could do something reasonable or not, morally good or morally evil, but if it did evil, the evil might be very slight.

Since reason does not know any single, all-fulfilling end, the child could not possibly order itself to such an end. Thus, one need not wonder what sort of issue the pagan child of seven ventures its soul upon. Its early acts very likely have little order to one another; some are consistent with integral human fulfillment and others not, but none so sophisticated or broad in scope as to settle the orientation of the child's life as a whole.

Appendix 2:   Arguments for fundamental freedom

Why do proponents of fundamental freedom think they are justified in positing it? On their own account, it is not part of experience, so experience cannot directly justify supposing it real. Moreover, there does not seem to be any philosophical argument which would show that there is fundamental freedom, and its proponents do not cite Scripture, the Fathers, or subsequent teaching of the Church to justify positing fundamental freedom. Rather, they offer indirect arguments based on experience. The logic of the case for fundamental option is an argument for a hypothesis.

Proponents of fundamental freedom seem to be arguing that certain aspects of self-determination and moral responsibility, affirmed by Christians on the basis both of faith and experience, cannot be accounted for by free choice alone. Free choice and the freedom of self-determination as the total self-disposition of the person are thought to differ in two important ways.

First, as proponents of fundamental freedom see it, whereas free choice is an object of human self-consciousness, one's total self-disposition cannot be objectified and must remain transcendental. In other words, they think one cannot be directly aware of and cannot adequately describe and talk about total self-disposition. Second, again as proponents of fundamental freedom see it, free choice is limited because what is chosen always is very limited, while a person's total self-disposition must be all-embracing. One's whole existence in its relationship to reality (God) cannot be identified with choosing this possibility or that one.

In support of the first point, a philosophical argument along the lines indicated by O'Connell (see question B above) often is proposed. The assumption which underlies this argument is that subject and object must be distinct and opposed. Hence, if one's total self were an object for consciousness, there would be no subject to dispose of this totality. So total self-disposal cannot be objectified. Free choice, however, is an object of consciousness. Therefore, free choice cannot be identical with the fundamental freedom by which one totally disposes of oneself.

Many proponents of fundamental freedom add a supporting theological consideration. The Council of Trent teaches that "no one can know with the certitude of faith, which cannot admit any error, that he has obtained God's grace" (DS 1534/802). If free choices were the locus of a person's self-determination, then presumably a person could know with considerable certitude whether his or her disposition toward God is loving or not. Hence, they argue, the really significant self-disposal must not be located in free choice. Therefore, fundamental freedom must be posited to avoid the certitude Trent excludes.[55]

In support of their second point, proponents of fundamental option offer the following considerations, which they think differentiate free choice and fundamental option. The former is limited to determination among particular possibilities. Moreover, free choices are spread over one's life; one makes different choices at different times. Thus, free choices lack over-all unity; they do not make up one's morally significant life, any more than the parts of a body without the soul would make up a person. By contrast, morally significant self-determination settles a person's whole destiny in reference to God; it organizes one's life as a whole and makes one be a good or bad person. Therefore, they conclude, fundamental freedom must be posited as distinct from freedom of choice.[56]

An additional aspect of the limitation of free choices, often stressed by proponents of fundamental freedom, is that free choices concern particular, transitory acts, whereas self-determination must have a more lasting, even if not absolutely permanent, character. O'Connell, who identifies free choice with agency and fundamental freedom with personhood, says: ". . . agents, by definition, are changeable beings. As actions change, so the doers of actions change. Persons, however, perdure beyond the life-span of any individual action. It follows from this, then, that agents are preeminently 'do-ers,' while persons are more clearly understood as 'be-ers.' Human beings, inasmuch as they are agents, exercise their existence through action. But humans-as-persons exercise their reality precisely by being."[57]

Glaser argues that particular choices, such as those made by persons with a "habit of serious sin," can quickly and repeatedly alternate. In human interpersonal relationships, one does not find a genuine, mature, personal love, life, and commitment which allow for a weekly or even daily transition from affirmation to rejection. Therefore, the profound reality of sin and grace must not be tied to free choice, but rather to fundamental freedom.[58]

All of these arguments for fundamental freedom have been answered in question E or appendix 1. The heart of the matter is that an adequate understanding of free choice, along the lines articulated in chapter two, renders fundamental freedom an unnecessary hypothesis. Moreover, to posit the self as a metaphysical reality inaccessible to consciousness leads to irresolvable problems like those evident in Kant's theory of freedom.[59]

Notes

1. Assuming a certain theological view of venial sin, someone might object that venial sins are not opposed to God's law but only beside it, not offenses against charity but only lacking in charity. The view of St. Thomas, along these lines, is criticized in question F. But the problem of light matter as it emerged in Catholic tradition involved the assumption that every venial sin is somehow opposed to God's law, that even a venial sin requires a remedy and repentance, and that its remission (at least through temporal punishment after death) is required. See Eugene F. Durkin, *The Theological Distinction of Sins in the Writings of St. Augustine* (Mundelein, Ill.: Saint Mary of the Lake Seminary, 1952), 121–38, for a clear account of Augustine's view of this matter.

2. Although one cannot agree entirely with the analysis, suggestive indications about the affinity between Lutheranism and theories of fundamental option which have emerged since 1960 in Catholic moral theology are provided by James F. McCue, "*Simul iustus et peccator* in Augustine, Aquinas, and Luther: Toward Putting the Debate in Context," *Journal of the American Academy of Religion,* 48 (1980), 81–96.

3. A clarification of the central idea of fundamental option, based in particular on the work of Louis Janssens: Eugene J. Cooper, "Notes and Comments: The Fundamental Option," *Irish Theological Quarterly,* 39 (1972), 383–92; another, based on several other authors: Felix Podimattam, O.F.M.Cap., "What Is Mortal Sin?" *Clergy Monthly,* 36 (February 1972), 57–67. A sympathetic summary of current theories of fundamental option: J. A. O'Donohoe, "Sin (Theology)," *New Catholic Encyclopedia,* 17:610–11. A critique: Theodore Hall, O.P., "That Mysterious Fundamental Option," *Homiletic and Pastoral Review,* 78 (January 1978), 12–20; (Feburary 1978), 29–50; also see Joseph Boyle, Jr., "Freedom, the Human Person, and Human Action," in *Principles of Catholic Moral Life,* ed. William E. May (Chicago: Franciscan Herald Press, 1980), 237–66.

4. Bernard Häring, *The Law of Christ: Moral Theology for Priests and Laity,* vol. 1, trans. Edwin G. Kaiser, C.Pp.S. (Westminster, Md.: Newman Press, 1961), 352–64, developed a fundamental-option theory along these lines, precisely to account for the difference between grave and light matter, by reducing light matter to that which is likely to belong to an imperfect act (362). The underlying assumption—not spelled out in so many words (357–62)—seems to be that the love of charity is a choice and that only a conscious, explicit choice to disobey God is a mortal sin.

5. Although it does not deal with the distinction between grave and light matter, a seminal article which influenced much later thinking clearly illustrates this point: Pierre Fransen, S.J., "Towards a Psychology of Divine Grace," *Lumen Vitae,* 12 (1957), 208. He distinguishes freedom of choice, which he calls "free will," from "fundamental liberty." The former is experienced: "We know by experience what I have called free will, that liberty by means of which man can to a certain degree order his life. He gets up, he eats, he reads a book rather than go for a walk, he refuses an invitation, he is obstinate, persistent, or accepts an excuse. Even children very early possess this possibility of choice. It is freedom in the usual sense of the word. All the same, it may be asked whether *as such* it merits the name of liberty. Animals have it also, if we can judge by their behavior . . . ." Thus Fransen confuses freedom of choice with mere physical freedom and contingency of behavior.

6. See John W. Glaser, S.J., "Transition between Grace and Sin: Fresh Perspectives," *Theological Studies,* 29 (1968), 263–65.

7. Josef Fuchs, S.J., *Human Values and Christian Morality* (Dublin: Gill and Macmillan, 1970), 93.

8. Glaser, op. cit., 261–62.

9. Ibid., 265.

10. Timothy E. O'Connell, *Principles for a Catholic Morality* (New York: Seabury Press, 1978), 62.

11. Karl Rahner, S.J., *Foundations of Christian Faith: An Introduction to the Idea of Christianity,* trans. William V. Dych (New York: Seabury Press, 1978), 93–106; "Theology of Freedom," *Theological Investigations,* vol. 6, *Concerning Vatican Council II,* trans. Karl-H. and Boniface Kruger (Baltimore: Helicon, 1969), 190–93. Rahner, however, does not so sharply separate fundamental freedom from free choice, for he recognizes self-determination and moral responsibility in free choices (*Foundations,* 93–101) and accurately presents the importance of free choice in the Christian tradition: "Freedom," *Encyclopedia of Theology,* 544–45; *Hearers of the Word,* rev. ed., J. B. Metz (London: Sheed and Ward, 1969), 104–8. Rahner's theory of fundamental option is related primarily not to moral principles but to theological anthropology; for him fundamental freedom of the will corresponds to the preconceptual orientation of intellect to God: "Theology of Freedom," 178–86. The limitations of Rahner's metaphysics lead to difficulties, however. He identifies the right deployment of fundamental freedom with charity and at the same time with the (metaphysically posited) underlying orientation of the finite person in his or her transcendence with respect to every finite being—"The 'Commandment' of Love in Relation to the Other Commandments," *Theological Investigations,* vol. 5, *Later Writings,* trans. Karl-H. Kruger (Baltimore: Helicon, 1966), 445–51; "Theology of Freedom," 180. Hence, "no" and "yes" to God are not parallel (*Foundations of Christian Faith,* 102); the "no" always presupposes the more basic "yes"; thus it becomes a mystery whether and how a really basic "no" to God is possible (102–6). At times, Rahner sounds Kantian in denying the access of consciousness to the real working of freedom; he explains phenomenal free choices as a synthesis of original (fundamental) freedom and imposed (empirical) necessity (96–97 and 104; cf. "Theology of Freedom," 193–95). Unfortunately, just to the extent that Rahner approaches Kant's distinction between the phenomenal and noumenal, with necessity (and inevitable guilt) consigned to the former and freedom identified with the very reality of the latter, his position suffers from the incoherence of Kant's attempt. See Lewis White Beck, *A Commentary on Kant's Critique of Practical Reason* (Chicago: University of Chicago Press, 1960), 191–94; John R. Silber, "The Ethical Significance of Kant's *Religion,*" in Immanuel Kant, *Religion within the Limits of Reason Alone* (New York: Harper and Row, 1960), lxxxvi–cvi. If Rahner and other proponents of fundamental option who are more or less influenced by Kant do not hold Kant's whole position and so do not have precisely Kant's problem of the two standpoints and their relationship, nevertheless, like Kant, those who hold for fundamental freedom do have the problem of explaining the relationship between it and particular free choices, and they no more solve this problem than Kant did. Just as with Kant himself, their theory both raises the difficulty and renders it insoluble in principle. For a fuller critique of Rahner's philosophy: Cornelio Fabro, *La svolta antropologica di Karl Rahner* (Milan: Rusconi, 1974), esp. 178–94.

12. Richard A. McCormick, S.J., "Personal Conscience," in *An American Catholic Catechism,* ed. George J. Dyer (New York: Seabury Press, 1975), 189–93, presents a compact statement of the version of fundamental-option theory he accepts. Unlike those who take a more Kantian approach to fundamental freedom, McCormick thinks fundamental liberty is self-determination in and an aspect of concrete human choices, and he says such fundamental self-disposition is conscious (189). Yet he makes a radical distinction between freedom of choice and fundamental freedom in maintaining that grave matter together with full freedom of choice is not enough for mortal sin, and that regardless of

deliberate free choice, no venial sin can be fully free since in venial sin "only peripheral freedom is involved" (192). Thus McCormick leaves the relationship between fundamental option and particular free choices no less mysterious than do other proponents of fundamental freedom.

13. Fransen, op. cit., 209, thinks that the fundamental option continually interacts with the "perceptible and conscious actions of every moment"; only in the fundamental option are the interiority and human significance of exterior activity; it is "therefore like the soul of our daily action." O'Connell, op. cit., 63–64, says the fundamental option is the deeper meaning of some, perhaps one in a hundred, ordinary decisions; he also talks as if acts were symptoms of one's fundamental option. Fuchs, op. cit., 101–4, refers to the relationship, but never says what it is.

14. Probably the clearest attempt to explain grave matter as that which is likely to provide an occasion for making or reversing a fundamental option: Josef Fuchs, S.J., *Theologia Moralis Generalis*, pars altera (Rome: Pontificia Universitas Gregoriana, 1968/69), 15–18 and 137–52, especially the emphasized conclusion (140–41).

15. Less cautious proponents of fundamental option strongly hint or explicitly draw the conclusion that mortal sins are not a very common occurrence: Podimattam, op. cit., 67; Ralph J. Tapia, "When Is Sin Sin?" *Thought*, 67 (1972), 223–24; and (with respect to sexual matters) Charles E. Curran, *Contemporary Problems in Moral Theology* (Notre Dame, Ind.: Fides Publishers, 1970), 15–26, 167–68, and 174–80.

16. Fuchs, ibid., 22–23, says that the grace of Christ works in us so that "we may love God above all (fundamental option)" and be able to express this love with particular acts, internal and external. Timothy E. O'Connell, "Changing Roman Catholic Moral Theology: A Study in Josef Fuchs," Ph.D. diss., Fordham University, 1974, 297–300, cites other places (including some unpublished material) in which Fuchs says the option is faith-charity-hope, but denies that this is any single act and asserts that single acts are only expressions of this option.

17. Fransen, op. cit., 214, adopts St. Augustine's contrast of the two loves—love of self to the forgetfulness and denial of God and love of God to the forgetfulness of self; he considers the good fundamental option to be the option for grace (217, 224). As for bad acts, they are not truly free: "Every action which is truly free, every good action, fully responding to the truth of what we are and should be, frees us further. Every bad action, that is to say, false and deceitful, freely degrades that same liberty. In a certain sense, *we are not free; we freely become so.* That is our vocation as men, which has to be fulfilled in the totality of each life" (211). With true liberty Fransen contrasts "the mechanical and empty automatism of evil" (228). Thus, while Fransen wished to leave room for mortal sin, his conception of fundamental freedom precludes an evil fundamental option; consequently, in the end the good option seems to be the only one possible. The implication would be that all sins are defective as human acts, a position Fransen surely did not wish to adopt. But he does reduce the core of all sin to pride understood as "the petty vanity of the bourgeois" (214) and speaks of grace as "the cure for our egoism" (216). These views would fit well the denial of any wrong fundamental option.

18. Karol Wojtyla, *The Acting Person*, trans. Andrzej Potocki, ed. Anna-Teresa Tymieniecka (Dordrecht: D. Reidel, 1979), 108–15, clearly describes the phenomena of self-determination, which are by no means unavailable to self-consciousness.

19. Fransen, op. cit., considers fundamental an option for grace (217, 224) which "is expressed in faith, hope and charity and is incarnated in a *vocation*" (231). But he nowhere explains how the theological virtues—and, in particular, the act of faith in which there is a fully conscious free choice—are expressions of the supposedly more basic option. It is perhaps significant that Fransen did not supply evidence for fundamental option from Scripture and the Church's teaching; the Council of Trent's account of justification leaves no room for any option on the part of the one justified subsequent to preparatory acts (which surely are not Fransen's option) yet prior to and more basic than the act of faith which justifies (see DS 1526–32/798–801).

20. Trent's proposition was carefully framed precisely to allow for the position that one not only can conjecture (as most hold) but can know for certain that one is in grace. See Michel Guérard des Lauriers, O.P., "Saint Augustin et la question de la certitude de la grâce au Concile de Trente," in *Augustinus Magister: Congrès International Augustinien* (Paris: Etudes Augustiniennes, 1954), 1057–67. The false assumption that Trent teaches "that man cannot have any real and absolute certitude about the state of his own conscience and his state of grace" served as a premise in a 1955 argument of Karl Rahner's that the "ultimate quality of a free decision" is an "unreflectable" reality: *Theological Investigations*, vol. 3, *The Theology of the Spiritual Life*, trans. Karl-H. and Boniface Kruger (Baltimore: Helicon, 1967), 108. This false assumption together with the fallacious inference from the inability to know grace to the inability to know one's sins became the basis for the most common theological argument for fundamental freedom.

21. See Eugene J. Cooper, "A Newer Look at the Theology of Sin," *Louvain Studies*, 3 (1971), 287.

22. For example, Franz Böckle, *Fundamental Moral Theology* (New York: Pueblo, 1980), 110–11, agrees with what he takes to be a widespread opinion that there is no way to distinguish in practice between *really* grave and light matter, so that any labeling has only the character of an "index." Like other proponents of fundamental freedom, Böckle insists that it cannot be grasped in consciousness, but only by transcendental reflection (106), yet he maintains in the end that "our individual acts should be judged on the basis of our fundamental human attitude" (112), as if this attitude were somehow knowable. I suppose that Böckle might say one can conjecture one's fundamental attitude by the preponderance of one's acts, but such a defense not only is circular but also invites people to say to themselves: "I am pretty good on the whole, so I can cheat a little by deliberately choosing what I used to think of as mortal sins without separating myself from the love of God."

23. O'Connell, op. cit., 80–81. The significance of such fundamental-option theories in allowing what otherwise would be mortal sins is clear in the influential essay of Charles E. Curran, "Masturbation and Objectively Grave Matter: An Exploratory Discussion," *Proceedings of the Catholic Theological Society of America*, 21 (1966), 97–102. As an ethics of right attitude, such fundamental-option theory is like Pharisaism, which was not overly exacting; see Hugo Odeberg, *Pharisaism and Christianity*, trans. M. M. Moe (Saint Louis: Concordia, 1964), 29: "Pharisaism is indeed far more lenient in its appraisal of the moral life than is Christianity, and this precisely because it attaches such great significance to the right attitude of the mind. One need not be unduly anxious because of one's sins against the divine will if one has once determined to do what is right. For God is merciful, indulgent, and gracious, and He Himself supplies what may be lacking on the part of men seeking righteousness in the matter of fulfilling the moral duty."

24. Sacred Congregation for the Doctrine of the Faith, *Declaration on Certain Questions Concerning Sexual Ethics* (Washington, D.C.: United States Catholic Conference, 1976), 10–12 (68 *AAS* [1976] 88–89). With respect to grave matter in the area of sexuality, the document states: "Now according to Christian tradition and the Church's teaching, and as right reason also recognizes, the moral order of sexuality involves such high values of human life that *every* direct violation of this order is objectively serious" (emphasis added). A helpful theological commentary: Georges Cottier, O.P., "La sexualité et le péché," *Nova et Vetera*, 52 (1977), 241–68, esp. 258–67.

25. Canon 7 is central; it teaches that divine law requires the confession of each and every mortal sin, including secret ones (DS 1707/917). In defining this truth, Trent bases itself primarily upon the Church's constant tradition, which included a homogeneous development: José A. Do Couto, S.C.J., *De Integritate Confessionis apud Patres Concilii Tridentini* (Rome: Analecta Dehoniana, 1963), esp. 150–69.

26. The weight of Trent's teaching in this present argument is not undercut by the well-known fact that the discipline of penance developed in the Church. Nor will it do to neutralize Trent's teaching by saying the received conception of sin was merely the framework of the doctrine, not the proposition taught. Moreover, if an unknowable fundamental option against God is essential to mortal sin, then Trent's solemn teaching on the necessity for integral confession could not *in principle* be fulfilled, and the faithful would have been directed to fulfill a meaningless norm. If, on the other hand, "mortal sin" is redefined so that it is only the phenomenal act which need not separate one from the love of God, then Trent's teaching on mortal sin is being rejected.

27. See Cooper, "A Newer Look at the Theology of Sin," 275–307, for a clarification of the way in which this development has occurred; O'Connell, op. cit., 77–82; Bernard Häring, *Free and Faithful in Christ: Moral Theology for the Clergy and Laity*, vol. 1, *General Moral Theology* (New York: Seabury Press, 1978), 396–410. Häring suggests (402) that he only objects to a recent excessive emphasis on quantitative considerations, and that his own approach is compatible with the Council of Trent. But he openly rejects (408) the teaching reaffirmed by the Sacred Congregation for the Doctrine of the Faith: *Declaration on Certain Questions Concerning Sexual Ethics*, loc. cit.

28. See Louis Monden, S.J., *Sin, Liberty and Law* (New York: Sheed and Ward, 1965), 44–62, for a drawing out of pastoral implications; on his view the penitent confesses particular acts only to serve as a *sign* of contrition, and these acts themselves are at most *symptoms* of a wrong fundamental option. Monden minimizes the importance of material integrity—the confession of all mortal sins—by pointing to cases in which absolution may be given without it (48). But he neglects the fact that these are cases where integral confession is *impossible* for some special reason, and the will to confess when and if it becomes possible to do so must be presumed for genuineness of contrition and the reality of the sacrament (see DS 1676/897, 1679–83/899–901, 1706–8/916–18). Also see Häring, *Free and Faithful*

in Christ, 435. O'Connell, op. cit., 81, gives his idea of what a confession would be like if a penitent were adequately sophisticated in theology: "Father, this is what I have done. I don't know for sure if it was a fully human act, a fundamental option. I cannot even be certain that it was a human act, totally devoid of those impediments which affect the mind and the will. But I know what I did, and I know that it was gravely harmful to my neighbor. I repent it. And I want the forgiveness of Christ, which may already have been given to me and which I may already have accepted, to be incarnated and renewed in this sacrament." It is perhaps significant that O'Connell limits the appropriately relevant content to serious sins against justice, thus suggesting that many other sins—for example, in the sexual domain—are not part of the content.

29. Charles E. Curran, *Contemporary Problems in Moral Theology,* 48–68, "reinterprets" Trent to eliminate the aspects of the sacrament of penance—including its juridical structure and the requirement to confess all mortal sins in species and number—inconsistent with the new theory of sin. At least in his early works, Rahner talked of the need for self-examination, precisely that choices might be in accord with love of God: *Hearers of the Word,* 104–8. Later—for example, "Theology of Freedom," 193–96—he insists that the fundamental option is in principle inaccessible to one's self-examination. In essays of about the same time, he treats as a purely hypothetical question whether the theological nature of sin ever is realized at all: "Guilt–Responsibility–Punishment within the View of Catholic Theology," *Theological Investigations,* 6:211–12. But, all the same, he continues to write as if guilt might be discerned by conscience in particular acts (210, 213). Thus for Rahner examination of conscience cannot reach to the actual situation of a person's freedom, but only to the objectively guilty character of actions, which despite their objective character can express a *positive* response to God: *Foundations of Christian Faith,* 104. Rahner still treats penance as if the confession of sins were appropriate (422), yet it is clear that all one could confess would be actions having an *objectively* bad character, whose ultimate moral quality would necessarily remain unknown.

30. Those who hold for a final option might object to this formulation. But a final option is distinct from the forms of fundamental option considered here. It will be treated (18-F). Fuchs, *Theologia Moralis Generalis,* pars altera, has the courage of his convictions and cites with approval (142) the opinion that one can make a fundamental option against God in the depth of one's soul without ever doing a materially grave act. Since fundamental option on his theory is unavailable to conscious reflection (141), the implication is that someone can be on the way to hell and unable by the most sincere self-examination to discover anything which requires repentance.

31. The view that lightness of matter is reducible to imperfection of the act, central to fundamental-option theories, is not new. Some medieval theologians held this position, but the consensus of the great theologians, including St. Thomas, formed in conscious opposition to it. See Ioanne Velez Puyada, S.I., *El Pecado Venial "Ex Genere Obiecti" de Pedro Lombardo a Santo Tomás* (Madrid: Pontificia Universitas Gregoriana, 1971), 59–73.

32. If anyone defends Thomas by saying that by "law" he refers only to the law of charity, his explanation is saved only by being rendered completely inane.

33. Collegii Salmanticensis Fr. Discalceatorum, *Cursus Theologicus,* tr. xiii, disp. xviii, dub. 1, sec. II–III.

34. See P. DeLetter, S.J., "Venial Sin and Its Final Goal," *Thomist,* 16 (1953), 32–70.

35. See *De malo,* q. 2, a. 5, ad 7; *S.t.,* 2–2, q. 4, a. 4; q. 10, a. 4. This argument against Thomas' position also is exemplified by the challenge based on Trent's teaching that by God's grace sinners do acts prior to justification which prepare for it (see DS 1526–27/798). If a person can have only one ultimate end at a time, what is the single ultimate end of the sinner in doing such acts? If it is the true ultimate end, then the sinner already is justified, for (according to Thomas) only charity directs good acts to this end (cf. *S.t.,* 2–2, q. 23, a. 8), and being in mortal sin is incompatible with charity (cf. *S.t.,* 2–2, q. 24, a. 12). But if the preparatory acts are directed to some other ultimate end, how can they lead to justification?

36. See F. X. Durrwell, C.Ss.R., *In the Redeeming Christ: Toward a Theology of Spirituality,* trans. Rosemary Sheed (New York: Sheed and Ward, 1963), 81–116. Heinrich Zimmermann, "Faith," *Encyclopedia of Biblical Theology,* 243–57; C. H. Pickar, "Faith (In the Bible)," *New Catholic Encyclopedia,* 5:793–96.

37. It seems clear that in the Johannine writings, sin is basically infidelity, flight from faith's light: Eugene J. Cooper, "The Consciousness of Sin in 1 John," *Laval Théologique et Philosophique,* 28 (1972), 237–48. For a detailed exegetical study of Johannine texts which shows that faith as a human act is central in the reception of the grace of begetting and also the basis of the Christian life, see Matthew Vellanickal, *The Divine Sonship of Christians in the Johannine Writings,* Analecta Biblica,

72 (Rome: Biblical Institute Press, 1977), 105–213, esp. 149–52 and 190; the sonship is manifested in the life of faith: 227–63, esp. 261–63; summary, 353–58.

38. The centrality of the act of faith in Christian life also is stressed in the Protestant tradition. See, for example, Karl Barth, *Church Dogmatics*, vol. 4, *The Doctrine of Reconciliation, Part I*, trans. G. W. Bromiley (Edinburgh: T. and T. Clark, 1956), 740–79, summarized (757–58) by Barth: "Like love and hope from other aspects, faith is *the* act of the Christian life to the extent that in all the activity and individual acts of a man it is the most inward and central and decisive act of his heart, the one which—if it takes place—characterises them all as Christian, as expressions and confirmations of his Christian freedom, his Christian responsibility, his Christian obedience. On whether or not this act takes place depends whether these acts are rightly done from the Christian standpoint." It would be difficult more clearly to characterize faith as the fundamental option of Christian life without using the expression.

39. Häring, *Free and Faithful in Christ*, 197; also see John H. Wright, S.J., "The Meaning and Structure of Catholic Faith," *Theological Studies*, 39 (1978), 716–17.

40. Some claim that the position that there is no parvity of matter in the area of sexual sins is a modern development. In the sense in which it is meant, this claim certainly is false. St. Thomas already clearly made the point that the only possible kinds of venially sinful acts in the domain of sex are legitimate, noncontraceptive marital acts which are engaged in with unreasonable desire—for example, intercourse chosen more for self-gratification than for the shared experience of marital unity (*De malo*, q. 15, a. 2). Any kind of sexual act other than legitimate, noncontraceptive, marital intercourse always is grave matter (see *S.t.*, 2–2, q. 154, aa. 4, 12).

41. See M. Huftier, "Péché Mortel et Péché Veniel," in *Théologie du Péché*, ed. Ph. Delhaye et al. (Tournai: Desclée, 1960), 395–401.

42. For helpful discussions with references, see Dionigi Tettamanzi, "La Dimensione Ecclesiale e Sociale del Peccato del Cristiano," *La Scuola Cattolica*, 107 (1979), 489–511; Karl Rahner, "Forgotten Truths about Penance," *Theological Investigations*, vol. 2, *Man in the Church*, trans. Karl-H. Kruger (Baltimore: Helicon, 1963), 166–70; "Penance as an Additional Act of Reconciliation with the Church," *Theological Investigations*, vol. 10, *Writings of 1965–67 2*, trans. David Bourke (New York: Herder and Herder, 1973), 125–49. Although objections can be raised to certain aspects of Rahner's view on the matter, especially with respect to his thesis that the forgiveness of the Church toward the sinner is the *res et sacramentum* of the sacrament of penance, his argument and references nevertheless support the point that the relationship with God is injured and restored in the human communion of the Church. Rahner's acceptance of fundamental option is hard to reconcile with this very incarnational and Catholic conception of mediated grace.

43. Huftier, op. cit., 403.

44. See St. Augustine, *Exposition on the Book of Psalms*, 81 (80), 20.

45. See Maurizio Flick, S.J., and Zoltan Alszeghy, S.J., "L'opzione fondamentale della vita morale e la grazia," *Gregorianum*, 41 (1960), 593–619. The problem with which they were primarily concerned was why people without the help of grace cannot long avoid mortal sin.

46. Ibid., 577–99.

47. Ibid., 599–600.

48. Ibid., 600–601.

49. Ibid., 601–3.

50. Ibid., 603–6.

51. Ibid., 604.

52. Probably the main source of this view was the Neoplatonic element (treated in chapter 13, appendix 1), in St. Augustine's thought about sin: Frederick L. Miller, "The Fundamental Option in the Thought of St. Augustine," *Downside Review*, 95 (1977), 271–83. Augustine, however, was too faithful to Scripture to suggest that one only commits mortal sin by a formal rejection of God, or that one might continue to love God while rejecting the divinely given order of created goods to one another.

53. For a richer and more adequate discussion of human action in its aspect of self-determination, see Wojtyla, op. cit., 105–48.

54. *Summa theologiae*, 1–2, q. 89, a. 6; Flick and Alszeghy (op. cit., 601) erroneously refer to q. 90, a. 6.

55. See, e.g., Fuchs, *Human Values and Christian Morality,* 105.

56. See, e.g., ibid., 100; O'Connell, op. cit., 62.

57. O'Connell, op. cit., 60.

58. See Glaser, op. cit., 260–61.

59. See Joseph M. Boyle, Jr., Germain Grisez, and Olaf Tollefsen, *Free Choice: A Self-Referential Argument* (Notre Dame and London: University of Notre Dame Press, 1976), 110–21.

CHAPTER SEVENTEEN

SUFFICIENT REFLECTION
SINS OF WEAKNESS

Introduction

The conditions for mortal sin—grave matter, sufficient reflection, and full consent—were stated in chapter fifteen. Then, in chapter sixteen, the problem of grave and light matter was considered at length. The present chapter will clarify what is meant by sufficient reflection and then examine sins of weakness. Weakness somehow limits responsibility. The question is whether, even in the presence of sufficient reflection and the definite, free choice which constitutes full consent, it can make venial what would otherwise be a mortal sin. It need hardly be said that the questions treated in this chapter are important for the pastoral work of a priest.

Question A: What is needed for sufficient reflection?

1. "Conscience" has several meanings (see 3-A), among them awareness of the pressures of the superego and the demands of social convention; but this is not enough for sufficient reflection. Sufficient reflection is awareness that a choice would be seriously wrong, taking "seriously wrong" in a sense determined by moral truth. Persons instructed in the Catholic faith will recognize seriously wrong acts as mortal sins, either because the Church's teaching identifies them as such or because they know a seriously evil act might be a mortal sin and realize that to choose what might be a mortal sin is to commit mortal sin.

2. The requirement of sufficient reflection is met ideally under certain conditions. These include awareness of the inherent value of being morally good and of the reasonableness of conforming to conscience both in general and in this particular case; and understanding of the intelligible goods at stake in the possibility under consideration, of their relevance to divine goodness, and of the relationship between human fulfillment in general and fulfillment in Jesus.

3. This ideal knowledge is accessible not just to those who have studied theology but to ordinary, well-instructed Christians, even though they may not be able to articulate what they know. Nor need they be highly spiritual persons, already so formed by upright choices and virtues that they are instinctively repelled by the very thought of doing wrong. Well-instructed children and recent

converts can have rich moral insight into Christian faith, without having that holiness which makes the Christian manner of judging second nature.

4. Even if it is not met ideally, the requirement of sufficient reflection can be met adequately in either of two ways. **First, even a person without faith can have sufficient insight into moral truth to judge that making certain kinds of choices can be gravely immoral. Second, the requirement of sufficient reflection can be met adequately if a person sees the intelligible good, the grave duty, and at least implicitly the religious significance of accepting some moral authority which proposes norms as truths.** Those who see the grounds for accepting a moral authority can also perceive that a possible choice would seriously violate a norm proposed by this authority. They are therefore in a position to reason: I ought to follow norms proposed by this authority (for instance, the Church); to choose in this way would violate a norm proposed by this authority (for instance, to choose this sexual act would violate a norm taught by the Church in Jesus' name); therefore, I ought not to make this choice.

For example, a child, normally around seven years old, can grasp the moral truth that it is right to be obedient to parents and others set in authority by parents, and can believe that disobedience is offensive to our heavenly Father. (Under what conditions the child's duty to obey is grave and at what point children become able to recognize this gravity are difficult questions which need not be treated here.[1]) Similarly, some adult Catholics see in much of the Church's moral teaching only the supreme level of social convention, but they do realize that the Church has the words of eternal life, that it is right to try to live a Catholic life, and that obedience to the Church is what God asks of them.

5. There is no reason to think that those who only adequately meet the requirement of sufficient reflection will comprehend, even with faith's light, the grave immorality of what the Church's teaching characterizes as such. Indeed, they may very well not see why a particular act—say, masturbation or perjury in a minor matter—should be taken seriously. But they do grasp that the matter is one in which the Church's teaching demands obedience, and they are further convinced that it is right to obey the Church's teaching. Knowing this teaching excludes an act and realizing one ought to live by this teaching, such persons commit sin if they freely choose to do the act.

6. It might be supposed that when the requirement of sufficient reflection is fulfilled only adequately, failure to see how the act is wrong in itself allows an individual to treat the Church's moral teaching on the matter as if it were Church law. If this were the case, every moral teaching would be open to change and exception as law is. But a faithful Catholic who thinks of the Church's moral teaching as if it were Church law will not consistently treat it as such. True, one who accepts most of the Church's moral teaching as the conventions of the Christian community will not be able to distinguish clearly between Church laws and the moral norms which the Church teaches. But such a person can understand and accept that some norms proposed by the Church are absolute, and that their violation for any reason whatsoever constitutes unfaithfulness to the Church and her Lord.

7. The requirement of sufficient reflection is not met at all if a person grasps neither the seriousness of the matter in itself nor the moral foundation of the

authority which proposes the norm excluding it.[2] For example, four-year-old Mary can be taught that it is a mortal sin to play in the middle of the highway, so that she realizes she acts wrongly in disobeying and even calls this a "mortal sin." But she cannot realize the serious wrongness of disobedience at the level of moral truth, and so she cannot reflect sufficiently to commit a mortal sin. Similarly, mere feelings of guilt and consciousness of breaking the Church's rules do not demonstrate that one has the awareness of grave matter required for adequately sufficient reflection; one must also be aware that one is being unfaithful to the Church to which one ought to be faithful.

8. Understanding of the various factors involved in moral truth can range from absolutely minimal to full and rich. The fuller and richer sufficient reflection is, the greater the responsibility of the sinner. Other things being equal, the guilt of a mortal sin is greater or less depending on how much insight one has into the factors which make it wrong.

It might be supposed that a confessor or counselor should try to assess these degrees of responsibility and inform the penitent or client of this assessment. However, this is unnecessary and likely to be misleading. Each person's conscience accepts norms according to his or her own capacity. Individuals bring the same standards into play in judging their failings as in making their choices. Thus, confessors and counselors need not instruct anyone to adjust his or her standards downward; rather, they should educate toward a better understanding of moral truth, which will lead to a more profound awareness of guilt if this truth is violated.

In considering the wrongful actions of others, we must maintain the important distinction between material sin and formal sin, that is, between the moral unacceptability of what is done and the possible guilt of the person doing it. The requirement of sufficient reflection is the most important factor which enables us to maintain this distinction. There simply is no way to know whether others grasp the moral truth and choose contrary to it. Perhaps they more or less sincerely believe that what they are doing is right; even if this belief is mistaken through their own fault, the extent of that fault cannot be determined.

Hence, the Christian can abide in every instance by the injunction, "Judge not," without thereby being reduced to tolerant acceptance of everything people say and do. For example, acts of racial discrimination or killing the unborn can be rejected firmly, without ultimately judging and condemning persons who do such acts. Only God knows whether they grasp the wrongness of what they are doing with minimally adequate sufficient reflection. However, insofar as Christian teaching includes the proposal of an integrally human way of life, all who share the responsibility for handing on this teaching must bear witness to the moral truth about wrongful actions. To do so is in no way condemnatory or judgmental.

Question B: How can the will be weakened by strong emotion?

1. We know from experience that will and emotions do not directly interact: We can feel strong emotion yet will contrary to it. The experiences of resisting temptation and of freely choosing to give in to it both show that emotion does not directly affect the will (see *S.t.*, 1–2, q. 10, a. 3; q. 77, a. 1). Nor does the will directly affect the emotions. We cannot change our feelings simply by choice; affection cannot be elicited or sadness banished at will (see *S.t.*, 1, q. 81, a. 3).

Someone might object that strong emotion can directly affect the will even though the

413

fact and extent of such an effect cannot be verified by experience. This objection can be answered only by an analysis of what is meant by "will." Since will is a spiritual power, it cannot be moved directly by nonspiritual factors. As an appetitive power proper to persons, who transcend the world of nonspiritual causality, will is determined only by intellectual judgment proposing something as intelligibly good or, in the case of free choices, by its own self-determination concerning which judgment to follow.

The will can indirectly affect the emotions. One can choose what to think, what to imagine, and what to do. By such choices, one can alter one's emotional actuations. Thus, one who wishes to love God wholeheartedly, including emotionally, can meditate upon his goodness, and especially upon those evidences of it which are sensibly moving. One who wishes to banish sadness can think of happy things and, especially, can engage in some activity which is not too difficult and is fulfilling to the whole person—in other words, can do the most enjoyable thing possible which also is genuinely worthwhile and in all respects good to do.

2. **However, emotions do affect the will indirectly** (see *S.t.*, 1–2, q. 9, a. 2; q. 77, aa. 1–2). If a present experience, a memory, or a phantasm arouses emotion, one's attention is drawn to it. If the emotion is strong enough, the ordinary wandering of attention stops and attention is fixed. Once this happens, one thinks about what one is attending to. If one sees some intelligible good in a possible course of action which would satisfy the emotion, one spontaneously wills the course of action and carries it out, unless some reason comes to mind for not doing so. Thus, emotion starts the process which leads to action by way of spontaneous willing. If a course of action is naturally suitable, emotion need not be strong for it to lead to intelligent, appropriate acts done by spontaneous willing.

3. Even when one acts by choice, there are two ways in which emotion influences the will by its effect on attention. **First, it causes one to attend to certain possible courses of action and ignore others.** One chooses only among possibilities which seem interesting and really possible for oneself; but a course of action must have some emotional basis, either immediate or more or less remote, in order to achieve this status in one's estimation. Second, the force of strong emotion can compel one to take note of a possible course of action even after one has rejected it—as, for example, when a man deliberately skips lunch yet, as he grows more hungry, keeps on thinking about stopping work and eating after all. **Emotion's power to compel the will to reconsider a possibility previously rejected as unacceptable explains persistent temptations to commit certain sins of weakness.**

4. Strong emotions not only can recall attention to a possibility but can distract one from certain of its aspects and those of its alternative which were previously considered. Suppose someone has decided to skip lunch for several reasons: to complete a task, to lose weight, and to do penance. Hunger and images of a pleasant lunch may become so distracting that finally only the intention of doing penance remains in view. If one now consents, one is not making the same choice one would have made at first. Since the choice now bears on only part of one's previous resolution, one is not exactly setting that resolution aside; yet one's choice to have lunch is certainly inconsistent with the original resolution not to have it.

Underlying every choice is some emotion. Very often, however, one is not especially conscious of emotions. One becomes aware of them only when they are unusual enough in their strength or some other respect to call attention to themselves by their physiological consequences. The ordinary desire to eat or drink is not noticed as an emotion; the craving of a person dying of hunger and thirst is noticed. The emotional satisfaction of walking across campus is not usually noticed; the joy with which one walks on a beautiful day in spring is noticed.

Similarly, every sinful choice involves emotion. One would not choose to determine oneself otherwise than in a fully reasonable way except that emotions dispose one to act otherwise. Each mode of responsibility excludes certain emotions from serving as nonrational principles of self-determination. But it does not follow that every sin is a sin of weakness. If one considers possibilities with an upright conscience and decides to do what is right, one normally has little or no difficulty directing one's attention to carrying out one's good decision. Sin of weakness becomes possible only when the strength of emotion is such that one's normal will to act reasonably is rebelliously resisted by emotion.

The situation is analogous to that in a deliberative assembly. Within the rules of procedure, members are entitled to propose anything they please. Many proposals are voted down, because they would not be in the common interest. Usually, the negative vote is accepted and the proposal disposed of. But at times the desire of some to have their own way is so great that they keep bringing up a rejected proposal, insisting on its acceptance lest the work of the assembly be bogged down and its harmony be disrupted. Under these conditions, there is a tendency to give in for the sake of peace. Similarly, the temptation to commit a sin of weakness arises when emotions are strong and unruly enough to resist a reasonable decision, distract attention from other matters, and keep demanding reconsideration for a rejected proposal.

In the fallen human condition, there is hardly any member of any assembly who is altogether impartial, who is not somewhat unreasonable and disruptive. The same thing is true of the emotions of fallen humankind. The whole human emotional complex is distorted by the fear of death consequent upon original sin (see 14-G). The "normal" human condition is somewhat abnormal and perverse. This state of affairs is what is called "concupiscence," which refers to a residual effect of original sin (see DS 1515/792). Consequently, very often emotions are not easy to integrate, and one experiences in one's members a law at odds with the law of one's mind (see Rom 7.23). Hence, emotional resistance to reasonable decisions cannot be accepted as humanly normal and healthy, even though in our actual condition it is virtually universal and not pathological.

Some contemporary psychologies, based upon a denial of free choice, tend to reduce the whole moral problem to the dimensions of emotional health and sickness, maturity and immaturity.[3] However, sickness and immaturity can be distinguished from sinful weakness and malice. Those who are emotionally sick or immature experience emotions which are not well integrated even at the level of sentient nature. For example, the neurotic has emotions out of proportion to the situation which arouses them, and the smooth flow of behavior as a whole tends to be disrupted. The adolescent likewise experiences emotional extremes which cause distress and cannot easily be explained by the actual situation and the content of consciousness. Thus the conscious and the unconscious minds are not functioning harmoniously in cases of emotional sickness and immaturity.

In cases of sinful weakness and malice, by contrast, the emotions can be perfectly well proportioned to the situation which arouses them and integrated into a smooth pattern of behavior, and so they can be explained by the actual situation and content of consciousness. One need not assume any hidden condition creating disharmony between the conscious and unconscious minds. The disharmony primarily is within consciousness itself, between the law of one's members and the law of one's mind—that is, between the emotionally appealing possibility which promises sentient satisfaction and the freely eligible possibility which reason proposes as intelligibly good (see *S.t.*, 1–2, q. 75, a. 2; q. 77, a. 2; q. 91, a. 6).

Obviously, in most of us both types of disorder and disharmony often are present in some proportion. This fact complicates matters and helps render plausible determinism's explaining away of human moral responsibility. However, one must reject this rationalization, for it is absolutely at odds both with reason and with faith. Immoral acts, including sins of weakness, are not a product of emotional immaturity and/or neurosis. Just to the extent that they are done by free choice, immoral acts are a product of nothing other than one's self freely choosing to be less than one could and ought to be.

Question C: What kinds of sins of weakness are there?

1. Even in the absence of unusual emotional pressure, circumstances sometimes mitigate guilt (see *S.t.*, 1–2, q. 73, a. 7). To be sure, emotion is present, but if it is not abnormally strong, the mitigation of guilt is not attributed to it. Sin in such cases is not a sin of weakness.

For example, one woman becomes a prostitute to satisfy her expensive tastes; she uses her income for self-indulgence. Another woman becomes a prostitute to provide better opportunities for her aged parents and illegitimate child; she works only two nights a week, to spend most of her time and energy caring for her family. The second woman's sin is not a sin of weakness; strong emotion does not qualify the choice by which she commits herself to this way of life. But classical moral theology would say that in the second case circumstances diminish guilt. Since on my account of human action, the action is specified by all the intelligible factors which condition choice, I hold that the two sins differ in kind (cf. *S.t.*, 1–2, q. 18, a. 6).

2. Sometimes wrongful behavior is nonvoluntary. Perhaps it results from coercion or from some factor which so affects an individual's mind that he or she begins to act without choosing to do so and without even having had the possibility of so choosing (see *S.t.*, 1–2, q. 6, a. 5; a. 7, ad 3). Since there is no consent at all in such cases, personal sin is excluded. This sort of wrongful behavior is not a sin of weakness either.

For example, Titus is physically dragged to an altar of pagan sacrifice, his fist held closed by a stronger person, then forced open to drop a bit of incense on the votive fire. Or Maximus is given a hypnotic drug, told to do the same thing, and does it without any choice at all. Or Paula is brought to the temple by force; she has every intention to resist, but when her throat is pricked with a knife, she winces and opens her hand—in this case knowing what she is doing, acting by spontaneous will, yet still without any choice at all.

If there is no choice, there is no morally significant human act—except insofar as the behavior or omission might be consequent upon some prior choice—and so there is no sin. Hence in all these cases of coercion one is not dealing with sin, and so there is no question of sin of weakness.

Cases in which circumstances mitigate guilt or wrongful behavior is nonvoluntary border on and are easily confused with sins of weakness. The remainder of this chapter is concerned with cases in which there are acts done through definite choices but under unusual emotional pressure. In such cases there is consent. But how full is this consent, if the sinner chooses to sin only after emotions become abnormally aroused? If weakness mitigates guilt, can it mitigate guilt to the point that a sin which otherwise would be mortal is no longer such?

3. There are four kinds of cases in which one sins through weakness in grave matter. These differ according to the relationship between emotion and choice involved in each.

Although one can sin through weakness in light matter, only sins of weakness in grave matter raise important pastoral questions, so only such sins will be analyzed here. Still, the analysis may be applied, mutatis mutandis, to sins through weakness in light matter.

4. **First, sometimes emotion inhibits a person from making or carrying out a morally required choice.** For example, sadness or fear can lead to hesitation and delay in regard to something which should be done. This constitutes a sinful omission through weakness. But as long as there is no definite choice to omit what one should do, the sin cannot be mortal.

Probably for this reason, the classical treatises on moral theology generally ignored sins of weakness of this sort. However, they are not insignificant. If the obligation which is not being satisfied is a grave one, a person unable to act because of emotional pressures has a responsibility to try to change the situation in ways which will make it possible to reduce and/or overcome the inhibiting emotions. For example, one might have an obligation to seek additional strength by natural or supernatural means: rest, the help of friends, medical advice, prayer, the reception of the sacraments, and so forth.

5. **Second, weakness can render venial a sin which otherwise would be mortal.** This plainly occurs if emotion distracts a person from the grave wrongness of a course of action (see *S.t.*, 1–2, q. 77, a. 2). The emotion can be fear, anger, desire, hostility, or sadness. How distraction occurs was described in B above. The action here is akin to behavior which is nonvoluntary due to coercion or an abnormal state of mind, except that in the present case one does choose. One gives in to the emotion, but not until reflection has ceased to be sufficient for mortal sin. In other words, one chooses to do what one had realized would be seriously wrong, but only after one has stopped attending to its serious wrongness. Although such acts are not in themselves mortal sins, a person has a grave obligation to try to avoid situations in which emotional pressure will overwhelm reflection in this way.

One can understand the psychology of this type of sin of weakness if one considers examples in which someone chooses not to do an immoral act, with both moral motives (it is against conscience) and nonmoral motives for the choice. Perhaps the nonmoral motives have been purposely magnified in one's thinking to reinforce one's good purpose. However, as emotion mounts, attention is drawn to more of the appealing aspects of what one ought not to do and to fewer of the motives against it. At some point, it is possible to lose sight of the moral objection to the action to such an extent that one no longer is aware of the act as seriously wrong. One then chooses to do it, setting aside nonmoral motives. Sufficient reflection and full consent are not present together; hence, sins of weakness of this sort are venial.

For example, a firefighter on duty in a dangerous situation can be tempted to abandon his responsibilities and flee for safety. At first he resists this temptation partly by the thought that it would be dereliction of duty to give in to it and partly by the thought that his comrades will look down on him if he flees. As fear rises, a point can come when he forgets duty and chooses to flee, willing to accept shame rather than risk life. Again, a wife who is being abused can resist striking back due both to fear of the consequences and to an upright refusal to act vindictively, but choose revenge when anger blinds conscience: "I do not care if it hurts me worse than it does him; I'm going to get even with him for this!"

6. **Third, sometimes strong emotion causes a person to act in a manner which is inconsistent with his or her previous upright character.** Thrust into an unusual situation and perhaps lacking prior relevant experience, an individual freely chooses to do what is wrong, knowing it to be so. Isolated sins of weakness of this sort can occur in all sorts of matters and under the influence of every kind of emotion. The strength of the emotion and the unusualness of the situation mitigate guilt in such cases but do not eliminate it. If all the conditions for mortal sin are fulfilled, there is no reason to suppose that the sin is only venial (see *S.t.*, 1–2, q. 77, aa. 6–8). Still, those who sin through weakness in this way very often repent quickly and sincerely.

For example, a student who previously has been honest is panicked by the prospect of a difficult examination, has an opportunity to purchase a stolen copy in advance, and decides to do it, although still considering the act gravely wrong. Again, a girl whose attitudes are in favor of life finds herself pregnant, is quite depressed but still realizes the gravity of abortion, and chooses that way to solve her problem. Again, a usually mild person is aroused to anger, realizes the evil of taking revenge, but freely chooses to do it.

7. Fourth, sometimes one sins through weakness in a way similar to the preceding in that a choice is made in a grave matter with sufficient reflection, but with this difference: that the sinner is not in an unusual situation and is not inexperienced. **Rather, the act is part of a pattern of temptation, struggle, sin, repentance, and renewed temptation. Sin of weakness of this type can be called "quasi-compulsive."** Because it is common and seemingly intractable, sin of weakness of this kind most often presents a challenge to pastoral ministry. The remainder of this chapter is therefore devoted to its detailed consideration.

Scripture indicates that passion which leads to a sin one otherwise would not or might not commit does lessen guilt. God's mercy is great because he knows human frailty (see Ps 78.38–39; 103.11–18). Peter's denial of Jesus is a sin of weakness (see Mk 14.27–31, 66–72; Jn 13.38; 18.15–18, 25–27; 21.15–17).

Scripture also suggests that passion does not eliminate guilt, nor even always make venial the guilt of what would otherwise be a mortal sin. David's sin clearly is one of weakness, of the third type. By his adultery and homicide, David merited death, for he had utterly spurned the Lord (see 2 Sm 12.13–14). St. Paul regards sins of the flesh—at least, some of them—as sins of weakness of the third or fourth types (see Rom 7.14–25); nevertheless, those who do the works of the flesh will not inherit the kingdom of God (see Gal 5.16–21).

The magisterium never has dealt in general with the question of the moral responsibility which remains when guilt is diminished by weakness. Condemned propositions suggest that one cannot suppose that sin of weakness would never be mortal (see DS 2151/1201, 2241–53/1261–73).

St. Thomas does treat clearly the questions whether sins of weakness, committed because of strong emotion, are diminished in guilt, and also whether they are still mortal sins. He holds that they are diminished in guilt, yet still can be mortal. In support of this view, Thomas refers to St. Paul: "While we were living in the flesh, our sinful passions, aroused by the law, were at work in our members to bear fruit for death" (Rom 7.5). Thomas also points out that crimes such as adultery and homicide often are done out of passion, and clearly are mortal sins.

Thomas considers cases in which strong emotion excludes deliberation and choice; he sets these cases aside. Where deliberation remains possible, one can set aside or block the emotional cause of temptation; what one pays attention to is within one's own power. Thus, Thomas takes for granted that while moral responsibility remains, the sin remains mortal if the matter is grave. The only exception he allows is when strong emotion so controls reason that one no longer has power to resist; one is then temporarily insane (see *S.t.*, 1–2, q. 77, a. 8).

Question D: What three conditions define quasi-compulsive sin of weakness?

1. **First, although one who sins in this way confronts the same sort of temptation repeatedly, most of the time he or she desires to avoid committing the sin.** The reality of this will-not-to-sin is evidenced by some real effort. For example, the sinner goes to confession, prays, tries to avoid the occasions of sin, and in general takes steps to try to keep the temptation from arising.

2. This first condition is very important. By contrast, the sin will no longer be one of weakness if the sinner decides, when in a normal state of mind, to abandon further efforts to resist the temptation. So, for instance, a Catholic who deliberately adopts, reluctantly but more or less permanently, an alternative sexual lifestyle, knowing it to be excluded by the Church's constant and very firm teaching, is no longer a sinner through weakness. Rather, the will to do what is recognized as morally wrong is now constant.

3. **Second, when the quasi-compulsive sinner through weakness experiences temptation, he or she resists at first, knowing the matter is grave and consent ought not to be given.** A choice is made not to sin; there are efforts to distract attention by thinking about something else, by engaging in a suitable activity, by praying, and so on. Yet emotion is powerful enough to frustrate these efforts; attention is drawn back to the sinful possibility. In this way, the sinful possibility becomes fascinating.

4. This second condition not only makes it clear that the sin will be one of weakness but also clearly separates it from sin of the third type (described in C), where the sinner is not so experienced in struggling with and giving in to passion. The quasi-compulsive sinner has reached a kind of wavering equilibrium between a good will and a sinful will. Good will rejects the sin most of the time, but bad will gives in to it when passion is strong. Even when this sort of sinner falls into a cycle of great regularity, which discourages resistance, the transition from good will to sin is more or less prolonged, not sudden.

5. **Third, this sort of sinner does not lose sight of the grave immorality of the possible act, as does the second type of sinner** (described in C) **who is distracted by emotion from its serious wrongness.** Still, the possibilities proposed for choice do tend to become impoverished, until they might be formulated as follows: Either I can continue to struggle (seemingly indefinitely, with no victory over temptation in sight), or I can surrender to the temptation, do

what is sinful now, but soon regain my normal state of mind and repent. At this point, quasi-compulsive sinners often give in to temptation, choosing to do the evil act which will satiate desire and still it. But they make their choice with the provision that afterwards they will repent, not persist in sin.

6. This third condition is especially characteristic of quasi-compulsive sin. The sinner regretfully takes a short break, as it were, from virtue, from the will to resist, and from God: "I'll be back soon, Lord." The alternative to sinning seems very bleak: endless temptation. In many cases, furthermore, and especially when the sin is in the sexual domain, the sinner is discouraged by the suspicion that a sin of thought has already been committed. Thus, although the quasi-compulsive sinner freely determines his or her self by a choice which is understood to be seriously wrong, such a person also and at the same time truly chooses to make a contrary choice—namely, to repent soon after the sin is committed. Moreover, the sinner perhaps chooses to sin now as much to escape the torment of temptation as to enjoy the satisfaction of the sinful act.

7. It is important to notice that quasi-compulsive sins of weakness, as defined by the preceding three conditions, still admit of considerable variety. Although they are motivated mainly by desire, one might also think of examples of such sins motivated by other emotions, such as hostility. As for the desires which lead to quasi-compulsive sins of weakness, often they are sexual, but desires for food, alcohol, and other drugs can also motivate sins according to this pattern.

8. Sometimes people commit sins of passion at regular intervals without any real effort to resist desire when it arises. Though they may make some gesture of repentance each time, they are not quasi-compulsive sinners through weakness, for they have no real purpose of amendment. Some persons who behave in this way probably do not commit mortal sins, even though what they do involves grave matter. Either they lack the maturity of conscience to grasp in a minimally adequate way the gravity of what they choose; or they really do act compulsively, without free choice; or, while aware that what they choose is evil in some sense, they no longer realize at the time of choice that it is contrary to moral truth. If their guilt is not genuine but is only a sense of violation of superego and social convention, their gestures of repentance might be adequate even though they have no genuine purpose of amendment.

Appendix 1 considers mitigating factors in moral consciousness. Many such factors can be at work in the case of the quasi-compulsive sinner through weakness.

For example, the adolescent boy may only slightly grasp the moral foundation of his own act of faith, and may perceive the mortal sin of masturbation almost entirely in terms of a risk of punishment and an obligation to go to confession; his conscience with respect to the guilt involved might largely consist in superego guilt and self-disgust for failure to keep the rules of the Church. Moreover, his surrender to temptation might be followed almost instantly by the execution of the choice and remorse.

By contrast, a mature person striving to overcome alcoholism might understand very well the intrinsic evil of self-destructive drinking and have a good insight into its sinfulness. His or her surrender to temptation might require intermediate thought and action—for example, a trip to a liquor store—and might lead to a more or less extended period of insobriety.

Quasi-compulsive sins of weakness often are said to be "habits of sin." To the extent that this expression suggests regularity in pattern, it is correct. However, it can be misleading in two ways. First, classical theology would have considered a sin habitual only if one were resigned to it and committed it regularly without resisting the temptation. One who is an habitual sinner in this sense is in much worse moral and spiritual condition than the quasi-compulsive sinner, other things being equal. Second, the modern psychological notion of habit primarily applies to acts done without a definite choice in each instance. The quasi-compulsive sinner does make a choice. Therefore, much of the psychology of habit is irrelevant to his or her situation.[4]

Question E: Are all sins of weakness which meet the usual conditions for mortal sin in fact mortal sins?

1. Pastoral treatment of quasi-compulsive sinners through weakness has become increasingly mild in this century. This development long antedated Vatican II. Faithful theologians began to suggest that perhaps under certain conditions quasi-compulsive sins of weakness might not be mortal sins. This seemed a plausible view inasmuch as the quasi-compulsive sinner goes on fighting the good fight, is anguished by failures, and often shows other signs of a real and serious Christian commitment. In recent years, even many bishops who affirm received Catholic teaching on matters such as contraception have urged pastoral approaches which seem reasonable only if it is supposed that quasi-compulsive sins of weakness need not be mortal sins despite meeting all three conditions for mortal sin. This sort of view also underlies much thinking about fundamental option (criticized in 16-E).

2. However, the pastoral practice formed by classical moral theology during a period of several centuries uniformly treated sins of weakness in grave matter as mortal. It does not seem possible to admit an implicit error in the pastoral practice of the whole Church which bound the consciences of the faithful under pain of mortal sin. Such practice teaches implicitly, and this binding and universal moral teaching meets the conditions for the infallibility of the ordinary magisterium (which will be explained in 35-D).

St. Paul confronts the problem of weakness experienced by Christians after their baptism. He recognizes the ambivalence of the condition of the Christian who must still struggle to overcome weakness. But he makes no concession to the possible view that sins of weakness might not be mortal provided one struggles against them. Rather, his emphasis is upon the real possibility of avoiding evil, a possibility which comes not from oneself but from the power of the Spirit (see Rom 6.12–8.17).[5]

Similarly, the writer of Hebrews emphasizes that our Lord is a compassionate high priest who can sympathize with our weakness. But this emphasis is to stress the sympathy he has because he himself was tempted, and so will be prompt to help us when we are tempted. The point is that sin can be avoided. Hebrews contains exhortations to people who might sin through weakness; if they do, the sin is considered most serious (see Heb 2.14–18; 4.15–16; 6.4–8).

3. **Moreover, in treating the question of certain sins of weakness, recent documents of the magisterium implicitly assume that, as long as there is a free choice—together, of course, with sufficient reflection and grave mat-**

ter—there is mortal sin. They also state that responsibility ought to be presumed.

4. For example, in its *Declaration on Certain Questions Concerning Sexual Ethics,* the Sacred Congregation for the Doctrine of the Faith says of a typical case of quasi-compulsive sin of weakness: "On the subject of masturbation modern psychology provides much valid and useful information for formulating a more equitable judgment on moral responsibility and for orienting pastoral action. Psychology helps one to see how the immaturity of adolescence (which can sometimes persist after that age), psychological imbalance or habit can influence behavior, diminishing the deliberate character of the act and bringing about a situation whereby subjectively there may not always be serious fault. But in general, the absence of serious responsibility must not be presumed; this would be to misunderstand people's moral capacity."[6]

5. The same position is developed at greater length in the teaching of Pius XII on the formation of Christian consciences in young people. His discourse on this subject acquired special importance because Vatican II incorporated it by reference and so made it part of its own teaching concerning the responsibility of Catholics to form their consciences in accord with the teaching of the Church (see DH 14; GS 16).

Pius XII, in a discourse on the correct formation of the Christian consciences of young people, rejects various false principles and draws the following relevant conclusions:

> Therefore, being conscious of the right and of the duty of the Apostolic See to intervene authoritatively, when necessary, on moral questions, We declare to educators and to youth: the divine commandment to be pure in soul and body applies without diminution also to today's youth. The youth of today has also the moral obligation and the possibility of keeping itself pure with the aid of grace. We reject, therefore, as erroneous the claim of those who consider inevitable the failings of the age of puberty, considered by them of no great import and almost as if they were not a grave fault, because, they add, passion cancels the liberty which is required to make a person morally responsible for an act.
>
> On the contrary, it is required from a wise educator that, without neglecting to impress on his youthful charges the noble qualities of purity so as to induce them to love and desire it for its own sake, he should at the same time clearly inculcate the commandment as it stands, in all its gravity and earnestness as a divine order. He will thus urge them to avoid immediate occasions, he will comfort them in the struggle, of which he shall not hide the hardness, he will induce them to embrace courageously the sacrifice demanded by virtue, and he will exhort them to persevere and not to fall into the danger of surrendering from the very beginning and thus succumbing passively to perverse habits.[7]

6. There can of course be a lack of sufficient reflection or of free choice in particular cases. The Sacred Congregation mentions immaturity of adolescence (which can persist), psychological imbalance, and habit. The possible effect of immaturity was explained (in A and D): Some individuals in respect to some matters lack sufficient maturity of conscience to grasp in a minimally adequate way the moral truth concerning the gravity of what they choose. Psychological imbalance and habit can lead an individual to act without choosing (so that the

behavior is not a morally significant act) or to choose only after losing sight of the gravity of the matter (so that the actual choice is only a venial sin).

7. If, however, one does assent to the judgment that a certain matter is grave and simultaneously chooses to do it, then one commits a mortal sin, even though the choice is made reluctantly, is motivated by passion, and is conditioned by the intention of repenting soon after.

8. The following consideration shows why this is so. Mortal sin is a self-disposition incompatible with love of God, because (for the Christian) contrary to the fundamental commitment of faith (see 16-G). When, however, a Christian is aware—truly aware, at the level of moral truth—that a choice concerns grave matter, he or she is also aware that this choice cannot be made without being unfaithful, that is, without acting against the claims of faith. One knows that in making such a choice, one will surrender the protection of one's upright fundamental option. If one then gives in to temptation, the sinful choice is a self-determination at odds with the commitment of faith and so incompatible with the love of God by which one should respond in faith to him.

9. **Thus, whenever the usual conditions are really fulfilled, mortal sin is committed. By definition, these conditions are fulfilled, assuming grave matter, in all sins of weakness of the third and fourth kinds: isolated sins of weakness inconsistent with previous upright character and quasi-compulsive sins of weakness.** Despite the mitigation of guilt, all such sins of weakness are mortal sins.

10. To deny this is at least implicitly to deny something of the reality of free choice and moral responsibility. One would have to suppose that in making choices people do not do what they are willing to do but something else which they cannot even know. This line of thinking points back to the mysteries of the indefensible theories of fundamental option (criticized in 16-D and 16-E).

11. The recent documents of the magisterium cited above also make it clear that those who appear to be quasi-compulsive sinners in grave matter must generally be presumed really to be sinning mortally. It is hard to see how one could have reasonable grounds for setting aside this presumption if the conditions which define "quasi-compulsive sin of weakness" seem to be met, for in any such case the individual seems to have minimally sufficient understanding of the gravity of the matter and also thinks he or she gave in to the temptation despite this awareness.

12. Normally, then, both confessor and sinner should suppose that apparent quasi-compulsive sins of weakness in grave matter really are mortal sins. All mortal sins must be confessed and so, therefore, must these. If one truly doubts whether one has made a sinful choice, one is not obliged to confess it. But usually this is not the case with quasi-compulsive sinners, who know that at a certain point they gave in to temptation.

A particular penitent who also accepts probabilism and who sincerely regards as solidly probable a milder theological opinion concerning the presumption of grave guilt in cases of apparent quasi-compulsive sin of weakness need not be considered in bad faith and must not be refused absolution if he or she continues in other respects to resist the temptation and avoid serious sin. However, anyone who understands what has been explained in this question, who is wholly faithful to the Church's teaching, and who understands what was explained about probabilism (in 12-D) will realize that apparent quasi-compulsive sins of weakness usually must be presumed to be mortal sins and should be confessed as such.

13. Although one may doubt whether one has committed a mortal sin, one does well to confess anything one suspects is a mortal sin. This is particularly true of a quasi-compulsive sinner, for once such a person adopts the view that seeming mortal sins might not be such and need not be confessed, he or she may well stop attempting to refrain from such actions. But then, the sins no longer will be sins of weakness and will certainly be mortal.

14. A good confession demands sincere contrition, which includes a real purpose of amendment. Contrition should not be considered insincere simply because, in sinning, the person also consciously intended to repent later. Rather, what is at issue as far as sincerity is concerned is whether the sinner really wills to avoid and reject the sin, to live in the future in unbroken faithfulness. And this is shown by readiness to make a real effort to deal with the occasions of sin.

15. Similarly, purpose of amendment is not a matter of speculation. One must simply decide to stop sinning. To decide this, one must believe it possible. Future sin must not be accepted as likely, for this would be to suppose that grace is insufficient or sin not a matter of free choice. Still a discouraged individual may not be able to help feeling that future sin is likely, while nevertheless having a genuine purpose of amendment. This, once more, is shown by readiness to do what is possible to deal with the occasions of sin.

Even if there is some grasp upon moral truth, the mentality of apparent quasi-compulsive sinners through weakness at least involves inadequately integrated elements of superego and social convention. These are essential underlying assumptions in the proposition: I can sin now and repent shortly. This state of mind is not one of presumption contrary to the virtue of hope; as St. Thomas already pointed out, it is characteristic of sin of weakness and mitigates it (see *S.t.*, 2–2, q. 21, a. 2, ad 3).

However, to sin with an intention to repent is to gamble, and to gamble with right and wrong is to suppose that evil is a naughty deed one can repair by accepting one's spanking, or a breaking of rules one can make good by following relevant rules. Quasi-compulsive sinners through weakness must learn what mortal sin really is. Then they will see how inappropriate are their attitudes toward it. This growth in insight will open the way to instruction about the larger realities of Christian life: To overcome sin one must pursue holiness; to pursue holiness one must discern one's personal vocation and commit oneself to it.

This growth in insight also is necessary if the sinner through weakness is to clarify his or her own mind concerning the sinful acts. It is important to understand the intrinsic point of the Christian norm, and the inherent meaning of its sinful violation. Moreover, most people have only a vague notion of what the conditions for mortal sin mean, and instruction on this score probably will not be grasped until it becomes personally relevant. However, when a person of sufficient age and intelligence realizes the need for it, he or she can come to understand what it means to reflect sufficiently and consent fully. In learning this, one learns more clearly what freedom and moral responsibility are.

Question F: Can the quasi-compulsive sinner through weakness simply stop sinning?

1. The answer with respect to all sins involving grave matter must be "Yes." Otherwise, we would be faced with the absurdity of a mortal sin (which implies freedom and responsibility) which is simply inevitable (which excludes freedom and responsibility). Two things must be kept in mind to understand this point.

2. First, although quasi-compulsive sinners really do choose to do what they recognize to be grave matter, still, as was explained, someone might seem to commit such a sin yet not actually do so. In the concrete it is often difficult and sometimes impossible, even for the sinner, to know whether the conditions for mortal sin have been met. One cannot tell whether apparent quasi-compulsive sinners who continue sinning are doing all they can. Especially if effort is intensified and some progress made, there is some reason to suspect that the apparent quasi-compulsive sinner is guilty only of venial sin.

3. Second, no sinner can simply stop sinning through his or her unaided power. In our fallen condition, without grace we could not help making free choices which would be mortally sinful; alienated from God, we cannot enjoy even that fulfillment which is naturally suited to us. However, God's grace is sufficient that those united to Jesus and enjoying the gift of his Spirit can certainly choose to resist every temptation to mortal sin (see *S.t.*, 1–2, q. 109, aa. 8–9).

Catholic teaching concerning the sufficiency of grace becomes clearer if one recalls that the Christian lives by the Spirit. To be adopted as a child of God truly transforms one inwardly; one has the power of the Spirit by which to live a life worthy of a member of God's family. "No one born of God commits sin; for God's nature abides in him, and he cannot sin because he is born of God" (1 Jn 3.9).[8]

4. Scripture teaches: "My grace is sufficient for you" (2 Cor 12.9). God does not demand the impossible (see Mt 11.30; 1 Jn 5.3). Those who are children of God love his Son; those who love him can keep his commandments (see Jn 14.23). God provides both the desire to do his will and the very free act by which one does it (see Phil 2.13).

5. The Fathers of the Church, especially St. Augustine, insist very clearly and firmly that God gives sufficient grace. "A man, helped by God, can, if he will, be without sin" (FEF 1720). "God, therefore, does not command what is impossible, but in commanding he also admonishes you to do what you are able, and to ask his help for what you are unable to do" (FEF 1795). Even the most hardened sinner is offered help enough to repent, if only the grace is accepted (see FEF 2097, 2232). A fortiori, grace must be sufficient for one who only sins through weakness.

6. The Council of Trent teaches definitively that sufficient grace is given so that mortal sin can be avoided altogether and God's commandments can truly be fulfilled (see DS 1536/804, 1568/828). **To assert that someone who repeatedly commits mortal sins cannot respond to God's grace and simply stop committing them, given willingness to stop, is to deny a defined truth of faith.**

7. Behavior which would be gravely sinful if freely chosen but is not gravely sinful because not freely chosen with adequate understanding of its gravity may be

inevitable in Christian life. Even the upright person commits at least some venial sins which are not fully deliberate. From the very beginning of a person's life in Jesus, however, and no matter what remnants of the fallen condition of humankind or one's own past sin might remain, mortal sin is altogether avoidable.

It is useful to reflect upon the question: What is the place of sin, especially sin of weakness, in Christian life?

Every sort of mystique of sin must be avoided. Sin has no place in Christian life, as if mortal sin were in any way a necessary or appropriate experience or phase of development. There is never a time when it is at all suitable or in any way good for one who has been adopted as a child of God to be alienated from him. Moreover, the psychospiritual value of common experiences of sinners should not be overestimated. The intense experiences of guilt and forgiveness of those who commit quasi-compulsive sins of weakness are not in themselves conducive to the development of a genuine spiritual life. The intensity of these experiences is connected far more with the guilt of superego and social conformity than with an awareness—which is much more conceptual than emotional—of the real guilt which consists in the state of sin itself.

Given these cautions, a sound principle for this reflection can be stated: God permits evil only because he can bring good out of it. Hence, even serious sin in Christian life is an occasion of some great good, often including a good to be realized in the sinner's own life (see *S.t.*, 1–2, q. 79, a. 4).

A true understanding of the guilt of sin serves as a point of departure for a more grateful and deeper love of God, just as the love of lovers reconciled after a quarrel often is deeper than before. A correct understanding of the reality of quasi-compulsive sin of weakness leads directly to genuine humility. One knows that one cannot stop sinning by oneself but certainly can with God's grace, and one therefore seeks and accepts this grace. The first principle of Alcoholics Anonymous is precisely this: I realize my life is out of control and that I need the help of a higher power.

If there were no temptation to sins of weakness, many people would lack the occasion to develop beyond the levels of superego and social convention, to think seriously about what it means to live a Christian life, and to undertake to organize life in the form of personal vocational commitment. The occurrence of the temptation, even though it sometimes is consented to, thus provides an important opportunity for growth in the Christian life. Certainly, no quasi-compulsive sinner through weakness is likely to achieve a real and lasting victory over such sin, without also being helped to develop a more mature conscience and to undertake the responsibilities of Christian life at a deeper level.

Those who try to make the living of the Christian life less burdensome by denying the grave sinfulness of many sexual sins are making a serious mistake. The person committing sexual sins freely, even without subjective guilt, is left at a rather infantile level of Christian existence. Such a person never will grow up spiritually, as must one who faces these sins for what they are and wins victory over them. Moreover, the sinfulness of these acts is not eliminated by its denial. Even people following such opinions in good faith experience in their spiritual lives many ill effects.

These effects probably account in part for the fact that these acts are recognized as grave sins. For instance, sexual sins committed mainly for pleasure and relief of tension involve introducing and constantly reinforcing a split between one's conscious self (which feels tension and pleasure) and one's body (which is an object used for self-gratification). This dualism of self and body is false and it leads to false beliefs and attitudes with respect to spiritual reality. For the dualist, spiritual reality either is reduced to unreality, as objects and experience divide the real, or spiritual reality is separated from the bodily and regarded as a higher and purer realm. This latter view is incompatible with the Incarnation and so is radically anti-Christian.

God could have redeemed us without human cooperation. He also could have done so by the life, death, and glorification of Jesus without our cooperation. He chose, however, not to redeem us without us, evidently in order to allow us to share in the nobility of his redemptive work. This work is no less noble when we begin where we must, with ourselves. As Vatican II teaches: "Christ obeyed even at the cost of death, and was therefore raised up by the Father (cf. Phil 2.8–9). Thus he entered into the glory of his kingdom. To him all things are made subject until he subjects himself and all created things to the Father, that God may be all in all (cf. 1 Cor 15.27–28). Now, Christ has communicated this power of subjection to his disciples that they might be established in royal freedom and that by self-denial and a holy life they might conquer the reign of sin in themelves (cf. Rom 6.12). Further, he shared this power so that by serving him in their fellow men they might through humility and patience lead their brother men to that king whom to serve is to reign" (LG 36).

Healed by contrition and reparation, the wounds of sin can be important powers of love and service, powers one would not wish to be without, however strongly one hates the sins whose commission occasioned their acquisition. United with our sinless Lord Jesus and with the sinners he calls us to help him save, we hope one day to stand in the Father's presence and say: Thank you, Father, for allowing us to share in your work of redemption. And to Jesus each of us should hope to say: Thank you, Lord, for allowing me to share in your work of my redemption.

Summary

As a condition for mortal sin, sufficient reflection requires awareness that an act would be seriously wrong by the standard of moral truth, not just superego or social convention. Sufficient reflection is ideally present when one grasps the inherent value of being morally good and the reasonableness of conforming to conscience in general and in this particular case, and understands the intelligible goods here at stake, their relevance to divine goodness, and the relationship between human fulfillment and fulfillment in Jesus.

Sufficient reflection is adequately present if one either understands that the choice might be gravely wrong or sees the intelligible good, the duty, and at least implicitly the religious significance of accepting some moral authority, such as the Church, which proposes norms as truths. This means for Catholics that, although they may not see why an act which the Church's teaching forbids is wrong (and may in general not distinguish between the Church's teaching and its law), they nevertheless know that the Church forbids the act, and they believe they ought to obey the Church's teaching. The requirement of sufficient reflection is not met at all, however, if one grasps neither the true wrongness of the matter in itself nor the moral foundation of the authority which says it is wrong.

Weakness in the face of strong emotion has a considerable bearing on the question of moral responsibility. Although the will and the emotions do not directly interact, will can shape emotions indirectly (for example, one can choose what to think, and so alter emotion by what one thinks about), and emotions likewise can affect the will indirectly. Emotion begins the process which leads to action by spontaneous willing. Furthermore, even when one acts by choice, emotion can influence the will by causing one to attend to certain possible courses of action and ignore others, and by causing one to reconsider a possible course of action after having first rejected it.

These considerations are relevant to sins of weakness. (Wrongful behavior whose guilt is mitigated by circumstances, but where emotion is not abnormally strong, is not a sin of weakness; nor is truly nonvoluntary behavior, which is not sin at all.) Sins through weakness involving grave matter pose an important pastoral problem, and the analysis of this chapter focuses on them.

Such sins occur in four different cases. First, where emotion keeps one from making or carrying out a morally required choice (this is a sinful omission, but not mortal sin since there is no definite choice). Second, where emotion distracts one from the grave wrongness of an action (again, there is no mortal sin, but one has a grave obligation to try to avoid such situations). Third, where strong emotion leads one to act in a manner inconsistent with previous upright character (if all the conditions for mortal sin are present, there is no reason here to suppose one commits only a venial sin). Fourth, where wrongdoing in face of strong emotion is not a more or less isolated occurrence, but part of a pattern—temptation, struggle, sin, repentance, renewed temptation. Sins of this last kind can be called "quasi-compulsive" sins of weakness. They present a common and difficult challenge to pastoral ministry.

Three conditions define quasi-compulsive sin of weakness. First, although the individual confronts the same sort of temptation repeatedly, most of the time he or she desires to avoid the sin; there is evidence of a real will to stop sinning. Second, when confronting temptation, the individual resists at first, knowing that the matter is grave and consent ought not to be given. Third, he or she does not lose sight of the grave immorality of the possible act, but giving in to temptation, does so with the intention of repenting later. Such sins admit of considerable variety; desire (for sexual pleasure, for food, for alcohol, and so on) is the most common motivation, but emotions like hostility can also play this role.

In this century, pastoral treatment of quasi-compulsive sinners through weakness has been increasingly mild. Often it is suggested that, although the conditions for mortal sin are met, such people do not really sin mortally. But the longstanding pastoral practice of the Church and recent documents of the magisterium do not support this view. True, there can be a lack of free choice or sufficient reflection in particular cases. But if the usual conditions are met, one must suppose that when the matter is grave mortal sin has been committed, even though the action was motivated by passion and done reluctantly, with the intention of repenting.

Furthermore, a quasi-compulsive sinner through weakness can simply stop sinning mortally. Otherwise, one is in the position of saying that a mortal sin, which implies freedom and responsibility, is inevitable, a trait which excludes freedom and responsibility. In our fallen condition, none of us could long avoid mortal sin without God's grace. As it is, however, God gives everyone sufficient grace to avoid mortal sin entirely. This position, found in Scripture and the Fathers, is taught definitively by the Council of Trent.

Appendix 1:   Degrees of awareness in sufficient reflection

Further clarification is needed for a deeper insight into the problem of sufficient reflection and grades of responsibility. The awareness which fulfills the requirement for sufficient reflection can be of absolutely minimal adequacy, or it can be full and rich. The fuller and richer the awareness, the greater the responsibility.

Awareness of moral truth demands understanding of relevant basic human goods. If one's moral basis for the act of faith itself is in an insight into human goods such as religion and truth, the depth with which one grasps these goods affects the extent of one's understanding of the moral truth that one ought to be faithful to the Church's teaching. A mature Christian need only reflect upon his or her life from childhood to the present to realize that the meaning of religion as a good has unfolded gradually and probably will unfold much more in the future. Many others, even including those older and more intelligent, probably understand this good far less than oneself. If so, their infidelity would not have as grave a significance as would one's own.

Awareness of moral truth also demands some understanding of the inherent reasonableness of loving all human goods and acting for integral human fulfillment. One can have a great deal of insight into this without having any of the sophistication required to articulate it reflexively. Some people are much more clearheaded than others about moral truth; some grasp very little in morality except at the levels of superego and social convention. Once more, one can reflect on one's own growth in insight and realize that other people experience similar growth, but some far less than others.

Awareness of moral truth does not exist in isolation in the intellect; it is always surrounded by a more or less completely integrated (or nonintegrated) cognitive and affective context. In other words, some people see little or no connection between their thinking in general and their moral thinking; for others, insight into moral truth is closely knit with the remainder of experience and knowledge.

Similarly, some people have a working understanding of the moral weight of only some of the human goods and modes of responsibility, and so are able to have many desires and interests, many goals and purposes in life, which remain for them in a "free area," like the free area of behavior upon which superego and social convention make no demands. The more totally integrated one is, the more one realizes that to violate conscience is to violate reality, genuine community, reason and sense, and one's self. Thus, some people can know that something is gravely wrong yet feel that doing it is not very important, while others who have the same intellectual awareness of grave wrong will have a total personal awareness of the absolute importance of avoiding such a thing.

Besides the preceding variable conditions of awareness of moral truth, there are other mitigating factors in moral consciousness, which lessen the practical force of the judgment of conscience that something would be seriously wrong.

An extremely important factor is the number of live options and practical alternatives one enjoys. For example, a person brought up in a city slum typically confronts many temptations to do what is morally evil. When the genuine conscience of moral truth begins to work, the individual realizes that doing evil is wrong. Few young people in such a situation, including those involved, think it right to take dope, and "right" here is not just a matter of superego or social convention. The practice is recognized as self-destructive and foolish, socially damaging, and a flight from reality. But the temptation is present and has great appeal, partly because the individual in these circumstances faces so much discouragement about any possibility of living a good and fulfilling life. Moreover, merely being told of possibilities does not change matters. A young person in the slums finds it hard to be interested in goods he or she has not adequately experienced, very hard to believe it worthwhile to share in goods other than those conspicuously enjoyed—often by immoral people.

Sometimes limited intelligence and emotional obstacles generated by lack of loving care in infancy make it very difficult for individuals to rise above the levels of superego and social convention and gain much insight into moral truth. Such individuals can accurately apply the moral categories of conventional morality, yet experience little moral force in these conventions, since they neither embody the compulsion of superego, nor the authority of community (for one alienated from that community), nor the appeal of moral truth (for one who is virtually blocked from understanding this truth).

Abnormal psychological conditions, which are manifold in type and degree, can limit or distort moral consciousness in many ways. If what a paranoid believes about the intentions of other people were true, his or her actions would not be as unreasonable and morally defective as they seem. Yet even the most extreme abnormalities can leave some grasp on moral truth and thus some responsibility to make right choices. Psychotics sometimes argue that their condition exempts them from moral responsibility for their actions. Such a rationalization would be unnecessary if there were not, in fact, awareness of responsibility, which can be awareness at the level of moral truth.

All these mitigating factors in moral consciousness introduce endless variations in the degree to which someone can understand and appreciate the moral truth that would be violated by a wrong choice in grave matter. In reality the evil of a mortal sin the same in kind can be present in various people—or in the same person at different times—in endless degrees, which only God can judge.

It does not follow that a confessor or moral counselor ought to try to assess these degrees, to determine at some point that mitigating factors eliminate grave moral responsibility, and to inform the penitent or person counseled of this opinion. People assess themselves and do so in their own terms; their ability to examine their consciences after the fact is not likely to differ much from their ability to apply their consciences when they are about to choose.

Therefore, for the confessor or counselor to deny grave responsibility will not be taken as a judgment concerning what he or she personally considers grave responsibility, but as a denial of what the penitent or person counseled regards as such. But to deny this reality, whatever precisely it is, is only likely to encourage an evasion of whatever responsibility there is. In this way, well-intended efforts to unburden a person of guilt can be damaging to moral growth.

All moral guidance is like the raising of children. A good parent does not present children with special moral standards reduced to suit them. Doing so would guarantee that they would never become able to make morally mature commitments, since moral truth is one. However, one does not expect children to grasp the existential world and respond in an adult way, any more than one expects them to grasp and respond in an adult way to the natural environment. In either case there is only one reality; children must be helped to grow up within it and learn to accept it.

Appendix 2:   The gravity of quasi-compulsive sins of weakness

There appear to be only three important lines of argument against the conclusion reached in question E, that sins of weakness in grave matter of the third and fourth kinds always are mortal.

First, it can be argued that when sins of weakness and the need to struggle against them are considered in Scripture, in traditional pastoral practice, and in the recent teaching of the magisterium, the main point is to insist upon the necessity of the struggle and the inescapably grave guilt involved if one surrenders entirely—for example, refuses even during sober periods to seek help to overcome alcoholism. The question of the guilt of the sinner fighting the good fight but not yet winning is not directly confronted. Therefore, the argument concludes, nothing in these sources really shows that sins of weakness of the fourth type always are mortal sins. Sinners have been allowed to think of them as such, since this belief has helped them in their struggle, but the theoretical question remains open.

But this line of argument implies that past pastoral practice was based either on a mistake or on deception. Neither is acceptable. The faithful were told that the choice to do certain things, even under the pressure of strong emotion, is a mortal sin. The inability of the Church as a whole to mistake God's mind and will, the certitude that what is bound on earth also is bound in heaven—this excludes mistake in a matter of this sort. A fortiori, deception is excluded; pastoral practice in the whole Church cannot have involved a noble lie told for the spiritual welfare of the faithful.

If surrender to such temptations in some circumstances were not mortal sin, Christian teaching could easily have made this fact clear, and Christians could have been reassured that consistent faithfulness during normal states of mind is sufficient for salvation. Such reassurance would remove much of the fear and trembling, much of the subjective concern, from Christian life. But the contrary of such reassurance seems to be given (see Lk 9.23; 13.24; 1 Cor 9.27; Phil 2.12; 3.12–16). Anxiety concerning salvation is opposed not by any such reassurance but rather by the assurance of hope: Since God is faithful, the seemingly impossible demands of Christian life can be met by human persons, weak in themselves but strong by the all-powerful Spirit (see Jn 14.10–18; 15.1–8; Rom 8.14–17).

A second line of argument arises from reflection upon pastoral experience in the light of modern thinking about the limits of human freedom and responsibility. Many quasi-compulsive sinners go through the cycle of sin and repentance time and again, sometimes in a very regular pattern through many years. Sound and pastorally experienced moral theologians have doubted for a long time that such sinners really are alternating repeatedly between mortal sin and grace. Even fairly soon after considering the statement of Pius XII, quoted in question E, they tended to exclude the likelihood of grave guilt in at least some cases of quasi-compulsive sin of weakness.[9]

The answer to this line of argument is threefold.

In the first place, modern thinking about the limits of freedom and responsibility does help us see that many acts involving grave matter do not involve sufficient reflection and a definite choice. But no psychological insight shows in the least that when one really does know—at the level of moral truth, not merely superego and social convention—that a matter is grave and when one really does choose to do it, one is not really determining oneself inconsistently with charity. Many theologians apparently confused two very different questions: (1) whether the usual conditions for mortal sin are met; (2) whether these conditions are sufficient for mortal sin. Psychology and experience can throw light on the first question but not the second.

Furthermore, some apparent quasi-compulsive sinners through weakness might not be committing repeated mortal sins, for the conditions might well not in fact be met, even if the sinners themselves think they are committing mortal sins. Others might not really be sinners through weakness; perhaps they have abandoned a serious struggle against sin, and carry out a pretense of struggle, putting up token resistance to temptation only to satisfy superego and social convention. Pastoral intuitions could reflect these facts without accurately interpreting them. Pastoral intuitions also could be mistaken. How can anyone know that a person cannot sin mortally and repent sincerely on a regular basis for years? Analogies with other interpersonal relationships do not necessarily hold for one's relationship with God, since in other relationships one can be endlessly ambivalent without being insincere, whereas the relationship with God is susceptible to only limited ambivalence.[10]

Finally, perhaps some whose pastoral intuitions suggest to them that quasi-compulsive sinners through weakness cannot be guilty of grave sin are misled by a false assumption concerning the frustration experienced both by such sinners and by confessors committed to helping them. The false assumption is that the frustration is a sign of impossibility, and the impossibility a sign that the sin cannot be mortal. However, failure and frustration need not signify impossibility; perhaps they signify inadequately directed effort.

A third line of argument against the conclusion reached above is as follows. As has been explained (16-G), the gravity of an act depends upon its inconsistency with specific implications of one's act of faith. However, it is not easy to see how certain quasi-compulsive sins of weakness, committed as such, interfere with the life of the Church or with the carrying out of one's Christian duties. A plausible argument can be made that any sexual sin, accepted as an integral part of one's lifestyle, will have an impact incompatible with implications of faith. But, it might be suggested, at least certain quasi-compulsive sins of weakness, when specified to be the kinds of acts described in question D, should be considered light matter.

In considering this suggestion, one wonders what would happen if the Church were to teach that the specific kind of act chosen in a quasi-compulsive sin of weakness is light matter—for example, that when the act of fornication was chosen as *fornication now to end temptation with repentance immediately afterwards* it is not the matter of grave sin. One suspects this act would become very attractive, but many who tried to commit it would not in fact meet the conditions of quasi-compulsive sin of weakness.

Beyond this, there is an intrinsic reason why such acts should not be considered light matter. As has often been pointed out, classical modern moral theology was too interested in isolated acts and insufficiently aware of the profound dynamisms of moral life. If acts are considered in their context, one can more easily see why acts gravely wrong in kind must remain so even if they are chosen as quasi-compulsive sins of weakness.

The person who freely commits sexual sins in adolescence also phantasizes other sins, later continues to indulge such phantasy and begins to carry it out, approaches adulthood with adolescent attitudes toward sexuality, and never learns how to integrate sexual activity in sincere self-giving. The sexual sins of adults cannot be isolated from the sexual struggle of the adolescent, for the more obviously evil sexual sins of adulthood are an outgrowth of an inadequate or abandoned moral effort at an earlier stage. Thus, one must either maintain the entire traditional norm or accept its entire reversal; the dynamic unity of sexual life permits no middle position.

Notes

1. However, I think that some authors are too quick to conclude that preadolescent children are totally incapable of sin. See, for example, Robert P. O'Neil and Michael A. Donovan, *Sexuality and Moral Responsibility* (Washington: Corpus Books, 1968), 4–25. These and other authors uncritically assume that the results of psychological studies of what children can say about theoretical ethical problems are a sound basis for inducing what they can think about the practical question of their duty to obey. (See chapter three, appendix 1, for discussion of the psychological data.) O'Neil and Donovan also rely on the theological theory of Thomists who hold that one who cannot commit a mortal sin cannot commit a venial sin. This theory both presupposes St. Thomas' way of distinguishing between grave and light matter (criticized in 16-F) and oversimplifies his position by assuming that even the child brought up in the faith must begin moral life with an option for an ultimate end.

2. In the absence of sufficient reflection, a person still can have theoretical knowledge which does not guide action and can have action-guiding cognition at the lower levels of superego and social convention. Such cognition, which is inadequate for sufficient reflection, has been called (confusingly) "conceptual" in contrast to the relevant "evaluative" cognition. See John C. Ford, S.J., and Gerald Kelly, S.J., *Contemporary Moral Theology*, vol. 1, *Questions in Fundamental Moral Theology* (Westminster, Md.: Newman Press, 1964), 224–28 and 270–75. The knowledge of moral truth required for sufficient reflection also is conceptual, but it includes some concepts and propositions in addition to those included in theoretical knowledge or in action-guiding cognition at the lower levels which fall short of knowledge of moral truth.

3. See, for example, Erich Fromm, *Man for Himself: An Inquiry into the Psychology of Ethics* (Greenwich, Conn.: Fawcett Publications, 1965), 18–46 and 232–38. Fromm is right in thinking that the basis of morality is human fulfillment, wrong in reducing this fulfillment to health broadly conceived.

4. Concerning the difference between "habitus" in St. Thomas and "habit" in modern psychology, see Servais Pinckaers, "Virtue Is Not a Habit," *Cross Currents*, 12 (1962), 65–81.

5. See F. Prat, *La Théologie de Saint Paul*, 43 ed. (Paris: Beauchesne, 1961), 1:268–84; 2:81–90; Lucien Cerfaux, *The Christian in the Theology of St. Paul* (New York: Herder and Herder, 1967), 446–66.

6. Sacred Congregation for the Doctrine of the Faith, *Declaration on Certain Questions Concerning Sexual Ethics* (Washington, D.C.: United States Catholic Conference, 1976), 10 (68 *AAS* [1976] 87). Anyone who claims that the Congregation in this document has departed in any significant way from received Catholic positions (in particular, the teaching of Pius XII on the presumption which must be made in cases of sin of weakness) will find a conciliatory interpretation blocked by the criticisms dissenting theologians leveled against the document shortly after its publication. For a summary of some of these, see Richard A. McCormick, S.J., *Notes on Moral Theology: 1965–1980* (Washington, D.C.: University Press of America, 1981), 674–78.

7. Pius XII, "De Conscientia Christiana in Iuvenibus Recte Efformanda," 44 *AAS* (1952) 275–76; *The Pope Speaks: The Teaching of Pope Pius XII*, ed. Michael Chinigo (New York: Pantheon Books, 1957), 97. Outside the quoted passage, this translation omits some paragraphs, which only add force to the message.

8. See Ignace de la Potterie, S.J., and Stanislaus Lyonnet, S.J., *The Christian Lives by the Spirit* (Staten Island, N.Y.: Alba House, 1971), 181–82.

9. Ford and Kelly, op. cit., 201–47.

10. This disanalogy often is overlooked by proponents of fundamental option. See, for example, John W. Glaser, S.J., "Transition between Grace and Sin: Fresh Perspectives," *Theological Studies*, 29 (1968), 260–61. Moreover, by treating agape as the term of a process of psychological maturation (269), Glaser seems to reduce all sexual sin to immaturity and thus to deny the very possibility of a mortal sin in the domain of sexual behavior.

CHAPTER EIGHTEEN

THE WAY OF SIN TO DEATH

Introduction

The five preceding chapters have clarified the nature and kinds of sin, and the conditions for mortal sin. This chapter will trace the relationship of various elements which make up a sinful life. Rather than being fixed and static, such a life is a continuous movement, from the moral indeterminacy of imperfection, through various stages of moral degeneration, to the ultimate disaster of eternal alienation from God. But its stages do not succeed one another with iron necessity; instead, a sinful life is a life of free choices, and its "stages" need not follow in precise sequence.

Analyzing the way of sin, we come to understand something of the power of evil. One might imagine the stage at which the moral consciousness of the child begins to dawn as a plain, the way of sin as an interstate route proceeding with many curves downward into the valley of death, and the way of Jesus as a hiking path with many switchbacks proceeding upward to the golden ridge of eternal life.

However, two mistakes must be avoided. First, one must not suppose that this process becomes automatic at any stage. If the downward road to hell is smooth, still sinners do not follow this road as if it were a railroad and they were cars without brakes. Rather, one reaches the end of this road only by freely staying on it, normally by making repeated wrong choices. At each point of choice, with the grace of God a right choice could have been made, and the right choice would have amounted to applying the brakes to halt the dynamics of sin. Second, the metaphor of the road must not be pressed too far. The dynamics of sin not only depend upon free choices, but also admit of shortcuts on the downward route and dramatic translocations from a point near the gates of hell to the very gates of heaven.

Question A: What is imperfection?

1. Jesus demands holiness of his followers. We are to be perfect as the Father is perfect (see Mt 5.48), to love God with our whole minds and hearts and souls and strength (see Mk 12.30), to love one another as Jesus loves us (see Jn 13.34; 15.12). (The call to holiness and the way it can be answered will be treated in 27-E and 28-E.)

2. Charity is central to holiness. The movement of Christian life toward perfection consists in perfecting charity. If one's charity were perfect, one's whole being would express and serve it (see LG 40 and 42).

3. Still, according to the more common opinion in modern Catholic theology, imperfection is not sin.[1] There can be dispositions and attitudes in a Christian which, without being sinful, fall short of perfection. This lack is not the privation which constitutes evil, for that which is merely imperfect has nothing specifically immoral about it. It simply is not what it would be if the ultimate holiness of the Christian vocation had already been realized.

4. **We must distinguish two types of imperfection. One is inevitable inasmuch as people only gradually constitute themselves existentially; they do not determine themselves rightly until they make the choices by which this is done. Such imperfection can be called "moral immaturity." The other type of imperfection is inevitable in fallen humankind—in everyone but Jesus and Mary—inasmuch as people have predispositions which block perfect integration in charity. Imperfection of this kind can be called "moral disintegrity."**

5. Being truly human and like us in everything but sin, Jesus himself was subject to the imperfection of moral immaturity. He was capable of moral growth, and progressed from the indeterminacy of childhood innocence to the determinacy of absolute and total self-oblation: "Although he was a Son, he learned obedience through what he suffered; and being made perfect he became the source of eternal salvation to all who obey him" (Heb 5.8–9).[2]

Having loved his own in the world, Jesus showed his love to the end (see Jn 13.1), at which alone he was able to announce: "It is finished" (Jn 19.30), and to deliver himself to glory, for at the end nothing remained to be perfected in him—nothing remained which did not wholly express and serve his love of the Father and of his fellow men and women.

Like that of any child, the humanity of Jesus had its limitations and its initial moral indeterminacy. His emotions naturally drew him to sensible goods appropriate to his determinate sentient nature. His understanding of intelligible goods initially led him spontaneously to will and act for a variety of specific objectives without any overall organization of his life. Doubtless, his early choices, although uniformly morally good, involved no all-embracing self-commitment.

6. The moral immaturity of Jesus was neither sin nor disintegrity. Rather, it was an inevitable consequence of the fact that he could only live his perfect human life by living it through, could exist in the mature perfection of integral love only after having made all the choices he had to make. By these choices he disposed in the form of finished holiness every aspect of himself which lay in his power to dispose.

7. All human beings are subject to the imperfection of moral immaturity. Unlike Jesus and Mary, however, we are also subject to the imperfection of moral disintegrity. By heredity and environment, nature and nurture, our natural dispositions are affected by the consequences of original sin and the personal sins of other people. Concupiscence inclines us to sin even before we make personal choices, and our sins will in their turn block perfect holiness not only in us but in others.

8. Unless we abort by mortal sin our divine life begun with baptism, living faith, once it is affirmed by a choice, is present in us as the fundamental option

which can organize Christian life. In fact, however, much of one's life is organized by desires, objectives, and commitments which have nothing to do with faith. To the extent that our lives are not yet integrated with faith, they are morally immature. To the extent that our desires and objectives are distorted by the effects of sin, they involve the imperfection of disintegrity.[3]

9. In sum, Christian holiness in this life is that ideal condition in which, being formed by living faith, all of the self one is capable of disposing through free choice expresses and serves charity (see *S.t.*, 2–2, q. 24, aa. 4–5, 8–9; q. 184, a. 3). Perfection requires the dedication of the whole self to Christ: "Whatever you do, in word or deed, do everything in the name of the Lord Jesus" (Col 3.17). Imperfection is characteristic of actions which, though morally good in themselves, are not integrated by the act of living faith. If they are in no way a consequence of the effects of sin exerted through heredity and environment, such actions are merely immature. To the extent that they are in some way affected by sin, however, they express disintegrity and present an obstacle to holiness. Even so, they are not themselves sins unless the distortion comes from bad will on the part of the person who does them.

Growth toward perfection involves more than existential integration. The other dimensions of the person also must be brought into complete conformity with living faith.

Much of one's thinking can be more or less inconsistent with faith. Sincere Christians hold many opinions—for example, ones they consider science of various sorts—incompatible with their faith. The contradictions are not explicit, and so they remain unnoticed. Many such false opinions have practical implications. One's redemption is incomplete as long as one's whole mind is not suffused by the light of Jesus, so that no darkness remains in it.

Further, both choices and intellectual judgments depend upon sentient nature. This dimension of the person is skewed by the common human inheritance, so that experience and emotion do not readily fall in line with the better self of the Christian. Moreover, early training and the constant input of a perverse cultural environment add to the difficulties one faces. One's whole soul is won over to Jesus only by a lifelong, constant struggle.

Finally, thinking and commitments are only principles of a full human life; words and deeds are needed to express the human person. Words and deeds are instruments; by them a person has the power to communicate with others and to change the world. Unfortunately, the available instruments are more or less recalcitrant to the purposes of one who wishes to manifest divine truth and love in the world. Language and the media of action have been shaped by the sinful uses to which things have been put. The Christian must wrestle with words and must work with tools which are not well adapted to serve Jesus' cause. It takes one's whole strength to work with the culture which exists and try to purify and renew it so that it will be better adapted to the redemptive work of the redeemed community.

In short, it is one thing for the love of God to be poured forth in one's heart; it is another to love God with one's whole heart and mind and soul and strength. Perfection requires that all one's choices be integrated with living faith; that all one's thinking be consistent with it; that all one's sentient dispositions and actuations be at the disposal of Christian love and truth; and that all one's powers have at hand suitable means for manifesting divine truth and love in the world. At every step of the way, the advance of love will meet and have to overcome the residues and effects of sin—original sin, one's own sin, and the sins of other individuals and groups. Initial conversion is only a beginning; one becomes a Christian little by little (see AG 13).

Question B: What are the sources of temptation?

1. **Because of imperfection, one can be tempted even without having committed prior personal sin. Some of these temptations are from within oneself, while others arise from other people. In the case of one who has already sinned, prior sin gives rise to still other temptations. Some mainly concern the coherence of one's life, while others concern one's relationship with God.**

As the Epistle of James suggests (1.14), passion is a general source of temptation. One could not choose wrongly unless there were some nonrational principle by which unreasonable proposals seem appealing, and emotion provides this principle (as was discussed in 7-G, 13-D, and 17-B). The First Epistle of John offers another point of view, according to which all temptation is reduced to the sinful world: "For all that is in the world, the lust of the flesh and the lust of the eyes and the pride of life, is not of the Father but is of the world" (1 Jn 2.16). It is plausible to think that here "lust of the flesh" refers to inordinate desires for sensual satisfactions (see Eph 2.3; 1 Pt 2.11; 2 Pt 2.10, 18), that "lust of the eyes" refers to inordinate desires for possessions, and that "the pride of life" refers to status seeking (see *S.t.*, 1–2, q. 77, a. 5).[4]

2. The temptations which come from within oneself even without prior personal sin reflect the spontaneous demands which emotions make when they cannot be satisfied by fully reasonable choices. To some extent, such temptations arise from the imperfection of immaturity. Thus it can be supposed that Jesus' hunger after fasting was a contributing factor in his temptation. In us, moreover, such temptations also arise because of the skewed emotional make up of fallen humanity (see *S.t.*, 1–2, q. 91, a. 6). For instance, the ordinary child is more insecure and demanding than ought to be the case.

3. Temptations of this sort have a social dimension in that two or more people can be tempted together. Besides such temptations and apart from any personal sin of one's own, though, evil in others presents a special challenge to the individual. The evil of the sins of friends tempts one to sin out of sympathy or solidarity, while the evil of the sins of enemies tempts one to sin for self-protection or in pursuit of legitimate objectives which they block.

When the New Testament authors speak of the "world," they generally refer to human society conditioned by sin. Paul speaks of the distractions of the "world" (see 1 Cor 7.29–35), while the Gospels speak sharply of the opposition between the Christian and the "world" (see Mt 5.14–16; Jn 17.14–17). The "world" is a source of temptation, and the Christian in the world must take care not to belong to the world (see Jn 15.19; 17.11; 1 Jn 4.4–6). As experience teaches, even children are tempted to do what their own inclinations might not suggest, to please their friends and to cope with their enemies, to conform to their world rather than to transform it.

4. A person who has sinned is subject to temptations based on his or her sinful state. First, one is tempted to integrate one's whole personality with one's sinful self (see *S.t.*, 1–2, q. 75, a. 4; q. 85, a. 1; q. 88, a. 3). But the self determined by sin is inherently unstable. While aspects of the self which have not been corrupted press for repentance, the self as determined by sin presses for its own consistent expansion. To be comfortable in sin, it is necessary to rationalize, to pretend that

the good which is violated is not good or that the violation cannot be avoided. A person in sin must cultivate dishonesty in order to defend an indefensible position.

"Truly, truly, I say to you, every one who commits sin is a slave to sin" (Jn 8.34)—this saying applies especially to this source of temptation. Slavery to sin, due to sin's own inner dynamism, can be appropriated in a special way to the Devil (see 1 Jn 3.8–10). Even the child is tempted to lie in order to conceal disobedience, and in lying often commits a more serious offense than the original one. Similarly, false and self-deceptive claims that the good was impossible and the evil not really intentional abound in the excuses offered by children.

5. Finally, given prior personal sin, an individual is tempted to distort his or her relationship with God. The distortion can be in the direction of pharisaism: limiting the relationship to a safe, legal minimum. Or it can be in the direction of zealotry: seeking God's favor by contending against evil—in others. Both responses reflect efforts to externalize sin and project it away from oneself, so that one can face God. A further temptation, even more radical, is to flee from the light, to refuse any longer to believe in the love one will not accept (see Jn 3.19).

Normally, when we say someone or something "tempts," we think of the subject as an agent which inclines to sin. In this sense of tempting, we must not say that God is a source of any temptation: "Let no one say when he is tempted, 'I am tempted by God'; for God cannot be tempted with evil and he himself tempts no one; but each person is tempted when he is lured and enticed by his own desire" (Jas 1.13–14). Yet God permits those he loves to be tried, so that they might prove their love (see Dt 13.3; Tb 12.13). In such temptations God provides sufficient grace that one can endure and win the victory (see 1 Cor 10.13).

The petition of the Lord's Prayer that we not be put to the trial (see Mt 6.13; Lk 11.4) perhaps refers to the extraordinary test of the last days. Still, it can appropriately be taken as asking that all temptations, which inevitably are painful and burdensome to those who love God, be mitigated.[5] When temptations come despite this constant prayer, one can be confident that they are permitted for one's own good: "Count it all joy, my brethren, when you meet various trials, for you know that the testing of your faith produces steadfastness" (Jas 1.2–3; cf. 1.12). One who never fights never wins (see 2 Tm 2.5).

Question C: How do venial sins lead to mortal sins?

1. The lives of Christians manifest both the imperfection of immaturity and the imperfection of disintegrity. Many desires and objectives are pursued without reference to living faith. This generates temptations and inevitably leads to venial sins. Some are recognized as sins; others are done with some awareness of their unreasonableness but no clear grasp of their sinful character; and still others are done more or less without moral reflection.

2. Venial sins can lead to mortal sins in four ways. All are similar in that they involve the venial sin's effect of opening up mortally sinful options or providing grounds for choosing them. Yet they are distinguishable.

Christian writers always have recognized that venial sins are serious, especially because they somehow lead to mortal sin. However, from the time of St. Augustine, who suggested the metaphor that many drops make a river and many grains a lump (see FEF 1846), the explanation of the relationship between venial and mortal sins usually has lacked the clarity one might wish. St. Thomas Aquinas is more helpful in indicating how sins can be causally related (see *S.t.*, 1–2, q. 75, a. 4; q. 84, a. 1; q. 88, a. 3). Although he is not concerned exclusively with the relationship of venial to mortal sins, his ideas can be adapted to explain this matter.

3. **First, venial sins can supply new options, fresh occasions, for sinning mortally.** By lying and disobedience, for example, children and young people gain liberty to go places and do things which offer occasions of mortal sin. Similarly, venial sins committed in acquiring wealth confer the power to be self-indulgent, while venial sins of defect in diligence in forming conscience free one to consider gravely wrong possibilities without at first attending to their full danger.

4. **Second, venial sins involve committing oneself to certain goods in whose enjoyment one grasps further sinful possibilities which might otherwise have remained unknown.** For instance, children's sins of impurity, which can be venial because of lack of sufficient reflection, make similar acts live options even after their gravity is known. Venially sinful acts of stealing can foster a taste for easy possession. One accustomed to deliberate lying takes a stance toward relevant goods which paves the way for mortal sins of lying.

5. **Third, venial sins often create situations which it is difficult to escape without mortal sin.** For example, venial sins committed in seeking popularity give rise to companionships with people who do not respect Christian faith and so lead to temptations to compromise faith in order to avoid embarrassment. A venial sin of carelessness can lead to an accident, which easily generates a temptation to sin mortally by evading grave duties—for example, by leaving someone injured at the scene. Venial sins of waste place people in a position of need, so that they are tempted to grave sins of theft.

6. **Fourth, venial sins often generate objectives one is tempted to pursue through mortal sins.** Venial sins of self-indulgence may accustom one to a standard of living which one is tempted to maintain by such means as theft, prostitution, or immoral methods of family limitation. Venial sins of status seeking may place one in a position where one is tempted to do whatever is necessary to acquire the status one craves—deny one's faith, cheat, offer illicit sexual favors or bribes, lie under oath, and so on.

This consideration of the seriousness of venial sin and its dynamic relationship to imperfection (from which it arises) and to mortal sin (to which it tends) makes clear the wisdom of using all available means to combat venial sin from the very beginning of moral life. One of these means is an early and regular use of the sacrament of penance (see 32-D).

Question D: What are the seven capital sins?

1. St. Gregory the Great formulated the familiar list of seven capital sins or sinful dispositions: pride, covetousness (or avarice), lust, gluttony, anger, envy, and sloth. These are best explained by St. Thomas Aquinas (see *S.t.*, 1–2, q. 84, aa. 3–4).[6] They are sins or sinful dispositions which lead to other sins. They are committed for their own sake, while other sins are committed because of them.

2. Thus, the capital sins are not necessarily the worst sins, nor are they always mortal. Furthermore, since many kinds of sins are omitted from the list of capital

sins, it is not a good format for examination of conscience. It is, however, a useful diagnostic tool for Christians in examining their lives insofar as they are sinful.

3. In looking at one's life, one finds much that is not perfectly integrated with living faith, not only because of immaturity but because of the disintegrity of imperfection and (at least) venial sin. Although a sinner's life cannot be perfectly integrated as a saint's can be, still a sinful life has some regular patterns. Consideration of the capital vices helps in locating the strategic points where sin is in control.

4. Self-examination is likely to be more fruitful if one temporarily sets aside temptations to commit serious sins of weakness, which are obvious, and concentrates instead on less obvious sinful dispositions. Using the list of capital vices, one can identify sinful inclinations one is likely to follow without much of a struggle. If ignored, these dispositions inevitably give rise to temptations to commit mortal sins, according to the fourth way described in the preceding question by which venial sins lead to mortal sins.

5. **Some of the capital vices are sinful dispositions which compete with love of God and neighbor, apparently providing alternative modes of fulfillment—though of course the alternatives are spurious and far inferior to true fulfillment.** So pride is a disposition to fulfillment in status and the respect of others; lust and gluttony are dispositions to fulfillment in immediate sensory gratifications; avarice is a disposition to fulfillment in possessions (see *S.t.*, 1–2, q. 84, a. 4; 2–2, q. 118, a. 7; q. 148, a. 5; q. 153, a. 4; q. 162, a. 8).

6. **The other capital vices are sinful dispositions which provide a defense of one's imperfection and sinfulness.** They are directed against the true good, insofar as it threatens one's sinful self (see *S.t.*, 1–2. q. 84, a. 4). So sloth is a disposition to avoid a more intense moral and spiritual life, which would require one to give up one's sins and overcome imperfections (see *S.t.*, 2–2, q. 35). Envy is a disposition against the true good of others, whose goodness makes unwanted demands on oneself (see *S.t.*, 2–2, q. 36). Anger, as a capital sin, is a disposition to harm and destroy, especially those things which pose a threat to one's sinful self; one cannot stand whatever gets in the way of having what one wants, least of all any spiritual or moral authority perceived as interfering with doing as one pleases (see *S.t.*, 2–2, q. 158, aa. 2, 6, 7).

One is likely to miss the point of this analysis of sinful character if one does not use some imagination to translate it into contemporary terms. One need not be analytically precise in this sort of reflection. The following translation is offered by way of example.[7]

Pride: One's life is a quest for status. Given this sinful aim in life, one tries to get through school in order to gain a respected position—to be a doctor, a priest, or a businessman. In one's work, one tries always to move up the ladder. One's identity depends upon the relationships one has with other people. One wants to be respected and liked, not be looked down on, considered odd, or regarded as a nuisance.

Covetousness: One looks for fulfillment in possessions. Given this sinful aim in life, one wants good clothes and a car. One would like a nice house in a good neighborhood and fine furniture. One wants to be well to do, not in need of anything. One spends much time and effort taking care of one's things. To have what one wants seems more important than being a better sort of person. The external is vital—for example, the wedding or the ordination ceremony is very significant, careful preparation for marriage or ordination less so.

Lust: One must have instant gratification. Given this sinful aim in life, one wants orgasms when one feels the inclination. But lust is not limited to sexual pleasure. One wants food and drink which will be pleasant; one wants to be amused and entertained constantly; one wants to feel no pain; one wants everything one wants right now. Even in prayer, one wants to feel one is getting something out of one's prayer; the liturgy must make one feel better.

Gluttony: One must always have more in order to have a good margin for security. Given this sinful aim in life, one wants to have a constantly rising standard of living. One wants to be well insured and to have a large savings account, to make sure of being cared for in retirement. One wants to have more time for oneself, and so carefully avoids becoming committed. One wants to live as long as possible, and so at once sets aside any commitment or good work which threatens health.

Envy: One wishes there were no truly better people around. They make it difficult to maintain the fiction that being better is not really possible. Sometimes they even offer criticism; one wishes people would not be so "judgmental." One prefers friends who are mediocre morally and spiritually; they are regular folks with whom one can feel comfortable.

Anger: One cannot stand anyone or anything which gets in the way. Thus obstacles to gaining status, to having things, to instant gratification, and to security are resented. Especially resented are spiritual threats: Do not tell me what the Church teaches about this matter; I follow my own conscience. One resents anyone in authority who tries to limit one's freedom to do as one pleases.

Sloth: One tries to keep one's mind and heart closed. One avoids experiencing anything or doing anything which would threaten the fragile equilibrium of one's sinful life. One likes the status quo. Since a largely immature conscience, more concerned with superego guilt feelings and rule keeping than with moral truth, makes only limited demands, one clings to this sort of conscience. One escapes into intense activity—hard work, social life, organizational matters, pastoral responsibilities—to avoid the recollected moment of truth.

Question E: How does persistence in mortal sin lead to final impenitence?

1. **The traditional list of sins against the Holy Spirit was drawn from various works of St. Augustine: impenitence, obduracy in sin, presumption, despair, rejection of the known truth, and envy of the grace others enjoy.**[8] **There is in these a certain dynamism and progression, by which sinners become increasingly unlikely to seek forgiveness.** In this sense sin can be said to become less and less forgivable, though absolutely speaking forgiveness remains a possibility until death. Here we shall follow but adapt the treatment given by St. Thomas Aquinas, with impenitence divided into initial and final impenitence.[9]

It is a matter of Catholic teaching that every sin can be forgiven during this life, using "can" in an absolute sense. The grace of God always is available and the power of the Church is not limited, so that one who is willing to accept forgiveness always can have it (see DS 349/167). Nevertheless, certain texts of Scripture indicate that some sins cannot be forgiven. Obviously, "cannot" must be used in a restricted sense in these texts (see *S.t.*, 2–2, q. 14, a. 3).[10]

One passage is a saying attributed to Jesus which contrasts sins committed against himself with blasphemy against the Holy Spirit. The latter sin is unforgivable (see Mt 12.31–32; Mk 3.28–29; Lk 12.10). A plausible interpretation of this saying is that blasphemy against the Holy Spirit attributes his work to some other power (such as the Devil). But the present work of God can be recognized only by the work of the Spirit. Therefore, if one insists on refusing to recognize the Spirit at work, God cannot communicate; one has effectively sealed oneself off. Obviously, if one gives up one's defense—as God's grace prompts one to do—the sin becomes forgivable.

In a similar way, one can understand the sin which is called deadly in the First Epistle of John (5.16). It can be taken to be a willful refusal to believe (see Jn 3.18, 36; 8.24; 1 Jn 5.10). Since forgiveness of sins comes through faith, one who refuses to believe cannot be forgiven; whereas those who believe are forgiven their sins and made children of God (see Jn 1.12–13). Apostasy also can be regarded as a sin which cannot be forgiven (see Heb 6.4–6; 10.26–31). Since the Church has the power to forgive sins, one who rejects the Church likewise rejects the source of forgiveness.

In all of these cases, what is in question is a sin which is more radical than most mortal sins, for it blocks the means of forgiveness.

2. By initial impenitence one chooses to commit a mortal sin and remain in it indefinitely. Going beyond sexual sins of weakness, for instance, people sometimes enter into sinful relationships which they mean to continue indefinitely (see *S.t.*, 1–2, q. 78, a. 2; 2–2, q. 14, a. 1). Again, a person in business may commit a sin of fraud with no expectation of repenting and making restitution.

3. By obduracy one resists the grace of repentance, very much as if it were a temptation. "Obduracy" is the hardening of heart often mentioned in Scripture and sometimes attributed to God inasmuch as it is a reaction to his continuing efforts to win back the sinner (see Jn 12.31–50). In no way, however, does God cause the sin of refusing to repent. Obduracy arises when, for example, a sinner hears a sermon, notices someone giving a good example, is moved by an image of our crucified Lord, or in some other way is led to think about his or her condition, but, rather than turning from guilt, instead turns his or her attention to something else.

If there is a family member, a friend, a coworker, a teacher, or someone else who reminds the sinner of his or her state, the reminder is resented, and the sinner looks for a reason to find fault with and condemn this person. This reaction is the beginning of the sin of envy of the grace which others enjoy. Moreover, the sinner looks to a new morality, to proportionalism, to the claim that the sin really is necessary rather than free, or to some other rationalization in an effort to deny its sinful character without repenting. Perhaps he or she goes from one confessor or counselor to another, seeking one who will approve the sin. This self-blinding by rationalization is the beginning of the sin of rejection of the known truth.

4. By presumption the sinner, aware of persisting in grave sin, takes the position that God will overlook the sin despite this persistence (see *S.t.*, 2–2, q. 21). "I can always count on God's grace, and I will repent in my own good time." Sometimes sinners turn legalistic and attempt to live a spotless life—except of course for the grave sin in which they persist—or do works of charity and become active in regard to social issues, or take enthusiastic part in the liturgy, as if to provide spurious evidence that their generally good life outweighs the

small area in which they are sinners. At this stage mistaken theories of fundamental option tend to be appealing.

5. By despair the sinner abandons hope for salvation. Often despair accompanies loss of faith; the sinner gives up both belief and hope regarding heavenly fulfillment. Despair can occur, though, without loss of faith (see *S.t.*, 2–2, q. 20). The presumptuous sinner who has counted on eventual repentance may experiment with "repentance" by seeking an experience of forgiveness without having a genuine purpose of amendment. Since the attempt is insincere, it fails; but, rather than blaming his or her own insincerity, the sinner blames God for withholding grace, and reasons: If grace is unavailable, then the situation is hopeless. So presumption gives way to despair. Again, a sinner who has relied on false theology and pseudospirituality may come to realize their speciousness, lose the support they provided, and thus find his or her presumption changed to despair.

6. By rejection of the known truth the sinner who has been evading truth comes to evasion's final stage: The darkness of sin is preferred to the light of faith (see Jn 3.19–21). This step could be taken at any time, even with the first choice to commit mortal sin. If one despairs without simultaneously abandoning faith, one is in a terrible state, believing in heaven and expecting hell. Reluctant to remain in this state but unwilling to repent, which indeed seems hardly possible by now, the sinner at this point abandons faith. Typically, this step is rationalized by an argument drawn from evil: The evil in the world shows that God is not good and loving, and faith is therefore false and must be abandoned.

Mortal sin does not at once destroy faith, unless it is a sin against faith. But every unrepented mortal sin sets up a crisis of faith. One in mortal sin who still believes is existentially torn between the lie of sin and the truth of God which condemns this lie. Christians who admit their sin can receive God's merciful forgiveness, but only if they will accept it and renew their commitment of living faith. For a Catholic, this means the confession of the sin or the desire to confess it when possible (see DS 1542–1543/807). To pretend one is not in sin when one is, is to make oneself a liar, to practice self-deception, to resist God's mercy, and ultimately to make shipwreck of one's faith (see *S.t.*, 2–2, q. 10, aa. 1, 3; q. 15, a. 1).

7. By envy of the grace others enjoy, the sinner regards those who believe and hope in God and strive to live faithfully as dangerous enemies (see *S.t.*, 2–2, q. 36, a. 4, ad 2). Possessing a residue of faith and Christian life even after rejecting faith, people in this state are like runaway children who not only suffer from amnesia but do not wish to remember their identity. Perhaps they try to lead others into sin or become militantly antireligious, attacking faith as superstition, doing volunteer abortion counseling, or seeking to discourage young people who think they have vocations to the priesthood or religious life.

8. By final impenitence, the sinner resists every grace and persists in sin until death. "Desire when it has conceived gives birth to sin; and sin when it is full-grown brings forth death" (Jas 1.15).

Those in despair or tempted to it must be reassured that forgiveness is possible whenever one is wholeheartedly ready to accept God's mercy. Those who think they know by experience that repentance is impossible for them can be helped to see the source of this mistake. False conceptions about divine causality and grace need to be cleared up; these remain remarkably prevalent even though they have been submerged by widespread silence about predestination.[11] A pastor whose hope is genuine and wholly free of anxiety can greatly help people with intact faith who are tempted to despair.

The obduracy which is basic to the sins against hope and faith is not easy to challenge directly. Yet the hardened heart and darkened mind are not totally insensitive and blind. Especially at moments of crisis—such as a serious illness, a death in a family, a major failure in one's projects—obdurate persons are shaken and can be reached. Those who are obdurate and know it must be encouraged to continue to participate in the life of the Church in other respects, yet discouraged from receiving the sacraments, since they are unwilling to receive them with good dispositions.

If obdurate persons are encouraged to receive the sacraments without repentance, they are being scandalized—that is, led into the worse state of the sin of presumption. For this reason, priests should be very careful in dealing with difficult marriage cases and should not give sacramental absolution without individual confession except in the extraordinary circumstances for which this practice is authorized.[12]

Question F: Is there a final option at the moment of death?

1. Some think that at the moment of death everyone has one last chance to dispose of himself or herself forever. Ladislaus Boros, S.J., has been a leading proponent of this idea.[13]

2. According to Boros, at the moment of death one makes the first totally personal choice about one's eternal destiny. It would not do for death to catch people, as it were, and freeze them either in grace or sin forever. This is particularly so because the acts which one can do in one's lifetime are limited in their personal character by one's limited knowledge, by passion, and by the limited possibilities with which any act deals.[14]

3. The hypothesis that in the moment of death one at last has a fully free, totally self-determining choice, a choice like that of the angels, seems to Boros also to solve many other theological questions, such as the fate of those who die in original sin only. Above all, he thinks his theory assigns the limited and imperfectly personal choices one makes in this life the limited and merely relative significance they deserve.[15]

Boros describes this final option. In death, the individual is fully free and conscious. Man's deepest being, his universe, splendid humanity "comes rushing towards him."

> Being flows towards him like a boundless stream of things, meanings, persons and happenings, ready to convey him right into the Godhead. Yes; God himself stretches out his hand for him; God who, in every stirring of his existence, had been in him as his deepest mystery, from the stuff of which he had always been forming himself; God who had ever been driving him on towards an eternal destiny. There now man stands, free to accept or reject this splendor. In a last, final decision he either allows this flood of realities to flow past him, while he stands there eternally turned to stone, like a rock past which the life-giving stream flows on, noble enough in himself no doubt, but abandoned and eternally alone; or he allows himself to be carried along by this flood, becomes part of it and flows on into eternal fulfillment.[16]

It seems clear that Boros imagines an option with no real choice.

4. **The hypothesis of a final option shares a central difficulty of other theories of fundamental option: It assumes that one can and must make a**

direct choice between God and creature. Describing this choice metaphorically, Boros contends that one can choose to be either eternally fulfilled or eternally turned to stone. Of course, this is no real choice. Who would choose to be turned to stone? At one point, Boros tries to answer this objection and another closely related to it, namely, that his notion makes the present life insignificant and guarantees that everyone reaches heaven. His reply is that Jesus speaks of legions of fallen angels, and their choice was precisely that of the final option.[17] However, Boros only assumes, not shows, that the angels' choice was such as he imagines.

5. Like proponents of fundamental freedom, Boros does not grasp the significance of the free choices we make from day to day. He does not see how we really determine our identities by the lives we live.[18] He therefore assumes that it is inexplicable for probation to end at death without a final option. The real question is not this, however, but how mortal sin can be repented during this life, since free choices of themselves tend to persist, and every mortal sin involves accepting separation from God.

6. Besides these difficulties which it shares with fundamental-option theories, the notion of a final option has difficulties of its own. There is no basis in experience for thinking that people make or are in any condition to make a choice at the moment of death. In practice, Boros attributes the final option to the disembodied spirit, but then it is no longer the final option of life but the initial option after death. Boros cannot admit this, however, for, as he says himself, it would "be contrary to the Church's teaching on the inalterability of the state a man reaches through his death."[19]

7. Nothing in Scripture supports the idea of a final option, and there is much against it. The gospel's warnings emphasize the importance for eternity of one's condition at death. This condition and therefore one's fate are being settled now: "Behold, now is the acceptable time; behold, now is the day of salvation" (2 Cor 6.2).[20]

8. From a rational point of view, it is very hard to see what sort of choice one could have as a final option. At one point Boros suggests it is to make or refuse an ultimate act of self-surrender, to resign oneself with faith to destruction or resist the ultimate self-emptying of death.[21] Initially this has some plausibility; it gives the option some content which is not wholly other-worldly. Upon further reflection, though, what sense does it really make to speak of self-surrender in the moment of death? Before death one can commend oneself to God and give up the ghost, resigning oneself to a foreseen but not yet present inevitability, or one can refuse to do so. But such resignation, if it occurs, must occur before death. At the moment of death, if one were perfectly aware, one would realize that the inevitable was now present. And what option remains to one aware that the absolutely inevitable is now at hand?[22]

Question G: Do impenitent sinners end in hell?

1. Scripture seems to say so. Various passages suggest that some people do persistently refuse to surrender themselves to God's love (see Mk 9.43–48; Jn

5.27–29; 2 Thes 1.7–10; Rv 20.9–15; 21.8). As everlasting happiness is promised those who do the works of love, so everlasting punishment is promised those who fail to do them (see Mt 25.31–46). There is no reason to take one of these promises seriously and treat the other as a mere figure of speech.[23]

2. Nevertheless, some theologians have recently proposed that hell is a terrible possibility, but only a possibility—one which could turn out never to be realized. In support of this, they say the Church has never definitively taught how many people will go to hell or that any particular individual (for example, Judas) is in hell. Thus, they suggest, hell might turn out to be like a three-dollar bill: a real possibility yet never actually real.[24]

3. Against this suggestion stands the teaching of the Church, which faithfully reflects the data of Scripture (see DS 76/40, 411/211, 801/429, 858/464, 1002/531, 1306/693). **Not only in her more formal teaching, but in the whole history of Christian teaching and preaching, the Church has proposed hell as the real fate of impenitent sinners.**[25]

All Christian teaching until now has proposed hell as a possibility which, unfortunately, sometimes is actualized. If this teaching were inaccurate, the faithful would have been massively misled on a matter of great interest and importance. One can imagine such a deception being practiced as a noble lie by someone not perfectly faithful and true; one cannot imagine it practiced by Jesus, teaching both in person and through his Church.

4. Moreover, contrary to the view that the Church has not definitely taught that anyone is in hell, a solemn statement of the Fourth Lateran Council asserts that the damned will suffer perpetual punishment with the Devil (see DS 801/429; cf. Mt 25.41). In other words, the Devil is in hell. Vatican II continues to affirm the reality of Satan, together with the truth that Christ has freed us from his power (see SC 6; LG 16, 48; AG 3, 9; GS 2, 13, 22). If some nonhuman person really is in hell, however, there is no reason to suppose no human person will join it.

One also must ask: How real a possibility is hell if it is a possibility which never is realized? If theology can provide any reasons whatsoever for thinking the possibility is never realized, these reasons actually will be arguments for the unreality of hell. For instance, to argue from God's love to an empty hell actually is to argue that God's love is incompatible with anyone ending in hell, and this is to argue for the impossibility of hell. If hell is to remain a real possibility, there can be no theologically convincing argument against populating it, because we have no independent source of evidence on this matter.

5. **Furthermore, the alternatives to a populated hell are theologically unacceptable.** To suppose that hell will turn out to be empty is to suppose either that everyone will repent before death, or that those who fail to repent before death will do so after death, or that those who have not repented will be annihilated, or that those who have not repented will be included in heavenly communion despite this.

6. There is no reason to think everyone repents before death. As for repentance after death, this hypothesis is incompatible with the Church's teaching. Moreover, it is also incompatible with the character of freedom of self-determination. Paradoxically, it is only because we are imperfectly integrated, existentially not all of a piece, that we are able to repent—able, that is, to reverse the thrust of our

self-determination contrary to the thrust of a previous immoral choice. But we are imperfectly integrated only during this life, and so the possibility of repentance is also limited to this life (see *S.t.*, sup., q. 99; *S.c.g.*, 4, 95).

If those who are eternally opposed to Jesus are in this state by their own choice, why can they not alter their choice? Is this fixation, at least, not a punishment arbitrarily imposed by divine power? The answer is "No." Freedom of choice is a capacity of self-determination (see 2-H). As such, one's free choices of themselves are constitutive of a self and are permanent. The present possibility of changing one's mind depends upon the present complexity and variability of human nature. A person completely integrated with his or her freely chosen self would have reason to continue in it and no reason to alter it. Presumably, after death persons are in this situation; therefore, they can no longer change their minds (see *S.t.*, 1, q. 64, a. 2).

7. The hypothesis of annihilation also is incompatible with the Church's teaching, as well as with God's love of all that is good (see Wis 11.24); for, although the damned abuse their freedom, their reality and their freedom remain great goods. Finally, the inclusion of the unrepentant in heavenly communion is ruled out by God's love itself. The unrepentant sinner is self-limited against God's goodness; and God would not force himself on one who freely rejects him.

Even if there were some sort of case to be made for the theory that hell might be empty, still there is no room for any Christian to accept such a theory as a practical supposition for living his or her own life, or to propose it to others for living their lives. There is no room for a practical supposition of this sort because for us, here and now, salvation is a task to be worked out.[26] One who looks at matters practically cannot assume that a real possibility is not really possible for oneself. And only a person obdurate in sin and tempted to presumption is likely to think of things in a different practical perspective. For with genuine hope, one can wait without anxiety, confident that God, who has brought one to repentance, will preserve one in his love until the end (see Rom 8.35; 2 Tm 4.8).

Question H: In what does hell consist?

1. Central to the misery of hell is loss of one's share in heavenly fellowship, which is the natural consequence of refusing to remain and grow in friendship with God (see *S.t.*, 1–2, q. 87, aa. 3–4; sup., q. 98, a. 2; *S.c.g.*, 4, 93). In contrast to the life communicated to those who accept Jesus as Lord, hell is eternal death (see Jn 5.29; 8.24). Hell is exclusion from the heavenly banquet (see Mt 22.11–14) and from the heavenly kingdom (see Rom 6.23; 1 Cor 6.9–10; Gal 5.19–21; 2 Thes 1.7–10; Heb 10.26–31).

2. Because it is a free choice by which one determines oneself, mortal sin tends to last. But the essence of mortal sin is separation from God. **Thus the central misery of hell, separation from God and exclusion from communion in heavenly fulfillment, is nothing else than the reality of mortal sin—that is, the lasting guilt which the sinner assumes by sinning and refusing to repent** (see DS 443/228a, 1002/531, 1306/693). Eternal death is a self-made judgment (see Jn 3.18–19; 12.47). It is sin's inherent outcome (see Rom 6.21).

Love of God must be accepted by a creature with freedom, and this freedom must for this very reason be faithful to the goods proper to the creature. If an angelic or human

448

person constitutes a self which is radically closed against his or her own true good, then that self is not compatible with love of God.

The more we love God, the more clearly we realize that he makes no arbitrary rules to trip us up and imposes no arbitrary punishments to make us suffer. Our evildoing diminishes his glory in ourselves. His concern about the sin of creatures is with the harm they do themselves and the misery they inflict on one another. The latter must be permitted for the time being; those who suffer unjustly will receive their compensation. Meanwhile, as God's children love him more purely, as they rid themselves of remnants of adolescent rebellion, they realize how ideal a Father he is. And so perfect love engenders confidence and excludes anxiety (see 1 Jn 3.18–22; 4.17–18).

3. **Besides loss of fellowship in the heavenly kingdom, those in hell are said also to suffer from "fire."** Beyond the fact that "fire" connotes painful experience, the Church's teaching leaves open the precise nature of this suffering.[27] There is no need to think of this painful experience as being especially created for sinners and imposed on them.[28] Given the unity of the human person, it is only reasonable to suppose that the essential misery of permanent unfulfillment will have natural consequences at the level of experience.

4. One is free to imagine that for the damned the fire of hell will consist partly in their unwanted perception of the new heavens and new earth, where everything will bespeak the triumph of God's love in Jesus. One may also imagine that it will consist partly in the unsatisfying existence of persons who have sinfully chosen very limited goods rather than the integral fulfillment they should have preferred. Sinful experiences—which even in this life are inherently unsatisfying despite their appeal—would comprise a wretched existence for one condemned to go on reliving the same experiences forever, especially in a society composed exclusively of obdurate sinners.

Might not the fire of hell be understood as the way in which heavenly fellowship and the new heavens and new earth, suited to the blessed who share in divine life, will be perceived by those alienated from this life? If one refused to go to a party, somehow found oneself on the edge of it, yet still maintained one's stubborn refusal to share in the celebration, then the party itself and everything which pleased the participants would be an irritant. The situation of those in hell, perhaps, will be somewhat like this. Everything will be suited to the joy of the blessed; everything will bespeak the triumph of Jesus. Those who are pilgrims now, often in a painful and hostile world, will be at home. But those perfectly comfortable with the world as it now is will find the home of the blessed in no way satisfactory and to their taste.

Question I: Does God cause anyone to go to hell?

1. God does judge. And hell is a punishment, in that it is a real evil consequent upon wrongdoing and deservedly suffered. It appears, then, that God sends sinners to hell. But is this so? And, if so, in what sense?

2. God chooses to impose other punishments besides hell. These are medicinal, intended to discourage persons from self-injury by wrongdoing and to encourage them to rectify their lives. Sin is separation from God and violation of his loving plan; punishment shows sinners what they are doing to themselves. Thus God permits humankind to experience the consequences of sin. The terrible

reality of death brings home to us what sin means. Unlike the angels, we experience something of the reality of hell in this life, while we still have the opportunity of avoiding endless separation from God.

3. God also corrects in the sense of bringing it about that the disorder inherent in sin, which disturbs the harmony of humankind's relationship with him, is rectified by the proportionate work of the redemption (see *S.t.*, 3, q. 48, aa. 2, 4; q. 49, aa. 1, 3). Jesus knew punishment, not as if he himself had sinned, but because he suffered sin's consequences and reconciled humankind with God, restoring the harmony sin had destroyed (see Is 53.4–12; Mt 20.28; Col 1.19–20; 2.14; Heb 9.24–28; 1 Pt 2.24). One who accepts a share in the redemption experiences a judgment of expiation accomplished in Jesus (see Rom 3.25–26; 2 Cor 5.19).

4. **Nothing, however, requires us to suppose that hell is imposed on sinners by God's choice, except insofar as God accepts this outcome as incidental to his creating of persons who have the great dignity of freely determining themselves either to accept communion with him or reject it.**

A legalistic outlook leads to the view that hell is a punishment God arbitrarily threatens and might equally arbitrarily waive. If one sees in moral requirements true conditions of human fulfillment and in moral choices self-constitution, then hell is seen as the persisting self-mutilation of moral evil. In other words, the Christian appreciation of human dignity in the freedom to love God by respecting the truth of one's own humanity implies as its reverse the ultimate seriousness of persistent immoral choice. Moreover, in the Christian context, to deny hell is to deny that one's faith in Jesus or rejection of him makes any ultimate difference.

5. Without excluding created freedom, God "desires all men to be saved and to come to the knowledge of the truth" (1 Tm 2–4; cf. *S.t.*, 1, q. 19, a. 6, ad 1). Jesus comes to save, not to condemn (see Jn 3.17; 12.47). His teaching discriminates only because it compels everyone to make a decision. By his words Jesus does judge between those who accept and keep them and those who do not (see Jn 5.22; 9.39). But the principle of discrimination is the truth, and the agent of condemnation is the individual who rejects it (see Jn 12.47–48).

6. This understanding of the sinner's self-condemnation is already suggested in the first nine chapters of Genesis, which make it clear that God creates everything good, that evil comes from creatures' abuse of their freedom, and that punishment for sin is not arbitrarily imposed by God. Human punishment often has the character of a more or less vengeful reaction, but God's punishment can have nothing of this character.

7. Nevertheless, hell as a punishment can be understood by analogy with the ultimate in human punishment. Sometimes society accepts the determination of criminals to live as outlaws, nonmembers cut off from participation in society itself. This acceptance is fair, and its fairness is the principle which justifies such practices as permanent imprisonment, banishment, and capital punishment. (The latter is not unfair, but seems to violate the good of life and can be ruled out on this ground.) The freedom of criminals who cut themselves off from society is respected in treating them as nonmembers.

8. Hell is similar, except that God has no choice to hold or not hold persons responsible. If a created person constitutes a self which is not open to his or her own good, that self is not compatible with heavenly communion. God can do nothing about this without either coercing the individual—and so destroying freedom and the self which it has constituted—or else annihilating the individual.[29] However, evil is the privation, while the freedom and the being of the damned remain good to the extent that they are real; and God, loving these goods which manifest his own goodness, cannot destroy them.

9. Might God not temper his justice with mercy toward the damned? Perhaps by easing their suffering, but not by ending their hell, for mercy presupposes a choice, and with respect to their alienation from him the damned leave God no choice. His justice ultimately consists in being faithful to his gifts of being and freedom, and God simply cannot be unfaithful (see 2 Tm 2.12–13). God tries every means to win the love of sinners who initially reject him but still might repent (see *S.t.*, sup., q. 99, aa. 2–3). In our Lord Jesus we see how far he goes: "God so loved the world that he gave his only Son" (Jn 3.16). Anyone who ends in hell simply refuses to yield to the powerful wooing of this divine love.

Summary

Although the stages of a sinful life do not follow one another with iron necessity, there is a typical progression to the process of moral degeneration.

The first stage, imperfection, is not itself sin. It is of two kinds: moral immaturity, which existed even in Jesus, and moral disintegrity, present in the predispositions of fallen humanity which block perfect integration in charity. Holiness is that state in which, formed by living faith, the self expresses and serves charity; imperfection, by contrast, marks actions good in themselves which are not integrated with living faith.

Because of imperfection, a person can be tempted to sin even without having committed prior personal sin. Some temptations come from within—from the spontaneous demands of emotions which cannot be satisfied by fully reasonable choices. Others come from other persons, as a result either of one's sympathy with or opposition to them. But one who has committed prior personal sin is subject to further temptation as he or she tries to integrate the whole personality with the sinful self—an effort which naturally leads to rationalization and dishonesty. One who has committed prior sin is also tempted to distort his or her relationship with God—by pharisaism, zealotry, or, more radically, fleeing from divine truth.

Temptation leads to venial sins, and they in turn lead to mortal sins: by supplying new options for sinning mortally; by introducing one to experiences which make one aware of further sinful possibilities which might otherwise have remained unknown; by creating situations difficult to escape without mortal sin; and by generating objectives one is tempted to pursue by mortal sin.

The so-called capital sins have special significance because they lead to other sins; the list of capital sins is thus useful for spiritual self-analysis. Four compete with love of God and neighbor by providing apparent alternative modes of fulfillment—in status and the respect of others (pride), in sensory gratification (lust and gluttony), in possessions (avarice). The others are defenses, as it were, of one's imperfection and sinfulness—against a more intense moral and spiritual life (sloth), against the goodness of others which makes demands on oneself (envy), against whatever stands in the way of getting what one wants (anger).

Through the sins against the Holy Spirit the sinner becomes increasingly unlikely to seek forgiveness. By initial impenitence one chooses to commit a mortal sin and to remain in it, and perhaps also in a situation or relationship conducive to further sins. By obduracy one resists the grace of repentance. By presumption one supposes that God will overlook one's persistence in sin. By despair one abandons hope for salvation. By rejection of the known truth one abandons faith. By envy of the grace others enjoy one regards believers striving to live faithfully as enemies. By final impenitence one resists every grace and persists in sin until death.

Some theologians have argued that everyone has one last chance at the moment of death to dispose of himself or herself forever. This has the same fatal difficulty as other fundamental-option theories: It assumes that one can and must make a direct choice between God and creatures, and overlooks the importance for self-determination of one's ordinary free choices. The theory has no support in experience, in reason, or in Scripture.

Scripture seems to say that impenitent sinners end in hell. Some theologians nevertheless argue that hell might turn out to be a possibility which is never realized. This cannot be reconciled with the Church's teaching. Furthermore, the alternatives to a populated hell (everyone will repent before death, those who fail to repent before death will do so after death, those who do not repent will be included in heavenly communion, the unrepentant will be annihilated) are theologically unacceptable.

The central misery of hell is nothing else than the reality of mortal sin. For hell is separation from God, and this is the essence of mortal sin (a free choice which, like any choice, lasts). The Church also teaches that those in hell suffer some painful experience, "fire," whose precise nature is, however, left open.

It cannot be said that God imposes hell as a punishment. God does impose other, medicinal punishments, intended to discourage people from self-injury by wrongdoing and encourage them to rectify their lives. God also punishes in the sense of bringing it about that, through suffering, persons participate in the work of redemption. But the case is different with hell. If a person freely constitutes a self radically closed against his or her own true good, that self is not open to heavenly communion; and God can do nothing about this without coercing the individual and so destroying freedom and the self it has created.

Appendix 1:   The reality and limited role of the Devil

It is not only taken for granted throughout the Bible but definitively taught by the Church that there exist, besides divine and human persons, other persons normally not visible in bodily form but able to act in our world—namely, good and bad angels (see DS 800/428, 3002/1783).

452

It is an important part of this teaching that these persons are created and wholly dependent upon God for their being; they have no independent reality over and against him. Nevertheless, although all are good insofar as they are creatures, some are bad insofar as by their own free choices they have determined themselves wrongly, and so exist in a certain disharmony with God, whose love would have shared with them his own perfect life (see DS 286/—, 325/—, 411/211, 797/427, 800/428).

It follows that the reality of the Devil and of demons cannot be denied; they are not merely mythical beings or the personification of evil. At the same time, the Devil must not be thought of as an absolute principle of evil opposed to the all-good God; there is no such principle. The Devil is in its entire positive reality good; its being remains relative to God and its evil limited by the scope of its own created (and still in itself good) freedom (see *S.t.*, 1, q. 63, aa. 4–5; q. 64, a. 1).

There is more systematic perversity in the world than human sin accounts for. The demons account for this excess: "For we are not contending against flesh and blood, but against the principalities, against the powers, against the world rulers of this present darkness, against the spiritual hosts of wickedness in the heavenly places" (Eph 6.12). Vatican II teaches that the Devil had a role in the fall of Man and that its work helps to account for the monumental struggle which makes up human history (see GS 13; AG 9). Evil spirits still are at work in the world, seeking to damage the redemptive work (see 1 Pt 5.8; Rv 12.7–9). The Devil tries to lead Christians into sin (see 1 Cor 7.5; 2 Cor 2.11; 1 Thes 3.5; 1 Tm 3.7, and so on).

The Gospels present the redemptive life of Jesus as an encounter with and victorious struggle against the Devil. Jesus is tempted by the Devil, delivers many people from evil spirits, and ultimately overcomes the Devil by his passion and death (see Lk 22.3, 31, 53; Jn 13.2, 27; 14.30; Col 1.13). Hence, we are freed from the power of the Devil (see SC 6; cf. *S.t.*, 3, q. 48, a. 4; q. 49, a. 2). No Christian can be conquered by the Devil without his or her own free choice to do what is evil (see Eph 4.27; Jas 4.7). The Church has firmly rejected tendencies to exaggerate the role of diabolical activity in temptation (see DS 2241–53/1261–73).

In accordance with an extensive theological tradition one can think of the sin of Satan as the first evil in creation, and so regard all other evil as somehow mysteriously related to it; in this view, one thinks of the diabolical realm as if it were a kind of perverse, wretched imitation of the kingdom Jesus is bringing to fulfillment (cf. 1 Jn 3.8–10). On this view, every temptation and sin can be credited to the work of the Devil (see *S.t.*, 1, q. 114, aa. 2–3; 3, q. 8, a. 7). It instigates to sin and then seeks the sinner's condemnation, so as to gain the lost soul for itself (see Rv 12.9–10).

Inasmuch as the power of the evil spirits has been broken by the victory of Jesus, one ought not to assume diabolical activity when other explanations are possible (see *S.t.*, 1–2. q. 80). Still, in regard to temptation, those temptations which arise from one's own prior sins are fittingly ascribed to the Devil, since by one's sins one somehow surrenders oneself into the power of the Devil. Also, an awareness that there are evil spirits still at work in the world will inhibit anyone from too quickly assuming that every spiritual inspiration is a good gift of the Holy Spirit. One must put spirits to the test; those only can be trusted whose suggestions contain nothing incompatible with sound doctrine and moral truth (see 1 Jn 4.1–3).

Appendix 2:   Covetousness and pride as roots of all sin

In Scripture two dispositions are mentioned especially as the root of all sin— covetousness and pride (see 1 Tm 6.10; Sir 10.13).

Coveting money really amounts to love of liberty and power to do as one pleases (see *S.t.*, 1–2, q. 84, a. 1). One who has this liberty and power is easily able to do evil; one who seeks it is looking for the opportunity to do evil. Moreover, love of money leads to injustice to others. The Marxist analysis of social evil is not wholly wrongheaded, although it is oversimplified. There was no money at all in the earliest human societies, but Man sinned from the beginning. Moreover, diabolical evil is not materialistic.

There is a "lust" or covetousness which is identified with idolatry (see Eph 5.5; Col 3.5). Idolatry is characteristic of paganism and is the source of all pagan vices (see Wis 14.27; Rom 1.21–23). It is not merely an honest error in religion; rather, it is a humanly contrived religion, intended to provide gods which can be manipulated and which make few moral demands. "Coveting" is used in an extended sense to refer to all wrongful desire (see Rom 7.7; 1 Cor 10.6–10). Thus covetousness and idolatry come together in the human will to have what one wants rather than what God wants. Wrongful desire and the displacement of God from his unique supremacy always go together (see Gn 3.5–6).

Regarded in this way, covetousness and idolatry are seen to be aspects of the same basic attitude involved in sinful pride. The Jewish sage who identified pride as the reservoir or root of all sin also identified the source of the pride with which he was concerned: "The beginning of man's pride is to depart from the Lord; his heart has forsaken his Maker. For the beginning of pride is sin, and the man who clings to it pours out abominations" (Sir 10.12–13). "Pride" here clearly means much more than status seeking, arrogance, boasting, or a haughty attitude. It is not primarily a defect in relationships with other people, but unwillingness to submit to God.

Christian humility is a basic mode of Christian response and the foundation of all the other Christian virtues (see 26-D). As opposed to it, pride, which can be understood to include the disobedience and rebelliousness which are opposed to meekness, is the fundamental obstacle to Christian moral and spiritual growth. Pride, as opposed to humility, is an unreadiness to seek and accept everything from God; affirmatively, pride is a will to be self-reliant and self-responsible—to be a divine person come of age, as it were, instead of a "mere" child of God.

Although pride, thus correctly understood, is fundamental to all sin, one must be very careful not to confuse this disposition with more specific ones or to draw false conclusions about the spiritual life.

One confuses this disposition with others if one supposes that the fundamental evil of pride is especially present in interpersonal relationships with other people, and that one can avoid pride by taking a self-depreciating attitude or by being careful to remain one of the mediocre crowd. The example of Jesus clearly stands against this misunderstanding. He frankly asserts his own status for the glory of the Father (see Jn 8.45–57). Similarly, in Jesus every Christian can boast and have great confidence (see Heb 3.6, 14). The mark of the legitimate pride of the Christian is that nothing is claimed as if it were one's own; one's boast is in the Lord from whom alone one's goodness comes (see Rom 5.11).

Furthermore, that pride which is basically opposed to humility is not the capital sin of pride—status seeking. One does not commit this sin of asserting one's autonomy except in wrongly choosing something else. Hence, one does not commit other sins for the sake of opposing oneself to God. One does not decide to disobey God and then think of some disobedience to commit. One rather thinks of some sin to commit—not because it is a sin, but because it has the appeal of the limited good it offers—and then, ordinarily very reluctantly, one decides to disobey God (see *S.t.*, 1–2, q. 71, a. 6; q. 72, a. 4; q. 75, a. 2).

Hence, the pride which is a capital sin is not the root of all sin (see *S.t.*, 2–2, q. 132, a. 4). One must oppose this specific pride, but one also must oppose every other form of sinfulness. It would be a mistake to assume that if one does not seek one's fulfillment in social status and the respect of other people, then one is essentially humble and a good Christian.

Notes

1. See J. J. Farraher, S.J., "Imperfection, Moral," *New Catholic Encyclopedia*, 7:396–98, for a survey of positions and references to some important works. James C. Osbourn, O.P., *The Morality of Imperfections* (Westminster, Md.: Carroll Press, 1950), 1–35, argues that St. Thomas had no place for imperfection (conclusions, 225–31). He could be correct; if so, St. Thomas missed something important. However, Thomas surely recognized the purely negative, nonprivative reality of immaturity. If he did not recognize imperfections of disintegrity as distinct from venial sins, this lacuna can be explained by his lack of clarity about the role of faith as a fundamental option whose requirements for an integrally Christian life can be at odds with particular acts good in themselves and innocently chosen—for example, interests and activities of adolescents which distract them from seeking and embracing their personal vocations.

2. For a theological commentary on this text, see Walter Kasper, *Jesus the Christ* (London: Burns and Oates, 1976), 208–15; also see Jean Galot, S.J., *Who Is Christ? A Theology of Incarnation*, trans. M. Angeline Bouchard (Chicago: Franciscan Herald Press, 1981), 376–79. Someone who resists attributing imperfection to Jesus (when the imperfection in question neither involves nor presupposes sin) seems to be afflicted with a trace of Apollinarianism, for to be a perfect human is reached only through learning obedience and freely accepting God's will, as Jesus did.

3. In modern theology, the problem of imperfection emerged in a legalistic context in which each choice was considered in isolation. In that context, it is very difficult to understand how Christians called to perfection can choose the less good, the less specifically Christian, without sin. But when one considers Christian life as a whole which ought to be organized by the fundamental option of living faith, one can see at once that many morally good acts are chosen without reference to faith. Such acts need to be integrated and, to the extent that they are conditioned by sin, they can resist integration in the specific pattern of a particular, personal vocation. This view of the problem of imperfection already was adumbrated by Etienne Hugueny, O.P., "Imperfection," *Dictionnaire de Théologie Catholique*, 7:1286–98, but by overlooking the fact that the specific requirements of perfection become known only gradually Hugueny tends to reduce all imperfection to venial sin.

4. See H. Schönweiss, "epithymia," *New International Dictionary of New Testament Theology*, 1:456–58.

5. See Heinrich Seesemann, "peira, etc.," *Theological Dictionary of the New Testament*, 6:28–32.

6. See *De malo*, q. 8, a. 1, which introduces a remarkable treatise on the capital sins. For the history of the background and development of the list of capital sins, see Morton W. Bloomfield, *The Seven Deadly Sins* (N.p.: Michigan State College Press, 1952), 43–89.

7. For a less free updating of the capital sins, see Bernard Häring, *The Law of Christ: Moral Theology for Priests and Laity*, vol. 1, trans. Edwin G. Kaiser, C.Pp.S. (Westminster, Md.: Newman Press, 1961), 374–82.

8. For bibliography: Antony Koch, *A Handbook of Moral Theology*, vol. 2, *Sin and the Means of Grace*, ed. Arthur Preuss (St. Louis: B. Herder, 1919), 92–95; Emmanuel Doronzo, O.M.I., *De Poenitentia*, tom. 4, *De Causis Extrinsecis* (Milwaukee: Bruce, 1953), 41–72.

9. St. Thomas, *De malo*, q. 3, a. 14; *Summa theologiae*, 2–2, q. 14, aa. 1–2. This list became standardized through Peter Lombard; see St. Thomas, 2 *Sent.*, d. 43, q. 1, a. 2.

10. See C. Bernas, "Sin against the Holy Spirit (in the Bible)," *New Catholic Encyclopedia*, 13:247–48.

11. There is a Catholic doctrine of predestination, witnessed in Scripture (see Rom 8.30), taught by the Church (see DS 621/316, 1567/827), and explained by St. Thomas (*S.t.*, 1, q. 23). This doctrine neither excludes free choice (see DS 622/317) nor admits that anyone is predestined to hell, but it insists on the absolutely essential point that no one is saved except by God's grace, which always antecedes any human contribution (see DS 1525–26/797–98).

12. See John Paul II, *Familiaris Consortio*, 74 *AAS* (1982) 184–86; Eng. ed. (Vatican City: Vatican Polyglot Press, 1981), 158–61 (sec. 84). Unfortunately, some theologians have encouraged the faithful to settle their freedom to marry by a private judgment of their own, using such weak criteria with

respect to their first marriage as "tolerance or intolerance of common life." See John R. Connery, S.J., et al., "Appendix B: The Problem of Second Marriages: An Interim Pastoral Statement by the Study Committee Commissioned by the Board of Directors of the Catholic Theological Society of America: Report of August 1972," *Proceedings of the Catholic Theological Society of America*, 27 (1972), 233–40 (criteria, 236–37). Several plausible criteria also are suggested—for instance, fidelity or its absence from the beginning, which might be a basis for a legitimate case for nullity in a tribunal. But tolerance of common life clearly could not; its acceptance would mean that every couple who are divorced and wish to remarry were never married, since they obviously have not tolerated common life.

13. Boros is not the only proponent of final option. Louis Monden, S.J., *Sin, Liberty and Law* (New York: Sheed and Ward, 1965), 19–44, spells out a version of final option. His argument depends heavily upon stressing the limitations of the freedom in ordinary choices, so that he virtually denies moral responsibility in the course of one's life. Others defend final option with arguments in general similar to those of Boros: Piet Schoonenberg, S.J., *Man and Sin: A Theological View* (Notre Dame, Ind.: University of Notre Dame Press, 1965), 30–36; Roger Troisfontaines, S.J., *I Do Not Die* (New York: Desclée, 1963), 147–88. For further references and some general, critical remarks, see Gisbert Greshake, "Towards a Theology of Dying," in *The Experience of Dying*, Concilium, 94, ed. Norbert Greinacher and Alois Müller (New York: Herder and Herder, 1974), 80–85.

14. Ladislaus Boros, S.J., *The Mystery of Death* (New York: Herder and Herder, 1965), 86–99.

15. Ibid., 127–28; cf. Monden, op. cit., 20–33.

16. Boros, op. cit., ix. Troisfontaines, op. cit., 152–53, also supposes that the final option is an unmediated (that is, direct) one between accepting and rejecting the divine invitation to communion.

17. Boros, op. cit., 98.

18. A telling critique of Boros' theory, especially in respect to its angelism: Matthew J. O'Connell, S.J., "The Mystery of Death: A Recent Contribution," *Theological Studies*, 27 (1966), 434–42. O'Connell's critique of Boros would be equally cogent against others, such as Troisfontaines, who makes it clear (op. cit., 156–60) that he thinks of the final option as an act of the angel-like separated soul.

19. Boros, op. cit., 4.

20. Another theological argument for final option is that this hypothesis solves the problem of children and retarded persons who die unbaptized (thus eliminating the awkward theological construct, limbo, which is not required by definitive Church teaching), and also that final option will cover the case of persons who never hear the gospel; see Troisfontaines, op. cit., 174–77, for a concise statement of this argument. With respect to those who have not heard the gospel, the argument has been weakened by Vatican II's teaching (see LG 16) that grace is given by way of preparation for the gospel, and that those who "strive to live a good life" thanks to this grace can be saved. This teaching seems to favor the view that people can be saved by an implicit desire for friendship with God, which amounts to faith so far as they are concerned. As for those who die unbaptized without the use of reason, they are no less disposed in themselves to grace than are infants who are baptized; and it seems to me that the real, human effort of the Church to carry out Christ's mandate to baptize constitutes a real relationship of the gospel to them, by which their baptism is incipient. As I explained in chapter fourteen, appendix 2, this beginning of baptism does not render less necessary the completion of the sacramental rite when that is possible, for a beginning is such only by pointing toward its completion.

21. Boros, op. cit., 68–81.

22. Karl Rahner, *On the Theology of Death* (New York: Herder and Herder, 1961), 35–39, attempts to argue that dying must not only be passive but also active. In doing so, he assumes that death is decisive for one's eternal status either by one's own act or by God's free decree (37–38). There is another possibility: that dying (and whatever happens afterwards) eliminates the dissonance between the self constituted by choice during one's life and other aspects of the personality, and that this dissonance is a necessary (not sufficient) condition of repentance during life. Rahner's a priori argument that since the person involves freedom, dying also must involve it, since dying affects the whole person, proves too much if it proves anything. For, as Greshake points out (op. cit., 83), there is also passivity in the beginning of life. Being conceived affects the whole person. Bartholomew J. Collopy, S.J., "Theology and the Darkness of Death," *Theological Studies*, 39 (1978), 22–54, esp. 33–39, offers profound reflections to clarify the arbitrary character of the model of death proposed by Boros and Rahner.

23. See Jean-Marie Fenasse and Jacques Guillet, "Hell," *Dictionary of Biblical Theology*, 2d ed., 233–35, esp. "Christ Speaks of Hell" (234).

24. See William J. Dalton, S.J., *Salvation and Damnation* (Butler, Wis.: Clergy Book Service, 1977), 75–83.

25. For a brief, clear dogmatic treatment of hell: E. J. Fortman, S.J., *Everlasting Life after Death* (New York: Alba House, 1976), 157–81; also Michael Schmaus, *Dogma*, vol. 6, *Justification and the Last Things* (Kansas City: Sheed and Ward, 1977), 249–59. A classic apologetic treatment, still worth study: Paul Bernard, "Enfer," *Dictionnaire Apologétique de la Foi Catholique*, 1:1377–99. A fuller treatise: M. Richard, "Enfer," *Dictionnaire de Théologie Catholique*, 5:28–120. An evangelical Protestant work, popularly written, but worthwhile as a witness to the post-Reformation tradition and departures from it: Jon E. Braun, *Whatever Happened to Hell?* (Nashville: Thomas Nelson, 1979), 80–129.

26. Karl Rahner, "Hell," *Encyclopedia of Theology*, 602–4, wishes to insist at least on this practical possibility on which the Christian must count "without any sly look at a possible apocatastasis" (604). At the same time, he disposes of the teaching of Jesus rather too easily as being "in keeping with the theology of his time" (602). He also seems to assume without argument the incompatibility of a threat with a realistic statement about what will happen if the threat is not heeded, when he says that "what Scripture says about hell is to be interpreted in keeping with its literary character as 'threat-discourse' and hence not to be read as a preview of something which will exist some day" (603). The very logic of any honest threat seems rather to require, among other things, a preview of something which may well happen.

27. Gregory IX, for example, simply says (DS 780/410) that actual sin is punished with the torture of perpetual *gehenna*, which leaves the nature of this fire as open as the New Testament does. To say the Church's teaching leaves open the nature of the fire of hell is not to say there is no such thing. Scripture, the Fathers, and the Church's teaching through the centuries are too uniform in using the language of "fire" to allow us to dispense with it when we do not know what the experience of hell is. For all we know, ordinary burning might be mild by comparison, since pain is no mere sensation, but a complex psychological experience. See Roger Trigg, *Pain and Emotion* (Oxford: Oxford University Press, 1970).

28. See Charles Journet, *The Meaning of Evil* (New York: P. J. Kenedy and Sons, 1963), 186 and 200; Fortman, op. cit., 172–74. The Sacred Congregation for the Doctrine of the Faith, "Letter on Certain Questions concerning Eschatology," 71 *AAS* (1979) 942; *L'Osservatore Romano*, Eng. ed., 23 July 1979, 7, restates the traditional doctrine in a way which devalues any "picture" or "imaginative representation" yet maintains the truth of faith: The Church "believes that there will be eternal punishment for the sinner, who will be deprived of the sight of God, and that this punishment will have a repercussion on the whole being of the sinner." Thus one need not think in terms of imposed pain of any sort; the positive suffering is a repercussion consequent upon self-determined separation from (instead of communion with) God.

29. See Joseph A. Bracken, S.J., "Salvation: A Matter of Personal Choice," *Theological Studies*, 37 (1976), 410–24, for an unfolding of this line of thought. Although somewhat weakened by an acceptance of final option and by an inadequate grasp upon the principle of morality (evil conceived as gross egoism), Bracken's discussion is helpful in respect to the central point: Hell is not a punishment arbitrarily imposed, but a condition of the sinner freely persisted in forever.

CHAPTER NINETEEN

FULFILLMENT IN JESUS AND HUMAN FULFILLMENT

Introduction

So far we have mainly considered common principles of morality: free choice, conscience, and natural law and its applications. Although included in the teaching of faith, these principles are accessible to unaided reason. Beginning with this chapter, our focus shifts to the principles proper to Christian morality. These presuppose and build on the common principles of morality, but what they add can be known only with the light of faith. (Some principles already treated, especially in the chapters on sin, can also be known only by faith.)

The first moral principle refers to integral human fulfillment (see 7-F). As far as experience indicates, integral human fulfillment—a perfect human community with all of its members flourishing in all the human goods—is only an ideal. But faith teaches that this ideal is realizable and, indeed, that it is being realized as part of God's larger plan for his creation.

Men and women who strive to do God's will reach heaven. Heaven is a perfect community of divine and created persons, freely living in fellowship. Heaven will include not only superhuman goods but also rich fulfillment in human goods. The risen Lord Jesus is the key reality around whom God is building the heavenly community; only in Jesus can all creation, including humankind, come to fulfillment.

Thus, integral human fulfillment is fulfillment in Jesus. The hope for this fulfillment cannot help but affect the entire lives of those animated by it. Herein lies the ultimate significance of realizing human goods and of the first principle of morality which guides choices toward these goods. Here, too, we find the full meaning of an upright life: Jesus "fully reveals man to man himself and makes his supreme calling clear" (GS 22; cf. GS 24). This calling is to live in unity with Jesus and to work to bring others into community with him. Thus, the fulfillment of all things in Christ—and our personal part in it—is a basic principle of Christian morality.

Other proper principles of specifically Christian morality will be discussed in subsequent chapters. All, however, are either included in the complex reality treated in this chapter or can be understood only by reference to it. The present chapter thus provides a foundation for the remainder of this volume.[1]

Question A: What is the relationship between human fulfillment and God's purpose in creating?

1. Vatican I definitively teaches that the world is created for the glory of God (see DS 3025/1805).[2] The glory of God primarily is his very divinity and perfection. But his intrinsic glory as supreme being is manifested outwardly, like the light that streams from the sun (see Is 60.1–3; Rv 21.23). It is realized in the minds of intelligent creatures, who recognize what God is and does, and appreciate and praise him (see Eph 1.11–14).[3]

2. But God does not create to acquire praise and honor for himself; he does not use us for his fulfillment. While Vatican I is anxious to exclude the idea that human happiness is the be-all and end-all of creation—which would make God a mere servant of the fulfillment of creatures—it also holds that God creates "to manifest his perfection through the goods which he makes creatures share in, not to increase his happiness nor to acquire anything" (DS 3002/1783; translation supplied). To suppose God gains anything at all by creating us would be to suppose God needs us, in which case he would not be God.

3. God depends on nothing else, and his actions must be understood as motivated ultimately by his love of his own, fully actual goodness. However, God also knows that his goodness can be manifested, expressed, communicated, and shared with creatures. His free choice to create the universe, including ourselves, is thus an act of pure generosity.

4. Plainly, the whole universe is the greatest created good, because it is the fullest created expression of God's goodness. Human fulfillment is only a part of this whole and, as such, not ultimate. But it does not follow that God uses us for an ulterior purpose; rather, we and our fulfillment are important parts of the self-expression God intends in creating (see *S.t.*, 1, q. 44, a. 4; q. 47, a. 1; q. 65, a. 2; *S.c.g.*, 3, 20–22).

5. **In sum, the purpose of the whole of creation is divine goodness, considered insofar as it can be expressed in creation. Our fulfillment is to be like God, to manifest his goodness in our being and actions. We are called to live for God's glory, not merely our own happiness. This is not because God is using us, but because our happiness is only part of that larger expression of God's goodness which is the whole of creation.**

6. Therefore, rather than being alternative purposes, God's glory and human fulfillment are inseparably joined. Whatever takes away from human dignity takes away from God's glory, because it takes away from the expression of his goodness (see *S.c.g.*, 3, 69).

God, perfect in himself, creates all things not to acquire anything, but solely to express his goodness (see *S.t.*, 1, q. 19, aa. 2–3; q. 20, aa. 1–2; q. 44, a. 4; *S.c.g.*, 1, 74, 83). God creates by a completely free decision, cares for and blesses all things he makes, preserves them in being, and orders them with gentleness (see DS 3001–3/1782–84). Reflecting upon God's power, the book of Wisdom finds in it the ground of his mercy and willingness to forgive. God's mercy is absolutely universal:

> For you love all things that exist,
> and have loathing for none of the things which you have made,

for you would not have made
anything if you had hated it.
How would anything have endured
if you had not willed it?
Or how would anything not called
forth by you have been preserved? (Wis 11.24–25)

The wonder of creation—the coming forth of things from God by his simple word—leads us to marvel at God's power: We believe in God, the Father almighty, creator of heaven and earth. But the total gratuity of the creative act, God's utter freedom in choosing to create, his generosity in blessing his creatures, his constant care for all things—all these make it clear that creation is the work and expression of God's love.

This is an important matter, which deeply affects our attitude toward God and shapes the spirit in which we live our lives for his glory. If we have any sense of being used, we will be resentful. Only if we correctly understand what it means to say the world is made for God's glory will we realize that in acting for the glory of God we are freely cooperating, by works which are themselves his gifts, in receiving from God a share in his own perfection. And only if we realize this truth will we feel toward God the wonder and gratitude we ought to feel, and so be able to live with the dedication and joy of true followers of Jesus.

Question B: How is the fullness of the Lord Jesus related to God's purpose in creating?

1. The revelation of the mystery of the fullness of Jesus clarifies how God is actually bringing about the communication of his goodness which is his purpose in creating: the plan "to unite all things in him [Christ], things in heaven and things on earth" (Eph 1.10). **God's glory, the self-manifestation which he wills, is not merely comprised of many different creatures; the whole has unity, the unity of the Lord Jesus. All else will find its proper place in Jesus' fullness.**[4] Since he is both God and man, the fulfillment of all things in him unites God's uncreated perfection with his created glory. The remainder of this question considers the complex reality of the fulfillment of everything in Jesus from several points of view.

In the Old Testament it is frequently said that God fills the earth, Jerusalem, and the temple. Without becoming mixed with his creation, God's glory, name, and presence fill and fulfill his creatures. With the Incarnation, God is present in a new way: "For in him [Christ] the whole fulness of deity dwells bodily" (Col 2.9). Jesus holds the first place in God's plan (see Col 1.15–20). Because he is both God and man, the Lord Jesus can integrate all of reality (see AG 3).

2. The good which God communicates in Jesus is himself. Insofar as he is God, Jesus unites his fellow human beings with the Father: "The glory which you have given me I have given to them, that they may be one even as we are one, I in them and you in me, that they may become perfectly one" (Jn 17.22–23; cf. *S.t.*, 1, q. 43, aa. 1–3, 6). Insofar as he is man, Jesus achieves his human fulfillment by living a perfect human life in which God's goodness is manifested in a unique way: "I glorified you on earth, having accomplished the work which you gave me to do" (Jn 17.4). God crowns Jesus' holy life with its creaturely fulfillment by raising Jesus from the dead (see 1 Cor 15.20–28; Heb 4.5–10).

3. Insofar as he is God, Jesus communicates to us a share in his divine fullness (see Jn 1.16). Insofar as he is man, he is "the first-born of all creation" (Col 1.15) and is completed by creation united under his headship (see Eph 1.9–10, 22–23; LG 7).[5] The whole reality of creator and creation thus comes to harmonious unity in the Lord Jesus; absolute fullness resides in him: "It pleased God to make absolute fullness reside in him and, by means of him, to reconcile everything in his person, both on earth and in the heavens making peace through the blood of his cross" (Col 1.19–20; NAB).[6]

4. Those who love God find their own fulfillment in the fellowship of everlasting life in Jesus. Everlasting life includes both a share in his divinity and in the creaturely fulfillment of his resurrection. Everlasting life is the ultimate end of human persons. Christians share by baptism in Jesus' divinity and by the Eucharist in his resurrection life. Hence, although the everlasting life of Christians will be perfected later, they begin to attain their ultimate end even now (see Jn 1.12–13; 3.5; 6.47, 54; Rom 8.14–19; Eph 2.6–7; Col 1.9–23; 3.1–4; 1 Jn 3.1–2).[7]

5. Jesus' fullness extends through the blessed to all things: "For all things are yours . . . and you are Christ's; and Christ is God's" (1 Cor 3.21, 23). Christ's fullness extends not only to humankind but also to the rest of creation. Because the world is "intimately related to man and achieves its purpose through him" (LG 48), it will share in human fulfillment, for which it now waits (see Rom 8.19; cf. *S.t.*, sup., q. 91, a. 1).

6. The fullness of deity present in Jesus will be communicated, "that God may be everything to every one" (1 Cor 15.28). **Yet, contrary to a pantheist conception, the created reality of human beings and other creatures will not be swallowed up in God.** Creatures will remain creatures. Created persons sharing in Jesus' fullness will know their creator, not be absorbed by him (see 1 Cor 13.12). The heaven in which they will find fulfillment is a city, that is, a fellowship (see Heb 12.22–24).

Jesus entered the heavenly sanctuary, not with the blood of an animal sacrifice, "but his own blood, thus securing an eternal redemption" (Heb 9.12). By Jesus' resurrection, the kingdom of God—the communion of truth and life, of justice, love, and peace—is established. Admission is free for the asking; one need only accept it as a child accepts a gift (see Mk 10.15; Lk 18.17). The only thing necessary is communion with Jesus (see Lk 10.38–42). The power to become children of God and to share in the fullness of life present in Jesus is given to believers in him (see Jn 1.10–16). "He who believes has eternal life" (Jn 6.47).

Question C: How can human persons be united with Jesus in order to find fulfillment in him?

1. The intimate communion with creation which God initiated in Jesus transcends his relationship with the people of the old covenant: "From his [Jesus'] fulness have we all received, grace upon grace. For the law was given through Moses; grace and truth came through Jesus Christ" (Jn 1.16–17). Jesus pours out his fullness to the Church (see Eph 1.22–23; LG 7), and so in the Church we share

in the fullness of Christ (see Col 2.9–13; *S.t.*, 3, q. 8, a. 1; q. 69, a. 5). Human members of God's family, the Church, are joined with Jesus in three distinct ways.

2. First, the fullness of deity which resides in Jesus in bodily form is communicated to members of the Church by the Holy Spirit. Those who believe in Jesus are begotten by God (see Jn 1.12–17), and this begetting is very real: God gives his gifts that we might be "partakers of the divine nature" (2 Pt 1.4); the word of God, which gives rebirth, is divine semen (see 1 Pt 1.23); the Christian is a child of God, truly of God's stock (see 1 Jn 2.29–3.1; 3.9). **The new People of God enjoy familial intimacy with the Father because through Jesus and in his Spirit we receive the right to commune in divine life, "to become children of God"** (Jn 1.12; cf. *S.t.*, 3, q. 8, a. 3; q. 23, aa. 1–2).

3. **There is a second profoundly mysterious aspect of the unity between the Lord Jesus and human persons joined with him in the Church: bodily union.** The bodies of Christians are members of Jesus (see 1 Cor 6.15). This bond is sacramental but no less physically real on that account (see *S.t.*, 3, q. 8, a. 2; q. 56, a. 1; sup., q. 76, a. 1).

4. **A third aspect of the unity between the Lord Jesus and human persons joined with him in the Church is community in human acts.** Jesus revealed God's kingdom by human words and deeds and sought acceptance in faith; on our part, faith requires human acts which are obedient and cooperative (see DV 4–5). Although the gift of the Spirit is distinct from and far transcends the human acts by which we respond to Jesus in faith, our response is nevertheless the condition for receiving the higher unity with Jesus in divine life (see Jn 20.31; *S.t.*, 1–2, q. 108, aa. 1–2).

5. Created persons who make up the Church are fulfilled, not absorbed, by their threefold union with our Lord Jesus (see GS 11, 21–22). In him we are to become one perfect man (see Eph 4.11–13), able to commune with God without ceasing to be the distinct human persons we are. Thus God's purpose in creating is achieved: His perfection is manifested in humankind fulfilled, which realizes the glory of God.[8]

Vatican II speaks often of the Church as the "People of God" (see LG 9–17). This expression, rooted in the Old Testament in which Israel is God's chosen people, can be helpful, but it also suggests the limitation of intimate communion before the fullness of God's revelation in our Lord Jesus. Another expression, which the Council also uses, is more suggestive of intimacy: "family of God." The supreme exemplar of the unity of the Church is the divine family, the Trinity (see UR 2). Priests "gather God's family together as a brotherhood of living unity, and lead it through Christ and in the Spirit to God the Father" (PO 6). In Jesus the human family is called to be the family of God (see GS 32, 40, and 92). The unity of the family of God's children strengthens and perfects the unity of the human family (see GS 40, 42, and 43).

Because human persons are not naturally children of God, it requires a second birth of the Holy Spirit for them to become so (see Jn 3.3–8). Without at all lessening the realism of the relationship, this rebirth can be considered adoptive incorporation into the divine family; by it we share the image of the eternal Son, and he becomes the firstborn of many brothers (see Rom 8.14–15, 29). God's adopted children share in his Spirit, whose presence is a pledge of all the divine good to which they are heirs (see Rom 8.14–17; Gal 4.6–7; Eph 1.13–14).

Question D: What is the perfection of our sharing in the divine life of Jesus?

1. After death we shall begin to exercise our status as members of the divine family in a new way. This life is a pilgrimage and death a homecoming to the Father's house, a house which Jesus prepared for his followers (see Jn 14.2–3). The human love between Jesus and his friends causes both him and them to long for this reunion (see Jn 16.20–22; Phil 1.23).

2. **By being with Jesus, his friends will share in a mature way in the divine life which naturally belongs to the Word of God:** "Beloved, we are God's children now; it does not yet appear what we shall be, but we know that when he appears we shall be like him, for we shall see him as he is" (1 Jn 3.2). St. Paul parallels this statement, emphasizing the difference between present immaturity and heavenly maturity: "When I was a child, I spoke like a child, I thought like a child, I reasoned like a child; when I became a man, I gave up childish ways. For now we see in a mirror dimly, but then face to face. Now I know in part; then I shall understand fully, even as I have been fully understood" (1 Cor 13.11–12). God's human children will then be grown-up members of his family.

3. In 1336 Pope Benedict XII defined that this heavenly knowledge of God will be intuitive and face-to-face vision, without the mediation of any creature. **The divine essence, God himself, will show himself openly and clearly.** The blessed will take great joy in this experience of God; by it they will possess eternal life and peace (see DS 1000/530; cf. *S.t.*, 1, q. 12, aa. 1–7; *S.c.g.*, 3, 25–63).

4. Sometimes this doctrine of the beatific vision is understood in a way which would make our sharing in divine life a limited sort of activity, appealing perhaps to intellectuals but not to many others. Heaven is thought of as consisting in an endless gazing upon the divine essence, an individual and ecstatic act of contemplating a magnificent object.

This conception of vision is impoverished by a Neoplatonic theory of the ultimate principles of reality, and by the assumption that the human intellect as such will be perfected by grasping these principles.[9] In other words, it assumes that human fulfillment is in the exercise of one human capacity, and this limitation precludes a richer intimacy with God. But since God is the source of everything beautiful, delightful, and satisfying, a human experience of him in himself will fulfill every good desire and more (see *S.t.*, 1–2, q. 4; *S.c.g.*, 3, 63; but cf. *S.t.*, 1, q. 62, a. 9; 1–2, q. 3, a. 8; 2–2, q. 181, a. 4). Nor need such an experience be purely static and passive, for God's life is not simply the being of an intelligible object.

5. Scripture offers a far richer prospect of heaven than this. **Perhaps most important, it insists upon the mysteriousness of the vision of God.** "It does not yet appear what we shall be" (1 Jn 3.2); it is "what no eye has seen, nor ear heard, nor the heart of man conceived" (1 Cor 2.9). In this life we live in the Church's womb, as it were, no more able to fathom heavenly experience than an embryo is to anticipate mature human relationships.

6. It is significant, too, that in Scripture "see" and "know" usually have a richer connotation of total personal experience than in everyday speech or in expressing a narrow concept of the beatific vision.[10] In John, "to see" often means to experience or to participate in (see Jn 3.3, 36; 8.51). Eternal life, even here and now, consists in knowing God and Jesus Christ (see Jn 17.3).[11]

7. Nor does Scripture express heavenly intimacy with God in cognitional terms alone. Jesus went to his Father's house to prepare a dwelling for his followers (see Jn 14.2–3). God's family on pilgrimage is traveling home and will live there at peace in the family dwelling (see Heb 4.10–11; 11.13–16). God's family will enjoy a refreshing sabbath (see Rv 14.13), but this need not be thought of as inactivity. Rather, it will be like a vacation after labor. The family reunion will be a fulfilling living-together (see Rv 21.3–4).

The desire to "see" God is not peculiar to the New Testament (see Ex 33.18–23); in the Old Testament context, one can hardly suppose that the experience sought was an exclusively intellectual vision. "Know" often is used to mean experience (see Ez 25.14). A husband knows his wife in having sexual intercourse with her (see Gn 4.1, 17, 25). To know God often means to recognize his status and authority, to adhere to him (see Jer 31.34; Hos 4.1–2). Similarly, for God to know someone is for him to establish a special relationship with that person (see Jer 1.5).

Beatific knowledge of God cannot be restricted by our experience of the limits of our human capacities. The beatific vision is a sharing in the intimacy of the Trinity (see Mt 11.25–27; Lk 10.22; Jn 10.14–15). This knowing will involve likeness to God; it is God's own knowing shared by his adopted children (see 1 Cor 13.11–12; 1 Jn 3.2). To enjoy this intimate, active communing with God, one must share in his own nature.[12] How, then, can we be on the right track if we think of the beatific vision as the exercise of capacities which belong to human nature? To the extent that the measure of this beatific knowing is God's own knowing, we do not know what it is in itself, since concepts drawn from anything else do not yield understanding of God in himself.

To suppose that the beatific vision is properly a fruit of the divine nature in which created persons are made to share is not to exclude from eternal life an appropriate and fulfilling exercise of human capacities. As God, our Lord Jesus certainly lived his divine life fully throughout his earthly life. Yet the Church teaches that during Jesus' earthly life his human soul also enjoyed the knowledge the blessed will enjoy in heaven (see DS 3645/2183, 3812/2289). If we think of the beatific vision essentially as an exercise of human capacities, it becomes difficult to understand how Jesus lived the human life he did.[13]

Question E: What is the perfection of our bodily union with Jesus?

1. The fulfillment of human persons united with Jesus is not limited to mature sharing in divine life. Their union with him in bodily life and in human action will also be perfected. In this way the created humanity of the divine Word becomes the medium for the salvation of the humankind whose fulfillment was blocked by sin.

2. **The perfection of our bodily union with Jesus will be sharing in his resurrection life.** St. Paul insists on the close relationship between Jesus' resurrection and the resurrection of those who live and die in him. The Father

"who raised the Lord Jesus will raise us also with Jesus and bring us with you into his presence" (2 Cor 4.14). That Christians will rise to share in the glorified life of Jesus follows from their present relationship to him (see 1 Thes 4.13–17). "If we have died with him [Jesus], we shall also live with him" (2 Tm 2.11). He is the first fruits in a heavenly harvest of life (see 1 Cor 15.20–23).[14]

3. Because the bodily relationship between the Christian and Jesus is so real, the New Testament sometimes regards the Christian's resurrection as having already taken place (see Eph 2.5–6; Col 3.1–4). The baptized are one flesh with the risen Lord, and they somehow share in his accomplished resurrection. Perhaps we have some inkling of this in the situation whereby humankind as a whole visited the moon when two astronauts did; but the unity of Christians with Jesus is greater, and so our present participation in resurrection far transcends a merely vicarious sharing or any form of projection or transference.

4. St. Paul, in the richest synthesis of his teaching on the resurrection, makes it clear that the new risen life, though different from and better than our present life, will be really bodily and not merely ghostly (see 1 Cor 15.12–56).[15] Persons now and persons then will have two things in common: that they are bodily and that they are not dead (see *S.t.*, sup., q. 79, aa. 1–2; *S.c.g.*, 4, 79–89). Paul's doctrine of the resurrection did not receive an enthusiastic reception, since it seemed foolish to those Greek thinkers who considered the body as at best a mere vehicle for the soul and at worst an obstacle to spiritual fulfillment (see Acts 17.31–32; 1 Cor 1.18–25). The doctrine still encounters difficulties with people who share this dualistic view of the human person.[16]

5. Resurrection life will also be different, in ways we do not positively understand, from the mortal life of human bodies in this world. The bodies of the blessed will be glorious, immortal, and spiritual—that is, heavenly and suited to persons who share in divine life.[17]

Jesus promises resurrection to those who share in the Eucharist (see Jn 6.54–57). But the resurrection includes all humankind, not only those living in Jesus (see Acts 24.15). The creeds make the doctrine of general resurrection very clear, and the Church is at pains to exclude any doubt about whether it is a realistic renewal of individual life in one's own body (see DS 76/40, 684/347, 801/429, 854/464). As St. Thomas Aquinas points out, even if one's soul were to enjoy salvation in another life, still such a disembodied existence would hardly amount to the salvation of a human person, for the human person is bodily. The soul is only a part of the bodily person: "My soul is not I" (see *S.t.*, 1, q. 75, a. 4; 1–2, q. 4, aa. 5–6).[18]

The New Testament's teaching on resurrection and marriage (see Mk 12.18–27) makes it clear that resurrection will occur, and that future life will not be merely a continuation of present life. Since God will transform the conditions of life, people will be immortal; generation will no longer be appropriate. In commenting on the New Testament's teaching on the resurrection of the body and marriage, John Paul II makes it clear that the resurrection perfects the person. The spiritualization of the person in the resurrection will eliminate all inner conflict; this "does not, however, signify any 'disincarnation' of the body, nor, consequently, a 'dehumanization' of man." What is involved is not a victory of spirit over body, but a perfect participation by what is physical in the person in what is spiritual. This spiritualization will be the fruit of the divinization of the whole person, "of the communication of God, in his very divinity, not only to man's soul, but to his whole psychosomatic subjectivity."[19]

Question F: What is the perfection of our cooperation with the human acts of Jesus?

1. We shall see in chapters twenty-two and twenty-three how one cooperates with the human acts of Jesus in living out one's fundamental option of faith in this life. However, this aspect of a Christian's unity with Jesus—namely, fellowship in human acts and human goods—is also to be perfected in heaven. **Christians have very often overlooked the place which properly human goods and actions have in heavenly fulfillment.**

2. Jesus speaks in parable of heaven as a wedding feast (see Mt 22.1–14; 25.1–13). This figure is beautifully developed in the last, visionary book of the New Testament (see Rv 19.7–9). The blessed in God's presence are also envisaged as sharing in an endless liturgy (see Rv 7.15). The Last Supper is clearly carried out in anticipation of the heavenly banquet: "I tell you I shall not drink again of this fruit of the vine until that day when I drink it new with you in my Father's kingdom" (Mt 26.29; cf. Mk 14.25; Lk 22.15–18).

3. Plainly, to conceive of heavenly fellowship as an endless wedding banquet calls attention to fulfillment in human goods. At a banquet bodily life is enriched by plentiful food and drink, while a wedding feast especially celebrates the vigor of life and its renewal. Music and dance, joyous performances done without a sense of burdensome effort, express play and skill. Practical business is set aside; the play of the mind and sheer communication are celebrated in conversation. Tensions are banished, and the companionship is warm. The hosts mingle with the guests; the home is open for hospitality. As St. Augustine says: "How great will be that happiness, where there will be no evil, where no good will remain hidden, where there will be leisure for the praises of God, who shall be all in all!" (FEF 1788).

4. Sin is excluded from human life in heaven, and with its exclusion every existential evil is likewise excluded: "Behold, the dwelling of God is with men. He will dwell with them, and they shall be his people, and God himself will be with them; he will wipe away every tear from their eyes, and death shall be no more, neither shall there be mourning nor crying nor pain any more, for the former things have passed away" (Rv 21.3–4). War will be at an end (see Is 2.4), and God's children will find comfort in his everlasting arms (see Is 66.11–14).

5. As was explained (in 2-E), choices are spiritual entities which last. Although Jesus offers his body once for all on Calvary, his sacrificial act of obedience and mediation lasts forever (see Heb 7.25–28; 10.11–14). Mary becomes the mother of God by her assent to the divine proposal presented to her by the angel, but her assent does not cease; it is now the principle of her maternal relationship to all who are united with Jesus (see LG 63). Similarly, by the human acts which they do now, in cooperation with the grace of the Spirit, Christians constitute themselves in communion with the redemptive act of Jesus.

6. **As was explained** (in 18-I), **the act of a person who dies in mortal sin is never left behind. Similarly, the works of those who die in the Lord accompany them** (see Rv 14.13). The brilliant white dress of finest linen worn by the Lamb's Bride at their wedding "is the righteous deeds of the saints" (Rv 19.8; cf. 1 Cor 3.14; GS 39).

7. Little attention was paid before Vatican II to the fact that human acts last in heaven and that the blessed are fulfilled in their properly human goods. But the Council teaches that, even though "earthly progress must be carefully distinguished from the growth of Christ's kingdom," still, "to the extent that the former can contribute to the better ordering of human society, it is of vital concern to the kingdom of God":

> For after we have obeyed the Lord, and in his Spirit nurtured on earth the values of human dignity, brotherhood and freedom, and indeed all the good fruits of our nature and enterprise, we will find them again, but freed of stain, burnished and transfigured. This will be so when Christ hands over to the Father a kingdom eternal and universal: "a kingdom of truth and life, of holiness and grace, of justice, love, and peace" [*Preface of the Feast of Christ the King*]. On this earth that kingdom is already present in mystery. When the Lord returns, it will be brought into full flower. (GS 39)

In short, the Council teaches that heaven and earth are not entirely separated; the kingdom is here, though invisible, and present human acts become part of it. When the Lord returns, the moral lives Christians live in communion with his redemptive act will be completed by rich fulfillment in all the human goods: The holy will be happy.

Question G: How does the human contribution to the fullness of Jesus constitute a gift to God?

1. We saw in question A that God creates for his own glory, but not as if by creating he acquired something for himself. Creatures cannot give God anything not already his; it is impossible to enrich him from whom all goods come (see Acts 17.25; Jas 1.17). Still, human goods can in some sense be shared with the divine persons, so that the communal life of heaven involves a certain mutuality. The possibility of this sharing can be understood by considering the idea of sacrifice.

2. Sacrifice is central to all religion. The very notion of sacrifice involves a gift offered to God (see *S.t.*, 2–2, q. 85, a. 3, ad 2; 3, q. 48, a. 3).[20] To the one who offers sacrifice it is important that God accept the gift. While the Old Testament sets forth an elaborate ritual of sacrifice, the prophets criticized allowing mere ritual to displace love, faithfulness, and good works (see Jer 7.21–23; Hos 6.6). By contrast, willing obedience and a contrite spirit are gifts which God will not reject (see Ps 40.7–9; 51.19).

3. In forming the new covenant, Jesus, by virtue of his obedience, "gave himself up for us, a fragrant offering and sacrifice to God" (Eph 5.2). In particular, the concept of sacrifice is implicit in Jesus' institution of the Eucharist,

and the Church definitively teaches that in the Mass a real sacrifice is offered to God (see DS 1751/948). But, as the very prayers of the rite make clear, Catholics who participate in the Mass offer Jesus' sacrifice with him, joining with it the offering of their own lives (see SC 48). Furthermore, the theme of praise and thanks runs throughout the Bible and Christian liturgy; these are due to God for his goodness and greatness, and they are true gifts to him. Indeed, Christian life itself is a living, spiritual sacrifice (see Rom 12.1; 1 Pt 2.5). Thus, human goods, immanent in a Christian life, can be given to God.

4. **From one point of view, giving human goods to God can be understood as putting them at the service of all that God intends in creating.** Obedient service fulfills the Father's providential plan, builds up Jesus' body toward ultimate fulfillment, and cooperates with the Holy Spirit's sanctifying work. The lives of Christians contribute to the fulfillment of the mission the Father gave Jesus, and in the accomplishment of this mission, he "delivers the kingdom to God the Father" (1 Cor 15.24); not that Jesus' reign will end (see 2 Pt 1.11; and the *Credo*, DS 150/86), but that his mission will in all respects be complete.

5. **From another, deeper point of view, we must believe that, when we wish to do God's will and please him, our efforts are received by him with satisfaction, and we somehow return good to the Lord for the good he has given us.** According to St. John of the Cross, the bride and the Bridegroom—the soul and the Son of God—show each other their riches "in order to celebrate the feast of this espousal, and they mutually communicate their goods and delights with a wine of savory love in the Holy Spirit."[21]

While it is wrong to suppose that God needs anything or that we can in any way enrich him, it is also wrong to imagine that God cannot be given anything by us, if this supposition is based upon characteristics which make human beings unreceptive to gifts. Whatever the assumed characteristics might be, they cannot be attributed to God in the same sense as to anyone else. For example, God is not like the person who has everything, for whom it is impossible to find a suitable present. Nor is he like the person who is so important that any gift we offer will never reach him.

The situation of the child who gives to a parent, while only an analogy, throws some light on this matter. The child has nothing of its own. But a child can take something which its parents allow it to use and bring this as an offering. The child's gift somehow expresses what is the child's own: a loving and obedient heart. In sharing human goods with the divine persons, we give them what is theirs with a heart which also belongs to them and with love they first give us. Nevertheless, the free giving itself is truly ours; we can withhold it, and our choice not to withhold this gift pleases our heavenly Father.

Question H: How is the task of Christian life related to the fullness of Jesus?

1. The human fulfillment already accomplished in Jesus and in him begun for all creation must be completed in our lives. Jesus already reigns in heaven (see Eph 1.20–22; Phil 2.9–11). From there he sends his Spirit (see Jn 15.26–27; Acts 2.33) and continually builds up the Church (see Eph 4.11–13). Vatican II passes smoothly from fulfillment already accomplished in Christ to fulfillment yet to be

realized by our carrying out our own task in this world: ". . . the promised restoration which we are awaiting has already begun in Christ, is carried forward in the mission of the Holy Spirit, and through him continues in the Church. There we learn through faith the meaning, too, of our temporal life, as we perform, with hope of good things to come, the task committed to us in this world by the Father, and work out our salvation (cf. Phil 2.12)" (LG 48).

2. **Though already justified, we still must work out our salvation. God's kingdom, already present on earth in a hidden way, must be the central concern of Christians. By doing God's will on earth, Christians not only contribute in an important way to earthly progress but also to the growth of the kingdom.**

3. One can begin to see why this is so by considering the Incarnation. The Incarnation itself initiated the time of fulfillment. When sin spoiled the original goodness of humankind, the personal relationship between the divine persons and the human family with which they wish to share their life was interrupted. The Incarnation of the Word is a bridge by which God spans the troubled waters of this disrupted relationship. From this point of view, Christian fulfillment was already present at the very beginning of Jesus' life: "Jesus came into Galilee, preaching the gospel of God, and saying, 'The time is fulfilled, and the kingdom of God is at hand'" (Mk 1.14–15; cf. Lk 11.20).

4. Sin affected the whole of humankind and the human world; except for Jesus and Mary, it pervaded every dimension of each human being. Both the human as a whole and each individual are complex realities, composed of many elements more or less incompletely united with one another. Hence, while redemption is fully present in the risen Lord Jesus, divine truth and life have still to reach from him to all people at all times and places (see Mt 28.19–20). God's kingdom is like leaven or a mustard seed; only gradually does it come to its fullness (see Mt 13.31–33). The work of saving humankind begins with the preaching of the gospel—something to be done at all places and times (see AG 8–9)—but only little by little does the gospel permeate a culture and draw back the human from alienation to fulfillment. Thus, the restoration of all things to God in Jesus is a gradual, incremental process.

5. Like humankind as a whole, each human being exhibits a similar multiplicity, alienation, division, and conflict (see GS 13). However, God's love is poured forth in the heart of any person who does not refuse the gift of the Spirit. When this happens, the act of living faith exists in what had been a sinful human mind and will, and, just to this extent, the person is redeemed—justification is an accomplished fact: accomplished, of course, by God's gift, not by the merit of the one who receives it.

6. Yet even a heart animated by living faith and so justified nevertheless remains largely unsanctified. We can still choose without reference to living faith, and so we still face the task of integrating our choices with faith by our personal vocational commitments. An electric company generates power in a powerhouse and transmits it to us by wires, but nothing happens unless we plug into the system; the Holy Spirit generates holiness in Jesus and communicates his holiness

to us by the sacraments of the Church, but nothing happens unless we do our other actions in continuity with our acts of receiving the sacraments.

7. **It is thus the task of a Christian life to integrate everything which has yet to be saved with the redemption which has already been accomplished. In this way one comes to fulfillment in Jesus, while contributing one's life to his fullness** (see *S.t.*, 3, q. 69, a. 5).

8. Christians cannot ignore the significance of their lives in this world. Although we cannot see the kingdom, except by the eye of faith, it is already here. The new creation, in which fulfillment already is realized in the risen Lord Jesus, and this world, in which it remains to be realized through human acts, are not altogether separate.[22]

9. The remainder of this volume will examine in detail the principles of this specifically Christian way of life. First we shall consider the relationship which God establishes with humankind by revelation; then we shall see how Jesus' human life is the principle of Christian life. On this foundation we shall consider the make up of the Christian, the specific norms of Christian morality, and the sacraments as organizing principles of Christian life.

Jesus will come again in glory to judge the living and the dead (see DS 150/86). This judgment will be part of a cosmic transformation whose outcome will be the ultimate, lasting situation which God planned from the very beginning (see Eph 1.9–10). The coming judgment will apply to everyone and to all that everyone has done (see 2 Cor 5.10). Judgment will be according to the quality of one's works (see Rom 2.5–11). Nothing will remain obscure; everything will come to light (see 1 Cor 4.4–5).

This judgment will involve no uncertain estimation and no arbitrary sentence. Rather, it will discriminate on the basis of performance with impartial objectivity. The wicked ". . . will answer, 'Lord, when did we see you hungry or thirsty or a stranger or naked or sick or in prison, and did not minister to you?' Then he will answer them, 'Truly, I say to you, as you did it not to one of the least of these, you did it not to me.' And they will go away into eternal punishment, but the righteous into eternal life" (Mt 25.44–46). What Christians are doing now not only will affect their own eternal fulfillment; it also, in a mysterious way, even now affects our Lord Jesus. The establishment of God's kingdom on earth thus will be a revelation of something which already exists (see Col 1.13; LG 5, 9).

Summary

At this point we turn to the principles proper to Christian morality. These presuppose and build on the principles of common human morality, treated up to now, but what they add can only be known with the light of faith. The first moral principle refers to integral human fulfillment; but integral human fulfillment, as we shall see, is fulfillment in Jesus.

Vatican I definitively teaches that the world is created for the glory of God. This does not mean God exploits us for his own fulfillment, for that would mean he somehow needed us. Rather, God's free choice to create is an act of pure generosity. He creates us, as the Council says, "to manifest his perfection through the benefits he bestows on creatures." We are fulfilled in manifesting his goodness in our being and actions.

God's self-manifestation in creation has unity, the unity of the Lord Jesus: Creatures will find their proper place in Jesus' fullness. But there is also a certain reciprocity here. Insofar as he is man, Jesus is completed by creation united under his headship. Despite this mysterious unity, however, creatures sharing in Jesus' fullness will not ultimately be absorbed in God, as pantheism would have it; heavenly fulfillment is instead to be understood as a fellowship.

The members of the Church are joined with Jesus in three distinct ways. First, the fullness of deity present in Jesus is communicated to members of the Church by the Holy Spirit—we become children of God. Second, there is real bodily union—a profoundly mysterious reality clearly taught in the New Testament. Third, we are united by human acts—by the redemptive act of Jesus and by our response of faith and the life of faith. Each of these three modes of union with Jesus is a present fact which, however, has yet to be perfected.

Our sharing in the divine life of Jesus will reach perfection in heaven, in the beatific vision. This ought not to be understood as a purely intellectual experience, an individual act of contemplation. Scripture offers a far richer prospect, suggesting total personal experience in community with others.

Our union with Jesus in bodily life will also be perfected in heaven. St. Paul makes it clear that the new, risen life will be truly bodily, though also different from the mortal life of human bodies in this world, inasmuch as the bodies of the blessed will be suited to persons who share in divine life.

Similarly, our union with Jesus in human acts will be perfected in heaven. Jesus' metaphor of heaven as a wedding feast underlines the aspect of fulfillment in human goods. As we have seen, human acts are spiritual entities which last; cooperating with the grace of the Holy Spirit, Christians constitute themselves now by human acts in communion with the redemptive act of Jesus. Vatican II teaches that the kingdom, though invisible, "is already present in mystery" in this world, and our human acts become part of it.

Although creatures cannot give God anything he does not already possess, there is a sense in which human goods can be shared with the divine persons. Giving human goods to God can be understood as putting them at the service of God's intention in creating; the lives of Christians contribute their part to accomplishing the mission which the Father gave Jesus. Moreover, we must believe that when we seek to do God's will and please him, he receives our efforts with satisfaction—somehow we return him good for the good he has given us.

Thus, the task of Christian life is this: to complete in our lives the human fulfillment already accomplished in Jesus and in him begun for all creation. God's kingdom, already present on earth in a hidden way, must be the focus of service in Christian life. The Incarnation initiated the time of fulfillment, but divine life and truth must still reach from the Lord Jesus to all people at all times and places, and this is a gradual process. Much the same is true of the salvation of each individual: Justification is an accomplished fact, but there is a great deal in each of us that has yet to be sanctified by the lifelong task of integrating our choices with our commitment of faith and our personal vocational commitment. In this way one comes to fulfillment in Jesus, while contributing one's life to his fullness.

Appendix: Questions about bodily unity with Jesus and resurrection

Baptism and the gift of the Spirit forge the bodily unity of Christians with Jesus (see 1 Cor 12.12–13). The unity is in him, based upon his individual, resurrected body (see Rom 12.4–5). Real unity with the bodily death and resurrection of Jesus is brought about in baptism; this bodily unity of the Christian with the individual body of the Lord Jesus makes of the Church a physical whole (see Col 1.22; 2.12, 17; 3.1–4, 15). Maintaining this bodily communion depends upon the sacrament of the Eucharist (see Jn 6.53–57).[23]

When Jesus himself compares his relationship with his disciples to that of a vine to its branches (see Jn 15.1–8), one might suppose that this instance of organic unity is only a metaphor for the unity of the Spirit and for existential solidarity by faith and love. But St. Paul's development of the thesis that Christians are members of Jesus' body goes far beyond the metaphorical.[24] Even so, there is a tendency to take the thesis as a figure of speech, since otherwise one confronts an apparently grave difficulty: If Christians really are united with Jesus in bodily unity, how can his and their organic individuality be maintained?

Modern individualism blocks understanding here. We tend to think persons are in all respects units completely separate and isolated from one another, that each hidden self-consciousness demarcates a self-enclosed entity, which can send signals to others but never really commune (become one) with another. We assume that if there really were communing, individuality necessarily would be forfeited. In fact, this is not so. Biologically, individuals of a species share concretely in common life; their independence is relative and a matter of degree. Not individuals but only species evolve. In species which reproduce sexually, the one act of generating a new individual involves the dynamic unity of a male and female. Such real unity takes nothing away from the individuality of each male and female. They exercise other functions separately, and play distinct roles even in the sexual act.

Now, the bodily unity of Jesus with his members in the Church is not unlike this real, physiological unity. The author of Ephesians himself suggests this when he compares the unity of wife and husband with that of the Church and Jesus (see Eph 5.22–33). The one-flesh union of marriage, which is most perfectly actualized in fruitful sexual intercourse, illuminates the bodily unity of Jesus with the Church. Like husband and wife, Jesus and his members do not lose their individuality, and they play distinct roles. Because of this bodily unity, members of Jesus already share in his resurrection life (see Col 3.1–4).

The whole of the created world is related to humankind and will be involved in the fulfillment of Christians (see Rom 8.19–22). On the one hand, some passages of Scripture seem to suggest that the physical universe will be utterly destroyed (see 2 Pt 3.7–12). On the other hand, God created things good and to last (see Wis 1.14; 11.24–25). The close relationship of the cosmos with human persons suggests that the new heavens and new earth which will renew the present ones (see Rv 21.1), will have been transformed along with human bodily life. The whole cosmos is destined to share in the same sort of total renewal initiated in the resurrection of the Lord Jesus (see GS 39).[25]

Certain texts in the New Testament seem to suggest that the coming of the Lord, the resurrection, the transformation of the universe, and the final judgment would come very soon. Some of these are sayings on the lips of Jesus himself (see Mt 24.34; Mk 9.1; 13.30; Lk 21.32). Others are not (see 1 Thes 4.15–17; 1 Pt 4.7; Rv 3.11; 22.20). At the same time, Jesus is said to have stated that not even he knew the time of the end, for this knowledge was reserved to the heavenly Father (see Mt 24.36; Mk 13.32; Acts 1.7). A passage in the

Second Epistle of Peter (3.8–9) often is taken as an attempt to square the delay in the coming of Jesus with a previous common expectation that it would occur shortly. However, no one could have supposed that the project of spreading the gospel to the whole world could be carried out quickly (see Mt 24.14; Mk 13.10). Paul also suggests a long period of activity for the Church (see Rom 11.25).

This difficulty could be resolved if we took the relativity of time much more seriously than it usually is taken. Time actually is a relative measure which depends upon a definite physical system and also upon various factors within the system. Time is not an absolute precondition of all existence, uniform for all things and all conditions. With this point in mind, we might ask how the present age and the new age of the Lord Jesus can possibly be related within the same temporal scheme. In some ways, the new age already has begun— using "already" to refer to it from within our present temporal framework. In other ways, the new age will not arrive until the end of the world—again using "will not arrive" and "end" to refer from within our present temporal framework to a reality of a different order.[26]

Notes

1. This chapter mainly concerns topics usually treated in eschatology. A good, recent textbook on this area: E. J. Fortman, S.J., *Everlasting Life after Death* (New York: Alba House, 1976). Also helpful: Michael Schmaus, *Dogma*, vol. 6, *Justification and the Last Things* (Kansas City: Sheed and Ward, 1977), 151–274.

2. Two important articles by one author clarify many of the points considered in this question: Philip J. Donnelly, S.J., "St. Thomas and the Ultimate Purpose of Creation," *Theological Studies*, 2 (1941), 53–83; "The Doctrine of the Vatican Council on the End of Creation," *Theological Studies*, 4 (1943), 3–33.

3. On the concept of glory in Scripture and its place in the djvine plan for creation, see S. Aalen, "doxa," *New International Dictionary of New Testament Theology*, 2:44–48.

4. A helpful introduction to the idea of the fullness of Jesus (*pleroma Christi*): George T. Montague, S.M., *The Living Thought of Saint Paul: An Introduction to Pauline Theology* (Milwaukee: Bruce, 1966), 182–203.

5. For indications of support in the Fathers for an eschatology along the lines sketched in this question and especially for support of the present point, see Georges Florovsky, "Eschatology in the Patristic Age: An Introduction," *Greek Orthodox Theological Review*, 2 (1956), 27–40, esp. 30. For a systematic theological development of this eschatology: Bertrand de Margerie, S.J., *Christ for the World: The Heart of the Lamb: A Treatise on Christology*, trans. Malachy Carroll (Chicago: Franciscan Herald Press, 1974), esp. 238–52, 275–300 (where the idea of Church as coredeeming spouse is developed), 435–42, 486–507. Note the statement (492) that the "growth of the Church, the Body of Christ, signifies in the last analysis that Christ grows through it. Incomplete, in a sense, He grows toward His full eschatological stature . . . ."

6. The theological point made here depends upon reading Ephesians 1.23 as an affirmation that the Church somehow fulfills or completes Christ. Unfortunately, this verse is one of the most disputed in the New Testament. For a concise summary of possible interpretations and argument favorable to the one I accept: Roy Yates, "A Re-examination of Ephesians 1.23," *The Expository Times*, 83 (1972), 146–51. In classic studies, J. Armitage Robinson laid out the argument for this interpretation and invoked in its favor the authority of all but one of the ancient translations of the Bible and the comments of three Fathers (Chrysostom, Origen, and Jerome): "The Church as the Fulfilment of the Christ: A Note on Ephesians I.23," *The Expositor*, 7 (1898), 241–59; *St. Paul's Epistle to the Ephesians*, 2d ed. (London: Macmillan, 1922), 42–45, 87–89, 100–101, 152, 255–59. The most extensive commentary by a Catholic exegete contains much useful background: A. Feuillet, P.S.S., "L'Eglise plérôme du Christ d'après Ephés., I.23," *Nouvelle Revue Théologique*, 78 (1956), 449–72, 593–610; he argues convincingly that the concept of *pleroma* used by the author of Ephesians arises from the Old Testament rather than from pagan thought, but does not accept my reading of Ephesians 1.23. The most extensive commentary by a Protestant exegete: Marcus Barth, *Ephesians*, Anchor Bible, 34 and 34a (Garden City, N.Y.: Doubleday, 1974), 153–59, 192–210; cf. 440–41, 484–96. Barth recognizes the argument for the interpretation I prefer (see esp. 206, n. 324), but rejects it on theological grounds (which are countered in 23-E, below, with accompanying notes). However, an exegesis fully in

harmony with Catholic theological presuppositions (which does not hesitate to consider *pleroma* as all-inclusive community nor to think Jesus as man to be fulfilled by his members) is my chief source: Pierre Benoît, O.P., *Jesus and the Gospel*, vol. 2, trans. Benet Weatherhead (London: Darton, Longman and Todd, 1974), 51–92, esp. 84–91. Louis Bouyer, *The Church of God: Body of Christ and Temple of the Spirit*, trans. Charles Underhill Quinn (Chicago: Franciscan Herald Press, 1982), 252–57. See also George A. Maloney, S.J., *The Cosmic Christ: From Paul to Teilhard* (New York: Sheed and Ward, 1968), 26–36 and 60–68. For a theological development of Benoît's view: Yves Congar, O.P., *Jesus Christ*, trans. Luke O'Neill (New York: Herder and Herder, 1966), 131–44.

7. See Bonaventura Mariani, O.F.M., "Il Nuovo Testamento e il Fine Ultimo dell'Uomo sulla Terra," *Divinitas*, 20 (1976), 282–312. If it sounds odd to say that Christians really begin to attain their ultimate end in this life, this is because the theology of happiness formulated under Neoplatonic influence chiefly by St. Augustine overlooked or misconstrued the evidence of the New Testament on this question and located the ultimate end of human persons exclusively in the vision of God after death (see 34-A).

8. Cf. St. Irenaeus, *Against Heresies*, iv, 20, 7. For the development of the Christian understanding of the unity of the Christian with Jesus, see Emile Mersch, S.J., *The Whole Christ: The Historical Development of the Doctrine of the Mystical Body in Scripture and Tradition*, trans. John R. Kelly, S.J. (Milwaukee: Bruce, 1938); he gives a specific treatment of St. Irenaeus (227–43), and a fine summary of the synthesis of St. Cyril of Alexandria (337–58) to whose thought the theology presented here is quite close. For a detailed study of some relevant aspects of Cyril's thought, see Walter J. Burghardt, S.J., *The Image of God in Man According to Cyril of Alexandria* (Woodstock, Md.: Woodstock College Press, 1957), esp. 105–25. For the scriptural witness to the unity of the Christian with Christ, see also the valuable work of an Anglican scholar, Ernest Best, *One Body in Christ: A Study in the Relationship of the Church to Christ in the Epistles of the Apostle Paul* (London: S.P.C.K., 1955).

9. On Augustine's Neoplatonism: Robert J. O'Connell, *St. Augustine's Early Theory of Man, A.D. 386–391* (Cambridge, Mass.: Belknap Press of Harvard University Press, 1968), esp. 203–26. On the influence of this Neoplatonism on Augustine's conception of the vision of God and his understanding of nature and grace: Eugene TeSelle, "Nature and Grace in Augustine's Expositions of Genesis I, 1–5," *Recherches Augustiniennes*, 5 (1968), 95–137.

10. See Rudolf Schnackenburg, "Vision of God," *Encyclopedia of Biblical Theology*, 947–52.

11. An exegesis of 1 Jn 3.2 which utterly rejects the metaphysical interpretation of an intellectual vision of the divine essence: Matthew Vellanickal, *The Divine Sonship of Christians in the Johannine Writings*, Analecta Biblica, 72 (Rome: Biblical Institute Press, 1977), 340–47.

12. The position taken here departs from Thomism and the intellectualism common in the Western tradition. But it is close in some ways to the thinking of some of the Fathers of the East and was developed in Orthodox theology by Gregory Palamas. He distinguishes God's essence and energies, the latter not being a creature but communicated divinity; he also rejects the Western view that human capacities are made for the vision of God. See V. Lossky, *The Vision of God* (Bedfordshire, Eng.: Faith Press, 1963), 9–27 and 124–37.

13. In current theology many questions are being raised about the received teaching concerning the beatific knowledge of Jesus as man during his earthly life. An introduction to this discussion: E. L. Mascall, *Theology and the Gospel of Christ: An Essay in Reorientation* (London: SPCK, 1977), 121–94, esp. 160–69. If, as I suggest, the heavenly vision of God is not in any case an exercise of specifically human capacities, then the received teaching is preserved and the difficulties about the knowledge of Jesus dissolved.

14. See F. X. Durrwell, C.Ss.R., *The Resurrection: A Biblical Study*, trans. Rosemary Sheed (New York: Sheed and Ward, 1960), 269–90.

15. See the helpful study: Ronald J. Sider, "The Pauline Conception of the Resurrection Body in I Corinthians XV, 35–54," *New Testament Studies*, 21 (1975), 428–39. Also: Jacob Kremer, "Paul: The Resurrection of Jesus, the Cause and Exemplar of Our Resurrection," and Maurice Carrez, "With What Body Do the Dead Rise Again?" in *Immortality and Resurrection*, Concilium, 60, ed. Pierre Benoît and Roland Murphy (New York: Herder and Herder, 1970), 78–91 and 92–102.

16. An exegetical study which firmly clears away modern prejudices to recapture the realism of St. Paul's teaching on the bodily union of Christians with Jesus: John A. T. Robinson, *The Body: A Study in Pauline Theology* (Philadelphia: Westminster Press, 1952), 49–67.

17. "Spirit" here does not mean immaterial, but transformed by divine life: Durrwell, op. cit., 91–107.

18. St. Thomas Aquinas, *Super primam epistolam ad Corinthios lectura*, xv, 2: ". . . now since the

soul is part of the body of man, it is not the whole man, and my soul is not I; and so even though the soul should reach salvation in another life, still not I, nor any man."

19. John Paul II, "The Resurrection Perfects the Person: Address at the General Audience, 9 December 1981," *L'Osservatore Romano,* Eng. ed., 14 December 1981, 3.

20. See Mariasusai Dhavamony, *Phenomenology of Religion* (Rome: Gregorian University Press, 1973), 195–211; Roland de Vaux, *Ancient Israel,* vol. 2, *Religious Institutions* (New York: McGraw-Hill, 1965), 447–56. For a simple and yet profound catechesis on the concept of sacrifice in relation to the Eucharist, see Clifford Howell, S.J., *Of Sacraments and Sacrifice* (Collegeville, Minn.: Liturgical Press, 1952), 81–123.

21. St. John of the Cross, *The Spiritual Canticle,* in *The Collected Works of St. John of the Cross,* trans. Kieran Kavanaugh, O.C.D., and Otilio Rodriguez, O.C.D. (Garden City, N.Y.: Doubleday, 1964), 527.

22. The conception of the relationship between Christian life and the fulfillment of everything in Christ articulated here is in some ways similar to the vision of Pierre Teilhard de Chardin. See, for example: *The Divine Milieu* (New York: Harper and Row, 1965), 57–58, 61–62, and 121–28. There are similarities in the understanding of the problem and of St. Paul; moreover, Teilhard (and others thinking along similar lines) influenced Vatican II's documents, especially *Gaudium et Spes,* which are at the basis of the present theological reflection. Still, the conception articulated here differs from Teilhard's vision, for reasons both philosophical and theological. Philosophically, I think his metaphysics of evolution is far too ambitious; it is another example of metaphysical systematization which soars beyond both data and clear sense. Theologically, I think his theology, in trying to ensure that nature and grace are not separated and opposed (a sound effort), mistakenly tends to commingle them, thus failing to do justice to the mystery of the constitution of the Christian on the model of Jesus. This last point will be developed further in chapters twenty-four and thirty-four.

23. A development of certain aspects of this point: Gustave Martelet, S.J., *The Risen Christ and the Eucharistic World* (New York: Seabury Press, 1976), 117–79.

24. See Benoît, op. cit., 58–67.

25. See De Margerie, op. cit., 102–3, 248, and 410–22.

26. See Pierre Benoît, "Resurrection: At the End of Time or Immediately after Death?" in Benoît and Murphy, eds., op. cit., 103–14.

CHAPTER TWENTY

THE RELATIONSHIP
BETWEEN GOD AND SINFUL HUMANKIND

Introduction

The communion with God which is central to Christian life begins with his initiative of revelation, accepted by faith. Classical scholastic theology and the popular piety of former times both tended to subordinate revelation and faith to redemption. Sin loomed large in Christian consciousness, often larger than God's plan for creation's fulfillment in Jesus and humankind's participation in divine fellowship. This tendency in Latin Christianity was only accentuated in Protestant thought. More recently, the pendulum has swung the other way. The reality and extent of sin and humankind's need for redemption have been greatly downplayed.

If not pushed to its extreme, either view can be stated in an orthodox manner. Still, better than an orthodox version of either view is a balanced position which integrates both. In outline, this is not difficult to sketch. Fundamentally, God has created for his own glory, that is, to manifest his goodness. Sin and the overcoming of sin are only secondary aspects of his plan. However, Christian life must be lived in the world as it is, thoroughly conditioned by the reality of sin and the need for salvation. In this world, for us as for Jesus, glory presupposes the cross. For sinful humankind, both human fulfillment and fellowship in divine life require redemption. As matters stand, revelation is a call to repentance and faith a conversion from sin to justification.

This chapter will clarify the relationship which God initiates with humankind by revelation—the relationship into which we enter by faith. Although the relationship was antecedent to the fall of Man and so does not absolutely presuppose sin, nevertheless, given sin, God's revelation is redemptive and the response of faith begins our cooperation in redemption. Therefore, after reflecting on revelation and faith, we shall consider the need for redemption and the form redemption takes. This chapter provides a basis for the close study, in chapters twenty-one and twenty-two, of our Lord Jesus and his life. Then chapter twenty-three will begin the treatment of specifically Christian life, whose essence is the following of Jesus.

Question A: What is divine revelation?

1. **Revelation is a communication of God to humankind. By it he makes himself known as personal and invites us to share intimately in his life.**[1]

2. As Vatican I and Vatican II teach, God manifests himself in creation (see DS 3004/1785; DV 3). But neither council calls this "revelation." This manifestation, which can be grasped by the natural light of reason, scarcely provides a basis for knowing whether God is personal.[2] It is inadequate to establish a relationship of intimacy between him and us (see *S.t.*, 1–2, q. 109, a. 1; 2–2, q. 1, a. 1; q. 2, aa. 2–4).

3. Hence, as Vatican I solemnly teaches, besides manifesting himself in creation and so making some knowledge of himself accessible to humankind by natural reason, God has also chosen ". . . to reveal himself and the eternal decrees of his will to the human race in another and supernatural way, as the Apostle says: 'In times past, God spoke in fragmentary and varied ways to our fathers through the prophets; in this, the final age, he has spoken to us through his Son' (Heb 1.1–2)" (DS 3004/1785). By this revelation even certain truths naturally accessible to reason are known with certainty and without error (see *S.t.*, 1, q. 1, a. 1; *S.c.g.*, 1, 3–5). But it is not on their account that supernatural revelation is absolutely necessary. Rather, "It is necessary only because God, out of his infinite goodness, destined man to a supernatural end, that is, to a participation in the good things of God, which altogether exceed the human mental grasp; for 'eye has not seen, ear has not heard, nor has it so much as dawned on man what God has prepared for those who love him' (1 Cor 2.9)" (DS 3005/1786). Thus by supernatural revelation, especially God's revelation in the Incarnation of the Son, we come to know God, not simply as creator but also as three persons who invite us into fellowship with themselves (see *S.t.*, 1–2, q. 62; 2–2, q. 2, a. 3; q. 4, a. 7).

God freely chose to call human persons to share in his own divine life; this calling involves a special, supernatural, and personal communication by God to those he wishes to call (see DS 3004–5/1785–86). Vatican I's teaching on the necessity of revelation so that human persons might reach heaven precludes the view that what one can know by reason alone is sufficient for living a Christian life.

It is important to notice that while the words "natural" and "supernatural" are not found in Scripture as a pair, the distinction they mark is in the New Testament. It is the distinction between human begetting and divine begetting (see Jn 1.12–13), for only they can enter the kingdom who are begotten, not merely of flesh and blood, but of water and the Spirit (see Jn 3.3–8). Persons human by nature are children of God by adoption (supernature) and so are called to everlasting life (see Rom 8.14–17; Gal. 4.3–7; Eph 1.4–6; 1 Jn 3.1–2).

4. Because it is personal communication, revelation does not essentially consist in information which could be obtained in some other way (see *S.t.*, 2–2, q. 1, aa. 4–5). At the same time, although not limited to propositional truths, it includes such truths: God tells us that he is our God and we his people, that he loves us, and much more (see Jer 31.33; Hos 1.6, 9; Rv 21.3; LG 9–17). These are truths to be believed. It would be nonsense to say one has faith in God but does not believe such propositions. More than this truth and that, however, God reveals himself (see *S.t.*, 2–2, q. 1, aa. 1–2). So faith, while it includes assent to truths, is also more than that.

5. God does not depend on anything apart from himself, but revelation does: There would be no revelation without a human recipient who grasps the communi-

cation (see *S.t.*, 2–2, q. 171, aa. 1, 4–5; q. 174, a. 6). Hence, while God primarily reveals himself, his revelation is not identical with him. Though it manifests God in a personal way, revelation belongs to the created world and can be grasped in human terms. Yet its content remains mysterious and draws the believer into the mystery. Otherwise it would not point us toward God and initiate a personal relationship with him.

6. **Revelation is a set of created entities; God's personal communication is carried out by human words and deeds.** By a human mediator God supplies a set of verbal expressions which call attention to and explain what he is doing, while what he does substantiates the truth of the discourse he provides (see DV 2). Thus, God adapts a certain set of created entities to serve as signals to us.

7. Since revelation is a particular set of created entities which can be grasped humanly, it should not be said that it is ineffable or that no human expression is adequate to it. This confuses revelation with God and implicitly denies that God has succeeded in revealing himself.[3]

8. Moreover, since revelation comes to human beings in a human form and a social context, one cannot say its content is given to the mind by some sort of nonconceptual intuition. On the contrary, the content of revelation is conveyed publicly in words and deeds, which can be observed and grasped by human beings together in community. For example, God's revelation in Jesus was experienced and appropriated by the Twelve. Faith comes to others through hearing the gospel of Christ preached by those appointed and sent to proclaim it (see Rom 10.13–17).[4]

Even as God reveals himself, his inner reality remains hidden and mysterious, as Vatican I teaches (see DS 3016/1796). In this life "we see in a mirror dimly" (1 Cor 13.12). This mirror is the relationship God has established with us. We still know him not in himself, but as one who is, in a way we cannot comprehend, all he must be to sustain with us the relationship into which he has drawn us. And even though Jesus is God, the truth he reveals still must be accepted by faith (see Jn 1.12–14). God for us is he whom we have met in Jesus.

As personal communication, divine revelation is not completed in the utterance of words or the performance of deeds, but only by a people's hearing of the words and response to the deeds. Thus the apostolic witness is to "that which was from the beginning, which we have heard, which we have seen with our eyes, which we have looked upon and touched with our hands, concerning the word of life" (1 Jn 1.1). With the death of the last apostle, the appropriation of what God reveals in Jesus was completed.[5] Now we expect no further public revelation (see DV 4).

9. Since revelation occurs in the world of the human and is humanly accessible, it includes many familiar things. God could not, for example, have revealed himself to Moses without using existing language and institutions, such as the institution of covenant. However, to attract our attention and initiate a special, personal relationship, revelation also requires a distinctive signal; it must include elements—words and deeds—which cannot reasonably be interpreted as anything except divine communication. This is to say that it necessarily includes signs and wonders: states of affairs brought about by God without the usual conditions which, if present, would dispose people to regard these happenings as

part of the normal course of events (see *S.t.*, 1, q. 105, aa. 6–7; 2–2, q. 6, a. 1; q. 171, a. 1). In the face of signs and wonders, the Israelites could not reasonably refuse to accept what they experienced as the words and deeds of God (see Ex 4.1–9).[6]

Revelation occurs in a world in which humankind already has some awareness of God—incomplete and partly mistaken but nevertheless real. If this were not so, missionaries could not make clear that the gospel message they bring is not merely a human message but a message from God, for "God" would have no meaning to those to be evangelized. This prior awareness of God is based on the fact that everything created depends upon him for its borrowed reality.

Revelation, however, is more than this natural awareness; it is essentially connected with the miraculous (see LG 5; DV 4; DH 11). Miracles and the fulfillment of prophecies are presented to experience in such a way that certain states of affairs can be discriminated from the normal order of things and reasonably accepted as signals—conveying personal communications—from God (see DS 3009/1790). Vatican I definitively teaches that external signs can render revelation credible, that one is not moved to faith exclusively by inner experience, that miracles are possible, that accounts of miracles in Scripture must not be dismissed as fables and myths, that miracles can be recognized with certainty, and that the divine origin of the Christian religion can be established by them (see DS 3033–34/1812–13). Anyone who denies the miraculous implicitly denies that divine revelation really has occurred.

Events which can be called "miraculous" in a strict sense are signs of an especially striking type. But God's revelation is not a sequence of isolated, spectacular occurrences. Once he gains the attention of those with whom he wishes to communicate, God sets up a continuing process of conversation, many of whose elements, taken by themselves, might seem perfectly natural. But the whole process hangs together with a systematic unity. Vatican II explains: "This plan of revelation is realized by deeds and words having an inner unity: the deeds wrought by God in the history of salvation manifest and confirm the teaching and realities signified by the words, while the words proclaim the deeds and clarify the mystery contained in them" (DV 2). In this way, God, who is naturally known by the relationship of all created things to him, becomes personally known by the relationship which those who believe in him have with him in the order of salvation.

Question B: What is it to have faith in a human person?

1. To understand what faith in God means, we must begin with other cases of interpersonal belief. Most things we think we know are taken on faith: in scientists, in communications media, in parents, in teachers, and so on. Even in a field such as physics, most of what even experts "know" is accepted on faith from others. And virtually everything known about human history is accepted on faith in witnesses, living and dead.

2. In principle, most propositions accepted on faith could be investigated and shown to be true or not true. A physicist with enough time and resources could verify the work of other physicists. The testimony of witnesses to a past event could often be verified by examining other witnesses, reviewing the evidence, and so on. But when it is a question of a personal relationship based on faith, verification is not possible even in principle.[7]

For example, a young couple who meet and get to know one another exchange confidences, hopes, and declarations of affection. "I love you," together with all that is most personally interesting and valuable in such conversation pointing toward intimacy, must be taken on faith if it is to be accepted at all. Here faith admits no verification proportionate to its certitude. What seems inconsistent with the expression of love always can be explained away; what seems in accord with it also can be accounted for even if the declaration of affection is insincere.

3. One's faith in another is not an experience of that person. On the contrary, although expressed by words and deeds, the other's inner self remains hidden, while everything which can be experienced is secondary to the reality one grasps in faith: the self of the other. With faith one accepts the truth of what another says about himself or herself, especially in making a commitment, and so accepts the person. In doing so, one proceeds to hope: to expect that the other will fulfill expressed intentions. And one proceeds to love: to commit oneself to communion and to carry out that commitment. Without faith there can be no intimacy.

4. The faith between a couple getting married is an especially suitable example of interpersonal faith. Their premarital faith in each other is fulfilled by the faith involved in their mutual marital commitment. Because this faith is motivated by the very marital communion it mutually accepts, it is like the living faith of a Christian. Even in the case of marriage, for those who are faithful to it, living faith cannot be falsified, because persons who refuse to judge and condemn each other always have reason to continue to believe in one another. Faith deepens as life unfolds. Communion in action constantly confirms it. Eventually the faithful couple become almost transparent to each other, yet the mystery also remains.

The mutual faith of a couple in love usually is mixed with emotion and the whole complex psychology of the romantic relationship. Most elements of such a relationship are nonessential. One can imagine a couple who have never met marrying one another by proxy, thus committing themselves to a lifelong union. The faith of each essentially bears upon the other's expression of commitment, which includes both a proposition (that one is making a commitment) and a promise (to keep this commitment). The couple cannot make the mutual commitment without faith. If they really do make and accept the marriage vow, they have faith in one another. A similar faith is essential to all genuine interpersonal communion.

5. From the preceding, one gathers the following points about the faith required for interpersonal relationships. **This faith cannot be replaced by any other sort of cognition. It concerns the person and also the propositions which he or she expresses, for the person is, in part, the self-knowledge which such propositions contain. It is the beginning of intimacy and points toward greater intimacy. Thus it always refers to the future. It leads to a common life in which each partner depends on the other to fulfill commitments; in other words, faith demands fulfillment in action. Finally, for the faithful, faith cannot be falsified.**

Question C: What is it to have faith in God?

1. What God reveals is not merely some fact about himself or some event or circumstance we can expect to befall us. Instead, God makes himself personally

known, revealing himself first through the mediation of human persons and then perfectly through his Son, our Lord Jesus. There is no God beyond him who reveals himself; and now we have a way to him. This way is Jesus (see Eph 2.18; 3.12).

2. **Faith is the acceptance of this personal communication. It is the beginning of our intimacy with God; without it we cannot share in the fellowship of divine family life.** The entire Bible makes it clear that faith in God is necessary. Nothing can replace it—neither human wisdom nor religious experience nor good works (see 1 Cor 1–2; Gal 3.1–9).

3. As was explained in A above, God reveals himself by words and deeds (see DV 2). Deeds are not just happenings—they are actions which carry personal meaning. Unless substantiated by deeds, any set of words might reasonably be regarded as more or less empty talk. But revelation contains deeds, especially miracles and fulfilled prophecies, which everyone can understand (see Mk 2.10–11; DS 3009/1790, 3034/1813). At the same time, without the words which interpret them, God's deeds in our world might seem merely odd and inexplicable events.

4. Now, to have faith in God is to accept his revelation, and revelation must be accepted as it is actually given. **Thus, faith includes both welcoming God's deeds and assenting to the truth of the words by which he gives propositional expression to the mystery contained in the deeds.**[8] Vatican II teaches: "'The obedience of faith' (Rom 16.26; cf. 1.5; 2 Cor 10.5–6) must be given to God who reveals, an obedience by which man entrusts his whole self freely to God, offering 'the full submission of intellect and will to God who reveals' [DS 3008/1789], and voluntarily assenting to the truth revealed by him" (DV 5; translation amended). The Council thus makes it clear that by faith one personally submits to God and for this very reason assents to revealed truth (cf. *S.t.*, 2–2, q. 2, aa. 1–2; q. 4, a. 2).

5. This revealed truth is heard when the gospel is preached: "So faith comes from what is heard, and what is heard comes by the preaching of Christ" (Rom 10.17). The word of God comes to us in human words. Thus, a definite body of truths articulated in human language constitutes the actual content of divine revelation as it is presented to us (see *S.t.*, 2–2, q. 1, aa. 6–10). In wholeheartedly accepting these truths and in no other way do we believe in God, for this is how we welcome God's deeds, take his promises to be true (see DS 1526/798), and enter into relationship with him as he has made himself present to us: in Jesus Christ and in salvation history, which centers upon Jesus.[9]

Vatican II reaffirms the traditional conviction that God's revelation in Jesus is definitive and will be transcended only when faith gives way to vision:

> . . . Jesus perfected revelation by fulfilling it through his whole work of making himself present and manifesting himself: through his words and deeds, his signs and wonders, but especially through his death and glorious resurrection from the dead and final sending of the Spirit of truth. Moreover, he confirmed with divine testimony what revelation proclaimed: that God is with us to free us from the darkness of sin and death, and to raise us up to life eternal.
>
> The Christian dispensation, therefore, as the new and definitive covenant, will

never pass away, and we now await no further new public revelation before the glorious manifestation of our Lord Jesus Christ (cf. 1 Tm 6.14 and Ti 2.13). (DV 4)

To attempt, as some do, to reduce revelation and faith to some sort of nonconceptual, nonpropositional, mysterious contact between God and the soul of the believer is to deny that revelation really has occurred, that God really communicates himself to us in the medium of Jesus' created words and deeds, that the Incarnation really is the fullness of revelation.

We believe by hearing. "If what you heard from the beginning abides in you, then you will abide in the Son and in the Father" (1 Jn 2.24). "O foolish Galatians! . . . Let me ask you only this: Did you receive the Spirit by works of the law, or by hearing with faith?" (Gal 3.1–2). "So faith comes from what is heard, and what is heard comes by the preaching of Christ" (Rom 10.17). The faith is professed aloud by one who seeks baptism (see 1 Tm 6.12) and by all who sincerely say the Creed.

It is a common faith (see Ti 1.4), because there is only one true faith (see Eph 4.5). One who keeps it and stands firm in it can be proud of so doing (see 2 Tm 4.7). When imposters moved by godless passions, people devoid of the Spirit, create divisions in the Christian community, the faithful must remember "the predictions of the apostles of our Lord Jesus Christ" (Jude 17). "Beware lest you be carried away with the error of lawless men and lose your own stability" (2 Pt 3.17).

Catholics find the living Jesus in the words and deeds of the Church teaching and working in the world today (see DV 7–10). For the Church is the Mystical Body of Christ, and his Spirit continually vivifies and builds up the Church (see LG 7–8). Jesus is present when the Church teaches (see Mt 28.20), and so heaven validates the Church's earthly decisions (see Mt 16.19; 18.18).

6. Vatican I teaches explicitly and definitively that one must assent to all the truths the Church proposes as revealed: "Moreover, by divine and Catholic faith everything must be believed that is contained in the written word of God or in tradition, and that is proposed by the Church as a divinely revealed object of belief either in a solemn decree or in her ordinary, universal teaching" (DS 3011/1792). No doubt some truths of faith are more important than others (see *S.t.*, 2–2, q. 1, a. 6, ad 1; 2–2, q. 11, a. 2, ad 3). But while assigning those more value, faithful Catholics accept even the least central truth of revelation as a precious part of God's total message.[10]

Still, there is more to revelation than the propositional truths included in it. Only by the fellowship of those who hear God's word and adhere to it, who benefit from his saving deeds and respond to them, can the message of God's revelation in the Lord Jesus remain in the world and be delivered to the whole of humankind, to every member of which it is personally addressed. Vatican II teaches: "Therefore the apostles, handing on what they themselves had received, warn the faithful to hold fast to the traditions which they have learned either by word of mouth or by letter (cf. 2 Th 2.15), and to fight in defense of the faith handed on once and for all (cf. Jude 3). Now what was handed on by the apostles includes everything which contributes to the holiness of life, and the increase in faith of the People of God; and so the Church, in her teaching, life, and worship, perpetuates and hands on to all generations all that she herself is, all that she believes" (DV 8). In this way, revelation remains alive in the world not only in the teaching and belief of the Church, but also in the liturgy and the holiness generated by sharing in it, and in the guidance of the Church's pastors and the cooperation of her members in living the truth in love.

The whole rich experience of God revealing himself abides in the Body of Christ, the Catholic Church. St. Irenaeus refers to this whole reality as the true gnosis: "The true gnosis is the doctrine of the apostles, and the ancient organization of the Church throughout the whole world, and the manifestation of the Body of Christ according to the successions of bishops, by which successions the bishops have handed down the Church which is found everywhere; and the very complete tradition of the Scriptures, which have come down to us by being guarded against falsification, and which are received without addition or deletion; and reading without falsification, and a legitimate and diligent exposition according to the Scriptures, without danger and without blasphemy; and the pre-eminent gift of love, which is more precious than knowledge, more glorious than prophecy, and more honored than all the other charismatic gifts" (FEF 242). Divine revelation is total personal communication, and the Church hands it on totally.

From the riches of this whole, the Church always can bring forth new truths and make the faith bear fruit (see LG 25). In doing this, the Church does not suppose that she can add anything to God's revelation (see DV 4 and 10). Nor does the Church suppose that revelation occurs apart from the fleshly signs, the words and deeds, which God uses. Rather, the Church believes that the Spirit, who teaches nothing on his own, continues to unfold the revelation of God in the Lord Jesus and so to lead humankind to the full truth of God himself (see Jn 16.13).

7. **The commitment of faith is the fundamental option of Christian life** (16-G). This fundamental option is a unique case of morally upright commitment. A morally upright commitment to intimate friendship always makes demands. Thus, it is inherent in faith, as a commitment to personal friendship with God, to make practical demands on those who believe. This is why, as Vatican II teaches, the "split between the faith which many profess and their daily lives deserves to be counted among the more serious errors of our age" (GS 43).

The People of God are in a disastrous situation when they exhibit lack of fidelity, mercy, and remembrance of him (see Hos 4.1–3), that is, lack of living adherence to his word. The faith which saves is the faith which works through love (see Gal 5.6). Not everyone who says "Lord, Lord" will enter heaven; it is necessary to do the Father's will and build one's life on the solid foundation of faith (see Mt 7.21–27; Lk 6.46–49). One who listens to God's word but does not act on it is like a person who looks in a mirror, "and goes away and at once forgets what he was like. But he who looks into the perfect law, the law of liberty, and perseveres, being no hearer that forgets but a doer that acts, he shall be blessed in his doing" (Jas 1.24–25). Clearly there is no room for the notion that faith is a gift which makes no demands.

While the gift of faith makes demands, it also carries with it the power to fulfill these demands. Against the view that a justified person "is not bound to observe the commandments of God and of the Church, but is bound only to believe," the Council of Trent teaches definitively that those who are justified can and must keep all the commandments of God and the Church (DS 1570/830; cf. DS 1536/804). It is not compatible with this teaching to suggest that any Catholic is unable to live up to the moral requirements of faith (see DS 1568/828).

8. In sum, God reveals himself by sensible signs, chiefly by the bodily existence and the words and deeds of his Son. Faith is no aconceptual intuition, nor is it the acceptance of some ancient information. Rather, faith is the hearing of God's word and adhering to it, the full human and personal experience of the personal relationship God seeks to initiate with all humankind. Catholic faith is

adhering to God in the Catholic Church by accepting the belief of the Church, worshipping according to this belief, and trying to live up to it in the whole of one's life.[11]

Question D: How does a person make an act of faith as a personal commitment?

1. **In making an act of living faith (that is, faith motivated by love of God), one makes a free choice to accept God's personal communication** (see *S.t.*, 2–2, q. 4, aa. 3–5; cf. q. 2, aa. 3, 9). **This choice is made for the sake of the human goods of truth and religion.** By the commitment of faith, one causes oneself to share in the human goods of the Christian community. The act of faith also contributes intrinsically to constituting, from the believer's side, the intimate relationship with God.

In living faith one makes a human free choice to accept God's proposal of intimate communion. Those who accept Jesus are given "power to become children of God" (Jn 1.12). St. John Chrysostom comments that the power is like that given an authorized agent, and that it is received in baptism. If one uses this power properly, then with the grace of God one has it in one's own free will to become a child of God.[12] The first Christian act of an adult who is being baptized is the act of living faith which those seeking baptism ask of the Church (see DS 1531/800).[13]

By any commitment one makes oneself be a person of definite identity, for free choice is self-determination. As a human free choice made for the sake of the human goods of truth and religion, a person's commitment of faith is likewise self-determining. Thus, by this human free choice, one makes oneself share in the human goods of Christian community, such as religion and truth—for example, one becomes a catechumen, associates with members of the Church, participates in some of their religious acts, such as prayers, and receives instruction in the faith.

Now, in the act of living faith, one's acceptance of God's proposal is transformed by being made out of love of him. The transformation occurs by God's gift, the love poured forth in our hearts through the Holy Spirit, and not by a self-creative act of our own. Thus we participate in divinity by our own free choice—not, however, by constituting ourselves divine, but by God's so constituting us (see *S.t.*, 1–2, q. 113, aa. 3–4). The act of living faith is the fundamental commitment of Christian life, the first act which is both divine and human in one who is drawn into and enters adoptive divine childhood by this very act. Since this act is primary, its make up is the paradigm for every other act of Christian life.

2. To understand the role of human goods in the act of faith it is necessary to bear in mind that any human choice whatsoever is directed to some basic human good. The Council of Trent teaches that, prior to living faith, a person prepares for it with God's help by listening to the gospel proclaimed by the Church, recognizing the Church's credibility, and believing it with a human credence (see DS 1526/798, 1530/800). In this way, as Vatican I expressly teaches, the acceptance of God in faith is a reasonable, free human act (see DS 3009–10/1790–91, 3033/1812). Such an act of reasonable submission, which is not suspended when the gift of faith is received, is directed to the human goods of truth and religion. Thus, converts come to the Church and seek faith from her in baptism because they think her teaching true and her way of life a sound path to peace with God. These are the same general goods sought more or less adequately by every religious person.

3. The content of faith includes many propositions which are not evident and seem false to nonbelievers. The factors making it possible to give responsible assent to these are twofold. First, because human relationships in general depend so heavily on faith, it is universally accepted that testimony ought to be believed, provided the one offering it seems competent and honest. This general norm of believing grounds a cautious receptivity and open-mindedness on the part of an upright person toward the gospel. Second, when carried out as it should be, the preaching of the gospel is accompanied by signs sufficient to show that, despite its extraordinary content, those who proclaim it are sincere and qualified in the field of religious truth, that is, the truth concerning humankind's relationship with God. Thus the hearer has good reason to believe but still has a choice, and so believes freely (see *S.t.*, 2–2, q. 2, a. 1, ad 1, 3; a. 9, ad 2, 3).

There are provisional grounds of faith which finally matures into absolute acceptance of God's self-revelation (see Mk 8.22–26; Jn 4.6–42). Jesus normally did signs in response to an incipient faith, and by means of these signs elicited faith in his revelation. Faith is given to provide eyes to see and ears to hear if one is willing to accept it (see Mt 16.5–12). But no cogent sign is offered to the closed-minded who are not prepared to receive God's saving love (see Mt 16.1–4; Lk 12.54–56). Confronted with facts, people do not automatically believe in the relevant way (see Mk 16.11–14; Lk 24.11, 37, 41).

4. The obligation to believe existed from the beginning of the human race. The very relationship of creature to creator is enough to require assent as soon as it is clear that one is being approached by God. Furthermore, as Vatican II teaches, God's love in creating implies a call for human response: "From the very circumstance of his origin, man is already invited to converse with God" (GS 19). Even by the light of natural reason human beings can know themselves to be creatures (see DS 3004/1785). They should admit this truth and live in accord with it.

5. In sum, every human person has a duty of conscience to seek the truth, especially religious truth, and embrace it when found (see DH 2, 10). Given the gospel's message and the evidence of its credibility, a reasonable person ought to accept its truth. Yet the truth of faith is not evident; one can refuse to assent and one's choice to assent remains free (see DS 1525/797, 1554/814). Thus, a person makes an act of faith as a personal commitment by choosing in accord with an upright conscience to accept the gospel's message. **In accepting the gospel, one makes the fundamental option to be a Christian.**

6. To refuse to believe is a sin. The only reason for this sin is a pre-existing state of sin. The explanation of the parable of the sower (see Mk 4.13–20) suggests that whether revelation is received and flourishes depends on the antecedent dispositions of the recipient. St. John makes the same point more bluntly: Those whose deeds are wicked love darkness, while those who act in truth come into the light and believe in Jesus (see Jn 3.17–21).

The explanation for unbelief is clear and it is simple: Sin and rationalization block openness to God's truth. "For every one who does evil hates the light, and does not come to the light, lest his deeds should be exposed. But he who does what is true comes to the light, that it may be clearly seen that his deeds have been wrought in God" (Jn 3.20–21). One who sins does not love himself or herself properly, and so cannot remain open to infinite goodness of which one's own goodness is a participation (see *S.t.*, 2–2, q. 25, a. 7). Those who oppose Jesus are willfully blind to the truth (see Jn 9.39–41). Faith is demanding. One who loves God is going to keep his commandments (see Mt 19.16–21; Jn 15.10). One unwilling to keep the commandments will be unable to believe, for that would mean doing God's will.

7. God's word is an indestructible seed. Unlike human things, which can be lost or destroyed, it stands firm (see 1 Pt 1.23–25). Hence, once we have received faith, it will not be taken away from us. **We will remain partners of Jesus as long as we do not rebel against the truth accepted in faith** (see 2 Tm 2.11–13). Unfortunately, though, "By rejecting conscience, certain persons have made shipwreck of their faith" (1 Tm 1.19). But that is a very different thing from "losing" one's faith, if this means simply suffering such a loss, without any fault on one's own part.

8. Since, as Vatican I teaches, God "strengthens with his grace those whom he has brought out of darkness into his marvelous light (see 1 Pt 2.9), so that they may remain in this light," those who have accepted the faith under the teaching authority of the Church "can never have any just reason for changing that faith or calling it into doubt" (DS 3014/1794; translation amended; cf. DS 3036/1815). To deny this is to reject not only Vatican I but the Council's premise: that God is faithful and never abandons anyone unless that person first abandons him (see DS 3014/1794, 1537/804).

The very fact that faith is personal acceptance of God excludes one from picking and choosing among the truths of faith, obeying some of its demands while disregarding others. God's truth is one and his will is one. We receive his one truth in many doctrines and moral norms. Assuming the usual conditions of responsibility (reflection and consent) are met, to deny any one doctrine or moral norm—to deny, not merely to violate—is to make a commitment incompatible with faith. One can continue to think one has faith; one can continue to behave in many respects like a good Catholic; one will be counted as a Catholic by those who take polls. But one has become an infidel, and this has happened not by loss of faith, but by unfaithfulness to God (see *S.t.*, 2–2, q. 5, a. 3; q. 11, aa. 1–2).

Question E: In what sense is the act of faith a gift of God?

1. As the Council of Trent teaches, living faith is more than a human act; it requires a divine gift, infused at baptism (see DS 1530/800). Vatican I definitively teaches that by living faith "with the inspiration and help of God's grace, we believe that what he has revealed is true—not because its intrinsic truth is seen with the natural light of reason—but because of the authority of God who reveals it, of God who can neither deceive nor be deceived" (DS 3008/1789; cf. 3032/1811). Vatican II likewise teaches that "the grace of God and the interior help of the Holy Spirit must precede and assist" faith, while the same Spirit by his gifts "constantly brings faith to completion" (DV 5). **Thus faith is both a human act and a divine gift.**

2. Scripture teaches that no one comes to faith without being moved by God: "No one can come to me unless the Father who sent me draws him" (Jn 6.44). Faith in Jesus is supported by the testimony of God the Father and the Spirit of truth (see 1 Jn 5.6–9).

3. However, this inward teaching by God does not add anything to the outwardly expressed content of faith (see *S.t.*, 2–2, q. 6, a. 1). That content is made up of the openly communicated propositions by which we grasp the created, revelatory realities, especially Jesus' humanity and career. Nothing in the Church's teaching or Scripture suggests that God's inward testimony adds to, alters, or in any way constitutes the content of faith.

On the contrary, Jesus manifested the whole content of revelation to his chosen witnesses (see Jn 15.15). The Spirit adds nothing to this content, but helps those to whom it is given to appropriate it (see Jn 14.26; 16.13–15). St. Paul's teaching that Christian wisdom is revealed through the Spirit (see 1 Cor 2.10–16) does not support a different position, for Paul states that the content of "words not taught by human wisdom but taught by the Spirit" (1 Cor 2.13) derives from "my speech and my message," and this message has "demonstration of the Spirit and power" (1 Cor 2.4).[14]

4. Even God's self-identification as God is a particular truth—a primary item in the content—which is revealed (see Ex 3.14; Dt 5.6; Jn 8.24, 58). One who accepts this truth accepts all the rest. Thus, all the Spirit need certify is the identifying truth: for example, that Jesus is Lord (see Cor 12.3; 1 Jn 4.15). **In other words, God moves one to recognize him communicating in the revealing medium: God's words and deeds at the Exodus and on other occasions, and definitively in the words and deeds of Jesus during his earthly life.**

5. The certitude of faith cannot be accounted for by the factors which make it possible as a free human act but only by the fact, which is itself a teaching of faith, that it is a divine gift (see *S.t.*, 2–2, q. 4, a. 8; q. 6, a. 1). The believer is aware of this absolute certitude, and this awareness is itself a datum which is an important sign of the divine source of faith.

6. **Moreover, one's share in divine life by living faith is due wholly to God's gift.** The transformation effected in us when the act of faith is made out of love of God does not come about by our own self-creative act; rather, the love of God is poured forth in our hearts by the Holy Spirit.

7. There is no incompatibility between faith's being a human act and its being a divine gift. Insofar as we share by faith in divinity, our love and the love of the Spirit are one; in this respect, it is exclusively by God's gift that we accept him in faith. Insofar as we remain human persons in supernatural friendship with God, the Spirit's giving of the gift is his, and our acceptance of the gift is ours; in this respect, we accept God in faith by our own free choice. But this free choice, like everything else of ours which is salvific, also is God's grace.

Question F: How does human sin affect the relationship of revelation and faith?

1. The relationship of revelation and faith is deeply affected by sin and God's redemptive work in overcoming it. Once sin has been committed, the human race is desperately in need of redemption. This need is experienced as misery, a misery which intensifies the human desire for fulfillment. On their own, however, human beings seem only to make their situation worse. An act of restoration and renewal by God is needed (see *S.t.*, 1–2, q. 109, aa. 2–3, 8).

2. Sin and its effects, precisely as evil, are privations. Privations are real in that they are objective facts, but not real as are the things God creates (5-A). Evils are real absences of perfections which should be present.

3. This understanding of evil shapes the whole Jewish and Christian attitude toward sin and redemption. Since evil is not a mere illusion but a reality contrary to God's good will, he cannot ignore it. But neither can he annihilate it, as if it were a positive power opposed to himself. Rather, because evil is privation, it must be overcome by restoring wholeness, making good what is lacking.

4. Sinful humankind exists in a self-mutilated condition. Only God can redeem by a radical restoration, a work of re-creation, which salvages all the good of creation, including that distorted by sin, while leaving behind only the privation of evil and those who resolutely cling to it even as the new heavens and new earth are being created (see Is 26.18–19; Rv 21.1–8). The work of redemption is exemplified by the creation of a new heart in the sinner and by the resurrection of the body, dead as a consequence of sin.

5. Even without sin, there would have been a discontinuity between time and eternity, this life and the next life. But with sin, the present heavens and earth affected by evil will pass away, to be succeeded by a re-creation which brings redemption to completion. In this restoration by God, everything good will be harmoniously integrated in Jesus, while radical evil will be excluded.

6. **God's revelation is thus received in the fallen human condition as an offer of reconciliation extended only for a limited time.** Faith in this revelation is conversion toward God; friendship with God begins by the justification—the straightening out—of the sinner. For us, the healing of sin and elevation to divine life are inseparable (see *S.t.*, 1–2, q. 113, aa. 1–4).

A good which suffers evil is not in its residual, positive, good reality what it would be if evil were not in it (5-A). But all the positive reality of human persons and their world, to the extent that it remains, is good, even in its distorted condition. God cannot simply demolish this good. The will of the sinner and even the act of sin, insofar as it is an expression of intelligence and freedom, are goods. God cannot eliminate them without annihilating what he made, without hating something which shares in his own life. This is impossible. And so God cannot simply make a fresh start, as if sin never existed.

God neither ignores evil as if it were illusory nor seeks to annihilate it as if it were a positive power opposed to himself (see Wis 11.23–26). Evil must be overcome by restoring wholeness, by making good what is lacking, because it is privation. To try to segregate oneself from evil or destroy it is not to overcome evil. Thus God saves by Jesus, in whom he personally meets evil and by undergoing it draws the wounded good back to the fullness of being the Father intended it to enjoy when he created it.

The great hostility of the Pharisees to Jesus lies in the fact that they do not accept his strategy for salvation. Rather, they seek to keep clear of evil by strict observance of the law. Today no one holds the concept of ritual purity. However, its contemporary equivalent is present in every effort to identify evil with some things as against other things, instead of identifying it with a defective and sinful attitude toward things. Every modern ideology which ignores the reality of sin and seeks to overcome evil by economic, technological, military, or some other kind of power implicitly conflicts with the Christian conception of evil as privation and of redemption as restoration to wholeness.

Question G: Why does God make humans cooperators in his redemptive work?

1. One must consider why God redeems in order to see why he makes humans cooperators in his redemptive work. God is a loving Father but not a foolishly indulgent one. Passages in the Old Testament concerning God's wrath are too numerous to mention. He loves justice and hates wickedness (see Ps 45.8); he hates evildoers (see Ps 5.6); he hates those who worship idols (see Ps 31.7). This is no mere peculiarity of the Old Testament mentality; we are warned in the New Testament of God's wrath from the first preaching of John the Baptist (see Mt 3.7) to nearly the last pages of the Christian apocalypse (see Rv 14.10).[15] **Thus, God can neither ignore nor tolerate the self-mutilated condition of fallen humankind.**

Of course, "hates" and "is angry" are said of God in senses different from those in which they are said of ourselves. But this does not mean that these attitudes are simply excluded from God. Without imagining that we understand God in himself, in our relationship with him we must not be one-sided. To suppose God does not hate and is not angry leads to a dilemma. On the one hand, one can suppose that he does not love either and is not pleased with the gifts of those who love him. This position would destroy any possible personal relationship with God. On the other hand, one can suppose that God indiscriminately loves good and evil, is pleased indiscriminately by the gifts of those who love him and the sins of those who do not. This position would maintain a personal relationship with God at the cost of destroying the significance of human life, for in the end it would make no real difference what we did.

It often is said that God hates the sin but loves the sinner. This is true, but it must be understood correctly. In sinning, we determine ourselves wrongly; we really embrace the privation which makes the sin evil and make this evil part of ourselves. Hence, the sin God hates is not something altogether separate and apart from the sinner he loves. This is why God's love of sinners does not simply accept them as they are, but is redemptive; if sinners do not resist, God transforms them by overcoming evil in them and bringing them to the wholeness of holiness which alone is unconditionally lovable.

2. If one understands evil as privation, it is easy to see why God really hates evil, is angry with sinners, and punishes them, and also why he loves sinners, is pleased when they acknowledge their guilt, and mercifully redeems them. God hates with precision: he precisely hates the evil which deprives evildoers of the good he wishes them to have (see *S.t.*, 1, q. 20, a. 2, ad 4). Hating nothing he has made (see Wis 11.24), God rejects the evil by which sinners mutilate themselves without rejecting anything of the good sinners still enjoy.

3. God is jealous in his love and angry when his children alienate themselves from him by following other gods and other goods (see Ex 20.5; 1 Cor 10.22). God is angry with sinners because he loves them. Out of this love he redeems them. He spares all things because they are his; he works to separate sinners from their sins (see Wis 11.26–12.2).

4. Still, unlike an indulgent father, God does not intervene to prevent the natural consequences of his children's wrongdoing. He allows us to bear responsibility for our sins. He does this because he respects our dignity. To do otherwise would be to treat us as children too immature to be responsible for our choices.

The indulgent human father, by denying the reality of evil and constantly intervening to assume responsibility for the actions of his children, takes from them their own responsibility, prevents them from learning by experience that life is serious, and so deprives them of the dignity of living as mature men and women. God does not do this. Rather, like the broken-hearted father who can hardly restrain himself from trying to help, but who holds back so that his children will be able to live their own lives, God punishes. This punishment is not the creation and arbitrary imposition of evils. It is the natural and inevitable unfolding of sin.

God created human beings and provided sufficiently for their well-being. He gave them the power to share in his own life, promised them freedom from the horror of death, and supplied guidance for living a humanly good life in this world. As the Council of Trent teaches, Man sinned and "through the offense of this sin, he incurred the wrath and the indignation of God, and consequently incurred the death with which God had previously threatened him and, together with death, bondage in the power of him who from that time had the empire of death (see Heb 2.14), that is, of the devil" (DS 1511/788).

This language is of a sort we do not often hear today. It is worth noticing that in other times Christians have found such language quite natural and pleasing. Why does it strike us so differently today?

The privation account of evil, which faith teaches, is opposed by two rival accounts: a radical dualism which gives evil the same sort of reality as good and a radical monism which makes all evil relative and ultimately only apparent (5-C). According to faith, evil is real, though not real as the things God creates are, but only as a privation of goodness. Sin and its consequences are deprivations—brought upon sinners by their own freedom—of the fulfillment which they could and should have enjoyed.

Even among believers, this privation account of evil often is lost to clear view. In the Reformation and the period since then, many Christians have verged toward a dualistic theory of evil. While talking of sin, they also have talked of human corruption which even God's grace does not repair, but only covers over. Christians who did not go so far as to think and say such things nevertheless tended in practice to divide the world into two groups: we friends of God and those enemies hopelessly lost because they do not belong to our ecclesial community.

While this attitude existed among Christians, secular humanists more and more rejected free choice and ultimate moral responsibility. They developed optimistic world views according to which evil is only relative, a mere passing phase. If religion and superstition could be forgotten, if knowledge and technology could be unleashed, if the present stage of evolution or dialectical unfolding could be hastened toward its goal, if neurotic feelings of guilt and hostility could be dissolved, if defects in the social structure could be put right—if some, or all, or some similar things were done, then there would be no more evil. Today even faithful Christians are greatly influenced by such optimistic world views.

5. God created Man in his own image, able to act freely and responsibly, like him not only in being but in causing. The causality of human persons bears not only on other things but themselves, for in choosing freely human persons are, in a limited but true sense, self-makers under God (2-B). God wished Man to live richly in this world, then to live still more richly in a heavenly communion in which created persons would dwell together with the Trinity in intimate friendship, forever sharing their goods with one another.

6. Once sin entered the world, this splendid plan could only be realized if sinful Man were somehow able to live a humanly good life in this world. Yet now

humankind had to struggle with a nature wounded by sin against an environment similarly damaged. Given sin, a good human life must acknowledge its reality, will to avoid it, accept its consequences as well-deserved punishment, and strive to repair everything good it has distorted (see *S.t.*, 1–2, q. 87, aa. 6–7).

7. In conclusion, by making us cooperators in his redemptive work, God makes our lives by his grace serve as a sacrifice and prayer, which he accepts and answers by his re-creative act. **If he redeemed us without our cooperation, we would be deprived of our dignity by having redemption imposed on us. True, only God redeems, and he does this by creating all things anew. However, for the sake of human fulfillment, he makes us cooperators in his work:** "For we are his workmanship, created in Christ Jesus for good works, which God prepared beforehand, that we should walk in them" (Eph 2.10).

8. Thus, God redeems sinful Man by continuing to do him good, making known his continuing love, and also by recalling sinful humans to friendship, providing them the means to respond, and supporting them individually and in fellowship in living holy lives, which help to overcome sin and its consequences. God does all this in a preliminary way in the Old Testament, and definitively and completely through Jesus and his Church.

9. Because faith is necessary for justification and the overcoming of all the humanly devastating consequences of sin, fallen human beings have a further reason to believe which Man did not have in the beginning. Anyone who has made an act of faith and is tempted to abandon the way of Jesus because of its difficulty should realize that the act of faith and fidelity to it are not only morally required but are in one's own interests. The alternative is failure to be fulfilled, now and eternally, both as a human individual and as one called to membership in the divine family. By contrast, even in the fallen human condition it is possible with faith to live a fulfilling life, a life heroic as Jesus' was, and to share in his eternal glory.

By faith one enters into the new creation which God has begun with the resurrection of Jesus. Since one's existence is new, one's life must be renewed to conform to this new existence (see Gal 6.14–16). Everyone who professes Jesus' name must abandon evil (see 2 Tm 2.19). God's word demands that those who hear it adhere obediently to it (see Rom 16.26; Jas 1.23–25). The word of God is divisive; it demands a response, and everyone must render an account (see Heb 4.12–13).

Redemption does not mean one is translated at once to glory, nor that one is put to sleep. Life must go on, and it should be both humanly fulfilling and suited to one's new status. We had lived foolishly, disobediently, as slaves of passion. But we are not slaves working for our own liberation (see Ti 3.3–7). We are freed by the grace of God to live a humanly fulfilling life: "For we are his workmanship, created in Christ Jesus for good works, which God prepared beforehand, that we should walk in them" (Eph 2.10). Christian life is part of God's gift.

By baptism one receives the gift of living faith; one is created anew as another Christ, as a child of God (see Gal 6.15). Dying to sin, one rises with Christ to new life; therefore, sin must be expelled from one's whole person, which should be devoted to upright life (see Rom 6.11–18). The vital point is that by the gift of living faith one becomes a child of God with a hope of forever sharing intimately in his life. "And every one who thus hopes in him

[Jesus] purifies himself as he is pure" (1 Jn 3.3). One ought to live a life worthy of the calling one has received, a life worthy of a child of God (see Eph 4.1).

Unfortunately, we human persons are not very consistent. We accept the gift of redemption and the hope of glory, yet continue to act as if we still were slaves of sin, of death, of the law, and of the devil. Thus we must be warned: "Not every one who says to me, 'Lord, Lord,' shall enter the kingdom of heaven, but he who does the will of my Father who is in heaven" (Mt 7.21).

We are comforted to read that when one believes that Jesus is the Son of God, "God abides in him, and he in God" (1 Jn 4.15). We conveniently forget that faith without works is dead (see Jas 2.14). We are comforted to read that "no one can say 'Jesus is Lord' except by the Holy Spirit" (1 Cor 12.3). We conveniently forget the words of our Lord Jesus: "Why do you call me 'Lord, Lord,' and not do what I tell you" (Lk 6.46).

The demand to live the life of the child of God one is and to live the life of human fulfillment for which one has been liberated is not arbitrary. It is a logically necessary consequence of one's acceptance of redemption and new life in Jesus. If we do not live the life of good deeds which God offers us as part of his loving gift, we are tragically untrue to ourselves. The *ought* of every Christian moral norm is the same as the fundamental *ought* in "One ought to accept redemption." It appeals to one's reasonableness, and it is a guide to one's own true self-interest.

Summary

Revelation conveys God's communication to humankind, inviting us to share intimately in his life. Although we can have some knowledge of him simply by natural reason, supernatural revelation includes truths about God which we could not otherwise know at all. God's personal communication is carried out by human words and deeds—it is not ineffable, not beyond the capacities of human expression, and not apprehended by some sort of nonconceptual intuition. Revelation occurs in the world of the human and is humanly accessible. To attract our attention and initiate a special relationship, it is also distinctive; it includes elements—signs and wonders—which cannot reasonably be taken for anything but divine communication.

To understand what faith in God means, we need to begin with other cases of belief in a person. Most of what we know is taken on faith—in parents, teachers, scientists, historians, "experts" of many kinds. Faith in the sense of assenting to propositions is generally subject to verification, but this is not true of the faith which is the basis of an interpersonal relationship. Such faith is acceptance of what other persons say about themselves, especially when they make commitments, and so is acceptance of them. Thus it is not subject to verification proportionate to its certitude. Faith in another is the beginning of intimacy and leads to further intimacy; it demands fulfillment in action.

What God reveals is not just some fact about himself or us—it is himself, revealed most perfectly through his Son, Jesus Christ. Faith is acceptance of this communication; it is absolutely necessary and the beginning of our intimacy with God. It includes welcoming his deeds and assenting to the truth of his words. It means accepting God as he reveals himself. But, as it is presented to us, the content of divine revelation is a definite body of truths articulated in human language and proposed by the Church. One must therefore assent to all the truths the Church proposes as revealed. Moreover, because faith is the fundamental option of Christian life, it is normative. One must act on one's faith, obeying God's will as he has revealed it. Thus faith makes demands, but it carries with it the power to fulfill them.

An act of living faith includes a free choice to accept God's proposal of intimate communion, and this is a choice for the sake of the human goods of truth and religion. The act is both free and reasonable: free because the truth of faith is not evident, so that one can refuse to assent; reasonable because, when the preaching of faith is carried out as it should be, it is accompanied by signs sufficient to show that one has good reason to believe. One who believes fulfills a duty of conscience to seek the truth and embrace it when found. Moreover, once we have faith, it will not be taken away from us; we can betray and abandon faith, but this is not a blameless "loss" of faith.

At the same time, living faith is not only a human act but a divine gift (though God's inward teaching or prompting adds nothing to the outwardly expressed content of faith). God moves one to recognize him communicating in the revealing medium—most perfectly, in the words and deeds of Jesus—and all else follows from this. The absolute certitude of faith cannot be accounted for by the fact that it is a human act, but only by the fact that it is a divine gift. Moreover, it is wholly by God's gift that one shares in divine life by living faith.

Given the fact of sin, humankind needs redemption. Given humankind's self-mutilation by sin, our redemption calls for a radical restoration, a work of re-creation, which only God can accomplish. In God's restoration, everything good will ultimately be integrated in Jesus, while what is radically evil will be excluded. But because this world will pass away, God's offer of reconciliation is extended only for a limited time. Faith in this revelation—this offer of reconciliation—is conversion and justification.

God, though a loving Father, is not a foolishly indulgent one. Scripture testifies that he hates evil and is angry with evildoers. This is understandable if we recall that evil is a privation, an absence of what ought to be present; God hates the evil which deprives evildoers of the good he wishes them to have. He rejects nothing of the good sinners still enjoy but, respecting our dignity, he calls upon us to change the evil self-determination of sin and does not intervene to prevent all the natural consequences of our wrongdoing.

This respect for human dignity is characteristic of all God's redeeming work. Though only he finally can redeem, he makes us cooperators with him. Our response to God's revelation—his offer of reconciliation and intimacy with him—should be the living of holy lives, which will help to overcome sin and its consequences. Fallen human beings thus have, in their need for redemption, a ground for faith which Man in the beginning did not have; and the act of faith and fidelity to it are not only morally required but in our own best interest.

Appendix 1:   The conditions for sound interpretation in Catholic theology

Catholic theology begins from faith in God, whose revelation in Jesus abides in the belief and life of the Church.[16] Only in the living Church is the fullness of revelation to be found. "Consequently," Vatican II teaches, "it is not from sacred Scripture alone that the Church draws her certainty about everything which has been revealed" (DV 9). This priority of the Church as the starting point for theology is peculiarly Catholic. As St. Augustine says: "Indeed, I would not believe in the gospel myself if the authority of the Catholic Church did not influence me to do so" (FEF 1581).

Catholic theology proceeds from the Church's living belief and teaching to study Scripture and other expressions and evidences of God's revelation. These expressions—which I call "witnesses of faith"—must be carefully interpreted, so that the Church will have a rich and accurate sense of her own identity, based upon an abundant memory of her own continuous life. Moreover, Catholic theology seeks to understand revelation ever more fully by asking what light it sheds upon reality, and especially what implications it has for life. These theological studies constantly demand the work of interpretation. Interpretation is at present the subject of many studies and debates; it has become a large and complex question.[17] A few clarifications are provided here.

"Interpretation" sometimes is used to refer to the acts of expressing and receiving involved in every communication, even the most simple and immediate. For example, it can be said that when one wants salt and says, "Please pass the salt," one interprets one's desire by means of the expression, and that when someone near the salt hears this request and responds to it, the one responding interprets "Please pass the salt." However, such simple and immediate instances of communication—although, like everything else, they can be subjected to endless study—do not involve interpretation in the sense in which it is especially necessary and difficult in theology. Instances of simple and immediate communication must be presupposed by all complex and mediated communicating. The bulk of human communication is simple and immediate. Even in such communication misunderstandings can occur, but for the most part immediate communication is effortless and fully effective.

In a stricter sense, "interpretation" refers to an effort of mediation, an intervention into the flow of direct and simple communication to facilitate communication when it otherwise would be ineffective and to correct misunderstandings which have occurred. Someone asks in English for salt and is not understood by a table companion who speaks no English. Perhaps the request is interpreted by a gesture. People who think others have misunderstood their words or deeds often say "in other words" or "that was not meant to hurt you," and try again to convey the intended proposition or soothe the hurt feelings.

As the examples show, interpretation can be helpful in all aspects of personal communication, not only in facilitating an accurate grasp of propositions expressed in language. A nonlinguistic communication such as a touch sometimes needs interpretation ("Excuse me"); actions often require many words to make their significance clear. Moreover, language itself not only expresses propositions, but also is a means for communicating requests ("Grant, we beseech you"), commitments ("I do believe"), images and feelings (much poetry), and so on. Efforts of interpretation appropriate to every possible aspect of personal communication are at times necessary in theological work, since God reveals himself to the whole of us fleshly persons.

In the case of language which expresses propositions, the fact that interpretation is possible and sometimes needed makes it clear that the propositions which are expressed and the language by which they are expressed are not the same. For example, someone can express the truth that snow is white in many languages and even in various ways in the same language. The proposition is a particular truth one can know about snow; it picks out and corresponds to the state of affairs of snow being white. No matter how many ways the proposition is expressed, it remains in itself what is meant by all the linguistic expressions. Thus a proposition is not part of language; it is a nonlinguistic entity. And one proposition can have many and varying expressions in language; for example, the proposition that snow is white is as much one as snow's being white is one, although the same proposition is expressed in many languages.[18]

Words often have many meanings, and even long and complex linguistic expressions sometimes are ambiguous. Moreover, the same linguistic expression can have different meanings at different times and in different places. A word such as "person," which is important in theology, has more than one meaning. Words such as "love" and "law" are ambiguous no matter where and when they are used; usually the context in which they occur helps to make clear what they mean. However, a linguistic context which suffices to eliminate ambiguities in a communication between two persons speaking to each other might not be sufficient if the discourse is recorded or transcribed and later heard or read by someone remote in time and place—that is, by someone whose knowledge of the language might be imperfect and who lives in a very different extralinguistic context.

Language only expresses propositions when a certain extralinguistic context is given. "God loves us" means one thing when said by a believer in a theological discourse, another when said by an atheist who has experienced some tragedy and is speaking ironically. Temporal and spatial references included in propositions descriptive of present events— "It's raining" said by a person gazing out the window to someone in the same room—often are not expressed in language. In general, language is used to express only what cannot be assumed from the extralinguistic context. Thus this context must be taken into account.

Some who notice these characteristics of language think it follows that propositions vary as the language in which they are expressed varies, and that propositions true at one time and place will be false at other times and in other places. This conclusion does not follow. Propositions are not linguistic entities. The limitations of language, including its variability, cause obstacles to accurate and easy communication and require careful interpretation. But the very fact that an interpreter can know that expressions used at some remote time and place had a different meaning than they would have if used now shows that what the expressions originally meant has not changed. The interpreter tells us what the expressions meant, using other expressions.

Moreover, if the propositions signified by certain expressions were true, subsequent variations in the meaning of the expressions does not affect the truth of the propositions, but only the ability of the expressions to communicate truth without interpretation. The proposition that it is raining, expressed by the person gazing out the window, includes many unmentioned determinations. The proposition is that rain is falling at a certain place, at a certain time, and so forth. If this proposition is true, it will be true always and everywhere, for rain did fall at that place and time and so forth.

The preceding point is very important for theology, since some are misled by a confusion between propositions and their expressions to conclude that truths of faith are not more than their linguistic expressions. Hence, they think that received Christian teachings are open to diverse and incompatible interpretations to complete their meaning at different times and places, much as their linguistic expressions require different efforts at interpretation in diverse extralinguistic contexts.

The fact is that truths of faith need nothing added to them to be true, but always need further truths of faith added to them to develop God's relationship to his people as he wishes it to develop. As explained previously, the Church always can bring such fresh truths from the riches of revelation. Since every such new truth is an aspect of the one truth revealed by God in the Lord Jesus, no authentic development of doctrine ever can contradict what the Church believed and taught in earlier times and other places.

Of course, since language is as variable as it is and since linguistic expression of truths of faith never can communicate these truths without an adequate extralinguistic context, anyone who tries to interpret old doctrinal expressions while ignoring the most important part of their extralinguistic context—the living Church handing on her whole self to all generations—is likely to misinterpret them. Within the Church, what was revealed by God in Jesus and handed on by the apostles is constantly communicated by the teaching, life, and worship of the whole People of God (see DV 8). For the most part, this communication is simple and immediate—for example, when children are brought up in a good Catholic family. Usually no interpreter is required to facilitate the genuine and fruitful reception of God's message by such children.

Yet parents and others who communicate the faith in this simple and direct way must themselves be formed by preaching and assisted by other forms of teaching, ultimately under the guidance of the bishops united with the pope. At this level, at least, obstacles to communication and breakdowns in it must be dealt with in a methodical way. Interpretation becomes essential to resolve difficulties and correct mistakes which otherwise would impede the handing on of the faith or corrupt the message of God. But the necessary work of interpretation can only make its contribution if carried out with a clear awareness that the linguistic expressions to be interpreted are only partial expressions of the truths the Church believes, and that the truths which the Church believes are only part of the whole reality which she herself is—the whole reality of humankind's relationship to God.

This awareness of the context of expressions to be interpreted is likely to be overlooked in the study of sacred Scripture, and so is not least urgent in this study. The Bible contains accounts of the signs by which God reveals himself. It also describes the hearing and reaction with which these revealing signs were received. Because of the personal character of divine revelation, much more than the expression and grasping of propositional truths is involved. The Bible richly reflects this whole communication in all its aspects. For this reason, Scripture contains prose and poetry of many kinds which permanently enshrine many aspects of God's shaping of his people by his living word.

If one applies historical-critical methods to the study of the Bible on the assumption that it is no different from any other ancient set of writings, one is hardly likely to assist effectively in the work of handing on God's revelation to which the sacred texts bear witness. One must take into account the ecclesial community to whose culture the Bible belongs. Since much of the text is for use in celebration and for shaping action, a sincere attempt to live out the biblical message and regular liturgical use of the text are as essential to understanding it as appropriate responses of infants to their parents are to their growing understanding of an adult world.[19]

These remarks are not intended to suggest that careful literary and historical study is unnecessary for the interpretation of Scripture. One must distinguish literary forms, learn about the extralinguistic context, and understand the language originally used and its limits. Since few but experts can do this, most of us must rely for guidance on the best available commentaries. In other words, we must trust experts for a correct understanding of God's word, which is essential to our Christian life.

Catholics will trust fully only those experts who conform in their work to the guidance offered by the magisterium—the living teaching office of the Church made up of the pope and the bishops in communion with him. For, as Vatican II teaches: "The task of authentically interpreting the word of God, whether written or handed on, has been entrusted exclusively to the living teaching office of the Church, whose authority is exercised in the name of Jesus Christ. This teaching office is not above the word of God, but serves it, teaching only what has been handed on, listening to it devoutly, guarding it scrupulously, and explaining it faithfully by divine commission and with the help of the Holy Spirit; it draws from this one deposit of faith everything which it presents for belief as divinely revealed" (DV 10; cf. LG 25; DS 3020/1800, 3070/1836). As the pope and bishops are servants and not masters of God's word, so Catholic Scripture scholars must be servants and not masters of this same word as it is received "whole and alive within the Church" through the service of the successors of the apostles (see DV 7).

The propositions which are asserted by the sacred writers are certainly true (see DV 11). But if one attempts to disengage these propositions asserted in Scripture, one must be on guard because of the many other aspects of the whole reality which is communicated. Moreover, to tell whether a proposition is asserted or not, historical and psychological information often is necessary, and sometimes it simply is not available.

In any effort to disengage from sacred Scripture the truths of faith asserted there, one must bear in mind the Church's solemn teaching: ". . . in matters of faith and morals affecting the structure of Christian doctrine, that sense of sacred Scripture is to be considered as true which holy Mother Church has held and now holds; for it is her office to judge about the true sense and interpretation of sacred Scripture; and, therefore, no one is allowed to interpret sacred Scripture contrary to this sense nor contrary to the unanimous agreement of the Fathers" (DS 3007/1788; cf. 1507/786). It is important to understand what this basic rule does not mean and what it does mean.

Sometimes in the liturgy and even in the teaching of the Church, phrases and longer passages from Scripture are used with a sense which no one supposes is that of the text in its actual context. This practice is called "accommodation." Even nonbelievers quote Scripture in this fashion; for instance, they often use "the truth will make you free" (Jn 8.32) to proclaim a secular humanist faith in merely human science and technology. The Church's accommodated use of Scripture should not be considered her holding of its true sense.

Again, because Catholic theology begins from the present teaching of the Church and examines Scripture and other witnesses to revelation in the light of living faith, one is easily led to find in Scripture propositions which are not there—for example, to find in the Gospels the truth that Jesus is a divine person existing according to both divine and human natures. But this truth of faith is articulated fully only in the fifth century by the Council of Chalcedon (see DS 301–2/148). It is compatible with the truths about Jesus asserted in the Gospels, but the teaching of Chalcedon adds to earlier formulations of faith and makes Christian knowledge of our Lord more complete and more precise. Thus, the Church's developed doctrine, formulated in concepts not available to the biblical writers, is not to be taken as the true sense of Scripture.

At the same time, it is a mistake to think that the Church holds a certain interpretation of Scripture to be a true meaning of it only if a proposition asserting that interpretation is defined. The Church teaches much more than it proposes in solemn definitions (see 35-D).

The Church holds an interpretation to be correct when this interpretation is presented in her constant and universal teaching as one which the faithful should accept. For example, the use which the Church makes of Romans 1.20 in her teaching on the possibility of knowing God by the natural light of reason makes clear what the Church holds to be the true meaning of this statement of Paul's.

Often scholars say the literal meaning of the text is what the original author intended to communicate or what the initial audience would have understood. But the Church does not consistently use this principle in her own interpretation of Scripture. There are several reasons for not doing so.

In the first place, in some cases virtually nothing is known about the original author and audience; in these cases, the ideal is impractical. Moreover, even under these conditions, a text does carry some meaning.[20] This, of course, is not to say that available information should be ignored, since it can supply relevant aspects of the extralinguistic context.

What is even more important, speakers and writers often communicate more than they intend. An author writes a sentence, rereads it, and comes to understand "what I meant to say"—a proposition not previously articulated. Thus the connotations and implications of any limited linguistic expression carry a true, fuller meaning (*sensus plenior*) which can be discovered only by considering the expression in the widest linguistic and extralinguistic context in which it is being used.[21] Since the Church reads Scripture as a witness of divine revelation, which lives and works through the long course of the history of salvation, each passage is understood in the context of the whole of Scripture and tradition, the whole history and life of the Church. Correct interpretation of Scripture finds its true sense in harmony with all the truths of faith which the Church believes and teaches (see DV 12).

Not only Scripture but all the other witnesses to the faith of the Church require careful interpretation. In general, the difficulties and principles of sound interpretation are similar, whether one is dealing with Scripture, the writings of the Fathers of the Church, conciliar or papal documents, or other expressions of revelation.

For instance, accurate interpretation of the documents of a Council such as Trent requires that one take into account what concepts were available to the Church at that time, what challenges it confronted and dealt with, what range of views existing among Catholics it wished to respect, and what meanings the technical expressions of theology had for Catholic thinkers who had been formed in the various schools faithful to the Church.

Still, it is far easier to disengage propositions asserted in conciliar teaching than those asserted in Scripture. The canons and decrees of Trent were intended to express either true propositions or suitable precepts. The Council does not attempt to convey in its decrees the extrapropositional dimensions of divine revelation as Scripture does in its varied forms of discourse.

As in reading Scripture, so in reading Trent, one must begin from the living faith of the Church. One cannot assume that the decrees of Trent never say more than the Fathers meant to say, because their expressions are part of the whole tradition of Catholic teaching. The extrapropositional dimensions of revelation always remain a source for the development of doctrine. But legitimate development will be stifled if existing expressions of the truths of faith are interpreted in a way which rigidly excludes finding in them a true, fuller meaning. Of course, this fuller meaning must be compatible with and even somehow implicit in the truth of faith articulated and expressed in the existing formulation.

Appendix 2:   The unalterability of the truths of Catholic faith

When theologians consider one truth in the light of another, by the dialectical method of disciplined meditation and discussion, they are often said to be engaged in the work of interpretation or of investigation of the meaning of the truths of faith. But one must distinguish between the effort to facilitate a given communication and the investigation of the ulterior significance of truths already formulated and accepted. The former is called "interpretation" in the strict sense discussed in Appendix 1; it is the chief work of positive theology. The latter might better be called "understanding" as in "faith seeking understand-ing"; this is the work of systematic theology.

The two tasks obviously are closely related and often confused. One reason for this is that theological reflection often begins from written documents, especially Scripture; documents are open both to interpretation and to understanding by systematic reflection. The interpreter of the Bible seeks to facilitate communication of what the language actually expresses; this is the quest for the literal sense of Scripture. Systematic reflection by disciplined meditation considers what Scripture literally communicates in one place and compares it with what it communicates in another (for example, by comparing the Old and New Testaments), or compares what Scripture literally communicates with other truths pertaining to faith and Christian life. Such systematic work is said to discover various spiritual or figurative (more-than-literal) senses of Scripture. In fact, the effort is to understand the realities which pertain to faith by the meditative comparison of one truth with another.

Confusion between interpretation and theological understanding not only occurs in the study of Scripture but also in treatments of defined doctrines and other truths of faith. For example, to interpret the Church's teaching on original sin is to try to determine the literal sense of the documents in which this teaching is expressed, such as the decree on the subject of the Council of Trent (see DS 1510–16/787–92), and to rearticulate what the documents assert in such a way that someone today can understand them accurately and thus accept or reject what the Church actually teaches, not some other propositions. But systematic theologians sometimes say they wish to offer a fresh interpretation of original sin, when they actually mean they wish to propose a new theological understanding of the states of affairs picked out by the propositions which the Church teaches.

Interpretation helps us know exactly what God has revealed, precisely what he wishes to communicate to us, especially in the Incarnation, the words and deeds, the death and resurrection of Jesus. Theological understanding helps us discover what difference this revelation makes to all of created reality and what difference it makes or should make for our own lives, so that we can consciously and responsibly praise God for what he is doing and cooperate with him in doing it. Notice that one might say: Theological reflection helps one to discover what revelation means for all of creation and for our own lives. But this use of "means" does not refer to the meaning of linguistic expressions which interpretation seeks; rather, it refers to relationships in reality itself.

This distinction between interpretation and theological reflection of a systematic sort points to a very important aspect of theological method: The quest for understanding of the faith presupposes the acceptance of the truths of faith (see *S.t.*, 1, q. 1, aa. 2, 5, 8). As the International Theological Commission states: ". . . theology can only be done in a living communion with the faith of the Church."[22] Theology is bound by the word of God in Scripture and in tradition; it is bound by the confessions of the belief of the Church in this and previous times; it is bound by the documents of tradition; and it is bound by pastoral and missionary responsibility, for theologians should take account of the impact of their publications on the belief of the faithful, on the proclamation of the gospel, and on catechesis.[23]

A dialectical method similar to that of theology can be used by one who does not accept the truth which God has revealed; in such a case, the discipline is a kind of philosophy. Or the method can be used by one—such as a believing Jew or Protestant—who does not think that the truth of divine revelation is present intact in the belief and teaching of the Catholic Church; in such a case, the discipline is theology, but not Catholic theology. One who is not a believer can try to interpret the Bible, using "interpret" in the strict sense of finding its literal meaning. But one cannot undertake to understand what one believes, using "understand" in the sense of systematic reflection, unless one believes some propositions.

Although this position might seem self-evident, some today deny it. Noticing that faith is a personal relationship with God, they exclude from faith itself all propositional content. To the extent that faith pertains to the mind, they reduce it to a kind of experience of God, a preconceptual and extrapropositional religious sense. The propositions which the Church believes and hands on as truths of faith are, on this view, only symbols or inadequate representations, which never fully express faith itself (see C, above, and accompanying notes).

This view presupposes the possibility of a more than sentient preconceptual and extrapropositional contact with reality. I indicated in chapter two, appendix three, why this presupposition is implausible. The teaching of Vatican I on faith (see DS 3008–20/1789–1800, 3031–43/1810–18) takes for granted throughout that faith itself includes the acceptance of some definite propositions. The nonpropositional notion of faith was put forward by certain theologians—referred to as "modernists"—around the beginning of this century.[24] St. Pius X rejects this view (see DS 3484–86/2081–85). That assent to some definite propositions is essential to faith is obvious from the New Testament itself (see Acts 2.41; Rom 10.9–17; 1 Cor 15.1–8; 1 Tm 4.6; 2 Tm 4.1–5; and many other places).

Those who advocate a nonpropositional notion of faith should be asked several questions. First, precisely what is faith on this view, and how can one tell whether one has it or not? Second, can an individual refuse to believe? If so, how? Third, how can anyone communicate the faith? How can any group hold the same faith? Fourth, how can any proposition symbolize or express faith? Exactly what is the supposed relationship between faith and expression? Fifth, how can one tell whether one or another expression is more or less appropriate?

Careful reflection upon such questions will make it clear that, although Christian faith is much more than assent to a set of propositions, anything called "faith" which does not include propositional content will be something completely different from what is called "faith" in the Bible and in the whole of Catholic tradition. It is possible for a person, like Plato, to carry on dialectical inquiry without accepting many propositions as certainly true; indeed, Plato perhaps assumed as truths which could never be contradicted only the things which must be so if dialectical inquiry is to be possible and worth carrying on. But usually those who engage in dialectic are not purely seekers of wisdom as Plato was; rather, they think that in some way they have ultimate truth.

Christians believe God has given humankind wisdom in the person of our Lord, Jesus Christ (see 1 Cor 1.18–2.16); Catholics believe that truths which belong to this wisdom are present in the belief and teaching which come to us in the Church from the apostles (see DS 1501/783, 3006/1787; DV 7–10). Therefore, Catholic theology is a dialectical reflection which begins not only from the belief that the quest for wisdom is possible and worthwhile, but also from the belief that God has mercifully responded to humankind's quest for wisdom. In theology, every past linguistic expression is open to examination and improvement; every proposition which does not somehow pertain to faith is open to denial if it should turn out to be incompatible with a truth of faith; every truth of faith is open to development as the Church gradually grows in understanding of God's revelation in Jesus. But not every proposition is open to denial, for then the proposition that God has revealed himself would be open to denial, and one's inquiry would not be theological.

Similarly, in Catholic theology, the truths the Catholic Church proposes for belief cannot be denied. Some today, however, seem to reject certain truths of Catholic faith, yet say they do not deny what the Church believes, but only reinterpret it. What are we to make of this?

Certainly, more careful interpretation of the documents of faith can throw new light on old truths without contradicting them. But some people actually do deny the factual content of faith and continue to accept only certain general propositions entailed by the Church's beliefs. They seem to feel a need to eliminate from faith everything which is factually unique, since the factually unique cannot be reduced to a phase in a rational system. For example, some writers say they reinterpret the doctrine of the resurrection of Jesus; they fail to affirm (or they even deny) that he is not dead now; they accept a general proposition, such as that Jesus plays a vital role in the religious lives of his followers, which is entailed by the traditional teaching; and they claim that their account of the role Jesus plays in the lives of his followers is a reinterpretation of the traditional doctrine of the resurrection—a reinterpretation which at last arrives at its true meaning, after nearly two thousand years of naive misunderstandings.

This procedure is deceptive. Catholic faith is not simply belief in a system of general propositions, but in the flesh and blood reality of the revelation of God in the Lord Jesus.[25] We cling to the Word Incarnate, to the intactness of his mother's virginity, to the bloody reality of his death, to his fleshly risen life, to his bodily presence in the Eucharist, to the death-dealing effect of our first parents' sin, to the life-giving power of our Lord's risen body for our dead bodies, and to the confident hope that we shall embrace him in the flesh. Catholic faith is not afraid of what is too concrete to be intelligible. We kneel before matter: the Word made flesh.

Vatican I already condemns anyone who "says that as science progresses it is sometimes possible for dogmas that have been proposed by the Church to receive a different meaning from the one which the Church understood and understands" (DS 3043/1818). In a famous statement at the beginning of Vatican II, John XXIII calls for a suitable restatement of Catholic teaching. But he points out that this is only possible because "the deposit or the truths of faith, contained in our sacred teaching, are one thing, while the mode in which they are enunciated, keeping the same meaning and the same judgment, is another."[26] By making this statement its own (see GS 62), Vatican II enhanced its importance.

However, this statement of Pope John's often has been mistranslated and misrepresented. He is making it clear that the propositional truths of faith are distinct from their linguistic expression. The phrase, "keeping the same meaning and the same judgment," usually is omitted by those who misinterpret this statement, because it would block the misinterpretation.

This phrase is a clear allusion to the classic statement of St. Vincent of Lerins (see FEF 2174) which Vatican I cites when it teaches that the "meaning of the sacred dogmas that has once been declared by holy Mother Church, must always be retained; and there must never be any deviation from that meaning on the specious grounds of a more profound understanding" (DS 3020/1800; cf. 3043/1818). Plainly, John XXIII is not opening the door to a merely verbal fidelity which would give the Church's definitions of faith and her common, even if nondefinitive, ways of expressing her belief a meaning different from the one the Church understood when those expressions were used prior to the opening of Vatican II.

Anyone who claims only to reinterpret the Church's beliefs yet seems to deny any aspect of them should be asked: Is yours the only reinterpretation of this doctrine or are there possibly others? In any case in which the deceptive procedure is used, there can be plural stories, each of them inconsistent with the others. The next question is: By what standard is your reinterpretation to be judged better or worse than any alternative? If the answer is: By the standard of the witnesses of faith, interpreted as the Church understands them, then one is dealing with a legitimate theological effort. If the answer is: By the standard of modern science, or by the standard of credibility to the contemporary mind, or by the standard of relevance to current problems, or anything of this sort—anything except the witnesses of faith understood as the Church understands them—then one is dealing with something other than a legitimate theological effort.

Often enough, those who claim to reinterpret the Church's beliefs but really deny them fail to ask themselves the question about a standard; they offer no decision procedure for one who wishes to compare and critically evaluate so-called reinterpretations. In the absence of a decision procedure, reinterpretation is not science, not dialectic, not a disciplined form of inquiry at all. Rather, it is a form of storytelling, a poor kind of fiction.

Notes

1. A useful introduction to many of the points treated in this chapter: Michael Schmaus, *Dogma*, vol. 1, *God in Revelation* (New York: Sheed and Ward, 1968). A more specialized treatise on revelation: René Latourelle, S.J., *Theology of Revelation* (Cork: Mercier Press, 1968), esp. 313–424.

2. On the possibility and limits of knowledge of God by rational reflection: Germain Grisez, *Beyond the New Theism: A Philosophy of Religion* (Notre Dame and London: University of Notre Dame Press, 1975), 241–72.

3. For an explicit statement of the position here rejected, see Gabriel Moran, "The God of Revelation," in *God, Jesus, and Spirit*, ed. Daniel Callahan (New York: Herder and Herder, 1969), 3–15, esp. 12: "The danger to which faith is continually exposed is that God will no longer be sought but that his revelation will be identified with something finite. The distinctive character of Judaic-Christian revelation is that God has left us no revelation."

4. St. Thomas Aquinas teaches clearly that while the assent of faith depends upon an interior grace directly given by God, the content of faith must be received by hearing the gospel preached (see *S.t.*, 2–2, q. 6, a. 1). In his early commentary on the *Sentences* (1, pro., q. 1, a. 5), Thomas teaches that the habit of faith demands more than the light of faith, because faith must be specified to definite content received by preaching, just as the light of principles naturally known must be specified through sense experience. For a clear explanation of the basis in divine transcendence for the limited role of experience in Christian faith: Robert Sokolowski, *The God of Faith and Reason: Foundations of Christian Theology* (Notre Dame and London: University of Notre Dame Press, 1982), 133–42.

5. Concerning apostolic reception as not only normative for us but constitutive of revelation: Latourelle, op. cit., 369–72.

6. Concerning miracles: Grisez, op. cit., 326–42, 357–65, and the works cited, 404, n. 24.

7. Although acceptable as far as it goes, an analysis of belief which omits the irreducibility characteristic of specifically interpersonal faith is inadequate. See, for example, Bernard J. F. Lonergan, S.J., *Insight: A Study of Human Understanding* (New York: Philosophical Library, 1957), 703–18. Various works of Gabriel Marcel are suggestive with respect to the specific quality of interpersonal faith. See, for instance, "From Opinion to Faith," in *Creative Fidelity*, trans. Robert Rosthal (New York: Farrar, Straus, 1964), 120–39. Also: Richard L. Purtill, *Reason to Believe* (Grand Rapids, Mich.: William B. Eerdmans, 1974), 71–79, on the nature of faith.

8. While not denying that in revelation God's self-communication is mediated by finite entities, some Catholic authors talk of faith as if it were a knowledge-experience of God without any ecclesially determinable content, and as if beliefs were always generated only as a product of theological reflection upon this protean faith. See, for example, Richard P. McBrien, *Catholicism*, vol. 1 (Minneapolis: Winston Press, 1980), 24–29, 45–48, 60–62, 73–76, and 232–37; Gerald O'Collins, S.J., *Foundations of Theology* (Chicago: Loyola University Press, 1971), 24–30. Although O'Collins makes many sound points, he mistakenly thinks of propositions as if they were constructed expressions of some more fundamental grasp of reality, rather than as integral parts of the interpersonal relationship of revelation and faith. Such analyses set up a false dichotomy between the personal and the propositional. An important underlying factor is the supposition, developed by Karl Rahner, that there is a universal, transcendental relation of revelation-faith between man and God: "Revelation," *Encyclopedia of Theology*, 1460–66. The argument for this hypothesis is that God wills all to be saved, and faith is required for salvation (see LG 16; AG 7). So far, so good, but the further step that there is no faith without accessible revelation is not evident and not warranted by Vatican II's teaching, which seems rather to point to a faith merely *implicit* in the effort of upright persons to follow conscience as it

leads them toward God. Certainly, *Dei verbum* deals exclusively with what Rahner calls "predicamental revelation." Thus, the views of revelation which McBrien calls "subjective" and "mediating" (op. cit., 222–23) can be set aside inasmuch as they depend on an unnecessary theological hypothesis. Faith is not a knowledge-experience of God without any determinable content, but a personal acceptance by a conscious, free choice of him revealing himself; at the limit, for one who has not heard the gospel, this acceptance is merely implicit in the openness to truth and religion of upright persons pursuing these goods as best they can.

9. Edward Schillebeeckx, *Christ: The Experience of Jesus as Lord*, trans. John Bowden (New York: Seabury Press, 1980), 29–79, stresses the role of religious experience, but fails to clarify what he means by "experience." Thus, his treatment is profoundly ambiguous. Sometimes, it might be understood as asserting that revelation is only completed when God's words and deeds are appropriated in faith (78): "So for believers, *revelation* is an *action of God* as *experienced* by believers and *interpreted* in religious language and therefore expressed in human terms, in the dimension of our utterly human history." But more often Schillebeeckx's treatment seems to overlook and even deny the essential role of true propositions (62): "Religion is not concerned with a message that has to be believed but with an experience of faith which is presented as a message." Thus, he seems willing to relativize doctrine to some sort of ineffable religious experience (63): "What the Christian community will be concerned to say in constantly changing situations, through constantly new forms of expression, even in philosophical concepts of a very complicated kind, is ultimately no more than that in Jesus Christ it experiences decisive salvation from God." Such a treatment of revelation allows individual theologians to substitute whatever opinions please them for the sacred dogmas declared by the Church, understood as the Church understood and understands them, and in this respect is at odds with the definitive teaching of Vatican I (see DS 3020/1800, 3043/1818).

10. See Pius XI, *Mortalium animos*, 20 AAS (1928) 13–14; *The Papal Encyclicals*, 201.9. Vatican II teaches that there is an order or hierarchy of truths of faith, since they are more or less close to the central mystery (see UR 11), but this teaching in no way undercuts the fact that every truth of faith is accepted on the same principle—namely, that it belongs to divine revelation, its explanation, or its defense—and so the denial of any one truth of faith is equally infidelity toward God revealing. On this point, see J. T. Ford, "Hierarchy of Truths," *New Catholic Encyclopedia*, 16:208, especially the quotation from Archbishop Andrea Pangrazio's Vatican II speech proposing and explaining the idea. Denis Carroll, "Faith and Doctrine," *Irish Theological Quarterly*, 46 (1979), 111–22, summarizes views of Karl Rahner, P. de Letter, and Olivier Rabut which would accept as consistent with faith a deliberate denial of some truths of faith—a "lightening of the burden." The arguments summarized rest on blurring the significance of the hierarchy of truths of faith and ignoring the distinction between ignorance (of some doctrine by a believer) and denial (of a doctrine by one limiting the commitment of faith). These positions are very similar to indefensible theories of fundamental option (criticized in 16-E) and more or less approximate the modernist conception of faith condemned by Pius X (see DS 3484/2081).

11. Of course, this is not to say Christianity is not a religion of the Spirit. But Spirit and institution are not exclusive, and Christianity from its origin is institutional, public, and social: B. C. Butler, O.S.B., "Spirit and Institution in the New Testament," in *Studia Evangelica*, ed. F. L. Cross, 3 (1961), Texte und Untersuchungen, 88 (Berlin: Akademie-Verlag, 1966), 138–65.

12. St. John Chrysostom, *Commentary on Saint John the Apostle and Evangelist: Homilies 1–47*, trans., Sr. Thomas Aquinas Goggin, S.C.H. (New York: Fathers of the Church, 1957), 100–101 (homily 10).

13. See *The Rite of Christian Initiation of Adults*, sec. 75. A theological account of faith as a human act: Benoît Duroux, O.P., *La psychologie de la foi chez saint Thomas d'Aquin* (Paris: Téqui, 1977).

14. It might be objected that in Galatians Paul takes a more radical view. But, however Galatians is understood, the teaching of Romans must be considered to present a more rounded and balanced expression: John W. Drane, "Tradition, Law and Ethics in Pauline Theology," *Novum Testamentum*, 16 (1974), 167–78.

15. The significance of Scripture's use of "hatred" and "wrath" in reference to God often is explained away by saying that such dispositions are attributed to God anthropomorphically. This is true, but anthropomorphic expressions still need to be understood, not dismissed. Otherwise, all the personal traits of God—for example, that he is a loving Father—will be dismissed, for all of them are anthropomorphic. The problem is to purify words used of God of their unsuitable connotations and elements of significance, while retaining some real significance. In this case, "hatred" and "wrath" signify absolute opposition between God's holy will and evil, and God's wrath is real because evil is

real, even though it is a privation, not a positive reality. What must be excluded is any disposition on God's part to alienate and destroy creatures mutilated by evil. Rather, his hatred of evil is subordinate to his reconciling and healing love of creatures mutilated by it; he eliminates the privation by restoring the subject of evil to wholeness. See *Theological Dictionary of the New Testament*, O. Michel, "miseō," 4:683–94, esp. 686–87; Gustav Stählin, "orgē: E. The Wrath of Man and the Wrath of God in the NT," 5:419–47.

16. See Pius XII, *Humani generis*, 42 *AAS* (1950) 586 (DS 3886/2314), *The Papal Encyclicals*, 240.21; Yves M.-J. Congar, O.P., *A History of Theology*, trans. and ed. Hunter Guthrie, S.J. (Garden City, N.Y.: Doubleday, 1968), 226–75, esp. 270–71.

17. One of the most influential works on interpretation: Hans-Georg Gadamer, *Truth and Method* (New York: Seabury Press, 1975). This work contains much information and insight. But Gadamer's position is faulty insofar as he falls into post-Hegelian relativism. He explicitly states (406–7 and 483) the self-referential criticism which shows the untenability of this relativism. (This line of argument is articulated in Grisez, op. cit., 217–25.) But Gadamer does not understand the logic of self-reference and mistakenly thinks that the performative character of the inconsistency, which (as Gadamer rightly notes) is not self-contradiction, allows the relativist to escape. On the logic of self-reference, see Joseph M. Boyle, Jr., Germain Grisez, and Olaf Tollefsen, *Free Choice: A Self-Referential Argument* (Notre Dame and London: University of Notre Dame Press, 1976), 122–38, esp. 127–30, where we criticize evasions of the sort Gadamer attempts.

18. See Richard L. Cartwright, "Propositions," in *Analytic Philosophy*, 1st series, ed. Ronald J. Butler (New York: Barnes and Noble, 1962), 81–103. Cartwright replies to criticisms: "Propositions Again," *Noûs*, 2 (1968), 229–46. Anyone who tries to talk about historicity, interpretation, development of doctrine, the infallibility of teachings and irreformability of definitions (two entirely different things), and other such topics without the necessary logical equipment is sure to fall into great perplexity and likely to make serious errors.

19. See the important article: George T. Montague, S.M., "Hermeneutics and the Teaching of Scripture," *Catholic Biblical Quarterly*, 41 (1979), 9–12. (This article is based on the author's presidential address at the 1978 meeting of the Catholic Biblical Association.)

20. Ibid., 6–7, and the works cited.

21. See Pierre Grelot, *The Bible Word Of God: A Theological Introduction to the Study of Scripture*, trans. Peter Nickels, O.F.M.Conv. (New York: Desclee, 1968), 317–29 and 368–90, for a balanced treatment of the *sensus plenior;* see also Raymond E. Brown, "The *Sensus Plenior* in the Last Ten Years," *Catholic Biblical Quarterly*, 25 (1963), 262–85, for fuller bibliography on this subject.

22. International Theological Commission, *Theses on the Relationship betweeen the Ecclesiastical Magisterium and Theology*, June 6, 1976 (Washington, D.C.: United States Catholic Conference, 1977), thesis 7.2.

23. Ibid., thesis 3. For a theological critique of more radical views of pluralism, including Karl Rahner's: José Luis Illanes Maestre, "Pluralismo teológico y verdad de la fe," *Scripta Theologica*, 7 (1975), 619–84.

24. A classic statement of the modernist conception of faith, revelation, dogma, and theology: George Tyrrell, *Through Scylla and Charybdis*, or *The Old Theology and the New* (London: Longmans, Green, 1907), 265–307. A historical and critical treatment of modernism: J. Riviere, "Modernisme," *Dictionnaire de Théologie Catholique*, 10:2009–47; a recent, comprehensive treatment: Ramón García de Haro, *Historia Teológica del Modernismo* (Pamplona, Spain: EUNSA, 1972). A brief introduction with an extensive context: Avery Dulles, S.J., *Revelation Theology: A History* (New York: Herder and Herder, 1969), 83–89.

25. Although his thought is marked by certain Protestant presuppositions a Catholic cannot accept, the point made here is brilliantly clarified in a scriptural study of Paul's anthropology: Ernst Käsemann, *Perspectives on Paul* (Philadelphia: Fortress Press, 1971), 17–29.

26. Ioannes XXIII, "Allocutio habita d. 11 oct. 1962, in initio Concilii," 54 *AAS* (1962) 792.

CHAPTER TWENTY-ONE

GOD'S REDEMPTIVE WORK:
COVENANT AND INCARNATION

Introduction

Having considered revelation, faith, and redemption, we turn now to the actual working-out of redemption in which Christian life participates. The first move is God's. He establishes a covenant community and prepares for his decisive act: the Incarnation and the resurrection of the Word. This chapter therefore treats the preparatory stages of redemption and the make up, the "constitution," of Jesus as redeemer. Chapter twenty-two will consider his redemptive life, death, and resurrection. Chapter twenty-three will take up in a general way the subject which the remainder of the book will develop in detail: the lives of Christians in the Church as their participation in the fulfillment of redemption.

Question A: What are the constant characteristics
of God's redeeming work?

1. God's redeeming work is prompt and ceaseless. No sooner had Man sinned than God held out the promise of redemption (see Gn 3.15; DV 3). "From that time on he ceaselessly kept the human race in his care, in order to give eternal life to those who perseveringly do good in search of salvation (cf. Rom 2.6–7). Then, at the time he had appointed, he called Abraham" (DV 3). The preliminary stages of God's redemptive work include essential features found also in redemption's culmination, accomplished in Jesus. But in Jesus certain limitations of the early stages are transcended.

2. In the typical case of Abraham, God makes a human being his helper in the work of redeeming. Abraham hears God's call and listens, receives God's commands and follows them (see Gn 12). Thus the relationship of friendship with God, shattered by Man's sin, is reestablished. Abraham's response to God is credited to him as saving faith (see Rom 4.1–9). The relationship is sealed by a covenant, a treaty in which permanent friendship is pledged and promises are made concerning the fulfillment of mutual responsibilities (see Gn 15; 17.1–14). Abraham is now God's ally, in a position to cooperate in redeeming others. Thus, when God is about to wipe out sin-filled Sodom and Gomorrah, Abraham intercedes, bargaining like a merchant of the Middle East with a fellow trader (see

Gn 18.16–32). The wicked do not escape, but Abraham's intercession at least saves his kinsman Lot (see Gn 19.29).

3. **The divine initiative, the genuineness of the relationship, the forming of a covenant community, and the element of intercession—these are constants in God's redeeming work.** Since Man is in sin, God must take the initiative; since those called must share in redemption, the relationship must be real; since humankind lives in community and is called to heavenly communion, there must be a community in friendship with God involving permanent responsibilities; and since those in friendship with God participate in his redeeming work (and, if they are to deal rightly with their sinful fellows, must help to save them), they engage in intercession.

4. Redemption by God does not mean that anyone is paid (see *S.t.*, 3, q. 48, a. 4; q. 49, aa. 1–3). True, the general notion of redemption is that of reclaiming something, as one reclaims a pawned article or buys the liberty of a slave. If one sold oneself into slavery and someone else purchased one's freedom, one would be redeemed and would have a redeemer. Man sold himself into slavery by sin; God redeems by freeing people from sin so that they no longer are slaves. However, in the redemption of the Israelites from Egypt, we see an important difference in the concept of redemption as it applies to what God does. God's work is not a commercial transaction; God neither pays nor is he paid.

5. This holds true throughout the history of redemption. God is not paid by another who redeems; God is the redeemer (see Jn 3.16–17; Rom 8.32). Nor are others who participated in redemptive work rewarded with any payment or ransom (see Is 45.13). Above all this is true in Christian redemption: "But thanks be to God, who gives us the victory through our Lord Jesus Christ" (1 Cor 15.57). God gives us the victory, he does so through Jesus, and it is truly ours.

6. These constant features characterize God's redemptive work throughout history. But salvation history also is marked by development. In the Old Testament, God's redemptive work is an ever-growing communication of his love. The promise of this communication points toward fulfillment in the New Testament: God's sharing of his own Spirit, by which human beings are made adopted members of the divine family (see Jn 1.16–17; Gal 4.3–7).

The Old Testament is a progressive revelation. Abraham is called to be God's friend (see Is 41.8). The Israelites are chosen not because of their greatness, but "because the Lord loves you, and is keeping the oath which he swore to your fathers" (Dt 7.8). Therefore, Israel is called to love "God with all your heart, and with all your soul, and with all your might" (Dt 6.5). Only God's personal circumcision of the hearts of his people makes it possible for them to fulfill this vocation (see Dt 30.6). God's love and kindness are so great that they endure forever (see Ps 118.1–4, 28–29).

God loves his people like a faithful husband who continues to love his unfaithful wife. God promises to repair human infidelity by his own action, overcoming sin by a gift of his Spirit (see Ez 36.25–28). The Messiah who is to come will be anointed with this Spirit (see Is 61.1; Lk 4.16–21), poured out like refreshing water, healing everything (see Is 32.15–20; 44.3). The effect of the gift of God's Spirit is that his people will have new hearts, capable of loving him faithfully (see Jer 31.33–34; Ez 36.26–27).

Question B: How is the covenant relationship to be understood?

1. Like almost everything else God uses in establishing community with us, covenant existed as an ordinary human institution before being taken up for his special purposes.[1] **Treaties were needed to cover relationships outside natural communities; such a treaty was a covenant.** It had one essential component: the stipulation of some definite responsibilities which shaped the relationship.

2. The format of a typical covenant is as follows. There is a preamble setting out who is granting it (both parties can give covenant to each other or a superior can grant covenant to an inferior—for example, a powerful king to a vassal). A historical prologue often follows describing prior relationships; this history identifies the parties in relation to each other and provides the basis for the further relationship to be established by the covenant. The responsibilities of the relationship—often only a set of duties imposed on the inferior party—are then stated. Unlike the impersonal expressions of a legal code, the stipulation as to what must be performed has a personal character: "I" and "you." Provisions generally follow for public reading of the covenant, so that those it binds will bear it in mind and fulfill it. Finally, the covenant is completed by a ceremony which puts it into effect and brings the relationship to life. This ceremony often involves an oath and an invocation of divine vengeance if the covenant's stipulations are violated.

3. Chapters twenty and twenty-four of Exodus present the relationship between God and Israel as a covenant.[2] The former chapter begins with identification and history, God's acts in the exodus providing the basis for the relationship to be established. Then follow stipulations—the Ten Commandments. These require the people's exclusive loyalty to God; they also regulate relationships among God's people, since they must maintain their unity to stay in common allegiance to their covenant Lord. God does not take the customary oath, but swears by himself; witnesses are excluded, since God has no need of gods to guarantee his relationship with anyone (see Heb 6.13–18).

4. Chapter twenty-four of Exodus completes the account of the covenant. (The intervening chapters contain details of the law.) The agreement is read, and the people accept it. The covenant is sealed with the blood of bulls, sprinkled partly upon the people and partly on the altar. This blood is life, the very principle of vitality (see Gn 9.4). Thus it brings the covenant to life, puts it in force.[3] After this, Moses and the other leaders beheld the God of Israel and had a meal in his sight—a sign of living together in the community which had been formed (see Ex 24.1–11).[4]

5. It is important to notice that God redeems first and then offers the covenant. **Although the covenant contains stipulations requiring a certain style of life, their fulfillment is not a condition for entering the relationship but a requirement arising from the relationship one freely accepts.** God provides law so that his people can cooperate freely in their valued personal relationship with him. Law is not a burden but a blessing and a real necessity for developing an

orderly life in common, especially for people recently freed from slavery and used to arbitrary treatment.[5]

6. Unlike a human code of law, however, God's commands, considered precisely as such, are not backed by imposed sanctions and enforced by a penal apparatus of police, courts, jails, and the like. Rather, in refusing to keep God's law, failing to love him, following other gods, one inherently invites disaster, since other gods are false and powerless to save (see Ps 115.4–8; Wis 13.11–19).[6]

7. The reason why the requirements of life within the covenant are not impositions is that they follow from what God's people are. Humankind is made in God's image and shares in responsibility for creation (see Gn 1.26–29). Even after sin, the children of Man share in God's glory and enjoy an almost godlike status (see Ps 8.5–10). Under the covenant, the challenge of being like God persists and is heightened for his people: "You shall be holy; for I the Lord your God am holy" (Lv 19.2). Created in God's image and recalled from sin to his friendship, human persons are expected to be as pure and holy in their lives as God is in his. God's people are expected to follow him.

In leaving Egypt, Israel responded to God's call (see Hos 11.1). The people were led by Yahweh and walked after him (see Ex 13.21–22). The experience of following God hidden in the pillar of cloud or of fire is never forgotten. Israel always is called to follow her Lord, as a betrothed to follow her bridegroom (see Jer 2.2), as a flock to follow its shepherd (see Ps 80.2).

In a covenant relationship, a vassal follows in the retinue of his lord. To love one's lord is to be ready to fulfill one's covenant undertakings. One walks along with the leader under whose command one must be prepared, if necessary, to do battle. When the Israelites commit themselves to living in accord with the covenant, their promise is not to "follow other gods" (see Dt 6.14), but to follow Yahweh, "to walk in all his ways" (Dt 10.12; cf. Jos 22.5).

When Israel is unfaithful, it is like a whore (see Ez 23.1–10), who follows the enemy's army. Sinners should turn back to their true Lord and follow him faithfully as they did in the exodus (see Hos 2.17). Then they will enjoy fully the power of his protection and the gentleness of his love.

To be safe is to stay close to God, to walk with him (see Mi 6.8). He takes the orphans, widows, and others who specially need help into his own family; he shakes the earth with his steps and makes rain fall when it is needed (see Ps 68.6–9). To such a protector, Israel prays: "Make me to know your ways, O Lord; teach me your paths" (Ps 25.4). Being kind, the Lord guides back to the safe path those who stray (see Ps 25.8–9). "Who is the man that fears the Lord? Him will he instruct in the way that he should choose" (Ps 25.12). "Fear" here means readiness to listen and follow.

The law is a guide to survival: "She is the book of the commandments of God, and the law that endures for ever. All who hold her fast will live, and those who forsake her will die. Turn, O Jacob, and take her; walk toward the shining of her light" (Bar 4.1–2). "Blessed are those whose way is blameless, who walk in the law of the Lord" (Ps 119.1). God marches with his people, and they have nothing to fear; they go off on their own and experience disaster (see Dt 31.8, 16–19). When they abandon God, his people are forced from their inheritance into exile (see Lv 26.33–41). But even then, a voice cries out in the desert, calling for a superhighway to be constructed for God and his people: "Every valley shall be lifted up, and every mountain and hill be made low; the uneven ground shall become level, and the rough places a plain" (Is 40.4). Yahweh will lead his people back from exile.

Question C: How does the covenant relationship deepen and transform morality?

1. **First, the relationship of the old covenant draws all human life into its context—the context of the relationship with God.** Harmony with God, religion, is universally recognized as a human good even outside the covenant relationship, but apart from that relationship it need not be considered the most basic form of harmony. However, the revelation recorded in the Old Testament at once makes it clear that this relationship has primacy. If its perfection is pursued consistently and diligently, every other human good will be served; but if harmony with God is not placed first, nothing else in life will go well. This point is made explicitly in the summary of the law and demand that God be loved above all else (see Dt 6.1–9).

2. **Second, the relationship into which Yahweh draws Israel causes God's people to share in some way in his qualities.** Throughout the Old Testament, the primary characteristics displayed by God are loving-kindness and faithfulness; Yahweh is a God of mercy and truth. Moreover, God makes it clear that he wills to act toward humankind not only in conformity with sound human standards of morality but in a way which goes beyond them. He also makes it clear that his people are to imitate him: "You shall be holy; for I the Lord your God am holy" (Lv 19.2). The rest of the chapter which opens with this injunction shows the practical significance of Yahweh's character for the morality of Israel.[7]

3. **Third, the covenant relationship deepens the moral insights available to humankind.** The richness of almost all the basic human goods is unfolded in many ways as human possibilities are opened up. The dignity of human persons, the sanctity of life, the pricelessness of wisdom, and so on are shown ever more clearly in the Old Testament, as the implications of the teaching that human beings are created in God's image and likeness are explored (see Gn 1.26–27; 9.6; Ps 8.5–6; Wis 7.13–8.8; Sir 15.11–20).

4. **Finally, the covenant community provides a fresh perspective for criticizing all conventional morality.** No society's accepted moral standards, not even those of Israel, are beyond question; God judges the ways of all humankind and finds them wanting. Such moral criticism, carried out only gradually in the Old Testament, is pressed farthest by the prophets. Moreover, in the face of repeated disasters to God's people themselves and nearly universal pessimism in pagan thought about the human condition, the prophets proclaim their hope for a new Jerusalem in which all nations would find salvation.[8]

Question D: How does the new covenant perfect the old?

1. The new covenant replaces the old. Jesus "has obtained a ministry which is as much more excellent than the old as the covenant he mediates is better, since it is enacted on better promises. For if that first covenant had been faultless, there would have been no occasion for a second" (Heb 8.6–7). A central theme of St. Paul's Epistles to the Romans and Galatians is that God's redemptive plan is accomplished, not by the law, but only "through faith in Jesus Christ for all who

believe" (Rom 3.22; cf. Gal 3.19–29). Yet the new covenant is not a new beginning of God's redemptive work (see DV 3–4). Jesus does not abolish, but rather fulfills, the law and the prophets (see Mt 5.17)—that is, the requirements and promises of the old covenant.⁹ As St. Thomas Aquinas points out, the community of the old covenant is a shadow of the communion realized in the Church of Christ (see *S.t.*, 1–2, q. 107, a. 2; cf. Col 2.17).

2. As was explained (in 20-G), God includes human cooperation in his redemptive work in order to preserve and enhance the dignity of fallen humankind even as he renews creation by his divine act of re-creation. Including human cooperation in his plan, God began by allying himself with human persons as they were, affected by sin and its consequences. For fallen men and women, the initial covenant relationship could not be perfect. As sinners, they were inevitably ambivalent toward God; as members of a humankind divided by sin, they were necessarily members of one human group locked in conflict with other groups. As chapter nineteen explained, God's plan for humankind includes both integral human fulfillment and a share in divine life. Fallen persons could not at once grasp perfectly either of these realities. The law of the old covenant served as a monitor to educate those to whom it was given in preparation for humankind's mature relationship with God in Jesus (see Gal 3.23–26).

3. **The Incarnation of the Word is the key to God's redemptive plan.** (Here this fact is taken as a starting point; its fittingness will be clarified to some extent by what follows.) In his human life, the Word justifies fallen humankind by his perfect obedience to the Father, which calls for the response of the divine act of re-creation begun in Jesus' resurrection, and forms the divine-human communion which God planned from the beginning (see Eph 1.7–23; Phil 2.6–11; Col 1.19–22).¹⁰ As man, the Word Incarnate needed a community and culture in which to be born. As chapter twenty-three will show, Jesus lived his life on earth only by understanding himself in terms developed in prior salvation history. Just as Mary was providentially prepared to be the mother of the Word made man, the old covenant providentially prepared Israel to be his nation (see Rv 12.1–5). Thus, before the perfect covenant God established with humankind in Jesus, an imperfect covenant was needed to shape the culture which humanly formed him.¹¹

The Word Incarnate is not simply a man of his culture, for God created this culture, just as he wished it, to serve as a medium of his work of revelation. God relates history to his own saving purposes (see Rom 11.30–32). The center of salvation history, the Incarnate Word, is not cast adrift in the stream of human history. Jesus completes what God all along intends (see Jn 19.28–30; 2 Cor 1.20; and all the New Testament references to the fulfillment of the Scriptures). Rather than Jesus being reducible to his culture, his culture is more appropriately reduced to him.

4. In sum, the central reason for the imperfection of the old covenant is that God simply could not complete his redemptive work all at once.¹² For the sake of the human cooperation included in his plan, the old covenant had to be a preparation for the fulfillment of God's promises in Jesus. Necessarily imperfect, the old covenant could not by itself justify fallen humankind. Those subject to the law of the old covenant could be saved by God's grace and by faith. But that law

itself, though it made God's people acutely conscious of their sinfulness, did not give them power to live good lives (see Rom 3.20; Gal 3.21–24).

5. **Fundamentally, the new covenant perfects the old in a way that goes beyond its human aspects to God's giving us a share in his own divine life.** The people of the old covenant was genuinely and closely allied with God. Yet in a very real sense, in his absolute transcendence God remained a foreign power. A share in the Spirit of God was promised and hoped for, yet it was not given by the law and the way of life it shaped. **The old covenant's inadequacy to heal humankind's alienation from God had to be overcome by a covenant which established intimate personal communion with him.** Jesus established this new covenant. In it, God does dwell with humankind, and men and women become his friends, even his children (see Jn 1.12–18; Rom 8.14–17; Heb 8.6–13). The promised Spirit is given, and by his power God's children can live not only humanly good but even supernaturally holy lives (see Rom 8.1–17).

If one might ask how Man even at the beginning could have conceived of sharing in divine life in a way that made it clear that this is truly worthwhile and involves no infringement on human interests, one certainly must ask how sinful Man could have conceived of such a thing. The Incarnation of the Word shows how this can be done. In Jesus God becomes humanly accessible (see *S.t.*, 3, q. 1, a. 2).

Even at the beginning, Man must have stood in awe of God. Sinful men and women hide from him in guilty fear. Although he seems friendly, might his friendship not be withdrawn, with dire consequences for humankind? The Incarnation of the Word disposes of this difficulty. There can be no suspicion now that God involves himself in the human either sporadically or with dubious intentions, for by becoming one of us he himself has entered lastingly and unreservedly into the human situation.

Even the best of those chosen by God, an Abraham or Moses, was himself enmeshed in sin. Established on such a person, a community of friendship with God always remained unstable. With the Incarnation of the Word, however, divine life becomes part of creation and can no longer be expelled. God's Spirit becomes present in creation in a new and personal way, the Word Incarnate being, as it were, a conduit through which the Spirit flows permanently into the created world.

6. Since the plan of God for divine-human communion, described in chapter nineteen, could not be revealed at once to the men and women of the old covenant, their cooperation in God's redemptive work necessarily was limited by hope for success in their pursuit of objectives in this world: the inheritance of the promised land, many descendants, national greatness, and so forth. In a humankind divided by sin, the covenant community had to be one group; other human groups inevitably were their competitors and foes.

7. Under these conditions, it is understandable that those under the old covenant tended to make certain mistakes. Not all the elements of integral human fulfillment seemed to them as important as those goods whose realization they sought. The implications of Yahweh's unique divinity and universal lordship did not easily transform the attitude of his people toward the remainder of humankind.

8. The fact that those under the old covenant were made acutely aware of sin yet not enabled to live holy lives had certain consequences. The relationship the

old covenant formed was unstable on the part of Israel. Not only its sacrifices and sin offerings, but the covenant itself, needed renewal (see Heb 8.7–13; 10.1–18). Reverencing the law but not fulfilling it, men and women were tempted to try to lessen their responsibilities by treating as adequate a certain manageable set of outward performances. As Jesus' conflicts with Pharisees and Zealots make clear, this legalistic mentality led to a false conception of evil, as if it were a positive reality to be avoided by precautions, isolated in certain classes— "sinners" and "pagans"—or destroyed by the violence of war. The apparent need to choose between some elements of human good and friendship with God was inevitable for fallen humankind and not wholly overcome by the old covenant.

The prophets longed for a better age in which friendship with God and complete human fulfillment would coincide. In such an age all the earth would know God (see Is 11.9). His pardon would be effective and would give everyone the power to live rightly (see Jer 31.31–34). Everlasting justice would be introduced (see Dn 9.24). The nations would come together at the Lord's holy mountain (see Mi 4.1–3).

The need was felt for a better type of redemptive community than that established by the old, restrictive covenants: The new covenant must be open to all men and women. Furthermore, while dealing with evil as a reality, the community must not try to set aside some part of the good things made by God as if evil were peculiarly present in them nor may it treat those involved in sin as enemies to be destroyed. Only in such a new covenant could faithfulness to God and love of all human fulfillment coincide. In a world marked by the reality of sin and its consequences, however, the lives of truly good people are at the mercy of those who persist in evil. How can anyone live in such a world without resorting to the evils necessary to cope with it?

There is only one possibility. Members of the new redemptive community must have solid assurance that they will really be fulfilled by being faithful to God and to their own integral fulfillment. If this happy outcome cannot be realized in a world broken by sin, however, it could be perfectly realized in another world. The solution to the problem thus is for God to establish his perfect communion of friendship, his kingdom, as a reality not of this sinful world. Men and women living in this world will be invited to live also in the invisible kingdom and for the sake of fulfillment there. Yet a real bridge between this world and the invisible community will be needed, together with sufficient grounds for confidence that the invisible is not a myth.

The Word, eternally with God and a coprinciple of creation, "became flesh and dwelt among us" (Jn 1.14). God and his love became visible; a common life of divine and human persons was inaugurated, involving vastly greater intimacy between God and human beings than under the law of Moses. Jesus is the bridge between this broken world of human experience and the new creation, free of sin, which is being built up with him as its head (see *S.t.*, 3, q. 26).

9. **Jesus, being both God and man, shows that there is no need to choose between human good and friendship with God. Moreover, the eternal kingdom proclaimed by the gospel provides an object of human hope sufficient to motivate Jesus' disciples to follow him lovingly, for the kingdom includes all the things for which a good person would long. Jesus makes it clear that his kingdom is not of this world and that it is a more inclusive reality than anyone previously could have imagined.** Limitations on openness to various human goods, set by the law of the old covenant and by its misunderstanding, are overcome. The boundaries of the covenant community are extended

to include all nations, so that the new covenant can coincide with the entire community of humankind, to whose integral fulfillment moral truth points.

10. The grace of the Holy Spirit, given through Jesus, supplies the power to overcome sin and live a genuinely holy life. Not conceived legalistically, the law of the new covenant is primarily interior (cf. *S.t.*, 1–2, q. 106, aa. 1–2). Former moral compromises, such as permission for divorce, can be set aside (see Mk 10.2–12). The full requirements of moral truth for human fulfillment, not merely a legalistic minimum, can be met. Evil is more easily understood as the privation it really is, and evil is overcome in the only way it can be—as Jesus does, by healing love for those mutilated by sin and its consequences. Because it really overcomes sin, the new covenant in Jesus' blood is made once for all and is everlasting.

11. In conclusion, the new covenant perfects the old primarily by establishing intimate divine-human communion through the God-man, Jesus Christ (see appendix 1). This communion in divine life has implications for human moral life and bodily life. Restored to friendship with God, those who enter into Jesus' covenant are enabled to live upright lives. Although in this fallen world such lives remain difficult and seem humanly unrewarding, those who live in Jesus can be good persons in this world and can hope for the fulfillment their goodness deserves when it is answered by God's re-creative act, begun in Jesus' resurrection.

12. The moral implications of the new covenant, briefly described here, will be articulated in detail in chapters twenty-three through twenty-eight. The central principle of what follows is this: In his human life, Jesus deals with evil as a good man and child of God should. In doing this, he not only shows us how to live good human lives in the fallen world, but makes it possible for us to do so. He does this by making his own redemptive action present to us, so that our lives can be lived in cooperation with God's redemptive work accomplished in him.[13]

A true man, yet free of sin, the Incarnate Word shows what human life in a sinful world ought to be. No one who believes in him can suspect his motives; they are entirely pure. He adds immeasurably to creation, to the glory of God, by manifesting God's goodness and love in an unprecedented fashion. He carries on God's redeeming work, not only by an almighty fiat from above but also by human action (see *S.t.*, 3, q. 46, aa. 3, 12; q. 47, aa. 1–2). Proceeding in this way, the Word Incarnate becomes a potential friend to all other men and women. We can love and trust him as we can no one else. We can ally ourselves with him. And insofar as we do this, our sinful existence can be greatly reformed in our personal relationship with him, and our good acts can contribute to a worthwhile cause: his redeeming work (see *S.t.*, 3, q. 8, a. 1; q. 69, a. 5).

As we shall see, it is almost impossible for a truly good human life in this sinful world to appear fulfilling. Jesus' life, considered as objectively as possible, hardly seems so. If we believe in him, however, we look beyond his earthly life. We see that, while he lived a very restricted existence and died a miserable death, he was at the same time bringing into reality the human dimension of the heavenly fulfillment of which he is the first principle (see Col 1.15–22).

By his Incarnation and life among us, the Word of God provides us with the model of the Son of Man sharing gloriously in divinity. Looking to him, we are confident that our own lives, however compelling contrary appearances might be, are not wasted when our good efforts fail, not defeated when evil prevails, not ended when death comes. Thus we can be confident that it is not vain to choose rightly, for neither the inevitable self-limitation which comes with choosing nor the suffering which comes with choosing rightly in a sinful world will last. Really though invisibly, fulfillment in a communion of love is already ours. We rejoice in hope.

Question E: How are the human and the divine united in Jesus?

1. The Council of Chalcedon, which provides the most precise formulation of Christian faith in the Word Incarnate, uses the words "person" and "nature" to set aside certain errors. It does not define what a nature is but takes it for granted that when two subjects can truly be said to be the same kind of something, they are of one nature.

2. With respect to the two natures in Jesus, the Council insists that he is in them "without any commingling or change or division or separation; that the distinction between the natures is in no way removed by their union but rather the specific character of each nature is preserved and they are united in one person and one hypostasis" (DS 302/148).[14] **In excluding commingling, Chalcedon denies that Jesus' divinity and humanity are mingled with each other or mixed together.** If they were, something of the reality and integrity of either or both natures would be lost. Thus, the definition protects the truth that Jesus is both God and man, and excludes the idea that he is a hybrid, partly human and partly divine but not entirely either.

3. The Second Council of Constantinople later makes it clear that the two natures are united in the hypostasis (the person), and that the person is the divine Word (see DS 424–30/216–20). In affirming that the Word is God from God and that the Incarnate Word is one person, we must deny that Jesus is a human person. Yet in denying this we do not say that Jesus lacks anything which belongs to the positive reality and perfection of a human person. Rather, we say that Jesus' human, creaturely reality and perfection are not primary in him as our human, creaturely reality and perfection are primary in us.[15]

4. In our experience, any entity which is of a certain nature by that very fact cannot possibly be an entity of any other nature. This is how finite natures are: They exclude one another. Thus one tends to suppose that Jesus, if he is truly human, cannot be divine, and vice versa. But this assumption is false. **Divine nature is not exclusive, though the fact of the Incarnation of the Word is the only evidence we have for this.** And this fact is a datum of faith, which remains a mystery to us. We do not understand what God is in himself.

Great difficulties arise if one forgets that language used with respect to God is relational. This point was treated in chapter two, appendix three.

"Nature" said of the divinity of Jesus cannot be used in the same sense as "nature" said of his humanity. For his human nature is the same as ours, and one of the essential characteristics of our nature is that it excludes our being anything of another nature—"nature" said again in the same sense. For example, one could not be human and a horse, since to be either excludes being the other and likewise excludes being any other kind of thing we understand. Clearly, whatever divinity is, the same does not hold true of "nature" said of God.

Similarly with "person" (see *S.t.*, 1, q. 29, aa. 3–4). There is a vast literature about the consciousness of Jesus. It usually takes for granted a remarkable familiarity with God, as if we knew what divine knowing is and as if God were a conscious self much like ourselves. In sober fact, we do not know what the inner life of God is like.

Moreover, even with respect to ourselves the concept of person has much that is mysterious about it. Our person includes not only our conscious subjectivity, but our bodiliness as well (see *S.t.*, 1, q. 75, a. 4; sup., q. 75, a. 1). "Me" serves better than "I" to indicate what belongs to our person, for someone who is careless bumps me, thoughts occur to me, my conscience bothers me, and people who disapprove what I write criticize me. "Me" somehow unites all these. There seems to be no particular difficulty in supposing that Jesus' subjectivity has the same general character of mysterious inclusiveness, with the difference that he also somehow knows: The Father begets me.[16]

5. Keeping in mind that we do not and cannot understand what God is in himself, we shall avoid the mistake of thinking we understand God's nature or, in particular, the divinity of Jesus. Avoiding this mistake is also important to understand the relationship between the goods proper to Jesus according to his two natures, for these goods are nothing but his full being.

6. If this mistake is avoided, we shall not think we understand what divine goodness and love are in themselves, nor imagine some conflict between them and human goodness and love. **The Incarnation of the Word is our assurance that it is not necessary to choose between the human and the divine, for the human nature the Word assumed was not thereby annulled** (see GS 22).

7. If a choice between loving God and loving human goods were necessary, it is evident that the Lord Jesus, being God, could not have made the wrong choice, would have chosen loving God, and thus could not have loved human goods. But anyone who could not naturally and spontaneously love all the basic human goods would not have an intact human nature, for love of these goods is nothing but human nature's built-in disposition toward its own fulfillment. Jesus, however, has an intact human nature and so loves human goods. Therefore Jesus, though a divine person, did not have to prefer—or, more accurately, could not prefer—the love of God to the love of basic human goods.

In his Incarnation, the Word as man accepts the conditions of human coming to be and human life. The Incarnation does not take place all at once—not that at any moment the Word is incompletely united with his humanity, but that this humanity, like our own, comes to be only gradually, and so, if one may speak thus, cannot be assumed faster than it becomes. Moreover, the Word becomes flesh not in an ideal humanity, in which his divinity would at once demand his human fulfillment, but in flesh like our own sinful flesh (see Rom 8.3). In this sense, in becoming man, Jesus "emptied himself, taking the form of a servant, being born in the likeness of men" (Phil 2.7; cf. Rom 8.3).[17]

Question F: How are the divine and human aspects of Jesus' actions related?

1. Jesus does many things, such as the miracles performed in his own name, which cannot be attributed to him only as God or only as man, but must be said to

be done by him who is God and man precisely insofar as he is one person in both natures. It may not be said that Jesus lacks either a human or a divine nature, that these natures are homogenized or commingled into one, that either nature is changed, or that the two are divided or separated. Similarly, it may not be said that Jesus lacks either a human or a divine will or willing, that these capacities and operations are commingled or collapsed into one, that either power or actuation is changed by their unity in him, or that they are divided or separated (see DS 556–57/291–92). Therefore, the problem is: How can we understand the acts of Jesus—for example, the raising of Lazarus from the dead (see Jn 11.1–44)—of which clearly it must be said that they are done by him insofar as he is one person in two natures?

Some Greek-speaking Christians of the seventh century tried to answer this question by saying that the actions of Jesus are simply divine-human actions, not actions in which the divine and human remain distinct. This attempt to merge the two natures of Jesus at the level of operation blurred the distinction between his divinity and humanity. Therefore, it was strongly condemned, first by the Council of the Lateran in 649 and later by the Third Council of Constantinople.

Although not an ecumenical council, the teaching of the Council of the Lateran, convened by Pope Martin I, became recognized as having great authority. This council rejected the attempt to merge Jesus' divine and human wills and their willing by saying: "If anyone, following the wicked heretics, foolishly takes the human-divine operation, which the Greeks call *theandric*, as one operation and does not profess in accord with the holy Fathers that it is twofold, that is, divine and human; or if he professes that the very neologism *divine-human* which has been established designates one operation but does not indicate the wonderful and glorious union of both operations: let such a one be condemned" (DS 515/268; translation amended).

A generation later, the Third Council of Constantinople enlarged on the matter. It insisted that Jesus has two wills and actuations of will, not divided, changed, separated, or commingled. The two wills are not opposed, but his human will is compliant and obedient to his divine will: "For it was necessary for the human will to move itself, but in obedience to the divine will, as the great wisdom of Athanasius has taught; because just as his human nature is said to be and is the human nature of God the Word, so too the natural will of his human nature is said to be and is God the Word's very own, as he himself says: 'I have come down from heaven not to do my own will, but the will of the Father who sent me' (Jn 6.38)" (DS 556/291).

The humanity of Jesus as a whole is not annulled by being assumed, so neither is his will. It follows that there are in him two actuations of will, since each nature does what is proper to itself. This position is necessary since otherwise what is created would be absorbed into the divine or the divine degraded to the level of creatures. Both miracles and sufferings belong to the same person:

> In every way possible, therefore, we uphold our denial both of commingling and of division and in this concise utterance we may express the entire matter: We believe that one of the Holy Trinity who, after the Incarnation, is our Lord Jesus Christ, is our true God; and we assert that both his natures clearly appear in his one hypostasis. In it throughout the whole ordered conduct of his life he gave evidence of both his miracles and his sufferings, not just in appearance, but in actuality. The difference of natures within the same person is recognized by the fact that each nature, in communion with the other nature, wills and carries out what is proper to itself.

Accordingly, we hold that there are two natural wills and operations concurring in harmony for the salvation of the human race. (DS 558/292; translation amended)

Thus, while the Council rejects a unity of actuations, it also rejects separation, and maintains evidence of both human and divine natures and actuations in the whole life of Jesus.

2. Certainly Jesus' actions, such as the raising of Lazarus, are unified as actions. But the willing which is the heart of the action is twofold, and the work and its effect are both human and divine. The problem is to clarify this complexity.

3. To begin with, the distinct actuation of both the divine and human wills in Jesus, upon which the Church's teaching insists, necessarily follows if the Incarnate Word really lives a life. Will is only a capacity for willing; a will without its appropriate willing would be null. Of course, it is equally necessary to maintain the real unity of Jesus in "the whole ordered conduct of his life" (DS 558/292), for otherwise one would have to suppose that the Incarnation is incomplete, as if it took place only at certain moments or in certain aspects of him and his life. It seems to follow that one should not suppose certain acts of the Incarnate Word to be human and others divine; all are both.

4. Chapter twenty-two will consider the human aspect of Jesus' life. As a man, he makes a commitment to the human good of friendship with God, discerns his unique human vocation with respect to this good, and lives out this vocation. His whole life is a well-integrated system of human acts. But the divine will of the Incarnate Word can hardly have remained inoperative with respect to anything he did humanly, whether the performing of miracles or the accepting of sufferings. Thus, the whole life of the Lord Jesus was both divine and human at the same time. How, then, are these distinguished, as the teaching of faith requires?

5. This question can be answered as follows. **Insofar as he is God, Jesus reveals the Father in the medium of his human nature and life as man.**[18] **Insofar as he is man, the Word responds to the Father in a manner appropriate to a man in perfect communion with God.**[19] In other words, Jesus' life has the character of a revelatory sign because it proceeds not only from the Incarnate Word's human willing but also from his divine willing, and it has the character of a human response to God revealing because it proceeds not only from the Word Incarnate's divine willing but also from his human willing.

6. These two distinct aspects of the life of the Word are not separated. Included in the revelation of God in Jesus is the appropriate human response to God revealing; part of what God wishes to communicate to us is how we ought to relate to him. At the same time, Jesus as man knew his life to be a medium of revelation and intentionally conducted it as such.[20] Part of what he wished to accomplish in his human response to God was to make himself a transparent medium of God's revelation, so that his human brothers and sisters could join in his response.

With respect to the life of Jesus as a medium of revelation, Vatican II teaches: "The Word made flesh, sent as 'a man to men,' 'speaks the words of God' (Jn 3.34), and completes the work of salvation which his Father gave him to do (cf. Jn 5.36; 17.4). For this reason Jesus—to see whom is to see the Father (Jn 14.9)—perfected revelation by fulfilling it through his whole work of making himself present and manifesting himself: through his words and deeds, his signs and wonders, but especially through his death and glorious resurrection from the dead and final sending of the Spirit of truth. Moreover, he confirmed with divine testimony what revelation proclaimed: that God is with us to free us from the darkness of sin and death, and to raise us up to life eternal" (DV 4; translation amended).

Revelation is personal communication. Human persons communicate by listening as well as speaking, undergoing as well as doing. This is also true of God, above all of God revealing in Jesus. Therefore, God is revealed in the medium of Jesus' total humanity, in its every actuation, expression, and undergoing. Likewise, precisely because God reveals in and through Jesus' human life, nothing appears in Jesus which is not part of his human life—his divinity never blazes forth—although his human life often does manifest more than human power and bring about supernatural effects, as when he performs miracles in his own name, forgives sins, institutes the Eucharist, and so on.

Summary

One finds essential features of God's redemptive work even in its preparatory stages. The initiative is God's, but he takes a human being as his helper; he enters into a relationship of friendship with this person, sealing it with a covenant; the human collaborator acts as an intercessor with God for other human persons. However, redemption by God does not mean he either pays or is paid; God is the redeemer, and he freely gives us his victory. In the Old Testament God's redemptive work is an ever-growing communication of his love, pointing toward his sharing of his own Spirit.

Covenant existed as a human institution before God used it for revelatory purposes. It had one essential component: the stipulation of some definite responsibilities to shape a social relationship. This is found in God's covenant with his chosen people. The commandments are the covenant's stipulations, requiring the Israelites' exclusive loyalty to God and regulating relationships among them for the sake of their unity and common allegiance to God. It is important to notice that God redeems first and then offers a covenant. Fulfillment of its stipulations is not a condition for entering into the relationship but a requirement arising from the relationship. God's commands are not backed by imposed sanctions; rather, failure to keep God's law of itself invites disaster.

The old covenant relationship deepens and transforms morality. All human life is drawn into its context, and the primacy of the human good of religion is made clear. The relationship causes God's people to share in his qualities, including those which are more than human. Moral insights are deepened, and the richness of human goods is unfolded. A fresh perspective is provided for criticizing all conventional morality.

The new covenant replaces the old by perfecting rather than abolishing it. To make it possible for fallen humankind to cooperate in God's redemptive work, he began by allying himself with human persons as they were. Given human sinfulness, this initial alliance necessarily was imperfect. Moreover, the Incarnation of the Word is the key to redemption. A covenant shaping a human community in preparation for this perfect divine communication necessarily was imperfect by comparison with it.

Necessarily imperfect, the old covenant could not by itself justify fallen humankind. While those subject to its law could be saved by God's grace and by faith, the covenant did not empower them to live good and holy lives. By contrast, the new covenant communicates a share in divine life. In Jesus the Spirit is given, and fallen human persons are transformed into God's children.

Because of the limitations of the old covenant, the hope of God's people under it was limited by their this-worldly goals and alienation from other communities. Not all the elements of integral human fulfillment seemed to them as important as their particular goals. Thus, Israel often was unfaithful and tempted to legalism. Some groups mistakenly conceived evil as if it were a positive reality. Insofar as this mistaken idea was adopted, there appeared to be a need to choose between friendship with God and some elements of human good.

Jesus, being both God and man, makes it clear that there is no need to make such a choice. His new covenant remedies all the defects of the old covenant. The kingdom Jesus proclaims is not of this world, and it holds out hope sufficient to motivate his followers. He excludes moral compromises, rejects legalism, assumes a true concept of evil in confronting it, and universalizes the communion of the new covenant to include all humankind. All this is effective for fallen humankind only because the grace of the Holy Spirit, given through Jesus, supplies the power to overcome sin and live a genuinely holy life.

The new covenant's perfection of the old has moral implications. Those who live in Jesus can be good persons in this world and hope for the fulfillment of their goodness through God's re-creative act, begun in Jesus' resurrection. Chapters twenty-three through twenty-eight will show in detail how Jesus makes it possible for us to live good human lives in this fallen world.

The divine and human natures are united in the person of Jesus without commingling (mixing with each other), separation, or change. Finite natures exclude one another, but evidently this is not the case with the divine nature. Nor, as the case of Jesus shows, are divine goodness and love alternatives to human goodness and love. Jesus did not have to choose between loving God and loving human goods.

Plainly, some things Jesus does cannot be attributed to him only as God or only as man, but as one person in both natures. Indeed, his whole life was both human and divine. This complexity can be clarified as follows: As God, Jesus reveals the Father in the medium of his human life; as man, the Word responds to the Father in the manner appropriate to a man in perfect communion with God. There is no separation here. God is revealed in every aspect of Jesus' life; but nothing appears in Jesus which is not part of his human life.

Appendix 1:   How the Incarnation reveals the personal life of God

In the New Testament, God makes known and shares his own inner communion. Christians know the distinct divine persons.

The wisdom of God has been with him from the beginning of creation; she plays on the surface of the earth where she finds delight in the sons of men (see Prv 8.31). This wisdom is or includes God's Spirit (see Wis 1.4–7; 7.7, 22; 9.17). The Spirit, the creative power of God, which renews the face of the earth (see Ps 104.30), makes divine wisdom able to penetrate and pervade all things, to transform them gently and inwardly. Wisdom "renews all things; in every generation she passes into holy souls and makes them friends of God, and prophets" (Wis 7.27). The love of God becomes his gift of his own wisdom and Spirit, which establish communion between God and his people.

This communion becomes manifest in Jesus. "God so loved the world that he gave his only Son" (Jn 3.16). Not because human hearts were ready: "But God shows his love for us in that while we were yet sinners Christ died for us" (Rom 5.8). "In this the love of God was made manifest among us, that God sent his only Son into the world, so that we might live through him" (1 Jn 4.9).

Jesus is not only a work of God's love, an expression communicated out of love. The very love of God comes to us in Jesus, our Lord (see Rom 8.39). The Word of God, his eternal wisdom in person, comes "full of grace and truth" (Jn 1.14). Jesus and his Father are one (see Jn 10.30). With his Father's love, Jesus, "having loved his own who were in the world, he loved them to the end" (Jn 13.1).

The Father's love of the Son is total: "The Father loves the Son, and has given all things into his hand" (Jn 3.35). The love of Jesus for his followers is the same: "As the Father has loved me, so have I loved you" (Jn 15.9). Jesus wishes his love to be communicated perfectly: "Abide in my love" (Jn 15.9). About to die, Jesus prays to the Father and expresses the meaning of what he is doing for those who will believe in him: "I made known to them your name, and I will make it known, that the love with which you have loved me may be in them, and I in them" (Jn 17.26).

The revelation of God's love is a total personal communication. Jesus gives nothing other; he gives himself filled with grace and truth so that of his fullness we may all receive (see Jn 1.16). Coming down from heaven, filled with divine life, Jesus gives himself as living bread, gives his flesh as food to be eaten, and thus communicates the Father's life, which also is his own, to all who partake of him (see Jn 6.33, 48–58).

The Incarnation of the Word is due to the power of the Holy Spirit (see Mt 1.18; Lk 1.35). Jesus is endowed with the Spirit and has power to baptize with the Spirit (see Mk 1.7–10; Jn 1.32–33). Jesus "utters the words of God, for it is not by measure that he gives the Spirit" (Jn 3.34). He announces that the Father gives the Spirit freely, for the asking: "If you then, who are evil, know how to give good gifts to your children, how much more will the heavenly Father give the Holy Spirit to those who ask him!" (Lk 11.13).

From within Jesus flows the Spirit, as living water (see Jn 4.10; 7.37–39). The Spirit is the Spirit of truth, of divine faithfulness; he will come to stay (see Jn 14.17). Jesus and the Father send the Spirit (see Jn 15.26). By his power, sins are forgiven (see Jn 20.22–23). When Jesus has been glorified, the promised Spirit comes and the new family of God is formed (see Acts 2). The love of God is sealed by his personal gift of himself, for the Spirit fills Christians and dwells in them permanently as in his own home (see Rom 8.9; 1 Cor 3.16; 6.19; 2 Tm 1.14).

Appendix 2:   The personal unity of the life of the Word Incarnate

There remains a puzzle of considerable theological significance. The human life of Jesus is a creature among creatures. As such, like every creature it is referred to God the creator, who is a single principle of created realities. In other words, in one respect the humanity and human life of Jesus belong no more to the Word than to the Father and the Holy Spirit; yet only the Word is man, and, clearly, the revelatory life of Jesus somehow must be the personal life of the Word (see DS 535/284, 801/429).

It will not do to try to escape the puzzle by denying that as a creature the life of Jesus is the work of the Trinity. Scripture makes it clear that the Incarnation, including the whole life and destiny of Jesus, is the work of the Holy Spirit. Jesus is conceived by the power of the Spirit (see Lk 1.35); he acts by the power of the Spirit (see Mt 12.28); he is raised by the power of the Spirit (see Rom 1.4; 8.11). Jesus is Christ (Messiah; the anointed) because he has the Spirit (see Lk 4.21). At the same time, Jesus makes it clear that his work is not separable from his Father's work as creator (see Jn 5.17). The Trinity is undivided in work, which is attributed now to one person and now to another.[21]

Still, the Gospels make it clear that Jesus regards himself as Son not only insofar as he is man, but also insofar as he is God, and thus make it clear that in a special sense he reveals as Son and primarily reveals the Father, while concomitantly revealing himself as Son and the Spirit as their common gift (see Mt 11.25–27; Lk 10.21–22; Jn 5.16–30; 7.14–18; 8.28–30, 54–55; 12.20–50; 14.1–14; and so on).[22]

This puzzle can be clarified to some extent if one bears in mind the distinction between creation and revelation. Everything depends upon God the creator. But among the things created, certain ones serve as the given component of a sign by which personal communication is carried out. Now, the life of Jesus as creature must be distinguished from this same life as revealing sign.

As creature, it proceeds from the Trinity, and in a way immediately from the Holy Spirit who, as it were, being the term of God's inner life is nearest the beginning of his outward manifestation in creation.

But as revealing sign, Jesus' life communicates God personally, as Scripture shows (see, e.g., Jn 14.6–11; 17.20–23). Only the unity of the personal relationship to the Father of the Word Incarnate according to both his natures makes it possible for him to communicate God personally by revealing the distinction and unity between himself and the Father. The unity of this personal relationship would be impossible if the life of Jesus as revealing sign—in which his human relationship with his Father is carried on—were not the personal life of the Word Incarnate. And so, in this respect, Jesus' life, rather than proceeding from the Trinity, is the personal life of the Word, revealing the Father, and so both himself as Son and the Spirit, as distinct persons.

If one puts matters as I have just done, many questions are likely to be raised concerning the relationships between the creative causality of the Trinity, the revelatory work of the Word, and the human life of Jesus as man. But there is not much point in trying to speculate about these relationships. They are simply aspects of the action-dimensions of the mysteries of the Trinity and the Incarnation, and we can no more understand the mysterious unity and complexity at the level of action than at the level of being. Just as "nature" cannot be said in the same sense of the divine and human natures, neither can "will" and "operation" have one sense said of principles of the life of Jesus considered as divine revelation and as human response. It is useless to try to speculate about divine realities in themselves, for we know God only insofar as we are related to him in creaturely dependence and in the relationship he establishes with us by revelation.

St. Thomas gives the most acceptable alternative to the solution sketched above to the problem of the personal unity of Jesus' life. Holding with the faith of the Church that in Jesus there are both divine and human operations, he tries to explain the unity of Christ's action by saying that "the divine nature uses the operation of the human nature as its own instrument in operation, and likewise the human nature shares in the operation of the divine nature, as an instrument shares in the operation of the principal actor."[23] This formulation seems somewhat appropriate for expressing the aspect in which the human life of Jesus ought to be attributed to the Word as the medium in and by which he reveals. But even here the formula can be misleading, and it is quite misleading if it is taken as a complete account of the situation. I will consider the latter of these two points first.

It is telling that Thomas says "the divine nature uses" rather than "the Word uses." This sort of expression is seldom found in Thomas' works. He very well knows that natures are principles by which actions are done, while persons act. In all strictness, the divine nature does not do anything; to say that it does is to use the word "nature" in a way which removes the only sense it has in its use in reference to God.

If Thomas had focused more sharply on the fact that the human life of Jesus is lived by the person who is the Word, according to the human nature which really is the humanity of the Word, he would have realized that the human life of Jesus not only must be considered an expression of his divinity but also a noninstrumental human response to God's love. Toward the Father, the Incarnate Son lives the human life of Jesus as the Son of Man, who forms the children of Man into a redeeming community, the Church.

Even insofar as the Incarnate Word reveals the Father in the human life which is his as man, the human willing of Jesus is not in any ordinary sense a mere instrument of his divine willing.[24] Thomas realized that "instrument" is said here in a special sense.[25] For if the idea of instrument is pressed too far, two implications follow. First, the unity of the person of the Word would be denied. Since one's own willing is not something one uses but something one does, if the human willing of Jesus is used by the Word, then it is not done by him, but by someone else—which faith forbids. Second, the full truth of the humanity of Jesus would be denied, since he would lack the freedom and responsibility of one who lives a morally significant human life as his own, not as someone else's life.

Apart from these arguments, it is important to set aside an idea about instrumental causality Thomas probably never entertained, but which probably is in the minds of some who use this language today. People often imagine that a human person is really a thinking and choosing subject hidden somewhere inside the head. The person tends to be identified with consciousness, and consciousness is imagined to be hidden within. This picture is part of modern mind-body dualism. According to this view, one's bodily performances already are instrumental to one's real inner self. The body is imagined to be a tool.

In this context, to talk of the humanity of Jesus and its operations as instrumental to his divinity suggests that the Word is once more removed from the outward behavior of Jesus. One almost imagines that the Word is not man, but is only sending messages to the human self which proceeds somewhat like a hypnotized subject to execute them. Obviously, this view of the situation altogether deprives the Word of his human life.

How ought we to think of the relationship? No image can begin to convey it. I think the words which best express it are these: "That which was from the beginning, which we have heard, which we have seen with our eyes, which we have looked upon and touched with our hands, concerning the word of life—the life was made manifest, and we saw it, and testify to it, and proclaim to you the eternal life which was with the Father and was made manifest to us" (1 Jn 1.1–2). This clear and realistic language totally negates the very image I also wish to reject. For him who had touched Jesus, the Word is given us in his sensible body and outward behavior, which is no less God's in being human and no less completely human in being God's.

Notes

1. On covenant: Delbert R. Hillers, *Covenant: The History of a Biblical Idea* (Baltimore: Johns Hopkins University Press, 1969), 28–70. A helpful brief treatment: William G. Most, "A Biblical Theology of Redemption in a Covenant Framework," *Catholic Biblical Quarterly,* 29 (1967), 1–19; also G. E. Mendenhall, "Covenant," *The Interpreter's Dictionary of the Bible,* 1:714–23.

2. The treaty form of the covenant is more perfectly exemplified in Deuteronomy, chaps. 5–28. See Dennis J. McCarthy, S.J., *Treaty and Covenant: A Study in Form in the Ancient Oriental Documents and in the Old Testament* (Rome: Pontifical Biblical Institute, 1963), 109–40. However, the parallelism between the account in Exodus and the forming of the new covenant makes it appropriate to prefer Exodus for the present study.

3. See F. Laubach, "Blood," and G. R. Beasley-Murray, "Sprinkle," *New International Dictionary of New Testament Theology,* 1:220–25.

4. Some scholars dispute this interpretation of Ex 24.1–11, but others support it. See, for example, John Bright, *The Kingdom of God: The Biblical Concept and Its Meaning for the Church* (New York: Abingdon Press, 1953), 228; for this and the ratification ceremony in general: John E. Huesman, S.J., "Exodus," *Jerome Biblical Commentary,* 3.67.

5. For a good treatment of this point and criticism of the excessive polemic of Luther against the law, see Karl Barth, *Ethics,* ed. Dietrich Braun, trans. Geoffrey W. Bromiley (New York: Seabury Press, 1981), 89–93.

6. There is a false theology which reduces the legal aspect of commandments to a purely secondary and questionable development from a purely "personalistic" covenant morality. This theology fails to recognize the grounding of commandments as a whole in wisdom and reality. For a helpful analysis: Jon D. Levenson, "The Theologies of Commandment in Biblical Israel," *Harvard Theological Review,* 73 (1980), 17–33.

7. The transforming impact of revelation on morality is made clear especially in this respect but also in others by Matthew J. O'Connell, S.J., "The Concept of Commandment in the Old Testament," *Theological Studies,* 21 (1960), 351–403.

8. Blocks of prophetic material contain criticism of the morality of the pagans (see, e.g., Is 13–23; Jer 46–51; Ez 25–32). The proclamation of a universal hope for salvation is found not in any general speculation about the human condition but in the vision of Jerusalem, saved by Yahweh, serving as the principle of salvation for the nations (see, e.g., Is 60). On these points, see B. D. Napier, "Prophet," *Interpreter's Dictionary of the Bible,* 3:910–20; Gerhard von Rad, *The Message of the Prophets* (New York: Harper and Row, 1972), 100–101, 258–63.

9. False notions of opposition between the Old Testament and the New Testament, between Matthew and Paul, are firmly set aside by careful exegetical work. See, for example, A. Feuillet, "Loi de Dieu, loi du Christ et loi de l'Esprit d'après les epîstres pauliniennes: Les rapports de ces trois lois avec la Loi Mosaique." *Novum Testamentum,* 22 (1980), 29–65.

10. Arianism and present theological opinions like it in denying that Jesus is God have the practical significance of denying that by communion in Jesus Christians truly are united with God: Alasdair I. C. Heron, "Homoousios with the Father," in *The Incarnation: Ecumenical Studies in the Nicene-Constantinopolitan Creed, A.D. 381,* ed. Thomas F. Torrance (Edinburgh: Handsel Press, 1981), 58–87. The explanation of redemption on the basis of the Incarnation of the Word and the obedience as man of the Incarnate Word already is found in the recapitulation theory of Irenaeus: J. N. D. Kelly, *Early Christian Doctrines,* rev. ed. (San Francisco: Harper and Row, 1978), 170–74; more fully, with useful references: Andrew J. Bandstra, "Paul and an Ancient Interpreter: A Comparison of the Teaching on Redemption in Paul and Irenaeus," *Calvin Theological Journal,* 5 (1970), 43–63.

11. See Pierre Grelot, "Relations between the Old and New Testaments in Jesus Christ," in *Problems and Perspectives of Fundamental Theology,* ed. René Latourelle and Gerald O'Collins, trans. Matthew J. O'Connell (New York: Paulist Press, 1982), 186–99. It is an error to contrast the old and new laws as if the old concerned only outward behavior and the new only interiority. The precepts of the old law called for inner holiness; the new law also has an outward aspect: Edward Kaczynski, *La legge nuova: L'elemento esterno della legge nuova secondo S. Tommaso* (Rome: Francescane, 1974).

12. For an excellent, brief account of the limitations of the morality of the old covenant: L. Johnston, "Old Testament Morality," *Catholic Biblical Quarterly,* 20 (1968), 19–25. For an introduction to the historical evidence of the actual situation of the people of the old covenant: William

Foxwell Albright, *From the Stone Age to Christianity: Monothesism and the Historical Process*, 2d ed. (New York: Doubleday Anchor Books, 1957), 200–333.

13. Thus, Jesus is not a new lawgiver, a new Moses, but is the very embodiment of the Torah: J. M. Gibbs, "The Son of Man as the Torah Incarnate in Matthew," in *Studia Evangelica*, ed. F. L. Cross, 4 (1965), Texte und Untersuchungen, 102 (Berlin: Akademie-Verlag, 1968), 38–46.

14. For the significance of Chalcedon in its historical context, see Aloys Grillmeier, S.J., *Christ in Christian Tradition*, vol. 1, *From the Apostolic Age to Chalcedon (451)*, 2d ed. (Atlanta: John Knox Press, 1975). For a summary of current erroneous accounts of Christ, see Jean Galot, *Le Christ, Foi, et Contestation* (Chambray: C.L.D., 1981), 9–88; critique, 141–83. These errors have been specified and condemned by the Congregation for the Doctrine of the Faith: *Declaratio ad fidem tuendam in mysteria Incarnationis et Sanctissimae Trinitatis a quibusdam recentibus erroribus*, 64 *AAS* (1972) 237–41; *Origins*, 1 (23 March 1972), 666–68. Moreover, the validity and possible authentic development of traditional Christology has been reaffirmed by leading theologians: International Theological Commission, *Select Questions on Christology* (Washington, D.C.: United States Catholic Conference, 1980).

15. For a sound, systematic treatment of the Incarnation, with a good review of scriptural data and brief history of the development of the doctrine in the Church: Jean Galot, S.J., *Who Is Christ? A Theology of Incarnation*, trans. M. Angeline Bouchard (Chicago: Franciscan Herald Press, 1981), 41–313.

16. A theological development consonant with my view: Walter Kasper, *Jesus the Christ* (London: Burns and Oates, 1976), 163–96. A philosophical treatment of person: Germain Grisez, *Beyond the New Theism: A Philosophy of Religion* (Notre Dame and London: University of Notre Dame Press, 1975), 343–53 and 365–69.

17. See J. Schneider, "omoîōma," *Theological Dictionary of the New Testament*, 5:195–97, for a clarification of the meaning of "in the likeness of" in Phil 2.7 and Rom 8.3.

18. Karl Barth and certain other Protestant theologians have developed the position that there is an intrinsic, necessary relationship between Jesus' divinity and the revelatory character of his life, death, and resurrection. Although not worked out in a way entirely consistent with Catholic faith, this theological insight seems correct in substance and extremely important. See Wolfhart Pannenberg, *Jesus: God and Man*, trans. Lewis L. Wilkins and Duane A. Priebe, 2d ed. (Philadelphia: Westminster Press, 1977), 127–41.

19. Current erroneous Christologies undermine the revelatory value of the life of Jesus for they deny it to be the human life of the divine Word. In reaction, Galot, *Who is Christ?*, 319–35; *Le Christ, Foi, et Contestation*, 197, denies that Jesus behaves as a man toward God; in doing so, he undermines the value of the life of Jesus as revelatory—as formative and exemplary for the Christian community. In affirming that Jesus is both true God and true man, Catholic faith denies the meaningfulness of such an either/or. A valuable, recent work which treats in a fully faithful way all of the principal questions of Christology: Lucas F. Mateo-Seco et al., eds., *Cristo, Hijo de Dios y Redentor del hombre: III simposio internacional de Teología de la Universidad de Navarra* (Pamplona, Spain: EUNSA, 1982).

20. See Joachim Jeremias, *New Testament Theology: The Proclamation of Jesus* (New York: Charles Scribner's Sons, 1971), 42–75, for an exegesis of relevant texts concerning the mission of Jesus to reveal the Father and his human awareness and commitment to this mission.

21. See Kasper, op. cit., 252–53.

22. See Louis Bouyer, *The Eternal Son: A Theology of the Word and Christology* (Huntington, Ind.: Our Sunday Visitor, 1978), 414–19.

23. *Summa theologiae*, 3, q. 19, a. 1. On this point, cf. 3, q. 13, a. 2; q. 43, a. 2. Thomas also treats the unity of Jesus' operation without using the language I criticize: *S.c.g.*, 4, 36. On his conception of instrumentality: *S.t.*, 3, q. 62, a. 1, ad 2; *S.c.g.*, 2, 21; *De veritate*, q. 24, a. 1, ad 5. The essential truth of what Thomas wishes to say (spelled out most clearly, perhaps, in *De veritate*, q. 27, a. 4) is that the humanity of Christ is a true causal principle without being a per se cause of those effects Jesus is able to bring about precisely insofar as he is not only human but also divine.

24. Galot, *Le Christ, Foi, et Contestation*, 170–83, deals with the subject of this appendix in a way quite similar to that followed here; he expressly denies (177) that the human nature is instrumental.

25. See Colman E. O'Neill, O.P., "Christ's Activity," in St. Thomas Aquinas, *Summa Theologiae*, vol. 50, *The One Mediator (3a 16–26)*, trans. Colman E. O'Neill, O.P. (New York: McGraw-Hill, 1965), 234–36.

CHAPTER TWENTY-TWO

GOD'S REDEMPTIVE WORK
IN JESUS' HUMAN LIFE

Introduction

Having considered the preparatory stages of God's redemptive work and the make up of Jesus and his action, we turn now to the culmination of God's redemptive work in the human life, death, and resurrection of the Word Incarnate.

Question A: Does Jesus have a fundamental option?

1. It would seem that Jesus does not have a fundamental option. For the fundamental option of Christian life is the act of faith, as was explained (16-G). But as the New Testament makes clear, in some way Jesus knew God to be his Father: He was aware "that the Father had given all things into his hands, and that he had come from God and was going to God" (Jn 13.3). Knowing he had no choice about being indissolubly linked with the Father, he could not make an act of faith and so, it seems, had no fundamental option.

2. Moreover, if Jesus had a fundamental option, it would seem that he could have refused to make the commitment he ought to have made. But that would have been sin, and Jesus could not sin. So again it appears that he had no fundamental option.

3. **Yet Jesus did make a basic commitment by a free choice** (see *S.t.*, 3, q. 40). He obediently accepted death (see Phil 2.8). "Although he was a Son, he learned obedience through what he suffered" (Heb 5.8). In doing so, he constituted himself the one mediator between God and humankind, for he gave himself for us (see 1 Tm 2.5–6). This giving presupposed a basic commitment.

4. Jesus could make a basic commitment without its being a fundamental option because the two are not exactly the same. Every commitment has certain characteristics (see 9-E). It is a large choice which bears primarily upon existential goods, and it goes beyond any limited project to establish one in open-ended relationship with another individual or a group. A basic commitment is the most inclusive commitment a person makes. A morally mature person's basic commitment organizes his or her entire life and in the case of a good person establishes, at least implicitly, a virtuous relationship with God and every human being of good will (see 8-I).

5. Jesus is "like us in every respect except for sin" (DS 301/148, 554/290). Making a basic commitment need neither presuppose nor include any sin. At the time of his public life, Jesus was a mature individual who lived a well-ordered life. Therefore, to hold that Jesus did make a basic commitment raises no difficulty.

6. **But Jesus' basic commitment could not be a fundamental option as ours is.** Our fundamental option is the act of faith. Faith is conversion from sin toward God and acceptance of the grace of adoption as children of God. "Fundamental option" connotes these features of our basic commitment of faith, and they are excluded from Jesus' basic commitment.

7. Nevertheless, contrary to the argument proposed at the beginning of this question, Jesus as man did make a basic commitment bearing upon his relationship with the Father. True, his commitment cannot have been to accept his filial relationship, since for him this is a fact about which he, unlike us, has no choice at all (see Mt 11.25–27; Lk 10.21–22). But one who has made an act of faith still can and must choose whether to live up to it. **Likewise, Jesus, although he made no act of faith, had a basic choice about how to live his human life.**[1] This life was not a given; his human heart was not predetermined to live it. For him really to live it required self-determination: He humbled himself and became obedient (see Phil 2.8).

The basic choice which Jesus faced can be explained as follows. As a small child of four or five, his willing of the good of religion and other human goods would have been very much like that of a baptized Christian child being brought up in the faith. As yet there was no choice; the good of friendship with God the Father was willed by spontaneous willing. The difference in Jesus' case was that he had not grown up knowing God only as "Lord" and "creator" but also, in a special way, as "my Father"—a familiar manner of thinking and speaking which Jesus significantly retained all his life.[2]

Reaching the age at which choices are made, Jesus, like a child raised in faith, made many good choices about many things, all in harmony with his spontaneous willing of friendship with the Father. At some point, generally around the time of puberty, many children experience a more or less conscious crisis of faith; either explicitly or implicitly they must choose whether they will keep their faith and live it. For Jesus, this commitment would have been similar to, yet not exactly the same as, a Christian child's first free choice to live in faith. That Jesus did make such a commitment is expressed by the story of the finding in the temple (see Lk 2.49).[3]

8. Similarly, the objection based on sinlessness can easily be resolved. Since human nature admits of sin, as man Jesus could choose sinfully. But if Jesus had chosen sinfully, the sin would have been that of the Word, and God cannot sin. Therefore, Jesus not only in fact never committed a sin; he could not possibly have done so (see DS 291/—, 556/291).[4] **Still, as man Jesus deliberated in a human way; the alternatives to right choices did occur to him.** He considered possibilities it would have been wrong for him to choose, recognized them as such, and rejected them for this reason. Therefore, although he did not sin, he "in every respect has been tempted as we are" (Heb 4.15). Thus, Jesus could and did make a basic commitment, clearly articulated in some of his choices, for example, his free acceptance of death, expressed by the evangelists: "Abba, Father, all things are possible to you; remove this cup from me; yet not what I will, but what you will" (Mk 14.36; cf. Mt 26.39; Lk 22.42).

The New Testament teaches that in some way Jesus was aware of God as his own Father.[5] Jesus was aware "that the Father had given all things into his hands, and that he had come from God and was going to God" (Jn 13.3). How did he know this?

We ought to hold that the knowledge of Jesus as man which is relevant to his human choices and actions was not radically different from the knowledge of the great prophets and holy men, for Jesus is a man like us in all things save sin (see DS 301/148, 554/290). Wishing to insist upon Jesus' divinity and give him the honor due him, many have attributed semidivine knowledge to Jesus as man.

But one must take care to avoid the commingling of divine and human knowing, which faith forbids. Moreover, Jesus as man is more honored and the very point of the Incarnation of the Word better recognized if we attribute to him no more in the way of special gifts than faith requires. For then Jesus' action is more clearly human, and he is more fulfilled and God more glorified in it.

Luke indicates that Mary conceived by the power of the Holy Spirit, knew she was doing so, and was told that the child "to be born will be called holy, the Son of God" (Lk 1.35). The synoptic Gospels all indicate that at the very beginning of his career Jesus accepted baptism from John, and received heavenly confirmation of his status (see Mt 3.17; Mk 1.11; Lk 3.22). It also is possible that Jesus as man received nonverbal communication from the Father. That Jesus received divine information in such ways is in line with what the Old Testament tells us about the modes of divine revelation.[6]

With information received in the ways indicated, perhaps on many occasions throughout his earthly life, Jesus was in a position to be humanly aware of who he is and what he was to do. The Gospel narratives bear witness that Jesus knew the Scriptures thoroughly and used them constantly. His awareness, guided by basic information received by direct revelation, was enriched by this study. Thus, it seems unnecessary to suppose that as man Jesus had any mode of knowing in principle inaccessible to other men and women.

Nevertheless, since we do not know what God's inner life is like, we cannot comprehend Jesus' divine and human self-consciousness. Therefore, we cannot rule out the possibility that his human knowledge includes unique modes of access to reality, including God. Of course, these would have to be within the radical possibility of human nature. But we cannot tell whether human nature includes possibilities which are realized in this life in no one but Jesus.

However, we can be sure that Jesus' human awareness did not include knowledge of future contingencies which would have precluded his living the life he lived. Knowledge of future contingencies which will be determined by one's choices is impossible before one makes them, for such knowledge would leave one no choice to make. Therefore, because Jesus' choices helped to determine a great deal of the future, he had to be humanly ignorant of a great deal of the future. Perhaps this explains how Jesus, contrasting his human awareness with the providential knowledge he shared as Word with the Father, could say of the coming end: "But of that day or that hour no one knows, not even the angels in heaven, nor the Son, but only the Father" (Mk 13.32).

It is difficult for us, who firmly believe in the divinity of Jesus, to accept without qualification all the implications of his humanity. Jesus insofar as he is man is a creature among creatures; if he were not, then nothing in creation would be the Word—the Incarnation would not have occurred. St. Thomas endorses the correctness of this manner of speaking (*S.t.*, 3, q. 16, a. 8; cf. aa. 1, 2, 6).

It is necessary to keep in mind that Jesus' humanity is a concrete and actualized one, not anything less than the totality of the Lord Jesus save only his eternal reality as Word. There is a heresy, Docetism, according to which Jesus truly is God, but only apparently human. Walter Kasper, after discussing theological versions of this heresy, remarks:

> It would be wrong however, to see the temptation to Docetism merely in theology and to overlook its much more dangerous subliminal influence on faith and the life of the Church. In the history of Christian piety the figure of Jesus had often been so idealized and divinized that the average churchgoer tended to see him as a God walking on the earth, hidden behind the façade and costume of a human figure but with his divinity continually 'blazing out', while features which are part of the 'banality' of the human were suppressed. In principle we can scarcely say that the doctrine of the true humanity of Jesus and its meaning for salvation have been clearly marked in the consciousness of the average Christian. What is found there often amounts to a largely mythological and Docetist view of Jesus Christ.[7]

Kasper is right, and the tendency he is talking about explains the reluctance of many to accept the simple statement that Jesus as man is a creature among creatures. It also helps explain resistance to the thesis that Jesus as man had to make a basic commitment.

Question B: What is Jesus' basic commitment?

1. **Jesus had to choose—and did choose—to live his human life in fulfillment of the unbreakable communion between him and the Father. This choice is his basic commitment.**

2. Scripture testifies that his basic commitment was a religious one: "My food is to do the will of him who sent me, and to accomplish his work" (Jn 4.34; cf. Jn 5.30). Our Lord Jesus is represented as understanding his own commitment to be that of absolute obedience to God: "Lo, I have come to do your will" (Heb 10.9; cf. Ps 40.7–9). A commitment to doing God's will is a commitment to the good of religion, that is, to that human fulfillment which consists in harmony between humankind and God. It is also a commitment to the persons involved: to humankind and to God.

3. A Christian's act of living faith can be compared with Jesus' basic commitment. Jesus committed himself to live as the Son he knew himself to be. This basic commitment was not a fundamental option, as question A explained, for he did not turn from sin and accept divine adoption. By our act of faith, we first accept revealed truth, then turn from sin and accept divine adoption, and finally commit ourselves to live as the children of God we thus become. Only in this last respect is our act of faith exactly the same as Jesus' basic commitment. With him we say to the Father: Not my will, but your will be done.

4. The accounts of Jesus' temptations clarify various aspects of his basic commitment.[8] They show that by this commitment he is determined to live his human life in absolute obedience to the Father, to do and undergo everything with confidence in the Father's loving power, and to do absolutely nothing which would involve the least compromise with evil. These aspects of his basic commitment correspond to the faith, hope, and uncompromising love of God which ought to mark the lives of Jesus' followers.

The Gospels describe temptations of Jesus (see Mt 4.1–11; Mk 1.12–13; Lk 4.1–13). These descriptions help us understand the existential identity Jesus established by his basic commitment. It is reasonable to think that the sacred writers included these portrayals of temptation precisely for this reason.

According to the accounts, Jesus is led into the desert by the Spirit, where he fasts for some time. The devil appears and suggests first that Jesus, if the Son of God, turn stones into bread. Jesus replies that man does not live by bread alone, but by every word of God. The choice here is between satisfying a natural appetite, hunger, and carrying out the fast which had been chosen for religious motives. There is nothing inherently wrong in eating, but it would be wrong to break one's fast out of mere hunger once one committed oneself to it in one's effort to do God's will. Therefore, Jesus refuses to break his fast. The reason for not breaking the fast is that he lives by the word of God—he considers what he is doing to be the Father's will for him at this moment.

The agony in the garden (see Mt 26.36–39; Mk 14.32–36; Lk 22.39–42) has a very similar structure. Jesus faces death. He naturally fears it and the thought of avoiding it occurs to him. He sees the considerable human value in survival and would like very much to live, if it were only God's will. But he firmly accepts death, rather than try to escape or otherwise avoid it.

The devil also tempts Jesus by suggesting that he throw himself from the pinnacle of the temple, with the expectation that God will send angels to protect his Son. Jesus answers that one ought not to tempt God. What is the issue here? Everyone committed to doing God's will knows that in doing it he or she can count on God's power. The consequence of this confidence is that as soon as any act seems to be what God wills, one undertakes to do it even if it seems absurd, useless, or impossible. God's ways, however, are mysterious; often it is very difficult to see how his providence is at work in one's life and to wait for the time when he will exercise his power to make one's effort fruitful. It quite naturally occurs to anyone at times to ask God for some hard evidence of his loving care and support. The temptation to jump off a high place with the expectation that God will protect one would be a spectacular instance. Jesus thinks of asking the Father for some sign of his reliability, but promptly rejects this possibility. The reason is that one ought not to tempt God—that is, to put his faithfulness to the test.

The same temptation is expressed at the time of the crucifixion when some suggest that Jesus save himself by invoking the divine power in which he trusts or which he enjoys as Son, and so win the faith of those who do not accept him (see Mt 27.39–44; Mk 15.29–32; Lk 23.35–37). Why not take a short cut to glory? The choice is to endure and wait for God to act in his good time. The trust in God which Jesus shows in his own basic commitment by rejecting any such temptation is very like Christian hope which waits for Jesus himself to come.

Finally, Satan claims dominion over the world. He offers to turn it over to Jesus if Jesus will worship him. Jesus refuses, saying that worship is due God alone. According to the New Testament, Satan does have some power in the world; he is called its "prince" (see Jn 14.30). This power is not described as a matter of rights, but as a de facto situation. Sinful humankind is considered to be in Satan's bondage, for Man in sinning abdicated human dominion and allowed Satan to usurp the role of lord of creation which had been given Man under God (see *S.t.*, 3, q. 48, a. 4; q. 49, a. 2). To do anything wrong for the sake of one's end, however good, is to submit to Satan's dominion.

The temptation, as presented, is to do something wrong—that is, to worship Satan—in exchange for which he will surrender dominion, thus accomplishing the good end of liberation Jesus has in view. Jesus refuses. It is not in accord with God's will that the Son of Man gain the whole world for God by doing anything wrong, since anything wrong is a violation of one's own human good, which God loves, and so contrary to God's will.

Jesus' most intimate and loyal followers hope and expect that he will establish some sort of earthly kingdom, destroy all God's enemies, and so accomplish redemption. Jesus refuses to do so (see Lk 9.54–55; Acts 1.6–8). One week Jesus enters Jerusalem triumphantly, and the people expect him to bring about redemption in the manner to which the history of Israel had accustomed them: by power (see Mk 11.1–11; Jn 12.12–19). The next week Jesus is overwhelmingly rejected because he wants to be the wrong sort of king (see Mk 15.6–14; Jn 18.38–40).

Question C: What is Jesus' personal vocation?

1. Jesus' basic commitment and our act of faith share the principle: "Your will be done." But God's will for each individual differs, for he gives each one different gifts and tasks. These God-given gifts and tasks constitute a personal vocation, a calling to accept the gifts and use them to complete the tasks. The appropriate response to this vocation is a commitment or group of commitments, by which one undertakes to carry out God's will in one's own life.

2. By any commitment one accepts a certain social role with its responsibilities. Thus commitments must be carried out by many particular choices over a long period of time. Because the commitments by which we undertake to do God's will in our lives carry out his calling, these commitments themselves are called our "personal vocation" insofar as they fulfill our basic commitment to do his will.

3. Like us, Jesus had a personal vocation, unique gifts and tasks by which to do the Father's will. John's Gospel clearly expresses this personal vocation. "I did not come to judge the world but to save the world" (Jn 12.47). "I came that they may have life, and have it abundantly" (Jn 10.10). "I have come as light into the world, that whoever believes in me may not remain in darkness" (Jn 12.46). "For this I was born, and for this I have come into the world, to bear witness to the truth" (Jn 18.37). **In short, Jesus' personal vocation was to overcome sin and communicate divine life to fallen humankind by establishing a new and lasting covenant. In doing this he both gave the covenant and mediated it to us.** In John's formulation: "I am the way, and the truth, and the life; no one comes to the Father, but by me. If you had known me, you would have known my Father also; henceforth you know him and have seen him" (Jn 14.6–7).

4. The Johannine expression of Jesus' unique vocation belongs to a developed theology. Although caution is required, the Synoptics provide hints which suggest how Jesus himself might have conceived of his vocation. Unlike us, he could not discern his unique calling by considering someone he knew as a possible model. However, Scripture contained the promise of God's kingdom, which it was Jesus' task to fulfill.[9] Meditating upon Scripture, Jesus found several sketches of the hoped for leader and savior, the one who would inaugurate the reign of God and free Israel from its misery and subjection. At least three of these sketches—those of Messiah, Son of Man, and Suffering Servant—seem to have helped Jesus discern his unique vocation.[10]

At the time of Jesus faithful Jews were looking forward to the coming of a great leader, a king anointed by God himself, who would gather together and completely liberate Israel. The anointed one ("Messiah" means anointed) would have the Spirit or power of God to set up God's kingdom and overcome all his enemies. At times, too, it was expected that the Messiah would have the office of a priest, that is, of one who would mediate between God and his people, offer sacrifice on their behalf, and direct their religious life.[11]

"Son of Man" is sometimes used in the Old Testament simply to refer to any human being or to human beings collectively. In the book of Daniel, chapter seven, however, the expression becomes a kind of name or title of office. To some extent the reference seems to be to an individual and to some extent to the whole of God's people. This Son of Man is an other-worldly figure, to whom the Father has given the power of kingship. The Son of Man judges the world, overcomes the wicked, and reigns in exaltation with the just.[12]

"Servant of God" is used broadly to refer to persons who have a special mission to God's people. This general concept also serves as a basis for a prophetic development, especially in the "Suffering Servant" songs (see Is 42.1–4; 49.1–6; 50.4–9; 52.13–53.12). A prophet, a spokesperson for God, is to reassemble and teach Israel, with which he also is mysteriously identified. By patiently and humbly enduring suffering, this special Servant carries out God's will, not only saving the Jews but justifying all of sinful humankind.

5. These three roles have certain common features. All have mysterious aspects, but they are generally concerned with the coming of God's kingdom, the execution of his will, and the liberation of his people from the reign of Satan— that is, from sin and all its evil consequences. In particular, an individual who fulfilled any one of the three roles would be a leader identified with and acting on behalf of the nation. Still, as they emerge from the Old Testament and from certain extra-Scriptural writings in circulation in Jesus' time, the roles of Messiah, Son of Man, and Suffering Servant of Yahweh hardly seem compatible with one another.

6. In reading the Scriptures, which he approached with sufficient knowledge of his own status in relation to God the Father, we may suppose that Jesus recognized his unique vocation: to fulfill the Scriptures by carrying out God's saving will in a life melding all three of these apparently incompatible roles into one unique role greater than the sum of its parts.[13]

Question D: By what types of acts does Jesus carry out his personal vocation?

1. We fulfill our personal vocations by making and carrying out many quite limited choices in the course of our lives. Jesus similarly must implement his largest choices—his basic commitment and acceptance of his vocation—by smaller ones. Ultimately, he does this primarily in his willing acceptance of death. But he lives before he dies, and it is worth noticing what he does to carry out his mission prior to its bitter end.

2. He has a hidden life, during which, no doubt, he prepares in many ways for his public activity. Furthermore, the Gospels, especially Luke's, indicate that even during his busy public life he often slipped away by himself to pray (see Lk 5.16). **It was important to him to commune with the Father; undoubtedly in such prayer Jesus discerned clearly what steps he should take.**

3. Jesus teaches not like the typical rabbi, but with authority (see Mt 7.28–29; Lk. 4.32); he is not simply expressing his own views but teaching what God wishes taught. **He announces the kingdom.**[14] **In doing so, he also clarifies what**

is required to share in it. The good news of the availability of renewed friendship and communion with God does have an important condition attached to it: One must be prepared to let go of one's sins. Children of God leave darkness behind (see Jn 1.5–12). Those who cannot bring themselves to do this must reject the gospel, whereas anyone who accepts the gospel is required to live in a new way, with new values, which Jesus both teaches and exemplifies (see Mt 5–7).

4. Jesus makes a frontal attack on Satan's kingdom, the sin-death complex, by driving out demons, curing illnesses, raising the dead, and forgiving sins.[15] **These acts of healing and forgiving both elicit faith and are a response to it.** Sometimes, especially in John, his miracles are regarded as signs to encourage belief (see Jn 2.11; 10.38; 11.41–42); Jesus wishes to show that faith brings salvation. However, he refuses to produce signs to satisfy the skeptical (see Mt 16.1–4). His signs presupppose a certain disposition of openness; challenged by them, his enemies only take greater offense at Jesus (see Jn 11.45–54). This disposition of openness is a kind of faith, a willingness to take Jesus honestly for what he is. He provides signs for those in this condition in order to transform their disposition into acceptance of God's love present in him (see *S.t.*, 3, q. 43, a. 1). His signs culminate in his own death and resurrection.

Jesus is friendly toward sinners (see Mt 9.9–13; Lk 7.34; 15.1–2; 19.7). He protects the sinner, not to condone the sin, but to save the sinner for life (see Jn 8.2–11). Forgiveness comes even without being sought, and it is followed by the healing which is sought; the visible healing demonstrates the divine reality of forgiveness (see Mt 9.1–8; Mk 2.1–12; Lk 5.17–26). Jesus also shows that the sin-death complex is broken by driving out demons (see Mk 1.23–28; Lk 4.33–37). His critics say he does this by the power of the devil (see Mt 9.34; Lk 11.14–20). Jesus points out the illogic of the position: Evil does not destroy itself.

Typically, Jesus works in response to faith. He forgives sins on this basis (see Lk 7.48–50). His cures are generally performed on this basis (see Mt 9.28–29). In Nazareth, he cannot do many miracles because of lack of faith (see Mt 13.53–58). Gentiles also are cured because of their faith in Jesus (see Mt 8.5–13; 15.21–28). A person with faith is cured by Jesus even prior to his knowing about it, the miraculous healing power being drawn out of him by faith (see Lk 8.45–48). The faith in Jesus of those who cannot see him leads him to cure their blindness, so that they come to see (see Mt 20.29–34; Mk 10.46–52; Lk 18.35–43).

Many of the miracles of Jesus, like that of opening blind eyes, signify the total redemption which they partially bring about. For example, the cleansing of lepers is an act of healing and compassion; it involves associating with those who are cast out and it returns them to the community (see Mk 1.40–45). The miracle of the multiplication of the loaves, which is the only miracle described in all four Gospels, in many ways shows how the Son of Man undoes what Man has done. Jesus is a spirit of truth, not deceit; he offers life-giving food, not the food of death. He draws people together instead of separating them (see especially Jn 6).

The account of the raising of Lazarus (see Jn 11.1–44) is an especially rich miracle story. John describes the engagement of all of the human powers of Jesus, and at the same time makes it clear that he is acting to manifest God's love. The miracle is a response to the faith of Martha and Mary; it arouses faith in the disciples. The miracle shows that God's friendship is given; it also promises the coming resurrection.

5. **Finally, Jesus begins to gather a group which can accept God's reign**

and carry on Jesus' own work of service.[16] He tells the first four whom he calls that instead of catching fish, they will be fishers of men, will gather humankind into the kingdom (see Mt 4.19). The Twelve were called by Jesus to be his companions, to preach, cure, and cast out demons as he did (see Mk 3.14–15). They were to be his witnesses, to receive God's revelation in him (see Lk 24.46–49). They were sent to carry his mission throughout the world (see Mt 28.18–20). Their lives, like his, would be given in service (see Jn 21.15–19). They would overpower evil in this life and gain eternal life for their work (see Lk 10.18–20).

Question E: What is the main issue in Jesus' conflict with the leaders?

1. In many ways, Jesus claimed direct divine authority; he did not subordinate himself to the old law and its interpretative developments. By his words and deeds, Jesus made it clear that God is ready to save all who accept the gospel with faith, even if they have not kept the stipulations of the law. Those who conceived holiness as separation from the unclean necessarily insisted on the legalistic fulfillment of the law and opposed Jesus' more profound fulfillment of it. Thus, emphasizing this conception of the holy, many of the leaders inevitably considered Jesus' teaching and activity a serious religious threat.[17]

2. Moreover, in the minds of at least some of them, there seems to have been a further ground for opposing Jesus. There is a certain tension in the old law (21-D). Although it establishes a community in friendship with God, this community is limited: There is a tendency to understand it in the context of conflict between God's chosen people and other nations with their false gods.

3. The prophets attempted to resolve this tension in favor of openness to all humankind and all human goods (see Is 56.6–8; also Jon and Ru). In the time of Jesus, however, many of the leaders overlooked this and instead regarded much of God's creation as beyond redemption. Hatred for evil which cannot be redeemed is justified. Thus, although there is no such statement in Scripture, Jesus was not misrepresenting the manner in which some actually lived out the law when he said: "You have heard that it was said, 'You shall love your neighbor and hate your enemy.'" Conflict was inevitable between this teaching and his own, radically different command: "Love your enemies and pray for those who persecute you" (Mt 5.43–44). To those who defined good and evil by the difference between us and them, his approach to evil was scandalous, almost blasphemous, for it seemingly mixed what is God's with what is Satan's.[18]

As Vatican II teaches, while "authorities of the Jews and those who followed their lead pressed for the death of Christ (cf. Jn 19.6); still, what happened in his passion cannot be blamed upon all the Jews then living" (NA 4).[19] Jesus, Mary, and all his first followers were faithful Jews. However, those elements of the Jewish leadership who shared with Roman authorities in responsibility for killing Jesus were motivated by considerations understandable in the framework of their distortion of the imperfect vision of the Old Testament. Very similar but less understandable errors about the nature of evil and the way redemption must be accomplished have been made by many Christians, who proceeded to try to destroy evil by killing Jews, heretics, and others, rather than by a process of healing beginning with personal conversion.

4. This conflict came to a head over the cures which Jesus did on the sabbath (see Mt 12.9–14; Mk 3.1–6; Lk 6.6–11). The Pharisees are outraged: They perceive that Jesus is breaking through one of the boundary lines which they consider to separate the good (which is God's) from the bad (which is Satan's and includes sick people as well as their illnesses). Jesus is operating from a very different fundamental conception of good and evil (see Mt 15.1–20; Mk 7.1–23), according to which evil is privation, and human fulfillment, such as the curing of the sick, belongs to God. So he cures; and some of the Pharisees begin to plot how to destroy him.

5. In effect, these Pharisees, with their tactic of segregating things and persons in order to avoid evil and their identification of themselves with goodness (being on God's side of the line thus drawn), had consigned a great part of creation to Satan (see Mt 9.9–13; Lk 5.27–32).[20] **God wished to redeem the whole; but his love was too indiscriminate to suit such Pharisees, and it therefore had to be resisted** (see Jn 9.1–41). **It was this resistance that moved Jesus to fury** (see Mt 23.1–35), **while such Pharisees for their part were moved to an exercise of destructive power: exerting pressure against those who would have believed Jesus and seeking his death** (see Jn 11.45–53; 12.42–43).[21]

6. Naturally, anyone whose activities might lead to instability posed a threat to the Jewish leadership, and the Pharisees who opposed Jesus surely used this fact for their own purposes. Moreover, it seems that the high priest Caiphas and his associates had reasons of their own for wishing not only to silence Jesus but to discredit him (see Mt 26.57–66; Jn 11.45–53). Thus the method of execution was important. His condemnation and execution as a criminal were sought, not simply as a form of public, social degradation, but because this type of death would seem to show that Jesus had been rejected by God. The criminal hanged on a tree is cursed (see Gal 3.13).[22]

Question F: How does it come about that Jesus freely accepts death?

1. **Jesus freely accepts death because in doing so he carries out his personal vocation.** Yet if one thinks about it, this is puzzling for two reasons. First, how can death accomplish anything? This question will be answered in G, below, where it will be explained how Jesus' death is redemptive. Second, how could accepting something carry out one's vocation? Usually, the side effects of one's choices are not the way one accomplishes one's central purpose in life. Still, the present question will show that Jesus' acceptance of death does just this, and will explain why his acceptance of death was inevitable given his faithfulness to his vocation.

2. Describing the death of Jesus, St. John writes: "Jesus, knowing that all was now finished, said (to fulfil the scripture), 'I thirst.' A bowl full of vinegar stood there; so they put a sponge full of the vinegar on hyssop and held it to his mouth. When Jesus had received the vinegar, he said, 'It is finished'; and he bowed his head and gave up his spirit" (Jn 19.28–30). One could hardly say more clearly that Jesus' earthly life was not just ended but completed by his death. His life was not

cut short by death; rather, just insofar as it was freely accepted, his death belonged to the main human act of his whole life. It best expressed and carried out his basic commitment. To the extent possible for any man, this act accomplished what Jesus had committed himself to.[23]

3. By affirming its intentionally redemptive character, Scripture and the teaching of the Church make it clear that in accepting death Jesus does carry out his personal vocation. The Creed affirms: "For our sake he was crucified under Pontius Pilate; he suffered, died, and was buried." The Church solemnly teaches that by his passion and death Jesus merited salvation for us and reconciled us to God in his blood (see DS 1347/711, 1513/790). It also teaches that the passion and death of Jesus made satisfaction to the Father, that is, somehow made up for sin (see DS 1529/799, 1689–90/904). This teaching is solidly based upon the New Testament, especially the Epistles of St. Paul.

4. For all that, Jesus' death remains puzzling. Why did he have to die like this? Why should the Father have willed such a thing? One wonders precisely how Jesus' dying was humanly fulfilling for him. It is comparatively easy to understand how other things he did fit into his personal vocation. But how did accepting death make sense in relation to the self-identity he had established by his basic commitment and refined by carrying out his personal mission? Was he in fact simply obeying the Father blindly?

5. It is important to be clear about what needs explaining here. Foreseeing that he would be killed, Jesus continued with his work and did nothing to avoid the consequences he foresaw. He accepted death but he did not choose it. (As was explained in 9-F, one does not will accepted side effects in the same way one wills what one chooses.) Hence, the human act which needs explanation is not a choice by Jesus to kill himself, not a suicide, for there was no such choice; rather, it is his free acceptance of death (see *S.t.*, 3, q. 22, a. 2, ad 1; q. 47, a. 1).

6. Before asking why Jesus humanly accepts death, a prior question should be considered. Why did the Word not become Incarnate as a nonmortal person? The answer is that this condition, so different from that of sinful humankind, would have negated the very purpose of the Incarnation. The race of Man is not simply lifted out of sin willy-nilly but, in Jesus, redeems itself in cooperation with God (see *S.t.*, 3, q. 1, a. 1, ad 2; q. 46, a. 3; q. 50, a. 1). To reunite sinful humankind with God, the Word accepts the human condition as it is, to the extent he can do so—that is, in everything but committing sin. Thus he accepts all the effects of sin which are not aspects of alienation from God. In short, the Word becomes mortal flesh in order really to be one of us (see Phil 2.6–8; *S.t.*, 3, q. 14, a. 1).

7. The question remains: How does it come about that Jesus freely accepts the death he suffers? To carry out his mission, Jesus had to present himself more and more openly as the redeemer for whom Israel hoped. But even the apostles did not fully understand what kind of redeemer he meant to be. Jesus' emergence as a popular figure undoubtedly frightened the Jewish leadership and disposed them to cooperate in killing him. Moreover, in proposing to be a leader who engulfs enemies in love rather than destroys them, Jesus lost much of the support he had. Thus he was in an extremely vulnerable position.[24]

8. As question E explained, for both Jesus and his adversaries, their opposition was a matter of principle; neither side could compromise. Understanding evil as he did, Jesus could deal with violence only by suffering it; understanding evil as they did, his adversaries could deal with evil only by destroying it, unless they could keep clear of it in some other way. Thus, Jesus was ready to suffer death if necessary, and his adversaries were ready to kill him if necessary.

9. Jesus' personal vocation demanded that he not avoid the decisive encounter in Jerusalem. Going there to celebrate the Passover and preach in the temple was important to him. Moreover, Jesus could not draw back even before the hostility of the religious leaders without abandoning them to their sins. This he would not do, for his personal vocation required him to call all Israel to repentance.

10. He went to Jerusalem for the last time knowing he would be killed. He could have remained away or, as the hostility grew intense, escaped before disaster befell him. **Sooner or later, however, he had either to give up his work and go into hiding, protect himself by miraculous acts, or accept being killed. The first would have betrayed his vocation. The second would have nullified the point of the Incarnation, for a redemption depending on constant miracles would not be a human work as is one which in general accepts the human condition and its consequences, nor would it be suited to elicit a free human response. Thus, only the acceptance of death remains as an option compatible with Jesus' faithfulness to his personal vocation.**

The Synoptics tell us Jesus considered giving his life for others an essential part of his mission: "For the Son of man also came not to be served but to serve, and to give his life as a ransom for many" (Mk 10.45; cf. Mt 20.28). Jesus repeatedly predicts his passion and death (see Mt 16.21–23; 17.22–23; 20.18–19; 26.1–2; Mk 8.31; 9.31; 10.32–34; Lk 9.22, 44; 18.31–33). According to most of these texts, he also predicts his resurrection. The narrative of the institution of the Eucharist at the Last Supper also makes it clear that Jesus meant to shed his blood to establish a new and lasting covenant between God and humankind, so that the alienation which is sin would be overcome and communion made perfect (see Mt 26.26–28; Mk 14.22–24; Lk 22.19–20).[25]

John has Jesus allude repeatedly to his death. The Son of Man must be "lifted up" (Jn 3.14). A time is coming when the dead will hear the Son of Man (see Jn 5.25–28). When he is lifted up, his divinity will be revealed (see Jn 8.28). "For this reason the Father loves me, because I lay down my life, that I may take it again. No one takes it from me, but I lay it down of my own accord. I have power to lay it down, and I have power to take it again; this charge I have received from my Father" (Jn 10.17–18). The moment of death is the great hour of the life of Jesus; when it comes, he is glorified. Dying like a seed planted in the earth, he rises to a fruitful new life (see Jn 12.23–24).

Question G: How is Jesus' acceptance of death redemptive?

1. The Gospels indicate that in sharing the Passover with the Twelve in Jerusalem Jesus was carrying out a positive choice on his part, a choice which immediately involved his free acceptance of death (see Mt 26; Mk 14.1–31; Lk 22.1–38; Jn 13–17).[26] To the extent that Jesus outwardly does anything to carry out his redemptive commitment, he does it at the Last Supper. (His suffering and death the following day are experiences which he undergoes, things which happen to

him.) Still, the events of Friday cannot be separated from those of Thursday night, nor can the Last Supper be separated from its consequences. In sum, Jesus makes a choice to celebrate the Passover in a certain way, knowing this will lead to his betrayal, passion, and death; he does what he has chosen to do, and the expected consequences ensue; and the whole process, rather than being a series of isolated acts, is for him one act which includes its foreseen and accepted consequences.

2. It is therefore to the accounts of the Last Supper, and especially the institution of the Eucharist, that we must turn for maximum insight into Jesus' fulfillment of his redemptive commitment (see Mt 26.26–29; Mk 14.17–25; Lk 22.14–20; 1 Cor 11.23–25). The new Roman Missal provides a standardized formula which sums up the common and essential elements:

> On the night he was betrayed, he took bread and gave you thanks and praise. He broke the bread, gave it to his disciples, and said: Take this, all of you, and eat it: this is my body which will be given up for you. When supper was ended, he took the cup. Again he gave you thanks and praise, gave the cup to his disciples, and said: Take this, all of you, and drink from it: this is the cup of my blood, the blood of the new and everlasting covenant. It will be shed for you and for all so that sins may be forgiven. Do this in memory of me. (Eucharistic Prayer III)

This formula makes it clear that Jesus was offering himself in sacrifice, that he was establishing a new covenant by his blood, and that he wished his eucharistic words and deeds to be repeated in his memory.[27]

Jesus commands his followers to do the Eucharist in memory of him. "Memory" is not just musing recall; in the context of the covenant, one who remembers God and his law lives according to it, while one who forgets follows other gods. As the celebration of the Passover kept the old covenant alive, so the celebration of the Eucharist would keep the new covenant alive—until Jesus comes. Thus he makes his sacrificial act not just an example to be followed but, more basically, a communal act embracing in itself all the subsequent acts done by his followers in fulfilling this command of his. Those who share the Lord's Supper share his covenant-forming commitment; they are to do the Eucharist in memory of him (see *S.t.*, 3, q. 73, a. 3; q. 79, aa. 5–6).

3. Briefly stated, Jesus' free acceptance of death, considered as a human act, is redemptive in the following way.[28] **Because Jesus' basic commitment is to do the Father's will, his free acceptance of death, required by his vocation, is a gift to the Father. The Father receives and approves this gift and in return raises Jesus from the dead. The gift and response together perfect the relationship of friendship between Jesus as man and the Father; this relationship displaces the alienation from God of fallen humankind. This new relationship is more than the friendship of the old covenant, for by it Jesus, as Word Incarnate, communicates divine life to his human brothers and sisters. The human action of Jesus in the Last Supper, completed by his passion and death, provides human persons with both the opportunity and the incentive to turn from sin, accept renewed friendship with God, receive the gift of the Spirit, and live as children of God with hope of eternal life. The Mass makes Jesus' gift of himself present to us so that we can cooperate with him in it. The**

sacrament of the Eucharist allows us to experience our communion with Jesus in human and divine life. This statement of the way Jesus' death is redemptive is compact. The remainder of this question unfolds some aspects of this endlessly meaningful reality.

4. Every authentic gift expresses self-giving. Sacrifice, however, is fundamentally the giving of a gift to God.[29] Thus, even though surrendering the gift and destroying it are part of sacrifice, its very essence is the gift of self (see *S.t.*, 2–2, q. 85). Jesus' death is a sacrifice offered to the Father (see Heb 9.24–28; 10.8–22). Abstracted from its human meaning, death is of no value; but to accept it as Jesus did—freely and in fulfillment of his personal vocation—supremely expressed his basic commitment and carried out his mission (see *S.t.*, 3, q. 22, a. 2; q. 47, a. 2; q. 48, aa. 3–4). He showed his love for the Father most fully by accepting the tragic situation as his will. Given its full human meaning, his acceptance of death is the supreme act by which he fully gave himself up to the Father.

5. Still, human action alone, even Jesus' sacrifice, does not overcome sin and establish the new covenant between humankind and God. Jesus' earthly life does serve the true cause of God and humankind by inaugurating God's reign, yet Jesus' human life and death does not by itself establish the kingdom—realize it in power and glory. Ultimately, this requires a new creation, which is essentially God's act. The resurrection is the divine response to the human act of Jesus. It begins the new creation, which is God's ultimate answer to sin and its consequences (see *S.t.*, 3, q. 53, aa. 1, 4).

It also puts Jesus in a position to continue, though now invisibly, human activity which is effective in liberating us from sin and making us grow in God's love. In heaven Jesus intercedes for us (see Heb 7.25). He sends the Spirit and communicates divine life to us by the Spirit (see Jn 7.37–39). He unites our present lives in a real, though mysterious and invisible, way in himself (see 2 Cor 5.15–18) and exists as the principle of ultimate fulfillment.

6. Jesus' act of freely accepting death reveals the new covenant. It makes known to fallen humankind the bond of communion with God which was formulated, as it were, in the Incarnation (see *S.t.*, 3, q. 48, a. 6, ad 3; q. 49, aa. 4–5). Jesus' human life is that of the Word revealing the Father, and his death most clearly manifests God's love (see Jn 3.16–17; Rom 5.6–8), for in the dying of Jesus God reveals that he is trying to give himself to us (see *S.t.*, 3, q. 46, a. 1, ad 3; a. 2, ad 3; a. 3).

7. Jesus dies as a priest who offers himself (see *S.t.*, 3, q. 22, aa. 1–3). His sacrifice is not simply the act of an individual but is done to establish the new community of God's people. Because his dying does overcome humankind's alienation from God, it ratifies a new and lasting covenant. Blood is life, and Jesus' blood unites the divine and human parties to this covenant and puts it in force.

Life is sacred to God, who is the Lord of life. Blood has religious uses because it is more than an organic substance; it is thought of as having life and life-giving power present in it. The blood of the covenant brings the covenant to life; the bond between the two parties is in force, for the blood shared between them joins them in a common life. The blood of sacrifice is life offered to God. Since one's own life depends upon one's herd, even if one offers an animal, one is offering something of one's own life. The blood of the Passover is a marking of God's own with a sign of life, so that the angel of death will leave them alone.

The establishment of the Mosaic covenant is narrated in Exodus 20 and 24. The structure of our Mass obviously has the same pattern. The word of God is read, for the Scriptures contain salvation history and stipulate how we are to live. The faithful accept this word, by saying, "Thanks be to God," "Praise to you, Lord Jesus Christ," and (at some Masses) the Creed. The consecration makes present Jesus' shedding of his blood, which puts the covenant into effect by reuniting sinful humankind with God. (Since blood contains life, it makes the word of God and our word of faith come to life; the blood of Jesus makes a perfect bond since he is both God and man.) Finally, by our offering and by the communion we receive, the common life instituted by the covenant is shared and enjoyed by God and his adopted children.

8. It was for us and for our salvation that Jesus came down from heaven. Hence, Jesus' sacrifice would be pointless if we could not receive its fruits. To enable us to do so he formed his human relationship with the Father as a new covenant. Acting as the head of the new People of God, Jesus carried out his redemptive work in a way that would enable us to accept it. Thus, an important aspect of the redemptive character of Jesus' free acceptance of death are those characteristics by which it moves us to turn from sin, gives us an example to follow, and offers us a vision of hope to guide our lives toward heavenly fulfillment in him.

9. Jesus crucified puts in an especially cogent manner the choice which all human beings must make between moral good and evil. Like the two thieves, one must either sympathize and ally oneself with him or take one's place among those who oppose him (cf. Lk 23.39–43). If we make the commitment we should, our commitment is united with his in the Eucharist, which he has given us at least partly for this purpose.

10. Jesus' free acceptance of death is also redemptive insofar as it provides us with a moral example to follow. Jesus is not the only one who, by living a good life in a sinful world, will reap a bitter harvest. Anyone who truly lives a good life will be hated (see Wis 2.12–20; Jn 15.18–19), for, as we saw (14-G), one of original sin's effects is to take away the moral motivation of genuine human community and make moral goodness costly. Jesus, by dying as he did, presents us with a telling example, probably the most horrifying possible, of the situation of a good person in this sinful world.

11. By dying obediently, Jesus leaves no doubt that he loves God (see Jn 14.31). But the case is also an *experimentum crucis:* the acid test of God's love. What will happen to this innocent man? The answer, of course, is that God's love is revealed (see Jn 13.31–35). Jesus is lifted up on the cross only as a stage on the way to being lifted up in glory to the Father's right hand (see Jn 3.14; 8.28; 12.32–34; Acts 2.33; 5.31). In this glory, the kingdom of God announced by Jesus begins to be realized.

12. So it becomes clear that the life of one who does what is possible to remain in friendship with God, even if a disaster in this world, is not ultimately pointless. Living the truth in love in this sinful world is both necessary and, by God's re-creating love, sufficient to reach and enjoy fulfillment. Knowing this to be so, a

Christian can, in hope, make morally good choices which a person without hope would hardly make. Moreover, considering themselves members of an invisible communion of love, Christians are able to distinguish between the arbitrary self-limitation of sin and the unavoidable self-limitation entailed in any choice, and to accept the latter, confident that it is compensated by membership in the Mystical Body of Christ (see 1 Cor 12–13).

If one looks without faith at the life and death of Jesus, the whole thing makes little sense. To begin with, one cannot make any sense of the basic commitment of Jesus, and his personal vocation seems like a confused mixture of conflicting myths. At best, one might abstract certain segments from the Gospels and consider Jesus a man who had good intentions, but was too gentle for his contemporaries. The abstraction will have to leave out a good deal. By many human standards, Jesus is not a very good man. If he lived today, he would strike most people as too radical, too single-minded, too uncompromising, and at times too harsh. He also would seem too idealistic, too childlike, and too emotionally tender.

He begins his mission with apparent enthusiasm and high hopes. But his neighbors in Nazareth do not take him seriously (see Mt 13.54–58; Mk 6.1–6). At times his own family think he is going crazy (see Mk 3.20–21). His teaching very often is badly misunderstood. It leads to polarization (see Lk 12.49–53). When he insists upon essential points, many of his followers begin to leave (see Jn 6.66–67).

His primary project is to gather together the Jewish people to form them into the nucleus of the new kingdom (see Mt 15.21–28; Mk 7.24–30). But those whom he wishes to bring together are like stubborn children, unwilling to play any game (see Mt 11.16–19; Lk 7.32–35). At the very time of his entry into Jerusalem, Jesus must observe that the real significance of his presence among the Jews has been ignored (see Lk 19.41–44). He wanted to gather up the people as a mother hen gathers her chicks, but his love has been rebuffed (see Mt 23.37–39; Lk 13.34–35).

Jesus has all the skills in arguing that any rabbi could ask for. In debate he regularly comes out on top. His opponents are finally reduced to silence (see Mt 22.46; Mk 12.34; Lk 20.40). However, they do not concede anything. Rather, they appeal to a different kind of "argument." They set out to have him killed.

The heartbreaking story of how his closest associates behave is familiar. One collaborates in having him killed. Most flee when danger becomes great. Peter, who seemed so sturdy, panics and disappears from the scene. Near the cross are John, Mary, and a few other women.

The life of Jesus is that of a martyr, but apart from faith it does not make a very satisfying martyr story. Compare Jesus with Socrates. Socrates largely and obviously succeeds in what he is trying to do. When he is condemned to death, he still has many supporters. His close followers stand by him. The prospect of death does not phase him, for he believes he will be better off dead. His actual death is easy and dignified. Although he had his oddities and died a martyr's death, Socrates obviously was a well-rounded and fulfilled human being.

Jesus knows his own great gifts. He has absolute purity of feeling and insight. How utterly frustrating his life must have been! Of course, he foresees that glory awaits. But he does not have the experience beforehand. He is like the first man to rocket into space, knowing in theory that all will be well, but lacking the reassurance of someone else's prior success in such an adventure.

It is important to consider what the life of Jesus looks like when it is considered without faith. Our lives are to be like his.

Summary

The fundamental option of Christian life is the act of faith. But Jesus' knowledge of his relationship with the Father rules out an act of faith for him, as the impossibility of sin on his part rules out a choice not to make a commitment he ought to make. Still, Jesus was capable of making a basic commitment, for his human heart was not predetermined to live his human life. Thus, he had to make a basic choice.

He chose to live his human life in fulfillment of the unbreakable communion between him and the Father. This is his basic commitment. It is a commitment to do God's will, and so a commitment to the human good of religion. A Christian's act of living faith and Jesus' basic commitment are the same in one respect: Both are commitments to live in obedience to the Father. The Christian chooses to live as an adopted child of God, while Jesus committed himself to live as the Son he knew himself to be.

By giving individuals different gifts and tasks, God calls each one to carry out a personal vocation. One's commitment to it settles in many ways one's social role and personal responsibilities. Like each of us, Jesus had a personal vocation. As John's Gospel expresses it, he was to overcome sin and death, and communicate divine truth and life to fallen humankind. In the Synoptics there are indications that Jesus discerned his personal vocation by combining and transforming three roles sketched out by the prophets as they looked forward to the inauguration of God's kingdom—the roles of Messiah, Son of Man, and Suffering Servant. As part of his vocation, Jesus was to establish the new covenant and become head of the new family of God.

In living out his personal vocation, Jesus sets about doing what a human individual can to accomplish God's will that humankind be freed of evil and fulfilled in human and divine goodness. Although ultimately he does this primarily by his willing acceptance of death, his life before then also carries out his mission. Its significant elements include prayer, by which he communes with the Father and discerns what steps to take; the proclamation of the kingdom and the call to repentance, conversion, and reconciliation; acts of healing and forgiving; and the gathering of followers as the nucleus of the new People of God.

Conflict with the leaders was inevitable. They regarded much of God's creation as beyond redemption; they took a narrow, exclusive view of the community in friendship with God. But Jesus enjoins love for one's enemies and prayer for one's persecutors; he proclaims a community of friendship with God potentially open to all. The conflict comes to a head over Jesus' cures on the Sabbath—his adversaries correctly perceiving that in acting as he did, he was expressing an understanding of good and evil radically different from theirs.

Jesus' earthly life was not just ended but completed by his death, which best expressed his basic commitment and fulfilled his vocation. But his death was not a suicide: He foresaw and accepted it, but he did not choose it. That Jesus died at all was a consequence of the Incarnate Word's acceptance of our mortality—something necessary if the human race was to cooperate in its own redemption. That he died a violent death was precipitated by his unavoidable conflict with those who felt threatened by his way of dealing with evil. He could have avoided death by abandoning his mission and so betraying his vocation, or by protecting himself with miracles and so nullifying the Incarnation. Instead, he accepted death, as the only option compatible with faithfulness to his vocation.

He accepted death in freely choosing to go to Jerusalem to share the Passover with the Twelve. The crucifixion and the Last Supper cannot be separated, and indeed, insofar as Jesus outwardly does anything to carry out his redemptive commitment, he does it on the latter occasion. The accounts make it clear that he was offering himself in sacrifice, that he was establishing a new covenant in his blood, and that he wished his words and deeds on this occasion to be repeated in memory of him.

Jesus' free acceptance of death was redemptive in the following way. Since his basic commitment is to do the Father's will, his acceptance of death in carrying out this vocation is a gift to the Father. Receiving and accepting this gift, God in turn raises Jesus from the dead. This gift and acceptance constitute a new relationship between Jesus as man and the Father, and this relationship displaces the alienation from God of fallen humankind. This new relationship is more than the friendship of the old covenant, for by it Jesus as Word communicates divine life to his human brothers and sisters.

The human action of Jesus in the Last Supper, completed by his passion and death, provides human persons with a new incentive to turn from sin. Moreover, Jesus is a kind of test case, and his resurrection is testimony that the life of one who strives to remain in friendship with God is not pointless. Thus Christians can live good lives even in this fallen world, firm in hope that life in union with Jesus will in the end mean fulfillment in him.

Appendix 1:   The use of the Gospels as sources

Modern scholarship makes it clear that one cannot obtain a biography of Jesus from the New Testament. The materials in it were derived from various sources and handed down orally and in writing for some time, being developed for use in the early Church, primarily in its work of preaching and teaching.[30] Therefore, it is appropriate to indicate briefly the extent to which and the grounds on which I rely upon the historical accuracy of the Gospel narratives.

Vatican II makes a clear statement on this matter. Although this statement is not definitive, it is recent and balanced. Expressing the mind of the Church, it ought to be accepted with religious assent by all Catholics (see LG 25). The Council says:

> Holy Mother Church has firmly and with absolute constancy held, and continues to hold, that the four Gospels just named, whose historical character the Church unhesitatingly asserts, faithfully hand on what Jesus Christ, while living among men, really did and taught for their eternal salvation until the day he was taken up into heaven (see Acts 1.1–2). Indeed, after the ascension of the Lord the apostles handed on to their hearers what he had said and done. This they did with that clearer understanding which they enjoyed after they had been instructed by the events of Christ's risen life and taught by the light of the Spirit of truth. The sacred authors wrote the four Gospels, selecting some things from the many which had been handed on by word of mouth or in writing, reducing some of them to a synthesis, explicating

some things in view of the situation of their churches, and preserving the form of proclamation but always in such fashion that they told us the honest truth about Jesus. For their intention in writing was that either from their own memory and recollections, or from the witness of those who themselves "from the beginning were eyewitnesses and ministers of the word" we might know "the truth" concerning those matters about which we have been instructed (cf. Lk 1.2–4). (DV 19)

Here the Church affirms both the substantial accuracy of the Gospels and their complex literary development and character.

When Jesus made various choices and carried them out is of little importance for understanding his life as a structure of human acts. The important questions are what his fundamental choices and intentions were and how his various actions, including acceptance of suffering and death, carried out his basic commitment. This sort of information is contained sufficiently in the Gospels. For, as C. H. Dodd says: "What emerges is a lively picture of the *kind* of thing that Jesus did, the *kind* of attitude which his actions revealed, the *kind* of relations in which he stood with various types of people he encountered, and the causes of the friction between him and the religious leaders." Details may be argued. "But taken together, these stories, told from many different points of view, converge to give a distinct impression of a real person in action upon a recognizable scene. When we add the wealth of sayings transmitted as such without any narrative setting, the total picture is enriched and given color and depth."[31]

The Church teaches that all Scripture is inspired by the Holy Spirit and provided for our instruction (see DV 11). Throughout the Gospels, Jesus offers himself as a model. His life can provide no principle for our own lives unless we can understand it as a structure of human acts centering in his basic commitment. It follows that we must be able to obtain what we need for the purposes of moral theology from the Gospels.[32]

Of course, only the propositions asserted by the sacred writers are certainly true, and so careful interpretation of the Gospels is necessary (see DV 11–12). For this reason one cannot ignore the work of Scripture scholars. At the same time, one must be careful in selecting the scholars one will believe.[33]

Appendix 2:   Further aspects and other theories of redemption

If the account in question G begins to render intelligible the human significance of Jesus' free acceptance of death, it also provides a basis for clarifying some other aspects of the work of redemption.

First, Jesus' death redeems inasmuch as it is meritorious. By dying, Jesus merits his own glorification and ours as well, insofar as we are united with him by faith. Jesus accepts death because of sin and on behalf of sinners; he offers himself as sacrifice in obedience to the Father (see Jn 1.29; 10.18; 14.31; Rom 4.25; 5.6–21; 1 Cor 15.3; 2 Cor 5.15; Eph 5.2). Given the human meaning of Jesus' death, it is understandable why God is pleased with this sacrifice. Not that the death as such pleases him; but the love expressed by the gift is wholly acceptable. Moreover, as a great gift freely given, it deserves an appropriate response from God. Thus, Jesus' death is meritorious (see *S.t.*, 3, q. 48, a. 1).[34]

Second, Jesus' death redeems inasmuch as it satisfies or makes up for our sins. His redemptive act pays the price and ransoms us (see Mk 10.45; 1 Cor 6.20; 7.23; 1 Tm 2.6; Ti 2.14; 1 Pt 1.18–19; Rv 5.9). Without Jesus and what he does, the human situation is quite hopeless. He comes into the world, lives and dies, and transforms our hopeless situation. This real transformation, which is somewhat understandable in terms of the human significance of Jesus' acceptance of death, is the making up for our sins. Just this real effect of what Jesus does is the paying of the price. One need not suppose that God collects a payment; rather, he does the redemptive work and in his Son pays the price. The privation of sin really is healed and filled in by love. Like a healed wound, forgiven sin is transformed (see *S.t.*, 3, q. 48, a. 2).[35]

Third, Jesus' death redeems inasmuch as by dying he *wins victory* over Satan (see Jn 14.30; Col 1.13; 1 Jn 3.8) and also over sin and death (see Rom 5.21; 6.6–23; 8.3; 1 Cor 15.20–58). This follows from the fact that what Jesus does makes a real contribution to undoing the situation in which original sin placed humankind (see *S.t.*, 3, q. 48, a. 4; q. 49, aa. 1–3). By reestablishing communion with God in a real human community, Jesus in principle overcomes everything involved in and consequent upon sin.

Certain mistaken ideas about redemption also ought to be set aside. Probably most people do not consciously hold these ideas in a straightforward way, but remnants survive in almost everyone's mind.[36]

One false idea is that Jesus had to die to pay the devil a ransom, so that the devil would release fallen humankind from captivity to evil. This idea attributes too much in the way of power and rights to the devil, and erroneously suggests that he gains something from the act of Jesus. If the devil acquires anything at all in this situation, it is only the sins of the enemies of Jesus, not Jesus' human act of freely accepting death. The act of Jesus does release us from the bondage of the devil, but the devil gains nothing from God or from Jesus. The redemption is more like a commando raid to rescue prisoners than the paying of ransom to buy their release (see *S.t.*, 3, q. 48, a. 4, ad 2; q. 49, a. 2).

Another false idea is that God's anger at sinful humankind had to be appeased. The picture is that of a vengeful tyrant, who has been greatly offended and would like to kill somebody. The trouble is, he cannot find anyone worth killing: The people who offend him are such vermin that it is beneath his dignity to bother wiping them out. But then there appears a real man among the offending group. So the tyrant delightedly kills him, getting the revenge he wants. This act calms the tyrant's anger and puts him in a better frame of mind. When clearly spelled out, this idea is so crude that anyone can see its absurdity as applied to God.

Another false idea is that the death of Jesus pays God a debt, a price he demands for accepting fallen humankind back into his friendship. This idea is an improvement in some ways on the two preceding ones. Also, as I have explained, it is true that by dying Jesus somehow makes up for our sins and merits God's love for us. However, the idea still is mistaken to the extent that it suggests that God needs to be reconciled to humankind rather than humankind to God. It also errs in suggesting that Jesus' death benefits God, whereas it is his gift to us: "For God so loved the world that he gave his only Son, that whoever believes in him should not perish but have eternal life" (Jn 3.16).

Finally, there is the idea that Jesus died as a scapegoat. This notion is that humankind deserved punishment for sin, but Jesus took the place of sinners, received their punishment, and so relieved them of having to be punished themselves. Up to this point, the idea is just right enough to find support in certain passages in Scripture and to be understandable in accord with faith as a whole (see *S.t.*, 3, q. 1, a. 2; q. 22, a. 3; q. 48, a. 2; sup., q. 12, a. 2). But the scapegoat idea often is developed badly, in a way that separates the death of Jesus from our lives. Punishment is viewed legalistically, as something arbitrarily imposed. Our redemption then, would not make any real change in us or demand any real change in our lives.[37] This view is incompatible with Catholic faith.

Notes

1. See Jean Galot, S.J., *Who Is Christ? A Theology of Incarnation*, trans. M. Angeline Bouchard (Chicago: Franciscan Herald Press, 1981), 376–84.

2. For the significance of Jesus' use of "Abba," see Joachim Jeremias, *New Testament Theology: The Proclamation of Jesus* (New York: Charles Scribner's Sons, 1971), 61–68. Note the conclusion (68): The use of this word "expresses the ultimate mystery of the mission of Jesus. He was conscious of being authorized to communicate God's revelation, because God had made himself known to him as Father."

3. The passage (Lk 2.41–52) about the finding in the temple has been identified as a biographical apophthegm—i.e., a narrative built around and emphasizing a particular saying. In this case, the saying is in v. 49. Thus, one should not naively consider the passage as a detailed report of an interesting event in Jesus' childhood, but as the sacred writer's expression of an important fact about Jesus' life relevant to his mission, death, and resurrection. What it expresses is that Jesus did shape his life toward his Father's service by a basic commitment. This being so, questions which could be raised about the details of the story, which might be taken to undermine its basic historicity, can be dismissed as irrelevant. See Joseph A. Fitzmyer, S.J., *The Gospel According to Luke*, Anchor Bible, 28 (Garden City, N.Y.: Doubleday, 1981), 438–39.

4. See Galot, op. cit., 384–92, for a different approach and reference to some other views. Galot seems to me inconsistent insofar as he is realistic about temptation but does not wish to admit that Jesus had a choice between good and evil. Such a choice does not entail that Jesus could (without qualification) sin, but only that as man he could have sinned. On my view the absolute sinlessness of Jesus follows solely from the fact that the acting person is the Word.

5. For a critical, Catholic evaluation of the New Testament evidence of Jesus' awareness of his own identity, see Jacques Guillet, S.J., *The Consciousness of Jesus*, trans. Edmond Bonin (New York: Newman Press, 1972), 43–46, 102–39, and 177–94.

6. For a generally similar treatment of Jesus' human knowledge, including his knowledge of God, see Galot, op. cit., 336–75.

7. Walter Kasper, *Jesus the Christ* (London: Burns and Oates, 1976), 199.

8. See C. H. Dodd, *The Founder of Christianity*, (New York: Macmillan Paperbacks, 1970), 123–24. A helpful discussion: Samuel Parsons, O.P., and Albert Pinheiro, O.P., "Appendix 4: The Temptation of Christ," in St. Thomas Aquinas, *Summa Theologiae*, vol. 53, *The Life of Christ*, ed. Samuel Parsons, O.P., and Albert Pinheiro, O.P. (New York: McGraw-Hill, 1971), 187–94.

9. On Israel's expectation, see James Muilenburg, *The Way of Israel: Biblical Faith and Ethics* (New York: Harper Torchbooks, 1961), 128–50.

10. A detailed exegetical study taking into account recent scholarship: Eduardus Dhanis, S.I., *De Testimonio Iesu circa Seipsum*, 7th ed. (Rome: Pontificia Universitas Gregoriana, 1970), 24–124; an even more recent work by a Protestant scholar: John Gray, "The Messiah, the Servant of Yahweh and the Son of Man," and "The Kingdom of God in the Mission of Jesus," *The Biblical Doctrine of the Reign of God* (Edinburgh: T. and T. Clark, 1979), 274–357. The narrative of the profession of faith by Peter (see Mt 16.13–20; Mk 8.27–33; Lk 9.18–22) presents in one situation the relevance and distinction of the three roles, since Jesus, already identified as Son of Man, now is recognized through a gift of faith as Messiah, and proceeds to reveal himself as Servant—much to Peter's dismay. On "Messiah," "Son of Man," and "Servant": Louis Bouyer, *The Eternal Son: A Theology of the Word and Christology* (Huntington, Ind.: Our Sunday Visitor, 1978), 168–82; Dodd, op. cit., 99–118.

11. On the precise conception of "Messiah" relevant to Jesus and the grounds for considering historically true his acceptance of the title in this relevant sense: H. P. Kingdon, "Messiahship and the Crucifixion," in *Studia Evangelica*, 3 (1961), ed. F. L. Cross, Texte und Untersuchungen, 88 (Berlin: Akademie-Verlag, 1966), 67–86.

12. In Daniel, the figure of the Son of Man probably is symbolic. However, in later Jewish apocalyptic literature, the expression took on reference to a real, hoped-for redeemer. Thus, Jesus' use of it cannot be limited by its more limited sense in Daniel. See Louis F. Hartman, C.Ss.R., and Alexander A. Di Lella, O.F.M., *The Book of Daniel*, Anchor Bible, 23 (Garden City, N.Y.: Doubleday, 1978), 98 and 219. It also is important to bear in mind that the Old Testament sketches were transformed creatively in their fulfillment. Thus, the eschatological character of the "Son of Man" in Daniel cannot be assumed a priori as a limit on the sense of the role assumed by Jesus. See Elizabeth Kinniburgh, "The Johannine 'Son of Man,'" in *Studia Evangelica*, 4 (1965), ed. F. L. Cross, Texte und

Untersuchungen, 102 (Berlin: Akademie-Verlag, 1968), 64–71; O. Michel and Howard Marshall, "Son of man," *New International Dictionary of New Testament Theology,* 3:613–34.

13. For a brilliant reading of the Old Testament context of the significance of Jesus' life and work, which shows (although that was not the author's expressed purpose) how Jesus may have developed his self-understanding: Louis Bouyer, *The Church of God: Body of Christ and Temple of the Spirit,* trans. Charles Underhill Quinn (Chicago: Franciscan Herald Press, 1982), 175–234, esp. 225–26. See Jeremias, op. cit., 250–99, for a clarification of the interrelationship of the roles. Although not the expected earthly kind, Jesus truly is the anointed savior sent by God, who consummates his mission in the role of God's Servant and is exalted as Son of Man. While many scholars would not grant the historicity of the Synoptics' indications concerning Jesus' titles, Gustaf Aulén, *Jesus in Contemporary Historical Research,* trans. Ingalil H. Hjelm (Philadelphia: Fortress Press, 1976), after summing up much recent scholarship on this matter, concludes (118–19): "There is actually fairly wide agreement in regard to Jesus' attitude—that is, to Jesus as the enigmatic representative of the kingdom of God. Whatever may be the case with the titles, it remains clear that Jesus acted with total sovereignty on behalf of God, enigmatically sovereign in both word and deed. And compared to this fact, the question of the titles seems secondary." Aulén goes on to quote approvingly Jacob Jervell, who warns against supposing that Jesus represented himself as less than the Messiah, when "the fact is that Jesus claimed to be something more than the Messiah, something that could not be expressed by this title."

14. See Jeremias, op. cit., for a treatment of the central theme of Jesus' preaching. He proclaims the reign of God (96–108), which is good news for the poor—that is, for sinners ready to accept God's mercy (108–21) during the time of grace prior to the consummation of the world and the hour of judgment (122–58). See also Xavier Léon-Dufour, S.J., *The Gospels and the Jesus of History,* trans. John McHugh (New York: Desclee, 1968), 114–16, 228–38; Dodd, op. cit., 53–79.

15. See Jeremias, op. cit., 85–96, for a development of this aspect of Jesus' work, significantly treated under the heading: "Overcoming the Rule of Satan."

16. See ibid., 159–78 and 231–40, for a treatment of Jesus' gathering of his own community and sending of messengers to expand his individual effort; Dodd, op. cit., 81–97. For the argument that Jesus did indeed found the Church on the apostles, see B. C. Butler, O.S.B., "Spirit and Institution in the New Testament," in *Studia Evangelica,* 3 (1961), ed. F. L. Cross, Texte und Untersuchungen, 88 (Berlin: Akademie-Verlag, 1966), 138–65; David M. Stanley, S.J., "Authority in the Church: A New Testament Reality," *Catholic Biblical Quarterly,* 29 (1967), 555–73.

17. See John Bowker, *Jesus and the Pharisees* (Cambridge: Cambridge University Press, 1973), 1–45. Bowker's study shows that the opposition between Jesus and Pharisees is subtler than many have supposed, but likewise makes it clear that the notion that there was no irreconcilable difference is indefensible. The latter notion, suggested by some liberal scholars, seems to be generated partly by their apologetic purposes and requires one to write off as valueless (not merely critically examine) the New Testament witness: Ralph Marcus, "The Pharisees in the Light of Modern Scholarship," *Journal of Religion,* 32 (1952), 153–64.

18. Birger Gerhardsson, *The Ethos of the Bible,* trans. Stephen Westerholm (Philadelphia: Fortress Press, 1981), 42–45, points out that Jesus' teaching and practice necessarily conflicted with the implicit exclusivity of Torah-centered piety. See Jeremias, op. cit., 204–18, for a discussion of Jesus' rejection of the oral tradition and criticism of the Torah itself.

19. See C. Witton-Davies, "'The Jews' in the New Testament," in *Studia Evangelica,* 6, ed. Elizabeth A. Livingstone, Texte und Untersuchungen, 112 (Berlin: Akademie-Verlag, 1973), 655–65; also, although somewhat dated and not entirely acceptable in its interpretation, a courteous and enlightening apologetic work by a Jewish rabbi: Samuel Umen, *Pharisaism and Jesus* (New York: Philosophical Library, 1963).

20. Although dated, a work of A. T. Robertson, *The Pharisees and Jesus* (New York: Charles Scribner's Sons, 1920), contains a still valuable reflection on the opposition between Jesus and the Pharisees which arose because of his "intolerable association with publicans and sinners" (76–81).

21. See D. Müller, "Pharisee," *New International Dictionary of New Testament Theology,* 2:810–14, for a fuller treatment of the opposition between Jesus and the Pharisees, consistent with that sketched here. See also Aulén, op. cit., 55–74, for a summary of recent scholarship on this issue; although not entirely supportive, it leaves room for the interpretation I accept.

22. For the political motives of the Sadducean leaders and the significance of crucifixion (although missing the connection between the two), see T. A. Burkill, "The Trial of Jesus," *Vigiliae Christianae,* 12 (1958), 1–18.

23. For a good summary treatment within a Thomistic framework of the scriptural evidence concerning the causes and motivations involved in Jesus' death, see Richard T. A. Murphy, O.P., "Appendix 3: Causes of Christ's Death," in St. Thomas Aquinas, *Summa Theologiae*, vol. 54, *The Passion of Christ (3a 46–52)*, ed. Richard T. A. Murphy, O.P. (New York: McGraw-Hill, 1965), 194–201. For a plausible interpretation which makes use of the concept of martyr, see John Downing, "Jesus and Martyrdom," *Journal of Theological Studies*, 14 (1963), 279–93. If the conclusion is accepted, of course, it does not exclude Jesus' acceptance of his death as a sacrifice, since that is in no way inconsistent with martyrdom.

24. See Kingdon, op. cit., 77–86; Dodd, op. cit., 130–38.

25. See Jeremias, op. cit., 276–99, for an exegesis of texts to show that Jesus announced his suffering and death and voluntarily accepted them in his role of Servant, offering himself in atonement.

26. It is necessary to study the narratives as unified wholes to understand what Jesus was doing. Although his book must be regarded with reserve, see Edward Schillebeeckx, *Jesus: An Experiment in Christology*, trans. Hubert Hoskins (New York: Seabury Press, 1979), 298–312, for a helpful treatment of this particular point. See also Aulén, op. cit., 150–51, for a concise summary argument, which seems to go beyond many of the critical opinions reviewed earlier in the book, 74–82.

27. For a good summary with extensive bibliography: Brian Byron, *A Theology of Eucharistic Sacrifice*, Theology Today, 35 (Hales Corners, Wis.: Clergy Book Service, 1974), esp. 37–53.

28. An exegetical study which substantiates all of the major elements of the following summary: F. X. Durrwell, C.Ss.R., *The Resurrection: A Biblical Study*, trans. Rosemary Sheed (New York: Sheed and Ward, 1960), 59–107.

29. On sacrifice: Robert J. Daly, S.J., *The Origins of the Christian Doctrine of Sacrifice* (Philadelphia: Fortress Press, 1978), 53–83; *Christian Sacrifice: The Judaeo-Christian Background before Origen* (Washington, D.C.: Catholic University of America Press, 1978), provides a much richer treatment, including the Fathers to Origen (summary, 491–97).

30. See Joseph A. Fitzmyer, S.J., "The Biblical Commission's Instruction on the Historical Truth of the Gospels," *Theological Studies*, 25 (1964), 386–408, including (402–8) a translation of the whole of this important document, which can serve, as it were, as an advance commentary on Vatican II's statement on the historical value of the Gospels (cf. DV 19).

31. Dodd, op. cit., 36.

32. See Fitzmyer, op. cit., 406; the Biblical Commission's Instruction points out: "From the results of the new investigations it is apparent that the doctrine and the life of Jesus were not simply reported for the sole purpose of being remembered, but were 'preached' so as to offer the Church a basis of faith and of morals." And Fitzmyer points out (401) that it is the form of the words and deeds of Jesus that the evangelists give us which is inspired by the Holy Spirit.

33. See Bouyer, op. cit., 151–67; E. L. Mascall, *Theology and the Gospel of Christ: An Essay in Reorientation* (London: SPCK, 1977), 65–117. For a treatment of the life of Jesus by a critical Catholic scholar: Léon-Dufour, op. cit., 193–258. For a very helpful treatment by a non-Catholic critical scholar: Robert M. Grant, *A Historical Introduction to the New Testament* (New York: Harper and Row, 1963), 284–377. For a summary of much recent critical scholarship on the life of Jesus, see Prosper Grech, "The Critical Problem and Hermeneutics," in *Problems and Perspectives of Fundamental Theology*, ed. René Latourelle and Gerald O'Collins, trans. Matthew J. O'Connell (New York: Paulist Press, 1982), 105–32. Aulén, op. cit., 17–120; the body of work they treat shows that former scepticism is being overcome, and the sort of historical claims required by the present project cannot be dismissed as absurd, even though in details the present chapter cannot pretend to meet critical standards.

34. See Colman E. O'Neill, O.P., "The Merit of Christ," in St. Thomas Aquinas, *Summa Theologiae*, vol. 50, *The One Mediator*, ed. Colman E. O'Neill, O.P. (New York: McGraw-Hill, 1964), 238–44.

35. For a detailed study which shows that this interpretation of how Jesus' death satisfies for sin is authentically Thomistic: Romanus Cessario, O.P., *Christian Satisfaction in Aquinas: Towards a Personalist Understanding* (Washington, D.C.: University Press of America, 1982), 188–218. This account is to be contrasted with that which attributes to Jesus' divinity the power of his death to satisfy for the infinite offense of sin, or which regards his death as paying to God the price of capital punishment for the sins of other humans.

36. A very instructive study: Stanislaus Lyonnet, S.J., and Léopold Sabourin, S.J., *Sin, Redemption, and Sacrifice: A Biblical and Patristic Study* (Rome: Biblical Institute Press, 1970), summarized 290–96. Also see Kasper, op. cit., 113–21 and 252–68.

37. See Lyonnet and Sabourin, op. cit., 225–44, for a treatment of this idea and its historical origins, around the time of the Reformation, among both Protestant and Catholic writers. It is part and parcel of modern legalism.

CHAPTER TWENTY-THREE

GOD'S REDEMPTIVE WORK
IN THE LIVES OF CHRISTIANS

Introduction

We have seen (19-B) that integral human fulfillment is fulfillment in Jesus. In the intervening chapters, we have seen how God is working to accomplish his plan of salvation, which reaches its climax in Jesus' free acceptance of death and his glorious resurrection. But God carried out his saving work in Jesus' human life in such a way that we can be united with him. The present chapter will therefore unfold the implications of Jesus' life for Christian life, focusing on our own human acts—the subject of moral theology. Indeed, the remainder of the book will do this, for the present chapter provides an overview whose important details will be treated in subsequent chapters through chapter thirty-three.

The central actions which organize a Christian's life are, in practice, the sacraments, which will be treated explicitly in chapters thirty to thirty-three. In the present and following chapters, up to twenty-nine, however, the sacramental perspective will remain implicit; the treatment will first provide a preliminary synthesis, and the chapters on the sacraments will then provide the final, unifying vision of the way of the Lord Jesus.

Thus, the present chapter is an overview of the following points. By their fundamental option of faith Christians are united with Jesus in a communion they celebrate in the Eucharist. Their common vocation is to follow Jesus by fulfilling his commandments, particularly his command to love others as he has loved them. Each Christian also has a personal vocation which involves prophetic responsibility—that is, the duty to share with other men and women the marvelous gifts the Christian receives in baptism and the Eucharist. This prophetic responsibility means that Christians must know, accept, and try to fulfill a single, harmonious set of true moral standards. Catholics are helped to do this by the Church's moral teaching, to which a faithful Catholic conscience conforms in detail.

Question A: How do fallen men and women enter into Jesus' redemptive act by making faith in him their fundamental option?

1. By freely accepting death, Jesus establishes the new covenant. To make his sacrifice redemptive for sinners, he enables them to enter into it. We have seen

(22-G) some of the ways in which Jesus presents sinners with the new opportunity to repent and fresh grounds for the hope without which one cannot live a good life in this fallen world.

2. If sinners accept the new option Jesus offers, they not only repent and undertake to live a good life but enter into the community of the new covenant. To enter into this community is to accept the relationship with God present in it. To accept God's revelation in Jesus is the act of Christian faith. Faith as a human act is a free choice one makes (20-D). This free choice is a commitment to Jesus and his covenant community, as well as to the human goods for which this community cooperates.

3. First among these goods is the good of religion itself—friendship with God. But all the goods which fulfill human persons are included as well, for all of them will be realized in the fulfillment of everything in Jesus. Thus, the commitment of Christian faith is a basic one: It is a commitment to all human goods and persons, to integral human fulfillment (8-I). This basic commitment, considered as conversion from sin and acceptance of membership in the covenant of Jesus, is a fundamental option (16-G).

4. As mediator between God and humankind, Jesus is unique. His gospel provides a unique reason for repentance and hope. Thus, Christian faith must be a personal faith in Jesus, an immediate relationship with him. The fundamental option of faith really does unite Christians immediately with Jesus because in making it they enter into the covenant community, the Church, in which he is personally present. The gift of faith is received in baptism, which will be treated (in 30-H).[1]

5. The new covenant of Jesus is far superior to the old covenant (21-D). Those who share in the new covenant are not merely God's loyal servants, but his adopted children, whom the grace of the Spirit enables to follow Jesus in living as children of God should (see Rom 8.12–17). The reality of the Christian's sharing by adoption in divine life will be treated more fully (24-C).

By faith in Jesus one accepts God's offer of a share in his life. "For this is the will of my Father, that every one who sees the Son and believes in him should have eternal life" (Jn 6.40; cf. Jn 1.11–12).

Jesus mediates a personal relationship which begins with himself but extends beyond him: "He who believes in me, believes not in me but in him who sent me. And he who sees me sees him who sent me" (Jn 12.44–45). Thus, Christians are God's adopted children (see Rom 8.15–17), begotten by God. The source of power for their rebirth is the Incarnate Word (see Jn 1.12, 14).

6. In sum, sinners are redeemed by being united with Jesus. This unity is threefold: in divine life, in human acts, and in bodily life (19-C). This threefold unity with Jesus is the full and exact meaning of "entering into his redemptive act." Since the present work focuses on the moral dimension of Christian life, our primary interest is in Christians' unity with Jesus in human acts. Unity in action is cooperation. The primary and best example is found in the Sacrifice of the Mass. Therefore, the next question will consider how the Mass unites Christians with Jesus in a single cooperative action.

Vatican II begins its teaching on the Church by calling attention to God's methods of redemption:

> At all times and among every people, God has given welcome to whosoever fears him and does what is right (cf. Acts 10.35). It has pleased God, however, to make men holy and save them not merely as individuals without any mutual bonds, but by making them into a single people, a people which acknowledges him in truth and serves him in holiness. He therefore chose the race of Israel as a people unto himself. With it he set up a covenant. Step by step he taught this people by manifesting in its history both himself and the decree of his will, and by making it holy unto himself. All these things, however, were done by way of preparation and as a figure of that new and perfect covenant which was to be ratified in Christ, and of that more luminous revelation which was to be given through God's very Word made flesh.
>
> "Behold the days shall come, saith the Lord, and I will make a new covenant with the house of Israel, and with the house of Judah. . . . I will give my law in their bowels, and I will write it in their heart: and I will be their God, and they shall be my people. . . . For all shall know me, from the least of them even to the greatest, saith the Lord" (Jer 31.31–34). Christ instituted this new covenant, that is to say, the new testament, in his blood (cf. 1 Cor 11.25), by calling together a people made up of Jew and Gentile, making them one, not according to the flesh but in the Spirit. (LG 9)

This passage explicitly mentions three aspects of the life of a Christian which follow from its being life within the covenant. First, the Christian lives within the covenant community, the Church; one's Christian life is not primarily that of an individual before God. Second, one enters into the new covenant not by the flesh (by birth as a Jew) but by the Spirit (by the grace of justification which gives living faith). Third, in the new covenant, one receives a law which must be lived, and it is all the more effective because it is written on the heart of every Christian, not merely inscribed on stone or in the Torah.

Question B: How are Christians united with Jesus' redemptive act in the Mass?

1. We have seen that the human meaning of all other aspects of Jesus' redemptive act can be understood in relation to his free acceptance of death (22-G). We have also seen how the Last Supper as a human act was related to the events of the following day and to the resurrection. It remains to show how the Mass and the sacrifice of the cross, considered as human acts, are one and the same, differing only in the manner of offering.[2]

The General Instruction of the Roman Missal (Introduction, 2) recalls that the Council of Trent teaches definitively that the Mass is a true sacrifice (see DS 1739–42/938–39). The Instruction also quotes Vatican II on the point that our Lord instituted the Eucharist to perpetuate the sacrifice of his body and blood through the centuries until he comes again (see SC 47). The doctrine is expressed in the prayers of the Mass. The Instruction then states: "In this new missal, then, the Church's rule of prayer corresponds to the Church's enduring rule of faith. It teaches us that the sacrifice of the cross and its sacramental renewal in the Mass are one and the same, differing only in the manner of offering. At the Last Supper Christ the Lord instituted this sacramental renewal and commanded his apostles to do it in memory of him. It is at once a sacrifice of praise and of thanksgiving, a sacrifice that reconciles us to the Father and makes amends to him for the sins of the world."

2. As spiritual realities, choices last (2-E). The choice which served as the vehicle, as it were, of Jesus' free acceptance of death—an act sufficient in itself to bind humankind to God forever—did not cease with the end of the Last Supper or with his death. It still remains a determinant of his glorious human identity (see Heb 9.11–12, 24–28; 10.5–14). The choice which he executed by going to Jerusalem, eating the Passover, and accepting the consequences still exists (cf. *S.t.*, 3, q. 22, a. 5).

3. Eating the Passover and celebrating the Eucharist at the end of the meal were religious acts of Jesus in which the Twelve also shared. Except for Judas, they were Jesus' friends, and, while not clearly understanding what he was doing, they wanted to be with him in it. By cooperating with him, through receiving and consuming his body and blood, they took part in his redemptive act.

The eucharistic sacrifice is a sign, for it does signify the bloody consequences of Jesus' choice. But the sign here is not merely a symbol with a purely cognitive relationship to what it symbolizes. The first Eucharist is Jesus' very carrying out of the choice in making which he concretely accepted death. Thus the sign expresses the existential reality.

4. As part of his eucharistic action, Jesus includes the command: "Do this." Thus he brought it about that the Mass in each of its performances concretely actualizes the eucharistic sacrifice he offered. **In other words, in commanding the repetition of his eucharistic action, Jesus establishes a real, existential relationship between his own choice, which led to his death, and the act of the priest consecrating in the Mass. In short, the Mass today continues to carry out the basic, redemptive commitment of Jesus.** This is done now in a different manner than on Good Friday, but its present carrying-out is really part of what Jesus was doing then, because the priest does now what Jesus then told him to do (see *S.t.*, 3, q. 64, a. 5, ad 1; q. 78, a. 1; q. 83, a. 1, ad 2, 3).

5. Thus, as Vatican II teaches (see SC 47), the Mass perpetuates the sacrifice of the cross until Jesus comes again. The Mass makes the sacrifice of the cross present so that we can share in it. The faithful ought to offer Jesus not only through the priest but with him, and so learn to offer themselves as well (see SC 48).

6. It follows that all of Christian life proceeds from and prepares for the Eucharist (a point to be discussed more fully in chapter thirty-three). Christians live in order to have prayers and works, joys and sufferings, to bring to the Offertory; having known Jesus in the breaking of the Bread, Christians come forth from Mass and enter into other activities in order to love and serve the Lord. In the Mass Christians are united with Jesus in his sacrificial act, which thus should be the overarching act of each Christian's life as a whole.

It is in the Mass that persons already Christian by baptism become fully joined to Jesus by cooperating in his human act and thus linking their own lives (made up of their own acts) with his. The Eucharist contains our Lord himself:

Through his very flesh, made vital and vitalizing by the Holy Spirit, he offers life to men. They are thereby invited and led to offer themselves, their labors, and all created things together with him.

Hence the Eucharist shows itself to be the source and the apex of the whole work of preaching the gospel. Those under instruction are introduced by stages to a sharing in the Eucharist. The faithful, already marked with the sacred seal of baptism and confirmation, are through the reception of the Eucharist fully incorporated into the Body of Christ.

Thus the Eucharistic Action is the center of the congregation of the faithful over which the priest presides. So priests must instruct them to offer to God the Father the divine Victim in the sacrifice of the Mass, and to join to it the offering of their own lives. (PO 5; translation amended)

Jesus' redemptive act is community forming. By faith one accepts God's communication of redemptive love. This love requires one to live as God's children should live.

Question C: What does it mean to follow the way of the Lord Jesus?

1. Here we reach the heart of this entire work, for it is now possible to explain clearly what it means to follow the way of the Lord Jesus. The idea of following Jesus seems mysterious. Confronted with it today, many people say to themselves: But Jesus is God and he lived a long time ago in a culture very different from ours. Others have thought that imitating Jesus means trying to discern and adopt his style of outward behavior. Such notions obscure the relevance of Jesus to the serious responsibility of living a Christian life. Moreover, they have no basis in Scripture, which makes it clear not only that we must follow Jesus but what this means.

2. Since God the Father is the font of all holiness, the first principle of Christian living is imitation of the Father. "As obedient children, do not be conformed to the passions of your former ignorance, but as he who called you is holy, be holy yourselves in all your conduct; since it is written, 'You shall be holy, for I am holy'" (1 Pt 1.14–16).

3. It follows that one must love one's neighbor as the Father does (see 1 Jn 4.7–11), be compassionate as he is compassionate (see Lk 6.36), and love enemies as he loves them, forgiving everything (see Mt 5.43–45; Lk 6.35). In a word, one must be perfect, as the Father is perfect (see Mt 5.48).

4. Taken seriously, this is a breathtaking challenge. We are called to give ourselves as unreservedly to God—to be perfect—as he gives himself to us in Christ. It is natural for children to be like their father, but how can we live up to this demand when our Father is God? God shows us the path of life in which we must walk (see Ps 16.10–11; Acts 2.28). It is not easy to find the way of life, but God gives us knowledge of salvation and guides our feet into the way of peace (see Lk 1.79). The way is our Lord Jesus (see Jn 14.6).[3]

5. Under the law, "the way into the sanctuary [of heaven] had not yet been revealed" (Heb 9.8; NAB). But Jesus himself is at one and the same time the way and also God's faithfulness and life, by which one is brought along the way and rewarded at its end. He is unique: "I am the way, and the truth, and the life; no one comes to the Father, but by me" (Jn 14.6).[4] Since he is the light of the world, no follower of his need walk in darkness; he is for Christians the new pillar of fire, the light of life (see Jn 8.12). If we go on walking in darkness while imagining we are

in communion with Jesus, we lie; but if we walk in his light, we are in communion with him and one another (see 1 Jn 1.6–7).

Jesus is the way of love. "And this is love, that we follow his commandments; this is the commandment, as you have heard from the beginning, that you follow love" (2 Jn 6). The way of Jesus is dependable teaching: "Anyone who is so 'progressive' that he does not remain rooted in the teaching of Christ does not possess God; while anyone who remains rooted in the teaching possesses both the Father and the Son" (2 Jn 9; NAB).

Jesus is a living lesson to be learned: "Take my yoke upon you, and learn from me" (Mt 11.29). St. Paul takes up this idea and points out that pagan lust has no place in Christian life: "You did not so learn Christ!" (Eph 4.20). Jesus is taught and learned; he is proposed as a norm. One must grasp the truth in him "and put on the new nature, created after the likeness of God in true righteousness and holiness" (Eph 4.24).

6. In the book of Acts, Christianity itself is at first distinguished from the traditional faith by the simple title "the way" (Acts 9.2; 18.25; 24.22). The way Jesus' disciples must follow means self-denial, for it is the way of the cross (see Mk 8.34). This way is not followed for its own sake, but for Jesus' sake and the gospel's (see Mk 8.35). The true disciple looks forward to the establishment of God's kingdom and contributes to the redemption of others by ecclesial service (see Mk 9.1; 10.42–45).[5]

7. Although the Church and the eternal kingdom are not absolutely identical, the kingdom is already present in mystery in the Church and growing visibly there (see LG 3). We are privileged to live now as members of God's pilgrim people, for the Church, united with God in the new and everlasting covenant, is the nucleus of the heavenly city of God (see Heb 8.7–13; 11.13–16; Rv 21.1–7; cf. *S.t.*, 3, q. 8, aa. 1, 4).

8. The covenant includes the practical requirements of the communion it establishes. Hence, the way to be sure of one's relationship with Jesus is to "keep his commandments. He who says 'I know him' but disobeys his commandments is a liar" (1 Jn 2.3–4; cf. Jn 15.10). The mandate to the apostles is to make disciples and baptize them, "teaching them to observe all that I have commanded you" (Mt 28.20). What does Jesus command? "This is my commandment, that you love one another as I have loved you" (Jn 15.12).

9. **In sum, Scripture makes it clear that following Jesus means keeping his commandments, particularly his commandment to love one another as he loves us.** To keep his commandments is to follow him because his commandments are the stipulations of the new covenant Christians enter by faith in him and celebrate in the Mass. To be a Christian is to be united with Jesus by a love which is not so much a matter of sentiment as of faithfulness to covenant responsibilities. In this respect, a Christian's relationship with Jesus is very like the love of a husband and wife for one another: To love faithfully is to live a life pleasing to one's covenant partner.

10. This scriptural teaching can be expressed with precision using theological language. The Christian's act of faith not only agrees with Jesus' basic commitment—to do the Father's will—but also corresponds in two ways to Jesus' personal vocation. First, by faith the Christian turns from sin and accepts the grace won by Jesus' redemptive act; second, accepting this grace the Christian

shares in the divine life Jesus mediates. As the fundamental option of Christian life, faith is a basic commitment; it requires each Christian to find and accept a personal vocation. In carrying out their personal vocations, Christians cooperate with Jesus by completing his redemptive work in themselves and mediating his truth and love to others. In doing this, Christians fulfill Jesus' commandment to love others as he loves them.[6]

11. This analysis enables us to give an exact sense to the expression: "the following of Jesus." It does not mean doing exactly what Jesus did; that is both impossible and unnecessary. Thus, the fact that Jesus is God and lived a long time ago is no obstacle to following him. Nor does following Jesus mean imitating him in superficial ways. **For us Christians, to follow Jesus means to accept and carry out our own personal vocations faithfully.** In doing so, we effectively cooperate with Jesus by completing in our own lives the commitment we share with him: to do the will of our heavenly Father.

One who takes up his or her cross and follows Jesus shares in his redemptive work. But often we wish to work with someone less because we want to get a job done than because we love that person and wish to share his or her company. So it can be with Jesus. Gratitude for what he has done for us grows into admiration for him as a man, and admiration for him grows into personal affection. Like a wife who loves her husband or an athlete who loves his coach, one often is more ready to act because of personal loyalty than because one understands the objective in view.

This aspect of the moral motivation of Christian life is essential to its growth toward perfection. It can be observed throughout the writings of St. Paul, who once had other values: "But whatever gain I had, I counted as loss for the sake of Christ. Indeed I count everything as loss because of the surpassing worth of knowing Christ Jesus my Lord. For his sake I have suffered the loss of all things, and count them as refuse, in order that I may gain Christ and be found in him" (Phil 3.7–9). Paul wants to know how to share in Jesus' sufferings, for he has been grasped by Jesus, and others should imitate Paul as he imitates Jesus (see Phil 3.10, 12, 17).

Question D: How do Christians carry out their common vocation to follow Jesus?

1. Imitating God means following Jesus, and following Jesus means joining him in his redeeming work. "Therefore be imitators of God, as beloved children. And walk in love, as Christ loved us and gave himself up for us, a fragrant offering and sacrifice to God" (Eph 5.1–2). Being redeemed by Jesus, one who accepts him in faith loves him with gratitude. This love requires keeping his commandments (see Jn 14.21); but he commands that we love one another as he loves us—that is, with a redeeming love (see Jn 15.12).

2. The only way a human being can make good his claim to be a Christian, one with Jesus, is "to walk in the same way in which he walked" (1 Jn 2.6). To follow Jesus is to make one's own his commitment to redeem: "If any man would come after me, let him deny himself and take up his cross and follow me. For whoever would save his life will lose it; and whoever loses his life for my sake and the gospel's will save it" (Mk 8.34–35). Jesus did not come to be served but to serve, to give his life for redemption. His followers must do likewise (see Mt 20.25–28;

Mk 10.43–45). **A commitment to Jesus is a commitment to help him do what he does: to communicate divine love by apostolic activity** (see Jn 13.12–17).

3. The redemptive commitment of Jesus is a social act, a community-forming commitment which one joins by making the act of living faith. We are not redeemed passively, but in Jesus are provided a way by which to accept redemption freely, become God's children, and share in the dignity of the Son of God by acting as his collaborators in redemption.

4. Yet even children of God continue to live in a sinful and largely unredeemed world, where ultimately there are only three choices: to join the world, and so abandon Jesus; to seek either to destroy evil or wholly segregate oneself from it, and so betray him by becoming a zealot or a Pharisee; or to try to convert the world with the love of Jesus, and so share in his fate. One will share his fate because not all of the sinful world accepts salvation, and that part which rejects it hates Jesus and his followers (see Jn 15.16–18; 16.1–4). "For what credit is it, if when you do wrong and are beaten for it you take it patiently? But if when you do right and suffer for it you take it patiently, you have God's approval. For to this you have been called, because Christ also suffered for you, leaving you an example, that you should follow in his steps" (1 Pt 2.20–21).

Initially, the demand of Christian life does not seem so great. Guided by the Spirit, the Christian is not constrained by the law (see Gal 5.18). One need only avoid serious sin, by which one would separate oneself from God's love, and freely undertake some works of love. Since one's needy neighbor is identified with Jesus, works of love are required; whatever fulfills a human need contributes to the fulfillment being accomplished in Jesus (see Mt 25.31–46).

Because Jesus did not live a pleasant life of self-satisfaction, however, neither may we: "Let each of us please his neighbor for his good, to edify him" (Rom 15.2). Furthermore, a Christian who marries and has a family must fulfill his or her responsibilities in a world in which marriage and family life are culturally adapted to practices which are sinful; a Christian in business must face dishonest competition; a Christian in any responsible position must carry out his or her responsibilities even though others become slack about theirs. Eventually, the real situation becomes clear. The way of the cross is the only way to live without evil. One must be with Jesus or against him; one helps in his redemptive work or interferes with it (see Lk 11.23).

5. Following Jesus takes priority over everything else in life for a person who is serious about this commitment. One may not love one's closest family in preference to Jesus (see Mt 10.37; Lk 14.26). One must sacrifice everything, even a part of one's body, if that is what it takes to avoid temptation (see Mk 9.43–48). The kingdom is so precious that one must give up one's whole livelihood for it (see Mt 13.33–46). Living thus, one becomes an image of Jesus and spreads his savor throughout the world (see Mt 5.13–16). Having been redeemed by Jesus, one must live redemptively; such is the vocation of every Christian.

6. Not only must those who have this vocation respond to God's love as Jesus does, they must share in his work of revelation. To cooperate with Jesus in revealing God's truth and love by one's own Christian words and deeds is to live an apostolic, redemptive life.

7. By living a redemptive life in union with Jesus, one prepares a suitable

sacrifice to join with his in the Mass. One's whole Christian life becomes liturgy. Sacrifice is a gift to God. The gift God wants from us is a good life, lived in union with the good life of Jesus, and the service he wishes us to perform is to cooperate in Jesus' redemptive work.

To live one's Christian vocation is to live in Jesus. "In Jesus" the whole new creation exists (see 2 Cor 5.17). "He died for all, that those who live might live no longer for themselves but for him who for their sake died and was raised" (2 Cor 5.15). Every Christian shares in and contributes to Jesus' single redemptive act. In one's own life one completes what is lacking in Jesus' sufferings (see Col 1.24). But is the redemptive act of Jesus not sufficient? Certainly, but as Jesus is in Christians and they in him, so his redemptive act is in their lives and by their own commitment their lives are in his redemptive act (see *S.t.*, 3, q. 8, aa. 1, 3).

Vatican II teaches: "The apostolate is carried on through the faith, hope, and charity which the Holy Spirit diffuses in the hearts of all members of the Church. Indeed, the law of love, which is the Lord's greatest commandment, impels all the faithful to promote God's glory through the spread of his kingdom and to obtain for all men that eternal life which consists in knowing the only true God and him whom he sent, Jesus Christ (cf. Jn 17.3). On all Christians therefore is laid the splendid burden of working to make the divine message of salvation known and accepted by all men throughout the world" (AA 3). A few paragraphs later, the Council adds that the Church's apostolate and that of every member is primarily to manifest the message of Jesus by words and deeds—by one's own revealing life—and to communicate his grace (see AA 6).

Question E: Why does every Christian have a unique personal vocation?

1. Besides his basic commitment to do the Father's will—to reveal the Father and to respond as a man should to God's love—Jesus had a personal vocation (22-C). In this unique role he became the new Man, the saving Christ of humankind, the sacrificial Lamb who in his blood reconciles all humankind to God and forms us into God's own human family.

2. Plainly, his personal vocation is not ours. Rather, each of us, in light of his or her personal gifts and unique situation, must make personal vocational commitments—a specific set of commitments made in the context of the basic commitment of faith. In other words, one's response to Jesus in faith must be a commitment to take up a personal cross, which takes a unique form. One's personal vocation must be executed in particular acts very different from those which made up the life of Jesus yet very much influenced by him: We must try to do what he would if he were in our place.

3. "Vocation" has often been used to refer only to the special calling of some to the clerical or religious life. Vatican II sometimes speaks of "vocation" in this sense, but also takes note of marriage as a Christian vocation (see GS 52). Even so, the concept of vocation is still that of a state of life rather than precisely that of a unique personal vocation. In even more general terms, the Council uses "vocation" to refer to the whole destiny which God has in mind for human beings in Jesus (see, e.g., LG 39, GS 11).

4. However, the Council also uses "vocation" to refer to the specific commitments, including any undertaken within one's state of life, which each and every Christian should make to shape his or her life into a responsible carrying-out of the basic commitment of faith (see LG 11, 46; PO 6; GS 31, 43, 75). So, for example, in a truly Christian home, "husband and wife find their proper vocation in being witnesses to one another and to their children of faith in Christ and love for him" (LG 35). Such specific witnessing within the context of one's state of life is a true Christian vocation and apostolate.

The different Christian states of life are complementary. If clerics are ordained for sacred service, the laity are commissioned for the complementary role of commitment to human goods other than the good of religion itself (see AA 6–7). The Council clearly distinguishes the secular, clerical, and religious states of life:

> A secular quality is proper and special to laymen. It is true that those in holy orders can at times engage in secular activities, and even have a secular profession. But by reason of their particular vocation they are chiefly and professedly ordained to the sacred ministry. Similarly, by their state in life, religious give splendid and striking testimony that the world cannot be transfigured and offered to God without the spirit of the Beatitudes.
>
> But the laity, by their very vocation, seek the kingdom of God by engaging in temporal affairs and by ordering them according to the plan of God. They live in the world, that is, in each and in all of the secular professions and occupations. They live in the ordinary circumstances of family and social life, from which the very web of their existence is woven.
>
> They are called there by God so that by exercising their proper function and being led by the spirit of the gospel they can work for the sanctification of the world from within, in the manner of leaven. In this way they can make Christ known to others, especially by the testimony of a life resplendent in faith, hope, and charity. (LG 31)

Thus personal vocation within each state of life is one's calling to a particular share in the single, all-embracing apostolate of the Church.

5. In his encyclical, *Redemptor hominis,* John Paul II refers to the teaching of St. Paul in emphasizing the principle of personal vocation:

> For the whole of the community of the People of God and for each member of it what is in question is not just a specific "social membership"; rather, for each and every one what is essential is a particular "vocation." Indeed, the Church as the People of God is also—according to the teaching of St. Paul mentioned above, of which Pius XII reminded us in wonderful terms— "Christ's Mystical Body." Membership in that body has for its source a particular call united with the saving action of grace. Therefore, if we wish to keep in mind this community of the People of God, which is so vast and so extremely differentiated, we must see first and foremost Christ saying in a way to each member of the community: "Follow Me."[7]

Not only do all Christians share the common vocation to follow Jesus and not only do particular Christians share the vocation to particular states of life, but each Christian also has a personal vocation: his or her unique way of following Jesus.

6. One should not think of personal vocation solely in terms of large-scale commitments. The child who undertakes to become more like Jesus each day is making a commitment to implement faith; such a simple commitment is a basic one for personal vocation. It is later defined and articulated in a more sophisticated way, but it need never be replaced.

7. Similarly, a person who enters religion or marriage as a major vocational commitment must make various other commitments—for example, to justice in civil society, to groups of friends, and so on. **And after taking one's religious or marital vows, one still has occasion to make additional commitments compatible with them. These need to be united to form a single, integrated identity. If they are, then the whole, complex self formed by commitments is determined by faith and is one's personal response to God's unique vocation.**

8. God creates to manifest his infinite goodness. The multiplicity and diversity of created entities is important, for each embodies a facet of perfection absent in all the rest: God creates no mere duplicates (see *S.t.*, 1, q. 47, aa. 1–2; *S.c.g.*, 2, 39–45). Jesus' humanity is the most excellent of creatures, but it is very limited. As Jesus needs the Father and the Spirit to complete the uncreated part of the total fulfillment which centers in him, so he needs each of us, in all his or her uniqueness, to complete the created part of this total fulfillment.

As man, Jesus accepted all the conditions of human existence except sin. It is one of the conditions of human existence that in making choices one limits one's life to a very narrow and partial fulfillment of human possibilities. Under the condition of sin, this aspect of self-limitation, inevitable in choice, makes moral goodness very unappealing (14-G). Jesus accepted an impoverished human life for himself (22-G). And though he perfectly fulfilled his personal vocation, his earthly life did not immediately touch the human lives of all men and women in all times and places, which are to be redeemed and brought to fulfillment in heaven.[8]

For his own human completion, Jesus depends upon his Church. As the members of the Church receive human completion by sharing in Jesus' human life, so he receives his human completion by sharing in the human life of each one of us (see Eph 1.22–23).[9] Together we build up his body and "we all attain to the unity of the faith and of the knowledge of the Son of God, to mature manhood, to the measure of the stature of the fulness of Christ" (Eph 4.13). In doing this, members of the Church also complete one another.

No Christian by himself or herself should seek to be a complete person, any more than Jesus did. Only all together, united with one another in him, do we form the one complete human Son of God. "Nor is there any ground," Leo XIII teaches, "for alleging that Jesus Christ, the Guardian and Champion of the Church, needs not in any manner the help of men. Power certainly is not wanting to Him, but in His loving kindness He would assign to us a share in obtaining and applying the fruits of salvation procured through His grace."[10]

9. Jesus needs each of us and our unique gifts and opportunities to complete the universal work of redemption. It is through us that Jesus comes to the people of our time. It is in our lives that the human goods in our culture are to be gathered up and redeemed. Jesus' sacrifice, offered to the Father, is an unsurpassable gift, but without our self-gift, united with his, both the homage of creation to God and the gratitude of redeemed humankind to the Father are incomplete. Through Jesus we share divine life by his gift to us of his own Holy Spirit. The Spirit's work is to

sanctify the whole of creation—utterly to renew the face of the earth. This work can only be completed by our acceptance and use of the Spirit's power to attain sanctity within our unique vocations (see LG 41).

St. Paul's chapter on love (see 1 Cor 13) often is read as if it stood by itself. It does not. It is the centerpiece and principle for the solution of a serious problem Paul treats with great care (see 1 Cor 12–14). He does not state the problem explicitly. But from the argument he gives toward its solution, the difficulty apparently was that many of the Christians at Corinth thought that their particular contributions to Christian life were the most important. Like children putting on a show, each of these people wished to dominate the assembly (the church gathered for liturgy or prayer) with his or her own favorite type of active participation.

Paul explains (1 Cor 12) that the Spirit gives Christians diverse gifts. These gifts are all one in coming from the Spirit, but all different in the personal capacities and roles to which they lead. The situation is like that of an organic body. The parts of a body do not all have the same function, but each is vital for the good of the whole. None of the parts of the body can get along without the rest. Consequently, the welfare and fulfillment of every part of the body is bound up with the welfare and fulfillment of the whole. So it is with Jesus. The Church is his single whole body; we are its many diverse members.

The hymn to love (1 Cor 13) carries the argument to its completion. Love solves the problem of unity and multiplicity. Paul states some of the implications of love: It generates all the virtues and heals all the vices which affect interpersonal relationships; moreover, love is always in season and will never become unnecessary. Paul follows his chapter on love with a practical discussion of the various gifts; he provides directions for rightly ordering the Church of Corinth. Near the end of this chapter of directives he states its binding force: "If any one thinks that he is a prophet, or spiritual, he should acknowledge that what I am writing to you is a command of the Lord" (1 Cor 14.37).

Question F: Why should Christians follow the same moral standards in carrying out their different personal vocations?

1. In one sense, Christians with different personal vocations follow different moral standards—for example, a Catholic priest and a married layman must follow different standards inasmuch as their lives differ. But where the morality of a single kind of choice is in question, all Christians should agree in the truth of the same moral norm. Moral norms, after all, are truths, not rules imposed on us or changeable laws. **Moral truth is one because it directs all men and women to the only complete good: fulfillment in Jesus. Moreover, the prophetic character of each Christian's personal vocation demands that all Christians know, accept, and do their best to live according to the same moral standards.**

2. A prophet is one who speaks before others. True prophets of the Old Testament received divine revelation and uttered the Lord's word to his people. Their work supplemented the Torah and kept its truth alive, especially by the reiteration and application of its moral implications. The prophets exhort, admonish, threaten, promise; in God's name they demand that sinners repent and commit themselves anew to the covenant.[11]

3. A person is personally called to prophetic responsibility and is obliged to

make a commitment to fulfill it. The prophet's task is a demanding one. It is given him whether he wants it or not; he has no discretion about the content of his message; he must not only speak God's message but live it out. His audience is invariably more or less resistant; often he is killed or otherwise persecuted.

4. Old Testament prophecy constantly points toward Jesus and prepares the way for him. Although the title of prophet seems inadequate in the case of Jesus, who was himself the fulfillment of all prophecy, he nevertheless acted as a prophet in many ways. Moreover, the role of prophet continues after Jesus' ascension. With the Spirit's coming to the Church, all who belong to Jesus share in prophecy, and some are especially gifted in this respect.

5. Vatican II teaches that Jesus continues to carry out his prophetic office, "not only through the hierarchy who teach in his name and with his authority, but also through the laity. For that very purpose he made them his witnesses and gave them understanding of the faith and the grace of speech (cf. Acts 2.17–18; Rv 19.10), so that the power of the gospel might shine forth in their daily social and family life" (LG 35). As prophets of Jesus, all Christians are called to communicate him in speech and in action. Revelatory deeds and words should make up the life of every Christian; those who meet a Christian should come to know God's saving truth and love through the experience, just as those did who met Jesus during his earthly life (see AA 6).

6. The role of prophet requires that one's faith and one's life be clearly of a piece. As ever in revelation, deeds and words can only work if they work together. Moreover, since Christians must proclaim the faith together, in one and the same Spirit, they must live the same kind of life, according to the pattern of Jesus. Jesus' disciples are known and make him known by their love (see Jn 13.34–35; 17.22–23; 1 Jn 4.7). Divergent and conflicting moral standards reduce the Church's witness to Jesus to confusion and babel.

In his encyclical, *Sapientiae christianae,* on the duties of Christians as citizens, Leo XIII develops this point in a perspicuous and compelling way. After quoting Vatican I's exhortation to the faithful, calling upon them to help repel errors and spread the pure light of faith (DS 3044/1819), Leo adds: "Let each one, therefore, bear in mind that he both can and should, so far as may be, preach the Catholic faith by the authority of his example, and by open and constant profession of the obligations it imposes." In this work, Leo explains, the laity also play a part, but they must not act individualistically:

> The faithful would not, however, so completely and advantageously satisfy these duties as is fitting they should were they to enter the field as isolated champions of the faith. Jesus Christ, indeed, has clearly intimated that the hostility and hatred of men, which He first and foremost experienced, would be shown in like degree toward the work founded by Him, so that many would be barred from profiting by the salvation for which all are indebted to His loving kindness. Wherefore, He willed not only to train disciples in His doctrine, but to unite them into one society, and closely conjoin them in one body, "which is the Church" (Col 1.24), whereof He would be the Head. The life of Jesus Christ pervades, therefore, the entire framework of this body, cherishes and nourishes its every member, uniting each with each, and making all work together to the same end, albeit the action of each be not the same (cf. Rom 12.4–5). Hence it follows that not only is the Church a perfect

society far excelling every other, but it is enjoined by her Founder that for the salvation of mankind she is to contend "as an army drawn up in battle array" (Sg 6.9).[12]

Leo proceeds to draw out the implications; emphasizing the importance of unity of mind, he cites St. Paul's exhortation (see 1 Cor 1.10), and adds: "The wisdom of this precept is readily apprehended. In truth, thought is the principle of action, and hence there cannot exist agreement of will, or similarity of action, if people all think differently one from the other."[13]

7. The life of the Church is a participation in divine love. The many believers must live with a single mind and heart (see Acts 4.32). Certainly there is room for plurality, but Christian plurality can involve no inconsistency. Rather, it must be the richness of many gifts united in the one body of the Lord Jesus (see 1 Cor 12–13). Not the cacophony of a stage full of soloists all playing at once but the rich harmony of a symphony orchestra provides the appropriate metaphor for Christian life.

8. The Church's unity is modeled upon that of the Trinity (see UR 2), who always act outwardly as one God (see DS 1331/704). If the Church is to communicate God's truth and love by her outward life before the world, her members must provide an image of the unity of God's action. To be sure, the image cannot have the absolute unity of its model; but its clarity and effectiveness will be needlessly diminished by conflict among the members.[14]

9. Therefore, Christian moral standards must be articulated and shared by all even in their details. To lend substance to the truth they profess, all must adhere to the same plan of life and act together. The Church must have only one mind: the mind of her Lord Jesus.

Christians who live their lives among others must communicate God's truth and love to them by revelatory words and deeds. Vatican II teaches: "For, wherever they live, all Christians are bound to show forth, by the example of their lives and by the witness of their speech, that new man which they put on at baptism, and that power of the Holy Spirit by whom they were strengthened at confirmation. Thus other men, observing their good works, can glorify the Father (cf. Mt 5.16) and can better perceive the real meaning of human life and the bond which ties the whole community of mankind together" (AG 11). The divisions among Christians seriously interfere with this sign, which ought to be given to nonbelievers (see UR 1).

To be prophetic, Christian life must really be humanly good, not merely conventionally good. The sinful world knows and understands its own; its own tell it nothing new. Supernatural truth is not at once recognizable by the world. The truly fulfilling for human persons, however, is something even sinful persons can recognize and wonder at. The purity and courage of Maria Goretti, the noble loyalty and truthfulness of Thomas More— even men and women who are children of this generation can grasp the sign in such virtue.[15]

Free choice as such is not ultimately intelligible; there is no sufficient reason for any free choice. However, when a person acts out of self-interest and when people choose according to expediency, then all the world can explain such acts and lives: Nothing is done which does not serve the individual's desires or the group's conception of its common interests. Each truly Christian life points to something beyond this world. In doing so, it is a powerful sign. It makes credible the words of faith which explain it.

Of course, not all of us are saints. Many of us are miserably weak and sinful. How can our lives bear witness to the truth and love of God? Despite our sins, they can. The Catholic is called to repentance and the sacrament of penance (see DS 1542–43/807). The sins we must confess do not communicate the truth and love of our Lord Jesus. But the line of people waiting to go to confession and the tears of grateful penitents help to make the Church a sign which challenges the unbelief of the world.

Vatican II teaches that the primary condition for effective missionary activity is interior renewal. All the faithful are duty-bound to share in the expansion of the Mystical Body, so that they can bring it to fullness as quickly as possible (see AG 36). The primary responsibility in the spreading of the faith is to lead a fully Christian life. Such a life will make the Church appear as Jesus intended her to be: a sign lifted before the nations, the light of the world (see AG 36; cf. Is 11.12; Mt 5.13–16).

Question G: Why must Catholics conform their consciences to the teaching of the Church?

1. One's life as a Catholic is communal, not individualistic. Members of the Church are members of God's family, commissioned to communicate his truth and life to the world. The Church's moral teaching is necessary for her members to reach the same, or at least harmonious, judgments of conscience, so that their common life in Jesus will fulfill the law of love of God and neighbor. Every member of the Church has a role to play in handing on, unfolding, and applying her moral teaching, but not all have the same role. None, however, may treat Catholic moral teaching as if it were merely a set of human rules.

2. Vatican II teaches on this matter in its document on religious liberty. Foreseeing that this document might be misinterpreted as denying the responsibility of Catholics to live up to their own faith, the Council includes an article emphasizing just this responsibility (see DH 14).

3. The Council begins by urging all members of the Church to work to spread the faith. The first thing to do is to pray for others, so that they might come to the truth and be saved. Then Catholics must form their consciences correctly and live the Christian life as a sign; all those who propose to live redemptively toward others have the responsibility of giving prophetic witness.

> In the formation of their consciences, the Christian faithful ought carefully to attend to the sacred and certain doctrine of the Catholic Church. The Catholic Church is, by the will of Christ, the teacher of the truth. It is her duty to give utterance to, and authoritatively to teach, that Truth which is Christ himself, and also to declare and confirm by her authority those principles of the moral order which have their origin in human nature itself. Furthermore, let Christians walk in wisdom in the face of those outside, "in the Holy Spirit, in unaffected love, in the word of truth" (2 Cor 6.6–7). Let them be about their task of spreading the light of life with all confidence and apostolic courage, even to the shedding of their blood. (DH 14; translation amended)

Finally, the Council insists that members of the Church know and proclaim her teaching, using all means compatible with the gospel itself. Thus the virtuous lives of Catholics who live according to consciences formed by the Church's teaching will be matched by kindly words articulating the meaning of their behavior.

4. The logic of Vatican II's teaching is plain. Every person has a conscience, precisely as a God-given means of finding divine truth. **Catholics enjoy the marvelous grace of having received the truth for whose attainment conscience is given. Having the truth, they must live by it and also share it with others. It is in one's own best interests to live in the truth and to live redemptively toward others. Our Lord Jesus provides the Church as the teacher of his truth; the Catholic, favored by hearing this truth, must conform to it.**

5. For her members, the Catholic Church is the supreme moral authority under God. Catholics ought to conform their consciences to her teaching in every question, every detail, every respect. If they are faithful, they will: not only because they hear the Lord Jesus' voice, speaking for the Father, in the teaching of the Church, but because by their conscientious commitment of faith they have accepted the Church as their own, more than humanly wise, moral guide (3-F).

6. Having made the judgment of conscience that one ought to listen to a certain moral advisor and follow whatever advice one receives, one then violates one's conscience in listening to this advisor yet acting contrary to the advice. Of course, the initial commitment can be something different—to accept the advice if it happens to accord with one's own opinion. But that is something different, for it is an important aspect of the act of Catholic faith that one has more confidence in the ability of the Church as a whole to discern moral truth than in the insights of any part of the Church or isolated individual, including oneself.

Some argue that the conformity of conscience to the Church's teaching is only for immature Christians, who are literally "children" of the Church. The mature Christian is spiritual and "judges all things, but is himself to be judged by no one" (1 Cor 2.15). Thus, the argument concludes, a Christian come of age must be autonomous, not dependent on Church authority in moral matters.

This argument rests on a confusion between the Church's moral teaching and law. Mature persons are more and more free of the constraint of law, for they readily do what is right without constraint. But one never outgrows the requirements of moral truth; those who seek autonomy from the Church's teaching separate themselves from the reality God reveals. St. Paul's text should not be misunderstood. His point is that all Christians insofar as they are embued with the truth of the apostolic message and endowed with the Spirit can judge any merely human wisdom.[16]

7. Conforming to the Church's teaching does not leave the conscience of a Catholic with nothing to do. It is necessary to make the Church's teaching one's own, and this work of appropriation is a task for conscience. One must also add to the Church's teaching anything compatible with it which is necessary to find and fulfill one's personal vocation. And, in carrying on this creative work, one must develop new moral norms to unfold the Church's teaching, when nothing in it tells one precisely what to do.

8. Furthermore, with conscientious docility Catholics must exchange views with fellow believers concerning the proper mode of together fulfilling our Lord's law (see GS 43). As part of this, Catholics should frankly and confidently make

known to their bishops whatever difficulties they encounter in accepting Jesus' moral teaching and living up to it. Bishops for their part should examine such difficulties, provide guidance and help, and so carry out their responsibility (see CD 16). (For a fuller discussion of the work of the Catholic conscience, see 27-D).

In its teaching quoted above, Vatican II makes a general reference to, and thus incorporates, the teaching of Pius XII on the right formation of Christian conscience in the young. (This note in DH 14 is numbered 35 in the official text, 57 in the Abbott edition. See GS 16, note 10 in the official text, 37 in Abbott.)

Pope Pius states that to go along the way of salvation "means, in practice, to accept the will and the commandments of Christ and to conform one's life to them, i.e., each single act, inner or exterior, which the free human will chooses and decides upon." Then he asks: "But where shall the educator and the youth find in each individual case with ease and certainty the Christian moral law? They will find it in the law of the Creator imprinted in the heart of each one as well as in revelation, that is, in all the truth and precepts taught by the divine Master. Both the law written in the heart, that is, the natural law, and the truth and precepts of supernatural revelation, have been given by Jesus the Redeemer into the hands of His Church as humanity's moral treasure, so that the Church may preach them, intact and protected against any contamination and error, to all creatures, from one generation to another."[17]

Today, Pope Pius goes on to point out, some object to this teaching which the Church has proposed for centuries. They wish to leave matters to the individual's conscience. But this position leads consciences off the way of Jesus: "The divine Redeemer has given His revelation, of which moral obligations are an essential part, not to individual men but to His Church, with the mission to lead men faithfully to accept that sacred deposit." Moreover, divine assistance to avoid error is promised not to individuals but to the Church. Therefore, individualistic autonomy of conscience is incompatible with God's providential plan of salvation.[18]

In morals, as in faith, a faithful Catholic never will permit his or her own opinions, any seemingly cogent deliverances of experience, even supposedly scientific arguments, or the contradictory belief of the whole world outside the faith to override the Church's clear and firm teaching. As one realizes that one's own opinion in any doctrinal matter can be in error, that the world cannot know the generosity of God's love, that reason cannot grasp the truths of Trinity and Incarnation, and that experience cannot perceive Jesus in the Eucharist; so one realizes that one's opinion in any moral question can be mere rationalization, that the world does not know how to live in God's love, that reason cannot grasp the way of Jesus, and that, although one cannot experience it, he lives in one's liturgy of obedience to faith.

Summary

In making his unique contribution to our redemption, Jesus proceeded in a way which enables us to enter into what he did. We do this by the act of faith, our fundamental option to turn from sin and accept the gift of Jesus' new covenant. Membership in the community of the new covenant, the Church, comes in baptism, which brings those who receive it into immediate union with Jesus. This bond of union includes sharing in his divine and bodily life, as well as cooperation with his human acts. The most important of his human acts is made present to us in the Eucharist.

Thus, in the Eucharist we are united with Jesus' redemptive act. Choices last; the choice which Jesus executed in going to Jerusalem, eating the Passover, and suffering the consequences still exists. As the Twelve took part in Jesus' redemptive act through eating the Passover with him, so we now do the same through the Mass. For Jesus, by commanding the repetition of his eucharistic action, establishes a real, existential relationship between his choice and the act of the priest consecrating in every Mass. In short, the Mass makes the sacrifice of the cross present so that we can share in it. All of Christian life proceeds from and prepares for the Eucharist.

The following of Jesus is a central yet mysterious principle of Christian life. Scripture makes it clear that God's children must be holy as he is holy, and Christians can do this by following the way of the Lord Jesus. Following him means keeping his commandments, for these are the stipulations of the new covenant. Faithfulness to Jesus as a partner in covenant is required of each Christian, who thus is called to love others as he or she has been loved by Jesus.

Hence, to follow Jesus is neither to do exactly what he did nor to imitate the style of his behavior in superficial ways. Rather, Christians are called to join him in his redeeming work, share his commitment to do the Father's will, and accept the responsibility of communicating divine truth and love to others. To follow Jesus is to cooperate with him in his redeeming work.

Carrying out this apostolic responsibility in a sinful and largely unredeemed world, however, one who follows Jesus will share his fate. Yet for one who is serious about being a Christian, following Jesus takes priority over everything else. Christians love others as Jesus has loved them only by helping him redeem others as he first redeemed them. By living a life of redemptive love in union with Jesus, one prepares a suitable sacrifice to join with his offering in the Mass.

Jesus' personal vocation is plainly not ours. Each of us has his or her own personal vocation distinct from though dependent upon his: to try to do what Jesus would if he were in our place. "Vocation" has often been used to refer only to a calling to the priesthood or religious life. Vatican II uses "vocation" in a broader sense—state of life in general—in discussing marriage as a Christian vocation. But the Council also refers by "vocation" to all the specific commitments an individual makes to carry out the basic commitment of faith. This is personal vocation: the individual Christian's unique way of following Jesus. Jesus needs the special contribution each of us can make to complete the created part of the total fulfillment which centers in him: he needs us to extend his redeeming work to our contemporaries and our culture.

While Christians have unique personal vocations, their prophetic responsibility requires that they live these in accord with the same standards. All Christians share in prophecy, for all are to communicate Jesus in speech and action. This requires consistency between faith and life. Moreover, since Christians must proclaim the faith together, they must live the same kind of life, according to the pattern of Jesus. The pluralism of Christian life lies in a harmonious diversity of gifts, not in inconsistency and much less in dissent. Christian moral standards, even in their details, must be known and accepted by all.

The life of Catholics is communal, not individualistic, for members of the Church are members of God's family. The Church's moral teaching is necessary for its members to reach harmonious judgments of conscience, so that their common life in Jesus will fulfill the law of love of God and neighbor. Vatican II teaches on this matter in its document on religious liberty: Conscience is a God-given means of finding moral truth.

In finding this truth, Catholics enjoy a special help; they are guided by the Church, which by Jesus' will is the teacher of truth. Having been helped by the Church to know moral truth, Catholics must live by it and share it with others. For her members, the Church is the supreme moral authority under God; by their conscientious commitment of faith they have accepted the Church as their more than humanly wise moral guide, to whose teaching they will conform their consciences. This does not leave the conscience of a Catholic with nothing to do, however. One must make the Church's teaching one's own, and one must add to this teaching what is necessary to find and fulfill one's personal vocation.

Appendix 1:   The liturgical character of Christian moral life

God is not always pleased with sacrifices offered to him. "I hate, I despise your feasts, and I take no delight in your solemn assemblies" (Am 5.21). "Bring no more vain offerings; incense is an abomination to me" (Is 1.13). "For in the day that I brought them out of the land of Egypt, I did not speak to your fathers or command them concerning burnt offerings and sacrifices" (Jer 7.22).

"But this command I gave them, 'Obey my voice, and I will be your God, and you shall be my people; and walk in all the way that I command you, that it may be well with you'" (Jer 7.23). "He has showed you, O man, what is good; and what does the Lord require of you but to do justice, and to love kindness, and to walk humbly with your God?" (Mi 6.8). "He who keeps the law makes many offerings; he who heeds the commandments sacrifices a peace offering" (Sir 35.1).

The authentic liturgy is the one to which good works are brought: "Consequently, when Christ came into the world, he said, 'Sacrifices and offerings you have not desired, but a body have you prepared for me; in burnt offerings and sin offerings you have taken no pleasure. Then I said, "Lo, I have come to do your will, O God," as it is written of me in the roll of the book'" (Heb 10.5–7).

Unwanted gifts and useless service are not gifts and service at all. Unless it is the center of genuine Christian living, even the Mass, like the sacrifices which the prophets condemned, can become a hypocritical substitute for Catholic life, an anodyne which makes us forget our unfaithfulness to Jesus and his Church (see *S.t.*, 3, q. 80, a. 4).

The Epistles sometimes introduce the theme of sacrifice when the transition is made from doctrinal topics to moral exhortation.[19] For example: "I appeal to you therefore, brethren, by the mercies of God, to present your bodies as a living sacrifice, holy and acceptable to God, which is your spiritual worship. Do not be conformed to this world but be transformed by the renewal of your mind, that you may prove what is the will of God, what is good and acceptable and perfect" (Rom 12.1–2). "Bodies" here means persons and lives as a whole, but perhaps especially connotes particular actions. One is to ignore whatever "new morality" happens to be current and judge instead by the standards of Jesus.

Jesus looked forward to a time when "true worshipers will worship the Father in spirit and truth" (Jn 4.23). Since the Christian has died and lives a hidden life in Jesus, he or she should offer everything to God the Father in thanksgiving (see Col 3.3, 17). "Religion that is pure and undefiled before God and the Father is this: to visit orphans and widows in their affliction, and to keep oneself unstained from the world" (Jas 1.27).

"Like living stones be yourselves built into a spiritual house, to be a holy priesthood, to offer spiritual sacrifices acceptable to God through Jesus Christ" (1 Pt 2.5). The Mystical Body of Jesus is God's living temple, and the sacrifice called for in this temple is the good lives of the priestly people united with their high priest, Jesus (see 1 Pt 1.22–2.10). In Jesus we are becoming "a dwelling place of God in the Spirit" (Eph 2.22).

Appendix 2:   The human authenticity of the faithful Catholic conscience

To nonbelievers, Catholics might appear to be untrue to themselves when they form their consciences by the Church's teaching. The nonbelieving world in general denies the reality of moral guilt, yet it knows this reality. Hence, the world fails to appreciate the blessing Catholics enjoy in having a secure means of knowing what is morally true; the world flees from moral standards—especially those proclaimed clearly and uncompromisingly by the Church—which call in question the world's own sin. The nonbeliever's challenge is: "You Catholics are abdicating your own consciences and enslaving yourselves to the opinions of your popes and bishops." This challenge must be answered.

The first point to make is that everyone who lives responsibly relies at times on the moral advice of others. For example, any person entering an especially responsible job must make many judgments about how to handle problems which arise. The sensible person looks for a colleague who is experienced, upright, and willing to talk, and seeks his or her guidance.

According to Catholic faith, humankind existing in a world sinful and redeemed is very much in need of wise advice from Jesus. He is our colleague: more experienced, certainly upright, and (through the Church) willing to talk. In this way we learn in the light of faith much moral truth—some of which we could know even without faith and can come to understand for ourselves once it is taught us by the Church. Without faith, we could not know it so easily, nor be so sure of it, nor gather it without a mixture of mistaken opinions (see DS 3005/1786).

Moreover, from our Lord Jesus we learn what we otherwise could not know: our true destiny of fulfillment in him. From Jesus we receive the power of the Spirit and the guidance to walk after Jesus to glory. Without faith, we could not know at all this truth which Jesus himself is, and so we would not know how to live in the only right way possible in this sinful world.

As in other choices of moral advisors, so in our commitment to Jesus and our adherence to his truth taught by the Church, we are led by conscience to seek the truth from Jesus and to accept his moral guidance as he speaks to us in the Church. Still, it will be objected, one abdicates personal responsibility by submitting unreservedly to the Church's teaching and not testing each moral norm she proposes by one's own reason and experience. One who is upright would never submit so completely to any other moral advisor.

The last point is correct. There are limits to the trust one can place in a merely human moral guide, and it would be irresponsible to go beyond these limits. But we believe that our Lord teaches in and through the Church and gives us the word of the Father. Hence, our submission to the Church's teaching is not submission to mere human opinions, but to the very word of God (see 1 Thes 2.13).

By faith we are certain that in faith we accept God and through faithfulness live in communion with him. Otherwise, faith would be null, since it is inherently normative. One is no more intellectually irresponsible in submitting unreservedly to the Church's moral teaching than in submitting unreservedly to any of the fundamental doctrines which go beyond reason and experience: the Trinity, the Incarnation, the adoption of children of God, the bodily presence of Jesus in the Eucharist, and so on.

But does it not degrade Catholics, place them in the position of immature children, that even the details of their intimate, personal lives are regulated by Church teaching? This would be the case if the Church were a political society. If her moral teaching were a code of law, its all-inclusiveness would be totalitarian. It is precisely this misconception—that Catholic moral teaching is a code of law—and reaction against the resulting appearance of totalitarianism, which lead some to reject the Church's teaching. But if moral teaching is a light from God, and if nothing is good or worthwhile apart from one's relationship to God, then humble acceptance of the whole of the Church's moral teaching, including those points which touch one most intimately, is in no way degrading.

Notes

1. On faith and baptism in Scripture, see F. X. Durrwell, C.Ss.R., *The Resurrection: A Biblical Study*, trans. Rosemary Sheed (New York: Sheed and Ward, 1960), 311–19 and 332–38.

2. See Brian Byron, *A Theology of Eucharistic Sacrifice*, Theology Today, 35 (Hales Corners, Wis.: Clergy Book Service, 1974), 37–70, for a generally helpful treatment with a good bibliography. Byron lacks understanding of the lastingness of human acts and is unable to explain the unity of Calvary and the Mass in fully existential categories, and so unfortunately reduces the Mass to a symbolic likeness of the one sacrifice.

3. A treatment of the imitation of Jesus and the apostles as the way of proceeding from one's natural status of image of God to one's heavenly destiny: Ceslaus Spicq, O.P., *Théologie Morale du Nouveau Testament*, vol. 2 (Paris: J. Gabalda, 1965), 688–744.

4. Jesus is not simply a human mediator, pointing the way to God by his law, but the very embodiment of the Torah: J. M. Gibbs, "The Son of Man as the Torah Incarnate in Matthew," in *Studia Evangelica*, 4 (1965), ed. F. L. Cross, Texte und Untersuchungen, 102 (Berlin: Akademie-Verlag, 1968), 38–46.

5. See Ernest Best, *Following Jesus: Discipleship in the Gospel of Mark*, Journal for the Study of the New Testament Supplement Series, 4 (Sheffield, Eng.: JSOT Press, 1981), 246–50 (summary).

6. In other words, the following of Christ is more than passive participation in the fruit of his redemptive sacrifice; it is sharing in the work of redemption as an active cooperator in the life of his co-redemptive Church. Bertrand de Margerie, S.J., *Christ for the World: The Heart of the Lamb: A Treatise on Christology*, trans. Malachy Carroll (Chicago: Franciscan Herald Press, 1974), 257–312, develops this point very well in the context of his systematic theology of Jesus.

7. John Paul II, *Redemptor hominis*, 71 *AAS* (1979) 317; *The Papal Encyclicals*, 278.86.

8. See Paolo Molinari, S.J., "Our Incorporation in Christ and Our Participation in His Work of Redemption," *Christ to the World* (1970), 388–93.

9. Marcus Barth, *Ephesians*, Anchor Bible, 34 and 34a (Garden City, N.Y.: Doubleday, 1974), comments at length (153–59, 192–210, 440–41, 484–96) on problems related to Eph 1.21–23. He admits very substantial support for the interpretation I follow (see 206, n. 324), but rejects it. Max Zerwick, *The Epistle to the Ephesians* (New York: Crossroad, 1981), 43–45, briefly and authoritatively summarizes the various views, admits the possibility of the interpretation I follow, but prefers one which considers the relevant fullness to be that which Christ communicates to the Church. Both seem to pay little attention to Jesus' humanity and to focus almost entirely upon his divinity. Barth, for instance, says: "In sum, it is most unlikely, and certainly not proven by Eph 1.23, that Paul believed in an implementation of God or the Messiah by the church. He who does the filling is God or Christ. That which is filled by God is Christ, the church, or all things—never God. And that which is filled by Christ is the church and the world." Similarly, in arguing against the view that Eph 4.13 means that Christ is not full until all the saints have been incorporated into him, Barth relies (491) on an argument based on the unacceptability of the late Gnostic notion "that the deity is filled up, completed, restored,

or perfected when the spirits of men enter or return into unity with the formerly split and deprived All-Father, the One-and-All." The unsatisfactoriness of such lines of argument is that while the sacred writer admittedly cannot be understood to mean that God is completed by anything or anyone, the Word Incarnate as man must be as open to completion as any other human individual, for otherwise he would not be like us in everything except sin. Moreover, this interpretation is in line with the obvious fact that like any other head incomplete without its body, any other leader incomplete without his army, Jesus as man would be incomplete if no one took up his or her cross and followed him.

10. Leo XIII, *Sapientiae christianae*, 22 *ASS* (1889–90) 391; *The Papal Encyclicals*, 111.14. The context of the quoted passage is an explanation of the Christian's responsibility to live a prophetic life in cooperation with the redemptive work of Jesus.

11. See "prophet," *Dictionary of the Bible*, 2d ed., 468–74; C. Brown, "Prophet," *New International Dictionary of New Testament Theology*, 3:74–79. Gerhard von Rad, *The Message of the Prophets* (New York: Harper and Row, 1972), 30–59, articulates several salient aspects of the prophetic role: the prophet has a personal vocation to which he must respond by a free commitment; he often makes this commitment reluctantly; in it he enjoys a special relationship to God; this relationship carries with it heavy responsibility; the prophet does not always bear his responsibility gladly; God rebukes him for this; the prophet suffers in carrying out his responsibility; his message is often ill-received; and prophets often come to a hard end at the hands of those to whom they are sent.

12. See Leo XIII, *Sapientiae christianae*, 22 *ASS* (1889–90) 392; *The Papal Encyclicals*, 111.16–17.

13. Ibid., 393;111.19. This entire encyclical provides powerful support for the argument of this and the next questions. In many places, Leo remarkably anticipates the perspective of Vatican II's teaching on the apostolate of the laity.

14. See Paul VI, *Paterna cum benevolentia*, 67 *AAS* (1975) 5–23 (*Apostolic Exhortation on Reconciliation within the Church*), for a description of the effort of some to bring about a revolution comparable to the Protestant revolt in the Church, the damage this process does to the Church as sign, and the large role in this process of false "pluralism" in dissenting theology.

15. On Christian life as sign: René Latourelle, S.J., *Christ and the Church: Signs of Salvation* (Staten Island, N.Y.: Alba House, 1972), 18–38, 254–64, and 285–319.

16. See Rudolf Schnackenburg, "Christian Adulthood According to the Apostle Paul," *Catholic Biblical Quarterly*, 25 (1963), 354–70.

17. Pius XII, "Nuntius Radiophonicus de Conscientia Christiana in Iuvenibus Recte Efformanda," 44 *AAS* (1952) 272.

18. Ibid., 273.

19. For an explanation of the sacrificial character of Christian life, by which the whole of it is to be rational worship: Raymond Corriveau, C.Ss.R., *The Liturgy of Life: A Study of the Ethical Thought of St. Paul in His Letters to the Early Christian Communities* (Brussels: Desclée de Brouwer, 1970). Also Robert J. Daly, S.J., *The Origins of the Christian Doctrine of Sacrifice* (Philadelphia: Fortress Press, 1978), 53–83; *Christian Sacrifice: The Judaeo-Christian Background before Origen* (Washington, D.C.: Catholic University of America Press, 1978), 230–56, 493–95, for the evidence that the sacrificial aspect of Christian life is in living as one ought more than in martyrdom.

CHAPTER TWENTY-FOUR

CHRISTIANS: HUMAN CHILDREN OF GOD

Introduction

The last chapter provided an overview of how the Christian cooperates in God's redemptive work in Christian life. Now we begin to examine specifically the central principle of Christian morality: Christian love. Within Christian life, love of a special sort is both the supreme standard and the highest good.

Love is not something secondary or incidental in God. God is love (see *S.t.*, 1, q. 20, a. 1). The Holy Trinity is a communion of persons in one being, one common life. Because of his love and by means of it, God communicates his love to created persons and so makes them share personally in his own life. Christian love is the new nature of a Christian who is a child of God by adoption.

Christian love often is confused with other loves. Many reduce it to sentiment or benevolence. But it is quite distinct from these loves, which, even if they are virtuous, are merely human (see *S.t.*, 1–2, q. 109, a. 3, ad 1; 2–2, q. 23, aa. 1, 4; q. 24, aa. 2, 12). Still others identify Christian love exclusively with God's love for us. This reduction also misses the full significance of Christian love by which we are transformed inwardly and made in truth children of God, sharers in the fullness of divinity present in Jesus in bodily form.

Aspects of human nature relevant to morality were examined in chapters two through twelve, and no extended treatise on human nature itself is required here. The present chapter will instead be devoted mainly to clarifying how God's human children really share in his life. The model on which to understand the Christian is Jesus. He shares our human nature without detriment to his divinity; we share his divine nature without detriment to our humanity. In the Christian as in Jesus, the two distinct natures, human and divine, are united without being mingled or confused in any way.

The love of God is the principle which heals sin and all its consequences, which were considered in chapter eighteen; it is the principle of the redemptive work of the Lord Jesus, which was considered in chapter twenty-two; it is the principle of all the virtues and precepts of the way of Jesus, which will be considered in chapter twenty-six; it is the principle which is nourished in us into eternal life by prayer and the sacraments, which will be considered in chapters twenty-nine through thirty-three; and it is the principle of the Church and her gospel, which will be considered in chapter thirty-five. The love of God which begins in the present life remains forever (see 1 Cor 13.13). More than anything else, this love unites our present Christian life with everlasting life. This unity will be the main subject of chapter thirty-four. Thus the present chapter is a key one.

Confusions about the make up of the Christian have often led to the supposition that something of humanity must be sacrificed for the sake of Christian life. However, the human and divine aspects of the Christian, being on diverse planes, remain distinct and uncommingled. There can be no conflict between them, and no need to limit or compromise either for the sake of the other.

Hence, these grave confusions, which have contributed so much to the flourishing and power of secular humanism during the past hundred years, can be set aside definitively, and the complex but harmonious unity of the Christian and Christian life clarified, as Vatican II already begins to do (see LG 36; GS 22, 32, 38–39, 40, and 45; AA 7).

Question A: What is human love?

1. Although "love" cannot mean precisely the same thing in God's case as in ours, God has chosen to use the language of love to reveal himself to us. Since we know the meaning of this language primarily from the experience of human love, some analysis of human love is necessary to understand the love which God is and in which he calls us to share.[1]

2. The good of each thing is that which fulfills its possibilities in such a way that it becomes more and more what it can be (5-A). But everything requires in itself a principle by which it is disposed toward its good. In creatures without cognition (for example, plants), the requirement is met by blind tendencies which under suitable conditions have their effect automatically. Creatures with cognition can to some extent anticipate what will be fulfilling and can act on this anticipation to bring about their own good.

3. Corresponding to cognition and based upon it, there must be a disposition which underlies tendencies both to suitable action and to rest when action has realized the good to which it is directed. Such a disposition is what love most basically is, and the capacity for such dispositions is the ability to love (see S.t., 1, q. 80, a. 1; 1–2, q. 6, a. 2; S.c.g., 3, 1, 2, 22).

In animals which have only sentient cognition, the ability to love is a basic aspect of emotional make up, which sometimes is called "sense appetite" or "the passions of the soul." Human persons also have an emotional make up corresponding to sentient cognition. In addition, they have an ability to love corresponding to intellectual knowledge of good. This ability is the basic power of will, which sometimes is called "rational appetite" (see S.t., 1, q. 80, a. 2; 1–2, q. 6, aa. 1–2; q. 22, a. 3; 2–2, q. 24, a. 1).

4. **Thus love is a basic disposition which adapts one to a known good** (see S.t., 1–2, q. 26, aa. 1–2; q. 28, a. 5). In human persons there are two fundamentally different modes of love: (1) emotions in respect to sensible goods; and (2) rational concern or caring in respect to intelligible goods, such as the forms of human goodness (treated in 5-D). Other emotions and volitions are based upon love or closely related to it, since their whole function is to enable creatures with cognition to fulfill themselves by action (see S.t., 1–2, q. 25, aa. 1–2, q. 28, a. 6).

Two other dispositions most closely related to love are desire and satisfaction. Often "love" and "desire" are used interchangeably, but there is a difference. Love of an anticipated good which is not yet realized arouses desire and leads to action. If the loved good is achieved by the action, desire is replaced by satisfaction—an emotion of pleasure at the sentient level or the joy of accomplishment at the intellectual level. Thus love is the constant, underlying disposition toward fulfillment whether anticipated or achieved (see *S.t.,* 1–2, q. 25, a. 2; q. 26, a. 3; q. 27, a. 4).

Emotions are often thought of as sentiments or feelings which are consciously experienced, and indeed they often do give rise to sensations of which one is aware, especially if the emotion is unusual or particularly strong. Moreover, it is not implausible to think of desire and satisfaction as more or less directly experienced. However, what is essential to emotions is not that one has a feeling, but that one is disposed to behave in certain ways. Hence, it makes perfectly good sense to talk about subconscious and unconscious love, hatred, anger, and so forth, as Freud and others have done. Since the emotion of love is in play only when it arouses desire or issues in satisfaction, it is not a feeling one can isolate in experience. One knows what an animal loves by what it pursues and rests in; similarly, one knows one's own emotional love and that of other persons by observing what arouses an urge and gives pleasure.

Just as emotional love is not primarily a conscious state, so volitional love is not primarily an experience. Neither is it a kind of knowledge or—in any ordinary sense of the English word—an action. Volitional love begins as a caring about or a basic interest in intelligible human goods. This caring or basic interest presupposes some understanding of these goods as goods—that is, as modes of human fulfillment. This love makes appealing various possible ways of intelligently acting to realize these goods. Sometimes one acts intelligently yet spontaneously, without deliberation, to realize a good understood and cared about volitionally (9-B). In other cases, different possibilities come to mind and one must choose which course of action to take, which possible good to try to realize. In any case, volitional love is not one's action—not something one does—but one's disposition of caring about understood goods. This disposition both makes appealing possible ways of acting intelligently and makes satisfying actions which go well.

5.   Abstract as it may seem to call love a disposition toward a fulfilling good, we do use the word this way: People "love" steak and they "love" truth. Even more often, we speak of loving people, ourselves and others. But the two things, loving something and loving somebody, are not separate; they are different aspects of the same thing.

Thus, to be disposed to a fulfilling good is to be disposed to the person fulfilled by that good. St. Thomas distinguishes between these two aspects of love, calling the disposition to that which is good "love of concupiscence" and the disposition to the person "love of friendship." This terminology misleads if it is mistaken to mean two different kinds of love—for example, selfish love and love which is altruistic (see *S.t.,* 1–2, q. 26, a. 4; 2–2, q. 23, a. 1).

6.   **Love is always in the first place a disposition to the fulfillment of the one loving; for love disposes to fulfillment through action, and every action is a fulfillment of the one who acts.** This ought not to be rejected moralistically as an expression of selfishness; rather, it is a basic fact about created persons (see *S.t.,* 2–2, q. 25, a. 4; *S.c.g.,* 3, 153). Moreover, Jesus promises the richest personal fulfillment to those who accept and follow him—the Beatitudes are one example (Mt 5.3–12)—while the Church condemns the view that one should love God with no hope of reward and no fear of punishment (see DS 2351–57/1327–33). Thus love is a disposition to the loving person's fulfillment, and the best love is a disposition to one's perfect fulfillment.

7. **Still, neither emotional nor volitional love is of itself limited to caring about the good only insofar as it is one's own.** Individuals are not made for fulfillment in isolation; they are made for some form of common life and for fulfillment there (see *S.t.*, 1, q. 47, a. 1; q. 60, a. 5).

That this is true at the emotional level is obvious by the disposition which leads animals to propagate and care for their young (see *S.c.g.*, 3, 24). Among all human individuals, natural sympathy shapes many spontaneous acts directed toward the protection and satisfaction of others. This fact tends to be ignored because it is so obvious, and because one begins to notice emotions when conflicts arise.

The same thing is true at the volitional level. Understandable goods do not have anyone's proper name attached to them. For example, one can notice and be interested in the possibility of rectifying injustice or protecting life whether or not the injustice is against oneself or the life threatened is one's own. Very often, someone who finds great fulfillment in a certain good is especially anxious to share it with others. For example, those who live joyfully in Jesus are most eager to make him known to others.

In all these cases, what one does is fulfilling to the one who does it. But in none of these cases need this fact be the reason for acting. Animals care for their young without self-consciousness; they simply cannot be selfish in their motives. A pedestrian who spontaneously reaches out to stop another from stepping off a curb into the path of an oncoming car is acting in an equally unselfconscious way.

Those who dedicate themselves by generous commitment to work—often very difficult and thankless work—for human life or the spreading of the gospel no doubt realize that their own goodness and holiness are realized in their lives, and hope for ultimate fulfillment in heaven. Yet one need not make one's commitments precisely for the sake of one's own fulfillment; one sometimes makes choices out of sheer fascination with a possible good, and only subsequently realizes how acting for and sharing in the good is fulfilling. An example is a child's interest in a field of study, in a hobby, or in collecting funds for a charitable cause, such as helping children in some faraway country. Even when one does make commitments with one's own fulfillment in view, this purpose need not render one's commitment to another's good ungenerous or selfish. The real question is how one's most fundamental commitments relate to and establish order among one's own interests and the interests of others.

8. How does one love another person? The active, transitive verb tends to confuse. In loving another, one does not do something to the other, either outwardly or even invisibly (for example, by feelings or wishes). Rather, love of other persons is simply an aspect of love as a disposition to fulfillment. For one cannot love a good without loving someone for whom it is fulfilling. **Thus, to the extent that the goods to which one is disposed by love are actualized in other persons, one loves other persons.**

9. Emotional love of another is a compound of various degrees of sympathetic or natural love of the other's own good and care about the other insofar as the other is identified with oneself. All of these affections are mingled and brought to focus upon the other. What is involved can be exemplified not only in emotional love of another person but also in emotional attachment to a pet animal.

10. Volitional love of another person adds to love, as a disposition, the beginning of action toward its fulfillment. One's intelligent concern for or caring about the forms of human goodness is potentially a disposition toward integral human

fulfillment. To begin to realize this potentiality, commitments are necessary. A commitment is a self-disposition through choice toward fulfillment with some particular person or group of persons. One committed to another is concerned for or cares about that person in particular. Considered as a particularization of the basic disposition toward the human goods, a commitment is a form of love; considered as an action, the same commitment is more fulfillment than love.

11. Persons who make a mutual commitment such as marriage are both united and distinguished in doing so. They are united by the common bond formed by their mutual choices. But like all other choices, commitments are self-determining, and so each partner's distinct personhood is actualized in his or her choice. Such love disposes toward the simultaneous increase of unity and distinction. Only in the distinctive fulfillment of the man as husband and the woman as wife can they achieve common fulfillment as a couple. Indeed, each partner wills the fulfillment of the other as distinct, for each wills that the other make the self-determining commitment by which the bond is formed. Each also wills the distinct fulfillment the other enjoys in their shared life.

Both selfish and unselfish love bond persons together or unite them, but in different ways. Selfish love involves nonacceptance of the real mutuality of the relationship. One who loves selfishly would reduce the other to a possession, a mere function of one's own fulfillment—a kind of appendage. Unselfish love between or among persons is marked by their focusing affection on one another with sympathy and fairness. The unity established is not by absorption but by a communality of interests and fulfillments (see *S.t.*, 1–2, q. 28, aa. 1–4). The closer the unity between those loving unselfishly becomes, the more their own identities and fulfillments are realized and appreciated.[2]

Genuine community is formed by unselfish love which unites two or many persons. Those who share in community are one insofar as they love the same good; they are disposed together to a common fulfillment. The one which is the real community is also many insofar as it fulfills its members in their diverse and complementary possibilities. In true community, unity is not lessened by the ever-increasing uniqueness of the members, and their individuality is not compromised by the ever-growing solidarity of their common life. Both the uniqueness of each individual and the solidarity of all increase as the good loved in common is effectively desired, pursued, and enjoyed by each and all.

Individualism and collectivism are two opposed, destructive movements in societies. Individualism would destroy society by eliminating its unity, by breaking its members up into a collection of selfish individuals all trying to reduce one another to functions of themselves. Collectivism would destroy society by eliminating its members in an attempt to overcome selfishness by eliminating selves. People very often suppose that the only solution is a compromise between individualism and collectivism: libertarian anarchy up to a point, beyond which selves become slaves.

The explanation of unselfish love shows that such a compromise is not a real solution at all, and that the only sensible option is to embrace both the one and the many: a fellowship of persons whose distinct personalities will be fulfilled by their common life. The bond of such a society is its common love, its common disposition to cooperation for goods which fulfill all and are personally sought with unselfish love by each for others.

Question B: What is the relationship
between the Trinitarian reality of God and
his self-communication to created persons?

1. The Church teaches that there is one true God, Father, Son, and Holy Spirit, one in being but three in persons.[3] The Father is not begotten; the Son is begotten of the Father; the Holy Spirit proceeds from the Father and the Son. None of the persons is identical with either of the others. The three persons are one God, not three gods; for they are one divine reality, a single entity, not three entities. There is multiplicity only in what is distinguished by the opposition of personal relationships: for example, of Father and Son to each other. Because of their unity, each person is wholly in each of the others. The Father, the Son, and the Spirit are not three principles of creatures, but one principle—one creator (see DS 1331/704).

2. Since we must understand God as a unity of three distinct persons, we can think of him, as the terms "Father" and "Son" require, as being familial. As familial, the divine persons are most perfectly united and most perfectly distinct. The ideal of love, in which unity and multiplicity are both at their ultimate, is best realized here; or, better, our ideal of love comes from this divine exemplar, proceeding from "the Father, from whom every family in heaven and on earth is named" (Eph 3.14–15).

3. Inculcating brotherly love, the First Epistle of John makes the point: "He who does not love does not know God; for God is love" (1 Jn 4.8). While the context indicates that the sacred writer is thinking of God's love manifested in the Incarnation and redemptive act of the Son, still it seems warranted also to take the verse as an expression of the reality of the Holy Trinity which is truly revealed in Jesus.

Ceslaus Spicq, O.P., in summarizing his analysis of many Johannine texts, particularly those bearing upon the love of Father and Son, says:

> There is so complete an identity between Christ's love and the Father's love that we can conclude from one to the other. It is more than a matter of manifestations and marks of love, as if God and Jesus were acting with one and the same heart. The relationship between the Father and his only Son springs from a reciprocal, permanent, and eternal charity (Jn 17.23–24). Everything that Christ has revealed about the intimate life of God is summarized in its being an exchange made within the mutual relationship of knowledge and love between God and his Son. The union of the two persons seems to be accomplished in *agape* [note: Jn 17.22-23, 26]. Thus one arrives at conceiving of a substantial charity which is God (1 Jn 4.10). Love is of the same nature as God.[4]

What is said here of the Father and the Son surely must be extrapolated to include the Holy Spirit. The inner reality of the Holy Trinity, it seems clear, is a communion which is infinite love (cf. *S.t.*, 1, q. 37, a. 1).

4. The mystery of the Holy Trinity is a mystery of love. More specifically, it is a mystery of the communicability of divinity. That there are three divine persons in the one only God shows that divinity is not a monad—a self-enclosed absolute unit, which could neither be many without exploding into an infinity of particles

nor gather the many into itself without absorbing them into an indistinguishable whole. God is not so. He is one in three, three in one. He is love, the perfect exemplar of love, the absolute reconciliation of the one and the many. This reconciliation is what philosophy always seeks and never finds; it is what sinful created persons always long for and never enjoy—until the Word becomes flesh and makes enduring love present in the world.

5. This has practical implications. Since God's very constitution is love, sharing in his love is sharing in his life.

Every Christian doctrine has a normative aspect. God's revelation demands a response from us, and everything God reveals should help to shape our response. In many cases, reflection has not made clear the practical significance of the most basic truths of faith, although their significance has been communicated more or less effectively to unreflective understanding by other means, especially by the words and deeds of the liturgy. The present chapter clarifies the practical significance of one of the most central doctrines of Christian faith, namely, the teaching on the Holy Trinity.

6. Non-Christians who think of God as absolutely and noncommunally one tend to suppose that the human relationship with God must take either of two forms: Either human beings must always remain extrinsic to God or they must be absorbed into him. The first possibility is reflected in Aristotle's thought, the second in some Eastern thought.

7. Although God established a personal relationship with Israel, it lacked the intimacy of Christian communion with God in the Lord Jesus (21-D). The sacramental communion of the old covenant was a meal which God deigned to permit in his sight (see Ex 24.11). The communion of the new covenant is a meal in which God not only takes part but gives himself (see Mt 26.26–29; Jn 6.53–58).

8. In sum, God is not a solitary being, nor an impersonal ocean of divinity. The Trinity, the one only God, is a communion of persons eternally one in love. **Although apprehended only by the indirect light of faith, this mystery shows that divine life is not in principle incommunicable and that it is not necessarily communicated at the price of the dissolution of selfhood. A divine Father who has a natural Son is a God who can extend his family by adoption.**[5]

Furthermore, the divine exemplar of love is a model for our brotherly and sisterly love. Teaching the importance of love of neighbor, Vatican II explains: "Indeed, the Lord Jesus, when he prayed to the Father, 'that all may be one . . . as we are one' (Jn 17.21–22) opened up vistas closed to human reason. For he implied a certain likeness between the union of the divine persons, and the union of God's sons in truth and charity. This likeness reveals that man, who is the only creature on earth which God willed for itself, cannot fully find himself except through a sincere gift of himself" (GS 24). The divine family of the Trinity is the model for the human family called to become the extended family of God.

Love always involves a gift and depends upon initiative. Someone must make the first move. Often, who does so is dictated by who can do so—for example, parents love their children into being. Analogously, in the life of God, the Father has the initiative in begetting the Son, and the Father and Son have the initiative in breathing forth the Spirit. By free choice, God has the initiative in creating the world. The Incarnate Word has the initiative in redeeming the fallen world.

Initiative establishes priority—of course, one must realize that initiative and priority are diverse within God from his initiative and priority toward creatures. But if one bears in mind the analogous sense of the statement, one can say that love always establishes order, and the order once established is never lost. The basic priority is built into the interpersonal relationship; to deny it or to try to reverse it is to negate what the relationship really is.

Among the persons of the Trinity, the priority apparently holds in the salvific and sanctifying missions of the Son and Holy Spirit: "The words that I say to you I do not speak on my own authority; but the Father who dwells in me does his works" (Jn 14.10). The Holy Spirit ". . . will guide you into all the truth; for he will not speak on his own authority, but whatever he hears he will speak" (Jn 16.13).

Such priority clearly does not mean that the Father is superior and the Son inferior. The Holy Spirit is not deprived of freedom in teaching because he does not speak on his own. Something similar is manifested in Jesus' washing of his disciples' feet (see Jn 13.12–16) and his subsequent remarks about their status as friends rather than slaves (see Jn 15.14–15). Of course, love does not eliminate real differences. But neither does the order which love necessarily implies entail that the one who has initiative is in a higher caste than the one who first receives.

One concrete example illustrates the tremendous significance of this point. St. Paul teaches: "Wives, be subject to your husbands, as to the Lord" (Eph 5.22). This teaching does not consign Christian wives to an inferior position. In the marital relationship, the husband has priority in giving, based upon the actual dynamics of the psychobiology of sex. In the maternal-filial relationship, as Paul remarks elsewhere, women have priority to men (see 1 Cor 11.12). The consequence of the priority of the husband in giving to his wife is that he must sacrifice himself for her: promote her security and fulfillment, not his own comfort, success, and pleasure (see Eph 5.25). For her part, a wife cannot proceed autonomously, as though she did not need her husband. The abuse of the male role is to dominate and exploit, to use one's wife for one's own ends. The abuse with which wives respond to this exploitation is refusal to submit: an irresponsible declaration of liberty.[6]

Question C: How intimate a communion does God establish with us?

1. God's love makes us his children: "See what love the Father has given us, that we should be called children of God; and so we are" (1 Jn 3.1). As his children, we are called to share intimately and fully in his own life: "beloved, we are God's children now; it does not yet appear what we shall be, but we know that when he appears we shall be like him, for we shall see him as he is" (1 Jn 3.2).[7] To be reborn as a child of God is to be begotten of the Spirit. The Spirit is the principle of adoption by which we call out to God: "Abba!" (see Rom 8.15). "It is the Spirit himself bearing witness with our spirit that we are children of God" (Rom 8.16). God lovingly chooses those whom the Spirit will adopt in order that the Son might be the firstborn of many (see Rom 8.29).[8]

2. This way of speaking suggests a parity between the eternal Son and God's adopted children. How seriously are we to take this suggestion?

3. Certainly we are not to take it in any way which would eliminate the distinction between the natural Sonship of our Lord, who is a divine person, and the adoptive sonship or daughtership of Christians, who remain human persons. Nevertheless, the personal communion in which Jesus wishes his disciples to remain is based upon a strict analogy with his Father's love for him: "As the Father has loved me, so have I loved you; abide in my love" (Jn 15.9). Jesus wants it

known that the Father loves his followers as the Father loves him (see Jn 17.23). It is the Father's very love for Jesus which is to live in Christians (see Jn 17.26).[9]

Divine love transforms created persons into partners in communion who are related to the divine persons much as the divine persons are related to one another. This transformation is not imposed upon anyone. That divine life which is the eternal Word is revealed to humankind as a light to be accepted in faith; if it is accepted, human persons are reborn as children of God who share in the faithful love of God which is fully present in the Word Incarnate (see Jn 1.4–16).

Thus, if we are faithful: "God abides in us and his love is perfected in us. By this we know that we abide in him and he in us, because he has given us of his own Spirit. And we have seen and testify that the Father has sent his Son as the Savior of the world. Whoever confesses that Jesus is the Son of God, God abides in him, and he in God. So we know and believe the love God has for us. God is love, and he who abides in love abides in God, and God abides in him" (1 Jn 4.12–16).

A mutual abiding-in, the unity of love, is established by God with his adopted children. On John 15.9, Spicq comments:

> The great revelation of this verse is that the charity of the Father, the Son, and the disciples is on one and the same level and flows from one to the other without any interruption. As the Father has loved me, so have I loved you. You, yourselves, remain in this *agape*. The verse implies that charity is a bond; charity creates the union between those who love one another. It tells us that "to be in Christ" (v. 2) means to be in his love. Above all, it presents the relationship of the Father to the Son as the type and source of Christ's relationship to his own disciples. There is so great a disproportion between the Son and the disciples that the statement is truly stupefying, but it is no arbitrary parallel or comparison. It is precisely the love most proper to God which reaches men through the intervention of Christ. God loves men in Christ, and they participate in his love and live from it in the most real sense.[10]

Now, as is argued above (and in appendix 1), God's proper love is his very constitution as one only God in three divine persons. If it is correct that the love which is proper to God is extended to us in Jesus, then it follows that in him—through having been reborn by the Spirit—the very constitution of God includes us.

4. Human love is not an action but a disposition to that which fulfills. The mutual love of two or more human persons simultaneously perfects their identities and joins them in communion (see A above). Similarly, to abide in God's love is to be drawn within the unity of God. This unity is so perfect that the divine persons, though utterly distinct, are also wholly in one another (see *S.t.*, 1, q. 42, a. 5). The Father and Son are expressly said in Scripture to be in one another (see Jn 10.38; 14.11), and the Church teaches that this is mutually true of all three persons (see DS 1331/704).

5. **In some way, God brings Christians into this divine unity.** Jesus prays for all who will believe in him: ". . . that they may all be one; even as you, Father, are in me, and I in you, that they also may be in us, so that the world may believe that you have sent me. The glory which you have given me I have given to them, that they may be one even as we are one, I in them and you in me, that they may become perfectly one, so that the world may know that you have sent me and have loved them even as you have loved me" (Jn 17.21–23).[11] Not only our Lord Jesus, but the Father and the Spirit as well, dwell in Christians (see Jn 14.17, 23).

581

6. Commenting on 1 John 4.17, where it is asserted that Christians are in this world as Christ is, Ceslaus Spicq, O.P., says: "The clause is not about qualities and virtues or even about states and modes of being in heaven and on earth, but simply about *being*. The burden of the comparison rests on the verb 'to be.' Just as he *is*, so we *are*. Who is he? He is the object of the disciples' faith, Christ himself, precisely the incarnate Son of God. Jesus is God and man. Similarly, in this world, Christians are both men and gods.""[12] **Human persons remain always of human nature and always creatures; yet by a free self-giving of the divine persons, a self-giving which always presupposes their own interpersonal relationships, human persons also in a real way share—"share" in an irreducible sense—in divinity.**

7. Although it may seem strange to us to speak of the divinization of human beings, the Fathers of the Church speak this way. St. Irenaeus says that Jesus "became what we are, so that he might bring us to be what he himself is" (FEF 248). St. Athanasius says of the Word: "He became man so that we might be made God" (FEF 752; cf. 780, 788). St. Basil the Great describes the effect of the gift of the Spirit by saying the Christian is "made God" (FEF 944). St. Augustine says Christians are deified by grace (see FEF 1468).[13]

Pope Pius XII warns us not to suppose that this intimate unity means that the Christian ceases to be a creature. Divine attributes cannot be predicated univocally of created persons (see DS 3814/2290). This warning cannot be ignored, but it also is true that communion by love in God's life is a mystery which can no more be reduced to any other way of speaking than to that excluded by Pope Pius. In other words, what is revealed about the sharing of Christians in the unity of God is an irreducible truth. One ought not to try to fit it into other categories.[14]

8. In sum, there is a true sense in which it can be said of created persons who enjoy the grace of adoption that they are God. Thus we can say: "Mary is God, and Joseph is God, and Peter is God . . . ." Clearly, though, in saying this one is not using the word "God" in precisely the same way one uses it in saying the Holy Trinity is God. That is probably why the Fathers prefer to say ". . . is made God," not simply ". . . is God."

It will help to clarify what has just been stated if one considers the question: What does St. Paul mean when he speaks of the love *of* God which "has been poured into our hearts through the Holy Spirit who has been given to us" (Rom 5.5)? Many interpreters take "love of God" to mean God's love for us rather than our love for God. However, St. Thomas takes "love of God" here to refer to our love (see *S.t.*, 2–2, q. 24, a. 2). The Council of Trent refers to this passage in Paul when it teaches about the charity which is infused by the Holy Spirit into hearts and inheres in them (see DS 1530/800, 1561/821).

The First Epistle of John speaks of love in a somewhat similar passage, in which it is clear that the love in question is our love: "Beloved, let us love one another; for love is of God, and he who loves is born of God and knows God. He who does not love does not know God; for God is love" (1 Jn 4.7–8). Making reference to Romans 5.5, Spicq comments on the passage just quoted, saying that while Paul's meaning is somewhat unclear, in this Epistle it is clear "that the Christian himself is the lover, for he has become capable of loving divinely." Spicq also says that since the phrases "he who has been begotten by God" and "he who loves" are equivalent, "it is clear that the child of God has received a faculty or power of loving which is inherent in the divine nature he has come to share."[15]

In Spicq's view, no sharp distinction should be made between "love of God" meaning God's love and the same phrase meaning our love. Rather, the phrase "represents a genitive of quality, 'the love that is truly divine,'" already mentioned in 1 Jn 3.17. Before being subjective or objective [that is, in this context, God's love of us or our love of God], love exists in itself as a distinct entity. It is possessed or shared by various persons and consequently has various manifestations, although it always keeps its own nature and essential laws. Perfect, authentic, full *agape* is described in 1 Jn 4.10. God possesses it supereminently and essentially (v. 8). He communicates it to his children, whom it enables to love their brothers and to love him. Love creates the stable union among all those who share the same divine nature."[16]

Of course, Spicq does not mean that love is a something prior to God in which he shares. God is his own love. The important point Spicq is making is that the love of God which is poured forth in our hearts is a disposition to the divine goodness which God is, the goodness which God communicates first in creating, and ultimately in divinizing created persons. By this disposition created persons receive their own inherent capacity to act according to the divine nature in which they share by God's grace.

Thus, in some true sense one can say of certain created persons—those in whom Jesus lives and who live in him—that they not only exercise human capacities in an appropriate and fulfilling way, but somehow also act in union with Jesus according to the divine nature in which they share. This conclusion seems to be supported by a remarkable passage in St. John of the Cross:

> Having been made one with God, the soul is somehow God through participation. Although it is not God as perfectly as it will be in the next life, it is like the shadow of God. Being the shadow of God through this substantial transformation, it performs in this measure in God and through God what He through Himself does in it. For the will of the two is one will, and thus God's operation and the soul's is one. Since God gives Himself with a free and gracious will, so too the soul (possessing a will the more generous and free the more it is united with God) gives to God, God Himself in God; and this is a true and complete gift of the soul to God.
>
> It is conscious there that God is indeed its own and that it possesses Him by inheritance, with the right of ownership, as His adopted son, through the grace of His gift of Himself. Having Him for its own, it can give Him and communicate Him to whomever it wishes. Thus it gives Him to its Beloved, who is the very God who gave Himself to it. By this donation it repays God for all it owes Him, since it willingly gives as much as it receives from him.[17]

The exchange of love, initiated by God in creating humankind, comes to its fulfillment in such unity.

Question D: How does the act of faith link the Christian as a human person with his or her share in the divine nature?

1. We shall approach this problem from the point of view of the Council of Trent, which in its Decree on Justification treats the relationships between the free choice by which a Christian makes the act of faith and the love by which he or she shares in divine life.

2. God's love has not been bestowed on a faithful humankind. From the

beginning all human beings were enmeshed in a web of sin, which alienated humankind from God (see Rom 3.9–19). God's love is shown all the more splendidly because he sent his only Son to die for us godless ones (see Rom 5.6–8). And so love comes not only as a deifying principle but, first of all, as a healing principle. It straightens out what is crooked; it justifies—that is, puts right. God's love is a gift of justification (see *S.t.,* 1–2, q. 109, a. 1; q. 113, a. 2).

3. Justification is by faith in Jesus (see Gal 3.1–9, 26). One's human life becomes a life of faith in Jesus (see Gal 2.20). The believer "is a new creation" in Jesus (2 Cor 5.17). The life of such a person must be that of the "new nature, created after the likeness of God" (Eph 4.24).

4. The intrinsic principle by which anything is such as it is, is called a "formal cause." Roundness is the formal cause of the shape of a ring, whiteness of the color of snow, and so on. What is the formal cause of the justification of the Christian? According to Trent, it is the "justice of God, not the justice by which he is himself just, but the justice by which he makes us just" (DS 1529/799). Sinners are justified by a rightness which is not merely attributed to them, but which they receive within them as their own, in a measure determined by the will of the Holy Spirit and their own disposition and cooperation (see DS 1529/799). God's love is poured into hearts by the Holy Spirit and remains in them (see DS 1530/800). Christians would not be justified without this inhering love given by the Spirit (see DS 1561/821).

5. From this point of view, the love of God is a principle by which the sinner is made right, the Christian is made a child of God. This love is not identical with the uprightness of God, nor is it identical with the Holy Spirit. It is the Christian's own love, which, although received as a gift, remains in the Christian as a transforming principle. A Christian's living is straightened out and conformed to Jesus by this principle, as a ring is shaped by its own roundness (see *S.t.,* 1–2, q. 110, a. 1; q. 113, a. 2, ad 2; a. 7).

6. One is justified by faith in Jesus in the following sense. Faith is the beginning of salvation (see DS 1532/801). The sinner must turn to Jesus and hear him (see *S.t.,* 1–2, q. 113, a. 4). Otherwise, he or she cannot become a Christian and so cannot become a child of God in Jesus. Yet even after one is justified, grace can be lost by mortal sin, without the loss of faith. When this happens, faith is called "dead faith" because it is loveless, not saving faith (see DS 1544/808; *S.t.,* 2–2, q. 4, aa. 3–5). **The faith which saves is that which one seeks and receives in baptism; it is infused along with hope and charity at the same time sins are remitted** (see DS 1528/799, 1531/800). This is the living faith which works through love (cf. Gal 5.6) and keeps the commandments faithfully (see DS 1531/800).

7. **Although living faith is wholly God's gift to us, it is also our own human act.** God's love does not destroy but perfects the unique reality of those he divinizes. God wishes that in sharing his life we be ourselves (see *S.t.,* 1–2, q. 113, a. 3; 2–2, q. 2, a. 9; q. 23, a. 2). As St. Irenaeus says: "Not merely in works, but even in faith man's freedom of choice under his own control is preserved by the Lord" (FEF 245). For anyone capable of free choice, there is the possibility of

refusing God's love. Moved and helped by God, therefore, one must cooperate by accepting his proposal of intimacy (see DS 1525/797, 1554/814).

8. This proposal comes to us in Jesus; it is his gospel. The first work of living faith is to accept God's proposal, an acceptance which justifies. This is the human person's own act by which he or she enters into the kingdom announced by the gospel. It is done by the person's free choice. Now, just as one must have love to have living faith, one must have living faith, which involves a free choice, to have love: "Whoever confesses that Jesus is the Son of God, God abides in him, and he in God" (1 Jn 4.15). Such acknowledgment is certainly not an act of dead faith. Thus, living faith presupposes love, and love presupposes living faith (see *S.t.*, 1–2. q. 113, aa. 4, 7; 2–2, q. 2, a. 9; q. 4, aa. 1–3, 7). How can this be?

9. As was explained (in 20-D), one is prepared to accept the gospel because it is credible; seeing that one ought to believe it, one chooses to do so. Before receiving God's love, one makes this choice for the sake of some human good, such as avoiding God's punishment and enjoying his favor. Having accepted God's proposal and thereupon received his gift of love, however, one is disposed by this love toward the divine goodness which God is and which he shares with his children. Thus, one has an additional reason, his goodness, for choosing to listen to God and adhere to him faithfully. One's choice is thereby transformed, not as if one chose to assent to a different gospel, but by being a differently motivated choice to assent to the same gospel. **Not merely out of love of a human good but out of love of God, one chooses to adhere to God revealing himself in Jesus and to be faithful to God by living according to the gospel.**

10. This clarifies how God's love invites, respects, and ultimately divinizes a human being. An adult enters freely, by his or her own human choice, into intimate communion with God. Since one remains a distinct person, this free commitment remains one's own act.

11. Still, as long as faith is living, this act is really proportionate to God's love and responsive to it. The human person is not accepting communion on unequal terms. As St. John of the Cross explains, the good shared by God and the soul is common to both. Moreover, one who adheres to God with living faith is not seeking eternal life with God for the sake of something—a merely human good—other and less than God, but for the sake of the divine goodness by which one hopes to be fulfilled with God.

12. By God's love poured forth in our hearts through the Holy Spirit who is given to us, we are disposed to love supernaturally and spontaneously the superhuman good, namely, divine goodness (see *S.t.*, 1–2, q. 62, a. 1; q. 109, a. 3). We are disposed supernaturally, because we share by adoption in the divine nature; by the Spirit's gift we share in the love of God, which is the power to act according to the divine nature.

13. By this power we freely choose, out of love of God and not merely out of love of a human good, to accept God's proposal of intimate communion. Our first act done by the love of God poured forth in our hearts through the Holy Spirit is our act of living faith, an act by which we freely accept this gift and our own participation in divinity.

14. In sum, God gives himself to us altogether gratuitously (see *S.t.*, 1–2, q. 109). We become his children only by his grace, his utterly free election. Yet, since we accept God in faith, we are his children by our own free choice. If we faithfully persevere in love until death, this free choice of ours will last forever. God's love for us is always his, our love for him will always be ours. The respective freedoms by which uncreated persons and created persons enter into communion with one another retain and always will retain their mutual distinctness. Thus, the love which is the Holy Spirit and the love of God inhering in us constitute a communion in divinity among persons and persons who remain absolutely distinct.

The stress placed here upon the role of free choice—the suggestion that the point of insertion of the human participant in divinity precisely is in the choice—is likely to raise a question about the situation of Christian infants. They surely share in divine life but appear not to make any free choices. The question is twofold. What about their situation now? What about their situation if they should die without ever making a free choice?

In considering this difficulty, one must bear in mind that revelation on the whole obviously is addressed as saving truth to those who can understand it and make choices; it is not personally addressed to infants. Therefore, how God cares for them is not likely to be clear in the sources of revelation, and endless controversies about the fate of infants seem to show this to be so.[18] One must always remember that in theology one proceeds on faith, and one does not know how many other ways of doing things God might have in the reserves of his infinite wisdom and love.

The social character of Christian life is relevant to the problem. Christian life is not individualistic. We are sinners in Adam and sons of God in Jesus. Children who cannot act at a specifically human level naturally are members of society in their families, through their parents or guardians. The Church is the mother of all her children. Thus the infant does in some sense share in an act of faith which is in some way its own, appropriate to its age and condition: the faith of the Church. When we say, "We believe . . . ," we include in the "we" our baptized infants and others who for whatever reason cannot make a free choice, but are somehow incorporated in the Church.

Question E: Can divine goodness and human goods be alternatives for choice?

1. In the past, much popular Christian piety suggested that loving God meant preferring him to created goods. Vatican Council II teaches otherwise. Declaring that human dignity "is rooted and perfected in God," the Council says it is the Church's teaching that Christian hope for eternal happiness with God "does not lessen the importance of earthly duties, but rather adds new motives for fulfilling them" (GS 21; translation supplied). This would hardly make sense if divine and human goodness were alternatives between which one had to choose.

Vatican II lists and discusses many elements which make up the order of this world, as we live in it here and now. About these elements, it teaches:

> All of these not only aid in the attainment of man's ultimate goal but also possess their own value. This value has been implanted in them by God, whether they are considered in themselves or as parts of the whole temporal order. "God saw all that he had made, and it was very good" (Gn 1.31). This natural goodness of theirs takes on a special dignity as a result of their relation to the human person, for whose

service they were created. Last of all, it has pleased God to gather together all things, both natural and supernatural, into one in Christ Jesus "that in all things he may have the first place" (Col 1.18). This destination, however, not only does not deprive the temporal order of its independence, its proper goals, laws, resources, and significance for human well-being but rather perfects the temporal order in its own intrinsic strength and excellence and raises it to the level of man's total vocation upon earth. (AA 7; translation amended)

This teaching would make no sense if there could be a direct conflict between supernatural love of God and natural love of human goods. There can be no such conflict. This point is part of what is meant by the saying that grace perfects nature and in no way mutilates it.

2. Furthermore, a negative answer to the question is required by the nature of divine love itself. God's love is all-inclusive; it is the very source of every other good. But the love of God given us by the Spirit is a share in God's own love. **Our supernatural love is therefore all-inclusive as God's love is. It embraces all genuine human goods; in no way are they an alternative to divine love.**

3. This can be explained more fully as follows. First and foremost, God loves the primary and perfect instance of goodness: himself. However, God's goodness includes every possible good, for he is infinitely good. His goodness is manifested in his work of creation and redemptive re-creation (see *S.t.*, 1, q. 4, a. 2; q. 7, a. 1; q. 19, a. 3; *S.c.g.*, 2, 23–24; 3, 16–22). God does not act to acquire glory, for he needs nothing (19-A). Rather, the glory of God is this communication of divine goodness.

4. In loving himself, God loves creatures, for the good of everything other than God is implicit in his goodness and becomes explicit by God's free, creative choice. God does not need to choose between created goods and himself; indeed, he cannot do so. His love extends to all possible created goods so far as they would be goods; his gratuitously creative choice makes some of these possibilities be (see *S.t.*, 1, qq. 19–20).

The creative work of God can be seen as love in the following way. God expresses his goodness in creating. As a real expression, creation must be wholly distinct from the creator, established in its own being, set apart from the creator. What truly is made must truly be other than its maker. But also as a real expression of its creator, creation is as it were a mirror reflecting his goodness, with human persons the very image of God within this mirror. What truly is made must truly be one with its maker. Nor can this bond of unity be dissolved. The created world continues to exist only insofar as it is preserved in God's love and gives him glory—although, of course, God's image in creation is mutilated by sin. For his part, God is faithful in his creative love; he hates nothing he has made, and so preserves all things and does everything possible to bring them to their fulfillment (see Wis 11.17–26). Thus the relationship of creator and creature is a unity in multiplicity, a reflection of the love which God in himself is.

5. Love is expressed in works (see 1 Jn 3.16). Living faith requires that one do the works of love (see LG 41). If one loves God, one loves what he loves, and he loves the goodness of all he makes (see Jn 8.42). God would hardly love human persons, however, if he cared nothing for the fulfillment of the human desires which he himself placed in their hearts. But these desires are directed to human goods. Therefore, by loving as God loves—that is, by holiness—one loves the goods which humanly fulfill, and "a more human way of life is promoted even in

this earthly society" (LG 40). Thus one's own fulfillment cannot be excluded by supernatural love of God.

First and foremost by this love we love God as he loves himself. We are glad God exists; we are moved to express joy in praise: "Some God!" In loving God, we also love everything else insofar as it is good, for insofar as it is good, God's goodness is in it as manifested and shared. Our love for creatures does not cause them to be real, but it causes us to care especially for what God creates and re-creates in Jesus: "Some world!" The world consists to a great extent in possibilities which can be realized by human acts. And so the Christian is moved to say: "Some opportunities!" Human wisdom enriched with the wisdom of the Spirit says: "Some playground for the children of God!" (cf. Prv 8.30–31).

In other words, the Christian's love is fixed upon the total reality of completion in Jesus (19-B). This completion includes divine and human persons, communing in perfect fellowship, fulfilled with every good. If we seek this kingdom, all else is added (see Mt 6.33), for to seek the kingdom is to begin to share in it, and to this initial share will be added everything which belongs to heavenly fulfillment.

6. A negative answer to the present question is also required by the nature of human free choices. Choices become necessary when particular possibilities for satisfying various interests come into conflict. When this happens, some interests can be satisfied and others cannot; some of one's basic thrusts toward fulfillment will issue in joy and others will not. In morally good choices, none of these thrusts toward fulfillment is constricted or suppressed, but in morally bad choices some are.

7. In morally good choices, one acts toward human goods in a way which is compatible with the all-embracing divine love. There can be no possible need to choose between love of God and anything one can rightly choose. A martyr, for example, does not choose God over the human good of life, but rather chooses the human good of religious faithfulness over the human good of preserving life at the cost of the human evil of infidelity toward God.

8. In acting immorally, one obviously does not choose in a way compatible with loving divine goodness. Even here, however, a person does not make a choice between divine goodness and human goods. Recall that a choice is not evil because of the real good which is sought but because one limits and mutilates good and so fails to be open to integral human fulfillment (see *S.t.*, 1–2, q. 72, a. 1; q. 73, a. 1; q. 75, a. 2). The positive good chosen in an immoral choice is by no means incompatible with divine goodness. Rather, divine goodness includes every good in its fullness, even those goods for whose sake sinners choose wrongly.

9. Moreover, immoral choices cannot reasonably be understood as opting for human goods over divine goodness. For divine goodness cannot be considered in deliberation as a possible object of choice. Even when one accepts divine adoption by making the act of faith, what one chooses is chosen insofar as it is humanly good—that is, as an instance of the good of religion. Insofar as divine adoption transcends the human good of religion, it is not chosen by the Christian, but received entirely as a gift. Since we cannot choose divine goodness, it makes no sense to speak of our choosing something else in preference to it.

10. **It necessarily follows that sin separates the sinner from God's love, not by being a choice of a human good in direct preference to love of God, but by**

being a choice which is not compatible with a will toward integral human fulfillment.[19] One need not and cannot directly choose between supernatural and natural love, between divine goodness and basic human goods. But one must choose among human goods, and one can do this in a way God cannot love. People who do so can know that they are breaking off their communion with God; and this is so of anyone who deliberately commits a mortal sin.

11. Thus, there is a sense in which a sinner can be said selfishly to prefer a limited, human good to the love of God (see *S.t.*, 1–2, q. 77, a. 4; 2–2, q. 25, a. 7). However, this does not mean that divine goodness and human goods can ever be alternatives for choice. There simply is no room for human beings to make such a choice. In principle, therefore, the Christian is in no way inhibited from loving every human good to the fullest extent of its goodness.

Question F: How are the divine and the human united in the Christian?

1. As was explained above in question C, the Christian, like Jesus, is both human and divine. This is the basis of the relationship between divine and human goodness in Christian life explained in question E. In Christian life, the human and the divine are distinct but not opposed, united but not commingled.

2. Several serious consequences follow from confusing or commingling grace and nature. First, it becomes impossible to delineate the likeness of the Christian to Jesus and of Christian life to his life. Second, because the supernatural is made to appear an alternative form of human fulfillment as such, it seems that the price of holiness is a more or less drastic dehumanization. Third, considered in itself, the natural order appears incomplete and therefore lacking in autonomy; for example, a natural desire for heavenly beatitude is posited, and the supposition that there is such a desire raises endless, insoluble theological difficulties. Fourth, the Christian's share in divine life tends to be reduced to a mere metaphor, so that it can be fit within the finite bounds of created human nature.

3. By pressing the likeness of the Christian to Jesus and of Christian life to his life as far as possible, chapters twenty-five and twenty-six will provide a map of the way of Jesus which avoids exaggerating (or denigrating) either its supernatural and other-worldly aspects or its human and this-worldly aspects (see 1-G). The intention will be to do greater justice than was done by either classical moral theology or the new moral theology to the complex unity of Christian life as both human and divine, this-worldly and other-worldly. Chapter thirty-four will return to an explicit treatment of this point.

4. The make up of the Christian is, to be sure, not that of Jesus. Jesus is a divine person; all things are made through him, and he is before all else that is; with the Father and the Spirit, he is the creator. We are human persons; we are creatures. Jesus becomes man by his own choice; he assumes humanity. We become divine by being begotten by the Spirit, who by the Father's will adoptively makes us members of the divine family.

5. The union of the divine and human in Jesus is hypostatic; that is, the two natures are united in his unique, divine person. In us, the union of divine and

human cannot be hypostatic, for human personhood is finite and as it is given cannot include divine life. **Divine life is in us as a disposition to fulfillment in divinity; it is the love of God which is poured forth in our hearts and inheres in us. Receiving this gift by faith, we act in faith both according to our divine love and according to our natural human love. Divine and human are thus united in the Christian dynamically, not hypostatically. Nevertheless, this union is real and is without commingling; likewise, the distinction of the divine and human in us is real and is without any opposition.**

Jesus is one person with two natures; so are we. His humanity is assumed into the unity of his divine person. Our divinity is received into the unity of our human free choice. As Jesus is, so we are in this world (see 1 Jn 4.17).[20] In considering the make up of the Christian and the make up of Christian life, this analogy must be carried through and taken seriously. If not, all sorts of difficulties arise analogous to those which arose in Christology in the early centuries of the Church.[21]

Of course, our make up is not exactly the same as that of our Lord. He is an uncreated divine person; we are created human persons. He is Son of God by nature, we children of God by adoption. But unlike ordinary cases of adoption, in which a person of human nature adopts a child of human nature, thus changing the child's parentage but not its nature, God's adoption of us makes us share in his divine nature. For all practical purposes, a human adoptive parent removes the adopted child from its natural family. But God does not remove us from our natural, human family. Thus God's adoption of us endows us with the infinite riches of his goodness without requiring us to renounce the finite, but very real riches, of our human heritage.

6. This account of the Christian's make up is of fundamental importance for understanding Christian moral principles. It safeguards the integrity of human goods, precluding any supposed need to negate the human in order to make way for the divine. Moreover, on this account the natural law remains valid for Christian morality, as is required by Catholic moral teaching. As chapters twenty-five and twenty-six will explain, Christian morality completes the morality of the natural law by specifying it, not by making extrinsic additions to it.

7. Furthermore, because by this account the Christian's divine life by adoption is no mere metaphor, any tendency to think of grace as merely covering over sins is excluded. By reason of their real deification, Christians can live like Jesus in this world and hope with a well-founded hope to share fully in his eternal fullness.

Summary

Because God reveals himself in the language of love, we must reflect on human love to understand the love which God is and which he calls us to share. Love, basically a disposition to a known good, is of two fundamentally different kinds: in respect to sensible goods, an emotion; in respect to intelligible goods, rational concern or caring. While love is always first of all a disposition to the fulfillment of the one who loves, it is not limited to caring about one's own good. Insofar as goods to which one is disposed by love are actualized in other persons, one loves them. Emotional love is affection focused upon another with whom one identifies in some way. Volitional love of another person is a disposition established by commitment to a common fulfillment. Mutual volitional love disposes those who share in it to a simultaneous increase in both individual perfection and communion.

God is a unity of three distinct persons. The ideal of love, unity and multiplicity at their ultimate, is best realized in God. The mystery of the Trinity, in which the one and the many are absolutely reconciled, is a mystery of love, specifically a mystery of the communicability of divinity. Since God's very constitution is love, sharing in his love means sharing in his life. It is not true either that human beings must always remain extrinsic to God or that their communion with him means being absorbed into God; instead, the mystery of the Trinity shows both that divine life is not in principle incommunicable and that loss of individual selfhood is not necessarily the price of its communication.

God's love makes us his adopted children, called to share intimately and fully in his life; the Spirit is the principle of this adoption. Although the natural sonship of our Lord and our status as adopted sons and daughters are distinct, the communion Jesus intends for his disciples is nevertheless based on a strict analogy with his Father's love for him: Jesus wants it known that the Father loves his followers as the Father loves him. To abide in God's love is to be drawn within the communion of God. In this situation human persons, though always remaining human, really share in divinity. While it may seem strange to speak of the divinization of human beings, the Fathers of the Church do not hesitate to speak in this way.

The act of living faith is the principle of our sharing in the divine nature. We are justified by faith in Jesus—justified, as Trent teaches, by a rightness which is not merely attributed to us but which we receive as our own: God's love is poured forth into our hearts and remains in them. Living faith is wholly God's gift to us, but it is also our own human act. Initially, seeing the credibility of the gospel, we choose to believe for the sake of some human good; but having done so, we receive the gift of God's love, and our choice is transformed, becoming an act of living faith made for love of God. This is how a person enters freely, by human choice, into intimate communion with God.

Formerly, much popular Christian piety suggested that loving God meant preferring him to created goods, but this is not the teaching of Vatican II. God's love is all-inclusive; the love of God given us by the Spirit is a share in God's love. Our supernatural love is therefore all-inclusive as God's love is, embracing all genuine human goods. In loving himself, God loves creatures, whose goodness becomes real by his creative choice. Since God loves human persons, he loves the goods which fulfill them; to love as God loves, therefore, we also must love the goods which fulfill us humanly.

In morally good choices, we act toward human goods in a way compatible with God's all-embracing love of them. In a morally evil choice, a sin, we act in a way incompatible with a will toward integral human fulfillment. Because every immoral act disrupts communion with God, one must say that in sinning one prefers a limited, human good to the love of God—but not as if love of divine goodness and love of human goods were incompatible or were alternatives for choice.

591

In Christian life, as in the life of Jesus, the human and divine are distinct but not opposed, united but not commingled. Commingling of grace and nature makes it impossible to delineate the likeness of Christian life to the life of Jesus, makes holiness appear a kind of dehumanization, destroys the autonomy of the natural order, and reduces the Christian's share in divine life to a mere metaphor. At the same time, the make up of the Christian is not that of Jesus. In him the union of the divine and human is hypostatic—a union in his unique, divine personhood— while in us divine life is a dynamic principle, a principle of free choices and the life which flows from them. This account is essential for understanding Christian moral principles; it safeguards the integrity of human goods, precluding any supposed need to downgrade or deny the human for the sake of the divine, and preserves the validity of the natural law.

Appendix 1:   The Trinity of divine persons as love

The mystery of the Trinity perplexes us and is beyond our understanding. If one omits part of the doctrine, one eliminates the perplexity but also misses the revealed reality; if one holds all of the doctrine but mistakenly thinks one understands it, one turns the perplexity into absurdity and also misses the only clue we have to the revealed reality. Thus it is important both to keep the doctrine intact and to realize the limits of one's understanding of it.

One might omit part of the doctrine by supposing that the Father really is the one God, and that the Son and the Spirit are divine beings of a lower type. Or one might hold the equality of all three persons, but suppose each to be a particular something, just as three human individuals are equal as human persons, but each is a distinct particular. The former mistake would eliminate the threeness of persons; the latter would eliminate the unity in being, and substitute three "gods" for the one only God.

The propositions which the Church articulates in her teaching are closely based upon, although they develop, propositions expressed in Scripture. If one assumes that the expressions in these statements mean precisely what they would mean outside the context of revelation, then the mystery is reduced to absurdity: How can three distinct entities be identical with something one? This reduction to absurdity is avoided if one bears in mind that what is said of God always is said relationally. We do not know what God is in himself, but we do know that he reveals himself to us as the one only God, the God of Abraham and our God, and also as the Incarnate Son who relates personally with his heavenly Father, with whom he sends a Holy Spirit who is God with us (see Jn 14.16; 16.7).

"Person" said of Father, Son, and Spirit certainly does not mean what "person" said of human individuals means. This situation is not new; it did not arise because of modern developments in the understanding of human persons; it has been true since the doctrine first was articulated and will be so always. Yet as long as we call parents and children "persons," we can hardly avoid saying that the one revealing himself as Father and Son is one God in distinct "persons." Since they must be called "persons," their Spirit also must be, lest his divinity be denied.[22]

Appendix 2:   The mystery of the Christian's share in divine life

Is our sharing in the love which God is—the sharing which inheres in us as our own love of God—itself something created or is it the very creator himself? I answer: Neither.

It is not the very creator himself, for only the Trinity creates. Everything other than the Trinity proceeds from the Father, Son, and Spirit together by their free choice (see DS 1330–31/703–4). The love of God which is poured forth in our hearts by the Holy Spirit does not proceed from him as the Son proceeds from the Father or as the Holy Spirit proceeds from the Father and the Son: that is by an eternal procession without which God cannot exist. The love of God poured forth in our hearts by the Holy Spirit proceeds from him—he having been sent by the Father and the Son—through a gracious act of the free will of the Trinity. In this respect, our share in divine love is like a creature.

Yet I do not see how this love can be a mere creature. How can it be something created? Surely, nothing created can be the very love which God is. If Christians do not share in this very love, in what sense are they really adopted children of God? Every creature participates in God's being, since every creature is some manifestation of God's goodness and love. But not every creature participates in the very divine nature; not every creature is an adopted member of the eternal Father's family. How could any created gift bring about this unique transformation in created persons?[23] For we remain created persons. In this respect, adopted children of God are altogether other than the divine persons, who are identical with their very divinity. We are not and never can be personally identical with the divine nature. We are children of God by adoption, by participation in his love.

Therefore, I think the love of God poured forth in our hearts through the Holy Spirit is neither something created nor the very creator himself. Like things created in being the Trinity's free gift, like the divine persons in being uncreated, this love of God which inheres in us also is diverse from both. It is unique, in a category all by itself, for this love makes created persons sharers in divine life. As question D explained, the opposing relationship between the Trinity's freedom in bestowing their love on us and our freedom in consenting to share in it guarantees that there can be no confusion between the divine persons and us created persons, and also that there can be no absorption of our created personhood into the love which makes us adopted children of God.

This position, so far as I know, never has been asserted before.[24] For this reason, this position should be entertained with great caution. It ought not to be proposed as if it represented the Church's teaching. But I believe it articulates an understanding of the relevant truths of faith, consistent with the Church's teaching, which might one day be accepted as a legitimate development of this teaching.

Prior to the time of St. Thomas, it had been suggested that the grace by which a Christian shares in divine life is the Holy Spirit himself. St. Thomas (with others around his time and since) insists that there must be something inherent in the Christian, assumes that everything other than the Trinity is some created entity, and concludes that grace is a created quality inherent in the Christian's soul.[25]

From the supposition that sanctifying grace is a created entity together with the principle that everything created as such relates to God as to a unitary principle, it follows that the Christian life of which grace is the principle involves a single relationship to God, not personal relationships with the Father and the Son and the Holy Spirit. However, Scripture, the Fathers, and liturgical texts all seem to indicate that Christians relate to the distinct divine persons. All this evidence had to be written off to appropriation—that is, to a manner of talking as if there were distinct relationships when there really are not.[26]

To many theologians, the Council of Trent seemed to have adopted the teaching of St. Thomas on grace. Trent certainly makes it clear that grace and/or charity inheres in the Christian. But Trent does not say that this principle of divine life in the Christian is caused or created; Trent rather says that it is infused (see DS 1528–31/799–800, 1561/821). And it must be noticed that Trent's main concern is to exclude an account of justification which would allow for no real transformation of the justified person—a position precisely the opposite of that taken here.

In recent years, many Catholic theologians have tried to articulate some theory by which the Christian really can be related to the indwelling divine persons in distinct ways which many theologians after Trent, drawing out implications of the Thomistic theory, had to write off to appropriation.[27] It seems to me that by denying conclusions logically consequent upon the theory of created grace, these recent theologians implicitly deny the theory, but fail to face this implication of their position.

Although the solution proposed here sounds self-contradictory, I am confident that it is not. The doctrine of our adoption as children of God, as I understand it, is very like the doctrines of the Incarnation and the Trinity. In all three cases, unity and multiplicity, which seem absurdly opposed, are perfectly reconciled. Is Jesus God or not? If he is God, must he not be the Father; if he is not the Father, must he not be other than God? In the sense in which this question first arose—in the minds of the Jews who listened to our Lord—Jesus neither is God (the Father) nor not-God (a created person). Is Jesus a man or not? If he is a man, must he not be a human person; if he is not a human person, must he not be God in merely human form? In the sense in which this question first arose—in the minds of many early Christians—Jesus is neither a man (a human person) nor not a man (God veiled in flesh not his own).

Similarly, is the love of God in us by which we are his adopted children something uncreated or something created? I am suggesting that it is neither in the sense in which the question has been asked since St. Thomas. It is neither the creator (the Trinity) nor a mere creature (something other than divine life); it is uncreated (a true sharing in divine life) and yet inherent in us by the free choice of the Trinity (and so a sharing by the grace of adoption, not by nature).

If this explanation of God's love and our sharing in it is correct, still the warning of Pope Pius XII, referred to in question C, must be borne in mind. The intimate unity which Christians enjoy with God by the love of God given by the Spirit does not make created persons cease to be created persons. Nothing which is said of the Holy Trinity can be said in exactly the same sense of created persons. Communion with God is no pantheistic merging into him. God loves us by an act of his sovereign freedom. We enter into communion with him freely. Giving and receiving forever unite and forever distinguish. We are God's adopted children.

Appendix 3:   Other accounts of Christian love

Without articulating and criticizing in detail other accounts of Christian love, I wish very briefly to point out how different this chapter's account is from some other views.

Some think love of God is simply a desire to get to heaven. True, such a desire follows from love of God, but love of God is much more, for it is a sharing in divine life. Others think love of God is simply friendship with him. True, the concept of friendship has application here. But to reduce love of God to friendship is to miss this love's supernatural meaning.

Others think love of God is just love of neighbor, and to love one's neighbor is just to satisfy his or her human needs. This view often underlies the proportionalist idea that one who loves God will be prepared to do anything necessary in a given situation to satisfy a neighbor's needs. But love of God cannot be reduced to love of neighbor, although supernatural love of God entails love of neighbor.

Some think love is a particular act rather than a disposition to action. This view makes one think of God's love for us as his act and our love for him as our act, and our loves for our neighbors and ourselves as so many other acts. This view is based upon a misunderstanding of what love is. The model of the Trinity shows that love is not primarily an act directed at a person as shooting is an act directed at a target. Rather, it is a communion of persons which in no way lessens their mutual distinction. Among finite persons, whose fulfillment in communion is a gift and/or an accomplishment, love is a disposition to this fulfillment. Such a disposition can be shared by many persons.

Some think "love" means exactly the same thing when it is said of love of God and love of the basic human goods. This view misses the wonder and mysteriousness of the revelation of divine love and God's invitation to sinful creatures to share in it. Moreover, it inevitably leads to unsolvable conflicts between love of God and love of basic human goods. The false, forced option between secularist humanism and fideistic supernaturalism depends in no small measure upon the logical working out of the implications of this view.

Moreover, because natural human love always requires some fulfilling good other than the love itself, one who thinks of heaven as the consummation of divine love and does not sufficiently distinguish between natural and supernatural love either will think of heaven as empty or will posit some particular form of human fulfillment to make heavenly happiness humanly interesting. The former approach, a vacuous heaven, makes all talk of love of God pointless. The latter approach, a heaven described in terms of some specific human fulfillment, introduces a division between that human good and all others. This division will make love of God seem a humanly limiting thing.

Others think love of God is experienced closeness to God. If one does not have the sentiment, one does not love God. The fact is that love of God makes possible experiences of communing joyfully with him, but these are particular favors without which it is possible to love God. Emotionally, one can feel angry at God and alienated from him yet still love him; the evidence will be that one is prepared to accept and to do his will despite one's feelings.

Still others think love of God is exclusively his love—his eternally free, totally gratuitous, saving love of sinful humankind. Except for its exclusivity, this view is basically correct, and those thinkers who have developed it have unfolded most beautifully a fundamental and essential part of Christian teaching about God's love. But this view, which so perfectly protects those who hold it from false mysticism and pantheism, is dreadfully incomplete. God loves sinful humankind like a faithful husband whose love brings his unfaithful wife back to loving him faithfully. Thus God's love which is poured forth in our hearts by the gift of the Spirit also inheres in us, as the Council of Trent teaches.

Love of God is something greater than desire for heaven, friendship with God, benevolence toward one's neighbor, actions God and we do, a disposition of one's heart to rest in God rather than in created goods, experienced intimacy with God, and God's loving-kindness toward sinful humankind. The love of God makes us desire heaven, makes us friends of God, makes us do good to our neighbors, makes us interact with God, disposes our hearts to rest in God, allows us to taste his sweetness, and gratuitously redeems us. It does more. It makes us children of God, adopted children who freely consent to be members of the divine family, and who therefore enjoy the glorious liberty to be fully ourselves, full human persons.

Notes

1. A helpful elementary treatment of the Thomistic analysis, followed here, of knowledge and love: James E. Royce, S.J., *Man and His Nature: A Philosophical Psychology* (New York: McGraw-Hill, 1961). This book is adequate, no more complicated than necessary, and has helpful bibliography.

2. Gabriel Marcel has clarified the central aspects of interpersonal existence. Unfortunately, his work is diffuse. A good starting place: *Homo Viator: Introduction to a Metaphysic of Hope*, trans. Emma Craufurd (New York: Harper Torchbooks, 1951), esp. 13–28.

3. A basic introduction to Catholic doctrine on the Trinity: Ronald Lawler, O.F.M.Cap., Donald W. Wuerl, and Thomas Comerford Lawler, eds., *The Teaching of Christ: A Catholic Catechism for Adults* (Huntington, Ind.: Our Sunday Visitor, 1976), 174–85; a fuller treatment: E. J. Fortman, *The Triune God* (Philadelphia: Westminster Press, 1972).

4. Ceslaus Spicq, O.P., *Agape in the New Testament*, vol. 3, *Agape in the Gospel, Epistles and Apocalypse of St. John* (St. Louis: B. Herder, 1966), 166. Also see Matthew Vellanickal, *The Divine Sonship of Christians in the Johannine Writings*, Analecta Biblica, 72 (Rome: Biblical Institute Press, 1977), 302–16; Raymond E. Brown, S.S., *The Epistles of John*, Anchor Bible, 30 (Garden City, N.Y.: Doubleday, 1982), 194–95, 515, 549–53.

5. See Matthias Joseph Scheeben, *The Mysteries of Christianity* (St. Louis: B. Herder, 1946), 141–48. Note the assertion (142): "Not God's creative power, but His generative power enables us to apprehend that the generation of adoptive children is possible." Scheeben does not go so far as to say that Christians are transformed by receiving a share in the uncreated divine nature, but his analysis points in that direction, and what he says is helpful toward articulating the point of view taken in this chapter.

6. For a very helpful treatment of this point, see Stephen B. Clark, *Man and Woman in Christ: An Examination of the Roles of Men and Women in Light of Scripture and the Social Sciences* (Ann Arbor, Mich.: Servant Books, 1980), 39–45 and 72–87.

7. For exegesis of 1 Jn 3.1–2, see Brown, *Epistles of John*, 387–96 and 422–27.

8. The doctrines of divine election and predestination, firmly rooted in Scripture (see Rom 8.28–30) do not mean that anyone is predetermined to do evil (see DS 1567/827) but that there is a grace which is truly sufficient and it is really entirely God's gift (see DS 2306/1296). Thus understood, predestination is an essential element of Catholic teaching, although it has been downplayed since the Reformation in reaction to distorted interpretations of it. For a brief summary, see A. G. Palladino, "Predestination," *New Catholic Encyclopedia*, 11:714–19; a longer treatment: R. Garrigou-Lagrange, O.P., *Predestination* (St. Louis: Herder, 1946). For a summary of St. Augustine's teaching on this matter, with references: Eugène Portalié, S.J., *A Guide to the Thought of Saint Augustine*, trans. Ralph J. Bastian, S.J. (Chicago: Henry Regnery, 1960), 213–23. A key text in St. Thomas: *S.t.*, 1, qq. 22–23; esp. q. 23, a. 1; see also *S.c.g.*, 3, 163; *De veritate*, q. 6, a. 1.

9. This central truth of Christian faith and life is the kernel of the doctrine, richly unfolded by Emile Mersch, S.J., *The Whole Christ: The Historical Development of the Doctrine of the Mystical Body in Scripture and Tradition*, trans. John R. Kelly, S.J. (Milwaukee: Bruce, 1938); note especially the treatment of Jn 17.21–23 in the work of St. Athanasius (276–77), St. Hilary (301–4), and St. Cyril of Alexandria (345–53).

10. Spicq, op. cit., 35; also see Brown, *Epistles of John*, 520–26 and 553–60, and on mutual indwelling (or "abiding/remaining in") 259–61 and 283–84.

11. For an exegesis of this passage, with references to much other exegetical work on it, see Raymond E. Brown, S.S., *The Gospel According to John (xiii–xxi)*, Anchor Bible, 29a (Garden City, N.Y.: Doubleday, 1970), 769–79. At the end of this section of commentary, Brown remarks parenthetically: "From the viewpoint of a later and more precise theology, one might like to have a sharper differentiation than John provides between God's incarnation in Jesus and God's indwelling in the Christian—in other words between natural Sonship and general Christian sonship. That such a distinction was not strange to Johannine thought *may* be indicated by John's custom of referring to Jesus as the *huios* or 'Son' of God, while the Christians are designated as *tekna* or 'children'; but no sharp differentiation is apparent in the verses we are considering." My contention is that some later and more precise theology, in making the necessary distinction between God's Incarnation in Jesus and his indwelling in the Christian, has made altogether too sharp a differentiation, so that the Johannine realism of Christians' deification is reduced in practice to a mere metaphor.

12. Spicq, op. cit., 143; also see Brown, *Epistles of John*, 528–30 and 561.

13. See Victorino Capánaga, O.R.S.A., "La Deificación en la Soteriología Agostiniana," in *Augustinus Magister: Congrès International Augustinien* (Paris: Etudes Augustiniennes, 1954), 2:745–54. Deification was downplayed in later Western Christianity, although it has a solid basis in Scripture and the Fathers of the Church: Petro B. T. Bilaniuk, "The Mystery of *Theosis* or Divinization," in *The Heritage of the Early Church*, ed. D. Neiman et al., Orientalia Christiana Analecta, 195 (Rome: 1973), 337–59. Although Protestant in interpretation, Patricia Wilson-Kastner,

"Grace as Participation in the Divine Life in the Theology of Augustine of Hippo," *Augustinian Studies*, 7 (1976), 135–52, very helpfully shows how Augustine adopted and altered the Eastern teaching on divinization, thus leading to the Western theory of grace in which deification is downplayed.

14. Just as attempts to explain the Incarnation of the Word in other categories inevitably fail, so do attempts to explain in other categories the sharing of God's adopted children in his life. In both cases, the revealed fact is a contingent one about God, and the predication is relational, as all contingent predication about God is. The proposition does not convey what God is in himself, but rather that whatever his always-mysterious inner reality is, God is what he must be to bring about realities related to him as are his Incarnate Son (Jesus) and his adopted children (Christians). See Bernard Lonergan, S.J., *De verbo incarnato* (thesis altera ad decimam), ed. 3 (Rome: Pontificia Universitas Gregoriana, 1964), 252–55.

15. Spicq, op. cit., 124.

16. Ibid., 137.

17. St. John of the Cross, *The Living Flame of Love*, 3, 78, in *The Collected Works of St. John of the Cross*, trans. Kieran Kavanaugh, O.C.D., and Otilio Rodriguez, O.C.D. (Washington, D.C.: ICS Publications, 1979), 641.

18. On theological problems and possibilites in respect to infants: P. J. Hill, "Limbo," *New Catholic Encyclopedia*, 8:762–65; E. J. Fortman, S.J., *Everlasting Life after Death* (New York: Alba House, 1976), 143–55.

19. St. Thomas, *S.c.g.*, 3, 122, rejects the argument against simple fornication that it injures God, saying that this "would not seem to be an adequate answer. For we do not offend God except by doing something contrary to our own good."

20. The New American Bible translates 1 Jn 4.17: "Our love is brought to perfection in this, that we should have confidence on the day of judgment; for our relation to this world is just like his." This translation makes "his" appear to have God for its reference and renders the passage irrelevant to the point for which I cite it. However, the exegesis of Spicq quoted in question C supports the use I make of the passage. Also see Wilhelm Thüsing, *The Three Epistles of St. John*, and Alois Stöger, *The Epistle of St. Jude* (New York: Crossroad, 1981), 83–84; Alfred Marshall, *The R.S.V. Interlinear Greek-English New Testament* (London: Samuel Bagster and Sons, 1975), 934 and 943.

21. An extensive treatise on the development of Christology and on the various heresies: Aloys Grillmeier, S.J., *Christ in Christian Tradition*, vol. 1, *From the Apostolic Age to Chalcedon (451)*, trans. John Bowden, 2d ed. (Atlanta: John Knox Press, 1975); also J. N. D. Kelly, *Early Christian Doctrines*, rev. ed. (San Francisco: Harper and Row, 1978), 138–62, 280–343.

22. Karl Rahner, S.J., *The Trinity*, trans. Joseph Donceel (London: Burns and Oates, 1970), 103–20, questions the suitability of the concept of "person" in the doctrine of the Trinity. In this questioning, he stresses the otherness of God, but he seems to fail to bear in mind this otherness when he deals with God's unity. Rahner claims the concept of person is not used of God in the New Testament and the early Fathers. I think this claim is mistaken, since the lack of the word "person" is not the same as the lack of the concept of person. The concept is used in all New Testament talk about Father and Son. For a fuller development of this line of criticism, see Jean Galot, *Le Christ, Foi, et Contestation* (Chambray: C.L.D., 1981), 142–64.

23. See Louis Bouyer, Cong. Orat., *Introduction to Spirituality*, trans. Mary Perkins Ryan (Collegeville, Minn.: Liturgical Press, 1961), 152–56.

24. However, the position taken here is very similar to the views of some theologians of the Eastern Church. See Vladimir Lossky, *The Mystical Theology of the Eastern Church* (London: Hames Clarke, 1957), 162–63: "In the tradition of the Eastern Church grace usually signifies all the abundance of the divine nature, in so far as it is communicated to men; the deity which operates outside the essence and gives itself, the divine nature of which we partake through the uncreated energies." Again (172): "In the theology of the Eastern Church, as we have already remarked, the Person of the Holy Spirit, the giver of grace, is always distinguished from the uncreated grace which He confers. It is the energy or procession of the one nature: the divinity . . . in so far as it is ineffably distinct from the essence and communicates itself to created beings, deifying them." On the uncreated energies, see 67–90. Also, see John Meyendorff, *A Study of Gregory Palamas*, trans. George Lawrence (London: Faith Press, 1964), 217–18: "The divine life—which is deifying grace when it is granted to man—therefore belongs to the divine nature even when men benefit from it (by grace and not by nature); hence it constitutes the means of a communion both personal and real with God, a communion which does not involve the impossible confusion of the natures. It is therefore just the opposite to an 'intermediary'

between God and man; that would be the case with a created grace, for then it would be an intermediate nature, neither divine nor human. Whatever name one gives them—grace, divine life, light, illumination—the energies or divine acts belong to the existence of God himself; they represent his existence *for us*. It is therefore not only justified but necessary to apply thereto the attributes proper to the divine Being . . . ." For a compact statement of this Eastern view, together with many indications which might be followed up by historical research: M. Edmund Hussey, "The Persons-Energy Structure in the Theology of St. Gregory Palamas," *St. Vladamir's Theological Quarterly*, 18 (1974), 22–43, esp. the summary, 26. For helpful indications of the consistency of this Eastern theology with Catholic faith: Louis Bouyer, *Le Consolateur: Esprit-Saint et vie de Grâce* (Paris: Editions du Cerf, 1980), 421–49.

25. Cf. St. Thomas, In 2 *Sent.*, d. 26, q. 1, a. 1; *De veritate*, q. 27, a. 1; *S.t.*, 1–2, q. 110, a. 1 and 2.

26. For some essential background and indications of the problem I am trying to resolve: Henri Rondet, S.J., *The Grace of Christ: A Brief History of the Theology of Grace* (Westminster, Md.: Newman Press, 1967), esp. 209–48 and 365–77; Robert W. Gleason, S.J., *Grace* (New York: Sheed and Ward, 1962), esp. 101–71 and 223–40. A recent effort to solve the problem within a Thomistic framework: Fernando Ocáriz, *Hijos de Dios en Cristo: Introducción a una teología de la participación sobrenatural* (Pamplona, Spain: EUNSA, 1972). A systematic treatise, without the history and problematic: Michael Schmaus, *Dogma*, vol. 6, *Justification and the Last Things* (Kansas City: Sheed and Ward, 1977), 3–81.

27. These recent efforts cannot be dismissed as an aspect of theological excess. Even as conservative a theologian as Reginald Garrigou-Lagrange, O.P., *The Trinity and God the Creator: A Commentary on St. Thomas' Theological Summa, 1a, q. 27–119* (St. Louis: B. Herder, 1952), 311, in defending the Thomistic position that the missions of the Son and Spirit are more than appropriations, invokes the support of certain Greek Fathers: "The Greek Fathers regarded the missions as prolongations of the processions *ad extra;* they thus distinguished the missions from creation. They said that the sending of the persons of the Son and the Holy Ghost differs from creation as to live differs from to command. And they based the communication of divine life, by which we are elevated to the order of grace, not on creation but on the divine missions. In this way they distinguished between the natural order and the order of grace as they distinguished between creation and the missions of the divine persons."

CHAPTER TWENTY-FIVE

CHRISTIAN LOVE
AS THE PRINCIPLE OF CHRISTIAN LIFE

Introduction

Lives take shape gradually; only by living our lives do we realize the possibilities open to us. This is true of Christian life as well as human life generally. In this chapter we shall consider Christian love as the principle shaping Christian life.

We have already seen, in the preceding chapter, that Christian love—which is also called "charity"—is that in Christians by which they are adopted members of the divine family, sharers in the love which is God's very life. Now our focus is upon charity as the principle by which Christians act as children of God. In this respect, charity in the Christian is the first principle of specifically Christian morality. It motivates faith itself, and faith is the fundamental option, the basic human act, of Christian life (24-D).

The present chapter will concentrate on charity as a principle of Christian morality, while chapter twenty-six will consider how it transforms the modes of responsibility into Christian modes of response.

Question A: Is Christian love a human act?

1. Since specifically Christian love is a Christian's own share in divine life, it must somehow transform his or her human life. But is Christian love itself a human act?[1] It would seem so, since there is a commandment to love God and neighbor (see Mt 22.34–40; Mk 12.28–31; Lk 10.25–27). Moreover, charity is a virtue, and virtues are dispositions to good actions; hence, it seems that there must be acts of Christian love, corresponding to the virtue of charity.

2. According to St. Paul, however, "God's love has been poured into our hearts through the Holy Spirit who has been given to us" (Rom 5.5). **What the Holy Spirit primarily gives us is the status of God's adopted children, by which we share in the divine nature** (see Jn 1.14–16; Rom 8.14–17; 2 Pt 1.4). **Participation in the divine nature is not a human act. Therefore, Christian love itself is not a human act, although it is related to human acts.**

3. Moreover, even infants, who are altogether incapable of human acts, receive the gift of charity and are transformed by it (see DS 1513–14/790–91,

1524/796). With the help of God's grace, adults must prepare themselves for the gift of charity by prior human acts, but these acts are not themselves charity (see DS 1525–26/797–98; *S.t.*, 1–2, q. 112, aa. 1–2; q. 113, a. 3, ad 1; 2–2, q. 24, a. 2).

4. Charity is a disposition toward fulfillment in divine life (see 1 Jn 3.1–2). As such, it is not something one is asked to do but something one is asked to remain in (see Jn 15.9; 1 Jn 4.7–16). Love of God is not a human action, and is presupposed rather than directly commanded.

5. The commandment to love God and neighbor affirmed in the Gospels is a command to integrate one's entire self and all one's interpersonal relationships with charity: "to love with one's whole . . . ." This requires human acts done out of charity. The perfection of Christian life according to charity can therefore be required, even though charity itself cannot be (cf. *S.t.*, 2–2. q. 44, aa. 4–6). Furthermore, the commandments indicate which acts must be done, and so, as far as human acts are concerned, love of God in deed and in truth (see 1 Jn 3.18) is reducible to keeping his commandments (see Jn 14.21; 15.10; 1 Jn 2.3–5; 3.21–24). Love of neighbor fulfills the commandments by avoiding harm to and serving one's neighbor (see Mt 7.21; 25.31–46; Jn 13.34; Rom 12.9–21; 1 Jn 3.11–17).

6. As to the virtue of charity, it is a disposition to good actions, as question B will explain. But the fulfillment to which it is most properly and specifically directed is not a human act but the divine act of seeing God as he is (see 1 Jn 3.2). Only the Spirit of God knows this depth of God and disposes human beings to it by a love transcending human nature (see 1 Cor 2.6–16; *S.t.*, 2–2, q. 24, a. 2).

7. The primary human act to which charity disposes Christians is their very act of faith. By faith they accept the gift of love which is their share in divine life (see 24-D). Faith, the fundamental option of the Christian, requires each member of the Church to find and accept his or her personal vocation. Hence, every act of Christian life is an act of charity insofar as it carries out one's personal vocation.

8. As will be explained in question E, Christian morality adds some specific norms to general human moral requirements. Acts of Christian life formed by these specific norms are called "acts of charity" in an especially appropriate sense. For example, deeds required by Christian mercy, insofar as it goes beyond fairness, are called "works of charity."

9. Acts of religious devotion, such as a prayer expressing love toward God, also are called "acts of charity"; in this sense, the offering of oneself with Jesus in the Eucharist is the most perfect act of charity. But all such acts of religious devotion are good human acts only inasmuch as they serve the human good of religion. If this good is not truly served as faith requires, then the human act is not an act of charity, for it has no real relationship with the gift of divine love.

Charity is a disposition toward fulfillment in superhuman, divine goodness. The most basic choice in Christian life, the choice to accept Jesus with living faith, is made out of this love. It follows that the love of God which inheres in the Christian is analogous to simple volition. It is a principle of action toward heavenly fulfillment similar to one's natural and necessary disposition toward human fulfillment.

However, the love of God poured forth in our hearts must not be regarded as merely another simple volition of an additional human good, inserted in us alongside the love of human life, knowledge of truth, and so on. Divine goodness and human fulfillment are not direct alternatives. The love of God includes and transforms all the natural forms of simple volition. Hence, out of love of God, Christians act both for the human fulfillment to which they are naturally disposed by simple volition and also for fulfillment in divine goodness.

The morally significant acts of Christian life are always inspired both by love of God and by love of some human good. According to the latter principle, they always are acts suited to human nature, although many of them, beginning with the act of living faith, can be done only by grace. A correct understanding of this matter obviates the illusion that in loving God above all things one must set aside or downgrade anything which pertains to true human goodness.

If one supposes that charity itself is a human act, one is likely to try to find some action with which charity can be identified. If no such action can be found, one is likely to become discouraged about one's spiritual life. If one identifies some particular experience or performance with charitable love of God, one is likely to cultivate this experience or performance to the detriment of other dimensions of human life which might be equally or more essential to a life of charity.

For instance, if it is supposed that, so far as human acts are concerned, charity is reducible to keeping God's commandments by serving one's neighbor, then the mystical dimension of Christian life is removed and Christianity is reduced to ethical behavior. This reduction is a mistake, because the good of religion also is a human good. Charity requires appropriate acts pertaining to this good, such as prayer and sacrifice, just as it requires appropriate acts pertaining to other goods.

Question B: Why does Christian love require moral goodness?

1. As question A showed, charity itself is not a human act; rather, it is a disposition to more than human fulfillment in God's intimate life. Still, since Christian life is formed through the act of faith by charity, the human acts of Christian life can be called "acts of charity." These acts must be morally good; they must issue from a will toward integral human fulfillment. That this is so is obvious. But why is it so? Why should a child of God be required to live in view of merely human fulfillment?

2. Moral goodness is not required as a necessary condition or a means for gaining or receiving charity. Charity is a gift of God, a gift which justifies fallen human beings and enables them to live virtuous lives (see *S.t.*, 1–2, q. 113, aa. 7–9). Without God's grace, no one merits anything (see *S.t.*, 1–2, q. 114). It is no part of Catholic faith to suppose a person can be justified by good works, as if the prodigal son could earn his father's love (see DS 1523–31/795–800).

3. Having received the gift of divine love, however, one both can and must fulfill the moral requirements of the commandments (see DS 1536–39/804). Salvation by God's grace requires a good life not as a means but as an integral part. "For we are his workmanship, created in Christ Jesus for good works, which God prepared beforehand, that we should walk in them" (Eph 2.10).

Love fulfills the law (see Rom 13.8–10). Saving faith is the faith which works through love (see Gal 5.6–14). One must act upon the saving word, not merely listen to it (see Jas 1.22–25). One must not merely say, "Lord, Lord," but must build on sound foundations and do the will of the heavenly Father (see Mt 7.21–27; Lk 6.46–49).

4. One way of clarifying this is to say that, as children will obey their father out of love for him, so charity requires that we obey our heavenly Father; but,

since part of the good he wills is the living of humanly good lives, our charity—
our love of God—obliges us to be morally good. This is correct, but it can be
misunderstood. The connection between loving God and being morally good is
intrinsic. It is not an extrinsic requirement, arbitrarily imposed, which God might
reverse or simply waive (like a father who promises a child a bicycle for doing a
certain job, then gives the bicycle even though the job has not been done).

**5. God is perfect goodness. Every other good reflects and participates in
his perfect goodness. Loving God is thus inseparable from loving created
things to the full measure of their goodness. But one who does not love human
fulfillment to the extent this is in his or her own power is failing to love a
created thing as it should be loved and so failing in love of God. The
requirements of morality, however, are simply the implications of love of
human fulfillment to the extent it is within human power. Therefore, one is
obliged to meet the requirements of morality if one is to love God with
charity.** One whose love of God is sincere and consistently carried out will detest
what is morally evil and cling to what is humanly good (see Rom 12.9).

6. From this point of view, loving one's brothers and sisters in Jesus is simply a
matter of being consistent with oneself: "If any one says, 'I love God,' and hates
his brother, he is a liar; for he who does not love his brother whom he has seen,
cannot love God whom he has not seen. And this commandment we have from
him, that he who loves God should love his brother also" (1 Jn 4.20–21; cf. Jn
15.12). Sharing in the same divine love should mean sharing human goods; failure
to do the latter indicates either that the former is unreal or that one is behaving in a
manner dreadfully inconsistent with one's status as a child of God.

7. Precisely insofar as one determines oneself by one's free choices, moral
evil harms not only others but oneself: It is a kind of self-mutilation or existential
suicide. One who loves God loves those whom he loves. But God, although he
loves morally evil people insofar as they are not wholly evil, simply cannot love
their moral evil. To love as God loves, therefore, one must hate oneself insofar as
one is morally evil. But if one freely chooses to be and to remain morally evil, one
is loving oneself as morally evil. Thus, one who chooses to be and to remain evil is
not loving as God loves and cannot love God.

8. To sum up in a negative manner: A human being simply cannot be open to
infinite goodness if he or she is closed against that share in it which is his or her
own personal fulfillment. As human free choice and divine love cannot be at odds
in Jesus, so in the Christian: "No one born of God commits sin; for God's nature
abides in him, and he cannot sin because he is born of God" (1 Jn 3.9). One cannot
be disposed to infinite goodness by divine love if one is closed by a morally evil act
to that participation in infinite goodness present in the human fulfillment which
moral evil negates (see *S.t.*, 2–2, q. 25, aa. 1, 4–5).

The requirement to love one's neighbor also can be drawn from the general principle
that love of God entails love of all the human goods, and these are realized only in the whole
human family. Often one cannot do much to promote these goods except in a few persons,
but one can always reverence the goods of persons. Hence, St. Paul teaches: "Owe no one
anything, except to love one another; for he who loves his neighbor has fulfilled the law.
The commandments, 'You shall not commit adultery, You shall not kill, You shall not steal,

You shall not covet,' and any other commandment, are summed up in this sentence, 'You shall love your neighbor as yourself.' Love does no wrong to a neighbor; therefore love is the fulfilling of the law" (Rom 13.8–10). Thus love of God demands service to all the basic human goods, at least the service of not violating the commandments which protect them. If people do love one another in a fully generous and sound way, they promote one another's true good. Thus human goods will be made to flourish abundantly. The act of faith, by which Christians give themselves to God, will not be a package without contents, but a package full of human good things.

Question C: Are the moral requirements of Christian love expressed by the commands to love God and neighbor?

1. **The direct answer is: Partly but not completely.** Love of God and love of neighbor express the moral implications of Christian love to the extent that norms expressed in the Old Testament law remain true for Christians.[2] However, while these two commands sum up the moral implications of Jewish faith, Christian love not only summarizes but fulfills the law and the prophets. Love of God and love of neighbor do not fully express the moral implications of Christian love.

2. The synoptic Gospels contain accounts of Jesus' specific teaching on the commands to love God and neighbor. Jesus is variously reported to have been asked by a hostile Pharisee which is the great commandment (see Mt 22.34–40), by a friendly scribe which is the first commandment (see Mk 12.28–34), and by a minimalist lawyer what one must do to gain eternal life (see Lk 10.25–29). In reply, he cites the familiar injunction to love God (see Dt 6.5) and adds to it the command to love one's neighbor, which also belongs to the Old Testament (see Lv 19.18).[3]

3. All the accounts make it clear that love of God and love of neighbor are so closely linked by Jesus that they can be taken as a single, complex norm. Insofar as they express the foundation for the whole law and prophets, they must be considered a formulation in religious terms of the first principle of morality (see *S.t.*, 1–2, q. 99, a. 1, ad 2; q. 100, a. 3, ad 1; 2–2, q. 44, aa. 1, 3).

In both the Old Testament and the New, the claims which love makes upon human persons always presuppose God's merciful and faithful love for sinful men and women. God loves first; he offers the covenant. This fact creates a new situation for human moral life. The new situation is what transforms the basic requirement that one's will be toward integral human fulfillment into the commandments of love of God and neighbor. For all human hope of fulfillment depends upon God's mercy and faithfulness, and the human contribution to this fulfillment is to do good—or, at least, to avoid harm—to one's human fellows, particularly to members of the covenant community.

In the context of the covenant, faith is acceptance of and commitment to the covenant relationship, hope is confidence that God will carry out his part of the covenant faithfully and fulfill all his promises, and love is the readiness to carry out one's own part in the covenant. Thus, the command to love is the demand to keep the commandments, to do the will of God. There is no special and separate act of loving God; love is a disposition to the goods shared in the covenant community with God. It includes both his honor (by exclusive worship of him) and the well-being of the community (which is ensured partly by human effort and respect for the goods protected by the commandments regarding one's neighbor, but mainly by divine care and intervention).

4. Under the impetus of the belief that Yahweh is the God of all creation and so of all nations and peoples, love of neighbor tended to expand in the Old Testament beyond any set boundaries. By the parable of the Good Samaritan, appended to one Gospel's treatment of the first commandment (see Lk 10.30–37), Jesus teaches that the neighbor is whoever is prepared to do good to others and implies that the commandment of love enjoins unrestricted concern for human fulfillment. **In sum, the commandments to love God and love neighbor remain within the framework of the old covenant, while the parable of the Good Samaritan hints at a fulfillment of the law and the prophets which goes beyond them.**

Some proponents of the so-called new morality have opposed the love commandments to specific moral norms and invoked the text of the Gospels as a premise in their argument for proportionalism. However, in the context of the law and the gospel, the commandments of love by no means suggest that one might rightly override specific moral norms to pursue what intuitive sympathies might lead one to identify as a greater good or lesser evil in particular cases. Indeed, virtually the same question about the way to heaven which introduces the commandment of love in one context (see Lk 10.25) in another context (see Mt 19.16) introduces the discussion of voluntary poverty which presupposes the keeping of the specific commandments, of which the command to love one's neighbor is given as a sort of summary (see Mt 19.18).

Question D: What does Christian love add
to the love commands of the Old Testament?

1. The purpose of the Old Testament law and prophets was to overcome sin and establish communion between God and his people, as well as among human persons themselves. Thus, love of God and love of neighbor as oneself were indeed the basis of the law and the prophets (see Mt 22.37–40).

2. By the fact of the Incarnation, however, Jesus himself embodies perfect love. Christian life is a sharing in the fullness of love, the personal divine-human communion which Jesus is. Although the law of Moses pointed to this fulfillment, the consummation of the divine-human relationship is reserved to Jesus; the enduring love present in him brings to its climax the love story begun in the Old Testament (see Mt. 5.17; Jn 1.14–17).

3. Not only does Jesus fulfill the law of love, he enables us to fulfill it, too. His love is unique in magnitude and unselfishness, and he commands us to love as he does (see Jn 13.34–35), with a willingness to lay down our lives for our brothers and sisters (see Jn 15.12–14; 1 Jn 3.16). These characteristics of Jesus' love result from a more fundamental principle: His human love for us is rooted in his divine love, which he receives in being begotten by the Father and which he shares with us. Thus he says: "As the Father has loved me, so have I loved you; abide in my love" (Jn 15.9).

4. Having been made children of God, Christians are to love their heavenly Father and one another as divine children. **The requirement to love as Jesus**

loves us is new, as the new and eternal covenant is new. As God's sons and daughters, Christians must love as the Son does (see *S.t.*, 1–2. q. 98, aa. 1–2; q. 107, aa. 1–2).

Clearly, the Christian requirement of love is in some way old and in some way new. The First Epistle of John says: "Beloved, I am writing you no new commandment, but an old commandment which you had from the beginning; the old commandment is the word which you have heard. Yet I am writing you a new commandment, which is true in him and in you, because the darkness is passing away and the true light is already shining" (1 Jn 2.7–8). Love always has been a requirement of life in covenant with God, but in the new covenant love is present in a new way.[4]

Jesus' love is not merely an example to imitate. Christian love is received and carried out only in the Church, by real unity with Jesus who is the Church's initiator and head. One loves as Jesus loves only by being united through baptism with his redemptive act, experiencing this unity in the Eucharist, and living it out in one's daily life. For this reason, Christian love is the unity of the Church, which binds together its many members and harmonizes their diverse gifts (see 1 Cor 12.12–13.13).

In Jesus, God is our neighbor; through him, human persons become—or, at least, are called to become—members of the divine family. Hence Christian love of God includes love of neighbor, and Christian love of neighbor includes love of God. What one does to one's fellows, one does to the Son of Man, who will separate those to be welcomed into the kingdom from those to be excluded (see Mt 25.31–46).

5. Although primarily a disposition to fulfillment in divine life, Christian love also requires moral goodness, as question B showed. Hence, Christian love disposes both to divine and human goodness—that is, to the perfect accomplishment of the divine-human communion which God is building up upon Jesus (see *S.t.*, 2–2, q. 23, aa. 1, 4). The hope which springs from Christian love will only be satisfied when the fulfillment of all things in Jesus is accomplished, when Jesus hands over the kingdom to the Father, and God is all in all (see 1 Cor 15.20–28; Eph 1.7–10, 22–23; Col 1.18–20).

6. The first principle of all human morality is: In voluntarily acting for human goods and avoiding what is opposed to them, one ought to choose and otherwise will those and only those possibilities whose willing is compatible with a will toward integral human fulfillment (7-F). Such fulfillment is more than an ideal; it is being accomplished in the fulfillment of all things in Jesus (19-B). **Thus, Christian love transforms the first principle of morality into a more definite norm: One ought to will those and only those possibilities which contribute to the integral human fulfillment being realized in the fulfillment of all things in Jesus.**

In the New Testament, one finds several normative statements which are equivalent to the first principle of morality specified in the light of Christian faith.

For example: "Therefore be imitators of God, as beloved children" (Eph 5.1). The idea is that inasmuch as we are children of God, we ought to be like our heavenly Father. Conceptually, this norm is distinct from the first principle of morality specified in the light of Christian faith. However, the author of Ephesians immediately explains how the Christian can put into practice the imitation of God the Father: "And walk in love, as Christ loved us and gave himself up for us, a fragrant offering and sacrifice to God" (Eph 5.2). The sacrificial gift which Jesus made out of love is the act by which the ideal of integral human fulfillment becomes a real possibility, to be realized through the divine power bringing all things to fulfillment in Jesus (see Eph 1.9–10, 22–23; Col 1.15–22). Hence, in fact Christians can imitate God by moral acts only by cooperating with the redemptive love of Jesus and so contributing to fulfillment in Jesus.

Similarly, the norm that Christians should walk according to the Spirit (see Gal 5.16) is in practice equivalent to the normative requirement of Christian love, since the Spirit transforms Christian moral life by communicating divine love. Likewise, the norm of Christian love is not something separate from Jesus in his concrete totality (see LG 42). Love disposes one to that good which will be accomplished in the fulfillment of all things in Jesus.

Again, since what the Church teaches is nothing else than the revealed truth received from Jesus, it follows that an injunction to live according to the Church's teaching is in practice equivalent (for believing Christians) to the first principle of morality. Hence, no different general principle is proposed when Paul says: "What you have learned and received and heard and seen in me, do" (Phil 4.9).

Question E: Are there specific norms knowable only by faith whose fulfillment is strictly required by Christian love?

1. The love command of the New Testament adds a new incentive to pursue human goods in a morally upright way. In the light of Christian faith, integral human fulfillment is more than an ideal; its realization is included in the Christian's hope for the fulfillment of everything in Jesus. The gospel also proposes certain counsels of perfection in a specifically Christian style of life, but the fulfillment of these is optional; they are not strict moral requirements.

2. Of course, Christian love strictly requires the fulfillment of all true moral norms—all the specific norms which direct action toward integral human fulfillment. All such norms, according to the account proposed in chapters four through ten, follow from the basic human goods and the first principle of morality, whose primary specifications are the modes of responsibility. Although faith's teaching clarifies and calls attention to these principles of natural law, all of them can in principle be known without faith. Divine goodness and human goods are not alternatives for choice, and all moral choices are between human goods (24-E). Hence, it seems that there is no room for specific norms, in principle knowable only by Christian faith, whose fulfillment is strictly required by Christian love.[5]

3. Nevertheless, it seems there are specifically Christian moral norms. St. Paul, for example, calls upon Christians to conform their lives to the mind of Jesus rather than to the world (see Rom 12.2), to walk according to the Spirit rather than the flesh (see Gal 5.13–26). Matthew's Gospel describes Jesus as presenting a strikingly distinctive set of norms, which as a body go beyond anything in the Old Testament as well as in any other religion or philosophy. For example, his demands for forgiveness and love of enemies, while suggested by others, are at the core of a distinctive way of dealing with evil, most perfectly illustrated in Jesus' own life, passion, and death (see Mt 5.38–48; Mk 8.31–33; Lk 9.22). Moreover,

he calls on anyone who wishes to follow him to take up a personal cross (see Mt 16.24; Mk 8.34; Lk 9.23).[6]

4. An adequate answer to this question requires a synthesis of both the preceding points of view. On the one hand, there are no specific norms other than those required to direct action to the fulfillment of the possibilities proper to human nature as such. Charity does not dispose to any human fulfillment other than that in basic human goods. A Christian's will, enlivened by charity, chooses and acts rightly only by its disposition toward integral human fulfillment. Thus, the principles of Christian morality are none other than those of natural law, treated in chapters four through ten (cf. *S.t.*, 1–2, q. 108, a. 2). But, on the other hand, there are specific moral norms knowable only by Christian faith.[7] Charity strictly requires the fulfillment of these norms because they are moral truths whose fulfillment is necessary for human fulfillment itself.

5. This answer to the question is paradoxical. One begins to resolve the paradox only by recognizing that humankind is fallen and redeemed. Original sin transforms the human situation in many ways, making moral uprightness seem unattractive and the irrationality of immorality seem unimportant (14-G). This actual situation and its humanly acceptable solution is known fully only in the light of Christian faith. The gospel teaches how sin and its consequences can be overcome and how human acts can contribute to this as cooperation with God's plan. It also teaches how the Christian's life contributes not only to earthly progress but to integral human fulfillment within everlasting life.

6. **The teachings of faith neither conflict with any of the general principles of morality nor add any new principles to them. Yet faith does generate specific norms proper to Christian life.** It does this by proposing options both possible for and appealing to fallen men and women—options which either cannot be conceived without faith or would lack sufficient appeal to be considered in deliberation in the absence of Christian hope. Specific moral norms are generated only when proposals are articulated as appealing possibilities for choice. Thus, by advancing fresh proposals, faith generates specific norms which could not be known without it.[8]

7. An analogy helps clarify this. Dietetics sets down general norms for an adequate, balanced diet. To work out specific diets for various difficult cases, a dietitian must consider the problems each abnormal condition poses. Thus, a dietitian preparing a diet for an individual suffering from a certain disease— ulcers, say—produces a specific set of norms which are fully in accord with the general norms but also add to them: for example, by excluding certain foods which are generally permitted, by setting a special pattern and frequency for meals, by specifying how food is to be prepared, and so on.

8. Christian morality is like this. The human race is in a pathological condition. At the same time, it must be in training to accomplish the spectacular feat of reaching integral fulfillment. The facts of the human condition must be taken into account in considering the practical implications of the true, general requirements of human morality. If the facts—which are only fully disclosed by revelation—are ignored, people will behave more or less unrealistically.

9. **In taking the actual human condition into account, divine revelation proposes specific norms, which can be derived from the general norms of human morality, yet are unknowable without the light of faith. Christian norms add to common human moral requirements from within, by specifying them, not from without by imposing some extrahuman demand upon human acts.** Rather than ignoring or violating the general requirements of human morality, one who lives by Christian faith fulfills them.

10. Every true moral norm sets a requirement whose fulfillment Christian love demands. Even in the fallen human condition, many of these requirements are known very widely. The conventional moralities of all peoples contain much truth, especially in directing action toward substantive human goods by the cooperation of small groups such as the family.

11. Yet without the help of divine revelation, no widely accepted morality is free of gaps, misunderstandings, and false norms (see DS 3004–5/1785–86). These defects appear especially in dealing with moral evil and its consequences, and in interacting with individuals and groups beyond one's own clan, tribe, caste, or nation. All the great moral and religious teachers of humankind have recognized these deficiencies in conventional moralities and sought to remedy them by radical reflection and more original and disciplined ways of life than those which suggest themselves to common sense.

12. Socrates and the Buddha, for example, in their distinct ways, considered the human situation with unusual clearsightedness. Like all men and women, they were given the grace necessary to live uprightly even in this fallen world. Unlike some, they apparently accepted it; unlike many, they reflected on the human condition with wisdom and tenacity. They sought a way for men and women to live uprightly in a world broken by sin. Since what they sought is found only in cooperation with God's redemptive work, even such good and wise men did not find the true plan for a good human life. Rather, they imagined a world in which redemption by human effort would be possible, a world different from ours in important ways—for example, in respect to the human significance of death and the need for human effort toward a better life in this world. (This point is treated more fully in the appendix to chapter twenty-six.)

13. Thus, without Christian faith even the wisest men did not discover the true way to live in the fallen world. Morally good possibilites often lack appeal, and appealing possibilities often lack the human goodness demanded by the upright consciences of men like Socrates and the Buddha. The distinctiveness of Christian morality is clearest in its linking together seeming opposites.[9] For example, one must love enemies, but absolutely refuse to compromise with them; one must suffer for the sake of uprightness, but not passively regard the world as broken beyond human effort to repair; one must concede nothing to anyone's moral error, yet judge no one wicked.

14. Beyond such norms, each of which by itself might in principle be known by reason alone, Christian faith proposes actions inconceivable except in its light. Because Jesus' redemptive act is cooperation with God's work, known only by revelation, it is a specific kind of human act inconceivable apart from revelation.

Jesus served the good of religion and the whole of humankind in a unique way by choosing to do what he did. While the life of Jesus as man is entirely within the framework of human goods and the moral principles proper to human life, the specific norm according to which he accepted his personal vocation could not have been formulated except by him.[10]

15. Moreover, Jesus' life is not only an inspiring example but a real principle of the new covenant. Those who enter this community by faith are really freed from the fallen human condition. Since they are aware of God's redemptive work, kinds of acts otherwise impossible become possible for them. Chief among these are the acts by which one finds and commits oneself to one's personal vocation. Doing this will involve the specific acts of helping Jesus communicate divine truth and love to humankind and of preparing the sacrifice, united with his in each Mass, which merits God's re-creative work, by which alone integral human fulfillment will be realized.[11]

16. In sum, there are certain specific norms, knowable only by faith, whose fulfillment is strictly required by Christian love. An important example is that one should find, accept, and faithfully carry out one's personal vocation. Or, in the language of the gospel: "If any man would come after me, let him deny himself and take up his cross daily and follow me" (Lk 9.23).[12]

Inasmuch as we, although children of God, remain human persons with moral responsibility to act in ways consistent with integral human fulfillment, the perfect unity (without loss, separation, or commingling) of the divine and human in the being of Jesus and in his life is the standard to which our own being and lives must conform. Jesus "fully reveals man to man himself and makes his supreme calling clear" (GS 22). The words and deeds of Jesus manifest the perfect love of God and the perfect human response to this love; it is the truth contained in this manifestation which the Spirit teaches (see Jn 14.26). The Spirit gives to Jesus' followers his mind and renews their hearts in conformity with his sacred heart.

The reality of the Incarnation—that Jesus is a man as we are human, in everything except sin—demands that human nature in him not be nullified. By this very fact, human nature in us is recalled to the perfection toward which God originally ordered it when he made man and woman in his own image and likeness (see GS 22, 34, 38, 45). Therefore, the requirements of natural law—the humanly intelligible conditions for human fulfill-ment—remain in Jesus and are satisfied in him. Insofar as he is our norm, these requirements of our own humanity become demands of Christian love. For this reason, Vatican II teaches that the perfection of charity which comes from following Jesus and living in him is a holiness by which "a more human way of life is promoted even in this earthly society" (LG 40). Christian holiness is not an alternative to true humanism and involves no escape from human responsibility to pursue human goods in this world.

Question F: Must the modes of responsibility be transformed so that all one does might contribute to a suitable response to God's gift of Christian love?

1. Question E showed that there are some specific norms knowable only by faith whose fulfillment is strictly required by Christian love. But all the acts of a Christian's life should be done out of Christian love. If they are, together they will

make up an appropriate response to God's gift of love. If the moral acts of Christian life are to have this character, all of them must be shaped by specifically Christian norms drawn from specifically Christian principles. Thus, the modes of responsibility must be transformed into modes of Christian response. This question will explain this point.

2. Chapter twenty-three showed that Christian life begins with the fundamental option of faith in Jesus, that by this option Christians enter into his covenant and commit themselves to cooperate in his redemptive act, and that each Christian's share in this cooperation is his or her personal vocation. **Ideally, every act of Christians will help carry out their personal vocations: "Whatever you do, in word or deed, do everything in the name of the Lord Jesus, giving thanks to God the Father through him" (Col 3.17). Thus, every act of Christian life should be specifically Christian; in every act one should live one's faith in response to God's call.**

3. If this requirement of Christian love is met, all of a Christian's life will differ specifically from the life of a non-Christian. When Christians ask themselves what they are doing, they should say: I am living my faith, following Jesus, and fulfilling my personal vocation by doing this or that—for example, by fixing dinner, making a sale, studying this chapter, going on a picnic, voting in the election, and so on. One's entire human life will be a life of faith in Jesus (see Gal 2.19–20).

4. Lived in this way, every act of Christian life will be eucharistic—that is, a sacrifice of praise and thanksgiving. God's gifts of faith and love initiate our life as his children. Our actions should make up a life which thanks him for his gifts. If one abides in Jesus, the fruit of God's love in one's life will be abundant (see Jn 15.1–8). This fruit, produced by God's grace and one's own work, is to be offered in the Mass with Jesus' sacrifice (23-B).

5. By such a life, one contributes to the fulfillment of everything in Jesus, as the first principle of Christian morality requires one to do. This fulfillment will be accomplished only by God's re-creative act. But one's own Christian life here and now prepares the material of the heavenly kingdom (see GS 38). Just as the sacrifice of the cross remains in the risen Lord, so the sacrifices of all who take up their crosses and follow Jesus remain and will be fleshed out again when God creates the new heavens and new earth (see GS 39).

6. The sacrifice Christian love requires is service: Christians are called to love others as they have been loved (see Jn 15.12). Jesus' life reveals the Father because of the love with which Jesus acts, and his teaching interprets the meaning of his acts in precisely these terms. Likewise, Christians living as children of God cooperate in Jesus' redemptive act by the apostolic work to which they are personally called. In doing this, they reveal God's truth and love, and make these gifts available to others.

7. Furthermore, since they respond to God's gifts, prepare the materials of the heavenly kingdom, and reveal God's truth and love to others, all the acts of Christian life contribute to one's personal sanctity. By enlisting all aspects of the self in the service of love, one integrates them with the divine life poured forth in

one's heart by the Spirit's gift. The charity which motivates faith is implemented in the Christian's life, and the acts done out of love cause it to pervade one's whole self. Doing human acts which engage all dimensions of oneself, one more and more fulfills the command to love with one's whole mind and heart and soul and strength. Then every act of Christian life will contribute to true self-fulfillment—holiness.

8. Thus, although not itself a human act, charity utterly transforms the whole of the Christian's life. To make sure that every choice will fit into such a life, specifically Christian norms must direct every choice one makes. Where are these norms to be found? In Jesus. His words and deeds reveal how to live a good human life in this fallen world; only his life is perfect in sacrifice, preparation of the human contribution to the kingdom, communication of God's life to others, and personal holiness.

9. The Gospels do not provide a complete and detailed moral code. Although the sacred writers do teach specifically on some important matters, the specific moral teaching of the New Testament clearly is insufficient to form Christian conscience on many matters. Yet God's revelation in Jesus cannot be inadequate to our needs, for he provides it precisely to meet them.

10. The solution to the problem is that new specific norms always can be derived from more basic principles (10-B). **Clearly, however, the principles of natural law known by unaided reason cannot by themselves generate specifically Christian norms. The modes of responsibility must be transformed in the light of faith into modes of Christian response to God's gifts.** This transformation is exemplified in Jesus' life and explained in his teaching. Chapter twenty-six will examine it in detail.

The Christian transformation of the human modes of responsibility by no means nullifies them. Jesus is the perfect man, and one who follows him does not become less human but more (see GS 41). As the principle and model of renewed humanity, Jesus responds to all authentic human aspirations (see AG 8). Still, he does bring something new to human hopes (see GS 22): He becomes the norm of a new morality, as human values and the way to pursue them are freshly understood in the light of the redemption.

The uprightness of Christian lives is their human moral goodness, but in the only specific form in which, under existing conditions, human moral goodness can be realized. This way of life is marked by redemptive love which overcomes evil by suffering and forms human community by faith and hope, according to which one looks to divine intervention to render the community's common effort fruitful and so validate one's commitment to membership in the community.

The transformation of the modes of responsibility into the Christian modes of response is one essential aspect of the transformation St. Paul describes when he speaks of dying to sin and rising to new life in Jesus (see Rom 6.3–11). Christians must not live like pagans, but must "put on the new nature, created after the likeness of God in true righteousness and holiness" (Eph 4.24). The new nature is that renewed in Jesus; the modes of Christian response are his perfectly human way of responding both to human evil and to divine redemptive love.

Question G: Does the new law surpass the old law by giving Christians something besides better guidance for living?

1. The new law does more than just specify the old. **Central to the new law is the gift of the Holy Spirit. By this gift the Christian is nurtured to maturity in Jesus—that is, to everlasting life. Thus, unlike the old law or any other law for fallen men and women, the new law not only indicates the right way—that of Jesus—but empowers one to follow it and draws one along it** (see *S.t.*, 1–2, q. 98, a. 1; q. 107, a. 2). It is no mere extrinsic word of exhortation, guidance, challenge, and condemnation; placed in the mind, written in the heart, it is effective in overcoming sin and uniting God's people with him (see Jer 31.31–34; Heb 8.7–10; 10.15–18).

2. The Old Testament anticipates this. The prophets looked to the time when God would give a new law written in the heart (see Jer 24.7; Bar 2.30–35; Ez 11.19–20; 18.31). The psalmist prayed that God would bring about a change in heart (see Ps 51.12; 119.32). The renewal was to be accomplished by an outpouring of the Spirit of God (see Is 32.15; Ez 39.29).

3. Jesus announces that the Father will give the Spirit to those who ask (see Lk 11.13). At the Last Supper, he promises to send the Holy Spirit (see Jn 14.16–17, 26; 16.7–14). The Spirit will complete Jesus' work, for he will remain permanently with Christians, lead them to the fullness of Jesus' truth, and bring the struggle against evil to a victorious conclusion. The promise of the Spirit is fulfilled at Pentecost (see Acts 2.1–4); thus the hope of the prophets is vindicated (see Acts 2.16–21).

4. The law of the Spirit frees Christians from sin and death (see Rom 8.2), for the Spirit dwells in Christians, pours God's love into their hearts (see Rom 5.5), and makes them God's children (see Rom 8.14–17). In other words, what is most central in the new law is not a commandment to love or a requirement to do works of fraternal charity, but the actual gift and endowment by the Spirit of the reality and effective power of divine love, which one accepts in living faith (see *S.t.*, 1–2, q. 106, a. 1). This is why the new law is expressed not so much outwardly as in the inner transformation of those who receive it (see 2 Cor 3.2–8).

St. Paul no sooner explains that Christians are liberated from slavery to the yoke of the law than he warns that the freedom of the children of God to which Christians are called is not freedom to do as one pleases. It is a freedom from sin and a power to do the works of love (see Gal 5). This warning of Paul's still is necessary today and it is so important that further explanation is useful.

In every law except the new law of Jesus, there are two aspects which must be distinguished. On the one hand, to the extent that it truly is law and not merely arbitrary imposition of an exploiting human authority, a law indicates what is necessary or appropriate for action to contribute to human fulfillment. In other words, every true law is a norm which shapes the actions of individuals and groups toward the good to be realized by and shared in through these actions (see *S.t.*, 1–2, q. 90, aa. 1–2; q. 91, a. 4). On the other hand, except for the new law of love, fallen humankind experiences even true law as a more or less unwelcome demand. One who has done wrong perceives the law as the source of reproach to conscience, usually the reproach of society. One who is tempted perceives the law as a curb on inclination. Even one who wants to do what is right perceives the law as a standard difficult to live up to.

When most people think about law, this second aspect—its burdensomeness—is foremost in their minds. Moreover, exploiting human authorities also call their impositions "laws." The arbitrary demands of unjust authorities, such as Nazi decrees, unjust Supreme Court decisions, and so on are put forth with the trappings of legality. As a result, law is perceived as even more burdensome than it truly is.

5. Any law short of the new law of transforming love seems alien to fallen humankind, the imposition of a burden which cannot be fulfilled (see *S.t.*, 1–2, q. 106, a. 2; q. 107, a. 1, ad 2). This is true even of natural law, for, although it is written in the heart, its dynamism toward human fulfillment is at odds with the stunted dispositions of fallen persons and with the compromises of conventional morality (see *S.t.*, 1–2, q. 94, a. 6; q. 107, a. 4).

6. Christians, however, undergo a real transformation: from the fallen condition to the condition of the new humanity of Jesus. In them, the natural law written in the human heart by the creator and the law of love poured forth in the heart of the redeemed by the Holy Spirit form a harmonious principle of living. This principle is the law of Jesus (see Gal 6.2). The natural law continues to indicate what is necessary and appropriate for human action to contribute to human fulfillment, which will be included in the fulfillment of everything in Jesus. But its indications are now clearer, insofar as a heart renewed by love is freed from the self-deception and rationalization generated to protect the sinful self. And now, too, the love of God provides its impetus toward divine goodness, to be enjoyed by the blessed sharing in it both divinely and humanly.

The law of the Spirit, the new law of love, does not nullify or replace natural law, although the new law does redeem natural law from its aspect of alien imposition (see *S.t.*, 1–2, q. 100, a. 1; q. 107, a. 2, ad 1; q. 108, a. 3, ad 3). As long as the human heart is alienated from itself by sin, even the law written in the heart must be experienced as an alien imposition. When the gift of the Spirit creates a new heart in men and women, the law written by God from the beginning upon the human heart begins to be experienced as the inclination of the real self.

7. The natural law disposes toward friendship with God as one form of humanly fulfilling harmony; living faith superabundantly satisfies this natural disposition (see *S.t.*, 2–2, q. 44, a. 1). At the same time, the new law of love disposes one toward a human life in perfect harmony with God's will; thus it disposes one to the perfect carrying-out of the natural law, since God wills integral fulfillment for his human children.

8. The disposition to fulfillment in Jesus comprehends and exceeds the human requirement to choose consistently with integral human fulfillment. Hence, love fulfills all the commandments (see Rom 13.8–10; 1 Cor 13; Gal 5.14–23).

9. Insofar as Christians are true to their calling, they are altogether freed from law in its burdensome, alien aspect.[13] The share in divine love communicated to them by the Spirit is a disposition to divine goodness and so to everything good, for every good comes from God, participates in his perfection, and contributes to the fulfillment of all things in Jesus. To hearts formed by divine love nothing that

is good is alien (see Phil 4.8–9), and right ways of acting—that is, ways to the good—are spontaneously preferred. Thus St. Paul stresses that the Christian is liberated from the law: One who lives by the Spirit spontaneously does what is conducive to good; law's demands are satisfied without being made (see *S.t.*, 1–2, q. 106, aa. 1–2).

Question H: In what senses can Christian love be called "grace"?

1. Charity can be called "grace" in two senses. These are designated by some uses of the terms "sanctifying grace" and "actual grace."

2. **"Sanctifying grace" refers to that in Christians by which they are transformed into adopted children of God.** The share in divine life which God offers created persons is a real regeneration, a second birth. Christians possess a new life which is their own (see Rom 6.4); they are new creatures (see 2 Cor 5.17), new men and women re-created in justice, holiness, and truth (see Eph 4.24). This new life is "grace" because it is a divine gift, "sanctifying" because it really transforms a person with the holiness of divine life.

3. As was explained in chapter twenty-four, the love of God by which Christians love him must also be understood as a disposition which is their own and really transforms them. The Church has not taught, and theologians do not agree, whether this love and sanctifying grace are in the Christian one and the same reality or two realities.[14] **Thus one is free to call charity "sanctifying grace."** Furthermore, at least for the purposes of moral theology, no distinction is needed between charity and sanctifying grace. Rather, the supposition here is that, insofar as the gift of divine life (sanctifying grace) bestowed on the Christian is distinct from the uncreated gift (the Holy Spirit), it can be identified with that love of God which "has been poured into our hearts through the Holy Spirit who has been given to us" (Rom 5.5).

4. The expression "actual grace" is used in various contexts with diverse references. The common element lies in the fact that the various realities referred to move people to act in ways which positively contribute to God's redemptive work.

5. Thus, "actual grace" can refer to God's causality, insofar as God brings sinners to conversion and causes the good deeds of saints. It can refer specifically to the work of the Holy Spirit in Christians, helping them in their weakness and nourishing their holiness. Sometimes "grace," in the sense of "actual grace," refers to created entities conducive to anyone's salvation or the good of the Church. A pious thought, a chance encounter, or even a difficulty which conduces to holiness is called a "grace."

6. **Since charity impels one to deeds of love** (see 2 Cor 5.14; 1 Jn 3.18), **it is a dynamic principle of Christian life in the ways explained in this chapter. Thus, it also can be called "actual grace."** If charity is considered in this way, it is not necessary to posit still other supernatural principles in the soul underlying the acts by which Christians living in God's love grow in holiness and progress toward salvation. This avoids the insoluble puzzles which arise from thinking of

actual grace as a mysterious, created force which somehow moves persons to make their free choices.

7. There is an underlying principle of unity which explains why the word "grace" is used with several different meanings. In Christian language, "grace" always refers to God's gifts, but not all God's gifts are called "grace." Rather, the word's use is restricted to God's gifts insofar as they are related to his personal revelation and contribute to our salvation.[15]

8. In summary, fallen men and women cannot hear and accept God's word unless he first causes them to be open to it, sends someone to communicate it, and draws them to conversion. These gifts of God's mercy and his causing of them are called "actual grace." When the sinner is prepared to accept God's self-communication, his love is poured forth in the heart by the Holy Spirit. This love not only overcomes sin but makes the person who accepts it with faith an adopted child of God. As a principle of sharing in God's own holiness, it is called "sanctifying grace." The new life of the adopted child of God is an appropriate response to his gift. Yet this response, while it is the Christian's own action, also is God's gift: "For we are his workmanship, created in Christ Jesus for good works, which God prepared beforehand, that we should walk in them" (Eph 2.10). Hence, every good act of Christian life, the charity which impels to it, and God's causing of it also can be called "actual grace." United with Jesus' sacrifice, Christians' holy lives merit the re-creative act by which God will complete his work of salvation. This ultimate achievement of God's love will bring about the fulfillment of everything in Jesus. This divine act and the perfection each Christian hopes to receive in it can be called "beatifying grace."

God's causality as a principle of conversion and Christian life is the primary reality called "actual grace."[16] The Church firmly, constantly, and definitively teaches that no one becomes an adopted child of God, no one lives up to this status, and no one reaches heaven except by the work of God. This work of God, an utterly free gift on his part, brings about in us everything which heals sin and contributes to sanctity unto eternal life (see DS 1525–26/797–98, 1541/806, 1544/808, 1546/809, 1551–53/811–13, 1568/828, 1572/832). At the same time, God's work in us in no way eliminates our own free choice; we must cooperate with God's grace (see DS 1525/797, 1528–29/799, 1541/806, 1554/814).

The problem raised by this teaching is: If God does it all, how can we freely and responsibly do anything? If we really make a difference, how can one suppose that the whole process and outcome of our redemption and sanctification are from first to last God's work?

The seeming paradox is contained in Scripture itself. We are God's handiwork with a life prepared for us to live (see Eph 2.10). Only those drawn by the Father come to Jesus (see Jn 6.44). On the other hand, there are constant exhortations, including ones urging and insisting that grace be used well (see Rom 2.4–11; 2 Cor 6.1). Christians are to "work out your own salvation with fear and trembling" (Phil 2.12), which would make no sense if they could not do anything about it. Clearly, everything is God's work and something also is ours.

Neither set of texts can be taken in isolation, nor should complex ideas be split up (see *S.t.*, 1–2, q. 109, aa. 2, 5–6, 9–10; q. 111, a. 2; q. 113, a. 3). For example: "He who abides in me, and I in him, he it is that bears much fruit, for apart from me you can do nothing" (Jn 15.5). The first two phrases make it clear that we do something, indeed, a great deal, if we live in Jesus; the last phrase by itself might be taken to mean the opposite. Paul says: "But by the grace of God I am what I am, and his grace toward me was not in vain. On the contrary, I worked harder than any of them, though it was not I, but the grace of God which is with me" (1 Cor 15.10). In these two sentences, the paradox appears twice.

In popular Catholic thought and piety, the difficulty often is clouded over and the truth of the gospel and the Church's teaching greatly obscured by the supposition that God does a good deal and we do the rest. The relationship is imagined to be like any ordinary cooperation. This sense often is given to the saying: Work as if everything depended on yourself; pray as if everything depended on God. The assumption is that in fact what depends on us does not depend on God. This is false, and to suppose it is true is to dishonor God, to reduce his mysterious reality, and to claim for oneself what is not one's own—namely, exclusive credit for what one does by one's own free choices.

At least two things lead people to segregate divine from human action. First, to the extent that "grace" means divine causality, one is confronted with the mystery of the compatibility between God's causing all creatures and created persons making created free choices. This mystery is insoluble, for we do not know what God is in himself and do not know what it is for him to cause. "Cause" is used in a unique sense of him, and so we have no basis for the troublesome supposition that if God causes a choice it cannot be free. God creates, gives reality to, human persons making free choices (see *S.t.*, 1, q. 19, a. 8; 1–2, q. 9, a. 6). We do not know how he does it, but neither do we know how he creates raindrops falling on our heads. This case is an instance of a general problem discussed in chapter two, appendix three.

Another factor which leads people to divide divine and human acts is that it often is supposed that actual grace is a created entity other than human acts themselves—not an obvious entity such as a mother, a retreat, or a chance encounter, but a mysterious psychic or spiritual entity, like an unconscious impulse. Now if actual grace were this, if it helped us by unconscious pushes and tugs, it would be incompatible with human free choice. Then it would be true that the more such impulses did, the less we did, and the more we did, the less they did.

Fortunately, nothing in Scripture or Catholic teaching requires us to believe in spiritual pushes and tugs. Therefore, while grace remains mysterious, we can be confident that there is nothing absurd in the idea that God's grace bestows our whole Christian life on us—everything we are and do and have, absolutely everything—and that a very important part of what God bestows is a human nature, human abilities, human freedom, human choices, human acts, human flourishing, and the sublime gift of our personal share in his own divine life which transforms our humanity and everything which belongs to it into the fulfillment of an adopted child of God. Therefore, we ought to pray because everything depends on God; we ought to work because our work is an important part of God's good gift to us.

Summary

Participation in the divine nature is not a human act, and so charity itself is not a human act, although it is related to such acts. As a disposition to fulfillment in divine life, charity is not something one does but something one is to remain in. As the principle of our response to the commandment to love God and neighbor, charity is a disposition to good human acts; but the fulfillment to which it is directed is not a human action. Thus certain actions are called "acts of charity" not because they are themselves charity but because they are closely related to it.

Moral goodness is not a condition or means for receiving charity, for charity is purely a gift of God. Having received this gift, however, one can and must live a morally good life. Such a life means loving human fulfillment. For every other good reflects and participates in the goodness of God, and one who does not love human goods as they should be loved is failing in love of God.

The moral implications of Christian love are partly but not completely expressed by the commands to love God and neighbor. Closely linked by Jesus, the two requirements can be taken as a single, complex norm, a formulation in religious terms of the first principle of morality. They remain, however, within the framework of the old covenant, while the parable of the Good Samaritan begins to suggest a fulfillment of the law and prophets which goes beyond them.

Jesus himself embodies perfect love. Christian life is a sharing in the fullness of love, the personal divine-human communion which Jesus is. His love is unique in magnitude and selflessness, yet he commands us to love as he does. This requirement to love as Jesus loves—that is, as divine children—is new. We are empowered to do this by charity, divine love poured forth in human hearts by the Holy Spirit. Christian morality transforms the first principle of all human morality—that we ought to will only those possibilities which are compatible with a will toward integral human fulfillment—into a more definite norm: To will only what contributes to the integral human fulfillment being realized in the fulfillment of all things in Jesus.

The principles of Christian morality are none other than those of natural law. Yet there are specific Christian moral norms. This is so because humankind's actual situation as fallen and redeemed can be fully known only by faith. Since faith proposes new options, it generates specific norms which could not be articulated without it. Thus, Christian norms add from within to common human moral requirements by specifying them, not from without by imposing some extrahuman demand upon human acts.

Without faith, people can still know moral truths, but their knowledge is inadequate in many ways. Great religious and moral teachers—upright and clearheaded men such as Socrates and the Buddha—were aware of the human need for redemption. But even they could not find the way to live a wholly realistic and good human life in the actual human situation. This way is revealed only in Jesus. Only by faith can one recognize this way and know that one must follow it.

Christian moral life is cooperation with Jesus' redemptive act. Since every act of a Christian's life should carry out his or her personal vocation, everything should be transformed by charity. Christians should be able to say at every moment that what they are doing is a specifically Christian act: following Jesus by doing this or that. Thus, every act of Christian life will be a response to God's gifts (an act of sacrifice and thanksgiving), a preparation of the materials of the heavenly kingdom, a revelation of God's truth and love to others, and a contribution to true self-fulfillment (holiness). To guide choices so that they will fit into such a life, specifically Christian norms are needed. These are found in the Gospels, not as a detailed moral code, but implicit in the moral principles exemplified and taught by Jesus. These specifically Christian principles transform the modes of responsibility into modes of Christian response.

The new law does more than just specify the old. For central to the new law is the gift of the Holy Spirit. Thus the new law not only tells one how to live, it empowers one to live in this way. This outpouring of the Spirit of God, anticipated in the Old Testament, is promised by Jesus and fulfilled at Pentecost. The action of the Spirit is the reality and effective power of divine love, poured forth in human hearts. Although even natural law seems a burdensome, alien imposition to fallen humankind, Christians, formed by divine love, are freed from law in its burdensome aspect. If they are faithful to this gift, Christians will spontaneously prefer right ways of acting and find nothing good alien.

Charity can be called "grace" in two senses. "Sanctifying grace" is that in Christians by which they are transformed into adopted children of God. Since the Church has not taught, and theologians do not agree, whether or not charity and sanctifying grace are the same reality, one is free to call charity "sanctifying grace," and no distinction seems needed for the purposes of moral theology. As for "actual grace," the term refers to various realities which move people to contribute to God's redemptive work. First among these is God's causality, but, as a dynamic principle of Christian life, charity also can be called "actual grace."

Appendix 1:   The Christian lives by the Spirit

St. Paul clearly and forcefully affirms that Christian life is a life of perfect freedom: "For you were called to freedom, brethren . . . . If you are led by the Spirit you are not under the law" (Gal 5.13, 18). Some Jewish Christians wished everyone to adhere to the law of Moses. Paul passionately rejects this imposition: "For freedom Christ has set us free; stand fast therefore, and do not submit again to a yoke of slavery" (Gal 5.1).

The prophets and holy men of Israel had praised God's law as a wonderful gift which helped one to walk with him. Paul rejoices that Christians are at last rid of the law: "Sin will have no dominion over you, since you are not under law but under grace" (Rom 6.14). Indeed, the law was a gift from God, but a very limited one. It did make clear what is right, but to make this clear to sinful people only aggravates their sinfulness. Not only is evil more serious when committed contrary to an express command of God, but sinful people given commands are stirred to rebellion (see Rom 7.7–12). As chapter twenty-one explained, the stages of redemption prior to Jesus involved inner tensions which rendered them unsatisfactory and required that they be surpassed.

The old law had a role. It was a monitor which boxed people in and forced them to learn their sinfulness (see Gal 3.23–24). Like a treatment which brings a disease to the point of crisis, the law was imposed to bring out all the bitter consequences of sin (see Gal 3.10). Christians naturally were glad to be free of all the detailed regulations and observances of the Mosaic law. But Paul is not primarily interested in such details. The example of the law he gives is from the Ten Commandments: "You shall not covet" (Rom 7.7). It is this sort of law which was more a burden than a blessing, and it is from this sort of law that Christians are gloriously liberated.

Paul was not the first to recognize the limitations of the law. Unless one has been inwardly renewed, it is a curse to know precisely what is right and wrong. So the psalmist prays: "Create in me a clean heart" (Ps 51.10). "I will run in the way of your commandments when you enlarge my understanding" (Ps 119.32). The prophets look forward to the time when God will give the people a heart to know who he is and who they are, a heart able to live as they should (see Jer 24.7; Bar 2.30–31). "And I will give them one heart, and put a new spirit within them; I will take the stony heart out of their flesh, and give them a heart of flesh, that they may walk in my statutes and keep my ordinances and obey them; and they shall be my people, and I will be their God" (Ez 11.19–20). The law, even the Ten Commandments, is no help at all unless one has the heart to love God. Nothing imposed from without can make a person holy (see *S.t.*, 1–2, q. 98, a. 1, ad 2; q. 107, a. 1, ad 2).

Jesus teaches that God will give what we need; we must pray persistently, and the heavenly Father will answer (see Mt 7.7–11). One can ask the Father for anything in Jesus' name and be confident of receiving what one asks so that one's joy may be full (see Jn 16.23–24). God knows how to give his children good things; he will "give the Holy Spirit to those who ask him" (Lk 11.13). One who has faith in Jesus will be able to live as he did and even to do greater works than his, for Jesus will ask the Father, and the Father will send the Spirit to those who wish to walk with Jesus (see Jn 14.12–16).

Accordingly, St. Paul teaches that Christians are freed from the condemnation of the law. They enjoy a new law. "For the law of the Spirit of life in Christ Jesus has set me free from the law of sin and death" (Rom 8.2). The prophetic promise was that the new law would be placed within God's people, written upon their hearts (see Jer 31.33). The dead, dry bones of God's people would be re-created: "I will put my Spirit within you, and you shall live" (Ez 37.14). By his gift of the Spirit, made at the request of Jesus, the Father fulfills this promise.

The new law of Jesus is not simply a higher and more perfect ideal, one which makes no compromises with human hardheartedness. It is not a code, not an external imposition. Instead, it is an interior transformation. The Spirit pours forth the love of God in our hearts (see Rom 5.5). We are changed from subjects under a law to members of the divine family, with all the rights and privileges pertaining to this status (see Gal 4.6–7). Children of God do not have to take orders from anybody; they enjoy absolute liberty and can do just as they please (see Rom 8.14–21).

"No one born of God commits sin; for God's nature abides in him, and he cannot sin because he is born of God" (1 Jn 3.9). Love of neighbor fulfills the entire law (see Gal 5.14). One who loves fulfills not only the Ten Commandments but any other commandment there might be (see Rom 13.8–10). Charity is not simply a matter of doing a little something extra now and then. It unifies all the virtues and excludes all the vices; one who receives this gift needs nothing else for perfection (see 1 Cor 13). One who has the Spirit is free of inclination to do wrong; life in the Spirit bears fruit in every virtue and good work (see Gal 5.16–23).

St. Paul teaches that the new covenant is one "not in a written code but in the Spirit; for the written code kills, but the Spirit gives life" (2 Cor 3.6). St. Thomas Aquinas teaches that this saying holds true even of the precepts of the gospel and the law of the Church. Any exterior requirement imposed upon a person is deadly (see *S.t.*, 1–2, q. 106, a. 2).[17]

If all this is so, do Christians still need moral teaching? Obviously, there is moral teaching, throughout the New Testament and the whole tradition of the Church. Nor does it consist merely of optional guidelines. Paul lists sins and then says: "I warn you, as I warned you before, that those who do such things shall not inherit the kingdom of God" (Gal 5.21). The First Epistle of John no sooner asserts that a child of God cannot sin than it warns against committing murder (see 1 Jn 3.12). Jesus explicitly insists that the commandments are to be kept and taught (see Mt 5.17–20). Why are Christians still confronted with moral law?

The unhappy fact is that Christians can sin, can evict the Spirit from their hearts. When we are lawless and unruly, then the law still serves its purpose: It makes clear to us what we are (see 1 Tm 1.8–11). Moreover, the human personality is complex. Even if we do not evict the Spirit, sin remains in the recesses of our selves (see Rom 8.23). We have our treasure in earthen vessels, and death is still at its work in us (see 2 Cor 4.7, 12). One's unredeemed part fights the Spirit (see Gal 5.16–17). Christian moral teaching marks out the way we must walk to conform to the perfect image of God which is given us in Jesus.

The liberty we receive as Christians is not liberty to do good and evil indiscriminately. Freedom from the law is not a permit for fuzzy thinking in morals, nor for slackness and laxity. The liberty we receive is the power of the Holy Spirit, the power of God's own love. Using this power with faith, we can do anything whatsoever. Therefore, we can fulfill perfectly every requirement of perfect fulfillment (see *S.t.*, 2–2, q. 183, a. 4). We can love enemies, die as martyrs, even live without orgasms.

Good parents need no law against murdering children. Faithful spouses need no law against committing adultery. Fair-minded people need no laws against injustice. One who lives by the Spirit finds out what is right and willingly does it; for such a person, law might as well not exist. One who perfectly loved God above all things would necessarily love every creature just as it should be loved, and so would necessarily love every human good properly. For such a person, any act which would violate a human good would be out of the question. Insofar as, but only insofar as, they approach this ideal, children of God may do just as they please because nothing pleases them which would displease the Father by mutilating the good he wills in them and creation as a whole.

Christians who live by the Spirit are freed from sin, death, the law, and Satan. But they are not robbed of their humanity. The Spirit does not take away human judgment and choice; if he were to do this, grace would destroy nature rather than heal and perfect it. God redeems us in a way which respects our dignity as responsible persons. Therefore, the Christian who lives by the Spirit and without the law still needs to learn what is right and still must choose it. Even Jesus had to know the Father's will and commit himself to it.

Appendix 2:   The humanity of Jesus and the natural law

The explanation in question E undermines two common objections launched from different theological perspectives against Catholic teaching concerning natural law. Some Catholic theologians have suggested that natural law is more or less irrelevant, since human persons never exist in a state of pure nature. Many Protestant theologians argue that natural law is no longer relevant and trustworthy, because fallen humankind which follows nature merely conforms to its own corruption. The answer in both cases is that in our Lord Jesus human nature is found as it should be; the law present in every human heart is fulfilled in him in an exemplary way. The theological articulation of moral norms and virtues provided in chapter twenty-six will be based upon him, not upon any abstract pure nature nor upon nature as we find it in ourselves and in sinful humankind generally.

Still, one should distinguish between human nature understood as that which is actually given (even in Jesus) and human nature understood as that fulfillment of which human persons are radically capable. If one takes the former, static concept of nature as normative, one either must reject natural law or develop an unacceptable theory (4-F). When it is admitted that the human nature which is given differs in diverse historical conditions, the conclusion inevitably follows that human nature—and so any morality based upon it—changes.[18] However, if one takes the latter concept of nature as normative and articulates it by a description of the various basic categories of human goodness, then one can develop a dynamic theory of natural law, by which one can account both for the continuity and the legitimate unfolding of human moral insight.

Despite this distinction, which takes us some way toward answering objections against Catholic moral teaching insofar as it articulates the requirements of natural law, the human condition subsequent to the fall does obscure the real possibilities of human persons. Moreover, the changes which occur in conventional morality as one moves through diverse times and places, humanly organized as diverse cultural units, raise doubts as to what is the real core of human possibility.

The concretization of the norm of Christian morality in the character of Jesus provides a remedy for these difficulties. In him, human persons see what a man can be. His good life is not rendered ambiguous by mixed motives; his human commitments are not limited by compromises with sin. The possibilities of human nature, which are known naturally (up to a point and with more or less mixture of error), are revealed in Jesus and become accessible to every man and woman by faith which accepts him in his total, Incarnate reality.[19]

Moreover, Jesus is not a mere historical figure out of the past. He remains—the same yesterday, today, and forever—a standard by which to reject false teaching (see Heb 13.7–9). This remaining is real because Christian life is not merely an independent life modeled upon his, but is a real, communal sharing in the central action of his life. This point was explained in chapter twenty-three.

The Stoic philosophers, who so strongly shaped the more noble secular moral standards of Greco-Roman culture at the beginning of Christianity, articulated a moral ideal in terms of the cardinal virtues of wisdom, justice, temperance, and fortitude. St. Paul confidently asserts the autonomy of the culture centered upon Jesus, whose death and resurrection struck the "wise" as foolish. God "is the source of your life in Christ Jesus, whom God made our wisdom, our righteousness and sanctification and redemption" (1 Cor 1.30).

Human culture is rooted in the basic human goods, and any culture more or less adequately serves them (see GS 53). In Jesus, the Word of God enters into history as the perfect man and reorganizes the wreckage of human community into a culture worthy of human dignity (see GS 38). Christian holiness, therefore, conforms to human nature (see LG 40). Yet, in Jesus human morality also is renewed and transformed. Wisdom and justice (righteousness) take on a new depth and meaning. Self-control yields to sanctification and fortitude to redemption, as limited goods are embraced by the prospect of glory and human evils are overcome by the might of God's intervention. Stoicism has long since died out with the classical culture to which it belonged; Jesus' way to a renewed humankind remains.

Appendix 3:   Self-affirmation, self-denial, and charity

The relationship between love of God and Christian morality has sometimes been explained differently than here, in such a way that divine love is thought to impose requirements upon human action which in no way conduce to the fulfillment of human persons as such. For example, it has been said that charity is an unselfish, personal love of communion with God, by which one finds more pleasure in God and his interests than in oneself and one's own interests. Many Christians have tended to suppose that the proper self-interest of human persons in their own fulfillment constitutes alienation from God.

Two kinds of confusion underlie this sort of mistake. One lies in failing to recognize that divine goodness and human goods are so utterly diverse that there simply can be no direct competition between them. The other lies in confusing the self whose identity is defined by sin with the true human self.

The first confusion is apparent as soon as anyone begins talking about God's interests, as if God had a set of interests of his own. Truly, in the sense that human individuals (including Jesus as man) have a self, God has none. His love of his own goodness cannot be a source of selfishness, for he can gain nothing from others. His love of others is all-embracing, altogether nondiscriminatory, and purely generous. It follows that when the love of God which is poured forth in our hearts by the Holy Spirit is turned upon ourselves and our fellow human beings, the result is a reconciliation of ourselves with our own true interests, not an alienation of ourselves from our own interests in favor of "God's interests" (see *S.t.*, 1, q. 60, a. 5; 2–2, q. 25, aa. 4, 7).

The second confusion is apparent as soon as anyone recognizes the sense in which Jesus does and does not have a normal, human self. What he lacks is the sort of self we sinners have insofar as we are sinners, namely, a self whose identity is defined in part by sinful commitments and sinful divisions from others. However, Jesus really has a human self in the sense that he can and does make that sincere gift of himself without which no human individual is able to find his or her true self (see GS 24).

St. Paul's statement, "I have been crucified with Christ; it is no longer I who live, but Christ who lives in me," should not be detached from what follows immediately: "The life I now live in the flesh I live by faith in the Son of God, who loved me and gave himself for me" (Gal 2.20). Paul's point is that one whose life is lived in communion with the redemptive act of Jesus does not constitute his or her own identity by an independent basic commitment, but only has existential identity by sharing in Jesus' redemptive act.

Similarly, the point of saying that Christians live no longer for themselves but for Jesus (see 2 Cor 5.15) is that a Christian has no private, personal life. The redemptive community formed by Jesus embraces the totality of one's life. In respect to the new covenant, one has not the private sphere and liberty one retains as a member of other societies, such as the family and civil society. One's whole human life falls within one's responsibilities as a member of the body of Jesus.

Appendix 4:   Charity as one of three theological virtues

To understand the sense in which charity is and is not a virtue, one needs a distinction between two senses of the word "virtue." In a broad sense, any lasting disposition to good acts is a virtue; in this sense, charity is a virtue (see *S.t.*, 2–2, q. 23, aa. 2–3). In another and more specific sense, a virtue is an aspect of character integrated around morally good choices, which constitutes an enduring disposition toward good acts. In this more specific sense, charity is not a virtue.

All love is a disposition toward fulfillment (24-A). However, not all love is a virtue; not all love is an enduring disposition, and not all love disposes toward humanly good fulfillment. For example, a passing love for a particular, sensible good is not a virtue, and even a lasting disposition, such as love of the feeling of alcoholic intoxication, will not be a virtue, since it is not in accord with human fulfillment. However, a love which both is lasting and disposes to actuations of one's capacities which will truly be humanly fulfilling is a virtue in the broad sense.

Charity, although it primarily disposes one to fulfillment in divine life, also disposes the Christian to integral human fulfillment. Faith primarily is an act, but insofar as it is a lasting gift on God's part and an enduring commitment on the part of the believer, it has the character of a lasting disposition; this disposition is good insofar as it is a disposition to accept charity and the life of friendship with God which flows from it. Thus faith is a virtue. Hope is an attitude of trustful confidence in God's faithfulness; this attitude is necessary for life according to faith; hence, the constant disposition of hope in God also has the character of virtue.

Although faith, hope, and charity can be called "virtues" in the sense explained, it is important to realize that they dispose to more than human fulfillment. They affect choices and human moral actions, but they also affect other parts of the personality. While certain human acts, done with the help of grace, are necessary to prepare one to receive these virtues, faith, hope, and charity are acquired not by human acts, but by the gift of the Spirit (see DS 1525–31/797–800; see *S.t.*, 1–2, q. 62, a. 1; 2–2, q. 6, a. 1; q. 24, a. 2).

Very often faith, hope, and charity have been thought of as if they were separate acts. It seems more nearly correct to think that in living faith, the three concur in a single act. St. Paul closely and dynamically links the three (see Rom 5.1–5; Gal 5.5–6). Also, there are suggestions in the First Epistle of John that faith is a consequence of love (see 1 Jn 5.1). Since faith, hope, and love are received together and since faith usually is considered the basis (see Rom 5.1–5), the priority of love can hardly be understood unless in living faith the three concur in one and the same act.

The act of faith-hope-love can be viewed in this way: By faith we accept the truth of God's self-revelation; acceptance of his truth makes us hope with confidence that he will fulfill the personal relationship he has initiated; this hope enables us to be disposed in love to live according to his will and so come to perfect communion with him. The act also can be viewed in this way: By love we share in God's own life and are disposed to fulfillment in it; the experience of this love and its dynamism makes us hope with confidence for fulfillment; this personal trust in God renders our faith in his revealed truth absolutely certain and unshakable.

This second way of viewing the dynamic unity of the three aspects of our personal relationship with God could clarify how justifying faith differs from preparatory acts of faith, why believing in God out of love of him justifies, and also how God testifies and the Spirit convinces. For if the assent of living faith is the first human act we do out of the love of God poured forth in our hearts through the Holy Spirit, then I see no reason to suppose that anything other than the gift of this love is required to make us certain beyond human certitude that what appears to be divine revelation most surely and truly is so: God's proposal of communion is surely true, for we find ourselves beginning to live in it.

Someone might ask: How can this view be reconciled with the Council of Trent's teaching about the faith of a person in mortal sin? Trent definitively teaches that by every mortal sin one loses grace or charity, but not faith except by sin contrary to it (see DS 1544/808, 1577–78/837–38). The faith which remains when one is in mortal sin is "true faith, granted it is not a living faith" (DS 1578/838). One remains a child of God although a prodigal one. I think this teaching is a very important reason why Catholics have tended to suppose that there are three distinct acts of the theological virtues, not one single act.

My answer is that when one continues to believe in God while standing against him in sin, one's act of faith obviously cannot be motivated by love. Yet on the account just now sketched, the past experience of God's love still can have its effect by the medium of hope. The past experience of love together with God's grace is sufficient to keep alive confidence in his mercy, and this confidence can preserve certitude that what is revealed truly is God's absolutely trustworthy communication. Even if I sin mortally, I know who is unfaithful.

Notes

1. Catholic authors generally do not ask this question directly. However, the position rejected here is stated clearly by some Protestants. See, for example, Karl Barth, *Ethics*, ed. Dietrich Braun, trans. Geoffrey W. Bromiley (New York: Seabury Press, 1981), 451–60. Barth flatly states (454): "Love is the epitome of the obedience of the sinner saved by grace. Deification is not the issue, but this is." Again (456): "For loving is an action, the action which takes place in the commitment that we have described by the terms law, authority, and humility and which is the underlying meaning of these concepts." What Barth is talking about here, I call "faith."

2. The fact of continuity makes it very worthwhile to understand the idea of *commandment* in the Old Testament. See Matthew J. O'Connell, S.J., "The Concept of Commandment in the Old Testament," *Theological Studies*, 21 (1960), 351–403. Much recent critical work on the life of Jesus

gives the love commands a more ultimate place in his ethic than I do. See Gustaf Aulén, *Jesus in Contemporary Historical Research,* trans. Ingalil H. Hjelm (Philadelphia: Fortress Press, 1976), 17–54. However, the account provided of the moral significance of the love commands differs little from the content chapter twenty-six will derive from the Beatitudes: that one must seek and expect everything from God, utterly submit to his will, give up everything else for his kingdom, and be wholehearted about it; that one must will and do good to everyone, even enemies.

3. See the generally helpful exegetical study: Pheme Perkins, *Love Commands in the New Testament* (New York: Paulist Press, 1982), esp. 10–25 and 104–21. Theological interpretations in this volume, especially those drawn from recent work of Schillebeeckx, must be treated critically.

4. A note in the *New American Bible* to 1 Jn 2.7–11 provides helpful exegesis: "The law of fraternal charity is based on human nature itself and is confirmed by the divine positive command to the Israelites (Lv 19.18). Through Christ, however, a new and higher relationship with neighbor (verses 8, 10) is achieved as a result of the new relationship with the Father: that of sons of God (cf. Jn 1.12) and brothers of Christ (Lk 8.21)."

5. In recent years some Catholic theologians, emphasizing only this side of the problem, have concluded that Christian morality can add no normative content to the general human norms which belong to natural law. See Timothy E. O'Connell, *Principles for a Catholic Morality* (New York: Seabury Press, 1978), 199–208, and 227, note 11; Bruno Schüller, S.J., "Christianity and the New Man: The Moral Dimension—Specificity of Christian Ethics," in *Theology and Discovery: Essays in Honor of Karl Rahner, S.J.,* ed. William J. Kelly, S.J. (Milwaukee: Marquette University Press, 1980), 307–27, ably answered by Richard Roach, S.J., 328–30, and Mary Rousseau, 331–35. Edward Schillebeeckx, *Christ: The Experience of Jesus as Lord,* trans. John Bowden (New York: Seabury Press, 1980), 586–600, admits a distinctive specific normative content for Christian morality, but gratuitously reduces it to the status of an ideal, always subject to situational exceptions—note his treatment of divorce, 592–93. At the same time he supposes that all strictly binding norms or commands are mere conventional impositions of only relative value—note his definition of "paraenesis" (904). Underlying these assertions is a question-begging division which leaves no place for moral norms as truths and so no place for the conception of conscience and natural law so clearly reaffirmed by Vatican II (see 3-B and 7-A).

6. For systematic exegesis which establishes the point made in this paragraph: W. D. Davies, "Ethics in the New Testament," *Interpreter's Dictionary of the Bible,* 2:167–76; Matthew Vellanickal, "Norm of Morality according to the Scripture," *Bible Bhashyam: An Indian Biblical Quarterly,* 7 (1981), 121–46.

7. See William Cardinal Baum, "The Distinctiveness of Catholic Moral Teaching," in *Principles of Catholic Moral Life,* ed. William E. May (Chicago: Franciscan Herald Press, 1980), 3–17. Baum correctly points to a solution to the problem in a Christocentric and sacramental understanding of Christian life: "Revelation, therefore, plays a constitutive part in the formulation of moral teachings and moral theology. The purpose of these teachings is to identify the way of life that is in accordance with the truth of revelation and Redemption" (6). See also Hans Urs von Balthasar, "Nine Theses in Christian Ethics," in *Readings in Moral Theology, No. 2: The Distinctiveness of Christian Ethics,* ed. Charles E. Curran and Richard A. McCormick, S.J. (New York: Paulist Press, 1980), 191–93, where the primacy of Jesus in Christian life is clearly stated. Although he denies at one point (39) that Jesus has given any new specific precept, Edouard Hamel, S.J., *Loi Naturelle et Loi du Christ* (Bruges: Desclée de Brouwer, 1964), 11–43, offers a synthesis of virtually all the elements of a proper solution to the problem, and articulates and cogently criticizes the more important, inadequate positions.

8. Joseph Fuchs, S.J., "Is There a Specifically Christian Morality?" in Curran and McCormick, eds., op. cit., 14–16, recognizes that Christian realities do determine the intentionality, the concrete conduct, and the ways of conduct of those who undertake to live Christian lives. Yet he fails to see that in doing all this, faith specifies moral requirements unknowable without it, requirements whose fulfillment is strictly demanded (and made possible) by Christian love. Fuchs' failure to see the implications of the facts he recognizes is explained by his assumptions about both human acts and moral norms. He fails to see that acts with different intelligible content, even if they are behaviorally the same, are different moral acts. Thus he misses the impact of a Christian "intentionality," displacing it into the mysterious realm of fundamental freedom. He also thinks of moral norms as if they were a limited set of available rules. For this reason he thinks that features of Christian action not related to norms knowable without faith are somehow transmoral. Both of these defects follow from the influence on Fuchs of classical moral theology's legalism and inadequate theory of natural law.

9. Joseph Ratzinger, "Magisterium of the Church, Faith, Morality," in Curran and McCormick, eds., op. cit., 176–78, clearly sees this aspect of the solution and rejects the false notion that Christians have simply adopted whatever conventional morality they encountered.

10. Hans Küng, *On Being a Christian*, trans. Edward Quinn (Garden City, N.Y.: Doubleday, 1976), 552, affirms Jesus as norm: "We might then summarily define Jesus' unique significance for human action in this way: with his word, his actions and his fate, in his impressiveness, audibility, and realizability, he is himself *in person* the *invitation*, the *appeal*, the *challenge*, for the individual and society. As the standard basic model of a view of life and practice of life, without a hint of legalism or casuistry, he provides inviting, obligatory and challenging *examples, significant deeds, orientation standards, exemplary values, model cases.* And by this very fact he impresses and influences, changes and transforms human beings who believe and thus human society." Yet Küng denies that there is any specific normative content to Christian ethics (541–49), for he fails to see that a model is followed only by grasping and willing its intelligibility. In place of Christian norms, Küng accepts (534) a pragmatic principle: "The *morally good* then is what 'works' for man, what permits human life in its individual and social dimensions to succeed and to work out happily in the long run, when freedom and love are engendered." Specific norms are hypothetical imperatives and only relatively valid: "All these precepts and prohibitions are valid therefore, not however for their own sake, but for the sake of realizing the greater good" (537). In practice, Küng holds (540) "the non-evidence, uncertainty and vagueness of the norms and of the pluralism of the ethical systems resulting from this," and so embraces a form of cultural relativism: ". . . we must be content to say briefly that *knowledge of the good, its norms, models, signs, is conveyed to the individual by society*" (541).

11. Dionigi Tettamanzi, "Is There a Christian Ethics?" in Curran and McCormick, eds., op. cit., 20–49, provides a rather helpful summary of the controversy concerning the distinctiveness of Christian ethics; he also states (49–57) most of the essential elements of the solution, although without all the precision one might wish, especially with respect to the distinction and relationship between grace and nature in human moral life. Similarly: Ph. Delhaye, "Questioning the Specificity of Christian Morality," in ibid., 234–69; his critique is especially valuable for pointing out the inadequacies of various partial solutions and the need for a balanced position in accord with the call of Vatican II for renewal in moral theology. The following studies also are helpful: Ferdinando Citterio, "Morale autonoma e fede cristiana: Il dibattito continua," *Scuola cattolica*, 108 (1980), 509–61, esp. 542–61; 109 (1981), 3–29, esp. 26–29; Teodoro López and Gonzalo Aranda, "Lo específico de la Moral cristiana: Valoración de la literatura sobre el tema," *Scripta Theologica*, 7 (1975), 687–767; Bernhard Stoeckle, "Flucht in das Humane? Erwägungen zur Diskussion über die Frage nach dem Proprium christlicher Ethik," *Internationale katholische Zeitschrift (Communio)*, 6 (1977), 312–24; Georges Cottier, O.P., *Humaine raison: Contributions à une éthique du savoir* (Friburg: Editions universitaires, 1980).

12. Charles E. Curran has argued that a distinctively Christian ethic would necessarily involve several false presuppositions, such as exclusion of non-Christians from the order of salvation, a doctrine of total corruption of human nature, a sharp separation of nature and grace, and of creation and redemption. See *Catholic Moral Theology in Dialogue* (Notre Dame, Ind.: Fides Publishers, 1972), 1–23. None of the presuppositions he points to underlies the solution to the problem proposed here. Richard A. McCormick, S.J., *Notes on Moral Theology: 1965 through 1980* (Washington, D.C.: University Press of America, 1981), 299–303, offers several telling criticisms of Curran's position, but himself fails to see how Christian faith can propose specific norms unknowable without it, without introducing anything into the human from without. Like most who have dealt with the question, McCormick fails to see that faith can generate new norms by proposing new kinds of acts; he takes for granted that all the possibilities for human acts are given beforehand.

13. Emphasis on this truth, combined with a fundamentally sound understanding of the specificity of Christian ethics, tends to cloud the issue concerning specific norms. See, for example, Yves Congar, O.P., "Réflexion et Propos sur l'Originalité d'Une Ethique Chrétienne," in *In Libertatem Vocati Estis*, ed. H. Boelaars and R. Tremblay (Rome: Academia Alfonsiana, 1977), 31–40. However, truth of a practical order remains when it is spontaneously fulfilled, and can be articulated with precision (see 26-D–K).

14. See S. González, S.J., *De gratia*, in *Sacrae Theologiae Summa*, ed. 4, vol. 3 (Madrid: B.A.C., 1961), 603 (tr. III, a. 196).

15. See Gerhard Trenkler, "Grace," in *Encyclopedia of Biblical Theology*, 340–44; E. M. Burke, "Grace," in *New Catholic Encyclopedia*, 6:658–72.

16. Concerning actual grace: Michael Schmaus, *Dogma*, vol. 6, *Justification and the Last Things* (Kansas City: Sheed and Ward, 1977), 9–41; Henri Rondet, S.J., *The Grace of Christ: A Brief History of the Theology of Grace* (Westminster, Md.: Newman Press, 1967), 313–64. While the answer to this question differs from St. Thomas by denying the distinction he makes between sanctifying grace and charity, as well as in other ways, the present view agrees with him in considering God's own causality, not something created, as the central reality of actual grace: *S.t.*, 1–2, q. 111, a. 2. For a textual analysis of St. Thomas' theology of grace, which reveals its complexity and stages of development, and clearly differentiates it from subsequent competing theological developments: Bernard J. F. Lonergan, S.J., *Grace and Freedom: Operative Grace in the Thought of St. Thomas Aquinas*, ed. J. Patout Burns (New York: Herder and Herder, 1971), 21–40 and 139–45. A treatment of actual grace in some ways like mine, yet one with which I cannot wholly agree: Charles R. Meyer, *A Contemporary Theology of Grace* (Staten Island, N.Y.: Alba House, 1971), 151–81.

17. On this point and the subject of this appendix as a whole: Ignace de la Potterie, S.J., and Stanislaus Lyonnet, S.J., *The Christian Lives by the Spirit* (Staten Island, N.Y.: Alba House, 1971), 145–74, esp. 162–63.

18. For a statement and critique of this mistaken move, which one finds in Karl Rahner and others, see John Finnis, "The Natural Law, Objective Morality, and Vatican II," in May, ed., op. cit., 139–42.

19. Thus, Vatican II teaches that Jesus "fully reveals man to man himself" (GS 22). For a commentary on this text, see John Paul II, *Redemptor hominis*, 71 *AAS* (1979) 271–72, 274; *The Papal Encyclicals*, 278.22 and 25.

CHAPTER TWENTY-SIX

MODES OF CHRISTIAN RESPONSE

Introduction

Morally good actions always conform to a will toward integral human fulfillment (7-F). This first principle of morality is implemented by the modes of responsibility articulated in chapter eight; these exclude ways of willing which fall short of this ideal. Integral human fulfillment is more than an ideal, for it will be realized in the fulfillment of all things in Jesus (19-B). Thus, in the light of faith, the first principle of Christian morality emerges: To will those and only those possibilities which contribute to the integral human fulfillment being realized in the fulfillment of all things in Jesus.

In the fallen world one can live a life fully in accord with this Christian standard only by cooperating with Jesus in his redemptive work. To make one's choices fit into such a life, the modes of responsibility must be transformed in the light of faith into modes of Christian response to God's gifts. The impetus of charity makes the modes of Christian response more than requirements for morally good action; in the Christian, living by the Spirit, they are true dynamic tendencies to respond to God's gifts with a life like that of Jesus.

We have seen why the transformation of the modes of responsibility will be found exemplified in Jesus' life and explained in his teaching (25-F). The present chapter proposes to show how this is so by identifying and clarifying these modes of Christian response, which correspond to the eight Beatitudes.

Question A: How are the modes of Christian response related to the Beatitudes?

1. Along with obvious differences, there also are similarities between the role of the Ten Commandments in the Old Testament and that of the Beatitudes in the New. As God gives the Ten Commandments to Moses, and then the rest of the law is unfolded from them, so Jesus gives the Beatitudes to his followers, and then the rest of the moral implications of the new covenant are unfolded. The Beatitudes provide a properly Christian moral framework. Although their relationship to the rest of the moral content of faith has never been clarified in detail, they have had an important place in moral instruction throughout Christian history. These are extrinsic, but not insignificant, reasons for taking the Beatitudes as organizing principles in analyzing Christian norms and virtues.

2. Of greater importance is a theological consideration. Although the New Testament provides no detailed moral code, one can expect to find in Jesus' teaching and example the basic guidance needed for Christian life (25-F). St. Matthew's Gospel is in a special way the New Testament book of moral teaching.[1] The Sermon on the Mount is the primary synthesis of such teaching, and the Beatitudes are placed at the start of this synthesis (see *S.t.,* 1–2, q. 108, a. 3). Hence, it is reasonable to suppose that the Beatitudes express specifically Christian moral principles.[2]

The beatitude form is found in many other places in the Old and New Testaments. Beatitudes are especially common in the wisdom literature (see, e.g., Sir 25.7–11). Psalms begins with a beatitude: Happy the person who follows the law of the Lord, not the way of sinners (see Ps 1.1–2). There are a number of beatitudes scattered throughout the Gospels (see, e.g., Mt 16.17; Lk 1.45; Jn 20.29) and several in Revelation (see 14.13; 16.15; 19.9; 22.7, 14).

The Beatitudes with which we shall be concerned are the eight stated at the beginning of the Sermon on the Mount (see Mt 5.3–10). Some commentators believe they find a ninth (in Mt 5.11–12), but sound scholars agree with the tradition in regarding these verses as an expansion of the eighth Beatitude, not as an additional one.[3] Luke places the sermon on a plain and has four beatitudes together with four corresponding woes (see Lk 6.20–26). Luke's version will not be considered here.

It is significant that in his expansion on the ancient creeds, the Credo of the People of God, Paul VI mentions the Beatitudes in his summary of Jesus' teaching. Our Lord proclaimed and established the kingdom, gave us the new commandment to love one another as he loves, and "taught us the way of the Beatitudes of the gospel: poverty in spirit, meekness, suffering borne with patience, thirst after justice, mercy, purity of heart, will for peace, persecution suffered for justice sake."[4] Thus the Pope suggests that the Beatitudes be taken as the model summary of the specifically Christian content of Jesus' moral teaching.

3. Reflection on the Beatitudes confirms this view. The Beatitudes propose norms of Christian life which are clearly more specific than the first principle but do not deal with definite kinds of acts (as, for example, the Ten Commandments do). **In other words, they are Christian moral principles at a level, midway between the general and the particular, corresponding to that of the modes of responsibility. Thus, the Beatitudes express, in language suited to the audience, the modes of Christian response, which transform the modes of responsibility.**[5]

4. The beatitude formula ("Blessed are . . .") is not so much a prayer as a declaration of fact. Beatitudes are propositions asserted as true. They state conditions under which people will share in or be fulfilled by goods, and they describe the goods in question. Thus they state the connection between certain dispositions or actions and the fulfillments to which these lead. Since those who do good merit the fulfillment in which their good action is a participation, the beatitude formula is suited to express the blessing enjoyed by those whose actions are meritorious inasmuch as their attitudes are pleasing responses to God's gifts (see *S.t.,* 1–2, q. 69, a. 1; q. 114, aa. 1, 4, 10).[6]

5. The Beatitudes of the Sermon on the Mount express principles of Christian moral life as blessings. This is so because these modes of Christian response

transform the modes of responsibility. The latter limit the inclinations of one's flesh; the former rejoice in the inclinations of a mind led by the Spirit (see Rom 7.22–8.9). The latter forbid what does not conform to a will toward the ideal of integral human fulfillment; the former commend what is characteristic of a will, enlivened by charity, hoping confidently for the reality of the fulfillment of all things in Jesus. Still, the modes of Christian response are like the modes of responsibility in proposing eight distinct conditions met by a person whose life is oriented toward true human fulfillment.[7]

For the poor in spirit and the persecuted, the blessing is the kingdom of God; for the sorrowing, it is consolation; for peacemakers, being called children of God; and so forth. Most commentators, ancient and modern, agree that these are all the same reality, conceptualized in a way proportionate to each of the dispositions whose fulfillment is promised. There is some discussion whether the promised blessing in every case is eschatological. Since there is considerable continuity between Christian life in this world and heaven, especially with respect to goods (34-E), one can consider the blessings mentioned in the Beatitudes to pertain both to this life and to life in the fully realized kingdom.

6. As Matthew's account of Jesus' ministry begins with Beatitudes proclaiming the blessings enjoyed by his followers, it ends with woes proclaiming the doom which awaits his adversaries, the scribes and Pharisees. Just as his apparently wretched followers are really fortunate, his apparently flourishing adversaries are really miserable. Thus, both Beatitudes and woes express the true state of those to whom they are addressed.[8] Yet the woes correspond only imperfectly to the Beatitudes. While there is only one way to be good, there are many ways to be bad, and Jesus highlights only one style of life opposed to his. Still, the woes correspond to the Beatitudes sufficiently that reflection on the former will help to clarify the meaning of the latter.

Question B: How are the modes of Christian response related to the Christian moral virtues?

1. Unlike passages in which Jesus is portrayed as calling for faith or articulating a love command, the Sermon on the Mount presupposes these principles, for here Jesus is described as instructing his own disciples concerning the way of life they have undertaken in following him. As question A explained, the Beatitudes articulate eight distinct modes of Christian response. These are not specific actions but ways of acting—or, better, distinct aspects of the unique way of Jesus. **The characteristics for which disciples are called "blessed"—such as poverty of spirit and mercy—are traits of a Christian's character. In other words, they are Christian virtues.**

2. Virtues are aspects of the character of a good person (7-H). A good person's character is his or her whole self integrated around a set of upright commitments. These commitments are upright because they fulfill true moral norms. Thus, virtues embody the skeleton of moral truth in the flesh and blood of a good life.

3. The distinctive norms of Christian morality are not a set of requirements added from without to the conditions one must fulfill to live a good human life

(25-E). On the contrary, Christian norms direct one to those humanly good options which one must accept if one is to live uprightly in the fallen world. In other words, Christian norms specify the requirements of moral truth in accord with the actual situation of humankind fallen and redeemed.

4. Any analytic treatment of virtues unavoidably seems to suggest that the virtuous character is less an organic unit than is the case. But since a morally good person is not split in two, we need not suppose that there are two sets of virtues in the Christian, one at the natural level and the other at the supernatural level. Christian virtues simply specify common human virtues further, thus making them genuine virtues in the present, fallen and redeemed, human situation. **Hence, every true virtue present in a Christian will include the characteristically Christian way of being a morally good person.**

Many sound Catholic theologians discuss human and Christian moral virtues. All agree that these are dispositions to morally good acts, and that Christian moral virtues dispose one to acts which are transformed by charity. Beyond these basic propositions, there is little agreement about human and Christian moral virtues, and no explicit, authoritative Church teaching on the subject. What follows clarifies the virtues within the framework of the assumptions of the present work.[9]

Choices are determinations of the self (2-E). They are spiritual entities. Of themselves, they endure. Some choices are more comprehensive than others, in the sense that they extend to a larger part of one's life. Among the more comprehensive choices are commitments, by which one settles one's relationships with some other person or persons and with some one or more basic human goods. The fundamental commitment of Christian life is the act of faith, by which one commits oneself to cooperate in the redemptive, community-forming act of Jesus (16-G). The commitments of one's personal vocation, by which one forms one's unique, Christian identity, give personal determinacy to one's act of faith (23-E).

The personal identity established by one's commitments is an enduring disposition to morally good or bad acts. Insofar as it is a disposition to morally good acts, it is virtue. Thus, the essence of the moral virtue of Jesus is his disposition to live his life in fulfillment of his basic commitment and unique personal vocation. The essence of Christian moral virtue is the disposition to live one's Christian life in accord with faith by carrying out one's personal vocation.

5. As question A explained, the Christian modes of response transform the modes of responsibility, inasmuch as the former incline one toward fulfillment in Jesus, whereas the latter only articulate requirements which must be met if an upright will is to follow reason against wayward inclination. In other words, in the modes of Christian response, the normative principles which can be expressed in propositions already are embraced by a Christian's will and at least somewhat embodied in his or her character.

6. To see why this is so, it is helpful to recall how Christian norms become known by adults who are converted to the faith. Such a person first discovers the Christian way of life as a happy solution to the seemingly hopeless human situation. The norms of Christian morality are accepted as true inasmuch as they are part of the gospel accepted in faith. Faith is a fundamental option, given with the Christian love which both motivates faith and is accepted by it. Thus, one who understands and assents to Christian moral norms already has a precommitment to

live by them. Moreover, except for the abnormal condition of a Christian living in mortal sin, charity impels those who accept Christian standards to fulfill them by the Spirit's power.

7. Thus, the integral self of a Christian, formed by divine love, is marked by dispositions which lead to a Christian fulfillment of the human modes of responsibility. Insofar as any virtue is perfected, the norm it embodies ordinarily is fulfilled without its coming to consciousness as a demand opposed to inclination. This is why Christians are liberated from the law, including the moral law insofar as it makes demands on the self. People who love God perfectly may do as they please, for nothing will please them except doing God's will.

8. Because Christian modes of response are more specific than the common modes of responsibility and their corresponding virtues, one finds in Christians states of character which are vicious only by specifically Christian standards. Although the same dispositions might not appear particularly praiseworthy by common human standards, they would not be judged vicious.

For example, by the common human standard of impartiality, those who are careful to be perfectly fair with others meet the norm of impartiality, although they are equally exacting in making certain that their own rights are fully respected by others. To be as precise in requiring and obtaining what one ought to have as one is in giving others their due in no way violates the requirement of impartiality. A person who regularly behaved in such a fashion would neither be praised for kindness and generosity nor criticized for any significant moral failing.

However, as question H will explain, the Christian specification of the mode of responsibility which requires impartiality transforms it into the Christian mode of response which is marked by mercy or loving-kindness toward others. This mode of response demands that one meet others more than half way. One must do one's duty and go beyond it. Hence, Christians who regularly insist on their rights, simply because these are their rights (not because insistence in a particular case is necessary to fulfill some commitment), fall short of the relevant Christian mode of response. This shortcoming includes the sort of thing one might call "stinginess" or "niggardliness." This is not a humanly admirable quality, but neither is it a vice by common human standards as long as it does not lead to unfairness of some sort.

9. We must therefore speak, somewhat paradoxically, of "Christian vices." These are dispositions incompatible with specifically Christian modes of response but not with the common human modes of responsibility and virtues. Christian vices are less drastically opposed to the Christian modes of response than common human vices (for example, stinginess is less opposed to Christian compassion than injustice is). But it does not follow that such vices are mere imperfections, unattractive but morally acceptable.

The Christian vices appear to lack appropriate names which fit them precisely, although a variety of negative traits can be mentioned in the area of each of the modes of Christian response which seem to meet the notion of a Christian vice. This difficulty ought not to prevent one from attempting to understand these traits with precision. Such understanding is likely to be especially valuable for the examination of conscience of persons who are avoiding grave sins (which usually violate common requirements of the modes of responsibility) and are striving for the holiness to which every Christian is summoned (see Mt 5.48; LG 40, 42).

Question C: How are the modes of Christian response related to the gifts of the Holy Spirit?

1. The gifts of the Holy Spirit belong to the messianic endowment of Jesus (see *S.t.*, 1–2, q. 68). During his earthly life he was filled with the Spirit (see Lk 4.1) and throughout his ministry accompanied by the Spirit. He acted by the power of the Spirit (see Lk 4.14) and, finally, through the Spirit offered himself to God (see Heb 9.14). For us to be children of God means receiving the Spirit and, like Jesus, being led by the Spirit (see Rom 8.14–16; Gal 5.25).

The Holy Spirit himself is the primary gift to Christians; sent by Jesus and the Father, he is God's loving gift of himself (see LG 39–40). The Spirit's first gift distinct from himself is that love by which sinful human persons are inwardly transformed into loving children of God (see Rom 5.5; 8.14–16; LG 40 and 42). The Spirit is not communicated to individual Christians in their separateness, as if to be a private possession. Rather, he is the Spirit of Jesus shared with his Church, and received by each member of the Church (see LG 7).

It follows that the effects of redemption accomplished by the Spirit primarily are gifts to the Church. Hence, St. Paul teaches that the one Spirit gives many gifts, each gift appropriate to the member of Jesus to whom it is given for the building up of the one body, the Church (see 1 Cor 12). However, the primary and greatest gift is that charity by which the entire body and all of its functions become an integrated whole, and every good work, every fruit of God's redeeming love manifested in Jesus, is brought to fulfillment (see 1 Cor 13).

2. The Fathers and Doctors of the Church have thus taught that every Christian shares in the endowment of the Spirit promised in Isaiah to the Messiah: "And the Spirit of the Lord shall rest upon him, the spirit of wisdom and understanding, the spirit of counsel and might, the spirit of knowledge and the fear of the Lord" (Is 11.2). Until recently, translations generally used in the Church have mistakenly added a seventh "spirit," piety. These seven aspects of the messianic endowment have been called, in a special sense, the "gifts of the Holy Spirit."[10]

3. St. Thomas Aquinas, following St. Augustine, closely relates the Beatitudes to the gifts of the Holy Spirit. He considers that the Beatitudes express the acts of Christians in accordance with the gifts by which lesser goods are set aside, obstacles overcome, and heavenly fulfillment attained. On this analysis, the gifts correspond to the first seven of the eight Beatitudes (see *S.t.*, 1–2, q. 69, aa. 1, 3). The view of Augustine and Thomas on this point is accepted here.

4. Thomas also holds, however, that the gifts are distinct from Christian virtues, since virtues dispose one to act by reason enlightened by faith; while gifts dispose one to be moved by the Spirit rather than act humanly (see *S.t.*, 1–2, q. 68, a. 1). Not all Catholic theologians agree with Thomas in making this distinction, and the Church has not settled the issue.[11] It would seem, however, that his position on this point is unsatisfactory.

5. The difficulty with Thomas' account is in the notion that human powers are actuated by the gifts of the Holy Spirit in a manner which reason enlightened by faith and human love enlivened by charity cannot account for. Thomas seems to admit an element of divine activity into the process of human action and to treat it as a principle on the same level with the principles of human action. (If it were not

on the same level, it would not be an alternative to the movement of reason.) This appears to be a case of commingling.

6. Therefore, it seems better to link the gifts of the Holy Spirit more closely with the specifically Christian virtues. These virtues are already transformed by faith and charity. They might be regarded as virtues to the extent that they are dispositions to human acts, though of a specifically Christian sort, and as gifts insofar as their relationship to faith enlivened by charity makes them specifically Christian. **Or, and perhaps preferably, the gifts of the Holy Spirit might be identified with charity considered precisely insofar as it is the gift of the Holy Spirit which transforms the moral requirements articulated in the modes of responsibility into the characteristically Christian inclinations (or modes of response) proclaimed "blessed" in the Beatitudes.**

St. Thomas summarizes the great diversity of theological opinion up to his time concerning the gifts. Some did not distinguish the gifts from virtues, in particular from the specifically Christian virtues by which one is conformed to Jesus. The common view was that the gifts are like virtues at least in being enduring dispositions and in having relevance for human acts.

Thomas' position is that the Christian needs the gifts as lasting dispositions distinct from the virtues. Human persons are naturally disposed to act according to reason, and the virtues perfect this disposition. But as a child of God, the Christian needs to be disposed to be divinely moved. The gifts are created qualities made present in the soul together with charity (and never apart from it) which provide an inherent receptiveness to divine leading, so that the Christian led by the Spirit is inwardly drawn, not violently dragged (see *S.t.*, 1–2, q. 68, aa. 1, 3). In providing this explanation, Thomas regards movement by reason and by the Spirit as alternatives, thus suggesting that the gifts of the Spirit account for actuations of the Christian's human powers which have no adequate natural principle (see *S.t.*, 1–2, q. 68, a. 2; cf. a. 1, ad 3, 4).[12]

It is true that Christian life, insofar as it is lived not only according to human nature but also according to a share in divine nature, is a participation in the activity of the Holy Spirit. It also is true, of course, that divine causality is presupposed by every actuation of human powers, and that such an actuation, if salvific, is caused by grace, which may be attributed to the Holy Spirit. Moreover, Christian life presupposes faith and is formed by it, and living faith has a certitude and force it could not have were it not motivated by charity. The same is true of all virtuous acts which make up the life of faith. Also, the human modes of responsibility and virtues are specified in the Christian to become modes of Christian response, and this transformation is accounted for by charity, which is the gift of the Spirit.

However, Thomas' position should not be accepted without qualification. The opposition he sets up between being moved by reason and by the inspiration of the Spirit appears to be a mistake, based upon commingling. If so, there are no nonmiraculous actuations of human powers which cannot be accounted for by the relevant human principles as these are affected and transformed by living faith.

Someone might object that this position is incompatible with Christian experience, which testifies to many sorts of acts which spontaneously arise without free choice (for example, the experience of loving knowledge in contemplative prayer) and also some sorts of acts which seem to elude rational principles (for example, some charismatic behavior experienced more as a happening than a doing, and undergone without understanding by the person who is subject to it).

However, such phenomena do not falsify the view defended here. As chapter nine explained, many human acts proceed by spontaneous willing, without free choice. There also are spontaneous acts of intellect which presuppose no willing at all. In the context of living faith, spontaneous acts of these sorts are possible. As effortless and not chosen (or even, in some cases, not willed at all), such acts will seem in a special sense to be gifts, to be "infused contemplation." Moreover, charity not only affects the mind but also transforms the whole person. Hence, a Christian might at times experience behavior altogether lacking a rational principle (and so not a human act) which is closely integrated with Christian life—for example, by being connected with acts of prayer and worship.

Question D: What mode of Christian response corresponds to the first Beatitude: "Blessed are the poor in spirit, for theirs is the kingdom of heaven" (Mt 5.3)?

1. People whose primary love is charity are disposed to divine goodness before all else. **Perceiving God's goodness as real quite apart from their own effort and action, they understand that their undertakings and achievements are only a share, given freely and generously by God, in his fullness.** Thus, the basic Christian mode of response is to *expect and accept all good, including the good fruits of one's own work, as God's gift.* This way of acting is faith's specification and charity's fulfillment of the first mode of responsibility: *One should not be deterred by felt inertia from acting for intelligible goods.*

"Poverty in spirit" was most often understood by the Fathers, and is still understood by many scholars, to mean humility of mind and will, which disposes one to recognize one's need for God's gifts, as a poor person is aware of his or her need; to ask for them without being deterred by the implied acknowledgement of one's lowly status and dependence; and to be grateful, as a self-confident and proud person cannot be, for everything received.[13]

In the fallen human condition, the lack of confidence that action for good will make much difference is the primary obstacle to fulfillment of the first mode of responsibility. An important aspect of the discouraging situation is that one realizes that even if one does act for good, others are unlikely to do so; hence, the good which might be achieved with their cooperation and cannot be achieved without it will hardly be realized no matter how hard one tries. Even before Jesus, divine revelation deepens the mode of responsibility and provides some hope, which encourages people to pursue the good (8-A).

However, many people who lack humility are energetic and ambitious. How do they manage to display such dispositions? The answer usually is that they are motivated by a desire for personal satisfaction or some particular goal. These motives are at least dangerous; they are likely to lead to unfairness, excessive attachment, and the expedient use of questionable methods; in extreme cases the energetic and ambitious person becomes a zealot or a fanatic. So in this fallen world the merely lazy person does not seem vicious; most of the actual alternatives to laziness are worse. The energetic often are oppressors.

Christian revelation, accepted with living faith, changes this prospect. One has grounds for a much greater hope, one which transcends death and all evil. Good acts will last forever. But there is a point in pursuing goods in this way only if one avoids all the usual, questionable motives for doing so, for the heavenly fulfillment certainly will not be available unless one is fair to others, detached, and unwilling to use bad means. The success of one's undertakings is guaranteed, instead, by divine power and love. God will give success as he did to Jesus by raising him from the dead.

2. A person who responds in this way will not violate the first mode of responsibility; he or she will not be a lazy and unprofitable servant but an industrious and diligent one. As a servant, however, the Christian can be energetic without falling into the vices which often mark a person of energetic disposition: devoted to the coming of the kingdom without zealotry and fanaticism, counting on God for success and crediting successes to him.

3. **The virtuous disposition present in this mode of Christian response is most often called "humility."** Childlike simplicity, which recognizes need, asks, and willingly receives, is an aspect of humility. So is thankfulness, the basic Christian attitude of gratitude, for in humility one recognizes that everything good comes from God and one's whole life must be a eucharistic return to him of all he has given. The Christian vice opposed to humility is called "pride." However, the Christian vice referred to by "pride" must not be identified with haughtiness nor limited to the status seeking by which it is manifested toward others. It is best understood as Pelagian self-reliance, the presumptuous assertion of autonomy, and a disposition of ingratitude toward God.

4. In excoriating the scribes and Pharisees, Jesus prefaces a series of woes with criticism of their various forms of status seeking, expressions of their pride, and concludes: "Whoever exalts himself will be humbled, and whoever humbles himself will be exalted" (Mt 23.12). The poor in spirit do not seek status. They recognize this as a delusory activity which falsifies a Christian's relationship to God and other human beings.

5. The Magnificat, Mary's triumphant song of fulfillment, illustrates Christian humility. God has looked upon his lowly handmaid and lifted her up; thus, "All generations will call me blessed; for he who is mighty has done great things for me" (Lk 1.48–49). Paul similarly expresses Christian humility in declaring that he is what he is by God's grace, which has not been fruitless (1 Cor 15.10).

6. According to St. Augustine, the gift of the Spirit corresponding to the first Beatitude is fear of the Lord: that is, childlike reverence toward him.[14] St. Thomas teaches that this fear is related to the virtue of hope, for by it we are open to the Spirit and unwilling to withdraw ourselves from the help of him on whom we totally and utterly depend (see *S.t.*, 2–2, q. 19, aa. 1, 9).

Humility is a virtue praised throughout the Bible. Jacob exemplifies it in his recognition of his own unworthiness, his dependence upon God, and God's generous gifts (see Gn 32.8–13). In the wisdom literature and prophetic writings of the Old Testament, the poor and oppressed are seen to stand in special need of God's intervention. Incapable of providing for themselves, they have, for the most part, been abandoned by the rich and powerful. God's intervention is promised repeatedly, and all who suffer injustice look forward to the day of salvation (see Ps 72; Is 11.4). This hope at least partly explains the affinity in the New Testament between the gospel and the poor, weak, afflicted, and outcast—including sinners who recognize themselves to be such. All these persons realize their need for God's intervention, and so they are ready to receive the gospel of Jesus. Thus, his message is especially directed to them (see Mt 11.5; Lk 4.18–21).[15]

There are intrinsic, even if not absolutely necessary, connections between wealth and pride, poverty and humility. The wealthy can afford to be proud. Their resources give them power, and power gives a sense of control and independence. But the seer tells the wealthy: "You say, I am rich, I have prospered, and I need nothing; not knowing that you are wretched, pitiable, poor, blind, and naked" (Rv 3.17). When St. Paul teaches a lesson in humility, he stresses that those to whom he writes have nothing they have not received, and so they have nothing to boast about, yet they are utterly complacent because, as he says ironically, "Already you have become rich!" (1 Cor 4.8). The poor, by contrast, realize their own powerlessness. Thus the poor are disposed to be humble—poor in spirit as well as in material things; they are ready to accept the gift of the kingdom. Since this gift is given freely to those open to it, the poor are blessed, for the kingdom is theirs (see Lk 6.20).

Since humility is characteristic of those who are poor, who are lowly—that is, in the lower stratum of society—the voluntary lowering of oneself in status suggests an understanding that wealth and superiority really are poverty and weakness. To lower oneself is a condition of or an expression of making oneself open and receptive, and receptivity is a condition of fulfillment by God's gifts. Hence, those who humble themselves are exalted.

This feature of humility—self-abasement—has been stressed so much in Christian thought that what is even more central, namely the disposition of receptivity toward God, often is overlooked. This is unfortunate, since some Christian preaching and catechetics encourages self-abasement as if it were a value in itself, whereas it is only morally significant if it means accepting one's total dependence upon God (see *S.t.*, 2–2, q. 161, aa. 2–3).

The centurion who realizes his unworthiness that Jesus enter his home shows humility not by this realization alone but by his recognition of his need for help: "Only say the word, and my servant will be healed" (Mt 8.8). The passage in which Paul speaks of Jesus' self-emptying, so that he might humble himself to the extent of accepting death, makes the point that this was the way to God's exalting act; by emptying himself Jesus put himself in position to be made Lord (see Phil 2.6–11). From this Paul draws the conclusion: "God is at work in you, both to will and to work for his good pleasure" (Phil 2.13). The point is the same in Paul's account of his humiliating and mysterious thorn in the flesh. It led him to beg relief, and his prayer was answered with the assurance: "My grace is sufficient for you, for my power is made perfect in weakness" (2 Cor 12.9). Paul adds that he boasts of his weakness, so that the power of Christ might rest on him.

Jesus teaches that a childlike attitude of humility is a necessary condition for entering the kingdom. The children are to be welcomed, for the kingdom belongs to them, since only those who accept God's reign like little children can share in it (see Mt 19.13–15; Mk 10.13–16; Lk 18.15–17). The wise and prudent, prophets and kings, desired the revelation of God in Jesus, but it was hidden from them. It is reserved for mere children and for the humble disciples of Jesus; it comes as a gift from the Father through him (see Mt 11.25–27; Lk 10.21–22).

When the apostles begin to worry about status, Jesus warns them that they must become as children and be prepared to serve children and the childlike (see Mt 18.1–5; Mk 9.33–37; Lk 9.46–48). Goods are attained only by being accepted as God's gifts, and they can be passed on only to others who are similarly willing to accept them.

The inculcation of humility as a necessary disposition of Christian life, not as an optional extra, is a standard part of New Testament catechesis (see Rom 12.16; 1 Cor 13.4; Eph 4.1–2; Col 3.12; Jas 4.6, 10). Christians are urged to be eager for the milk of the Spirit like newborn babes (see 1 Pt 2.2), and to be humble toward one another (see 1 Pt 3.8; 5.5).

Question E: What mode of Christian response corresponds
to the second (or third) Beatitude:
"Blessed are the meek,
for they shall inherit the earth" (Mt 5.5)?[16]

1. People whose primary love is charity are disposed to divine goodness above all else. **But God's goodness is real and abundant enough to satisfy everyone, and one's efforts to participate in it can be submissive to his universal, salvific plan and will without any loss or delay to one's personal fulfillment.** Thus the second mode of Christian response is to *accept one's limited role in the Body of Christ and fulfill it.* This way of acting is faith's specification and charity's fulfillment of the second mode of responsibility: *One should not be pressed by enthusiasm or impatience to act individualistically for intelligible goods.*

In the fallen human condition, the apparent impossibility of genuine community makes openness to community seem pointless. If one tries to allow for the participation of others, one is likely to find them sluggards, or willing to cooperate only as long as it is in their own interest, or unfaithful to responsibilities they accept. One who strives to share collaboratively in the pursuit of goods is doomed to many disappointments. The establishment of the covenant provided an opportunity for an obedient faith, within whose framework this mode of responsibility could to some extent be fulfilled (8-B).

However, many who lack meekness are quite submissive to social requirements; they seem to fulfill this mode of responsibility. How do they come to show such a disposition? The usual answers are either that they are too lazy to exercise personal initiative or that they find the security and support of others the easiest way to realize most of their own interests. These motives for docility are questionable; they are likely to lead people to cooperate in doing things they know to be wrong. At best, they reduce community to an arrangement in which the members use one another.

The acceptance of salvation through Jesus by living faith transforms this situation. By this acceptance, one enters into a genuine fellowship, in which integral human fulfillment is being achieved. Of course, faith demands both energetic, apostolic dedication and a life less directed toward one's own satisfaction than toward the building up of the Church. One who accepts a place in this fellowship cannot expect to be a well-rounded person, a self-fulfilling individualist, or a superstar. However, one can be confident that one's team spirit will contribute to the fulfillment of God's redemptive plan. One accepts the role of a servant of the body of Jesus, and personal fulfillment is found in that role.

2. **The virtuous disposition present in this mode of Christian response can be called "Christian dedication." The meek person recognizes his or her personal vocation, knows its limits, sees in it God's will, and accepts it with resignation and love.** Such persons accept their individual and limited roles in the cooperative work of redemption and dedicate their lives to fulfilling these roles. Opposed to dedication are lukewarmness and minimalism. People with these dispositions are not prepared to put their whole lives at the service of the redemptive work and are discontented with their lot in life.

3. The Beatitude's promise—of the inheritance of the land—is the promise of the covenant. Thus this blessing is the fulfillment of God's people as a community. Individually, the meek lack power, but they are docilely submissive to God.

Performing the service God asks of them, they will share in the fellowship of the kingdom, where the promise of empowerment will be fulfilled superabundantly.[17] To serve Jesus is to reign.

4. Excoriating the scribes and Pharisees, Jesus says: "You shut the kingdom of heaven against men; for you neither enter yourselves, nor allow those who would enter to go in" (Mt 23.13). Having some power, the scribes and Pharisees lack the meekness to serve God in the way required to lead the whole of Israel into the kingdom. Instead, they lock the door (the gate which Jesus is) and take away the key (knowledge of him) (see Lk 11.52; Jn 10.9; 14.6). They bar the people from their inheritance.

5. Jesus' role is one of complete submission to the Father and also of full cooperation with him (see Jn 5.19–30). Jesus says nothing on his own and acts in the role of servant (see Jn 12.49; 13.12–17), even though he is entitled to the name of the Lord: "I am" (Jn 8.58). Neither Jesus nor the Holy Spirit operates autonomously or individualistically (see Jn 14.24; 16.13). They work in a perfect communion of love with the Father.

6. Here is the characteristic most proper to Christian dedication. Going beyond the obedience of the Old Testament, which for all its nobility still involved an element of servitude, the meekness of the New Testament transcends servility and disposes those who share in divine community: "You are my friends if you do what I command you. No longer do I call you servants" (Jn 15.14–15). Moreover, Christian dedication is directed primarily to the fulfillment of one's personal vocation, not, as was the case with the pious Jew, to the observance of a common and burdensome law.[18]

7. According to St. Augustine, the gift of the Holy Spirit corresponding to the second Beatitude is piety or godliness: "Godliness corresponds to the meek, for he who seeks in a godly frame of mind honors Holy Scripture and does not find fault with what as yet he does not understand, and therefore he does not oppose it— which is to be meek."[19] St. Thomas, pointing out that by piety one has an attitude of filial reverence and dutifulness toward God as Father, cites St. Paul: "You did not receive the spirit of slavery to fall back into fear, but you have received the spirit of sonship. When we cry, 'Abba! Father!' it is the Spirit himself bearing witness with our spirit that we are children of God" (Rom 8.15–16; *S.t.*, 2–2, q. 121, a. 1).

The Beatitude concerning the meek is drawn from the Old Testament. It is a promise that those who follow the Lord and trust in him will not lose out. They need not be upset with the apparent success of evildoers (Ps 37.8–11). In English "meek" connotes a lack of irritability; a hot-tempered person hardly would be called "meek." While this quality is not central to the scriptural concept, neither is it absent. How does it fit in with Christian dedication?

One who accepts and strives to fulfill his or her personal vocation inevitably encounters much frustration. Frustration naturally causes anger. However, a dedicated person recognizes that frustration is an essential part of any Christian vocation, and so accepts it with resignation. Resignation—the acceptance of frustration as part of God's will for oneself— is calming. Hence, lack of irritability is an essential, although secondary, element in Christian dedication and meekness.

But what is more central is confidence in God to put right the social wrongs which would arouse vexation and a tendency to violent rebelliousness. This core of meekness is illustrated in Moses, who is said to be the meekest man in the world, because he accepts and fulfills the role God assigns him (see Nm 12.3).

Meekness is characteristic of Jesus. Although sinless, he accepts baptism to fulfill his role perfectly (see Mt 3.15). John the Baptist also accepts his limited role in the plan of salvation and is ready to yield prominence to Jesus when the time comes (see Mt 3.11; Mk 1.7; Lk 3.16; Jn 3.28–30). When he enters Jerusalem for the last time, Jesus comes not as the warrior-king, but as a meek leader responding to God's redemptive love (see Is 62.11; Zec 9.9; Mt 21.4–5).

Most significant is the passage in which Jesus presents himself as an example: "Come to me, all who labor and are heavy laden, and I will give you rest. Take my yoke upon you, and learn from me; for I am gentle [meek] and lowly in heart, and you will find rest for your souls. For my yoke is easy, and my burden is light" (Mt 11.28–30). Those tired of the struggle to do good in a fallen world are promised relief when they join with Jesus and submit to his yoke. It is light because it is accepted without resistance in his dedicated carrying out of the Father's will.

Meekness is commended by name in a number of places in the catechetical instructions contained in the Epistles (see Gal 5.23; Eph 4.2; Col 3.12; 2 Tm 2.25; Ti 3.2; Jas 1.21; 3.13). More important than these references is the theme of mutual responsibility, love, and submission, which runs through the social catechesis (see, e.g., Eph 5.22–6.9; Col 3.18–4.1; 1 Pt 2.13–3.8). One who has entered into Jesus fulfills his or her role with a dedication which precludes an individualistic approach to life.

Question F: What mode of Christian response corresponds to the third (or second) Beatitude: "Blessed are those who mourn, for they shall be comforted" (Mt 5.4)?

1. The hearts of people whose primary love is charity are fixed upon God. Every other good is pursued only in the context of the basic relationship of friendship with God. **Disposed to goodness itself, they are freed from the pursuit of particular goods except insofar as these contribute to the fulfillment of everything in Jesus.** Thus the third mode of Christian response is to *put aside or avoid everything which is not necessary or useful in the fulfillment of one's personal vocation.* This way of acting is faith's specification and charity's fulfillment of the third mode of responsibility: *One should not choose to satisfy an emotional desire except as part of one's pursuit and/or attainment of an intelligible good other than the satisfaction of the desire itself.*

In the fallen human condition, the universality of futility conceals the specific futility of acting out of motives which one realizes to be nonrational. When degradation is universal, one might as well do what is degrading. Death is an awesome reality; one might as well live for the moment or gain what satisfaction one can in pursuing particular objectives, even if their attainment will be unsatisfying. If the dead are not raised, eat, drink, and be merry, for tomorrow you die (see 1 Cor 15.32). The revelation of the Old Testament provided some help in overcoming this attitude (8-C). Moreover, by the time of Jesus, many pious Jews believed in the resurrection to come (and many still do today).

However, many people who lack detachment are quite self-disciplined. How do they manage to develop such a disposition? The answer is that the self-control of the person without detachment usually is in the service of one major nonrational motive which is thoroughly rationalized so that its true character is not obvious. For example, many hardworking and tightly controlled people are bent on achieving fame and reputation. These goals, when considered reflectively, clearly are of value neither to the one who attains them nor to anyone else. Also, to some extent, such persons avoid nonrational action out of prudential motives. People avoid excess, follow a healthful regimen, and lead generally orderly lives because they are afraid of the consequences of not doing so.

The light of faith transforms one's view of this present life. One who accepts Jesus with living faith now has a real purpose in life, and this purpose is adequate to organize the whole of life. In it, integral human fulfillment can be found. Therefore, one should put aside everything else as irrational: not only behavior which has been indulged in without any rational motive but even behavior which could have a rational motive but has no place in one's personal vocation.

2. Some suggest that those who mourn, referred to in the Beatitude, are contrite sinners comforted by God's forgiveness. Although "those who mourn" certainly include the contrite, the concept has often been taken far more widely, as embracing the Christian's entire attitude toward this world.[20] As St. Augustine remarks concerning this Beatitude, those who turn to God no longer take pleasure in things which previously pleased them, and "until there comes about in them the love for what is eternal, they feel the sting of sadness over a number of things"; they are comforted by the Holy Spirit so that "disregarding the temporal they may enjoy eternal happiness."[21] One who follows Jesus is a stranger and pilgrim in this world—a world which is passing away. Along with rejoicing in hope of fulfillment in Jesus, Christians mourn the dying world from which they must detach themselves.

3. **The virtuous disposition present in this mode of Christian response is referred to as "detachment."** Detachment is the surrender of every good which does not contribute to the carrying out of one's personal vocation. Habitual self-denial is an aspect of such detachment, and following the counsels of poverty, chastity, and obedience is an important means. "Worldliness" and "anxiety" often signify opposed dispositions. One who follows nonrational motives suffers a kind of enslavement; but the fruit of detachment is an important aspect of the liberty of the children of God (see Gal 5.16–24).

4. Detachment is one of the requirements of discipleship indicated when Jesus tells those who propose to follow him that they must take up their crosses. In Matthew and Mark this precept is immediately preceded by his first prediction of his passion and death and by his reproof to Peter, who used human standards rather than God's. Jesus then insists on the necessity of self-denial for following him and on the uselessness of gaining the whole world while losing one's soul. He also promises the reward of heaven to those who follow him (see Mt 16.24–28; Mk 8.34–39; Lk 9.23–27).

5. In excoriating the scribes and Pharisees, Jesus condemns their avarice and impurity: "You cleanse the outside of the cup and of the plate, but inside they are full of extortion and rapacity" (Mt 23.25). The covetousness Jesus condemns in his opponents is the extreme opposite of the detachment he blesses in his disciples.

In Luke, a similar woe is complemented by an explicit call for generosity: "But give for alms those things which are within; and behold, everything is clean for you" (Lk 11.41).

6. According to Augustine, the gift of the Holy Spirit corresponding to this Beatitude is knowledge. Christian liberation gives a genuine insight into values in the light of the gospel.[22] St. Thomas teaches that by this gift one is enlightened both to discern what belongs to faith and to judge earthly things by its light, in this way knowing where one's true good lies and how secondary or unimportant everything else is by comparison (see *S.t.*, 2–2, q. 9, aa. 3–4).

While a certain asceticism was commended in the Old Testament—and moderation and self-control were taught—the promises initially were of this-worldly goods. Only in the New Testament can one find the conception that the kingdom is not of this world, that the Messiah is the Suffering Servant. Christian other-worldliness provides a new ground for discipline: "Beloved, I beseech you as aliens and exiles to abstain from the passions of the flesh that wage war against your soul" (1 Pt 2.11).

The detachment Jesus teaches is radical. If one's eye or hand offends, detach oneself from it (see Mt 5.29–30). One is to be entirely carefree, with no concern even about the necessities of life, since God will provide what is truly necessary (see Mt 6.25–34). Seek the kingdom and everything else will follow: "Fear not, little flock, for it is your Father's good pleasure to give you the kingdom. Sell your possessions, and give alms; provide yourselves with purses that do not grow old, with a treasure in the heavens that does not fail, where no thief approaches and no moth destroys. For where your treasure is, there will your heart be also" (Lk 12.32–34). The worldly rich man is a fool; his soul will be required of him, and he cannot take with him the goods he has accumulated (see Lk 12.16–21). Jesus teaches that one must be detached from everything, including life itself (see Mt 10.28; Lk 12.4–6). His own death is a necessary condition for his resurrection, and so he gladly lays down his life (see Jn 12.25).

Jesus tells the rich man, who has kept the commandments, to sell all he has and follow him. And he goes on to explain that riches are a burden and an obstacle (see Mt 19.16–24; Mk 10.17–25; Lk 18.18–25). Paul drives home the lesson of detachment with respect to everything one does in this world; from the use of marriage to the use of the world's goods, one must proceed as if one were not even involved with these things: "For the form of this world is passing away. I want you to be free from anxieties" (1 Cor 7.31–32). Here is what is most characteristic of Christian detachment. It is not so much a negative attitude as a disposition of liberty from impediments to living toward heaven.

Question G: What mode of Christian response corresponds to the fourth Beatitude: "Blessed are those who hunger and thirst for righteousness, for they shall be satisfied" (Mt 5.6)?

1. People whose primary love is charity have a disposition of complete and enduring love which can be touched by no evil and thus has nothing whatsoever to fear: "There is no fear in love, but perfect love casts out fear" (1 Jn 4.18), even fear of punishment. **One who abides in God has absolute confidence; even childlike fear gives way to a reverent boldness.** Thus the fourth Christian mode of response is to *endure fearlessly whatever is necessary or useful for the fulfillment*

of one's personal vocation. This way of acting is faith's specification and charity's fulfillment of the fourth mode of responsibility: *One should not choose to act out of an emotional aversion except as part of one's avoidance of some intelligible evil other than the inner tension experienced in enduring that aversion.*

In the fallen human condition, evil and suffering are prevalent; fear becomes a dominant motive in human life. The great masses of people struggle for survival, driven to action and kept in check by terror of pain, suffering, and death. Lesser fears, with few exceptions, are controlled by greater ones. Since fear of death is so great, courage in the face of death is regarded almost universally as an exceptional and excellent quality. The revelation of the Old Testament provided considerable help in overcoming this attitude (8-D). Sheer terror gives way to reverential fear of God and faith in him. Courage develops into the magnificent faithfulness of the Old Testament martyrs and the heroic fidelity of many other holy persons, especially several of the great prophets.

However, many people who lack faithfulness seem to have considerable courage. How do they manage to develop this disposition? Generally by falsely estimating the significance of evil, especially the evil of death, thus neutralizing normal réactions of fear. For example, the value and personal quality of bodily life itself often are downplayed to make death seem insignificant. Either a better, disembodied, and perhaps nonpersonal existence is expected after this life or permanent escape into darkness is accepted as an escape from misery. Many people also manifest courage out of excessive commitment—for instance, out of fanatical dedication to a cause or out of love of honor.

The light of faith transforms the understanding of evil and of human hopes to overcome it. One who accepts Jesus with living faith does not diminish the value of human goods threatened by evil and does not distort the reality and seriousness of evil in order to make it more bearable. Like the Jew, the Christian instead trusts in God. Courage becomes a function of faithfulness. The faithfulness of God guarantees salvation, while the faithfulness of the believer demands that no repugnance, suffering, or obstacle be allowed to lead to violation of the basic commitment which forms the whole of one's life. Belief that Jesus already has won the victory and awareness that one's fidelity is essential to bear witness to him transform courage into Christian faithfulness.

2. **The virtuous disposition present in this mode of Christian response is the faithfulness and heroism characteristic of the martyr yet required of all Christians, who must be ready to suffer martyrdom at any time if that is necessary.** Patient endurance of lesser evils and sufferings is also an important aspect of Christian faithfulness. Opposed to this disposition are weakness of faith, faintheartedness in the face of non-Christian standards, reticence about one's faith, embarrassment about practicing it, and so on.

3. To those who hunger and thirst for goodness, Jesus gives living water; his own food is doing God's will (see Jn 4.14, 34). He himself is "the bread of life; he who comes to me shall not hunger, and he who believes in me shall never thirst" (Jn 6.35). The condition for permanent satisfaction of the most urgent human appetites, on which survival itself depends, is faith in Jesus.[23] One who has these appetites will hardly notice obstacles to satisfying them, and so will be heroically faithful to his or her personal vocation.

4. Having transformed water into wine at Cana, Jesus finishes his redemptive work by transforming the bitter wine of his heroic suffering into the blood and water of saving grace. The human appetite for goodness is now satisfied by the

Eucharist and by the union with God which the Eucharist gives (see Jn 6.53–58).

5. What is most distinctive about Christian faithfulness is that it is fidelity to Jesus and his Church. From this comes firmness based on the conviction that the only real evil to be feared has been destroyed: "I have said this to you, that in me you may have peace. In the world you have tribulations; but be of good cheer, I have overcome the world" (Jn 16.33). In light of this assurance, there should be no concern in Christian hearts; they are to be filled with joy and peace (see Jn 14.1, 27–31).

6. In the face of persecution Christians are certain they cooperate with the Holy Spirit in bearing witness to an already triumphant Lord (see Jn 15.18–16.4). The resurrection quickly confirms the promise, brings peace, grounds faith (see Jn 20.19–29). It is not the mere fact of the resurrection—which induces terror (see Mk 16.6–8)—that effects this result, but the living presence of Jesus and the confirming gift of the Spirit (see Lk 24.36–49).

7. In excoriating the scribes and Pharisees, Jesus condemns their false assiduousness: "You traverse sea and land to make a single proselyte, and when he becomes a proselyte, you make him twice as much a child of hell as yourselves" (Mt 23.15). Taking shelter in legalism because of their infidelity to the law's purpose, even its servants who endured great hardships on its behalf achieved only counterproductive results by Jesus' standard.

8. According to St. Augustine, the gift of the Holy Spirit corresponding to this Beatitude is fortitude.[24] St. Thomas points out that by this gift the Christian not only does good things but lives with an insatiable desire, suggested by "hunger" and "thirst," for what is truly good (see *S.t.*, 2–2, q. 139, a. 2).

The Old Testament already saw a considerable development of the virtue of faithfulness. Much of what is contained in the New Testament does not, in any explicit way, add anything to this heritage. For example, the great eschatological discourse (see Mt 24; Mk 13; Lk 21.5–36) clearly is written to encourage faithfulness in time of persecution; present suffering means God's help will soon arrive. But this discourse contains nothing on the required response which might not have been known from the Old Testament. Similarly, speaking of the genesis by charity of Christian virtues, Paul notes in the area of faithfulness love's power to trust, to hope, and to endure (see 1 Cor 13.7)—all fully illustrated in the Old Testament.

Christian faithfulness is not mere courage, not true grit. Suffering for the sake of future joy belongs to faithfulness as such (see Jn 16.21–22; Heb 12.2). But for the Christian, suffering must be accepted with present joy, since it unites one with Jesus (see Col 1.24; Jas 1.2–4; 1 Pt 1.6–7).

Because of the importance of personal vocation in Christian life, faithfulness for the Christian demands not only endurance but an active effort. One must put Jesus' teaching into practice, building upon the solid foundation of charity (see Mt 7.24–27). Good fruit is required; united with Jesus one will bear it abundantly (see Jn 15.1–8). Hence, Christian faithfulness demands creativity, by which one not only is able to do works like those of Jesus, but works even greater than his (see Jn 14.12), works which with faithful initiative build Jesus to his full stature and complete his sufferings (see Eph 4.11–13; Col 1.24).

Because of the positive aspects of both detachment and faithfulness, the two dispositions virtually merge into one. The Christian must be utterly carefree, without the concerns which arise from attachment to transient goods, with joy in suffering because it is a way of sharing here and now in everlasting fulfillment. Hence, the law of the cross links self-denial and the taking up of one's cross in the fulfillment of each Christian's personal vocation: "If any man would come after me, let him deny himself and take up his cross and follow me. For whoever would save his life will lose it; and whoever loses his life for my sake and the gospel's will save it" (Mk 8.34–35).

Question H: What mode of Christian response corresponds to the fifth Beatitude: "Blessed are the merciful, for they shall obtain mercy" (Mt 5.7)?

1. People whose primary love is charity are disposed to divine goodness before all else. But God practices no partiality and is utterly and absolutely faithful; he is unconcerned with justice to himself, for his own goodness is absolute. **One identified by charity with the universal good can and will take the same totally disinterested and selfless attitude.** Thus the fifth Christian mode of response is to *be merciful according to the universal and perfect measure of mercy which God has revealed in Jesus.* This way of acting is faith's specification and charity's fulfillment of the fifth mode of responsibility: *One should not, in response to different feelings toward different persons, willingly proceed with a preference for anyone unless the preference is required by intelligible goods themselves.*

In the fallen human condition, the prevalence of unfairness and the harshness of living conditions are important obstacles to the fulfillment of the fifth mode of responsibility. To survive in a situation of struggle and scarcity one needs some reliable companions, and one must meet some standard of fairness in dealing with them. But beyond the circle of one's own group, one is hardly likely to be treated impartially and can hardly afford to treat others impartially. For practical purposes, people must be divided into friends and enemies; one is virtually compelled to do good to one's friends and to treat one's enemies as they seem to deserve. Even apart from the New Testament, divine revelation greatly deepens the mode of responsibility, by making clear the universal need for mercy, God's universal granting of it, and the general obligation to imitate his example (8-E).

However, many people unwilling to go beyond the requirements of strict justice seem very conscientious in matters of fairness. What is the basis of this disposition? The answer generally is that people are careful about rights and duties within an established framework of conventional morality, but set some very arbitrary limits. For example, many secular humanists who are very careful to be fair in many matters establish arbitrary criteria of quality of life, by which they are willing to kill certain groups of persons. If one can impose upon others one's ideology, one can afford to be fair within the framework of this ideology. Those who make the rules normally want the game played by them.

Christian revelation, accepted with living faith, transforms the understanding of human goods and human community. Human goods can and will be realized in the fulfillment of everything in Jesus; there, too, everyone willing to accept a place has one. All the boundaries of existing societies therefore dissolve. Moreover, the fulfillment which consists in commitment to goods and the handing on of redemption to other persons clearly is far more important than the actual share in a good which one receives.

2. **The virtuous disposition present in this mode of Christian response is Jesus-like mercy, generosity, compassion, service to others.** This is a disposition to require of others not even that to which fairness entitles one and to be

available to them without any consideration of what is fair. The vice opposed to this virtue is a legalistic attitude toward others; one tries to protect one's interests by appealing to a framework of fairness which establishes rights and limits responsibilities.

3. "Mercy" as the Beatitude uses it means not only forgiveness but the generous doing of good to others without counting the cost to oneself.[25] The new law of retaliation is to turn the other cheek; the new law for settling disputes is to give more than is demanded; the new law for service is to double what is asked; the new law for lending is to give without reservation; the new law for forgiveness is to love enemies, treat them as friends, and so seek the redemption of persecutors (see Mt 5.38–48). While the Christian must protect what is essential to fulfilling his or her personal vocation, self-interest is entirely excluded.

4. With the parable of the merciless official (see Mt 18.23–35), Jesus makes it inescapably clear that Christians, who are aware of their need for God's mercy and have received it, are bound by the Golden Rule itself to extend this same mercy to others. Universality and perfection are most proper to Christian mercy. The Christian has obligations to everyone and makes claims on no one. This flows from the fact that Christian life is a participation in God's own life and love, and the Christian is called to communicate Jesus' redemptive love to others.

5. Even to the apostles it came as a tremendous surprise that God was so impartial as to make his new family wholly universal. Peter remarks on this with wonder: "Truly I perceive that God shows no partiality, but in every nation any one who fears him and does what is right is acceptable to him" (Acts 10.34–35).

Paul likewise: "God has consigned all men to disobedience, that he may have mercy upon all" (Rom 11.32; cf. Eph 2). The perfection of God's mercy in Jesus is that he gave his own Son that we might become adopted children. Having given us the Spirit, is it possible he will withhold anything less (see Rom 8.14–34)?

The Word Incarnate is filled with enduring love, and of his fullness the Christian shares (see Jn 1.14, 16). Christian mercy must share in his life: "Give no offense to Jews or to Greeks or to the church of God, just as I try to please all men in everything I do, not seeking my own advantage, but that of many, that they may be saved. Be imitators of me, as I am of Christ" (1 Cor 10.32–11.1). Having been redeemed, sharing in God's own justice, the Christian must be altogether impartial in sharing redemption with others. Only so is the requirement of impartiality fulfilled by one who knows himself or herself to be a child of God.

Hence, the example of Jesus who forgives enemies who are killing him even as he dies in agony on the cross (see Lk 23.34) is followed by the first martyr, Stephen. Stephen commends his spirit to Jesus, as Jesus to the Father, prays for his persecutors, and gives bold testimony, for he is filled with the Holy Spirit and clearly sees Jesus standing at the right hand of God (see Acts 7.54–60). Similarly, in catechetical instruction the doctrinal point that Christians are saved by God's mercy is followed by an injunction to live blamelessly among the pagans, despite their mistreatment, so to contribute to their conversion (see 1 Pt 2.9–12).

6. In excoriating the scribes and Pharisees, Jesus says: "You tithe mint and dill and cummin, and have neglected the weightier matters of the law, justice and mercy and faith" (Mt 23.23; cf. Lk 11.42). Unless their justice goes beyond narrow legalism, Christians cannot enter the kingdom (see Mt 5.20).

7. According to St. Augustine, the gift of the Holy Spirit corresponding to the fifth Beatitude is counsel. He takes it that this gift makes us realize that it is in our own best interests, for us to be merciful.[26] For St. Thomas the gift has a higher meaning; it is a divine practicality, which directs the Christian in mercy transcending ordinary human standards (see *S.t.*, 2–2, q. 52, aa. 2, 4).

It is worth noting that in the work of social justice, nothing truly can be achieved without mercy. As John Paul II says: "A world from which forgiveness was eliminated would be nothing but a world of cold and unfeeling justice, in the name of which each person would claim his or her own rights vis-a-vis others; the various kinds of selfishness latent in man would transform life and human society into a system of oppression of the weak by the strong, or into an arena of permanent strife between one group and another."[27]

This is so because in any society, there will be a large body of persons unwilling to act fairly or in error about what fairness demands; hence, a general balance can be achieved only if some substantial group of persons is willing to make voluntary compensation to rectify unfairness. Force and violence can achieve nothing, and no legal system can begin to cut fine enough to attain justice. Traditionally, those who especially devoted themselves to the works of mercy undertook to fulfill this Christian responsibility. Because of the scale of modern social structures, Christians today can fulfill it as they should only by cooperation organized on a larger scale.

Question I: What mode of Christian response corresponds to the sixth Beatitude: "Blessed are the pure in heart, for they shall see God" (Mt 5.8)?

1. People whose primary love is charity are disposed to divine goodness above all else. **Since this goodness includes every other good in its true measure and worth, love of God itself draws one to love as one should and turn away from loving as one should not. In this life, charity leads to continuous conversion; those who love God always have reason for sorrow that they do not love as they ought.** Therefore, the sixth mode of Christian response is to *strive to conform one's whole self to living faith, and to recognize and purge anything which does not meet this standard.* This way of acting is faith's specification and charity's fulfillment of the sixth mode of responsibility: *One should not choose on the basis of emotions which bear upon empirical aspects of intelligible goods (or bads) in a way which interferes with a more perfect sharing in the good or avoidance of the bad.*

In the fallen human condition, the prevalence of misery and disappointment, especially disappointment with other people, breeds hopelessness. If everything is vanity, if life is a story full of sound and fury but without ultimate meaning, then it is no more absurd to pursue immediate satisfactions, which one can experience, than to pursue true goods, for even if the former pursuit blocks the latter, the latter is pointless. Furthermore, lack of self-control is very common, and those who act irrationally in violation of the third mode of responsibility are very likely to give up the struggle and adopt a policy of satisfying desire as much as possible. Thus they are predisposed to violate this mode as well. Even apart from the New Testament, divine revelation deepens this mode of responsibility (8-F). The struggle against pseudoreligion provides a paradigm for a sharp distinction between true goods and the merely empirical aspects of goods pursued for their own sake.

However, many people who are not pure in heart seem to avoid substituting apparent for true goods; they seem to have a serious, realistic, and clearheaded grasp on human goods. How do they manage to have such a disposition? To some extent it is a matter of ideology. One can develop a view of reality which virtually negates the value of human experience; one finds such views not only in idealistic philosophies such as Plato's, but also in the grim practicality of the Marxist. More generally, many people settle for the apparent good with self-deception only in one area of life (for example, in the sphere of intimate, personal relationships) but live quite realistically in other areas, which they place in the service of the satisfaction they seek (for example, in experiences of superficial and unreal love or friendship).

Christian revelation, accepted with living faith, transforms one's understanding of the attainability of true human goods: All can be realized in fulfillment in Jesus. Hence, one need not settle for mere appearances. But, at the same time, any way of acting which does not contribute to one's Christian life—that is, any commitment or choice not positively integrated with faith—leads toward some experience of good which is less than one could be pursuing. In other words, for the Christian, any act not formed by living faith is an unreasonable pursuit of a merely apparent good. But to the extent that one falls short of the perfection of charity—which we all do—one's life is not wholly integrated with living faith. The reality of this situation must be admitted, since only by admitting it can one strive for perfection.

2. **The virtuous disposition inherent in this mode of response is single-minded devotion to God, essentially including a sense of sin and a process of continuing conversion.** The devout life consists in having no commitments which do not constitute part of one's personal vocation, seeking in every act only to fulfill one's commitments, recognizing one's failures in realizing this ideal, turning away from whatever underlies these failures, and so living ever more completely in faith's light and by its power. Mediocrity and insincerity constitute the vicious disposition opposed to this virtue: One desires to be a Christian but is unwilling to surrender totally to Jesus, though this is an inherent requirement of Christian life.

3. The purity of heart envisaged in the Beatitude goes far beyond the ritual purity initially required for one to come into God's presence in the liturgy (see Lv 11–16).[28] Jesus declares that true purity is interior (see Mt 15.10–20; Mk 7.14–23). Purity comes ultimately from the word of truth (see Jn 15.3) and from holiness of life in Jesus. The perfection of charity "issues from a pure heart and a good conscience and sincere faith" (1 Tm 1.5). Thus Christians must strive to love God with every part of themselves. Such striving is the work of the pure in heart (see Mt 22.37; Mk 12.30; Lk 10.27).

4. The First Epistle of John clearly expresses the twofold attitude central to Christian devotion. On the one hand, insincerity can be avoided only if one admits sin; a person who does not admit it is a liar, self-deceived, devoid of truth. Admitting sin is essential to being forgiven (see 1 Jn 1.8–10). On the other hand, no one begotten of God acts sinfully; sin belongs exclusively to the devil, while God's children are immune to it (see 1 Jn 3.7–9). In short, Christians recognize the reality of sin in their lives and, with it, their constant need for conversion and mercy; but Christians also recognize the reality of divine love at the center of their lives and, with it, their real power to attain perfect holiness.

5. In excoriating the scribes and Pharisees, Jesus places special emphasis on their hypocrisy (see Mt 23.27–28; Lk 11.44; 12.1–3). Far from being irreligious, the Pharisees are devout; but their devotion—and this is Jesus' quarrel with them—is not and does not even try to be total devotion to God. Primarily self-serving, it involves grave self-deception concerning their own uprightness, since they claim perfection by a standard which is false and which they ought to know is false (see Mt 12.22–42; 15.1–14; Lk 18.9–14; Jn 9.40–41).

6. According to St. Augustine, the gift of understanding corresponds to the sixth Beatitude.[29] St. Thomas explains that by understanding one is free from vain imagining and from a limited and erroneous understanding of Christian life, and so helped toward perfection (see *S.t.*, 2–2, q. 8, aa. 6–7).

Jesus condemned the hypocrisy of religious acts done for the sake of human respect (see Mt 6.5, 16). One cannot serve two masters (see Mt 6.24; Lk 16.13). One must follow Jesus without putting family duties, such as burying the dead, first (see Mt 8.21–22; Lk 9.59–62). Yet Jesus does not take his own out of the world; rather, he wishes them to live in the world lives consecrated in divine truth (see Jn 17.15–19). The invitation to the heavenly banquet is given to all, but those are excluded who would rather fulfill an incompatible commitment (see Mt 22.1–10; Lk 14.15–24).

The passage on the coin of the tax shows that Christian life does not preclude fulfilling secular commitments and responsibilities. However, these are of an order altogether different from that of the commitment of Christian faith. Hence, one gives to earthly authority only what is due it—material goods and services. Devotion is reserved to God (see Mt 22.15–22; Mk 12.13–17; Lk 20.20–26).

Christian life is founded upon Jesus who is not wishy-washy, not "yes" and "no," but only "yes." He demands total devotion and gives the Spirit as the pledge of fulfillment (see 2 Cor 1.17–22). Sincere love is now a real possibility, since the Holy Spirit has been given, yet we are not yet perfect (see Phil 3.12–16). The danger to the Christian is falling away from sincere devotion to Jesus (see 2 Cor 11.3).

Paul writes that as a Christian he has a new sense of values. Jesus is wealth, and nothing else really matters. To be in Jesus with the rightness which comes from faith in him is all-important. One must experience the power which flows from his resurrection and be shaped in the form of his death (see Phil 3.7–11). Then Paul adds thoughts distinctively Christian: "Not that I have already obtained this or am already perfect; but I press on to make it my own, because Christ Jesus has made me his own. Brethren, I do not consider that I have made it my own; but one thing I do, forgetting what lies behind and straining forward to what lies ahead, I press on toward the goal for the prize of the upward call of God in Christ Jesus. Let those of us who are mature be thus minded; and if in anything you are otherwise minded, God will reveal that also to you. Only let us hold true to what we have attained" (Phil 3.12–16). Those whose hearts are set upon worldly things will end in disaster. Our citizenship already is in heaven (see Phil 3.20). Thus mature Christian spirituality is a progress toward perfection.

Question J: What mode of Christian response corresponds
to the seventh Beatitude:
"Blessed are the peacemakers,
for they shall be called sons of God" (Mt 5.9)?

1. People whose primary love is charity love divine goodness above all else.
There is no evil mutilating this goodness, and so no principle of opposition and
conflict, which arise solely from evil[1] and its distorting consequences. **To love
goods mutilated by evil with divine love is to love them as good, not as evil,
and so to separate them from their evil and restore them to wholeness. Hence,
the effort to live according to divine love will be universally conciliatory.** The
seventh mode of Christian response is therefore to *respond to evil with good, not
with resistance, much less with destructive action* (see Lv 19.17–18; Mt 5.38–41;
Rom 12.17–21). This way of acting is faith's specification and charity's fulfillment of the seventh mode of responsibility: *One should not be moved by hostility to
freely accept or choose the destruction, damaging, or impeding of any intelligible
human good.*

In the fallen human condition, injustice is common. The prevalence and ineluctability
of evil breed resentment. The sense of vindication is part of the experience of justice, and so
it can be sought as an apparent good. Emotionally, the release of pent-up negative feelings
in destructive behavior bears some resemblance to the sense of vindication, even when this
relief is itself not experienced as the appearance of justice—for example, even when it is
felt to be a wrong balancing another wrong. Even apart from the New Testament, divine
revelation provides some relief for this frustration by promising divine rectification (8-G).

However, many people who are not particularly conciliatory seem to avoid acting
irrationally out of hostile feeling. How do they manage to develop a disposition of self-
restraint? The answer is that most people restrain themselves out of self-interest. Revenge
is unprofitable, and since the tendency to it is so common, there is a general interest in
making it costly. To do so is an important part of the function of criminal law and of many
less formal devices of social control. Unfortunately, however, there are limits to self-
restraint imposed by self-interest. Hence, in most people the tendency to irrationally
destructive action is not eliminated; rather, it is channeled. Petty spitefulness, taking out
resentments upon the weak and those in subordinate positions, purposeful injury by
omission (which is not so easily recognized as malicious), and gross revenge when
operating beyond the limits of ordinary controls (as in warfare) are all extremely common.

Christian revelation, accepted with living faith, transforms one's understanding of evil
and of the possibility of coping with it. Evil is not necessarily ineluctable. The victory over
it has been won; redemption has been accomplished in principle in Jesus. The full
implication of the character of evil as privation is that zealotry is no more able than
pharisaism to deal with it. The privation as such cannot be confronted. Resistance to evil is
useless and an effort to destroy it worse than useless, since such an effort only succeeds in
destroying the residual good.

2. **The virtuous disposition present in this mode of Christian response is
the conciliatoriness which seeks the redemption of enemies** (see Mt 5.43–44).
An essential aspect is the patient endurance which is a fruit of the Spirit (see Gal
5.22). This virtue also includes certain aspects of mildness. One opposite
disposition is comprised of defensiveness and aloofness: the tendency to try to

avoid evil instead of carrying on a redemptive ministry to those enslaved by it. Another opposite is the tendency to fret about evil rather than respond to it with good. Discouraged about the prospects for the conversion of those who seem obdurate in error or sin, yet unwilling to harm them, the Christian all too easily falls into an attitude of passive resentment.

3. Elaborating on the point of this Beatitude, Jesus says: "Love your enemies and pray for those who persecute you, so that you may be sons of your Father who is in heaven; for he makes his sun rise on the evil and on the good, and sends rain on the just and on the unjust" (Mt 5.44–45).[30] Jesus fulfilled this command himself, making peace through his blood (see Col 1.19–20).

4. Accepting responsibility for spreading peace by communicating Jesus' peace to others is most proper to Christian conciliatoriness (see 2 Cor 5.16–21). Reverence for enemies and refusal to judge their ultimate state of soul are a foundation for peacemaking (see GS 28). Ultimately, however, peace can only be attained by making love universal, and so the Christian must try not only to live in love but to bring others to share in it (see GS 78).

5. Jesus castigates the scribes and Pharisees as blind guides leading the blind; they employ a false casuistry in their effort to save others and gain their own salvation (see Mt 23.16–22). This false casuistry is a way of evading the duty to respond to evil with the healing love which alone would overcome it. By contrast, Jesus himself is the sun of justification, who really dissolves darkness and guides the feet of human beings on the way of peace (cf. Lk 1.78–79).

6. According to St. Augustine, the gift of the Holy Spirit corresponding to the seventh Beatitude is wisdom: "Wisdom corresponds to the peacemakers in whom everything is in order and there is no emotion to rebel against reason, but all things obey the spirit of man just as it obeys God."[31] St. Thomas points out that wisdom is the power of putting in order, and that this power is what peacemaking, the restoration of right order, requires. Also, wisdom is appropriate to Jesus, the eternally begotten Word and wisdom of the Father (see *S.t.*, 2–2, q. 45, aa. 1, 6).

The sacred writers of the Old Testament declared that only righteousness would bring true peace (see Ps 72.1–3; 85.9–14; Is 32.16–18; Jer 6.13–16).[32] They looked forward to peace in the time of redemption (see Is 9.5–6; Hos 2.20). This promise of conciliation and peace is fulfilled in Jesus (see Mt 28.9; Lk 2.14; Jn 14.27; 20.19, 26). His peace is the forgiveness of sins for which the prophets hoped (see Jn 20.19–23). The infant Church spreads this peace to the nations (see Acts 10.34–36, 43), for the redemption accomplished in Jesus is not for Israel alone. Rather it is the reconciliation of all humankind with God and the overcoming of all enmity between nations (see Eph 2.13–18).

One aspect of the Christian attitude toward peacemaking is the conviction that evil is utterly powerless. This conviction is represented in a symbolic way in the book of Revelation, which comes to a climax when Jesus comes forth to do battle with evil. As soon as he appears, evil is vanquished; no battle is necessary (see Rv 19.11–21). The victory over evil already has been won. Hence Christians can be peaceable; no one can frustrate their hope (see 1 Pt 3.8–17).

Question K: What mode of Christian response corresponds
to the eighth Beatitude: "Blessed are those
who are persecuted for righteousness' sake,
for theirs is the kingdom of heaven" (Mt 5.10)?

1. People whose primary love is charity love divine goodness above all else.
Since divine goodness is incompatible with the destruction of anything, one
who loves it will not be willing to destroy, damage, or impede any good, even
to overcome evil, but will be prepared instead to undergo evil in order to
bring the evildoer into touch with goodness without defect. Thus the eighth
mode of Christian response is to *do no evil that good might come of it, but suffer*
evil together with Jesus in cooperation with God's redeeming love. This love will
overcome all evil and achieve integral human fulfillment in the fulfillment of all
things in Jesus. This way of acting—the Christian way of achieving success—is
faith's specification and charity's transformation of the eighth mode of responsibility: *One should not be moved by a stronger desire for one instance of an*
intelligible good to act for it by choosing to destroy, damage, or impede some other
instance of an intelligible good.

In the fallen human condition, compromises seem essential if one is going to be at all
effective in pursuing human goods and avoiding evils. If one refuses to do evil—for
example, to kill—one seems to surrender not only oneself but all one's dependents to being
victimized by those who will not hesitate to do evil. The law of Israel had ambiguous
implications for this dilemma (8-H). On the one hand, it deepened a sense of the dignity of
human persons and their goods, and it called in question confidence about human value
judgments. But it seemed also to validate a conventional morality which authorized doing
some evils.

Some people who are not self-sacrificing nevertheless condemn pragmatic craftiness
and maintain that there are absolute standards of morality. How do they manage to develop
such respect for human goods? In some cases the answer simply is that they condemn the
craftiness of others, or the doing of evil for the sake of goods they consider inadequate.
Thus diplomats of the liberal democracies reject the Machiavellianism of the Commu-
nists—and vice versa. Many people reject the use of craft in private affairs, but consider it
justified in any sort of public or official matter. This position makes sense for those who are
in power.

There are certain other instances in which moral norms are conceived of as having an
absoluteness of their own, and observing them is thought of as being the sole human good.
A position of this sort can demand that moral norms be obeyed regardless of consequences:
Let right be done though the heavens fall! The trouble with this is that in absolutizing
morality, it treats the substantive goods of human persons as of no ultimate consequence.
Some Stoics, for example, held both the absoluteness of moral requirements and the
acceptability of suicide. A position of this sort is a form of fanaticism; lacking humane
concern for the substantive goods of the person, it violates authentic morality despite its
noble moralism.

Christian revelation, accepted with living faith, transforms the understanding of human
goods and the possibility of realizing them. Faith teaches that integral human fulfillment
can be realized, despite evil, in the fulfillment of all things in Jesus. One must respond to
evil with good; in doing so, one can live consistently with integral human fulfillment. Such
a life will inevitably involve suffering evil, and one will have to forgo the immediate

attainment of those goods and avoidance of those evils which cannot be attained or avoided without adopting bad means to good ends. However, one will accept the suffering of evil precisely in order to overcome it. Jesus' resurrection shows this strategy to be effective.

2. **The virtuous disposition present in this mode of Christian response is self-oblation, the offering of oneself to God as a living sacrifice.** The opposite disposition is the fragile rectitude of the person who does not wish to sin but seeks fulfillment in this world. Such a person might consistently respect all the other modes of responsibility, but sooner or later will be tempted to violate the eighth one. At this point one either accepts a share in Jesus' self-oblation or separates oneself from him by irreverently violating a human good.

3. Christian self-oblation is not self-destruction; it aims at true human self-fulfillment. "For whoever would save his life will lose it; and whoever loses his life for my sake and the gospel's will save it" (Mk 8.35; cf. Mt 16.25; Lk 9.24; 17.33; Jn 12.25). No sooner does Jesus reveal the awful mystery of the cross than he reveals the wonderful mystery of the resurrection. In a world fallen and redeemed, human fulfillment is only possible by sharing in the fulfillment of the risen Lord Jesus. If we die with him, we shall rise with him (see Rom 6.5). As his wounds and pierced side remain to him as badges of glory, so we shall rejoice forever in the fulfillment our present sufferings merit.

4. Jesus makes it clear that those persecuted for the sake of righteousness are persecuted for his sake, since he is righteousness. "Blessed are you when men revile you and persecute you and utter all kinds of evil against you falsely on my account. Rejoice and be glad, for your reward is great in heaven, for so men persecuted the prophets who were before you" (Mt 5.11–12). "Indeed all who desire to live a godly life in Christ Jesus will be persecuted" (2 Tm 3.12). Anyone who responds to evil with good and refuses to do evil for the sake of good does not belong to this world. The world will hate and persecute every true Christian because of Jesus (see Wis 2.1–20; Jn 15.18–21; Phil 1.27–30; 1 Pt 3.13–17; 1 Jn 3.16; Rv 13.10).[33]

5. The last and longest woe in Jesus' excoriation of the scribes and Pharisees condemns them for their impending murder of him, a murder which puts them in the line of those who murdered the prophets. This murder will not save Jerusalem as the leaders hope; they will fail to gain their end. They will find their temple empty, and Jesus, who came to save Jerusalem, will not return until he comes in judgment (see Mt 23.29–39).

6. Because there are only seven gifts of the Holy Spirit, St. Augustine does not assign a gift corresponding to Christian self-oblation. In his view, this last Beatitude returns to the first, forming a kind of circle.[34] At the same time, it illuminates the perfection of Christian life and shows in what it consists (cf. *S.t.,* 1–2, q. 69, a. 3, ad 5; a. 4, ad 2). Perhaps we could say there is a gift of the Spirit corresponding to this Beatitude, but one without a common name like "wisdom" or "fear of the Lord." Rather, it is a unique gift proper to each Christian, by which he or she is disposed to share creatively and in a personal way in Jesus' suffering. To offer God that unique gift which is oneself, each Christian requires an impetus of divine love which is his or her own special gift of the Spirit.

Readiness to suffer death for the sake of God is a great virtue. But, as Jesus points out, it is a virtue which existed throughout the Old Testament. The prophets were also martyrs. Faithful unto death, they died out of loyalty to God and to the truth of God which it was their mission to communicate.

Christian self-oblation differs. It is not required only of some persons, when they must either die for their faith or renounce it. The demands of Christian morality extend to all the human goods. Hence, the possibility of martyrdom is not limited to the case in which one might be forced to choose between suffering evil and violating a specifically religious good. Anyone who tries to live a Christian life will suffer evil (see 2 Tm 3.12). Thus, slaves are instructed: "For one is approved if, mindful of God, he endures pain while suffering unjustly. For what credit is it, if when you do wrong and are beaten for it you take it patiently? But if when you do right and suffer for it you take it patiently, you have God's approval. For to this you have been called, because Christ also suffered for you, leaving you an example, that you should follow in his steps" (1 Pt 2.19–21).

To be a Christian is to have a vocation to suffer, because suffering is inevitable as a consequence of doing what is right. Accepted out of love—in awareness of God's "presence"—such suffering becomes an acceptable gift to God. Hence, Christian self-oblation is the offering of one's whole life, united with Jesus in suffering, as a gift to God.[35]

The greatest love is not a love for God which cares nothing for human goods; the greatest love is a love for God which is fulfilled by one's laying down one's life for one's friends (see Jn 15.13). "By this we know love, that he laid down his life for us; and we ought to lay down our lives for the brethren" (1 Jn 3.16). The friends for whom Jesus laid down his life included his followers, who also were enemies of God in need of redemption, and his opponents, who also were called to be his friends. Paul's wonder that Jesus died for godless men (see Rom 5.6–10) is based on personal experience, since he had persecuted Jesus (see Acts 8.1–3; 9.4; 1 Cor 15.9). Christian self-oblation is aimed at the redemption of others— one's inimical friends and potentially friendly enemies.

Summary

The modes of Christian response are faith's specification and charity's fulfillment of the eight modes of responsibility. The modes of responsibility, treated in chapter eight, forbid what does not conform to a will toward integral human fulfillment. The modes of Christian response are ways of acting characteristic of a person whose will, enlivened by charity, is directed in hope toward the fulfillment of everything in Jesus. These principles of Christian moral life are the blessings proclaimed in the eight Beatitudes.

These Christian moral principles are more blessings than demands, because living faith which makes them known also leads one to fulfill them. Thus, the modes of Christian response are not only norms but virtues. The difference between common human virtues and Christian ones is the difference between good acts formed by the modes of responsibility and good acts formed by the modes of Christian response. Christian virtues specify common human virtues in light of the fallen and redeemed human situation. Since the Christian modes of response are more specific than the common modes of responsibility, one finds in Christians states of character vicious only by specifically Christian standards— "Christian vices."

St. Augustine and St. Thomas teach that the gifts of the Holy Spirit correspond to the first seven Beatitudes. The gifts belong to the messianic endowment of Jesus in which every Christian shares; they are principles of life in the Spirit. Although Thomas takes a different position, the view suggested here is that the gifts can be identified with charity insofar as it is the gift of the Holy Spirit which transforms the moral requirements articulated in the modes of responsibility into the modes of Christian response called "blessed" in the Beatitudes.

Taking the Beatitudes as the framework, then, what are the Christian modes of response?

1. *To expect and accept all good, including the good fruits of one's own work, as God's gift*—for the "poor in spirit" understand that their achievements are only a share, given freely and generously by God, in his fullness. The virtuous disposition is humility; the Christian vice is pride. The corresponding gift of the Spirit is fear of the Lord, which Thomas links to the virtue of hope.

2. *To accept one's limited role in the Body of Christ and fulfill it*—for the "meek" understand that submissiveness to God's will involves no loss or delay to their personal fulfillment. The virtuous disposition is "Christian dedication," while lukewarmness and minimalism are opposed to it. The corresponding gift of the Spirit is piety or godliness, an attitude of filial reverence and dutifulness toward God.

3. *To put aside or avoid everything which is not necessary or useful in the fulfillment of one's personal vocation*—for those who "mourn" (not contrite sinners but those who turn from transient goods to fulfillment in Jesus) understand that to be disposed to goodness itself frees one from the pursuit of particular, finite goods for their own sake. The virtuous disposition is detachment; worldliness and anxiety are opposed dispositions. The corresponding gift of the Spirit is knowledge, by which one discerns what belongs to faith and judges everything by its light.

4. *To endure fearlessly whatever is necessary or useful for the fulfillment of one's personal vocation*—for those who "hunger and thirst for righteousness" understand that they have nothing whatsoever to fear. The virtuous disposition is the faithfulness and heroism characteristic of the martyr, though required of all Christians, while weakness of faith and faintheartedness in the face of non-Christian standards are among the Christian vices. The corresponding gift of the Spirit is fortitude.

5. *To be merciful according to the universal and perfect measure of mercy which God has revealed in Jesus*—for those who "are merciful" understand that they are to be disinterested and selfless as God is. The virtuous disposition is mercy, compassion, service to others on the model of Jesus, while the opposed vice is a legalistic attitude toward others. The gift of the Spirit is counsel: for Augustine, realization that it is in our best interests to be merciful; for Thomas, a divine practicality directing to a life of mercy which transcends human standards.

6. *To strive to conform one's whole self to living faith, and purge anything which does not meet this standard*—for the "pure in heart" understand that in this life charity requires continuous conversion. The virtuous disposition is single-

minded devotion to God, including a sense of sin and continuing conversion, while the Christian vice is reflected in mediocrity and insincerity. The corresponding gift of the Spirit is understanding.

7. *To respond to evil with good, not with resistance, much less with destructive action*—for "peacemakers" understand that the effort to live according to divine love must be universally conciliatory. The virtuous disposition is the conciliatoriness which seeks the redemption of enemies; one opposed disposition is the tendency to shun evil instead of carrying on a redemptive ministry to those enslaved by it. The corresponding gift of the Spirit is wisdom, the power of putting in order as peacemakers do.

8. *To do no evil that good might come of it, but suffer evil together with Jesus in cooperation with God's redeeming love*—for "those persecuted for righteousness' sake" understand that one must undergo evil in order to bring the evildoer in touch with perfect goodness. The virtuous disposition is self-oblation, the Christian vice the fragile rectitude of the person who does not wish to sin but seeks fulfillment in this world. Since there are only seven gifts of the Spirit, Augustine assigns none here; however, one might say there is a corresponding gift, unique to each Christian and disposing him or her to offer God the unique gift of himself or herself.

Appendix: The upright who have not heard the gospel

In view of question D through K's explanations of why a Christian life-style is necessary to live uprightly in this fallen world, someone might suppose that all who are not formed by the gospel in a self-conscious Christian life are necessarily immoral. But this is false.

Each society's conventional morality is based upon a limited set of accepted goals, a requirement of fairness necessary for a common life, and the exclusion of certain types of behavior which are unreasonable in view of the common purposes (4-E). Conventional moralities represent workable compromises between human aspirations for fulfillment and the hard realities of the fallen human condition. Such moralities are an aspect of culture which defines "the world" over against Jesus. For this reason, the Fathers of the Church were right in regarding the standards of pagan morality as norms of immorality and the pagan virtues as vices.

Nevertheless, the Church clearly teaches that God provides every person with the opportunit for salvation (30-H). Such salvation comes only by the grace of Jesus; somehow those who have not heard the gospel can be united with Jesus by living faith. In short, upright pagans also receive the gift of the Spirit and share in divine love. How can this teaching be reconciled with the position that there is a specifically Christian normative content to morality, different from the specific content of conventional moralities, which can be grasped only in the light of the mystery of the redemption?

The starting point for answering this question is that persons who follow sincere consciences which are in error through no fault of their own are morally upright. They do not close themselves against integral human fulfillment; rather, they choose consistently with it. For instance, people who first conceived the idea of enslaving their defeated enemies rather than torturing them to death probably acted uprightly; similarly, many religious aberrations, such as human sacrifice, probably have been accepted out of an earnest but mistaken will to please God.

Moved by God's grace, people in every state and condition can use their ability to make free choices in a way which is upright—given the options and the moral demands as they see them. Of course, people also can choose to violate their own consciences. Any society will be shaped by the interplay of both good and bad choices, although those who are vicious are likely to have greater wealth and power, and thus will exercise greater influence in shaping the common life.

Those who are upright seek God insofar as they understand how. They receive the gift of divine love which enlivens their love of human goods and makes them conscious of the unsatisfactoriness of the human condition and the inadequacies of conventional morality. Thus is born the restless heart, ready to welcome the gospel, disposed to grope toward it, and able to begin in some inadequate way to outline some aspects of Christian truth.

Under appropriate conditions, upright persons who have not heard the gospel have emerged and made an impact upon the consciousness of a society; some have become great historical figures. It seems reasonable, for example, to assume that Socrates and the Buddha were such persons. Their emergence depended upon factors in addition to their moral character—for example, on their intelligence and articulateness, on their social positions in societies at a certain stage of civilization, on their having some extraordinary associates and followers, and so forth. All such moral leaders are at odds with their own societies' conventional moralities.

Despite the nobility of such moral leaders, their thought involved serious errors and their moral teaching fell short—according to objective standards of Christian morality—of marking the way toward integral human fulfillment.[16] Neither Socrates nor the Buddha, for example, adequately appreciated material creation, and so neither proposed a moral ideal which gave due emphasis to the pursuit and enjoyment of human goods in this world. Both tended to confuse moral evil with the human condition of bodiliness; for both, evil cannot so much be overcome as escaped by a kind of knowledge which transcends the concrete limits of space and time, sentient desires, and death. In short, neither Socratic philosophy nor Buddhism is adequately and integrally redemptive; neither gathers humankind into a community in friendship with God.

To offer these criticisms is not to detract from the nobility of moral leaders such as Socrates and the Buddha. Their lives very likely were holier and more pleasing to God than are the lives of most self-conscious Christians; indeed, they seem to be great saints. Yet they lived in semidarkness; they did not perceive the true significance of the shadow of death; objectively, their ways are not the way of our Lord Jesus, which is the only way of peace which is wholly wise, wholly enlightened, wholly life-giving.

According to Catholic faith, which is true to divine revelation recorded in Scripture, all grace is through Jesus and all who are saved will rejoice in his fullness (see LG 14; *S.t.*, 1–2, q. 106, a. 1, ad 3; 2–2, q. 2, a. 7, ad 3).[37] There is only one heaven, the fulfillment of all things in Jesus; there is no world of ideas for Socratic disembodied minds and no nirvana into which Buddhists will be dissolved without their unwanted individual selves. The precious gift which has been received by those who live in Catholic faith is this: "He has made known to us in all wisdom and insight the mystery of his will, according to his purpose which he set forth in Christ as a plan for the fulness of time, to unite all things in him, things in heaven and things on earth" (Eph 1.9–10). The work of redemption ultimately is a divine work. But by the Incarnation, God also has made it a fully human work.

Through the Church and explicit Catholic faith, we are blessed with the opportunity to cooperate consciously in God's work. We are friends of God, for we know what he is about (see Jn 15.15). Working with Jesus, we build up his fullness in this world; ours is the dignity of confidants and intimate fellow workers with the architect and Lord of the world which will never end. If we are faithful, after death we shall find ourselves at home in heaven. Socrates and the Buddha also will find themselves there, but for them it will be an unexpected wonderland. (Concerning the way in which those who have not heard the gospel can be members of the Church, see chapter thirty, appendix two.)

Notes

1. See John P. Meier, *The Vision of Matthew: Christ, Church, and Morality in the First Gospel* (New York: Paulist Press, 1979), 42–51. Some have attempted to deny that the New Testament really contains moral teaching except incidentally to the gospel, but this view is not sustained by historical evidence: W. D. Davies, *The Setting of the Sermon on the Mount* (Cambridge: Cambridge University Press, 1964), 94–108.

2. For a plausible argument for this point based on literary genre, see Hans Dieter Betz, "The Sermon on the Mount: Its Literary Genre and Function," *Journal of Religion*, 59 (1979), 285–97. For an argument that the centrality of the Sermon on the Mount is a key to St. Thomas' moral thought, see Servais Pinckaers, O.P., "Esquisse d'une morale Chrétienne: Ses bases: la Loi évangélique et la loi naturelle," *Nova et Vetera*, 55 (1980), 108–11; a fuller treatment by the same author: *La quéte du bonheur* (Paris: Téqui, 1979).

3. See Neil J. McEleny, C.S.P., "The Beatitudes of the Sermon on the Mount," *Catholic Biblical Quarterly*, 43 (1981), 1–13.

4. 60 *AAS* (1968) 433–45.

5. Paul Hinnebusch, O.P., "The Messianic Meaning of the Beatitudes," *The Bible Today*, 59 (1972), 707–17, explains clearly and simply the Old Testament roots of the spirituality of the Beatitudes, defends the view that their promise begins to be fulfilled in this world, and sees them as "a portrait of Jesus himself" (717) expressed not only in words but in his life.

6. On the beatitude formula as it is used in the New Testament, see F. Hauck, "makarios," *Theological Dictionary of the New Testament*, 4:367–70.

7. Robert A. Guelich, "The Matthean Beatitudes: 'Entrance-Requirements' or Eschatological Blessings?" *Journal of Biblical Literature*, 95 (1976), 415–34, provides a scholarly and insightful examination of the Beatitudes, which, however, suffers from an unnecessary opposition between ethical requirements and blessings. He assumes that meritorious activity which meets an ethical requirement for ultimate blessedness is not itself a grace and part of the eschatological blessing insofar as this is already realized. To this assumption one must oppose Eph 2.10.

8. See Meier, op. cit., 163, esp. n. 177. The correspondence between Beatitudes and woes in Matthew not only seems obvious from their content and the neatness of the inclusion, but from their evident relationship to Lk 6.20–26, where blessings and woes are paired somewhat as the blessings and curses of the covenant are in Dt 28. Of course, the Beatitudes of the new covenant correspond precisely neither to the stipulations nor to the blessings of the old, for in Jesus the requirements of friendship with God are one with the fulfillment of these requirements.

9. The implications of the theological framework developed in this work point to an understanding of virtue rather different from that of St. Thomas and more like that of St. Bonaventure. See W. D. Hughes, O.P., in St. Thomas Aquinas, *Summa theologiae*, vol. 23, *Virtue*, trans. and ed. W. D. Hughes, O.P. (New York: McGraw-Hill, 1969), 245–48.

10. Leo XIII, *Divinum illud munus*, 29 *ASS* (1896–97) 652–54; *The Papal Encyclicals*, 140.9, gives "gifts of the Holy Spirit" a wide sense, in which the Spirit himself is the primary gift, but also says: "More than this, the just man, that is to say he who lives the life of divine grace, and acts by the fitting virtues as by means of faculties, has need of those seven *gifts* which are properly attributed to the Holy Ghost. By means of them the soul is furnished and strengthened so as to obey more easily and promptly His voice and impulse. Wherefore these gifts are of such efficacy that they lead the just man to the highest degree of sanctity; and of such excellence that they continue to exist even in heaven, though in a more perfect way. By means of these gifts the soul is excited and encouraged to seek after and attain the evangelical beatitudes, which, like the flowers that come forth in the spring time, are the signs and harbingers of eternal beatitude." This seems to be the most explicit, important teaching of the magisterium on the gifts. It does not require that they be regarded as distinct from the Christian virtues; indeed, Pope Leo seems to consider the gifts as aids in attaining the Beatitudes. If so, it seems entirely fitting to identify the gifts with charity considered insofar as it is a gift of the Holy Spirit which transforms modes of responsibility into modes of Christian response.

Chapter 26   Notes

11. See Iosepho A. de Aldama, S.I., *Tractatus IV: De virtutibus infusis*, in Patres Societatis Iesu Facultatum Theologicarum in Hispania Professores, *Sacrae Theologiae Summa*, vol. 3, ed. 4 (Madrid: B.A.C., 1961), 729–30.

12. A helpful, nontechnical study of the gifts as Thomas understands them: Robert Edward Brennan, O.P., *The Seven Horns of the Lamb: A Study of the Gifts Based on Saint Thomas Aquinas* (Milwaukee: Bruce, 1966), 1–33. Brennan's notes suggest the extent of theological indeterminacy on this subject.

13. See Jacques Dupont, *Les Béatitudes*, tome III, *Les Evangélistes*, 2d ed. (Paris: J. Gabalda, 1973), 399–411, 458–71. Mary's Magnificat perfectly exemplifies humility. Some deny that it should be attributed to Mary. However, see the powerful exegetical argument in defense of the historicity of Luke's narrative on this point (and of the infancy narratives generally): René Laurentin, *Les Evangiles de l'Enfance du Christ: Vérité de Noël au-delà des mythes* (Paris: Desclée, 1982), 13–22, 445–49, 451.

14. St. Augustine, *The Lord's Sermon on the Mount*, Ancient Christian Writers, 5; trans. John J. Jepson, S.S. (New York: Newman Press, 1948), 19.

15. See Léon Roy, "Poor," *Dictionary of Biblical Theology*, 2d. ed., 436–38; John L. McKenzie, S.J., *Dictionary of the Bible*, 681–84.

16. The order of the second and third Beatitudes varies; the R.S.V. and the N.A.B. put that concerning the sorrowing in second place. Here, the Beatitude concerning the meek is put in second place, because this order, being that of the Vulgate, is followed in most past Catholic writings. Nothing vital hangs upon this point. Also, I prefer the "meek" of the R.S.V. to the "lowly" of the N.A.B. John P. Meier, *Matthew* (Wilmington, Del.: Michael Glazier, 1980), 40, accepts "meek" as an appropriate translation, avoids reducing meekness to humility, warns against taking "meekness" to mean softness, and helpfully characterizes the meek: "The truly meek are, in the Bible, the considerate, the unassuming, the peaceable towards both God and man. They do not push their own plans to the detriment of God's saving plan."

17. See Dupont, op. cit., 473–545.

18. Fred L. Fisher, *The Sermon on the Mount* (Nashville: Broadman Press, 1976), 31, illustrates meekness with the example of a football team; the disciplined players docilely follow signals. The meek Christian accepts a position in Jesus' kingdom on earth, and following his signals plays this position as perfectly as possible.

19. St. Augustine, loc. cit.

20. See Dupont, op. cit., 545–55.

21. St. Augustine, op. cit., 14.

22. Ibid., 19.

23. See Dupont, op. cit., 355–84.

24. St. Augustine, loc. cit.

25. See Dupont, op. cit., 604–32.

26. St. Augustine, op. cit., 19–20.

27. John Paul II, *Dives in misericordia*, 72 *AAS* (1980) 1225; *The Papal Encyclicals*, 279.153. A more general argument that justice must be transformed into mercy is presented earlier in the encyclical (1215–16; 117–22), where the Pope explicitly asserts that Jesus challenged those faithful to the Old Testament to go beyond its requirements.

28. See Dupont, op. cit., 557–603.

29. St. Augustine, op. cit., 20.

30. See Dupont, op. cit., 633–64.

31. St. Augustine, loc. cit.

32. See Heinrich Gross, "Peace," *Encyclopedia of Biblical Theology*, 648–51.

33. See Dupont, op. cit., 329–55.

34. St. Augustine, op. cit., 16–24.

35. See Dietrich Bonhoeffer, *The Cost of Discipleship*, rev. unabridged ed. (New York: Macmillan, 1959), 76–83. While Catholic readers will note certain Lutheran positions in it, this work is excellent, and much of it is relevant to the present chapter.

36. A survey of moral systems considered as types of wisdom alternative to Christian faith: Jacques Maritain, *Moral Philosophy: An Historical and Critical Survey of the Great Systems* (New York: Charles Scribner's Sons, 1964), esp. 71–91.

37. To deny this proposition, as some do, leads to the relativization of Jesus, who comes to be regarded as only one way of religious relationship with the transcendent; that, in turn, leads to denial of the authority of Scripture and of the Incarnation itself. See Lucien Richard, O.M.I., *What Are They Saying about Christ and World Religions?* (New York: Paulist Press, 1981), 44–73. It is unclear why anyone would be interested in such a ghost of religion—which is no more acceptable to a serious Hindu than it is to a serious Christian.

CHAPTER TWENTY-SEVEN

LIFE FORMED BY
THE MODES OF CHRISTIAN RESPONSE

Introduction

How do the modes of Christian response shape a Christian's life into an orderly unity? The present chapter will seek to answer that question, but only as it pertains to Christian moral principles. A comprehensive answer must also take up many specific issues, which belonging to the special treatises of moral theology, are not considered here. What is crucial at this point is that the style of Christian life is both distinctive and admits of striking diversity. In the present chapter we shall see why this is so.

Question A: What is the underlying principle which unifies the modes of Christian response?

1. Anyone comparing the general modes of human responsibility with the specifically Christian modes of response will notice that the distinctions among the latter are far less clear than those among the former. Yet the Christian modes of response include the human modes of responsibility and transform them. Why, then, do the Christian modes form so tight a unity that they seem almost to merge, rather like double images which fuse when a lens is focused?

2. Logically, the Christian modes are distinct among themselves. From a conceptual point of view, each requires something different from the others. Still, in many Christian acts one clearly sees the various modes exemplified together. For instance, the missionaries among the North American martyrs undertook the work of mercy of spreading the gospel, carried out their mission with single-minded dedication, lived as peacemakers among their enemies, and laid down their lives for Jesus. In fact, all the modes of Christian response come to bear upon every act of Christian life. All demand what each demands, all exclude what each excludes.

3. To see why this is so, it will be helpful to recall the relationship between the principles of morality and God's redemptive work in Jesus. The first principle of morality is that one's willing should always be that of a will toward integral human fulfillment. Revelation tells us that this fulfillment is more than an ideal; it is to be realized in the accomplishment of God's plan for the fulfillment of all

things in Jesus. By the gift of charity, God's adopted children are disposed toward this greater good which will include their human fulfillment. Thus, the first principle of Christian morality is always to will in a way which contributes to human fulfillment as part of the fulfillment of all things in Jesus (25-D).

4. Charity, one's share in the divine nature, in no way limits or nullifies one's human nature. Hence, the modes of responsibility which specify the first moral principle are still valid for Christian life. The fallen human condition, however, sets special requirements which must be met if one is to live uprightly (25-E). In the fallen condition, persons confront death, lack the support of a genuine human community, and so see little point in an upright and energetic pursuit of human goods. Thus, without the grace of Jesus, it is in practice impossible for fallen men and women to live consistently good lives. They are constantly tempted to deal with evil inappropriately—for example, by destructive methods or renunciation of human hope for a good life in this world.

5. Jesus' way of dealing with evil is uniquely appropriate to the actual human condition. Encountering evil with healing love, he meets all the requirements of moral goodness. He faces the human condition with absolute realism, rejects violence, yet sets to work to change things for the better insofar as this is possible through human action. On the basis of these characteristics alone, Jesus' life is morally exemplary and his cause worthy of support. But his life and especially his death and resurrection also are revelatory. They show that humankind can escape evil and share in the realization of all human hopes by living in union with Jesus. For in accepting Jesus' self-offering, God has made it clear that Jesus' human life is cooperation with the divine redemptive work, which will be completed through the re-creation of the broken world.

6. With these principles in mind, one can understand the precise difference between the modes of responsibility and the modes of Christian response. The modes of responsibility are moral principles excluding ways of willing incompatible with a will toward integral human fulfillment. The modes of Christian response are norms for action which actually will contribute to the realization of integral human fulfillment. **The modes of Christian response take into account what must be done if one is to live an upright life and realize human goods in the fallen human condition. They direct men and women to commit themselves to a definite kind of action—that begun by Jesus.** Moreover, the modes of Christian response not only prescribe good acts, but include a precommitment to do them and, by the gift of the Spirit, the power to carry out this commitment (26-B).

7. In sum, the modes of responsibility remain valid moral principles which, even in the fallen human condition, require human action in accord with integral human fulfillment. Their indications are all met perfectly in one human act: the sacrificial act of Jesus. In this completely virtuous act Jesus overcomes all the disharmonies of sin—within the individual, among the principles of human actions themselves, among human individuals and groups, and between humankind and God. Hence, Jesus' act includes both the norms for the choices essential to these existential harmonies and their virtuous fulfillment. These norms and

their realization are the modes of Christian response. Thus, the modes of Christian response, in transforming the modes of responsibility, merge like so many images of human goodness coming to focus in one perfect image.

Question B: How do the modes of Christian response shape the life of each Christian following Jesus?

1. Chapter twenty-three treated God's redemptive work in the lives of Christians. That treatment considered faith as the fundamental option of Christian life, the commitment included in faith to follow Jesus, and personal vocation as each Christian's way of fulfilling this commitment. The present question will add an explanation of the role of the modes of Christian response in shaping Christian lives, in all their rich diversity, according to the perfect model of Jesus.

2. As question A explained, Jesus' redemptive act perfectly embodies all the modes of Christian response. This act is social and covenant forming; each Christian enters into it by the act of faith. It follows that the act of faith itself is formed by all the modes of Christian response. By baptismal faith, Christians humbly accept God's revelation, meekly seek salvation in the Church, renounce Satan, undertake to follow Jesus, escape the web of hatred and injustice by forgiving their enemies, set about to overcome the residue of sin in their lives, are reconciled to God, and prepare to offer themselves with Jesus in the Eucharist.

3. However, while the Christian's act of faith embodies the Christian modes of response insofar as this act is one with the redemptive act of Jesus, the likeness of each Christian's life to Jesus' life is still more obvious in the commitments of personal vocation which implement faith. In these, one accepts one's own part in the cooperative action Jesus began; one carries on his work of revealing divine truth and love to others.

4. The readiness to accept one's life as God's gift is the work of humility, for humility disposes the Christian to listen for and hear God's call. One's individual vocation is a very limited part of the life of the Church; meekness is needed to accept one's limited place obediently and to resign oneself to its inevitable frustrations. Commitment to one's vocation requires detachment from every other possibility of individual fulfillment; it also demands faithfulness despite obstacles and temptations to swerve from one's calling. Each vocation imposes responsibilities for the salvation of others; the fulfillment of these responsibilities is a continuous work of mercy. One's vocation puts all one's powers to work and demands mortification of anything which interferes with this work; this single-minded devotion is purity of heart. Through carrying out one's vocation, one makes some contribution to overcoming sin and its consequences; even in this life, the peace of Jesus begins to be realized. But, in the end, every Christian must expect to share in Jesus' fate, for the ultimate success of redemptive work requires that one undergo the evil one cannot conquer, and look to God's re-creative work for vindication of one's hope.

5. **Since all Christian vocations are ways of cooperating with Jesus' redemptive work, all are alike in embodying the modes of Christian response.** Thus, distinctively Christian ways of acting are common to all truly

Christian lives and markedly present in the lives of the saints. **Yet, since personal vocations are different roles in the drama of salvation, each uses diverse gifts to carry out one part of God's plan, and so Christian lives are unique.** Each saint embodies the Christian virtues in a personal way.

6. Every single act of a Christian's life should help to carry out his or her personal vocation. One's whole life, in all its complexity, should come down to doing always and only one thing (25-F). Thus, particular deeds will only be ways of living one's faith by carrying out the personal vocation which implements it. Insofar as Christians do live their lives in this consistent way, the modes of Christian response which shape their vocational commitments also will shape each and every choice they make. In everything they do, they will act in Jesus and respond with him to the Father's love.

7. Thus, the Christian modes of response are aspects of a tightly unified, Jesus-like character. Nevertheless, since they remain conceptually distinct, the Christian modes of response provide distinct principles for reflection. One can proceed from each to formulate norms, just as one can generate specific norms from each of the common human modes of responsibility.

Various approaches in moral and spiritual formation have emphasized one or another of the modes of Christian response. There is nothing wrong with such an emphasis, if the true model of Christian life—the character of Jesus—is not distorted. Whether one begins by emphasizing humility or mercy, detachment or conciliation, one will reunite all of the other aspects, since all the dispositions of Christian life are rooted in the same, central redemptive act. Of course, a form of spirituality will run into trouble if it is nourished by personal idiosyncrasies or ideology drawn from extragospel sources. In such a case, humility, for example, sometimes has been mistaken for a sort of servility alien to Christian dignity. Again, mercy sometimes is reduced to a secular humanistic beneficence, ready to use violence to liberate the oppressed.

Question C: How do the Christian modes of response lead to specific Christian norms?

1. Specific norms can be derived by considering the relation of the willing involved in each kind of action to the intelligible goods which actions of that kind bear upon (10-B). This consideration is carried out in the light of the first principle of morality and the modes of responsibility. Because the modes of Christian response should shape all the actions of a Christian's life, they also must lead to specific norms.

2. Like the modes of responsibility, the modes of Christian response determine the moral character of kinds of action by evaluating the ways in which one's will in doing them relates to human goods. However, there are two special features of the derivation of Christian norms. First, the actions of a Christian's life always are specifically different from those possible without faith (25-E). Second, the modes of Christian response are themselves affirmative norms of a very general kind, for they direct that every action of a Christian's life be a way of living redemptively in Jesus.

3. In practice, individual Christians need not derive all the specific Christian

norms for themselves. Some important ones are found in the New Testament and the Church's constant and universal teaching—for example, injunctions to fast and give alms, to do good to persecutors, to correct erring fellow Christians in a certain way, and so on. Many other specific norms can be gathered from the lives of those honored as saints, rules approved for religious·families, practices commended in pastoral exhortations, and so on. Such norms often can be adapted to determine precise responsibilities for those Christians to whose options they are relevant.

4. **Most of the affirmative responsibilities of Christian life follow quite clearly from the commitments which constitute one's personal vocation.** Whenever one recognizes some kind of action as appropriate to carry out one's vocation, doing that kind of action becomes obligatory unless there is another good option or some reason for not doing it. Of course, at times the richness of options or difficult conflicts can make it hard to see how one ought to proceed in accord with one's vocation.

5. In such cases, reflection on the factual situation and its possibilities in the light of the Christian modes of response often leads to a solution. This solution will be a new and appropriate kind of action together with a norm requiring that it be chosen. For example, pressed either to swear falsely or to commit treason, St. Thomas More saw it as his duty to avoid both by a careful refusal to speak his mind, which entailed his suffering the penalties of loss of position, property, and personal liberty.

6. When individual Christians—or even the Church as a community—finds it necessary to seek solutions by deriving new moral norms, it is important to bear in mind that Christian morality does not negate any moral truth known without the light of faith. **Hence, if a norm of common morality is absolute, any Christian specification of it will also be absolute.** An act which is always immoral for anyone is always immoral for a Christian. Otherwise, Christian norms could direct one to act in a manner incompatible with integral human fulfillment. It is necessary of course to keep in mind that an absolute norm determines the morality of a kind of act morally described, not a kind of act behaviorally described.

Blasphemy, for example, is wrong. Understanding "blasphemy" as the choice to demean what one believes to be divine, the norm of common morality already is absolute. The Christian norm of morality cannot change this moral determination, although the norm is more specific insofar as God and humankind's relation to him are better understood. However, in a culture which is not Christian, certain patterns of behavior will be counted "blasphemy" which in the light of Christian faith really are not such. For example, the Jewish leaders considered blasphemy what Jesus did not (see Mt 26.65; Jn 10.36). Therefore, what the standards of conventional morality consider blasphemy can be obligatory for a Christian, yet the specifically Christian norm on this matter does not change the negative moral determination of the norm of common morality against blasphemy.

7. **Moreover, even when a norm of morality for a kind of action considered without faith is nonabsolute, a similar action done within Christian life will have further specifications.** In view of these, the corresponding

Christian norm can be absolute. For example, even without faith one can know that marital faithfulness until death is a moral responsibility. But a Christian's marital commitment is a richer act than is that of a person without faith. Christian marriage necessarily is a vocational commitment to which Jesus is a party; the sacramental bond of marriage shares in and contributes to his unbreakable union with the Church. The result is that the nonabsolute norm of morality holding even nonbelievers to faithfulness in marriage until death is replaced by an absolute norm of Christian morality.

8. Christian reflection also sometimes leads to a specific moral judgment which seems to reverse an apparently sound norm. When this occurs, Christian morality is not overriding any moral truth knowable without faith. Rather, the Christian action is different in kind, because faith provides new options and enriches existing ones with new meaning (25-F). The result is that many nonabsolute norms articulated without faith, although true for the realities they take into account, prove inadequate for Christian life. What would be approved or even required by upright judgment without faith often must be rejected by Christian standards. The opposite also is true.

For example, common morality enjoins that family members compose differences in religious practice in a way likely to promote the family's solidarity. The norm is nonabsolute, but sound at its level of specification, since apart from revelation religion is not superior to essential social solidarity, and since the good of religion in general does not generate any specific requirement of exclusive worship in one form. Christian revelation, however, is divisive (see Lk 12.52), for it puts the claims of Jesus above those of family solidarity, requires that any form of religious practice incompatible with the gospel be avoided, and even demands a profession of faith when failure to make such a profession would be equivalent to denial by silence. Thus, the specifically Christian norm about religious differences and family solidarity sometimes requires what the nonabsolute norm of common morality would correctly exclude.

Again, according to a nonabsolute norm of common morality, divorce is wrong, for although marriage is not in itself sacramental and absolutely indissoluble, the relationship is morally unbreakable. However, according to a more specific norm of Christian morality—the so-called "Pauline privilege" (see 1 Cor 7.15)—a Christian can accept as definitive the refusal of a nonbelieving spouse to live in a marriage in a manner compatible with the Christian partner's observance of the duties of Christian life. (Thus Christian norms specify the common requirements of marital faithfulness in two seemingly opposite ways, but both are understandable if one bears in mind the distinction between marriage in general and specifically Christian marriage.)

Question D: How does each Christian's conscience function in forming his or her unique life?

1. A Catholic conscience should conform absolutely to the Church's teaching (23-G). However, this teaching is not sufficient by itself to settle any question about precisely what one should do. The Church does propose some norms which absolutely exclude certain kinds of action, such as killing the innocent. Moreover, the Church firmly teaches that one must live one's faith by faithfully carrying out one's vocational commitments. But the Church does not assign her members their

personal vocations and cannot teach anyone which precise actions are required day by day to carry out vocational commitments. The specific, affirmative norms the Church proposes—either to all the faithful or to certain groups—can help one to find one's vocation and to make the judgments of conscience required to carry it out. But these affirmative norms are necessarily nonabsolute, for they are never so fully specified that they can provide the immediate basis for any judgment of conscience.

As Vatican II teaches, the pastors of the Church do not have concrete solutions to every problem of conscience which arises, nor is that their mission. The laity are to make conscientious judgments of their own, enlightened by Christian wisdom and paying close attention to the Church's pastors (see GS 43).

2. For instance, the Church's teaching indicates many duties which are serious and normally inescapable, but it points out no specific positive duty which might not under some conditions yield to some other responsibility. Moreover, a positive duty which is required in a general way—say, the duty of parents to educate their children in the faith—must be carried out in some specific way, and this way must be chosen in accord with a norm of Christian judgment more specific than any the Church can teach. One must be able to conclude: This is what I should do to carry out my commitment of faith and the vocational commitments I have made to implement it.

3. Thus, a Christian of mature conscience is not satisfied with knowing that one possibility is forbidden and another permitted. He or she looks for the right choice: what is holy, pleasing to God, and perfect. **The Christian's conscience is no mere negative norm or monitor, leaving the positive determination of behavior to nonmoral inclination. This is so because the point of Christian life is not just to avoid sin but to cooperate in redemptive work, and to do this affirmatively according to one's unique personal vocation.**

If an individual reaches moral maturity shortly before or around the time he or she makes major vocational commitments, his or her conscience seems to be working a good part of the time. "What ought I to be and to do?" becomes an engrossing question. Once one has made one's commitments and settled into the life they require, conscience is less busy.

Superego and social convention extend to only a selected part of one's behavior. At these immature stages, much of life remains in a "free area," in the sense that morality is not felt to apply to it and one considers oneself at liberty to do as one pleases. Even when the third level of conscience begins to emerge, it does not develop all at once and extend to the whole range of one's choices. Thus, for some time (perhaps for many people for the whole of their lives) many choices are without moral significance for good or ill.

This situation is not changed at once by the fact that one has Christian faith. The boundaries of the area of liberty seem different for Christians, but many people with genuine faith sincerely assume that there is no moral or religious stake in many choices.

4. Thus, whenever a Christian really wonders, "What should I do?" no preexisting norm will be specific enough to give the answer. An adequate norm must embody but further specify one or more preexisting norms, so that all the intelligible aspects of the possibility will be taken into consideration. In many actual judgments the affirmative norm, "This is what I should do," is very complex, because of the intelligible complexity of the options under considera-

tion. Although such a norm remains universal (it would apply to any exactly similar case), it may be that there never has been nor will be another case to which the norm applies, and the norm will have to be developed to fit this sole instance.

5. Moreover, even when a sufficiently specific norm is found or developed to fit the options under consideration, conscience still has its proper task to perform. This task is not to bring into play some incommunicable and mysterious moral determinant. The only factors which determine the moral character of choices are the intelligible relationships between the willing involved in available options and the human goods proposed actions would bear on. A sufficiently specified norm takes all these moral determinants into account (10-D).

6. In reaching the judgment, "This is what I should do," conscience directs the choice referred to by "this" as an instance of the kind referred to by "what." This kind of action has been morally characterized by the specific norm one takes to be adequate for the case. If one is conscientious in taking a norm to be adequate, prudence is required to make two prior judgments: (1) that one has reflected far enough in reaching the specific norm; and (2) that of the options considered good at the end of moral reflection one is to be preferred.

7. Even in making these two prudential judgments, a Catholic's conscience receives valuable assistance. By identifying certain kinds of actions and omissions—those inconsistent with faithfulness to one's Christian commitments—as grave matter, the Church's teaching facilitates the judgment that one has reflected adequately in reaching the specific norm one is about to follow. For if reflection has established that choice of a certain kind of action would not be a mortal sin, and if a norm commends it as good, then one can act on the norm with prudent certainty. Even if further reflection would bring to light additional morally relevant features of the situation, these would not detract from faithfulness in following Jesus according to one's personal vocation.

8. Also, the Church's indications as to what might be more perfect facilitate the judgment of personal preference. This is the prudential judgment among options which still appear good after all relevant moral determinants have been rationally examined. Because human action involves the whole person, at this point preference for one option is rightly settled by nonrational inclination. One who not only has the mind of Jesus but also his heart will be affected by his nonbinding wishes—such as the counsels of perfection—and by preferences indicated by the Church.

9. If it seems that there is no good option rather than too many good options, a mature Christian conscience will not at once define the issue by the possibilities which first present themselves. Since conscience is governed by the basic commitment of faith (specified by a personal vocational commitment), it must search out or invent ways to carry out the commitment. The person of mature conscience seeks additional information and thinks of fresh possibilities. The source of moral ingenuity or creativity thus lies in commitment; love looks for and finds a way to serve the good to which the Christian is dedicated.

Question E: Does the Christian conscience demand perfection?

1. Vatican II teaches that every Christian is called to the perfection possible in this life (see LG 40–42). This perfection is holiness, and charity is its heart: "The Lord Jesus, the divine Teacher and Model of all perfection, preached holiness of life to each and every one of his disciples, regardless of their situation: 'You therefore are to be perfect, even as your heavenly Father is perfect' (Mt 5.48). He himself stands as the Author and Finisher of this holiness of life. For he sent the Holy Spirit upon all men that he might inspire them from within to love God with their whole heart and their whole soul, with all their mind and all their strength (cf. Mk 12.30) and that they might love one another as Christ loved them (cf. Jn 13.34; 15.12)" (LG 40). **The Christian conscience demands that one live according to the calling one has received** (see Eph 4.1). **Therefore, the Christian conscience demands perfection.**

2. Charity is the heart of Christian perfection, but it does not constitute perfection by itself. One must grow in charity (see *S.t.*, 2–2, q. 24, aa. 4–8; q. 184, a. 3, ad 3). This happens when charity is bodied out by prayer, the sacraments, and a morally good life shaped by these principles.

3. Holiness cannot be separated from love of neighbor; one can only find oneself by giving oneself (see GS 24). Because love is the law of human perfection, love demands the transformation of this world (see GS 38). Thus, Christian perfection requires that this world be built up by fruitful activity (see GS 34). Moreover, this activity cannot be limited to the promotion of religion. It must include cultivation of the many human goods, for here and now we "make ready the material of the celestial realm" (GS 38).

The love which is at the heart of Christian life is not a mysterious something hidden in the depths of one's inner self. Rather, it is the disposition to total fulfillment in divine and human life. Charity rules all the means of attaining holiness, because it organizes and enlivens the whole of Christian life, which is communion in divine life, and this very living and flourishing whole is holiness (see *S.t.*, 2–2, q. 184, aa. 1, 3).

The perfection of Christian life is perfection of the whole interpersonal relationship with God, with other persons, and with the remainder of creation. God initiates a friendship with creatures; holiness is the blossoming of this friendship. In this blossoming, nothing of divine goods is held back by God, and nothing of created goods may be held back by those who love him. All one's life, all society, everything good, beautiful, and true must be drawn into this friendship. Charity excludes no human good, but rather requires the cultivation of every good of the human person: "By this holiness a more human way of life is promoted even in this earthly society" (LG 40). The idea that the perfection to which Christians are called in this life is exclusively spiritual and religious—that holiness has little to do with the body and secular human goods—is radically mistaken. Indeed, this idea is at war with Christianity, which is centered upon the Word made flesh.

In Jesus the mystery of humankind takes on new light. Jesus, "by the revelation of the mystery of the Father and his love, fully reveals man to man himself and makes his supreme calling clear" (GS 22). For Jesus makes clear that the new law of love can be fulfilled by the Spirit's power, that human persons are called to integral human and divine fulfillment, that the way to this fulfillment requires love and service also of bodily goods, that the way leads through death to resurrection, and that heavenly fulfillment will enhance individuality and every aspect of human potentiality (see *S.t.*, 2–2, q. 25, a. 5; 3, q. 56).

4. **Since every Christian is called to perfection and perfection includes love of all human goods, the demand for perfection extends to the whole of moral life.** As question C explained, the Christian modes of response are moral principles of the specific norms reached by a Christian conscience. They require that every choice conform to charity and contribute to the living out of redemption. Since the requirements of charity demand perfection, a fully mature Christian conscience demands perfection in every act. Thus, in every act one ought to carry out the fundamental redemptive commitment of the act of faith (see DS 1535/803). In other words: "Whatever you do, in word or deed, do everything in the name of the Lord Jesus, giving thanks to God the Father through him" (Col 3.17).

5. As the previous questions of this chapter have made clear, Christians must implement their fundamental option of faith by finding, accepting, and committing themselves to their personal vocations. It follows that Christians respond to the universal call to holiness in no other way than by responding perfectly to the personal call each one receives to play his or her unique role in God's all-embracing plan of salvation. A perfect response to one's personal vocation is sanctifying, because in carrying it out with all one's resources one brings one's whole mind, heart, soul, and strength into the service of God's plan.

Vatican II confirms this conclusion by explaining how holiness can be reached in diverse conditions and states of life and summing up: "All of Christ's faithful, therefore, whatever be the conditions, duties, and circumstances of their lives, will grow in holiness day by day through these very situations, if they accept all of them with faith from the hand of their heavenly Father, and if they cooperate with the divine will by showing every man through their earthly activities the love with which God has loved the world" (LG 41).

John Paul II builds upon the teaching of the Council about vocation and also treats personal vocation as an essential principle of Christian moral life. We must remember, he teaches, that efforts at renewal are authentic only insofar as they are ". . . based on adequate awareness of the individual Christian's vocation and of responsibility for this singular, unique and unrepeatable grace by which each Christian in the community of the People of God builds up the Body of Christ. This principle, the key rule for the whole of Christian practice—apostolic and pastoral practice, practice of interior and of social life—must with due proportion be applied to the whole of humanity and to each human being." After exemplifying the principle with respect to several states of life, he adds: "It is precisely the principle of the 'kingly service' that imposes on each one of us, in imitation of Christ's example, the duty to demand of himself exactly what we have been called to, what we have personally obliged ourselves to by God's grace, in order to respond to our vocation."[1]

Question F: To what extent are Christians obliged to forgo their rights?

1. The gospel's demand for perfection clearly requires that Christians forgo their rights in some circumstances (see Mt 5.39–41). To what extent is this requirement binding on a Christian's conscience in his or her relationships with others, with society, and especially with the Church?

2. There are three possible ways of regarding one's rights. One can be concerned to claim them precisely because they are one's own. One can be

concerned to claim them for the sake of justice. Or one can be ready to claim or forgo them the better to fulfill one's commitments. Only the third way is appropriate for Christians (see *S.t.*, 2–2, q. 72, a. 3).

3. In the fallen human condition, people often are most concerned to protect their rights simply because they are theirs. Because ·this bias toward self is virtually universal and in this instance is concerned with what one is justified in demanding, conventional morality approves this approach. Still, it violates the fifth mode of responsibility, since it leads one to act out of love of self rather than love of justice. A person who loved justice would not be concerned with rights precisely as his or her own but would instead be concerned impartially with the justice to be done, and so would be concerned with the rights of all who suffer a similar injustice.

4. As for those who take the second approach and are concerned to defend their rights on principle, they do have a social consciousness and they pursue their own rights for the sake of justice to all who are similarly situated. Indeed, they do this even in cases where they would otherwise consider it too much trouble to defend their rights. Based as it is upon an impartial love of justice, this approach conforms to the common requirements of moral responsibility.

5. **Christians, however, must seek and accept everything as a gift from God. In imitation of Jesus, who did not cling to his right to divine honor, they ought to pursue others' interests in preference to their own** (cf. Phil 2.1–11). **Transforming justice into mercy, they should voluntarily forgo their rights and more than fulfill their duties** (see Mt 5.38–42). Overcoming evil with good, they should forgive injuries (see Mt 5.43–48; Rom 12.21). Living redemptively, they should suffer evil meekly so that good might come from it (see Mt 5.10–11).

6. Christians therefore ought not to be concerned about their rights but about the responsibilities entailed by their personal vocations. St. Paul, for example, did not accept support from the Corinthians, though he was entitled to it, for he wished them to receive the gospel entirely as a gift even from its human agent (2 Cor 11.7–9). In sum, Christians should seek to vindicate their rights when this is required to fulfill their responsibilities, but not otherwise.

For example, a bishop ought to defend his right to preach the gospel and to minister to his flock; Christian workers ought to seek just compensation for the support of their families and the work of the Church; Christian nurses should defend their right to exemption from assignments to participate in abortions. Christians may make establishing and protecting justice in society a part of their vocational commitment. But if they do, they will prove that their concern for justice is redemptive by preferring to act in defense of rights whose violation does not affect them personally.

Because Christians should claim their rights when doing so fulfills the responsibilities of their personal vocations, there often will appear to be little difference between the behavior of conventionally moral persons and that of Christians in exacting rights. If one has the mind of Jesus in this matter, however, in certain cases one's behavior will be strikingly different.

Question G: How can Christian norms require preference for certain persons?

1. Most ethical systems take it for granted that, except for those with whom one has a special relationship, one need only avoid harming others. But Christian responsibility extends to all humankind. "Neighbor" is not a predefined category but includes all who need redemption—in other words, all without qualification. A conscience formed by the demands of charity must therefore pursue the salvation of all, and this salvation includes their human fulfillment.

2. How, then, can a Christian rightly prefer certain persons? Of course, this question cannot be taken to ask how a Christian can rightly practice unfair discrimination. Nor should it be taken to ask how a Christian can rightly have a stronger attachment to some persons—for example, to friends and family. Rather, the question is how Christians can rightly have policies of preferring to benefit some persons rather than others by their good actions. For example, how does one justify the policy of preferring to do good to those who are of the household of the faith?

3. **The answer essentially is that there is an order in charity, grounded in the Trinity.** Among human persons, some are direct media of salvation for others. Priority of love among members of the Church is required by her mission, while individuals fulfill their general redemptive responsibility by fulfilling specific responsibilities to specific persons according to their personal vocations.

4. This can be explained as follows. Charity is a disposition toward fulfillment in divine life. Fulfillment in divine life is a communion of persons among whom there is a definite order; thus, there is an order in charity. No one comes to the Father except through the Son (see Jn 14.6); and, since Jesus loves his human brothers and sisters as the Father loves him (see Jn 15.9), it follows that the natural unity of the Father and the Son is the precondition of the communion of human persons in divine life. United in Jesus, not as isolated individuals, human beings share in divine life and become God's children (see Jn 1.12; 17.20–26). The Spirit who pours forth charity (see Rom 5.5) is the Spirit of the Son (see Gal 4.6). Thus, in their relationships with each other and with us, the divine persons are not interchangeable.

5. There is likewise an order in charity among human beings (cf. *S.t.*, 2–2, q. 26, aa. 6–8). All who are saved are saved by being united with Jesus as members of his Mystical Body, the Church (see Eph 2.11–22). But within the Church there are different roles and a definite order—for example, the apostles and prophets provide a foundation (see Eph 2.20). Thus, in their relationships with one another and with those outside the Church, human persons are not interchangeable.

6. **The order inherent in charity explains why so much emphasis is placed upon fraternal charity among Christians.** Jesus demands that his disciples love one another (see Jn 13.34). The First Epistle of John repeatedly stresses the love of believers for one another. Love among Christians has a certain priority over their love for others: "As we have opportunity, let us do good to all men, and especially to those who are of the household of faith" (Gal 6.10; cf. 1 Pt 2.17).

7. This priority is not partiality and discrimination. The love which Christians have for one another is the necessary precondition for the revelation and effective communication of divine love to others (see Jn 13.34–35). The priority of love within the Church is determined by the Church's mission of service in the redemption of humankind. Only if divine love is present in the Church can the Church communicate divine love to the world. Moreover, the intensity of love in the Church conditions her effectiveness in saving the world as the intensity of heat in a furnace conditions its effectiveness in heating a building.

8. Charity requires that all human goods be pursued in every upright way by some Christian or group of Christians, for by their lives Christians prepare the material of the heavenly kingdom (see GS 38–39). Most goods can be pursued effectively only by a limited group who mutually commit themselves to their pursuit. Hence, charity requires such commitments—for example, of this man and this woman to one another in marriage.

9. In making such commitments, one assumes definite responsibilities to definite persons. As part of one's Christian life, all such commitments belong to one's personal vocation. Charity requires Christians to carry out their personal vocations. Therefore, charity requires that Christians make a policy of preferring to benefit some persons rather than others by their good actions. Parents, for example, must raise their own children before going off to engage in missionary activity on behalf of people in a distant land. Even Jesus' personal vocation included a special responsibility for Israel (see Mt 15.21–28).

Charity is community forming; love builds up the Church (see 1 Cor 8.1; Eph 4.15–16). This follows from the nature of charity as a communion of divine and human persons. For this reason, one ought not to think of Christian love individualistically, as if it were a bond only between individuals—individual souls and God, or any other pair as "I" and "thou." The relationship of love begins with a single "I" in only one case: that of the Father from whom everything proceeds. In this case, it immediately unfolds into the "we" of the Father and the Son together, from whom as a single source the Spirit proceeds, and then by generous freedom into the "we" of the creator who says: Let us . . ..

In loving with charity, then, one always loves as part of a fellowship and loves many persons in communion. As a member of the Church carrying out her apostolic mission to the world, one loves unbelieving humankind. As part of his created family loving its source, one loves God. This characteristic of charity solves the problem, often raised, of how love can be universal without being diluted to such an extent that it becomes a mere abstract philanthropy, like that of secular humanists who love humankind in general but are willing to sacrifice certain individuals. By Christian charity, one's love, on whatever scale, is engaged in a real and cooperative work. The larger the scale of this work, the greater the demand for charity in deed and in truth among those who share in the more immediate relationships necessary to carry it out.

Question H: How can a conscientious Christian make any vocational commitment other than to follow the counsels of perfection?

1. The Catholic Church has constantly taught that virginity or celibacy dedicated to God, poverty, and obedience are recommended as counsels of

perfection; that life in accord with these counsels is a special, divine gift; and that those who commit themselves to such a life by vows or similar promises act with a freedom and generosity which exceed duty (see LG 42–44; PC 1, 12–14). There is a foundation for this position in Scripture: St. Paul, for example, clearly favors Christians remaining unmarried, but in no case insists on this as a definite obligation (see 1 Cor 7.1, 7, 8, 28, 32–35, 38, 40; *S.t.*, 1–2, q. 108, a. 4; 2–2, q. 186, aa. 1, 3–5).

2. This appears puzzling. Every Christian is called to perfection. It would seem that if an act is conducive to perfection, it is obligatory; if not, it is excluded as inappropriate. But if this is so, there are no acts which a Christian can undertake which would be better than the acts required by specific Christian moral norms. Apparently, there is no room for a way to perfection which need not be followed by every conscientious Christian. If so, however, every vocational commitment except that of following the counsels of perfection falls short of the standard of a fully mature Christian conscience.

3. Nevertheless, the counsels cannot be obligatory for all, for otherwise they would in no sense be counsels. Thus a puzzle, but it can be solved. The account of Christian norms and conscience given here shows why the counsels are not obligatory norms.

4. **Carrying out the counsels becomes obligatory for some by their commitment to the religious life. Until one discerns that this form of life is one's vocation, there can be no obligation to fulfill the counsels.** As counsels, they call the attention of all to an especially suitable and noble possible form of Christian vocation, and in doing so help some Christians recognize that it is part of their personal vocation to follow them. Without the counsels, few would be likely to think of this possibility and even those few probably would not appreciate its excellence.

5. St. Thomas gives a partial account of the reason why Christian morality includes counsels as well as precepts (*S.t.*, 2–2, q. 184, a. 3; q. 186, a. 7). He explains that the counsels are only counsels, not precepts, because they concern means to perfection rather than perfection itself. Everyone is called to the complete integration of self with divine love. The counsels indicate one way of fulfilling this precept, but only one way (see *S.t.*, 2–2, q. 184, aa. 3–4). Therefore, they are not obligatory. Nevertheless, for those who can accept them, they are an easier and more apt way than a personal vocation outside their framework. Thus, the counsels indicate a better way, and for those who make the commitment to fulfill them, it is part of their Christian responsibility to do so (see *S.t.*, 2–2. q. 186, a. 2).

6. Another partial account of the reason why Christian teaching offers the counsels as advice rather than proposing them as precepts is that Christianity fulfills, not nullifies, God's plan for humankind. That plan includes the blessing: "Be fruitful and multiply, and fill the earth and subdue it" (Gn 1.28). In the life of the Church, the special value of the religious state is to be a sign of the reality of the invisible kingdom of Jesus (see LG 44). However, this value is realized provided some members of the Church commit themselves to life according to the

counsels and faithfully fulfill this commitment. Hence, there is no need for all Christians to follow this particular way of life; many can continue to find an authentic Christian vocation in marriage and secular occupations.

7. However, the question remains: If life according to the counsels truly fosters charity in a special way, how can the choice of such a life not be strictly obligatory for those capable of this commitment?

8. "Capable of this commitment" can be understood in two ways, which must be distinguished to answer this question. In one way, the phrase refers to a capacity to follow a judgment of prudence that life according to the counsels is to be preferred for oneself. In a second way, it refers to a capacity to determine this preference.

9. A person capable of the commitment in the first sense has made the prudential, discerning judgment: "God is calling me to live according to the counsels." For such a person, the choice of this life is strictly obligatory, not by virtue of the counsels, but by virtue of a specific norm: One ought to accept and commit oneself to whatever one discerns to be one's personal vocation.

10. A person capable of the commitment in the second sense is not yet sure what his or her vocation is. Because life according to the counsels is not necessary for any particular Christian's salvation and not appropriate for all Christians in their communal building up of the Mystical Body, no specific norm ever requires anyone to undertake this life. But one at the point of making the relevant vocational commitment considers this way of Christian life as one good option among others. Since commitment to such a life is an open option for free choice, the person is capable of making it. Yet, since the counsels are not precepts, the capability of making the commitment entails no obligation to make it.

11. Still, the question remains: If the counsels entail no obligation, how do they help one reach the prudential judgment discerning one's vocation? The answer is that when reflection ends with two or more good options, as question D explained, one rightly attends to one's nonrational inclinations. **The counsels come into play at this point by affecting one's feelings about the option of life according to them. They affect one's feelings by making it clear that this way of life is especially pleasing to Jesus, toward whom one not only has the volitional commitment of faith but the emotional affection which belongs to human friendship.**

12. What occurs here is not mysterious; it is an instance of a familiar experience. People often express their preferences to others, yet make it clear that they do not wish this expression to be taken as binding. For example, a husband talking with his wife about plans for a wedding anniversary celebration might say: "I think it would be fun to go away for a weekend together, but if you'd rather have a little party with the children, that's fine with me too." Such advice will affect the wife's feelings and might or might not be decisive in settling which option she chooses. The probability that she will choose the vacation is greater than if her husband had not offered his counsel, yet this might not be sufficient to make this option seem to her the one to be preferred. She would violate the spirit in which the advice was given if she nevertheless said to herself: I am more inclined to the party,

but ought to please my husband, and so have an obligation to choose the weekend vacation.

Some light can be thrown on the counsels by a passage in which Paul holds that every new Christian ought to stay in the condition in which he or she is at the time of conversion—the married are to stay so, the single so, the slaves so, the uncircumcised so (see 1 Cor 7.17–24). The vital thing is to make the most of one's condition, not to be in this or that state of life. With little time before one leaves this world, one does well to simplify, not complicate, the job one must do. Thus, it seems that to make the most of their opportunity, all who have not made incompatible commitments and begin to consider the option of life according to the counsels should prefer it.

On the other hand, one must consider the saying, with respect to celibacy or virginity: "He who is able to receive this, let him receive it" (Mt 19.12). This often is taken to mean that one must be careful to assess one's ability to live according to the counsels before committing oneself to doing so. Many who attempt such an assessment reach inconclusive results. Thus, it seems that many to whom Paul's advice is directed should not follow it.

However, "He who is able to receive this, let him receive it" is misunderstood when it is taken to call for self-assessment of capacity to live according to the counsels. This cannot be ascertained in any direct way, for it is a matter of one's future development and depends on God's grace. Hence, when people try to make such an assessment, they embark on a reflection in principle interminable. In doing this, moreover, they make the serious error of supposing their ability to fulfill commitments will depend on their own power, rather than on God's grace, which a humble Christian always will confidently ask for and gratefully receive.

The true meaning of "He who is able to receive this, let him receive it" is indicated in the answer to the main question above. One has the capacity to accept this teaching when one has made a prudential judgment discerning life according to the counsels as the option to be preferred. The counsels themselves help one to reach this judgment. If a person considers the option and prayerfully allows the counsels to have their proper effect on inclination yet still feels a preference for another way of living a good Christian life, then he or she does not reach the prudential judgment, "God is calling me to this life," and so should make no commitment to it.

It also is worth noticing that worries about the difficulty of fulfilling a commitment to live according to the counsels are to a large extent ungrounded in the realities of Christian life. As Paul's advice makes clear, a young person who chooses the religious life keeps the comparative simplicity of childhood and avoids most of the complexity of adult, secular life. (This observation is not intended in any pejorative sense.) Like the life of a child, the life of a religious is celibate (and so unburdened with the responsibilities and distractions of spouse and family), is without personal property (and so unburdened with the responsibilities and temptations of ownership), and is without individual autonomy (and so unburdened with the responsibilities and temptations of setting and striving for one's own goals in life). Thus, rather than being especially difficult, life according to the counsels actually is a simpler and easier way to live a good Christian life.[2] St. Thomas also points out this personal advantage of this way of life.

At this point, someone is likely to object that if life according to the counsels really is an easier way to live a Christian life, then it is not superior. One would do better to worry less about personal sanctity and accept the greater burdens of a more complex life, thus contributing its goods to fulfillment in Jesus. This objection is plausible but fallacious. It presupposes that the choice of what is harder is better, and it takes for granted that the easier way to lead a fully Christian life is easier in all respects. Neither assumption is correct. To work out one's salvation within the framework of the counsels is not easy by human standards. It is especially difficult at the outset, whereas married life is easy at the beginning and becomes harder as it unfolds. More important, the more difficult is not necessarily morally superior. Fulfilling the law of Jesus is both better and easier than fulfilling the law of Moses (see Mt 11.28–30; Rom 7.1–6; Gal 4.21–5.6).

Summary

Although logically distinct, the modes of Christian response all point in one direction and guide every action of Christian life. Their unity is explained by the fact that the various modes of Christian response are aspects of Jesus' one redemptive act. By dealing with sin realistically, this act not only passes the test of the modes of responsibility but contributes to the realization of integral human fulfillment.

Since Christians enter into Jesus' redemptive act by faith, this fundamental option embodies the modes of Christian response. They are embodied even more clearly in commitments of personal vocation and the particular choices made to implement them. Thus, insofar as Christians faithfully carry out their personal vocations, the modes of Christian response will mark each and every choice they make.

Like the modes of responsibility, the modes of Christian response lead to specific norms. But because Christian life is a specific type of human life, Christian norms are more specific than those of common morality. In practice, individual Christians need not derive all the specific Christian norms for themselves. The Church's guidance and the claims of personal vocation go far to indicate what each Christian needs to do. Moreover, the moral absolutes of common morality hold true in specifically Christian morality. As for the nonabsolute norms of common morality, they sometimes give place to absolute ones in Christian morality. In other cases, the Christian specification of such norms remains nonabsolute, but may characterize as wrong what common morality commends, and vice versa.

While a Catholic's conscience should conform absolutely to the Church's teaching, and this excludes certain choices, still the Church's teaching can never say by itself what one positively should do. It points out no specific positive duty which might not yield in some circumstances to some other responsibility. Thus, a conscience wholly faithful to the Church's teaching has work to do in every choice, for one must always choose what one will do, not just what one will not, and this often requires a very complex affirmative norm. A mature Christian conscience is not satisfied with knowing one possibility is forbidden and another permitted; it seeks instead for the right choice.

To find it, not only an adequate norm but prudence is required. Prudence judges the right time to end moral reflection and determines which of two or more morally good options is to be preferred. In difficult situations it also can play a creative role by proposing fresh possibilities.

Vatican II teaches that every Christian is called to the perfection possible in this life. Charity is the heart of Christian holiness but it does not constitute perfection by itself. One must grow in charity by prayer, the sacraments, and a morally good life whose perfection includes the human goods. Since perfection includes love of all human goods, the demand for perfection extends to the whole of moral life. Christians respond to the universal call to holiness in no other way than by responding to the call of personal vocation, in whose carrying out Christian perfection is realized.

The gospel's demand for perfection clearly requires that in some circumstances Christians forgo their rights. People are often concerned about their rights simply because they are theirs, and conventional morality approves this, though it violates the fifth mode of responsibility. Less often, people are concerned for their rights as a matter of justice and take the same view of the rights of others; this conforms to the requirements of common human morality. But Christians, imitating Jesus, should voluntarily forgo their rights, when this can be done without injury to their responsibilities, and should more than fulfill their duties.

Since Christian responsibility extends to all human beings, inasmuch as all need redemption, how can a Christian give preference to certain persons, such as fellow Christians? Part of the answer is that there is an order of charity, grounded in the Trinity. As there is a definite order among the divine persons, so there is an order of charity among human persons. All who are saved, are saved by being united with Jesus as members of the Church, within which there are different roles and a definite order. This order inherent in charity explains why so much emphasis is placed on fraternal charity among Christians. The order of charity likewise requires preference for certain persons whenever this is a responsibility of one's vocation.

Another puzzle arises from the Church's teaching that life according to the counsels is recommended but not obligatory. But if such a life, as the Church further teaches, is conducive to perfection, it must be obligatory; however, if it is obligatory, the counsels are not "counsels" but obligatory norms for all Christians.

The beginning of an answer is that carrying out the counsels only becomes obligatory by a commitment to the religious life; until one discerns that this form of life is one's vocation, there is no obligation to fulfill the counsels. Furthermore, as St. Thomas points out, the counsels are means to perfection but not perfection itself; they are one way, but not the only way, of fulfilling the precept of complete integration of self with divine love. Moreover, the mission of the Church as a whole requires both that some live according to the counsels and that others respond to different vocations.

The question remains: Why is life according to the counsels not strictly obligatory for those capable of making this commitment? The answer is that one becomes capable of the commitment only by discerning that one's vocation is to follow the counsels. They help one to discern this, but do not prescribe it.

Appendix 1:   Jesus as Christian moral principle: unique but intelligible

If moral norms always are about kinds of action (and so are logically universal propositions, although more or less specified), how can specifically Christian norms make reference to one's personal vocation, which is a share in the redemptive act of Jesus? Here is determination to something unique. Does not Christian morality in this way really go beyond the boundaries of reason and become personal in a sense that no other human morality is? In other words, is it really true that Christian morality specifies common moral requirements? Or does it not add something concrete which understanding cannot grasp? Is this not the point at which each Christian is personally led by the Spirit through the opacity of the concrete, which reason never penetrates?[3]

The answer to this objection is that Christian life does center upon Jesus, who is a unique individual, yet Christian morality does not go beyond what is intelligible in the light of faith into the opacity of the concrete.

The modes of Christian response already proceed from the level of normative principles to that of norms, although they are very general norms. This is so because the modes of Christian response are determined by factual considerations about the human condition and the real possibility of realizing integral human fulfillment by making human action into a cooperation in the redemptive work of God.

God and integral human fulfillment are both unique entities, not classes with many members. However, neither is a particular thing, a singular item. When normative principles or specific norms make reference to them, the reference is based upon something intelligible—for example, the intelligibility of the good of religion and the reasonableness of acting in a way consistent with integral human fulfillment. So references such as these to what is unique do not go outside the domain of the intelligible. Of course, faith adds to rational knowledge, and so the factual considerations which transform the modes of responsibility into modes of Christian response go beyond reason in the sense that they are contributed by the light of faith. But they do not go beyond reason by adding something concrete and purely intuitive. The truth about God and the human condition which Christian faith teaches is intelligible in the light of faith.

But it will be objected that when the modes of Christian response make reference to the redemptive act, the reference is to a particular act by a particular individual, namely, Jesus of Nazareth. Christian religion is not simply a question of living in a certain kind of way; it is a matter of living with and in Jesus, of sharing his life and death and resurrection, of cooperating in living toward his ultimate fulfillment. All this is true and very important. But it does not mean that Christian morality goes beyond the intelligible to something extrarational as suggested by the original argument.

Jesus himself had to understand what he was humanly doing in order to commit himself to it (see 22-C). He understood the human condition and the divinely offered solution to it. He knew himself to have an opportunity to live a good human life in the sinful world, and in doing so to constitute a new human community in friendship with God. This opportunity was in fact unique. But as a commitment he had to make, his redemptive act was an intelligible possibility whose moral determinant—its rightness—followed from its perfect consistency with integral human fulfillment.

In the light of faith, Christians also understand the rightness of what Jesus does. Moreover, the determination of one's personal vocation is a consequence of applying normative principles to the intelligible possibilities. The possibilities are limited by one's factual situation, but the rightness of one's commitments is not determined by nonintelligible factors.

Of course, one's communion with Jesus does go beyond what understanding can grasp even in the light of faith. One's communion with him is more than cooperation in human action. It also is sharing in his divine fullness and being joined with him in bodily solidarity. Both of these are immensely important in the total personal relationship Christians have with Jesus—and with one another. In the obscurity of divine love and creaturely materiality the reality of Christian life is completed in ways which no moral norm can direct.

However, precisely for this reason, these other dimensions of Christian life do not add something concrete to Christian moral requirements. Communion in the Spirit and in the sacramental flesh do not displace the order proper to Christian moral life. When human action is transcended, so are moral requirements; but when human action is in question, Christian moral norms (which are intelligible in the light of faith) never are transcended.

Appendix 2: Life according to the counsels of perfection

Within the common Christian vocation, the Church recognizes certain important distinctions among states of life as elements in personal vocation. In particular, tradition teaches that the status of the religious—which involves a communal life and the vows of poverty, chastity, and obedience—is especially suitable for those called to it; this form of life has been called a "state of perfection" (see *S.t.*, 2–2, q. 184, a. 4). The concept of state of perfection often has been misunderstood, with bad effects for other states of life. However, the unique value of the religious state ought to be recognized. Nothing in this chapter about the common vocation of Christians and the personal vocation of every Christian is inconsistent with full appreciation for the religious state of life.

There are several misunderstandings of the religious state which need to be set aside.

First, the religious is not special in living a life entirely shaped by a fundamental commitment to the good of religion. The redemptive commitment of Jesus, in which every Christian shares as the fundamental commitment of his or her own life, is to the human good of religion—of friendship with God and the fulfillment in communion of divine and human persons. In contrast with nonbelievers, who might organize their lives by a morally upright fundmental commitment to justice or by a selfish commitment to certain aspects of personal self-integration, every Christian is primarily a religious person.

Second, as Vatican II teaches (see LG 39–42), every Christian is called to holiness. God's will for all is sanctity (see 1 Thes 4.3; Eph 1.4). What is central to holiness is the love of God; it "governs all the means of attaining holiness, enlivens them, and brings them to fulfillment" (LG 42; translation supplied). The precept of charity is radical and total: One must love God with one's entire mind, heart, soul, and strength (see Mt 22.36–37; Mk 12.29–30; Lk 10.25–28). If one fulfilled this precept, one would be perfect. Thus, since this precept is addressed to all; all are called to personal perfection (see *S.t.*, 2–2, q. 44, aa. 3–6; q. 184, a. 3).

Third, the religious is not special in living a life which is more divine, while other Christians live a life which is more human. Everyone who lives in God's love lives a life (sin apart) altogether divine, and every human person lives a life altogether human. Moreover, every Christian is called to be one with Jesus both in revealing God's love to others and in responding to God as humankind should.

Fourth, the religious is not special in living a life which is more other-worldly, leaving to others the task of living a this-worldly existence. All Christian life is lived in this world and must contribute something to the realization of human goods—which include the great good of religion—here and now. At the same time, everything one does out of love of God is destined to last forever, and contributes even now to the hidden but real growth of the invisible kingdom of Jesus.

The true distinction between the religious state and other Christian states of life is hinted at by Vatican II when it says that there are diverse gifts of the Spirit: "He calls some to give clear witness to the desire for a heavenly home and to keep that desire green among the human family. He summons others to dedicate themselves to the earthly service of men and to make ready the material of the celestial realm by this ministry of theirs" (GS 38). Again, the Council teaches that the religious state reveals to all believers that heavenly goods are already present now. Life in the religious state provides a kind of preview of resurrection life in the heavenly kingdom (see LG 44).

The whole of Christian life is marked by a tension between fulfillment-already-realized and fulfillment-not-yet-realized. These are not contraries—that is, qualities incompatible with one another. Rather, they are the relative opposites inherent in the fact that Jesus is risen and the new creation already is being built up in him, yet life goes on in this world and sin with all its effects still must be overcome. Jesus has come, yet Jesus is still to come. Christian life has its meaning from both comings.

What Vatican II says about the religious state amounts to this: So far as possible in this world, those in the religious state live in accord with fulfillment already realized. By contrast, other Christians live much more in accord with the reality of the kingdom as a project still to be completed. The difference is one of polar (or relative) opposition, like that between north and south. If this way of understanding the distinction is right, one should expect to find various degrees of the religious state and its opposite—a conclusion which seems to be verified by the Church's liberality in approving various religious life-styles.

The explanation just given of the specific character of the religious state can account for the three vows. In heaven, the work of creation will be complete, and no new members of the communion will be called for. Hence, there will be neither marriage nor begetting (see Mt 22.23–33; Mk 12.18–27; Lk 20.27–40). Consecrated virginity is appropriate insofar as the heavenly situation already is real. In heaven, the need for scarce means to achieve ends will no longer obtain, and so there will be no problems of property. A life of communal poverty, without private ownership of goods, seems eminently suited to manifest this aspect of heaven (see Mt 19.16–22; Mk 10.17–22; Lk 18.18–23). Finally, in heaven the self-determination of the saints will already have been achieved, and so they will be able to live with spontaneity without the burden of making major decisions. The obedience of religious life can be regarded as a sign of this situation.

Appendix 3:   The present theology and received Catholic teaching

This chapter completes the treatment of the normative principles of Christian morality. This treatment is grounded in Christian revelation—preserved, unfolded, and defended in the Church's teaching. Yet to the extent that I offer a theology, my account of normative principles is a construct which goes beyond the data of faith. The perceptive student will wonder to what extent the account I offer will generate normative judgments in accord with the Church's specific teaching on matters such as sexual activity, social justice, and so on.

In general, there is likely to be agreement but not perfect identity between the normative implications of the principles articulated here and the specific norms proposed by the Church.

There is likely to be agreement, because the principles articulated here are not the result of autonomous philosophical reflection; I have tried to understand the gospel, not simply impose preconceived ideas on it. (Although I engaged in philosophical reflection on moral questions for twenty years before undertaking the present theological work, my philosophical reflection also was conducted in the light of faith.) Likewise, the Church's moral teaching is very closely based upon divine revelation, for it either is drawn directly from revelation or has been developed by the reflection of twenty centuries of Christians (and more centuries of faithful Jews), who were striving with God's grace to live their lives in the light of faith.

There also is not likely to be perfect identity between the normative conclusions one will reach by systematic reflection and the specific norms received in the Church. To a great extent, the nonidentity will not be discrepancy; there will be a difference but no conflict. Systematic treatment provides a means for dealing with every possible question about individual and social morality; the Church's teaching is limited to actual questions which have been important to Christians up to the present. Thus the normative implications of the system will extend beyond the boundaries of received teaching, without necessarily conflicting with it.

To some extent, however, there are going to be inconsistencies, and for two quite different reasons. First, no theological system is perfect. I expect errors to be found in the system I have articulated, and some of these errors will lead to false normative conclusions. Where there appears to be an inconsistency between the implications of the system and Catholic moral teaching, it is clear that anyone would be prudent to assume the error is mine. As history amply demonstrates, any theologian or group of theologians is far more likely to be wrong about any question than is the magisterium.

Still, the teaching of the Church is one thing, and teaching received in the Church is another, as I will explain in chapter thirty-five. Not all received teaching has been proposed infallibly, and teaching which has not been proposed infallibly might possibly require refinement and correction in its details. There is a possibility of legitimate development, including the correction of errors on some points. One purpose of theological reflection is to assist such refinement of the Church's teaching. I believe such refinement is possible and appropriate, for example, with respect to capital punishment and (in a slightly different way) war.[4]

Dissent from a moral norm proposed authoritatively, although not infallibly, within the Church cannot be justified unless one can appeal to a superior theological source (35 G). Insofar as the normative principles for moral-theological reflection which I have outlined are an interpretation of the data of revelation contained in Scripture, they provide some basis for justifying dissent from some moral teachings in the Church.

Notes

1. John Paul II, *Redemptor hominis*, 71 *AAS* (1979) 318–19; *The Papal Encyclicals*, 278.87.

2. This point often has been made by saintly religious. See, for example, St. Thérèse of Lisieux, *Story of a Soul*, trans. John Clarke, O.C.D. (Washington, D.C.: ICS Publications, 1976), 218, on obedience: "O Mother, what anxieties the Vow of Obedience frees us from! How happy are simple religious! Their only compass being their Superiors' will, they are always sure of being on the right road; they have nothing to fear from being mistaken even when it seems that their Superiors are wrong."

3. For a clear example of the position outlined here and criticized in the remainder of this appendix: Hans Küng, *On Being a Christian*, trans. Edward Quinn (Garden City, N.Y.: Doubleday, 1976), 530–53. Much rather confused writing about the need for discernment, which treats it as a substitute for conscientious reflection, seems to embody a similar view.

4. A treatment of the problem in ethical theory: Germain Grisez, "Toward a Consistent Natural-Law Ethics of Killing," *American Journal of Jurisprudence and Legal Philosophy*, 15 (1970), 64–96.

CHAPTER TWENTY-EIGHT

THE PRACTICABILITY OF CHRISTIAN MORALITY

Introduction

The last three chapters have clarified the norms of Christian living. Essentially, these say Christians must live like Jesus and cooperate in his redemptive act. But a large question remains: Is this practicable, or is it a wonderful but impracticable ideal?

Some argue that taking Christian morality too seriously is likely to have bad psychological and social consequences. Others say Christian morality should be taken literally but without rigorism; perfection is a very high ideal, and it is imperfection but no sin to fall short.

Classical moral theology was anxious to avoid rigorism. That concern is understandable and reasonable; it complements concern for conformity with moral norms. Norms which cannot be fulfilled by all or nearly all are likely to discourage many from even trying to live up to them. Yet Christian life is for all; thus, it seems to follow that its standards cannot be too high. The present chapter addresses these matters.

Question A: In what sense do the Christian modes of response articulate ideals?

1. There are several senses in which Christian morality can be said to propose an ideal. To begin with, norms which are admittedly demanding can be called "ideals," insofar as they are principles of faithful and determined effort. Purity in thought in sexual matters, for instance, can be called "an ideal." This is not to deny that deliberate violation of such purity is a sin. Rather, it is to point out that most people attain purity only by a determined struggle, sometimes marred by more or less serious failures due to weakness. Christian morality does propose ideals in this sense, for the modes of Christian response only gradually gain control of the imagination and emotions.

2. Integral human fulfillment remains a mere ideal for humankind, if natural human capacities alone are considered. Moreover, even with grace, perfect love of God—love with one's whole mind, heart, soul, and strength—remains an ideal in this life. A person proceeds toward this goal of Christian striving only by determined effort throughout a lifetime.

3. Again, Christians ought to bear witness to Jesus by their common life in a loving community whose practice lends support to the gospel it proclaims. Yet the imperfections of the Church are insurmountable for any individual Christian, and the perfection of life in a Church fully conformed to the heart of Jesus is an ideal. The Church should be a perfect image of Jesus, but the sinfulness of her members makes it more or less difficult to discern him there. Individuals can only work to build up the Church and pray that the Spirit will make their work fruitful.

4. **Granting that Christian morality proposes an ideal in the above senses, the Christian modes of response must still not be reduced to mere ideals. They are to govern our lives as binding norms, not counsels.**[1] As was shown in previous chapters, they articulate the requirements for a life lived in accord with the love of God and in union with Jesus' redemptive act. For Christians, such a life is not optional (see Mt 25.31–46; 1 Jn 3.16–17), since every Christian is bound to pursue holiness, which primarily consists in perfect charity (see LG 42).[2] Nor is being a Christian optional. The truth which every person is obliged to seek, embrace when found, and live when accepted is Christian faith (see DH 1–2). Specifically Christian moral norms are therefore not mere ideals.

5. Some moral theories lend support to the opposite idea, for they begin by trying to formulate norms for a society whose every member is perfectly upright, then try to adapt this wonderful system to the world as it is. Kant's philosophy suggests this, and many theologians influenced by him try to interpret Christian morality along these lines.[3]

6. That this approach is mistaken is shown by the fact that requirements to love enemies and undergo evil with redemptive intent are among the highest norms of Christian morality. In a perfect community, however, they would make little or no sense. Only when the day of the Lord comes will his own no longer need to suffer for his sake. Meanwhile, such requirements make it clear that Christian morality does not propose an ideal designed for life in a perfect community—one to be adjusted by compromising with the realities of life in this broken world. Christian norms for dealing with evil show that Christian morality is meant for this world as it is.

Sometimes it is argued that the norms of Christian morality cannot be taken literally. Are Christians to pluck out their eyes in order to avoid occasions of sin which they could avoid if they were blind? Is the saying of the Liturgy of the Hours in choir to be forbidden in favor of saying it in one's room? Are we to offer no resistance to a kidnapper who is trying to snatch one of our children?

Some suggest that while the teaching of Jesus was meant to be taken literally, it was aimed at the brief interim before an expected, early end of the world. Others urge that if Christians need not pluck out offending eyes, neither need they remain faithful in a marriage which has hopelessly broken down—for example, if the other party has obtained a civil divorce and remarried.

There is a difference between taking teaching literally and taking it out of context and misinterpreting it. Christian moral teaching, especially the Gospels, certainly must be taken literally, but it also must be understood accurately.

Hyperbole—exaggeration for rhetorical effect—is found in many illustrative examples in the Gospels. But if one reads statements in their wider context, one can distinguish what is hyperbolic from what is not. In the catechesis in the Epistles, there is nothing about plucking out offending eyes. But the teaching on divorce is stated by St. Paul with the explicit assertion that it comes from Jesus (see 1 Cor 7.10–11). Similarly, the modes of Christian response articulated in the Gospels also enter into the more prosaic formulations of the Epistles, as was shown in chapter twenty-six.

Of course, there are cases in which the precise norm could not be disengaged if one had only the text of the New Testament.[4] But the Bible exists in the Church, and the Church has constantly read and interpreted it. Hence, one can look to tradition to clarify many obscure points.

For example, one might not be certain whether the Christian prohibition of oaths (see Mt 5.33–37) is an absolute or a nonabsolute norm. The tradition makes it clear that the norm is nonabsolute. Christians ought to be consistently honest, speaking as it were always under oath. If they are perfectly honest, they never have occasion to take an oath on their own initiative. However, if a process—for example, in court—requires an oath, then Christians are permitted to acknowledge publicly that they are bound by faithfulness to God's truth also to speak truly under these conditions.

By applying the norm of the Church's understanding of the New Testament's moral teaching, one can be certain that this teaching was not intended only for the interim before the momentarily expected second coming of Jesus. The Church always has taken this teaching to be the message to be conveyed to all nations and times. If the New Testament's specific moral norms could be dismissed as an interim program, there would be nothing revealed there for us.

It also is worth considering that, with respect to what is at issue here, it makes no difference whether the world is expected to end momentarily or go on indefinitely. Suppose Jesus asked us to live by his standards for, say, one month. If, however, one can live up to Christian moral norms for one month, one can as well live up to them for two, and so for the whole of one's life—which, after all, will end quite soon, whether or not the world does.

Question B: Is it possible to fulfill the norms of Christian morality?

1. "Possible" and "impossible" have many meanings. It is necessary to give them a precise sense in discussions of moral norms.

2. To begin with, one cannot be morally responsible for anything about which it is impossible to make a choice, except to the extent that one's present voluntariness (other than choice) is conditioned by a past failure to choose or to make a right choice. This is important, for if one is not responsible, one certainly is not guilty. One cannot repent what one, after all, does not will, and if one is not guilty, one need not amend.

3. Under what conditions is it impossible to choose something which has the characteristics of an imaginable choice? There are several (see *S.t.*, 1–2, q. 13, a. 5).

4. First, a choice is obviously impossible if the imaginable action never occurs to one. Thus, integral Christian morality is impossible to people who have never heard the gospel.

5. Again, the choice is impossible if one cannot see any point at all in doing the imaginable action. A small boy told by someone other than his parent or a person in authority to give up still more of his share of a candy bar to his sister, who has

already taken more than her share for herself, will find it impossible to accept the suggestion, for he will see no point in it.

6. Finally, it is impossible to choose an imaginable action, even if it occurs to one and seems interesting, if one can think of no way to begin doing it. Someone who cannot read German and is given a book in that language might imagine reading the book and might be curious about its contents, but would still find it impossible to choose to read it. Similarly, someone who is depressed and is told, "Pull yourself together and cheer up!" cannot choose to do so, for lack of any idea how to begin. Again, an adolescent boy told simply to "avoid the occasions of sin" of impurity is likely to have the same sort of difficulty.

7. On these grounds, it can be impossible for some people to fulfill Christian moral norms. **But in a strict sense Christian morality is not impossible. The obstacles noted above can be overcome.** Ignorance and failure to see the point of living up to Christian norms can be removed by the preaching of the gospel and Christian education. Furthermore, a person who receives sound Christian moral instruction and spiritual direction is never confronted with a requirement of Christian morality which cannot be chosen because he or she cannot even imagine how to begin. Thus, such people could choose to put Christian norms into practice. If they do not, moral responsibility and guilt follow.

8. Ordinarily, when Christian moral requirements are said to be "impossible," one of two things is meant. First, it may be that the Christian norm is absolutely incompatible with a contrary commitment which the individual (or many individuals) will not give up. For example, Christian norms concerning honesty in business are impossible for people who are in tight competition with dishonest rivals, are determined to continue and survive in business, and simply cannot do so while remaining honest themselves. Second, it may be that the Christian norm is difficult to integrate into one's life, so that, although one usually wills to fulfill it, one sometimes surrenders to temptation and violates the norm by a sin of weakness. For example, someone struggling against sexual temptation, alcoholism, or a volcanic temper might say in a discouraged frame of mind that the Christian standard is impossible.

9. In such cases, "impossible" is not used in a strict sense. The individual knows what is good, sees the point in choosing it, and knows how to do at least something toward fulfilling the requirement. In fact, however, he or she chooses freely not to respond to the good and gives in to temptation. Calling Christian norms "impossible" may then be an exercise in self-deception, designed to evade moral guilt.

Nothing is impossible with God (see Jer 32.17, 27; Mt 19.26; Lk 1.37). Those who are dead in sin can be raised to new life. The miracle of moral regeneration is demonstrated by miracles of bodily regeneration (see Mt 9.1–8; Mk 2.1–12; Lk 5.17–26). With faith, one is borne up; without faith, one sinks in one's sins. The Council of Trent definitively teaches: "If anyone says that the commandments of God are impossible to observe even for a man who is justified and in the state of grace: let him be anathema" (DS 1568/828). One can keep the commandments, for one can choose to do what one can and pray for God's grace to make the impossible possible. He will give this grace (see DS 1536–39/804). (This point was treated more fully in 17-F.)

10. Nonbelievers and those who speak of Christian norms as impossible in the loose sense frequently argue that Christian morality is incompatible with human nature. When everyone else is cheating, it is unnatural to be honest, even to the point of losing one's livelihood and means of supporting dependents. It is unnatural to live without sexual satisfaction. It is supremely unnatural to love enemies, retaliate with kindness, and accept suffering willingly for the benefit of those who inflict it on oneself.

11. There is some foundation to this argument. Christian responses are incompatible with fallen human nature; children of Adam as such, merely natural men and women, cannot avoid sin (see DS 227/105, 242/133, 245/138, 1552/812; *S.t.*, 1–2, q. 109, a. 8). However, human nature is not static; its sinful condition is open to radical transformation. Human nature is truly renewed by the redemptive sacrifice of Jesus (see Eph 4.17–24). The word "impossible" ought to be excluded from the vocabulary of Christian life.

In Jesus, the old nature is put to death and a renewed one given (see Rom 6.1–11). Jesus liberates from the confines of fallen human nature, and his Spirit provides a new principle of life (see Rom 8.7–11; Ti 2.11–13). Human nature truly is renewed (see *S.t.*, 1–2, q. 106, a. 2; q. 107, a. 4). God's grace is sufficient both to convert the sinner and sustain the faithful in their weakness (see 1 Cor 10.13; 2 Cor 12.9).

Some suggest that the whole of Christian morality—or, at least, many norms traditionally received as binding precepts—is subject to a law of "gradualness," so that willful violations are acceptable provided one looks forward to living according to the norm at some time in the future.⁵ This idea is not clear, and so it is not easy to evaluate.

The suggestion certainly is compatible with traditional teaching concerning kinds of acts which are light matter or those which admit parvity in cases in which the matter is in fact small. Here the willful violation—the deliberate venial sin—is compatible with charity. But the suggestion does not comport with constant Catholic teaching concerning kinds of acts which are grave matter.

Perhaps implicit in the suggestion is some form of defective fundamental-option theory, such as was criticized above (16-D). Or, more broadly, it might be assumed that sins of weakness of one or more kinds can be committed by a free choice without that free choice being self-determining. (This view was criticized in 17-E.)

Whatever "law of gradualness" means, there are several things it should not be taken to mean if it is to be compatible with Catholic teaching. It must not be taken to mean that received moral norms characterizing various kinds of acts as grave matter merely mark out an ideal to be achieved in the future. Rather, such norms must be regarded as commands of Jesus demanding that difficulties be overcome right along. The process of gradualness has no place unless one accepts divine law with a sincere heart and seeks the goods which are protected and promoted by the moral truth clarified in Jesus and proposed to us in the Church's moral teaching. Thus, the law of gradualness cannot be identified with a theory of gradations of the law, as if there were in divine law various levels or forms of precept for various persons and conditions.⁶

Question C: Does the fulfillment of the norms
of Christian morality
involve a process of growth toward perfection?

1. Even sinners, moved by God's grace, can cooperate in their own conversion (see DS 1526/798, 1557–59/817–19, 1676/897, 1705/915). Those who live in God's friendship, by his gift of living faith, are inclined and empowered by the charity which motivates their faith to do the works of love. The norms of Christian morality call for and shape these works. Thus, since the fullness of charity is perfection, the gradual fulfillment of the norms of Christian morality constitutes growth toward perfection (see *S.t.*, 2–2, q. 184, aa. 1–4).

2. The Council of Trent makes this point clear.

Therefore, in this way the justified become both friends of God and members of his household (see Jn 15.15; Eph 2.19), advancing from virtue to virtue (see Ps 83.8), renewed (as the Apostle says) day by day (see 2 Cor 4.16), that is, by mortifying the members of their flesh (see Col 3.5) and showing them as weapons of justice (see Rom 6.13, 19) unto sanctification by observing the commandments of God and of the Church. When faith works along with their works (see Jas 2.22), the justified increase in the very justice which they have received through the grace of Christ and are justified the more [cf. DS 1574/834; 1582/842], as it is written: "He who is just, let him be just still" (Rv 22.11), and again: "Fear not to be justified even to death" (Sir 18.22), and again: "You see that by works a man is justified, and not by faith only" (Jas 2.24). Indeed, the holy Church begs this increase of justice when she prays: "O Lord, give us an increase of faith, hope, and charity." (DS 1535/803)

To seek perfection in Christian life is to seek to do one's every act as a morally good act informed by living faith—to do everything for the glory of God (see 1 Cor 10.31), to try always to contribute here and now to the fulfillment of everything in Jesus, and so to merit a share in this fulfillment (see DS 1545–49/ 809–10).[7]

Charity can and should grow (see 2 Thes 1.3). But if Christian love is primarily a sharing in divine life, how can it grow?

Considered in itself, the love of God which is poured forth in the heart of a Christian is not subject to more or less. One either is a child of God or not; one either shares in the divine nature or not; one either abides in the love of the Lord Jesus or not. But love is a principle of joy and of desire, and joy and desire lead to expressions and actions. When we consider the divine goodness already realized in God himself and in the creation in which he pours it forth, we rejoice; our joy leads to praise and thanksgiving. When we consider the divine goodness still to be realized in its participations, when God is all in all, then we desire the good yet to be and detest the evil which blocks it. Our desire for good and hatred of evil lead to petition and contrition.

Every act based upon the desire and joy which flow from charity is an act which builds up friendship with God, an act of religion. The primary act of religion which pervades all others is the will to do what God wills one to do. Love of God most centrally means this: conformity to his will. St. John of the Cross makes it clear that really Christian mysticism is nothing but this: the union which "exists when God's will and the soul's are in conformity, so that nothing in the one is repugnant to the other."⁸

3. **The "growth" of charity should not be understood as if the divine gift itself were subject to intrinsic change. Rather, this expression designates the process by which a person receives charity more perfectly by becoming more and more fully integrated with respect to it** (see *S.t.*, 2–2, q. 24, aa. 4–5). The primary act of charity is living faith. Charity grows as the whole of one's life is increasingly organized by faith and lived through the power of love. There is an analogy in the way the sun's heat grows more intense in summer: not that the sun becomes hotter, but that the earth shares more fully in its warmth.

4. This explanation clarifies why a good life is necessary to attain holiness. Holiness is not a reward, as if it were some sort of payment, for good works. Rather, as one made holy by God's gift of living faith puts mind, heart, soul, and strength to work in the service of love, the whole self is transformed according to the likeness of Jesus. Thus, St. Paul teaches: "Man believes in his heart and so is justified, and he confesses with his lips and so is saved" (Rom 10.10), for those who sincerely confess their faith in word and deed gradually become perfectly at one with the grace by which they were justified, and so perfectly at one with Jesus.

5. Many faithful Christians mistakenly think that they need work for holiness only in certain special areas of their lives—for example, in prayer and in pious practices. They do not realize that charity, which is the heart of holiness, is a divine gift, and that perfection consists, not in acquiring charity, but in integrating the whole of one's life with the charity poured forth in one's heart by the Holy Spirit (see *S.t.*, 2–2, q. 184, a. 2, ad 2). Prayer, the sacraments, and other specifically religious acts are vital principles of this integration. But no part of one's life can be regarded as a free area. Nothing can be withheld from the purging and transforming fire of God's love.

Because prayer, the sacraments, and various pious practices mediate between charity and all the rest of one's being, these specifically religious acts often and rightly are called "means of grace"; they mediate God's gifts to one's whole mind, heart, soul, and power of action. However, the expression "means of grace" often is misunderstood in two ways.

First, sometimes Catholics have tended to think that religious acts precisely as human acts cause grace. This is an error to which Luther and others rightly took violent exception, but it is not the error of Catholic teaching itself (see *S.t.*, 1–2, q. 109, a. 9; 3, q. 62, aa. 1, 3–5). The true Catholic position is that the sacraments contain and confer grace because God has provided them as cooperative acts by which we can share in the redemptive work which primarily is the doing of the Holy Spirit.

Second, very often Catholics have thought of prayer, the sacraments, and other specifically religious acts not just as means but as mere means—tools which are not built into the work, stages in the process which fall away before it reaches fruition. This view is false. Prayer is the basis of one's personal relationship with God; it is no more a mere means than sexual intercourse is a mere means for the cultivation of conjugal love. The Eucharist contains Jesus and fulfillment in him; only the appearances to the contrary need drop away. And the same thing is true by analogy of every "means" of grace.

No doubt the most serious mistake one can make is to think one can do anything whatsoever to attain holiness which is not first, last, and always God's gift (see Eph 2.8; Jas 1.16–17). The whole of Christian life is based upon God's revelation. This communication

689

is utterly gratuitous, and in no way required by our created nature for its proper integrity and proportionate fulfillment (except insofar as fallen humankind can attain fulfillment only by a grace which deifies at the same time it heals). The gift of this communication can be received by humankind and by each person only because of God's gifts of the Incarnation of the Word and sending of the Spirit.

Anything we do that increases our own holiness is itself a special gift of God to us. Growth in perfection which is our work is no less God's grace (see DS 1545–46/809). Indeed, the reason why we can do something is that God wishes his gifts also to be our merits (see DS 248/141, 1548/810). He not only wants to give us fulfillment in divine life; he also wants us to have this fulfillment in a way which will fulfill us as human persons, ennoble us by making use of our own capacities, fully respect us by appealing to our own intelligence and freedom (see *S.t.*, 1–2, q. 113, a. 3; q. 114, a. 1; 2–2, q. 23, a. 3).

Growth in holiness is more obviously God's gift in some cases than in others: "My grace is sufficient for you, for my power is made perfect in weakness" (2 Cor 12.9). When acts cannot be elicited at will, but come about spontaneously, then one is more conscious of their character as graces. Yet the most competent work one does in carrying out one's Christian vocation is no less a gift of God than is the miraculous outcome which crowns one's best but failing effort. The first lisped prayer of the child, if it is sincere, is no less a grace of contemplation than is the supreme mystical experience of a John of the Cross.

Clarity about this point should block any temptation to quietism—that is, the erroneous idea that grace perfects sloth. Progress toward holiness is entirely grace. For this very reason it is our work too: "O Lord, you will ordain peace for us, you have wrought for us all our works" (Is 26.12).

One progresses toward perfection by the means of holiness God has provided. Yet these means are in no sense to be regarded as techniques. Holiness is in no sense a human product. Our part is to pursue human goods and to deal with evil as best we can. The pursuit of human goods ought first but not exclusively to be the pursuit of the human good of friendship with God. Evil is dealt with by healing and integrating love, in union with the redemptive sacrifice of Jesus.

It is noteworthy that although he constantly faced the demand that he be an effective Messiah by other people's standards, he rejected this demand and accepted the role of the Suffering Servant (see Mt 16.13–28; Mk 8.27–39; Lk 9.18–27). Like him, we must use the strength and breath God gives us to go about doing good to the extent we can, but in the end freely accept suffering and death.

Question D: Why is growth toward Christian perfection often stunted?

1. Christian moral norms specify the common norms of morality. Those who are aware of them and could fulfill them but fail to do so are guilty of moral evil. Any morally evil act or omission is a sin. Failures in respect to the Christian modes of response—in respect to humility, dedication, detachment, faithfulness, mercy, devotion, conciliatoriness, and self-oblation—are thus sins.

2. Of course, not all sins are mortal sins. But failures in Christian modes of response are not mere shortcomings, imperfections, less than ideal yet nonetheless good ways of acting. These sinful failures block growth toward perfection. Many will be inclined to consider this view too strict—rigoristic. To see why it is not, we need to consider in the remainder of this question how people do organize their lives. We shall go on in question E to consider how Christians

should organize their lives. Then in question F the issue about rigorism will be resolved.

3. Many people probably do not organize their lives beyond the structuring which is based on spontaneous willing—a structure comprised of likes and dislikes, definite goals and objectives, and choices strictly within this limited framework. People can live their entire lives in the context of a conventional morality without reflecting on life's meaning, taking a personal stand with respect to basic human goods, and so establishing a personal identity by commitments. Even free choices, which always presuppose a framework of existing likes and dislikes and a set of accepted goals, can largely be understood in terms of these prior factors. Hence, without commitments, the radical character of the capacity for free choice does not become apparent. This helps explain why free choice is fully appreciated only in the Jewish and Christian tradition (see chapter two, appendix four).

Even before a child makes any free choice, his or her life has a certain degree of intelligible order. The intelligible goods are willed by simple volition, and possible actions understood as conducive to these goods are willed by spontaneous willing. Moreover, having acted and experienced a participation in an intelligible good, children can spontaneously will to have and enjoy experiences of that sort. Thus, children come to have likes and dislikes, and tend to do what they like and avoid what they dislike.

A child of four or five can plan and carry out a project of some complexity to try to obtain something he or she wants. For example, a child can try to obtain several items in order to have a party. Such a scheme involves ordering a number of actions to definite goals, all of which are subordinated to a complex act in which the desired satisfaction will be attained. Children of this age also are able to do and refrain from doing a variety of things out of obedience. Obedience is accepted as a means to attaining or retaining the conditions necessary for satisfying many likes and dislikes.

This development of children prior to their first choices is not without moral significance for later life (9-B). The likes and dislikes children develop, their patterns of scheming, their relations to those who make demands, and thus the whole organization of their lives will be the framework within which choices will be made. Children will not choose anything they cannot think of as a live option. They will find difficulty in choosing anything which runs too heavily against their established identity.

The patterning of the child's life continues after he or she has begun to make choices. To the extent that these choices are morally good ones, the developing likes and dislikes, the increasingly large projects, and the general organization of a child's whole life will remain open to integral human fulfillment. But to the extent that these choices are morally bad ones, the child will develop likes and dislikes, adopt objectives, relate to authority, and thus organize a life which is more or less nonrationally limited and indisposed to wholehearted love of intelligible goods.

4. Some people, however, take more control of their lives and cause themselves in a more radical sense by making commitments. These are free choices of a special sort (see 9-E). In making commitments, people do more than assert likes or adopt well-defined goals to be achieved by projects (however large and complex). They take a stand with respect to an aspect of one or more of the existential goods and also in relation to one or more other persons. When it is made, the commitment may demand very little by way of outward performance,

perhaps no more than a symbolic gesture; but the commitment remains to shape many later choices.

5. People form and join genuine communities by commitments. They also establish their own identities by commitments, deciding, for example, to undertake some special way of life through dedication to a good: to be a scholar or a priest, for instance. Commitments obviously introduce a new dimension of organization into life. True, the possibilities for commitments are more or less limited by what one already has become. But commitments can come into conflict with many existing likes and dislikes, can demand the abandonment of old projects and the development of new ones, can lead to the recognition of genuine authorities.

6. Moreover, because of their open-ended involvement with intelligible human goods, commitments provide a principle for living creatively. A person whose life is shaped by commitments has far greater scope—and a different sort of scope—for creativity than one who lacks commitments. He or she tries to think of ways to serve goods and thus, confronted with particular situations, thinks of possibilities which do not occur to people who view the same situations merely in terms of their likes and dislikes and projects.

7. Christian faith is a commitment. It is the acceptance of participation in the redemptive act of Jesus (see 23-A). As a commitment with potential significance for every interest and relationship, the act of living faith should organize life and generate continuous growth toward Christian perfection. Yet for a number of different reasons no growth may be apparent. What follows outlines a common situation which at least partly accounts for this lack of growth in the lives of many Christians.

Children are—or should be—instructed in the faith as a covenant which has moral implications. One who believes must keep the commandments. However, the commandments are not easy to keep, especially if the intrinsic connections between faith and these moral requirements are not made clear and if there is no vital community to support the efforts of its members.

The specifically Christian modes of response are preached, especially and universally in the liturgical readings. The faithful know that some demand is being made by this teaching, yet to a great extent they remain unclear about what is required. Occasional gestures toward fulfillment seem sufficient. Thus, humility is served by an occasional self-deprecating remark when one is tempted to brag, mercy by occasional donations to charities, and conciliatoriness by trying to get along with an especially obnoxious associate at work. In practical terms, what else exactly can one make of these rather frightening sayings one hears on Sundays?

Meanwhile, one has developed—as every child does develop—a whole set of likes and dislikes, and a variety of projects. These make their own demands. Whatever specifically Christian moral teaching might mean, it is only a set of nonabsolute norms, and these are in practice limited by one's existing plan of life.

8. The life of a person reaching the end of adolescence is likely to be organized more or less as follows. Strong likes and dislikes control a great part of action. Among these are the liking for pleasure in experiences and for personal gratification in accomplishments, especially in relations with other people: gratification in

helping them, in winning their admiration, receiving their praise, defeating them in competition, and so on. Some of these likes and dislikes lead to the selection of very long-term projects: typically, the setting of a career objective, understood as a state of affairs in which it will be possible to obtain maximum gratification.

9. There may also be genuine commitments apart from faith which open up areas for personal, creative development yet also render it more or less likely that tensions will arise between the resulting loyalties and loyalty to the Church. That happens if these commitments which are not integrated with faith sometimes make demands inconsistent with the Church's teaching.

10. Faith itself may very well remain an overarching commitment, and the Christian life of such a young person is by no means necessarily insignificant. There can be a real effort to live within the framework of the Church's essential moral teaching. Yet faith is insulated from much of life. Religion is a concern, but only one concern among many. Most of the time, specifically Christian teaching simply has no relevance. What does self-oblation have to do with successfully completing the program of training which is required for a career one will enjoy? What has mercy to do with football weekends?

Under these conditions, even choices which unquestionably have the character of commitment can be colored by mixed motives to such an extent that they do little to organize life in accord with faith. Thus, a young couple might marry, yet regard marriage more as a project of mutual gratification than as a way of living their Christian lives together. Similarly, some men enter the priesthood as a project for self-fulfillment rather than as a way of service.

11. Wholly or in part, a life organized along these lines lacks the structure of personal vocation. **The commitment of faith is more or less isolated and in competition with many other cares and interests. The possibility of mortal sin, at least from time to time, is considerable, and there is also a real possibility of determined refusal to repent, which can lead to loss of faith. Even where this does not happen, however, and even in a life with few or no mortal sins, the lack of affirmative and thorough organization by faith blocks any significant growth in holiness.** Living faith hardly touches most everyday activities, which at best coexist with faith in a more or less peaceful relationship.

Question E: How does commitment to one's personal vocation promote growth toward perfection?

1. Living faith requires that it be lived out. Commitment to a personal vocation specifies how to do this in a way suited to one's own abilities and opportunities. But neither progress in holiness nor even minimal perseverance in grace is guaranteed by the fact that a Christian's life is organized in response to a personal vocation. One still can be radically unfaithful. Once life is organized in this way, nevertheless, one who is not radically unfaithful is almost compelled to make progress, slowly or quickly, toward holiness. There are several reasons for this.

2. **First, in trying to live out a vocation, one attempts to place the rest of oneself in the service of the source of the vocational commitment—namely,**

living faith. But integration of the self with living faith is precisely what is meant by progress toward holiness. One loves God with all one's mind and heart, soul and strength, by putting one's whole self to work carrying out commitments made out of this love. At first, of course, the commitments themselves are imperfect. But the effort to live them out brings their imperfections to the surface, and thus gives one the opportunity increasingly to purge them of the mixed motives by which they were originally contaminated.

3. Second, as one tries to live out a personal vocation, residual elements of other systems for organizing the self are challenged. For instance, a serious married man with hobbies is required either to fit them into his family life or give them up. If rightly subordinated to Christian family responsibilities, these interests are brought within the sphere of faith.

4. Third, when the whole of life is viewed as a personal response to one's unique vocation, the implications of the Christian modes of response begin to become clear. Understanding life in terms of a commitment of faith to God, one is likely to begin to ask him for things and to realize that goods come from him; thus humility develops. Knowing one's life to be a response to a call, one sees that one should accept one's role and its difficulties with resignation; detachment and faithfulness begin to take on definite meanings. One's Christian vocation implies responsibilities exceeding what others could justly expect of one; so the imperatives of mercy take shape.

5. Fourth, the inescapable, intrinsic dynamics of Christian transformation become operative. To avoid mortal sin and its occasions, to get rid of dispositions to sin and temptations, it is necessary to deepen and purify one's Christian commitment, seek to overcome evil with good, and accept suffering for Christ's sake. For example, a married couple come to find the precise shape of their own cross in the needs of sick or defective children, in difficulties about finances, in the problem of family limitation, in all the stresses and strains of their common life. For every person who sees life in terms of personal vocation, a time comes when actual moral options narrow down and the possibility of being a Christian without fully responding like one no longer exists.

6. Problems of the same sort arise for a person whose life is not organized as a response to a personal vocation, but he or she is not prepared to meet them. Discouragement comes easily. A search is launched to determine the absolute minimum required by morality, and even that minimum is breached more or less knowingly and deliberately. Even so, the possibility always remains that a person struggling along in a marginally Christian life of this kind will recognize its inadequacy and undertake to renew his or her commitment to Jesus.

Personal vocation has been discussed (in 23-E). But it is necessary to clarify here how one's Christian vocation can organize one's whole life. The religious life does this job most simply.

A person who enters upon the religious life undertakes a major commitment which clearly implements the commitment of faith. The decision probably is made with certain mixed motives. Nevertheless, preparation for taking the vows and living in accord with them brings the commitment to bear against the individual's likes and dislikes. The vow of obedience tends to remove the possibility of developing projects which will provide means for one's own gratification. Other commitments must be held in abeyance or subordinated to the commitment to religious life. In being subordinated to it, they are also brought under the commitment of faith. Thus, rather quickly, an individual who enters religion (assuming a sound community with an adequate formation program) organizes all—or at least much, and increasingly much—of his or her life to implement the commitment of living faith. The simplicity and effectiveness of this way of organizing a Christian life is one reason why religious life is a very apt means for pursuing holiness.

In simpler and less affluent cultures and societies than ours, the commitment to Christian marriage could function for those who undertook it in a truly Christian spirit very much as does the commitment of the religious vows. A couple who committed themselves to indissoluble faithfulness, to a common effort of mutual sanctification, and to having and raising children for God lived their faith in the form of marriage and family life. A simpler culture left them few other commitments to make. Many faithful husbands worked simply to support themselves and their families; their social life and community involvements were oriented toward the welfare of their families. Many faithful wives had no life except that of family and church. Given faithfulness to the marital-parental commitment, virtually the whole of life was brought under the sway of faith working through love. (This is not to express nostalgia for a bygone age. Such cultures had their own problems. They did, however, provide a setting for the commitments of Christian personal vocation very different than that provided by our complex culture. This difference should not be ignored.)

In our society, where greater complexity and affluence make for greater liberty, everyone has more choices and so has a more complex task if the whole of life is to become the fulfillment of a personal vocation. A special difficulty is that in a pluralistic society those with faith associate and cooperate with those without faith, and thus tend to acquire worldly attitudes toward various activities. The association and cooperation cannot be excluded, but Christian life will be blocked from its proper integration if commitments are made which do not affirmatively express faith. Moreover, Christian integration will be blocked if there is room for activities in the service of likes and dislikes, projects aimed at various desired states of affairs, which fall under no commitment at all.

Question F: How can the requirement that Christians live according to the modes of Christian response escape rigorism?

1. We have seen how people organize their lives and how Christian life can be most perfectly organized—namely, as a personal response to one's personal vocation. We also have seen (in 27-C) that the modes of Christian response generate norms which specify strict moral responsibilities—that is, ones whose violation is sinful. These two points make it possible to clarify how Christian morality, although strict, avoids the rigorism classical moral theology rightly feared.

2. The obligation to live the Christian life is limited by blameless limitations on a person's understanding of its responsibilities. Not just children and people who have been inadequately instructed suffer from such limitations, but, to one degree or another, every Christian—except Mary—of every age and condition.

3. This is so because the modes of Christian response are very general. They

make a definite demand upon conscience only when a person can recognize an option as an instance of a kind of act which a specifically Christian norm enjoins. The capacity to do this consistently, in turn, depends on two factors.

4. First, one must be living one's life as a Christian vocation and must be conscious of doing so. This is an obligation: "Whatever you do, in word or deed, do everything in the name of the Lord Jesus" (Col 3.17). But the obligation can be fulfilled only gradually, as one lives one's Christian life, so that the formation of oneself by commitments and the integration of self with living faith constitute what is necessarily a lifelong process.

5. Second, one must not be following any norms except Christian ones. A possible course of action will not be recognized as an instance of a kind of act enjoined by Christian norms if one innocently limits nonabsolute Christian norms by other genuine (although not yet specifically Christian) norms thought to be controlling. But that is inevitable in the life of a Christian who has not reached perfection.

For example, many Christians who would never deny their faith are reticent when it is challenged in polite society, although they actually ought to speak out boldly in its defense. Often the omission is without sin. The nonabsolute norm of polite intercourse in pluralistic society is to avoid acrimony by avoiding religious debate. The nonabsolute Christian norm is to proclaim the faith—a responsibility which varies in its specifications according to one's condition and state in life. Many sincere Christians are not clear about how they are required by their personal vocation to proclaim the faith, and they do not know how to do it without acrimony. So they innocently limit their affirmative responsibility to speak up by nonabsolute norms of etiquette accepted uncritically from the common culture.

6. **Thus, even for Christians, a more or less extensive part of the body of specifically Christian norms is subjectively beyond reach. This state of affairs depends upon conditions which need not be blameworthy and which cannot be removed by general instruction, but only by individual spiritual and moral development.** Hence, the general moral instruction of the Church concerning sin (especially mortal sin) usually treats only the minimal moral responsibilities common to every Christian or very important for those in certain states of life.

7. At the same time, the specifically Christian moral norms have never been neglected by the Church. They have been constantly proposed by the reading of the New Testament in the liturgy and by personalized modes of instruction (for example, spiritual direction in connection with the sacrament of penance) permitting individuals to grow in understanding and fulfillment of the responsibilities of Christian life. Each faithful Christian's sense of sin grows gradually as the exigence of specifically Christian moral norms becomes clear.

When classical moral theology insisted upon the need for a serious effort to strengthen oneself against temptation and avoid occasions of sin, it implicitly insisted upon a responsibility to fulfill specifically Christian modes of response. In practice, the view taken here is not more rigoristic, for it does not suggest that there is grave matter where the Church has not said so, and does not even suggest that imperfection is venial sin until the obligation to move toward perfection is recognized.

What classical moral theology lacked was a clear understanding of the intrinsic and dynamic relationship between the demands of natural law and the life of Christian perfection. These were thought of as two worlds, each complete in itself, existing on different levels. In reality, the relationship is more organic, like that of an animal's vegetative and sentient life. For an animal, unlike a plant, a complete system of growth, nourishment, and reproduction without sensation and emotion is quite impossible. The animal's vegetative life is the foundation for its higher, sentient life. But, at the same time, only by unfolding into the full, animate life of its kind can any animal long survive and flourish even in its most basic vegetative functions. Similarly, Christian life specifies human life, and human life can be lived as it should be only if one becomes Christian and proceeds toward Christian perfection.

8. Rigorism is relative. It is asking too much to expect fallen men and women as such to live as children of God. But it is not asking too much to expect God's adopted children to do so by living in Jesus (see Jn 15.4–7). Since Christians can do the works Jesus does and greater, this is a realistic expectation—not, of course, because human beings can manage it by human power, but because the Father gives those who believe the power of the Holy Spirit (see Jn 14.12–17). Mary and the other saints are only human beings; what God has done in them he wishes to do in us, for his will is our sanctification (see 1 Thes 4.3; 1 Tm 2.4; 2 Tm 1.9; Ti 2.11).

9. The gift of the Spirit is love. **Love makes possible—even easy and joyous—what would otherwise be impossibly difficult. Without minimizing the requirements of Christian life, without compromise, love finds a way: the way which is Jesus, the way of the cross, the way to resurrection and eternal life.** Following this way, Christians moved by the Spirit create new and beautiful lives, which they offer to God. In exchange for the gift of his Son and his Spirit, his own truth and love, we return to the Father the gift of our own lives, lives truly human but also, with Jesus and in his Spirit, truly divine.

Today it is often suggested that Christian life is bound to lead to psychological disaster. The strain of fulfilling the standards of Christian marital morality, for example, is pointed to as a cause of marital disharmony and a reason for approving contraception. This objection, though insubstantial in theory, is formidable for people engaged in pastoral activity, and so it deserves some consideration.

The psychological difficulties which arise for those who try to live according to Christian moral standards probably stem from two sources. First, if one lacks insight into the personal and human value of fulfilling the Christian norm, one undertakes to live up to it, if at all, only for the sake of ulterior considerations, such as fear of mortal sin and the threatened punishment of hell. Second, if one lacks a helpful and supportive community and yet tries to do anything which is very difficult, the strain can become unbearable. It is hard to follow a way of life at odds with that of almost everyone one meets each day.

The remedy for the first source of difficulties is a closer personal relationship with Jesus and more adequate instruction, especially in Christian moral principles. The faithful need to be helped to see the intrinsic connections which form a tight chain between their act of faith and their motives for making it, on the one hand, and the difficult requirements of Christian life, on the other. If they are not so instructed, they might undertake to live according to Christian standards out of obedience to the Church's teaching for the sake of attaining heaven and avoiding hell, but this undertaking will be unnecessarily burdensome and can lead to psychological difficulties.

This does not mean that the hope of heavenly reward should be de-emphasized. Quite the contrary. The morality of Christian love demands that this motive be greatly emphasized. If one loves one's father, one does what he wishes in order to obtain the rewards he promises, when it is clear that he wishes one so to act. Likewise, if we love Jesus we will be eager to gain our heavenly reward, for he has made it clear he desires this for us.

Rather, the point is that the meaning of this heavenly reward as human fulfillment needs to be explained to Christians who find it hard to live their faith. They can be helped by understanding the intrinsic relationships between life in this world and heavenly fulfillment (which was the subject of chapter nineteen), the reason why Christian life in this world must be difficult if it is to be worthwhile (which was the subject of chapters twenty-two and twenty-three), the way in which faithfulness to the Church's teaching helps Jesus complete his redemptive work on earth (which was treated in chapter twenty-three), the beauty of the gift one can offer to God by living a life like that of Jesus (which was the subject of chapters twenty-five through twenty-seven), and the process of growth in holiness which truly is possible and necessary (which will be the subject of chapters twenty-nine through thirty-three). Understanding these things, those who love Jesus and yet find it hard to live up to their faith will nevertheless find the effort meaningful, not meaningless suffering.

The Church's teaching never has left these intrinsic connections wholly obscure, but they need to be made clearer, and they can be and are being made much clearer today. If priests and teachers whose own love is ardent will do the work necessary to understand these matters deeply and to convey richly and abundantly what they come to understand, good fruit can be expected for Christian life.

The other problem of a psychological kind arises from lack of an adequate, supportive community. "Bear one another's burdens, and so fulfil the law of Christ" (Gal 6.2). Here, too, the Church always has offered help and still does. Yet much more is needed. The Church is made up of sinners struggling for salvation. It needs to have something of the character of a flourishing chapter of Alcoholics Anonymous. Its members suffer repeated experiences of shipwreck. It needs to have something of the character of those groups who by mutual support and common effort have survived shipwreck and sailed to safety in small boats over thousands of miles of open sea. Its members feel weakness and loneliness. It needs to have something of the character of the mother whose capacious lap and soft breast offer comfort to her little ones. The Catholic Church in modern times has shown less of these qualities than have various Protestant churches. Much work is needed to make the Church the home and family it ought to be.

Question G: Why is hope indispensable to living a Christian life?

1. Hope is related to faith and charity (see *S.t.*, 1–2, q. 62, aa. 3–4; 2–2, q. 4, a. 1). By faith we accept God's love in the form of covenant communion; by this love we are disposed to fulfillment in divine life. By hope we count on God to fulfill the covenant he has made with us in Jesus—to bring us to fulfillment in Jesus by making us faithful as he himself is faithful.

2. Hope is the orientation of one's entire Christian life toward the reality of the unseen fulfillment in Jesus, which already exists in him and is being built up as we live our lives. We look for completion yet to come, for we wish to be part of heavenly fulfillment and to be aware of being part of it (see *S.t.*, 2–2, q. 17, aa. 1–2, 6). Like all the saints before us, we now know the real meaning of our lives only by faith. The great cloud of witnesses (see Heb 11.1–4; 12.1) is composed of all those who showed their absolute confidence in God's faithfulness to his promises.

They lived by faith, which was effective in shaping their lives in that it told them precisely what they could hope for and gave them grounds for believing in the reality of what was unseen.

3. The world as we know it is passing away (see 1 Cor 7.31; GS 39). Our heavenly home already exists, and we only wait to be taken into it. By hope we live in accord with this reality, which is altogether opposed to the realism of common sense.

St. Paul clarifies the reality in which Christians live. Heaven must not be set aside as "other-worldly," for a sense of its present reality is a key to living a Christian life now: "For we know that if the earthly tent we live in is destroyed, we have a building from God, a house not made with hands, eternal in the heavens. Here indeed we groan, and long to put on our heavenly dwelling. . . . He who has prepared us for this very thing is God, who has given us the Spirit as a guarantee" (2 Cor 5.1-2, 5).

4. Christian realism has not only individual but social dimensions; one fully formed by the Christian modes of response is not solely concerned with individual salvation. But even though Christians are bound to do all they can, consistent with uprightness, to bring about human fulfillment here and now and overcome evil in this world, there are limits. Faithful Christians, in order to mitigate social evils, will not do what they believe wrong, for they are convinced that these evils do not compare in significance with the heavenly fulfillment to come: "I consider that the sufferings of this present time are not worth comparing with the glory that is to be revealed to us" (Rom 8.18).

5. This is not hope for a purely individualistic salvation. It is a hope for humankind as a whole and indeed for the whole universe (see Rom 8.19–25). Christians most perfectly fulfill social responsibility when they work energetically and unselfishly to spread God's redemptive truth and life to all humankind. By the same token, the Christian who is content to treat the faith as if it were a private possession fails in love of neighbor (see *S.t.*, 2–2, q. 17, a. 3).

6. Jesus' redemptive work does not simply cancel out sin and restore this world to what it was. While it makes possible a good life in this world, there are many respects in which such a life cannot be humanly fulfilling, since it is lived amid the consequences of sin and involves suffering the consequences of faithfulness to Jesus. **It will very often seem—and worldly wisdom will insist— that the only reasonable course is to do something evil, in order to avoid a greater evil or bring about a greater good. In such cases, it is only by hope that goodness is possible.** By hope one realizes that one's good act is invisibly fruitful, that its fruit will last, and that one who loses everything for Jesus' sake in this world will be most richly fulfilled in him in heaven.

In announcing the kingdom of God, Jesus urged that we look forward to it (see Mt 24.44–51; Mk 13.32–37; Lk 12.35–48). While waiting, he taught us to persevere until the end (see Mt 10.22; Mk 13.13; Lk 21.19). After the resurrection of Jesus, the early Church looked forward longingly to his return (see 1 Cor 16.22; Phil 3.20; Rv 22.20). Christians waited in hope (see Gal 5.5; Ti 2.13). What they hoped for was salvation, eternal life—a share in the resurrection and glory of Jesus himself (see Rom 5.9; 6.22; 8.17; Gal 6.8; Phil 3.20–21; 2 Thes 2.13).

If one is faithful to the end, one can be confident that one's hope will be fulfilled (see

Heb 6.11). The basis for assurance is the faithfulness of God to his promises, and the fact that Jesus already has entered glory (see Heb 6.13–18). "We have this as a sure and steadfast anchor of the soul, a hope that enters into the inner shrine behind the curtain, where Jesus has gone as a forerunner on our behalf, having become a high priest for ever after the order of Melchizedek" (Heb 6.19–20). The blood of Jesus assures our entrance into heaven "by the new and living way which he opened for us through the curtain, that is, through his flesh" (Heb 10.20).

Our hope extends through the Eucharist from this world into the invisible kingdom which is growing, and in which the real results of our present lives are being built into fulfillment. Getting results here and now is of no great importance (see Mt 16.26; Mk 8.36; Lk 9.25). The Christian lays up treasure in heaven (see Mt 6.20–21; Lk 12.33–34). The reality of a Christian's life is not apparent. It is hidden with Jesus, and will appear only when he comes (see Col 3.3–4).

The confidence of the Christian is not in himself or herself. The basis of confidence is that one has experienced God's love, and one knows by faith that the power of the Holy Spirit is available (see Acts 1.8; Rom 15.13). With such confidence, when seemingly most alone, one knows that one is in the company of the divine persons (see Jn 14.16–18).

Summary

Christian morality can be called an ideal in certain senses. Its norms demand faithful and determined effort; perfect love of God requires a lifetime of striving; individuals cannot overcome the imperfections of the Christian community, the Church, but can only work to build it up and pray their work will be fruitful. Still, the Christian modes of response are not mere ideals; they are principles of binding norms, not counsels. Certain moral theories err in seeking to formulate norms for a society of perfectly upright people and then adapting these to the world as it is. Christian norms, such as loving enemies and suffering evil redemptively, are meant for this world precisely as it is.

Christian norms can be fulfilled. Granted, people are not morally responsible for anything they truly cannot choose (because it never occurs to them, because they can see no point to it, or because they can think of no way to begin doing it), and in this sense Christian norms are impossible for some. But in this sense, also, the impossibility can always be overcome. In any case, when people say Christian morality is "impossible," they usually mean that they do not wish to surrender some contrary commitment or that they often fail in their efforts to live up to Christian norms. Some say Christian morality is incompatible with human nature, and indeed it is at odds with our fallen condition. But human nature is truly renewed by Jesus' redemptive act, and Christian norms are not impossible for those open to this radical transformation.

Christian norms express the requirements of charity; but since the fullness of charity is perfection, gradual fulfillment of these norms constitutes growth toward perfection. This does not mean charity, a divine gift, is itself subject to change; rather, one receives charity more perfectly as one's life is increasingly organized by faith and lived according to love.

Failures in respect to the Christian modes of response are sins. To see why this is not a rigoristic view, one must consider the different ways in which people organize their lives.

For many, this probably does not go beyond a structuring based on spontaneous willing—likes and dislikes, goals and objectives—and choices in this framework. Some, however, take more control over their lives by making commitments, which establish their identities.

Christian faith is a commitment which should generate constant growth toward perfection. Yet growth is not apparent in Christians for whom their faith, though a genuine concern, is only one concern among many, and is more or less insulated from the rest of life. Wholly or in part, the lives of such persons lack the structure of personal vocation.

Commitment to a personal vocation does not guarantee progress in holiness or even perseverance in grace—one can still be radically unfaithful—but one who is not radically unfaithful is almost compelled to make progress. To live out a vocation, one must place oneself in the service of the source of the vocational commitment, living faith; but growing integration with living faith is precisely what is meant by progress toward holiness. The effort leads one to challenge the residual elements of other systems by which one may have structured one's life. The meaning of the Christian modes of response becomes clearer and more definite, and the dynamics of Christian transformation become operative as one confronts problems in accord with these Christian norms.

The obligation to live the Christian life is limited by blameless ignorance of what that entails—ignorance from which every Christian suffers to some extent. One recognizes one's responsibilities as a Christian only as one lives one's Christian life. Inevitably, a Christian will sometimes take some other norm as controlling in a particular situation, overlooking the Christian norm. Thus, a more or less extensive body of Christian norms is always subjectively—and blamelessly—beyond one's reach.

This state of affairs cannot be remedied by the Church's general instruction, which usually focuses upon minimal moral responsibilities, but only by individual spiritual and moral development. Yet the Church has never neglected the specifically Christian moral norms; they have been constantly proposed by the reading of the New Testament in the liturgy and by personalized instruction such as spiritual direction in connection with the sacrament of penance. Perhaps it is asking too much—rigorism—to expect fallen men and women to live as children of God, but it is not too much to ask of God's adopted children.

Hope is indispensable to living as a Christian. By hope one orients one's entire Christian life to unseen fulfillment in Jesus, already existing in him and being built up as we live our lives. Hope deters us from attempting to overcome evil with evil. Hope is not purely individualistic; it is hope for humankind as a whole and indeed for the whole universe.

Appendix: Christian morality and social responsibility

Some argue that even if it is possible to fulfill specifically Christian moral norms, doing so would be socially destructive. Hence, while Christian morality might be a realistic guide for private life, it is unrealistic as a guide for those who must bear the weight of social responsibility. For example, what would happen to a nation which refused to carry on war in its modern forms?

Three things should be borne in mind in thinking about this question. First, it is largely hypothetical. People with real Christian convictions seldom gain and stay in positions of great worldly power. Second, Christian norms do not altogether rule out carefully restricted uses of defensive force. The exclusion of violence is a nonabsolute norm, but Christians also are required to fulfill their responsibilities by defending the weak, and this can justify the use of deadly force and cooperation in such activity. Third, the Machiavellianism of nonbelieving politics also leads to human disasters of great scope. If deterrent strategies eventually lead to a large-scale thermonuclear war, as seems likely, it will be clear that the world might have been better off if some participants in current power struggles had formed policies more in accord with Christian standards.

Throughout history, those who seriously tried to live in accord with Christian moral norms have been accused of social irresponsibility. In ancient times, refusal of service to the pagan gods by the Christians was blamed for the decline of the fortunes of the Roman empire in its confrontations with barbarians. Today, advocates of violent revolution condemn as squeamish Christians who resist their approach. The argument is that one should be more concerned about human misery and less about moral purity. Those who refuse to dirty their hands in the cause of revolution are said to lack compassion.

This line of argument might be telling against a Stoic, who so exalts the importance of moral rightness as to make a veritable idol of this human value: "Let right be done, though the heavens fall!" A person who takes this view and who makes no clear connection between moral uprightness and perfect human fulfillment is in an embarrassing position. Even a sound rational morality, which cannot show that integral human fulfillment is more than an ideal, asks a great deal when it demands that palpable human misery be endured for the sake of an ideal possibility.

However, Christian faith proposes that fulfillment in Jesus is the real future of humankind. Morally upright action in this life is not demanded for its own sake, as if morality were the ultimate value. Rather, moral goodness is necessary for the sake of human fulfillment, of which it is an essential element. The upright acts of men and women will contribute to fulfillment in Jesus; these acts are destined to last forever.

Christians also resist doing what they believe evil because they realize that the seemingly rational methods of violence really will not prove effective in dealing with human misery. Revolutionary violence leads immediately to tremendous misery; Marxism, for instance, has inspired acts, including abortions, which already have caused hundreds of millions of deaths and much suffering. At the same time, such methods do nothing to overcome evil, for evil is not an obstacle to be demolished or a problem to be solved, but a privation to be healed by redeeming love.

Those who conform to the mind and heart of Jesus by refusing to do evil in an effort to overcome evil are not afraid of dirty hands so much as they are reluctant to cut off the hands of the unjust to prevent their unjust deeds. Deprived of hands, the unjust can find hooks to use in creating misery even more efficiently. The Christian way is to allow one's own hands to be pierced, and then with pierced palm to shake the hand of the evildoer. In washing from himself the blood of one who will not do violence, the evildoer is offered a new opportunity to look at his own hands, and to allow them to be cleansed of evil.

Notes

1. This point is more than a theological conclusion, for it is part of the ordinary teaching of the Church. See, for example, Leo XIII, *Exeunte iam anno*, 21 *ASS* (1888) 327–28; *The Papal Encyclicals*, 108.10: "By the infinite goodness of God man lived again to the hope of an immortal life, from which he had been cut off, but he cannot attain to it if he strives not to walk in the very footsteps of

Christ and conform his mind to Christ's by the meditation of Christ's example. Therefore this is not a counsel but a duty, and it is the duty, not of those only who desire a more perfect life, but clearly of every man *always bearing about in our body the mortification of Jesus'* (2 Cor 4.10). How otherwise could the natural law, commanding man to live virtuously, be kept?" On the preceptive and practicable character of the law of Christ, see Edouard Hamel, S.J., *Loi Naturelle et Loi du Christ* (Bruges: Desclée de Brouwer, 1964), 11–43; Augustine Stock, O.S.B., *Counting the Cost: New Testament Teaching on Discipleship* (Collegeville, Minn.: Liturgical Press, 1977), 26–60; Servais Pinckaers, O.P., *La quéte du bonheur* (Paris: Téqui, 1979).

2. On St. Paul's teaching of the universal call to Christian perfection: Ignace de la Potterie, S.J., and Stanislaus Lyonnet, S.J., *The Christian Lives by the Spirit* (Staten Island, N.Y.: Alba House, 1971), 197–219.

3. This paragraph is not intended to be a description of Kant's methodology, but a simplified indication of the implications of his approach, especially as it influenced the development of situation ethics and compromise theories of Christian morality. Kant sets up the model of a kingdom of ends, which he does not intend as a plan for society but uses to generate norms: Immanuel Kant, *Foundations of the Metaphysics of Morals*, trans. Lewis White Beck (Indianapolis: Library of Liberal Arts, 1959), 56–59. Then, when he deals with specific normative matters, Kant introduces casuistical questions which make norms nonabsolute without providing any method of limiting exceptions: *The Metaphysical Principles of Virtue*, introduction by Warner Wick (Indianapolis: Library of Liberal Arts, 1964), 71; examples: 84, 88, and so on. For a clear example of theological situationism influenced by Kant: Helmut Thielicke, *Theological Ethics*, vol. 1, *Foundations*, ed. William H. Lazareth (Philadelphia: Fortress Press, 1966), 609–67. This sort of theology has influenced Catholics, for example: Charles E. Curran, *Catholic Moral Theology in Dialogue* (Notre Dame, Ind.: Fides Publishers, 1972), 209–19; Curran distances himself from more radical, Protestant theories of situation ethics.

4. For exegesis of New Testament moral teaching in conformity with this Catholic principle of interpretation, see Rudolf Schnackenburg, *The Moral Teaching of the New Testament* (New York: Herder and Herder, 1965). Jesus' moral teaching is both strictly binding and practicable: 73–89.

5. See, for example: Boniface Honings, "Christian Conscience and *Humanae Vitae,*" in *Natural Family Planning: Nature's Way—God's Way,* ed. Anthony Zimmerman, S.V.D., et al. (Milwaukee: De Rance, 1980), 204–5.

6. John Paul II, *Familiaris Consortio,* 74 *AAS* (1982) 123–24; Eng. ed. (Vatican City: Vatican Polyglot Press, 1981), 67 (sec. 34).

7. See *The Rites of the Catholic Church,* trans. International Commission on English in the Liturgy (New York: Pueblo, 1976), 444–45, for a recommended form for examination of conscience which articulates one meaning of "perfection." The heading is coordinated with and divided against headings which organize responsibilities toward God and neighbor, and thus is concerned primarily with personal vocation and moral responsibilities toward oneself.

8. St. John of the Cross, *The Ascent of Mount Carmel,* II, 5, 3, in *The Collected Works of St. John of the Cross,* trans. Kieran Kavanaugh, O.C.D., and Otilio Rodriguez, O.C.D. (Washington, D.C.: ICS Publications, 1979), 116. Cf. St. Thomas Aquinas, *Summa theologiae,* 2–2, qq. 82–85.

CHAPTER TWENTY-NINE

PRAYER: THE FUNDAMENTAL CATEGORY OF CHRISTIAN ACTION

Introduction

Christian life requires perfection, and growth toward perfection occurs in the day-to-day observance of Christian moral norms. Charity, the central principle of Christian holiness, grows insofar as it is the principle of morally good lives integrated with faith in Jesus.

Such lives must be shaped by prayer and organized by the sacraments (see *S.t.*, 2–2, q. 82, a. 3; 3, q. 65). This chapter considers prayer in general, types of prayer, and certain questions concerning prayer; chapters thirty through thirty-three treat the sacraments. Underlying this treatment is the teaching of Vatican II: "Each must share frequently in the sacraments, the Eucharist especially, and in liturgical rites. Each must apply himself constantly to prayer, self-denial, active brotherly service, and the exercise of all the virtues. For charity, as the bond of perfection and the fulfillment of the law (cf. Rom 13.10; Col 3.14), governs all the means of attaining holiness, enlivens them, and brings them to fulfillment" (LG 42; translation amended).

Although there are norms concerning them, prayer and the sacraments are not themselves normative principles. But they are basic principles of Christian living. Prayer brings God's revelation to bear upon all one's thinking and even upon nonintellectual processes and the subconscious. The sacraments are central acts of faith. When the acts of daily life are integrated with the sacraments, living faith becomes operative in the whole of life.

This and the next four chapters are subject to a number of important limitations which the reader should bear in mind.

First, this is not a dogmatic treatise on prayer and the sacraments. Many problems which are important in such a treatise will be passed over here without mention. Moreover, the moral-canonical problems about valid and worthy administration and reception of the sacraments do not fall within the study of Christian moral principles.

Second, to a great extent these chapters cover material generally studied in works on spirituality. An adequate moral theology, however, cannot make any clear distinction between morality and spirituality. Therefore, these chapters must be continuous with the preceding ones, and the treatment cannot be organized and developed as is customary in works on spirituality. Still, works on spirituality contain much helpful detail which does not pertain to principles. Hence, this part, although necessary to the whole, may appear a rather summary treatment of spiritual theology.

Third, Christians are called to live with originality and creativity. We are not bound by hundreds of detailed precepts. Hence, there are many optional forms of spirituality accepted by the Catholic Church—various types of prayer, methods of meditation, forms of penance, diverse devotions, and so forth. On the whole, the present treatise will ignore this rich diversity—not because it lacks value, but because it is not a matter of Christian moral principles—and concentrate on the common spirituality the Church herself provides for all her children.

Question A: What is prayer?

1. Christianity begins in God's self-revelation, by which he makes himself known and offers an intimate share in his own life. Our first responsibility is to listen to God with open hearts.

The starting point for humankind's relationship with God is the reception of his revelation with living faith. By faith one is moved toward God, by love one is disposed to fulfillment in his goodness, and by hope one confidently relies upon him to bring one to fulfillment. Faith, hope, and charity are not three separate acts; rather, they are three aspects of one complete act.[1] For this reason, in its teaching on perfection, Vatican II says: "Every person should walk unhesitatingly according to his own personal gifts and responsibilities in the path of a living faith which arouses hopes and works through charity" (LG 41; translation amended).

2. Even before hearing God's word, one might be moved by the grace of the Spirit to be ready to hear it and, as it were, be aware of the awesome silence enveloping the whole world and the constant talk which fills it. Only when God's word is proclaimed to people and they hear it, however, do they become able to make their first contribution to the relationship: to listen. Listening is more than hearing; it is receptive hearing, hearing with a kind of attentive passivity. Such listening is the beginning of prayer, and there is no real prayer without it. **All Christian prayer consists in hearing God's word, thinking it over, and responding to it.**

3. St. Francis de Sales summarizes the teaching of the Fathers on prayer. While they often speak of "prayer" in a narrow sense, to signify petition, they also use it in a wider sense, to signify all the acts of contemplation ("contemplation" meaning loving thought of any sort about divine realities). Two formulae have become classic. One defines prayer as a conference or conversation or discussion with God, the other as a lifting of the mind and heart to God. De Sales seems to prefer the former, for he comments: "If prayer is a colloquy, a discussion, or a conversation of the soul with God, then by prayer we speak to God and God in turn speaks to us. We aspire to him and breathe in him; he reciprocally inspires us and breathes upon us."[2] This seems a more adequate conception of prayer than that which stresses ascent to God. **Thus, prayer will be considered here as the Christian's side of divine-human conversation.**

De Sales provides a metaphor: Prayer and the sacraments are two sides of a ladder reaching to heaven. Prayer calls down God's love and the sacraments confer it. The rungs are the various degrees of charity by which one moves from virtue to virtue, either ascending toward union with God or descending again with help for one's neighbors.[3] The value of this metaphor is in its linking of prayer and the sacraments, personal sanctification and apostolate. Of course, like all metaphors, this one limps. Its suggestions about directions of movement are at least unclear and perhaps misleading.

4. As Vatican II points out, prayer and the reading of Scripture go together. The former is the human side and the latter God's side of one and the same conversation. In listening to the Scriptures we listen to God, and in praying we respond to him, as Ambrose says (see DV 25; GS 19).

Thus, just as "talking" in one sense refers only to one's own part in a conversation, but in another sense refers to the entire conversation, including listening, so "prayer" in one sense refers only to one's own part in communication with God, but in another sense refers also to hearing and assimilating what he reveals.

5. To a great extent, prayer consists in remembering: remembering what God has said and done, especially what he has made known and available to us in Jesus. So essential to one's sense of identity is it to hold many things in one's heart that loss of memory is a kind of loss of self. This is true also of one's identity as a child of God; faith is a holding fast to gifts received.

6. At the same time, one knows one's identity in and by living it out. This also applies to faith: "For if any one is a hearer of the word and not a doer, he is like a man who observes his natural face in a mirror; for he observes himself and goes away and at once forgets what he was like" (Jas 1.23–24). Hence, prayer also projects Christian life; it shapes action in accord with faith. It is the principle of continuity, by which one's past relationship with God is kept fresh and made to yield still more abundant fruit.

Question B: Why is prayer necessary?

1. Prayer is divinely commanded. Scripture not only commends but enjoins it (see Mt 7.7–11; 26.41; Lk 18.1; Col 4.2–4; 1 Thes 5.16–18). There is a profound reason for this.

2. Scripture and the Holy Eucharist are paired as two tables of the new law; they are two forms in which the Word of God comes to us (see DV 21, 25, 26; AA 6; AG 6). **God's words and acts together give us himself in personal wholeness. Hence our side of the relationship requires prayer—the conversation with God who speaks to us in Scripture—just as much as it requires reception of the Eucharist.** By both of these acts, we accept and assimilate the bread which has come down from heaven.

The general point that prayer is necessary for our side of the relationship of revelation and faith includes all the specific ways in which prayer is required to live the Christian life. Speaking of self-control, for example, Leo XIII explains why faith and prayer are necessary to cultivate this virtue: "The virtue of which we speak, like the others, is produced and nourished by divine faith; for God is the Author of all true blessings that are to be desired for themselves, as we owe to Him our knowledge of His infinite goodness, and our knowledge of the merits of our Redeemer. But, again, nothing is more fitted for the nourishment of divine faith than the pious habit of prayer, and the need of it at this time is seen by its weakness in most, and its absence in many men. For that virtue is especially the source whereby not only private lives may be amended, but also from which a final judgment may be looked for in those matters which in the daily conflict of men do not

707

permit states to live in peace and security. If the multitude is frenzied with a thirst for excessive liberty, if the inhuman lust of the rich never is satisfied, and if to these be added those evils of the same kind to which We have referred fully above, it will be found that nothing can heal them more completely or fully than Christian faith."[4] Pope Leo then goes on to exhort clerics to lead exemplary lives thoroughly formed by prayer, because otherwise their learning, teaching, and preaching cannot be fruitful.

3. Acts of prayer are human acts by which one fulfills and determines oneself. These acts last; they build up one's Christian personality. As a man and woman become husband and wife more and more perfectly by constant, loving communion, so human persons and the indwelling Trinity become more and more perfectly united by constant prayer.

4. The analogy with the interpersonal relationship of husband and wife sheds further light on the need for prayer. The whole common life of a married couple depends on mutual understanding, which in turn requires conversation. Such conversation cannot always be directed to some practical object. Sometimes they must converse simply to commune, a communing which reaches a peak in the play of love. As marriage requires such communing, Christian life requires prayer (see *S.t.*, 2–2, q. 82, a. 2, ad 2).

Because prayer is a fulfilling human act, it ought not to be engaged in as if it were labor or bitter medicine to be taken in small doses only for the sake of its health-giving effects. Like play, prayer is essentially a leisurely activity, something worth doing for its own sake (see *S.t.*, 2–2, q. 82, a. 4). However, this does not mean prayer should be playful in the sense that one should engage in it only when and as long as one finds it pleasant, nor that one may engage in it in a careless manner. If one ought to be conscientious in labor and take pride in work well done, even when done for some ulterior end, how much more ought one to be conscientious in the best form of leisure activity and seek to do it well.

Question C: How does the Christian's life of prayer depend on the Holy Spirit?

1. St. Paul teaches that Christians need and receive the special help of the Holy Spirit to pray as they ought: "Likewise the Spirit helps us in our weakness; for we do not know how to pray as we ought, but the Spirit himself intercedes for us with sighs too deep for words. And he who searches the hearts of men knows what is the mind of the Spirit, because the Spirit intercedes for the saints according to the will of God" (Rom 8.26–27).

2. This passage is frequently taken to mean simply that the Spirit causes us to ask as we should and stirs right desires in us.[5] There seems no reason, however, for excluding a more straightforward meaning of the Spirit "himself intercedes for us."

3. We have good grounds for thinking of ourselves as having distinct personal relationships with each of the three divine persons (24-C). The Holy Spirit is the gift given by the Father to those who ask (see Lk 11.13). The General Instruction to the Liturgy of the Hours teaches: "The unity of the Church at prayer is brought about by the Holy Spirit, who is the same in Christ (see Lk 10.21), in the whole Church, and in every baptized person."[6]

According to the promise of Jesus, the Spirit comes and remains (see Jn 14.16–18). He is not only with us as a principle, but present in person. The children of God are not left in loneliness like orphans. The Spirit instructs (see Jn 14.26). He defends and guides (see Jn 16.7–14; Gal 5.25). Because of the presence of the Spirit, we have a concrete realization that we are children of God (see Rom 8.16). We cry out to God: "Father!" (see Rom 8.15). The Spirit makes up for our infantile condition by helping us in our weakness (see Rom 8.26–27). He takes a personal interest in our growth in the Christian life (see Eph 4.30).

4. The work of the Spirit in the Christian's life of prayer might be explained as follows. Prayer is the basic act of Christian life. It is normally a work of living faith—in other words, a work of charity. In praying, God's children act toward him according to the divine nature which he has begotten in them through the gift of the Spirit, as St. Paul also teaches: "For all who are led by the Spirit of God are sons of God. For you did not receive the spirit of slavery to fall back into fear, but you have received the spirit of sonship. When we cry, 'Abba! Father!' it is the Spirit himself bearing witness with our spirit that we are children of God" (Rom 8.14–16). However, as undeveloped, embryonic children of God (see 1 Jn 3.2), we are not yet capable of acting fully by ourselves according to the nature we have from the Father; we do not yet "see him as he is," that is, experience the fullness of divine life.

5. **The Spirit, who "is the Lord, the giver of life, who proceeds from the Father and the Son," therefore somehow mediates our relationship with them, supplying what we simply cannot supply ourselves, as a pregnant mother mediates her unborn child's relationships with its human father, with other people, and with the world at large, doing for it what it cannot yet do for itself.**

6. Prayer is the fundamental category of Christian life, and the Christian's life of prayer depends on the Holy Spirit in the way explained. Therefore, the Christian's entire life is supplemented by the work of the Spirit. Since this mysterious communion between Christians and the Holy Spirit pertains to them precisely as children of God—that is, according to the divinity they share in by adoption—it is distinct from their cooperation by human acts with God's redemptive work in Jesus.

7. Hence, the fact that the whole of Christian life is lived in the Spirit in no way means that the Holy Spirit fulfills any of the Christian's human responsibilities. Rather, just as Jesus' communion as Word with the Spirit is no substitute for his faithful fulfillment as man of his personal vocation, so Christians' life in the Spirit leaves them with undiminished moral responsibility.

God allows us to share in his life by degrees rather than all at once, not because he is grudging or because he lacks the power to overcome evil and divinize us without our help, but because he is generous and has the power to make us cooperators to some extent in his work of redeeming and divinizing us.

The Father loves us and desires our fulfillment in his own life with creative intensity: "This is the will of God, your sanctification" (1 Thes 4.3). He sends us the help we need to accomplish what we cannot do for ourselves. First the Word, then the Holy Spirit. Through them we receive from the Father the gift of our own powers, our own responsibilities, our own actions, and our own merits.

But over and above all this, the Spirit in person unites the Church, and so the Church comes to her Lord in communion with him. Likewise, the Word in person will unite all things in heaven and on earth (see Eph 1.10) and deliver the kingdom to the Father (see 1 Cor 15.24). Therefore, it seems that we can say without detracting from their equal divinity that the Spirit prays with us and on our behalf, and likewise that our Lord Jesus intercedes for us not only insofar as he is man but also (although in a different sense) insofar as he is the eternal Son.

Question D: What characteristics should mark Christian prayer?

1. First, like everything else, prayer should be centered on Jesus. Christian prayer is prayer with, through, and in him. As Incarnate Word and our high priest, our Lord brings heavenly conversation to earth. "He joins the entire community of mankind to himself, associating it with his own singing of this canticle of divine praise" (SC 83).

2. Jesus is both the model and the principle of our prayer.[7] He teaches us to pray (see Mt 6.5–13; Lk 11.1–4); his Spirit in us causes us to do so with the familiarity he taught us to employ (see Rom 8.15; Gal 4.6); one does not reach the Father except through Jesus (see Jn 14.6; Rom 5.2; Eph 2.18; 3.12). The conclusion of all the eucharistic prayers—"Through him, with him, in him"—is most fitting, since the eucharistic prayer is the central prayer of Christian life.

The General Instruction of the Liturgy of the Hours provides a chain of references to the New Testament which illustrate the abundance of Jesus' personal prayer.[8] Jesus prayed often. His daily work flowed from prayer. He also took part in public prayers and used the standard forms of prayer—for instance at meals. The decision in which he accepted death was formed and executed in prayer as an offering to the Father (see Jn 17; Heb 5.7).

Jesus commands us to pray (see Mt 5.44; 7.7; 26.41; Mk 14.38; Lk 6.28; 10.2; 11.9; 22.40, 46). St. Augustine beautifully summarizes the centrality of Jesus in Christian prayer: "God could give no greater gift to mankind than to give them as their head the Word through whom he created all things, and to unite them to him as his members, so that he might be Son of God and Son of man, one God with the Father, one man with men. So, when we speak to God in prayer we do not separate the Son from God, and when the body of the Son prays it does not separate its head from itself, but it is the one savior of his body, our Lord Jesus Christ, the Son of God, who himself prays for us, and prays in us, and is the object of our prayer. He prays for us as our priest, he prays in us as our head, he is the object of our prayer as our God. Let us then hear our voices in his voice, and his voice in ours."[9]

3. Because it is a human act, prayer should be done in accord with the Christian modes of response. Some of these are especially relevant and have been emphasized in Scripture.

4. **Thus, Christian prayer must first of all be humble** (see Lk 18.9–14). Humility is so necessary because, without it, we are not ready to accept the gifts which God is always trying to give. We imagine we can do without them. But unless one holds out one's hand, nothing can be given to fill it.

By teaching his followers at the outset of his model prayer to think of God as their Father, Jesus shows the relationship between childlike humility and asking God in prayer for what one needs, namely, awareness of dependence, readiness to receive, confident hope, and persistence in expecting needed goods (see Mt 6.9–13; 7.7–11; Lk 11.1–4; 18.13).

According to a plausible interpretation, the point of the parable of the publican and the Pharisee is not so much the former's self-abasement and the latter's conceit (these are significant but secondary factors) as the former's readiness to receive the pardon for which he is praying and the latter's failure to realize that he still needs pardon and continuing conversion. The Pharisee trusted in himself, was self-righteous (Lk 18.9–14). In Luke this parable is followed immediately by the pericope on the children, which says that to enter God's kingdom one must accept it as a child.

5. **Christian prayer should be filled with a spirit of joyous thanks.** This requirement is emphasized especially in several of the Epistles (see Eph 5.4; Phil 4.6; Col 2.7; 4.2; 1 Thes 5.18; 1 Tm 2.1; 4.3–5). Paul begins his own letters with thanks to God (see Rom 1.8; 1 Cor 1.4–5; and so on). The necessity for gratitude follows from the requirement of humility, together with the fact that those who are united with Jesus already have so much to be thankful for. Christian prayer is formed by the conviction that Jesus lives in glory and will soon return to finish what he has begun.

"Prayer" in the narrow sense is prayer of petition; the Lord's prayer is a series of requests (see *S.t.*, 2–2, q. 83, aa. 9, 17). Petition and thanks naturally go together; one who asks must express thanks for what already has been received and, in advance, for the next, hoped-for gift. Similarly, one who willingly and gratefully receives gifts readily asks for further gifts. Both asking God for all one needs and thanking him for all he gives are appropriate expressions of dependence on God, and thus essential consequences of the childlike attitude which belongs to Christian humility (26-D). One might say that prayer is necessary to receive the goods God wills to give precisely because by this act one determines oneself into an attitude of humility—one holds out one's hand to accept (see Mt 15.21–28; 17.14–21; Mk 7.24–30; 9.14–29).

6. **Prayer must be vigilant and attentive** (see Lk 21.36; Col 4.2). Otherwise, it rapidly deteriorates into a mere external exercise, which makes little difference to one's heart. St. Benedict's dictum with respect to the Liturgy of the Hours (see SC 90), that one's mind should be attuned to one's voice, is valid for all prayer. Without attention, one merely goes through the motions.

7. **Christian prayer must also be persevering and confident in our Father's goodness** (see Lk 11.5–13; 18.1–8; Jn 14.13; 16.23; Rom 12.12; 1 Pt 4.7). One cannot expect gifts unless one really wants them. Nor is one who fails to persevere in asking very eager to receive. Similarly, people who are sincere in giving high praise will naturally repeat it over and over. For example, husbands and wives who are truly in love do not tire of saying so. Perseverance is essential because prayer is interpersonal communion, and the communion is meant to last forever.

Jesus illustrates this point with the parables of the friend who borrows bread at night (see Lk 11.5–8) and the woman who pesters the unjust judge until he responds to her petition (see Lk 18.1–8). Most charmingly, the point is shown in the narrative of the miracle performed for the persistent Canaanite woman; ready to liken herself to a puppy receiving scraps at the table, her humble faith obtains from Jesus the cure she desires (see Mt 15.21–28; Mk 7.24–30).

People who understand how prayer determines a person into a proper disposition to receive God's gifts will not complain that they get little or nothing out of praying in certain ways prescribed or highly commended by the Church. Children frequently stop listening to their parents when the experience ceases to be gratifying, but often it is at just that point that they would benefit greatly from listening.

8. **Christian prayer must be sincere, not for show** (see Mt 6.5–8). Authentic prayer is offered to God in spirit and in truth (see Jn 4.23). In Christian prayer God's children converse with their Father; such conversation calls for privacy for an individual. A group, too, needs a certain apartness—a focus on what is being done rather than on how it is being perceived—lest what should be an act of prayer become a performance for the benefit of nonparticipants.

In view of this, it is easy to see how alien to the spirit of prayer is any liturgical format or development which turns the carrying out of the sacred acts into an artistic spectacle, however well executed, directed more toward a congregation as audience than from an ecclesial community to the Lord. One should participate in the liturgy for the sake of the liturgical act itself, not for the sake of one's impact on other participants or outside observers. Liturgy should be done well as a participatory act, but not become a performance for any audience—except God.

9. **Jesus himself teaches that prayer should be constant** (see Lk 18.1). This precept was followed by the early Church (see Acts 2.42) and was renewed by St. Paul (see Rom 12.12; Eph 6.18; Phil 4.6; Col 4.2; 1 Thes 5.17–18).

Beyond the requirement of perseverance in prayer, what can this demand for constancy be taken to mean? Some have maintained that the requirement is that one engage continuously in explicit acts of prayer—or an explicit state of prayerful awareness—at least at the margin of one's consciousness. Various methods have been developed in an effort to attain this objective.

St. Thomas realistically rejects this idea (see *S.t.*, 2–2, q. 83, a. 14). One can give one's full attention to only one thing at a time, and Christian life includes many acts besides prayer which ought to be given their due. However, one can maintain a constant desire to be in communion with God when an appropriate opportunity arises; one can avoid missing prayers; one can keep alive between times the devotion nourished during periods of prayer; one can pray through the prayer of others, as by benefices and stipends, and by sharing in the constant, liturgical prayer of the whole Church.

To all these ways in which prayer can be constant without its becoming a constant distraction from other important activities, one can add the true sense of the adage: To work is to pray. Not all work is prayer. But when one's work in fact carries out the will of God which one has discerned and accepted with loving firmness in prayer, then indeed to work is to pray, and to fail to give one's whole heart and attention to one's work is to nullify prayer.

Question E: Are prayers always answered?

1. Jesus says, "Every one who asks receives" (Lk 11.10) and, "Ask, and you will receive" (Jn 16.24). Yet often we ask in his name, without receiving what we ask for.

2. A partial explanation might be that one has not yet prayed long enough, but at times such an explanation is clearly irrelevant. Parents pray for their children's safety—surely a legitimate request—but the children sometimes die in accidents. The same is true of liturgical prayer as well: The Church prays for unity, but unity does not come. The Church prays for peace, but persecutions and wars continue.

3. The solution is along the following lines. God is a loving Father, and he does

hear and answer our prayers. The First Epistle of John says: "This is the confidence which we have in him, that if we ask anything according to his will he hears us. And if we know that he hears us in whatever we ask, we know that we have obtained the requests made of him" (1 Jn 5.14–15). However, God responds wisely. Therefore, he does not always give us exactly what we ask for. Wise parents do not give their children sweets every time they ask, for otherwise the children would be malnourished and would have rotten teeth. Instead, the parents provide a balanced diet and offer other forms of gratification, such as cuddling.

4. The principle emerging here was at work in Jesus' own prayer and the Father's way of answering it. Jesus prayed that the cup of suffering might pass him by (see Mt 26.39–44; Lk 22.39–44). But he was crucified. He had, however, couched his request in conditional form, as we should do: "Nevertheless, not as I will, but as you will" (Mt 26.39; cf. Lk 22.42). One who loves God prays first of all: "Your will be done" (Mt 6.10). Thus, a sacred writer can say of Jesus and his prayer: "In the days of his flesh, Jesus offered up prayers and supplications, with loud cries and tears, to him who was able to save him from death, and he was heard for his godly fear" (Heb 5.7). Obviously, Jesus' passion and death occurred; he was not saved from death in the precise way he requested. Yet he was saved from death: "He has risen from the dead, and behold, he is going before you to Galilee" (Mt 28.7).

5. We must trust that God deals similarly with our requests. Though our prayers are often not granted in the specific form in which we make them, the safety and well-being of those for whom we pray will nevertheless be secured, provided only they come to fulfillment in Jesus, in which every human good will be enjoyed together with the blessed vision of God.

6. Still, this solution to the traditional problem about petitionary prayer only leads to a more fundamental and metaphysical difficulty. If we are always to pray that God's will be done, what is the point of praying? As Jesus himself says, God already knows what we need (see Mt 6.32; Lk 12.30). Moreover, his providence embraces everything, and his will of all the good that ever will be done is clearly antecedent to our own upright desires (see Wis 11.20–22; Rom 11.33–36).

7. St. Thomas answers this difficulty by saying our prayers do not alter God's plans but fulfill them (see *S.t.*, 1, q. 19, a. 5, ad 2; 2–2, q. 83, a. 2; *S.c.g.*, 3, 95–96). **God has disposed not only that goods be given us, but that they be given in answer to our prayers.** Our prayers also are part of the providential design; God wills them so that we might have a share in bringing about even his redeeming work.

8. This answer seems sound, provided it is not misunderstood. As we have already seen, prayer is an essential and basic dimension of our interpersonal relationship with the divine persons. By acts of prayer we form ourselves into the relationship and begin to make our proper contribution to the bond of friendship. This is a real relationship, whose reality should not be diluted by positions erroneously derived from the metaphysical thesis that God is all-knowing and unchanging.

9. It is certainly true that ignorance, error, or change of any sort must be

713

excluded from God. But also to be excluded are any sort of comprehensive knowledge and unalterability which we can understand (see *S.t.*, 1, q. 13, a. 5; *S.c.g.*, 1, 30). **If we mistakenly suppose that God is all-knowing and unchanging in some sense we can fathom, prayer will indeed seem pointless. However, the presumption that we know what God is must be set aside, and his utter mysteriousness kept in mind.** We do not know what God is in himself, but we know it is right to think of him as Father. Our prayers matter greatly to him; our petitions and gratitude are required if he is to develop the intimate relationship he desires with us.

Question F: Why should liturgical prayer be the center of each Christian's prayer life?

1. To answer this question, it is necessary to recall what liturgy is. The sacred liturgy of the Catholic Church is her worship of God. Prayer is an integral part of worship but not the whole of it. Worship adds to prayer behavior appropriate to complete—at least symbolically—the interpersonal communing of prayer. For example, the Mass is a prayer completed by the offering of gifts and receiving of the Eucharist.

In the Mass, the behavior which completes prayer is more than symbolic; the communing of prayer is really perfected by the sacrifice and sacrament of the Eucharist. Just as marital love goes beyond the communing of conversation into the behavior by which love is made, so worship of God goes beyond the communing of prayer into the behavior by which the relationship with God is really accepted and developed. Now, any true lovemaking is preceded, accompanied, and followed by loving thoughts and words; similarly, all true worship is preceded, accompanied, and followed by prayer. Indeed, prayer is so essential and determinative of acts of worship that worship can be considered prayer in action.

2. Members of the Church can worship apart from the liturgy, individually or in groups, but then their acts of worship, as excellent as they may be, constitute worship in the Church rather than worship by the Church. For example, when the faithful carry out a devotional exercise such as the stations of the cross, they are engaged in true worship in the Church, but this act of worship is nonliturgical and does not constitute the worship of the Church.

3. Pius XII, in his great encyclical on the liturgy, *Mediator Dei*, explains that the Church acts in union with Jesus, who remains present to her in many ways, in particular when she offers prayers of praise and petition through him to our heavenly Father. He concludes with this clear statement of what the liturgy is: "The sacred liturgy is, consequently, the public worship which our Redeemer as Head of the Church renders to the Father, as well as the worship which the community of the faithful renders to its Founder, and through him to the heavenly Father. It is, in short, the worship rendered by the Mystical Body of Christ in the entirety of its Head and members."[10] Vatican II assumes this formulation into its own more complex teaching, which equally emphasizes liturgy's aspects as worship and as redeeming and sanctifying act. In both aspects, the liturgy is primarily Jesus' action, and he is always present in it (see SC 7).

4. The human life of the Incarnate Word is both a revelatory sign and an appropriate human response to revelation (21-F). These two aspects mutually

714

include one another, without becoming in any way confused. By the Incarnation, furthermore, the work of redemption, which is God's work, also has been made human work, and thus a divine-human cooperation. Jesus consummated his human part of the work by his freely accepted death on the cross (see Jn 19.30), but his entire life expressed the commitment which led to this final act and prepared for it. Thus his whole life must be considered part of his redemptive act. This act, considered both as revelatory sign of God's love and as human response to it, is made present to us in the Church's liturgy, especially and centrally in the sacrifice and sacrament of the Eucharist (see SC 10; *S.t.*, 3, q. 62, a. 5; q. 83, a. 1).

5. As a revelatory sign, the redemptive act presented in the liturgy is sacrament; it does what it signifies, because God's revelation is really effective communication of himself to us. As a human response to God's love, the redemptive sacrifice in which we participate in the liturgy is perfect worship, as Pius XII stresses. In the Spirit we are united with Jesus, the head of the Church, and through him we worship the Father.

6. In conclusion, there are two reasons why the liturgy ought to be the center of each Christian's prayer life. First, in its essentials the liturgy is not created by the Church, but prescribed for the Church by Christ. By instituting the sacraments, Jesus provides his Church with God-given worship. Humility accepts what God gives, and humility is the primary characteristic of Christian prayer. The liturgy should therefore be accepted humbly as the principle of any effort of personal prayer.

7. There is, however, a second and more basic consideration. The whole of Christian life is to be lived in communion with Jesus. **Liturgical worship is Jesus' redemptive act made present for us to participate in, both as beneficiaries and as subordinated coredeemers of ourselves and others. Therefore, the prayer which is to form the remainder of one's life must flow from and return to the liturgy as to its vital center, and in particular from and to the Eucharist as to its heart.**

The liturgy, because it is the work of the whole Church, must have and does have a formal character, which some who dislike it call "objective" and "impersonal." They mistakenly regard this quality as a defect, which they attempt to remedy either by "personalizing" the liturgy or by promoting other forms of prayer and devotion in place of it. However, the formality of the liturgy is no defect. Rather, this very quality is one of its important strengths, for in virtue of it the liturgy unites the whole Church with Jesus in a single harmonious choir together performing the same worship. To accept the demands of the liturgy upon oneself is to adapt oneself to life in the Spirit, to submit one's subjectivity to communion in Jesus. This acceptance itself is an important act of humility and obedience—the virtues which are basic modes of Christian response.

Therefore, if we find ourselves insincere in doing the liturgy, if we miss in liturgical prayer the gratification of authentic self-expression, the remedy is not to tamper with the liturgy, but to change ourselves until we conform to the liturgy. We should not conform our voices to our minds, but rather our minds to our voices, as St. Benedict says (see SC 90). If one's personal life is not lived in a Christian way, the liturgy itself becomes isolated and loses its essential point—namely, to be the medium by which we participate in redemption both passively and actively. If the liturgy is isolated, it quickly falls either into sterile formalism, coldly going through meaningless motions, or into fruitless emotionalism, which provides nothing but the apparent good of religion, stopping with the experience instead of proceeding to the whole reality of cooperation with God.

Question G: What is the role of sacramentals and devotions in Christian life?

1. Two things are fundamental in Christian life: the liturgy and one's personal vocation. By the liturgy one participates in the redemptive work of God in our Lord Jesus. By accepting one's personal vocation and carrying it out in daily life, one makes one's own contribution to fulfillment in Jesus, in union with his redemptive act.

2. Sacramentals and devotions are subordinate and instrumental to these two fundamental things. **Sacramentals extend the liturgy into personal, daily life, while devotions foster the personal assimilation of divine realities and prepare one to participate more fruitfully in the liturgy.**

3. Sacramentals are acts which are somehow related to the sacraments. They are done by the Church and are effective by the prayer of the Church as an articulation of the sacraments (see SC 60). Some are directly associated with the sacraments. For example, various acts included in the liturgy of the Eucharist, such as the priest's washing of his hands, which go beyond the essentials are sacramentals. Others are less directly related to the sacraments. For example, holy water recalls baptism; the ashes of Ash Wednesday prepare for penance; the anointing of kings is perhaps related to confirmation.

4. "Sacramental" is very often taken to refer to particular objects: holy water, candles, palms, and so on. This is not wrong, but it can be misleading if it is forgotten that the objects have a likeness or relation to sacraments only insofar as they are blessed by the Church's prayer and/or used in a way which is somehow connected with the central liturgical rites.[11]

One can most easily understand sacramentals if one compares them to various aspects of other human relationships. A couple could consummate their marriage in a few minutes. Normally, they do not hurry so. The joyous occasion is given an appropriate setting and elaborated into a honeymoon. People having a dinner party do not settle for McDonald's. The young couple bring home souvenirs; they extend their honeymoon into their later life by recalling it and using items connected with it. Company takes home a gift, perhaps a bit of dessert for the next day's lunch. Similarly, with sacramentals the Church elaborates the sacraments and extends them out into daily life (see SC 61).

5. Devotions are essentially specifications of worship which provide a personalized focus and pattern suited to the needs of particular individuals and groups. They are rather like the optional extras on an automobile: Not essential for everyone, they nevertheless personalize the essentials in a way which can be extremely important to different people according to their diverse needs.

6. Each devotion focuses attention on some particular religious truth or truths, some particular religious value or values. The special focus calls for specific acts of mind and will, specific emotions, and specific practices. Such specification is needed, for revelation and Christian values as a whole can only be assimilated by people little by little and with help which suits their widely differing temperaments, levels of maturity, personal vocations, and so forth.

As specifications of Christian devotion as a whole, the devotions must conform to the principles of the whole—in other words, they must be in accord with Catholic teaching, worship, morality, and law.[12] If devotions meet this criterion, they ought never to be despised or treated with disrespect; condescending attitudes toward other peoples' devotions are wrong. The liturgy itself ought not to be adapted (except as the Church has stipulated) to suit personal inclinations and needs. The necessary adaptation should be achieved not within the liturgy but by adding appropriate devotions to the liturgy. Thus, the present poverty of popular devotional life is one factor which impedes sound and fruitful completion of the liturgical renewal mandated by Vatican II.

Prior to Vatican II, the comparative dryness and tendency to formalism in the Church's proper worship made a rich devotional life essential by way of compensation.[13] Yet even with the reform of the liturgy, popular devotions remain necessary. Vatican II itself, precisely in reforming the liturgy, warmly commends them, provided they conform to the principles of the Church's worship as a whole, and somehow derive from and lead to the liturgy (see SC 13).

Question H: Why is personal prayer necessary in addition to liturgical prayer?

1. It should not be supposed that, because the liturgy is central in Christian prayer life, there is no need for personal prayer (see SC 12). On the contrary, the personal life of good deeds which God has prepared for each Christian (see Eph 2.10) is required to complete his or her unique share in the redemptive work; and this personal life must be shaped by personal prayer, just as Jesus' life was.

2. It is precisely because prayer is necessary for the self-determination of each Christian's personality that the liturgy, the Church's common, public prayer, is not adequate by itself for any particular person. **Private prayer and devotions are also needed, to specify for the individual what is common to all.** In this way individuals personally assimilate the bread from heaven which is in the first place nourishment for the whole Church.[14]

3. God's wisdom and love, most perfectly revealed in Jesus' life, constitute the model of Christian life as well as its motive and goal. To conform to this model, one must examine it closely and make it one's own; one must put on the mind of our Lord Jesus (see Rom 13.14; 1 Cor 2.16; Phil 2.5). This begins with prayer and is completed by putting into practice what one has come to understand in prayer. That is why the methods of meditation which have been most strongly recommended generally terminate in a practical resolution.

The prayers composed by the Church for liturgical use also provide an excellent model for personal prayer. Prayers are to be offered—supplications, prayers, intercessions, and thanksgivings—for all humankind (see 1 Tm 2.1–2). The prayer formula most often used by the Church includes all these elements: Almighty, eternal God (prayer), who has given such and such a benefit (thanksgiving), grant, we beseech you (supplication) to give us such and such, through Jesus Christ, your Son, our Lord (intercession). A complete prayer involves not four different prayer-acts, but one act with all of these aspects.

If Christians try to engage in activity of any sort without forming it by prayer, their efforts are likely to have several bad results for their relationship with God. First, being aware only of one's own effort, one loses humility; self-gratification in the activity rapidly dominates. Second, being interested in what one is doing, one has definite goals and a passionate drive to succeed in attaining them. Without prayer, one will lose meekness, and so will shunt others aside and become angry or discouraged in the face of obstacles. Third, the strain of activity demands refreshment and recreation. If one does not find it in prayer, one is tempted to find it in self-indulgent escapism, thinking that one is entitled to compensation for all the good one is doing. Fourth, one will take success or failure much too seriously. One will not realize that even the most important work, such as pastoral activity, belongs to this passing world, and that the real treasure is elsewhere. Fifth, one will fail to form one's action by faith; one will become fixated on particular objectives and begin to seek a kingdom and justice other than God's.

Summary

Prayer begins with listening to God's revelation. Of the two classic definitions of prayer—a conversation with God, a lifting of the mind and heart to God—the first seems more adequate, because it takes into account not only the human act but God's reciprocal act. Prayer and the reading of Scripture go together, as the two sides of the same conversation. To a great extent, prayer consists in remembering God's words and deeds, especially what he has communicated to us in Jesus. At the same time, prayer issues in action; it shapes one's life in accord with faith.

Scripture insists on the need for prayer; it is as necessary as reception of the Eucharist. For acts of prayer are human acts by which one determines oneself; they build up one's Christian personality. Any interpersonal relationship depends on mutual understanding, and that requires conversation. So, too, our relationship with God.

In order to pray, Christians need and receive the special help of the Holy Spirit. Although we are God's adopted children, we are now, as it were, his embryonic children, not yet fully capable of acting by ourselves according to the nature we have from the Father. Thus, the work of the Spirit is required to mediate our relationship with God, supplying what we cannot supply ourselves. The Spirit likewise helps Christians in their entire lives, but this help in no way diminishes their own moral responsibility.

A number of characteristics should mark Christian prayer. It should be centered on Jesus, who is the model and principle of our prayer. It should be done in accord with the Christian modes of response. It should be humble, filled with a spirit of joyous thanks, vigilant and attentive, persevering and confident of the Father's goodness, sincere and constant.

Jesus tells us, "Ask, and you will receive" (Jn 16.24), yet often we do not receive what we ask for. Part of the explanation concerns the fact that God is not only a loving Father but a wise one: He answers our prayers by giving us what we need, not necessarily what we want. Thus, as Jesus shows, our prayer ought always to be conditional: If it be God's will.... That, however, points to a more fundamental problem: If we ought always to pray that God's will be done, and God already knows what we need, what is the point of praying? St. Thomas answers that our prayers do not alter God's will but fulfill it. To this it should be added that, as we cannot attribute ignorance, error, or change of any sort to God, so, too, we cannot attribute to him any sort of comprehensive knowledge and unalterability we can understand. We know that prayer is essential to our interpersonal relationship with God; we err in supposing that we know what God's knowledge is, and that it is such as to render prayer unnecessary or irrelevant.

Liturgical worship should be the center of each Christian's prayer life. Other acts of worship by members of the Church are worship in the Church but not worship by the Church. Jesus' redemptive act is made present to us in the liturgy, especially the Eucharist, and we participate in it there.

Sacramentals and devotions also have a role to play in the Christian's prayer. Sacramentals are acts somehow related to the sacraments—extensions of the sacraments into daily life. Devotions are specifications of worship, focusing attention on some particular religious truth or truths, and accommodating the diverse needs and vocations of particular individuals and groups.

Personal prayer is required in addition to liturgical prayer, for it shapes one's unique participation in Jesus' redemptive act. The liturgy is not adequate by itself for the self-determination of any particular person; private prayer and devotions are necessary in order to personalize for each what is common to all. One's conformity to the model of Jesus begins in prayer and is completed by putting into practice what one has learned there.

Appendix 1:   The experience of communion with the Spirit

The First Epistle of John makes it clear that fellowship with the Spirit has a definite empirical aspect. The Spirit makes us know that Jesus remains in us (see 1 Jn 3.24). The Spirit makes it clear to us that we are in God and God in us (see 1 Jn 4.13). How does he do this?

In seeking to answer this question, one is tempted to look for the extraordinary and to ignore the ordinary manifestation of the Spirit in Christian life. Faith itself really is quite remarkable, for by it we can adhere with absolute assurance and steadiness to our heavenly Father, accept and defend the mysterious truth of our Lord Jesus, and remain relatively calm amidst great difficulties (see 2 Cor 5.16–6.10; Heb 11; 1 Jn 4.1–6). Faith is aroused and sustained by the Spirit (see LG 12). Thus, people conscious of the firmness and effective power of the living faith that is in them have empirical evidence of the gift of the Spirit (see *S.t.*, 2–2, q. 6, a. 1).

The prophets hoped for the Spirit to enable God's people to keep his word. Christians who cooperate with grace can experience this power of the Spirit in their lives. Thus anyone who lives a Christian life and experiences growth in likeness to Jesus has personal experience of the continuing presence of the Spirit (see *S.t.*, 1–2, q. 106, a. 1; q. 112, a. 5).

Of course, at times there are extraordinary manifestations of the presence of the Spirit (see 1 Cor 12.8–10). But living faith working through love is a greater gift and a surer experience of the fellowship of the Spirit than is any extraordinary occurrence, since such occurrences can be the work of spirits other than the Holy Spirit (see 1 Jn 4.1).

In the past, many Christians lacked reflective awareness of the presence and work of the Spirit. Devotion to one's guardian angel, while excellent in itself, sometimes served as a substitute for the devotion we ought to have to the Holy Spirit. He is ever at our side; we are committed to his care by God's love; he lights, guards, rules, and guides us in the way of the Lord Jesus. Today, in contrast with the past, some may be pressing to excess a desire for intense, explicit awareness of the presence of the Spirit. In my view, each of the three divine persons should be present in our religious experience somewhat differently from the others.

The Father revealed himself as the transcendent God; we ought to be aware of his presence in creation, in the given realities of faith and Christian life, and in the demands which Christian morality makes upon our consciences. The Son revealed himself to us by coming among us as man, as another man like us; we ought to be aware of his presence in the Liturgy, in the leaders and fellow members of the Church, in the needs of all men and women. The Spirit reveals himself to us as a mentor in living the divine life; we ought to be aware of his presence as God with us, alongside us in our Christian lives.

A young brain surgeon assisting in a delicate operation is adequately aware of the more experienced colleague, who is the chief of the operating team, if the younger surgeon collaborates smoothly and adaptably. The junior physician cannot do this effectively if he or she pays attention to the elder colleague as he or she would to a dinner companion or to the chief of staff's address to a conference. Not yet face to face, but already side by side, the Christian rejoices in the experience of the Holy Spirit.

By this analogy I by no means wish to suggest that the adopted child of God is equal to the uncreated Spirit. Since he is the natural Spirit of God and we the adopted children, the fruit of our common work primarily is his. The Spirit is the soul of the Church; the Church is our mother in Jesus, the mother of all God's little ones. We might well think of ourselves as embryonic children, snug in the womb of the Church, dependent for our divine life upon the Spirit, much as a natural embryo depends for all its life and functioning upon its mother.

In heaven we hope to enjoy in the exercise of our native human capacities a great awareness of the divine persons with whom we will be sharing our entire lives, including our lives as the particular human individuals we are. But even now we have some experience of the three divine persons with us. It varies from the experience we all have at times of God's closeness in our prayers and our daily work to the experience of a martyr like St. Stephen (see Acts 7.55–56) or a mystic like St. John of the Cross.

Appendix 2:   Sacred Scripture in the liturgy

Because the redemptive act of Jesus is the culminating revelatory sign and because Scripture is the primary literary expression of divine revelation, it is appropriate that the liturgy, which makes the redemptive act present to us for our participation, make abundant use of Scripture. Because God's revelation in Jesus also includes the perfectly appropriate human response to his love, Scripture is used in the liturgy not only as the means by which God speaks to us, but also as the means by which we in turn speak to him. God speaks to us especially in the Liturgy of the Word; with Jesus we respond most especially in the psalms and other scriptural prayers of the Liturgy of the Hours (see SC 6, 7, and 83–84).

The revelation of God's redeeming love is proclaimed in the words of Scripture and carried out by the deeds of the sacraments (see SC 6); the worshipping response of Jesus as head and the Church as his body is expressed in words certainly acceptable to the Father, since drawn from Scripture, and carried out by a liturgy of Christian life united with the redeeming life of our Lord Jesus (see Rom 12.1–2).

As divine communication, the liturgy brings heaven to earth, most especially by the real presence of Jesus in glory in the Eucharist; as human response, the liturgy brings the earthly Church and all of her participating children into the heavenly courts, to sing with the angels (see SC 8; also, the ending of all Prefaces). Thus a real continuity between Christian life in this world and in heaven is attained in the liturgy.

The reading and hearing of Scripture within the liturgy is, in a special sense, sacramental. It is Jesus "himself who speaks when the holy Scriptures are read in the Church" (SC 7). This presence, of course, is mediated by the one who proclaims the word in the name of the Lord, and who makes his own role clear by the concluding assertion:

"This is the word of the Lord" or "This is the gospel of the Lord." If Jesus appeared to us "live" on a television screen and we heard him through its speaker, we would not doubt that he speaks to us now and we hear him doing so. God has chosen instead to use the better instrument of a living human person. We ought not to allow this medium to detract from our sense of the real presence of Jesus when we listen to him speaking in the liturgy.

Science is not in science books; it is in the minds and activities of people who do science. Operas are not in their printed scripts, but only in their staged performances. Similarly, the communication which is revelation and faith is not actual in the text of Scripture as a literary document but rather in the careful reading and prayerful hearing of the word, primarily in the liturgy, and then by extension in personal prayer. For this reason, study of Scripture which is in continuity with the liturgy—as the faithful study of Scripture can and ought to be—is itself an important form of prayer (see DV 21 and 25).

Appendix 3:   Not every Christian is called to contemplative prayer

One can speak of "contemplative prayer" in a wide and a strict sense. In a wide sense, it refers to the loving effort to hear, understand, and assimilate what God has revealed, and to respond to him with attentive praise, thanks, and practical deliberation in the light of faith. Contemplative prayer in this wide sense can be called "meditation." In a strict sense, "contemplative prayer" refers to what St. Teresa of Avila calls "prayer of recollection" and other types of mystical prayer, up to and including what she calls "spiritual marriage." In other words, "contemplative prayer" in the strict sense is what modern writers in spiritual theology call "infused contemplation."[15]

While every Christian certainly is called to meditation, it would appear that the gift of contemplative prayer in the strict sense is an aspect of their personal vocations for only some. This is important, for, if it is correct, a great deal of modern writing in spiritual theology is misleading and potentially discouraging to the vast majority of Christians—who are not called to contemplative prayer in the strict sense—although it is pertinent and helpful to some.

Meditation, as defined above, is broader than the systematic mental prayer to which the word "meditation" is sometimes limited. Thoughtful and loving participation in the liturgy is meditation, as are prayerful reading of Scripture apart from the liturgy, devout saying of vocal prayers such as the rosary, thoughtful effort to discern God's will in an important decision, examination of conscience, and other forms of prayer, including systematic efforts to arouse devotion.

As we have seen, both liturgical and personal prayer are essential to Christian life. It follows that meditation in its many forms—what is here called "contemplative prayer in the wide sense"—is essential to Christian life.[16]

Moreover, every Christian life must not only be prayerful but must have other characteristics usually treated as aspects of the contemplative life. Basically, a Christian must strive to overcome every fault and conform totally to God's will—must strive, in other words, for perfection. Secondarily, every Christian ought to have some compelling experience of God's presence and all-powerful love in his or her life. This experience can, however, take many forms, and is by no means limited to those described by the great doctors of mysticism.

Everyone can experience the unshakable firmness of his or her own living faith and the power the Spirit gives to fulfill the law of Jesus. One need only abide in Jesus and desire with the Spirit's help to do the Father's will to have these experiences. (One who is impenitent in mortal sin certainly does not experience the Spirit's power to do what is right, and one who is obdurate is likely to begin to have some doubts in matters of faith.)

There are many other modes in which one can have an awareness of the personal relationship one has by living faith with the Spirit, the Son, and the Father. Devout participants in the liturgy often sense the presence of Jesus—for example, when they listen to or proclaim the word of God, receive or consecrate the Eucharist, receive or give absolution in the sacrament of penance, and so forth. Those who find and accept their personal vocation with living faith and try to fulfill it with constant fidelity very often are aware of the hand of God in their lives, to make things work out and to bring good out of evil. Those who share with the right dispositions in the work of the Church often experience the almost palpable presence of our Lord through his Spirit.

A life directed toward contemplative prayer is an excellent gift for those called to it. It is a special form of religious life (see *S.t.*, 2–2, qq. 180–82). This style of Christian life is a true and simple way to holiness. It yields extraordinary fulfillment, in the form of intense intimacy with God, in an important human good, that of religion. Furthermore, it is a true apostolate of great importance, for it serves the Church by providing the constant nourishment of prayer and the example of prayerfulness, while proclaiming to nonbelievers that the kingdom we seek is not of this world.[17]

However, the call to contemplative prayer in the strict sense is not universal. In support of this view one can cite the testimony of St. Teresa, a doctor of the Church whose authority is also relied upon by writers in spiritual theology who maintain that everyone is called to "infused" contemplation.

St. Teresa generally refers to the various forms of prayer grouped here as "contemplative prayer in the strict sense" as "favors," because they are experienced as gifts of the Spirit. At times she speaks of them as if they were charismatic gifts, given more for the benefit of others than for the spiritual welfare of the recipients. Thus: "He doesn't grant them because the sanctity of the recipients is greater than that of those who don't receive them but so that His glory may be known, as we see in St. Paul and the Magdalen, and that we might praise Him for His work in creatures."[18] The point is important, for everyone is called to holiness (see LG 39–42), but if the relationship between holiness and favors is not essential, not everyone is necessarily called to contemplative prayer in the strict sense.

While saying that favors are quite helpful if one happens to receive them, Teresa also says that God "is not obliged to give them to us as He is to give us glory if we keep His commandments. Without these favors we can be saved, and He knows better than we ourselves what is fitting for us and who of us truly loves Him."[19] The only thing essential to Christian perfection is perfect conformity of one's will to God's will. This is possible without favors: "There are many holy persons who have never received one of these favors; and others who receive them but are not holy."[20]

Teresa explains with great clarity that not all souls are suited to contemplation. Considering the life of Carmelite nuns, which is directed toward contemplative prayer, she says: ". . . it is important to understand that God doesn't lead all by one path, and perhaps the one who thinks she is walking along a very lowly path is in fact higher in the eyes of the Lord. So, not because all in this house practice prayer must all be contemplatives; that's impossible. And it would be very distressing for the one who isn't a contemplative if she didn't understand the truth that to be a contemplative is a gift from God; and since being one isn't necessary for salvation, nor does God demand this, she shouldn't think anyone will demand it of her."[21]

True, a few chapters later Teresa seems to contradict this statement by suggesting that all (Carmelite nuns) are called to the contemplative state. However, it seems to me her point is that no one is excluded from the favors of contemplation, no one is forbidden to strive for the greatest intimate experience of God, and no one who so strives will go unrewarded. Precisely how each one's striving will be rewarded is another matter: "You must always proceed with this determination to die rather than fail to reach the end of the journey. If even though you so proceed, the Lord should lead you in such a way that you are left with some thirst in this life, in the life that lasts forever He will give you to drink in great plenty and you will have no fear of being without water. May it please the Lord that we ourselves do not fail, amen."[22] In other words, all—that is, all Carmelite nuns—share in a life directed toward contemplative prayer in the strict sense, but in some cases the hoped-for fruit will be given in this life only in respect to the one thing necessary: never to fail the Lord.[23] The favors of contemplation will be received only in heaven.

When one experiences effortless, spontaneous, and especially moving states of prayer, one is more than usually conscious that prayer and all of Christian life is a grace. One tends to forget that excellence in any line of activity—for example, participating in a sport, doing theology, or writing poetry—flowers into acts with these qualities. It would be surprising if experts in prayer did not at times experience such gifts. As for the so-called infused character of contemplation, one can reduce this quality to the common character of Christian life as divine grace, based upon what truly is infused—namely, the love of God poured forth in our hearts by the Holy Spirit—together with the unique experienced qualities of some forms of prayer.[24]

St. Augustine's conception of the relationship between this life and heaven was heavily influenced by Neoplatonism. Many mystical writers also express themselves within a Neoplatonic conceptual framework. Thus they aim at a pure union with God, a union in which the "earlier stages" of prayer are left behind and human action is minimal. An aspect of the Neoplatonic influence on Christian life is the emphasis upon an individualistic, interior spiritual life. One withdraws from other people and from action into oneself, and within oneself seeks to ascend to God.

In modern times, the one-sidedness of a Neoplatonically influenced view of spiritual life has been distorted further by the common, dualistic conception of the human person. Many people suppose that their souls are hidden somewhere inside them, and that God is hidden somewhere inside their souls. Christian spirituality is systematically misinterpreted in line with this view; for example, St. Paul's statement that our Lord Jesus lives in him (see Gal 2.19–20) is taken as a motto for the pursuit of interiority, whereas it should stand for the transformation of one's whole life in Jesus. Jesus lives in us when we participate in the liturgy, when we share in the work of the Church, when we do the works of love, as well as when we engage in meditation.

The ideal of Christian life taken for granted by many modern writers of spiritual theology is that of the religious living in a cloister. This ideal involves exclusive dedication to the good of religion; every other human good is regarded as mere means. The religious life is excellent, but married people with families and professions ought also to be dedicated to other human goods, not only as means to more intense intimacy with God, but also as their contribution to fulfillment in the Lord Jesus—that is to say, as part of the ultimate end itself.

Notes

1. See St. Thomas Aquinas, *De veritate*, q. 28, a. 4, c.

2. St. Francis de Sales, *Treatise on the Love of God*, trans. John K. Ryan, vol. 1 (Rockford, Ill.: Tan Books, 1974), 268.

3. St. Francis de Sales, *Introduction to the Devout Life*, trans. John K. Ryan (Garden City, N.Y.:

Doubleday, 1972), 42. A recent theological treatment of the central role of prayer and the sacraments in Christian morality: Ramón García de Haro and Ignacio de Celaya, *La Moral cristiana: En el confín de la Historia y la Eternidad* (Madrid: Rialp, 1975), 136–44.

4. Leo XIII, *Exeunte iam anno,* 21 *ASS* (1888) 330; *The Papal Encyclicals,* 108.13.

5. See, for example, St. Thomas Aquinas, *In Rom.,* viii, 5, 692–93.

6. See "General Instruction," *The Liturgy of the Hours,* 1:27.

7. For excellent developments of this point: Gabriel M. Braso, O.S.B., *Liturgy and Spirituality,* trans. Leonard J. Doyle, 2d ed. rev. (Collegeville, Minn.: Liturgical Press, 1971), 68–78; Yves Congar, O.P., *Jesus Christ,* trans. Luke O'Neill (New York: Herder and Herder, 1966), 86–106.

8. See *The Liturgy of the Hours,* 1:22–24.

9. Ibid., 26; St. Augustine, *Discourse on the Psalms,* 85, 1.

10. Pius XII, *Mediator Dei,* 39 *AAS* (1947) 528–29; *The Papal Encyclicals,* 233.20.

11. A good treatment of sacramentals: Colman E. O'Neill, O.P., *Meeting Christ in the Sacraments* (Staten Island, N.Y.: Alba House, 1963), 323–53.

12. See P. F. Mulhern, "Devotions, Religious," *New Catholic Encyclopedia,* 4:833–34.

13. See Braso, op. cit., 194–208.

14. See Pius XII, *Mediator Dei,* 39 *AAS* (1947) 533–37; *The Papal Encyclicals,* 233.31–37; *Mystici Corporis Christi,* 35 *AAS* (1943) 234–37; *The Papal Encyclicals,* 225.87–90.

15. Vatican II frequently uses the words "contemplate" and "contemplation": SC 2, 103; LG 6, 41, 46, 64, 65; PC 5, 7, 16; DV 7, 8; GS 8, 15, 56, 57, 59, 82, 83; CD 35; AG 15, 18, 40; UR 15, 17, 21; PO 13. Many of these uses refer simply to thinking, even secular thinking, about something; others refer to a prayer act, but to one which is either plainly not contemplation in the strict sense or not clearly such; some refer to the "contemplative" in the technical sense; perhaps a few refer to contemplation in the strict sense (see PC 5; AG 18; UR 15), but in contexts concerned either with a certain vocation or with a particular function of the Church as a whole. Contemplation in the strict sense may be essential to the life of the Church, but it does not follow that it is essential for every Catholic, any more than the sacraments of matrimony and holy orders are.

16. St. Thomas, *Summa contra gentiles,* 4, 22, makes it clear that contemplation in the wide sense is essential to Christian life, since the Holy Spirit leads us with the cooperation of our own intelligence and freedom. Spiritual writers who use a chapter like this to support the thesis that everyone is called to "infused" contemplation distort its obvious sense, with the discouraging implication that only a very small number of Christians (those who receive this gift) are led by the Spirit.

17. See "Instruction on the Contemplative Life and on the Enclosure of Nuns" ("Venite seorsum"), 15 August 1969, in *Vatican Council II: The Conciliar and Post Conciliar Documents,* ed. Austin Flannery, O.P. (Northport, N.Y.: Costello, 1975), 656–75. This document says that "a certain degree of withdrawal from the world and some measure of contemplation must necessarily be present in every form of Christian life" (661). The Sacred Congregation cannot refer here to contemplation in the strict sense, for it talks about something essential to every form of Christian life, not about a universal invitation to "infused" contemplation.

18. St. Teresa of Avila, *The Interior Castle,* I, 1, 3, in *The Collected Works of St. Teresa of Avila,* trans. Kieran Kavanaugh, O.C.D., and Otilio Rodriguez, O.C.D. (Washington, D.C.: ICS Publications, 1980), 2:285.

19. Ibid., IV, 2, 9 (326); the passage referred to earlier in the paragraph is in III, 2, 11–12 (313–14).

20. Ibid., VI, 9, 16 (417).

21. St. Teresa of Avila, *The Way of Perfection,* XVII, 2 (in the cited edition, 99).

22. Ibid., XX, 2 (114).

23. *The Interior Castle,* V, 3, 7 (350–51).

24. A good treatment of this point: Louis Bouyer, Cong.Orat., *Introduction to Spirituality,* trans. Mary Perkins Ryan (Collegeville, Minn.: Liturgical Press, 1961), 76–81.

25. See Thomas Verner Moore, *The Life of Man with God* (New York: Harcourt, Brace, 1956), 217–28, for descriptions of persons who apparently lead very holy lives without contemplative prayer in the strict sense.

CHAPTER THIRTY

SACRAMENTS IN GENERAL AND BAPTISM

Introduction

The sacraments are divine-human cooperative acts in which God, Jesus as glorified man, the Church acting by her minister, and the recipient join in the work of justification and sanctification. As basic human and Christian acts of the one who receives them, the sacraments give a divine character to a human life.[1]

A preliminary synthesis of the elements of Christian life was provided by chapters twenty-three through twenty-nine. Now this synthesis will be completed by showing how the sacraments function as organizing principles of Christian life. Thus, the consideration of the sacraments in this and the next three chapters will provide the final, unifying vision of the way of the Lord Jesus.

The present chapter considers the sacraments in general, emphasizing their relevance to the Christian moral life.[2] It also treats baptism, the sacrament of entry into Christian life. The three chapters which follow discuss the sacraments of confirmation, penance, anointing, and the Eucharist as Christian moral principles which in distinct, simultaneous, but harmonious ways organize all the subsequent actions of a Christian's life. They do not determine what is right and wrong, but they do shape a Christian life toward its perfection in this world and toward eternal fulfillment in Jesus.

The Council of Trent teaches that all true justification—that is, all sanctifying grace—begins through the sacraments, once begun increases through them, and when lost is regained through them (DS 1600/843a). This implies that even nonbelievers who are saved receive grace by some sort of relationship to the sacraments.

Trent also teaches that the sacraments are seven, no more and no less, and all were instituted by Jesus (DS 1601/844). These sacraments of Jesus differ essentially from the sacraments of the old law (DS 1602/845). They are not all equally important; some are more basic than others (DS 1603/846). Not all are necessary for each individual, but the sacraments as a whole are essential for salvation; those who do not receive them must at least somehow desire them (DS 1604/847). Faith by itself is insufficient, and the sacraments do more than merely nourish faith (DS 1605/848).

Trent further teaches that the sacraments of Jesus contain the grace which they signify and confer this grace on those who do not obstruct it (DS 1606/849). The grace received in the sacraments certainly is a gift of God, but when one receives the sacraments properly, God always gives the grace he has promised (DS 1607/850). Faith by itself is not sufficient to obtain grace, but the sacramental rite itself (properly performed and received) does confer grace (DS 1608/851).

Trent also teaches that baptism, confirmation, and holy orders imprint a character on the soul—an indelible spiritual sign—so that these three sacraments cannot be repeated (DS 1609/852). Not every Christian has the power to preach the word and to administer all the sacraments (DS 1610/853); for certain of those acts, ordination is necessary. The minister must also intend at least to do what the Church does in the sacrament (DS 1611/854). In other words, the minister of a sacrament acts for the Church; the sacrament is an action, the minister an agent authorized to do this action. The minister need not personally be holy; he can be in mortal sin without invalidating the sacramental act (DS 1612/855).

Finally, Trent teaches that the accepted and approved rites customarily used by the Catholic Church in the administration of the sacraments cannot without sin be belittled or omitted by ministers as they see fit, nor may any individual pastor (bishop) change the rites (DS 1613/856).

Question A: How are the sacraments related to God's redemptive work in Jesus and in Christians?

1. During his earthly life, Jesus gathered a group of men, the Twelve, to be the foundation of the Church. He formed and prepared them to continue his work. At the Last Supper, he carried out the very action by whose choice he also freely accepted the suffering and death which followed the next day—namely, the action of giving himself to his chosen band in the appearance of bread and wine for humankind. Moreover, he directed the Twelve to do the same thing on his behalf (22-G).

2. Included within Jesus' single act of self-oblation are the subsequent actions performed to fulfill his command by the apostles, their successors, and their successors' priestly assistants. **Thus, in the Eucharist—and, by association with the Eucharist, in all the other sacraments—Jesus' redemptive act is made present to us, available for our cooperation and effective for our sanctification** (see *S.t.*, 3, q. 65, a. 3; q. 78, a. 1; q. 83, a. 1).

3. As extensions into the present of Jesus' unique redemptive act, the sacraments have all its complexity. They reveal and communicate the divine life which they signify, while at the same time responding to it with appropriate human worship (see *S.t.*, 3, q. 61, a. 1; q. 62, a. 1). Furthermore, these two aspects mutually include each other.

4. As revelatory, the sacraments have the complexity of every revelatory sign: They involve mutually complementary words and deeds. Likewise, as acts of worship, they involve the complexity of all such acts: They involve mutually complementary prayers and rituals of worship (see *S.t.*, 3, q. 60, aa. 5–7).

5. As one can imagine that God could have redeemed and deified human beings without the Incarnate Word (that is, without any really adequate creaturely cooperation), so one can imagine that Jesus could offer us the benefits of his redemptive work without any adequate cooperation on our part. He could, for example, simply have extended forgiveness and a share in divine life to those who would accept them, perhaps without their even knowing explicitly what they were receiving (as in fact seems now to be the case with nonbelievers who are saved). Or he might have arranged that news of what he had done be proclaimed abroad, with

the provision that those who believed and trusted in him would passively receive the benefits of his work (this is the classic Protestant conception).

6. In line, however, with the basic reason for the Incarnation itself—the ennobling of humankind and, thereby, the greater glory of God—Jesus arranged from the beginning to make sinful men and women his co-workers in their own redemption and the redemption of their brothers and sisters.[3] To make this cooperative work possible in a way wholly suited to our needs and capacities, he instituted the sacraments (see *S.t.*, 3, q. 46, a. 3; sup., q. 34, a. 1).

The life of Jesus as the principle of Christian life was treated in chapters twenty-two and twenty-three. The present discussion relates the sacraments to the redemptive act of Jesus which is their principle.

To redeem humankind and confer a share in divine life on created persons essentially is work only God can do. Redemption demands re-creation; deification can occur only by a divine begetting. However, God did not wish to redeem us and deify us without our free consent and willing cooperation. He is trying to bring us up to the dignity of mature children of God, not make puppets of us.

His problem was how to make human persons able to cooperate in their own redemption and deification. God's solution to this problem is the Incarnation, the human acts of Jesus, culminating in his self-oblation on the cross, and the divine response of the resurrection and glorification of Jesus. Jesus in glory indissolubly unites in himself the whole power for good, the total capacity to achieve fulfillment, of creator and creature. His potentiality is for the totality of goodness which God wills. He is in process of realizing this capacity. Its ultimate realization will be the fulfillment of everything in our Lord Jesus (19-B).

The new covenant principally is Jesus in glory. What he does, the Father and the Spirit also do; the divine persons are perfectly unanimous—that is, of one mind and purpose. The forgiveness of sin and the begetting of created persons to divine life is at our disposal, not as if re-creation and divinization were acts within creaturely power, but because we are united with our Lord, who in glory acts both as God and as man. Through him God has put himself at the disposal of his creatures (see *S.t.*, 3, q. 62, aa. 1, 3, 5).

The human life of Jesus centers in his personal commitment to do the Father's will, and specifically to carry out his personal vocation. Replacing Adam who separated humankind from God, Jesus reconciles humankind to God, to the extent that human action can do so. In doing this, he accomplishes two things at once. First, he provides a community-forming human act—thus a principle homogeneous to us, something we can "plug into." In this respect, his human life is the revelatory and communicative work of the Word Incarnate. But second, he acts toward God precisely as a human being, in his situation, should act. He does all in his human power to be a perfect Son.

Consequently, the divine act by which he is raised from the dead and established in glory as Lord of the universe is not imposed on creation willy-nilly. The Word Incarnate has freely consented to and fully cooperated with God's plan. He has merited his role as Lord in power (see Rom 1.4). By accomplishing redemption in this way, God enriches creation and wonderfully achieves his glory, which is the expression of his goodness. Had God redeemed and divinized us without the action of Jesus, creation would be so much the poorer, and the manifestation of God's goodness the less (see *S.c.g.*, 3, 69).

Thus, the glory of the Word Incarnate detracts nothing from the Father and the Spirit, but rather equally glorifies all three persons. The same will be true of our glory. Hence, there is no need to be anxious when sacramental doctrine attributes much to the work of created persons. To attribute much to ourselves is to attribute more to God, for we are and have nothing but sin which is not his gift.

Question B: Why are the sacraments Christian moral principles?

1. From one point of view, the sacraments are dramatic performances according to a script supplied in outline by Jesus and produced and directed by his Church. Considered this way, they are correctly defined as a kind of sign (see *S.t.,* 3, q. 60, a. 1; q. 64, a. 3).

2. Morality, however, is much more concerned with actions than with outward performances. Thus, insofar as they are principles of Christian life, the sacraments ought mainly to be considered as acts.[4] Doing so makes it possible to see how the human acts involved in the sacraments organize all the rest of one's Christian life. This is the approach emphasized here, with the notion of the sacraments as signs having a subordinate role.

3. **Insofar as they involve human acts, the sacraments are cooperative actions in which God the Spirit, Jesus the Lord in glory, the Church by her ordained minister, and the recipient (unless the recipient cannot act) join to accomplish the justification and sanctification of human persons, by extending to them the redemption (from the consequences of sin) and glorification already accomplished by God in Jesus with his human cooperation.**

4. The sacraments permit us to become conscious participants not only in the benefits of Jesus' human redemptive act but in the act itself. They do this by joining several human acts—the redemptive human act of Jesus, the human act of the ordained minister on behalf of the Church, and (normally) the human act of the recipient—to the divine act of restoration and divinization. This divine act first restored Jesus from the dead and glorified his humanity. It is still having its effect in the world, where Jesus' Spirit is gradually renewing the face of the earth (see *S.t.,* 3, q. 61, a. 1, ad 3; q. 62, a. 5; q. 63, aa. 1, 6; q. 64, a. 1, ad 2; q. 64, a. 6, ad 2; q. 64, a. 8).

5. **The recipient's sacramental act is a moral principle because it organizes the rest of his or her life.** A Christian life begins with baptism and is structured by the other sacraments in several distinct but compatible ways, which will be explained when each sacrament is considered.

Of course, the cooperation involved in the sacraments is not that of coequal partners. It is not like the cooperation of a husband and wife in generating and raising children, but more like the cooperation of mother and infant in nursing. The divine act and the human acts which together constitute a unified sacramental act are infinitely different, and even the various human acts which are done by our Lord in glory, the minister for the Church, and the recipient are diverse in kind. God allows us to cooperate in his work, but our role is a subordinate one, ours by his merciful condescension.

The situation is like that of a mother who makes bread for her family and has her small children help. One holds his finger carefully at a place where the mother puts it on the recipe. She could as well or even better use a ruler to keep her place. Another holds the pans to receive the formed loaves. The mother could as well set the pans on the counter. A third watches the clock until the big hand reaches a certain designated point. The mother could more confidently use the automatic timer on the range. Yet the children do help. As a result, they can proudly present their father with a sample of bread when he comes home from work: "We helped mama make it!"

By enlisting the children's help, the mother actually made more work for herself. She could more easily have baked the bread in the evening after they were all in bed. But she is interested not so much in making bread as in making men and women. Similarly, in redeeming us from sin and perfecting us to glory, God is interested in raising mature members of his family. Our cooperation is not a necessary means to attaining his objective. Rather, it is part of his objective. By the gift of this cooperation God causes us freely to determine ourselves as the humanly fulfilled divine children he wishes us to be forever.[5]

Question C: What is the relationship between the sacraments as acts and as signs?

1. Once the sacraments' essential character as cooperative acts is clear, one can proceed to clarify several other aspects of their complex reality. For instance, as outward performances, they have a symbolic dimension which will no longer be necessary in heaven (so that, like faith and hope, they will be surpassed).

The sacraments also involve something permanent, insofar as they restore and perfect fallen human persons. Thus, baptism, confirmation, and orders give a permanent character. Penance gives reconciliation, which in principle is meant to last. Anointing prepares the body for resurrection. The Eucharist and matrimony establish loving interpersonal communion which is a beginning of heavenly fulfillment. In all the sacraments, furthermore, we are united with Jesus, drawn from our present unstable situation into his present and lasting glory.

2. Defining the sacraments as signs emphasizes their transient, symbolic dimension, which belongs to them as outward performances. This dimension is generally and correctly said to be important because we humans are bodily and learn by experience, and because the tremendous realities involved in the sacraments would be too great for us without the mediation of symbolism. Therefore, it is said, God kindly provides a simple, sensible sign suited to our condition (see *S.t.*, 3, q. 60, a. 4; q. 61, a. 1).

3. Though perfectly true, this ought not to be misunderstood. As Trent teaches, the sacraments are more than signs of faith; they really contain and confer the grace which they signify. Like the glorified Jesus, whose acts they are, the sacraments are complex realities, and their bodily dimension is not what is most important about them. At the same time, this bodily, symbolic dimension is not a mere means, something extrinsic to their sacred reality. Rather, like the body of Jesus in glory, it is an essential part of the sacraments' redeeming and sanctifying power.

4. One might imagine the work of sanctification as occurring through the soul's purely spiritual and interior communion with God. This in fact is how Protestants faithful to the theology of the Reformation do think of it. The difficulty is that this excludes any social act. Human beings are in communion only by way of bodily cooperation. Unless they do something together as an outward performance—at least something symbolic like uttering words and making gestures—they cannot do anything together which is a human act. Eliminating the sacraments thus eliminates the possibility of effective cooperation between our Lord in glory and human beings joined with one another (see *S.t.*, 3, q. 62, aa. 1–2).[6]

5. **The outward, symbolic dimension of the sacraments is best understood in light of their essential reality as cooperative divine-human acts. Human beings wish to contribute to their own salvation; they wish to do something to be saved. In the sacraments, God makes this possible.** Having effected redemption in principle by the Incarnation of the Word, where creation, represented by the humanity of Jesus, cooperates in its own re-creation, God carries redemption through to completion in the sacraments. In these divine-human acts created and fallen persons collaborate with Jesus in their own reconciliation and sanctification.

6. Considering the sacraments as signs, one might paraphrase and expand a familiar definition as follows: A sacrament is a meaningful performance instituted by Jesus to communicate the fruits of his redemptive act to human persons, so that they will receive these fruits as gifts in whose receiving (for themselves) and giving (to others) they can consciously and freely cooperate.

Another analogy might be helpful, one more complex than that of the mother making bread, since both the divine-human cooperation and the symbolic aspect of the sacrament are represented.

Imagine an operating room. A man is undergoing surgery; his blood is being circulated by a heart-lung machine concealed behind a one-way mirror; and he is conscious, since the anesthetic blocks pain only. He has been told to blink his eyes when he begins to feel weakened. When he does so, an attendant who is facing the mirror grimaces. The person in control of the heart-lung machine which is sustaining life then adds a nutrient to the bloodstream. To do this, however, the nutrient must be provided. Some source outside the hospital is responsible for this.

The patient is like the recipient of the sacrament. The attendant who is authorized to signal for more nutrient is like the minister of the sacrament. The person operating the heart-lung machine is like Jesus, who now lives beyond the veil, but still acts to sustain our lives (see Heb 6.19–20). Finally, the source of the nutrient is God. Of course, he also is the source of all the other elements.

Question D: What is God's part in sacramental cooperation?

1. **God's work in the sacraments is not simply one role among many. Everything else, even the other actors, is a divine gift which is part of God's work.** He gives all these gifts, fills them with life and goodness, blesses them, and makes them holy.

2. "It is God who establishes us with you in Christ, and has commissioned us; he has put his seal upon us and given us his Spirit in our hearts as an guarantee" (2 Cor 1.21–22). We are baptized in the name of the Trinity (see Mt 28.19), not only into their family but by their power, for the divine authority given to the risen Jesus underwrites this act (see Mt 28.18; *S.t.*, 3, q. 64, aa. 1, 3).

The Father begins the work of salvation in us and brings it to perfection (see Phil 1.6). If we do anything, it is only because he does it in us (see Phil 2.13). He makes everything work together for the good of those who love him (see Rom 8.28), for he means to bring us to the perfection of Jesus himself in glory (see Rom 8.29). Thus prayer for the grace required to gain perfection appropriately is addressed to the Father (see Rom 15.5).

Jesus our Lord, in communion with the Father, makes charity abound (see 1 Thes 3.12). He is the head and source of the Church (see Col 1.18). Thus he is the author of life for us (see Acts 3.15). Moreover, our progress is toward his perfection; we grow up toward him, to conformity to his pattern (see Eph 4.15; 5.2). Insofar as he is God, our Lord himself brings about our transformation into his own likeness (see 2 Cor 3.18). Jesus in glory is in the process of filling the universe (see Eph 1.22–23). He holds in himself the total capacity for all the good which is to be, and he associates us with himself in realizing fulfillment (see Eph 2.6; Col 3.1).

During his earthly life, Jesus was always filled with the Spirit (see Lk 4.1; 10.21). He promised that the Father would give the Spirit to those who ask (see Lk 11.13). However, only through his resurrection is Jesus made Lord in power and enabled to impart the Spirit (see Jn 7.39; Rom 1.4).[7] He promises to send the Spirit, but must leave this life and be transformed by resurrection to do so (see Jn 16.7). When he appears as glorified Lord, he comes as one sent by the Father who is able to send human persons as he himself is sent, with the power of the Spirit: "'As the Father has sent me, even so I send you.' And when he had said this, he breathed on them, and said to them, 'Receive the Holy Spirit'" (Jn 20.21–22), and he handed over the authority to extend redemption to all humankind (see Mt 28.18–20).

3. The Church teaches that the sacraments contain and give grace (see DS 1310/695, 1451/741, 1606/849). (The Church does not precisely assert in her solemn teaching that the sacraments cause grace, though this is often said by theologians and in popular writing.[8]) They contain and confer grace because the divine action which justifies and sanctifies is present in them.

4. This divine action is not present in the sacraments as if the finite performance comprehended God's infinite love, but because God makes his love available to us in this way, as he makes it available in the words of Scripture and in the humanity of the Word, which the sacraments make present and effective for us. **As a human act, even as the human act of Jesus, a sacrament is effective only insofar as it is a mode of cooperation with God's action, which alone re-creates and divinizes.**

5. Thus sacraments are not merely human acts. In them the Spirit is united with the water and the blood of Jesus' redemptive death (see 1 Jn 5.6–9). The divine power of the Spirit, available to our glorified Lord to complete his work (see Jn 7.38–39; 15.26; 16.7; 20.22), does bring it to completion in us.

6. Finally, God's role in the sacraments not only makes them effective but reveals this effectiveness. They are revelatory signs, made up of words and deeds, which, though ours, are also Jesus' (cf. DV 2; SC 5–7). God not only reconciles and divinizes us, but makes it plain to us what he is doing by giving us evidence of it (see 1 Jn 5.6–11). For example, by providing the sacrament of penance, God manifests his forgiveness of a Christian's sins through the Church's words of absolution which the contrite sinner hears as divine pardon. Thus faith is nourished. God's revelation is effective. He communicates not mere information but his own truth and love: his very self.

The role of divine action in the sacraments explains why they both work from the very performance of the rite (*ex opere operato*) and work only by virtue of a divine response to the faith and prayer of the Church. The sacraments are effective whenever they are properly carried out and worthily received, because the covenant established in Jesus is real and effective—the gift of the Spirit to the Church is true and irrevocable. This is no more magical than is obtaining gold in exchange for a check, when someone keeps the account full of funds to draw upon. God has sworn and he will not renege.

At the same time, the Church never takes the Spirit for granted. His work is free and personal cooperation. Hence, in various invocations, such as the epiclesis which asks the Spirit to effect the consecration of the Eucharist, the Church (like a loving wife) gently asks the Spirit of her Lord to do what he has promised and is always ready to do.[9]

Question E: What is the human action of our glorified Lord in the sacraments?

1. Insofar as he is Incarnate—that is, insofar as he is man—our Lord's redemptive act is a perfect sacrifice (22-G). As a human act, Jesus' sacrificial act lasts, since human acts which determine a person endure (2-E). This point, already explained (23-B) as it pertains to the sacrifice of the Mass, is taught in Scripture (see Heb 7.22–28; 10.10–12). The death of Jesus is past, but the human commitment which led to his death remains forever.[10]

2. Since Jesus' human, redemptive act still exists, all the Masses done in remembrance—acts commanded by him at the Last Supper in the very act which carried out the choice that led to his death—are really performances of this same, enduring redemptive act (23-B).

3. Here, to "remember" does not mean returning to the past in memory, but keeping fully in view for its present relevance what is essentially permanent, though it began at a certain point in the past. In this context, remembering signifies much the same thing as when one is said to remember a friend by sending a gift to keep the relationship alive. This is not simply recalling old times but giving fresh expression to an enduring bond.[11]

4. Jesus' human activity ought not to be regarded merely as the instrument of the divine person. His human acts really are human acts of the Word. It is not that human acts are used by the divine nature, but that the divine person acts humanly according to his assumed nature and capacities (21-F, but cf. *S.t.*, 3, q. 64, a. 3).

Insofar as our Lord is the Incarnate Word, his human life, death, and resurrection all have the character of a revelatory sign. In him is revealed the mystery, the hidden plan of God (see Eph 1.9). During the time of his earthly life, he revealed the Father (see Jn 1.18). Now the mystery, which is Jesus himself in glory, is itself communicated to us (see Col 1.25–27), so that we can be formed into the great mystery, the whole Lord Jesus.[12]

This forming is accomplished in the Spirit by the action of Jesus in the sacraments. Whenever the sacraments are administered, they are always Jesus' human acts (see SC 6–7; *S.c.g.*, 4, 76). The Church also acts in the sacraments, but before she can act must first exist, and she exists only insofar as Jesus instituted the sacraments and formed the Church by them (see DS 1601/844; LG 7).

The washing of the feet of the apostles at the Last Supper (see Jn 13.3–10), the institution of the Eucharist and authorization of the apostles to do it in memory of him (that is, to keep his act always present—cf. 1 Cor 11.23–29), the conferral of the Spirit and power to forgive sins (see Jn 20.21–23), the authorization to proclaim the gospel and baptize into a gathering of the people of the new covenant (see Mt 28.18–20), and the sending of the Spirit at Pentecost (see Acts 1.4–5; 2.1–4) were acts in which Jesus instituted the sacraments by making the signs which brought the Church into being (see LG 9; SC 6).

5. The divine person, our Lord Jesus, continues to act not only divinely but humanly in the sacraments. They make the human actions of the Word visibly present. As every well-instructed Catholic child knows, the species of the Eucharist conceal our Lord's bodily presence; he is invisibly present there, with a presence which includes his whole being and action. Less often realized, however, is that Jesus is visibly present in the sacramental acts which are really his, although they are carried out by human persons acting as his agents (see *S.t.*, 3, q. 64, a. 4; q. 78, a. 1).

6. Thus, one's meeting with Jesus in the sacraments is not a symbolic contact or a purely spiritual encounter. One really meets the Incarnate Word (and thereby also meets the Father and the Spirit). This is real, human communion with God.[13]

Insofar as the sacraments are cooperative acts in which we are united with Jesus, we come to share morally by our commitments and performances in his redemptive act. However, there is another communion—that which derives from the bodily dimension of the human meeting, both in its substantial (hidden eucharistic) aspect and in its dynamic (sacramental performance-contact) aspect.[14] This bodily dimension of human meeting with God in Jesus gives the sacraments their unique importance, for without this we might follow Jesus by imitating him, but our Christian lives would not be the carrying out of his very own life. Because of the sacraments, we can do the very same works Jesus does and constantly enlarge upon them (see Jn 14.9–21).

It is primarily insofar as the sacraments are performances of the redeeming act of our glorified Lord Jesus that they effect what they signify, because they do this by making his act present and effective. Thus the sacraments both signify grace and communicate the grace which is God's response to the sacrifice of Jesus. Because the human, redemptive act of Jesus which exists now and is communicated in the sacraments began during his earthly life and will be wholly fulfilled only in his second coming, the sacramental sign also refers back to the passion and death of Jesus and ahead to the end of ages (see *S.t.*, 3, q. 60, a. 3; q. 62, a. 5).

Question F: What is the Church's role in the sacraments?

1. The sacraments are the supreme part of the Church's activity. **In them she offers her worship in union with our Lord to the Father. By them she confers upon her children his redemptive love, effective through the same Lord Jesus in the power of the Holy Spirit** (see SC 7, 9, 10, and 59). **Moreover, by providing authorized ministers to carry out the performance of the sacramental acts, the Church acts visibly as Jesus' agent** (see *S.t.*, 3, q. 64, a. 5; sup., q. 34, a. 1; *S.c.g.*, 4, 74).

2. In addition, three of the sacraments, baptism, confirmation, and orders, are sacraments of the Church not only because they are her acts, but because they inaugurate the recipients into her offices. Thus these sacraments make certain actions of her members official actions of the Church, actions themselves involved in sacramental cooperation.

3. The sacramental character conferred by these sacraments is precisely the recipient's permanent role in the Church, a role which ought always to be fulfilled worthily even if it is not (see DS 1609/852). While the precise differences among the three roles will be dealt with in considering these three constitutional

sacraments, some preliminary indications are in order here (see *S.t.*, 3, q. 63, aa. 1–3, 6; q. 64, a. 6).[15]

4. Baptism, confirmation, and holy orders all confer an identification with Jesus and a specific role in the Church by which one shares in his priesthood. The baptized share receptively, while the confirmed share in the profession of faith and apostolic work of Jesus. As for the recipients of orders, their role is further specified in that they are designated for specific ecclesial service to the scriptural word and the sacraments (see AA 6; *S.t.*, 3, q. 63, a. 6; q. 72, a. 5).

5. Through the bishops, and thus through the priests who share in the episcopal office, Jesus himself preaches and administers the sacraments (see LG 21; PO 2). "By sacred ordination and by the mission they receive from their bishops, priests are promoted to the service of Christ, the Teacher, the Priest, and the King. They share in his ministry of unceasingly building up the Church on earth into the People of God, the Body of Christ, and the Temple of the Holy Spirit" (PO 1). Acting not simply in Jesus' name but in the very person of Jesus, the ordained priest offers sacrifice and forgives sins by Jesus' redemptive act (see PO 2; LG 10; *S.t.*, 3, q. 78, a. 1; q. 82, a. 1).[16]

Many people think of the Church and her sacramental actions as an obstruction between Christians and God. The Church as institution, as visible society and agent through her ministers of redemption, seems to them a medium with which they should like to dispense. This is the view of Protestants faithful to the spirit of the Reformation.

However, this view is mistaken. Jesus is God, and the Church is no third something between Christians and Jesus. Rather, she is the very communion of Christians with Jesus in his Spirit, and so the Lord Jesus remains present in the Church (see LG 14).[17] The Church is the very body of Jesus, and the sacraments—far from being objects which obstruct the Christian's union with Jesus—are the means by which the Christian is incorporated into him. This great theme of Pius XII's encyclical on the Mystical Body is reaffirmed by Vatican II (see LG 7).

True enough, the present situation in which the Christian in the body is apart from the Lord is not wholly satisfactory (see 2 Cor 5.1–9). However, to wish to dispense with the sacraments before we attain to heavenly fulfillment is to wish to abort ourselves, for the sacraments are our present vital link with Jesus, just as the umbilical cord is the unborn child's vital link with its mother (and not an obstacle to its immediate relationship with her). Again (to change the analogy), the sacraments are the organs by which the Church, enlivened by the Holy Spirit, materially builds herself up as the body of Jesus (see Eph 4.16; also LG 8 and 11). The apostolicity of the Church establishes her structure as a visible society of human persons. It is Jesus himself who decided "that some should be apostles, some prophets, some evangelists, some pastors and teachers, for the equipment of the saints, for the work of ministry, for building up the body of Christ" (Eph 4.11–12). Jesus enjoined that his appointed ministers should be like him in serving (see Jn 13.12–16).

Defects in the minister of the sacraments create the impression that the Church herself is an obstacle between the Christian and Jesus. But the only obstacle is the deficient minister, whose failings obstruct the very communion his work ought to serve. Still, as Trent teaches, the scandal need not be fatal. Just as one can hear the true gospel from those who proclaim it with bad motives (see Phil 1.15–18), one can receive the sacraments fruitfully from sinful ministers (see DS 1612/855). It is enough that the minister of the sacrament be validly ordained and authorized to act for the Church, and that he intend to do what the Church does (see DS 1611/854).

Question G: What is the recipient's role in sacramental cooperation?

1. As was pointed out above, the Word became flesh so that creation might be enriched, for its own excellence and God's glory, by having a share in its own renewal and transformation into fulfillment in the Lord Jesus.

2. Similarly, through the sacraments Jesus now extends his redemptive act, crowned with divine glory and power, so that we created persons might be enriched for our own excellence and God's greater glory by having a personal share in our own justification and sanctification and those of our fellows.

3. From this point of view, the purpose of the sacramental economy is the action of the recipient (as well as the action of the minister as a personal act). This action is impossible without the sacrament. Sacraments are designed precisely to allow God's children to help him accomplish what only he can do.

4. By receiving the sacraments, we freely accept and grow in divine life; we are formed by a direct relationship with God who presents himself in the form of palpable actions; and we worship God fittingly in union with the redemptive act of our Lord in glory (see SC 59).[IX] In this way we are allowed to share in the priesthood of Jesus (see LG 10). **By sacramental cooperation, we participate in a divine act suited to us as children of God, by means of a human act suited to our condition as children who are not yet what we shall be.**

5. The actions of the recipients of the sacraments also have another aspect. The sacraments nourish Christian life (see SC 59). This life as a whole includes not only the acts by which the sacraments are received but acts by which all virtues are exercised (see LG 11). Thus, a Christian's acts of sacramental participation in Jesus' redemptive act comprise the medium which enables him or her to make the whole of life into a living sacrifice (see Rom 12.1).

6. **Precisely how the sacraments organize Christian life will be the subject of the remainder of this chapter (with respect to baptism) and of the next three chapters. However, the general and fundamental point is just this: The acts by which we receive the sacraments enable us to bring everything else in ourselves into perfect integration with charity.** Thus, we can live totally oriented toward God through Jesus as mediator, consciously and freely cooperating with Jesus as our firstborn elder brother, and abiding in Jesus as the unifying Lord whose fulfillment is the object of God's plan.

The obviously subordinate role of our actions in receiving the sacraments is one respect in which these actions are especially suited to us. Even though we are allowed to help in the work of God, the structure of the sacraments makes it clear to us that our contribution is insignificant in comparison with his, for we only bring about the symbol of what the Spirit does in the sacrament. If we did not have sacraments, we might well imagine that our role— for example, in believing—is more important than it is. In fact, the manner in which we cooperate with God in his salvific work clearly shows that our role is more like that of the children who help mother than that of the mother who, together with the father, raises the children.

Question H: Why is baptism the basic sacrament?

1. The Catholic Church teaches that baptism or the desire for baptism is essential for salvation (see DS 1524/796, 1618/861).[19] This is the same as the demand that one accept the Lord Jesus (by whom alone we are saved), that one have faith (which is the acceptance of Jesus), or that one enter the Church (which is the communion of those who accept Jesus and the community where those who seek Jesus find him).[20]

This teaching has been repeated very clearly by Vatican II. The missionary activity of the Church

> ... finds its reason in the will of God, "who wishes all men to be saved and to come to the knowledge of the truth. For there is one God, and one mediator between God and men, himself man, Christ Jesus, who gave himself a ransom for all" (1 Tm 2.4–6), "neither is there salvation in any other" (Acts 4.12).
>
> Therefore, all must be converted to him as he is made known by the Church's preaching. All must be incorporated into him by baptism, and into the Church which is his body. For Christ himself "in explicit terms... affirmed the necessity of faith and baptism (cf. Mk 16.16; Jn 3.5) and thereby affirmed also the necessity of the Church, for through baptism as through a door men enter the Church. Whosoever, therefore, knowing that the Catholic Church was made necessary by God through Jesus Christ, would refuse to enter her or to remain in her could not be saved." (AG 7; cf. LG 14)

2. **Baptism is personal union with Jesus** (see *S.t.*, 3, q. 68, a. 1; q. 69, a. 5). **Everything else follows from this.** Our Lord in glory is the new covenant, the new and everlasting bond uniting God and humankind. Sin is separation from God; baptism overcomes sin, for one who is united with Jesus cannot be separated from God. Baptism means receiving the Spirit and the charity he pours forth in one's heart; one shares in the Spirit by being united with Jesus whose Spirit he is (see DS 1530/800). Those who accept Jesus abide in him and the Father, who send the Spirit and abide in all who are united with Jesus. As a result, human persons are similarly bonded with one another (see Jn 17.20–23). Thus the Church is formed, for those who are members of the Lord Jesus and children of God are members of one another and brothers and sisters in the same divine family (see 1 Cor 12.12–13, 23–27).

3. Because one receives faith in baptism and by it is united with Jesus (see Gal 3.26–28), baptism makes one a child of God. Adam's children are reborn in Jesus (see DS 1523/795). Buried with him (see Col 2.12), they are reborn from the water of baptism, not as from the waters of a natural womb—to a merely human life—but as new people and part of a new creation (see 2 Cor 5.17; Eph 2.15–16). Baptism truly is a new birth (see Jn 3.5; Ti 3.5; 1 Pt 1.3); therefore, it gives one a new heart—a new inner self, a new personal being (see Is 32.15; Jer 31.33; Ez 36.26; Jl 3.1–2).

4. The new person one becomes by baptism is not simply a new and better self. One is clothed with Jesus (see Gal 3.27), one becomes the new man who is Jesus (see Eph 2.15; 4.24). He unifies all creation, first of all by forming his Church

(see Col 3.10–11; also LG 7 and 8). Thus the baptized form in him one body, the Church (see 1 Cor 12.27).

As Vatican II teaches, through baptism as through a door, men and women, as well as infants, enter the Church (see LG 14), for the Church is the communion of those who make up God's family by being united with Jesus (see LG 8–11). "Thus, by baptism, men are united to the paschal mystery of Christ: they die with him, are buried with him, and rise with him (cf. Rom 6.4; Eph 2.6; Col 3.1; 2 Tm 2.11); they receive the spirit of adoption as sons 'by virtue of which we cry: Abba, Father' (Rom 8.15), and thus become those true adorers whom the Father seeks (cf. Jn 4.23)" (SC 6; translation amended). Jesus is the mediator. By communion with him, one comes to the goal of baptism: adoption as a child of God.

5. **Baptism into the Lord Jesus is baptism into his reality, a sharing in his Spirit** (see Jn 3.1–21). This central truth about the Christian has already been treated at length. Those who form Jesus in his Church are God's adopted children, really sharing Jesus' status by the gift of his Spirit, who pours forth God's love into their hearts (see Rom 5.5; 8.14–17). The present gift of the Spirit is, as it were, a down payment (see Eph 1.13–14) on the full experience of divine family life which they shall enjoy as the fruit of Jesus' death (see 1 Jn 3.1–2). Inasmuch as the Spirit is the soul of the Church (see LG 7), baptism makes them one not only in body but in soul.

6. By baptism we are so closely united with our Lord that we already share in his resurrection and glory, although in an invisible way (see Eph 2.5–6; Col 2.12; 3.1–4).[21] Our dignity as divine children, to whom immortality and heavenly fulfillment are due, is not only future but present, waiting only to be revealed (see Rom 8.18–19). At the same time, resurrection is not yet complete in us (see 1 Cor 15.20–23). For the present, our resurrection is evidenced in this: We should and can live the life of good deeds which God has prepared for us (see Eph 2.6–10).

7. The special character received in baptism is something like citizenship in a political society. As members of the Church, the baptized are entitled not only to receive the Eucharist and everything else the Church has to give, but to share in common actions—that is, to participate in offering the Eucharist and in other acts which the Church does in common.

8. Jesus has given those who accept him the power to become children of God (see Jn 1.12–13). This power, as St. John Chrysostom suggests, is like that of an agent. It enables one who is being baptized both to become and to behave as a child of God.[22] If this insight is correct, an adult in receiving baptism both receives and exercises the baptismal character, both becomes a member of the Church and acts in that role, both receives the gift of living faith and commits himself or herself to Jesus with this faith.

9. As life is in a sense the most important human good, since only those who live can seek and enjoy other goods, baptism is in a sense the most important sacrament. **Christian life as a whole is present here in embryonic form. For baptism unites one with Jesus in his Church and confers the grace of divine adoption.** The other sacraments add nothing extrinsic, but rather, in their distinct ways, develop to full maturity what is present in embryo in baptism (see *S.t.*, 3,

q. 65). This explains why those whose lives are cut short (for example, an infant who dies soon after baptism) and those who blamelessly fail to appreciate the fullness of Catholic truth (for example, Protestants of good will) can enjoy a true sacramental life by baptism alone.

10. The embryonic richness of baptism is unfolded in the fullness of mature Christian life: into the fullness of the gift of the Spirit in confirmation, the fullness of communion with Jesus in the Eucharist, the fullness of overcoming sin and its effects in penance and anointing, the fullness of sharing in Jesus' priesthood in orders, and the fullness of the interpersonal communion of the members of Jesus' Body in matrimony. This no more detracts from the beauty and richness of the total gift received in baptism than appreciation of the physiology of an adult organism reduces one's sense of wonder at the perfection of the embryo, where all that will be is already present in its beginnings.

By baptism, sinful human persons are united with our Lord in glory, and so their sin (separation from God) is overcome (see *S.t.*, 3, q. 69, aa. 1–2). In Jesus, God's natural Son, they become adopted children of God, called to a life in this world and in eternity appropriate to their new being as members of the divine family.

In two passages in Colossians one finds the entire theology of baptism (see Col 2.9–14; 3.1–6). A movement of turning toward Jesus, which is aroused by the preaching of the gospel and the grace of the Spirit, brings one to baptism. There one receives living faith, which is a sharing in the communion with God. This communion is the new covenant, established in Jesus by his redemptive act and God's redeeming response to it. This covenant with God wipes away sin and makes one share in the fullness of deity present bodily in Jesus. In consequence, one has died to the former sinful life of fallen humankind; one has a new life to lead.

Certain aspects of this complex whole—the preaching of the gospel, conversion to Jesus, faith, and the forgiveness of sin—deserve further discussion.

From the point of view of the Church, the liturgy is not the whole of her work, but is its heart. To prepare people for participation in the Eucharist, the Church first must bring them in baptism to living faith. To do this, she must first preach the gospel of repentance and faith (see SC 9). As St. Paul teaches, faith in the heart justifies, but faith comes into one's heart only by the acceptance of the gospel, and one cannot accept it unless it is preached by those commissioned to do so (see Rom 10.10–17).

Conversion essentially is a turning toward the dawn which arises in the darkness, a dawn which is liberating (see Lk 1.78–79). One need only accept this new light in order to receive the power to become a child of God—not a servant, but a friend and member of the divine family (see Jn 1.12–13; 15.15). Jesus did not come to condemn the world, but to judge it mercifully, if only the world will accept him in faith (see Jn 3.17; 5.22–30; 12.47). Hence, the announcement of the kingdom and the call for repentance must be understood as a summons to mercy: "Awake, O sleeper, and arise from the dead, and Christ shall give you light" (Eph 5.14).

According to Trent's definitive teaching, a person capable of acting who hears the gospel and does not resist the grace of the Spirit is turned and turns toward God, by preliminary human dispositions of imperfect faith, hope, and love which prepare for baptism (see DS 1526–27/798, 1557–59/817–19). Grace is primary, but one can and must cooperate with it (see DS 1525/797, 1554/814). Thus it is correct to regard conversion both as the sinner's act: "Return to me, says the Lord of hosts, and I will return to you, says the

Lord of hosts" (Zec 1.3), and as God's act: "Restore us to yourself, O Lord, that we may be restored!" (Lam 5.21).

The call to conversion which the Church proclaims is a call to penance and the remission of sins (see Mt 28.16–20; Lk 24.47), and for this very reason it is an invitation to baptism. In baptism, the preliminary dispositions of conversion are accepted by the Church as the token of one's willingness to be united with Jesus. The person baptized receives perfect, living faith and hope, together with the love of God which is poured forth by the Holy Spirit (see DS 1528–30/799–800). Faith and baptism are closely bound together (see Mk 16.16; Acts 8.11–12; Gal 3.26–27; Eph 4.5; Heb 10.22–23). Acceptance of the gospel brings one to baptism; baptism itself makes one's acceptance of the gospel into a personal acceptance of the truth and love of God, a real beginning of eternal communion in the new covenant of Jesus.[23]

Therefore, it is in baptism itself that sin is taken away (see Col 2.13–14). Faith brings the remission of sin only insofar as it brings one to new life in Jesus. Therefore, baptism is the door of the spiritual life. By it one is initiated into communion with the death of Jesus, and thereby original sin and all actual sins are taken away, together with all the punishment due to sin (see DS 1314/696). Moreover, God's forgiveness of sin in baptism is most gracious and magnanimous, for the individual who is baptized need not outwardly confess his or her sins and need accept no personal responsibility to do penance for them (see *S.t.*, 3, q. 68, aa. 5–6). The heavenly Father welcomes his prodigal children with joy (see Lk 15.11–24).

Question I: What are the implications of baptism for Christian moral life?

1. Jesus taught that the faith which saves is not just intellectual assent and an initial willingness to do the Father's will, but a rocklike foundation (see Mt 7.24–27; Lk 6.47–49). The Christian's model is not the son who says "yes" to the father and then fails to do what is asked, but the one who executes the father's will even after saying "no" (see Mt 21.28–31). Jesus demands a faith which involves commitment (see Mt 10.37–39; Mk 8.34; Lk 14.25–27). Faith has moral implications because it is the fundamental option by which one enters into the new covenant (23-A).

2. One is not justified and deified due to one's works; salvation is by grace through faith (see Rom 3.21–22; DS 1532/801). "For by grace you have been saved through faith; and this is not your own doing, it is the gift of God—not because of works, lest any man should boast" (Eph 2.8–9).

3. No sooner is the gift given, however, than one must begin to live the new life one has received, completing the acceptance of the gift by acknowledging its moral implications (see Eph 2.10). To be sure, all that matters is that one is created anew (see Gal 6.15) by the gift of divine life received in baptism. **But precisely this re-creation includes a call to live as befits a member of God's family** (see Gal 5.13–6.10). Being baptized, we are trained by grace to live according to the Spirit (see Ti 2.11–3.8). Salvation is the work of grace, but this divine work includes as an essential part our own work: the living of a Christian life (see Rom 6.3–11).

4. Salvation is an indivisible whole. One accepts its fullness or one has none of

it. That is why Jesus teaches that not all those who receive the word are true disciples who will be saved, but only those who abide in it (see Mt 13.1–9; Mk 4.1–9; Lk 8.4–8; Jn 8.31–32). More even than for her unique motherhood by which she bore the Word of God, Mary, together with all like her, deserves praise for having heard God's word and kept it (see Lk 11.27–28). Keeping God's word means living by it. No one who acts in an unholy way is a child of God (see 1 Jn 3.4–10).

Because baptism does have moral implications—the requirement that one live a morally good life—the Church asks those about to be baptized whether they reject Satan, whether they reject sin so as to live as God's children, and whether they reject the glamor of evil and refuse to be mastered by sin.[24] Or again, the Church asks simply and bluntly: "Have you listened to Christ's word and made up your mind to keep his commandments?"[25]

In the case of the baptism of children, the Church explains to the parents what they are doing and asks for a commitment: "You have asked to have your children baptized. In doing so you are accepting the responsibility of training them in the practice of the faith. It will be your duty to bring them up to keep God's commandments as Christ taught us, by loving God and our neighbor. Do you clearly understand what you are undertaking?"[26] Trent definitively teaches that the person who receives the grace of baptism can and must keep the commandments, that the commandments to be kept include the Ten Commandments, and that Jesus is not only a trustworthy redeemer but also a lawgiver who must be obeyed (see DS 1536–39/804, 1568–71/828–31).

5. Even the baptism of John the Baptist, which was only with water and was directed only at eliciting repentance for sin, required practical fruits appropriate to one who turns away from evil (see Mt 3.8; Lk 3.8–14). Jesus, however, baptizes not merely with water but with fire and the Holy Spirit—in other words, by his redemptive act and by the adoption as divine children which is effected for all those who enter into it (see Mt 3.11; Mk 1.8; Lk 3.16; Jn 1.12–13; 3.5–8; Acts 1.5; 11.16). How much more, then, does his baptism require the keeping of all his commandments (see Mt 28.20; see *S.t.*, 3, q. 69, aa. 4–5)!

6. **Baptism with the Spirit not only requires us to fulfill the commandments but makes it possible for us to do so.** Freed from the law, Christians are able to live according to the Spirit. There is no longer any excuse for sin (see Rom 8.9–13).

In a beautiful passage concerning his own baptism, St. Cyprian of Carthage indicates how the new life is experienced. Before baptism, he had been wedded to sin as if it were part of himself: "But afterwards, when the stain of my past life had been washed away by means of the water of re-birth, a light from above poured itself upon my chastened and now pure heart; afterwards through the Spirit which is breathed from heaven, a second birth made of me a new man. And then in a marvelous manner, doubts immediately clarified themselves, the closed opened, the darkness became illuminated, what before had seemed difficult offered a way of accomplishment, and what had been thought impossible was able to be done. Thus it had to be acknowledged that what was of the earth and was born of the flesh and had lived submissive to sins, had now begun to be of God, inasmuch as the Holy Spirit was animating it" (FEF 548). Although the person baptized in infancy can be spared the reign of sin, the Christian child as well as the adult convert should enjoy the same experience of illumination and the power to attain goodness.

Enriched as much as possible with sacred Scripture, even elementary catechesis should aim at cultivating a prayerful acceptance of the Word of God. Among the truths of faith, three especially need to be inculcated and accepted as real: first, that heaven exists although it is invisible; second, that God has generously forgiven all our sins, and wills and enables us to be perfect; third, that one lives as a Christian not in isolation but in the midst of the Church, in real community with Jesus, Mary, and the saints from the beginning of salvation history until its end. A lively sense of these truths will protect one through one's whole Christian life against worldliness, pelagianism, moral indifference, and historicist relativism. These are the most dangerous current threats to faith.

Summary

The sacraments extend Jesus' redemptive act into the present, enabling us to cooperate in that act and also making it effective for our justification and sanctification. As extensions of Jesus' act, the sacraments not only reveal and communicate the divine life which they signify but also respond to God's redeeming love with human worship. Having planned from the beginning for us to be his co-workers in redemption, Jesus instituted the sacraments to make this possible in a way wholly suited to our needs and capacities.

Although correctly defined as signs of a sort, insofar as they are principles of Christian life sacraments ought mainly to be considered as acts. Indeed, they are cooperative actions, involving the Spirit, Jesus, the Church by her minister, and the recipient, joined to accomplish the salvation of human persons. They permit us to become participants not only in the benefits of Jesus' redemptive act but in the act itself. And they are moral principles because they organize a Christian life, which begins with baptism and is structured by the other sacraments.

While defining the sacraments as signs emphasizes their symbolic dimension, they are more than just signs of faith, for they contain and confer the grace they signify. All the same, their bodily, symbolic dimension is an essential part of their redeeming and sanctifying power. As created reality, represented by the humanity of Jesus, cooperates in its own redemption by the Incarnation, so the outward, symbolic dimension of the sacraments enables us to do something suited to our condition in order to collaborate with Jesus in our own reconciliation and perfection.

At the same time, everything else in the sacraments, even the other actors, is a divine gift which is part of God's work. As a human act, even as the human act of Jesus, a sacrament is effective only insofar as it is a mode of cooperation with God's action, which alone re-creates and divinizes. Furthermore, God's role in the sacraments not only makes them effective but reveals this effectiveness; in this sense they are revelatory signs.

The sacraments are also actions of Jesus. We have seen that, as a human act, Jesus' redemptive act still exists, since acts which determine a person last. Every Mass is really a performance of this same, enduring redemptive act. The divine person, the Lord Jesus, continues to act humanly in the sacraments, which make the actions of the Word himself visibly present. Thus, one's meeting with Jesus in the sacraments is not a symbolic or purely spiritual encounter, but a real meeting with the Incarnate Word, and so also with the Father and the Spirit.

The sacraments are actions of the Church as well—the supreme part of her activity, in which she offers worship to God and confers his love on us. Moreover, the sacraments of baptism, confirmation, and orders not only are acts of the Church but inaugurate the recipients into her offices, making certain of their actions official actions of the Church. Through them one shares, in distinct ways, in the priesthood of Jesus.

Finally, the sacraments are actions of the recipient, designed precisely to allow God's children to have a personal share in the renewal and sanctification he effects in them. The sacraments also nourish Christian life. The acts by which we receive the sacraments enable us to bring everything else in ourselves into perfect integration with charity.

Baptism is the basic sacrament. To receive or at least desire baptism is, as the Church teaches, essential for salvation. Baptism is personal union with Jesus, and from this all else follows: that it overcomes sin, that in being baptized one receives the Spirit, that through baptism the Church is formed. In receiving baptism, one does not simply become a new and better self—one becomes the new man who is Jesus, so closely united with the Lord that one already shares, though in an invisible way, in his resurrection and glory. It can be said of baptism that it is Christian life in embryonic form; the other sacraments add nothing extrinsic but in their several ways develop to maturity what is already present there.

One is not justified by one's works; salvation is by grace through faith. Nevertheless, having received the gift of divine life in baptism, one must begin to live according to the new life one has received—one must live a Christian life. Baptism not only requires this, however, but makes it possible. Freed from the law, Christians are able to live according to the Spirit. There is no longer any excuse for sin.

Appendix 1:   The symbolic aspect of the sacraments

As Vatican I teaches, God is a spiritual substance (see DS 3001/1782). This means that he is not bodily as we are and that his being is that of his personal reality. This truth often is misunderstood, for it is mistaken to mean that God is something like our own mind. God, however, is no more a mental than a bodily reality; he is beyond all such finite categories. Therefore, the bodily is no more alien to him than is the immaterial reality of thoughts and choices. The bodily resurrection and glorification of Jesus, his bodily presence in the Eucharist, and our own hoped-for bodily communion with him in heaven, which already mysteriously begins when we receive the Eucharist here on earth—all this argues that the bodily aspect of the sacraments is an intrinsic and indispensable part of the fulfillment God is accomplishing in Jesus.

Even so, although essential, the pure symbolism of the sacraments is secondary; it is determined to be precisely as it is only because of Jesus' choice to use some rather than other words and deeds as appropriate, expressive performances (see *S.t.*, 3, q. 64, a. 2).

The Eucharist being under two species symbolizes the separation of Jesus' body and blood in his passion and death, and allows us symbolically not only to eat his flesh but also to drink his blood. Yet the whole reality of Jesus in glory is present under both species. Similarly, the liturgical year provides a quasi-chronological experience of the complex reality of the redemptive act of Jesus and the re-creating response of God, although this reality is not essentially temporal, and the particular events we review each year are as particular events simply past. Other symbols could have been used. Yet symbols of some sort are necessary if we are to be able to cooperate with Jesus. The ones he in fact has provided serve us by giving us something to do to cooperate humanly with him; they serve him as appropriate tokens of the very same redemptive act (the basic human act which is shaped by his lasting commitments and choices) which he once carried out by all the performances of his public life culminating in his going to Jerusalem, eating the Passover with his friends, giving them his flesh and blood to eat and drink, and accepting the consequences of what he had done.

Once one understands clearly the essential yet secondary role of the symbolic dimension of the sacraments, one can see why the actual performance of the sacrament need not coincide temporally with the grace which flows from the cooperative act. One who is preparing for baptism perhaps already is in grace; similarly, one who comes with the right dispositions to sacramental confession. The sacraments of anointing and matrimony also perhaps have important effects upon those preparing to receive them worthily, by sanctifying preparation for death or engagement to be married.

Yet the actual reception of a sacrament remains vital, since in the performance one's cooperation really is carried through. By desiring the sacrament (even in an implicit way), by preparing for it (however remotely), one already is beginning the cooperation which culminates in the sacramental performance itself. If one is not somehow aiming toward this performance, then one is in no way humanly disposed to cooperate in the human redemptive work of Jesus, through which alone the remission of sin and deification are given us. For this reason, even those who have not heard the gospel are redeemed only by some sort of remote relationship to the sacraments. (Perhaps their sincere groping amounts to an implicit wish to receive them.)

Thus what appears to us at times an illogical sequence of events—for example, contrition and reconciliation, followed by an examination of conscience, sacramental confession, and finally absolution—is not really illogical, because it is not a sequence of events in a causal process but an assembling of the elements required to constitute the complex whole of the sacrament. A similar situation is narrated in Mark, when the woman with a hemorrhage first touches Jesus and is healed, then is noticed by him and nervously admits what she has done, and only finally is told: "Go in peace, and be healed of your disease" (Mk 5.34). He also tells her that her faith worked the cure, but the account makes it clear that healing power had gone out from Jesus (see Mk 5.30). Thus divine causality, the woman's faith, and the human act of Jesus combine in the cure.

Appendix 2:   The one Church
and those who do not hear the gospel

The Church's teaching on the necessity of baptism and membership in the Church raises the question of the status of those who blamelessly do not hear the gospel. The Church teaches that such persons can be saved, but not without somehow being led to faith (see AG 7). It seems that as the Church extends her effort to bring the gospel and baptism to those who have not yet had an opportunity to believe explicitly, such persons with God's grace can also stretch out their hearts gropingly to receive the word of God and consciously cling to Jesus (see LG 16).

The preceding consideration raises a question about the unity of the Church: In what sense are all people of good will, including those who have never heard the gospel, members of the Catholic Church? To answer this question, one must consider that the unity of the Church is complex, somewhat as the unity of the United States is.

The United States is many states which enjoy a certain independence relative to one another, but it also is one nation. People who are not citizens live in the United States; some have permanent status as residents and some do not. Some American citizens live abroad and perhaps never have lived in the United States. Some people think they are citizens but are not; others are citizens without knowing it. All this complexity does not mean that the United States is not really one nation, nor does it mean that everyone who somehow "belongs" to the United States enjoys all the privileges and immunities of American citizens residing in the United States and conscious of their status.

Since the unity of the Church is complex, the truth that there is no salvation apart from the Church is a subtle one (see DS 802/430, 1351/714). Trent teaches that one can be saved by baptism of desire (see DS 1524/796, 1604/847). In 1949 the Holy See teaches, and backs its teaching with an excommunication of those who obstinately reject it, that the saving desire can be merely implicit, but that it must be informed by perfect charity and have with it supernatural faith (see DS 3866–73). Vatican II teaches that God welcomes all who fear him and do what is right (see LG 9). To be saved one must be converted to the Lord Jesus, for there is no salvation except in him. Nevertheless, "God in ways known to himself can lead those inculpably ignorant of the gospel to that faith without which it is impossible to please him" (AG 7). No one can be saved outside the Church, but obviously some can be saved who are ignorant of the gospel and so who would not consider themselves Christians or be counted as such (see LG 16).

The universal salvific power of Jesus corresponds to the all-embracing salvific will of the Father, who "desires all men to be saved and to come to the knowledge of the truth. For there is one God, and there is one mediator between God and men, the man Christ Jesus" (1 Tm 2.4–5). God wants everyone to know Jesus, but his redemptive love comes to some even before they enjoy this great blessing, if they do what is right as God enlightens them to know what is right.

The whole human race from the beginning has been given helps sufficient for salvation (see LG 2). Historically, the roots of the Church reach back to the beginnings of revelation recorded in the Old Testament (see DV 3). Yet the whole of human history centers upon Jesus, for fulfillment in him is the destiny toward which all creation is directed. In becoming Incarnate, the Word gathers all history to himself and provides within history the central reference point to which everything else is relative (see GS 10, 38). In its all-embracing unity, the gathering together of humankind in the Lord Jesus is the work of the Holy Spirit, who was at work from the beginning, throughout the Old Testament, and who now dwells on earth permanently in Jesus' Church and impels her to her full expansion and ultimate, perfect, heavenly unity (see LG 4, 6; DV 2; AG 2, 4, 5, 7, 15; GS 10, 22; and so on).

Obviously, those whose awareness of Jesus is conscious and explicit, who knowingly commit themselves to him in faith, and who receive the sacrament of baptism into Jesus and bear the name "Christian" live within the unity of the Church (see UR 22–23). "Nevertheless, our separated brethren, whether considered as individuals or as Communities and Churches, are not blessed with that unity which Jesus Christ wished to bestow on all those whom he has regenerated. . . . For it is through Christ's Catholic Church alone, which is the all-embracing means of salvation, that the fullness of the means of salvation can be obtained. It was to the apostolic college alone, of which Peter is the head, that we believe our Lord entrusted all the blessings of the new covenant, in order to establish on earth the one Body of Christ into which all those should be fully incorporated who already belong in any way to God's People" (UR 3). Yet the Spirit is at work amid our separated brothers and sisters (see UR 3); we are united with them in Jesus and the Holy Spirit (see LG 15). Thus, while the Church constituted and organized in the world as a society subsists in the Catholic Church (see LG 8), still those Christians separated from the Catholic Church are not wholly separated from Jesus' Church (see LG 15), because they live in a real, "though imperfect, communion with the Catholic Church" (UR 3).

It follows that without excluding non-Christians and separated Christians from salvation in Jesus, we must find the oneness of the only Church of Jesus in the enduring unity of the Catholic Church (see LG 8). She alone recognizes the principle of unity and cooperation established by Jesus: the collegial episcopacy centered upon the successor of Peter, who is the vicar of the Lord Jesus and head of the whole Church (see LG 18). To put the matter bluntly: Christians who do not regard themselves as Catholics are so despite themselves, just insofar as they truly are Christians. (Although the purpose of this bluntness is clarity, not offensiveness, it obviously is not likely to be appreciated by our separated brothers and sisters.)

Once the preceding explanation is understood, one will realize that the possibility that people who have not heard the gospel can be saved in no way renders unnecessary the hearing of the gospel, explicit faith, baptism, and active membership in the Church. On the contrary, those who have not heard the gospel can be saved only because in some manner they are on their way to the baptismal font, so that their baptism already has begun.

Notes

1. For a wider treatment than I provide of sacramental theology, with a wealth of scholarship, see Bernard Leeming, S.J., *Principles of Sacramental Theology* (Westminster, Md.: Newman Press, 1956).

2. A great many of the moral-canonical questions about the administration of the sacraments are clearly treated by Nicholas Halligan, O.P., *The Ministry and Celebration of the Sacraments*, 3 vols.; vol. 1, *Sacraments of Initiation and Union: Baptism, Confirmation, Eucharist;* vol. 2, *Sacraments of Reconciliation: Penance, Anointing of the Sick;* vol. 3, *Sacraments of Community Renewal: Holy Orders, Matrimony* (Staten Island, N.Y.: Alba House, 1973–74). See also Pietro Palazzini, *Vita Sacramentale: I: Teologia Sacramentaria e Sacramenti dell'Iniziazione Cristiana* (Rome: Paoline, 1974); *II: Sacramenti della Maturitá Cristiana*, vol. 1, *Riconciliazione;* vol. 2, *Ordine Sacro e Matrimoni* (Rome: Paoline, 1976).

3. A helpful treatment of the Catholic conception of sacramentality: Karl Adam, *The Spirit of Catholicism*, trans. Justin McCann, O.S.B. (New York: Macmillan, 1931), esp. 176–92.

4. The Eucharist has been treated as action very suggestively (though not in every respect in accord with Catholic teaching) by the Anglican philospher-theologian, J. R. Lucas, *Freedom and Grace* (Grand Rapids, Mich.: William B. Eerdmans, 1976), 109–19.

5. For a conception of the significance of the sacraments remarkably similar to mine, see Bernard Bro, O.P., *The Spirituality of the Sacraments: Doctrine and Practice for Today,* trans. Theodore DuBois (New York: Sheed and Ward, 1968), 104–52; note the remarkable statement (124): "It is with an infinite delicacy that God does everything he can to depend on man in the work of salvation, in so far as he can without ceasing to be God [emphasis deleted]." A treatment of the sacraments which subordinates sign to action and emphasizes the primacy of God's work: Antonio Miralles, "Gracia, fe y sacramentos," *Scripta Theologica,* 6 (1974), 299–328.

6. See Josef Jungmann, S.J., *The Liturgy of the Word,* trans. H. W. Winstone (Collegeville, Minn.: Liturgical Press, 1966), 7.

7. See Lucien Cerfaux, *The Christian in the Theology of St. Paul* (New York: Herder and Herder, 1967), 292–95. This is not to say Jesus lacked divine power during his earthly life. But the power to bestow the Spirit at will seems to follow from the status of Jesus as Christ in glory (see Jn 16.7; 20.21–22).

8. See St. Thomas Aquinas, *Summa theologiae*, 3, q. 62, a. 1. Thomas' way of speaking has been adopted widely; it follows from his position that sanctifying grace is a created quality. I disagree, but even on my account one could say in a loose sense that the sacraments "cause" grace, since they bring it about that the divine nature is communicated and that the human person shares in and is more and more perfectly integrated with charity. E. Schillebeeckx, O.P., *Christ the Sacrament of the Encounter with God* (Kansas City, Mo.: Sheed, Andrews and McMeel, 1963), 4–5, says that grace is an encounter

(personal meeting) with God as seen from the human side. It seems to me this theory is far less adequate than that of St. Thomas, for it reduces the inward transformation of the human person affected by the Spirit. Indeed, I do not see how Schillebeeckx's conception can satisfy the requirement of the Council of Trent (see DS 1530/800, 1561/821) that grace inhere, for encounters do not inhere.

9. Joseph A. Jungmann, S.J., *The Early Liturgy to the Time of Gregory the Great*, trans. Francis A. Brunner, C.Ss.R. (London: Darton, Longman and Todd, 1959), 70, 218–20. To say that the Spirit acts is not to deny that both the Father and Jesus as Word also act in all the sacraments.

10. Schillebeeckx, op. cit., 55–56, fails to grasp the lasting character of human acts; thus, he attributes the enduringness of the redemption to Jesus' divinity. This position is a case of commingling, for it attributes a divine quality to something properly human.

11. A study of this important point about remembering: Bastiaan van Iersel, S.M.M., "Some Biblical Roots of the Christian Sacrament," in *The Sacraments in General: A New Perspective*, Concilium, 31, ed. Edward Schillebeeckx, O.P., and Boniface Willems, O.P. (New York: Paulist Press, 1968), 6–15.

12. See Cerfaux, op. cit., 474–94.

13. The phrase "Christ the sacrament" is a symptom that something is wrong. Christ is not a sacrament. One who sees him also sees the Father (Jn 14.9). The sacraments are not signs of a meeting with God; they are meetings by cooperation with God. They are signs (expressive performances or carryings-out on us and for our benefit) of the unique, complex, human, redemptive act of Jesus and the divine response to that sacrifice.

14. This point is put clearly: Odo Casel, O.S.B., *The Mystery of Christian Worship and Other Writings*, ed. Burkhard Neunheuser, O.S.B. (London: Darton, Longman and Todd, 1962), 14–15, 150–60. In general, Casel rightly understands the sacraments as acts and takes seriously the presence in them of Jesus' unique redemptive act. Unfortunately, he lacks the theory of action needed to explain what he rightly asserts. He also seems to overstate the similarity between the mystery of Christ and the pagan mysteries. However, his theory of the sacraments is much sounder than that of Schillebeeckx, who criticizes (op. cit., 55–56) Casel, wrongly assuming that human acts are events which pass away when their performance is finished. Schillebeeckx does not see that the suffering, death, and resurrection of Jesus are not in themselves acts of his, but foreseen consequences of his act, which is to eat the Passover, a meal which still continues in every Mass as the continuing performance of the very same choice Jesus was executing when he said: "Do this in memory of me." Jesus now executes his lasting self-determination by means of the performance of priests acting in his person according to his command.

15. On sacramental character, see Colman E. O'Neill, O.P., *Meeting Christ in the Sacraments* (Staten Island, N.Y.: Alba House, 1964), 110–18.

16. See John Paul II, *Dominicae Cenae*, sec. 8, 72 *AAS* (1980) 127–30; *L'Osservatore Romano*, Eng. ed., 24 March 1980, 7.

17. See Louis Bouyer, *Liturgical Piety* (Notre Dame, Ind.: University of Notre Dame Press, 1954), 178–79. Although somewhat dated by Vatican II's implementation of many of its ideas, this work remains an excellent treatment of the liturgy as the primary element of Catholic spirituality.

18. John Paul II, op. cit, sec. 7 (124–26; 6–7), makes the point that worship centered in the Eucharist springs from intimacy and gives all Christian life a sacramental style. In other words, Christian life as a whole is lived in cooperation with God who is present, very much as marriage is lived in cooperation with a spouse whom one loves because of communion in one flesh.

19. For a compact but rich historical study of baptismal theology, see Lorna Brockett, R.S.C.J., *The Theology of Baptism*, Theology Today Series, 25 (Hales Corners, Wis.: Clergy Book Service, 1971).

20. For theological reflections on baptism and entry into the Church in close harmony with the doctrine set out in the present question, see Louis Bouyer, *Christian Initiation* (New York: Macmillan, 1960), 60–97.

21. See Markus Barth, *Ephesians: Introduction, Translation, and Commentary on Chapters 1–3*, Anchor Bible, 34 (Garden City, N.Y.: Doubleday, 1974), 115–19 and 219–22; Eduard Lohse, *Colossians and Philemon* (Philadelphia: Fortress Press, 1971), 103–6 and 132–35.

22. St. John Chrysostom, *Homilies on the Gospel of John*, 1, 12.

23. If someone argues that the catechumen receives grace before baptism, I answer that perhaps grace is received before the rite of baptism is performed, but the sacrament begins earlier: when the

catechumen, moved by grace, begins to move toward the rite. The rite only completes the long journey of souls seeking Jesus and of him in his Church seeking them.

24. See *The Rites of the Catholic Church*, trans. International Commission on English in the Liturgy (New York: Pueblo, 1976), 98–99, 145–46.

25. Ibid., 109.
26. Ibid., 198.

CHAPTER THIRTY-ONE

CONFIRMATION, THE APOSTOLATE, AND PERSONAL VOCATION

Introduction

Baptism makes one a Christian and in doing so requires one to live as befits a child of God. The grace of the Spirit given in baptism empowers one to do this, as natural begetting empowers one to do what comes naturally to a human being.

While initiating Christian life, however, baptism does not organize it. That is left to confirmation, penance, anointing of the sick, and the Eucharist (see *S.t.*, 3, q. 65, aa. 1–2). In distinct but simultaneous and altogether compatible ways, these sacraments structure the lives of all who seek to live according to their membership in God's family. They add nothing from outside to baptism, but, as we saw in the last chapter, develop what it embryonically contains to a mature, organically differentiated, and fully functioning state.

The sacraments of holy orders and matrimony, to which only certain members of the Church are called, do not structure the lives of all. Hence they are not Christian moral principles in the same way as the other sacraments, and so they will not be treated in this volume.

The present chapter concerns confirmation's way of organizing Christian life. Confirmation is the sacrament of maturation, of strengthening, of the fullness of the Spirit, of complete conformity to Jesus (see *S.t.*, 3, q. 72, a. 1). The present treatment will show that it is a sacrament of transition—from divine life as a gift received, to divine life as a reality one lives out, expressing one's identity as a child of God and sharing in the revelatory work of the Church. At natural maturity, a child becomes an adult, able to be a parent to others; at confirmation, a child of God comes to share in the life of the Church as one not only redeemed by the Lord Jesus but redeeming with him (see *S.t.*, 3, q. 72, aa. 4–5).

Question A: How is confirmation a principle of Christian life?

1. The Council of Trent examined and condemned the opinion that confirmation was once no more than a catechesis of Christians nearing adolescence which equipped them to give an account of their faith before the Church. The Council insists instead that confirmation is a sacrament really distinct from baptism (see DS 1628/871). The Church firmly believes that confirmation is one of the seven sacraments instituted by Jesus.

2. The sacrament is normally administered by a bishop or by a priest specially authorized for the task, by anointing with chrism as a seal of the gift of the Holy Spirit (see DS 1317–18/697).[1] Concerning this sealing the Council of Florence teaches: "The effect of this sacrament is that the Holy Spirit is given in it for strength just as he was given to the apostles on Pentecost, in order that the Christian may courageously confess the name of Christ. And therefore, the one to be confirmed is anointed on the forehead, where shame shows itself, lest he be ashamed to confess the name of Christ and especially his cross . . ." (DS 1319/697). In speaking of confessing the name of Christ, the Council is referring to the specific aspect of Christian life which this sacrament consecrates (see *S.t.*, 3, q. 72, a. 9).

3. Vatican II develops and clarifies this. In a passage in which it moves from its treatment of baptism to confirmation, the Council teaches concerning the baptized: "Reborn as sons of God, they must confess before men the faith which they have received from God through the Church. Bound more intimately to the Church by the sacrament of confirmation, they are endowed by the Holy Spirit with special strength, and hence are the more strictly obliged to spread and defend the faith both by word and by deed as true witnesses of Christ" (LG 11; translation amended).

4. At the end of the first sentence just quoted, Vatican II refers to St. Thomas Aquinas' teaching on sacramental character. According to Thomas, this is a spiritual power by which one shares as an instrument in the Lord Jesus' priestly act and so participates in worship according to the rite of Christian religion (see *S.t.*, 3, q. 63, a. 2). This spiritual power is either passive (that of receiving divine gifts) or active (that of handing them on). Thomas makes it clear in a subsequent passage that baptism belongs on the "passive" side of this division and confirmation on the "active" side. In baptism one is made like an infant in divine life, with the capacity to do what is necessary for one's personal salvation. By confirmation one is made mature, with the power of professing the faith publicly, even before Jesus' enemies. Thus confirmation presupposes baptism (see *S.t.*, 3, q. 72, aa. 5–6).

5. **In sum, confirmation is a principle of the whole of Christian life considered under a certain aspect, namely, as a share in the Lord Jesus' revelatory mission which exists in the life of the Church as it communicates or hands on divine truth and love.** The confirmed are to live not just as God's adopted children in some general sense, but as children who take part in the family business: the extension of God's kingdom (see *S.t.*, 3, q. 72, a. 5).

Vatican II develops the concept of witness when it prescribes as a remedy for atheism a proper presentation of the Church's teaching and ". . . the integral life of the Church and her members. For it is the function of the Church, led by the Holy Spirit who renews and purifies her ceaselessly, to make God the Father and his Incarnate Son present and in a sense visible. This result is achieved chiefly by the witness of a living and mature faith . . . . This faith needs to prove its fruitfulness by penetrating the believer's entire life, including its worldly dimensions, and by activating him toward justice and love, especially regarding the needy" (GS 21). This passage does not mention confirmation, but it does develop the concept of witness of faith which is central to this sacrament. Elsewhere, the Council teaches explicitly that Christians must show by the example of their lives as well as by their words the power of the Spirit by whom they were strengthened through confirmation (see AG 11).

In such statements, Vatican II continues the New Testament's teaching that life in the Spirit is a life of mercy, for the law of Jesus is fulfilled not merely by saving one's own soul, but by bearing one another's burdens (see Gal 6.2) and preaching the gospel through one's deeds (see 1 Pt 2.12, 15). The Christian is not only to have divine life, but to communicate it, as Jesus himself does—to be the salt of the earth and the light of the world (see Mt 5.13–16; Mk 4.21–22; Lk 8.16).

Sts. Irenaeus and Cyprian of Carthage distinguish two functions of the Spirit, one of bringing to new birth, the other of bringing to maturity. They connect the second to the Spirit of prophecy, with which the Church must be endowed for the promulgation of the gospel. With this distinction, the effect of the laying on of hands is distinguished from the effect of baptism. St. Augustine ties the gift of the Spirit in confirmation to the growth of charity and the seven gifts of the Spirit mentioned in Isaiah.[2] These ideas are altogether consistent with the concept that confirmation commissions the faithful to share in the life of the Church handing on divine truth and love. For prophecy is a concrete work of continuing the communication of divine revelation. To accept responsibility for cooperating with the Spirit in handing on the faith is to grow in charity.

The teaching of St. Thomas that confirmation confers the power of doing what belongs to the spiritual fight against enemies of the faith has been criticized. It is claimed that the distinction between confirmation and the other sacraments, especially baptism and the Eucharist, remains unclear. The Eucharist also nourishes divine life while baptism also confers the Spirit, and both also confer strength.[3]

However, there is nothing unclear about the teaching of Thomas on this matter, although his military conception of the profession and spreading of the faith is somewhat restricted. If one grants that confirmation is the "sacrament of the mysterious influence of the Paraclete upon the life of each Christian enabling him to bear witness to Christ,"[4] one implicitly grants that the sacrament gives the power to fight enemies of the faith, for one cannot bear witness to Jesus without confronting and struggling against those who reject him. Baptism and the Eucharist do not specifically assign and strengthen Christians to fight enemies of the faith.

Question B: In what sense is confirmation the sacrament of the apostolate?

1. In defining "apostolate," Vatican II teaches that every member of the Church is called to share in it:

> For this the Church was founded: that by spreading the kingdom of Christ everywhere for the glory of God the Father, she might bring all men to share in Christ's saving redemption; and that through them the whole world might in actual fact be brought into relationship with him. All activity of the Mystical Body directed to the attainment of this goal is called the apostolate, and the Church carries it on in various ways through all her members. For by its very nature the Christian vocation is also a vocation to the apostolate. No part of the structure of a living body is merely passive but each has a share in the functions as well as in the life of the body. So, too, in

the body of Christ, which is the Church, the whole body, "according to the functioning in due measure of each single part, derives its increase" (Eph 4.16). (AA 2)

This makes two things unmistakably clear. First, the apostolate includes the Church's entire activity insofar as this is directed to extending redemption to all people. Second, every member of the Church has some share in the apostolate.

2. For a long time before Vatican II, there was uncertainty as to whether the apostolate includes only activities of a specifically religious character. If so, many thought that the apostolate would pertain primarily and properly to priests—indeed, only fully to bishops, as successors of the apostles—while the ordinary faithful would share in apostolic work only by helping priests and bishops. Vatican II clarifies this point.

3. The Church's work of salvation "is done mainly through the ministry of the word and of the sacraments, which are entrusted in a special way to the clergy." But the laity also have "their very important roles to play" in this ministry; "the apostolate of the laity and the pastoral ministry complement one another." There are in fact "innumerable opportunities" available to the laity for carrying out "their apostolate of making the gospel known and men holy. The very testimony of their Christian life, and good works done in a supernatural spirit, have the power to draw men to belief and to God." Good deeds, the Council further insists, must often be accompanied by the words of faith; to the extent of their ability and learning, the laity must explain, defend, and apply Christian principles (AA 6).

4. This suggests that here, as in other contexts, the revelatory activity which communicates divine truth and love is a complex of words and deeds (see DV 2). **In the present instance, every Christian is called upon to reveal Jesus by a faithful life, whose significance is to be explained in terms of Christian truth.**

5. Works of mercy toward persons and groups in great need are especially important if carried out in a really Jesus-like way (see AA 8). It would be a mistake, however, to limit the apostolate to specific types of acts. Works of mercy give especially effective witness to the love of God, but any good act which contributes to unfolding one's Christian faith and love can be apostolic. Indeed, the content of the apostolate of the laity necessarily includes a wide range of secular activities: "The laity must take on the renewal of the temporal order as their own special obligation . . .. Outstanding among the works of this type of apostolate is that of Christian social action. This sacred Synod desires to see it extended now to the whole temporal sphere, including culture" (AA 7).

6. Hence, there can be no intrinsic limit to apostolate. The Council teaches that it "should reach out to all men wherever they can be found; it should not exclude any spiritual or temporal benefit" which one can confer. And it should take the form of the spoken word as well as deeds, since there are many people "who can hear the gospel and recognize Christ only through the laity who live near them" (AA 13).

7. The laity are not restricted to doing apostolic works in confraternities, Catholic action groups, and the like. In fact, "A particular form of the individual

apostolate, as well as a sign especially suited to our times, is the testimony of a layman's entire life as it develops out of faith, hope, and charity. This form manifests Christ living in those who believe in him. Then by the apostolate of the word, which is utterly necessary under certain circumstances, lay people announce Christ, explain and spread his teaching according to their situation and competence, and faithfully profess it" (AA 16; translation amended). It is an important part of this pervasive apostolate, the Council explains, to act always with motives which are visibly Christian. In this way, good acts have their greatest apostolic effectiveness.

8. While the Council is speaking of the laity in all these texts, most of what it says applies equally to every Christian's life. More of course needs to be said in considering the specific form of the apostolate of the priest, who is ordained for the service of the word and the sacraments. **The point here is simply that, if one understands what the apostolate is and how confirmation is a principle of Christian life, it follows necessarily that confirmation is the sacrament which assigns and strengthens Christians to live their entire lives as their share in the Church's apostolate.**

Vatican II does not explicitly say that confirmation is the sacrament of the apostolate, perhaps because "apostolate" is too easily understood in a narrower sense than the Council wishes, and perhaps because the sacrament of confirmation is to be conferred even on infants in danger of death, and in such conditions it seems irrelevant to apostolic activity.[5]

Nevertheless, confirmation consecrates the Christian for living and speaking as a witness to Jesus, and such witnessing precisely is the common essence of the apostolate. And Vatican II does say that the lay apostolate ". . . is a participation in the saving mission of the Church itself. Through their baptism and confirmation, all are commissioned to that apostolate by the Lord himself" (LG 33). Again, the Council teaches: "The laity derive the right and duty with respect to the apostolate from their union with Christ their Head. Incorporated into Christ's Mystical Body through baptism and strengthened by the power of the Holy Spirit through confirmation, they are assigned to the apostolate by the Lord himself. They are consecrated into a royal priesthood and a holy people (cf. 1 Pt 2.4–10) in order that they may offer spiritual sacrifices through everything they do, and may witness to Christ throughout the world" (AA 3). These passages imply that confirmation is the sacrament of apostolate, although they stop short of saying this.

Question C: How are confirmation, apostolate, and personal vocation related to one another?

1. Confirmation consecrates a Christian to share in the apostolate. But an individual's specific apostolic responsibility is determined by his or her personal vocation. Confirmation therefore organizes the Christian's life to the extent personal vocation does. But personal vocation integrates all aspects of a mature Christian's life, and so the act of receiving and living in the sacrament of confirmation organizes every morally good act of the life of such a person.

2. In other words, confirmation includes a commitment to bear witness to Jesus—to give glory to God—by the whole of one's life. Thus it organizes everything else one does out of living faith into the unity of one's life. Personal

vocation is the personal specification of faith to one's own life (28-E). **Thus, personal vocation is the medium by which confirmation shapes the whole of one's life as apostolate.**

3. Nothing in a Christian's life is exempt from integration by living faith. St. Paul teaches: "Whether you eat or drink, or whatever you do, do all to the glory of God" (1 Cor 10.31). Again: "Whatever you do, in word or deed, do everything in the name of the Lord Jesus" (Col 3.17). There is a place in a Christian's life for every human good, provided it is pursued in a morally upright manner (see Phil 4.8). Hence, every act of Christian life should be done in Jesus' name, should give God glory, and so should carry out the apostolic commitment proper to confirmation.

4. Vatican II makes it clear that the Church's apostolate requires both that personal vocations be differentiated and that the members of the Church cooperate in carrying out their complementary vocations (see AA 3). In explaining this, the Council lays out the great principle of personal vocation. Each Catholic receives his or her own gift from the Spirit, and each gift is to be used to the fullest in making one's personal contribution to the whole, coordinated life and work of the Church.

Citing Scripture (Col 3.17), Vatican II points out explicitly that family concerns and secular affairs must be included within one's religious, apostolic program of life (see AA 4). "By its very nature the Christian vocation is also a vocation to the apostolate" (AA 2). Therefore, the whole of each person's life also is to be lived apostolically.

5. Personal vocation already has been discussed at length (23-E, 27-B, 28-E). Yet here it bears emphasis that both the very specific commitments of the mature and the rather general commitments of children, the largest commitments to a state of life consecrated by a sacrament or vows and the many smaller commitments concerning work and leisure—all these choices concerning one's style of Christian life should form a harmonious whole and organize one's day-to-day activities. To the extent that this is not just a lovely ideal but a living reality, the whole of one's life will make Jesus' light shine before humankind and give glory to God. Then all one is and does will flow from God's self-gift in the Lord Jesus and one's baptismal faith in him.

6. Because the whole of life should be lived in dedication to Jesus and as a contribution to the Church's apostolate, a mature Christian should not reserve any area or type of activity merely for self-indulgence. This does not mean the Christian is to be a workaholic or a fanatic. Christians are committed to fulfillment in respect to the full range of human goods. But there is no room in a mature Christian life for doing just as one pleases, except insofar as one is pleased to fulfill one's commitments. Every act for every good ought to contribute positively to the fulfillment of one's total personal vocation.

Charity extends not only to God and to one's neighbor but to oneself. But it does not follow that one's life should be divided into compartments—one for religious activities, one for service to others, and one for self-gratification. Rather, all of one's life should be consecrated to God as a living sacrifice of praise; all of it should be dedicated to Jesus-like service of others. In this way all of it will be fruitful in genuine self-fulfillment in this world and the next.

Christians need to make some use of their every part and ability in loving service, precisely so that they can love God with their whole reality. But a dedicated life cannot be well-rounded; no individual can aspire to be the whole Mystical Body. Does it follow that there is no room in life for spontaneity—that no time should be devoted to recreation? By no means. A well-integrated person with deep commitments fulfills them with considerable spontaneity. One who slavishly follows rules in a laborious way is perhaps less deeply committed, and certainly is less integrated with the goods to which such burdensome actions are directed. Moreover, everyone needs recreation, and a Christian makes commitments with this need in mind.

Question D: Why is strength the special grace of the sacrament of confirmation?

1. The teaching of the Church (see A above) shows that confirmation confers the Spirit especially to strengthen the Christian for courageous witnessing. Witnessing is one's personal vocation, considered as one's proper share in the apostolate of the Church. **Strengthening graces are needed to fulfill any Christian vocation consistently, for none lacks suffering and hardship. The martyr is a witness, and every Christian witness will be a martyr** (see *S.t.*, 3, q. 72, a. 4).

St. Stephen, the first martyr, closely followed Jesus. He boldly bore witness to Jesus, commended his spirit to him, prayed for his persecutors, and died with resignation (see Acts 7.54–60). Sts. Peter and John before the Sanhedrin also boldly bore witness, for they were filled with the Spirit (see Acts 4.8–21).

2. Reading the signs of the times in the light of faith, Christians relativize time by the standards of eternity. The Christian sees through the world and announces its passing character (see 1 Cor 7.29–31). Not hiding their hope, Christians challenge worldly powers and their evil ways (see LG 35).

3. Holiness comes by doing one's ordinary work in intimate association with Jesus according to God's loving plan (see AA 4). Although not meant as a condemnation of anyone, such simple holiness is rightly perceived by the wicked as a condemnation. The world's negative reaction is inevitable; every faithful Christian must be prepared for it (see Jn 15.18–25; 16.1–4; 1 Jn 3.12–13).

4. To fulfill one's Christian vocation also requires strength because of the intrinsic difficulty of any such vocation. Self-interest must be subordinated to the needs of the kingdom, as in the case of John the Baptist, who was content to fade away to make room for Jesus (see Jn 3.27–30). One must be prompt in setting aside security in order to be in communion with Jesus, as Levi was prompt in giving up his job (see Mt 9.9–13; Mk 2.13–17; Lk 5.27–32).

5. The strength of confirmation also is required because every Christian vocation demands unswerving fidelity. With respect to the elements of one's vocation, there is no room for experimentation and no room for writing off a commitment as a mistake and making a fresh start. True, the commitments which constitute one's vocation always are open to further specification. Moreover, projects chosen to fulfill one's vocation can be completed and sometimes may be abandoned. However, vocational commitments themselves specify what the Christian modes of response require of each individual. Hence, one cannot change

one's mind about any vocational commitment without violating the claims of Christian morality. Often, indeed, one's eternal life is at stake in being faithful to vocational commitments.

6. One who loves God willingly strives to fulfill perfectly even a small role in his story of salvation, for every role is important (see 1 Cor 12.19–22). The many different and limited personal vocations prepare for a rich diversity of relationships in heaven. For human acts, especially those which are vocational commitments, are not just means to an end. They are made to last. The good deeds of those who die in communion with Jesus will remain with them forever (see Rv 14.13).

The strength which the Spirit conveys in confirmation need not be considered some sort of supplement apart from charity, but can be identified with charity itself enlivening faith and hope. "Love bears all things, believes all things, hopes all things, endures all things" (1 Cor 13.7). In committing oneself in vocational choices, one who loves considers needs and dares to try to fulfill them, humbly confident that God will supply. In facing unexpected difficulties, one who loves creatively excogitates new approaches, because love finds a way.

Question E: How can one discern one's personal vocation?

1. We have seen that Christian conscience has an important, creative role to play in working out the specific affirmative norms which shape one's personal vocation and its execution in the course of life (27-D). We also have seen how the counsels of perfection contribute to prudence's work of determining one's personal vocation (27-H). The present question provides a clarification of the discernment necessary prior to making any vocational commitment.

2. There is no question of personal vocation unless one considers one's life in the light of faith, and with at least some awareness that one's fulfillment lies, not in individualistic well-roundedness, but in communion with the Lord Jesus and one's fellow Christians. With these suppositions, one also must know one's own talents and limitations—the special gifts the Spirit has given one. Further, one must think about the opportunities for service which are offered by the world in need of Jesus; one must attend to the points at which the life of Jesus in the Church can use one's hand and one's talents.

3. Having done all this, one still needs special help from the Holy Spirit. But this creates a problem. How can one distinguish between inspirations from the Holy Spirit and those from other sources? In traditional terminology, the problem is that of the discernment of spirits. Scripture, teaching that there is need for this (see 1 Jn 4.1–6; 1 Cor 12.10), takes solid faith according to the norm of apostolic teaching as a standard by which one can discern. Although this is central and basic, the problem requires closer examination.

4. It is important to be clear about what sort of problem discernment presents. The question is not how to know what is true in matters of faith or what is right in matters of morality. These questions can be settled by learning what the Church teaches and making a direct, reasoned application of it. The problem of discernment, by contrast, is one of recognition.

5. Quite apart from faith, people must be able to recognize their own good or bad motives. Also, without judging others, one must form probable opinions as to whether it is possible to rely on them and cooperate with them. Someone thinking of marriage, for example, must decide whether the other party is being completely forthright and is likely to live up to the responsibilities of married life.

6. The discernment Christians need in respect to vocation is only required because they are living within the structure of Christian faith, moral teaching, and Church order, and can take this structure for granted in forming their lives. Assuming all this, discernment is necessary whenever one must make an important judgment in a unique or fresh instance about whether to take something concrete as having a particular significance for one's Christian life.

7. **Discernment is practiced, first, by using the indications of one's faith, Christian moral convictions, and ecclesial life; then by prayerful preparation and close attention; and finally by following one's inclination or predominant impression.**

8. The New Testament offers guidance regarding the use of the framework of one's Christian life for discernment.[6] First, it is necessary to ask what faith suggests with respect to the alternatives. For instance, what sort of attitude toward Jesus and his self-oblation does the possible commitment suggest? (If the attitude is not in accord with his reality as faith makes it known, something is wrong.) Second, what fruits are to be expected? (Are they good or bad in the light of Christian moral teaching? Does that which needs judging seem to conduce to genuine charity, to generous love of neighbor? Or is it attractive because of the gratification it promises?) Third, what alternative offers the prospect of building up the Church, of making her apostolic work more effective?

9. Remaining options can be narrowed to one and moral certitude reached that one's discernment is conclusive by applying further, subjective criteria. Does the prospect of accepting and acting along the line of a particular possibility give a sense of light, joy, and peace? Do various signs in experience seem to confirm the discernment? Does one have a sense of recognizing God's will in it? As one reflects on such questions all options but one drop away. At this point, one's vocation is clear and one should make a commitment in accord with the Christian norm that one should follow God's clear call.

Because this process goes beyond general rules and even beyond reflection which one can articulate propositionally, it seems mysterious. A great deal has been written about it, under such headings as "discernment of spirits" and "being led by the Spirit," as though the Spirit were at work in instances of this sort but not in cases in which one sees the intelligible demands of duty and fulfills them or sees that certain kinds of acts are always wrong and avoids them. Actually, whenever one proceeds in the light of faith and strives to choose and act out of love of God, the Spirit of God is fully at work in one's heart. His work is not limited to filling the gaps between reflective acts of the mind.

Conversely, a process like the one used in eliminating options to arrive at one's proper vocation is conducted in many ordinary decisions. For example, one might consider taking a vacation, and after eliminating many possibilities for various reasons, have two left between which to choose. At this point, one imagines oneself taking each vacation, and chooses the one which has the best "feel." (The Spirit is at work here as truly as in one's discernment of one's vocation, provided that one's choice of a vacation implements one's vocation.)

Question F: What sorts of prayer are appropriate to Christian life as apostolate?

1. All sound forms of prayer are obviously appropriate in some way to every confirmed person. However, this question must be addressed with reference to confirmation's specific relevance to the fulfillment of one's personal vocation as one's own share in the apostolate. Considered from this special point of view, what forms of prayer are especially appropriate in Christian life?

We learn in the New Testament how necessary prayer is to the Christian life of witness (see Acts 1.14, 4.31; Rom 1.9; 12.12; and so on). Vatican II teaches that meditative prayer is essential for our participation in the apostolate: "Only by the light of faith and by meditation on the word of God can one always and everywhere recognize God in whom 'we live, and move, and have our being' (Acts 17.28), seek his will in every event, see Christ in all men whether they be close to us or strangers, and make correct judgments about the true meaning and value of temporal things, both in themselves and in their relation to man's final goal" (AA 4). This brief statement outlines an appropriate program of prayer directed toward the fulfillment of the responsibilities of the confirmed Christian.

2. **First, one must recognize God's presence.** Although he is always present, we tend to forget this, and we must not do so. It is necessary always to recall the source of all our responsibilities, powers, acts, and merits. It is always necessary, too, to remember that the value of our lives, especially insofar as they are apostolic, lies in their contribution to the fulfillment of everything in our Lord Jesus, not in their visible, this-worldly results, even when these results seem to have supernatural significance. Only by keeping one's heart set on heaven can one carry on important apostolic work with faithfulness in hardship, patience in frustration, and resignation to God's will in failure.

3. Second, one must seek God's will in every event. Nothing can happen without God's permission. If it happens to us, God wishes us to understand in faith the meaning which he wants us to attach to it. **In thus reflecting on the given facts, one finds one's personal vocation and its daily requirements.** The signs of the times, studied in faith, tell us of both the misery of sin and the possibility of redemptive work—work given us today as our task.

4. Third, one must see Jesus in everyone. He is present in some as at work, in others as in need, and in many, perhaps most, in both of these ways. The apostolic life is a life of service and cooperation. It is an important form of prayer to consider others with faith. Only by doing so does one see the full demands and opportunities of one's apostolate.

5. Fourth, it is necessary to judge rightly about the meaning and value of temporal things. To do this, one must develop a conscience fully formed at the level of moral truth, not determined by childish compulsions and inhibitions or restrained by social conventions which fall short of Christian truth. Without the light of the Spirit, one cannot solve one's problems and reach sound judgments. In many cases, of course, reflection reveals something needed for one's work. In prayer one confidently asks for everything necessary.

6. **Finally, one must make a continuing, conscious, and prayerful effort to distinguish one's own apostolic objectives from God's will.** Uprightly seeking to do God's work by pursuing certain specific goals in this life, we can easily forget that failure and frustrations as well as success and satisfactions are included in God's wise and loving plan. Forgetting this, we will be tempted to violate the Christian modes of response precisely in our apostolic efforts—for example, by discouragement and even infidelity when dedicated effort seems fruitless, by mercilessness toward those who seem to us to block God's will, and by compromising the gospel to make it more acceptable to those to whom we are seeking to proclaim it.

Question G: What is the role of friendship
with Mary and the other saints
in the apostolic life of every Christian?

1. The saints are models of Christian life whom the Church proposes for our imitation.[7] They are also intercessors on our behalf—again, a role in which the Church commends them to us. But, potentially, our relationship to the saints involves still more than this (see LG 48–50).

2. Each of the saints is in heaven because he or she shared in Jesus' redemptive commitment and lived a personal life which fulfilled this commitment in a clear and outstanding manner. Like Jesus himself, each saint was trying to do a job, a job which, like his, was never entirely done. The love which perfects God's family is strengthened when we love the saints, thank God for them (see LG 50), and with friendship carry on what they were trying to do.

3. For example, one who wishes to do apostolic work is a colleague of the apostles and of apostolic persons of all times, continuing what each of them wished to do and gave his or her life in doing. One engaged in theological labor for the Church works along with St. Augustine and St. Thomas and all the others who have done such work. One who seeks truly to reform the Church works with St. Catherine. One who strives to build up a genuine Christian humanism cooperates with St. Thomas More. This is more than just a pious thought. It is a fact which flows from the reality of membership in God's apostolic family.

4. **To the extent we share with saints not only in the common commitment of following our Lord Jesus but some more special form of serving him, it is appropriate that we develop a special closeness to some of them.** Their lives exhibit many more definite aspects of goodness and particular ways of holiness to imitate than we can find in the individual, though absolutely perfect, life of Jesus himself. Furthermore, since we share in their work, it is only to be expected that they do what they can to help us. These close personal relationships with real though invisible friends give our hope a concreteness and vivacity it otherwise lacks.

One who is conscious of the communion of saints, which gathers together God's children of every time and place, is not likely to be overly impressed with arguments based on the values of contemporary humankind. The "contemporary" world rapidly passes away; the relevance of today is the straitjacket of tomorrow. Do sixty-three percent of those questioned in some poll disregard the teaching of the Church on some matter? A serious situation to be sure. But why do members of this one generation imagine their judgment to be a reflection of anything but rationalization, when a far larger number of persons already has reached heaven by accepting this teaching and striving to live up to it, often with great sacrifices which showed a love of Jesus not so evident today?

5. Above all the other saints we honor Mary, the mother of Jesus, whom he gave us as our own mother. Her personal vocation is a unique exemplar for all other human beings called to share in Jesus' redemptive work (see LG 53). When the angel proposed that Mary be the mother of Jesus and she agreed, she showed how the work of redemption can depend upon the willing cooperation of human persons (see Lk 1.38). Her natural motherhood demonstrated the limited individuality of Jesus, his human dependence upon others. Her continuing work for our redemption exemplifies the manner in which all the holy commitments of Christians contribute to completion in the Lord Jesus and will last forever (see LG 65).

6. Since Mary's personal vocation was related in a unique way to that of Jesus, we should love her with a special love and share in carrying on her work. Thus, she is a model for our imitation and a helper in our lives. Although she was not a liberated woman, she is the model for all truly liberated men and women, for she lived and she lives in the glorious liberty which belongs to God's children—the liberty of a life of love according to the Spirit.

Mary also provides a special ground for our hope. God's faithfulness is the fundamental ground of hope; the resurrection of Jesus is the primary evidence of this faithfulness and the exemplar of our own resurrection to come. But without Mary one might doubt that God could bring human persons to share in divine glory. Mary is a created person just as we are. Her greatness depends entirely upon God's grace. What he has done for her he can do for us. Our limitations need not make us doubt. Even our sinfulness need not make us despair, for the same redeeming love which preserved Mary from sin and death can heal our sins and raise us from death to life.

Summary

Confirmation empowers one courageously to confess Christ, for in this sacrament, as Vatican II says, the recipients are "endowed by the Holy Spirit with special strength." Confirmation presupposes baptism. In baptism one becomes an infant in divine life, able to do what is necessary for personal salvation; in confirmation one is made mature, with the spiritual power—confirmation's sacramental character—to profess the faith publicly. Thus, confirmation is a principle of the whole of Christian life considered under a certain aspect, namely, as a share in the Church's work of communicating or handing on divine truth and love.

Vatican II teaches that every member of the Church is to share in the apostolate. The apostolate is not limited to the clergy, nor do lay people share in it only by helping bishops and priests. The witness of Christian life and deeds of mercy are capable of drawing people to God; indeed, any good act which expresses Christian faith and love can be apostolic. The Church's teaching about confirmation and about apostolate make it clear that confirmation is the sacrament of apostolate.

An individual's specific apostolic responsibility is determined by his or her personal vocation. Confirmation therefore organizes the Christian's life to the extent it is organized by personal vocation; personal vocation is the medium by which this sacrament structures the whole of one's life as apostolate. Every act in a Christian's life should be done in Jesus' name, give God glory, and so carry out the apostolic commitment proper to confirmation. The Church's apostolate requires that the personal vocations of Christians be differentiated but that Christians cooperate in carrying these out. Because the whole of life should be lived apostolically, a mature Christian should reserve no area or type of activity merely for self-indulgence; rather, every act for every good should contribute positively to carrying out one's personal vocation.

The strengthening graces of confirmation are needed to fulfill a Christian vocation consistently, for in one way or another every Christian witness will be a martyr. Christian holiness—fidelity to God's loving plan—is rightly perceived by the wicked as a condemnation; their negative reaction is inevitable, and every Christian must be prepared for it. Moreover, fulfillment of one's Christian vocation also requires strength because of the intrinsic difficulty of the vocation, which is contrary to limited self-interest and worldly security and precludes the abandonment of vocational commitments in the face of difficulties.

In making decisions about one's personal vocation, the help of the Holy Spirit is required, and this calls for discernment. Discernment is not concerned with what is true in matters of faith or morality, for this can be settled by learning and applying what the Church teaches; rather, the work of discernment is to recognize one's own motives and to form probable opinions about the possibility of relying on and cooperating with others. Discernment is practiced by using the indications of Christian faith, moral convictions, and ecclesial life, by prayerful preparation and close attention, and finally by following one's inclination or predominant impression. Subjective criteria (a sense of joy, peace, and so on) may be needed to complete the discernment but do not apply when there is the least counterindication from faith, Christian morality, or the requirements of Church order.

Certain forms of prayer are especially relevant from the point of view of personal vocation and apostolate. Such prayer should help one to recognize God's presence, seek God's will in every event, see Jesus in everyone, judge temporal things rightly, and distinguish one's own apostolic objectives from God's will.

The saints are our models and intercessors, but they also have another role of particular relevance from the perspective of our personal vocations and apostolate. Not only do we carry on in general what the saints were trying to do, we can appropriately view ourselves as the colleagues and co-workers of those whose apostolic work was the same or similar to ours. Above all the other saints we honor Mary, whose personal vocation is a unique exemplar for all other human beings called to share in Jesus' redemptive work.

Appendix 1:   The meaning of confirmation indicated in the new rite

The documents of the new rite of confirmation further develop the Church's understanding of this sacrament. The Introduction begins by stating its effect: "In this sacrament they receive the Holy Spirit, who was sent upon the apostles by the Lord on Pentecost. This giving of the Holy Spirit conforms believers more perfectly to Christ and strengthens them so that they may bear witness to Christ for the building up of his body in faith and love."[8] The *Apostolic Constitution on the Sacrament of Confirmation* develops the idea more fully. It begins by emphasizing that through this sacrament the faithful receive the Holy Spirit as a gift. The New Testament shows that the Spirit descended on Jesus and assisted him in his messianic mission. He promised his followers the gift of the Spirit and kept this promise on Pentecost. From then on the apostles laid hands upon the newly baptized to complete its grace with the gift of the Holy Spirit himself.[9]

Some might argue that the emphasis upon the gift of the Spirit tends to exclude any specific role for confirmation. For the Spirit already is received in baptism. But this objection is easily answered. It is one thing to receive the Spirit as the principle of one's own adoptive divinity, and it is something else to receive the Spirit as Jesus did after his baptism and as the apostles did on Pentecost. In the latter case, one has the Spirit as the principle of one's conscious living out of one's status as member of the divine family, and so as the principle by which one not only adheres to Jesus in faith, but reveals his truth to others— not only is redeemed by God's love, but hands on this same love.

A homily provided as part of the new rite of confirmation within Mass makes the preceding point clear:

> In our day the coming of the Holy Spirit in confirmation is no longer marked by the gift of tongues, but we know his coming by faith. He fills our hearts with the love of God, brings us together in one faith but in different vocations, and works within us to make the Church one and holy.
>
> The gift of the Holy Spirit which you are to receive will be a spiritual sign and seal to make you more like Christ and more perfect members of his Church. At his baptism by John, Christ himself was anointed by the Spirit and sent out on his public ministry to set the world on fire.
>
> You have already been baptized into Christ and now you will receive the power of his Spirit and the sign of the cross on your forehead. You must be witnesses before all the world to his suffering, death, and resurrection; your way of life should at all times reflect the goodness of Christ. Christ gives varied gifts to his Church, and the Spirit distributes them among the members of Christ's body to build up the holy people of God in unity and love.
>
> Be active members of the Church, alive in Jesus Christ. Under the guidance of the Holy Spirit give your lives completely in the service of all, as did Christ, who came not to be served but to serve.[10]

Thus, confirmation is an anointing with the Spirit to share in the public ministry of Jesus. By baptism, one shares by adoption in what he is by nature; by confirmation, one shares by commissioning in the redeeming work of Jesus. The confirmed have the power of the Spirit; they are equipped to be active members of the Church, which is a sign lifted up before the nations to hand on the truth and love revealed by God in Jesus (see LG 1; DS 3014/1794).

Appendix 2:   Scriptural indications about the sacrament of confirmation

The Church does not exclusively depend on Scripture to know what God revealed in Jesus (see DV 9). The total appropriation by the apostles of what they witnessed in the life of the Lord was expressed by their preaching, reflected in Scripture, but also was contained in their practices and the manner in which they organized the Church and its work of handing on the faith (see *S.t.*, 3, q. 72, a. 4, ad 1). Hence, even if it were clear that the New Testament cannot establish the institution of confirmation by Jesus, that would not be a reason to deny the Church's teaching that Jesus instituted this sacrament as well as others (see *S.t.*, 3, q. 72, a. 1, ad 1).

However, since some think they find little or no basis in the New Testament for confirmation, it is worth considering briefly what evidence there is in Scripture concerning this sacrament. The *Apostolic Constitution on the Sacrament of Confirmation* makes use of (and thus provides an ecclesial interpretation of) some relevant passages of Scripture.[11]

First, it is pointed out that the Holy Spirit assisted Jesus in his mission; Jesus himself taught that the words of Isaiah, "The Spirit of the Lord is upon me," referred to himself (see Lk 4.17–21). It seems that if confirmation is assimilated to this anointing of Jesus with the Spirit, then a solid basis for the distinction between baptism and confirmation is established, for baptism into Jesus makes us by adoption what he is naturally: a child of God. The anointing of Jesus with the Spirit was given for his temporal mission of revelation and worship of the Father; clearly, we also need a parallel gift and commissioning, distinct from baptism. This gift and consecration is received in confirmation.

Second, the document recounts the promises of Jesus to his disciples that he would send the Spirit, to help them specifically in their capacity as witnesses (see Lk 12.12; 24.49; Jn 14.16; 15.26; Acts 1.8). To these one might add the passage in which Jesus promises the Spirit to convict the world of sin, justice, and condemnation, and to help the apostles assimilate just what Jesus revealed, not something new and different (see Jn 16.7–15). This passage can reasonably be taken to bear on the apostolic task of assimilating and proclaiming the gospel. Thus, in the promise of the Spirit the orientation is strongly toward the ministry of the followers of Jesus, not simply toward their personal transformation.

Third, the document interprets the Pentecost manifestation as the fulfillment of the promises of Jesus. Those filled with the Spirit proclaim the works of God (see Acts 2.4), and begin to prophesy according to the promise of the messianic age (see Acts 2.17–18). The baptized also received the gift of the Spirit (see Acts 2.38). The document uses a reference to the laying on of hands as distinct from baptism (see Heb 6.2) to support the conclusion that from Pentecost on "the apostles, in fulfillment of Christ's wish, imparted the gift of the Spirit to the newly baptized by the laying on of hands to complete the grace of baptism."[12]

The texts used in this document and its interpretation of them provide a scriptural basis for the judgment that the sacrament of confirmation was instituted by Jesus when he promised the gift of the Spirit, that this sacrament was administered by the apostles from Pentecost on, and that confirmation always has been distinct from baptism.

The Pentecost manifestation is the central event narrated in the New Testament relevant to confirmation, for although the existence and distinctness of the sacrament is not established by the narrative of this event, the sacrament's substance is the gift of the Holy Spirit for the proclamation of the gospel, which begins with Pentecost. A footnote in the *New American Bible* (on Acts 2.1–41) calls in question the historicity of the Pentecost manifestation: "It is likely that the narrative telescopes events that took place over a period of time and on a less dramatic scale. The Twelve were not originally in a position to proclaim publicly the messianic office of Jesus without incurring immediate reprisal from those religious authorities in Jerusalem who had encompassed Jesus' death precisely to stem the rising tide in his favor; cf. Jn 11.47f. Once the 'new covenant' had acquired many adherents, public teaching could more easily be undertaken." But according to the narrative, the public proclamation was made at once, and "there were added that day about three thousand souls" (Acts 2.41).

Had the apostles not received the gift of the Spirit or had they lost this gift due to infidelity, then undoubtedly they would have reasoned that they could not carry out the mandate of Jesus to proclaim his gospel without immediately incurring reprisal from the religious authorities in Jerusalem who had brought about his death. But they did receive the gift of the Spirit and they were faithful. So why doubt that they considered themselves to be in a position to carry out Jesus' mandate, and that they explained the Pentecost manifestation along the lines narrated? The authorities, who had some difficulty securing Roman authorization and cooperation in the execution of Jesus (see Jn 18.28–19.22), doubtless found Pilate unwilling to do additional crucifixions in an effort to stem a movement which to him probably seemed more religious intoxication than political insurgence.[13]

Notes

1. See *The Rites of the Catholic Church*, trans. The International Commission on English in the Liturgy (New York: Pueblo, 1976), 296.

2. See Austin P. Milner, O.P., *Theology of Confirmation*, Theology Today, 26 (Hales Corners, Wis.: Clergy Book Service, 1972), 98–99.

3. Ibid., 70–73.

4. Ibid., 101.

5. *The Rites*, 194 and 324.

6. See Jacques Guillet et al., *Discernment of Spirits* (Collegeville, Minn: Liturgical Press, 1970), 44–53; National Conference of Catholic Bishops, *Statement on Charismatic Renewal* (Washington, D.C.: United States Catholic Conference, 1975), 1–3; St. Ignatius Loyola, *The Spiritual Exercises*, trans. Lewis Delmage, S.J., (New York: Joseph F. Wagner, 1968), 152–64. It is easy to make too much of discernment as conceived by Ignatius, who clearly assumes that all issues of right and wrong have been settled prior to this process.

7. For a sound theological treatment of the saints: Paul Molinari, S.J., *Saints: Their Place in the Church* (New York: Sheed and Ward, 1965). A remarkable work of lay theology by a leader of the charismatic renewal: Judith Tydings, *Gathering a People: Catholic Saints in Charismatic Perspective* (Plainfield, N.J.: Logos International, 1977).

8. *The Rites*, 298.

9. Ibid., 291–92.

10. Ibid., 307.

11. Ibid., 291–92.

12. Ibid., 292.

13. Someone who rejects this line of argument will, if consistent, reject the historicity of chapter four of Acts; once this is done, there will be no good reason to consider any part of the book anything but fabrication. Denial of the historicity of Acts will leave Christianity emerging at some later time with inexplicable vitality and momentum.

CHAPTER THIRTY-TWO

PENANCE, ANOINTING, AND THE LIFE OF SELF-DENIAL

Introduction

Vatican II favors the metaphor of Christian life as a pilgrimage. Christians follow Jesus' path through trials, oppression, suffering, and endurance to glory (see LG 7). The Church as a whole is like a pilgrim in an alien country, pressing on despite persecution, consoled by God, proclaiming Jesus, overcoming obstacles by the Spirit's power, faithfully revealing Jesus' truth and love until he comes in glory (see LG 8 and 9). The goal of the Church's pilgrimage is heavenly fulfillment, and only in this perspective can she be understood (see LG 48). Even the obligation to cultivate human goods in this world is grounded in the more fundamental Christian obligation to seek heavenly things (see GS 38, 57).

This pilgrimage by the Church and each of her members is a hard journey. Its successful completion is a certainty for the Church, but that is not necessarily the case for us individually. Disaster is possible. One can die along the way. And, regardless of what else happens, the day of the Lord is coming, a day of judgment which can spell doom (see LG 48). Eternal salvation is at stake at every moment of one's earthly pilgrimage. Each Christian must work out his or her personal salvation in fear and trembling (see Phil 2.12).

Despite the clear teaching of Vatican II, the passing character of this life and the reality of heaven and hell have in practice been deemphasized and sometimes ignored since the Council. Much attention—rightly—goes to faith and hope. But there is a tendency to pass over the need to build a life of Christian performance on a sound foundation of living faith. The teaching of the Council of Trent, that every Catholic "ought to keep severity and judgment in view as well as mercy and goodness" and none should acquit himself or herself (DS 1549/810; cf. Rom 2.4–11), receives scant acknowledgment in preaching and religious instruction, which frequently are one-sided at best.

In fact, however, the way of the Lord Jesus, the pilgrimage of Christian life, must be a way of self-denial. This is necessary for us not only as it was for him—to make up for the sins of others—but to make up for our own sins, to heal the effects of sin in ourselves, to strengthen ourselves for a more adequate effort, to free ourselves from all that holds us back on our journey. The sacraments of penance and anointing of the sick organize Christian life from this point of view.

Old Testament experience was shaped by the seemingly endless journey of God's people traveling toward their promised homeland. It began with Abraham, who was called by God to leave his home. He responded with faith. His traveling, like that of others called by God, was symbolic: "These all died in faith, not having received what was promised, but having seen it and greeted it from afar, and having acknowledged that they were strangers and exiles on the earth. For people who speak thus make it clear that they are seeking a homeland. If they had been thinking of that land from which they had gone out, they would have had opportunity to return. But as it is, they desire a better country, that is, a heavenly one. Therefore God is not ashamed to be called their God, for he has prepared for them a city" (Heb 11.13–16). Detaching themselves from what had seemed secure, God's people always were compelled to move on. Christians, too, must leave everything behind to follow Jesus and in him find fulfillment. To be a Christian is to be a member of a people perpetually on pilgrimage. Thus the injunction: "Set your minds on things that are above, not on things that are on earth" (Col 3.2).

For many people in the West, life has been comparatively comfortable since World War II. Pilgrimage means little in the jet age, especially if the world's troubles have little personal impact. Catholics must remember that the journey to heaven will be hard, obstacles must be overcome, much which is good must be left behind, the sacrifices to be made and the sufferings to be endured cannot be limited in advance, there is no insurance against the cross, the worldly environment through which we travel is hostile and can be seductive, and the Church is not a vehicle to spare her members the hardships of travel by transporting them while they sleep.

Perseverance is necessary, and a special grace is required for it (see DS 1572/832; *S.t.*, 1–2, q. 109, a. 10). This gift will be given to those who are faithful to the graces they receive. Yet we must be careful. Trent teaches that salvation is worked out not only in fear and trembling, but "in labors, in sleepless nights, in almsgiving, in prayers and offerings, in fastings, and in chastity"; Christians "should be in dread about the battle they must wage with the flesh, the world, and the devil" (DS 1541/806).

Question A: Why is the sacrament of penance necessary?

1. The Catholic Church definitively teaches that the sacrament of penance is necessary for those who commit mortal sin after baptism (see DS 1579/839, 1668/894).

2. Still, in order to be forgiven, is it not sufficient to be genuinely sorry for sin out of love of God, even apart from the sacrament? Trent "teaches that, although it does sometimes happen that this contrition is made perfect through charity and reconciles man to God before the sacrament is actually received, nevertheless the reconciliation must not be attributed to contrition exclusive of the desire for the sacrament included in the contrition" (DS 1677/898). In other words, some sort of desire for the sacrament is necessary for perfect contrition (see *S.t.*, sup., q. 1, a. 1; q. 6, a. 1; *S.c.g.*, 4, 72).[1]

3. The essential parts of the sacrament are the acts of contrition, confession, and satisfaction on the part of the penitent and the act of absolution on the part of the minister (see DS 1673/896). Absolution is the wiping out of sin; the bonds which held the sinner fall away. "The complete effect of this sacrament, so far as its full efficaciousness is concerned, is reconciliation with God, which, in devout men who receive the sacrament with devotion, is sometimes followed by peace

and serenity of conscience joined to a great consolation of soul" (DS 1674/896).

4. Although the sacrament of penance is similar to baptism in overcoming sin and conferring divine life, it is not simply a repetition of baptism. These sacraments differ in important ways.

Conversion, contrition, repentance, turning toward God—all the same thing—is not once and for all. If we sin mortally after baptism, a new and radical conversion is again needed. But even if we do not sin mortally, venial sins detract from friendship with God. Thus, continuing repentance is essential in every Christian life (see Rom 6.12–14; Eph 4.20–24; Col 3.1–17).

God desires the reconciliation of sinners. He does not wish any soul to be lost (see Mt 18.10–14; Lk 15.3–7). If we are faithful to Jesus, we will enjoy glory with him; if we are unfaithful, he will disown us, for he is faithful even when we are unfaithful. He keeps his promises even when we do not; he constantly seeks our free surrender to his love (see 2 Tm 2.11–13). For this reason, Jesus gave his Church the power to bind and loose. The Church from the beginning used this power to rescue sinners (see Mt 16.15–19; 18.15–18; Jn 20.22–23; 1 Cor 5.1–5; 2 Cor 2.5–11).

5. Repentance for grave sin committed after baptism requires not only that one give up one's sins and detest them (this is required also by baptism) but that one make, or at least in some way desire to make, a sacramental confession and receive the absolution of a priest. Moreover, the newly baptized person is freed by baptism not only from the guilt of sin but from all temporal punishment due to it; but those who receive forgiveness in the sacrament of penance are still obliged to do something by way of satisfaction for their sins (see DS 1542/807; *S.t.*, 3, q. 90, aæ. 2–3).

6. The requirement that grave sins be confessed gives this sacrament an essentially judicial character. The sinner stands trial, as it were—although pardon is guaranteed, provided the right dispositions are present. The unpleasant act of confessing, together with the need to do penance to satisfy for sin, make the sacrament of penance an arduous way to renew the integrity of baptism (see DS 1671–72/895; FEF 493).

To remit sins subsequent to baptism, it is not sufficient simply to recall one's baptism (see DS 1623/866). The requirement that Christians confess their sins to a priest is clearly taught by many Fathers of the Church: St. Cyprian of Carthage (see FEF 551, 569, 570), Aphraates the Persian Sage (see FEF 685), St. John Chrysostom (see FEF 1165, 1169), St. Ambrose (see FEF 1298), St. Augustine (see FEF 1480a), St. Cyril of Alexandria (see FEF 2121), and St. Leo the Great (cf. FEF 2184b).

Worthy reception of the Eucharist requires that those who have committed a mortal sin receive sacramental penance before receiving Holy Communion, unless they do not have access to a confessor and must celebrate Mass or participate in the Eucharist. A priest who celebrates Mass without having confessed should confess as soon as he can (see DS 1646–47/880, 1661/893).

During his life on earth, Jesus often showed his power to forgive sins (see Lk 5.18–26; 7.36–50). When he handed over his saving work to the apostles after his resurrection, he gave them the sacrament of penance as a means by which they might apply the merit of his death for the forgiveness of sin committed after baptism (see DS 1668/894).

The Catholic Church definitively teaches (DS 1670/894) that Jesus instituted the sacrament of penance when he said: "Receive the Holy Spirit. If you forgive the sins of any, they are forgiven; if you retain the sins of any, they are retained" (Jn 20.22–23). Some deny that Jesus instituted the sacrament of penance by this conferral of authority. However, the binding and loosing referred to in the passage quoted is involved in no other centrally important act of the Church—certainly not in baptism, where no judicial act is required.[2]

7. Still, why is it not enough to seek reconciliation with God in one's heart? The answer lies in the ecclesial aspect of sin and the sacrament of penance mentioned by Vatican II: "Those who approach the sacrament of penance obtain pardon from the mercy of God for offenses committed against him. They are at the same time reconciled with the Church, which they have wounded by their sins, and which by charity, example, and prayer seeks their conversion" (LG 11). Christians are not united to God in a purely spiritual way and as isolated individuals. Union with him comes about in the Church, through socially structured, visible actions. Sin, however, disrupts one's relationship with the Church, as well as with God. **Reconciliation therefore requires that the sinner be restored to God by being humanly reconciled with the Church. The sacrament of penance's human encounter and judicial aspect are indispensable to this human reconciliation** (see *S.t.*, 3, q. 90, a. 2; sup., q. 6, a. 1; *S.c.g.*, 4, 72).[3]

The ecclesial significance of mortal sin was discussed earlier (16-G). Corresponding to the ecclesial significance of sin is the ecclesial dimension of the sacrament of penance. The ancient Gelasian Sacramentary provides a formula for reconciliation which makes clear this aspect of the sacrament. The bishop prays: "Bestow, we beseech you, O Lord, on this your servant, fruit worthy of penance, that by obtaining pardon for the sins he has admitted, he may be restored unharmed to your holy Church, from whose wholeness he has strayed by sinning."[4]

The *Introduction* to the new rite of penance expands upon the ecclesial aspect of this sacrament: "'By the hidden and loving mystery of God's design men are joined together in the bonds of supernatural solidarity, so much so that the sin of one harms the others just as the holiness of one benefits the others' [reference omitted]. Penance always entails reconciliation with our brothers and sisters who are always harmed by our sins. In fact, men frequently join together to commit injustice. It is thus only fitting that they should help each other in doing penance so that they who are freed from sin by the grace of Christ may work with all men of good will for justice and peace in the world."[5] By mortal sin, one is unfaithful not only to God but to the Church. That is why the mortal sinner is excluded from Holy Communion. The absolution of the sacrament of penance readmits the sinner into perfect communion with the Church and by this very fact brings the sinner back to friendship with God.

The Church definitively teaches that to obtain remission of sins, confession of each and every mortal sin found during diligent self-examination is required by divine law (see DS 1707/917).[6] Also, the Church definitively insists that such confession is not impossible and that the requirement of it is no mere human tradition (see DS 1708/918).

The requirement of integral confession of sins in kind and number is implicit in the character of absolution, which is a judicial act in which the Church's power to bind and loose is exercised by pardoning the sinner. The judgment cannot be rendered without a statement of the case. Nor can appropriate penances be imposed if sins are not manifested (see DS 1679/899). All mortal sins, including the circumstances which alter their kind and seriousness, must be confessed. Venial sins need not but may be confessed (see DS 1680–81/899). Confessing one's sins seems burdensome but the burden is lightened for those who

768

receive the sacrament worthily by the great benefits received with absolution and also by confidence in the secrecy of the confessional (see DS 1682–83/900–901).

In any human interpersonal relationship, a sincere and open admission of wrongdoing, by its very difficulty for the one who makes it, goes some way toward making up for the wrong done; so in the sacrament of penance, honest and complete confession of sin by one truly contrite is itself a penitential act of considerable value. There is a tendency to evade the requirement of detailed, integral confession of sins. The likelihood that self-deception is involved should not be overlooked. One generally not only is embarrassed to speak openly of one's sins, but also is reluctant to make a perfectly clean break with them. If integral confession were not required, many of us would limit and so corrupt our contrition, thus settling for a feeling of repentance without its reality.

Question B: What is the contrition required for the sacrament of penance?

1. The Church has given a clear definition of contrition, precisely as an act of the recipient of the sacrament of penance. Trent teaches: "Contrition, which ranks first among these acts of the penitent, is sorrow and detestation for sin committed, with a resolution of sinning no more. Moreover, this spirit of contrition has always been necessary to obtain the forgiveness of sin, and thus, in the case of a man who has fallen after baptism, it is certainly a preparation for the remission of sins, if it be accompanied by trust in the divine mercy and a firm desire of fulfilling the other conditions necessary to receive the sacrament properly. Therefore, this holy council declares that this contrition implies not only abandoning sin and determining to lead a new life and beginning to do so, but also hating one's past life . . ." (DS 1676/897; translation amended). True contrition is the basic act of the penitent.

2. **Contrition includes within itself a firm purpose of amendment and the utter rejection of past sin. It requires a sincere intention to fulfill all the other conditions for the sacrament's worthy reception.** Lacking this intention, contrition is not sincere, and any feeling of sorrow is useless. Still, contrition does not by itself remit sins; of itself it is a preparation for the forgiveness of sins (see *S.t.*, 3, q. 85, aa. 1–3; q. 90, a. 2; sup., q. 1, aa. 1–2; q. 5, aa. 1–3; *S.c.g.*, 4, 72).

The *Introduction* to the new rite of penance stresses the need for sincere contrition. After quoting Trent's definition of it, the document goes on to identify contrition with conversion or repentance (*metanoia*): "a profound change of the whole person by which one begins to consider, judge, and arrange his life according to the holiness and love of God . . . ." Further: "The genuineness of penance depends on this heartfelt contrition. For conversion should affect a person from within so that it may progressively enlighten him and render him continually more like Christ.'"

3. **Trent teaches that a sorrow for sin based on awareness of its evil and fear of punishment, which includes the intention to amend, is a divine gift which leads sinners to grace by disposing them to seek forgiveness in the sacrament of penance.** Of itself, this type of contrition is not perfected by charity, and so it is called "imperfect contrition" or "attrition" (DS 1678/898, 1705/915).[8] Catholic theologians have long debated whether imperfect contrition which does not include as a motive love of God for his own sake is sufficient within

the sacrament of penance. This controversy was explicitly left open by a decree of the Holy See (see DS 2070/1146).

4. St. Thomas Aquinas takes the very reasonable position that genuine contrition and the conferral of charity are mutually dependent; a mortal sinner cannot love God as his child should without becoming contrite and cannot become contrite without again loving God as his child. The two things come together by the conjoining of God's grace and the sinner's free response which this grace creates. This can happen before the sacrament is received or when it is received, provided one approaches the sacrament with the right intentions (see *S.c.g.*, 4, 72; *S.t.*, sup., q. 1, a. 1; q. 5, a. 1, ad 2; q. 6, a. 1; q. 10, a. 3).

5. Reflecting on the issue, it seems obvious that a penitent must believe and hope in God. It is impossible to approach this sacrament with serious intentions without being confident that God acts in it and is ready to do everything necessary to restore one to grace. One must also have rejected sin and must desire to do what is right. In this desire, there is an at least implicit human love of God as the source of all good.

6. However, such love is not identical with charity. The latter is not a human act and experience but a divine gift (25-G). Although it does not seem possible to determine the precise moment at which this gift is conferred again on those who have committed mortal sin, the teaching on the sacrament of penance does make it clear that it is restored to those who receive the sacrament worthily at least as soon as absolution is administered.

7. If the preceding is correct, perfect contrition, by which one again begins to live as a child of God out of love of him, is not psychologically recognizable. Before receiving the sacrament one cannot be certain of having made an "act of perfect contrition"; one can only know with moral certitude that one is truly contrite for motives which are not purely selfish. One can know that one desires to submit wholly to God.

Question C: What does it mean to do penance for sin?

1. According to Catholic teaching on the sacrament of penance, even forgiven sin deserves some punishment (see DS 1689/904). Being sorry and being forgiven are not enough; something must be done to undo sin's existential consequences. Trent teaches that it belongs to God's mercy not to waive all punishment when he forgives sins. For in making satisfaction, a sinner learns the seriousness of sin, is deterred from future sin, healed of the self-mutilation of sin by acts of virtue, and overcomes the bad habits acquired in living sinfully (see DS 1690/904).

2. Thus the punishment required for forgiven sin should not be thought of as an evil which God imposes to get even with the sinner. It is, rather, a way of repairing the damages caused by wrongdoing. Mortal sin is a betrayal of the Church and a sort of adultery against God. Besides being sorry and being restored to communion, one must work to regain one's spiritual health and make up for the damage to the relationship (see *S.t.*, 3, q. 86, a. 4; sup., q. 12, a. 3).

The situation is like that of a man who has committed adultery, repented, and been forgiven. It still is necessary that by more generous love he give his wife more of himself to make up to her for that of himself which he wrongfully took from her (see *S.t.*, sup., q. 15, a. 1). The repentant adulterous husband must try to compensate in happiness for the misery he has caused. So we with God. Although God is neither hurt nor pleased by us in a merely human way, still our relationship does matter to him, and when we are unfaithful, we need to make amends.

3. In making reparation or satisfaction for our sins we are made like Jesus, who satisfied for our sins (see *S.t.*, 3, q. 49, a. 1; q. 62, a. 5; sup., q. 13). The reparation we make is not independent, isolated; it is made through him, for of ourselves we can do nothing (see DS 1689–91/904). But through Jesus, our satisfaction for sin is a real contribution to our own sanctification. In making this contribution, the sinner, degraded by sin, is ennobled. Thus the grace of God is the greater in not only forgiving the sin but ennobling the sinner into the likeness of Jesus.

4. **In sum, satisfaction for sin belongs to the sacrament of penance, and a "penance" is imposed for this purpose** (see DS 1692/905). **This, however, is only a token of the will to make reparation; above and beyond this token, all the repentant sinner suffers in life and accepts from God can serve as penance** (see DS 1693/906 *S.t.*, sup., q. 15, a. 2). The confessor may appropriately conclude the sacramental rite by praying that the passion of Christ, the intercession of Mary, and "whatever good you do and suffering you endure, heal your sins, help you to grow in holiness, and reward you with eternal life."[9]

Question D: How can the sacrament of penance be a principle of the whole of a Christian's life?

1. **The sacrament of penance plainly is a vital principle for the Christian lives of those who commit mortal sins.** But this function does not make it a principle of the whole of every Christian's life. However, this sacrament also is an apt way of overcoming venial sin. **Because venial sin is pervasive, in this function the sacrament can organize the whole of a Christian's life.** The present question will show how this is possible and even, in a certain sense, necessary. Questions E and F will treat two important aspects of the penitential ordering of Christian life.

2. Venial sins are of many sorts. Some involve grave matter but fall short of mortal sin because of defects in reflection or consent. Others are unknown faults, defects in voluntariness other than wrong choice (9-G). Yet all venial sins are real moral evils—privations in one's willing. Venial sins which involve morally wrong choices are, as it were, little secondary selves, morally split from one's better Christian self. Venial sins of other sorts are fragments of some such little self, somehow surviving as a parasite on one's Christian self.

3. Faith is the fundamental option of Christian life (16-G). Unlike mortal sins, venial sins do not violate specific requirements implied by this fundamental option. Still, they really deprive the Christian personality of perfect integration with living faith. Hence, they weaken the effectiveness of faith as a fundamental option and render its supremacy in life less absolute than it ought to be. The coexistence of living faith with venial sin is uneasy. If one deliberately persists in

venial sins, one will be likely to commit more serious sins (18-C). Thus, it is important that a Christian make faith fully effective as a fundamental option by treating venial sin of all sorts as a threatening evil to be overcome.

4. This struggle against venial sin is a strict requirement of Christian life, not something optional. It is demanded by the sixth mode of Christian response which inclines one to a devout life of striving toward single-mindedness or purity of heart (26-I). Although perfect love of God—love with one's whole mind, heart, soul, and strength—is an ideal, all Christians are called to work toward this perfection (27-E). This is so because Christian life means following Jesus by cooperating in his redemptive work, not least as it bears upon oneself.

5. While venial sins can be forgiven apart from the sacrament of penance, in time the confession of devotion became common for those seriously striving for perfection. This practice was attacked during the Reformation and vindicated by the definitive teaching of the Council of Trent, which commends it as a proper and advantageous practice of devout persons (see DS 1680/899, 1707/917).[10]

6. While acknowledging that venial sins can be expiated in other ways, Pius XII strongly commends use of the sacrament of penance: "But to ensure more rapid progress day by day in the path of virtue, We will that the pious practice of frequent confession, which was introduced into the Church by the inspiration of the Holy Spirit, should be earnestly advocated. By it genuine self-knowledge is increased, Christian humility grows, bad habits are corrected, spiritual neglect and tepidity are resisted, the conscience is purified, the will strengthened, a salutary self-control is attained, and grace is increased in virtue of the Sacrament itself."[11] Pope Pius considers opinions which tend to discourage frequent confession "most dangerous to the spiritual life."[12] In the context of an exhortation to clerics, but without limiting his statement to them, John XXIII recalls Pope Pius' teaching on this matter and says parenthetically that the pious practice of frequent confession is "necessary to the attainment of sanctity."[13]

7. Since Vatican II, the sacrament of penance often has been called "the sacrament of reconciliation." Reconciliation most properly is the restoration of mortal sinners to divine friendship and ecclesial communion. To speak of the sacrament as effecting reconciliation might therefore seem to suggest that its use to overcome venial sin is not appropriate. However, as was explained above, venial sin also is a real evil, which requires repentance and is healed only by God's mercy. While the better self of a Christian guilty only of venial sin need not be reconciled with God and the Church, his or her alienated, little, fragmentary selves need to be reconciled with God, the Church, and the better self of living faith. The *Introduction* to the new rite of penance makes it clear that the traditional practice is appropriate. Frequent confession of devotion "is not a mere ritual repetition or psychological exercise, but a serious striving to perfect the grace of baptism."[14]

8. John Paul II considers the Eucharist and penance together: "two closely connected dimensions of authentic life in accordance with the spirit of the Gospel, of truly Christian life." Without constant conversion the Eucharist is deprived of its full redeeming effectiveness, while communion with Jesus' perfect self-

oblation in the Eucharist arouses "the need to turn to God in an ever more mature way and with a constant, ever more profound, conversion." Pope John Paul also declares that Christ has a right to encounter sacramentally "each one of us in that key moment of conversion and forgiveness. By guarding and affirming the sacrament of Penance, the Church expressly affirms her faith in the mystery of the Redemption as a living and life-giving reality that fits in with man's inward truth, with human guilt and also with the desires of the human conscience."[15]

9. Theological reflection easily clarifies the reasons for the Church's strong encouragement of the use of the sacrament of penance to overcome venial sin. The sacraments' value is in making it possible for human persons to cooperate fittingly and consciously in their own redemption and that of others (30-B). The context of Pius XII's teaching on devotional confession is a warning against quietism, which leaves everything in Christian life to God's action and nothing to ours. Grace is primary, but Christians "should strive to reach the heights of Christian perfection and at the same time to the best of their power should stimulate others to attain the same goal,—all this the heavenly Spirit does not will to effect unless they contribute their daily share of zealous activity."[16] As a divinely given mode of cooperation with the grace of the Holy Spirit, the sacrament of penance most fittingly enables Christians to strive for their own perfection while making it clear that everything they achieve, including this very effort itself, is entirely the result of God's grace.

10. Moreover, sacramental penance is explicit and conscious cooperation with Jesus' redemptive act as it bears upon the recipient's own self. As John Paul II explains, the sacrament affords "a more personal encounter with the crucified forgiving Christ, with Christ saying, through the minister of the sacrament of Reconciliation: 'Your sins are forgiven'; 'Go and do not sin again.'"[17] Then too, in the sacrament the penitent sensibly experiences redemption: "In this sacrament each person can experience mercy in a unique way, that is, the love which is more powerful than sin."[18]

11. Furthermore, Christian life is not a lonely struggle for a sanctity which concerns only oneself. The entire life of faith is a life of membership in the Church. But even venial sin lessens the Church's vitality and stunts the fruitfulness she deserves of her members. The devotional use of the sacrament of penance responds perfectly to this reality. Confessing venial sins acknowledges their ecclesial dimension, and the Church herself forgives them by giving absolution through her ordained minister. More perfectly a member of the Church, the absolved sinner benefits more richly from the limitless and unending atoning power of Jesus. This power, present in the Church, is made available in the sacrament and has a lasting effect on the life of the penitent.[19]

12. The sacramental act of the recipient gains added value insofar as it is an act of liturgical worship. The practice of sacramental penance also has a unique revelatory value, for it manifests God's mercy and proclaims the Spirit's power to sanctify those who make faith in Jesus their fundamental option. In sum, the work of overcoming venial sin by frequent use of the sacrament of penance is a different and far richer Christian act than any other suited to this obligatory task.

13. In addition, the devotional use of the sacrament of penance has certain advantages which might be attained otherwise but in practice often are not. One's work toward perfection is likely to be more systematic and persistent if one receives the sacrament frequently. The sacrament also provides a context for individual spiritual direction, which is helpful for progress toward perfection. These incidental advantages partly explain the good effects of regular use of the sacrament pointed out by Pius XII.[20]

14. When Christians begin to strive for holiness, venial sin is pervasive in their lives. Much of this sin is not recognized as such; much of it consists of unknown faults. These defects impair the fundamental option of living faith and all other Christian commitments. As sin is gradually overcome, these commitments are reaffirmed over and over; they become purer and firmer by excluding more and more wrong options. Thus the sanctified personality of the Christian permanently bears in its healed wounds the marks of Jesus' cross and God's love. Because faith and the commitments which implement it shape one's entire Christian life, in perfecting these commitments the sacrament of penance becomes a principle of the whole of Christian life.

Question E: How does avoiding the occasions of sin contribute to the penitential ordering of Christian life?

1. One who repents mortal sins must avoid their occasions, because contrition requires a purpose of amendment, and a real purpose of amendment includes the will to avoid occasions of sin. But all who wish to live a Christian life must try to avoid occasions of sin. As the preceding question made clear, one must strive to avoid venial sin, and any failure to avoid an occasion of mortal sin will be at least a venial sin.

2. An occasion of sin is usually defined as any person, place, or thing likely to lead one into sin. This is not mistaken, but it is less helpful than it might be. In the first place, occasions of sin generally are considered only when grave matter is in question and the problem is how to avoid mortal sin. (Only this kind of case will be considered here, but what is said can be adapted to avoiding temptations to commit venial sins, such as habitual wasting of time, spontaneous cursing, angry shouting at the children, and so forth.) Furthermore, it is not so much persons, places, and things which are occasions of sins as one's relationship to them and what one does in respect to them.

3. Thus, an occasion of sin might better be defined as follows: It is a situation or action which in any way conduces to sin and which one can avoid or modify so that one will be less likely to be tempted to commit mortal sin or able more easily to overcome the temptation if it arises.

4. Some occasions of sin are situations. Living in a neighborhood where there are many homosexuals is an occasion of sin for someone with a homosexual disposition. Belonging to a club whose members for the most part reject Christian standards is an occasion of sin. Owning the means to commit sin is often an occasion of sin. Great wealth provides many opportunities for sins which poor

people and those of moderate means do not have; wealthy people thus live in an occasion of sin by the very fact of their wealth.

5. Other occasions of sin are actions. Working as a large-claims insurance adjustor is an occasion of sin, for parties to such business often exert pressure or offer bribes to obtain gravely unjust settlements. Hearing confessions is an occasion of sin for a priest, since, for example, he may be tempted by sympathy to compromise Christ's teaching. Glancing at the "entertainment" section of a newspaper can be an occasion of sin for someone addicted to pornography. Talking one's feelings over with someone to whom one is inappropriately attracted is often an occasion of sin, since it is likely to lead to a deepening of the relationship.

6. Some occasions of sin can be avoided entirely. A person whose job provides many opportunities to steal and who is tempted to do so may be able to find another job. A person can refrain from talking about his or her feelings toward other people when such talk may create the need to choose whether to sin or not. A person with a contraceptive device can dispose of it. Rich people can sell their possessions and give the money to the poor.

7. Other occasions of sin cannot be avoided entirely, but they can be modified. This can be done in two different ways: modification in the situation or action as it objectively exists or is done, and modification of the context or meaning of the situation, largely through taking a different stance toward it and/or thinking differently about it.

Suppose, for example, that an alcoholic finds it an occasion of sin to go to a party where drinks are served but cannot avoid being there. ("Cannot" here might be taken in the weak sense; avoiding company where drinks are served often is not possible in the sense that it is incompatible with some other responsibility.) Still, the alcoholic can modify this situation objectively, by ordering a nonalcoholic beverage which looks like a drink. He or she can also provide a modified context for the situation—for instance, by discussing it beforehand with a member of his or her Alcoholics Anonymous chapter.

8. Carried out conscientiously, the avoidance of occasions of sin will organize the whole of each Christian's life. **Major commitments will be made with the need always in view to avoid or modify occasions of sin. Moreover, since no one can conform to the accepted practices of a post-Christian culture without being constantly subject to occasions of sin, all who wish to follow Jesus must refuse to conform to these practices in many obvious ways.**

9. In sum, the avoidance of occasions of sin should shape the whole of each Christian's life, and this necessary task pertains to the sacrament of penance. Hence, constant effort to avoid sin's occasions can contribute to the ordering of Christian life by this sacrament.

Work on occasions of sin is a strict and grave moral obligation. This work cannot be precisely defined and limited; one must begin where one can and constantly expand the field of battle. Creative ingenuity is required for this process, and confessors must try to acquire this virtue.

In quasi-compulsive sins of weakness, the problem is to discover and avoid situations and actions which are avoidable and are associated with the beginning of temptation, and to modify various unavoidable situations and actions. Those told simply to avoid occasions of sin are likely to notice many unavoidable actions which are somehow conditions conducive to sin, but to overlook certain avoidable actions which regularly precede and initiate temptation.

This "overlooking" probably has a subconscious cause: If the sinner attended to these actions and avoided them as occasions of sin, then temptation would not occur and the satisfaction of the sinful behavior could not be obtained. Subconsciously, this satisfaction is desired even by a person whose conscious purpose of amendment is authentic and firm. Consequently, the sinner has a presentiment of rising emotion and could still resist by evasion, but does not. Instead, the action which is the immediate occasion of the temptation is done instead of avoided, emotion mounts, and the sin of weakness is committed again.

Question F: How does reparation for sin contribute to the penitential ordering of Christian life?

1. As question C explained, doing penance—that is, making reparation for sin—is an essential part of the sacrament of penance. One who has injured another by unfaithfulness and then been reconciled can best make up for the offense by whatever self-denial is needed to assure, so far as possible, that the offense will not be repeated. Thus, a determined effort to deal with occasions of sin is an especially suitable expression of penitential love of God.

2. Not only the self-denial involved in avoiding occasions of sin, but all forms of self-denial can serve as reparation. Since self-denial is required throughout Christian life, its penitential significance is another way in which the sacrament of penance can be a principle of the whole of Christian life. (The explanation of this point will help to clarify the significance of the prayer quoted at the end of question C above.)[21]

Christian self-denial does not mean despising or rejecting created goods insofar as they are goods. It flows from the insight that all human activity is infected by sin, that progress means the healing of this infection, and that healing sometimes requires radical surgery and involves unpleasant medicine: "Hence if anyone wants to know how this unhappy situation can be overcome, Christians will tell him that all human activity, constantly imperiled by man's pride and deranged self-love, must be purified and perfected by the power of Christ's cross and resurrection. For, redeemed by Christ and made a new creature in the Holy Spirit, man is able to love the things themselves created by God, and ought to do so" (GS 37). Thus all of one's life must be purged of the effects of sin.

3. "Self-denial" has various meanings. It can refer to detachment, moral practice, mortification, and resignation.

4. Detachment is the surrender of any interest, desire, or objective which would keep one from using all one's time, energy, and resources to love God and neighbor. It is self-liberation for service. To do everything for God's glory and in Jesus' name (see 1 Cor 10.31; Col 3.17) it is necessary to set aside any relationship, possession, or power which interferes with total dedication. Detachment was treated previously as one of the basic modes of Christian response (26-F).

5. Moral practice, asceticism in the strict sense, is a matter of doing good works which one would not choose for their own sake but which are done for practice or training, so that one can do other, more difficult good works when the

responsibilities of Christian life require them. The metaphors of pursuing a prize in a race and of training for war (see 1 Cor 9.24–27; Eph 6.10–17; Phil 1.27; 3.8–16; 1 Tm 4.7–10) suggest the model of asceticism in its narrow sense: arduous practice which trains one to resist temptations to sins of sensory gratification.

6. Mortification is the putting to death of sin so that one can fully live for goodness in Christ (see Rom 6.6–23; Gal 5.24). Physical practices are appropriate for this purpose, but so are spiritual forms of mortification. When one speaks of mortification, what is usually in question is an especially determined and systematic campaign against sin, not only mortal sin but venial sin. From a positive viewpoint, mortification is vivification; it is the use of every ability and part of oneself to contribute to fulfillment in Christ (see DS 1535/803). Mortification pertains to Christian devotion, treated previously (26-I).

7. Resignation is acceptance, out of love of God, of the evil that befalls one, insofar as every such occurrence must have been permitted by God, directed to some good by his wise and loving providence, and intended as a challenge to one's ingenuity or patience. When Christian, transforming love cannot at once heal an evil, it is the work of resignation simply to endure it patiently. This is especially necessary in regard to incurable suffering and death. Resignation is an aspect of Christian dedication and meekness, treated previously (26-E). As will be explained below, it is especially related to the sacrament of anointing of the sick.

8. Although the various aspects of Christian self-denial can be distinguished in this way, they are in fact closely related. The Christian's sharing in the cross of Jesus embraces all of them: "If any man would come after me, let him deny himself and take up his cross and follow me" (Mk 8.34; cf. Mt 16.24–28; Lk 9. 23–27).

9. Like Jesus, each Christian must live a life detached from many good things which would interfere with holiness and witness, must engage in moral practice, must accept suffering, death, and other evils with submission to God's will. Even if a person never committed a personal sin, self-denial in these forms would be necessary in Christian life. Like Jesus and Mary, one still could offer penance for the sins of others (see *S.t.*, sup., q. 13, a. 2). And, to become more like Jesus, we sinners must practice mortification.

10. All the various forms of self-denial are components of the work of penance for us who have an obligation to make up for our own sins. Detachment, asceticism, mortification, and resignation undo the moral effects of one's sins by reversing the subordination of love to self-assertion and submitting one's whole self to the requirements of love.

The situation can be clarified by the analogy of the adulterous husband. Even a faithful husband must give up some personal satisfactions for the sake of marriage, avoid the occasions of adultery, accept his wife's limitations, and so on. But an unfaithful, repentant, and reconciled husband must do all these things more generously and more thoroughly, if the marital relationship is to be restored to its full confidence and affection. Similarly, the repentant Christian must practice all the forms of self-denial and self-giving appropriate in Christian life, but now as forms of penance.

11. **Because no good act of the Christian can be done without self-denial of some kind and to some degree, and because every act of self-denial becomes**

part of reparation for the penitent Christian, every good act of Christian life is ordered to a penitential life. Insofar as doing penance is part of the sacrament of penance, the sacrament effects this ordering for those who receive forgiveness in it.

The suffering of tribulations as a condition for the coming of the kingdom was proclaimed in the Old Testament, for example, in Daniel. Thus Christians were not surprised by their sufferings (see Lk 24.26; Acts 14.22; 17.3; 1 Thes 1.6; 2.14–15; 3.2–3; 2 Thes 1.3–5; and so on). Suffering with Jesus is a condition of being glorified with him (see Rom 8.17–18; Phil 3.10–11). The apostolic life, to which every Christian is called (31-B), cannot be without suffering (see 2 Cor 4.7–12; Eph 3.1–19; Phil 3.17–19; Col 1.24–29).

The imitation of Jesus is an imitation of his self-denial. It also is an imitation of his endurance unto glory (see Heb 12.1–4). Vatican II teaches that we are made like Christ by baptism. "Still in pilgrimage upon the earth, we trace in trial and under oppression the paths he trod. Made one with his sufferings as the body is one with the head, we endure with him, that with him we may be glorified (cf. Rom 8.17)" (LG 7). The whole of Christian life is a putting on of the new man, created in God's image, and a putting off of the old self, with its illusions and false desires (see Eph 4.17–24).

To share in the divine nature with Jesus is to separate oneself from the corrupt world (see 2 Pt 1.3–11). Faithfulness to our Lord Jesus necessarily means division from others who do not accept him (see Mt 10.34–36; Lk 12.51–53). To sanctify themselves by suffering and to redeem the world, the followers of Jesus are left in the world, to which they do not belong (see Jn 17.15–16). Consecrated to the truth, Christians have God's Word to communicate; for this the unbelieving world inevitably hates them (see Jn 17.14).

Since Jesus' self-denial was entirely for others, we are likely to overlook the extent to which our struggle against our own sin and its consequences within us is a sharing in the passion of Jesus. Yet it is clear that there is an important aspect of Jesus-likeness in this struggle. So there is a great nobility in it which we tend to overlook. Perhaps we forget that as Christians and sinners we are split personalities: victims of our own freedom as sinners, but beneficiaries of God's grace as Christians united with Jesus in a redemptive work which we must carry out—first of all in ourselves.

There is a natural tendency to wish to avoid and forget about this painful, negative aspect of Christianity. One thinks one perhaps ought to be exempted from suffering. But although Jesus loved his mother dearly, he did not prevent her suffering along with himself, as Vatican II teaches: ". . . the Blessed Virgin advanced in her pilgrimage of faith, and loyally persevered in her union with her Son unto the cross. There she stood, in keeping with the divine plan (cf. Jn 19.25), suffering grievously with her only-begotten Son. There she united herself with a maternal heart to his sacrifice, and lovingly consented to the immolation of this Victim which she herself had brought forth" (LG 58).

Surely, the great sorrow any mother naturally feels at the death of her child was increased immeasurably in Mary's case by the following facts: Jesus was her only child; Joseph almost certainly already had died; the relationship between Jesus and Mary was unmarred by selfishness on either side; the killing of Jesus was unjust; the manner of his death was unusually cruel; Mary was present but unable to do anything tangible to help. God did not permit Mary to suffer so much except for the great good of the closeness to Jesus she achieved in this gift of suffering. This good and gift, like everything in Mary, are proposed to us as a model for our own lives.

Question G: What are the primary forms of penance?

1. **Fasting, almsgiving, and prayer were traditionally proposed as the three typical acts of penance** (see Tb 12.8–10; Is 58.3–10). While Jesus condemned abuses in these practices, insisting that they be done in a proper spirit and not for show, he by no means abolished or criticized the practices themselves. Rather, he taught that, done in a proper spirit, they are meritorious, and the Father will reward them (see Mt 6.1–18).

2. It is understandable that Jesus should have commended these three practices (see *S.t.*, sup., q. 15, a. 3). Sin is self-destructive, antisocial, and alienating from God. The self-restraint of fasting makes up to some extent for the destructive self-indulgence of sin; the mercy of almsgiving makes up for the damage done by sin to the Church's communion of love; loving praise of God and petition to him make up for the alienation from God and pride involved in sin.

3. Christian thought has never regarded these penitential practices narrowly or considered them arbitrary and irrational impositions. In keeping watch and praying, for example, one keeps a vigil, that is, denies oneself rest as a means to serve the Lord more perfectly (see Mt 26.36–41; Mk 13.33; Lk 21.36). Again, as St. Leo the Great points out, fasting and almsgiving go together; what one denies oneself is available for the needs of others.[22] **Essentially, then, the classic system of penance is: Give up what might be legitimately claimed as one's own, use it to serve others, and draw nearer to God by prayer.**

4. Paul VI's apostolic constitution on penance, *Paenitemini,* places traditional penance in a contemporary framework. Urging that internal conversion and external penance be closely linked, he makes three points: first, "that everyone practice the virtue of penance by constantly attending to the duties pertaining to his state in life and by patiently enduring the trials of each day's work . . . and the uncertainties of life"; second, that those especially burdened by infirmity, disease, or oppression should offer their misery; and, third, that priests and religious should follow Jesus more closely in his emptying of self.[23]

5. Although the legal obligation to fast and abstain has been considerably reduced by the Church in recent years, the obligation still exists, and, in any case, fasting and abstaining remain a highly relevant form of penance. Pope Paul suggests, for example, that Catholics in wealthy countries deny themselves sufficiently to make it clear they are not in conformity with their culture's attitudes and practices in regard to food and material possessions, while practicing charity toward others, especially the wretched in distant countries.[24] In the United States, the bishops have retained a minimal framework of the traditional discipline of penance, while urging works of mercy as especially appropriate penance.[25]

A person who completely organized his or her life by vocational commitments would have included the principles of penance to such an extent that no supplement of penance would be possible. But few if any of us are so well organized. Therefore, penances can be chosen in addition to those which fulfill some other commitment.

In the line of fasting, one obviously can give up unneeded food, drink, and sleep, according to older practices; one also can deny oneself free and unrestricted use of one's

779

time, energy, money, and possessions. One can give away things one likes; settle for less pay than one might obtain; take one's exercise in manual labor, as St. Paul did, rather than in a pleasant game or sport; deny oneself the pleasure of idle talk; allow others to have their way in matters of taste, as long as no question of principle is involved.

In the line of almsgiving, one can give money. But one also can give all sorts of help to others: truth which is not welcome and one's time and energy more fully than one is strictly required to do in the fulfillment of one's duties.

Prayer remains an important form of penance, especially in resignation, the acceptance of suffering and pain as God's will. To accept is to control one's feelings and actions as much as one can in a way that is fitting for a Christian. For example, if a woman loses her husband to death or a man loses his job due to some injustice, then they accept what has happened by understanding it in faith, judging it with hope, and acting with love toward themselves and others involved. The beginning of the whole process is prayer. Without prayer, there is no Christian resignation, and without Christian resignation, there is no Christian life. For a large part of any truly Christian life is disappointment, frustration, and pain.

Spiritual direction can be helpful for self-examination and for shaping a serious but moderate penitential life, as well as for a more regular and consistent use of the sacrament of penance itself.[26] Pilgrimages are inherently suited to the penitential dimension of Christian life. They symbolize the fundamental characteristic of Christian life as a journey still to be completed toward our heavenly home.

Question H: How does the sacrament of anointing of the sick complete penance?

1. The Council of Trent begins its treatment of this sacrament by linking it to the sacrament of penance. It calls the sacrament of anointing a "culmination not only of penance but of the whole Christian life which itself ought to be a continual penance" (DS 1694/907; *S.c.g.*, 4, 73). **According to this teaching, the sacrament organizes the whole of Christian life by shaping it into a penitential preparation for suffering and dying in the Lord Jesus.** Thus it is an important general principle of Christian morality.

The basis in Scripture for the Church's understanding of the anointing of the sick is the following brief passage: "Is any among you sick? Let him call for the elders of the church, and let them pray over him, anointing him with oil in the name of the Lord; and the prayer of faith will save the sick man, and the Lord will raise him up; and if he has committed sins, he will be forgiven" (Jas 5.14–15). Trent teaches that in this passage all of the essential elements of this sacrament are included (see DS 1695–96/908–9).

God answers all prayers of petition (29-E). Evidently, the restoration to bodily health promised in this sacrament often is accomplished through death and resurrection. But the restoration to spiritual health is always accomplished at once in one who receives the sacrament and puts no obstacle in its way.

2. The sacrament's effects are explained clearly in the *Introduction* to the new rite of the sacrament: "This sacrament provides the sick person with the grace of the Holy Spirit by which the whole man is brought to health, trust in God is encouraged, and strength is given to resist the temptations of the Evil One and anxiety about death. Thus the sick person is able not only to bear his suffering bravely, but also to fight against it. A return to physical health may even follow the

reception of this sacrament if it will be beneficial to the sick person's salvation. If necessary, the sacrament also provides the sick person with the forgiveness of sins and the completion of Christian penance."[27] Anointing brings to bear Jesus' redemptive work, to help the gravely ill person in every way appropriate in this ultimate situation. The temptation to despair before the terror of death is put aside. The soul is healed and, if it will be spiritually beneficial, the body, too (see *S.t.*, sup., q. 30, aa. 1–2).

As the culmination of penance, the sacrament of anointing normally presupposes a recipient whose sins have been forgiven through the sacrament of penance. Thus, a seriously ill person in need of reconciliation should if possible confess before receiving the sacrament of anointing. However, children old enough to be comforted by the sacrament of anointing may be anointed even if they are not yet ready for the sacrament of penance. Likewise, a dying and unconscious adult, if not certainly dead, should be anointed if there is any ground to believe that he or she would have desired to receive the sacraments. In all doubtful cases, including persons apparently but not certainly dead, the sacrament is administered conditionally.

3. The penitent goes from the sacrament of penance to lead a life of penance, a life of reparation for sin by renewal according to the gospel.[28] The suffering one endures and the good one does are consecrated for conversion unto eternal life.[29] This consecration, a promise as it were of continuing conversion, is renewed, perhaps for the last time, in the sacrament of anointing (see *S.t.*, sup., q. 29, a. 1; q. 30, a. 1).

4. Here one receives a special chance to be faithful to conversion. One's life is now consecrated to the ultimate penance: suffering and death with Jesus. One receives a special role in the Church, that of serving as a reminder to every Christian of what life is all about, what finally it means, and how all our lives will end.[30]

The Christian attitude toward suffering and death is at once totally realistic and completely mystical.[31]

On the one hand, suffering and death are recognized as unnatural, horrible, and final. They are consequences of sin; human persons and children of God should not have to endure them. Christian faith does not pretend that suffering and death are inherently natural, only conditionally evil, basically good, or remediable by cosmetics. The illusions of pagan mummification and secular humanist funeral practices are contrary to Christian realism.

On the other hand, Christian faith requires that suffering and death be accepted with hope. One must abandon oneself and one's loved ones to the mercy of God, confident that he can unite the death of Christians with that of the Lord Jesus, and so bring glory in resurrection for all who die in him. Death is not to last, contrary to the belief of sinners (see Wis 2). Paul clings to Jesus, "that I may know him and the power of his resurrection, and may share his sufferings, becoming like him in his death, that if possible I may attain the resurrection from the dead" (Phil 3.10–11). The attitude of every Christian should be that of Paul in prison: "It is my eager expectation and hope that I shall not be at all ashamed, but that with full courage now as always Christ will be honored in my body, whether by life or by death" (Phil 1.20).

5. Resurrection and glory are the greatest of goods, but the only way to them is by suffering and dying. Jesus completed his earthly life by this last act of full

sharing in the human condition—an act by which he loved to the end (see Jn 13.1). A person's whole life should be preparation for this passage. Without a final act of abandonment, a life lived in unity with Jesus by willingness to suffer with him and die for him is not complete. The sacrament of anointing consecrates one for this culmination.

Someone might challenge the preceding interpretation of the sacrament of anointing by arguing that it is not only for the dying, but for the sick in general. The new rite, following a prescription of Vatican II, uses the phrase "anointing of the sick" rather than "extreme (last) anointing" to refer to the sacrament. Moreover, the text in James seems to treat the sacrament as one of healing rather than consecration of dying.

Yet it seems the Council's action has been misinterpreted and the sacrament still ought to be regarded as a consecration of terminal suffering and dying. It is hardly likely that Vatican II wishes to contradict the solemn teaching of the Council of Florence: "This sacrament should not be given except to the sick whose death is feared" (DS 1324/700). Hence, Vatican II's actual statement should be considered carefully: "'Extreme unction,' which may also and more fittingly be called 'anointing of the sick,' is not a sacrament for those only who are at the point of death. Hence, as soon as any one of the faithful begins to be in danger of death from sickness or old age, the appropriate time for him to receive this sacrament has certainly already arrived" (SC 73). What the Council wishes to exclude is the postponement of the sacrament until the very moment of death.

The *Introduction* to the new rite for the anointing of the sick repeatedly uses the words "danger," "dangerous," and "dangerously" in referring to the condition of the person to be anointed.[32] It assumes that the illness must be judged serious when it says: "A prudent or probable judgment about the seriousness of the sickness is sufficient; in such a case there is no reason for scruples, but if necessary a doctor may be consulted."[33] This provision clearly takes for granted that anointing for a minor illness or psychological problem is inappropriate.

Objectively, a person is dying only when he or she has some specific condition which probably will cause death. Psychologically, whenever a person is in a condition such that death can reasonably be feared as a personal prospect—not simply as a general aspect of the human condition—the person is suffering unto death from his or her own point of view and from the point of view of dear ones. The sacrament of anointing becomes appropriate at this point. Perhaps the reasonable fear of death is based upon a serious (even if usually nonfatal) illness; perhaps it is based upon old age; perhaps it is based upon major surgery. In any of these cases, a prudent individual contemplates death as a personal prospect. The help of the sacrament is needed, and its revelatory value to others is real.

What, then, about the text of James which refers so strongly to health? The answer is that the Greek word (*egerei*) sometimes translated "restore . . . to health" (Jas 5.15; NAB) also means "raise" as in "He has been raised (*ēgerthē*), exactly as he promised" (Mt 28.6; NAB). Readers of the Greek text hardly would have missed the resonances of the verb, for "health" considered in the light of Christian faith is a rather different concept than proponents of anointing as a healing sacrament have in mind. Ultimately, health is attained only by resurrection.

The sacrament is not a gift of miraculous cures, as experience shows. It is a sacrament of faith that God will cure if that is good, but more especially that he will save, as the *Introduction* to the new rite explains: "The anointing of the sick, which includes the prayer of faith (see James 5.15), is a sacrament of faith. This faith is important for the minister and particularly for the one who receives it. The sick man will be saved by his faith and the faith of the Church which looks back to the death and resurrection of Christ, the source of the sacrament's power (see James 5.15), and looks again to the future kingdom which is pledged in the sacraments."[34] The health to which the sacrament of anointing is primarily directed is that which never will fail, the wholeness of friendship with God which heals even death (see *S.t.*, sup., q. 30, aa. 1–2; *S.c.g.*, 4, 73).

Summary

Repentance and reparation for sin—one's own as well as others'—are necessary elements in the pilgrimage of Christian life. The sacraments of penance and anointing of the sick organize Christian life from this point of view.

The sacrament of penance, or at least some sort of desire for it, is necessary for those who commit mortal sin after baptism. Its effect is reconciliation with God. The requirement of confession gives the sacrament an essentially judicial character. It is not enough simply to seek reconciliation with God in one's heart, for sin also disrupts one's relationship with the Church, and so reconciliation requires that the sinner be restored to God by being humanly reconciled with the Church.

Contrition, the basic act of the penitent, includes a firm purpose of amendment and rejection of past sins, along with a sincere intention to fulfill the sacrament's other conditions. "Imperfect contrition"—sorrow for sin based on awareness of its evil and fear of punishment, together with the intention to amend—is a divine gift which disposes sinners to seek forgiveness in the sacrament of penance. St. Thomas reasonably holds that perfect contrition and the conferral of charity are mutually dependent—they are given together—and this can happen before or when the sacrament is received. It is clear from the teaching on penance that the divine gift of charity is restored to those who receive penance worthily at least as soon as absolution is administered. Since charity is not psychologically recognizable, however, one cannot be certain of having perfect contrition before receiving the sacrament.

Even forgiven sin deserves some punishment. Something must be done to undo its existential consequences and to make up for the damage done to the sinner's relationship with God and the Church. The "penance" imposed in the sacrament is only a token of the will to make reparation; beyond it, all the repentant sinner does that is good and suffers in life can serve as penance. In doing penance, sinners are ennobled by being made like Jesus, who satisfied for all human sins.

Insofar as it is used to overcome venial sin, the sacrament of penance can shape the whole of a Christian's life. The struggle against venial sin is a strict requirement of Christian life, and the Church's teaching makes it clear that the sacrament of penance is the most appropriate—even in some sense the necessary—way to carry on this struggle. The sacrament of penance links in explicit and conscious cooperation the actions of the Holy Spirit, Jesus as man, the Church, and penitents themselves in overcoming their sins. Thus, overcoming venial sin by means of the sacrament is a different and far richer Christian act than any other suited to this obligatory task.

The avoidance of occasions of sin can pertain to the sacrament of penance. An occasion of sin is a situation or action which conduces to sin and can be avoided or modified so that temptation is less likely or more easily overcome. Where occasions of sin can be avoided, they should be. Many occasions cannot be avoided but can be modified: either by modification of the situation or action as it is objectively, or by modification of its context or meaning, by taking a different stance toward it. Since the avoidance of occasions of sin should affect the whole of a Christian's life, the constant effort to do so can contribute to the ordering of life by the sacrament of penance.

The reparation or satisfaction for sin essential to the sacrament of penance can transform all of the self-denial essential to Christian life. "Self-denial" signifies various things: detachment, moral practice (asceticism in the strict sense), mortification (the putting to death of sin), and resignation. All forms of Christian self-denial are aspects of the Christian's sharing in the cross of Jesus; all are components of the work of penance by which one submits one's whole self to the requirements of love.

Fasting, almsgiving, and prayer have traditionally been regarded as the three typical acts of penance. The self-restraint of fasting makes up for the destructive self-indulgence of sin, the mercy of almsgiving for its damage to the Church's communion of love, and prayer for the alienation from God it involves. Today the Church places these practices in a contemporary framework—urging, for example, that fasting and abstaining be a form of witness to Christian values in the face of the attitudes and practices of a consumer society.

To the sacrament of penance Trent links the sacrament of anointing of the sick, calling it a "culmination" of penance and of a penitential Christian life. Thus, the sacrament of anointing organizes Christian life by shaping it into a penitential preparation for suffering and death in the Lord Jesus, and is an important general principle of Christian morality. It helps the dangerously ill person in every way appropriate in this ultimate situation. Here one's life is consecrated to the ultimate penance, suffering and death with Jesus—the passage for which one's whole life should be preparation.

Appendix 1:   The distinction between restitution and penance

Although restitution pertains to the common responsibilities of Christian life rather than to Christian moral principles, I discuss the topic briefly to distinguish restitution from penance.

Restitution for harm done is an obligation which follows in strict justice from all personal wrongdoing which unjustly causes harm to anyone. Harm is actual, definite damage of any sort. It is distinct from the inherent moral evil of sin, which is made up for by penance. The moral evil to oneself, to one's relationship with other persons, and to God is built into sin; the need to satisfy for this moral evil by penance follows whether one has unjustly harmed anyone or not.

An example will clarify this distinction. Suppose I steal someone's car. Morally, I need to repent and do penance. But also, as a matter of justice, I have done the harm of taking another's property, and I must give the car back. Perhaps I am caught and the police restore the car to its rightful owner. Still, I must repent and do penance to get straightened out morally. Perhaps, however, the person from whom I stole the car is a billionaire; when, though not having been apprehended, I nevertheless repent and offer him the car, he tells me to keep it, since he never liked it anyway and hoped I would steal it. In this case, I do not have to make restitution or reparation of harm, since there is no injustice in keeping the car. But I still have to do penance, for my sin has upset the moral harmony within myself, with other people, and with God.

Restitution for harm is most often recognized as a moral obligation in matters of money and property. However, the obligation is wider. If a person harms others through bad example, he or she ought to try to help those scandalized to know that the example was bad and ought not to be followed. If a person harms another by careless, unfair talk, then there is an obligation to try to correct the erroneous impressions which have been given. Thus, whenever one repents of any sin, one needs to ask oneself who has been harmed, whether the harm was caused unjustly (willing accomplices in one's sins are not harmed unjustly, and so restitution is not due them), and whether and how restitution might be made.

One who does not conscientiously consider the obligation to make restitution is only half-sincere in repenting. Of course, restitution, although distinct in concept from penance, can also serve as penance, even as part of a sacramentally imposed penance.

The distinction between restitution and penance is important, however, and must be borne in mind when one acts with only venial guilt but causes serious harm to others. For example, the thoughtless word which does harm to another demands careful effort to remedy the harm, even if the thoughtlessness made the deed virtually blameless. In such a case, one need not repent as if of mortal sin, for one has not committed mortal sin. Still, the obligation to make restitution is real.

Appendix 2: Penance, indulgences, purgatory, and temporal punishment

The Catholic doctrines concerning purgatory and indulgences are based upon the Catholic doctrines of sin, penance, and the solidarity of the Mystical Body of our Lord Jesus. In other words, purgatory and indulgences have their place in Catholic moral life, because they are tightly tied into the sacramental ordering of life by the sacraments of penance and the anointing of the sick. Both doctrines—on purgatory and indulgences—are often misunderstood.[35]

Many people imagine that indulgences are remissions of sin. They are not. On the contrary, indulgences are of no use whatever unless sin itself has been repented and forgiven. Many people think of purgatory as a kind of short-term hell, suited to those who are sinners but not great enough sinners to be damned forever. On the contrary, purgatory is an initial stage of heavenly glory, suited to those who are saints but who need a moment to adjust their garments—that is, the good deeds in which they are dressed—before making their entrance into the wedding banquet which lasts forever.

Basic to both doctrines is the idea of temporal punishment. Once sin itself has been overcome by repentance and reconciliation, there remain existential effects of sin. These effects are taken care of by penance, provided one has a sufficient opportunity to do penance and does it. If one fails to do sufficient penance in this life, the rectification still necessary is somehow accomplished after death, in ways only God knows. This rectification after death is purgatory (see DS 1304/693, 1580/840, 1820/983).

Someone who dies in friendship with God is in a position utterly diverse from that of someone who dies at enmity with him. Even if some rectification is required, one who dies in friendship with God is welcomed into the kingdom. If some purification is needed, it is like the process of healing, not like the void of death (see *S.c.g.*, 4, 91). Therefore, purgatory is altogether diverse from hell, and the tendency to assimilate the two states is mistaken.

Still, some who die and many who live can use help in satisfying for sins. All the penance we can do either is not enough or would be too arduous for us. At this point, the solidarity of the Church comes to the rescue. Having been redeemed by being united with Jesus, our satisfaction for sin also can be achieved by his help and by the help of Mary and the other saints. By the will of Jesus, the Church, which has the power to make effective in heaven what it does on earth (that is, the power of binding and loosing), simply extends to the repentant sinner in need of help in penance the help abundantly present in the merits of Jesus and the saints. This extending of help is an indulgence.

Thus, indulgences are remissions of punishment, not absolutions of sin. They are an act by which Jesus in the Church, having forgiven sin, also takes away all or part of the moral consequences of one's having sinned (see *S.t.*, sup., q. 25, a. 1; q. 27, a. 1). The effect of the system of indulgences is that either the sacrament of penance or anointing together with a plenary (full) indulgence puts one in much the same position as a newly baptized person or one who died immediately after baptism without having committed any sin whatsoever.

The doctrine of purgatory reveals the importance of the penitential dimension of Christian life. The granting of indulgences makes it clear that this dimension need not and should not be onerous. Only sin is ultimately evil, and penance is not sin. It is an important aspect of unity with Jesus, who though sinless paid for sin.

Notes

1. This requirement raises a question about the forgiveness of sins for those in good faith who do not believe in the sacrament. This question can be solved by considering good faith a kind of implicit desire for the sacrament, just as with baptism.

2. See Paul F. Palmer, S.J., *Sacraments of Healing and Vocation* (Englewood Cliffs, N.J.: Prentice-Hall, 1963), 6–9.

3. Some historical background in respect to this point: Peter Riga, *Sin and Penance: Insights into the Mystery of Salvation* (Milwaukee: Bruce, 1961), 108–22.

4. *Gelasian Sacramentary*, 1, 38. See Palmer, op. cit., 34–36, for a summary of the view of certain theologians (which he accepts) that the *res et sacramentum* of the sacrament of penance is reconciliation with the Church.

5. See *The Rites of the Catholic Church*, trans. the International Commission on English in the Liturgy (New York: Pueblo, 1976), 344. The internal reference is to another document of Paul VI.

6. This canon of Trent's is doctrinal, not merely disciplinary, in nature. The teaching is based principally upon the constant tradition of the Church, which included a homogeneous development in the sacrament of penance of which the Fathers of Trent were not ignorant. For a very helpful history of this canon, see José A. Do Couto, S.C.J., *De Integritate Confessionis apud Patres Concilii Tridentini* (Rome: Analecta Dehoniana, 1963). Someone might object that the possibility in emergency situations of general absolution without individual confession shows that detailed confession of sins is not absolutely essential to the sacrament. However, the discipline of general absolution makes it clear that even in this case each and every grave sin must be confessed eventually if this becomes possible: *The Rites*, 355–57. Thus, in the exceptional cases in which general absolution is licitly received and validly received, only the sequence of confession and absolution is reversed. See Sacrae Congregatio pro Doctrina Fidei, "Normae Pastorales circa Absolutionem Sacramentalem Generali Modo Impertiendam," 64 *AAS* (1972) 510–14. Several sound commentaries clarify the theological point: Dionigi Tettamanzi, "In margine alle 'Normae generales' sull'assoluzione sacramentale generale," *La Scuola Cattolica*, 100 (1972), 255–89; Marcelino Zalba, S.J., "Commentarium ad normas pastorales circa absolutionem sacramentalem generali modo impertiendam," *Periodica de Re Morali, Canonica, Liturgica*, 62 (1973), 193–213; Jan Visser, C.Ss.R., "Le recenti norme circa l'assoluzione co-munitaria," *Seminarium*, 25 (1973), 572–96.

7. *The Rites*, 345.

8. For a very helpful account of the history of the concepts and controversies over contrition and attrition: P. de Letter, "Contrition," *New Catholic Encyclopedia*, 4:278–83.

9. *The Rites*, 363.

10. For practical guidance on the practice of devotional confession, see St. Francis de Sales, *Introduction to the Devout Life*, trans. John K. Ryan (Garden City, N.Y.: Doubleday, 1972), 111–14; Benedict Baur, O.S.B., *Frequent Confession: Its Place in the Spiritual Life*, trans. Patrick C. Barry, S.J. (London: St. Paul Publications, 1959), 23–47. The frequent reception of the sacrament should consecrate a genuine striving for perfection, and so sins should not be confessed without contrition, which necessarily includes a real purpose of amendment.

11. Pius XII, *Mystici Corporis Christi*, 35 *AAS* (1943) 235; *The Papal Encyclicals*, 225.88.

12. Pius XII, *Mediator Dei*, 39 *AAS* (1947) 585; *The Papal Encyclicals*, 233.177.

13. John XXIII, *Sacerdotii Nostri primordia*, 51 *AAS* (1959) 574–75; *The Papal Encyclicals*, 264.95–96.

14. *The Rites*, 347.

15. John Paul II, *Redemptor hominis*, 71 *AAS* (1979) 313–15; *The Papal Encyclicals*, 278.82–83.

16. Pius XII, *Mystici Corporis Christi*, 35 *AAS* (1943) 234–35; *The Papal Encyclicals*, 225.87.

17. John Paul II, *Redemptor hominis*, 314–15; 83.

18. John Paul II, *Dives in misericordia*, 72 *AAS* (1980) 1219–20; *The Papal Encyclicals*, 279.132.

19. See Bernard Leeming, S.J., *Principles of Sacramental Theology* (Westminster, Md.: Newman Press, 1956), 363–66.

20. Considering the importance of sacramental penance in a devout Christian life, one understands how sound is the practice of preparing children to receive this sacrament for the first time and encouraging them to do so before they make their first Communion. The Holy See has insisted that this practice be maintained: Sacred Congregations for the Clergy and for the Discipline of the Sacraments, "Sanctus pontifex," 65 *AAS* (1973) 410; "Declaration on First Confession and First Communion," in *Vatican Council II: The Conciliar and Post Conciliar Documents*, ed. Austin Flannery, O.P. (Northport, N.Y.: Costello, 1975), 241.

21. See Leeming, op. cit., 364–65, on the significance of this prayer and its relationship to absolution and to the permanence of the sacrament in the life of the person who receives it.

22. See St. Leo the Great, *Sermo* 13, *P.L.*, 54:172.

23. Paul VI, *Paenitemini*, 58 *AAS* (1966) 182; *Apostolic Constitution . . . on Penance*, *The Pope Speaks*, 11 (1966), 368.

24. Ibid., 369.

25. National Conference of Catholic Bishops, "Penance and Friday Abstinence," *The Pope Speaks*, 11 (1966), 356–61.

26. See Pius XII, *Menti nostrae*, 42 *AAS* (1950) 673–75; *Apostolic Exhortation to the Clergy of the Entire World* (Washington, D.C.: National Catholic Welfare Conference, 1950), 19–21.

27. *The Rites*, 583–84.

28. Ibid., 352.

29. Ibid., 363.

30. Ibid., 582. On this point especially, but also on other aspects of this sacrament, including its reservation to cases in which there is danger of death: Bertrand de Margerie, S.J., *The Sacraments and Social Progress*, trans. Malachy Carroll, (Chicago: Franciscan Herald Press, 1974), 94–123.

31. *The Rites*, 582–83.

32. Ibid., 584–85.

33. Ibid., 584.

34. Ibid.

35. On this matter: Paul VI, *Indulgentiarum doctrina*, 59 *AAS* (1967) 5–24; *Apostolic Constitution on the Revision of Indulgences*, in Flannery, ed., op. cit., 62–79. This theologically rich document gives a clear and well-developed account of its subject.

CHAPTER THIRTY-THREE

EUCHARISTIC LIFE
AS FULFILLMENT IN THE LORD JESUS

Introduction

The sacrament of the Eucharist is the supreme integrating act of Christian life. Christian life is eucharistic life, lived in preparing the gifts to be offered at Mass and in fulfilling the commission to go forth and serve the Lord. The Mass is the summit, daily or weekly, of each Catholic's life; everything else should prepare for it and follow from it (see *S.t.*, 3, q. 65, a. 3).

In the Mass, one participates even now in Jesus' glory. Likewise, by being integrated with the Mass, the rest of one's life constitutes even now an imperfect but real beginning of heaven, an incipient sharing in the ultimate fulfillment of everything in the Lord Jesus.

Because of the relationship between morality and charity, the morally good human acts of a Christian's life have meaning in many distinct ways beyond their basic human meaning and value. The supreme and integrating meaning of Christian life is, however, its character as eucharistic, as a gift offered to God in thanksgiving for everything he gives us.

Question A: How is the Eucharist both complex and simple?

1. The Eucharist is a complex, many-sided reality (see *S.t.*, 3, q. 73, aa. 2–4; q. 79, aa. 1, 2, 4, 6). **The Council of Trent lists five reasons for Jesus' institution of this most holy sacrament** (see DS 1638/875).[1] First, it is a remembrance of the works of Jesus, to be received to preserve his memory and proclaim his death until he comes (see 1 Cor 11.23–26). Second, it is spiritual food, to sustain and build up those who live with Jesus' life (see Mt 26.26; Jn 6.53–58). Third, it is to free us from daily defects and keep us from mortal sin. Fourth, it is a pledge or down payment on our future glory and everlasting happiness; by it we begin to be in heaven even during this life. Fifth, it is a symbol of the Mystical Body whose head is Jesus (see Eph 5.23); as Jesus wills, its worthy reception strengthens the bonds of faith, hope, and charity which unite members of the Church.

Essentially the same points are made by Vatican II at the beginning of its chapter on the mystery of the Eucharist: "At the Last Supper, on the night when he was betrayed, our Savior instituted the Eucharistic Sacrifice of his Body and Blood. He did this in order to perpetuate the sacrifice of the Cross throughout the centuries until he should come again, and so to entrust to his beloved spouse, the Church, a memorial of his death and resurrection: a sacrament of love, a sign of unity, a bond of charity, a paschal banquet in which Christ is consumed, the mind is filled with grace, and a pledge of future glory is given to us" (SC 47). The only difference between Trent and Vatican II is that the latter does not explicitly mention the role of the Eucharist in overcoming venial sin and keeping us from mortal sin, but says instead simply that in the Eucharist "the mind is filled with grace."

2. **Besides the rich complexity of its purposes, the Eucharist also involves another complexity, arising from the fact that it is a divine-human communion of love.** United in the human life of Jesus are the revelatory signs and the human response of the Word Incarnate (21-F). The Eucharist, as well as the other sacraments by relationship to it, make Jesus' human redemptive act present to us, inasmuch as this act exists in him as he now is in glory and is outwardly enacted in the sacramental rites (see *S.t.*, 3, q. 62, a. 5; q. 65, a. 3; q. 79, a. 1). Hence, the Eucharist as well as the other sacraments must be understood both as a revelatory sign, communicating divine truth and love to us, and as a human response of sacrifice in thanksgiving for the great good—namely, himself—which God shares with us in Jesus.

The structure of our Mass is like the structure of the making of the covenant of Sinai: The law is read to the people; they respond with an expression of acceptance and commitment; the agreement is sealed in blood; and a covenant meal is shared in the presence of God (see Ex 24.3–11). Similarly, we hear the word of God in the gospel and respond in faith; the baptismal commitment is consummated by sealing with the blood of Jesus; and he, both priest and victim, becomes our food in holy Communion. The difference between the ancient ceremony and the new rite of Jesus is that the Mass consummates an infinitely more intimate relationship: "For the law was given through Moses; grace and truth came through Jesus Christ" (Jn 1.17). The old covenant was an engagement between God and humankind; the new is marriage, fruitful in divine children.

3. In the liturgy of the Mass, we first receive the word of the Lord calling us to intimacy and guiding and shaping our lives; next we receive our Lord Jesus in Communion: him bodily, the power of his Spirit, and his life as principle of our lives; finally, we receive the commission to go forth to love and serve the Lord. We receive all these gifts inasmuch as the Mass is truly revelatory, truly communicative of divine truth and love.

4. In the liturgy of the Mass we also act. We give a gift, as human persons united with Jesus our head and priest. Since we are baptized, the human goods realized in us and the fruits of our work are already holy in God's sight, just as Jesus was already holy when he undertook his sacrificial life. At the offertory, we offer what we are and have, to be formed into Jesus at the consecration. With him, we then offer to the Father both Jesus and ourselves, now united as one. We make these offerings inasmuch as the Mass is truly a fitting response to God— acceptance of all he gives and a loving return of it all to him.

5. It should therefore be clear how complex the Eucharist is. But it is also simple. **Its complexity is not that of a multiplicity of unrelated purposes and disjointed parts, but of a very perfect, endlessly rich relationship: the**

communion of charity. God loves us, gives himself to us, gives us a perfect response, and we make this response our own through, with, and in our Lord Jesus. Thus we are fully ourselves but perfectly united with Jesus.

Near the beginning of his apostolic letter, *Dominicae cenae*, John Paul II reaffirms that

> ...Eucharistic worship constitutes the soul of all Christian life. In fact Christian life is expressed in the fulfilling of the greatest commandment, that is to say in the love of God and neighbour, and this love finds its source in the Blessed Sacrament, which is commonly called the Sacrament of love.
>
> *The Eucharist signifies this charity,* and therefore recalls it, makes it present *and at the same time brings it about.* Every time that we consciously share in it, there opens in our souls a real dimension of that unfathomable love that includes everything that God has done and continues to do for us human beings, as Christ says: "My Father goes on working, and so do I" (Jn 5.17). Together with this unfathomable and free gift, which is *charity* revealed in its fullest degree in the saving Sacrifice of the Son of God, the Sacrifice of which the Eucharist is the indelible sign, there also springs up within us a lively response of love. We not only know love; we ourselves *begin to love.* We enter, so to speak, upon the path of love and along this path make progress. Thanks to the Eucharist, the love that springs up within us from the Eucharist develops in us, becomes deeper and grows stronger.
>
> Eucharistic worship is therefore precisely the expression of that love which is the authentic and deepest characteristic of the Christian vocation. This worship springs from the love and serves the love to which we are all called in Jesus Christ [note omitted]. A living fruit of this worship is the perfecting of the image of God that we bear within us, an image that corresponds to the one that Christ has revealed to us. As we thus become adorers of the Father "in spirit and truth" (Jn 4.23), we mature in an ever fuller union with Christ, we are ever more united to him, and—if one may use the expression—we are ever more in harmony with him.[2]

Here the complexity of the Eucharist is reduced to its central simplicity, the simplicity of communion in divine love, of which the Eucharist is the sacrament (see *S.t.*, 3, q. 73, a. 3, ad 3; q. 75, a. 1; q. 79, aa. 1, 4). That love is revealed in Jesus' sacrifice, we respond to it, and by participation in this sacrament we grow toward the maturity of heavenly completion in our Lord Jesus by becoming ever more closely united, even during our earthly life, with him.

Question B: How is sharing in the Eucharist sharing in the sacrifice of Jesus?

1. The fundamental sacrifice of Jesus is his obedience to the Father's will (22-B). This leads him to the Last Supper. In celebrating this Supper, he freely accepts the death which reconciles humankind to God and merits the divine work of renewal that commences with his own resurrection.

2. In celebrating the Last Supper, Jesus also empowers the apostles—and priests of all times and places—to act on his behalf in expressing and making present his redemptive sacrifice. **Jesus' sacrifice is thus present for us in every Mass. The unity of Christians with Jesus, initiated in baptism, is expressed and perfected by their participation in the Mass** (23-B).[3]

3. An important point clarified by Vatican II is the universal priesthood of the

faithful, insofar as all are called to offer spiritual sacrifices (see PO 2). Of course, the ordained priest has a unique role and dignity, for through his ministry "the spiritual sacrifice of the faithful is made perfect in union with the sacrifice of Christ, the sole Mediator" (PO 2; cf. *S.t.*, 3, q. 82, a. 1). But the priest also offers Mass in the name of the people, and in this respect his celebration of the Mass would be pointless if the Christian life were not lived by the faithful. The offering must be the living sacrifice of "all those works befitting Christian men" (LG 10).

4. In speaking of the laity, the Council teaches that Jesus gives them the Spirit and urges them on "to every good and perfect work" (LG 34). If done in the Spirit, all the activities of life "become spiritual sacrifices acceptable to God through Jesus Christ (cf. 1 Pt 2.5). During the celebration of the Eucharist, these sacrifices are most fittingly offered to the Father along with the Lord's body. Thus, as worshippers whose every deed is holy, the laity consecrate the world itself to God" (LG 34; translation amended). This is, of course, true of all members of the Church, not just the laity.

5. Every Christian's life, to the extent it is truly Christian, not only contributes to the growth of the eternal kingdom and continues Jesus' redemptive work but completes his perfect sacrifice. Jesus offers the Father his obedience; we must share in this offering and live it out in our own lives. Such is eucharistic worship as sacrifice: the living of Christian life (see Rom 12.1–2). "Like living stones be yourselves built into a spiritual house, to be a holy priesthood, to offer spiritual sacrifices acceptable to God through Jesus Christ" (1 Pt 2.5).[4]

Jesus' free acceptance of death as the will of the Father is the sacrifice which seals the new covenant in blood—that is, in life, since blood is life (see Ex 24.8; Dt 12.23; Mt 26.28; Heb 9.11–22). Jesus' sacrifice is once and for all (see Heb 10.12); he offers this sacrifice in the heavenly sanctuary (see Heb 8.1–6; 9.24).

Central to this unique sacrifice is Jesus' perfect obedience to the will of the Father: "I have come to do your will" (Heb 10.9). Jesus' righteous act displaced Adam's sin as the principle of humankind's relationship with God and "leads to acquittal and life for all men" (Rom 5.18). Through and in Jesus, God reconciles the world to himself (see 2 Cor 5.18–19). The gift of himself which Jesus makes by his obedience to the Father is neither of himself alone nor for himself alone. It seals the covenant of love for all humankind, and includes all who ever will be united with Jesus as members of his Mystical Body.[5]

Jesus' redemptive sacrifice was explained (22-G) as a human act carried out both in the Last Supper and in the Mass (see *S.t.*, 3, q. 73, a. 5). An essential point to remember is that Jesus' human act is not what is done to him, but rather what he does in choosing to eat the Passover with his friends, knowing that in doing so he is freely accepting suffering and death. This human act is not a passing event, it is a lasting self-determination.

This clarifies the sense in which the Eucharist is done in remembrance of Jesus and is received to preserve his memory and proclaim his death (see 1 Cor 11.26; *S.t.*, 3, q. 82, a. 1; q. 83, a. 1).[6] There is no question here of recalling to mind a past event as past. Jesus' redemptive act is not something apart from him; it precisely is the human fulfillment of his earthly life. That fulfillment, a gift of obedience to the Father on behalf of all of us, exists in Jesus, accepted and sealed with glory. Its remembrance is a reexpression of an inherently atemporal, existential reality, much as the remembrance of a wedding anniversary is the reexpression of the reality of the bond of marriage itself.

What Jesus first actually does outwardly to carry out his redemptive commitment, he does in the Last Supper (22-G). But in doing what he then does, he commands others to carry out further performances of the same type to keep his redemptive act present. The consecrations of all Masses, carried out as executions of this command, were included in the single act of Jesus at the Last Supper. For this reason, the central moment in the Eucharist is the consecration.[7] In consecrating, the priest speaks in the very person of Christ, doing Jesus' own act—an act only Jesus personally can do—for him (see DS 1321/ 698), much as a proxy in a marriage ceremony acts for (not in place of nor as a mere delegate of) the absent party who alone can give marital consent.

The Council of Trent, in its teaching on the Mass, does not say that the sacrifice of the Mass precisely is the same sacrifice as that of the cross, nor does it say that the offering is the same offering. Rather, it holds that the unity of the Mass and the cross is in this: Jesus offered himself in a bloody manner on the cross, and now offers himself in an unbloody manner (see DS 1743/940). But Vatican II says: "As often as the sacrifice of the cross in which 'Christ, our passover, has been sacrificed' (1 Cor 5.7) is celebrated on an altar, the work of our redemption is carried on" (LG 3). To suppose that the two councils disagree, however, would be a mistake.

The sacrifice of the Mass and of the cross is one, yet they are many; the offering is unique, yet it is repeated. The central redemptive choice, by which Jesus as man is our saving Lord, is one and unique. The performances which express this choice are many. The first performance of it was in the Last Supper, which carried out Jesus' choice in which he freely accepted what he knew would be done to him—namely, arrest, mistreatment, and murder. The performances since then of what he commanded to be done in his memory also carry out that same choice. The unity of the sacrifice is primarily in the unity of the self-determining act of Jesus and secondarily in the ordered unity of the performances. The multiplicity of the sacrifice is in the multiplicity of the outward expressions of the same personal reality.

This situation is common in our experience. It is not unlike the multiplicity of performances which execute the marital commitment. In the rite of marriage, it is carried out by verbal expressions of consent; in subsequent consummating sexual intercourse, it is carried out in fitting bodily communion; in faithful abstinence with respect to any other potential sexual partner, the marital commitment also is outwardly realized and manifested. Even the wearing of a wedding ring is an act which expresses the same commitment. The fundamental marital act is the commitment which inherently lasts; the many expressions are not so many additional marriages.

It is similar with the offering of Jesus which marries humankind to God. It is one lasting act with many and somewhat varied outward expressions. Among these, the performances which are consecratory acts in Masses are special, for they were specifically included in the Last Supper, they continue that same sacred banquet, and they make Jesus in glory bodily present among us.

The making present of the redemptive act in the Eucharist provides us with a visible sacrifice, which we need in order to be able to participate as men and women in our Lord Jesus' human act (see DS 1740/938). As the *General Instruction of the Roman Missal* states: "The celebration of Mass, as the action of Christ and the people of God hierarchically structured, is the center of the entire Christian life for both the universal and the local Church, as well as for each of the faithful" (cf. SC 41; LG 11; PO 2, 5, and 6; CD 30; UR 15).[8] The Eucharist, therefore, is our sacrifice, too.

Question C: How is the Eucharist spiritual food for Christians?

1. Our communion with Jesus has three inseparable but distinct aspects (19-C). We share divine life with him by adoption and the Spirit's gift; this sharing begins in baptism (30-H). We are commissioned by anointing with the Spirit to live our own lives as a share in his revelatory, redeeming life; this communion in cooperative work is established by confirmation (31-A). And we are united bodily with Jesus and enlivened by his resurrection life; this is effected by the Eucharist (see LG 26; *S.t.*, 3, q. 73, a. 3, ad 2).

2. Ordinary bodily digestion involves ingesting food and transforming nonliving material into one's own living flesh. The Eucharist follows this pattern up to a point, then diverges remarkably. **We ingest Jesus' living, bodily self, but then he makes our mortal flesh come alive with his glorious resurrection life.** "For 'the partaking of the Body and Blood of Christ does nothing other than transform us into that which we consume'" (LG 26).[9]

3. The situation is not unlike the communion of marital love, which, as we shall see in question H below, is a sacrament of the communion of Jesus and the Church. From the communion of two in one flesh proper to marriage comes the special modality of a married couple's cooperative action and even of their sharing in divine life. **Similarly, communion with the Lord, at once bodily and mysterious, is necessary and effective in maintaining and perfecting the sharing in divine life and cooperation in human action which also unite us with Jesus** (see Jn 6.44–58).

4. Acts of marital intercourse engaged in worthily "signify and promote that mutual self-giving by which spouses enrich each other with a joyful and thankful will" (GS 49). Holy Communion works in a similar manner. Worthy reception of the sacrament signifies and promotes the mutual self-giving of our Lord in glory and of us, as well as the imperfect contribution which we make to his fullness (see Eph 4.15–16; *S.t.*, 3, q. 65, a. 3; q. 73, a. 3. ad 3; sup., q. 42).

People have difficulty in grasping this truth partly because of a tendency to separate personal reality from bodiliness. Many theologians whose accounts of the sacraments are not unorthodox nevertheless presuppose a false metaphysics, according to which the body is an instrument through which personal contact occurs.[10] They assume that the person is a spiritual subject, the thinking and choosing self, who uses a body, very much as one uses an automobile. This metaphysical assumption is called "body-self dualism."

But dualism is altogether false. A human person is not a mental self concealed in a body-object but a living human body who, among other things, thinks and chooses (see *S.t.*, 1, q. 75, a. 4; q. 76, a. 1). The theological proof of the falsity of body-self dualism is that the Word who was from the beginning and whom we proclaim is the very same reality as was seen and heard by the apostles (see 1 Jn 1.1–2). If body-self dualism were true, the apostles would never have seen the Word Incarnate, but only a bodily sacrament of him.[11]

Question D: How does the Eucharist transform Christian moral life?

1. Questions B and C treated the first two reasons the Council of Trent gives for Jesus' institution of the Eucharist. Trent next says that worthy participation in

the Eucharist protects us from mortal sin and overcomes venial sin. Vatican II puts this affirmatively by saying the Eucharist fills the mind with grace (see SC 47).

2. The point made in question B suggests how this is so. To participate in the Eucharist means that, having been united by faith and baptism with Jesus, one offers his sacrifice with him and so offers oneself as a gift to the Father. Thus, one way the Eucharist transforms Christian moral life is by demanding that one live faithfully and avoid mortal sin or repent promptly if one should fall into grave sin.

Thus St. Paul teaches: "As often as you eat this bread and drink the cup, you proclaim the Lord's death until he comes" (1 Cor 11.26). It follows that only those who have made the baptismal commitment of faith and are faithful to it may share fully in the Eucharist by receiving Holy Communion. Hence, Paul adds immediately: "Whoever, therefore, eats the bread or drinks the cup of the Lord in an unworthy manner will be guilty of profaning the body and blood of the Lord. Let a man examine himself, and so eat of the bread and drink of the cup" (1 Cor 11.27–28). This teaching warrants special attention when the sacrament of penance has fallen into widespread disuse, yet few who attend Mass hesitate to receive Communion.

3. From ordinary human experience, moreover, we know that the more we act lovingly toward anyone, the more we love that person. Giving gifts is an act of love, and we care most about those, such as our children, to whom we give the most. Small children for their part love in a certain way—they are affectionate—but their love for their parents matures as they grow up and do things for them. Any beneficent act presupposes love, but beneficence also nourishes and matures love. In doing good, we become involved in the one to whom we do it. Where one's treasure is, there one's heart is: One finds the good one has done in the person to whom one has done it, now another's but still one's own.

4. God similarly loves us so much because everything good in us comes from him; he hardly wishes ill to what is entirely his (see Wis 11.24–26).

5. This can be applied to the Eucharist. In the Eucharist, we first bring forward bread and wine, goods which God supplies from the bounty of nature and by the work of human hands. We offer these, blessing God in thanks. The priest prays quietly: "Lord God, we ask you to receive us and be pleased with the sacrifice we offer you with humble and contrite hearts." The gifts represent our very selves, created by God and shaped by our freedom in goodness due to God's grace. We ask God to receive us and be pleased with our self-offering.[12]

6. Far surpassing the initial offering of the gifts is the offering, to which it leads, of the sacrifice of Jesus. This is done by the priest who acts in Jesus' person and by all the faithful who offer him through and with the priest, while at the same time they offer themselves united and transformed in Jesus (see SC 48).

Vatican II makes it clear that priests must teach the faithful "to offer to God the Father the divine Victim in the sacrifice of the Mass, and with it to make an offering of their own life" (PO 5; translation supplied). The requirement and power to make this offering come from the Eucharist itself: "The other sacraments, as well as every ministry of the Church and every work of the apostolate, are linked with the holy Eucharist and are directed toward it. For the most blessed Eucharist contains the Church's entire spiritual wealth, that is, Christ himself, our Passover and living bread. Through his very flesh, made vital and vitalizing by the Holy Spirit, he offers life to men. They are thereby invited and led to offer themselves, their labors, and all created things together with him" (PO 5). Jesus' gift of himself to us calls forth our gift of ourselves with him to the Father. Conscious that God gives us so much, we wish to give him something in return.

Vatican II also clearly teaches that all acts fitting to a Christian become spiritual sacrifices pleasing to God (LG 10). The priestly commission of the faithful at large equips them to "...produce in themselves ever more abundant fruits of the Spirit. For all their works, prayers, and apostolic endeavors, their ordinary married and family life, their daily labor, their mental and physical relaxation, if carried out in the Spirit, and even the hardships of life, if patiently borne—all of these become spiritual sacrifices acceptable to God through Jesus Christ (cf. 1 Pt 2.5). During the celebration of the Eucharist, these sacrifices are most fittingly offered to the Father along with the Lord's body. Thus, as worshipers whose every deed is holy, the laity consecrate the world itself to God" (LG 34; translation amended). Through the Eucharist, everything fitting in one's life becomes a gift to God.

7. Thus, by a sort of virtuous circle, one loves God more as one gives him more, and, loving him more, one wishes to give him still more. In this way the Eucharist fills the mind with grace, overcomes venial sin, and keeps us from mortal sin (see *S.t.*, 3, q. 79, aa. 1, 4, 6).

8. There are many reasons for leading a good Christian life: To prepare the material of the heavenly kingdom (see GS 38), to be united more closely with the obedience of Jesus, to carry his redemptive love to others, to perfect our very selves in his love. **All these are gathered up in the supreme consideration: the virtuous circle of love. God has given us everything, and we must thank him with, through, and in Jesus. Thanking him, we love him more, and loving him more, we must live more perfectly to make a better gift.**

9. A loving father wants of his children only their own fulfillment in goodness. If they give their father this joy, mutual love and satisfaction grow, and the relationship becomes ever more perfect. The children strive ever harder to please their father; he rewards them with constantly growing approval. By the covenant love celebrated and nurtured in the Eucharist, it is like this between us and God.

In his great encyclical on the liturgy, *Mediator Dei*, Pius XII strongly emphasizes the theme of offering by all the faithful, which has been developed further by Vatican II. In one respect, Pius' treatment provides an explicit indication missing from the Council's documents—namely, that one offers oneself at Communion. In receiving Jesus, one ought to accept his love and offer oneself to his service.[13] This requirement of acceptance is expressed in the words: "Go in peace to love and serve the Lord."

John Paul II also suggests that the Eucharist orders Christian life subsequent to it toward fulfillment in Christ:

> To this sacrifice [of Christ upon the cross], which is renewed in a sacramental form on the altar, the offerings of bread and wine, united with the devotion of the faithful, nevertheless bring their unique contribution, since by means of the Consecration by the priest they become the sacred species. This is made clear by the way in which the priest acts during the Eucharistic Prayer, especially at the consecration, and when the celebration of the Holy Sacrifice and participation in it are accompanied by awareness that "the Teacher is here and is calling for you" (Jn 11.28). This call of the Lord to us through his Sacrifice opens our hearts, so that,

purified in the mystery of our Redemption, they may be united to him in Eucharistic communion, which confers upon participation at Mass a value that is mature, complete, and binding on human life: "The Church's intention is that the faithful not only offer the spotless victim but also learn to offer themselves and daily to be drawn into ever more perfect union, through Christ the Mediator, with the Father and with each other, so that at last God may be all in all."[14]

This summary indicates all of the aspects of the offering which draws our entire lives into the Eucharist and directs them by it.

Question E: How is the Eucharist a pledge of glory?

1. Gift giving is successful in building a relationship of love only if the recipent accepts and treasures the gift. If we offer our whole lives to God, will he accept? Why should this gift mean anything to him?

2. The answer is found in Jesus. His sacrifice is accepted: He is risen. Jesus' resurrection in glory, his establishment in power at the Father's right hand (see Rom 1.4)—this divine act is acceptance. In the Eucharist our gifts are united with Jesus' gift.

3. The Eucharist, however, unites us with Jesus as he truly is, not as he once was on earth or dead in the tomb. From the perspective of the end of history, all human life, the totality of human history, is one long preparation of the gifts which are to be offered to the Father in, through, and with Jesus for the final transformation in which the new city of God will come down from heaven (see Rv 21.1–2). Jesus' Spirit frees all human persons " . . . so that by putting aside love of self and bringing all earthly resources into the service of human life they can devote themselves to that future when humanity itself will become an offering accepted by God. The Lord left behind a pledge of this hope and strength for life's journey in that sacrament of faith where natural elements refined by man are changed into his glorified Body and Blood, providing a meal of brotherly solidarity and a foretaste of the heavenly banquet" (GS 38). **The virtuous circle of eucharistic devotion means growing intimacy with God, and this points toward perfect intimacy** (see SC 48). **The Eucharist is therefore the pledge of glory** (see Eph 1.14).

4. One can approach this truth in another way. The shedding of Jesus' blood has opened the way into the holy of holies (see Heb 10.19–21). In the Eucharist we share in this blood. Therefore, we pass through the veil, which is his flesh, into the temple of God. Again, Jesus not only died for us but also was raised for us (see 2 Cor 5.15).[15] In the Eucharist, we receive the resurrection life of Jesus (see Jn 6.54). In the Eucharist we therefore have the pledge (not simply a promise but a beginning) of heavenly glory (see *S.t.*, 3, q. 73, a. 4; q. 79, a. 2).

5. The mystery hidden for the ages from everyone is the mystery of Jesus himself, the mystery of God present among us, sharing in our human life and enabling us to share in his divine life. This mystery has been revealed to us, and we know—that is, have experience of—glory which is priceless, our communion in divine life. The Eucharist precisely is Jesus in us, our hope of glory (see Col 1.27). In view of this hope, we strive toward fulfillment in our Lord Jesus and are

impelled to work in the apostolate "with all the energy which he mightily inspires within" us (Col 1.29).

Question F: How does the Eucharist constitute the Church?

1. Like the fall of Adam and its consequences, Christian life is essentially social. People are God's adopted children insofar as they are Christians, that is, insofar as they are in Jesus (see Rom 8.9–10, 14–17, 35–39). Thus unity with Jesus is the principle of Christian unity.

2. The Eucharist, however, is primarily the sacrament of unity with Jesus. Therefore, it is also the sacrament by which the unity of the Church is built up and sustained. The Council of Trent stresses the role of the Eucharist as "a symbol of the unity and love" by which Christians are joined (DS 1635/873a). Vatican II teaches that the liturgy, and especially the Eucharist, "daily builds up those who are in the Church, making of them a holy temple of the Lord, a dwelling-place for God in the Spirit (cf. Eph 2.21–22), to the mature measure of the fullness of Christ (cf. Eph 4.13)" (SC 2; Flannery translation).

In his apostolic constitution, *Dominicae cenae*, John Paul II takes up this theme and clarifies it. The Eucharist builds up the Church (see LG 11). The sacrament involves both fraternal communion of the members of the Church with one another and the communion of Jesus with each participant. The latter is basic, for "in Eucharistic Communion we receive Christ, Christ himself; and our union with him, which is a gift and grace for each individual, brings it about that in him we are also associated in the unity of his Body which is the Church."[16]

3. **The Eucharist can build up the Church because it establishes a real communion of love, a true union which, nevertheless, leaves distinction intact, between each person and our Lord Jesus.** By the holy Sacrament, each of us abides in him and he in each of us (see Jn 6.56). **By making us one with him, furthermore, the Eucharist also establishes a bond of communion among us** (see Jn 17.20–23). This bond is ecclesial communion; it is constitutive of the Church (see *S.t.*, 3, q. 67, a. 2; q. 73, aa. 2, 4; q. 82, a. 2, ad 3).

4. It might be objected that the preaching of the gospel, faith, and baptism constitute the Church. They do indeed, but only in an initial, incomplete manner, which the Eucharist alone brings to completion. For example, though it is perfectly true that all the baptized are united in Jesus, baptism nevertheless unites Christians by admitting them to the Church, whose inner unity is only fully actualized by their communion in Jesus in the Eucharist (see *S.t.*, 3, q. 63, a. 6; q. 73, a. 3).

5. In considering the manner in which the Eucharist constitutes the Church, one ought not to overlook the union we gain in the Eucharist with the angels and saints in heaven. In Jesus we are united with them; in the Eucharist we share in a hidden way in their glory. Memory of the mother of Jesus and of the other saints and angels in the Eucharist honors them, stimulates our love for them, and so draws us closer to Jesus himself (see LG 48–50).

Baptism is important in the manner of an admission ticket, but it is fulfilled only in the Eucharist to which it admits. In its decree concerning ecumenism, Vatican II teaches:

"Baptism, therefore, constitutes a sacramental bond of unity linking all who have been reborn by means of it. But baptism, of itself, is only a beginning, a point of departure, for it is wholly directed toward the acquiring of fullness of life in Christ. Baptism is thus oriented toward a complete profession of faith, a complete incorporation into the system of salvation such as Christ himself willed it to be, and finally, toward a complete participation in Eucharistic communion" (UR 22). Catholics and other Christians share in the same baptism, but the unity of the Church is defective, because Christian communities which lack the sacrament of orders cannot share in the authentic and perfect celebration of the Eucharist.

Someone might object that stress upon the sacramentality of Communion tends to separate the Eucharist as sacrament from the Mass as sacrifice. The answer to this objection is that the consecration of the Mass, which expresses Christ's redemptive act in the present, is altogether directed to Communion in him: "Take this, all of you, and eat it.... Take this, all of you, and drink from it...." At the same time, Communion can unite us with our Lord Jesus in glory and build us up as his body only because Communion really is a sharing in his redemptive sacrifice which reconciles us with the Father.

Question G: How does the Liturgy of the Hours extend the Eucharist throughout the day?

1. The relationship between the Eucharist and the Liturgy of the Hours is clearly stated in the *General Instruction of the Liturgy of the Hours:* "The Liturgy of the Hours extends (see PO 5) to the different hours of the day the praise and thanksgiving, the commemoration of the mysteries of salvation, the petitions and the foretaste of heavenly glory, that are present in the eucharistic mystery, 'the center and apex of the whole life of the Christian community' (CD 30). The Liturgy of the Hours is an excellent preparation for the celebration of the Eucharist itself, for it inspires and deepens in a fitting way the dispositions necessary for the fruitful celebration of the Eucharist: faith, hope, love, devotion and the spirit of self-denial."[17]

2. As we have seen, the Eucharist, as a principle of Christian moral life, causes one to live the rest of life in preparation of the gifts to be offered at Mass and in execution of the dismissal mandate to love and serve the Lord. But this extension of the Eucharist, like all Christian activity, must be formed and structured by prayer. **The Church provides the Liturgy of the Hours to serve as the common act of prayer, suitable for shaping life in preparation for and following through upon the Eucharist.**

"Christian prayer is above all the prayer of the whole human community, which Christ joins to himself (cf. SC 83)."[18] The Lord Jesus and his body pray together, as if in chorus, to the Father. This communion in prayer will be clearer if those who pray the Hours study and meditate upon Scripture, in reading which our word and God's word are at one.

Additional aspects of the Liturgy of the Hours are to be noted. It constantly gathers and presents to the Father the petitions of the whole Church. All pastoral activity must be drawn to completion in the Liturgy of the Hours and must flow from its abundant riches. In this chorus of prayer, the Church more perfectly manifests what she is, for her identity as body of Jesus is kept continually in actuation; the injunction to pray without ceasing, which cannot be fulfilled by any one individual, is corporately fulfilled by the Church as a community.[19]

3. All aspects of the rich complexity of the Eucharist itself can be distinguished in the Liturgy of the Hours. In this Work of God, Jesus prays, his Church is united with him in prayer, and the whole course of life is sanctified (see SC 83–84). Participating in the Liturgy of the Hours, one not only fulfills a duty of the Church on her behalf but shares in the nobility of the Church, the bride of the Lord Jesus, who stands before God and sings to him (see SC 85). In this earthly choir of unending prayer, the endless liturgy of heaven is anticipated and experienced (see SC 8).

The revision of the Liturgy of the Hours after Vatican II is intended to make this prayer more accessible and fruitful, and also to make it a source of devotion and nourishment for personal prayer (see SC 90). The hope of the Church in revising the Liturgy of the Hours is that it might "pervade and penetrate the whole of Christian prayer, giving it life, direction and expression and effectively nourishing the spiritual life of the people of God."[20] This being so, it is unfitting if this prayer is restricted almost entirely to the clergy and religious. The Church wishes the worship of the Hours to be celebrated in parishes, to serve as family prayer, and to be recited by laypeople generally.[21]

Any supposition of conflict between personal, private prayer and the Liturgy of the Hours must be rejected. By using the variants provided by the Church, the Liturgy of the Hours can be adapted; on the other hand, by conforming minds to voices, those who pray can adapt themselves to this Liturgy, as they ought to do. In doing this, the Liturgy of the Hours attains its full impact as a principle of Christian moral life: "If the prayer of the Divine Office becomes genuine personal prayer, the relation between the liturgy and the whole Christian life also becomes clearer. The whole life of the faithful, hour by hour during day and night, is a kind of *leitourgia* or public service, in which the faithful give themselves over to the ministry of love toward God and men, identifying themselves with the action of Christ, who by his life and self-offering sanctified the life of all mankind."[22] The Hours are the suitable and ecclesially provided formative prayer of the liturgy of life to which every Christian is called.

Many people would accept and enter into the Liturgy of the Hours more willingly if they were not put off by the psalms, which are its backbone. They need to be reminded that these songs are divinely given; the Spirit provides them for us to use to respond to God's other revelations of himself. Moreover, the psalms contain all of the basic spiritual attitudes which we must seek to cultivate: humility, meekness and resignation, detachment, faithfulness, mercy, yearning for perfection, the will to make peace, and the surrender of oneself to the will of God.

The Liturgy of the Hours is entrusted in a special way to those in holy orders. They must say it for and on behalf of those they are called to serve. Moreover, in the Liturgy of the Hours they can find not only a source of devotion and strengthening of personal prayer, but nourishment for pastoral and apostolic activity. No one who hopes for apostolic fruitfulness should forget that success depends primarily upon the Holy Spirit, and so is most effectively achieved by prayer, rather than by anything else one might choose to do. Finally, since the Liturgy of the Hours is service of the word, faithfulness to it ensures the reception of the word, with its life and power, into the lives of those who ponder it.[23]

Question H: How does the sacrament of matrimony extend
the Eucharist into the basic
personal relationships of most Christians?

1. Most adult Christians are married persons. They prepare the gift to be
offered in the Eucharist in the mutual self-giving of marriage, while the love and
service of the Lord to which they are sent forth from the Eucharist begin in loving
and serving one another and their children (see GS 48).

2. Christian children are holy, and women are saved by bearing and raising
them (see 1 Tm 2.15). Most men, for their part, learn to love somewhat as they
ought in trying to fulfill their family responsibilities, subordinating selfish
interests to the needs of their spouses and the demands (often enough irresistible,
urgent, and unreasonable at the same time) of infants, difficult adolescents, and
even grown children. Members of families fulfill themselves as human persons in
and through their mutual relationships; then they offer this human fulfillment in
union with Jesus' sacrifice in the Church's eucharistic communion with God.

The Church never has doubted that marriage is a way toward heavenly perfection (see
DS 802/430). The Epistle to the Ephesians teaches that the love of husbands and wives for
each other ought to be appropriate to the two different roles.[24] The wife's love ought to be an
act of receptive submission and respect, which excludes any claim to "liberated" autonomy;
the husband's love ought to be an act of tender and perfect care and even, if necessary, of
absolute self-sacrifice, which excludes any temptation to domineering exploitation. Jesus
gave himself for the Church, to purify her in the baptismal bath for her marriage to himself,
a marriage celebrated in the Eucharist. Similarly husbands must sacrifice themselves to
make their wives' love perfect. Marriage foreshadows the union of Jesus with the Church
(see Eph 5.23–33; *S.t.*, sup., q. 42, a. 1).

3. However, every good act and upright relationship of every Christian
becomes eucharistic in essentially this same way. Why, then, does the marital
relationship have the special status of a sacrament, by which the Lord enters and
remains in the lives of married Christians (see GS 48)?

4. The marital covenant is the union of two in one flesh. This is a real union,
since the act proper to marriage is a single human function of the partners together.
Husband and wife share in it as incomplete coprinciples, each completed by the
other. This real unity of the marital covenant symbolizes the unity of our Lord
Jesus and the Church (see Eph 5.32), for the Church is his fullness (see Eph 1.23)
and he fulfills the Church (see Col 1.19–20). **The unity of the new covenant
which marriage signifies is accomplished in Jesus' sacrifice and actualized
for us in the Eucharist.**

5. All members of the Church share in the life of Jesus by participating in the
Eucharist. "Truly partaking of the body of the Lord in the breaking of the
Eucharistic bread, we are taken up into communion with him and with one
another. 'Because the bread is one, we though many, are one body, all of us who
partake of the one bread' (1 Cor 10.17). In this way all of us are made members of
his body (cf. 1 Cor 12.27), 'but severally members one of another' (Rom 12.5)"
(LG 7).

6. **By this sharing, the bonds of marriage and family life are incorporated within and transformed by the life of the Mystical Body of the Lord Jesus. Hence, the status of the marital relationship as a sacrament, by which our Lord in a special sense is included in every Christian marriage and family, is a consequence of the intrinsic relationship of marriage to the Eucharist, insofar as the former is a sign of that which the latter realizes.**

In marriage, the man and woman are fulfilled in three ways: by faithful love, by becoming parents, and by constituting a bond of communion with one another which both represents and realizes the communion which Christ establishes in the Eucharist (see DS 1327/702). Divine-human communion is perfect unity with full respect for and fulfillment of uniqueness; marriage should express and realize this ideal of love (see *S.t.*, sup., q. 42, a. 1; q. 49, a. 4).

The primary purpose of marriage—"primary" not in the sense of "most important," since the sacramental aspect is most important, but in the sense of "most specific"—is the having and raising of children, who are called to live forever in heaven (see DS 3704–5/ 2228–29). This common teaching of the Church, which basically is a fact of biology and anthropology, has not in the least been denied or qualified by Vatican II. While the Council does not use the words "primary" and "secondary," it neither repudiates the distinction nor denies the primacy, rightly understood, of having and raising children: This purpose distinguishes marriage from every other type of companionship (see GS 50; *S.t.*, sup., q. 49, a. 3).[25]

The Eucharist and the sacraments of anointing and matrimony consecrate the earthy foundation of human and Christian life. The Eucharist centers upon eating, nourishment, and survival itself. Anointing and matrimony more explicitly and pointedly bring to bear the consecration of the glorious life of the risen Jesus, who is present bodily in the Eucharist, upon the beginning and end of bodily life, as it comes from nothingness to being and the touch of eternal life, and as it goes from mortal life to fulfillment in the everlasting arms of Life himself.

Summary

The Eucharist is both complex and simple. Complexity is reflected in the five reasons listed by Trent for its institution by Jesus. But the Eucharist also involves another complexity. Like Jesus' life, this sacrament—as well as the other sacraments by their relationship to it—is a revelatory sign communicating God's truth and love, and also a human response of sacrifice in thanksgiving. Jesus acts in the Mass but so do we, with him offering to the Father both him and ourselves united with him. For all its complexity, however, the Eucharist is also simple. It is not a multiplicity of unrelated purposes and actions but the expression of the divine-human communion of love—God's self-communication to us and our response through, with, and in Jesus.

Jesus' fundamental sacrifice is his obedience to the Father's will. At the Last Supper he empowers the apostles and priests of all times to make this sacrifice present in the Mass. All Christians share in the universal priesthood of the faithful, since all are called to offer spiritual sacrifices; and, if done in the Spirit, all the activities of life become such sacrifices. But it is above all in the celebration of the Eucharist that these are offered to the Father in union with Jesus. The living of Christian life as a sharing in the sacrifice of Christ thus prepares for and flows from the Eucharist.

Our communion with Jesus has three inseparable but distinct aspects: sharing by adoption in his divine life, which begins in baptism; sharing in his revelatory life, for which we are commissioned in confirmation; and bodily union with him and enlivening by his resurrection life, effected by the Eucharist. In the Eucharist we consume Jesus' living, bodily self, while he causes our bodily selves to come alive with his glorious, resurrected life. This communion maintains and perfects the sharing in divine life and cooperation in human action which also unite us with him.

In ordinary human experience, the more one gives a person, the more one loves him or her, and the more one loves, the more one wishes to give. This "virtuous circle" is present also in the Eucharist. We bring gifts representing ourselves; this offering leads to Jesus' offering of himself, in which we share while at the same time offering ourselves united and transformed in him. The many reasons for leading a good Christian life are gathered up in this virtuous circle of love: God has given us everything, and we must thank him with, through, and in Jesus; the more we do, the more we love him, and the more we love him, the more perfectly we must live to make a better gift.

Still, why suppose that if we offer our lives to God, he will accept? The answer is found in Jesus. His gift is accepted; his resurrection in glory is God's acceptance of it. In the Eucharist, we are united to Jesus—Jesus as he is, risen in glory. Since we receive his resurrection life in the Eucharist, we have in this sacrament not simply a promise of heavenly glory but a beginning of it.

As the sacrament of unity with Jesus, the Eucharist is also the sacrament by which the unity of the Church is built up and sustained. By making us one with him it establishes a bond of communion among us. This bond is ecclesial communion, constitutive of the Church. Preaching the gospel, faith, and baptism also constitute the Church, but in an initial, incomplete manner which the Eucharist brings to fullness and completion.

The Eucharist is extended throughout the day by the Liturgy of the Hours. All one's life is to be lived as preparation of the gift one offers in the Eucharist with, through, and in Jesus and as execution of the dismissal mandate at Mass to love and serve the Lord. But Christian life must be formed and structured by appropriate prayer, and the Liturgy of the Hours is the common act of prayer provided by the Church for shaping life as an extension of the Eucharist.

For most Christians, too, the Eucharist is extended into their basic personal relationships by the sacrament of matrimony. The self-giving, love, and service of marriage and family life prepare the gift to be offered in the Eucharist and carry out its mandate. The marital relationship enjoys the status of a sacrament because, as the union of two in one flesh, the marital covenant symbolizes the unity of Jesus with the Church—the unity accomplished in us by the Eucharist. In other words, the marital relationship is a sacrament because of its intrinsic relationship to the Eucharist, as a sign of what the Eucharist realizes.

Appendix: The bodily presence of Jesus in the Eucharist

The Catholic Church is absolutely committed to a realistic and straightforward understanding of the bodily presence of Jesus in the Eucharist (see DS 1636–42/874–77, 1651–58/883–90; *S.t.*, 3, q. 73, a. 1, ad 3; q. 75, a. 1; q. 78, a. 1). It will not do to say that the difference between the Eucharist and the other sacraments is one of degree only, on the ground that the "complete humanity of Christ, glorified body as well as soul, is active in all the sacraments."[26] Jesus in glory is active—his actions are visible to us—in all the sacraments. But his own human self is bodily present in the Eucharist in a unique way (see SC 7).

Expounding the traditional teaching on the Eucharist—a tradition he says he personally received from Jesus (see 1 Cor 11.23)—St. Paul makes clear the realism of the Lord's bodily presence in this sacrament by pointing out the implications if one receives Jesus unworthily: "Whoever, therefore, eats the bread or drinks the cup of the Lord in an unworthy manner will be guilty of profaning the body and blood of the Lord. Let a man examine himself, and so eat of the bread and drink of the cup. For any one who eats and drinks without discerning the body eats and drinks judgment upon himself" (1 Cor 11.27–29). Just as unloving intercourse in marriage does not promote mutual self-giving, so the unworthy reception of Communion does not nourish the soul to eternal life. In both cases, one ought to realize what one is doing and respect the sacred reality of flesh.

The theology of "transfinalization" or "transignification" was a product of the development of understanding of the sacraments as revelatory signs and as actions. Much in this approach was excellent. However, it failed insofar as it presupposed body-self dualism and took inadequate account of the realism of Jesus' bodily presence in the Eucharist.[27]

One often encounters false statements such as the following: "Just as bread exists as bread only in relation to man, so what now is before him stands to him as the Body of Christ because of the new and essential relationship it has with him."[28] Implicit here is a denial of the mysterious but simple truth we believe. A bodily human individual does not stand as such to others because of his or her relationship to them; on the contrary, a bodily human individual stands as such to others because he or she is this bodily person. We must recognize the body of the Lord Jesus, as Paul says. We do not create him by the projection (by faith) of Jesus-bodiliness upon a piece of bread and a cup of wine.

In the Eucharist Jesus is present bodily, not merely "by virtue of the sign and the power of the sacrament but in his proper nature and true substance" (DS 700/355). This eucharistic presence is mysterious, because this being-with-us is unique in all reality (see *S.t.*, 3, q. 75, a. 1, ad 3; a. 4; q. 76, aa. 5–6).

However, there is nothing mysterious about the negative side of the situation (see *S.t.*, 3, q. 75, a. 2). We know exactly what it means to point at anything which is not bread or not wine and say truly: "This is not bread; that is not wine." In exactly the same sense that one can point at a cup of wine and say truly, "This is not bread," or point at a piece of bread and say truly, "That is not wine," one can point at the Bread after the consecration and say truly, "This is not bread," and to the Cup and say truly, "That is not wine" (see DS 1256/666). For after the consecration, Jesus himself is present whole and entire, body and blood, soul and divinity, under both species (see DS 1257/667, 1639–40/876; *S.t.*, 3, q. 76, aa. 1–2).

The whole substance—that is, the reality—of the bread is changed into the substance of Jesus' body, and the whole substance of the wine is changed into the substance of his blood, but since he now dies no more, body and blood are not separated from each other or from his human self and divinity (see DS 1642/877, 1652/884; *S.t.*, 3, q. 75, aa. 2, 4, 6, 8; q. 76, a. 2). It follows that we ought to worship the Eucharist, although the sacrament was instituted that we might receive Communion (see DS 1654/886, 1656/888).

Speculative theologians sometimes get into difficulties about this mystery by trying to understand it in categories other than those uniquely proper to it. But in the case of the Eucharist, just as seeing is not believing, so metaphysics is not believing. Believing is believing, and if one's sight or reasoning leads to a different conclusion than that of simple faith, one should conclude that sight and reason are untrustworthy (see *S.t.*, 3, q. 75, a. 1).

Less from professional theologians writing as such than in popular discussions and encounters with nonbelievers, one often receives the challenge: "If the Eucharist is understood realistically, then in receiving it you are engaging in cannibalism." How should this challenge be answered?

There are diverse reasons why people eat human bodies. In some instances, there is a moral or religious motive for consuming a human body (or some part of it)—for example, to share in the person's virtuous characteristics, or to keep the dead individual from reverting back into the dust from which he or she came. When such cannibalism is considered, one can see that the underlying motive is by no means repulsive; the trouble is that the method is ineffective. One does not gain courage by eating the dead heart of a noble warrior, nor preserve one's mother from hades by digesting her dead body.

Essentially, the Eucharist is unlike cannibalism because the Eucharist does what it signifies. The sacramentality of the presence of Jesus makes available at all times and places and to all individuals for eating the one, unique, living Body who is the glorified Incarnate Word. The cannibals eat the dead remains of a person; we eat Jesus alive and glorious, and our eating neither divides nor harms him. Rather, he transforms us by, as it were, inverse digestion.

Notes

1. The teaching of Trent on the Mass and Eucharist has been ignored and even denied in some recent catechetical materials, but also has been firmly defended by the magisterium. See Eugene Kevane, *Creed and Catechetics: A Catechetical Commentary on the Creed of the People of God* (Westminster, Md.: Christian Classics, 1978), 141–52.

2. John Paul II, *Dominicae cenae*, sec. 5, 72 *AAS* (1980) 119–21; *L'Osservatore Romano*, Eng. ed., 24 March 1980, 6.

3. For relevant exegesis: F. X. Durrwell, C.Ss.R., *The Resurrection: A Biblical Study*, trans. Rosemary Sheed (New York: Sheed and Ward, 1960), 35–77, 136–50, and 319–32; *In the Redeeming Christ: Toward a Theology of Spirituality*, trans. Rosemary Sheed (New York: Sheed and Ward, 1963), 54–63.

4. See Louis Bouyer, *Liturgical Piety* (Notre Dame, Ind.: University of Notre Dame Press, 1955), 76–78; Robert J. Daly, *Christian Sacrifice: The Judaeo-Christian Background before Origen* (Washington, D.C.: Catholic University of America, 1978), 498–508.

5. See St. Augustine, *City of God*, x, 6.

6. See Louis Bouyer, *Eucharist: Theology and Spirituality of Eucharistic Prayer* (Notre Dame and London: University of Notre Dame Press, 1968), 103–5.

7. See Pius XII, *Allocution to the International Congress on Pastoral Liturgy* (22 September 1956), 48 *AAS* (1956) 711–25.

8. *The New Order of the Mass*, introduction and commentary by J. Martin Patino et al., trans. Bruno Becker, O.S.B.; *Institutio Generalis Missalis Romani*, trans. Monks of Mount Angel Abbey (Collegeville, Minn.: Liturgical Press, 1970), 69.

9. The internal quotation is annotated by note 55; St. Leo the Great, Serm. 63, 7; *P.L.*, 54:357 C.

10. An example: E. Schillebeeckx, O.P., *Christ the Sacrament of the Encounter with God* (Kansas City: Sheed, Andrews and McMeel, 1963), 15: "When a man exerts spiritual influences on another, encounters through the body are necessarily involved." Statements of this sort signal the assumption that the person really is the "inward man" or "interiority" which uses the body as an expression and instrument by which to "manifest itself." The assumption is bad metaphysics. See Germain Grisez, "Dualism and the New Morality," *Atti del Congresso Internazionale Tommaso d'Aquino nel Suo*

Settimo Centenario, vol. 5, *L'Agire Morale* (Naples: Edizioni Domenicane Italiane, 1977), 323–30. A refutation of dualism and additional references to the literature: Germain Grisez and Joseph M. Boyle, Jr., *Life and Death with Liberty and Justice: A Contribution to the Euthanasia Debate* (Notre Dame and London: University of Notre Dame Press, 1979), 377–80. Theologians influenced by dualism will deny that they are dualists; they will insist upon the very close relationship of body and subject. This insistence would be unnecessary except for the dualistic assumption which they are rightly trying to overcome but wrongly cling to.

11. Hence the title of Schillebeeckx's work on the sacraments, which stops short of saying simply that Jesus is God and reduces him to a sacrament of encounter with God; this is hardly: "The Word became flesh" (Jn 1.14).

12. In the interest of affirming our offering of Jesus with him, which is not in the Offertory, some have denied the reality of offering at the Offertory. But this position is at odds with the liturgical action of bringing forward gifts. See Josef A. Jungmann, S.J., *The Early Liturgy: To the Time of Gregory the Great* (London: Darton, Longman and Todd, 1959), 117. It is not a case of either/or but of both/and; the offering we make in the Mass is complex and dynamic, not simple and static, as is wrongly assumed.

13. Pius XII, *Mediator Dei*, 39 AAS (1947) 555–56; *The Papal Encyclicals*, 233.92–94.

14. John Paul II, *Dominicae cenae*, sec. 9, 130–34; 8; the internal quotation at the end is from the *General Instruction on the Roman Missal*, 55 (ed. cit. above, 56).

15. A treatment of the unbreakable unity of the death and resurrection of Jesus as a redemptive principle: Lucien Cerfaux, *Christ in the Theology of St. Paul* (New York: Herder and Herder, 1959), 107–60. In itself, dying would be useless; God redeems by re-creating, as in the resurrection of Jesus.

16. John Paul II, *Dominicae cenae*, sec. 4, 119–21; 6.

17. *Apostolic Constitution on* and the *General Instruction of the Liturgy of the Hours*, *Liturgy of the Hours*, 1:29.

18. Ibid., 17.

19. Ibid., 9 and 31–34.

20. Ibid., 16.

21. Ibid., 34, 36, and 39.

22. Ibid., 18.

23. Ibid., 37–38.

24. This point often is rejected today. For a positive, philosophical exposition of the Christian conception: Robert E. Joyce, *Human Sexual Ecology* (Washington, D.C.: University Press of America, 1980), 63–85.

25. For a comparative analysis of texts to show that the teaching of Vatican II is not significantly different from that of St. Thomas: Germain Grisez, "Marriage: Reflections Based on St. Thomas and Vatican Council II," *Catholic Mind*, 64 (June 1966), 4–19. "Primary" is a technical, logical term; in this sense, the primary end of a bridge club is playing bridge, even if most people participate more for sociability than to play the game, and the primary office of a king is to rule, even if his personal interest is in exploiting the people. Vatican II did not change the received view, but neither did it use the expression "primary end" which had been widely misinterpreted.

26. Colman E. O'Neill, O.P., *Meeting Christ in the Sacraments* (Staten Island, N.Y.: Alba House, 1964), 58. On the whole this book is sound; perhaps the author did not mean what he says here.

27. A magisterial evaluation of this approach: Paul VI, *Mysterium fidei*, 57 AAS (1965) 753–74; *The Papal Encyclicals*, 273. A concise, current theological treatment in harmony with faith: James Quinn, S.J., *The Theology of the Eucharist*, Theology Today Series, 27 (Hales Corners, Wis.: Clergy Book Service, 1973), 62–91.

28. Thomas D. Stanks, S.S., "The Eucharist: Christ's Self-Communication in a Revelatory Event," *Theological Studies*, 28 (1967), 47. This article contains much that is excellent concerning the revelatory aspect of the Eucharist; unfortunately, the author apparently does not believe that Jesus is bodily present under the appearance of bread and wine.

CHAPTER THIRTY-FOUR

CHRISTIAN LIFE ANIMATED
WITH HOPE OF EVERLASTING LIFE

Introduction

We have seen why hope of everlasting life is necessary for living the Christian life (28-G). Christians have always held that hope gives meaning to the whole of their lives and distinguishes them from the lives of people without hope. Still, the relationship between life in this world and Christian hope for everlasting life needs to be clarified. Which of several possible accounts one accepts makes a great difference to the way one regards Christian life in this world.

This chapter criticizes two distinct Christian views of the matter as well as modern secular humanism. The latter denies the afterlife altogether, but does so partly to safeguard certain values originating in the Christian understanding of the dignity of human persons. By bringing to bear Vatican II's vision of Christian humanism, the inadequacies of the preceding views can be avoided. In the light of this vision, the chapter offers a fresh account of the relationship between life in this world and the fulfillment in our Lord Jesus for which we hope.

Question A: What difficulties are generated by the view that Christian life in this world is only a means to be used to reach heaven?

1. While no orthodox Christian may ever have held, entirely without qualification, that life in this world is nothing but a means to reach heaven, much Christian theology and popular piety have come close to saying this.[1] According to such a view, nothing one does in this life contributes directly to human fulfillment; the only human fulfillment is in enjoyment of God in heaven. Since the purpose of the present work is theological clarification, not a history of theology and spirituality, this unqualified position will be criticized here without considering its nuanced historical expressions.

2. Among those who contributed to this view was St. Augustine.[2] It is a question for historians exactly what Augustine had in mind, but he has been widely taken as saying that life in this world is only a means to reach heaven, and that heaven is an entirely other-worldly goal. According to this position, which became classic, only one human fulfillment should be sought for its own sake,

namely, the enjoyment of God in heaven. Since God alone is infinitely good, everything else is to be loved only as a means to heavenly peace in the beatific vision.[3] In outline, the argument is that human beings were made for perfect happiness, yet they will not find it in this life but only in the heavenly vision of God; any enjoyment short of this is no more than a distracting imitation of it; therefore, nothing in this life is to be enjoyed, and everything short of heavenly happiness should be used as a means to that end.[4]

3. Those who hold this view attach a special significance to certain specifically religious acts, of which mystical, contemplative prayer is the prime example.[5] These are not altogether extrinsic means to heaven but provide a foretaste of it—somehow they anticipate the beatific vision.[6] Such acts are thought to be best when human action ceases and divine action is passively experienced.

4. Other acts of a secular character are unlike the beatific vision. Insofar as they involve finite goods which have an immediate appeal and could be enjoyed, their chief significance is in being a source of temptation. One is in danger of sinful conversion from the supreme Good toward a finite good, in whose enjoyment one might wrongly and vainly try to rest content.

5. **The classical view leads to a sharp division within Christian life between religious and secular, supernatural and merely natural.** Life in a cloister is the way to holiness; life in the world is at best a more or less perilous compromise suited to those who are less generous. Saints are found almost exclusively among the religious and the clergy, not in ordinary families.[7]

6. **This sharp division has been harmful even to the religious dimension of Christian life.** The beatific vision was thought of as if it were a particular, created, human act of intellectual knowledge (see *S.t.*, 1, q. 12, aa. 1–2; 1–2, q. 3, aa. 1–2, 4–5, 8). But such an act would be an inherently individualistic and incommunicable experience. Moreover, hope for the enjoyment of this act does not of itself include hope for resurrection.[8] Hence, the latter, while never denied, lost much of its relevance in a piety directed toward saving one's soul. Heaven thus conceived had a certain appeal for intellectuals but seemed a boring prospect to many other Christians. They sought heaven more out of a desire to escape suffering, in this life and in hell, than out of any positive enthusiasm for disembodied, intellectual bliss.

7. **The sharp division in Christian life into religious and secular also tended to depreciate human goods other than religion.** Religion was confused with the divine life in which Christians share by adoption. As a result, the Christian religion was seen not as one good among others, but as a more than human fulfillment which radically devalues all merely human goods. This gave rise to false conceptions of self-denial and renunciation of the world, which at their worst threatened the Christian belief in the inherent goodness of creation and the dignity of human persons as human. Religion also tended to become totalitarian—a tendency expressed in the burning of heretics, the suppression of liberty for the sake of the security of religious institutions, and the hegemony of clerics in the Christian lives of the faithful.

8. Indeed, according to the classical view, it is hard to understand the value of nonreligious acts for the natural goods of human beings even as means to be used to reach heaven (see *S.t.*, 2–2, q. 181, a. 4; q. 182, aa. 1–2). Plainly, they do not bring about the beatific vision, and secular life is not a participation in heavenly glory. Nonreligious acts for human goods seemed necessary only insofar as Christian morality commands them. But if this were so, then Christian moral norms would not be based on human goods, as St. Thomas and other sound Christian thinkers affirmed (see, e.g., *S.c.g.*, 3, 121–22, 129). Rather, these norms would be—and were increasingly perceived as—arbitrary divine commandments constituting a kind of test, with heaven the reward for obedience and hell the punishment for disobedience.[9]

9. When someone requires others to do something to attain their end which nevertheless is not inherently necessary for attaining it, the requirement is an imposition. When moral norms are regarded as impositions, however, morality is reduced to legalism. Thus, given the tendency to perceive God's commandments voluntaristically, Christian morality became legalistic (1-D). Legalism fostered moral minimalism, the idea that it is not doing good which is most important but avoiding evil. It also generated resentment of God, inasmuch as morality seemed unreasonable. In these circumstances, anyone who set aside strict obedience was likely also to set aside the supposedly arbitrary principle of God's will in favor of the truly arbitrary principle of self-will.

The teaching of Vatican II, including virtually the whole of *Gaudium et spes* (see especially 21, 34, 39), liberates Catholics from the limitations and defects of the classic way of thinking. Life here and now is not merely instrumental. It is by no means extrinsic to fulfillment in the Lord Jesus.

Observing that the end (purpose) of a knife is to cut and the end of an eye is to see, Aristotle asked what the end of man is. His answer: To think about the best and highest things, the principles and the order of the universe, and to shape human life and society as reasonably as possible. St. Augustine later stated a great Christian truth in an immortal formula: Our hearts are made for God and never will rest except in him. That is true precisely in this sense: God knew what he was doing when he fashioned humankind; he knew we were to be his adopted children; and, in fact, human persons cannot live good human lives without redeeming grace, which also is deifying grace.[10] But St. Thomas Aquinas synthesized Aristotle's concern about the end of man with St. Augustine's articulation of our hunger for the destiny for which God created us. He concluded that human persons naturally desire the beatific vision and described heaven primarily in terms of intellectual knowledge of what God is.[11]

It seems to me that this conclusion and description contributed to many of the difficulties I am trying to surmount in this work. My contention is that the human heart is not naturally oriented toward adoption as a child of God and the heavenly inheritance which goes with this status. It is naturally oriented toward human fulfillment, which is found in human goods in which one naturally can participate more and more. No single complete good is naturally available to human persons as their determinate, ultimate end.

Of course, in choosing, one seeks a good loved for itself. In this sense, one always acts for an ultimate end—that is, an end not pursued as a means to some ulterior end. But an end ultimate in this sense need not be the complete good of the human person, as Thomas assumed when he tried to prove that one's will cannot be directed simultaneously to two or more ultimate ends (*S.t.*, 1–2, q. 1, a. 5). Rather, in loving various human goods for their own sake, human persons remain upright insofar as they remain open to integral human fulfillment. This fulfillment is naturally only an ideal, not a determinate goal to which all the acts of a good life contribute. Thus, on the theory of human fulfillment proposed in chapters five and seven, the view that the human heart is naturally restless is based on a mistaken theory of human goal-directedness.

The Church firmly teaches that human persons' calling to share in divine life is entirely gratuitous and supernatural (see DS 1921/1021, 1923/1023). Vatican I solemnly teaches that revelation is absolutely necessary only because God has called human persons to a supernatural end (see DS 3005/1786). Pius XII again rejects the theological opinion that God cannot create intellectual beings without ordering and calling them to the beatific vision (see DS 3891/2318). From this teaching it follows that God could have created human beings without such a calling, and, since God creates nothing by its nature destined to evil, that such human beings could have lived good lives.

We need not suppose that this possibility ever is anything more than a mere possibility. God knew what he planned when he created angels and human beings. But one can draw an important conclusion from the possibility, considering it as a pure hypothesis: If God had created human persons without calling them to adoption, and if human persons had lived good lives in such a condition, then human hearts would have been no more restless than they would need to be to keep humankind growing and progressing endlessly. But having been called to be adopted children of God and having fallen into the condition of prodigal children, human persons now have restless hearts which cannot rest except in God.

Therefore, rest in God is not an alternative, as Augustine perhaps thought (and as many who followed him certainly thought), to the effort to bring about and share in a full and rich human life in this world. The beatific vision which Scripture promises and the Church teaches us about is a mysterious and indescribable blessing which transcends merely human fulfillment. The beatific vision ought to remain mysterious to us, because it is utterly beyond human capacities. Moreover, the mysteriousness of what is essentially supernatural is important even humanly speaking, because it makes heaven intriguing to people of every taste and temperament, and prevents it from becoming an alternative to the love of human goods.

Heavenly fulfillment requires not only respect for human goods—which Augustine clearly realized—but dedication to them. Respect for human goods can be maintained merely by not attacking them; one respects life when one refrains from killing. Dedication demands positive service to human goods, a determined effort to promote them, and a great concern for human well-being in this world.

When I was a small child, every spring my parents bought each of the bigger children a kite to fly. The first time I received one for myself, I took it at once and eagerly unwrapped it, only to discover that when I had torn away the wrapping, only the sticks remained. I learned then that it can be a mistake to think that something is a mere means, when it might be an important part of the good one loves.

Human actions done in this life are destined to be an important constituent part of eternal life. Every human effort and success of those who love God will last forever. If everlasting life excluded human fulfillment or limited it to a single good—the good of the intellect—then love of God would be dehumanizing, and Christians would be immoral to hold and live their faith, and irresponsible and antihuman to propagate it. All our thinking about Christian life needs to be examined and perfected in the light of an inclusive conception of the destiny of creation: namely, the scriptural conception of everlasting life as fulfillment in the Lord Jesus rather than the theological conception of heavenly bliss as the end of man.[12]

Question B: What are the implications of the view that human fulfillment will be found exclusively in this world?

1. The problems of the view just criticized generated tensions which eventually led to the split between humanism and fideistic supernaturalism. This split became obvious during the Renaissance and Reformation as well as subsequently. This is not the place to trace these developments in detail. It is clear enough, however, that the qualified humanism of the Renaissance developed through the Enlightenment into the antireligious, secular humanism of the nineteenth and twentieth centuries.[13]

2. Radical Protestantism of the Reformation despaired of corrupt human nature. In response, humanism began to assert the autonomy and inherent worth of human life in this world—if necessary, even to the exclusion of the human good of religion. Badly distorted as it is, secular humanism nevertheless retains several elements of the Christian view of the human person. First, every version of secular humanism believes that life has a definite goal, usually thought to be some sort of ideal community in which all people will be fulfilled and individuals will be at liberty to do as they please. Second, secular humanists believe the fulfillment of humankind will be attained; it is not a mere ideal but a goal to be reached by human efforts.[14] Third, every secular humanism claims to reverence the dignity of human persons and calls for liberty and justice for all.

In its conception of Christian morality, recent Protestant situation ethics remains faithful to the most questionable aspects of the thought of the Reformation. Rudolf Bultmann provides a concise formulation of the voluntarism inherent in fideistic supernaturalism:

> The liberation which Jesus brings does not consist in teaching man to recognize the good as the law of his own human nature, in preaching autonomy in the modern sense. *The good is the will of God, not the self-realization of humanity, not man's endowment.* The divergence of Jesus from Judaism is in thinking out the idea of obedience radically to the end, not in setting it aside. His ethic also is strictly opposed to every humanistic ethic and value ethic; it is an ethic of obedience. He sees the meaning of human action not in the development toward an ideal of man which is founded on the human spirit; nor in the realization of an ideal human society through human action. He has no so-called individual or social ethics; the concept of an ideal or end is foreign to him. The concepts of personality and its virtues and of humanity are also foreign to him; he sees only the individual man standing before the will of God. Conduct moreover is not significant because a value is achieved or realized through action; the action as such is obedience or disobedience; thus Jesus has no system of values [italics in original].[15]

This view combines truth and error. The truth is that Jesus proclaims something more than the fulfillment proper to human nature and makes it clear that even this will be attained only by God's grace. The error is Bultmann's gratuitous exclusion of an authentic Christian humanism. His failure to make room for human fulfillment and to recognize its role in grounding moral truth is typical of radical Protestantism. This failure helped to elicit the antireligious response of the Enlightenment and of post-Enlightenment secular humanism.

3. Since all varieties of secular humanism affirm certain elements of the

Christian view of the person denied or ignored by classical Christian piety itself, secular humanism appeals even to faithful Christians, despite its rejection of faith. Ultimately, however, the implications of secular humanism are by no means benign. Its own inherent inadequacies frustrate and often grossly pervert its efforts to create on earth a kingdom of God without God.

4. **The goal of every secular humanism is a definite and objective state of affairs: the gradual and continuing perfecting of some aspects of persons in community.** The character of this definite goal has led to an ethics of effectiveness: **What contributes to the goal is good, what obstructs it is evil. This proportionalism has in turn had two effects. First, even the most basic human goods are attacked if they stand in the way of the approved program of progress.** Human life, for example, is destroyed in the name of revolutionary progress in the case of Marxism or, as in the case of the present policy on abortion in the United States, for the sake of individual convenience and social utility. **Second, existential goods, those realized in morally upright choices, are either ignored or treated as mere components of the goal to be achieved.** When pursued as parts of this goal, they also are often compromised for the sake of its other elements.

5. Still more fundamentally, free choice is denied, because a definite, future goal is taken to be the supreme human good. Only technical choices, those concerned with means to ends, are recognized. People who choose not to pursue the goal are considered ignorant, sick, determined by class bias, religious fanaticism, or the like. Secular humanists uniformly appeal to some sort of deterministic theory to account for those who do not share their views and goals.

6. In combination with the assumption that human fulfillment can be attained by human powers, such an explanation, which excludes free choice, entails the denial of radical evil. Secular humanist theories deny sin, both original and personal. They deny that there is any privation which only healing love can overcome. Evil which cannot be ignored or remedied by education and therapy must be dealt with by force. Thus, for a secular humanist ideology mass murder is the appropriate mode of response to intractable problems.

7. The exclusion of free choice also requires the radical reinterpretation of existential goods, which in reality can be realized only in free choices and community-forming commitments. Secular humanists regularly think of these goods as if they were mere psychological and sociological facts. Friendship, for example, is regarded as a set of psychological dispositions and experiences, rather than a bond of fidelity which can last regardless of such facts. The exclusion of free choice implies the exclusion of moral norms antecedent to human desires, and this leads to the loss of the distinction between authority and power. In consequence, justice is regarded as the product of the political process rather than the antecedent principle for forming, carrying out, and judging policies.

8. Secular humanist ideologies tend to politicize the whole of life. In practice, however, a private sphere of social existence cannot be eliminated. Free choice prevails here, but it is without the direction of any socially accepted norms. Thus secular humanism inclines individuals to pursue their own interests wherever and

however they can. Wherever a form of secular humanism becomes dominant, moral subjectivism and hedonism—escape from pressure, pain, and tension— prevail in private life.

For secular humanists the ultimate significance of this life is both absolute and nil. It is absolute in the sense that this life is the only life there is; whatever human fulfillment there ever will be must be had here and now. It is nil in the sense that this life points to nothing beyond itself; it is a tale told by a computer, full of clicks and beeps, signifying nothing.

Secular humanists seek to avoid the ultimate dreadful consequences of their view in one or both of two ways. Sometimes they emphasize the satisfactions people can enjoy here and now. This emphasis leads to hedonism. Hedonism leads to selfishness, to individualism, to hypocrisy, to vanity. As Americans, we can see what hedonism means; it is all around us and like a cancer is destroying our society. At other times, secular humanists seek to avoid the emptiness of life by claiming that the present is important as a means to a brighter future for humanity. They project the new heavens and new earth as a goal, and say that present toil and misery will bring this vision to reality—for example, by violent revolution. This emphasis leads to totalitarianism and brutal repression. Communism illustrates what this form of secular humanism does to human persons.

Either form of secular humanism spells death for humankind. The secular humanist prophet proclaims death and more abundant death. Having ridiculed the good news of Jesus for its promise of eternal life—"pie in the sky when you die"—secular humanism delivers the bad news of death by propaganda and other perverse uses of the media, and carries out the deeds which go with this poison: the destruction of untold millions of people already in this present century, the continuing destruction by abortion of tens of millions of Jesus' littlest ones every year, and the perpetually threatened poison of atomic warfare, by which the majority of the earth's population will probably one day die.

Question C: What are the implications of the view that heaven will inevitably follow this life, but that the positive meaning of this life is found entirely within it?

1. The unsatisfactoriness of both the preceding views has led to efforts at a synthesis in some form of liberalized Christianity.[16] Since Vatican II, certain products of this effort have become quite widely accepted among Catholics.[17] Teilhard de Chardin was one—and perhaps the single most important—precursor of this movement and contributed greatly to it.[18] More important than any Catholic thinker as the precursor of liberalizing Christianity among Catholics, however, were liberal Protestant theologians in the immense movement stemming from Schleiermacher and Hegel.[19] In wealthy countries, individualistic versions of secularized Christianity have had wide appeal, while in the less developed countries socialistic versions, promoted by various liberation theologians, have captured many people's imaginations. Proponents of liberalized Christianity often qualify their views sufficiently to avoid making obviously unorthodox assertions, but they cannot avoid giving a selective and exclusive emphasis to certain parts of Catholic truth while neglecting others.[20]

2. Certain features are common to all forms of liberalized Christianity. They rightly affirm the importance of both human fulfillment in this life and heavenly

fulfillment. They also rightly reject a merely instrumental relationship of the former to the latter. They fail, however, to give any other explanation of how hope for heaven positively affects the pursuit of human goods in this life. Partly to eliminate instrumentalism, heaven is considered inevitable while hell is ignored or denied. Life in this world thus becomes an early stage of eternal life, which will emerge by a homogeneous process of development. Admittedly, there is a great deal about the present life which is unpleasant and painful, but it is a matter of optimistic conviction that these unsatisfactory aspects will gradually and inevitably be overcome.[21]

3. No one can live with two ultimate orientations. One practical implication of liberalized Christianity's orientation to this world is that its adherents generally ignore heaven. Hope for heaven plays a certain role at the emotional level, namely, in mitigating inevitable suffering, especially in the face of death. Since its role is only emotional and has no practical relevance for morality, eternal life eventually comes to function only as a symbol, not as a reality. Thus, liberalized Christianity often psychologizes heaven, taking it as a way of regarding life in this world, suggesting that it does not matter whether or not the myth is really true, and so on. (Those who deny the bodily resurrection of Jesus must also deny it for Christians, and vice versa; generally, however, they claim only to be engaged in reinterpreting the "resurrection experience" and "resurrection hope" in terms of their "existential" meaning.)

4. **Views of this sort empty Christian life of moral seriousness.** Classical piety's challenge is rejected as legalism; what really matters is the challenge of promoting human welfare in this world. **As for human goods, they need not be treated as inviolable, as received Christian teaching demands; one can instead conform in good conscience to the moral norms of the secular humanists among whom one lives. But because this world is not ultimate, there is no need to strive for excellence in it and so no need to treat human goods with the ultimate seriousness assigned them by secular humanists.**

5. Logically, at least, the outcome of this compromise between classical piety and secular humanism is a style of life which embraces all the vices of the latter, without the cultural energy and individual ambition nurtured by its thisworldliness. Whatever the good intentions of its authors and however correct they may be on some points, much current work by Catholics in the moral and spiritual fields is blemished by the compromise of liberalized Christianity, including its tendency to empty life of moral seriousness.

Question D: How does the doctrine of fulfillment in the Lord Jesus make clear the incompleteness of the preceding views?

1. Completion in the Lord Jesus includes the perfection of the threefold unity of Christians with Jesus: unity in divine life, in human acts, and in bodily life (19-C).

2. Classical Christian piety emphasized only one of these, heavenly fulfillment in divine life in the beatific vision. It tended to deemphasize and even

depreciate human acts, except to the extent that the beatific vision was considered a human act and one's moral state at death settled one's eternal destiny. Faithful Christians always held the doctrine of the resurrection, but their idea of heavenly fulfillment made little of bodily life. As for the communal aspect of heaven, human communion in intimate life also tended to be ignored or considered only secondary.

3. **When what we hope for is conceived as fulfillment in Jesus, however, both human fulfillment and divine fullness are essential, for Jesus includes both.** Human goods, many of them impossible to realize without resurrection, contribute to the perfection of this communion. Fulfillment in Jesus is essentially communion of persons, not just many created minds contemplating the beauty of God and taking note of one another only incidentally, if at all.

That human acts and goods last in heaven is the other side of heaven's hidden but real presence to us as we live this life. Actions done to others affect Jesus; actions done in his name contribute to his completion. The union of Christian marriage not only symbolizes but in a real way shares in and contributes to the growing bodily union of Jesus and the Church; there will be no marrying in heaven, not because the communion which marriage realizes will be no more, but because the limitations of this good—its exclusivity and procreative function—will be transcended.

No faithful Christian doubts that children raised by married couples for our Lord will be good works present in heaven, nor that the spiritual children begotten by priests can last forever. Even now, our relationship with Jesus and with Mary and the other saints continues; if this were not so, prayer to them would be pointless. All our real relationships with others are built of a fabric of actions—of commitments and understandings. If heaven is to be the reunion for which we hope, then such actions must last. They will do so if we love one another faithfully and holily.

Of course, our actions also change the world in ways which seem merely transient. However, Vatican II's teaching that we will find in heaven the good fruits of our nature and effort enlarges belief in the resurrection. The new heavens and new earth will include the whole community of those risen in Jesus. Their bodily lives in this world did not stop at the surface of their skins. Rather, they lived into the environment and humanized it. So this world too must in some way be reconstituted, or else resurrection would be incomplete (see GS 39).

The prospect remains mysterious, and it is useless to ask questions about its details. The important point is that as life proceeds, the good works of Christians which seem to come and go, even those which fail in their worldly effect, are helping to build up the mysterious world of fulfillment in Jesus. The goods of human nature and the fruits of human work, gathered from all times and places, provide the material of the heavenly kingdom (see GS 38).

If human actions initiated in this world have enduring reality in heaven, the reality of the bodily resurrection also argues for continuing and expanded expressions of the selves formed by these enduring actions. Scripture suggests a continuing heavenly liturgy (see Rv 4); the whole Christian tradition reinforces this idea.²² Such acts will be human ones involving multitudes in social expression.

4. Secular humanism emphasizes certain human goods, but it altogether denies fulfillment in divine life. Implicitly, secular humanist ideologies also deny the intrinsic value of human bodily life, as well as the human fulfillment to be found in the existential goods realized in morally upright acts themselves.

5. **Fulfillment in Jesus does include the perfect human well-being which secular humanism falsely promises in this life. But it also includes as essential components divine life, immortal bodily existence, and all the reflexive goods summed up and embraced by the notion of eternal peace.**
Religion is a basic human good. Therefore, of itself the human heart can desire peace with God and his favor, but no human heart of itself desires to enjoy the good which is proper to the divine persons. This hope is a gift, which comes with the love of God "poured into our hearts through the Holy Spirit who has been given to us" (Rom 5.5).

The Christian promise occurred to no one apart from the gospel. Promising a fulfillment which satisfies and goes beyond every human wish, the gospel astounds anyone who reads it with fresh eyes. The subconscious never projected so wild a dream: human happiness plus a share in divine joy, which takes nothing from human happiness but rathers insures it as it crowns it.

Secular humanists think the hope of a more than human fulfillment necessarily detracts from the energetic pursuit of human fulfillment in this world. But the Christian promise removes this fear, because the promise is given in and by our Lord Jesus, who by his Incarnation shows that divine life is not at odds with human perfection. Jesus "fully reveals man to man himself and makes his supreme calling clear" (GS 22; cf. GS 38). God creates us with the power of free choice; he does not fix our hearts upon any of the limited goods which naturally contribute to our fulfillment (see *S.t.,* 1, q. 82, aa. 1–2; q. 83, aa. 1–2; 1–2, q. 10, a. 1). Therefore, the divine Word and we human persons can share one another's natures and lives without conflict. No trimming, no pushing out of shape, is required to fit together human and divine life.

6. While all forms of liberalized Christianity emphasize that heaven will include divine life and bodily human life, they ignore or deny human acts insofar as these constitute the self and interpersonal relationships. The existential goods become psychologized. This setting aside of the existential is necessary, for to acknowledge the significance of the use of free choice would also require the acknowledgment that eternal life is conditioned upon moral uprightness in this life (one must be good to go to heaven). It is impossible to take human acts with full seriousness and still regard human fulfillment as inevitable. Rather, in really taking human acts seriously, one must admit hell and make other concessions to classical piety. This is something liberalized Christianity tries to avoid.

7. **By contrast, conceiving of heaven as fulfillment in Jesus leads to the conclusion that human beings are included in heaven as members of Jesus who have freely constituted themselves in him by human acts in cooperation with God's free gifts.** Hell also is a real possibility, though one experienced only by those who willfully reject or abuse God's gifts. Among Christians, only those can evade God's mercy who are persistently unfaithful to their vocation to live their faith and share in Jesus' redemptive work.

Question E: How is Christian life in this age both continuous with and discontinuous from everlasting life?

1. In maintaining the moral seriousness of Christian life in the world, the classical view had the merit of orthodoxy. In effect, it affirmed (for those who are

saved) both continuity and discontinuity between this life and eternal life: essential continuity in regard to basic moral disposition and divine life itself, essential discontinuity in regard to the change from faith and mortal life now to the beatific vision and, in or out of the body, a spiritualized existence later. However, it failed to show how this life makes an intrinsic contribution to fulfillment in the Lord Jesus.

2. A more adequate view of the relationship between this life and the next must do three things: It must explain the relationship in view of the actual end of creation, namely, the fulfillment of everything in Jesus; it must clarify the continuity between this life and the next in regard to all three of the ways a Christian is united with Jesus; and it must consider more exactly in what the discontinuity consists. This question will do these three things as a basis for question F, which will show how this life is intrinsically related to everlasting life, but is not merely an early stage in a continuous process inevitably ending in heaven.

3. **The basic principle of continuity is this: The goods in which we participate during this life will also be included in fulfillment in Jesus.** This principle, not fully recognized in the classical view, has been clearly affirmed by Vatican II (see GS 39).

4. **There is also discontinuity, of two sorts. First, the discontinuity of maturation: Goods shared in imperfectly in this life will be shared in more perfectly in everlasting life. Second, a radical discontinuity: Evil, which now disrupts Christian life, will be eliminated from creation or wholly overcome.** Evil will be so completely removed from its basis in good that the separation will be final (last judgment), the universe will be created anew (the transformation of creation on the model of Jesus' resurrection), and those who have constituted themselves in alienation from God will be rendered permanently harmless (the condemnation of the wicked).

The coming of Jesus will be unmistakable; the reign of God already begun in him will become apparent in this world as he reveals himself in the glory and power of his resurrection (see Mt 24.27; Lk 17.20–35). The universe as a whole will be transformed, and new heavens and a new earth brought into being (see 2 Pt 3.11–13). The Church, the human race, and the entire world will be perfectly fulfilled in the Lord Jesus (see LG 48; GS 39).

The prayer of ages that God reign on earth as in heaven will be fulfilled; a new and beautiful community will be formed on earth, in which God will dwell with his people in lasting fellowship. "He will wipe away every tear from their eyes, and death shall be no more, neither shall there be mourning nor crying nor pain any more, for the former things have passed away" (Rv 21.4). "He who conquers shall have this heritage, and I will be his God and he shall be my son" (Rv 21.7). The treasures and wealth of nations will be found in the new community, and it will be illumined with the light of God himself (see Rv 21.23–26). The whole created world will share in this wonderful transformation (see Rom 8.19–22).

5. There is a fundamental continuity between this life and fulfillment in Jesus in respect to divine life, since the real share in divine life which Christians now

enjoy by the gift of adoption is intended to last. Since in this respect there is no evil to be eliminated, there is no radical discontinuity between the Christian's share in divinity in this life and in everlasting life. The divine life of the Christian need not be re-created: Charity does not pass away. There is, however, discontinuity of maturation in respect to divine life, since we now have faith, whereas then we shall be like God for we shall see him as he is.

6. There is also a fundamental continuity in respect to human acts. The Christian's acts of self-determination and faithful communion with and in Jesus will last. The discontinuity of maturation here concerns the fact that the saints will be confirmed in their faithfulness: Temptation and sin will no longer be possible. But there is also a radical discontinuity: Re-creation will eliminate imperfection and venial sin, defects in interpersonal communion, and, in general, all the existential effects of sin. Every source of disharmony and discontent will be overcome.

The ultimate elimination of all conflict and disharmony, the permanent establishment of perfect harmony, is expressed poetically: "The suckling child shall play over the hole of the asp, and the weaned child shall put his hand on the adder's den. They shall not hurt or destroy in all my holy mountain; for the earth shall be full of the knowledge of the Lord as the waters cover the sea" (Is 11.8–9). The whole richness of the many distinct aspects of creator and creatures, self and others, and dimensions of the self will be perfected in perfectly harmonious unity.

7. In respect to bodily life, there is a continuity between this life and everlasting life in two respects (see *S.c.g.*, 4, 79–81; *S.t.*, 3, q. 56, a. 1; q. 79, a. 2). First, one rises in one's own body; second, even now one shares by the sacrament of the Eucharist in Jesus' resurrection life, by which one will rise and live forever. The discontinuity of maturation is that in everlasting life one will share so fully in the resurrection life of Jesus as to have positive immortality. The radical discontinuity lies in the fact that God's re-creative act will eliminate all the evils consequent upon sin which extend beyond the existential domain. Death is the epitome of such evil, but every other sort of disorder will also be eliminated. Thus the blessed will be richly fulfilled in all the substantive human goods, and the present lack of correspondence between uprightness and success, moral goodness and human fulfillment, will come to an end.

Even now, the Christian is blessed with a share in God's knowledge. The disciples of Jesus are his friends, not his servants, for he makes known to them everything he has heard from the Father (see Jn 15.15). The plan of God is now clear: "For he has made known to us in all wisdom and insight the mystery of his will, according to his purpose which he set forth in Christ as a plan for the fulness of time, to unite all things in him, things in heaven and things on earth" (Eph 1.9–10). Perfect knowledge will be given (see 1 Cor 13.9–12).

Jesus is the resurrection and the life (see Jn 11.25), come to give life and more abundant life (see Jn 10.10). The Christian is promised: "He who eats my flesh and drinks my blood has eternal life, and I will raise him up at the last day" (Jn 6.54). And so in the new Jerusalem "death shall be no more" (Rv 21.4).

8. None of the preceding aspects of continuity and maturation is merely individual. The life of Christians is social, lived in the communion with Jesus which we call "Church." The Church herself lasts forever, but she will be perfected in glory. In other words, what is going to last is the whole Lord Jesus. The Mystical Body of Jesus will be perfected by growing to maturity, so that in him we shall form one mature person.

The goal of God's entire magnificent plan is a communion of divine persons and created persons, not a large number of separate relationships between a monadic deity and saved individuals. This communion is incipient in the Church. Hence, the Church is no mere temporary vehicle of the Christian's pilgrimage toward an altogether other-worldly heaven.

We are not adopted as isolated individuals, but as members of the Church. This is so because one and the same Holy Spirit communicates divine life to all God's adopted children. Thus he not only vivifies the Church but also unifies her. The Spirit is to the Mystical Body of the Lord Jesus as a soul is to an organic body (see LG 7). The unity in multiplicity of the Church is itself a reflection of the Holy Trinity, upon which the Church is modeled by the Holy Spirit (see UR 2). Thus the fellowship of adopted children of God in the life of the Church will last forever.

This point is made clear by Vatican II. The Church will achieve her fulfillment at the end of time, when she will include every just person (see LG 2). The Church is identified with the kingdom of God already present in mystery (see LG 3). The Church is the initial budding forth of the kingdom on earth (see LG 5). The fullness of the life of the Church is now hidden with the Lord Jesus; she will appear with her spouse in glory (see LG 6).

This is not to say that the Church and the kingdom are entirely identical. There is a difference, since the Church is fully visible in the present world, working toward fulfillment yet to be realized, while the kingdom is hidden and already realized in Jesus. But this distinction should not be exaggerated. Although not of this present world, the kingdom of God is very much in it. Some of the parables concerning the kingdom indicate that at present it includes both the good and the bad (see Mt 13.24–50), and many others show that the kingdom is growing slowly to maturity by divine power (see Mt 13.31–33; Mk 4.26–32). Also, when Jesus gives Peter his unique role, "church" and "kingdom" are used with the same reference (see Mt 16.18–19).

The heavenly Church (or the kingdom in its perfection) includes all created persons, angels as well as human persons, who enjoy eternal life with God (see DS 1000/530). We acknowledge in the Preface of every Mass the inclusion of angels. But as the communion of the adopted children of God, the heavenly Church does not include the cosmos, which is the environment of human persons, or those created persons who refuse to cooperate in the divine plan. Absolute fullness somehow includes all these, but they are not part of the extended family of God.[23]

Question F: Why is the living of Christian life in this age necessary for the realization of God's salvific purpose?

1. By now it should be clear why life in this age has a more than instrumental relationship to everlasting life. In this life, Christians engage in human actions which are intrinsically meaningful because of the human goods in which the actions enable them to share. The prime instance is the act of faith, by which Christians determine themselves to friendship with God and cooperate in forming God's human family in Jesus.

2. Secondarily, but not just instrumentally, Christians in this life engage in the

actions which make up the life of faith and so work out their unique Christian identities. They do this by carrying out their personal vocations, which in unique and complementary ways articulate and enrich their personal shares in the life of the whole Lord Jesus. In living their human lives in him, Christians collectively contribute to his human completion. Jesus gathers up and restores all things to the Father; thus all the human goods which are served in Christian life, including those considered secular, contribute to fulfillment in Jesus.

3. There is a further implication of the fact that the enduring share in divine life and bodily resurrection life now enjoyed by Christians is based on their human acts of living faith, sacramental participation, and faithful Christian living in general. Such actions are not merely instrumental. For example, the act of faith by which charity is accepted is intrinsically necessary to the reception of this gift, and the eating of Jesus' flesh in the Eucharist is intrinsically necessary to sharing in his resurrection life. Thus, even in the aspects of union with Jesus which transcend the existential domain, Christians accept and maintain their solidarity with him by human acts in this life, and this solidarity is to endure and mature.

4. Furthermore, the actions by which Christians cooperate in redemption with Jesus, and so with the Father and Spirit, are themselves permanently meaningful human actions done for the good of religion. Just as Jesus' doing of the Father's will is sacrifice, so life in Jesus is living sacrifice, offered to God as the response possible for human beings in this sinful age. God's response to this sacrifice is certain because he is faithful. This relationship of gift and response is not merely instrumental, as if human action could mechanically elicit God's re-creative work. Nevertheless, the discontinuity of re-creation is wholly unlike the effortless and inevitable continuity of maturation which the syntheses of liberalized Christianity envisage.

5. The reality called "merit" lies in this intrinsic relationship between human sacrifice and divine re-creative work. Merit is not control over God or a claim upon him apart from his mercy. To merit is instead to do one's part in friendship with God; he will respond by keeping his promises (see *S.t.*, 1–2, q. 114, aa. 1–4). God's re-creative work is a free gift on his part, not something which our work compels him to do; and yet we truly merit this work of God's mercy by the sacrifice of our lives in union with Jesus' sacrifice.[24]

6. As several previous chapters have explained, the point of the Incarnation, of the sacraments, and of the moral life of Christians as a whole is that God wishes to ennoble creatures by allowing them to share as much as possible in his work (see *S.c.g.*, 3, 69). Now the ultimate significance of this aspect of God's saving work is clear. **Since the fulfillment of all things in Jesus includes human selves, self-determined by free choices, and a communion of selves constituted by choices which are communion constituting, Christian life in this world is intrinsically necessary to the fullness of Jesus in its created aspects.** That is why creatures are not beatified without the toil of existence, the overcoming of evil, the work of redemption. Even God cannot create Jesus' life, which is to last forever, without Jesus' living of his life. The same is true of our Christian lives. **The heavenly kingdom is built by Jesus in the life of his Church on earth.**

Vatican II teaches that the secular calling of Christians is to dedicate themselves to the earthly service of others and in this way make ready the stuff of the heavenly kingdom (see GS 38; LG 44). Because this present world is deformed by sin and its consequences, it must give way to the new heavens and new earth; for this reason, historical progress is distinct from, and must not be confused with, the growth of the kingdom (see GS 39). Nevertheless, not only charity but the human acts which are its fruits will endure. Nor may these acts be imagined to survive in some disincarnate form. In the Christian cultivation of this world, there "grows the body of a new human family, a body which even now is able to give some kind of foreshadowing of the new age" (GS 39).

This last conception seems strange. However, the physical environment transformed by human work into a world of culture truly is the body of the human community, which is shared in common by the bodily individuals who communicate in it. Consider, for instance, the way a home bodies out its family or the soil those who live immediately by cultivating it. Hence, Christian hope for resurrection, which is not individualistic, must affirm that "after we have obeyed the Lord, and in his Spirit nurtured on earth the values of human dignity, brotherhood and freedom, and indeed all the good fruits of our nature and enterprise, we will find them again, but freed of stain, burnished and transfigured" (GS 39).

Hence, we ought not to imagine that the fulfillment for which we hope is a spiritual heaven far from human concerns and this material world. Christian hope, like that of secular humanists, is for heaven on earth; the new Jerusalem comes "down out of heaven from God" (Rv 21.2). The difference is that fulfillment in Jesus will be in "a new heaven and a new earth" (Rv 21.1), transformed by God's re-creative act. The good fruits of our nature and work—including our bodily nature and the work of our hands—will not be left behind, but recovered cleansed of the damage our sin inflicts upon them.

Question G: What attitude should Christians have toward the realization of human goods in this life?

1. Since all human goods share in divine goodness and express it, charity requires that all be loved (25-B). **Christian life should therefore develop out of love of human goods, insofar as they fulfill human beings in communion.** It follows that the lives of a good Christian and a decent nonbeliever will appear similar in many ways. But they will differ. The good Christian loves all the goods inclusively and openheartedly, sharing them indiscriminately and never treating any as mere means; this is to say that the fifth and eighth modes of Christian response, mercy and self-oblation, will characterize Christian life. The nonbeliever may possess similar qualities, but at best they will be expressions of the corresponding modes of responsibility. Moreover, the nonbeliever will set limits on their exercise, whereas in principle the Christian can set none.

2. Good Christians will also be as energetic as the most ambitious nonbelievers, but Christian life will not be absorbed in any limited goal. Both tasks and successes will be received with humility (the first mode) as gifts of God. Moreover, in dedication to their personal vocations, good Christians will accept limited roles willingly, will not grasp at other sorts of human fulfillment, and will resign themselves to limitations and frustrations (the second mode).

3. They will also be aware of the hidden meaning of this life, considering the

real and lasting significance of their efforts to be not so much in their observable outcomes as in their contributions to the reordering of goods in the fullness of our Lord Jesus. They will attach the highest importance not to success but to faithfulness until death—a faithfulness accompanied by detachment from everything which does not belong to one's vocation (the third and fourth modes).

4. Good Christians will take evil seriously insofar as it is a real privation which limits human fulfillment. But they will not despairingly regard evil as a positive force which requires either compromise (excluded by the sixth mode) or human retribution (excluded by the seventh mode). Since God's creative work—and only that—ultimately will eliminate evil or overcome it completely, the good Christian will regard evil as Jesus does, with utter repugnance but no misdirected hostility, with hatred for sin and all its effects but compassion toward those who are in sin insofar as they still can be saved.

5. Good Christians will see their lives as a process of perfecting themselves in God's love, building up the fullness of Jesus, and meriting God's re-creative act. Far from being devoid of human meaning, their lives in this world will be supported with fresh incentives (see GS 21, 34, 39, and 43). Aware that earthly progress is not to be confused with the growth of God's kingdom, they will avoid conforming to the contemporary world, hoping instead for the coming of Jesus and the fulfillment by divine re-creation of all things in him (see LG 42; GS 37, 39, and 45).

St. Paul writes movingly of his eagerness to reach his everlasting dwelling. He considers it a reality which is present but invisible, permanent rather than temporary. Fleshly life is waning, but the inner life, a self built up by deeds of love, is waxing. What is most important is that this mortal life be transformed by being drawn into immortal life (see 2 Cor 4.16–5.5). This view usually is considered other-worldliness, and in one sense it is. But the otherness of the other world must be understood accurately. It is the hidden reality of this world. Paul nowhere suggests that human fulfillment achieved now through a totally dedicated life in Jesus belongs to the present world, which is passing away.

Summary

Historically, much Christian theology and piety have tended to regard life in this world only as a means of reaching heaven. The result has been to divide Christian life into the religious and the secular, the supernatural and the merely natural. This is harmful even to the religious dimension of life: Heavenly fulfillment is reduced to the beatific vision, considered as a human act of knowledge—individualistic, incommunicable, and even unappealing to nonintellectuals. Religion is confused with the divine life in which Christians share by adoption; as a result, it is thought of as a more than human fulfillment which radically devalues human goods.

This view leads both to false ideas of renunciation of the world and to religious totalitarianism. Moral norms come to be regarded as arbitrary divine decrees, with heaven the reward for obedience and hell the punishment for disobedience—a view which fosters legalism, moral minimalism, resentment toward God, and, ultimately, subjectivism.

While the secular humanism which developed as the diametrical opposite of this retains elements of the Christian view of the human person, the goal of every secular humanism is a definite and objective state of affairs: the perfecting of some aspects of persons in community. Whatever contributes to this is good, whatever obstructs it, evil. Human goods are compromised or attacked when necessary to achieve the goal. Only technical choices are recognized, and self-determining free choice is denied. This also entails the denial of radical evil, of sin; and any evil which cannot be ignored or remedied by education or therapy must be dealt with by force. Existential goods are psychologized and politicized, while in the private sphere freedom is expressed in moral subjectivism and hedonism.

The unsatisfactoriness of both of these views has led to efforts at a synthesis in liberalized Christianity. This is individualistic in wealthy countries, socialistic in less developed ones, but all its forms have certain common features. While liberalized Christianity denies that human fulfillment in this life has a merely instrumental relationship to heavenly fulfillment, it provides no other explanation of the impact of hope on moral life in this world. Instead, heaven is considered inevitable, and hell is ignored or denied. Because of their orientation to this world, liberalized Christianity's adherents usually ignore heaven, invoking it only as an anodyne in the face of death and other evils beyond human control. Christian life is emptied of moral seriousness: So far as human goods are concerned, one can violate them as secular humanists do, yet one need not approach them with the ultimate seriousness of secular humanists.

In contrast with these views, the conception of everlasting life as completion in the Lord Jesus includes the threefold unity of Christians in Jesus: unity in divine life, in human acts, and in bodily life. Both human fulfillment and divine fullness are essential, for Jesus includes both. Realized human goods contribute to the perfection of everlasting communion—a true communion of persons united with one another in Jesus. Yet this fulfillment is seen as including not only perfect human well-being, but divine life, immortal bodily existence, and all the reflexive goods, summed up by the idea of eternal peace.

The basic principle of continuity between Christian life in this age and everlasting life is that the goods in which we participate now will be included in the fulfillment for which we hope. But there is also discontinuity, of two sorts: the discontinuity of maturation (goods shared in imperfectly now will be shared in more perfectly) and radical discontinuity (evil will be eliminated). Both continuity and discontinuity can be traced in respect to the elements of our threefold unity with Jesus.

Clearly, this life has a more than instrumental relationship to everlasting life, for the human goods which are served in Christian life contribute to the fulfillment of all things in Jesus. At the same time, the discontinuity involved in resurrection and re-creation rules out an effortless and inevitable maturation as envisaged by liberalized Christianity. All this helps clarify the meaning of "merit"—not that we gain a claim on God by what we do, but that if we do our part in friendship with God, he will respond by keeping his promises.

Since Christian life develops out of love of human goods, the lives of a good Christian and a decent nonbeliever will appear similar in many ways. But they are fundamentally different. Loving all the goods inclusively, the Christian will live a life characterized by mercy and self-oblation, the fifth and eighth modes of Christian response, while the good qualities of the nonbeliever will be expressions of the corresponding modes of responsibility. Moreover, the nonbeliever will in principle at least always set limits on the exercise of these, while the Christian can set none. Good Christians will receive success with humility, resign themselves to frustrations and limitations, be faithful to their vocations and detached from everything unrelated to them, and respond to evil by neither compromise nor violence.

Appendix 1:   Christian humanism and cultural progress in history

Proponents of liberalized Christianity are likely to argue that by minimizing or denying the discontinuity between this life and the next, their approach allows uniquely for an account of how Christian life transforms culture and history. However, the view proposed here also (and I think more adequately) allows for a Christian transformation of culture and the promotion of historical progress, while maintaining that redemption ultimately requires divine re-creation.

During his earthly life, Jesus drew people to himself and in doing so drew them together into the communion of his disciples. The followers of Jesus found the reason for their mutual relationship in their more basic interest in him. Similarly today, people who accept the faith have a common bond, but they truly become a working community when they celebrate the Eucharist. Its celebration requires common effort and a common place and property. People in a new neighborhood who do not know one another gather, build a church, and become one people. In former times, people scattered over a wide area created a town by building a church.

In meeting together, those baptized into Jesus and bonded to him and one another by Communion recognize one another as brothers and sisters. From this recognition grows love of neighbor and its works, the bearing of one another's burdens (see Gal 6.2; 1 Jn 2.8–11; 4.19–21).

The actual performance of the Eucharist requires the use of many things: the materials of the gifts, of the church building and furnishings, of vestments; the works of liturgical language, music, and art; the whole secondary system of things involved in preparing the liturgy, the sacramentals, and so forth. All of these uses transform what is used toward holiness. In this way, the Eucharist creates its own culture and begins to consecrate the whole world to the service of God (see LG 34).

One need not idealize the Middle Ages to notice that Christendom was far more humanistic in practice than it should have been according to theological theories. The best in Western civilization was generated during the centuries when faith flourished. Even today, the cathedrals which express the humanism of an earlier time dominate most of the great cities of Europe.

In forming culture, the Eucharist, which is profoundly social, is also shaping not only the lives of individuals but even the entire course of the world's history, directing the immense complex of human words and deeds, accomplishments and sufferings to the end appointed by God. Insofar as the Eucharist is a memorial which keeps present and effective—that is, available for our communal participation—the redemptive act of our Lord Jesus, the eucharistic act more than any other determines humankind to be what it is in response to the divine vocation. At the same time the reality of the eucharistic act in the world makes every moral evil, every refusal to accept communion with Jesus, into a more monstrous sin and a greater perversion of the power of humankind for fulfillment.

Hence, although history does not have an over-all pattern which we can interpret, it is not without sense. Still this sense is not single and unambiguous. The whole of history presents us with the vision of the field of the Lord, in which fine wheat is seen growing toward its maturity while, at the same time, weeds flourish with incredible vitality, seeming almost to overwhelm the wheat.

History has several stages. At first, with the dawn of creation, it had an unambiguous direction toward God. With the fall, this direction was changed to an unambiguous thrust away from God. Left to itself, humankind would have wandered endlessly in empty space. With the revelatory work which prepared for the coming of the Word and the repeated covenants between God and humankind, history was redirected into an orbit about the Incarnate Word. But with him, the course of history does not become a simple path of descent to our everlasting home. Those who share in the adventure of humankind's history struggle for the controls; the course of history is erratic, although it cannot be forced out of its orbit around our risen Lord. Eventually, he will return, come aboard the world, and take control of it.

Progress in the course of human history is not from the material to the immaterial, from the biological to the intellectual. The Word was made flesh, and now his flesh is wholly transfused with the glory of his divinity. Progress in history is not from the human to the divine; our Lord Jesus from the start is perfect man and true God, and the fulfillment of history is to be he himself, nothing else.

Progress in history is from the carnal to the spiritual, from creation alienated from God to creation fulfilled in him. This progress occurs within history, but it is not a progress of history. The integrity of the historical order is passing away. But behind the eucharistic species, hidden with God in the Lord Jesus, the new Jerusalem which will flourish from age to age already is being built up (see LG 6; GS 38–39).[25]

Appendix 2:   Fleshly reality lasts and its givenness is transcended

We expect to die; we watch history passing away and divinely scheduled for an eventual end. We look for resurrection and life everlasting. But in what sense is the fleshly reality of the Christian to last? Death is a profound transformation, in some sense a real destruction of the bodily person. Resurrection is a re-creation. While this re-creation is not creation out of nothing—since resurrection is resurrection from death—the death-resurrection sequence seems more discontinuity than continuity. Thus the resurrection life for which we hope seems only part of what is not yet, in no way part of present Christian life. But this is not so.

In the first place, Jesus already has the bodily life he will enjoy forever. By our union with him, we now share in resurrection life. On this basis, we already commune with God in glory by participation in Jesus' communing, although we do not individually have the full experience he enjoys. In the second place, we now are bodily incorporated in Jesus. If one puts these two considerations together, one sees more clearly that if bodily human persons are to enjoy any real solidarity with the Word made flesh, then some sort of bodily communion is not only fitting but seems necessary.

Our Lord provided for this need by the sacrament of the Eucharist, in which even now we are in bodily communion with him (see Jn 6.25–58). For this reason, we not only have already died with Jesus in baptism, but also have already risen with him and dwell with him in his completion (see Eph 2.5–7; Col 2.12–13; 3.1–4). This statement is not merely a metaphor; it is a statement of fact, and part of the fact is real, present, bodily communion with our Lord Jesus in his resurrection life. To the extent that this life is the present bodily life of a Christian, the Christian's present bodily life is part of what will last forever.

Moreover, resurrection is of one's own body, which is a unique, personal body. The Church clearly teaches this truth (see DS 325/—, 684/347, 801/429, 854/464), and it is a serious mistake to think—as I suspect many people do implicitly think—that at resurrection one's soul gets a new body very much as one's wrecked car is supplied with a new body, only the chassis being saved (see *S.c.g.*, 4, 79–81). My body is not all of myself, but it is an essential and intrinsic part of myself; if I did not live forever in my very own body, then I would not be saved.

Therefore, the aspect of the Christian's bodily reality in which this unique body is personal also is destined to last. What will not last is the mortal organic life which at present constitutes one's bodily self; this will be transformed into immortal organic life like— because still in full communion with—the glorious flesh of Jesus.

It also is worth considering how a Christian's present life bears upon his or her lasting reality. One of the attractions of secular humanism is its promise to liberate humankind from the givenness of the natural world which often constrains and will eventually put an end to all the creative efforts of human intelligence. In trying to fulfill this promise, contemporary humanist ideologies go so far as to reject the meaning and value God has given creation. The promise of liberation by unaided human effort and the rejection of all natural meaning and value are, of course, Promethean arrogance. Still, Christian faith makes it clear that in many respects God's plan for humankind exalts men and women beyond their most ambitious dreams. It is permissible to speculate—and the following is speculation—that the blessed will be more completely liberated from all the givenness of nature than secular humanists imagine.

Jesus rises from the dead by his own action. Jesus asserted he would raise up the temple of his body after it was destroyed (see Jn 2.19–21). He also said of his own life: "I have power to lay it down, and I have power to take it again" (Jn 10.18). St. Thomas explains that there is a certain sense in which, even in death, Jesus miraculously raises himself. Thus the resurrection of Jesus is not exclusively a divine work; it also is in some way a work in which Jesus' body and soul share by divine power (see *S.t.*, 3, q. 53, a. 4).

Having risen in glory, Jesus in heaven continues the work of building the new creation, of which he himself is the cornerstone (see LG 6–8). The coming of the Son of Man in glory, for which we hope, will complete this work, for he will raise the dead, judge, and complete the mission the Father gave him (see Mt 13.41; 16.27–28; 24.31–46; 1 Thes 4.16). When death, the last enemy, is destroyed, Jesus will hand over the kingdom to his Father (see 1 Cor 15.20–28), not as if he were resigning his kingship, but inasmuch as he will have finished the work of bringing all things to completion in himself.[26]

The book of Acts makes it clear that Christians, in unity with Jesus and never apart from him, can bring divine power to bear by miraculous acts, which also are their own human acts. For example, when Peter raises the cripple, he says: "I have no silver and gold, but I give you what I have; in the name of Jesus Christ of Nazareth, walk" (Acts 3.6). Peter both acts in the name of Jesus and gives what he himself has to give. Jesus had said: "He who believes in me will also do the works that I do; and greater works than these will he do, because I go to the Father" (Jn 14.12). Peter is doing a work Jesus does.

When Jesus comes again, the "human race as well as the entire world, which is intimately related to man and achieves its purpose through him, will be perfectly reestablished in Christ (cf. Eph 1.10; Col 1.20; 2 Pt 3.10–13)" (LG 48). The new heavens and the new earth are therefore the work of our Lord Jesus. Through him, as Word of the eternal Father, all things are created (see Jn 1.3). The new heavens and new earth also are part of creation; as such they are solely the work of the Trinity, and so the work of our Lord only insofar as he is the divine Word. But the new heavens and new earth are also his work as Incarnate Word, and so are brought about by his human act just as were his smaller-scale earthly miracles.

At present, we ourselves can unite our own lives to Jesus' life. In offering our lives with his sacrifice in the Eucharist, we do precisely this (see LG 7). So we too have a share in the re-creation of all things. Thus our Christian lives in Jesus not only make a material contribution to the new heavens and the new earth, they even share in the work of bringing this hope to fruition. For each Christian, an important part of this hope is for the resurrection of his or her own personal body.

And so there are two principles by which one's present bodily existence is to last. One of them is one's bodily incorporation in Jesus, which already is established and destined to last. The other is one's share in his work of bringing about the resurrection, a share by which one acts upon one's own present body, precisely as it is uniquely personal. In this respect death in Jesus not only surrenders but at the same time renders unbreakable one's own attachment to one's own body.

In our present life, we find ourselves constrained in many ways by the universe which was here prior to our arrival. Our bodily existence, in particular, is a pure fact. In heaven, we shall not be thus constrained, for having died with Jesus, we will have freely exchanged the mortal life we were given for a life we cooperate in re-creating. Only the Trinity is creator; we are and always shall be creatures. But in the re-created world to come, nothing which determines us will be given without our having freely willed it in advance.

Having freely accepted God's offer of a share in his own divine life, having freely constituted our human existential selves by our own choices, and having freely shared in the work of re-creating everything else in Jesus, we will be revealed fully as adopted children of God, whose whole being will express the glorious freedom proper to such children (see Rom 8.19–21).

Notes

1. See Louis Bouyer et al., *History of Christian Spirituality,* vol. 1, *The Spirituality of the New Testament and the Fathers* (New York: Seabury Press, 1963), 449–54. Frequently, the excesses of Christian spirituality have been in reaction against a false optimism of nonbelieving humanism. This appears to have been the case with the French school of spirituality: Emile Mersch, S.J., *The Whole Christ: The Historical Development of the Doctrine of the Mystical Body in Scripture and Tradition,* trans. John R. Kelly, S.J. (Milwaukee: Bruce, 1938), 542–54; Henri Bremond, *A Literary History of Religious Thought in France,* vol. 3, *The Triumph of Mysticism,* trans. K. L. Montgomery (London: S.P.C.K., 1936), esp. 294–358. The centrality of sacrifice in the spirituality of the French school easily led to a false opposition between human fulfillment and holiness; despite its undoubted contributions to Christian life, the imperfections of this type of spirituality inhibited development of an authentic Christian humanism.

2. For a good, brief treatment with references to the most relevant passages: Eugène Portalié, S.J., *A Guide to the Thought of Saint Augustine,* trans. Ralph J. Bastian, S.J. (Chicago: Henry Regnery, 1960), 271–73; also Etienne Gilson, *The Christian Philosophy of Saint Augustine,* trans. L. E. M. Lynch (New York: Random House, 1960), 3–10.

3. See St. Augustine, *The City of God,* x, 2–3; xix, 10–11 and 25–28. For a detailed and sympathetic study: Ragnar Holte, *Béatitude et Sagesse: Saint Augustin et le problème de la fin de*

l'homme dans la philosophie ancienne (Paris: Etudes Augustiniennes, 1962), 207–81. Only God is to be enjoyed; all else is to be used: *De doctrina christiana*, 1, 3–4. True, as Bouyer et al., op. cit., 487, point out, Augustine himself is the first to sense the inadequacy of this distinction; he is too good a Christian to deny the inherent goodness of the fulfillments proper to human persons as such. However, a system which must stretch its own categories to accomodate the minimal requirements of Christian humanism leaves something to be desired.

4. An alternative account of the ultimate end of human persons was given above (19-B); it puts the end in divine-human communion as the fulfillment of God's plan, which Christians enter even in this life, and this alternative is strongly rooted in Scripture: Bonaventura Mariani, O.F.M., "Il Nuovo Testamento e il Fine Ultimo dell'Uomo sulla Terra," *Divinitas*, 20 (1976), 282–312; Aelred Cody, "The New Testament," in *Heaven*, Concilium, 123, ed. Bas van Iersel and Edward Schillebeeckx (New York: Seabury Press, 1979), 34–42. A question historical inquiry must answer is: How did the theology of St. Augustine and other Fathers—in some ways dangerously influenced by Neoplatonism but still more balanced than its popularizations—come to have so strong a hold on Christian thought? I suspect the answer would be found at least partly in the great emphasis on the divinity of Jesus necessary to combat Arianism. With this emphasis, the humanistic implications of Christian faith tended to be obscured.

5. On St. Augustine's mystical theology, see Portalié, op. cit., 285–88; Bouyer et al., op. cit., 468–82; Vernon J. Bourke, "Augustine of Hippo: The Approach of the Soul to God," in *The Spirituality of Western Christendom*, ed. E. Rozanne Elder (Kalamazoo, Mich.: Cistercian Publications, 1976), 1–12.

6. In his early works, Augustine followed Neoplatonism in thinking that the vision of God is possible in the present life, but in his later works, guided by Scripture, he abandoned this view: Frederick van Fleteren, O.S.A., "Augustine and the Possibility of the Vision of God in This Life," *Studies in Medieval Culture*, 11 (1977), 9–16.

7. For a candid, balanced account: Yves M.-J. Congar, O.P., *Lay People in the Church: A Study for a Theology of Laity*, trans. Donald Attwater (London: Geoffrey Chapman, 1957), 379–99. A new form of Christian life, that of the secular institutes, has arisen from the more profound understanding of the religious significance of the secular: José F. Castaño, O.P., "Il carisma della secolarità consacrata," *Angelicum*, 53 (1976), 319–61.

8. Robert J. O'Connell, *St. Augustine's Early Theory of Man, A.D. 386–391* (Cambridge, Mass.: Belknap Press of Harvard University Press, 1968), 204, points out the difficulty Augustine, influenced by Neoplatonism, had with resurrection of the body; he shows (217–18) that in the *Confessions*, 4, 1, Augustine follows Plotinus to the extent of holding that human fulfillment by possession of God requires man to cease being human; later (284) he observes: "The doctrine of the body's resurrection forces a more sympathetic view of the bodily and the human." More influenced by Platonism than the other Fathers, Origen taught that souls were first created without bodies and became embodied as punishment for sin; for a summary, see J. N. D. Kelly, *Early Christian Doctrines*, rev. ed. (New York: Harper and Row, 1978), 180–83. A case can be made out that Augustine held a similar view in his early works: Robert J. O'Connell, S.J., "Augustine's Rejection of the Fall of the Soul," *Augustinian Studies*, 4 (1973), 1–32. Most Greek Fathers avoided Origen's excess, but their anthropology is marked by a tension between Platonizing spirituality, and Christian doctrines of the material as part of the good creation and of the resurrection of the body. For one example, see Gerhart B. Ladner, "The Philosophical Anthropology of Saint Gregory of Nyssa," Dumbarton Oaks Papers, 12 (Cambridge, Mass.: Harvard University Press, 1958), 59–94.

9. John Paul II, *Laborem exercens*, 73 AAS (1981) 589–92; *The Papal Encyclicals*, 280.22–27, articulates a true Christian conception of work as inherently fulfilling of persons and, building on Vatican II (644–47; 125–30), shows perspicuously how the activity of Christian life is inherently related to heavenly fulfillment. On the moral theology of work: Jean-Marie Aubert, "La Santificación en el Trabajo," in *Mons. Josemaría Escrivá de Balaguer y el Opus Dei: En el 50 Aniversario de su Fundación*, ed. Pedro Rodríguez et al. (Pamplona, Spain: EUNSA), 201–13; J. M. Casciaro, "La Santificación del Cristiano en Medio del Mundo," in the same volume, 101–59; José Luis Illanes Maestre, *La santificación del trabajo*, 6th ed. (Madrid: Palabra, 1980).

10. The *theological* tradition, stemming from Augustine, which imposes on the data of faith a commingling, Neoplatonic metaphysics is currently most often formulated by means of the concept of a "supernatural existential": Karl Rahner, S.J., *Theological Investigations*, vol. 1, *God, Christ, Mary and Grace*, trans. Cornelius Ernst, O.P. (Baltimore: Helicon Press, 1961), 297–317. In an essay reflecting upon the significance of Augustine's Neoplatonism, O'Connell, *St. Augustine's Early Theory of Man*, 279–89, brilliantly suggests some of the weaknesses of this theological tradition. For

those who find it difficult to distinguish Augustine's theology from the essential truth of Catholic faith, this entire work, especially the chapter on "Vision" (203–26), will be helpful. For a telling critique of Rahner's philosophy of man: Cornelio Fabro, *La svolta antropologica di Karl Rahner* (Milan: Rusconi, 1974). For a treatment by a faithful theologian of Vatican II's revolutionary teaching on earthly life in relation to heavenly life: Ermenegildo Lio, *Morale e beni terreni: La destinazione universale dei beni terreni nella "Gaudium et spes"* (Rome: Città Nuova, 1976).

11. See St. Thomas Aquinas, *Summa contra gentiles*, 3, 25 and 50–63; *Summa theologiae*, vol. 16, *Purpose and Happiness*, ed. Thomas Gilby, O.P. (New York: McGraw-Hill, 1969), q. 3, a. 8, and the editor's discussion, 153–55. For further discussion of the historical issue: Germain Grisez, "Man, the Natural End of," *New Catholic Encyclopedia*, 9:132–38. Even so, St. Thomas was careful to include in his description of heavenly beatitude, as constitutive of its perfection, elements of human fulfillment other than the intellectual vision of God: *S.t.*, 1–2, q. 4.

12. The present work is an attempt to begin to meet the need for such reexamination and perfecting of our thinking about this very important subject. The present effort is by no means a beginning without antecedents. Vatican II was preceded by a century and more of Catholic thought developing an integral Christian humanism. Much of this work contributed to the unfolding of theological reflection on history. A useful introduction to this area: James N. Connolly, *Human History and the Word of God: The Christian Meaning of History in Contemporary Thought* (New York: Macmillan, 1965). The work of Jacques Maritain deserves special mention; he did much to bring the revival of St. Thomas' thought toward fruition.

13. For a very clear and historically competent tracing of this history in its broad outlines: James Hitchcock, *What Is Secular Humanism? Why Humanism Became Secular and How It Is Changing Our World* (Ann Arbor, Mich.: Servant Books, 1982), 7–60. For a rich treatment of the philosophical development: Cornelio Fabro, *God in Exile: Modern Atheism: A Study of the Internal Dynamic of Modern Atheism, from Its Roots in the Cartesian "Cogito" to the Present Day*, trans. and ed. Arthur Gibson (Westminster, Md.: Newman Press, 1968).

14. Although defective in some respects, a powerful critique of utopianism: John Passmore, *The Perfectibility of Man* (New York: Charles Scribner's Sons, 1970), 190–259.

15. Rudolf Bultmann, *Jesus and the Word* (New York: Charles Scribner's Sons, 1958), 84. For an impartial summary of this trend of thought with further examples, see Edward LeRoy Long, *A Survey of Christian Ethics* (New York: Oxford University Press, 1967), 146–57. For a very different interpretation of one central Protestant tradition, that stemming from Luther and Melanchthon: Theodore R. Jungkuntz, "Trinitarian Ethics," *Center Journal*, 1 (Spring 1982), 39–52.

16. For a helpful analysis of the process of liberalization from the point of view of cultural history and sociology of religion: Peter L. Berger, *The Sacred Canopy: Elements of a Sociological Theory of Religion* (Garden City, N.Y.: Doubleday Anchor, 1969), esp. 155–71. For an analysis of recent liberalizing trends within a broader historical perspective: Hitchcock, op. cit., 115–38. For a closer view of tensions in the Catholic Church related to Vatican II: Jeremiah Newman, *Change and the Catholic Church: An Essay in Sociological Ecclesiology* (Baltimore: Helicon, 1965), 13–79 and 311–42. For a good summary view of the social and ideological environments of the modern world for Christian faith: Stephen B. Clark, *Man and Woman in Christ: An Examination of the Roles of Men and Women in Light of Scripture and the Social Sciences* (Ann Arbor, Mich.: Servant Books, 1980), 467–540, bibliography 672–73.

17. An effort has been made to find in the Fathers schemas to work out a theology along these lines: J. Patout Burns, S.J., "The Economy of Salvation: Two Patristic Traditions," *Theological Studies*, 37 (1976), 598–619. For a helpful survey of some of the literature: James J. Megivern, C.M., "A Theology of Incarnationalism," in *The Paradox of Religious Secularity*, ed. Katherine T. Hargrove, R.S.C.J. (Englewood Cliffs, N.J.: Prentice-Hall, 1968), 145–59.

18. There is a vast literature on Teilhard. A brilliant analysis of his thought in comparison with that of Marx and Engels, which reveals the fundamental similarity between them and the divergence of both visions' from orthodox Christianity: R. C. Zaehner, *Dialectical Christianity and Christian Materialism*, The Riddell Memorial Lectures, 40th ser. (London: Oxford University Press, 1971). An impressionistic but insightful critique of Teilhard, with references to other critical studies: Jacques Maritain, *The Peasant of the Garonne: An Old Layman Questions Himself about the Present Time*, trans. Michael Cuddihy and Elizabeth Hughes (London: Geoffrey Chapman, 1968), 112–26, 154–59, and 264–69. A careful and sympathetic—and for that reason all the more devastating—critique of Teilhard's Christology: Bertrand de Margerie, S.J., *Christ for the World: The Heart of the Lamb: A Treatise on Christology*, trans. Malachy Carroll (Chicago: Franciscan Herald Press, 1973), 68–120.

19. A very brief introduction: M. B. Schepers, "Liberalism, Theological," *New Catholic Encyclopedia*, 8:711–12. For introductions to many of the key figures, with helpful bibliographies, and treatments of other movements in modern theology: James C. Livingston, *Modern Christian Thought: From the Enlightenment to Vatican II* (New York: Macmillan, 1971).

20. For a survey of this process, see Ralph Martin, *A Crisis of Truth: The Attack on Faith, Morality, and Mission in the Catholic Church* (Ann Arbor, Mich.: Servant Books, 1982), 87–142. The magisterium has reacted to such trends; for some examples and references, see Candido Pozo, S.J., *The Credo of the People of God: A Theological Commentary*, trans. Mark A. Pilon (Chicago: Franciscan Herald Press, 1980), 155–66.

21. A helpful, brief theological articulation of the dialectic which leads to such a view: Christian Duquoc, "Heaven on Earth?" in *Heaven*, Concilium, 123, ed. Bas van Iersel and Edward Schillebeeckx (New York: Seabury Press, 1979), 82–91. Duquoc does not discuss hell and so takes no position on the question whether heaven is inevitable. His view, as expressed in this article, need not be read as contrary to Catholic faith. However, otherwise he clearly articulates a liberal position, which leaves unclear how hope of heaven affects life on earth. Edward Schillebeeckx, *Christ: The Experience of Jesus as Lord*, trans. John Bowden (New York: Seabury Press, 1980), argues (800) that hope of resurrection gives Christians boldness and liberty of action, but otherwise develops a liberalized eschatology, with an approving summary (756–57) of H. Kuitert's position on salvation in this world, and his own exposition (790–804) of a theory of final salvation. This is guardedly suggested (793) to be universalist. It is worth noticing that Schillebeeckx absolutely reduces (792) the divinization of man through grace to "God is the salvation of man," in this way apparently denying the truth of faith that the love of God poured forth into human hearts by the Holy Spirit *inheres* in them (DS 1530/800, 1561/821). At any rate, pervasive commingling in his view of the Christian makes it impossible for Schillebeeckx to distinguish the divine and human aspects of the Christian and Christian life, and hence blocks an adequate solution to the problem of the relationship between this life and heaven.

22. See St. Augustine, *City of God*, xxii, 30.

23. See Pierre Benoît, O.P., *Jesus and the Gospel*, vol. 2, trans. Benet Weatherhead (London: Darton, Longman and Todd, 1974), 58–67. The fundamentally social character of salvation according to authentic Christianity is stressed by Henri de Lubac, S.J., *Catholicism: A Study of Dogma in Relation to the Corporate Destiny of Mankind* (New York: Longmans, Green, 1950), 51–63.

24. A brief summary of the essential doctrine on merit: Michael Schmaus, *Dogma*, vol. 6, *Justification and the Last Things* (Kansas City: Sheed and Ward, 1977), 138–45.

25. Connolly, op. cit., is a useful introduction to modern theology of history. Also see Jean-Hervé Nicolas, O.P., "Le Christ centre et fin de l'histoire," *Revue Thomiste*, 81 (1981), 357–80.

26. See Pius XI, *Quas primas*, 17 *AAS* (1925) 595–600; *The Papal Encyclicals*, 197.7–16, on the universal kingship of Christ as man. By this encyclical the establishment of the feast of Christ the King was announced.

CHAPTER THIRTY-FIVE

THE TRUTH OF CHRIST LIVES IN HIS CHURCH

Introduction

Throughout this work the assumption is that theological reflection can begin from the teaching of the Church, and from Scripture and tradition as the Church understands them. Although common among Catholic theologians until recently, this assumption is denied today by many who challenge various points of Catholic teaching.

Because their denial would undercut the whole of the present work, this issue must be treated here, although it belongs more to ecclesiology than to Christian moral principles. The treatment remains a theological clarification, however, which assumes the truth of the Church's teaching rather than trying to prove it. Yet such a clarification, although not adequate as an apologetic addressed to non-believers, will help Catholics understand the issues and see through many poor arguments used by dissenting theologians. The present chapter deals with the problem constructively, by clarifying the infallibility of the Church and the authority of both Scripture and ecclesial teachings. Chapter thirty-six examines certain specific claims of dissenting theologians and shows that they are specious.

Question A: What is the origin of the infallibility of the Church?

1. Jesus chose apostles to be his companions and witnesses (see LG 19; AG 5). These apostles had a unique role as the authorized recipients of God's revelation in Jesus, for the appropriation of all Jesus communicated by his words and deeds was essential to complete the relationship in which revelation consists (DV 7).

2. Divine truth is really present in the words and deeds of Jesus and communicated by them in a humanly accessible form. The content of revelation enters human experience in the material media of spoken words and observable behavior, and not in some other, mysterious way (20-C). Jesus' humanity, rather than hiding his divinity, expresses it (see 1 Jn 1.1–3). There is no room in this expression for error on his part, for his life reveals insofar as it is the medium of the activity of the Word (21-F). Thus the apostles directly received God's revealing acts and testimony (see DV 4): In seeing Jesus, they saw the Father (see Jn 14.9).

3. Faith has absolute certitude from the divine testimony which grounds assent to revealed truth (20-E). Nevertheless, individual believers can make mistakes in matters of faith. For instance, St. Thomas Aquinas did not believe in Mary's immaculate conception, mistakenly thinking it incompatible with the universality of Jesus' redemptive work (see *S.t.*, 3, q. 27, a. 2, ad 2). Such a mistake is possible without any defect either in divine revelation or in the individual's faith, since individuals can err in identifying what does and does not belong to divine revelation—for example, by misunderstanding the content which is communicated (see *S.t.*, 2–2, q. 11, a. 2, ad 3).

4. Could the apostles have made this sort of mistake, despite having immediate contact with Jesus? Humanly speaking, they could. They very often misunderstood Jesus during his mortal life. Peter himself, although he recognized Jesus with divinely given faith as the Messiah, proceeded to draw wrong conclusions from his imperfect grasp of Jesus' mission (see Mt 16.13–23; Mk 8.27–33).

5. But Jesus promised and sent the Holy Spirit to assist the apostles (see Jn 14.16–17, 26; 15.26–27; 16.7–15; 20.21–22; Acts 1.5, 8; 2.1–4). The role of the Spirit and that of the apostles are parallel; both bear witness to Jesus and communicate the truth revealed in him (see Jn 15.26–27; *S.t.*, 2–2, q. 6, a. 1). The Spirit reveals nothing new but brings about the apostolic appropriation of God's revelation in Jesus (see Jn 16.13–15).[1]

6. **By this gift and only by it, God ensured that the apostles would and indeed could make no mistake in believing. Enlightened by the Spirit, they believed with absolute faith, itself a divine gift, all and only those things which God wished to make known to humankind through the life, death, resurrection, and ascension of the Lord Jesus.**

The apostle has the Holy Spirit (see 1 Cor 7.40). The apostles together with the Spirit are witnesses to divine revelation in Jesus (see Acts 5.32; 15.28). To accept apostolic teaching is to obey God (see Acts 6.7; Rom 1.1–6). By the Spirit, Jesus fulfilled his promise to remain forever with the apostles (see Mt 28.20). God confirmed their work with many miracles (see Acts 2.43; 3.1–10; 5.12–16; 9.32–42; 19.11–12; and so on).

Hence it was not unreasonable to demand that humankind accept the apostolic witness as the very word of God (see Mt 10.40; Lk 10.16; Jn 13.20; 1 Thes 2.13). Given the infallibility of the apostles' faith, the gospel they proclaimed could not possibly deviate from divine truth, and so it was not inappropriate to make the salvation or damnation of human persons hang upon their acceptance or rejection of apostolic testimony (see Mk 16.15–16).

7. In sum, not only did the apostles in fact make no mistake in their acceptance of revelation, it was not even possible for them to err in this. The exclusion of the possibility of error is what is meant by "infallibility." Although the word "infallibility" only came into use in the Middle Ages, the reality understood by this concept and expressed by this word certainly was present in the apostles' grasp of God's revelation in Jesus.

8. That the apostles were infallible in believing and preaching does not mean that all of them believed and preached exactly the same things. The diversity of individuals in fact makes possible a more rich and complete revelation. Each apostle could appropriate and find meaning in particular words and deeds of Jesus

which might have been overlooked by the others. The harmonious pluralism of apostolic faith is reflected in the unity in diversity of the New Testament which bears witness to that faith (see DV 19).

9. Thus, two things are true. First, any incompatibility among the beliefs of the different apostles was precluded by the unity of divine truth and the infallibility of the apostles in identifying what God revealed. Second, there nevertheless was need for their collegial unity and communication with one another so that they could proceed together in the full light of the whole of revealed truth. The apostles therefore conferred in Jerusalem (see Acts 15.1–29), and Paul submitted his preaching to the scrutiny of the other apostles "lest somehow I should be running or had run in vain" (Gal 2.2).

10. God's revelation in Jesus is a concrete reality, comprised not only of statements of propositional truths but of the whole of Jesus' human existence witnessed and shared in by the apostles. Thus, apostolic infallibility meant more than just the impossibility of making a mistake in identifying which propositions pertain to revelation and which do not. The apostles had also to be assisted so that they made no mistake in humanly appropriating other aspects of the personal revelation of Jesus. Without such assistance, human fallibility would have caused them to betray God's revelatory intention by their methods of operating, patterns of worship, and communal structures. Revelation would more or less have failed.

11. In Jesus' Church, apostles are primary (see 1 Cor 12.28; Eph 4.11); the Church is founded upon them, both at first and forever (see Eph 2.20; Rv 21.14).[2] Although the apostles were chosen to receive God's revelation in our Lord Jesus, this revelation was not for them alone but for all humankind, to which they were commissioned to spread it (see Mt 28.20). After Pentecost, they faithfully carried out this commission. They and their associates also committed the message of salvation to writing and left successors to carry on the work (see DV 7).

Vatican II teaches concerning the apostolic foundation of the Church, and the true, inclusive meaning of the Church's tradition: "Therefore the apostles, handing on what they themselves had received, warn the faithful to hold fast to the traditions which they have learned either by word of mouth or by letter (cf. 2 Thes 2.15), and to fight in defense of the faith handed on once and for all (cf. Jude 3). Now what was handed on by the apostles includes everything which contributes to the holiness of life, and the increase in faith of the People of God; and so the Church, in her teaching, life, and worship, perpetuates and hands on to all generations all that she herself is, all that she believes" (DV 8). It follows that to the extent that errors in belief and teaching can occur within the Church, these ought not to be attributed to the Church herself but rather to her individual members, whether they be popes, bishops, or others. The belief and teaching of the Church cannot err; beliefs and teachings within the Church can err, to the extent that they diverge from the norm of faith which is the common heritage of the Church as a whole.

12. Christian faith is not individualistic. Each believer enters into the faith of the Church: the apostolic, collegial grasp upon God's revelation in Jesus.[3] **Hence, the Church as a whole enjoys the prerogative of the apostolic faith in which it shares: infallibility. Unity with the apostles makes it possible for the Church to continue to carry out Jesus' mission through all generations** (see AG 4–5).

13. The apostolic college, under Peter's leadership, enjoyed infallibility in its

belief in and preaching of divinely revealed truth. Others shared in this gift to the extent that they received Christian faith through the apostles and built up the Church on their foundation. The episcopal college, with the successor of Peter at its head, continues the work of the apostles; it enjoys their secure gift of communicating divinely revealed truth (see DV 8; LG 25; DS 3071/1837).[4]

14. Thus, the infallibility of the Church, taught by Vatican II, is based upon the infallibility of the college of the apostles. Individual members of the Church can make mistakes concerning what is and is not included in divine revelation, and so concerning what is and is not to be believed with divine faith. The Church as a whole can make no such mistake (see *S.t.*, 2–2, q. 2, a. 6, ad 3; q. 5, a, 3, ad 2; q. 11, a. 2, ad 3). The absolute truth of God revealing, the absolute certitude of divine faith, and the unerring recognition by the Church of what pertains to faith converge to make the Church's human belief and teaching enjoy and manifest the unerring quality of divine truth itself.

In its teaching on the Church as the People of God, Vatican II makes the point that the Church as a whole shares in Jesus' prophetic office. Every member of the Church, not only bishops and priests, should bear living witness to Jesus, especially by living a Christian life and participating in the sacred liturgy. The Council then explains how the Church as a whole is equipped to do its work:

> The body of the faithful as a whole, anointed as they are by the Holy One (cf. Jn 2.20, 27), cannot err in matters of belief. Thanks to a supernatural sense of the faith which characterizes the people as a whole, it manifests this unerring quality when, "from the bishops down to the last member of the laity" [note to St. Augustine omitted], it shows universal agreement in matters of faith and morals.
>
> For, by this sense of faith which is aroused and sustained by the Spirit of truth, God's people accepts not the word of men but the very word of God (cf. 1 Thes 2.13). It clings without fail to the faith once delivered to the saints (cf. Jude 3), penetrates it more deeply by accurate insights, and applies it more thoroughly to life. All this it does under the lead of a sacred teaching authority to which it faithfully defers. (LG 12; translation amended)

This unerring quality, which belongs to the Church as a whole, excludes not only the making of mistakes but the very possibility of being mistaken in these matters: "in credendo falli nequit." "Matters of belief" includes moral norms: "de rebus fidei et morum." This unerring quality is what elsewhere is called "infallibility."

Thus Vatican II teaches that the Church as a corporate person is infallible in believing. This is not to say that the Church, even considered as a whole, lives up to its belief—that is another question. Nor is it to say that the laity as distinct from (much less as opposed to) the bishops enjoy infallibility in believing. Rather, the whole Church, including the bishops and under their leadership, including all who handed on the faith from the apostles and to whom we shall hand it on, clings to the faith unerringly, develops it, and applies it to life, thus bearing witness to divine truth and love. The Council continues in the same article to explain that the Spirit also enriches various parts and members of the whole Church with various appropriate gifts, to build up Jesus' body. But judgment as to the genuineness and right use of such gifts also belongs to those who preside over the Church (see LG 12).

In recent years, "sensus fidelium" often has been used to suggest that opinions of the faithful have an independent value as a witness to moral truth, so that when these opinions diverge from received Catholic teaching, this divergence is a sign of a need for revision in the teaching. In response to this misunderstanding, John Paul II carefully interprets the teaching of Vatican II that the faithful at large discern truth through a supernatural sense of faith: "The 'supernatural sense of faith' [note omitted] however does not consist solely or necessarily in the consensus of the faithful. Following Christ, the Church seeks the truth, which is not always the same as the majority opinion. She listens to conscience and not to power, and in this way she defends the poor and the downtrodden. The Church values sociological and statistical research, when it proves helpful in understanding the historical context in which pastoral action has to be developed and when it leads to a better understanding of the truth. Such research alone, however, is not to be considered in itself an expression of the sense of faith."[5] The sense of faith of which the Council speaks characterizes the People of God as a whole; by this very fact one cannot discover it in dissenting opinions, no matter how many subscribe to them at a particular time and place.

Writing to the Corinthians, St. Paul asserts that whether one is led by the Spirit can be detected from the faith one professes (see 1 Cor 12.3). The word of God did not come from the people; they must conform to it: "If any one thinks that he is a prophet, or spiritual, he should acknowledge that what I am writing to you is a command of the Lord. If any one does not recognize this, he is not recognized" (1 Cor 14.37–38). Salvation depends upon standing firm in the faith one received (see 1 Cor 15.1–2). Jesus is present in the Church (see LG 14), teaching through the apostle himself, for the apostle was made "teacher of the Gentiles in faith and truth" (1 Tm 2.7). Christians must hold fast to the faith (see Col 1.23), for it communicates Jesus, the fullness of wisdom (see Col 1.28). They must beware of being deceived by seductive philosophy which comes from human traditions (see Col 2.6–8). As children of God, Christians learn through apostolic instruction "how one ought to behave in the household of God, which is the church of the living God, the pillar and bulwark of the truth" (1 Tm 3.15).

As long as—but only as long as—individual Christians think with the Church, they share in its unerring sense of faith and enjoy the support and defense of this pillar and bulwark. For "the Spirit expressly says that in later times some will depart from the faith by giving heed to deceitful spirits and doctrines of demons, through the pretensions of liars whose consciences are seared" (1 Tm 4.1–2). Those who are misled have failed to obey the truth; if they had not disobeyed, they would have remained firm in the faith, for it is an indestructible seed, "the living and abiding word of God" (1 Pt 1.23).[6]

Question B: What in Scripture must be accepted as certainly true?

1. If the Church as a whole is infallible in believing and preaching its faith, still, apart from the apostles, all members of the Church as individuals can make mistakes in attempting to identify revealed truth. Acts by which the Church's belief is expressed must therefore be carefully distinguished from acts by which members of the Church, even popes, express their individual belief. The belief of the Church must be distinguished from belief within the Church. Infallibility essentially belongs to the former; it belongs to the latter only insofar as what is believed "within" the Church arises from and is true to the belief "of" the Church.

2. Sacred Scripture expresses and bears witness to divine revelation. It is "the word of God inasmuch as it is consigned to writing under the inspiration of the divine Spirit" (DV 9). Having been accepted and handed on by the whole Church, Scripture is both an expression and a norm of the Church's belief: The books of Scripture, that is, communicate the belief of the Church and not merely belief

within the Church. From the Church's infallibility in believing, it follows that Scripture can contain no error in its identification of divinely revealed truth.

3. Vatican II formulates anew and reaffirms the belief of the whole Christian tradition that Scripture, including all the books of both the Old and New Testaments, was written under the inspiration of the Holy Spirit. These books thus have God as their author; they contain his word. At the same time, in Scripture God speaks only in and through human writers who by his inspiration are also true authors of their own works. It should not be supposed that either cause, divine or human, must be limited to make room for the work of the other, since the two cause in diverse ways. The result is that these humanly written works—the word of God in human words—contain precisely what God wants in them. Vatican II says: "Therefore, since everything asserted by the inspired authors or sacred writers must be held to be asserted by the Holy Spirit, it follows that the books of Scripture must be acknowledged as teaching firmly, faithfully, and without error that truth which God wanted put into the sacred writings for the sake of our salvation [note 5 omitted]. Therefore 'all Scripture is inspired by God and useful for teaching, for reproving, for correcting, for instruction in justice; that the man of God may be perfect, equipped for every good work' (2 Tm 3.16–17, Greek text)" (DV 11). Since the assertions of the writers are assertions of God, the teaching of Scripture is without error. Hence, in identifying divine revelation by the norm of its own understanding of Scripture, the Church—infallible in believing—can make no mistake.

Vatican II does not use the word "inerrancy" in *Dei verbum*, 11, perhaps because this word had acquired undesirable connotations from its use in polemics and inadequate theological treatments of the problem. However, in teaching that everything asserted by the inspired authors is without error, Vatican II reaffirms constant Catholic teaching on the inerrancy of Scripture. When "inerrancy of Scripture" is used in what follows, it means precisely what *Dei verbum*, 11, affirms in the first sentence of the paragraph quoted above.

4. A fundamentalist rightly believes that what is asserted in the Bible is true, separates out what he or she takes to be asserted in the Bible, and holds these propositions. A theological liberal thinks some less important propositions asserted in the Bible are false, sets up what he or she considers to be adequate criteria of importance, and censors the Bible. **In contrast with both, Catholics believe that all propositions asserted in the Bible are true (because God is faithful), believe that the Church as a whole can make no mistake in identifying divine truth, and so work toward an ecclesial understanding of the Bible** (see *S.t.*, 1, q. 1, a. 10; 2–2, q. 5, a. 3, ad 2). Precluded by this are both the private interpretation of fundamentalism, which assigns the value of divine truth to those propositions which each individual extracts from the text for himself or herself, and liberalism's attempt to judge the truth of God's word by some extrinsic standard.[7]

To understand the teaching of *Dei verbum*, 11, concerning inerrancy, one must understand what assertions are. They are propositions proposed as certainly true; one asserts a proposition if and only if one expresses it in a way which definitely claims assent from those to whom it is addressed. This definition requires an understanding of what a proposition is.

A proposition is something thought which can be true or false. Propositions must be distinguished from language. If I say "The sun is shining" or "Sol lucet" or (tomorrow at this time) "Yesterday at this time the sun was shining," then I express the same proposition, although the language is different. Propositions usually are partly conveyed by the nonlinguistic context of communication.

Conversely, language often expresses no proposition. Scripture conveys much more than asserted propositions, for its concrete style provides many images and poetic symbols, which perhaps presuppose propositions but do not express any proposition. "Glory to God in the highest" does not express a proposition. Nor do many expressions in polite conversation—for example, "I am fine" is not a statement about one's health when it responds to a conventional "How are you?"

Language depends heavily upon context for its meaning. Therefore, it is relative to culture and has to be interpreted with this in mind. But propositional content is not relative to culture; its many conditions and limitations are built into it. Interpretation and translation attempt to disengage the propositional content from one linguistic vehicle and rearticulate it in another.

Very often, propositions are expressed in language without being asserted. One might wonder whether something is so; one might suggest a view as possibly true, or even as likely, yet not be prepared to assert the proposition. In reflecting upon and talking about common beliefs or the beliefs of other individuals, one very often expresses propositions without providing any clear indication whether one is asserting them. Sometimes, one does not even ask oneself whether one wishes personally to assert such propositions.

Moreover, the conventions of narration are different in different times and places, and even in the same culture in different social situations. Often, in telling a story one asserts only the main point, and fills in a background without taking care to be precise about the many subordinate details. If someone narrating in this manner is challenged on a factually erroneous statement, he or she is likely to say: "Well, that's only incidental. My real point is . . . ."

With these distinctions in mind, it is clear that *Dei verbum* is far from saying that every sentence in the Bible is true, since many of the sentences in the Bible express no proposition. Nor is it saying that every proposition articulated in the Bible is true, for many propositions articulated in the Bible are not asserted; in very many cases, the human authors either did not ask themselves whether the propositions they articulated were true, or did not propose them as true, or at least did not demand assent from their readers.[8]

5. Moral norms are proposed in Scripture.[9] But a genuine moral norm is a true proposition (4-H). **Thus some of the moral norms formulated in Scripture—namely, those asserted by the inspired authors—are inerrant moral teachings.**

6. In considering the moral teaching contained in Scripture, one must bear in mind that most moral norms are nonabsolute. Furthermore, most moral norms can be commended with varying degrees of force; only those proposed as certainly true and definitely to be followed are asserted in Scripture.[10]

7. For these reasons, instances in the Bible of norms which admit of exceptions or seem unsound do not argue against the truth of absolute norms which are proposed there as absolute and certainly true. For instance, what St. Paul says about women covering their heads in church (see 1 Cor 11.2–16) is subject to limitations implied by the context which do not condition what the Bible teaches about adultery (see Ex 20.14; Dt 5.18; Jer 7.9–10; Hos 4.2; Mt 5.27–32; 19.18; Mk

10.19; Lk 18.20; Rom 13.8–10; Jas 2.11). Moreover, nonabsolute norms proposed in Scripture as certainly true are not falsified by their exceptions, and Scripture itself generally indicates their limits clearly enough. For example, St. Paul's injunction, "Let every person be subject to the governing authorities" (Rom 13.1), is true but nonabsolute; many passages of Scripture make clear the limits to obedience, such as the prior claims of faithfulness to God.

8. Within the New Testament, Christian morality is presented as the perfection and superabundant fulfillment of the Decalogue.[11] In the Sermon on the Mount, Jesus broadens and deepens several of the commandments and demands their interiorization (see Mt 5.21–37). All the synoptics, moreover, present Jesus as affirming the commandments as a necessary condition for entering eternal life (see Mt 19.16–20; Mk 10.17–19; Lk 18.18–21). St. Paul, in asserting that Christian love fulfills the law, assumes the truth of the Decalogue and its permanent ethical relevance, extols the superiority of love, and rejects any suggestion which would empty love of its practical, normative implications (see Rom 13.8–10). This recognition of the continuing validity of the Decalogue indicates that the norms it contains are asserted by the human authors and so, too, by the Holy Spirit.[12]

9. The Ten Commandments have a unique place within the Mosaic law; they are represented as being the very words of the covenant, dictated by God (see Ex 34.27–28).[13] Their religious and liturgical significance makes them no less functional as a moral foundation for legal enactments.[14] The prohibitions of the commandments were no doubt understood more narrowly in their original context than in their unfolding in later Jewish and Christian tradition. **Still, no reasonable reading of the Decalogue can deny it the status of fundamental revealed moral truth—a status always recognized by common Christian practice in moral instruction** (see *S.t.*, 1–2, q. 100, aa. 1, 8; q. 107, a. 2, ad 1).[15]

10. To say that the Decalogue has the status of fundamental, revealed moral truth is not to deny that it needs interpretation and development. This process begins in the Old Testament itself and, as indicated, is continued in the New. However, this does not justify the claim that the Decalogue is mere moral exhortation to follow an existing code, which always must be read with proportionalist riders—for example, Thou shalt not commit adultery, unless it happens to be the lesser evil.[16]

Some commentators on *Dei verbum*, 11, have taken "for the sake of our salvation" to be a restriction upon the kind of assertions of the sacred authors which must be considered free of error. They say Scripture contains errors, but can be trusted to the extent that its content bears upon matters of faith and morals.

However, those who assert that Vatican II has limited biblical inerrancy to some part of the assertions contained in Scripture misinterpret the text of the Council's document. To some extent, mistranslation of the conciliar document explains the tendency to misinterpret it. The Abbott edition translation of *Dei verbum*, 11, for example, is misleading, for it makes "for the sake of our salvation" part of a restrictive clause. In the Latin text, however, this phrase is nonrestrictive. It indicates God's purpose in revealing without limiting the truth he reveals: "Cum ergo omne id, quod auctores inspirati seu hagiographi asserunt, retineri debeat assertum a Spiritu Sancto, inde Scripturae libri veritatem, quam Deus nostrae salutis causa Litteris Sacris consignari voluit, firmiter, fideliter et sine errore docere profitendi sunt."

The following considerations show that *Dei verbum*, 11, teaches that all propositions asserted by the inspired authors are true. First, inerrancy is concluded from the premise that the Spirit asserts what the human authors assert; therefore, to admit any erroneous assertion in Scripture is to admit a false assertion by the Spirit. Second, the Council's footnote five refers to passages in St. Augustine, St. Thomas Aquinas, the Council of Trent, and encyclicals of Leo XIII and Pius XII. These passages, most clearly those in Pope Leo's *Providentissimus Deus*, exclude altogether the possibility of error from all assertions in Scripture (see DS 3291–93/1950–52). (The passages cited also show that the concern of Scripture is to communicate truth relevant to salvation, not assorted information which in no way affects our relationship with God.) Finally, the history of *Dei verbum* shows that the Council's Theological Commission made it clear that the text was not meant to restrict the inerrancy of the Bible to some subset of the assertions contained in it.[17]

Precisely because the Council does reaffirm the inerrancy of Scripture, it proceeds directly to insist upon the importance of careful interpretation to find out what God wants to communicate—that is, what the sacred writers really intended. The result of careful interpretation will be to discern as asserted by the sacred writers only propositions which do pertain to faith or morals, at least in some indirect way. This outcome should be no surprise, since the Bible contains a witness to God's revealing words and deeds and an expression of their initial appropriation. The whole, considered together, richly hands on revealed truth, which is a personal communication directed toward establishing and perfecting a personal relationship between God and his adopted human family (20-C).

The primary truth revealed in the Bible is the firmness and faithfulness of God himself, who never abandons or betrays his people.[18] It is precisely God's fundamental truth which precludes error in the propositions asserted in the Bible. At the same time, the purpose of God in providing the Bible limits its propositional content to the truth which we need to know to form our relationship to him and our lives in response to his love.

Does this conclusion amount to the same thing as the position of those who take Vatican II's phrase, "for the sake of our salvation," to be a restriction upon the inerrancy of Scripture? Not at all. They assume that other propositions are asserted in Scripture and that these might be false. I deny this, and in denying it hold the point which the Church obviously is intent upon maintaining: The Holy Spirit inspires the whole of Scripture and makes no false assertions.

Moreover, in practice there is a great difference. When one supposes that the Bible contains some false propositions, one tends to ask oneself whether what one takes to be an assertion in the Bible is true, and one tries to answer the question by extrinsic criteria. This process will lead to the exclusion of propositions which are saving truths, but happen to be hard to understand and accept. When one supposes, as the Church does, that the Bible contains no assertions of false propositions, one tends to ask oneself how what one takes to be an assertion in the Bible can be true. To answer the question, one must try to discover what the statement means in its larger context and ultimate reference to salvation. In the last resort one will give up the supposition that apparently asserted propositions are really such. When necessary, one will do this with the help of what is found in other parts of the Bible, in the whole of tradition, and in current documents of the Church's teaching office.

Question C: What is meant by the "magisterium" of the Church?

1. Catholic faith teaches that the bishops are the successors of the apostles in respect to those apostolic functions which in the nature of the case could be handed on.[19]

2. Vatican I solemnly and definitively teaches that by the institution of Jesus himself the pope is the successor of Peter as head of the Church (see DS 3058/ 1825; *S.t.*, 2–2, q. 1, a. 10; q. 11, a. 2, ad 3). Vatican II confirms this teaching (see LG 18) and adds to it: "Just as the role that the Lord gave individually to Peter, the first among the apostles, is permanent and was meant to be transmitted to his successors, so also the apostles' office of nurturing the Church is permanent, and was meant to be exercised without interruption by the sacred order of bishops. Therefore, this sacred Synod teaches that by divine institution bishops have succeeded to the place of the apostles as shepherds of the Church, and that he who hears them, hears Christ, while he who rejects them, rejects Christ and him who sent Christ (cf. Lk 10.16)" (LG 20). As men in a special way empowered to exercise Jesus' prophetic office in the Church, bishops succeed the apostles as leaders of the Church and authorized spokesmen for the Lord Jesus.

3. **In communion with one another, the pope and other bishops together exercise this prophetic role, which many documents of the Church refer to by the word "magisterium."** Although this word has been given its technical sense only in modern times,[20] the reality to which it refers, according to the teaching of Vatican I and Vatican II, has existed in the Church since the apostles.[21] "Magisterium" is translated by both "teaching office" and "teaching authority." The teaching of the magisterium is said to be "authentic" and "authoritative," both expressions meaning essentially the same thing.

4. The intent in what follows is to clarify what "authority" means in this context and why our Lord Jesus establishes the bishops as a teaching authority within his Church, whose faith is infallible, as question A explained.

5. The revelation of God in Jesus is expressed and witnessed in Scripture and in the tradition of the Church—that is, in the whole life and reality of the Church who extends herself from generation to generation (see DV 8). Nevertheless, members of the Church as individuals are not infallible. In interpreting revelation they can err in belief, mistaking what belongs to revelation for what does not and vice versa.

6. Evidently, then, the infallibility of the Church as a whole needs an organ, an instrument by which it can be exercised. Vatican II teaches: "The task of authentically interpreting the word of God, whether written or handed on, has been entrusted exclusively to the living teaching office [magisterium] of the Church, whose authority is exercised in the name of Jesus Christ. This teaching office is not above the word of God, but serves it, teaching only what has been handed on, listening to it devoutly, guarding it scrupulously, and explaining it faithfully by divine commission and with the help of the Holy Spirit; it draws from this one deposit of faith everything which it presents for belief as divinely revealed" (DV 10).

7. Plainly, the magisterium has a great deal more to do than just ascertaining and expressing a consensus. **The magisterium has authority to decide—not in the sense of choosing but in the sense of judging—what belongs to revelation.** It is not above the word of God; revelation is complete in Jesus. But what is revealed must be unfolded and effectively communicated in each age. For this

work to be accomplished without deviation from divine truth, the magisterium exists to receive, guard, and explain that truth which the Church as a whole infallibly believes.

8. Inasmuch as the bishops share in divine authority, communicated to them by Jesus (see Mt 28.18–20), it is this—not scholarly competence and expertise nor administrative power—which qualifies them for their magisterial function. Their doctrinal decisions, judgments in matters of faith and morals, have the authority of truth, the personal truth revealed in Jesus. (Like the office of the bishops, the office of theologians and the charisms of the faithful at large do not stand above this truth, but must accept it with faith and serve it.)[22]

9. In sum, the foundation of the teaching authority of the bishops is twofold: first, the divine truth which they receive in faith and share as members of the Church; second, their special office of leadership, in which they carry out that part of the apostolic responsibility—to act sacramentally in Jesus' person—which belongs to the Church's permanent constitution.

One can imagine that Jesus might have initiated a redemptive community without providing any leadership role. However, no human society exists without leaders, whose activities unify the group. The authority of leaders derives from the fact that their official acts are directed to the common good; in them the interests of all members of the group make their demands upon each member. Had Jesus not provided leadership for the Church, leaders would have emerged, but their right to lead would always have been open to question. The Church herself could not establish this right, since the Church is not simply a voluntary human community, but a communion in Jesus with God.

For this reason it was fitting that Jesus created the apostolic office and the role of bishops as successors to the apostles. By means of the college of bishops, Jesus provided his Church, which is infallible in believing and proclaiming him, with a single, recognizable voice. Thus when the bishops speak with one voice, their preaching is not only teaching within the Church, but teaching of the Church. It is—and the whole Church can be sure it is—the word of God himself.

One can imagine a Church in which every member participated equally in the magisterium. However, if all exercised this office responsibly, all other goods would remain unattended, because the communication required for this single task (especially if everyone were involved) would absorb the whole of one's Christian life. One also can imagine a Church in which only theologically competent persons were ordained as bishops. However, scholars have their biases; in any society they form an elite more or less removed from the people at large: They "live in an ivory tower."

Furthermore, one always must bear in mind that the truth with which the bishops are concerned primarily is the personal truth of God revealed in Jesus. This truth includes but is not limited to true propositions. The methods of scholarship are not well adapted for discerning such truth; indeed, their habitual use tends to obscure it with an interesting but not always relevant pluralism of theories and arguments. To some extent, the truth of Catholic faith is contained in the lived reality of the Church, not yet articulated intellectually, but handed on (see DV 8). For managing the task of handing on a personal truth which in part has not yet been articulated, a man like Peter perhaps is a better choice than someone more learned and clever—even than one like Paul.

One aspect of the authority of the magisterium is shared by every member of the Church. Jesus amazed his listeners, because he taught with authority, unlike the scribes (see Mt 7.29; Mk 1.22; Lk 4.32). The scribes functioned as theologians; they dealt in scholarly opinions about the meaning of the law, which they studied as a given object. Jesus did not talk about divine revelation; he personally revealed the Father. His preaching was not reflection upon truth as an object, but direct communication of the personal truth of God to human persons.

One who accepts the revelation of God in Jesus enjoys a wisdom which surpasses that of scholarship: "I thank you, Father, Lord of heaven and earth, that you have hidden these things from the wise and understanding and revealed them to babes" (Lk 10.21). When a Christian mother tells her children of God, of Jesus, and of the following of Jesus, she shares in the authority of Jesus, for she hands on his personal truth. Insofar as her belief is one with the belief of the Church, Jesus speaks in and through her; her instruction is the word of Jesus, and it is received by her children with the light of the Spirit of divine truth.

In recent years, some have argued that authority is of two sorts: some authorities are qualified (to determine what is true) by their experience or scholarly competence, while other authorities are qualified (to decide what will be done) by their social status. The former must be respected because they are in a position to know better; the latter must be obeyed because of their official power to decide. To which of these categories does the teaching authority of the bishops belong? If to the former, their judgment depends on expertise, and can be challenged by theologians, who in general are more able scholars than most bishops. If to the latter, their decisions have only the force of law, not the force of truth; laws can bind in conscience only as long as one does not have a sufficiently good reason for setting them aside.

The authority of Jesus in revealing fits neither of these two categories. The division is inadequate. It leaves out of account the authority enjoyed by one who communicates personal truth to be accepted with personal faith. The teaching authority of the bishops derives from that of Jesus, and belongs to the same category as his authority.[23]

Question D: Under what conditions, apart from solemn definitions, does the Church teach infallibly?

1. Because individual members of the Church can err, and erring individuals can form movements of opinion, factions within the Church have often disagreed about what belongs to Catholic faith. Typically, all claim to express the same faith and to be committed to the attempt to live up to it, yet diverse parties dispute over the appropriateness of particular expressions and actions. This spectacle has always been repugnant to those who wish to live redemptively, for it diminishes the effectiveness of Christian life as a sign of divine love and truth. In such circumstances, the role of the magisterium is especially important. The unified witness of the bishops in matters of faith and morals enjoys the infallibility of the Church.

2. Vatican II clearly states the criteria for an infallible exercise of the magisterium by the bishops engaged in their day-to-day work of teaching: **"Although the bishops individually do not enjoy the prerogative of infallibility, they nevertheless proclaim the teaching of Christ infallibly, even when they are dispersed throughout the world, provided that they remain in communion with each other and with the successor of Peter and that in authoritatively teaching on a matter of faith and morals they agree in one judgment as that to be held definitively"** (LG 25; translation supplied). (The

Council's development of this text and use in a footnote to it of four earlier documents are considered at the end of this question.)

3. The development of the conciliar text makes it clear that the first condition—that the bishops be *in communion* with one another and with the pope—does not mean that they must act formally as a single body, in a strictly collegial manner. It is necessary and sufficient that they remain bishops within the Catholic Church. The voice of the Church is identified, and distinguished from various voices within the Church, by the sacramental ordination and bond of communion which unite the bishops who share in uttering the Church's teaching.

4. The second condition—authoritative episcopal teaching *on a matter of faith and morals*—requires that the bishops be acting in their official capacity as teachers, not merely expressing their opinions as individuals or as theologians. As for the subject matter of their teaching—"faith or morals"—the formula has a long history.[24] It is sufficient here to say that nothing in the pertinent documents limits "morals," in the sense intended by Vatican II, in such a way as to exclude specific moral norms, like that forbidding adultery.

5. The third condition—that the bishops agree *in one judgment*—identifies universality as a requirement for an infallible exercise of the ordinary magisterium. What is necessary, however, is the moral unity of the body of bishops in union with the pope, not an absolute mathematical unanimity such as would be destroyed by even one dissenting voice.[25]

6. Furthermore, if this condition has been met in the past, it would not be nullified by a future lack of consensus among the bishops. The consensus of future bishops is not necessary for the ordinary magisterium to have taught something infallibly or to do so now. Otherwise, one would be in the absurd position of saying that it is impossible for there to be an infallible exercise of the magisterium until literally the end of time; since at any given moment, one cannot tell what some bishops in the future might say.

7. The fourth condition—that the bishops propose a judgment to be held *definitively*—obviously does not refer to the formulation and promulgation of a solemn definition, since what is in question is the bishops' day-to-day teaching. The condition does mean at least this: that the teaching is not proposed as something optional, for either the bishops or the faithful, but as something which the bishops have an obligation to hand on and which Catholics have an obligation to accept. In the case of moral teaching, however, it is unlikely that those proposing the teaching will explicitly present it as something to be intellectually accepted as true; it is more likely that they will leave this demand implicit and will propose it as a norm which followers of Jesus must try to observe in their lives.

8. Vatican II's teaching on the infallibility of the ordinary magisterium is not new in substance. Catholics have always believed that the apostles and their successors enjoy an unfailing gift of truth in proclaiming Christ's teaching. As early as the fifth century, St. Vincent of Lerins tried to formulate the conditions for an infallible exercise of the ordinary magisterium (see FEF 2168 and 2174–75).

Very frequently the consensus of the Fathers of the Church is invoked in the Church's teaching as a witness of faith which cannot be contradicted.[26] The Fathers were bishops or closely associated with bishops; their writings as a body indicate what the bishops were teaching during the patristic period. The authority of the Fathers is an instance of the authority of the ordinary magisterium; their consensus in proposing a point of faith or morals to be held definitively makes it clear that the conditions for the infallibility of the ordinary magisterium were met.

9. If one considers that the Church as a whole is infallible in believing and handing on the faith, and also that the bishops as leaders of the Church are her legitimate spokesmen, then the infallibility of the teaching of the bishops under the conditions articulated by Vatican II follows. To deny it is to deny either that the Church is infallible or that the bishops really do exercise the role of apostolic leadership. For if they do exercise this role, they surely cannot all err and call upon the faithful as a whole to accept their error as the truth of the Lord Jesus.

An examination of the development in the conciliar process of the text from *Lumen gentium*, 25, discussed above makes clear two things the Council is not saying here: first, that a strictly collegial act is necessary for an infallible exercise of the ordinary magisterium; second, that such an exercise of the ordinary magisterium can occur only when something divinely revealed is proposed for acceptance with the assent of divine faith. Had the Council said either of these things, it would have limited the possibility of the infallible exercise of the ordinary magisterium of the bishops. In fact, it said neither.

The unity required of the bishops is unity in communion and judgment. The relevance to revelation required for infallible teaching is that the matter be one of faith or morals, either included in revelation or required to explain and safeguard what is expressly revealed.[27] Hence, if the teaching of the bishops meets the stated conditions, one cannot argue that it is not infallibly proposed merely because they did not formally act as a body or because one cannot see precisely how a particular point is included in or implied by divine revelation.

To understand the conditions enunciated by Vatican II, it helps to look at the four documents cited in note 40. The first is a passage from Vatican I's constitution on the Catholic faith: "Further, all those things are to be believed with divine and Catholic faith which are contained in the word of God, written or handed down, and which the Church either by a solemn judgment or by her ordinary and universal magisterium proposes for belief as divinely revealed" (DS 3011/1792; translation mine). Because this constitution concerns divine revelation, this solemn teaching is limited to matters divinely revealed, to be accepted with divine faith. Nevertheless, the passage has a bearing upon Vatican II's teaching on the infallibility of the ordinary magisterium. It makes it clear that one must believe not only those things which are defined, but also certain things taught by the ordinary magisterium.

In recent years, many have said or assumed: "This teaching has not been defined; therefore, it is not infallibly taught, and it could be mistaken."[28] This argument is incompatible with what Vatican I and Vatican II teach, for it overlooks the possibility that a teaching which has never been defined is proposed infallibly by the ordinary magisterium.

The note of Vatican II next cites a passage added to Vatican I's first schema *On the Church*, namely, a text drawn from St. Robert Bellarmine. Vatican I's document on the Church was never completed, but it has the weight of Vatican II's use of it to illustrate its own teaching. Rejecting limits on infallibility urged by some Protestants, Bellarmine writes: "Therefore, our view is that the Church *absolutely* cannot err, either in things absolutely necessary [for salvation] or in other matters which she proposes to us to be believed or to be done, whether expressly included in the Scriptures or not. And when we say, 'The Church cannot err,' we understand this to apply both to the faithful as a whole and to the bishops as a whole, so that the sense of the proposition, *The Church cannot err,* is this: that what all the faithful hold as of faith, necessarily is true and of faith, and similarly what all the bishops teach as pertaining to faith, necessarily is true and of faith."[29] Two things must be noted about this. First, Bellarmine refers both to things which are to be believed and to things which are to be done. Second, he does not limit infallibility to matters explicitly contained in Scripture or to matters which are absolutely essential for salvation.

The third document cited is Vatican I's revised schema for its never-completed constitution *On the Church of Christ,* together with a commentary by Joseph Kleutgen. The formula prepared in this schema would have defined the infallibility of the ordinary magisterium in terms very close to those in which Vatican II teaches it. Where Vatican II uses the expression "to be held definitively," Vatican I's formulation would have been "held or handed down as undoubted." Both expressions leave room for the infallible teaching of propositions not expressly revealed, if they are necessary to explain and defend revealed truth. Kleutgen's commentary discusses this point at length, arguing among other things that the Church can infallibly teach moral truths, whether or not they are included in divine revelation.[30]

The fourth text to which Vatican II's note 40 makes reference is a document of Pius IX (see DS 2879/1683), in which the same point is made as in Vatican I's subsequent solemn teaching: Faith is not limited to defined dogmas.

Question E: Does the Church infallibly teach some absolute moral norms?

1. Plainly, there is a substantial body of common Catholic moral teaching. Its expressions are found in the New Testament and the Fathers of the Church, in the lists of sins and penances used by confessors, in canon law (where no act was considered a crime unless it was assumed to be a grave sin), in the works of doctors of the Church such as St. Thomas Aquinas, in many catechisms, in numerous episcopal statements both individual and collective, in some conciliar documents including those of Vatican II, and in numerous documents of various sorts issued by the popes and their congregations. (It is evidence of the common character of this teaching that most of it was also handed on by Orthodox Christians and by Protestants, at least up to the nineteenth century.)[31]

2. It might be objected that much of this teaching is in the form of exhortation, that many nonabsolute norms are proposed without explicit qualifications, and that the teaching is not completely uniform on every matter on which it touches. All this is quite true. There is, however, no room for doubt that some kinds of acts were condemned absolutely and without exception, and approved by no Christian teacher during many centuries. One will not, for example, find Catholic bishops, except for some condemned as heretics, defending the moral acceptability of sexual relations apart from the marital act or of a choice to kill the unborn.[32]

3. Furthermore, there is a constant consensus about such matters among Catholic theologians in modern times, a consensus broken only since 1960. This consensus is important, because any indefiniteness in the tradition regarding the details of immoral kinds of acts, their immorality in every single instance, and

other matters was eliminated, either by explicit statements of the modern theologians or by the general principles they shared in common. This is especially true of the works in moral theology generally used in Catholic seminaries in the nineteenth and twentieth centuries, right up to Vatican II.[33]

Not all the principles shared by moral theologians during this period deserve the same respect as does the Church's substantive moral teaching, which they handed on. Moral theology was influenced by rationalism, and the theologians proceeded legalistically, with defective theories. But their shared principles do preclude suggestions that they did not all mean the same thing when they agreed, for example, that every act of adultery is intrinsically and gravely evil in its matter (and so is a mortal sin if done with sufficient reflection and full consent).

4. The consensus of modern Catholic moral theologians also shows that common Christian moral teaching was universally proposed by the bishops, since the theologians' works were authorized by the bishops for use in seminaries, and thus for the training of priests who communicated moral teachings in the confessional, in their preaching, in various forms of catechesis, in missionary evangelization, and so on. As authorized agents of the bishops during centuries when the latter were careful not to share their teaching authority with theologians whose views they did not accept, these approved authors in writing their manuals shared by delegation in the teaching authority of each and every bishop who sent his seminarians to seminaries in which these manuals were used as textbooks.

In many cases, documents of individual bishops, groups of bishops, and the Holy See refer to the theological manuals, which in later editions refer to them. Instructions from Rome are picked up by bishops, and the teaching of bishops often is supported by Rome. This situation does not show that the bishops failed to fulfill their individual responsibility as teachers. On the contrary, it shows the harmony of action which one would expect of the body of bishops teaching in communion with one another and with the pope, proposing what they had received and held to be Catholic moral truth.

5. Thus there is evidence that some absolute moral norms are proposed universally and authoritatively by the ordinary magisterium. Still, it is necessary to ask whether these are proposed as certain—as the single position to be held definitively.

6. The evidence supports an affirmative answer. Many norms were proposed not just as pious opinions, probable judgments, admirable ideals, or optional guidelines, but as essential requirements for anyone who wished to live in the state of grace. In other words, it has been the common teaching that acts of certain kinds are grave matter. On some matters, the magisterium allowed no differing opinions; probabilism was inapplicable. The conditions under which the teaching was proposed left no room for doubt in the minds of the faithful. But when the Church proposes a moral norm as one which the faithful must try to follow if they hope to be saved, she a fortiori proposes the teaching as certain.

7. In many cases, the norms proposed were set forth as divinely revealed. Very often the Ten Commandments were used as a framework for moral instruction, and numerous kinds of acts commonly held to be grave sins were assimilated to one of these norms. The faithful were taught, for instance, that any completed sexual act apart from marriage is forbidden by the commandment "Thou shalt not

commit adultery." Other passages in Scripture also were used or cited in condemning various kinds of sexual acts—for example, the story about Onan (see Gn 38.9–10) was often used to support the condemnation of contraception.

8. Prescinding from whether the evidence advanced to show that the moral condemnations of various kinds of acts are divinely revealed really does show this, the point here is simply this: When those who propose a teaching appeal to divine revelation to confirm the truth of what they propose, they are implicitly calling for an assent of divine faith and thus proposing the teaching as one to be held definitively.

9. In cases in which Scripture and common Catholic moral teaching plainly coincide—the exclusion of adultery, for instance—there is no room for doubt that the Church's ordinary magisterium has infallibly proposed a revealed truth.

10. In other cases, where there is room for reasonable argument about the interpretation of Scripture—as for example in the case of the Onan story and the condemnation of contraception—it is important to remember that those who invoked or alluded to particular texts in Scripture did not interpret them in isolation from the whole body of Christian moral convictions. These latter in turn were grounded more in the meditation of Christians upon the whole of divine revelation, contained both in Scripture and in the concrete experience of Christian life, than in an exact reading of isolated texts. Holding a body of moral convictions, which they were confident expressed God's wisdom and will for their lives, Christians invoked particular Scripture texts as witnesses to the truth and obligatory character of the moral norms they believed to belong to the law of God. Rather than a debatable interpretation of Scripture settling the moral teaching of the Church, the moral convictions of Christians often conditioned their interpretation of Scripture.

11. In either type of case, the ordinary magisterium proposed moral norms to be held definitively. If, however, all natural law is implicitly revealed (27-A), it follows that the moral norms which are to be held definitively are also revealed, if only implicitly. **Be that as it may, having been proposed with one voice by Catholic bishops as a requirement for eternal salvation, the whole body of common Catholic moral teaching concerning acts which constitute grave matter meets the requirements articulated by Vatican II for teaching proposed infallibly by the ordinary magisterium.**

In exercising the extraordinary magisterium, the Church also infallibly teaches in matters of morality. The purpose of this chapter does not require detailed consideration of this mode of teaching. However, some remarks about it are appropriate at this point.

Vatican I defines the dogma that when the pope speaks ex cathedra and defines doctrine, he has the infallibility of the Church, and so such definitions are irreformable—that is, they may not be rejected as expressions of false propositions. "Ex cathedra" means he is acting as pastor of the universal Church and defining a teaching on faith or morals to be held by the whole Church (see DS 3074/1839). As the spokesman of the Church, the pope under the stated conditions utters the teaching of the Church, not merely a teaching within the Church. The pope is the principle of unity for the bishops, much as the bishops are for the Church as a whole.

Vatican II restates the teaching of Vatican I concerning the infallibility of the Pope when he acts as the voice of the faith of the Church. It adds that the body of bishops also has the same infallibility when it exercises supreme teaching authority in union with the pope (see LG 25). In each case, what is in question is a mode in which the infallibility of the faith of the Church is manifested, for it is manifested in all the ways in which the faith of the Church as a whole is manifested.

Both Vatican I and Vatican II make it clear that in defining doctrine, there is no question of adding to divine revelation. To define is to identify infallibly a teaching as belonging to divine truth, and so the process of defining is subordinate to revealed truth (see LG 25; DS 3070/1836). The infallibility of the Church extends just as far as divine revelation extends—that is, it extends to all those things and only those things "which either directly belong to the revealed deposit itself, or are required to guard as inviolable and expound with fidelity this same deposit" (LG 25; translation supplied).

The clarification in the phrase, "or which are required to guard as inviolable and expound with fidelity this same deposit," was provided by the commission responsible for Vatican II's text; it excludes a restrictive theory of the object of infallibility, which would limit it to truths explicitly contained in already articulated revelation, and so prevent the Church from developing its doctrine and rejecting new errors incompatible with revealed truth.[34]

It is sometimes said that the Church has never defined any moral teaching, and this lack of defined doctrine in the moral domain is claimed to imply that the Church cannot define moral teachings. In fact, in its canons on matrimony, the Council of Trent excludes polygamy (which had been permitted in practice and defended in theory by Luther): "If anyone says that Christians are permitted to have several wives simultaneously, and that such a practice is not forbidden by any divine law (cf. Mt 19.4–9): let him be anathema" (DS 1802/972). Of greater interest, the same Council defends the Church's teaching on the indissolubility of marriage with two canons:

> If anyone says that the marriage bond can be dissolved by reason of heresy, domestic incompatibility, or willful desertion by one of the parties: let him be anathema. (DS 1805/975)

> If anyone says that the Church is in error when it has taught and does teach according to the doctrine of the Gospels and apostles (cf. Mk 10; 1 Cor 7) that the marriage bond cannot be dissolved because of adultery on the part of either the husband or the wife; and that neither party, not even the innocent one who gave no cause for the adultery, can contract another marriage while the other party is still living; and that adultery is committed both by the husband who dismisses his adulterous wife and marries again and by the wife who dismisses her adulterous husband and marries again: let him be anathema. (DS 1807/977)

One might argue that Trent does not define the indissolubility of marriage absolutely—for example, it does not say that marriage cannot be dissolved if both parties agree that different arrangements might promote the greater good of their growth toward personal fulfillment. This observation is technically correct.[35] No one in the sixteenth century had suggested anything so absurd, and Trent had enough real errors without inventing possible ones to condemn.

In any case, some moral teachings have been defined and others can be. What the Church defines already has been infallibly proposed by the ordinary magisterium; a definition only clarifies the situation and insists upon the boundaries of faith for members of the Church who are in serious error.

One might wonder why there have been few solemn definitions in the moral field. There are at least two reasons.

First, in the past moral norms have normally not been denied so much as they have been violated in practice. Exhortation to live up to accepted teachings has been more appropriate than definition of their truth. As a rule, the primary deviation of those who radically questioned Christian moral norms concerned matters of doctrine, and rejection of moral teaching was only incidental to this.

Second, canon law from the Middle Ages until 1917 codified moral formation in a manner analogous to the way in which the creeds and dogmatic definitions summarize and defend the truth of faith. The canonization of saints also is a mode of solemn and universal teaching; a canonization concretely presents moral truth which all Catholics are to hold. Similarly, the formal approval of the rules of religious communities by the Church constitutes solemn and universal moral teaching concerning the forms of life proposed in such rules.[36] Thus, the Church's moral teaching has not lacked an appropriate form of definition, but until now the dogmatic definition of moral norms as truths of faith seldom has been necessary.

Question F: Why must one give religious assent to teachings not infallibly proposed?

1. Plainly, there are times when bishops, including the pope, express private opinions on matters outside the area of faith and morals. There are also times when they speak or write on faith and morals, but make it clear that they are doing so as simple believers, private theologians, or civic leaders. Even within the context of official teaching, it is often the case that observations and arguments are put forward which are not part of the proposition proposed for acceptance by the faithful. In some cases, disciplinary directions are given: This opinion should not be taught; that one is hard to reconcile with faith. At other times, propositions are proposed tentatively: For instance, some bishops have questioned the morality of capital punishment without proposing their view as the judgment to be held definitively. In all these ways, statements by bishops, including the pope, can fail to meet the conditions required for teaching proposed infallibly by the ordinary magisterium.

2. We are not concerned with any such cases in the rest of this chapter. And it is worth noting that many standard theological works do not explicitly and clearly exclude all these cases before taking up the point to be discussed here. That point may be stated as a question: How are we to regard teachings by bishops, including popes, which could be recognized as truths proposed infallibly except for one thing, namely, that the entire collegium has not agreed in one judgment, either because there has always been some disagreement among the bishops or because most of the collegium has never addressed the issue?

How does it happen that such teachings are proposed at all? Why should a bishop or group of bishops (or a pope) insist that a certain point be accepted as certain, although the point is not part of common and universally received teaching, and other bishops either disagree or, at least, might disagree if they addressed the issue?

One case in which teachings are proposed firmly by some of the collegium yet rejected by part of it arises when some part of the collegium falls into error and begins to teach contrary to Catholic truth. As the history of the Church amply shows, this can happen even when a matter has been solemnly defined. It happens more easily when a received teaching has been proposed infallibly by the ordinary magisterium, but then is called into question.

The latter situation often has led to a resolution of an issue by a solemn definition. Until such a resolution is achieved, the part of the collegium which holds the truth (which eventually is vindicated) often is very firm in teaching it despite the equally firm contradiction of the truth by the remainder of the collegium. The Arian controversy is a paradigmatic example.

When this occurs, the main point or points in controversy already have been infallibly proposed. But usually many related points, not previously infallibly proposed, enter into the dispute. Some may never have been considered before, while others may have been open questions up to that time. Members of the collegium defending the true position during such a controversy will be forced to teach as truths to be held definitively not only the main point or points in controversy, but also the related propositions which contradict parts of the false position.

Another situation in which teachings are proposed firmly by some of the collegium and yet rejected, or simply ignored, by part of it arises when bishops find it necessary to draw from the faith conclusions about new questions. Vatican II points out, for example, that in missionary situations the encounter of the faith with the culture into which it is being introduced should lead to an enriching development in the understanding of faith and its application in life (see AG 22). The revealed truth remains the principle of judgment, but its preaching must make use of new ideas as well as new language, and Christian life must be lived in the institutions and opportunities offered by a changing world (see GS 44). In short, that "tradition which comes from the apostles develops in the Church with the help of the Holy Spirit" (DV 8).

3. In exercising their prophetic office, bishops preach and teach the faith which their people accept and put into practice. They not only repeat what they have received but clarify the faith with the help of the Holy Spirit, "bringing forth from the treasury of revelation new things and old (cf. Mt 13.52), making faith bear fruit and vigilantly warding off any errors" (LG 25). The "new things" which are brought forth should spring from faith itself and so be "in harmony with the things that are old" (DH 1). Yet, to fulfill their duty, bishops must venture to teach what has never been taught before, and sometimes they must propose this teaching as truth to be held definitively. In such cases, their teaching is official teaching within the Church and the faithful must accept it.

4. Nevertheless, in cases of this sort, bishops (including a pope) do not individually enjoy the gift of infallibly discerning what belongs to divine truth and what does not. Mistakes are possible. There is room for disagreement among bishops. Until the magisterium as a whole has spoken, one cannot be certain that such disagreement will not arise nor how it will be resolved. But until it is resolved the faithful must accept the teaching of the pope or, lacking such a teaching, that of their own bishop. What Vatican II says about "religious assent" concerns such a situation: "Bishops, teaching in communion with the Roman Pontiff, are to be respected by all as witnesses to divine and Catholic truth. In matters of faith and morals, the bishops speak in the name of Christ and the faithful are to accept their teaching and adhere to it with a religious assent of soul. This religious submission of will and intellect must be given in a unique way to the authoritative teaching of the Roman Pontiff, even when he does not speak ex cathedra. That is, it must be given in such a way that his supreme magisterium is reverently acknowledged, and the judgments proposed by him are sincerely accepted, according to his manifest

mind and will, which he expresses chiefly either by the type of document, or by the frequent proposal of the same teaching, or by the argument for the position" (LG 25; translation supplied).

5. Even in the situation envisaged, the bishops (and pope) teach in Jesus' name. As Pius XII points out, "He who hears you hears me" (Lk 10.16; cf. Mt 10.40; Jn 13.20) applies in such a case; if a pope makes a point of settling a matter disputed among theologians, it can no longer be treated as an open question (see DS 3885/2313; cited in OT 16). The judgment must be accepted sincerely and adhered to, provided the pope makes clear in one way or another that the truth is proposed as a position to be held definitively—that is, as certain.

6. When bishops, including the pope, individually venture to teach beyond the body of teaching which is commonly received and proposed, this may represent a first stage in the expansion or development of the belief of the Church as a whole, but it may also represent a false start. The outcome cannot be predicted in advance. Such a teaching does not at once express the belief of the Church as such; the Church's infallibility is not involved. Nevertheless, it might well be the case that the teaching faithfully expounds divinely revealed truth or is essential to safeguarding it. If so, the teaching which is noninfallibly proposed pertains in some way to revealed truth, although it cannot at once be recognized for what it is.[37]

In recent years, many theologians have assumed that nothing other than religious assent can be due to any teaching which is not solemnly defined. The explanation in question D of the infallible exercise of the ordinary magisterium shows how mistaken this assumption is. But even if this obvious blunder is avoided, a subtler one often is made: Any teaching which is not recognizable as infallible teaching—either because it is defined or because the conditions are met by which it can be recognized as proposed infallibly by the ordinary magisterium—is classified forthwith as noninfallible, and the conclusion is drawn that it could be mistaken.

However, as explained above, infallibility is not a characteristic of the truths believed but of the Church in believing. Divinely revealed truth carries its own objective solidity, and divinely given faith makes one who enjoys it absolutely confident in assenting. But individuals can mistakenly assent with faith to what is not divinely revealed, and fail to assent to what is. Infallibility is the gift by which the Church as a whole is protected from this kind of mistake. Thus the infallibility of the Church properly pertains to the Church's acts of believing and teaching.

Nevertheless, belief and teaching within the Church on matters of faith and morals normally will be the holding and handing on of divinely revealed truth, even though such belief and teaching, if not that of the Church as a whole, do not enjoy the charism of infallibility. Hence, what the teachers of the Church propose noninfallibly very likely is divine truth, whose acceptance is necessary for the salvation of those to whom it is proposed. Therefore, such teachings must not be brushed aside as "noninfallible, and so possibly mistaken." Dissenting theologians failed to do justice in this respect to the responsibility of religious assent.

7. Therefore, the teaching of bishops, including the pope, which is not proposed infallibly at a particular moment in history may on that account be categorized as possibly erroneous, but "possibly" refers here only to one's subjective lack of certainty whether one is confronted with revealed truth. Even if

the other conditions for a teaching proposed infallibly by the ordinary magisterium are met, lack of agreement by the collegium as a whole warrants the statement: "This proposition could be false." But the statement, "This proposition could belong to revealed truth," is also warranted by the nature of the subject matter, the role of the bishops in the Church, and the firmness with which a teaching is proposed by one who wishes it to be accepted as certain.

8. Much of the contemporary social teaching of the Church falls into this category when first proposed. The constant development of socioeconomic culture continually raises new questions which must be dealt with, sometimes by individual bishops or groups of bishops, sometimes by the pope. Mistakes can and will be made at the leading edge of such teaching. Nevertheless, when it is proposed as certain, conscientious Catholics are bound to make use of it in forming their consciences. This obligation is what Vatican II means by the expressions "religious assent of soul" and "religious submission of will and of mind" (LG 25).

9. The standard theological manuals in use until Vatican II employ these or similar expressions to refer to the assent which must be given to the teaching of the bishops, and especially the pope, when it is not clear that this teaching is infallibly proposed. Very often, however, the manuals attempt to analyze this assent legalistically, as if it were merely a duty of obedience owed by Church members to the governing authority of the Church.[38] The explanation given here shows the inadequacy of this analysis. For what is most fundamental to religious assent is the possibility that the proposition to which assent is given may in fact pertain to revealed truth.

10. If a proposition clearly does pertain to revealed truth, a person with faith will accept it in faith. When one does not know whether or not a proposition pertains to faith, however, one's assent with faith is conditioned. The attitude is this: If this proposition is a truth of faith, I assent to it as such; if not, I do not.

11. However, this attitude, which is fundamental to religious assent, is not itself assent. As the formula just suggested illustrates, it is a conditioned disposition to assent by one in no position to know whether the condition is fulfilled. Thus it is necessary to ask what else is involved in religious assent. On what grounds can one responsibly accept as true teachings proposed by one's bishop or the pope and form one's conscience by them, when these teachings are not independently evident and do not clearly pertain to faith?

12. **Even when it is not clear that the bishop's or pope's teaching is proposed infallibly, one has a good reason for assuming that his teaching pertains to divine revelation. This good reason is the reality of his divinely given office and the grace which accompanies it. One also accepts these latter realities with divine faith. Thus religious assent is a Christian act of human faith, which is grounded in divine faith itself.**

13. The alternative to making this act of human faith is to proceed individualistically in Christian life, with no sure interpreter of the word of God and no safe guide for living the Christian life. One who makes the act of human faith—that is, accepts teaching with religious assent even when it is not recognizable as infallibly

852

proposed—can proceed with confidence and a clear conscience. If the teaching should turn out to be in error, one has nevertheless followed the guidance which God has seen fit to provide.

Question G: What are the limits of the obligation of religious assent?

1. The question is precisely this: Considering the sort of proposition with which we are concerned here—a proposition which could be false but which also could pertain to divine revelation—what sort of reason could undercut the normal grounds for religious assent? (The concern here is only with propositions in the moral domain. Further complexities might be involved if one were to take into account the full range of matters about which the Church teaches.)

Obviously, religious assent is conditional, in the sense that one who assents in this way is aware that a norm which could be false but is a safe guide does not have the same status as an article of faith or a moral norm constantly and universally taught. While the norm might be a divinely revealed truth, it also might require correction by a later and better judgment. The individual teaching of one's own bishop, for instance, can be corrected and perfected by the teaching of the higher authority of the pope. And the teaching of a pope, when it develops the prior teaching of the Church, is open to correction by himself, by a later pope, or by an eventual consensus among the whole collegium including a pope.

Because this assent is conditional and open to correction, the standard theological manuals in use until Vatican II consider conditions under which one might rightly withhold or suspend the assent.[39] However, in discussing this problem, the manualists did not always consider clearly and distinctly the case in which only the agreement of the collegium as a whole is lacking for the proposition to be recognizable as one proposed infallibly by the ordinary magisterium.[40] Hence, they did not point out that a proposition not infallibly proposed, which for all we know could be mistaken, also might pertain to faith and have the solidity of divine truth.[41]

Even so, the manualists do not authorize public dissent.[42] They talk of withholding assent by a person who has competence and serious grounds to consider a point of teaching false. The suggestion generally is that even such a person must maintain silence or communicate the difficulty to the teacher (pope or bishop) concerned.

2. No moral theory can settle any issue with complete certainty by experience and purely rational analysis (1-C). It is impossible to demonstrate that a moral norm is false by confronting it with data, since the norm states what ought to be done, not what is the case.

3. Thus, experience and reason not themselves illumined by faith cannot undercut the confidence with which Catholics accept the moral norms proposed as certain by their own bishops or the pope. The fact that the bishop or the pope proposes a moral norm as certain is a sufficient ground for a Catholic to have human faith that the norm is a moral truth pertaining to God's plan for human fulfillment.

4. In considering a proposition proposed by the magisterium—especially one currently proposed by the pope—as a truth of Christian morality to be accepted as certain and followed as a necessary part of the way of salvation, the fundamental fact which theologians, as much as other Catholics, must always keep in mind is

that even if such a proposition is not proposed infallibly, it still might well pertain to divine revelation. Such a proposition deserves the conditional assent of faith: If this is a truth of faith, then I accept it as such. It is impossible to maintain this disposition while firmly rejecting the proposition.

5. Thus, there is a good reason to accept the norm, and there will be no good reason not to accept it except a reason founded on some clearer claim of faith. **In other words, the only good reason for doubting a norm proposed in the manner under discussion here will be a stronger authority drawn from faith itself.** Thus, a faithful Catholic is not in a position to think a moral norm currently proposed by the ordinary magisterium is false, unless there exists a superior source (such as Scripture, a defined doctrine, or a teaching proposed infallibly by the ordinary magisterium) which requires this conclusion.

6. History shows it is not unusual for one or a few bishops to become firmly convinced of an erroneous doctrine and to propose it to the faithful as certain. In such cases the faithful can look to the Holy See for a clarification, since there is a basis in Catholic faith for preferring the pope's judgment in such a matter.[43] In the case of papal teaching, the normal grounds for religious assent are unlikely to be undercut by a superior theological source (such as Scripture, defined doctrine, or a teaching infallibly proposed by the ordinary magisterium), since popes ordinarily try hard to avoid proposing as certain any moral norm which might be shown false from such a source.

In view of the complexity of many new moral problems, it is only after careful investigation that bishops in general and the Holy See in particular can responsibly pronounce on them a judgment to be held as certain. Such investigation ought to include consultation with persons who are expert. Moreover, the difficulties and opinions of the faithful at large should be investigated and taken into account.[44]

Nevertheless, the collegial magisterium has the responsibility for judging what faith requires of Catholics in their lives, and the pope has a supreme responsibility within the collegium. His judgment ought to be accepted by all and followed in practice. This submission most obviously is necessary if study of a disputed question tends to suggest that a moral norm has been proposed infallibly by the ordinary magisterium. Paul VI perhaps came to such a conclusion after he examined the results of the work of the Pontifical Commission on Population, Family, and Birthrate.[45]

Summary

The apostles had a unique role as the recipients of God's revelation in Jesus. By the gift of the Spirit, Jesus ensured that they would not make mistakes in believing. In their recognition of God's revelation, they were infallible—that is, the very possibility of error was excluded. But God's revelation was not just for the apostles. They were commissioned to spread it to all humankind. Founded on the apostles and continuing their mission, the Church as a whole also enjoys infallibility. Individual members can err about what is and is not included in revelation, but the Church as a whole cannot.

The books of Scripture, which express the Church's faith, have God as their author; they contain his word. Therefore, whatever the sacred writers assert must be recognized as true. Fundamentalism assigns the value of divine truth to the propositions each individual extracts from the Bible; theological liberalism attempts to judge the truth of God's word by some extrinsic standard. In contrast with both, Catholics trust that all propositions asserted by the sacred writers are true, but rely on the discernment of the Church in interpreting the Bible.

Scripture contains some inerrant moral teachings—namely, those asserted by the inspired writers. Because most moral norms are nonabsolute and can be commended with varying degrees of force, the presence in the Bible of norms which admit of exceptions or seem unsound does not argue against the truth of those norms proposed as certainly true and exceptionless. Specifically, the Ten Commandments, though needing interpretation and development, have the status of fundamental, revealed moral truth.

As successors of the apostles, bishops, in communion with one another and the pope, are authorized spokesmen for Jesus; their prophetic role is called the "magisterium." Since individual members can err in belief, the infallibility of the Church evidently needs such an instrument. The magisterium has authority to judge what belongs to revelation. Its authority is not that of scholarly competence or administrative power, but a participation in the authority of Jesus' communication of the personal truth of God.

Vatican II clearly states the criteria for an infallible exercise of the magisterium by the bishops engaged in their ordinary work of teaching. They must be in communion with one another and the pope; they must teach authoritatively on a matter of faith and morals; they must teach with virtual unanimity; and they must propose a judgment to be held definitively. To deny that the bishops teach infallibly under these conditions is to deny either that the Church is infallible or that they really exercise the role of apostolic leadership instituted by Jesus.

There is a substantial body of common Catholic moral teaching in which some kinds of acts are condemned absolutely, without any exception. A constant consensus, broken only since 1960, exists about such matters among Catholic theologians in modern times. It is expressed, among other places, in works whose authorized use—for training priests—shows that they contain moral teaching universally proposed by the bishops. The evidence further indicates that on many specific points this moral teaching was proposed definitively. Where Scripture and this teaching clearly coincide, there is no room for doubt that the ordinary magisterium has infallibly proposed a revealed truth. In other cases, its exercise clearly meets Vatican II's criteria for infallible teaching.

But how is one to regard teaching which could be recognized as infallibly proposed, except that the entire college of bishops has not agreed in one judgment? The question is particularly relevant when bishops confront new questions and teach what has not been taught before. Mistakes are possible, yet the faithful must accept such teaching. Here what Vatican II says about "religious assent" comes into play.

Even in such cases, where a teaching might possibly be erroneous, it also might possibly belong to revealed truth. This latter possibility cannot be ignored, and a faithful Catholic will of course be ready to accept in faith anything which turns out to be a revealed truth. This conditioned disposition to assent, together with one's acceptance with divine faith of the episcopal or papal office as divinely given and accompanied by grace, leads one to religious assent: a Christian act of human faith grounded in divine faith itself.

Because no systematic moral theory can settle any issue with complete certainty by experience and purely rational analysis, experience and reason not illumined by faith cannot undercut the moral certitude of Catholics in accepting the teaching of the bishops and pope. There will be no cogent reason not to accept their teaching except some clearer claim of faith itself. It may happen that one or several bishops become firmly convinced of an erroneous doctrine and propose it as certain; the faithful can then look to the Holy See for clarification. In the case of papal teaching, however, there is little chance of its being undercut by a superior theological source.

Appendix 1:   The apostle and the handing on of Christian revelation

All truth originates with the Father: "Of his own will he brought us forth by the word of truth that we should be a kind of first fruits of his creatures" (Jas 1.18). The Father first sends his Son into the world to bear witness to the truth (see Jn 18.37). The teaching of Jesus is not his own (see Jn 7.16–18). He teaches only and all that the Father has handed over to him (see Jn 8.26–28, 47). But he does not teach everything to everyone; only his chosen friends receive everything he has heard from the Father (see Mt 13.11; Mk 4.11; Lk 8.10; 10.23–24; Jn 15.15–16).

"Apostle" means one who is sent.[46] Jesus himself is an apostle of the Father (see Heb 3.1). As one authorized to carry out a mission, he has the full authority of the one who sends him to do what he is sent to do (see Mt 28.18; Jn 17.1–8). Like a minister or envoy sent with unconditional power by a government, an apostle's act within his sphere of authority is of itself the act of the one for whom he speaks.

The salvation announced by Jesus was confirmed to others by those who heard him (see Heb 2.3). God gave witness to their teaching by signs—miracles and gifts of the Spirit (see Heb 2.4). Jesus had chosen men to be his apostles, to bear witness to him (see Jn 15.16). When he first sent them out, he told them they would speak for him (see Mt 10.40; Lk 10.16). "He who receives any one whom I send receives me; and he who receives me receives him who sent me" (Jn 13.20). Subsequently, he sent them to convey his gospel and gave them all the authority necessary to act for him on earth (see Mt 16.18–19; 28.16–20; Mk 16.15–20; Lk 24.44–49; Jn 20.21–22; Acts 1.8).

"Apostle" can be used loosely for others sent to preach the gospel, but it applies in a special way to the Twelve.[47] Paul, although not one of the Twelve, was an apostle in the same sense as they, for he also had seen the risen Jesus and been sent to bear witness to him (see Acts 26.16–18; Rom 1.1, 5; 11.13; 1 Cor 9.1–2; 2 Cor 11; Gal 1.15–16; 2.8). Hence the Church is built on the foundation of the prophets and apostles (see Eph 2.20); the faithful are the living stones of this structure (see 1 Pt 2.5).

In the apostolic foundation, which Jesus himself lays, Peter has a special place; his confession of faith is the rock (see Mt 16.13–20; S.t., 2–2, q. 174, a. 6).[48] His faith wavers, but is strengthened by a special grace for which Jesus prays, so that Peter can firmly support the faith of the rest (see Lk 22.31–32). Peter's role is to be a service of love (see Jn 6.68–70; 21.15–17). In general, the work of the apostles is to serve the faith of others, just as Jesus served others and communicated God's truth and love to them (see Mt 20.24–28; Mk 10.41–45; Jn 13.12–17, 34–35).

After Jesus returns to the Father, the apostles proceed to carry out the work he set them. Peter takes the initiative in replacing Judas (see Acts 1.15). All are filled with the Spirit on Pentecost; Peter takes the lead in preaching (see Acts 2.14, 38–41). Before the Sanhedrin, the apostles claim their teaching and the witness of the Spirit are the same (see Acts 5.29–39). Peter takes the lead in accepting non-Jews as Christians (see Acts 10; 15.7–11). When the decision is adopted by all, it is asserted as the decision of the Spirit (see Acts 15.28). Paul also carries on the work of Jesus; the Lord comes to reassure him (see Acts 18.9–10; 23.11; 2 Tm 4.17).

The position of the apostles is unique, since they are original witnesses of Jesus (see 1 Jn 1.3). With the gift of the Spirit, they appropriate the revelation of God in Jesus, in this way completing the communication relationship, which cannot exist without a recipient (see Jn 14.26; 16.12–13).[49] The apostolic testimony is the necessary medium of our own faith in Jesus (see Acts 10.39–42). As a result, those who believe the apostolic testimony accept not the word of men, but the word of God (see 1 Thes 2.13). The apostle conveys the commands of Jesus (see 1 Cor 14.36–38). God appeals through the apostle and Jesus speaks in him (see 2 Cor 5.20; 13.3).

But the faith does not end with the apostles; it only begins from them its tradition through history until Jesus comes again (see Mt 28.20). Paul makes it clear that he only hands on what he has received (see 1 Cor 15.1–3; 2 Thes 2.15). Those who receive the teaching are to preserve it carefully (see 1 Tm 6.12; 2 Tm 1.14; 3.14). In a departing statement to the presbyters of the Church of Ephesus, Paul exhorts them to guard the flock and defend the faith (see Acts 20.28–31). That part of the apostolic task which is not unique is handed on to successors (see 2 Tm 1.6–8; 4.1–5).[50]

The Catholic Church firmly teaches that her bishops are the successors of the apostles of Jesus: "To the Lord was given all power in heaven and on earth. As successors of the apostles, bishops receive from him the mission to teach all nations and to preach the gospel to every creature, so that all men may attain to salvation by faith, baptism, and the fulfillment of the commandments (cf. Mt 28.18; Mk 16.15–16; Acts 26.17 f.). To fulfill this mission, Christ the Lord promised the Holy Spirit to the apostles, and on Pentecost day sent the Spirit from heaven" (LG 24).

The mission of the apostles lasts until the end of the world (see LG 20). In the bishops Jesus himself is present to believers to preach the gospel and administer his sacraments (see LG 21). The teaching office of the apostles belongs to the bishops (see DV 7). Vatican II asserts with great clarity the special role of the Twelve, of Peter, and of Catholic "bishops with Peter's successor at their head" (UR 2). Bishops are not merely appointed by men, but are appointed by the Holy Spirit and empowered to act by Jesus (see CD 2).

Appendix 2: A critique of some views on infallibility in general

Those who deny infallibility or attempt to limit it in ways not sanctioned by received Catholic teaching generally do not discuss the infallibility of the apostles. However, most of their arguments, if sound, would exclude apostolic infallibility. Therefore, I consider some of these arguments as objections to the infallibility of the apostles and respond to them on that basis. This procedure helps greatly to clarify what ultimately is at stake in some of the debates about infallibility.

Hans Küng argues that faith always is articulated in propositions—simple or complex articles of faith. He asserts that propositions of faith never are directly God's word but are at best God's word mediated in human language, perceptible and transmissible by human propositions. Propositions, Küng claims, always fall short of reality, are open to misunderstanding, are susceptible to translation only within limits, change their meanings as time goes by, and can be abused for ideological purposes.[51]

Küng makes several mistakes. First, he apparently assumes that the word of God is not revealed in human words. This position, if carried through to its final implications, would exclude revelation altogether, for revelation is accomplished by a set of created entities (20-A), such as the human words and deeds of Jesus, which were experienced by the apostles. Second, Küng seems to assume an individualistic conception of the act of faith; he nowhere makes it clear that infallibility is claimed for the faith of the Church founded on the apostles, not for the faith of any individual precisely as such. Third, Küng confuses propositions, which are nonlinguistic entities, with statements, which belong to language (see 20, appendix 1).

The propositions of apostolic faith certainly fell short of the reality revealed in Jesus, but the apostles also captured many aspects of this reality in nonpropositional modes of appropriation. The whole revelation falls short of divine reality itself, but cannot be faulted on that account; it is the self-communication God chose to give in the modality of the Incarnation, and is a sufficient way by which we can come to see God as he is. The propositions of apostolic faith were not open to misunderstanding; they were themselves understandings, and ones accurate by the Spirit's help so that revelation did occur successfully.

These propositions needed no translation, but were expressed linguistically with an accuracy underwritten by the Holy Spirit (see Acts 2.5–11; AG 4). The linguistic expressions which the apostles used in preaching could in time change their meaning; but since human persons can recognize such changes, they also can compensate for them. Moreover, the Church can correct misunderstandings which arise because of the ambiguities of language. As to the ideology-prone character of propositions, Küng only shows that we can abuse truths of faith if we do not live up to them. He is certainly right about this, but it shows nothing against the infallibility of the apostles in identifying truths revealed by God.

Küng also argues that although the Spirit of God who can neither deceive nor be deceived "acts on the Church," human beings who can both deceive and be deceived constitute the Church. The Spirit and the Church must be distinguished absolutely.[52] In arguing thus, Küng apparently denies that in the man, Jesus, God reveals himself, and that by the Spirit Jesus not only acts on but speaks in and through the Church. Küng seems allergic to the Incarnation and to the lasting results in human persons of our participation through Jesus in divine truth and life.

Küng does say that infallibility belongs to God's word: "to his word that became flesh in Jesus Christ; to the gospel message as such, which is the unerring faithful testimony of this salvation-event." But he denies that either Scripture or the Church is infallible.[53] Instead, the most he will grant is that the Church is "indefectible"—that it remains fundamentally in the truth despite all sorts of errors.[54]

His basic reason for taking this position is that he does not accept propositions as a medium of divine revelation; he thinks that in some mysterious way faith contacts Jesus directly.[55] If one does not imagine with Küng that one's faith is independent of the word one hears and of the Church's faith in it, then one will be unable to make sense of Küng's notion of indefectibility. For if not even the apostles knew what God revealed, then he tried to reveal in vain. And if the apostles knew but the Church as a whole does not know what God has revealed, then God has abandoned his own word.

In his most radical criticisms of "propositions"—linguistic entities he mistakenly identifies with propositional truth-claims—Küng actually maintains that every human proposition is historically conditioned and, as such, partly true and partly false.[56] This position, which Küng draws uncritically from a number of contemporary philosophers, is an instance of self-defeating relativism. Reduced to a straightforward formula, Küng's thesis on propositions amounts to this: "Here is an absolutely true proposition: No proposition is absolutely true." Like all relativists, Küng of course exempts his own relativistic thesis from the limitedness, inadequacy, and partial falsity which he claims afflicts the language we use to confess and preach our faith.

Peter Chirico does not deny infallibility altogether, but asserts that it can exist only with respect to what he calls "universal meanings." Underlying this position is a conviction that divine infallibility cannot be communicated to human persons, and so any infallibility the Church can have in believing and preaching revealed truth must be limited to areas in which human persons naturally can know without the possibility of error.[57] Chirico thinks that the Church somehow is in contact with Jesus, but he does not want to admit any infallibly certain identification of revealed truths, since for him the only infallibility admissible in human judgment is that by which one identifies the necessary conditions for any human communication whatsoever.[58]

Chirico's attempt to limit infallibility fails. He never makes a clear distinction between meanings and propositions, never clarifies what revelation tells us which we do not already know by human experience and reason, and gratuitously imposes on faith a theory of knowledge which limits human certitude to the conditions of the possibility of communication. In the last analysis, Chirico is prepared to admit as a truth of faith only what he is able to understand to be a saving truth; if he cannot see the value of some teaching of faith which cannot be established independently of faith, then he is prepared to reject it.[59]

Many theologians who disown Küng's frank attack upon infallibility nevertheless hold views not far from his. This will be so whenever anyone suggests that each and every expression of the faith of the Church can be evaluated by one's own faith (at least, if one is a theologian), and that one's own faith need not be measured by any public and communal standard. Although his writings are very obscure, I think Karl Rahner's acceptance as legitimate of a pluralism which he holds to preclude any new dogmatic definition implicitly subordinates the faith of the Church to the opinions of theologians, and so by a further implication denies the infallibility of the Church.[60]

Appendix 3:   A critique of some views on infallibility in morals

Besides recent denials and restrictions of infallibility in general, there also have been specific denials and restrictions of infallibility in the moral domain.

Rahner limits the possible range of infallible moral teaching drastically, by claiming it extends to "hardly any particular or individual norms of Christian morality."[61] Only universal norms of an abstract kind—perhaps he means: "Moral evil is to be avoided"— and the radical orientation of human life toward God could be proposed as dogmas. The reason he gives for this position is that concrete human nature is changeable, and the enduring universal nature of the human person yields little in the way of moral maxims.[62]

Rahner here obviously assumes a scholastic natural-law theory (criticized in 4-F). Assuming such a theory, any admission of dynamism in human life seems to require a corresponding admission of evolution in ethics. But Rahner never troubles to make clear what he thinks is changing and what constant in human nature. Does Rahner think, for instance, that life once was an intrinsic good of persons, but no longer is so, or might cease to be so some time in the future? One does not know; he never considers such a question, but contents himself with talking abstractly about "concrete human nature." If one does not claim that the basic human goods (5-D), eventually will no longer fulfill human persons, then one does not exclude the foundations of a permanently valid normative ethics, whose norms are grounded, not in a demand to conform to human nature, but in the vocation to unfold the possibilities of human persons.

Peter Chirico also excludes infallibility for all the Church's specific moral teaching. He asserts that infallibility has only to do with the "universal" (by which he apparently means very general), and so could concern only the process of Christian growth as such. No particular act always and everywhere contributes to or blocks this process. "It is the whole act taken in context of the life of the individual at his stage of development that determines whether he will or will not grow by it."[63] Chirico never shows that infallibility necessarily is limited to the universal; he himself wishes—commendably but inconsistently—to extend it to the belief that Jesus is God and man, that he died and is risen.[64]

But beyond this, Chirico makes no effort to show that certain kinds of acts, which always have been excluded by Christian moral teaching, are in fact compatible with growth in Christian love. Instead, he simply assumes a proportionalist theory of morality, and supposes that sometimes acts excluded by received Christian moral teaching will be helpful to "Christians in their march to the universal relatability of the risen Christ."[65] This last phrase seems to express Chirico's conception of the basic principle by which all acts ought to be evaluated. As standards go, it is rather vague. Imagine a young couple tempted to fornicate pondering whether the act would or would not help in their march to the universal relatability of the risen Christ.

Like Chirico, Gerard J. Hughes, S.J., assumes a proportionalist theory of basic moral norms. On this assumption, infallible teaching in the moral domain would be limited to two kinds of propositions. One kind, which could be true permanently, would not be informative—for example, "Murder is always wrong," where "murder" means unjust killing and leaves open whether a choice to kill the unborn or the aged should be considered unjust. The other kind, which might be informative, would be true only because of the consequences acts happen to have at a given time. A teaching excluding acts with all and only these consequences could be infallible, but Hughes argues that such a teaching would be useless. One always would have to appraise consequences for oneself to discover whether the teaching was relevant; it would be found so only if it agreed with one's own judgment of the case.[66]

Hughes' pervasive assumption of proportionalism undercuts his treatment of infallibility in morals. He assumes without proving that norms such as that excluding sexual intercourse apart from marriage are nonabsolute and based only on the bad consequences of such a practice.

A number of other theologians have suggested that moral norms cannot be proposed infallibly because any moral norm is expressed within a certain conceptual framework; when conceptual frameworks change, the moral norm can become invalid. An example of a norm in a conceptual framework is the belief of a primitive group concerning how they should worship God.

This suggestion fails for several reasons. First, it is never accompanied with evidence or arguments to show that basic moral principles are as dependent upon conceptual frameworks as are specific norms. Second, no proof is given that a true norm cannot be expressed in a rather inadequate "conceptual framework"—and the latter expression is none too clear. One would like to know what is inadequate about the conceptual framework in which the Christian tradition has, for example, rejected adultery, and how this inadequacy might invalidate the norm. Third, Christian moral norms are embedded within the framework of Christian faith and the description of the character of Jesus. It is not clear why this framework should be expected to change in the way that the beliefs of a primitive people can be expected to change.

Appendix 4:   Moral teaching in the New Testament

Joseph Fuchs, S.J., grants that there is some absolute and universally valid moral content in the New Testament, but he wishes to limit it to the commendation of values and attitudes, and to general principles—such as the requirements of fidelity and obedience to God, of the following of Christ, of life according to faith and baptism (or, in John, faith and love). He recognizes also that specific norms of behavior, which he calls "operative," are proposed in both the Gospels and the Epistles. These Fuchs admits to be absolute, in the sense of being objectively valid for their time, but he denies they are universally valid. Thus he refuses to accept arguments from the New Testament against justifying exceptions to those moral norms which set definite requirements, such as that excluding adultery.[67]

With respect to the Sermon on the Mount, for instance, Fuchs admits that it contains absolutely—that is, objectively—valid norms. He then goes on: "The question is: absolute validity, as what—as universal norms, or as models for the behavior of the believing and loving citizens of God's kingdom who will be ready for such modes of conduct, perhaps, under determined conditions not individually specified by the Lord? The latter interpretation seems probable from the context and manner of expression. In recent years there has been renewed and heated discussion of the Lord's word about the *indissolubility of marriage* (Mt 19.3–10). Regarding the scope of this word, it is asked: Is it a question of a moral imperative or of something more? Is the moral imperative to be understood as a norm to be followed as universal practice or as ideal? The discussion makes at least this much clear: The acceptance of an absolute in the sense of an objectively valid moral affirmation in Scripture does not necessarily involve recognizing it as an absolute in the sense of a universal norm."[68]

Fuchs, of course, is right in saying that the status of the norms in the Sermon on the Mount has been questioned, and that some interpreters regard them as ideals—that is, as counsels which Christians might try to live up to when they feel ready to do so. He also is right in saying that there has been much discussion of the Lord's word on indissolubility of marriage; such discussion has been going on for several hundred years. The question is: Does such questioning and discussion establish anything against the Church's teaching?

Rudolf Schnackenburg, a competent Catholic exegete who has written on the moral teaching of the New Testament, discusses the question of the practicability of the moral teaching of Jesus. He points out that the Catholic theological tradition "firmly maintains both the possibility and duty of carrying out the moral commands of Jesus, but has felt bound to draw certain distinctions between them."[69] Precepts in the Sermon on the Mount need to be interpreted and delimited, but the distinction between commandments and counsels does not apply to it. The grace and mercy of God are the solution to the problem of practicability. Schnackenburg draws his own conclusion after criticizing various exegetical theories: "So then we must let the words of Jesus stand in all their severity and ruggedness. Any mitigation, however well intended, is an attack on his moral mission. But how Jesus judges those who fall short of his demands is quite another matter."[70] In other words, the moral teaching of Jesus is not the proposal of an ideal. Correct interpretation will recognize nonabsolute norms and their limits; hyperbolic language will be taken for what it is. But the propositions which are disengaged are to be taken as normative for conscience, not merely as ideals for aspiration.

861

Schnackenburg also discusses the passage on indissolubility which Fuchs mentions (see Mt 19.3–9) together with its parallels (see Mt 5.31–32; Mk 10.11–12; Lk 16.18; 1 Cor 7.10–11), and concludes that the prohibition of remarriage is a universal norm; he does not even consider the possibility that this norm is an ideal.[71] Against the notion that this norm is an ideal stands the weight of Christian tradition, including the views of separated Christians who argued that the prohibition of remarriage admitted exception in cases of adultery. Their argument would have been unnecessary and pointless if anyone had thought the prohibition of remarriage a mere ideal.

Fuchs also discusses St. Paul's moral teaching. He begins by noting that Paul ascribes some moral norms to the Lord and others to his own insight. Fuchs next claims that Paul presupposes most of the moral norms he teaches, taking them from the moral wisdom of the good people of his time. From this Fuchs concludes: "Paul does not present himself as a teacher of moral living, still less as a teacher of specifically Christian norms of conduct." He thinks Paul took his moral ideas from Stoic, Judaic and diaspora-Judaic sources. Was this morality not historically and culturally conditioned? Fuchs takes Paul's teaching on the position of women in marriage, society, and the Church as a self-evident instance of directives conditioned by the times. Perhaps all of the moral teaching was binding only for Paul's own time? "For the affirmation that certain explicitly mentioned modes of conduct ban one from the kingdom of God, from companionship with Christ and from the life given by the Spirit remains true if these modes were to be judged negatively, in accordance with the moral evaluation proper to the age and accepted by Paul. Paul therefore did not teach such evaluation as thesis, but admitted it as hypothesis in his doctrinal statement on the Christian mystery of salvation."[72] Fuchs admits that these considerations do not show that the norms of behavior found in the New Testament are no longer valid today. Nevertheless, later in his article, he proceeds on the assumption that there are no universal and permanently valid moral norms in Scripture.[73]

The first thing to be noted about Fuchs' argument is that it is not valid. The fact that St. Paul adopts some moral norms from the existing wisdom of his time—especially from the Judaic wisdom which itself had developed in the light of faith—does not show that Paul does not present himself as a teacher of moral living. In the passage quoted from Fuchs, the sentence beginning, "Paul therefore did not teach such evaluation as thesis . . .," does not follow from anything which precedes it. The illicit deduction probably was made because of an assumption that moral norms bearing on properly human goods could not pertain directly to the message of salvation.

The second point to be noted is that Paul does propose some norms as counsels, others as prudential guides in particular situations, and others in other ways. There are several specific moral norms which appear to be presented as universal and categorically binding for Christians: "Do not be deceived; neither the immoral, nor idolaters, nor adulterers, nor homosexuals, nor thieves, nor the greedy, nor drunkards, nor revilers, nor robbers will inherit the kingdom of God" (1 Cor 6.9–10). This passage is used by the Council of Trent when it makes the point that the grace of justification is lost not only by unbelief, but by every mortal sin (see DS 1544/808).

Like Jesus himself, Paul was careful to discriminate what Christians had to accept from the earlier tradition of Israel. The diligence he shows in liberating his converts from unnecessary requirements of the law argues strongly that any demands Paul assumes from the Judaic tradition are believed by him to be essential for the salvation of Christians. Paul believes that the greatest possible transformation of human nature has occurred in Jesus; anything which survives this transformation can hardly be in his eyes a mere expression of the Jewish ethos.

The thesis that Paul borrowed heavily from Stoic and other popular morality of the time needs to be proved, and Fuchs offers no proof for it. Against it stand very substantial exegetical studies, which minimize the borrowings of the authors of the New Testament Epistles, including Paul, from Greek sources, and find in the Epistles a pattern of moral teaching which suggests that underlying them is a primitive Christian catechism, probably developed for the instruction of the catechumens and the recently baptized.[74]

Finally, it seems impossible to reconcile Fuchs' position with the use which the Church always has made and continues to make of the New Testament. The Epistles are read for the purpose of instructing the faithful. When the Epistle has been read, the lector affirms: "This is the word of the Lord." If Fuchs were correct, the Church should have the lector say: "These are words of Paul the Apostle, adopted from the Stoic, Judaic, and Diaspora-Judaic ethos, valid in his day absolutely, and perhaps, but not necessarily, relevant to you today. It all depends on whether these ideas correspond to the moral convictions of upstanding members of our present secular humanist, post-Christian society."[75]

Notes

1. See Ignace de la Potterie, S.J., and Stanislaus Lyonnet, S.J., *The Christian Lives by the Spirit* (Staten Island, N.Y.: Alba House, 1971), 62–68.

2. See International Theological Commission, "Apostolic Succession: A Clarification," *Origins,* 4 (19 September 1974), 193, 195–200.

3. For a powerful development of the original character of institutionalism in Christianity, see B. C. Butler, O.S.B., "Spirit and Institution in the New Testament," *Studia Evangelica,* 3 (1961), Texte und Untersuchungen, 88, ed. F. L. Cross (Berlin: Akademie-Verlag, 1966), 138–65.

4. For an interpretation of a phrase which has been used to refer to infallibility (see DS 3071/1837; DV 8), see Jerome D. Quinn, "'Charisma Veritatis Certum': Irenaeus, *Adversus Haereses* 4, 26, 2," *Theological Studies,* 39 (1978), 520–25. For a clarification of the concept of apostolic tradition, developed by St. Irenaeus, and the continuity of the apostolic faith in the Church through the succession of bishops, see Jean Daniélou, *A History of Early Christian Doctrine before the Council of Nicaea,* vol. 2, *Gospel Message and Hellenistic Culture,* trans. John Austin Baker (London: Darton, Longman and Todd, 1973), 139–56.

5. John Paul II, *Familiaris Consortio,* 74 AAS (1982) 85–86; Eng. ed. (Vatican City: Vatican Polyglot Press, 1981), 10–11 (sec. 5). A full theological treatment of this matter: Jesús Sancho Bielsa, *Infalibilidad del Pueblo de Dios: "Sensus fidei" e infalibilidad organica de la Iglesia en la Constitucion "Lumen gentium" del Concilio Vaticano II* (Pamplona, Spain: EUNSA, 1979).

6. For further clarification of "sense of the faithful": Hans Urs von Balthasar, *Elucidations,* trans. John Riches (London: SPCK, 1975), 91–98.

7. An extraordinarily suggestive article concerning a Catholic approach to the interpretation of Scripture: George T. Montague, S.M., "Hermeneutics and the Teaching of Scripture," *Catholic Biblical Quarterly,* 41 (1979), 1–17.

8. For a treatment of some of these matters, with references to other authors, see Pierre Grelot, *The Bible Word of God: A Theological Introduction to the Study of Scripture* (New York: Desclee, 1968), 106–37. Although written before Vatican II and questionable on some details, Grelot's treatment remains quite helpful.

9. For a summary of the evidence for this statement with respect to the New Testament, see the excellent article of a leading non-Catholic Scripture scholar: W. D. Davies, "Ethics in the New Testament," *Interpreter's Dictionary of the Bible,* 2:167–76.

10. This point is most obviously but not only true with respect to the problem of Old Testament teaching. See L. Johnston, "Old Testament Morality," *Catholic Biblical Quarterly,* 20 (1958), 19–25.

11. See Matthew Vellanickal, "Norm of Morality according to the Scripture," *Bible Bhashyam: An Indian Biblical Quarterly,* 7 (1981), 121–46, for a remarkably clear and balanced synthetic statement of the biblical teaching of moral truth, centrally in Christ, but also including specific and unchanging norms.

12. On the essential unity and continuity of the moral teaching of Scripture, see three articles by

A. Feuillet: "Loi ancienne et Morale chrétienne d'après l'Epître aux Romains," *Nouvelle Revue Théologique*, 92 (1970), 785–805; "Morale ancienne et Morale chrétienne d'après Mt V.17–20; Comparaison avec la Doctrine de l'Epître aux Romains," *New Testament Studies*, 17 (1970–71), 123–37; "Loi de Dieu, Loi du Christ et Loi de l'Esprit d'après les Epîtres Pauliniennes," *Novum Testamentum*, 22 (1980), 29–65.

13. See Edouard Hamel, S.J., *Les dix paroles: Perspectives bibliques* (Brussels: Desclée de Brouwer, 1969), 18–20.

14. See Gordon Wenham, "Law and the Legal System in the Old Testament," in *Law, Morality and the Bible*, ed. Bruce Kaye and Gordon Wenham (Leicester, Eng.: Inter-Varsity Press, 1978), 24–52; Delbert R. Hillers, *Covenant: The History of a Biblical Idea* (Baltimore: Johns Hopkins Press, 1969), 88–89.

15. For a very detailed study of this point in the Fathers of the Church, see Guy Bourgeault, S.J., *Décalogue et Morale Chrétienne: Enquête patristique sur l'utilisation et l'interprétation chrétiennes du décalogue de c. 60 à c. 220* (Paris: Desclée, 1971), 405–18 (summary of conclusions). An important textual study: Patrick Lee, "Permanence of the Ten Commandments: St. Thomas and His Modern Interpreters," *Theological Studies*, 42 (1981), 422–43.

16. Here is another instance of the question-begging tendency of proportionalists to claim that all limitations of nonabsolute moral norms and all precisions in understanding any moral norm support proportionalism. As was explained (10-C), the specification of moral norms is fundamentally different from the commensuration of human goods which proportionalism takes for granted without being able to perform. See Timothy E. O'Connell, *Principles for a Catholic Morality* (New York: Seabury Press, 1978), 129; Richard A. McCormick, S.J., *Notes on Moral Theology: 1965–1980* (Washington, D.C.: University Press of America, 1981), 528–29. McCormick and others beg the question by assuming without proving that moral texts proposed in Scripture are parenetic (exhortation) rather than paracletic (reaffirmation of duties). In other words, they say but do not even try to prove that what the Bible says on morality is like a pep talk rather than like *Humanae vitae*. Until they show this, merely asserting it proves nothing. Bruno Schüller, "Christianity and the New Man: The Moral Dimension—Specificity of Christian Ethics," in *Theology and Discovery: Essays in Honor of Karl Rahner, S.J.*, ed. William J. Kelly, S.J. (Milwaukee: Marquette University Press, 1980), 307–27, asserts that what is distinctive about Christian ethics is solely in its "paraenesis" which he sharply contrasts with "normative ethics." But Schüller fails to clarify what he means by "normative ethics" and so does not begin to prove it is not found in Scripture. Edward Schillebeeckx, *Christ: The Experience of Jesus as Lord*, trans. John Bowden (New York: Seabury Press, 1980), 586–600, makes a similar move; note his definition (904) of "paraenesis." By an inadequate, question-begging division between a "socio-culturally determined ethics" conceived as mere convention and the "utopian-critical goad" of the gospel conceived as an ideal subject to situational exceptions, Schillebeeckx leaves no room for moral truths knowable by reason, and so leaves no room for conscience and natural law as understood by the Church, including Vatican II (see 3-B and 7-A). Underlying this move is an uncritical acceptance and absolutization of post-Kantian dialectic: "Ethical norms were recognized as a cultural creation of mankind in search of a higher humanity" (657, to be read in the context of the whole of Part IV) which pervades and vitiates Schillebeeckx's Christological project. On "parenesis" and "paraclesis" see E. Hamel, "La théologie morale entre l'Ecriture et la raison," *Gregorianum*, 56 (1975), 317. O'Connell (op. cit., 129) stresses the liturgical and religious significance of the Ten Commandments, and the limitations which some exegetes see in the specific prohibitions, and concludes: "From all this, then, it is clear that the Decalogue did not present a particularly sensitive ethic, that the revelation of God's election of Israel neither included a revelation of moral specifics nor guaranteed that the people would quickly perceive the ideal of human behavior." After further discussion, he summarizes: "So the Decalogue was a tremendously important document, indeed a primary statement of Israel's life. But its importance was not precisely ethical." O'Connell's contrast between the religious and liturgical, on the one hand, and the ethical, on the other, is alien to both Jewish and Christian morality, which locates personal life within a community in covenant bonds with God. See William G. Most, "A Biblical Theology of Redemption in a Covenant Framework," *Catholic Biblical Quarterly*, 29 (1967), 1–18; Oswald Loretz, *The Truth of the Bible* (New York: Herder and Herder, 1968), 64–69. The true significance of the Decalogue can be judged more adequately by considering it within the framework of interpretation prescribed by Vatican II—that is, one must interpret the Old Testament in light of the New (see DV 15).

17. For a fuller discussion and references to relevant synodal documents: Augustin Cardinal Bea, *The Word of God and Mankind* (Chicago: Franciscan Herald Press, 1967), 184–91. Raymond E. Brown, S.S., *The Critical Meaning of the Bible* (New York: Paulist Press, 1981), claims (16) that

"critical investigation points to religious limitations and even errors" in the Bible, citing passages in Job (14.13–22) and Sirach (14.16–17; 17.22–23; 38.21) which he thinks "deny an afterlife" as an example. Brown claims that a sound and critical interpretation of Vatican II's teaching (in DV 11) supports his view, and cites the commentary of Alois Grillmeier, "The Divine Inspiration and the Interpretation of Sacred Scripture," in *Commentary on the Documents of Vatican II*, ed. Herbert Vorgrimler (New York: Herder and Herder, 1969), 3:214. However, Grillmeier's examination of the conciliar documents (211–14) shows that even before Paul VI's intervention the Theological Commission was explaining "the truth of salvation" (replaced by the nonrestrictive phrase "which God wanted put into the sacred writings for the sake of our salvation") as implying no material limitation of the truth of Scripture but only indicating its formal specification. Brown fails to notice that inerrancy is limited to what is *asserted* and even (18) paraphrases *Dei verbum* as saying that "everything in Scripture is asserted by the Holy Spirit," which is *not* what the document says. If one pays attention to what Vatican II actually says, one can solve problems posed by passages such as those in Job and Sirach. The former contains dialogue whose propositions can hardly be thought to be asserted by the sacred writer; the latter include propositions which deny afterlife according to some conception of it, but do not deal with the question of resurrection and so do not contradict New Testament teaching concerning the afterlife for which we hope.

18. A generally sound clarification of the idea of biblical truth: see Loretz, op. cit., 64–137. Loretz argues (sometimes too exclusivistically, 71–86) that in the Bible truth is always centered on God's faithfulness in the covenant relationship. But he does admit (90–91) propositional truths in Scripture about God, while insisting on the relationship of these to God's own solidity.

19. For a historical consideration of this point, with reference to the Fathers of the Church, see Louis Bouyer, *The Church of God: Body of Christ and Temple of the Spirit* (Chicago: Franciscan Herald Press, 1982), 318–26.

20. See Yves Congar, O.P., "Pour une Histoire Sémantique du Terme 'Magisterium,'" *Revue des Sciences Philosophiques et Théologiques*, 60 (1976), 85–98; "Bref Historique des Formes du 'Magistère' et de ses Relations avec les Docteurs," same journal, 99–112. The first of these articles clarifies the semantic point, the second the diverse modes in which the magisterium has functioned, particularly in relation to theologians. In regard to the latter, one should bear in mind that almost all the responsibility of bishops to teach is fulfilled by delegation to others. Nothing Congar shows indicates that theologians enjoy any teaching authority in the Church—that is, authority to which the faithful as such ought to submit their personal judgments—except by the bishops' delegation of it to them. Sometimes it will be delegated to theologians to such an extent that they, rather than the bishops themselves, appear to function collegially as the voice of the Church's faith. Then too, theologians as scholars can have the authority of their competence in matters which go beyond the boundaries of the teaching of the Church. Moreover, as Congar shows (104), certain theologians of earlier times, such as Godfrey of Fontaines, arrogated to themselves the right to judge episcopal and papal teaching. None of the foregoing facts falsifies what I say about the magisterium. The authority theologians exercise (usually as priests) by delegation is not theirs as theologians; the authority proper to them as scholars cannot judge the sacramental teaching authority of bishops which theology must presuppose; and the claim of theologians to authority superior to that of bishops (including popes) is not self-justifying and lacks grounds in any of the witnesses of faith.

21. See Grelot, op. cit., 58–61, for a concise but telling review of the New Testament data on the transition from the apostolic charism to that of the perennial ecclesial magisterium. Also see International Theological Commission, op. cit., 197–98; Bouyer, op. cit., 346–65.

22. For a helpful clarification of the role of the magisterium and theology's relationship to it, see Juan Alfaro, "Theology and the Magisterium," in *Problems and Perspective of Fundamental Theology*, trans. Matthew J. O'Connell, ed. René Latourelle and Gerald O'Collins (New York: Paulist Press, 1982), 340–56. Rejection of legalism is coupled with affirmation of revelation and the indispensable role of the hierarchy by Philippe Delhaye, "La collaboration de la Hiérarchie et de tous les chrétiens dans la formulation des normes morales," *L'Année canonique*, 22 (1978), 43–60.

23. For the authentic meaning of teaching authority in the New Testament and early Church, see David M. Stanley, S.J., "Authority in the Church: A New Testament Reality," *Catholic Biblical Quarterly*, 29 (1967), 555–72; J. N. Bakhuizen van den Brink, "Tradition and Authority in the Early Church," *Studia Patristica*, 7 (1963), Texte und Untersuchungen, 92, ed. F. L. Cross (Berlin: Akademie-Verlag, 1966), 3–22. The uniqueness of the authority with which the Church teaches often is overlooked, and it is usually simply assumed that this authority, if concerned with truth, must be that of expertise. However, sometimes this reduction is expressly (although gratuitously) asserted. See, for example, Bruno Schüller, S.J., "Remarks on the Authentic Teaching of the Magisterium of the

Church," in *Readings in Moral Theology: No. 3: The Magisterium and Morality*, ed. Charles E. Curran and Richard A. McCormick, S.J. (New York: Paulist Press, 1982), 16–20 and 31–32, n. 4.

24. See M. Bévenot, "Faith and Morals in Vatican I and the Council of Trent," *Heythrop Journal*, 3 (1962), 15–30; Piet Fransen, S.J., "A Short History of the Meaning of the Formula 'Fides et Mores,'" *Louvain Studies*, 7 (1979), 270–301. The formula in Vatican I and II certainly includes reference to specific moral norms under "mores," and in Trent and before, when "fides" was understood more existentially and less rationalistically, under "fides." See Teodoro López Rodriguez, "'Fides et mores' en Trento," *Scripta Theologica*, 5 (1973), 175–221; Marcelino Zalba, S.J., "'Omnis et salutaris veritas et morum disciplina': Sentido de la expresión 'mores' en el Concilio de Trento," *Gregorianum*, 54 (1973), 679–715.

25. At Vatican I, Bishop Martin of Paderborn, speaking for the Deputation of Faith, explained the unanimity required for the infallibility of the ordinary magisterium (which Vatican I teaches: DS 3011/ 1792) by using the following example: All Catholic bishops believed in the divinity of Christ before the Council of Nicaea, but this doctrine was not defined until then; therefore, up to that time it was taught by the ordinary magisterium: J. D. Mansi et al., ed., *Sacrorum conciliorum nova et amplissima collectio*, 51:224–25. As everyone knows, there hardly was anything like unanimity about this doctrine either before or even after Nicaea, except to the extent that those who denied it may have ceased to be Catholic bishops, having lost communion by their heresy.

26. See DS, Latin edition, index item *A 7 ad*, for a list of explicit appeals to the authority of the Fathers in Church teachings.

27. See John C. Ford, S.J., and Germain Grisez, "Contraception and the Infallibility of the Ordinary Magisterium," *Theological Studies*, 39 (1978), 264–69, esp. 268–69, n. 29. My own view is that everything infallibly taught is somehow included in revelation, for I consider revelation to be the living, personal reality communicated by Jesus and present in all its vitality throughout the Church and its entire history. Thus the seeming novelty of points needed to expound and safeguard what already is accepted as revealed does not prevent these points also from being parts of revealed truth—new shoots from the old vine.

28. Many theologians who disagree with received Catholic moral teaching are quite imprecise and ambivalent when they deal with the question of its possible infallibility. For example, Daniel C. Maguire, "Morality and Magisterium," in Curran and McCormick, eds., *Readings in Moral Theology: No. 3*, mentions and raises some difficulties about the infallibility of the ordinary magisterium near the beginning of his article (37–38), a few pages later ignores the infallibility of the ordinary magisterium and implicitly equates infallible teaching with defined doctrine (42–43), and then goes on to question the very possibility of infallibility, particularly but not only in the moral domain (43–45).

29. In Mansi, ed., op. cit., 579 C (translation my own).

30. Ibid., 53:313 AB (Vatican I's schema); 324–31 (Kleutgen's commentary). I gave reasons (7-B) for thinking all natural law is part of revealed truth. If this is accepted, an argument like Kleutgen's is unnecessary; if not, then his approach (and the important fact that Vatican II carefully leaves room for continuing to take it) closes the door against those who would argue that points of natural law fall beyond the Church's authority to teach on moral matters.

31. A marshalling of the evidence that the conditions for an infallible exercise of the ordinary magisterium have been fulfilled in the case of the norm excluding contraception: Ford and Grisez, op. cit., 277–86. This argument was criticized by an article in the same issue: Joseph A. Komonchak, "*Humanae Vitae* and Its Reception: Ecclesiological Reflections," *Theological Studies*, 39 (1978), 238–50. (Komonchak does not explicitly mention Ford-Grisez but had a year to study and reply to their article.) The heart of his reply is in the first full paragraph on 248; nothing else he says contradicts the Ford-Grisez thesis. Ford and Grisez had reserved the right to reply briefly in the same issue to Komonchak's critique, and did so by adding one footnote to their article, 292, n. 73.

32. This point can be seen with respect to any choice to kill the unborn (direct abortion): John Connery, S.J., *Abortion: The Development of the Roman Catholic Perspective* (Chicago: Loyola University Press, 1977), esp. 311. Those who talk as if the tradition never reached precision about what falls under the commandments ignore evidence, for example: *Catechismus ex decreto Ss. Concilii Tridentini ad Parochos, Pii V., Pont. Max., iussu editus* (Rome: Propagandae Fidei, 1839), 2:125–31 (on the fifth commandment). The treatment of murder carefully sets out cases which are not murder: (1) killing animals, (2) capital punishment, (3) killing in a just war, (4) killing in obedience to a divine decree, (5) accidental killing, and (6) killing in self-defense. Having done this, the unexceptionability of the commandment is asserted as clearly as one could ask: "These, which we have just mentioned,

are the cases not contemplated by this commandment; and with these exceptions, the prohibition embraces all others, with regard to the person who kills, the person killed, and the means used to kill. As to the person who kills, the commandment recognizes no exception whatever . . . . With regard to the person killed, the obligation of the law is no less extensive, embracing every human creature . . . . It also forbids suicide . . . . Finally, if we consider the numerous means by which murder may be committed, the law makes no exception . . . ." (This catechism has special status, since it was launched by the Council of Trent, published with the authority of many popes [first edition 1566] translated into many languages, used for centuries all over the Catholic world, and served as a model for many other modern catechetical works.)

33. For works consulted to bear out this point with respect to contraception: Ford and Grisez, op. cit., 279–80, n. 51. Probably almost all seminarians between 1850–1950 used one of these manuals. They were remarkably uniform, not only on contraception, but on anything involving grave matter, because probabilism had dissolved whatever differences existed before the Reformation about what constitutes grave matter.

34. See Ford and Grisez, op. cit., 264–69.

35. However, the canons are to be read in the context of the doctrinal introduction to the decree, which does assert indissolubility in general (DS 1797–1800/969–70). Pius XI, *Casti connubii*, 22 *AAS* (1930) 574; *The Papal Encyclicals*, 208.89, having cited the authority of Trent, concludes: "If therefore the Church has not erred and does not err in teaching this, and consequently it is certain that the bond of marriage cannot be loosed even on account of the sin of adultery, it is evident that all the other weaker excuses that can be, and are usually brought forward, are of no value whatsoever." Piet Fransen has worked carefully to show the limits of Trent's seventh canon on the sacrament of matrimony (the second of the two, I quote, concerning divorce on the ground of adultery). For a summary of his view with references to his fuller treatments: Piet Fransen, "Divorce on the Ground of Adultery—The Council of Trent (1563)," in *The Future of Marriage as Institution, Concilium*, 55, ed. Franz Böckle (New York: Herder and Herder, 1970), 89–100. While ingenious, his interpretations are not entirely consistent with the decree's doctrinal introduction which, even if not of the same dogmatic value as the canons, has unqualified value as a framework for sound interpretation of the canons.

36. The manualists commonly considered disciplinary decrees, canonizations of saints, and definitive approbations of religious communities to fall under the "secondary object" of infallibility— that is, to be included in things connected with revelation. For example: I. Salaverri, S.J., *De Ecclesia Christi*, in *Sacrae Theologiae Summa*, vol. 1, *Theologia Fundamentalis*, ed. 5 (Madrid: B.A.C., 1952), 720–37; Christiano Pesch, S.J. *Praelectiones Dogmaticae*, tom. 1, *Institutiones Propaedeuticae ad Sacram Theologiam*, ed. 6–7 (Freiburg: Herder, 1924), 385–92. I prescind from the question whether all the propositions asserted in such acts are proposed infallibly; I believe that the propositions of faith and the moral norms proposed in such solemn, magisterial acts are proposed infallibly.

37. Karl Rahner, S.J., "The Dispute Concerning the Teaching Office of the Church," in Curran and McCormick, eds., *Readings in Moral Theology: No. 3*, 113–16, quotes a 1967 document of the German bishops which seriously obscures the status of teachings proposed as certain but not proposed infallibly. By characterizing such teachings as "provisional" the German bishops use a modality more proper to law and planning than to the teaching of what the teacher believes to be true. Moreover, while they recognize the existence of nondefined but infallibly proposed teachings, they proceed to treat their "provisional" character as if it were identical with everything nondefined. The authority of such teachings is analogized to that of the statements of a physician or statesman, without attention to the disanalogy—that teaching noninfallibly proposed by the magisterium could pertain to divine revelation. Rahner attacks (118–20) a critic of this statement as self-destructive, on the ground that the critic rejects the authority of this statement while absolutizing just such teachings. But the attack is fallacious insofar as one need not absolutize noninfallible teachings to find this particular one seriously defective. In the same volume (96–101), the "Note of the Italian Episcopal Conference on the Conclusions of the Italian Moral Theologians" is more nuanced and less supportive of dissent. In a case of discrepancy such as this between the teaching statements of two conferences of bishops, one must look to higher theological principles, such as the teaching of Vatican I and II, to settle the issues.

38. See, for example, Salaverri, op. cit., 708–10. This understanding of the responsibility in terms of rights and duties partly arises from the documents he cites. Needless to say, Catholics do have a legal duty to assent, but they should understand the moral foundation of this duty, which is deeper than that to obey ecclesiastical laws.

39. Some references and brief summaries: Joseph A. Komonchak, "Ordinary Papal Magisterium and Religious Assent," in *Contraception: Authority and Dissent*, ed. Charles E. Curran (New York:

Herder and Herder, 1969), 105–16. Unfortunately, this treatment is biased in favor of dissent. For example, Komonchak never mentions that one manual he cites—Francisco A. Sullivan, S.J., *De Ecclesia*, vol. 1, *Quaestiones Theologiae Fundamentalis* (Rome: Apud Aedes Universitatis Gregorianae, 1963)—warns explicitly (344) that papal doctrine often is infallibly proposed because of the consensus of the universal magisterium, even if it has not been defined by any pope or council. Nor does he make it clear that an author as recent and respectable as Sullivan considers (348–52) it a tenable, though less likely, view that a pope in his ordinary teaching on matters of faith and morals always is teaching infallibly if he proposes a teaching to be held as certain. Like Sullivan, I do not consider this view true. In an article, "The Moral Implications of a Nuclear Deterrent," *Center Journal*, 2 (Winter 1982), 15, I commented on a statement of John Paul II as follows: "In a message (published in *L'Osservatore Romano*, English edition, 21 June 1982) to a special session of the United Nations for disarmament, John Paul II stated (p. 4): 'In current conditions, "deterrence" based on balance, certainly not as an end in itself but as a step on the way toward a progressive disarmament may still be judged morally acceptable.' Here the Pope spoke generally; I am concerned with the actual United States deterrent. Moreover, he did not say that deterrence *is* morally acceptable, but that it can be *judged* to be so—a possibility which remains open for persons of good will until its immorality becomes clear to them. Further, even if Pope John Paul had unqualifiedly affirmed the morality of the deterrent, it is not clear that he intended to speak as supreme teacher in the Church and to propose teaching to be accepted by the faithful as certain. Hence, there would be no difficulty in supposing him to have erred in this statement." Richard A. McCormick, S.J., "Current Theology: Notes on Moral Theology: 1982," *Theological Studies*, 44 (1983), 98, comments: "Here Grisez implies that a pope cannot err when he speaks as 'supreme teacher' about something 'to be accepted as certain.' This is a theologically false expansion of the charism of infallibility." McCormick commits an elementary logical fallacy. "When the pope is not speaking as supreme teacher and not proposing a teaching to be accepted by the faithful as certain, he can be mistaken" does *not* imply "When the pope is speaking as supreme teacher and proposing a teaching to be accepted by the faithful as certain, he cannot be mistaken." By McCormick's logic, "If someone is not a man, he cannot be a Jesuit" implies "If someone is a man, he must be a Jesuit." My point simply was that since John Paul's statement on nuclear deterrence does not even meet the conditions which call for religious assent (see questions F and G), there is *no difficulty in supposing him to have erred*—i.e., in withholding assent.

40. See Salaverri, op. cit., 711, who makes it clear that he is talking about a variety of sorts of propositions, and that some other authors are less clear about this than he himself is.

41. Even the most competent theologians who analyzed the obligation of religious assent seemed to be impeded by a somewhat legalistic emphasis on the acts of the teaching authority, which overlooked the possibility that noninfallible teaching can articulate revealed truth. See, for example, John J. Reed, S.J., "Natural Law, Theology, and the Church," *Theological Studies*, 26 (1965), 56–60; John C. Ford, S.J., and Gerald Kelly, S.J., "Doctrinal Value and Interpretation of Papal Teaching," in Curran and McCormick, eds., *Readings in Moral Theology: No. 3*, 4–7. (Curran and McCormick anthologized this 1958 treatment by Ford and Kelly of the relationship between the magisterium and morality, but omitted the 1978 treatment by Ford and Grisez, which Ford considered necessary to clarify and correct his own earlier view.) This defect in the classical treatment of the obligation of religious assent renders it susceptible to criticism. See, for example, Daniel C. Maguire, "Morality and Magisterium," in the same anthology, 49–58. As soon as one takes into account the possibility that noninfallible teaching might contain divinely revealed truth, such criticism loses its force.

42. Even Komonchak, "Ordinary Papal . . .," 110, admits: "The manuals are generally rather negative on the possibility of public dissent or disagreement." This is an understatement; he goes on to discuss only one—J. M. Herve, *Manuale Theologiae Dogmaticae*, vol. 1, *De Revelatione Christiana; De Ecclesia Christi; De Fontibus Revelationis*, ed. 16 (Paris: Berche et Pagis, 1935), 523—"who can be regarded as leaving any door open." But a reading of the page cited shows there is no such open door in Herve, as Komonchak himself virtually admits. What he does not mention is that Herve's discussion is mainly, although not wholly, concerned with decrees of the Roman congregations, not with papal teachings proper. A few pages later (112–13) Komonchak makes much of another author's— L. Lercher (F. Schlagenhaufen), *Institutiones Theologiae Dogmaticae*, vol. 1 (Innsbruck: Rauch, 1951), 297—statement that the Holy Spirit might prevent the Church from falling into error by helping the subjects of a decree detect the error and desist from giving it internal assent. Komonchak moves quickly (113) from this to: "Lercher does not exclude the faithful from the possibility of such dissent for the sake of preserving the Church from error." But Lercher (298) states: "If suspicion of error arises, which too quickly happens among those who trust in their own learning and are not favorable to the Holy See, there remains the obligation to be silent (20) and to accept a definitive and infallible judgment." The note (20) is: "As is evident the reasons for doubting may be made known to the Holy

See." It is hard to see how Komonchak thinks he finds here any room for dissent, since the procedure Lercher indicates no more constitutes dissent than passive resistance constitutes armed rebellion.

43. See Bouyer, op. cit., 369–90.

44. A very important statement of policy concerning two-way communication within the Church: Pontifical Commission for the Instruments of Social Communication, "Pastoral Instruction on the Means of Social Communication," in *Vatican Council II: The Conciliar and Post Conciliar Documents*, ed. Austin Flannery (Northport, N.Y.: Costello, 1975), 330–32. Part of the present difficulty is that while most of the faithful have no way to communicate effectively with the pastors of the Church, a small group of persons who are by no means representative have considerable access.

45. Hans Küng, *Infallible? An Inquiry* (Garden City, N.Y.: Doubleday, 1971), 31–63, makes a plausible case for this statement. Although many of his critics rejected his view that the teaching of *Humanae vitae* is proposed infallibly if anything is, no one provides any good reason for denying that Paul VI more or less clearly thought the teaching had been proposed infallibly by the ordinary magisterium.

46. See Michael Schmaus, *Dogma*, vol. 4, *The Church: Its Origin and Structure* (New York: Sheed and Ward, 1972), 132–99.

47. See Raymond E. Brown, S.S., "The Twelve and the Apostolate," *Jerome Biblical Commentary*, 795–99 (78.160–82).

48. See *Peter in the New Testament: A Collaborative Assessment by Protestant and Roman Catholic Scholars*, ed. Raymond E. Brown, S.S.. Karl P. Donfried, and John Reumann (Minneapolis: Augsburg Publishing House; New York: Paulist Press, 1973), 157–68.

49. See René Latourelle, S.J., *Theology of Revelation* (Cork: Mercier Press, 1968), 369–72.

50. See International Theological Commission, op. cit., 197–99; Daniélou, loc. cit.

51. Küng, op. cit., 157–61.

52. Ibid., 177.

53. Ibid., 218–19.

54. Ibid., 181–93.

55. Ibid., 192.

56. Ibid., 169–72.

57. Peter Chirico, S.S., *Infallibility: Crossroads of Doctrine* (Kansas City: Sheed, Andrews and McMeel, 1977), 57–72.

58. Ibid., 46–56.

59. Ibid., 219.

60. Karl Rahner, *Theological Investigations*, vol. 14, *Ecclesiology, Questions in the Church, The Church in the World*, trans. David Bourke (New York: Seabury Press, 1976), 66–84, esp. 80–81. Rahner's claim (74) that his position does not mean that "from now on the dogma hitherto defined will retrospectively dissolve" is unconvincing. His argument for this is based upon the reality of God's self-communication to us in Jesus, but he provides no reason to suppose that the "pluralism" he admits does not eliminate received dogmas as effective media of access (within the one, public faith of the Church) to this reality. For a critique of false notions of pluralism and of Rahner's view: José Luis Illanes Maestre, "Pluralismo teológico y verdad de la fe," *Scripta Theologica*, 7 (1975), 619–84.

61. Rahner, op. cit., 14.

62. Ibid., 14–15. Rahner's distinction (15) between "transcendental necessity in human nature on the one hand, and human nature as it exists in the concrete on the other" is not explained here, but seems to invoke a mode of necessity (posited in Kantian metaphysics) involved in the very conditions of the possibility of any thinking whatsoever. Even if one takes such metaphysics seriously, one should try (but Rahner does not bother) to show that the invariant conditions of human action (which include the basic human goods) are insufficient to exclude permanently certain kinds of acts, such as choices to kill unborn persons. Rahner also talks about change in concrete human nature, says it is too slow to detect in one lifetime, but provides no criteria for detecting it at all, and even suggests (16) there are none. One begins to suspect that the criterion for change in human nature will be an antecedent judgment that a norm is no longer going to be accepted—for instance, that having decided to replace the Church's very firm and constant teaching concerning contraception with a secular humanist evaluation of this practice, one will then say that in the contemporary world human nature has changed. For a devastating critique of Rahner's philosophy of man: Cornelio Fabro, *La svolta antropologica di Karl Rahner* (Milan: Rusconi, 1974), esp. 87–121.

63. Chirico, op. cit., 185.

64. Ibid., 68–83.

65. Ibid., 185.

66. Gerard J. Hughes, S.J., *Authority in Morals: An Essay in Christian Ethics* (London: Heythrop Monographs, 1978), 99–110.

67. Joseph Fuchs, S.J., "The Absoluteness of Moral Terms," in *Readings in Moral Theology: No. 1: Moral Norms and Catholic Tradition*, ed. Charles E. Curran and Richard A. McCormick, S.J. (New York: Paulist Press, 1979), 97–98.

68. Ibid., 98.

69. Rudolf Schnackenburg, *The Moral Teaching of the New Testament* (New York: Herder and Herder, 1965), 82.

70. Ibid., 88.

71. Ibid., 132–43.

72. Fuchs, op. cit., 99–100.

73. Ibid., 100–106.

74. See Philip Carrington, *The Primitive Christian Catechism: A Study in the Epistles* (Cambridge: Cambridge University Press, 1940), 88–89 (summary); Edward Gordon Selwyn, *The First Epistle of Peter: The Greek Text, with Introduction, Notes, and Essays* (London: Macmillan, 1958), 437–39 (summary); David Daube, *The New Testament and Rabbinic Judaism* (London: Athlone Press, 1956), 90–105, esp. 102–3: "Everything points to the existence of early Christian codes of duties in Hebrew, from which the participles of correct practice crept into the Greek of the epistles. Freedom in the spirit did not relieve the Church of the necessity of insisting on a definite moral order." Forcefully opposing pagan corruption and carefully prescinding from elements of the Judaic law not essential to Christian life, the apostolic Church appropriated the revelation in Jesus of what persons should be; the result was moral formation in the way of Christ which is valid always for anyone prepared to help transform human nature from its fallen condition into perfect conformity with his renewed image of God (see GS 22, 38, 41, and 45).

75. Some might challenge the Church's liturgical use of Scripture on the basis of Scripture scholarship. But modern Scripture studies developed under the influence of rationalism and suffered, just as did moral theology, from the influence of rationalist conceptions of method. See Dennis J. McCarthy, S.J., "God as Prisoner of Our Own Choosing: Critical-Historical Study of the Bible, Why and Whither," *Proceedings of the Fellowship of Catholic Scholars, 1979 Convention: Historicism and Faith*, ed. Paul L. Williams (Scranton, Pa.: Northeast Books, 1980), 17–47. Until the methodology is reconstructed from the ground up, a genuinely critical attitude requires a certain reserve. Moreover, such scholarship in the very nature of the case cannot be an exact science, and competent people are divided on fundamental issues. For example, there have been many changes since 1800 on the important question of the dating of the books of the New Testament, and the correct resolution is still argued: John A. T. Robinson, *Redating the New Testament* (London: SCM Press, 1976), 1–7 and passim; E. E. Ellis, "Dating the New Testament," *New Testament Studies*, 26 (1980), 487–502.

CHAPTER THIRTY-SIX

A CRITICAL EXAMINATION
OF RADICAL THEOLOGICAL DISSENT

Introduction

Catholics who wish to be faithful and consistent will attempt to conform their consciences exactly to the Church's moral teaching (23-G). There is a substantial body of received moral teaching which deserves recognition as infallibly accepted and handed on by the Church (35-E). Moreover, even teachings which are not proposed infallibly must be accepted with religious assent; this obligation admits of exception only if there is some superior theological source for a contrary judgment.

There were of course theologians who disagreed with these views. (There might still be such theologians when this book is read. Throughout this chapter, however, the statements and acts of dissenting theologians will be referred to as absolutely past. Unlike the truth the Church teaches, which always is current, dissenting opinions are mere historical facts the moment they are uttered.)

In general, such theologians took the position that faithful Catholics need not conform their consciences to the teaching of the Church if they have reasons for not doing so which are satisfactory to them; that apart from defined doctrines, few if any of which involve moral norms, Catholics need only take the Church's moral teaching into account as one factor among others; that theologians ought to judge moral issues by their own scholarly standards; and that theologians may, and even should, propose their conclusions as norms to be followed by Catholics even though they contradict the Church's constant and very firm moral teaching. This theological position is here called "radical theological dissent."

An example of such dissent was a statement published in 1968 after *Humanae vitae* by a group of theologians and other persons led by Charles E. Curran: "Spouses may responsibly decide according to their conscience that artificial contraception in some circumstances is permissible and indeed necessary to preserve and foster the values and sacredness of marriage."[1] It should not be supposed, however, that radical theological dissent was confined to the question of contraception or any other single issue or group of issues (for example, those pertaining to sexual morality). Within a dozen years of the publication of *Humanae vitae*, various theologians had asserted that anyone may responsibly decide according to his or her conscience that acts of any of the kinds the Church

871

has rejected as intrinsically evil are in some circumstances permissible and even obligatory to preserve and foster greater goods or avoid greater evils.[2] This general position embodied the adoption of the method of proportionalism, examined in chapter six.

The principal reasons for rejecting radical theological dissent have already been stated in chapters six, twenty-three, and thirty-five. The present chapter examines the dynamics and methodology of radical theological dissent more closely (using for this purpose representative documents and authors), considers some of its varieties, criticizes some of the more important attempts to defend it, and offers further reasons why it cannot be considered a source of moral guidance.

On May 15, 1961, Pope John XXIII issued the encyclical, *Mater et Magistra*, to reaffirm and develop the Church's moral teaching with respect to social justice. Pope John is aware that it is hard to apply this teaching, for each person has a deep-rooted and immoderate love of his or her own interests; many Catholics are heavily influenced by the current materialistic philosophy of life. He notes also that many people are preoccupied with an inordinate desire for enjoyment, a desire whose satisfaction is altogether incompatible with the ascetical style of life required of Christians.[3]

With these obstacles in mind, Pope John insists that when the magisterium speaks authoritatively in social matters, its judgment is to be obeyed promptly by Catholics: "The Church has the right and obligation not merely to guard ethical and religious principles, but also to declare its authoritative judgment in the matter of putting these principles into practice."[4]

In the fall of 1961, William F. Buckley, a Catholic layman who defended so-called conservative positions on socioeconomic questions, gave a lecture at Georgetown University. Buckley rejected as socialist a number of points taught by John XXIII in his recent encyclical. Moreover, while declaring himself a loyal Catholic, Buckley impugned the right of the magisterium to make judgments which would impinge upon the socioeconomic values sacred to his own class. Reducing his own view of the magisterium to an oversimplified slogan, Buckley drew enthusiastic applause when he declared the Church his mother but not his teacher: "Mater, si! Magistra, no!"

When Curran and his associates published their apologia for dissent after *Humanae vitae*, they used Buckley's dissent as one instance to show that even prior to the controversy over contraception there were "developing reinterpretations of the 'right to dissent' as proposed in the manuals."[5] Richard A. McCormick, S.J., used two social encyclicals, *Rerum novarum* and *Populorum progressio*, to exemplify his claim that the magisterium's teaching is only pastoral in character—that it is concerned only with prudential determinations which are open to change.[6]

In carrying out the work of this chapter, I necessarily call into question not only the truth of what many persons have said but also the rightness of their having said it. In doing this, I am not questioning anyone's ultimate personal sincerity. However, the obligation to presume sincerity on everyone's part by no means makes it uncharitable to challenge the claim of anyone whose opinions radically dissent from the Church's moral teaching to be engaged in theological activity which is legitimate according to the canons of both faith and scholarship.

Question A: Does the Church's teaching itself provide some justification for radical theological dissent?

1. The statement mentioned above, issued by Charles Curran and his associates on July 30, 1968, asserted: "It is common teaching in the Church that Catholics may dissent from authoritative, noninfallible teachings of the magisterium when sufficient reasons for doing so exist."[7]

2. It is important to understand that radical theological dissent was by no means limited to the Church's teaching on contraception. Curran, for example, had by 1978 asserted a generalized thesis: Dissent can be legitimate with respect to any specific moral teaching.[8] Although he did not himself defend exceptions on every specific norm, he did defend exceptions from the norms concerning abortion, sterilization, remarriage after divorce, and various other matters.[9] He pointed out that "the official teaching" on questions such as contraception, sterilization, masturbation, homosexual acts, adultery, euthanasia, and divorce had been challenged by at least some theologians, and he defended the legitimacy of their challenge even if he did not agree with them on every substantive issue.[10]

Earlier the so-called minority report of Paul VI's Pontifical Commission on Population, Family, and Birthrate (the "Birth Control Commission," as it became popularly known) had argued that a departure from Catholic teaching on contraception logically entailed a wider departure from the norms pertaining to sexuality—indeed, from the norms pertaining to all kinds of acts which received Catholic moral teaching excludes as always wrong.[11] The "majority reply" was that the approval of contraception would not lead to the approval of other kinds of acts excluded by received Catholic teaching.[12]

On 29 December 1975, the Sacred Congregation for the Doctrine of the Faith issued *Persona humana*, a declaration on sexual ethics, in which it reaffirmed received Catholic teaching that any sexual actuation outside marriage is grave matter; it referred to *Humanae vitae* for teaching concerning the norms of sexual life within marriage. This document, too, encountered much dissent.[13]

3. The common position of radically dissenting theologians was that in general the Church had been mistaken in teaching that acts of certain kinds are wrong regardless of circumstances, intentions, and consequences. Many theologians who shared this common position agreed with the claim made by Curran and his associates in 1968.

4. **However, an examination of the theological manuals cited by Curran and others in support of the claim that common teaching in the Church justified dissent shows that these authors do not justify dissent.**[14] All admit the possibility that one might not be obliged to assent to certain teachings—those neither defined nor proposed infallibly by the ordinary magisterium. But none asserts that theologians may publicly dissent from teachings proposed by the magisterium. Moreover, no Catholic theologian before Vatican II thought that theologians might rightly counsel the faithful to form their consciences by dissenting theological opinions rather than the Church's constant, firm, and currently reaffirmed moral teaching.

5. Challenged in their assertion about the teaching of the manualists, Curran and his associates were obliged to provide their own interpretation of these texts. They then fell back on the following position: "The perspective of the manuals

concerning assent and dissent suffers from serious philosophical and theological limitations. The manuals' analyses of the nature of assent is inadequate, and quite oblivious to the crucial questions raised by Newman in his *Grammar of Assent*."[15] Whatever else might be said of this, it constituted a repudiation of the earlier claim that the manualists testify to a common teaching which justifies dissent.

One further point about the teaching on dissent of the classical manualists—the "approved authors"—is worth noticing. In *Humani generis,* published in 1950, Pius XII wrote about dissent: "Nor must it be thought that what is contained in encyclical letters does not of itself demand assent, on the pretext that the popes do not exercise in them the supreme power of their teaching authority. Rather, such teachings belong to the ordinary magisterium, of which it is true to say: 'He who hears you, hears me' (Lk 10.16); very often, too, what is expounded and inculcated in encyclical letters already appertains to Catholic doctrine for other reasons. But if the supreme pontiffs in their official documents purposely pass judgment on a matter debated until then, it is obvious to all that the matter, according to the mind and will of the same pontiffs, cannot be considered any longer a question open for discussion among theologians" (DS 3885/2313; cited in OT 16). Most of the theological manuals cited by Curran and his associates were published before 1950 and so do not contain a reference to this document. But two of them, those by Francis Sullivan, S.J., and I. Salaverri, S.J., do contain this statement as part of their theology of the teaching of the ordinary magisterium.[16]

6. It was also claimed that Vatican II provides support for radical theological dissent. Curran and his associates pointed out that at the Council three bishops wanted an amendment to *Lumen gentium,* 25, to take into account the possibility that a scholar faced with a noninfallible teaching might not be able to give it internal assent. The conciliar commission dismissed the proposed amendment with the observation that one might consult the manuals about the matter.[17] But, as noted, Curran and his associates themselves repudiated the manualists as witnesses to the legitimacy of dissent.

One can assume that the commission of Vatican II which sent to the approved authors the three bishops concerned about scholars who could not assent to magisterial teaching referred, among other things, to the clear statement of Pius XII on the subject quoted above.

Having advanced this far, however, the argument of Curran and his associates next proceeded to claim that Vatican II nevertheless implicitly did what it does not explicitly do: "Post-Vatican II ecclesiology contemporizes the classic 'right to dissent' in a dialogic context. There is, first of all, the very experience of the Council."[18] After several more pages, a conclusion finally was reached: "*Lumen Gentium, Gaudium et Spes* and the *Decree on Ecumenism* of Vatican II articulate an ecclesiological atmosphere that differs basically from the rather hierarchological character of *Humanae Vitae.*"[19] "Ecclesiological atmosphere"—one expected a theological conclusion and suddenly found oneself in metaphysical meteorology.

7. **The fact is that nothing in Vatican II supports radical theological dissent.** According to Avery Dulles, S.J., "the Council in its formal teaching did not advance the discussion of dissent beyond where it had been in the previous generation." (He argued, however, that the Council worked indirectly "to undermine the authoritarian theory and to legitimate dissent in the Church."[20]) Similarly, Curran and his associates claimed that the documents of Vatican II were

"dated" the day they were published; they said one must not ignore the spirit of the Council in favor of its letter. In this vein, some theologians began at once to articulate and correct what they considered the defects of Vatican II.[21]

8. Although Richard A. McCormick, S.J., was not in the forefront of this movement, in 1977 he wrote: "Appeal is made repeatedly to no. 25 of *Lumen gentium,* but it is widely, even if quietly, admitted in the theological community that this paragraph represents a very dated and very discussable notion of the Church's teaching office."[22] As with the manualists, so with Vatican II, whatever else one may make of such a comment, it constituted an implicit but clear repudiation of the claim that Vatican II justified radical theological dissent. Evidently, if such dissent had any justification, it had to come from a source other than the Church's teaching.

As a matter of psychological and social fact, some of the statements of conferences of bishops after *Humanae vitae* had the effect of powerfully supporting radical theological dissent. But the theological question is not one of psychology and sociology. It is: What did the bishops say, what did they mean, and what implications do their statements have for the issues being treated here?

Very many statements were issued by individual bishops, particularly immediately after the publication of *Humanae vitae.* There is no collection of this vast body of material. However, reports at the time in *L'Osservatore Romano* and in various news services indicated that almost all of these statements affirmed and many defended the teaching reaffirmed by the encyclical. Only a handful of these statements of individual Catholic bishops contained negative reactions, and even fewer went so far as to contradict what *Humanae vitae* reaffirmed.[23]

Statements also were issued by or on behalf of various national hierarchies, and these have been collected.[24] If one reviews the collective episcopal statements, it becomes clear that most of this body of teaching is consonant with *Humanae vitae.* However, each of the documents has a unique character; all were composed as thoughtful responses both to the encyclical and to the pastoral problems raised by its reaffirmation of the received teaching.[25]

It is a mistake to speak of these episcopal statements as if they contributed a chorus of episcopal dissent to the dissent of some theologians who criticized the encyclical and rejected its reaffirmation of the received teaching on contraception. None of the episcopal statements denied the competence of the magisterium to propose specific moral norms, in themselves obligatory, on the morality of contraception. Moreover, none explicitly rejects the norms restated in *Humanae vitae.*[26]

One must admit, nevertheless, that not all these statements were fully consonant with *Humanae vitae;* some of them even made statements about conscience and dissent at odds with previous Church teaching. But the episcopal statements more acceptable to dissenting theologians not only diverged from the majority of the collective pastorals, which harmoniously support *Humanae vitae,* but conflicted with and canceled out one another.

Still, the residual discord within the magisterium was an abnormal situation which called for resolution. Points in dispute were aired fully at the Synod of Bishops in 1980, and substantial consensus was reached. This was expressed in a set of synodal propositions delivered to John Paul II with the request that he prepare a synthetic document. In response the Pope published the apostolic exhortation, *Familiaris Consortio,* resolving the discord within the magisterium concerning conscience and dissent in a way which clearly excludes radical theological dissent.

With respect to the pastoral work of priests and deacons, John Paul II teaches: "Their teaching and advice must therefore always be in full harmony with the authentic Magisterium of the Church, in such a way as to help the People of God to gain a correct sense of the faith, to be subsequently applied to practical life. Such fidelity to the Magisterium will also enable priests to make every effort to be united in their judgments, in order to avoid troubling the consciences of the faithful." In carrying out their complementary roles, pastors of souls and families must share in dialogue. "Theologians and experts in family matters can be of great help in this dialogue, by explaining exactly the content of the Church's Magisterium and the content of the experience of family life. In this way the teaching of the Magisterium becomes better understood and the way is opened to its progressive development. But it is useful to recall that the proximate and obligatory norm in the teaching of the faith—also concerning family matters—belongs to the hierarchical Magisterium."[27]

This papal teaching, synthesizing the consensus reached at the 1980 Synod, supersedes and so renders obsolete everything dissenting theologians found useful in the episcopal statements published in the wake of *Humanae vitae*.

Question B: Did those who engaged in radical theological dissent carefully consider the possible infallibility of the norms they denied?

1. The statement issued by Curran and his associates after the publication of *Humanae vitae* contained this assertion: "The Encyclical is not an infallible teaching." It went on to argue that documents of similar or even greater weight have been proven inadequate or even erroneous.

2. However, Curran and his associates did not consider whether the Catholic teaching reaffirmed by *Humanae vitae* might have been infallibly proposed prior to Paul VI's inquiry. Instead, they merely assumed that the teaching had not been proposed infallibly and concluded that dissent from it would be licit in view of what they considered sufficient reasons.[28]

3. Some signatories of the statement issued by Curran and his associates subsequently published a defense in which they explained and sought to justify their dissent. Here the possibility of infallibility in the ordinary magisterium was admitted.[29] But the authors went on to argue: ". . . those who defend the possibility of infallibility in teaching morality do not produce specific historical instances in which such teaching has been promulgated. According to the guidance of Canon 1223 [sic], No. 3, of the Code of Canon Law nothing is to be considered defined '*nisi id manifesto* [sic] *constiterit*' (unless it is manifestly clear). There is no specific moral issue where this condition can be shown to obtain."[30] This argument clearly proceeded on the assumption that any infallible moral teaching would have to meet the conditions proper to infallibly defined teachings. **This and similar arguments by other theologians overlooked the possibility that, though not defined, the moral norms which they rejected might have been infallibly proposed by the ordinary magisterium.**

The relevant canon is 1323, not 1223. What is more important, the first section of the same canon requires that teachings proposed as divinely revealed by the universal and ordinary magisterium, as well as those solemnly defined, must be believed with divine and

Catholic faith. This requirement is drawn, almost word for word, from Vatican I's solemn teaching on the same matter (see DS 3011/1792).

4. Some episcopal statements issued after *Humanae vitae*, while by no means stating or even implying that the bishops who joined in them dissented from the encyclical's teaching, discussed the possibility and the limits of licit dissent from authoritative teachings of the magisterium. In several cases, such statements proceeded directly from the nondefinitive character of *Humanae vitae* to the possibility of dissent.[31] No hierarchy raised the question of whether the received Catholic teaching has been proposed infallibly by the ordinary magisterium, and so none took a position on this question. In consequence, although what some of the hierarchies said about dissent seems to have assumed that the received teaching is not infallible, there is no warrant for supposing that many bishops meant to take a position on this question, which they simply did not address.[32]

Probably the most important statement by a national hierarchy concerning dissent was one published not after *Humanae vitae* but before it, by the bishops of West Germany in 1967.[33] By mid-1968 it had been widely disseminated; without doubt, it influenced virtually everything said about dissent in the episcopal statements after *Humanae vitae*. The German statement points out that teachings can be proposed infallibly by the ordinary magisterium, and that if they are, then there is no room for dissent. But it goes on to discuss "the possibility or the fact of error in *nondefined* [italics added] statements of doctrine on the part of the Church." Here a vital distinction is overlooked.

The German bishops proceed to explain why it is necessary to teach and preach in ways not always infallible; in such cases, they say, the faithful are in the position of people who must follow a fallible professional judgment—for example, that of a statesman or a physician—because it is the best judgment they can obtain. (This point is sound as far as it goes, but the German bishops fail to clarify the relationship between teachings proposed noninfallibly and divine faith; they also confuse matters by their analogy between the magisterium and other responsible leaders or professional persons.)

The German bishops next exclude the preaching and teaching of dissenting opinions, but acknowledge the possibility that an individual with adequate theological knowledge could reach a dissenting view "in his private theory and practice." (This admission need not go beyond the dissent admitted in chapter thirty-five. The difficulty, however, is that the German bishops do not make clear that in the moral field, at least, only a superior theological source could justify dissent.) They proceed to warn against subjectivism and rationalization, and they defend the authenticity of a person who submits his or her conscience with all docility to the Church's teaching.

In sum, what the German bishops say is not false, but it is incomplete and somewhat confusing. On the account (in 35-F) of teaching not proposed infallibly, one should not be surprised to find defects in the bishops' teaching when they noninfallibly taught about teachings which are not infallibly proposed.

5. Until the end of Vatican II, no Catholic theologian denied the infallibility of the ordinary magisterium under conditions such as those articulated by the Council (see 35-F). Many theologians clearly and forcefully defended the infallibility of the ordinary magisterium in moral matters.[34] Furthermore, up to the time this is written, no critic has shown any serious flaw in the detailed argument set forth in an article published in 1978 by John C. Ford, S.J., and the present writer to demonstrate that the received Catholic teaching on contraception

has been proposed by the ordinary magisterium in a manner which meets the conditions for infallible teaching articulated by Vatican II.[35]

About a decade before *Humanae vitae*, Karl Rahner, S.J., published a small book which included an essay entitled, "An Appeal to Conscience"; it is in a part of the book subtitled: "Dangers to Catholicism Today."[36] This essay on conscience is a response to situation ethics, which the Holy Office dealt with in 1956 (see DS 3918–21/—).

Responding to situation ethics, Rahner lays out received Catholic teaching on conscience and its formation. Conscience is the most immediate giver of moral norms; it must be followed even when in error. But one must form one's conscience carefully and distinguish it from mere subjective inclination. "And so man has a duty to do everything he can to conform his conscience to the objective moral law, to inform himself and let himself be taught and make himself prepared to accept (how difficult this often is!) instruction from the word of God, the magisterium of the Church and every just authority in its own sphere."[37] Conscience does sometimes lead individuals to actions unique to themselves, and individuals need to accept personal and mature responsibility. But this maturity requires that one accept binding norms which are valid for human persons as such. Moreover, morality is essential to Christian life; the fulfillment of the commandments is not just a field for faith to manifest itself.

Furthermore, the Church teaches these commandments with divine authority exactly as she teaches the other "truths of the Faith," either through her "ordinary" magisterium or through an act of her "extraordinary" magisterium in *ex cathedra* definitions of the Pope or a general council. But also through her *ordinary* magisterium, that is in the normal teaching of the Faith to the faithful in schools, sermons and all the other kinds of instruction. In the nature of the case this will be the normal way in which moral norms are taught, and definitions by Pope or general council the exception; but it is binding on the faithful in conscience just as the teaching through the extraordinary magisterium is.

It is therefore quite untrue that only those moral norms for which there is a solemn definition (and these are criticized from all sides in the "world") are binding in faith on the Christian as revealed by God, and must be accepted by him as the rule for his own behaviour; and of course it is equally untrue—and this is often unadmittedly expected—that the moral law preached by the Church must necessarily receive the assent (even if it is only theoretical) of the non-Christian world. When the whole Church in her everyday teaching does in fact teach a moral rule everywhere in the world *as* a commandment of God, she is preserved from error by the assistance of the Holy Ghost, and this rule is therefore really the will of God and is binding on the faithful in conscience, even before it has been expressly confirmed by a solemn definition.

A moral norm is by nature universal but, precisely as a universal law, is intended to be the rule for the individual case. And so when it is fully grasped and rightly understood and interpreted (that is, understood as the magisterium means it, not just as an individual thinks fit to interpret it), and bears on an individual case, then this unique individual concrete case is bound by the norm and obliged to abide by it. When, for example, the Church teaches that *every* directly induced abortion is morally wrong, that every sacramentally contracted and consummated marriage between two baptized persons is indissoluble, then this applies to every individual case quite regardless of the circumstances.[38]

Although clearer than others, Rahner's defense of the infallibility of the ordinary magisterium articulated the common view of Catholic theologians at that time.

Question C: What other grounds were proposed to support the legitimacy of radical theological dissent?

1. At first, the principal ground was the claim that the Church's own teaching justifies such dissent. Eventually, however, this was universally acknowledged not to be the case. Thus the concern of the present question is with other grounds which were advanced from time to time by various theologians. Since many simply repeated one another's views, only a few typical examples drawn from a vast literature will be considered.

2. Richard McCormick, more accurate than Charles Curran and his associates, did not claim that common teaching justified radical theological dissent. Instead, he claimed that Vatican II led to a renewed concept of teaching in the Church, one more open to participation by the whole Church and less legalistic with respect to the authority of the magisterium. Up to this point, as the analysis in chapter thirty-five makes clear, such views are unexceptionable.

3. McCormick further argued that the new concept of teaching had repercussions for the notion of the magisterium and its functioning.[39] First, by its teaching the magisterium must persuade, not just command. Second, McCormick argued that there was a developing theology "which emphasizes a docile personal assimilation and appropriation of authentic teaching as the appropriate immediate response, rather than an unquestioning assent." Third, the reflection of theologians is essential to the work of the magisterium.[40] McCormick also argued that if the magisterium's teaching must be accepted on its authority, not on the force of the arguments offered for it, dissent would be eliminated in principle, and one could do nothing but agree with everything the magisterium says.[41]

4. **Complementing this view of the limited authority of the magisterium was the thesis that theologians enjoyed a magisterium of their own to which the magisterium of the bishops in practice ought to be subordinate.** Avery Dulles asserted that the episcopal magisterium should not say anything without consulting theologians. Usually it should not speak in a binding way without the prior consensus of theologians. Lacking such consensus, the magisterium can at most propose its own theological opinion, while admitting that good Christians can disagree with it. Dissenters from Church teaching should not consider themselves disloyal, for there is no obligation to assent. For the same reason, nothing should be done to inhibit dissenters in expressing their views.[42]

5. McCormick developed his views in line with those of Dulles. He came to think that the congregations of the Holy See should be liberated from their single theological language and perspective; perhaps they should refrain from doing theology altogether, for the "temptation is almost irresistible for such groups to support the theological views of the officeholders whom they serve."[43] McCormick agreed with Dulles on the inadequacy of "the notion of tradition and the magisterium being followed by the pope and many bishops," since according to this view theologians could have only a subordinate and instrumental role, and "are not teachers in the Church or part of the magisterium."[44]

6. McCormick earlier insisted that the magisterium produce adequate reasons for received Catholic teaching.[45] The Holy Spirit is at work in the whole Church,

and so the whole must determine doctrine; the magisterium can propose doctrine, as Bernard Häring says, only with "proofs from human experience and with good arguments."[46] If the hierarchy does not listen to the theologians, its efforts to teach are counter-productive.[47] Eventually, McCormick laid down rules for the magisterium's use of theology: Bishops must not choose theological advisors by the criterion of their assent to received teaching; they must not teach against a significant theological consensus; they must not consider theological dissent objectionable.[48]

These views imply three things. First, McCormick and radically dissenting theologians generally were forgetful that faith is a presupposition of theology. Second, they not only tended to ignore the divinely appointed leadership role of the bishops and the pope, but also tended to deny them even the role which would belong to the managers of any human society, namely, the right and duty to make decisions, to pick advisors, to follow some advice and not other conflicting advice. Third, the radically dissenting theologians more and more posed as the Catholic theological community; those who did not join in radical dissent simply did not count, and their arguments could be ignored.

7. In evaluating McCormick's position, the first point to notice is that he made a simple logical mistake. The possibility of nonassent is by no means excluded by readiness to assent to an authoritative teaching proposed without convincing arguments. Anyone who trusts another can generally assent to what he or she says without convincing reasons—or despite unconvincing reasons—yet also sometimes have reasons for nonassent, namely, the existence of a positive reason for thinking a particular statement false. It is simply not the case, as McCormick supposed, that one must either admit the need for the magisterium to prove its case or else lapse into the obscurantism of agreeing with whatever the magisterium says just because it says it. For the basic requirement of assent, which is due irrespective of the magisterium's arguments, does not exclude the possibility of nonassent should the teaching proposed conflict with a superior theological source, such as Scripture or a Church teaching already infallibly proposed (35-G).

8. With respect to McCormick's earlier view, his position amounted to this: There is nothing about the sacramental office of the bishops, including the pope, which specifies that one's response to the magisterium be assent rather than dissent. Rather, the status of the magisterium requires that the faithful think over the reasons it offers. On this view: "Dissent from authoritative noninfallible teaching is but a single aspect of the learning process of the Church. That is, it is the terminus of a sincere attempt to assimilate authentic teaching."[49] Thus McCormick shifted the burden of proof: A Catholic needs no reason for dissenting, but should not assent unless he or she finds the magisterium's arguments adequate.

9. In effect, this position reduced the pope to the status of a private theologian. Any competent theologian deserves as much consideration as McCormick recommended be given the teaching of the magisterium. Having arrived at this view, McCormick reasonably went on to question whether bishops enjoy any special assistance of the Spirit if they neglect to use the human processes which any theologian would have to use to reach doctrinal judgments.[50]

McCormick provided a proportionalist rationalization for public dissent, saying it would be justified if other forms of dissent are ineffective and unopposed error by the magisterium would be very harmful.[51]

In other words, if the magisterium teaches and if theologians do not find its teaching persuasive, they can consider it in error, publicly dissent from it, and urge the faithful to follow theological opinion instead of the Church's teaching. McCormick did not specifically endorse the dissent of Curran and his associates, nor did McCormick subscribe to Curran's statement. But neither did McCormick disown that instance of dissent, the most obvious example of what he was talking about. In that instance, the dissenting statement was issued one day after *Humanae vitae* was published, and numerous signers subscribed to it.

How such a procedure was an expression of theological scholarship and why any theological work would need the endorsement of persons other than those who shared in doing it were unanswered questions. It seems clear that the statement of Curran and his associates had the character of a manifesto; the procedure was political rather than scholarly. It is surprising that McCormick could have tolerated such an operation; only a few years earlier he clearly explained "the inherent reasonableness of an authoritative magisterium," on the basis that while moral principles are intuitively clear, they are hard to articulate, and our perception of them is fragile and difficult.[52]

10. However, the position taken subsequently by both Dulles and McCormick denied the magisterium even the status enjoyed by established academic theologians. The latter can always and without challenge freely and firmly state their own views, definitely reject the positions of others, consult and collaborate with whomever they choose. In practice, the radically dissenting theologians not only operated independently of the Church's teaching authority but granted it a status inferior to that which they granted one another as professional academic theologians.

11. In view of the authority on moral questions with which this position would invest dissenting theologians, it became reasonable to ask why any faithful Catholic, including any bishop, should rely on their authority. The claim to authority which their position proposed was their scholarly competence. But there are many other scholars, Catholics and non-Catholics, believers and nonbelievers, whose scholarly competence is equal or greater. Every significant ideology has a body of competent scholars who articulate it. In most cases, these various bodies of scholars come to conclusions which differ from one another and, specifically, differ from the conclusions of the radically dissenting Catholic theologians.

12. Presumably these latter thought Catholics should attach special weight to their views because they were fellow believers and, for the most part, priests. **However, nothing in Catholic faith requires anyone to believe a theologian, even if he is a priest, in preference to a bishop or, particularly, in preference to the pope.** (Or to believe a body of theologians in preference to a body of bishops.) **On the contrary, Catholic faith urges that, inasmuch as the bishops are successors of the apostles, on matters of faith and morals the judgment of the collegial magisterium be accepted as normative for the Church.**

13. In the past and also at present, theologians have enjoyed an important status in the Church—a status entirely based, however, on their having placed

scholarship at the service of the word of God, under the guidance of the magisterium. Once their methodology surrendered this relationship and committed them to the view that their own reasoning was the only warrant for the truth of their judgments in moral matters, dissenting theologians, regardless of their intelligence and good intentions, lacked a basis for the status proper to Catholic theologians. There no longer was any reason for a faithful Catholic to rely on their authority.

Some urged that the dissenting opinions created a genuine probability against the received teaching, and that the faithful were, therefore, free to set aside the Church's teaching and to act according to the dissenting opinions. In making this claim, they invoked probabilism (12-D). There are two things to be said about this view.

First, it ignored the difference between the teaching authority of the Church and the value of theological reflection upon the Church's teaching. In classical moral theology, probabilism was never invoked in favor of theological opinions against the Church's teaching, but only in favor of one theological opinion against another (or others) in areas left indeterminate by the teaching of the Church.

Second, the authority of the Church's teaching ultimately rests on divine revelation and faith, and the magisterium's duty to articulate and defend this teaching rests on divine commission. The authority of theologians rests on three things: their use of the Church's teaching as the presupposition of their thought, their authorization by the magisterium to share in its work, and their scholarly accuracy in presenting what faith teaches and cogency in arguing from this teaching. When theologians dissented from the Church's teaching without a solid foundation for dissent in a superior theological source, they undermined their own authority.

Question D: How did dissenting theologians try to buttress their claim to an authority superior to that of the magisterium?

1. **One line of argument appealed to history.** Avery Dulles stated: "In the post-Tridentine Church, and in the Neo-Scholastic theology of the nineteenth and twentieth centuries, the dialectical tension between the charisms in the Church is virtually eliminated. All authentic teaching power is simply transferred to the episcopal order."[53] He argued at length that the situation in which popes and bishops determine points of teaching concerning faith and morals was a relatively recent development and a kind of aberration in the Church due to peculiar, modern conditions.

2. However, this is not the case. The status of the pope and bishops in the Church belongs to them as successors of the apostles. **There is no point subsequent to apostolic times at which they began to act as the teaching authority of the Church, for they were authorized by Jesus to play this role.** Tracing how they have done so and how the peculiar competence of the magisterium has been articulated at various times is a proper function of historical scholarship. But the fact that supreme teaching authority, however exercised and articulated, is vested in the pope and bishops as successors of the apostles goes back to the origin of the Church herself.[54]

One of Curran's colleagues, Daniel Maguire, made a statement very similar to Dulles'. However, according to Maguire, the trouble began earlier, with a shift to the juridical in the eleventh and twelfth centuries. He explained the effect of this shift: "After this transition there is a tendency to see the teaching acts of popes and bishops as divinely guaranteed. The teaching of Church officers seems to enjoy an inalienable presumption in its favor, a certain authenticity that other Christian teaching does not have. The magisterial role of the Church at large is neglected in the stress on the prerogatives of officers. The hierarchical emphasis was intensified in the panicked reaction to the Reformation."[55] Thus, Maguire considered the situation in which the hierarchy has unique teaching authority an aberration which has existed, unfortunately, for nearly half the life of the Church.

A Protestant scholar, Hans von Campenhausen, examined the relationship between magisterial authority and various other charisms in the early Church. Von Campenhausen thought that teachers and theologians had some independence through the second century but lost it in the third. He summed up: "In the course of the third century the exclusive authority of office attains its full stature. It is true that the right to co-operate and share in church decisions is nowhere absolutely denied to the congregation, and that in practice their influence shrank only gradually and step by step before the growing might of the clergy. But everywhere in governing circles we can see the effort to make the effectiveness of clerical authority as unrestricted, unqualified and exclusive as possible. These efforts were especially successful in the western Church, and Cyprian here marks the terminal point of the process. He formulates for the first time quite unambiguously—and with terrifying precision and candour—the principle that authority resides uniquely with the bishops."[56] Cyprian died in 258. On this analysis the situation in which the hierarchy has the kind of teaching authority it claims for itself in Vatican II (see LG 25 and DV 10) was an aberration which has existed for nearly seven-eighths of the life of the Church.

While von Campenhausen was an excellent scholar, I do not think he pushed back far enough. At the beginning of Mark's Gospel, Jesus appears in Galilee teaching. People are used to religious teachers, such as the scribes, who were the theological scholars of the day. Jesus is different. When he begins to teach: "They were astonished at his teaching, for he taught them as one who had authority, and not as the scribes" (Mk 1.22). This aberration from past teaching practice was handed on by Jesus when he said first to Peter and then to all the apostles: Authority is mine, and I authorize you to carry on my work (see Mt 16.17–19; 18.18; 28.18–20).

3. Another line of argument was that the magisterium made errors in the past in matters such as the Galileo case, the decrees of the Biblical Commission between 1905 and 1915, and the question of religious liberty. In light of this, it seemed that the magisterium, rather than the theologians, could be mistaken in regard to matters in dispute, and that the judgment of the latter.could reasonably be preferred to that of the former.

4. There are several possibilities with regard to alleged magisterial errors in the past. **In some cases there really were errors, but in matters of discipline or government, not doctrine. This kind of error is not at issue here. In other cases, it is arguable whether there were errors.** For instance, some theologians, assuming that past error on contraception had to be conceded, argued from this that there may have been errors in many other matters of received Catholic teaching, especially in respect to sex and innocent life. In the actual debate, however, such allegations of error were question-begging. Anyone who accepted

all of the Church's moral teaching simply did not concede the point assumed by these theologians. **In still other cases, there really were errors in teaching proposed in the Church with some authority, but the instances did not meet one or more of the conditions for a teaching proposed infallibly by the ordinary magisterium.** (A discussion of some instances of alleged error will be found in appendix 1.)

5. In respect to the real instances of error by the magisterium, Catholics of the time, including theologians, acted rightly in trusting the magisterium's judgment, for reasons explained above (35-F). If like cases were to occur again, it would be impossible at the time to recognize them with the clarity of hindsight. Responsibly following the possibly erroneous judgment of the magisterium is the same as responsibly following one's sincere conscience in other cases; it is possible to go wrong in this way, but one has no better norm than one's best judgment. Thus, when a faithful Catholic's best judgment is formed, as it should be, by the Church's noninfallible teaching, the Catholic might possibly be following a false norm. Yet God has provided no better norm for his or her current belief and practice.

6. It might be argued that people could avoid having to rely on the possibly erroneous judgment of the magisterium by instead following the judgment of dissenting theologians. But this, too, is question-begging. Moreover, it necessarily assumes either of two things: that it would be safer to trust the possibly erroneous judgments of dissenting theologians or that they, unlike the magisterium, are infallible without conditions or limits.

Some dissenting theologians appealed to the "sensus fidelium." However, Avery Dulles pointed out that most laypeople were uninterested in the "liberal" program for reforming the Church: "The majority of the faithful are probably unaware of the reasons for protecting the right of speculative theologians to hold new and untried theories; and they would probably oppose the admission of women to holy orders."[57] Dulles warned against confusing the *sensus fidelium* with majority opinion. Nevertheless, he thought that the hierarchy could not be relied upon exclusively, because of their "class interests and professional biases." What was needed, he thought, was a "pluralistic theory of authority in the Church."[58] This theory allowed theologians independence.[59]

7. The dissenting theologians did not of course claim to be infallible. They did, however, appeal to their own consensus against criticism which challenged the authority which they asserted for themselves. **But this appeal had no rational weight, since in scholarly disputes only evidence and reasons count in establishing credibility.** It appears that dissenting theologians were impressed by their consensus precisely because it was the agreement of a large part of those who held power in academic theology. The danger in this, from the point of view of scholarship, was in the consequent tendency to be closed-minded toward conflicting views regardless of the case presented to support them.

One reason often given for following radically dissenting opinions was that so many theologians accepted them. For example, Joseph Komonchak's main argument in criticizing the position John C. Ford, S.J., and I defend with respect to the infallibility of the Church's teaching on contraception was: "Finally, there is something like a *consensus theologorum* that the magisterial tradition behind *HV*'s condemnation does not constitute an infallible exercise of the teaching office."[60] McCormick, designating himself too much a specialist in moral theology to enter the argument, nevertheless adopted this argument from Komonchak.[61]

Since Komonchak's article appeared in the same issue of *Theological Studies* as the article written by Ford and me, and since Komonchak had a year to study our article before completing his own (and McCormick was reviewing both), the invocation of a *consensus theologorum* must mean they were confident that the conclusion defended by Ford and me was rejected and would continue to be rejected by theologians who had never read our argument. In other words, the attitude of Komonchak and McCormick was: Never mind arguments; our position is in power.

The refusal of dissenting theologians to consider arguments against their consensus was evidenced by later events. At the beginning of a book he published in 1982, Charles Curran discussed the relationship between magisterium and theology; in delimiting the subject to be treated, he blandly claimed "all admit that the investigations of theologians have not involved the infallible teaching office of the church."[62]

In the same year, Curran and McCormick published an anthology on the magisterium and morality from which they excluded serious work arguing that moral teachings have been proposed infallibly under the conditions stated by Vatican II (see LG 25; 35-D). However, this anthology included a paper by John Boyle contributed to the 1979 meeting of the Catholic Theological Society of America, in which he tried to deal with the problem posed for radical dissent by the article of Ford and me. Boyle tried to argue that "it is no simple matter to develop purely formal criteria for infallible moral teaching, as Grisez and Ford have attempted to do."[63] Thus he mistakenly suggested that the criteria were theological proposals; in fact, we merely drew Vatican II's criteria from the conciliar documents themselves.

A political attitude also was expressed by some theologians' constant references to "the majority" and "the minority" in the Birth Control Commission. Ten years after *Humanae vitae*, McCormick still talked about Paul VI's rejection of "the majority" opinion, saying it reflects a highly legal notion of the magisterium and that consultation becomes a disposable luxury when majority opinions are not accepted.[64] He missed the point that the Commission was not a legislature. It was intended to be a study group. Its members were supposed to marshall reasons and evidence for their views.

No one ought to believe any theologian. If the evidence and reasons make a good argument, one will understand it for oneself, and the authority of the theologian will be as irrelevant as a clean window opening upon a view. Only if someone has bad arguments will he seek to enhance them by invoking a *consensus theologorum*. Sixteen signatures did not transform a bad argument into a good one, and six hundred names did not make a manifesto into a theological proof.

Question E: Could morality be considered outside the field of authority proper to the magisterium?

1. The Church is competent in moral matters as well as dogmatic ones. **The inherent normativity of faith and the fact that the covenant is a way of life preclude barring the magisterium from the moral domain.** Moreover, the teaching of the three most recent councils agrees in asserting the Church's competence in faith and morals (35-D).

2. One defense of theological dissent, nevertheless, was the claim that the magisterium's authority in respect to morals is limited, so that it cannot propose

any specific moral norm as a truth to be held definitively. Charles Curran, for example, said that specific moral issues, such as contraception, "so removed from the core of faith can never be the place where the unity of the Church is to be found."[65] Joseph Fuchs, S.J., argued that since faith and love determine salvation, specific moral practices are "only a secundarium," so that various and incompatible moral norms may be accepted as Christian, provided only that in a given culture they are nonarbitrary and considered "right."[66]

3. To the objection that the Church has always held some specific moral norms as truths to be held definitively (for example, that adultery is always wrong) such theologians replied either that the norm is nonabsolute or that it refers only to certain instances—for example, in the case of adultery, to certain instances of extramarital intercourse, namely those in which such intercourse happens to be wrong. In cases in which it is right, these theologians said, extramarital intercourse involving a married individual simply should not be called "adultery." In other words: Adultery is always wrong, but extramarital intercourse by a married person is not always adultery.

4. Dissenting theologians who held that the magisterium cannot propose any specific moral norm to be held definitively usually adopted proportionalism, which was examined in chapter six. If proportionalism were true, the Church could only give general advice in moral matters; the determination of the right thing to do in each situation would still rest on taking all circumstances into account—a process of accounting which might make a lesser evil of the choice which in most cases would be morally wrong. Other inadequate moral theories, such as intuitionism (4-B), would also preclude the magisterium from teaching anything specific in the moral field.

5. It is true that many moral norms are nonabsolute. But, as was shown (10-C), some are absolute. The Church has always proposed norms of both sorts. The teaching on adultery is a clear example of an absolute norm. Only a dissenting theologian arguing his case would claim that Christian teachers, from Jesus to the present day, merely meant to say that it is always wrong to engage in wrongful extramarital relations.

In 1970, a group of Italian moral theologians met to discuss the relationship between morality and the magisterium. One of their conclusions was: "The establishing of norms having juridical force is not the characteristic function of the magisterium in the area of morality; that particular task is per se inherent in the function of governing, though it could entail a choice of a magisterial character."[67] In response to this, the Italian Episcopal Conference said:

> The formulation of this section is not readily comprehensible to the average reader. Because of its ambiguity, it readily lends itself to unacceptable interpretations. In reality it must be said that the moral magisterium is *per se doctrinal, with morally binding efficacy* for the formation of conscience and the conduct of life, but it can have different characteristics and functions. It can be definitively doctrinal, prudentially doctrinal, and so forth. In short, it can teach some norm, which interprets the Gospel law or natural law, as an absolute norm for all times and places, or it can present some norm as the *historical application* of an indeterminate and dynamic Gospel law.
>
> The historicity *of the origin and formulation* of many of the magisterium's moral

norms should not lead people to the conclusion that *all of them are always* historically conditioned insofar as their value is concerned, and hence changeable as cultures change.[68]

In offering this explanation, the Italian bishops explicate the teaching of Vatican II, to which they also refer (LG 12, 25; GS 50) in their document.

6. Moreover, as explained above (35-E), at least one specific moral norm has been solemnly defined: "If anyone says that Christians are permitted to have several wives simultaneously, and that such a practice is not forbidden by any divine law (cf. Mt 19.4–9): let him be anathema" (DS 1802/972).

7. **There are at least two reasons why the magisterium must teach the specific norms of Christian life actively and with certainty.**

8. **First, the Church has the task of guiding the faithful on the way to salvation.** People need and must be given help to follow Jesus uprightly; but uprightness depends upon moral honesty with oneself. The Church's specific moral teaching helps individuals by making them acutely aware of moral truth which they might otherwise evade and ignore—but not without moral responsibility, sometimes even grave responsibility, for doing so. The magisterium does for the faithful what true prophets always have done for God's people—what, for example, Nathan did for David.

9. **Second, the Church is a prophetic community.** Precisely as such, it must show people of good will that Christian life is the purest humanism, that Christianity is really committed to the human goods which true morality protects and which even the vicious often hypocritically acknowledge. The Church cannot fulfill this prophetic office unless the magisterium engages in quite specific moral teaching to shape a common life in which this teaching is put into practice, thus showing that Christian love really does redeem fallen humankind. For instance, in cultures which institutionalize divorce and lying, the Christian avoidance of such practices is testimony to the faithfulness and truthfulness of Jesus.

Some claimed that in a pluralistic age, absolute unity in Christian moral teaching no longer is appropriate. The "official teaching" ought to be regarded as one option, it was argued, and dissenting theological opinions as another legitimate option. Just as the law of the state allows consenting adults liberty to engage in sexual activities of their choice, provided they are done in private, and just as the state approves and facilitates abortion and remarriage after divorce, so (it was suggested) should the Church.

This argument neglected to notice that while every community can be pluralistic about whatever is not vital to its concerns, no community is pluralistic about what touches its essential purposes. Thus no state ever tolerates pluralistic approaches to the payment of taxes or to the assassination of public officials. The Church is pluralistic in many ways: It welcomes people who are Jews and Gentiles, people of all races, ages, levels of intelligence and culture, people male and female, and so forth. And none of these distinctions blocks one from enjoying full membership in the Church.

Moral norms are not an optional extra in any community. They express its very identity; they require what must be required for the community to live and hand itself on. Societies can be pluralistic with respect to morality only if and to the extent they concern themselves with certain limited aspects of life, as political society, for instance, concerns itself mainly with bare survival and mutual protection, and so need not insist upon all the norms of personal morality.

But the community of friendship with God concerns the whole of a person; nothing remains private in relation to God. The whole of chapters nineteen through twenty-seven tends to show that Catholic faith—which centrally constitutes the Church's identity— excludes the pluralism which would be admitted if radical theological dissent were accepted as a legitimate alternative to received Catholic moral teaching.

Hence, Christian morality necessarily embraces the whole of life and leaves nothing to individual arbitrariness. If the Church were a political society, it would have to be totalitarian or its morality would necessarily be a mere legal code of behavior—which explains what happened when state and Church were too closely connected. Since the Church is a communion of love, not of power, it can embrace the whole person without infringing upon his or her unique individuality.

Question F: Could radical theological dissent be construed as mere reformulation of traditional moral teaching?

1. The discussion up to this point has concerned radically dissenting theologians who said clearly that some of their positions on moral issues were inconsistent with the Church's moral teaching. In 1978, however, Richard McCormick took a new tack, maintaining that he and other theologians who disagreed with statements of the magisterium were not touching the substance of received Catholic moral teaching but only altering its inherently alterable formulation.

2. McCormick began by noting a "conceptual and destructive impasse" which tended to pit theologians and bishops against one another. Was there no solution? He suggested another way of looking at matters, one which "views the magisterium as the precious vehicle of our shared experience and knowledge." Still, the hierarchical magisterium is pastoral in character, for it makes prudential judgments when more basic principles must be brought to bear in changing times; the magisterium is philosophical-theological in character, for it uses a thought-system and language which are culture-conditioned and imperfect; the magisterium must address believers of various cultures and value perspectives. "Together these three characteristics mean that there is a difference between the substance of a teaching and its formulation. This was explicitly acknowledged by John XXIII and *Gaudium et spes*. If there is a distinction between the substance and formulation, there is also an extremely close, indeed inseparable connection. They are related as body and soul. The connection is so intimate that it is difficult to know just what the substance is amid variation of formulation."[69]

3. McCormick took premarital intercourse as an example. Various things have been said about it, among others: "It is morally wrong, scil., there is always something missing. Hence, it should be avoided." McCormick said this was the substantial teaching to which the Church is committed. The rest of the things which had been said, according to McCormick, were philosophical-theological and subject to change. They included: "It is intrinsically evil" and "There is a presumption of serious guilt in each act."

4. McCormick proceeded to draw three conclusions. First, the substance could not be identified with the formulation, and the magisterium must participate

in a teaching-learning process to arrive at suitable formulations. Second, "It is not a stunning theological putdown or an insuperably serious objection against an attempted formulation" to point out that it is incompatible with a recent statement of the Holy See dealing specifically and authoritatively with the matter. Third, the pope and bishops "should not formulate their teaching *against* a broad or even very significant theological consensus; for such a consensus indicates at least that the problem has not matured sufficiently to allow an authoritative formulation."[70]

5. In saying that substance and formulation are related as body and soul, McCormick defeated his own purpose (that is, to show that the substance of the Church's teaching was not being touched by theologians such as himself). If the two are so close ("inseparable"), it is impossible to change the formulation without changing the substance. (If, after all, body is separated from soul, the result is death.) Nor will it do to say that McCormick's analogy was merely a figure of speech, not to be taken seriously. He evidently meant it to be taken seriously, inasmuch as he was trying to make the substance of teaching inaccessible, that is, to exclude its being encapsulated as an objectively formulated truth. For this reason, he compared it to the soul.   ·

6. **McCormick's example of the substance-formulation distinction— what he said about fornication—suggests that he wanted the substance of moral teaching to consist in what was common both to received Catholic teaching and to the opinion of theologians who dissented from it.** The extent of the difficulties this raises is suggested by the fact that he omitted from his list of statements made at one time or another on the subject of premarital sex what the Council of Trent says in teaching that the grace of justification is lost by anyone who commits mortal sin: "This assertion defends the teaching of divine law that excludes from the kingdom of God not only those without faith, but also those with faith who are fornicators . . ." (DS 1544/808). If McCormick were correct, one would have to conclude that the substance of what Trent meant to say is merely that there is always something missing from premarital sex, and so it is to be avoided. In any case, McCormick provided no reason why the proposition he selected ought to be accepted as the substance of Christian teaching on fornication, when there are other propositions better grounded in Scripture and tradition to fulfill this role.

7. **Finally, McCormick failed to show how the "conclusions" which he drew about the relationship between the magisterium and the dissenting theologians followed from what he said about the substance-formulation distinction.** His first "conclusion," for instance, stressed the difference between substance and formulation, while the part of his argument noted above stressed their very close relationship, on the analogy of body and soul. Similarly, his second and third "conclusions" followed only if the magisterium does not have the responsibility to judge what formulation of the Church's faith is adequate to it. But the magisterium has always claimed precisely this duty, together with a corresponding right to reject theological formulations as inadequate to the faith which has been received and which must be handed on intact.[71]

McCormick's proposal with respect to substance and formulation was vulnerable not only in respect to its reasoning and its conclusions, but also in respect to its premises.

In 1969 McCormick had reported the first distinction he made—that between the doctrinal and the pastoral—as a proposal of Phillipe Delhaye, who had suggested that *Humanae vitae* was not teaching that contraception is wrong, but only giving pastoral guidance. McCormick had remarked that, if so, practically all the bishops and theologians of the world misunderstood *Humanae vitae*. Less than a decade later, however, McCormick suggested that all the teaching of the magisterium be taken as he had rightly noted *Humanae vitae* cannot be taken.[72]

McCormick's second premise—the idea that the magisterium itself is philosophical-theological in character—went back to a paper by Archbishop Robert Coffy of Albi (speaking as a theologian, not as a bishop), which McCormick had reported in 1977. According to Coffy: "Every understanding of the faith necessarily implies a theology. There are no sharp lines of demarcation between the faith and the theological understanding of the faith." According to McCormick's summary, Coffy had gone on to reject a conception of revelation "that allowed it to be encapsulated in objective formulated truths." It followed that the magisterium cannot "distinguish clearly between the true and the false." Truth was historical, and magisterial formulations were not beyond discussion. Therefore, theologians and the magisterium must serve the word of God together. The magisterium would do well to teach less and to allow a long maturing process for many questions.[73]

Coffy's argument depended upon equivocation between various meanings of "theology" (1-A). His assertion that truth is historical and his denial that the magisterium can distinguish between the true and the false were very like the position of Hans Küng, criticized in chapter thirty-five, appendix two. Moreover, Coffy seemed to reject the definitive teaching of Vatican I concerning the object of faith (20-C). If Coffy had been right, faith would be some sort of mysterious, aconceptual relationship to God.[74]

McCormick's third premise—that the magisterium has to talk to all sorts of people and to people with different value systems—certainly is correct. But all that this showed is that the same truth of faith must be articulated in different languages and developed to meet new problems. It by no means showed that the Church must accept the diversity of cultures and their value systems and bless all of it, good and bad alike, by calling it "diverse formulations of the same substance." When in Corinth, Paul did not say that the mind of Jesus is to do as the Corinthians were accustomed to doing. He had a different way of dealing with cultural diversity (see Rom 12.1–2; Gal 5.13–26).

The passage quoted from McCormick, in which he claimed that John XXIII and Vatican II accept the substance-formulation distinction as he articulated it, contained the distortion discussed in chapter twenty, appendix two. When John XXIII and the Council (see GS 62) say that "the deposit or the truths of faith, contained in our sacred teaching, are one thing, while the mode in which they are enunciated, keeping the same meaning and the same judgment, is another," they take for granted that one can find the truths of faith in very definite formulations—for example, in the teaching of the Council of Trent, in Scripture, and so forth. The phrase "the same meaning and the same judgment," often omitted by those who translate the statement, makes this point absolutely clear, for it would be nonsense to talk about sameness of meaning and of judgment if there were not two formulations, A and B, about which one could say two things: (1) "Both A and B mean X," and (2) "A and B agree in affirming X" or "A and B agree in denying X." The key phrase, "eodem sensu eademque sententia," is taken from Vatican I's definitive teaching on Catholic faith (see DS 3020/1800; cf. 3043/1818). Vatican I quotes the phrase from St. Vincent of Lerins who (in the fifth century) uses it to express the continuity which must be maintained as Catholic teaching develops (see FEF 2174).

Question G: Could radical theological dissent be construed as legitimate doctrinal development in the moral domain?

1. Catholic teaching plainly develops, and there is no reason to exclude moral doctrine from the process.[75] Much development is merely refinement or, as in the case of slavery, a movement from what was condoned without a firm judgment to a clear condemnation. Theologically speaking, however, these are not the really interesting cases of development.

2. The interesting cases are those in which development seems to involve a reversal. Simply to contradict what was previously taught, however, would in no sense be to develop it. Hence, those who suggested that radical dissent on a matter such as contraception could be regarded as licit development needed to show that their apparent negation of the Church's teaching was not a true contradiction.

3. Actual theological dissent on this matter, among others, obviously did contradict the teaching constantly proposed by the magisterium. But the developmentalists' claim was that the current official teaching did not adequately reflect the deeper truth of Christian tradition, which was being appropriately developed in the work of the dissenting moralists.

4. This approach had to confront a serious problem as to when the supposed development could have occurred. If the result of development was a practical reversal of specific normative demands, it had to have happened at some definite time. Those who argued for development seemed never to confront this problem. It is put aside here, not because it is unimportant, but because the discussion which follows will clarify it sufficiently.

5. The effort to show that a dissenting position really is a legitimate development usually took the following form.

> Specific norms express the practical demands of basic human values. Exactly what the various values demand can vary with circumstances which condition what is needed to protect and promote them. If the practical implication of a set of values at a certain period of history requires the absolute exclusion of a certain form of behavior as an immoral kind of act, then the Church rightly teaches that for those conditions such an act is always wrong. However, with changed circumstances, the practical implication of the same set of values can justify or even require that one engage in precisely that form of behavior. In such a case, the behavior comes to be a specifically different kind of act from the one formerly condemned. The Church should recognize this objective change and develop its teaching accordingly. The appearance of contradiction is an obstacle to this recognition; it arises because, although the same behavior is different from a moral point of view, it seems from a physical point of view that the Church would be approving exactly what it previously condemned. But this is an illusion, not a real difficulty.[76]

This account of development has merit. Many specific moral norms are nonabsolute (10-C). With respect to such norms, authentic development of the Church's moral teaching often will appear to be a reversal but will not really be such. The development of the Church's teaching on usury is a clear case in point.

6. **Still, development of this sort has limits. The belief that all specific moral norms are nonabsolute was based on an inadequate normative theory.** Thus, those who defended dissent from the Church's constant and very firm teachings concerning sex and innocent life and who claimed their dissent was a development of doctrine, virtually always assumed some sort of proportionalism.

7. The example of contraception illustrates the preceding very abstract analysis. In his important historical study of the Church's teaching on this matter, John T. Noonan, Jr., argued in conclusion that a development in the teaching was possible.[77] His case can best be understood in the form articulated above: Conception-preventing behavior under former social and economic circumstances was harmful to a set of basic human goods, and the Church rightly condemned it; today, the same sort of behavior perhaps serves these same goods; if so, it should be approved.

It is worth noticing that Noonan's book reached only this modest conclusion; he did not pretend to show that development had in fact occurred in the subject matter. The use of Noonan's work as if he had shown this required an additional premise—that the purported possibility of development rendered unreasonable the continuing affirmation of the received teaching. In other words, even if the theory of development applied to contraception—if the norm forbidding it were nonabsolute—it still would not follow from Noonan's work that the Church could or should change her teaching, for it would be necessary first to prove that the relevant change in fact had occurred.

8. The essential weakness of Noonan's argument was that conception-preventing behavior cannot be chosen for its conception-preventing effect without choosing to prevent a new life from coming into being; and such a choice violates the eighth mode of responsibility with respect to the good of human life: in this instance, the life of the unwanted baby whose coming to be the contraceptive choice is made to prevent. The specific norm taught by the Church is therefore absolute, and so it is not open to reversal.

9. In the many diverse formulations of Catholic teaching concerning contraception, reference to one or another particular type of behavior has not been the constant feature. From the earliest days of Christianity up to the present, conception-preventing behaviors have been of various sorts, ranging from coitus interruptus to the use of sterilizing drugs. The constant feature has been the deliberate choice of those who practice contraception to impede the coming to be of a new person. What has been condemned is precisely the deliberate attempt to impede a fresh realization of the basic good of human life.

Contraception is mentioned here only as an example; I have treated the issue in itself elsewhere.[78] But to forestall misunderstandings, two points perhaps should be noted.

First, while the specific malice of contraception arises from its antilife character, it also violates the other goods of marriage. As a reflexive good, love or friendship needs content. The acceptance of contraception modifies the content which makes marital love marital, and redirects sexual relationships to other goals. A sign of this is that as soon as contraception is culturally accepted, nonmarital forms of genital interaction also are approved.

Second, proponents of the view that the Church's teaching on contraception could develop to admit conception-preventing techniques very often argued: "The Church's teaching on the matter already developed when Pius XI and Piux XII approved rhythm. Its point is the same as contraception's. So the continued rejection of other methods of preventing conception can only be based on pure physicalism, which mistakenly makes a moral issue of outward behavior and neglects the significant identity of intent."

The short theological answer to this is that Christians always practiced sexual abstinence to avoid conceptions when they considered themselves morally obliged to do so, and the Church never condemned such abstinence, while it always condemned doing anything to impede the fruitfulness of sexual intercourse by those who choose to engage in it. The recent teaching on periodic abstinence merely adds that those meeting the responsibilities of parenthood in this traditional Christian way need not on that account abstain during those intervals which modern knowledge tells us are infertile.

This traditional discrimination between contraception and sexual abstinence is not based on physicalism, but rather on the morally significant difference in intention between these two approaches to new life. The critic assumed that intent is defined by the concrete outcome, so that contraception and abstinence are identical insofar as both are ways of avoiding pregnancy and, if successful, have the same factual result: Someone who would have existed does not exist.

But a closer consideration of intention is required here using necessary distinctions (9-C). Those who contracept (say, in an effort to fulfill a conscientious judgment that they should avoid pregnancy) necessarily adopt a proposal which includes the impeding of the beginning of a new life. This impeding of new life is a chosen means to their good end. Those who abstain in accord with a judgment of conscience that they should at present avoid pregnancy need not adopt a proposal which includes the impeding of the beginning of a new life. They make no choice to impede new life in any act of sexual intercourse which they think could lead to a new life, and no such choice is possible in other acts.

10. By contrast with the Church's teaching on contraception, various teachings on interest taking lacked such a constant element. They referred to a form of unfair behavior, and they defined this behavior in terms of economic institutions whose relationships to basic human goods vary under changing conditions of society and economy.

After he published a major work on contraception, John T. Noonan, Jr., went on to publish articles arguing: The Church once condemned the taking of interest (usury) just as severely as it condemned contraception; but the Church now approves the taking of interest; therefore, the Church can approve contraception. The question is: Did the condemnation of the taking of interest ever meet the conditions for the infallible exercise of the ordinary magisterium (35-D)? The answer is negative, for the following reasons.

As has often been argued by Catholic scholars, the teaching of Scripture and of the Fathers forbids charging interest on loans to the poor and condemns the greed of usurers, but this teaching does not condemn the taking of interest as such, and does not envisage a situation in which moderate rates of interest are established by money markets. The decrees of the councils and popes up to 1450 are aimed at the same evils attacked in Scripture and by the Fathers.[79]

In his study of scholastic theories of usury, published before the debate among Catholics on contraception began, Noonan himself rejected the view that the central Catholic teaching on the morality of taking interest had changed: "Moreover, as far as dogma in the technical Catholic sense is concerned, there is only one dogma at stake. Dogma is not to be loosely used as synonymous with every papal rule or theological verdict. Dogma is a defined, revealed doctrine taught by the Church at all times and places. Nothing here meets the test of dogma except this assertion, that usury, the act of taking profit on a loan without a just title, is sinful. Even this dogma is not specifically, formally defined by any pope or council. It is, however, taught by the tradition of the Church, as witnessed by papal bulls and briefs, conciliar acts, and theological opinion. This dogmatic teaching remains unchanged. What is a just title, what is technically to be treated as a loan, are matters of debate, positive law, and changing evaluation. The development on these points is great. But the pure and narrow dogma is the same today as in 1200."[80] Although Noonan's formulation of his point here is neither completely satisfactory nor precise, his idea is clear: The moral teaching on the taking of interest, proposed infallibly by the ordinary magisterium, has not changed at all.

The key to clarity in this matter is precision with respect to the concept of that usury which the Church condemns. The sin of usury is not simply the charging of interest on a loan, but the charging of interest on a loan in virtue of the very making of the loan, rather than in virtue of some factor related to the loan which provides a basis for a fair demand for compensation. Undoubtedly, there were many erroneous teachings about usury which never met the conditions necessary for an infallible exercise of the ordinary magisterium. But the main reason why the Church does not teach today on usury as she did in the Middle Ages is not that she has corrected such errors—much less changed her doctrine. The main difference is that the economic subject matter has changed; money and interest simply are not now what they were then.

Charles Curran, writing in 1978, admitted that the argument on the basis of development, which he himself supported before 1968, was attractive because it seemed necessary to facilitate change, but never was plausible. Those who argued against change, Curran admitted, had a clearer understanding of the radical character of the problem. He concluded: "One must honestly recognize that 'the conservatives' saw much more clearly than 'the liberals' of the day that a change in the teaching on artificial contraception had to recognize that the previous teaching was wrong."[81]

Question H: Why did some wish to change Catholic teaching?

1. The intent of the answer which follows is not to single out one theologian, Avery Dulles, for special criticism. Dulles did, however, provide an exposition whose principal elements appeared to be shared to one degree or another by many of his colleagues among the radically dissenting theologians. His position is therefore worth examining for the light it sheds on this movement as a whole.

2. While it appears that Dulles could find room in his theory of development of doctrine for the conception of development treated in the preceding question, he did not think it adequate. He wished also to allow for revisions of received teaching, including some which were admittedly incompatible with the principle of continuous and cumulative growth.[82]

3. Dulles did not provide a very precise answer to the question of how he wanted to change received doctrine. He held that God's saving work in Jesus Christ is the central mystery and that the primary or central truths of faith are those which express this mystery. With respect to other doctrines, he proposed a program of simplification, intensification, and concentration.

4. As an outcome of this process, not every Catholic would be expected to

affirm personally every proposition ever proposed definitively as a truth of faith. Only a minimum—to avoid "harmful deviations from the gospel"—would be imposed on all. For the rest, everyone would be at liberty to reject the Church's teaching, and certainly none would be expected to assent to anything in which he or she could "as yet find no meaning, relevance, or credibility."[83]

5. Dulles presented many arguments for accepting this program of change. Most started from true propositions—precisely the propositions which point to the need and possibility of genuine development. By themselves, however, none of these considerations lent any support to this radical proposal. For instance, Dulles pointed to the need to find better and more relevant ways of expressing Christian faith; he cited John XXIII in support of this unexceptionable premise. But the premise by no means showed that the Church should consider any of its definitively proposed doctrine, always assuming it is rightly understood, to be dispensable for those who do not agree with it. (No one, it should be noted, has ever said that every Catholic must be aware of and assent to every truth of faith. Most Catholics never hear of some defined truths—not because they are concealed but, typically, because the controversies which occasioned their definition are not currently live issues in the Church. The Church has only required that one not reject truths of faith and that one affirm those truths about which one has been instructed.)

6. Dulles' main reason for his program of change was simple: "to lighten the burden of assenting to doctrines handed down from the past."[84] This consideration is not trivial. In the modern world, Christian faith and moral teaching has not easily gained and held the allegiance of people who can choose other, immediately appealing options.[85] Liberalizing Christianity is one way of trying to meet this challenge. The updating of nonessentials and repackaging of essentials advocated by John XXIII is another approach to the problem.

7. Dulles invoked his general theory of change in support of the proposal for a new ecclesiology which would admit dissent otherwise inadmissible.[86] The essential claim which Dulles thought allowed change of the sort he advocated was that revelation itself is not a matter of propositions, that the content of faith remains transcendent (what "transcendent" means was not clarified), and that the categories used in definitions are human.[87]

8. Thus Dulles apparently embraced a view of revelation and faith criticized above (20-C). His account ignored the complex reality of human faith explained there. It seems clear as well that the position he held was one which has been solemnly condemned by Vatican I (see DS 3020/1800, 3043/1818).[88]

On the whole, radically dissenting theologians never tried to justify dissent by appealing to expressions of faith more authoritative than the teachings received and reaffirmed by the magisterium. At times, however, their remarks suggested arguments along this line. For example, in defending dissenting theologians, Walter J. Burghardt, S.J., said that an important part of a theologian's work was to subject every earthbound expression of faith to the test: "Does it square with, correspond to, adequately represent the Word of God? In doing so, we are not setting ourselves above the Pope or bishops; we are collaborating with them in a joint effort to understand what God says to us and what God wants of us."[89] Thus

Burghardt suggested that theological dissent was justified by the word of God, and implied that theologians had access to this word in a way which could test every "earthbound affirmation of Christian truth."

Unfortunately, Burghardt never explained what this access was. If he meant that theologians could read the Bible, he was right. But the theological dissent considered in this chapter almost never appealed to Scripture as a basis. How could it? Where in Scripture will one find any hint that contraception, homosexual behavior, adultery, abortion, and so on are sometimes good acts? Where will one find any hint that theologians have an authority to which bishops must submit? Perhaps Burghardt did not mean Scripture. Perhaps he meant that theologians had access to the word of God quite apart from the earthbound affirmations even of the Bible. But what was this access, and how could it be squared with a Catholic conception of revelation and faith?

9. The relevance of Dulles' proposal to the argument unfolded in the present chapter is twofold. **First, here one sees clearly just what was at stake in radical theological dissent on moral issues. The ecclesiology of Dulles, or something very like it, was required by Curran, McCormick, and others in order to justify their activities and positions. But this ecclesiology depended upon an untenable theory of revelation and faith. Second, one also sees in Dulles' wider proposal a similarity to radical theological dissent in the moral field. The aim in both cases was to lighten the burden of faith by allowing believers to say yes and no simultaneously—yes to the elements of Christian teaching they found acceptable, no to those they did not.**

10. It is no criticism of Dulles and his colleagues but merely a truism about the human condition that sinful humankind always wishes to have things both ways. This attitude, however, is clearly rejected—not only in the constricted domain of "religion" narrowly conceived but in regard to the whole of life—by Jesus, who demands a radical commitment of the total person to his whole person, including his Mystical Body, the Church. It is a heavy demand. Dulles and others showed human sensitivity in wishing to lighten it. Yet it is a demand of God's love. Those who accept it can fulfill it by the power of the Spirit, and so they find the burden of Christian faith light and their share in the cross of Jesus sweet.

This work has criticized many theories which were more or less widely supported by moral theologians. Subjectivist theories of conscience, proportionalism, the denial of the authority of Catholic moral teaching, untenable theories of fundamental option, the supposition that sins of weakness are not mortal sins, and the theory of an empty hell are only a half-dozen of the positions criticized. None of these theories is very plausible.

It is worth asking oneself: What was behind this multitude of theories? I think the answer is that all of them tended toward a single goal: To permit wills determined to act contrary to very firm and constant Catholic moral teaching to maintain that determination without giving up hope of reaching heavenly fulfillment.

But if all these theories had a single objective, why were there so many of them? Why did they proliferate so? One might suppose that they were simply different approaches, proposed by different individuals or schools. But in fact most of these theories were promoted by the very same people.

The multiplicity of theories is accounted for by the fact that Catholic moral principles are like a football team, whose defenses in sudden-death overtime might conceivably be breached in any number of different ways. The many implausible theories were so many different strategies for scoring. The success of any one strategy would have won the game. If this is so, why did the dissenting moral theologians not content themselves with a single, most promising line of attack? I think the answer is that they themselves suspected that none of these theories was very plausible. Thus the same author perhaps promoted a subjectivist theory of conscience, but defended proportionalism (which is incompatible with a subjectivist account of conscience) just in case the first theory did not succeed; he perhaps claimed that proportionalism really articulated the Catholic moral tradition (although it did not), yet just in case this claim was not admitted denied the authoritative weight of the tradition; he perhaps went on to argue in favor of some unintelligible sort of fundamental option, just in case his theory of norms failed to show that the sins to be permitted really were virtuous acts; he perhaps also argued that sins of weakness were not mortal sins, just in case the theory of fundamental option did not prevent them from really being self-determining acts; finally, as a last desperate effort, he perhaps defended the theory of empty hell, just in case everything else failed.

The dissenting moral theologian who proceeded in this way was like a man who wishes to jump from a height toward a deep pit, yet avoid falling into the pit. To break his fall, he deploys a safety net. It looks strong at first glance, but on examination it proves to be very weak; it almost falls apart under its own weight. Frantically, the man obtains more nets and deploys them, one beneath another. But all the nets are like the first one. None of them could bear the man's weight. Still, he has decided to jump, and jump he does.

Summary

Defenders of radical theological dissent held that in general the Church had erred in teaching that acts of certain kinds are wrong regardless of circumstances, intentions, and consequences. They held that dissent from any specific moral teaching is legitimate. Initially they maintained that either the Church's theological tradition or Vatican II justifies dissent. But neither does, and ultimately the dissenting theologians conceded this. With respect to Vatican II, they found it necessary eventually to reject its doctrine on the Church's teaching authority.

In repudiating various moral teachings, dissenting theologians either overlooked the possibility that they had been proposed infallibly by the ordinary magisterium or assumed that an infallible moral teaching would have to meet the conditions for infallibly defined teaching. The statements of several episcopal conferences published in response to *Humanae vitae* proceeded from the nondefinitive character of that document to the possibility of dissent. But no conference discussed whether the encyclical's teaching had been proposed infallibly by the ordinary magisterium and so none took a position on this question. However, this teaching and a substantial body of moral teaching on other matters has been infallibly proposed by the ordinary magisterium.

Some dissenting theologians proposed a new view of the magisterium as an agent whose task was to persuade, not teach certain truth; complementing this was the view that the theologians enjoyed a magisterium of their own superior to that of the bishops. Scholarly competence was the basis of their claim. But many other scholars, Catholics and non-Catholics, believers and nonbelievers, of equal or greater competence, differed from the radically dissenting Catholic theologians on most matters. Thus, once these theologians surrendered the status which comes from placing scholarship at the service of the word of God, under the guidance of the magisterium, Catholics had no reason to rely on them.

Dissenting theologians tried to buttress their claim by appealing to history. Contrary to one of their claims, there is no point after apostolic times at which the pope and bishops began to act as the teaching authority in the Church. They also argued that the magisterium had made errors in the past; but either the teachings in question were not erroneous, or the errors were in matters of discipline and governance, or the teachings did not meet the conditions for an infallible exercise of the ordinary magisterium. Finally, they appealed to the authority of their own consensus; but this had no rational weight, since only evidence and reasons count in scholarly disputes.

Sometimes it was said that the magisterium cannot propose any specific moral norm as a truth to be held definitively. Counterexamples, such as the norm forbidding adultery, were handled by saying that the norm either is nonabsolute or refers only to instances in which the behavior in question happens to be wrong. The view that the Church could give only general moral advice was usually accepted by those who adopted proportionalism, for proportionalism usually excludes moral absolutes. In fact, however, some specific moral norms are absolute (for example, the teaching on adultery) and at least one (against polygamy) has been solemnly defined. The magisterium must teach specific norms with certainty in order to foster moral honesty in the faithful and to fulfill the Church's prophetic office.

It was also argued that dissent did not touch the substance of Catholic moral teaching but only altered its changeable formulations. Typically, however, the "substance" was reduced to what was common both to received Catholic teaching and to the views of those who dissented from it, without showing any reasons why this should be taken as the "substance." Moreover, the magisterium has always claimed the right to determine what formulations of the Church's faith are adequate to it and to reject inadequate formulations.

Moral doctrine is plainly subject to genuine development. Many specific moral norms are nonabsolute. With respect to these, authentic development can appear to be a reversal (although not really such): for example, development in the Church's teaching on usury. However, some moral norms are absolute (for example, the norm excluding contraception) and so are not open to reversal.

It has been proposed that, apart from the primary or central truths of faith, the Church should pursue a program of doctrinal simplification and concentration. Only a minimum would be required for belief by all, while everyone would be at liberty to reject the rest of the Church's teaching. The purpose of this program was to lighten the burden of belief. But the underlying view of revelation and faith was solemnly condemned by Vatican I. As with radical dissent in the moral field, the intent was to allow believers to say yes and no simultaneously—yes to elements of Christian belief they found acceptable, no to those they did not.

Appendix 1:   Some examples of alleged errors in Catholic teaching

The Galileo case can be summarized from a recent work by an apparently competent and unbiased secular scholar, Stillman Drake.[90]

Galileo was born in 1564, just after the end of the Council of Trent, when the Church was fighting for her life. He became a professional mathematician and physicist. The standard understanding of the solar system was that the earth stands at the center, and the sun, other planets, moon, and stars revolve around it. Nicolaus Copernicus (1473–1543), a Polish astronomer, proposed a simpler account of the astronomical evidence: that the sun stands at the center and the earth and other planets revolve around it. Galileo accepted and supported this new theory.

The theory of the solar system was an important part of Aristotle's philosophy, in which physics and metaphysics were closely connected. Aristotle's philosophy had become an important instrument of Catholic theology. Moreover, the centrality of the earth in the universe and the special place of humankind in creation are symbolically related. For these reasons, Galileo's work was bound to draw the interest of the magisterium. The new theory superficially seemed incompatible with certain passages in Scripture, especially that in which God is said to have made the sun stand still (see Jos 10.12–13). If the sun always stands still, how could it have been made to do so by a miracle?

In 1616 the Holy Office looked into the matter. Its theological consultants found against the Copernican theory on the basis that it was repugnant to Scripture, and Cardinal Bellarmine, by the authority of the pope, told Galileo not to continue to hold and defend it as unqualifiedly true. Books trying to reconcile the new theory with the Bible also were forbidden, but it was not forbidden to examine the theory as a hypothesis and to make use of it scientifically. Galileo accepted the Holy See's decision and was personally reassured by Pope Paul V that all would be well. This reassurance was appropriate because some of Galileo's opponents were taking a much harder line than the Church's official decision.[91]

Sixteen years later, in 1632, Galileo published a book in dialogue form defending the Copernican theory. He did not say anything about the earlier decisions when he sought and obtained an ecclesiastical license to publish the book. In 1633 Galileo was tried by the Inquisition for violating an order not to teach the Copernican theory in any way. There is some evidence that this order was given him in 1616 during his meeting with Bellarmine, not, however, by Bellarmine, but by officials of the Inquisition acting without proper authorization. Galileo was convicted; he admitted disobedience; the Inquisition sentenced him to life in prison. He was never actually imprisoned, but was restricted in his movements and teaching, so that he spent the rest of his life under house arrest.[92]

If the preceding account is correct, there is a real doctrinal issue in the Galileo case. The issue is not in the proceedings of 1633, which were disciplinary in nature, but in the decision of 1616, when it was determined by the authority of Paul V that the Copernican theory is incompatible with Scripture. (One might argue that the position was not proposed as one to be held definitively, but I will grant that it was.) Moreover, the decision of 1616 obviously was false. Thus Paul V taught a false proposition and proposed it as a truth pertaining to faith to be held definitively. The ordinary magisterium erred.

However, nothing in the historical record shows that the bishops scattered about the world taught (or that many of them ever thought about) the proposition Paul V mistakenly taught. And Paul V's teaching certainly was not ex cathedra. The Galileo case is an example of a situation in which the magisterium must teach firmly on a new question and can make a mistake (35-G). The saddest aspect of the case is that officials of the Church seem to have gone beyond their authority (when they told Galileo not to teach the Copernican theory in any way) and to have been unjustly supported by the Inquisition in its disciplinary act of 1633.

It is worth noticing that Galileo's assertion directly bore upon an empirical truth—a question of fact about the physical world. Dissent from the Church's moral teaching bears directly upon moral norms—which are not matters of fact and which in themselves pertain to Christian life. The decision in the Galileo case could be and was undercut by growing factual evidence. No amount of factual evidence ever can falsify the Church's moral teaching. The mistake in papal teaching in the Galileo case was a naive reading of Scripture; this led to a serious injustice and considerable inconvenience for Galileo. If there were a mistake in the Church's teaching on the matters disputed by radically dissenting theologians, it would be in the very substance of a large segment of the Church's constant and very firm teaching, and this error would have misled all the faithful throughout the centuries, not only causing them inconvenience but wrongly binding them to a standard of life which was often violated with a sense of grave sin.

Between 1905 and 1915, the Pontifical Biblical Commission issued a series of decrees on matters related to the interpretation of Scripture and on factual questions about the Scriptures.[93] Today it is generally admitted that these decrees contain many errors. At least with respect to questions of doctrine, scholars were bound to submit to these decrees and to assent to them (see DS 3503/2113). In 1948, the authority of the decrees was officially modified by a letter of the secretary of the Biblical Commission to Cardinal Suhard (DS 3862–64/2302).[94] Thus we have a case of official mistakes officially rectified.

A careful reading of the document of St. Pius X, issued in 1907, which declared the force of the decrees of the Biblical Commission shows that these decrees primarily were disciplinary in character.[95] Their ultimate purpose was to protect the faith, but their immediate object was to regulate the work and teaching of scholars. They bound consciences to obedience, but it does not seem they had in general to be accepted as certainly true. Moreover, these decrees primarily were a matter between the Holy See and a certain group—scholars. For this reason, they did not have to be and were not proposed universally by the bishops of the world to the faithful.

The moral teaching of the Church with which the radically dissenting theologians took issue is not primarily disciplinary; rather, it is proposed as truth. Its immediate object is the formation of Christian life. It demands not only obedience, but personal appropriation as normative truth. It has been proposed universally by the bishops to the faithful as a whole. The mistakes in the decrees of the Biblical Commission, even to the extent that they are errors in teaching, are altogether different, and well within the bounds of possible error described above (35-F).

A final example. It often was argued that Vatican II changed the Church's teaching on religious liberty. Hence, the Church also could admit the liberty of Catholics to follow their personal judgments in sexual matters.[96] The first thing to notice about this argument is that it suggested that Vatican II teaches a liberty of conscience which is alien to its doctrine. Vatican II's true teaching on religious liberty concerns the just liberty of all persons in relation to political authorities. It has nothing to do with some imaginary liberty to call the Church "Mother" but ignore her teaching.

John Courtney Murray, S.J., the leading theological architect of Vatican II's teaching on religious liberty, argued that the new teaching would be an authentic and legitimate development of traditional Catholic teaching. His argument was that the question to which Vatican II addresses itself is a new one, because political societies and their relationship to religion have changed, so that now their chief duty toward religion is to protect the liberty of citizens in this area. Murray also was able to point out properly theological grounds for his argument.[97] Vatican II implicitly accepts Murray's argument and finds a basis in faith itself for what is novel in its teaching.

Appendix 2:   Authentic development in moral teaching

People who come to moral theology with a legalistic outlook tend to identify human acts with outward behavior. Thus changes in moral judgment due to change or unfolding of the meaning of an act seem to suggest that the same act now has a different moral value. If one who reaches this conclusion holds a scholastic natural-law theory (criticized in 4-F), he or she will assume that if the same act has a different moral value, the other term of the relationship which determines morality, human nature itself, has changed. Thus the historicity of action, a misunderstanding of what constitutes a human act, and a poor moral theory lead to the conclusion that human nature changes.

If one also assumes some form of proportionalism, one will suppose that moral norms are merely rules devised to protect and promote human goods in a particular historical context, and that these norms can change when necessary to promote the good or bring about less evil. It is easy at this point to suppose one can use as one's standard the relative importance given to the basic goods in the life-style of a given society.[98] The conclusion will be drawn that changing human nature demands a proportionalist transformation of all moral norms, including absolute ones.

The difficulty with this position is that although even basic human goods unfold new dimensions of meaning (7-D), all human persons have the same nature (see GS 29), and so each good has some invariant meaning. Thus, acts which include a proposal to destroy, damage, or impede some basic human good—for example, the life of an unborn child— can be precisely the same in kind insofar as they are opposed to the invariant aspect of the good of life, although they differ in kind insofar as they are done by people in different cultures and situations, who understand more or less fully the good of human life.

The fundamental requirements of Christian moral life which demand reverence for the basic human goods are not concerned with something merely instrumental. While these requirements gain new and deeper meaning as our understanding of the goods grows, they cannot be contradicted, because they express in a direct way the minimal demands of love in respect to these goods. Because they are truths, not mere rules, these norms cannot be changed.

The Christian norm forbidding adultery, for example, has a depth absent from the Old Testament norm, which was not understood to be protecting so great a good as the sacrament of marriage we know. The exclusion of adultery in itself, moreover, hardly begins to suggest what marital love means. Nevertheless, the absolute prohibition of adultery is always valid and it is extremely important. For this exclusion defines the marital relationship without limiting its power to develop new meaning. If one attempts to define marriage without excluding adultery one will have to invoke some specific, positive form of love. In doing so, one will limit what marriage can be. Such limitation will foreclose the human possibilities of marriage before exploring what is foreclosed.

Just as true negative propositions about God do not define him but preserve the silence in which he reveals himself, and just as definitive condemnations of heresies do not limit our relationship with God but preserve unbroken the line of communication we have with him, so absolute moral prohibitions do not limit human freedom to pursue the good but preserve intact our understanding and love of the basic human goods.

To assume that one can criticize and perhaps revise such moral norms by taking as a standard the relative importance assigned to the basic human goods in the life-style of a given society—for example, that of the contemporary nations of the West—is to lose one's historical consciousness. Historicity does not exclude but demands insight into the unity of each basic good of human persons, a real unity over time and place which cannot be limited without arbitrariness to the contingent conditions of the here-and-now which delimit one's present point of view. Only with insight into the unity of the human goods can the various ages and conditions of humankind be understood as a history—as the one universal history of salvation, to which our Lord Jesus is always and everywhere present—rather than as a disjoined succession of arbitrarily delimited sociocultural points of view.

To understand how negative norms protect human goods and so permit them to be creatively unfolded helps one understand another important aspect of legitimate development in Christian moral thought. Today everyone realizes that enslaving anyone—and buying and selling people in general—are great crimes; the Church condemns these and many other acts against the person (see GS 27). Surely, one thinks, slavery always was wrong. Yet the Church did not always condemn it, and many teachers in the Church at times defended it as licit. How could Christian morality be so inadequate?

The answer is that although the liberty violated by slavery does pertain to justice, and so is a good which always deserves reverence, the aspects of justice which involve liberty were much less well understood in times past than they have come to be in recent centuries. The chief obstacle to clarity was that much slavery was related to punishment, and penal servitude can be just. The errors involved in condoning slavery related to confusions between the public and private spheres, as well as misplacement upon children of responsibility for the wrongdoing of their parents or more remote ancestors.

Gradually, these matters were clarified. There are many reasons for this development of understanding; it was powerfully advanced by secular humanists. Secular humanism, one must remember, is a Christian heresy; the principles of the human individual liberty it promotes belong to the Christian conception of redemption and deification (see Gal 3.28; Phlm 15–16; Jas 2.12–13). However, Christians did not at once draw all the conclusions from their principles. (Secular humanists, of course, draw some false conclusions from them.)

The development of moral doctrine with respect to slavery was from condoning it to forbidding it. The change concerning slavery can be seen as possible because of the unfolding understanding of the human good; now that the development has occurred, we find it hard to see why it did not occur much sooner. The supposed development which radically dissenting theologians proposed would have been from forbidding kinds of acts to permitting them—indeed, in cases in which they were considered the "lesser evil," enjoining them. Such a change could not occur because the received prohibitions are based on aspects of the human goods which are already understood. One can no more learn something new which would lead one to find adultery good than one can learn something new which would lead one to find slavery good.

Appendix 3:   How academic theology became secularized

The kind of change discussed in question H, which some wished to admit into Catholic teaching, had been advocated by some Protestant theologians for more than a century. With the development of Renaissance humanism into modern secular humanism in the eighteenth century, unbelief began to dominate the intellectual culture of the West; perversely, this movement was called the "Enlightenment." By 1800, the Enlightenment, which had begun with the work of brilliant amateurs, became dominant in the universities of certain nations, especially Germany. Protestant theologians belonged to the academic world, and they found themselves in a difficult situation.

Modern scientific and historical studies had raised fresh questions for Christian faith, and theologians had to try to find answers. Rationalism had become dominant in theology, with the damage to Catholic theology described in chapter one. The effect on Protestant theology was even worse, since the Reformation had rejected the Catholic Middle Ages, and thus left Protestant theologians with an even poorer store of philosophical resources. Protestant theologians also were burdened with the difficulties inherent in the opinions of the Reformers to the extent that these opinions fell short of the fullness of Catholic truth.

For example, the development of historical and literary studies caused special difficulty for those committed to sacred Scripture alone as the norm of faith, and the theory of private interpretation made it difficult for an individual theologian to take advantage of the difference between his or her own faith and the faith of the Church universal. (This difference allows a Catholic in difficulties to suppose that while the Church's faith is true, it is sometimes hard to discern what it is.)

Moreover, having rejected the vows and religious life, Protestant theologians lacked the support Catholic theologians often received from their religious confreres. It is a truth of social psychology that an individual under pressure from one community important to his or her identity hardly can resist the pressure and continue to function in the community without great moral support from another community of similar or greater importance for his or her identity.

Under these conditions, it is not surprising that many Protestant theologians in the nineteenth century developed positions by which they intended to protect Christian faith but which in fact compromised it. Nor is it improbable that some such theologians substituted another fundamental commitment—to the assumptions of the Enlightenment—for Christian faith, and changed theology into a philosophy, perhaps even without realizing that they were doing so.

Their dialectic changed from one in which the truths of Christian faith could not be contradicted to one in which the ideology of the Enlightenment could not be contradicted, but otherwise things could seem to remain much as they had been. They still could treat Scripture with reverence, very much as philosophers treat the works of Plato with reverence. They still could call their courses "theology," publish books on theological topics, train young men for the ministry, and take for granted much of what Christians believe—as much of it as seemed at a given time to be unproblematic.

In this situation, many Protestant theologians began a process often called "reinterpretation." Much or all of the factual content of faith was denied; the residue was defended and explained much as any philosopher would defend his or her philosophy, but with the difference that this philosophy was claimed to be the "core" of the tradition: what Christian faith really means. Hegel provided the greatest example of this strategy, and he carried out his project so ingeniously that many philosophers since his time have been convinced that Hegel's philosophy contains all the claim to truth in Christianity that one need consider.

These remarks are intended neither as a polemic against Protestants nor as a condemnation of anyone. Many Protestants resisted the trend, and one hopes that those who did not, acted in accord with sincere consciences. Catholics also must admit that they did little to help their brethren face the challenge of the Enlightenment; indeed, Catholic theology only recently began to face this challenge, with results thus far quite mixed.

Until after World War II, the Catholic theological community was largely separated from the Protestant theological community and from the secular academic world in general. But a gradually growing movement toward academic professionalism, begun in Catholic theology much earlier, suddenly crystalized after World War II. Most Catholic theologians who wished to engage in scholarly research and writing wanted to be respected members of the academic profession; in theology this demanded status in the single theological community recognized as legitimate by the secular academic world.

It is not to be supposed that Catholic theologians thereupon rushed to sell their souls for academic respectability. The process was both subtler and, subjectively, more creditable. One became a member of a group, identified with it, accepted its ideals and methods. One then sincerely took a new look at the Church's received teachings, found them a burden not simply to oneself but to many other contemporary men and women who also more or less fully identified with secular humanistic values, and zealously undertook to renew and reform the Church to bring it into the twentieth century.

At the same time, the secularized theologian continued to have a loyalty to his or her Church. Many aspects of its faith and life—at least many aspects of its communal reality—remained important. These were defended by respectable theologians with considerable ingenuity and effort against secular humanism, which would have totally destroyed Christianity. Because of this work in defense of the faith, theologians who went very far toward secular humanism nevertheless sincerely believed themselves to be true moderates. They were fighting a hard fight on two fronts: against the obscurantism (as they saw it) of conservatives on the one hand and, on the other, against the irreligion of those who rejected the "core" of Christianity.

Protestants could proceed in this fashion without destroying their personal faith and their ecclesial communities, because Protestants considered faith essentially an individual experience. The only objective norm of faith accepted by orthodox Protestants was the Bible, and the Bible could always be interpreted to mean what it must and not to mean what it must not. By itself, the Bible is just a book; it cannot fight back.

A Catholic, however, could not proceed as secularized Catholic theologians proceeded without quickly getting into deep trouble. For a Catholic, the Church's faith is prior to each individual member's faith, and the Church's faith is articulated and defended by the living magisterium. Hence, the radically dissenting Catholic theologians set themselves in contradiction to the norm of their faith which, all the same, they nevertheless wished to acknowledge. Otherwise they would have had to admit to themselves and to the Church at large that they were no longer Catholic theologians.

Appendix 4:   Causes of the successes of theological dissent

This chapter has argued that the dissenting theologians were in error. If one agrees that they were, one wonders: What does such serious and widespread dissent mean? How could so many intelligent people—most of whom had enjoyed long formation in Christian faith and spiritual life—have gone so far wrong? This question is a deep and important one, which probably has no simple answer. I suggest some partial answers.[99]

First, the culture of the time was a factor. Secular humanism was dominant. In some respects, it developed aspects of Christian truth and goodness previously only partly appreciated in the Church. It also had the attraction of denying evil, thus ridding people of guilt without contrition. The secular humanist atmosphere made Catholics forgetful of heaven, reluctant to take up the cross, neglectful of the duty to live redemptively, and resentful of authority.

Second, the Church and Christian life were not all they might have been. In the doctrinal domain, important theological mistakes blocked full appreciation of human goods and a proper commitment to the building up of the human. Pervasive legalism also blocked understanding and adequate response to the great truths of faith. In this context, many poor arguments were used to defend received teaching and many questionable motives urged for obeying it. When the defects of such arguments and motives became apparent, the teachings themselves seemed to be called into question, although logically the truth of a conclusion is untouched by the weakness of arguments offered for it, and although historically the style of life proposed by Christian morality originated prior to the legalist emphasis upon sanctions as a motive for living it.

Some dedicated persons and groups in the Church had been too crafty, too concerned with good consequences. Such a concern led to a temptation to compromise the gospel and the rigorous demands of Christian life when this seemed necessary to obtain or hold the commitment to the Church of those who were most active, articulate, and influential in the world. If some of the Church's societies of religious in the past had catered to the needs of the nobility and rising merchant classes, in the twentieth century they strove to serve the leadership which emerged in mass society. No doubt, the intent was to exert in this way a benevolent and apostolic influence on society as a whole. Nevertheless, the question remains: Who was working to help bear the burdens of simpler believers who faithfully struggled to live according to the gospel?

The diocesan clergy did this to some extent. But the effectiveness of secular priests was limited insofar as they adopted contemporary expectations and values. Every confessor should have helped his penitents to bear the burden of confronting sin; a lazy priest spoiled by his own comfortable life was tempted to shrug off this burden. Celibacy should have freed priests for communion with the whole body of the faithful; but sometimes, at least, it was abused by being taken as an opportunity—and an excuse—for a more or less self-indulgent way of life, freed from certain irksome responsibilities and lived within the confines of a clerical fraternity which, good in itself, nevertheless tended to take on the characteristics of a club which obstructed rather than facilitated the communion of the Church as a whole.

Separated in spirit from their penitents, confessors in earlier times often had been harsh with them. After Vatican II this same separation led too many priests to accept misformed and troubled consciences as adequate Christian consciences, although these were consciences no father who is holy should have found acceptable in children he truly loved. Priests who were more genuinely fatherly would have been more like St. Paul.

In many ways, then, members of the Church were not bearing one another's burdens. The social dimension of living the Christian life had been emphasized insufficiently. Christian life must be possible. When individuals left to struggle alone seemed to make little progress, the temptation was very strong to suspect that the burdens were too great. The moralist does not want to make anything more difficult than it must be. Any possible way of lightening the burden of Christian life began to seem attractive. For this reason, theologians were drawn into dissent. They were trying to lessen the burden of faith.

One must admit that the attitudes of the theological community toward the magisterium were partly the fault of the magisterium. Unfair and harsh treatment by the magisterium of many theologians prior to Vatican II led to solidarity among Catholic theologians in a bond of common resentment. After Vatican II, the magisterium perhaps moved too far in the other direction. Bishops who absolutely rejected radically dissenting theological opinions nevertheless found it impossible to bring themselves to oppose dissenting theologians in any effective way.

In modern times, the Church provided many opportunities for the laity to become educated in the faith. But some of the laity were unwilling to make the sacrifices necessary to seize these opportunities. Many others, having received a more or less adequate Catholic intellectual and spiritual formation, no sooner left school than they ceased thinking about their faith and its practical implications. When challenges to difficult teachings began to seem acceptable, many lay people were all too ready to put to use their superficial theological knowledge to rationalize setting aside the moral truth taught by the Church. All too often, those most active in various Catholic movements appropriated the works of dissenting theologians and transmitted their opinions to wider audiences.

In addition to all the other factors which help to explain why so many joined the radically dissenting theologians, there is one which hardly can be discussed without giving offense. Once one adopted proportionalism, one no longer regarded willful deception of others as intrinsically evil. Deception became lying only in the absence of a proportionate reason to justify it.[100] It followed that when theologians adopted proportionalism, they could begin to feel justified in deceiving others when this seemed necessary to promote the greater good—for example, to bring about changes they considered necessary in the Church's teaching.[101]

Scholars usually trust factual statements of their colleagues and even assume, when there is too little time for critical reflection, that the arguments of colleagues are valid. For this reason, scholars who were neither proportionalists nor dissenters were impressed by the statements and arguments of their dissenting colleagues. Thus, the work of dissenters had a disproportionate force upon nondissenting theologians, especially those not immediately concerned with the moral field. In this way many basically sound theologians in other areas, such as Scripture and canon law, were persuaded to go along with dissenting colleagues.

Appendix 5:   An afterword on pastoral responsibility and solidarity

Certain logical preconditions for any authoritative change in the Church's moral teaching never were understood clearly by dissenting theologians. This teaching has been and still is widely accepted by the Church, especially by her leadership. Therefore, to change it one had to try to show it false or doubtful. To show a universal norm doubtful, one must show that in some case one ought to act contrary to it. To show this plausibly, one must make a case at least consonant with faith itself for setting aside the received norm. If one thinks one has made such a case, one must propose it to the leadership of the Church. This is what happened in the Birth Control Commission.

For this reason, the Commission was unable simply to tell Pope Paul to say that the received teaching on contraception was uncertain and no longer binding. They had to tell him to say that "in fulfillment of its mission the church must propose obligatory norms of human and Christian life."[102] They had to tell him to say that "responsible parenthood is a fundamental requirement of a married couple's true mission."[103] They had to tell him to say that "if they are to observe and cultivate all the essential values of marriage, married people need decent and human means for the regulation of conception."[104] They had to tell him to say that "the means which are chosen should have an effectiveness proportionate to the degree of right or necessity of averting a new conception temporarily or permanently."[105] Finally, although they did not have to tell Paul VI to say it, the proponents of contraception had to tell him that abstinence from intercourse is not always an adequate and morally acceptable means.

The official documents of the Birth Control Commission did not make clear precisely what these assertions implied concerning what the Pope would be doing if he approved contraception. However, Paul VI was fully informed by means of other documents about the implications of the official documents, along the following lines. To say the things proposed would amount to saying this: "Until now, I have been telling you that practicing contraception is a grave matter. Now I must tell you that you have a grave obligation to begin practicing it, if it is the method most suited to you for fulfilling your obligation to regulate conception. In other words, what it was a mortal sin to do last night might well be a mortal sin to omit tonight."

Moreover, Paul VI realized that the Church could not change its moral teaching only on contraception. Any plausible account of the change on contraception would consistently lead to change on other matters. So the Commission was implicitly telling Paul VI to say: "Until now I have been telling you that masturbation, fornication, homosexual relations, abortion, adultery, and so forth all involve grave matter. Now I must tell you that what was a sin until this moment might well be a sin to omit from now on. Sorry about this folks, but the Church can make mistakes."

Those who do not have responsibility for the Church's teaching can grasp Paul VI's problem only by putting themselves in his place.[106] The ordinary priest or theologian thinks about the problems of the faithful in living up to the teaching, and perhaps thinks about his or her own reasons and rationalizations for changing it. A pope must ask himself whether a proposed new teaching could possibly be true if it clearly requires the Church utterly to discredit her claim to communicate divine truth to humankind. (And, lest there be any doubt, the issue here is not the "image" of the Church but the truth of received Christian moral teaching.)

Thus, dissenting theologians undertook an impossible task. They could succeed in changing the norms only if they could change the character of the community. To accomplish this, they had either to convert the leadership to their view, or to assume leadership themselves and transform the Church by revolutionary action. Until *Humanae vitae,* the theological dissenters were attempting to convert the leadership. After that, they were primarily attempting to execute a coup, especially with respect to the Holy See. Later still, it appeared that they might be attempting to do both things—convert part of the leadership while undermining the authority of the part, especially the Holy See, which refused to be converted. Perhaps dissenting theologians did not see it that way, but I am concerned with the dynamics of their position and program, not with their intentions.

John Paul II has been a rock in the way of the dissenting theologians. His sophisticated conviction concerning traditional teaching has rendered hopeless his conversion to dissenting opinions. His popularity with the faithful has rendered hopeless any effort to convince the membership of the Church that he is not their head and appropriate spokesperson—whether or not they agree with what he says. And, obviously, John Paul II does not consider the doctrine of Vatican II dated and discussable, something which has to be set aside as to the letter in favor of its "atmosphere" or "spirit."[107]

Thus, each Catholic had to make a choice. One could accept the authority of Charles Curran, Richard McCormick, and other radically dissenting theologians; one could join them in setting aside many points of common Catholic moral teaching, the ecclesiology of Vatican II, and any responsibility to assent to the teaching of John Paul II when he repeats teachings one finds unsatisfactory. Or one could accept the authority of John Paul II and most of the bishops of the world; one could join them in affirming all points of Catholic moral teaching which have been held and handed down by the universal magisterium; one could accept the ecclesiology and help to carry out the program of Vatican II; one could bear effective witness to the love and truth of God revealed in our Lord Jesus by conforming one's conscience to the Church's teaching and by living according to one's Catholic conscience.

Bishops who stand firm with John Paul II and priests who stand firm with him and their own bishops are contributing to the true renewal of the Church according to the plan of Vatican II. Renewed according to this great vision, the Church, our mother and our teacher—she, the lovely, holy, and spotless bride of our Lord Jesus—will more effectively carry on her mission: To teach the gospel by the proclaimed word and prophetic deeds, to reveal redemption in the world of today so that those who do not flee the light of Jesus will receive life in his name, and creatively to unfold and hand on intact the precious faith of our fathers to our children.

Notes

1. Charles E. Curran et al., *Dissent In and For the Church: Theologians and "Humanae Vitae"* (New York: Sheed and Ward, 1969), 26 (cited hereinafter as *"Dissent"*).

2. Richard A. McCormick, S.J., summarizes the position, counting himself among those who hold it: *Notes on Moral Theology: 1965–1980* (Washington, D.C.: University Press of America, 1981), 709–11 (cited hereinafter as *"Notes"*). In an article, "The Moral Implications of a Nuclear Deterrent," *Center Journal*, 2 (Winter 1982), 20–21, I state: "The theologians Charles E. Curran led in dissent from *Humanae Vitae's* reaffirmation of the received teaching on contraception subscribed to a statement saying that 'spouses may responsibly decide according to their conscience that artificial contraception in some circumstances is permissible and indeed necessary to preserve and foster the values and sacredness of marriage.' Generalized, the position is: Christians may responsibly decide according to their conscience that any sort of act, although formerly excluded by Christian teaching as intrinsically evil, in some circumstances is permissible and indeed necessary to preserve and foster important human values on which it bears." Commenting on this, McCormick, "Current Theology: Notes on Moral Theology: 1982," *Theological Studies*, 44 (1983), 101–2, said: "During the course of his study Grisez mentions the 'theologians Charles E. Curran led in dissent from *Humanae vitae*.' They held that spouses may sometimes decide in conscience that contraception is morally acceptable. Of this Grisez states: 'Generalized, the position is: Christains may responsibly decide according to their conscience that any sort of act . . . in some circumstances is permissible.' Generalized, it means nothing of the kind. They did not say, nor can their statement be forced to say, that 'any sort of act' could be permissible in some circumstances. They said that contraception was not always a morally evil act. That leads to no generalization whatsoever about 'any sort of act.' It is painful to have to remind others that disputes are not clarified by misrepresentation." McCormick's summary of and truncated excerpt from my exposition hides the fact that the statement of dissent from *Humanae vitae* assumed and applied a general principle, which could be and was subsequently more generally applied. That was all I asserted by my statement beginning "Generalized." McCormick misrepresented my position by introducing the phrases, "means nothing of the kind," "be forced to say," and "leads to no generalization," for these phrases suggest that I asserted a logical implication which I did not assert. I entirely agree with McCormick that disputes are not clarified by misrepresentation.

3. John XXIII, *Mater et Magistra*, 53 AAS (1961) 454–56; *The Papal Encyclicals*, 267.229, 235.

4. Ibid., 457; 239. See Dario Composta, "Il magistero di fronte al diritto naturale," *Apollinaris*, 49 (1976), 79–105.

5. *Dissent*, 117; also 119.

6. McCormick, *Notes*, 744.

7. *Dissent*, 26.

8. Charles E. Curran, "Ten Years Later," *Commonweal*, 105 (7 July 1978), 429.

9. See Charles E. Curran, *New Perspectives in Moral Theology* (Notre Dame, Ind.: Fides Publishers, 1974), 41–42, 192–93, 211, 271–76.

10. Ibid., 19–22.

11. See *The Birth Control Debate*, ed. Robert G. Hoyt (Kansas City, Mo.: National Catholic Reporter, 1968), 55–59. The leaked documents are not exactly what they were purported to be. Moreover, the very use of the words "minority" and "majority" in this context conveys a conception of the work of the Commission evidently different from that of Paul VI. He sought from the advisory body a thorough study to see if it was possible that the received teaching might somehow be refined or limited. The number who subscribed to one brief did not make their case better; it clarified nothing for the Pope, who proceeded for two additional years to investigate the subject by other means.

12. Ibid., 75–77. Other documents of the Commission, not published by proponents of change, showed the extent to which theological literature by 1966 signaled the beginning of a shift of opinion in the whole field of sexual morality.

13. See McCormick, *Notes*, 668–82.

14. *Dissent,* 14, mentions the manualists referred to by Curran and his associates in an effort to substantiate their claim that common teaching accepted dissent. The authors say that I prepared an English translation of parts of these texts and add: "The translations prepared for the Chancellor [Cardinal O'Boyle] were selective, and thus somewhat distorted, and failed to indicate all the points favoring the possibility of dissent." There are two errors here. I did not prepare the English translation; that was done by Rev. Msgr. E. Robert Arthur. Second, the excerpts never were given anyone by me or with my knowledge without copies of the whole sections of the Latin texts from which they are excerpted. If this procedure was selective and distorting, one might wish that dissenting theologians had adopted it.

15. Ibid., 47–48. Perhaps when Curran and his colleagues gave Cardinal O'Boyle a list of names of approved authors who purportedly supported the legitimacy of dissent they did not expect him to look at the works cited.

16. See Francisco A. Sullivan, S.J., *De Ecclesia,* vol. 1, *Quaestiones Theologiae Fundamentalis* (Rome: Apud Aedes Universitatis Gregorianae, 1963), 354; I. Salaverri, S.J., *De Ecclesia Christi,* in *Sacrae Theologiae Summa,* vol. 1, *Theologia Fundamentalis,* ed. 5 (Madrid: B.A.C., 1952), 708, no. 669. The dissenters pointed out that this statement of Pius XII had been in the first schema of Vatican II on the Church, but was removed after that schema was roundly criticized. *Dissent,* 115, noted: "Apparently the warning was not dropped without opposition, for among the suggested *emendationes* distributed along with the second *schema* was that of five bishops who ask that the statement from *Humani Generis* be replaced in the text." Charles Curran, *Moral Theology: A Continuing Journey* (Notre Dame and London: University of Notre Dame Press, 1982), 6, asserted: "The Second Vatican Council expressly rejected that same sentence." He provided no evidence for this claim, because there is none; certainly the Commission's nonacceptance of an amendment proposed by five bishops is not the Council's rejection of the statement that amendment would have inserted. Avery Dulles, S.J., "The Two Magisteria: An Interim Reflection," *Proceedings of the Catholic Theological Society of America,* 35 (1980), 162, said about the statement: "The position of Pius XII to this effect in *Humani generis* (DS 3885), even though not explicitly repeated by Vatican II, still seems to stand, especially in view of its reaffirmation by Paul VI." I have searched the relevant conciliar documents pertaining to *Lumen gentium* and found no criticism whatsoever of the statement from *Humani generis.* There was much more on the magisterium in Vatican II's first draft, including a treatment of the ways in which members of the Church other than bishops share in it. Dissenting theologians who insisted on their share in the magisterium should, if consistent, have taken Vatican II's noninclusion of this material in *Lumen gentium* as evidence that the Council rejected the idea that anyone but bishops can share in the magisterium. Furthermore, if it were true that Vatican II expressly rejected Pius XII's statement in *Lumen gentium,* promulgated in 1964, this still would not have been the Council's last word on the matter, since the following year it cites (in OT 16, official note 31; Abbott note 46) the section of *Humani generis* (42 AAS [1950] 567–69) in which this statement is located as its primary reference for its own prescription that seminarians be taught theology "under the light of faith and with the guidance of the Church's teaching authority."

17. *Dissent,* 115–16.

18. Ibid., 119.

19. Ibid., 124. Antonio Acerbi, "Receiving Vatican II in a Changed Historical Context," in *Where Does the Church Stand?* Concilium, 146, ed. Giuseppe Alberigo and Gustavo Gutiérrez (New York: Seabury Press, 1981), 77–84, tried to give some theological plausibility to talk about the ecclesiological atmosphere or spirit of Vatican II. He appealed from the Council's documents to what he claimed the Council in the first place was: a spiritual experience. The trouble with this is that Vatican II, as a social entity, had no subjectivity and no experience of its own; the Council only existed in its acts. Each person even remotely involved no doubt had some spiritual experience of the Council, and anyone can generalize beyond his or her individual experience by drawing on publications. Unfortunately, the latter convey impressions of common or universal experience strongly conditioned by the media of communication, which were largely managed by atypical believers or nonbelievers. Thus, Acerbi's appeal from Vatican II's *acta* to a spiritual experience of the Council really (though doubtless unintentionally) was an appeal to the interpretations and opinions of a narrow group, including nonbelievers.

20. Avery Dulles, S.J., *The Resilient Church: The Necessity and Limits of Adaptation* (Garden City, N.Y.: Doubleday, 1977), 109. Concerning theological abuse of Vatican II: Philippe Delhaye, *La Scienza del bene e del male: La morale del Vaticano II e il "metaconcilio"* (Milan: Ares, 1981).

21. *Dissent,* 100–101.

22. McCormick, *Notes,* 667.

23. The scantness of negative reaction can be seen by examining the *New York Times,* the *National Catholic Reporter,* and *NC News Service* from 29 July through 31 August 1968. Not more than a half-dozen negative reactions by individual bishops are reported. The media did not give equal attention to the many bishops who affirmed the teaching as their own and defended it against the dissent.

24. For example, *Humanae Vitae and the Bishops: The Encyclical and the Statements of the National Hierarchies,* ed. John Horgan (Shannon: Irish University Press, 1972). Even this collection is incomplete; see the list of Martin Brugarola, S.J., "Presentacion," in Marcelino Zalba, S.J., *Las conferencias episcopales ante la "Humanae vitae"* (Madrid: Editorial Cio, 1971), 5–7.

25. See E. Hamel, S.J., "Conferentiae episcopales et encyclica 'Humanae vitae,'" in *De matrimonio coniectanea* (Rome: Gregorian University Press, 1970), 323–40.

26. Ibid., 340. A work favorable to dissent found "clear acceptance" in twenty-five documents from eighteen countries, "clear mitigation" in sixteen documents from thirteen countries, and an "uncertain" position in eleven documents from ten countries (see Joseph A. Komonchak, *"Humanae Vitae* and Its Reception: Ecclesiological Reflection," *Theological Studies,* 39 [1978], 249, n. 87). It also was seldom noted by dissenting theologians that various conferences which made hurried statements in 1968 subsequently issued more carefully prepared documents on relevant matters. For instance, the Canadian Catholic Conference, "Statement on the Formation of Conscience," 1 December 1973, corrected (without explicitly saying so) the statement issued five years before, to bring the teaching of the bishops of Canada into line with the received teaching on the Catholic conscience and its responsible formation. Again, in 1970 a group of Italian moral theologians claimed it appropriate for moral theologians to "help believing Christians to serenely follow their own sincere conscience even though in a given situation it cannot be clearly seen how their complete choice is to be reconciled with a particular goal that has been authoritatively proposed by the magisterium—provided that they seem to be on the road toward the ideal envisioned by the total teaching." (Quoted in Antonio di Marino, S.J., "Morality and the Magisterium," in *Readings in Moral Theology: No. 3: The Magisterium and Morality,* ed. Charles E. Curran and Richard A. McCormick, S.J. [New York: Paulist Press, 1982], 95.) To this the Italian Episcopal Conference responded that the "formulation readily inclines people to the error that in particular individual cases something is licit in conscience which may even have been declared illicit in absolute terms by the authentic magisterium. As it is formulated, this section cannot be accepted as a correct statement of a *moral-theology teaching that is faithful* to the magisterium of the Church. Hence it cannot be proposed in teaching moral theology without failing in the duty that theologians have to the magisterium, which entrusts them with the task of teaching" (ibid., 101).

27. John Paul II, *Familiaris Consortio,* 74 *AAS* (1982) 171; Eng. ed. (Vatican City: Vatican Polyglot Press, 1981), 138–39 (sec. 73).

28. *Dissent,* 25–26.

29. Ibid., 56.

30. Ibid., 63. Some of the dissenting theologians argued in the same way in independent works. See, for example, Daniel C. Maguire, "Morality and Magisterium," in *Readings in Moral Theology: No. 3,* who admits the category of infallible, ordinary magisterium (36), yet proceeds to argue as if it did not exist (42). Bruno Schüller, S.J., "Remarks on the Authentic Teaching of the Magisterium of the Church," in the same volume, 14–21, simply assumes that in its moral teaching the magisterium is not infallible.

31. Conferences of bishops which proceeded directly from the assumption of noninfallibility to consideration of dissent (in Horgan, ed., op. cit.): Austria, 61; Belgium, 65; Canada, 79; Scandinavia, 237–38; Switzerland, 259–60; United States, 276–77; West Germany, 306.

32. Among the few instances, the clearest examples are in the statements (cited in the preceding note) of the Austrian bishops ("Since the encyclical does not contain an infallible dogma . . ."), the Canadian bishops ("Since they are not denying any point of divine and Catholic faith . . ."), and the West German bishops ("a non-infallible doctrine of the Church's magisterium . . ."). Even in these cases, the documents provide no evidence that the bishops considered and rejected the possibility that the doctrine has been infallibly proposed by the Church in its ordinary magisterium. Hence, those who made these statements cannot be said to have rejected this possibility which they very likely never considered. Joseph A. Komonchak, "Ordinary Papal Magisterium and Religious Assent," in *Readings in Moral Theology: No. 3,* 90, said: "There is the possibility that some would maintain that the practical conclusions of *Humanae Vitae* are infallible not because of the encyclical but because of a constant tradition in the Church. Obviously, I have assumed throughout that the practical conclusions

are not infallible. In 1964 Pope Paul VI, by speaking of a possible duty to reform the tradition, implied that the tradition to that point was not irreformable. Nothing in the subsequent discussion can be said to have strengthened the force of the tradition. And in *Humanae Vitae* itself, Paul's quest for assent is built not upon the infallibility of the tradition or of his restatement of it, but upon the authority of the ordinary magisterium. This is also the assumption of the great majority of those bishops who have commented on the encyclical and its authoritative force." Komonchak was mistaken in saying that Paul VI in 1964 spoke of a possible duty to reform the tradition; rather, he referred only to certain statements of Pius XII, as Vatican II correctly indicates by referring to "certain questions" (GS 51, official note 14). In June 1964, the Commission Set up by the Holy See to Study the Problems of Population, Family, and Birthrate, was asked to consider the precise question of the "pill"; eventually all but one or two of the theological *periti* voted negatively on the question: "Whether in the moral consideration of methods the use of the 'pill' constitutes a special problem?" See Henri de Riedmatten, O.P., "Rapport Final," mimeograph, with a covering letter dated 27 June 1966, 8 and 18. Paul VI's quest for assent in *Humanae vitae* should be gathered from the official text (60 *AAS* [1968] 481–503) which refers (501, n. 39) to the whole of *Lumen gentium*, 25: "*AAS*, 57 (1965), 29–31." Moreover, note 39 is placed in *Humanae vitae* to include a reference to Vatican II's teaching on the light of the Spirit, which is mentioned in *Lumen gentium*, 25, especially in respect to *infallible* teachings. In talking of the "tradition" and ignoring the infallibility of the ordinary magisterium, Komonchak confused the issue. Moreover, he merely asserted, not proved, that most bishops commenting on the encyclical assumed its teaching on contraception to be noninfallible; even if they did, their assumption on an issue they did not consider, which was being misrepresented at the time by some theologians, can hardly constitute authoritative teaching on the point.

33. The text of the relevant segment of the document is in Karl Rahner, S.J., *Theological Investigations*, vol. 14, *Ecclesiology, Questions in the Church, The Church in the World*, trans. David Bourke (New York: Seabury Press, 1976), 85–88. Rahner, in a very influential article published soon after the publication of *Humanae vitae* (*Theological Investigations*, vol. 11, *Confrontations I*, trans. David Bourke [New York: Seabury Press, 1974], 263–87), ignored the category of teachings infallibly proposed by the ordinary magisterium, and in quoting (267–70) from the German bishops' letter of 1967 omitted from their remarks about dissent *only* the opening section in which they acknowledge this category. Thus Rahner was free to proceed (270) from the observation that *Humanae vitae* contains no ex cathedra definition to the conclusion that its teaching is in principle open to revision.

34. Some who defended *Humanae vitae* against dissent took the approach that even if not infallible, its teaching should be accepted as binding. See, for example, Austin Vaughan, "Msgr. Vaughan Answers Critics," *National Catholic Reporter*, 11 September 1968; a fuller development of this case: James J. Mulligan, *The Pope and the Theologians* (Emmitsburg, Md.: Mount Saint Mary's Seminary Press, 1968), 13–88. But others did make the case for infallibility. See, for example, Zalba, op. cit., 63–65, 93, 124–26, 130–32, and 179; *La regulación de la natalidad* (Madrid: B.A.C., 1968), 133–40; Joseph F. Costanzo, S.J., "Papal Magisterium and 'Humanae Vitae,'" *Thought*, 44 (1969), 377–412, esp. 410, n. 9.

35. See John C. Ford, S.J., and Germain Grisez, "Contraception and the Infallibility of the Ordinary Magisterium," *Theological Studies*, 39 (1978), 264–69. This argument was criticized by an article in the same issue: Joseph A. Komonchak, *"Humanae Vitae* and Its Reception," 238–50. (Komonchak did not explicitly mention Ford-Grisez but had a year to study and reply to their article.) The heart of his reply is in the first full paragraph on 248; nothing else he says contradicts the Ford-Grisez thesis. Ford and Grisez had reserved the right to reply briefly in the same issue to Komonchak's critique, and did so by adding one footnote to their article, 292, n. 73. The most pointed critique of Ford-Grisez: J. Piegsa, "Hat das ordentliche Lehramt zur Empfängnisregelung unfehlbar gesprochen?" *Theologie der Gegenwart*, 24.1 (1981), 33–41; ably answered: Rhaban Haacke, O.S.B., "Ein Widerlegungsversuch misslingt: Um das Lehramt und seine Aussage zur Empfängnisverhütung," in *Nicht Unfehlbar?*, ed. Johannes Bökmann (Abensberg: Josef Kral, 1981), 43–57. F. J. Elizari, "The Ten Years of 'Humanae Vitae,'" *Theology Digest*, 28 (1980), 33–34, digested from "A los diez años de 'Humanae vitae': Boletín bibliográfico," *Moralia: Revista de ciencias morales*, 1 (1979), 239–42, raised five points. The first three were anticipated by Ford-Grisez, the fourth ignores their use of Noonan (which considerably reduces the need to provide data about the tradition), and the fifth is a question-begging argument based on the authority of theologians and the confusion of some episcopal conferences after *Humanae vitae*. Garth L. Hallett, S.J., "Contraception and Prescriptive Infallibility," *Theological Studies*, 43 (1982), 629–50, tried to show that Catholic teaching on contraception (and, by implication, on all other disputed moral issues) could not possibly be proposed infallibly because, he claimed, it lacks any constant propositional content which could be true. His starting point was a theory of moral norms proposed by certain analytic philosophers, such as Kai Nielsen and R. M.

done previously in the spring of 1964.) Several of the members, including Cardinal Ottaviani, President of the Commission, argued strongly for such a consultation, but it was defeated eleven to four (ibid., 61) with all those favoring contraception against consultation. There also is a possibility that the brief of the theologians who opposed contraception was not made available to the cardinals and bishops of the Commission before their one common, decisive four and one-half day meeting; see John Cardinal Heenan, "The Authority of the Church," *Tablet*, 222 (18 May 1968), 489.

65. Curran, "Ten Years Later," 428. Christopher Mooney, "The Claim of the Church to be Guardian of a Universal Natural and Moral Law," in *True and False Universality of Christianity*, Concilium, 135, ed. Claude Geffre and Jean-Pierre Jossua (New York: Seabury Press, 1980), 23–32, virtually denies the competency of the magisterium in matters such as contraception. In doing so, he ignores the scriptural grounding of Christian sexual morality, the Catholic conception of natural law, and thus the anteriority of both to specific theologies of natural law, including that of St. Thomas. Of course, he also ignores the solemn teaching of Trent, which rightly interpreted makes the "claim" Mooney and many others would deny: Teodoro López Rodriguez, "'Fides et mores' en Trento," *Scripta Theologica*, 5 (1973), 175–221; Marcelino Zalba, S.J., "'Omnis et salutaris veritas et morum disciplina': Sentido de la expresión 'mores' en el Concilio de Trento," *Gregorianum*, 54 (1973), 679–715.

66. Joseph Fuchs, S.J., "The Absoluteness of Moral Terms," in *Readings in Moral Theology: No. 1: Moral Norms and Catholic Tradition*, ed. Charles E. Curran and Richard A. McCormick, S.J. (New York: Paulist Press, 1979), 102. McCormick, "Notes on Moral Theology: 1982," 73–74, summarizes and commends a later study by Fuchs along the same lines, which makes clear the relationship between Fuchs' view of the competence of the magisterium and his theories of fundamental option and the specificity of Christian ethics. (These theories were criticized in 16-E and 25-E.) Fuchs' conception of the relationship between the grace of salvation and human acts appears more like the view rejected by the Council of Trent in its Decree on Justification (esp. DS 1535–39/ 803–4) than like the position taught by Trent: It is necessary and possible to keep the commandments *of God and the Church* (which are *not* mere determinations by human experience, evaluation, and judgment), and this is not merely a consequence and sign of the grace of salvation, but a principle of growth in holiness and, by merit, of eternal life.

67. See Marino, op. cit., 93.

68. Ibid., 99–100.

69. McCormick, *Notes*, 744.

70. Ibid., 744–45.

71. See José Luis Illanes Maestre, "Pluralismo teológico y verdad de la fe," *Scripta Theologica*, 7 (1975), 619–84. McCormick, *Notes*, 778, urged the need to "reformulate what is defective" in *Humanae vitae* by eliminating from it the position that contraception always is wrong. He offered no indication concerning what he considered to be the substance of the received teaching on contraception, except that "technology can be of great assistance to us but should not be allowed to dominate us."

72. McCormick, *Notes*, 255.

73. Ibid., 657–58.

74. See Robert Coffy, "The Magisterium and Theology," in *Readings in Moral Theology: No. 3*, 212 and 214–15, for a translation of the relevant parts of Coffy's paper. Whereas Vatican I teaches that "by divine and Catholic faith everything must be believed that is contained in the written word of God or in tradition, and that is proposed by the Church as a divinely revealed object of belief either in a solemn decree or in her ordinary, universal teaching" (DS 3011/1792), Coffy, admittedly offering a possibly over-summary treatment, said (215): "To put it sharply, truths were conceived as coming from above and as lending themselves to definitive translations into formulas quite capable of expressing them perfectly. In this question, the magisterium could draw the line between what was truth and what was error." With more historical consciousness, Coffy claimed, it is now clear that truth is discovered gradually in history: "Revelation is not the transmission of immutable formulas, or statements. It is a mystery; the mystery of God." In arguing thus, Coffy overlooked the actual status of the truths God makes known about himself, for these are distinct from both the divine reality they reveal to humans according to their capacity and the culturally conditioned linguistic vehicles by which and in which these truths are expressed.

75. The work of Newman, although pioneering, remains fundamental. Those who invoke his name, however, seldom test their opinions, offered as development of doctrine, by the seven criteria of faithful development he proposes. See John Henry Newman, *An Essay on the Development of Christian Doctrine* (Westminster, Md.: Christian Classics, 1968), 169–206. For a more general summary of the

theology of development, with bibliography: J. H. Walgrave, "Doctrine, Development of," *New Catholic Encyclopedia*, 4:940–44.

76. This formulation is mine, not quoted from another author. It is a summary of a view implicit in the developmentalists' attempt to resolve the problem.

77. John T. Noonan, Jr., *Contraception: A History of Its Treatment by the Catholic Theologians and Canonists* (Cambridge, Mass.: Belknap Press of Harvard University Press, 1965), 532–33.

78. See Germain Grisez, "A New Formulation of a Natural-Law Argument against Contraception," *Thomist*, 30 (1966), 343–61; "Dualism and the New Morality," *Atti del Congresso Internazionale Tommaso d'Aquino nel Suo Settimo Centenario*, vol. 5, *L'Agire Morale* (Naples: Edizioni Domenicane Italiane, 1977), 323–30; "Natural Family Planning Is Not Contraception," *International Review of Natural Family Planning*, 1 (Summer 1977), 121–26; "Contraception, NFP, and the Ordinary Magisterium: An Outline for a Seminar," *International Review of Natural Family Planning*, 4 (Spring 1980), 50–58. See note 60, above, for a sampling of works by other Catholic theologians defending the Church's teaching. Richard A. McCormick, S.J., "Current Theology: Notes on Moral Theology: 1981," *Theological Studies*, 43 (1982), 104, stated: "Several theologians in Germany have informed me that there is only one (G. Ermecke) who still defends the formulations and conclusions of *Humanae vitae*." That statement is falsified by the collective work edited by Bökmann, and by the frequent, relevant contributions to *Theologisches*, a theological newsletter he also edits. On the Church's teaching about the morality of natural family planning: Marcelino Zalba, S.J., "Continentia periodica iam ab anno 1853 in Ecclesia probata fuerat," *Periodica de Re Morali, Canonica, Liturgica*, 70 (1981), 523–53.

79. See A. Vermeersch, S.J., "Usury," *Catholic Encyclopedia*, 15:235–38, and works cited by him; Thomas F. Divine, S.J., *Interest: An Historical and Analytical Study in Economics and Modern Ethics* (Milwaukee, Wis.: Marquette University Press, 1959), 5–11, 24–35, and 45–64.

80. John T. Noonan, Jr., *The Scholastic Analysis of Usury* (Cambridge, Mass.: Harvard University Press, 1957), 399–400.

81. Curran, "Ten Years Later," 426.

82. Dulles, *Resilient Church*, 51–54. Not all theologians were as sanguine as Dulles about the resiliency of the Church: Gustav Ermecke, "Die katholische Theologie in der Krise," *Münchener theologische Zeitschrift*, 32 (1981), 194–205. Concerning the philosophical foundations of liberalizing theological programs: Cornelio Fabro, *L'Avventura della teologia progressista* (Milan: Rusconi, 1974).

83. Dulles, *Resilient Church*, 52–57. Dulles did not ask the question: Which deviations from the gospel are harmless?

84. Ibid., 51.

85. See Peter L. Berger, *The Sacred Canopy: Elements of a Sociological Theory of Religion* (Garden City, N.Y.: Doubleday Anchor, 1969), 127–71. For a good summary of the social and ideological situation of faith in the modern world, see Stephen B. Clark, *Man and Woman in Christ: An Examination of the Roles of Men and Women in Light of Scripture and the Social Sciences* (Ann Arbor, Mich.: Servant Books, 1980), 467–540, 672–73 (bibliography), and 726–35 (notes).

86. Dulles, *Resilient Church*, 110–12.

87. Ibid., 52.

88. Ibid., 55–56, makes much of Vatican II's teaching (see UR 11) that there is an order or hierarchy in the truths of faith, since they differ in their relationship to what is fundamental. But this hierarchy does not allow one to dispense with some dogmas, for all of them, as aspects of one and the same personal relationship with God, must be held with the same act of faith. The Council instead intended to guide study: Catholics and other Christians can perhaps find ways of resolving their differences on less central questions if they develop their thinking on these matters by reference to the fundamentals held in common.

89. See Walter J. Burghardt, S.J., "Stone the Theologians! The Role of Theology in Today's Church," *Catholic Mind*, 75 (September 1977), 50. One who rejects Burghardt's view is not driven to blind obedience to arbitrary ecclesial authority: Philippe Delhaye, "La collaboration de la Hiérarchie et de tous les chrétiens dans la formulation des normes morales," *L'Année canonique*, 22 (1978), 43–60.

90. Drake's account was chosen as the basis for the summary of the Galileo case to avoid prejudicing the issue. However, J. J. Langford, "Galilei, Galileo," *New Catholic Encyclopedia*, 6:250–55, provides an account the same in all material respects. Jacques Maritain, *On the Church of*

Some key words

Absolutes, moral: moral norms which do not admit of exceptions (10-C). *See* Norm. All moral absolutes are negative norms. Nonabsolute norms are moral norms which admit of exceptions. Most specific norms are nonabsolute.

Analogy: primarily refers to language; the use of the same word in two or more sentences with meanings partly the same but partly different. The relationships among the meanings are based in one way or another on real relationships in the things referred to. One knows something analogously when one knows it only through the relationship something else has to it.

Appropriation: the Christian's intellectual and personal reception of revelation. The initial appropriation of God's communication by the apostles is necessary for revelation to occur (1-A and 35-A).

Authenticity: one of the existential or reflexive goods; the harmony within the person between practical reason, will, and behavior; also called "practical reasonableness" (*see* Goods; 5-D, 5-G, and 5-2.)

Authority: the capacity of some judgments and/or choices to elicit reasonable assent and/or obedience without conveying the intrinsic grounds for the judgment or choice (11-A–B). The authority of experts is based on their special knowledge or skill. The authority of leaders in society is based on the need for unity and coordination of activities within the society. The Church has two kinds of authority: authority in teaching and in governing (11-F–G and 35-C). The teaching authority of the Church can be exercised infallibly and is not reducible to the authority of scholarly expertise. *See* Magisterium.

Bad: lacking something appropriate, the opposite of good. *See* Evil, Privation (5-A). "Bads" are those things that are bad or evil. The most important distinction among bads is that between sensible and intelligible bads (5-B). The first refers to objects repugnant to sentient desire; the second to objects which lack something which is judged to be appropriate or which brings about such a lack. Badness is the precise lack in bad things that makes them to be bad.

Basic commitment: a commitment which has implications for all the choices in a person's life (8-I, 16-G, and 22-A).

Casuistry: the part of moral theology which deals with difficult cases; chapters 10 and 12 treat the principles of sound casuistry. This essential part of moral theology has a bad name because of its legalistic abuses.

Charity: the Christian's participation in divine life; the love of God poured forth in the hearts of Christians. One of the theological virtues insofar as it is a disposition to act—that is, to perform acts which carry out the Christian's basic commitment of faith (24-C, 25-A, and 25-4).

Classical moral theology: the moral theology which developed after the Council of Trent (sixteenth century) and persisted until Vatican II. It was characterized by rationalism, legalism, and minimalism (1-D and 4-G).

Commensurability: literally, the ability to be measured and compared. In ethical theory this term refers to the mistaken belief that basic human goods can be measured by some common scale or index; assumed by all forms of proportionalism (6-F). The denial of the commensurability of human goods is expressed by "noncommensurability." *See* Proportionalism; Values, hierarchy of.

Commitment: a large choice bearing on existential goods and one or more other persons; commitments integrate all or a great deal of a person's life (9-E and 28-D).

Consent, full: one of the three conditions for mortal sin; one consents fully to an act when one freely chooses to do it (15-C and 17-E). *See* Sin, mortal.

Consequentialism. *See* Proportionalism.

Conventional morality: the code of morality predominant in a culture. Conventional morality contains some moral truth but also error; its function is not to spell out the requirements of moral truth but only to provide guidelines for living together in society (3-A and 4-E).

Determinism: any theory which involves the denial that human beings can make free choices (2-B, 2-4, and 13-F–G). *See* Free choice.

Dialectic: a method of inquiry, distinct from the scientific method—in either the Aristotelian sense, the rationalist sense, or the modern, empirical sense. Dialectic proceeds by revising the propositions one thinks true in the light of the whole set of truths one accepts. This is the appropriate method for theology; but here, unlike other forms of dialectic, the truths of faith are taken as fixed and unrevisable (1-C and 1-5).

Dissent, radical theological: a mistaken view which tries to justify setting aside authoritative and even infallible Church teaching as the norm for Catholic belief and practice (36-A).

Double effect, principle of: a set of rules developed in classical moral theology for dealing with the application of generally stated norms to difficult cases; these rules flow from the psychological and moral difference between what is intended and the foreseen but not intended side effects of one's action (12-F and 12-3).

Empirical: what can be experienced; the methods used by modern physical and social sciences to study the physical and social worlds.

End: any purpose, goal, or ideal which can motivate human action; ends are contrasted with means (9-D). Means are instruments for achieving ends or are ways of realizing ends that can be realized in more than one way. Means are sought for the sake of ends; thus ends and means are relative to one another. There are ends sought for their own sake and not as means to any further end; these ends are the basic human goods (5-D). These goods are not concrete objectives or goals that can be fully realized, but are purposes such as friendship and knowledge in which actions can participate more and more.

Epikeia: a reasonable judgment that one may act against the letter of a law when such action is necessary to fulfill the lawgiver's intention; applies only to positive law (11-E and 11-G).

Evil: the bad; especially the morally bad, a privation in the existential order; primarily in a choice contrary to a moral norm. *See* Sin. The expression "lesser evil" is most often used in a proportionalist context in which the

Love: a disposition to fulfillment (24-A). The distinction between emotional and volitional love is theologically important. The former is love of sensible goods; the latter is love of intelligible goods. Divine love primarily is the Trinity itself as a perfect communion of persons (24-B). The love of God in human persons is charity—the love of God poured forth in our hearts, and thus the share in divine life of those in the state of grace.

Magisterium: the authority and role of the pope and other bishops, as successors of the apostles, to distinguish what belongs to revelation from what does not, and to guide the receiving, guarding, and explaining of revealed truth. The exercises of this responsibility are divided into extraordinary and ordinary. The extraordinary magisterium embraces all acts of solemnly defining truths of faith and morals, and all teaching of ecumenical councils. The ordinary magisterium is the role as day-to-day teachers of the pope and other bishops. Under certain conditions the exercise of the ordinary magisterium is infallible (35-C–D).

Matter of sin: what one does in sinning considered in abstraction from the sinner's knowledge of its moral status and volitional involvement in it. Moral theology's concern with the matter of sin is focused on the seriousness of what the sinner does (15-C). The standard of seriousness is the compatibility or incompatibility of the act with the fundamental option of Christian life (16-G). Those acts which when freely and knowingly undertaken are incompatible with faith or its specific requirements are grave matter. One who does such acts with sufficient reflection and full consent commits a mortal sin. Those acts which, although immoral, are not incompatible with faith or any of its specific requirements are not so serious; such acts are light matter; even when knowingly and freely chosen, they are only venial sins. *See* Parvity of matter.

Method, theological: a systematic way of proceeding in theology, which should be appropriate to the subject matter. Dialectic is the appropriate method for theology, since it does not suppose that the theologian stands outside the subject, but rather explores God's revelation as one who accepts it and shares in the Church's life of faith (1-C and 1-5).

Modes of Christian response: the modes of responsibility transformed by charity and in the light of the actual fallen and redeemed condition of humankind; they are ways of appropriately responding to God's gifts and to the needs of others with a life patterned after that of Jesus. Indicated by the eight Beatitudes, the modes of Christian response are the principles of specifically Christian norms (25-E–F and 26-A).

Modes of responsibility: intermediate moral principles which follow from the first principle of morality and are the source of specific moral norms which follow from them. The modes of responsibility rule out ways of willing which are somehow satisfying to part of the person but which fall short of a will toward integral human fulfillment (7-G).

Morality: the aspect of our lives which depends on our free choices, for good or ill (2-A). Morality in this sense is concerned with moral truth. However, the word "morality" often is used to refer to conventional morality—the rules for getting along in a society—and to sensitivity to the internalization of parental and societal attitudes, often called "superego" (3-A).

Neoplatonism: a world view which developed at the same time as early Christianity. Neoplatonism was admired by many Fathers of the Church, especially St. Augustine, and has had a profound influence on all Christian theology and piety. Its most influential notions are that the human mind has a natural affinity for the divine and that the human person is primarily spirit; these notions lead to thinking of human fulfillment as the other-worldly perfection of the soul in an intellectual activity which unites it to God, while other human goods and life in this world are downplayed (19-B and 34-A).

Norm: a standard of goodness which is not always met. A moral norm is a norm for free choices and other will acts. In other words, moral norms are the requirements for existential goodness (2-A).

Normative force: the practical requirement of a norm. Moral norms differ in normative force because the modes of responsibility exclude different inappropriate ways of willing (10-A).

Normative principle: a source of the distinction between moral good and evil. Other principles of moral life help organize it in respects other than the distinction between good and evil (2-A).

Objectivity of moral norms: the truth of moral norms founded on genuine moral principles. Objective moral norms are not based on individual or social preference, but on the inclusive and unselfish love of human goods (3-B, 7-F, and 25-B).

Occasions of sin: situations or actions which conduce to sin and can be avoided or modified so that temptation is less likely or more easily overcome (32-E).

Omission: the not-doing of something in a situation where it is in some way—not necessarily morally—called for. Omissions can be voluntary in all the ways in which doings can be voluntary (9-C).

Original sin: primarily, the sin of Man (Adam), by which he lost God's friendship for himself and for humankind as his family. Secondarily, the privation of friendship with God which each human person inherits insofar as he or she receives humanity from Man (14-I).

Participation: sharing in, especially sharing in divine life (24-D).

Parvity of matter: a falling-short of grave matter. There is parvity of matter in acts having grave matter but in such small degree that the act is not a true instance of its kind. Stealing has grave matter because of the injustice and harm involved, but the act of stealing an insignificant amount has parvity of matter. Where there is parvity of matter there can be no mortal sin. *See* Matter of sin.

Performance: the behavior which carries out a choice (2-E and 9-C).

Precept: an ambiguous word, which can refer either to a rule of law or to a moral norm. *See* Norm. Precepts are often contrasted in theology with counsels of perfection (27-H).

Principles: realities or truths on which derived realities and/or truths depend. Principles of morality lead to moral norms (4-B). The modes of responsibility are principles of specific moral norms (7-G and 10-B). First principles are

useful applications, for example, as applied to the ordering of ends and means, of sensible and intelligible goods, and of various human interests by moral principles.

Vocation: the personal responsibility which each Christian is called by God to carry out. The call to perfection by following Christ is the universal vocation of all Christians (23-D). The particular set of commitments each Christian should make to implement the fundamental option of faith is his or her personal vocation (23-E).

Voluntariness: the feature of human acts in virtue of which they depend on the will and are the personal acts of the one who does them; there are various sorts of voluntariness, and moral norms bear on them in different ways (9-A).

Voluntary: whatever proceeds from the will—that is, from what is sometimes called "rational appetite." Any interest in or desire for a good understood to be such is an act of rational appetite. Free choice is the central voluntary act. *See* Free choice.

Voluntary in cause: the voluntariness of an action one does not choose to do but does as the foreseen result of another act one chose to do. Sometimes used in magisterial pronouncements and by traditional moralists to refer to the acceptance of side effects (9-3).

Willing: refers to various volitional acts and dispositions. Simple willing is a basic interest in or caring about human goods; it is the disposition towards goods which underlies all other actuations of the will. Spontaneous willing refers to the willing of a definite possibility without considering alternative possibilities and so without choice. Executive willing is the willing of a possibility that emerges in the execution of a choice without any additional choice. Choices and the accompanying acceptance of side effects are the central acts of willing.

Names and subjects

Life: as a human good, 5-D, -H, -3, -4;
sacredness of, 8-H; secular humanism and,
34-B. *See also* Eucharist, sacrament of;
Jesus
Limbo, 14-2, 18 n.20
Lio, E., 1 n.28, 7 n.17, 34 n.10, 36 n.60
Liturgy: Christian life as, 23-1, 33-D;
Eucharist as center, 33-A; of Hours, 33-G;
as prayer, 29-D, -F, -H, -3; sacramentals,
devotions, and, 29-G; revelation in, 29-F,
-2, 30-A, -D, -E, 33-A; Scripture in, 29-2;
as symbol, 30-1; theological study and,
1-I. *See also* Christian life; Jesus; Prayer;
the sacraments by name
"Living faith," 20-D, 24-E, 25-B, -4
Livingston, J. C., 34 n.19
Livingstone, E. A., 22 n.19
Lohse, E., 30 n.21
Lombard, P., 18 n.9
Long, E. L., Jr., 4 n.6, 34 n.15
Lonergan, B. J. F., 1 n.4, 20 n.7, 24 n.14,
25 n.16
López Rodriguez, T., 7 n.13, 25 n.11,
35 n.24, 36 n.65
Loretz, O., 35 nn.16, 18
Lossky, V., 19 n.12, 24 n.24
Love: Christian, 20-E, 24-D, -3, 25-A, -D, -4;
commands of, 7-E, 23-C, 25-C–E; divine,
19-A, 20-A, 22-G, 24-B–E, -2; of
enemies, 25-C, 26-J; Eucharist and, 33-A,
-C, -D; human defined, 5-B, 24-A; law
and, 21-D, 25-G; marital and eucharistic,
33-H; modes of Christian response and,
25-F, 26-D–K, 27-B, 28-F; order in, 27-G;
penance and, 32-B; personal vocation and,
23-E; revealed in Jesus, 20-F, 21-I, 22-G,
25-D, 30-A; rigorism and, 28-F; sin and,
13-C, -1, 16-A, 18-H, 20-F, 21-A, -D,
22-C, -G, -2, 25-B, -G, -1, 27-E, 30-A,
-H, 32-D, 33-D; Trinity as, 24-B, -1. *See
also* Charity
Lowie, R. H., 7 n.22
Lucas, J. R., 30 n.4
Luijpen, W. A., 4 n.5
Lukewarmness, 26-E
Lukken, G. M., 14 nn.14, 24, 28, 34
Lust, 8-C, 18-D
Luther, M., 2-B, 16 n.2, 34 n.15
Lyonnet, S., 13 nn.2, 3, 5; 14 n.15; 17 n.8;
22 nn.36, 37; 25 n.17; 28 n.2; 35 n.1

MacBeath, A., 7 n.22
McBrien, R. P., 20 n.8
McCarthy, D., 1 n.14
McCarthy, D. J., 21 n.2, 35 n.75
McClear, E. V., 14 n.9
McCormick, R. A., 1 nn.11, 13, 15, 23, 27;
4 n.18; 7 nn.9, 10, 14, 18, 40; 8 n.2;
9 nn.2, 9; 10 n.1; 16 n.12; 17 n.6;
25 nn.7–9, 11, 12; 35 nn.16, 23, 28, 37,

39, 41, 67, 68; 36 Int., -C, nn.2, 6, 13,
22, 26, 30, 32, 39, 40, 41, 43–52, 61, 63,
64, 66, 69–73, 78, 93, 96, 100, 101; on
magisterium, 36-D; on natural law, 7-B,
-3; on proportionalism, 6-B–D, -F, -H, -1,
nn.1, 4–6, 8, 10, 11, 13, 14, 17, 19, 20,
22, 28, 29, 33, 34, 36–41, 43–49, 52–59;
on reformulation of doctrine, 36-F
McCue, J. F., 16 n.2
McDermott, B. O., 14 n.8
McDonnell, K., 4 n.13
McEleny, N. J., 26 n.3
Machiavelli, N., 10-F
Machiavellianism, 8-H
McHugh, J. A., 12 n.10
MacIntyre, A., 4 nn.1, 22
McKenzie, J. L, 26 n.15
Mackey, J. P., 14 n.19
Maclaren, D., 4 n.17
McNamara, R. S., 9 n.8
MacQueen, D. J., 13 n.18
Magisterium: conscience and, 3-E, -F, 4 n.12,
17-A, 23-G, -2, 35-E, -F, 36-A, -E;
defined, 35-C; infallibility of, 1 n.31,
35-D, -E, 36-B; interpretation and, 20-1,
36-F; law and, 3-F, 11-F; natural law and,
7-B, -3, 35-F, 36-E; of the pope, 35-C,
-E–G, -1, 36-C, -D; religious assent to,
35-F, -G; theological dissent from, 1-F,
6-H, 7-3, 20-2, 34-C, 35-2, -3, 36-A–G,
-3, -4; theology and, 1-A, -C, -E, -2, -5;
20-1, nn.22, 23; 27-3; 35-A, -1. *See also*
Church teaching; Teaching of the Church
Maguire, D. C., 35 nn.28, 41; 36-D, nn.30,
55, 96
Malice, sin of, 17-B
Malina, B. J., 14 n.27
Maloney, G. A., 19 n.6
Maly, E. H., 13 n.2
Man. *See* entries under Human
Mangan, J. T., 12 nn.6, 14
Manichaeism, 5-C, 13-E
Mansi, J. D., 35 nn.25, 29, 30
Marcel, G., 1 n.8; 2 n.8; 9 nn.10, 11; 20 n.7;
24 n.2
Marcus, R., 22 n.17
Maréchal, J., 1 n.4, 2 n.17
Mariani, B., 19 n.7, 34 n.4
Marino, A. di, 36 nn.26, 67, 68
Maritain, J., 4 n.1; 10 n.10; 13 n.7, 15;
26 n.36; 34 nn.12, 18, 90
Marriage, 24-B, 27-C, 33-H, 35-E
Marshall, A., 24 n.20
Marshall, H., 22 n.12
Martelet, G., 19 n.23
Martin I, 21 n.F
Martin, R., 34 n.20
Martyrdom, 26-G, -K, 31-D
Marx, K., 4 n.17, 5-C, -H, 13 n.12
Marxism, 1-3, 2-4, 13-F, -G, 26-I, 28-I, 34-B

Reverence for human goods, 8-H, 26-K
Revolution, 28-I
Rice, P. B., 4 n.1
Richard, L., 26 n.37
Richard, M., 18 n.25
Riches and detachment, 26-F
Riedmatten, H. de, 36 nn.32, 64
Riga, P., 32 n.3
Riggan, G. A., 14 n.9
Right reason, 7-F, -G
Rights, 7-F; 10-E, -2, nn.5, 6; 26-H; 27-F
Rigorism, 12-D, 28-D, -F
Riley, L. J., 11 n.11
Rites, the: anointing, 32-H; baptism for
    children, 31 n.5; Christian initiation of
    adults, 20 n.13, 30 nn.24–26;
    confirmation, 31-I, nn.1, 5, 8–12;
    penance, 28 n.7, 32 nn.5–7, 9, 14, 27–34
Riviere, J., 20 n.24
Roach, R. R., 1 n.14, 25 n.5
Robertson, A. T., 22 n.20
Robinson, H. W., 2 n.12
Robinson, J. A., 19 n.6
Robinson, J. A. T., 5 n.15, 19 n.16, 35 n.75
Rodríguez, P., 34 n.9
Rogerson, J. W., 2 n.12, 14 n.29
Rommen, H. A., 4 n.19
Rondet, H., 24 n.26, 25 n.16
Ross, J. F., 1 n.40
Ross, W. D., 2 n.23, 7 n.35
Rousseau, M., 25 n.5
Roy, L., 26 n.15
Royce, J. E., 14 n.18, 24 n.1

Sabourin, L., 13 nn.2, 5; 22 nn.36, 37
Sacrament(s): as acts and signs, 30-C;
    character received in, 30 Int., -C, 31-A;
    Church and, 30-F; as encounter, 30 n.8,
    33 nn.10, 11; Eucharist as central, 22-G,
    23-B, 29-F, 30-A, 33-A, -F; Jesus' human
    action in, 22-G, 23-A, -B, 30-A, -E, 33-B;
    liturgy and., 29-G; minister of, 30-F; as
    moral principles, 23-A, -B, 29-F, 30-B,
    31-C, 32-D, 33-D, 34-F, -2; recipient of,
    30-G; redemption and, 22-G, 23-A, -B,
    30-A, -D; revelation in, 30-A; Scripture
    and., 29-2. *See also* Liturgy; entries on
    each sacrament
Sacred Congregation for Catholic Education,
    1-E, -I, -2, nn.3, 21, 22, 30, 32–37, 47,
    51
Sacred Congregation for the Doctrine of the
    Faith, 16-E, nn.24, 27; 17-E, n.6; 18 n.28;
    21 n.14; 32 n.6; 36-A
Sacred Congregation for Relgious and Secular
    Institutes, 29 n.17
Sacrifice, 19-G, 21-B, -D, 22-G, -2, 23-B,
    -D, -I, 25-G, -I, 29-F, 30-A, -E, 33-A–D,
    -F. *See also* Eucharist, sacrament of; Jesus;
    Mass, sacrifice of
Saints, devotion to, 31-G

Salaverri, I., 35 nn.36, 38, 40; 36-A, n.16
Sánchez, M., 15 n.5
Sancho Bielsa, J., 1 n.10, 4 n.12, 35 n.5
Sanctification of the Christian, 18-A, 19-H,
    26-I, 28-C, 30-I, 32-D, 33-D. *See also*
    Christian life; Divine life of the Christian;
    Grace
Sanctifying grace. *See* Grace
"Sanctity of life," 8-H
Sapientiae christianae, 23-F, nn.10, 12, 13
Satisfaction: good and, 5-E; for sin, 22-2,
    32-A
Scandal, 9-F, -3, 12-G, 15-I
Scharbert, J., 8 n.4
Scharf, P., 3 nn.27, 29, 31, 32
Scheeben, M. J., 24 n.5
Scheler, M., 3 n.24, 5 n.3, 6 n.12, 7 n.24
Schepers, M. B., 34 n.19
Schillebeeckx, E., 1 n.10; 20 n.9; 22 n.26;
    25 nn.3, 5; 30 nn.8, 10, 11, 13, 14;
    33 nn.10, 11; 34 nn.4, 21; 35 n.16
Schlagenhaufen, F., 35 n.42
Schleirmacher, F., 34-C
Schmaus, M., 18 n.25, 19 n.1, 20 n.1,
    24 n.26, 25 n.16, 34 n.24, 35 n.46
Schnackenburg, R., 3 n.20, 19 n.10, 23 n.16,
    28 n.4, 35-4, nn.69–71
Schneider, J., 21 n.17
Scholastic natural-law theory, 4-F, -G, nn.19,
    20; 7-C; 35-3; 36-2
Schönweiss, H., 15 n.7, 18 n.4
Schoonenberg, P., 14 nn.14, 27; 18 n.13
Schüller, B., 6 n.1; 9 n.9; 25 n.5; 35 nn.16,
    23; 36 nn.30, 96
Scott, J. B., 4 n.19
Scripture: corporate personality in, 2-H, 14-I,
    19-B; and Enlightenment, 36-3; inerrancy
    of, 22-I, 35-B; interpretation of, 1-C,
    20-I, 35-B; liturgy and, 29-2;
    magisterium's teaching about, 1-C, -E,
    22-I, 35-B, -I, 36-I; moral teaching and,
    8-A–H, 25-E, -F, -2, 26-A, 35-B, -E, -4,
    36-E; prayer and, 29-A, -B, -3; theology
    and, 1-A, -C, -E, 20-I, 22-I, 35-B, -I, -2;
    use of in this work, 1-2, 22-I. *See also*
    Revelation; Theology; separate Scripture
    index
Second coming of Jesus, 34-E
Secular humanism: and fulfillment in Jesus,
    1-3, 34-B, -D; and good and evil, 5-C,
    20-G; liberalized Christianity and, 1-3,
    34-C, 36-4; origins of, 1-G, -3, 34-A, -B;
    on sin, 13-F, -G, 14-C, 34-B; slavery and,
    36-2; and theological dissent, 6-A, 36-H,
    -4
Seesemann, H., 18 n.5
Segundo, J. L., 1 n.27
Self-abasement, 26-D
Self-control, 8-C, 26-F
Self-deception, 8-F

Sacred Scripture

Denzinger–Schönmetzer

The Second Vatican Council

St. Thomas Aquinas

Secunda secundae

✝